PRACTICAL
CHRISTIAN
THEOLOGY

FOURTH EDITION

PRACTICAL
CHRISTIAN
THEOLOGY

Examining the Great Doctrines of the Faith

FLOYD H.
BARACKMAN

kregel
PUBLICATIONS

Grand Rapids, MI 49501

*Practical Christian Theology: Examining the Great
Doctrines of the Faith*

© 1981, 1994, 1998, 2001 by Floyd H. Barackman
First edition 1981
Fourth edition 2001

Published by Kregel Publications, a division of Kregel, Inc.,
P.O. Box 2607, Grand Rapids, MI 49501. Kregel Publications
provides trusted, biblical publications for Christian growth and
service. Your comments and suggestions are valued.

Scripture marked BV is taken from the MODERN LAN-
GUAGE BIBLE: THE BERKELEY VERSION IN MOD-
ERN ENGLISH. Copyright © 1945, 1959, 1969 by
Zondervan Publishing House. Used by permission.

Scripture marked KJV refers to English wording specific to
the King James Version of the Holy Bible.

Library of Congress Cataloging-in-Publication Data
Barackman, Floyd H.
    Practical Christian theology: examining the great doc-
trines of the faith / Floyd H. Barackman.—4th ed.
        p.   cm.
    Includes bibliographical references and indexes.
    1. Theology, Doctrinal. I. Title.
BT75.2.B33   1998   230-dc21   97-49304
                                              CIP

ISBN 0-8254-2380-5

Printed in the United States of America

5 6 7 8 9 / 09 08 07 06

To
my children,
Ruth and Philip,
their spouses,
and their posterity,
this book is
affectionately dedicated.

CONTENTS

PREFACE

The importance of studying Bible doctrine cannot be overstated. The decline in doctrinal teaching and preaching accounts for the widespread ignorance of basic biblical doctrine that prevails among the Lord's people today. God has given in His Word all the instruction that is needed for a holy, productive Christian life and ministry (2 Tim. 3:16–17; John 15:15; cp. Deut. 29:29). But to receive its benefits, we must decide to learn what this is, look to the Holy Spirit to give us understanding, search the Scriptures, and resolutely appropriate this truth to our lives.

The following pages present my understanding of the great doctrines of the Christian faith. Having been forged during more than fifty-five years of study and twenty-five years of classroom discussion at Practical Bible Training School (now Practical Bible College), Bible School Park, New York, this understanding continues to grow as the Holy Spirit gives further insight into His truth.

Although our understanding of divine things is incomplete, we who are saved can say that we know God's truth. Contrary to the epistemology of the world, spiritual understanding follows the acquisition of spiritual knowledge, which is received through the canonical Scriptures by faith (1 Cor. 2:12; Heb. 11:3). For instance, we know from the Scriptures that the Lord Jesus was virgin-born, yet we do not fully understand this unique event. Contrariwise, the world must understand a matter in order to know it, for its knowledge is acquired by the scientific method and requires empirical verification. For this reason, the world regards gospel believers as naive and unscientific when we claim certain knowledge of divine things, based on divine revelation.

Beginners are surprised that there is no textbook that satisfactorily answers all theological questions, and that scholars differ in their understanding of spiritual truth. While all gospel believers agree on what doctrines are Christian, they do not all have the same understanding of these teachings, despite their being taught by the Holy Spirit. Their differences of understanding spring from the fact that insight into divine truth is relative, being formed by an overall grasp of the Scriptures, religious training and conditioning, and other elements of life experience that affect comprehension. Thus I do not offer this work as being complete or final, but I trust that it will be used of God to give fresh insight into His truth and to stimulate study. Theologically, its slant is toward a modified Calvinism that rejects limited atonement. Also, it recognizes the various dispensations and covenants that God has given to mankind.

It is impossible to give credit to all who have contributed toward my understanding of these doctrines. If the reader should come upon the thoughts of others, with or without new garb, he or she should give credit to whom it is due. Ultimately, all praise must be given to our God—the living and true God—who has been pleased to give and to teach His people His self-revelation.

While many have encouraged me in this work, I wish to acknowledge two former Practical Bible Training School colleagues who are now with the Lord: Urban F. Cline and John L. Benson. I also thank the Reverend John C. Nippert for reading the manuscript of the present revision and his insightful remarks. Finally, I wish to recognize my wife, Ella, whose constant support through the years has done much to make this work possible.

This work rests upon the staunch conviction that the Bible, consisting of sixty-six canonical books, is the Word of God; that it was divinely given in inerrant, verbal form within the history of earthly place and time; and that its truth can be understood only as the reader stands in a right relationship with God and is taught by God the Holy Spirit. May it be the purpose of both author and reader not only to gain a greater understanding of God's unchanging truth but also to submit to its authority and to allow it to govern our lives for His glory. By this we lovingly show the Lord Jesus that we are His friends as well as His slaves (John 14:15; 15:14; 1 Cor. 6:20).

If the reader should have any doubt about his salvation from sin, he should read of its need, provision, reception, and assurance in chapter 10.

Introduction

1

INTRODUCTION

Before beginning our study of the contents of Christian systematic theology, we must consider the answers to several basic questions that are relevant to this subject: What are the requirements of this study? What is the meaning of Christian theology? Into what divisions is Christian theology usually divided? Why do we systematize Christian theology? What are the major parts of Christian systematic theology? What are the main beliefs of the major Protestant theological systems?

THE REQUIREMENTS FOR STUDYING CHRISTIAN THEOLOGY

- **We must be born again (John 3:3–7).**
Our rebirth through faith in Jesus and His atoning work brings us the divine renewal of our personhood and inner human nature, including our mind, and the spiritual capacity and capability that are necessary for understanding God's truth (cp. Eph. 1:18; 4:17–21, 23; 1 Cor. 2:12; Titus 3:5; Heb. 11:3; 1 John 2:20, 27).

HIGHER & LOWER CRITICISM

- **We must accept the divine authority of the Bible and its teachings (John 17:17; 2 Tim. 3:16–17; Ps. 119:105).**
It is our creatural duty to receive God's Word—the sixty-six canonical books of the Bible—and to align our thinking with what God, the Creator, says (Ps. 36:9; Rom. 3:4; cp. 1:18).

LET SCRIPTURE FORMULATE YOUR DOCTRINE

- **We must follow the inductive method of reasoning.**
This starts with the Scriptures and formulates doctrinal statements from them. By this method, we consider the truths given in the Bible and derive from them specific theological teachings and principles (cp. Acts 17:11; 2 Tim. 3:16). This objective approach allows God to instruct us through His Word. Observe that the mind, renewed by the Holy Spirit and taught from the Word, is the doorway to true biblical understanding and spiritual experience (Rom. 12:2; Eph. 4:17–24; Ps. 1:1–3).

- **We must rely on the teaching ministry of God the Holy Spirit.**
He alone can give us the right direction in theological study and clear understanding of God's truth, according to our spiritual needs and ministry (1 Cor. 2:10–12). This requires our being yielded to Him and our responding favorably to His Word (Ps. 119:18; Luke 8:18; John 7:17; 1 Tim. 4:13–16; 1 John 2:27).

- **We must seek to understand all the subjects that the Bible teaches and all that the Bible teaches about each subject.**
It is our duty to learn and to minister the whole counsel of God (Acts 20:27). We should

not be surprised that people who know the Lord differ in their understanding of biblical doctrine. While all gospel believers agree on what teachings are essential to the Christian faith (the Trinity, the deity of Christ, and so on), not all have an identical understanding of these doctrines. This variation is due to differences in the understanding of words, overall grasp of the Scriptures, religious training and conditioning, and life experiences. The input of these elements introduces variable and sometimes faulty features into our concept of biblical truth. This understanding, however, is subject to change as we grow in our spiritual life and gain more knowledge of biblical truth (Col. 1:10; 2 Peter 3:18). Also, the Holy Spirit teaches each child of God according to the needs of his spiritual development and the requirements of his Christian ministry. In this teaching process, the Holy Spirit gradually corrects the deficient or defective elements that we bring to biblical interpretation and gives us deeper and new insight into God's Word. This process continues throughout our Christian lifetime.

As much as possible, we must avoid subjectivism, which is the deliberate distortion of the ordinary meaning of Scripture to suit our interests or preferences. As far as possible, we must always allow the Bible to speak for itself rather than permit religious bias or preconceived unbiblical ideas to control our interpretation. Also, we must amiably allow others their views of theology although we may not agree with them.

THE MEANING OF CHRISTIAN THEOLOGY

THE ETYMOLOGY OF THEOLOGY

The word *theology* is derived from the Greek words *theos*, meaning "God," and *logos*, meaning "word," "discourse," or "doctrine." Theology is a discourse or teaching about God and the things of God. It is the science of God.

A DEFINITION OF CHRISTIAN THEOLOGY

Christian theology may be defined in two ways: in a *broad sense* it is the whole scope of Christian doctrine that is revealed in the sixty-six books of the Bible; in a *narrow sense* it is the Christian doctrine of God, or Theology Proper.[1]

Sometimes Christian theology is identified as *revealed theology*, based on truth that is revealed in the Bible. On the other hand, *natural theology* is a science of God that is based solely on what is revealed about Him in nature. The primary fault of natural theology is that it does not recognize any divine explanation for the things that make up nature or any revelation of the divine will for mankind.

THE DIVISIONS OF CHRISTIAN THEOLOGY

EXEGETICAL THEOLOGY

Being based on biblical interpretation, this theology is concerned with the study of the Scripture text. This division includes the study of biblical languages, textual criticism, biblical archaeology, biblical introduction, biblical hermeneutics (interpretation), and biblical theology. Biblical theology seeks to arrange systematically the truths revealed within the various periods of the Old Testament, like the Mosaic Period and the Monarchical Period, and those revealed in the writings of the New Testament authors, like those of the apostle John and of the apostle Paul.

HISTORICAL THEOLOGY

Being based on the history of doctrinal thought, this theology traces the origin, development, and spread of true Christian religion, together with its doctrines, institutions, and practices. It covers biblical history, church history, the history of missions, the history of doctrine, and the history of creeds and confessions.

SYSTEMATIC THEOLOGY

[handwritten: WATCH OUT WE DON'T TAKE PASSAGES OUT OF CONTEXT]

Being derived from exegetical and historical theology, systematic theology arranges the Bible's teachings and people's explanations of them in logical order under the heading of theological study. In addition to the systematic arrangement of doctrine, this division also includes Christian apologetics, polemics, and ethics.

PRACTICAL THEOLOGY

[handwritten: TAKE 1ST.3 AND APPLY]

Consisting of the practical application of theology, practical theology seeks to use that which is contributed by the other divisions of Christian theology in the salvation, sanctification, edification, education, and ministry of gospel believers. This division comprises homiletics (the art of preaching), church organization and administration, worship, Christian education, pastoral theology, and the work of missions.

Observe that *Practical Christian Theology* presents a study of systematic theology, together with its application to Christian life and ministry.

THE NEED FOR CHRISTIAN SYSTEMATIC THEOLOGY

Our need for a systematic form of Christian theology not only points to the practicality of theology but also motivates us in its study. This need is indicated by the following:

- **It is required by our minds.**

Our minds are not contented with an accumulation of facts. They seek to unify and systematize these facts by looking for the relation between them and arranging them in logical order. In our study of God, we not only learn what the Bible reveals about Him but we also organize this truth into a logical system. In this sense, theology is a science.

- **It is required by the composition of the Bible.**

The Bible is not formally organized into a systematic theology. It consists of a variety of literary forms, including history, prophetic utterances, visions, poetry, wisdom literature, biographical notes, and letters. The theological truths scattered throughout this literature must be gathered and assembled into a logical system. Although there are Scripture passages that extensively treat certain doctrines, none treats any doctrine completely. In this logical construction, we must take care that our deductions are based on God's Word and do not conflict with what God has revealed in the Scriptures.

- **It is required by life's questions and problems.**

The world must be shown that the Bible has the answers to the basic questions about the universe that unsaved people's philosophy does not have. These include those about origin (Where did man come from?), meaning (What is man?), purpose (Why does man exist?), relation (How is man related to everything that makes up the universe?), and destination (Where is man going?). Moreover, the Bible offers the solution to human spiritual problems that the world cannot provide. The Scriptures also present a rational, full, consistent worldview that honors God and that agrees with mankind's essential nature. Answering these questions and meeting this need require a systematic grasp and a clear presentation of Christian theology (cp. 1 Peter 3:15; 2 Tim. 3:15; 1 Cor. 1:18–25; cp. Acts 17:16–34).

- **It is required for spiritual living.**

The concept that Christian theology necessarily has a deadening effect upon our spiritual life is wrong. Correct, biblical belief rightly influences behavior (Prov. 23:7; Luke 6:43–45). Biblical Christian theology teaches us the kind of life we are to live (2 Tim. 3:16–17), shows us how to live it (Ps. 119:105; cp. John 14:16–17; Phil. 4:13; 2 Peter 1:3), and motivates us to live this way (cp. Eph. 4:1–5:21 with chaps. 1–3; Col. 3:1–17 with chaps. 1–2; Rom. 12:1–15:13 with chaps. 5–8).

- **It is required for Christian ministry.**

Christian theology teaches us what our divine mission on earth is—evangelizing the unsaved and teaching the saved (Matt. 20:19–20; 2 Cor. 5:19–20). In their ministries, the Lord Jesus and His apostles taught doctrine (Mark 4:2; Acts 2:42; 2 Tim. 3:10) and exhorted gospel believers to do the same (Matt. 28:19–20; 2 Tim. 2:2; 4:2; Titus 1:9; 2:1). Christian theology teaches us the nature, resources, goals, and operation of Christian ministry as well as the needs to which we are to minister.

THE MAJOR PARTS OF CHRISTIAN SYSTEMATIC THEOLOGY

Bibliology . . . . the doctrine of the Scriptures
Theology Proper . . . . the doctrine of God
Paterology . . . . the doctrine of God the Father
Christology . . . . the doctrine of God the Son
Pneumatology . . . . the doctrine of God the Holy Spirit
Angelology . . . . the doctrine of angels
Anthropology . . . . the doctrine of man
Hamartiology . . . . the doctrine of sin
Soteriology . . . . the doctrine of salvation
Zoeology . . . . the doctrine of the Christian life
Ecclesiology . . . . the doctrine of the Universal Christian Church
and the local church
Eschatology . . . . the doctrine of future prophetic events

THE MAJOR PROTESTANT THEOLOGICAL SYSTEMS

While it is primarily important for us to seek to understand what the Bible teaches about various theological subjects, we cannot ignore the theological systems that were developed during and after the Reformation era and upon which much systematic theological thinking rests. A summary of these systems follows.

CALVINISM

Calvinism is the system of theology that grew out of the study and writings of the Genevan reformer and pastor, John Calvin (1509–1564). Essentially, this is the development and Protestant form of the teachings of the Latin church father, Augustine (354–430).

Holding the Bible to be the Word of God, Calvinism seeks to build its system on the Scriptures. Its basic doctrine is the total sovereignty of God. Recognizing human responsibility, it associates this with the comprehensive plan of God. Obedience to God is man's supreme duty. While this was possible before the Fall, it can now be only by God's sovereign grace. In Christ, God redeems only the elect. The church, the ordinances of baptism and the Lord's Supper, and civil government are divine institutions. This is the theology of the Reformed, Congregational, and Presbyterian churches.

ARMINIANISM

Arminianism is the system of theology that grew out of the study and writings of the Dutch theologian, James Hermann, or Jacobus Arminius (1560–1609). He protested against the extreme form of Calvinism that prevailed at the close of the sixteenth century and that was defended by Calvin's son-in-law, Theodore Beza (1519–1605). Arminius saw what he believed were two great errors in Calvinism: *one,* it made God the author of sin; and *two,* it did away with genuine human freedom.

In their discussions with their opponents, the Arminians rejected five points of Calvinism as being unscriptural. They set forth their own position in the five articles of their "Remonstrance" of 1610.[2]

The two positions are contrasted in the following:

— CAN RELY ON LOGIC TOO MUCH

One: Calvinism teaches people's total depravity. This means that sin's ruin affects their entire person and hinders their ability to win and merit salvation.

Arminianism holds that all people, by divine grace, possess free will and have the capability of doing good, which God accepts.

Two: Calvinism teaches unconditional election. This means that God's choice of whom He would save was not determined by anything that He foresaw in people.

Arminianism holds that election and condemnation were conditioned upon divinely foreseen faith or unbelief of people.

Three: Calvinism teaches limited atonement. This means that Jesus died only for the ✓ elect whom God chose to save.

Arminianism holds that Jesus died for all people, but only gospel believers enjoy its saving benefits.

Four: Calvinism teaches irresistible grace. This means that the elect cannot successfully resist being drawn to God in salvation.

Arminianism holds that divine grace can be resisted to one's damnation. People have the final decision in their salvation. *PRSEVRATION*

Five: Calvinism teaches the perseverance of saved people. This means that, because they divinely persist in faith, gospel believers cannot lose their salvation. *— MOST DON'T ACCEPT THIS*

Arminianism, at first, held that perseverance was open to inquiry. "On this point the disciples of Arminius went further and taught the possibility of a total and final fall of believers from grace. . . . They moreover denied, with the Roman Catholics, that anybody can have a certainty of salvation except by special revelation."[3]

The student must beware of the logic of Calvinism, which sometimes leads to conclusions that go beyond what God has revealed in His Word. He must also beware of the reasonableness of Arminianism, which sometimes seeks to establish doctrine on purely human concepts, contrary to what God has revealed.

LUTHERANISM

While accepting the three ancient ecumenical creeds (the Apostles', the Nicene, and the Athanasian Creeds), Lutheranism differs from Calvinism in that it teaches the necessity of water baptism for salvation, the real presence of Christ's body and blood "in, with, and under" the bread and cup of the Lord's Supper, and the qualities of Christ's divine nature as belonging to His human nature. It differs from Arminianism, further, in that it teaches man's total depravity, the bondage of the human will to sin, and an unconditional predestination of the elect to everlasting life.[4] It holds that water baptism imparts faith to infants for their salvation.

SPURGEON · CALVINIST
MISODY - ARMENIAN

17

ANGLICANISM

While neither Roman Catholic nor Calvinistic, Anglicanism continues to preserve the old English Catholicism, rejecting the peculiar errors and abuses of Rome and holding royal supremacy in ecclesiastical as well as in civil matters.[5] Calvinistic elements persist in the evangelical section of the Church of England.

* * *

In our theological studies it is impossible to avoid a position that is to some degree in agreement with one or more of these theological systems. But as I see it, our purpose should be to strive for a position that is as objectively biblical as possible rather than to conform thoughtlessly to someone else's theological system.

THEOLOGICAL CREEDS

The doctrinal position of large segments of the Protestant church is stated in their historical creeds: Lutheranism in the Augsburg Confession (1530), Anglicanism in the Thirty-nine Articles (1571), Presbyterianism and early Congregationalism in the Westminster Confession of Faith (1646), and Methodism in the Twenty-five Articles of Religion (1784). Historically, Baptists have not had a common doctrinal creed, but they have universally adhered to certain principles that make them distinctive and have been willing to express their doctrinal convictions regionally as in the Philadelphia Confession of Faith (1742) and in the New Hampshire Confession of Faith (1833).[6]

As we study the doctrines of the Bible, we will develop our own theological model that is fashioned by our understanding of doctrinal truth. This model will be suited to our mental capacity and personality and to the ministry to which we are divinely called. We must be careful, however, not to allow ourselves to become locked into someone else's system of theological thinking so that this person, with his or her views, becomes our doctrinal mentor rather than God and His Word. We also must courteously allow others their doctrinal views that differ from ours, for we want them to extend this courtesy to us as well. As all of us look to the Holy Spirit to teach us new biblical truth, give us greater insight in truth we already know, point out to us error in belief that we hold, and enable us to live and serve by what we know, we shall "speak those things that become sound doctrine," "adorn the doctrine of God our Savior in all things," and be workers "approved unto God" (Titus 2:1, 10; 2 Tim. 2:15).

As we turn now to the great doctrines of the Christian faith, let us give ourselves anew to the Holy Spirit so that we allow Him to teach us these truths according to what the Scriptures say about them and the understanding that He wants us to have of them. God's truth is so profound that all of us have more to learn. May we be motivated in our quest for theological knowledge to learn more about our God—the true and living God—and His will for us so that we may fear, love, and obey Him throughout our Christian lifetime on earth for His glory (Deut. 29:29; 1 Cor. 10:31).

A Review of the Introduction

1. What are the basic requirements for the study of Christian theology?
2. Why must we rely on the Holy Spirit for an understanding of Christian theology?
3. What is the meaning of Christian theology in its broad and narrow aspects? Of doctrine?
4. Briefly explain exegetical, historical, systematic, and practical theologies.
5. Why is Christian systematic theology required by our minds, the composition of the Bible, and life's questions and problems?

6. How does Christian systematic theology relate to spiritual living and Christian ministry?
7. List the major parts of Christian systematic theology.
8. Give the primary doctrinal emphasis of Calvinism.
9. Give the primary emphasis of Arminianism.
10. List the five points of Calvinism to which the Arminians objected.
11. What was the Arminian position on these five points?
12. Which point of the Arminian position does the writer prefer?
13. How does Lutheranism differ from Calvinism and Arminianism?
14. In what way is the Baptist denomination different from others?
15. List the Baptist distinctives.
16. What must we be alert for in developing a doctrinal model?
17. Have you been born again through faith in Jesus and His atoning work?

Endnotes

1. The word *doctrine* is derived from the Latin words *doctor*, which means "teacher," and *doctrina*, which means "teaching." Doctrine means that which is taught, a teaching. Like theology, it can mean a body of instruction, or teaching, or the teaching of a particular subject within a body of truth.
2. I agree with four of these five points of Calvinism. Believing the Arminian view of an unlimited atonement (no. 3) to be more biblical, I reject the Calvinistic view of a limited atonement. See "His Humiliation: The Extent of Jesus' Atoning Work" under Christology.
3. Philip Schaff, *The Creeds of Christendom* (Grand Rapids: Baker Book House, n.d.), 1:519. See pages 509–23 for a fuller discussion.
4. Philip Schaff, "Lutheran Church," in *Schaff-Herzog Encyclopaedia of Religious Knowledge* (New York: Funk & Wagnalls Company, 1891), 2:1370f.
5. Schaff, *The Creeds of Christendom*, 1:622f.
6. See Appendix P: "Baptist Distinctions."

Bibliology

2

BIBLIOLOGY
The Doctrine of the Bible

The doctrine of the Scriptures—the sixty-six canonical books of the Bible—belongs to God's special revelation, and it is better to look at this before we consider Theology Proper. The importance of this study is indicated by the Bible's being the basis of Christian belief and conduct as well as the special means by which God makes Himself and His will known to mankind. One's belief about the Bible fashions one's view of God and the Christian faith.

THE CONTENTS OF THE BIBLE

ITS SUBSTANCE

Belonging to His special revelation, in contrast to His general revelation through nature, the Bible is God's message to mankind. It is His Word, the written form of His speaking (Heb. 1:1–2). It was produced by His breath, or by the activity of God the Holy Spirit (2 Tim. 3:16, lit. "all Scripture is God-breathed"). By the Scriptures, God tells all that is necessary for people to know about Himself. Also, by the Scriptures He gives exclusive information about the universe, angels, and humans, including their origin, meaning, purpose, unity, and destination (cp. Heb. 11:3).

ITS MAIN SUBJECT

The dominant theme of the Scriptures is the Lord Jesus Christ, God's promised Conqueror-Savior (Gen. 3:15; Luke 24:27, 44; John 1:45; 5:39). The Lord's messianic work was announced in the Old Testament by prophecy (Gen. 3:15; Isa. 11; 49:1–12; 52:13–53:12) and was portrayed by the OT ritual sacrifices (Heb. 7–10); it was established in the Gospels by His public ministry, death, and resurrection (Matt. 27–28); it was preached and applied in the Acts of the Apostles to those who trusted in Him and His atoning work (Acts 16:31–34); it was doctrinally stated and explained in the Epistles (Rom. 1:1–6); and its consummation was anticipated in the visions of Revelation (Rev. 19:11–21; chaps. 20–22), which revealed His second coming to earth, defeating His enemies, rewarding His people, and ruling over the earth for one thousand years.[1]

THE MAJOR DIVISIONS OF THE BIBLE

The Bible consists of two major divisions: the Old Testament (OT) with thirty-nine books and the New Testament (NT) with twenty-seven books. With *testament* meaning "covenant," these divisions are called "the old covenant," being related to the Mosaic covenant, and "the new covenant," being related to the new covenant that Jesus mediated, for these parts of the Bible set forth God's relationship with His people by these covenants.[2]

THE OLD TESTAMENT

Its Meaning

The Old Testament derived its name from the Mosaic covenant that God made with Israel at Mt. Sinai (Exod. 19:1–8; 24:8). Early Christians gave this title to this part of the Bible because the statement of this covenant and the history of Israel's relation to God under it make up almost all of this section of the Bible (Exod. 19–Mal. 4). The thirty-nine OT books were written during the period c. 1491–399 B.C.

Its Arrangement

In our English Bible the arrangement of the thirty-nine books of the Old Testament follows that of early Bible translations—the Greek *Septuagint* and the Latin *Vulgate*. This arrangement appears to have been governed by the contents of these OT books.[3]

A helpful analysis follows:

History		Teaching		Prophecy	
Legislative	*Executive*	*Poetry*	*Wisdom*	*Major*	*Minor*
Genesis	Joshua	Job	Proverbs	Isaiah	Hosea
through	through	Psalms	Ecclesiastes	Jeremiah	through
Deuteronomy	Esther	Song of		Ezekiel	Malachi[4]
		Solomon		Daniel	
		Lamentations			

Its Value

One: The Old Testament was the Bible of our Lord and His followers (Matt. 5:17–18; Luke 24:27; Acts 17:2).

Two: It gives us information about the existence of God (Gen. 1:1; Deut. 6:4; Isa. 40:10–31), the creation of the universe and of humans (Gen. 1–2), people's first sin (Gen. 3), and their salvation by faith in God's promise of the coming Savior (Gen. 12:3; 15:6; Isa. 45:17–25; 49:6–9; 55:1–7; Zech. 9:9; cp. Gal. 3:8).

Three: It emphasizes God's genuineness (Jer. 10:10), oneness (Deut. 6:4), power (Gen. 1), holiness (Lev. 11:44), mercy (Ps. 103:8), justice (Isa. 45:21), sovereignty (Ps. 103:19), and loving-kindness (Ps. 91:1–2; Jer. 9:24).

Four: It gives many prophecies about Jesus, like His birth, including His race (Gen. 15:5), tribe (Gen. 49:10), family (2 Sam. 7:12–13; cp. 2 Tim. 2:8), place (Mic. 5:2), and time (Dan. 9:25); His messianic works (Isa. 49:6–7; 52:13–53:12; 61:1–2); His coming earthly kingdom (Pss. 2:8–9; 72; Isa. 2, 11); and His defeating Satan and his allies (Gen. 3:15; Isa. 14:12–15; cp. Rev. 20:1–3, 10).

Five: It contains much, like the books of Psalms and Proverbs and the stories about people of faith, that encourages us who are saved, stimulates our devotion, and helps our spiritual growth (Heb. 11; cp. 2 Tim. 3:16; Rom. 15:4; 1 Cor. 10:11).

Six: It presents the history of God's dealings with the people of Israel, the reasons for their existence, and their future restoration to God and to their land (cp. Ezek. 36). God used those Israelites who had a personal relationship with Him to bear witness to His existence, to show the blessing of serving the true God, to be the writers and guardians of the OT Scriptures, to give birth to Jesus and, in time, to be the channel of divine blessing to the world (Gen. 12:3; John 4:22; Rom. 3:2; 9:4–5; 11:13–18).

Seven: It presents many details of Jesus' earthly, millennial rule that are not repeated in the New Testament (cp. Isa. 11:1–9). However, there is nothing revealed in the Old Testament about His present work of building the Church (Eph. 3:1–11).

THE NEW TESTAMENT

Its Meaning

The New Testament received its name from the new covenant, which replaced the old covenant of the Mosaic Law (Heb. 8:6–13; 10:9; 2 Cor. 3:6–14). Predicted in Jeremiah 31:31–34, the new covenant was mediated by Jesus' death and resurrection (Luke 22:30; Heb. 8:6; 9:15; 12:24). The New Testament not only tells us about Jesus' atoning death and resurrection, which made the new covenant effective but also elaborates on the covenant's salvational promises and states God's will for His people (the Dispensation of Grace), who are its recipients through faith in Jesus and His atoning work. The twenty-seven NT books were written during the period c. A.D. 45–95.

Its Arrangement

Like the Old Testament, the order of the twenty-seven NT books in our English Bible follows the arrangement of the Greek and Latin versions, which also appears to have been governed by their contents. The four Gospels were brought together into a collection, called "The Gospel." Also, the epistles of the apostle Paul were gathered under the title, "The Apostle." In time "The Acts of the Apostles" became the link between the two collections, and there were added the remaining NT writings that were recognized as having divine authority.[5] The NT arrangement is similar to that of the Old Testament:[6]

History		Teaching		Prophecy
Of Christ	*Of Church*	*Pauline*	*Non-Pauline*	*Visions*
The Gospel	The Acts	Epistles	Hebrews	Revelation
according to	of the	of Paul	James	
Matthew	Apostles	*to churches*:	Peter (2)	
Mark		Romans	John (3)	
Luke		Corinthians (2)	Jude	
John		Galatians		
		Ephesians		
		Philippians		
		Colossians		
		Thessalonians (2)		
		to associates:		
		Timothy (2)		
		Titus		
		to a friend:		
		Philemon		

Its Value

One: The New Testament fulfills, or anticipates the fulfillment of, all the truths that were foreshadowed by OT types and that were predicted by OT prophecies (Matt. 5:17–18; Luke 18:31; 21:22; Rom. 16:25–26).[7]

Two: It tells us of the Founder and the meaning of biblical Christianity, with its teachings, instructions, and practices (Luke 1:1–4; John 14:6; Eph. 4:20–21; 2 Thess. 2:15; 2 Peter 3:1–2).

Three: It tells how sinners can be delivered from the punishment, ruin, and bondage of their sins and be brought into a right relation with God (John 3:16–18; Rom. 3:9–26; Eph. 2:1–10).

Four: Comprising the Dispensation of Grace (Titus 2:11–14), it gives the teachings of the Lord and His apostles that state God's will for His people today (Gal. 6:2; Col. 3:16).

Five: It reveals the Lord's present program of building His Church (Matt. 16:18) and the various ministries of His people in this work (1 Cor. 3:8–9; Rom. 12:1–8).

Six: It gives more details of certain OT prophecies of future events (cp. Matt. 24; 2 Thess. 2:1–12; Rev. 13 with Dan. 7–9). It also reveals new future events as well (cp. 1 Thess. 4:13–17).

THE INSPIRATION OF THE BIBLE

We shall now consider how the Word of God was first produced. As we do, there are three theological terms that we must distinguish. These are revelation, illumination, and inspiration. According to its context, *revelation* refers either to God's activity of making known His truth (Gal. 1:12; Eph. 3:3; 1 Cor. 2:9–10) or to the truth that He has revealed (Rev. 1:1). On the other hand, *illumination* concerns God's activity of giving us an understanding of His truth (1 Cor. 2:11–12; 1 John 2:20, 27; Eph. 1:17–18). In contrast to these terms, *inspiration* has to do with the original production of God's truth in human words, whether spoken or written (1 Cor. 2:13; 2 Peter 1:21; 2 Tim. 3:16). It is to this last divine work that we direct our attention.

FALSE THEORIES OF INSPIRATION

It will help us to understand the divine inspiration of the Scriptures if we first look at several theories that present a false view of this doctrine.

Natural Inspiration

This false theory states that the Bible was written by people who had a high order of genius or creativity like that belonging to fiction writers, poets, and others with creative ability.

My objection to this theory is that it would make the Scriptures solely a human product, subject to error. *The true view* of inspiration is that it is the work of God the Holy Spirit in and through people (2 Peter 1:21).

Universal or Mystical Inspiration

This false theory holds that the Bible writers were inspired in the same way, although to a fuller degree, as Holy Spirit-filled people today are inspired to prepare a message or to preach a sermon.

My objection to this theory is that it fails to distinguish between the prophet who produced God's Word under divine inspiration and the preacher who proclaims God's Word by reading or reciting it, interpreting it, and applying it to the needs of his listeners. Not distinguishing between the divine production of Scripture and the human interpretation and application of it to others, this theory would make the Scriptures subject to human limitation and error. *The true view* of inspiration is that it was a particular work of the Holy Spirit in and through certain people (2 Peter 1:21; 1 Peter 1:10–11). His inspiring people, as we shall see, is not the same as His filling them, leading them, or illuminating them.

Inspired Concept Inspiration

This false theory teaches that God gave His spokesmen and Bible writers thoughts or ideas of divine truth and allowed them to express these in their own words as they remembered and understood them.

I object to this theory, for it would make the Bible a human product and subject to human error. *The true view* holds that divine inspiration, not being the product of human interpretation (2 Peter 1:20), is verbal, extending to each word of Scripture and to the grammatical form of each word (1 Cor. 2:13; cp. John 10:34–36; Gal. 3:6; Matt. 5:18).

Variable Inspiration

This false theory says that some parts of the Bible are more inspired than other inspired parts and that there are parts of the Bible that are not inspired at all.

I object to this theory, for the nature of divine inspiration is such that it does not admit degrees; it is absolute—either a text is inspired, or it is not. *The true view* teaches that divine inspiration is plenary, extending to every part of the Bible to an equal degree (2 Tim. 3:16). While some parts of the Bible are more "inspiring" (exerting an animating influence upon the reader), all parts are uniformly, divinely inspired to the same degree.

Dictation Inspiration

This false theory holds that every word of Scripture was dictated by God and that the Bible writers recorded these words as a stenographer would do.

My objections to this theory are that it does not account for the characteristic style of the Bible writers and that dictation does not protect one from error in hearing and recording words. *The true view* of divine inspiration is that the Holy Spirit prepared these writers for their work and then incorporated their literary style, vocabulary, individuality, intelligence, and temperament in producing through them the very words of God. When portions of the Bible were dictated in their production, divine inspiration governed both speaker and writer (cp. Jer. 36:4; Rom. 16:22).

THE TRUE VIEW OF INSPIRATION

Although this has been briefly stated under false theories of inspiration, the true doctrine of divine inspiration may be summarized as follows: *The Scriptures* are inspired in the sense that they are the product of God's breath, that is, a special work of the Holy Spirit (2 Tim. 3:16). *The speakers and writers of God's words* were inspired in the sense that they were acted upon by the Holy Spirit to produce through them God's truth in human language (2 Peter 1:21; cp. Num. 23:12; Deut. 18:18; 2 Sam. 23:2). Let us look more closely at what the divine inspiration of the Scriptures is.

Definitions

Divine inspiration is the activity of the Holy Spirit whereby He enabled certain people to receive God's special revelation and to speak it or to write it without error or omission in their language and style as the very words of God (2 Peter 1:21).

Plenary inspiration means that every part of the sixty-six canonical books of the Bible was the product of divine inspiration to an equal degree (2 Tim. 3:16).

Verbal inspiration means that divine inspiration extended to every word of the Scriptures and to its grammatical form (cp. Gal. 3:16).

Observations

One: Relating only to the original production of the Scriptures, divine inspiration is concerned with only the original utterances and writings of God's spokesmen and writers. Copies and translations of the original Scriptures contain errors (see "The Accuracy of the Original Writings" in this chapter).

Two: Divine inspiration, concerns God's spokesmen only when they spoke or wrote

His words under the influence of the Holy Spirit. It does not relate to their other actions and words of life (cp. 2 Sam. 7:3).

Three: Under divine inspiration the speakers and writers of God's Word were kept not only from every error of communication but also from any omission. Their utterances and writings were complete and accurate within their divinely determined limits. Also, they did not say or write more than what God intended for them to.

Four: While God did not approve every action or statement of angels and humans recorded in the Scriptures, divine inspiration secured an accurate (inerrant) biblical record of their actions and utterances (cp. Gen. 3:4).

Five: Our inability to understand how the Holy Spirit used fallible people to produce an inerrant record is not sufficient reason to deny His ability to do this and the fact that He did do this. Indeed, we do not fully understand any work of the Holy Spirit.

Six: Because of the sufficiency of the Bible for belief and conduct and the statements of Proverbs 30:5–6; 1 Corinthians 13:8; and Revelation 22:18–19, I believe that no special revelation has been given since the close of the New Testament Canon at the end of the first century. Consisting of sixty-six canonical books, the Bible is the complete written revelation of God. It is noteworthy that the world's religions and cults are doctrinally based on alleged extra revelation, in addition to the Bible (e.g. *The Book of Mormon*) or in place of the Bible (e.g. *The Koran*).

Seven: The Bible teaches that all divine special revelation has its source in the Father (Rev. 1:1), is transmitted through the agency of the Son (Rev. 1:1; John 1:1; Matt. 11:27), and is clothed in human language by the Holy Spirit's activity upon people (1 Cor. 2:13; 2 Peter 1:21) who were God's spokesmen (Deut. 18:18; Heb. 1:1–2). As the Revelator of the Father (Matt. 11:27), the Lord Jesus not only spoke the Father's words but also manifested by His earthly life and ministry the Father's character and works (John 12:49–50; 1:14; 14:9–11). Furthermore, having received the NT revelation from the Father, He conveyed it to His apostles and their associates by the Holy Spirit (John 16:13–15; 1 Cor. 2:13; Eph. 4:20–21; Rev. 1:1).

Eight: God rarely spoke through unsaved people (2 Chron. 35:21–22; John 11:49–51).

THE BIBLE'S TESTIMONY TO ITS OWN INSPIRATION

In addition to the confirmation of Christian experience, there is the witness of the Scriptures to their divine inspiration (2 Tim. 3:16).

The Inspiration of the Old Testament

Although not every book in the Old Testament bears specific witness to its divine inspiration, each one belongs to an OT section that does give this testimony. Following the arrangement of the Hebrew Old Testament *(Tenach),* there are three of these OT sections (Luke 24:44): *one,* the Law *(Torah),* consisting of the five books of Moses (the Pentateuch); *two,* the Prophets *(Naviim),* consisting of the "Early Prophets" (Joshua, Judges, 1 and 2 Samuel, and 1 and 2 Kings) and the "Latter Prophets" (Isaiah, Jeremiah, Ezekiel, and the Twelve Minor Prophets); and *three,* the Writings *(Kethubim),* consisting of poetical books—Psalms, Proverbs, and Job; the rolls—Song of Solomon, Ruth, Lamentations, Ecclesiastes, and Esther as well as the remaining historical books—Daniel, Ezra, Nehemiah, and 1 and 2 Chronicles.

This arrangement appears to be based on the prophetic rank of the writer. First, there are the writings of Moses, who was the greatest of the OT prophets, for the Lord spoke to him face to face (Exod. 33:11; Num. 12:7–8; Deut. 34:10). Next, there are the writings of those who were vocational prophets, like Isaiah and Jonah. Finally, there are the writings of those who had the prophetic gift but who followed other careers, like David and Daniel.

1. The testimony of Old Testament writers

Certain writers of each section of the Hebrew Old Testament bore witness to their divine inspiration: the Law (Exod. 20:1; 32:16; Lev. 27:34; Num. 36:13), the Prophets (Josh. 24:26–27; 1 Sam. 3:18–19; Isa. 1:1–2; Jer. 1:1–2; Ezek. 1:3), and the Writings (Ps. 45:1; Eccl. 1:16; 12:9). They also regarded other portions of the Old Testament as being divinely inspired: the Law (1 Kings 2:3), the Prophets (Neh. 9:20; Dan. 9:2, 10), and the Writings (2 Sam. 23:2; 1 Kings 4:29–32).

2. The testimony of Jesus

The Lord's regard for the Old Testament is a powerful witness to its divine inspiration.

a. He recognized the whole Old Testament (John 5:39; Luke 24:44–46) as well as its three primary sections as Scripture (Mark 7:8–13; Matt. 13:13–14; John 10:34–35).

b. In His recorded utterances, there are references to fourteen OT books: Genesis (Mark 10:6–8), Exodus (Luke 18:20), Numbers (John 3:14), Leviticus and Deuteronomy (Luke 10:26–28), 1 Samuel (Mark 2:25), 1 Kings (Matt. 12:42), Psalms (Mark 12:10), Isaiah (Luke 4:17–21), Daniel (Matt. 24:15), Hosea (9:13), Jonah (12:40), Zechariah (26:31), and Malachi (11:10).

c. He believed the historicity of such persons and events as Abel (Luke 11:51), Noah and the Flood (Matt. 24:37–39), Moses (John 3:14), David (Luke 20:41), Jonah and the fish (Matt. 12:40), man's creation and the divine institution of marriage (19:4–7), and the prophet Daniel (24:15).

d. He readily submitted Himself to the authority of the Old Testament (Matt. 5:17; 26:54; Luke 18:31). Although He broke scribal traditional law when it conflicted with the Father's will for Him (cp. John 9:16), He never violated God's law as given in the Old Testament (Matt. 3:17; 5:17; 17:5; John 8:29).

e. He had complete trust in the writings and teachings of the Old Testament. This is indicated by His appealing to them for God's will when He was tempted (Matt. 4:4, 7, 10), His referring to God's statement regarding marriage (Matt. 19:4–6), and His argument for the doctrine of the resurrection (Matt. 22:29–32).

f. He declared that the Scriptures could not be broken (John 10:35). In context, the Lord said that the Scriptures (Ps. 82:6), which He identified as the Word of God, could not be annulled as though its declarations were untrue.

3. The testimony of New Testament writers

In addition to the witness of Jesus in the Gospels, several NT writers gave evidence for the divine inspiration of the Old Testament.

a. They quoted from or alluded to all the OT books, except the Song of Solomon.[8]

b. They called the Old Testament "the Scriptures" (Luke 24:27, 44–45; Acts 17:11; 18:24; Rom. 1:2), even asserting that the Scriptures are "God-breathed" (2 Tim. 3:16).

c. They referred to each section of the Hebrew Old Testament as being God's Word: the Law (Rom. 10:5–7, 17), the Prophets (9:25; Heb. 10:15), and the Writings (Acts 1:15–16; 4:24–26).

d. The writer of Hebrews attributed to the Holy Spirit the authorship of two of his quoted OT portions (Heb. 3:7 with Ps. 95:7–11; Heb. 10:15 with Jer. 31:33).

The Inspiration of the New Testament

The divine inspiration of the NT books rests upon the authority of Christ and that which He delegated to His apostles (John 3:34–35; 12:49–50; Rom. 12:3; 15:15–16; 1 Cor. 14:37; 2 Cor. 5:20; 13:10; Gal. 1:1, 11–12; 1 Thess. 5:27; 2 Peter 3:1–2). Our Lord testified to

His own prophetic ministry (John 3:11, 34; 7:15–17; 8:28; 12:49–50; 14:10, 24). His apostles regarded their message as being from God (Gal. 1:11–12; Acts 1:2–3), as being the Word of God (1 Peter 1:25; 1 Thess. 2:13), and as being equal to that of the OT prophets (2 Peter 3:1–2). With this in view, let us examine the testimonies of Jesus and of His apostles regarding the NT writings.

1. The testimony of Jesus

Jesus anticipated His giving the New Testament revelation when He spoke to His apostles about His later communicating to them "many things" that they could not then bear (John 16:12–15). He indicated that He would do this by the Holy Spirit, to whom He would give the truth that He Himself would receive from the Father. That the New Testament had its origin in our Lord's prophetic ministry is further suggested by Acts 1:1; Ephesians 4:20–21; and Revelation 1:1–2. Upon His return to heaven, the Lord Jesus received the NT Scriptures from the Father, and by the Holy Spirit's inspiration He communicated portions of these to His apostles (Matthew, John, Peter, and Paul), to their associates (Mark and Luke), and to His half-brothers (James and Jude).

2. The testimony of New Testament writers

The apostle John testified to the divine inspiration of his writings in John 21:24; 1 John 5:6–13; 2 John 4; and Revelation 1:1–2; 21:5; 22:9. The apostle Paul bore witness to the divine inspiration of his own writings in 1 Thessalonians 4:2, 15; 1 Corinthians 2:13; 14:37; and 2 Corinthians 2:17, and to Luke's writings in 1 Timothy 5:18 (cp. Luke 10:7 with Deut. 25:4). Also, the apostle Peter spoke of the divine inspiration of his writings in 2 Peter 3:1–2 and of the apostle Paul's writings in 2 Peter 3:15–16. Finally, Jude testified to the divine inspiration of the apostle Peter's writings in verses 17 and 18 (cp. 2 Peter 3:5).

This witness to the divine inspiration of the Bible may not be convincing to unsaved people, whose understanding is affected by their sinful state and by their bent toward protecting their autonomy (independence of God) and philosophy (cp. Rom. 1:18; 8:7; John 3:19–20; 5:40; 1 Cor. 2:14). However, to those of us who are saved, it is sufficient for our belief and conduct (Ps. 119:105; 2 Tim. 3:15–17).

THE ACCURACY OF THE BIBLE

The diversity of texts among the translations and editions of the Scriptures that we have and among the original language copies that are extant raises questions about their accuracy. In our consideration of this theme, we must distinguish between the original Scriptures, all of which were inerrantly produced by divine inspiration and none of which we have today, and the copies and translations of the original Scriptures, which we have in abundance.

DEFINITIONS

Biblical accuracy is usually expressed by the adjectives "inerrant" and "infallible." While these are often used synonymously, there is a difference in their meaning. "Inerrant" emphasizes the absence of errors, while "infallible" emphasizes the incapability of making mistakes or errors, as in the revelation of spiritual truth or the biblical definition of doctrine.

Biblical Inerrancy

This is that quality of the original Scriptures, or autographs, that describes them as being without error in their recording of facts and in the inspired utterances and writings of God's spokesmen.

Biblical Infallibility

This is that quality of the original Scriptures that describes them as being without error in their record of the utterances, events, and facts of sacred history and in their intrinsic teachings. This asserts that all biblical teachings, based on the inerrant original Scriptures, are true and reliable.

THE ACCURACY OF THE ORIGINAL WRITINGS

The Bible Teaches Its Inerrancy
1. God is true, or real (John 7:28; 8:26).
2. God never lies (Titus 1:2; Rom. 3:4; Heb. 6:18).
3. God produced the Scriptures (2 Tim. 3:16).
4. The Lord Jesus is truth (John 14:6), bears witness to truth (John 8:14), and speaks truth (John 8:40).
5. The Holy Spirit, who enabled the original Scripture authors to write without omission or error (2 Peter 1:21), is the Spirit of Truth (John 14:17; 15:26; 16:13) and not a lie (1 John 2:27).
6. God's Word is truth (John 17:17), true (Ps. 119:160), perfect (Ps. 19:7), and pure (Prov. 30:5).

Jesus Affirmed This
Having thorough knowledge and understanding of God's Word,
1. He appealed to the Scriptures (Matt. 4:1–11; Luke 20:37–38; John 5:45–47).
2. He submitted to the Scriptures' authority (Matt. 5:17; Luke 4:18–19; 18:31).
3. He declared that the Scriptures are true (John 17:17) and cannot be broken (John 10:35).

Divine Inspiration Assured This

Both inerrancy and infallibility were rooted in the divine inspiration of the original Scriptures (2 Tim. 3:16; 2 Peter 1:21). This was that special work of God the Holy Spirit whereby He acted upon fallible people in such a way that He secured by them God's very words in human language. He enabled these people to receive the divine revelation and to convey it orally or to record it manually without error or omission as the very Word of God. Since divine inspiration relates only to the original production of God's Word (2 Tim. 3:16; 2 Peter 1:21), absolute inerrancy can be asserted only of the original writings of Scripture.

ERRORS IN PRESENT EDITIONS OF THE BIBLE

Despite the fact of the absolute inerrancy of the original writings of Scripture, it is recognized that changes and errors have intentionally and unintentionally entered the biblical text in its reproduction and translation.[9] For instance, there are two hundred thousand variant readings in five thousand Greek NT manuscripts, most of which concern word order, spelling, and the like. However, a study of this manuscript evidence reveals what most of the underlying text was. A hundred years ago only a thousandth part of the Greek New Testament was in question.[10] That most of these scribal changes and errors are known today and none affect primary biblical doctrine assures us of the reliability of present, unbiased, standard editions of the Scriptures. Thus, insofar as present standard editions of the Bible accurately represent the original writings, they are the Word of God and to this extent they are infallible and authoritative in their teachings and commands. Examples of copy and translation error and bias, as found in the King James Version, follow:

Real Errors and Biases

1. Scribal error

These are errors that entered the text of Scripture when it was copied, either from dictation of words that sound alike or from copying words or sentence endings that look alike (e.g. 2 Chron. 36:9 with 2 Kings 24:8, "eight" for "eighteen").

2. Translation bias

Any translation to some extent reflects the doctrinal views of the translator. Thus we find in Acts 2:38 the Anglican preference for baptism as being "for the remission of sins" rather than my preference "because of the remission of sins." The Greek preposition *eis* may be translated either way (cp. Matt. 12:41, KJV "at").

3. Printer error

An example of this is in Matthew 23:24, where we find "at" for "out."

4. Recited error

Under divine inspiration these were intentionally and inerrantly recorded in the Scriptures like lies (Gen. 3:4; 2 Kings 5:22), false charges (Job 22:5–11), wrong evaluations (Luke 7:39) and the like.

Apparent Errors or Difficulties

These are not proven errors but difficulties due to our lack of knowledge to resolve them or to our effort to accommodate Scripture to the opinions of men. Scholars who hold the inerrancy of the Scriptures have adequately answered the critics' objections and have demonstrated that there is no actual contradiction in the Scriptures.[11] Note the difficulties in the following areas:

1. Seeming contradictions

Proverbs 26:4–5. It is unprofitable to argue with a fool on his own level, yet there are times when he needs to be shown that he is a fool.

2. Chronology

Daniel 1:1 with Jeremiah 25:1. Possibly Daniel was using Babylonian reckoning of time.

3. Large numbers

See Numbers 2:32. Israel multiplied under repressive measures despite the Egyptians' attempts to check the male population (Exod. 1:12, 18). The Hebrew word *elaph,* meaning one thousand, also means "family" (Judg. 6:15) and "chief " (Zech. 9:7; 12:5–6). Without vowel pointing, it can be confused with *alluph,* meaning "chieftain" or "commander" of one thousand (Gen. 36:15–43). Judges 20:2 may refer to four hundred professional soldiers. Discrepancies between parallel passages may be due to scribal error (2 Chron. 36:9 with 2 Kings 24:8; 2 Sam. 10:18 with 1 Chron. 19:18). See also 2 Samuel 15:7 (Gk. LXX reads "four" for "forty").

4. Historical references

Second Kings 17:5–6 implies that Shalmanezer took Samaria. However, Assyrian records show that Samaria fell to Sargon II. Either Shalmanezer died while the siege of Samaria was in progress or Sargon's remarks refer to another time.

5. Moral issues

People's sinful acts were recorded, like Noah's drunkenness (Gen. 9:20–27), but these were not divinely approved. Rahab's faith, not her deceitfulness (Josh. 2:1–24), was commended (Heb. 11:31; James 2:25). Some things, like multiple wives (Gen. 29:16–28) and divorce (Deut. 24:1; Matt. 19:3–9), were permitted in pre-Christian times, but these were not God's ideal for His people (Matt. 19:4–6, 8).

6. *Statements in the Gospels*

Written by different men from different perspectives, yet under the influence of the Holy Spirit, the four Gospels do not all contain the same material. For an example, compare Luke 18:35 with Matthew 20:29. Perhaps the beggars were between the sites of ancient Jericho and the newer Roman Jericho.

7. *Old Testament quotations given in the New Testament*

As to their use of the Hebrew OT text, the NT writers were often divinely led to quote from the Greek translation of the Old Testament (*LXX,* Rom. 10:11 with Isa. 28:16), to paraphrase the quotation (1 Cor. 2:9), or to allude to it without quoting it (2 Cor. 4:6). Being directed by the Holy Spirit, they modified these references as He directed them.

8. *Conflict with scientific opinion*

Scientific opinion is based on people's assumptions of what they think is true and upon their interpretation of facts, guided by these assumptions. We cannot expect scientific opinion, which is based on observation, speculation, and experimentation, to be accurate regarding metaphysical matters. Science and its tools cannot deal with things like the creation of the universe or the existence of God. Only God's Word addresses these matters with authority and accuracy.

Regarding the conflict between statements of the Bible and the findings of scientists, E. J. Young wrote, "This does not mean that there are no problems; nor does it mean that the answer to every difficulty is immediately apparent. It does mean, however, that there are no actual contradictions. It is incumbent upon those who contend for the presence of actual errors in Scripture to prove their assertion. Merely to point out difficulties in the Bible will not suffice."[12]

The Holy Spirit has so overruled the transmission and translation of the Scriptures that present standard editions of the Bible are accurate in their teachings and serve God's purpose for His people (2 Tim. 3:15–17). We can unhesitatingly say that we have the Word of God insofar as these editions convey the truth of the original writings. The abundance of manuscript evidence indicates sufficiently what the divinely inspired original writings were so that present standard editions of the Scriptures give us a text that is trustworthy and authoritative.[13]

THE AUTHORITY OF THE BIBLE

Springing from the truth of the Bible's divine inspiration is that of its authority. Since the Scriptures are God's Word, they inherently possess His authority as His speaking.

ITS DEFINITION

The authority of the Bible has been described as that property by which the Scriptures demand faith in and obedience to all their declarations.[14] Being God's Word, the Scriptures inherently possess the right to command and to enforce obedience to their revelation of the divine will for mankind, both unsaved and saved peoples. This right is the Bible's authority.

ITS EVIDENCE

The fact of the Bible's authority is seen in the following:

The Divine Character of the Bible

Being God's Word, the Bible possesses many divine attributes (cp. Pss. 19:7–9; 119:39, 43, 62, 86, 89; John 17:17; Heb. 4:12; 1 Peter 1:25) and is involved in God's works (Ps. 33:6, 9; Heb. 4:12; John 5:45; 12:48; 2 Tim. 3:15; 1 Peter 1:23).

The Divine Inspiration of the Bible

Being the divinely inspired Word of God, the Bible is God's authoritative communication to man (2 Tim. 3:16; Heb. 1:1–2). This authority is manifest in the Old Testament by the recurring phrase, "Thus saith the LORD." It is also manifest in the New Testament by the authority expressed by Jesus' utterances (Matt. 11:27; 7:28–29; John 12:49–50) and by His apostles, who spoke in His name as His official representatives (John 20:21–23; Matt. 28:18–20; 1 Thess. 2:13; 2 Peter 3:2; Rev. 21:5).

The Submission of Jesus to the Scriptures

Although the Lord possessed all authority (Matt. 28:18), exercised authority (Luke 4:33–36), and taught with authority (Matt. 7:28–29), He appealed to the authority of the OT Scriptures (John 5:45–47; Matt. 23:23). He also submitted Himself to their authority during His earthly lifetime and in His messianic work (cp. Matt. 5:17; 26:52–56; Luke 18:31–33; 24:44).

The Recognition of the Lord's Apostles

The Lord's apostles recognized the authority of the Scriptures, both of the Old Testament (2 Tim. 3:16; Acts 2:14–36; Rom. 3:9–22) and of the New Testament (1 Thess. 2:13; 2 Peter 3:2).

ITS APPLICATION

This authority applies to all the areas of which the Bible speaks. It is the final authority in matters of history and science as well as belief and conduct. Since the Scriptures authoritatively express God's truth and His will for everyone, it is people's duty to learn this truth and to submit themselves to His will by believing and obeying His Word (see "The Dispensations of God" under Theology Proper). This response to God's Word exhibits our love for Him (John 14:15, 21, 23).

THE CANONICITY OF THE BIBLE

Canonicity concerns the right of any literature to be accepted as the Word of God. *Canon* refers, *one,* to the *standard* that a literary work must meet before it is recognized by God's people as Scripture and, *two,* to the *collection of books* that meet this standard. Let us consider in reverse order these two ideas that are associated with canon.[15]

THE FORMATION OF THE CANON OF SCRIPTURE

Here we are thinking of *canon* as a collection of books—the sixty-six books that comprise the Bible. The formation of the canons of the Old and New Testaments consisted of the production of their books by divine inspiration, these books being recognized by God's people as His Word, and their being gathered together into a collection.

The Old Testament Canon

As these thirty-nine books were written, they were immediately recognized as being inspired of God and were deposited at the side of the ark of the covenant, first in the tabernacle and later in the temple, along with the accumulative store of holy writings (Deut. 17:18; 31:9, 24–26; 1 Sam. 10:25; 2 Kings 22:8; 2 Chron. 34:14). The priests of Israel cared for these sacred writings and made new copies when they were needed (Deut. 17:18).

When the temple in Jerusalem was destroyed in 587 B.C ., the holy writings were carried to Babylon (cp. Dan. 9:2). Later, they were restored to their place in the second temple in Jerusalem (cp. Ezra 7:6; Neh. 8:1; Jer. 27:21–22).

Beginning with the writings of Moses, c. 1491 B.C., the Old Testament Canon was completed about 399 B.C., with Nehemiah and Malachi being the last to write. There was no further prophetic voice heard in Israel until that of John the Baptizer, c. A.D. 26 (Luke 3:1–2).

427 YRS. WITH NO WRITINGS PROPHECY
446 YRS. w/o WRITINGS

The New Testament Canon

Since there was no central place where these books were kept, the extent of their collection varied in different localities. The New Testament Canon closed with the writings of the apostle John at the end of the first century, but it was not until the fifth century that the whole New Testament Canon of twenty-seven books was universally received by the churches. This was due, in part, to the slow circulation of these books and to the wide distribution of Christian churches. In the West the canonicity of Hebrews was debated because of its uncertain authorship. In the East there was opposition to Revelation, because its authorship was questioned and its millennialism was challenged. In the West the Synods of Hippo (393) and of Carthage (397) recognized the canonicity of the twenty-seven books of the New Testament. The matter was settled in the East later.

Several factors helped to form the New Testament Canon: *one,* the influence of the incomplete canon of the heretic, Marcion, a native of Asia Minor who went to Rome in A.D. 140; *two,* the appearance of a number of noncanonical writings (see Appendix T: "Classes of Books Relating to the Biblical Period") that were held by many to be canonical; and *three,* the edict of the Roman Emperor Diocletian (303), ordering the Scriptures to be destroyed. This led to the sifting of the books that were to be preserved. Influenced by these factors, the early Christian believers were motivated to judge what literature was truly inspired of God.

THE TESTS OF CANONICITY

Throughout the time when the canonical books of the Bible were written and afterward, other literature was produced that some people regarded to be the Word of God (cp. Luke 1:1–3; 2 Thess. 2:1–5; see Appendix T: "Classes of Books Relating to the Biblical Period"). This led godly gospel believers to develop certain tests, based on the canonical books of the Bible, by which to judge the validity of these claims. Observe that the application of these tests does not impart canonicity, for the canonicity of any sacred literature is inherent, being determined by God. However, these tests enable people to recognize whether or not any other literature, alleged to be Scripture, is truly canonical. These tests follow in question form:

The Test of Divine Inspiration

Does the book claim to be divinely inspired? Is there any evidence of its inspiration?

The Test of Human Authorship

Is the book written, edited, or endorsed by an accredited agent of God, like a prophet, the Lord Jesus Christ, or one of His apostles? If not, did the writer have the gift of prophecy, like David and Daniel, or a relation to a prophet or an apostle, like Mark and Luke, that would raise his book to the level of their writings?

The Test of Genuineness

Can the book be traced back to the time and/or the writer from whom it professes to have come? This concerns the manuscript evidence for the book. Can the book be shown to have content that agrees with the time of which it speaks or in which it is alleged to have been written? This concerns the book's historicity. Archaeological discovery has revealed much about the history and culture of biblical times and has repeatedly shown the agreement of these features with the Bible.

The Test of Authenticity

Is the book factually true? It is noteworthy that Bible authors did not use the false philosophical and scientific opinions of their times. But they sometimes used popular expressions that are universally understood (cp. Isa. 11:12).

The Test of Testimony   NT recognized early on

Was the book universally recognized by the Jews and/or by the Christian church as being God's Word? Does the Holy Spirit bear inner witness to the born-again reader that the book is God's Word?

The Test of Authority

Does the book authoritatively demand faith in and obedience to its declarations? "Thus saith the LORD" and the like occur about 3,800 times in the Old Testament.

The Test of Agreement

Does the book agree doctrinally with the teachings of known canonical books? While there is progression in the Bible's revelation of doctrine, there is no positive contradiction.

The Test of Fulfillment

Is there any evidence in history or in the known canonical books for the fulfillment of this book's promises or predictions?

The Test of Endurance

Does the book convey God's message to each generation of His people in a fresh, living way (cp. 1 Peter 1:23–25)?

The Test of Spirituality

Is the content of the book of such spiritual character that it is in harmony with the dignity and majesty of God? Even those passages that deal with sexual sins do so in a way that shows the evil nature of these sins without titillating the normal reader.

May I repeat again that these tests are based on what is known of the sixty-six canonical books of the Bible. When these tests are applied to ancient or current noncanonical literature that asserts to be divine revelation, they readily show the falseness of its claim. They reveal that noncanonical literature does not meet the standard that is set by the Bible. Any literature that does not meet this standard is not God's Word.

The religious liberal's charge that we who believe the Bible to be God's Word are "bibliolaters," or Bible worshipers, is not true. We worship the God of the Bible, who has spoken this Word. "Bibliolatry" is not the problem with gospel believers that they who reject God and His Word imagine. The greater problem lies with those people who call God a liar (1 John 5:10).

We praise God for His self-revelation by the written Word. Like the psalmist of old, let us love God's Word and strive to meditate on the Scriptures day and night (Pss. 119:97; 1:1–2; cp. Col. 3:16). Besides teaching us about God and the way of salvation, they describe our spiritual resources, reveal His will, give us the object of practical faith, minister to our spiritual needs, and provide us the expectation of our glorious future (see under

Zoeology "The Maintenance of the Christian Life: The Bible"). All who do are blessed of God and lead productive lives (Luke 11:28; Ps. 1:3).

A Review of Bibliology

1. Essentially, what is the Bible?
2. What is the main subject of the Scriptures? How does the Bible present this?
3. Give the two major divisions of the Bible.
4. Why are these divisions named as they are?
5. Give the arrangement of the books of these two divisions.
6. What determined this arrangement?
7. Be ready to identify any biblical book according to the Bible's major divisions and the arrangement of each division (e.g., Romans: NT, teaching, Pauline, to churches).
8. Give the values of the Old Testament.
9. Give the values of the New Testament.
10. Why is the New Testament so important to gospel believers?
11. Briefly explain the terms *revelation, illumination,* and *inspiration.*
12. Briefly explain the false theories of biblical inspiration and give one objection to each theory.
13. Explain the divine inspiration of the Scriptures as indicated by 2 Timothy 3:16.
14. Explain the divine inspiration of the speakers and writers of God's Word as indicated by 2 Peter 1:21.
15. Define *verbal inspiration* and *plenary inspiration.*
16. What evidence is there for the divine inspiration of the Old Testament?
17. What evidence is there for the divine inspiration of the New Testament?
18. Explain the terms *inerrancy* and *infallibility* as they relate to the Bible.
19. To what extent are present-day standard translations of the Bible the Word of God?
20. What is the weakness of scientific opinion as this relates to metaphysical (spiritual) matters like the creation of the universe?
21. What is meant by Bible authority?
22. What makes the Bible authoritative?
23. In what ways did Jesus express His recognition of the Scriptures' authority?
24. What should our response be to the Bible's authority?
25. What is the meaning of *canonicity* and of *canon?*
26. Give the steps in the formation of the OT Canon.
27. During what time span were the OT books written?
28. Where were these OT books kept during this time?
29. Give the steps in the formation of the NT Canon.
30. During what time span were the NT books written?
31. Why did it take so long for the churches to agree upon the books of the NT Canon?
32. What leads us to believe that God is not giving us more Scripture today?
33. Give the tests of canonicity.
34. How were these tests devised?
35. If men did not impart canonicity to the Scriptures, what is its source?
36. Give the classes of books (canonical and noncanonical) that relate to the Old Testament Period (see Appendix T).
37. Give the classes of books (canonical and noncanonical) that relate to the New Testament Period (see Appendix T).
38. What is the value of this noncanonical literature?
39. Which of these noncanonical books are included in some versions of the Bible?

40. Why do we not accept this noncanonical literature as being God's Word?
41. Of what value are the Scriptures to the gospel believer?

Endnotes

1. The Lord Jesus' messianic work consists of all that He does as man in obedience to the Father and in the power of the Holy Spirit, including His atoning for sin, mediating the new covenant, saving gospel believers, building the Church, judging His enemies, and ruling over the earth (see "The Messianic Work of Jesus" under Christology).
2. God's covenants are His solemn declarations to certain people of what He promises to do for them. See "The Covenants of God" under Theology Proper.
3. See W. G. Scroggie, *The Unfolding Drama of Redemption* (London: Pickering & Inglis Ltd., 1953), 1:27. He places Job with the wisdom books, but later he says that it is "a poetical treatment of historical facts" (p. 93). "Legislative" refers to the giving of the Mosaic Law; "executive" to carrying out the law in the lives of the Israelites. The "major" and "minor" prophetic books are described as such for their length. For instance, in the KJV Daniel has 357 verses and Zechariah has 211 verses.
4. There are two kinds of prophecy that we must distinguish in our study: *One,* any communication from God by words through an inspired person (cp. Deut. 18:18; Heb. 1:1–2; 2 Peter 1:21) and, *two,* any prediction or vision about the future beyond the time of its being given. The prophetic books of the Old and New Testaments belong to the second as well as to the first of these kinds.
5. See F. F. Bruce, *The Books and the Parchments* (London: Pickering & Inglis Ltd., 1963), 107–13.
6. "Gospel" means "good news" about Jesus' earthly life and work, "epistles" are letters, and "churches" are local assemblies of professed gospel believers. "Prophecy" here includes both kinds: *one,* any communication from God by words through a divinely inspired person; and *two*, any prediction or vision that is given by God of future events.
7. Types are those OT persons, events, and things that portray NT truth. See F. H. Barackman, *How to Interpret the Bible* (Grand Rapids: Kregel Publications, 1991), 62ff.
8. Kurt Aland, Matthew Black, Bruce M. Metzger, and Allen Wikgren, eds., *The Greek New Testament* (London: United Bible Societies, 1966), 897ff.
9. See D. A. Carson, *The King James Version Debate* (Grand Rapids: Baker Book House, 1979), 21ff.
10. B. F. Wescott and F. J. A. Hort, *The New Testament in the Original Greek*, (New York: The Macmillan Co., 1941), 565.
11. See Gleason L. Archer, *Encyclopedia of Bible Difficulties* (Grand Rapids: Zondervan Publishing House, 1982).
12. M. C. Tenney, ed., *The Bible: The Living Word of Revelation* (Grand Rapids: Zondervan Publishing House, 1968), 109.
13. The accuracy of the Masoretic Hebrew OT text has been confirmed by the Dead Sea Scrolls. There are five thousand ancient copies of part of the Greek NT text, about fifty copies of the whole NT text, and eight thousand ancient copies in other languages. For standard English editions of the Bible, see Appendix Y: "The Kinds of English Bibles."
14. D. Martyn Lloyd-Jones, "The Authority of the Scriptures," *Eternity Magazine,* vol. 8, no. 4 (1957), 39.
15. *Canon,* derived from Heb. *qaneh* and Gk. *kanon,* was a reed, which was often used as a measuring rod; hence a rule or standard (Gal. 6:16), or limit (2 Cor. 10:13, 15–16).

Theology Proper

3

THEOLOGY PROPER
The Doctrine of God

We who are saved have the blessed privilege of knowing the one true and living God, who exists as three, eternal, simultaneous Persons. However, our knowing Him does not mean that we automatically understand Him.[1] Since He has been pleased to reveal some things about Himself in the Scriptures, it is our duty to search these out and to learn from them all that we can about Him. Before looking at the biblical doctrine about each Person of the divine Trinity, let us examine in this chapter the biblical truth that belongs to Them in common.

THE FACT OF GOD

People who believe in the existence of a god are theists in contrast to atheists, who do not believe that any god exists. Christian theists are people who believe in the true God, who has revealed Himself to mankind and who exists as three simultaneous Persons—the Father, the Son, and the Holy Spirit.

THE DEFINITION OF GOD

If by definition we mean a complete explanation of God, then He cannot be defined, for we who are finite cannot wholly explain the infinite One. On the other hand, God may be partly defined insofar as He has been pleased to reveal Himself.

When we define something, we may identify its *genus* (the kind of things to which it belongs) and describe its *differentiae* (its essential qualities, which distinguish it from all other members of its kind). For example, we may say that a stool belongs to the genus of seat and has qualities that distinguish it from the other kinds of seat like chair, bench, and recliner. While God is uniquely different from all the personal creatures whom He has made, we may say that, because He has personhood, His genus is Personal Being and that He is distinguished from other personal beings, like angels and humans, by those qualities that belong to His divine nature.

THE EXISTENCE OF GOD

How do we know that God exists? We cannot know this by the empirical evidence that the scientific method requires and that unsaved people demand (1 Cor. 2:9). The tools of science are not capable of detecting Him or other metaphysical (spiritual) realities like heaven and angels. We know of God's existence by His self-revelation by words and works (1 Cor. 2:10; see "The Revelation of God" in this chapter).

God's Self-Revelation by Words

Today, God's self-revelation by words is the Scriptures, which declare His existence. Assuming God's existence to be true, the Bible does not attempt to prove this by formal argument (Gen. 1:1). Actually, this kind of proof is unnecessary, for the Bible is God's Word (2 Tim. 3:16; cp. Heb. 1:1–2), and His creatures intuitively recognize His voice (Gen. 3:8; Rom. 1:18).

God's Self-Revelation by Works

This self-revelation is manifested by the universe that God has created and now governs. In Romans 1:18–20, the apostle Paul gives us several aspects of this witness of God's works to mankind.

1. God's witness of His existence to people's experience (Rom. 1:18)

God's dealing with unsaved people shows His existence. He deals with them in judgment (Rom. 1:18) as well as in beneficence (Matt. 5:45; Acts 14:17). Throughout history people everywhere have acknowledged God's hand upon them, thus, His existence (Exod. 12:31–33; Josh. 2:1–11; Dan. 4:34–37).

God's dealings with gospel believers also show His existence (cp. John 9:25). These dealings include His changing them (2 Cor. 5:17; Eph. 2:10; Col. 3:9–10), answering their prayers (John 14:13; Matt. 7:11), disciplining them (Heb. 12:6), caring for them (Matt. 10:29–31), and producing His moral character in their lives (Gal. 5:22–23).

2. God's witness of His existence to people's innate awareness (Rom. 1:19a)

People intuitively know of God's existence, for "that which may be known of God is manifest in them." Being made in His image, people are universally aware of the Creator's existence. This means that, apart from reason or sense perception, they have immediate, innate certitude of God's existence. Still, they do not know the Creator personally unless they have been born again, or saved (John 17:3). That people universally have this awareness is indicated by their impulse to worship one or more supreme beings or things (Acts 17:22–23).

3. God's witness of His existence to people's senses (Rom. 1:19b–20a)

The apostle Paul also declared that that which may be known of God has been shown to mankind (v. 19b). Although God is invisible, certain qualities of His nature "are clearly seen" (v. 20a). Everything in the universe that people can perceive with their senses has the impress of the Creator's handiwork upon it (Ps. 19:1) and bears witness to His power and deity (Rom. 1:20).

4. God's witness of His existence to people's reason (Rom. 1:20b)

The things that God has made not only bear witness of His existence to people's senses but also to their mind and reason (the process and conclusion of logical thinking). The apostle declared that the invisible things of God are "understood by the things that are made." Consider how this occurs in the following rational arguments for God's existence:

a. The cosmological argument

This points to an adequate Cause of all things. The existence of the universe requires a Creator as every house must have a builder (Heb. 3:4). Everything that makes up the universe is the result of a Cause that was sufficient to produce it. A product points to a producer.

Some say that the weakness of this argument is that the cause need not be omnipotent if the universe is finite. In reply, we observe that God's creating the universe instantly by command was an expression of infinite power. Opponents who reject God as the originating Cause of the universe say that matter is eternal and that the universe is a closed, self-contained, self-maintained, eternal system.

To the saved person the cosmological argument points to the conclusion that there is a Cause who is powerful enough to bring the universe immediately into existence and to sustain it. This Cause, we believe, is God. Declaring that the universe, excepting sin, was made by God, the Bible supports this conclusion (Gen. 1:1; Ps. 90:2).

b. The teleological argument

This points to an intelligent Cause. This argues from the design, order, and purpose that are manifest in the universe. These show an intelligent Creator who planned and constructed the universe.

Some say that the weakness of this argument is that the designer may be impersonal. Opponents to Christianity hold that design and order are products of evolutionary forces like chance mutation and natural selection. But the question remains, How can impersonal, chance forces produce a product that exhibits intelligence, design, order, and purpose, which these random forces themselves do not have? Everyone knows that these rational qualities belong to personal beings and are exhibited in their productions.

To the saved person the teleological argument points to the conclusion that the originating Cause of the universe possesses sufficient intelligence and purpose not only to devise but also to carry out His plan of creation. The Bible declares that this intelligent Cause is God (Pss. 19:1; 139:13–17).

c. The anthropological argument

This points to a personal Cause. This argues that humans' having personhood with self-awareness and moral self-determination points to a personal Creator who has these qualities.

Some say that the weakness of this argument is that this does not require a primary, personal cause but a personality producing force that need not be personal in itself. Opponents to the Bible believe that people's makeup is the product of chance, evolutionary development and that their idea of a god is the projection of their personality into infinity. Again, we who are saved assert that it has yet to be demonstrated that chance, impersonal forces can create personal beings. That personal beings produce personal beings is a daily occurrence on earth.

To the saved person, the anthropological argument points to the conclusion that the originating Cause of the universe is a personal, self-conscious, self-determining Being who is similar to mankind in His having personhood. The Bible supports this view with the revelation that this personal Cause exists as three divine Persons—the Father, the Son, and the Holy Spirit (Matt. 28:19)—and that God made man in His own image (Gen. 1:26–27).

d. The ontological argument

This reasons that since we have a concept of a perfect Being, this Being must exist. If He did not exist then He would not be perfect since existence is a quality of perfection.[2]

The weakness of this argument is that we cannot deduce real existence from abstract thought. The idea of God does not prove that He exists anymore than the idea of Martians proves that some kind of beings live on Mars. Opponents say that people cannot form a true conception of God.

To the saved person the ontological argument affirms that God is infinite and perfect, not because we can prove this but our mentality will not allow us to think otherwise.[3]

Observe that these four arguments do not prove with mathematical certainty the existence of God. But they do point to a superhuman Being whom Christians believe is the true God—the God of the Bible. While these arguments do not compel belief, they do give a rational explanation of our belief in God's existence (1 Peter 3:15; cp. Acts 14:15–17; 17:23–28).

God's self-revelation by means of His works is clear and efficient to the degree that all who do not respond to it in a suitable manner are without excuse (Rom. 1:20c; Acts 17:27). The problem is not people's ignorance of the Creator's existence but their unwillingness to accept this fact, which they innately know (John 3:19–20; 5:40; Rom. 3:11). Deceived by satanic philosophy and directed by rebellious hearts, unsaved people prefer to deny or to ignore the true God's existence rather than to acknowledge any responsibility to Him. Their hostility toward God is manifest in their attributing all things to chance or to false gods. But their course will bring them divine judgment (Acts 17:30–31; Rev. 20:11–15).

THE VARIOUS VIEWS OF GOD

Atheism
This denies the existence of God or of any gods.

Agnosticism
This holds that the existence and nature of God are unknown and unknowable.

Polytheism
This holds that there are many gods.

Zoroastrianism
This assumes that there are two distinct, eternal, irreducible realities—one good and the other evil, which oppose each other.

Pantheism
This believes that all things are merely aspects, modifications, or parts of the one eternal self-existing being or principle; that god is everything and everything is god.

Deism
This holds the existence of God but rejects His having any self-revelation or relation to the world. As pantheism accepts the immanence of God to the exclusion of His transcendence, so deism accepts the transcendence of God to the exclusion of His immanence (see "God's Attributes" in this chapter). For deism, God is like an absentee operator. Having made the universe as a vast machine, He allows it to run on its own by inherent natural law without His personal supervision. Deism claims that all truths are discoverable by reason and that the Bible is merely a book on the principles of natural religion, which are discernible by the light of nature.

Theism
This is the view that people hold who believe in a god.

Christian Theism
This is the view of us who believe in the true God as He is revealed in the Bible. In the following sections, we shall examine what God has revealed about Himself and about His relation to the universe.

THE REVELATION OF GOD

If God had not revealed Himself to mankind, there would be nothing that we would know or could say of Him. But, in His grace, He condescended to communicate truth about Himself, the universe, and mankind that could not be known in any other way. He did and is doing this by His works and words. James I. Packer wrote, "Revelation is a divine activity; not, therefore, a human achievement. Revelation is not the same thing as discovery or the dawning of insight or the emerging of a bright idea. Revelation does not mean man finding God, but God finding man, God sharing His secrets with us, God showing us Himself."[4]

ITS NECESSITY

God's self-revelation is necessary, for His transcendence (His being above the universe) makes Him inaccessible to His creatures unless He reveals Himself to them (Pss. 97:9; 113:4–6). Furthermore, the nature and state of mankind require God to take the initiative in His self-revelation if man is to know and worship Him. Let us look at people's need for divine revelation.

Mankind's Nature

By nature, humans are dependent creatures. This is in marked contrast to the self-existent Creator, who is infinitely greater and higher than mankind. Because of this, unaided people cannot see God (1 Tim. 6:16), find Him by searching (Job 23:3–9), or read His thoughts (Isa. 55:8). Even unfallen man required revelation of the divine will for his obedience to God (Gen. 2:16–17).

Mankind's State

Mankind's moral fall and subsequent sinful condition intensified their need for divine revelation, especially that which concerns salvation (2 Tim. 3:15), and for God to take the initiative in revealing Himself to them (cp. Luke 19:10; Gen. 3:8–9). Fallen people's powers of spiritual perception have been blinded by Satan (2 Cor. 4:3–4) and sin (1 Cor. 2:14; Eph. 4:17–19). Moreover, their minds are possessed by fanciful ideas that are nourished by Satan's lies and protected by humanistic assumptions (Rom. 1:21–25, 28; 1 Cor. 1:21). In fact, unsaved people suppress God's truth (Rom. 1:18), for being in rebellion against God, they do not want Him in their lives (John 3:19–20; 5:40; 12:37). But this spiritual state does not keep God from doing His sovereign work in the hearts of the elect, those people whom He has chosen to save (2 Cor. 4:3–6).

We who are saved have the desire and the ability to receive God's revelation and to profit from it (1 Cor. 2:9–12; Eph. 1:17–18; 4:23; Phil. 2:13). Therefore, we should strive to learn all that we can about our God and to respond to this truth in a manner that glorifies Him.

ITS KINDS

There are two kinds, or forms, of divine revelation: general and special. B. B. Warfield observed that these two kinds constitute a whole, each being incomplete without the other (cp. Ps. 19:1, 4 with v. 7):

> Without special revelation, general revelation would be for sinful men incomplete and ineffective, and could issue . . . only in leaving them without excuse (Rom. 1:20). Without general revelation, special revelation would lack that basis in the fundamental knowledge of God as mighty and wise, righteous and good, maker and ruler of all things, apart from which the further revelation of this great God's interventions in the world for the salvation of sinners could not be either intelligible, credible or operative.[5]

General Divine Revelation

General revelation is that communication that God makes continuously to all people by His works. This kind of revelation points to the existence of God and the creaturehood of man. Because of this revelation, the world is without excuse for its failure to acknowledge the true God, to seek Him, and to render to Him basic honors and service (Rom. 1:20; Acts 17:23–29).

1. Its means

God's general revelation is given by His works in His creating and governing the universe. His creating the universe manifests His eternality, power, divinity (Rom. 1:20), glory (Ps. 19:1), purpose (Rev. 4:11), wisdom (Ps. 136:5), and immensity (Isa. 66:1). God's government of the universe reveals His goodness in providing for man and beast (Act 14:17; Rom. 2:4; Ps. 104), His sovereignty in controlling nature (Job 38–41) and the affairs of men (Dan. 4:17), His holiness in expressing displeasure with wickedness (Rom. 1:18; 9:22; Ps. 9:16), and His mercy in dealing with His people (Rom. 9:15, 23; Ps. 103:13).

2. Its insufficiency

Contrary to the teaching of natural religion, general revelation is not in itself adequate to meet people's spiritual needs. It does not reveal God's will for them, particularly how they can become rightly related to their Creator and please Him. This does not imply that general revelation is defective, for it fulfills God's purpose in making known His existence to mankind and in showing their need to seek after the Creator, who visits sinners with terrible judgments. But general revelation does not show people everything that they should know about God and the universe. It says nothing about salvation for sinners and His will for His people.

3. Its effectiveness

The effectiveness of general revelation is seen in that all people are without excuse for their refusing to respond favorably to God's clear manifestation of Himself by the things He has made (Rom. 1:18–20). This favorable response includes fearing God, making an effort to seek Him out, and contacting Him (cp. Cornelius; Acts 10:22, 31).

Special Divine Revelation

Special revelation is that action by which God makes Himself known to people by some communication with them through personal manifestation and/or words. This completes general revelation by providing additional information about God and the universe, by making known God's will for mankind, and by revealing salvation through the Lord Jesus. While only the elect (those chosen to be saved) receive and understand God's revelation of words, as given in the gospel, God still has something to say to the nonelect by gospel appeals (Luke 24:47; Acts 17:30) and warnings of coming judgment (Acts 17:31; Rom. 2:3–9).

1. Its means

God has given special revelation in various ways throughout human history.

a. During the Old Testament period

During the early part of mankind's history, God spoke to people directly by voice alone (Gen. 3:8–9; 13:14), theophany (a visible manifestation of God's presence) and voice (Gen. 7:1; 18:13), dreams (Gen. 28:12–13), and wakeful visions (Gen. 46:1–4). Later on, God spoke indirectly through angels (Dan. 9:21; cp. Acts 7:53; Heb. 2:2) and human agents (Deut. 18:18; Jer. 18:18). Mankind's deteriorating spiritual condition may have required this. These human agents were the holy prophets (2 Peter 1:21; Heb. 1:1), the high priests of Israel (Num. 27:21), and certain wise men (Dan. 5:11; 1 Kings 3:5–12). It appears that the high priests received yes and no answers by the Urim and Thummim, which were carried in a pouch on their breastplate (Exod. 28:30; 1 Sam. 28:6). Such wise men as Solomon and Daniel had the prophetic gift, but they were not vocational prophets. In any case, all humans whom God used to make known His special revelation did so under divine inspiration (2 Peter 1:21).

b. During the New Testament period

During this time, God revealed Himself uniquely through the Lord Jesus Christ (Heb. 1:1–2; John 1:1, 14, 18; 1 Tim. 3:16). Unlike a temporary theophany, this special revelation was a permanent incarnation of God the Son. Assuming a complete, sinless human nature, the Lord Jesus revealed the Father by His holy character and moral excellence (John 1:14), His actions (John 14:8–10), His words (Heb. 1:2; John 3:34; 7:16–17; 8:26, 28, 38, 40; 12:49–50; 14:10, 24; 15:15; 17:8, 14), and His emotions (Mark 3:5; 10:21; Matt. 9:36). Although He was personally distinct from the Father, Jesus' life and ministry so manifested the Father that to see Him was to see the Father (John 14:9). Indeed, He was (and is) the Revelator of the Father (Matt. 11:27; John 1:18).

God also revealed Himself directly by dreams and visions (Matt. 1:20; 2:12, 22; Acts 9:4; 10:10–16; 22:17–18). Furthermore, He revealed Himself indirectly through His angelic servants (Rev. 1:1) and by Jesus' apostles and NT prophets through their utterances (Acts 13:1–3), teachings (1 Thess. 2:13; Eph. 4:20–21), and writings (John 16:12–15; 1 Cor. 2:10–13; Rev. 1:1–2).

c. Today

God is continuously revealing Himself in and through the sixty-six canonical books of the Bible. However, I do not believe that He has given any additional special revelation since the closing of the New Testament canon. More special revelation is not needed today since the Bible provides us with sufficient truth for our belief and conduct during the present dispensation (2 Tim. 3:16–17; see the warnings of Rev. 22:18–19; Deut. 4:2; Prov. 30:5–6; 1 John 4:1). More special revelation will be given during the Tribulation Age (Rev. 11:3) and the millennial Kingdom Age (Isa. 2:3; Joel 2:28).

It must be remembered that every religious or spiritual experience must be tested by the Scriptures to determine its spirituality and genuineness. These experiences are of God only so far as they conform to what the Bible teaches about their nature, content, and effect (see Matt. 5:16; John 3:21; 8:12; 15:5; Rom. 14:17; Eph. 5:8; Phil. 1:20–21; 1 John 1:7). Also, all literature that professes to be God's revelation must be judged by the tests of canonicity that are determined by the canonical books of the Bible (see "The Tests of Canonicity" under Bibliology). With the Bible in hand and the Holy Spirit filling our hearts, we who are saved can examine any alleged divine, special revelation and discern whether or not it is from God.[6]

2. Its aspects

God's special revelation has both active and passive aspects, as determined by its context. *Actively,* it is His communicating to mankind truth about Himself (cp. 1 Cor. 2:9–12). *Passively,* it is the truth about Himself that He communicates (cp. Rev. 1:1).

3. Its sufficiency

Complementing general revelation, special revelation completes God's self-disclosure by providing the truth that He would have people know and that general revelation does not give. Special revelation makes known God's gracious provision of salvation through Jesus (2 Tim. 3:15). It also provides the truth that His people need for their belief and conduct (2 Tim. 3:16–17). Furthermore, it explains more fully God's person and works as well as man's existence and world. God has not told us everything, but He has revealed what we need to know for obeying Him and for anticipating the future (cp. Deut. 29:29; John 14:1–3; 15:15; 1 Cor. 2:9–10; Rom. 15:13).

4. Its effectiveness

This is seen in the salvation of the elect (2 Tim. 3:15), their instruction in the things of God (2 Tim. 3:16–17), their sanctification in daily life (Ps. 119:11; John 15:3; Eph. 5:25–26), and their pleasing God (Heb. 11:5–6; 2 Cor. 5:9; 2 Tim. 4:6–8).

5. *Its reality*

Religious liberals deny the possibility of divine revelation in words, or what is called "propositional revelation." They hold that God's revelation cannot be expressed in human words or be inerrantly recorded by fallible men. They hold that God's revelation is non-verbal and existential, consisting of what one experiences in a personal, indescribable encounter with the Supreme Being. In reply, James I. Packer writes:

> Indeed, the Biblical position is that the mighty acts of God are not revelation to man at all, except so far as they are accompanied by the words of God to explain them. Leave man to guess God's mind and purpose, and he will guess wrong: he can know it only by being told it. Moreover, the whole purpose of God's mighty acts is to bring man to know Him by faith; and Scripture knows no foundation for faith but the spoken word of God, inviting our trust in Him on the basis of what He has done for us. Where there is no word from God, faith cannot be. . . . The need for verbal revelation appears most clearly when we consider the Person and work of Christ. His life and death were the clearest and fullest revelation of God that ever was or could be made. Yet it could never have been understood without explanation.[7]

Religious liberals and their theology ignore the work of the Holy Spirit in inspiration—His control in securing an inerrant, verbal record of God's special revelation through fallible men (2 Peter 1:21). They also ignore Hebrews 1:1–2, which describes God as speaking. God's special revelation is real, as the Bible shows and as countless numbers of people affirm. God has been pleased to reveal Himself by His works and by His words. Without this, there would be no way of our knowing that He exists and what He is.

THE NATURE OF GOD

Remembering our creaturehood, let us reverently seek to understand what God is and the kind of nature He has. Only the Holy Spirit can illuminate our hearts through the Scriptures regarding this deep truth, yet whatever He is pleased to teach us will be only a small part of what God is. If God were understood easily and fully, then He would be little more than what we are. But because He is limitless, we shall be learning about Him throughout eternity, as the experience of the holy angels indicates (Eph. 3:10; 1 Peter 1:10–12). However, it is important for us now to be learning all that is revealed about Him.

GOD'S CONSTITUTION

As incomprehensible as God's makeup is, it seems to consist of three personhoods with a single divine nature.

God Has Three Personhoods

God exists as three distinct, simultaneous Persons—the Father, the Son, and the Holy Spirit (Matt. 28:19), with each One possessing His separate personhood, which makes Him to be a person. Because personhood, in my opinion, is the divine image in humans, we have some concept of what this is and what some of its features are (see "The Nature of Mankind" under Anthropology).

The personhood of these divine Persons is indicated by Their having personal features like those that we find in ourselves. These include a unique selfhood with its self-awareness (Exod. 3:13–14; Lev. 11:44–45; Isa. 44:6; 45:22; 46:9) and self-determination—the ability to choose and direct one's affairs in a responsible way (Isa. 46:9–10; Rom. 11:33–34; Eph. 1:11), a sense of morality with its awareness of good and evil (Prov. 15:3; Rom. 2:5–6; 2 Tim. 2:13), and perpetuity (unending existence, cp. Ps. 102:12). Other features that often are attributed to personhood, like intelligence (Isa. 1:18; 55:9), emotion (John 3:16; Ps. 5:5), and the ability to communicate (Heb. 1:1–2) are not solely indicative of personhood since they belong to higher forms of animals as well as to personal beings.

God Has a Single Divine Nature

This single divine nature is that essence, with its qualities and powers, that makes the three Persons of the Trinity to be God.[8] The possession of the divine nature distinguishes God from other persons like angels and humans, who have their own distinctive natures. The substance of God's divine nature, which is uncreated and which underlies all His outward manifestations, is spirit (John 4:24). Being immaterial, this essential spirit is invisible (John 1:18; Col. 1:15; Heb. 11:27). In our thinking about this spirit nature, we must distinguish between the spirit substance, of which the divine nature consists, and the Holy Spirit, who is the Third Person of Trinity. Excepting John 4:24, all references to the divine Spirit in the Scriptures are to the Holy Spirit. Moreover, this divine spirit substance differs from angels, who are created spirits, and from the created human spirit, which is an essential part of man's makeup.

As we consider God's makeup, we must distinguish between the three personhoods and the one divine nature. There are three Persons—the Father, the Son, and the Holy Spirit, each of Whom possesses His own separate personhood. Each Person also possesses with the other Persons the one, undivided, divine nature. This makes each Person to be God, and Their sharing the one divine nature makes Them to be one God.

GOD'S ATTRIBUTES

Their Definition

God's attributes are those essential qualities that belong to the divine nature and that make the Persons of the divine Trinity to be the kind of Persons that They are. Although *perfections* may be a better term since *attributes* conveys the idea of assigning something to one, *attributes* is generally used. W. G. T. Shedd explained the relation between the divine nature and its attributes:

> The attributes are not parts of the essence, of which the latter is composed. The whole essence is in each attribute, and the attribute in the essence. We must not conceive of the essence as existing by itself, and prior to the attributes, and of the attributes as an addition to it. God is not essence and attributes, but in attributes. The attributes are essential qualities of God.[9]

For example, we must not think of God's nature as existing apart from His love or His love as something that is independent of Him and to which He must conform. Being a quality that is determined by His nature, divine love is what God is (1 John 4:8). On the other hand, He is much more than love, for no one attribute of His nature makes up the sum of what He is. He has, and therefore is, many other qualities as well.

Each attribute has its own sphere of expression within God's nature and does not modify or eclipse the other qualities that are present. Each one expresses itself freely and harmoniously with the others that belong to His nature. For example, in love the Lord Jesus wept over Jerusalem when He foresaw the judicial reaction of His holiness against the city's sins (Luke 19:41–44). His love did not stifle the judicial expression of His holiness, as later events have shown.

Their Classifications

Theologians have made various classifications of God's attributes: that based upon His moral qualities (moral and amoral), that based on His relation to the universe (absolute and relative, intransitive and transitive), and that based upon those qualities that He reproduces in personal creatures (communicable and incommunicable). In this survey of God's attributes, we shall not attempt to classify them formally.

God shares with His creatures only moral attributes like His love, righteousness, and holiness, which He reproduces in them. These were displayed in our Lord's human life (John 1:14) and are now reproduced in His people by the Holy Spirit (Gal. 5:22–23; Rom. 14:17; Heb. 12:10). We call the display of these qualities in our lives "godliness" and "Christlikeness," but our participation in these moral attributes does not make us to be God. We shall always be finite human beings, made morally and physically in the image of Jesus' glorified humanity (Phil. 3:21; 1 John 3:2).

Their Description

Although they are often listed as divine attributes, I do not consider *personality* and *spirituality* as belonging to these essential qualities of the divine nature. *Personality*, which I associate with personhood, is not a part of the divine nature. To my mind, personality is the total expression of one's personhood as it is affected by one's nature. Unlike love and holiness, *spirituality* is not an attribute of the divine nature. It describes God's nature as being spirit in substance. It has to do with the "stuff" of which the divine nature consists. Contrariwise, the divine nature does not essentially consist of love or holiness although it enables the Persons of the Trinity to express these qualities. Observe that, possessing the one divine nature, all three Persons of the divine Trinity have the same essential qualities to the same degree.

As we reflect upon these divine attributes, may God give us understanding and blessing. May this lead us to worship Him by giving Him praise for what He is.

1. Life *(the quality of being alive)*
   a. Function
      This quality makes God uniquely alive. Life itself is undefinable. We can describe what it does, but we cannot explain what it is.
   b. Comment
      1) God is alive (Jer. 10:10; 1 Thess. 1:9).
         He is alive in a way that nothing or no one else is. He is not only self-acting but also self-existent. This means that the ground of His activity and existence is wholly within Himself (John 5:26). He does not have need of or depend on anything outside Himself for His life (Acts 17:25). He is the "I AM" (Exod. 3:14).
      2) God is the source of all creatural life.
         (a) As the Creator of physical life
            All physical life has its source in God (Acts 17:25) and is maintained by Him (Job 12:10; 34:14–15). Thus as the Creator, God has an impersonal, metaphysical relationship with all His creatures.
         At creation, God gave all earthly creatures physical life (Gen. 1:21, 25–27; 2:7), which continues to be transmitted to their offspring by reproduction (Gen. 1:22, 28). Upon death all physical life that has its dynamic source in the spirit and soul of humans and animals (James 2:26; Gen. 35:18) returns to God (Eccl. 12:7; Job 34:14). We humans continue to

exist after our physical death (Heb. 12:22–23; Rev. 6:9–11) because of the perpetuity of our personhood. In time, the Holy Spirit will reanimate all human bodies with a new kind of life, by which they will ever be physically alive in the eternal state, whether in heaven or in hell (Rom. 8:11; 1 Cor. 15:44).

(b) As the Father of spiritual life

God the Father is the source of spiritual life (1 Peter 1:3), which in the Scriptures is called "everlasting life" and "eternal life." This is a new kind of life that He gives to all who trust in the Savior and His atoning work (1 John 5:11–12). Because of this paternity, God the Father has a personal, spiritual relationship with all saved people as their heavenly Father (Matt. 6:32; Gal. 3:26; 4:6). However, He is not our Father in the same way that He is the Father of God the Son. When He regenerated us, the Father did not impart to us His own inherent, divine nature with its divine life as He does to His Son and as we impart our human nature and life to our offspring. He is our Father in that He gave to us who are saved spiritual life. While God the Father is the source of this spiritual life (Rom. 6:23), the Lord Jesus is the expression and model of this new life (John 14:6; 1 Cor. 11:1). Also, the Holy Spirit is the imparter and energy of this new life (John 3:6; Gal. 5:25).

Spiritual life is more than everlasting existence. It brings to all who possess it new power (Phil. 4:13), new direction (2 Tim. 3:16–17), new purpose (1 Cor. 10:31), new knowledge (2:12), new associations (1 John 1:3), new character (Gal. 5:22–23), new desire (Phil. 2:13), new activity (Eph. 2:10; 5:17), new interests (Col. 3:1), new expectation (Titus 2:13), and new destination (Phil. 3:20–21).

We experience and manifest this new life by abiding in Jesus (John 15:4–5; Rom. 13:14) and by cooperating with the Holy Spirit (Gal. 5:22–23, 25; Eph. 5:18). These relationships require our submission, faith, and obedience.

2. *Unity (the quality of being one in number and parts)*

  a. *Function*

    1) This quality makes God to be one in singularity.

    This means that God is one in number. Having the one divine nature, the three Persons of the Trinity are one God, not three Gods (Deut. 6:4; 1 Tim. 2:5).

    2) This quality makes God to be one in simplicity.

    Being only spirit (John 4:24) and having no known essential parts, the divine nature is simple rather than complex. Also, it is undivided and indivisible.

  b. *Comment*

    1) God's singularity

    Israel worshiped the one, true God (Deut. 6:4). This was in striking contrast to their Canaanite neighbors, who honored ten gods. Unlike Israel, these pagans did not have one god who was big enough to look after all the needs of the universe. See Psalm 146:5–10.

    2) God's simplicity

    Having the divine nature that is spirit, the true God does not have parts as our human nature does. The biblical descriptions of God's human parts, actions, and characteristics are figurative expressions, called "anthropomorphisms" (Prov. 15:3; Jer. 9:20; 27:5; Isa. 42:1). These graphically convey truths about God with which we humans can identify and that we can understand.

    This singleness of the divine nature assures the unity and the equality of the three Persons of the Godhead in Their attributes and purpose (John 10:30, Gk. neuter gender, "one thing," not one person). Because They have the same qualities, powers, and purpose, all that is essentially true of one Person is also true of the Others. For example, while it is said that the Lord Jesus loves us (John 13:1; 15:9), the Father and the Holy Spirit also love us (John 14:21; Rom. 15:30). However, in Their dealings with the universe, these three Persons have different roles, or functions, as we shall see later.

(3.) *Immutability (the quality of being unchanging)*

    a. *Function*

    This quality makes God to be forever the same (Ps. 102:25–27).

    b. *Comment*

    Because of its immutability, God's nature never changes by development or degeneration as ours does. The qualities of God's nature are constant and eternal (James 1:17). Consequently, God is unchanging in His purpose, in His word, and in His attributes.

    1) In His purpose (Isa. 46:10)

    He will complete what He has planned to do. Also, He will never change His plan. This fact is challenged by God's repenting (a change of mind or attitude, leading to a change of action) on certain occasions (cp. Num. 23:19 with Gen. 6:6–7; Exod. 32:14; Amos 7:3). As Jonah 3:5–10 shows, when He repents, God responds differently towards people according to their change of attitude or behavior. Actually, this change in the divine response is not an essential change at all. Beneath this apparent change, God's nature and purpose always remain the same. It is man who changes in his attitudes and actions. God's responses to changeable people, whether in His acts of judgment or of mercy, always conform to His unchanging holiness and justice and follow a righteous course (cp. Rom. 9:14–18).

    2) In His word (Ps. 119:89)

    God does not and cannot lie (Num. 23:19; Titus 1:2). He freely fulfills His conditional promises when their requirements are met; He also fulfills all His unconditional promises. This truth provides the basis for our faith in Him, for His unchanging promises give us something to believe (Heb. 10:23).

    It is important to distinguish between those promises that are unconditional in their fulfillment and those that are conditional. God's keeping His conditional promises depends upon people's meeting the stated conditions. If they fail to do this, they will not experience what God has conditionally promised to do. God's immutability is seen in His abiding by the conditions of these promises.

    3) In His attributes (Mal. 3:6)

    The qualities of His unchanging nature are always the same. Because of this, God never changes.

    When God the Son assumed a created human nature, there was no change in His uncreated divine nature. He continues to possess all the unchanging attributes of Deity. United in His personhood, the divine nature and the human nature remain distinct, separate, and unmodified, making Him to be both wholly God and wholly man.

    God's immutability contributes to our stability (Ps. 102:28). He is always the same in loving His people and being with them, regardless of their circumstances (John 13:1; Isa. 41:10). Moreover, because He always hates sin and loves righteousness (Ps. 45:7), we can be assured that He will punish evildoers and will reward those who do His will (Rev. 3:19; 22:12).

(4.) *Infinity (the quality of being without limits)*

    a. *Function*

    This quality makes God to be without bounds in His nature and its attributes.

    b. *Comment*

    God's limitlessness is manifest qualitatively as perfection and quantitatively as fullness.

    1) *Qualitatively,* God is without limit in perfection or excellence.

    His qualities of nature are perfect in their character and expression (cp. Ps. 18:30;

Deut. 32:4; Isa. 40:25). They are free of any defect like a blemish or a lack of complete-ness. His excellence is a moral model for His people (Matt. 5:48; Eph. 5:1–2).

2) *Quantitatively,* God is without limit in fullness.

There is never any consumption or shortage of any of His attributes (Ps. 145:3). He always has a full, unlimited supply of each of these qualities. Because of this truth, God never tires or needs replenishment (Isa. 40:25–31). Thus He is able and willing to provide for our needs (John 7:37–39; James 1:17; 2 Peter 1:3).

5.) *Truthfulness (the quality of being true)*

    a. Function

This quality makes God to be true in His nature, words, and works.

    b. Comment

        1) The qualities of God's nature are genuine (John 17:3; 1 John 5:20).

He is everything that He has revealed Himself to be (Jer. 10:10). This is in contrast to false gods that differ from what they are alleged to be (Ps. 115:2–8).

        2) God's words are true (John 17:17).

His words are true in the sense that all that He says is factual and without error and all that He inspires men to speak or to write is without error. His words are absolutely trustworthy (Ps. 19:7–11). He cannot lie (Titus 1:2).

        3) God's works are real (Ps. 33:4; Rev. 15:3; 16:7).

All that He does is real. It is never deceptive, fraudulent, or something other than what He says about it or what it appears to be.

Daily, we should thank God for the privilege of knowing and belonging to Him—the true and living God. The true God deserves from His people more devotion, loyalty, and service than that which false gods receive from their followers (John 8:12). He is worthy of our complete commitment, obedience, and trust (Rom. 12:1–2; Gal. 2:20).

6.) *Faithfulness (the quality of being reliable and loyal)*

    a. Function

This quality makes God to be the worthy object of faith, for He is reliable in keeping His promises (Heb. 10:23) and loyal to His covenant people (Deut. 7:9).

    b. Comment

God is reliable in His declarations and promises (Num. 23:19; cp. 1 Thess. 5:24; 1 John 1:9).

        1) He will do what He says that He will do (Titus 1:2), for He cannot deny Him-self (2 Tim. 2:13) or lie (Titus 1:2). Review His great covenant promises (see "The Cov-enants of God" in this chapter). Again, observe the distinction between God's unconditional promises and His conditional ones. He does not keep His conditional promises without their conditions being fulfilled.

        2) God is loyal to His people (1 Cor. 1:9) in their trials (1 Cor. 10:13; 1 Peter 4:19), dangers (2 Thess. 3:3), and times of need (Heb. 2:17; 4:14–16).

As our Lord was faithful to the Father (Heb. 3:1–2; Rev. 19:11) so we who are saved should be faithful to God and to that which He has entrusted to our care and use (Luke 16:10–13; 1 Cor. 4:2).

7.) *Eternality (the quality of being infinite in duration)*

    a. Function

This quality makes God to be without beginning and without ending (Deut. 33:27; Isa. 57:15; Jer. 10:10).

    b. Comment

Time results from a succession of events.[10] It began with the creation of the uni-verse (Gen. 1:1–5) and will continue forever (Eph. 2:7, "ages").

1) From the divine standpoint, God is timeless, as His name "I AM" suggests (Exod. 3:14).

The whole of God's existence is one indivisible present (Ps. 90:4; 2 Peter 3:8). There is no succession of events among the Persons of the Trinity in their eternal internal relationships. On the other hand, God observes time in His dealings with the universe and its people and in carrying out His plan (Dan. 9:2, 24; Gal. 4:4; Acts 1:7). Being creatures who shall always experience the succession of events, humans will always be aware of time. We who are saved will ever be involved with the Father's future messianic programs for the Lord Jesus. These will consume time as the word "ages" in Ephesians 2:7 suggests.

2) From our time-conscious standpoint, God is endless (Ps. 90:2; Isa. 44:6; Rev. 1:8).

Existing from everlasting to everlasting, God is eternal. He has no beginning or ending.

God is sensitive to our restriction by time. He allows us enough time to do His will. What crowds us for time are those things that we take on that are in addition to or in place of His will for us (Matt. 6:34; Eph. 5:17; Rom. 13:11–14).

8. *Immensity (the quality of being spatially limitless)*

   a. *Function*

This quality makes God to be without measurable dimensions (1 Kings 8:27).

   b. *Comment*

Being spirit, God's nature is immeasurable. He cannot be contained in a box or be limited by a universe, regardless of their size (Isa. 66:1; Acts 7:48–49). This truth points to God's essential *transcendence,* which speaks of His being above, outside, separate from, and something other than the universe that He has created (Ps. 113:4–6).

Although He cannot be confined to our bodies, God is within us who are saved, for our bodies are His temples (1 Cor. 6:19). This truth should affect how we treat our bodies, where we go, and what we do. It should also encourage us when we desire to have something more or when we feel alone (Heb. 13:5–6).

9. *Omnipresence (the quality of being everywhere present)*

   a. *Function*

This quality enables God to be wholly present everywhere at once (Ps. 139:7–10).

   b. *Comment*

Although He transcends all spatial limitations, God is wholly present at every point in the universe simultaneously. This truth emphasizes His *immanence,* which speaks of His being everywhere present in the universe, although He is not a part of it or limited by it (Jer. 23:23–24). Unlike anything in this world, God's omnipresence does not occur by extension, multiplication, or division of the divine nature.

As a man the Lord Jesus is seated in heaven at the right hand of the Father (Heb. 1:3); as God He is present everywhere (Matt. 28:20). Although He dwells in heaven (Matt. 6:9), God is everywhere present, even in hades (Heb. *sheol*), which is in the heart of the earth (Ps. 139:8). By His presence and power He sustains and maintains the existence of all things and people outside Himself (Heb. 1:3; Col. 1:16–17).

While God is with all people metaphysically as their Creator, the Father, the Son, and the Holy Spirit have a personal relationship with each saved person as his Parent, Master, and Helper, respectively (1 John 1:7; see "Fellowship with God" in this chapter). We can be aware of God's presence intuitively by living in obedience to Him (John 14:21, 23), and rationally by claiming the promise of His presence (Isa. 41:10; Matt. 28:20).

10. *Omniscience (the quality of knowing everything)*
    a. *Function*
        This quality makes God to be fully aware of all things and gives Him complete understanding of everything.
    b. *Comment*
        Because of this quality God knows everything:
    Comprehensively, in that His knowledge embraces all knowable things, both actual and possible (Job 37:16). Regarding *actual things,* God knows all existing things in the past (Prov. 24:12), the present (Jer. 32:19; Prov. 15:3), and the future (Isa. 46:10). Regarding *possible things*, God knows all that is capable of existing or occurring but never does, for He has not decreed it (1 Sam. 23:12; Matt. 11:21, 23).
    Completely, in that He fully understands all that can be known about everything, like its nature, composition, condition, place, activity, needs, and relationships (Ps. 147:5).
    Independently, in that He never needs or receives information, as from an instructor or informer (Isa. 40:13–14).
    Simultaneously, in that He is aware of all things at once in their totality and in their every detail (Acts 15:18).
    Innately, in that His knowledge is inherent in His nature. It is not acquired by observation or reasoning (Isa. 65:24).
    God's *foreknowledge* (Acts 2:23; 1 Peter 1:2) is His knowledge of all actual things before they exist or come to pass. This foreknowledge is made certain, not by simple foresight but by the divine decree by which God has determined all existing things. His foreknowledge is equated with His *counsel* (plan or decree) in Acts 2:23.[11]
    As suggested by Romans 8:28–29, with "purpose" representing God's decree and preceding His "foreknowledge," the logical order of the components of His knowledge follows:

His Necessary →	*His Decree* →	*His Free Knowledge* →	*Reality*
Knowledge	His plan, embracing	His foreknowledge	The actual
Knowledge deter-	all actual things that	of all actual things,	things He
mined by His divine	He chose from all	determined freely by	brings to pass
nature, causing Him	possible things.	His decree without	or allows to
to know all possible		outside influence.	come to pass
things.			as He has
			decreed.

    Knowing all that can be known, God knows all about us—our thoughts, actions, conditions, circumstances, feelings, and motivations (Ps. 139:1–6). He is the searcher of our hearts (Ps. 7:9; Rom. 8:27; Rev. 2:23). While He wants us to pray about everything (Luke 18:1; James 4:2), He does not rely on this for His information (Matt. 6:8).

11. *Wisdom (the quality of know-how)*
    a. *Function*
        This quality gives God the ability to use His knowledge in ways that best accomplish His purpose.
    b. *Comment*
        Wisdom is the ability to apply knowledge in practical ways. It is knowing best what to do, how to do it, and when to do it. Being all-wise (1 Tim. 1:17), God knows how best to carry out His own plan as well as to give the best direction to His personal creatures for their lives (1 Cor. 1:21–25; Eph. 3:10; Rom. 12:2).
    We can rely on God's knowing what is best for us (Matt. 7:11; Rom. 12:2) and with confidence follow His direction for our lives (Prov. 3:5–6; Pss. 1:1–3; 16:11; John 8:12).

12. *Omnipotence (the quality of being all-powerful)*

    a. Function

This quality gives God all power, including the ability to carry out His plan. He is the Almighty God (Gen. 17:1).

    b. Comment

God has the skill and the strength to do all that He wishes (Isa. 40:26).

1) Some people have the skill but not the strength to do a certain work; others have the strength but not the skill. God has both. Nothing that He does baffles Him or tires Him (Isa. 40:28). Think of the immense power that He exercised in creating the universe instantly (Gen. 1:1; Ps. 33:6, 9).

2) There are some things that God decided not to do.

For example, He decided not to save everyone (2 Thess. 2:13) and not to destroy Nineveh (Jonah 3:10).

3) There are some things that He cannot do.

Morally, He cannot sin or look with approval upon sin (Hab. 1:13). He cannot lie (Titus 1:2; Heb. 6:18), be tempted with evil (James 1:13), or do anything that is contrary to His moral perfections (2 Tim. 2:13).

Logically, He cannot do anything that is irrational, like making a square triangle. W. G. T. Shedd observed that logical impossibilities are absurdities and, therefore, nonentities. God's power is involved in creating what is real.[12]

Being all-powerful, God is greater than our circumstances and needs and is able to help us as we look to Him in submission and faith (Eph. 3:20; Phil. 4:13; Heb. 13:5–6; 2 Chron. 14:11–12). "With God nothing shall be impossible" and "the things which are impossible with men are possible with God" (Luke 1:37; 18:27).

13. *Holiness (the quality of being set apart)*

    a. Function

Since the basic idea of holiness is the state or condition of being set apart, this quality makes God to be distinctive from the universe and to be separate from sin.

    b. Comment

1) *Amorally,* God is holy in that He is set apart from the universe.

This means that He is transcendent and exalted above all things (Isa. 57:15; Ps. 113:4–6) and is different from them (1 Sam. 2:2). Because God is amorally holy, all personal creatures must look up to Him (Isa. 6:1).

2) *Morally,* God is holy in that He is set apart from sin and from what is sinful.

Being omnipresent, God is in every place where sin is; being holy, He has no personal relation to sin (Hab. 1:12–13; Isa. 6:1–5). Being without sin, He is absolutely morally pure (1 John 1:5). Because of His moral purity and intrinsic goodness, God, together with His pure Law, or Word (Ps. 12:6; 19:8; 119:140), is the standard by which all moral evaluations are to be made (Rom. 3:20, 23).

Because God is holy, we who are saved are to live holy, or sinless, lives (1 Peter 1:14–16; 1 John 2:1) by separating ourselves from that which is sinful (Col. 3:8; 2 Cor. 6:14–7:1; 2 Tim. 2:19, 22; 3:1–5) and by doing His will in His strength (Rom. 6:11–13, 18–22; 12:2). We can now experience periods of moral holiness, or sinlessness, as we give ourselves to Jesus, abide in Him, and live in the power of the Holy Spirit (John 15:4–5; Rom. 8:4; 13:14; Gal. 5:16; Eph. 5:18).

14. *Righteousness and Justice*

Since both of these qualities are translations of the same words in their respective original languages, we shall consider them together. Their meaning is determined by the subject matter of the biblical texts in which they occur, and their contexts.

a. Righteousness (the quality of being right)
1) Function
    (a) This quality makes God to be righteous in character (Dan. 9:7, 16).
    (b) This quality requires God to do right in His actions (Ps. 145:7, 17).
2) Comment
    God's righteousness of nature determines the righteous character of the laws that He imposes on His personal creatures. It also requires God to do what is right in conformity to His own laws. Hence, God never does wrong; He always abides by that righteous standard that is determined by His nature and expressed by His laws. For example, God was right in forgiving the OT believers their sins because of the coming sacrifice of the Lord Jesus (Rom. 3:25–26).

We who are saved are to live righteous lives, that is, live in conformity to God's will for us (Ps. 11:7; Acts 10:35; Phil. 1:11; 1 John 2:29; cp. Eph. 2:10). We can do this, for we have been made righteous in Jesus (1 Cor. 1:30; Eph. 4:24) and have the Holy Spirit to help and to direct us (John 14:16–17; Gal. 5:16).

b. Justice (the quality of being fair)
    Because He is righteous, God deals fairly with everyone.
1) Function
    This quality requires God to do what is right judicially in His response to the actions of His personal creatures (Isa. 45:21). In all His dealings He is just or fair.
2) Comment
    Being righteous, God requires of His personal creatures obedience to His laws, or will; being just, He gives people what is due them according to their response to His laws. He exacts penalties from the disobedient and gives rewards to the obedient (Neh. 9:32–35; Acts 17:31; Rom. 2:6, 11; 2 Tim. 4:8). He also can justly forgive those who meet the conditions of divine forgiveness because of the atoning work of the Lord Jesus, which paid the debt of these sins (Rom. 3:24–26; 5:8; 1 Peter 2:24; 1 John 1:9).

We are to treat others fairly, regardless of their station in life. This means that we are not to be partial toward those of high rank or to ignore others of low rank (James 2:2–9).

(15) *Goodness (the quality of being and doing good)*
    a. Function
    This quality makes God to be morally excellent and to deal well with His creatures (Nah. 1:7).
    b. Comment
    God is good both qualitatively and actively (Ps. 119:68).
1) God is good qualitatively in that He is morally excellent (Mark 10:18; Ps. 25:8).
    This means that God *is good*. While *holiness* emphasizes God's sinlessness, or moral purity, *goodness* emphasizes His perfection, or His moral excellence and essential soundness.
2) God is good actively in that He deals well with mankind.
    This means that God *does good*. He bountifully bestows His gifts on those who seek Him (Ps. 103:1–5) and lavishly extends His mercy to all (Pss. 107:1; 145:9). God's active goodness, or beneficence, is the expression of His compassionate love in providing mankind with those things that are essential to life in this world (Matt. 5:44–45; Acts 14:17). Delaying His judgment, God is now exercising His active goodness for the purpose of giving sinners opportunity to trust in Jesus as their Savior from sin (Rom. 2:4; 2 Peter 3:9). He is also actively good toward His people in providing for their needs (Pss. 34:10; 84:11; 103:5; Matt. 7:11) and giving them good direction (Rom. 12:2).

We not only should praise God for His goodness to us (1 Tim. 6:17) but we should also seek to do good (1 Tim. 6:18; Eph. 2:10). This consists of our doing God's will (Eph. 5:17; Rom. 12:2), which includes our lovingly ministering to the needs of others (Titus 3:1; Gal. 6:9–10; 1 John 3:16–18). We can do these things effectively only as we are empowered and led by the Holy Spirit (Gal. 5:16, 22–23). This requires our submission to Him and reliance upon Him as our Helper.

16. Love (the quality of affectionate caring)
    a. Function
        God's love is an affection that moves Him to provide for the well-being of humans, regardless of their personal merit, worth, or spiritual state.
        1) His sacrificial love (John 3:16)
        This was graciously expressed to all unsaved people once and for all by the Father's giving His Son as a sacrifice for their sins (1 John 4:9–10).
        2) His compassionate love (Matt. 5:44–45)
        This is manifest in God's providing mankind with those things that are essential to life in this world (Acts 19:17; Matt. 5:44–45).
        3) His paternal love (John 16:27)
        This expresses God's fatherly affection for all saved people, whom He has brought into His family in response to their faith in Jesus and His atoning work (John 1:12; 3:16). Amazingly, the Father loves these people as He loves His own Son (John 17:23), and the Son loves them as the Father loves Him (15:9).
    b. Comment
        God's love for sinners must be distinguished from human friendship love, which spontaneously rises from pleasure in its object. Despite His hostility toward us when we were sinners, God graciously chose to love us, to provide a way by which to deliver us from our sins, and to bring us into a right relation with Himself (Rom. 5:7–8). Because of our sin-ruined condition and hostility toward God, there was nothing in us that attracted His love. He did not spontaneously love us or like us in our sinful state. He graciously loved us because He chose to do so, not because He was attracted to any delightful thing in us.

John 3:16 reveals several qualities of God's love. *It is universal,* for He loved the whole human race. *It is sacrificial,* for its great cost is seen in the Father's giving His Son (1 John 4:9–10) and in the Son's giving Himself for our sins (Matt. 20:28; Gal. 2:20). *It is gracious,* for He loved us when, as guilty sinners and enemies, we were undeserving of this love (Rom. 5:6, 8). And *it is beneficent,* for, because of this love and its expression in Jesus' sacrifice, God is ready to bring about the greatest good in the lives of all who trust in the Savior and His atoning work for their salvation (1 Peter 2:24–25; 1 John 4:9).

Observe that God's salvational, sacrificial love for the unsaved is transient. Stated in the past tense, God's love for the world was expressed in His giving His Son (John 3:16; Rom. 5:8). We must be very careful, when telling sinners of God's love, that we do not convey the false, sentimental idea that He likes them and somehow will spare them hell. Those who fail to receive the gift of God's love (divine forgiveness based upon Jesus' sacrifice) are left with only His wrath (John 3:36). On the other hand, God's parental love for His children is the same for all who are saved and is unchanging and everlasting (John 13:1; Rom. 8:35–39; Rev. 1:5).

In the Old Testament there is a special covenant love (Heb. *chesed*) that God has for His people. This is most often represented in the KJV by the words "kindness" (Neh. 9:17; Isa. 54:8, 10), "lovingkindness" (Pss. 69:16; 92:2; Jer. 9:24), and "mercy" (Pss. 100:5; 103:8, 11, 17). This love emphasizes God's faithfulness toward His covenant people. It is a steadfast love, committed to His fulfilling to them the promises of His gracious covenants.

We who are saved are commanded to express God's love to others, whether saved or unsaved, friend or foe (John 13:34; Matt. 5:44; see Appendix Z: "Our Loving God and Others"). The expression of this love, which is the badge of true discipleship (John 13:34–35), is our caring for others, including undeserving people, and our seeking to provide for their well-being, even at personal cost (1 John 3:16–18). Because of the qualities of this love (1 Cor. 13:4–7), we can do this only as we submit to and rely on the Holy Spirit to reproduce this love in our hearts and lives (Rom. 5:5; Gal. 5:22). Again, keep in mind that this is not friendship love, which finds pleasure in others. God does not ask us to like our enemies but to seek His blessing on them, to do good to them, and to pray for them (Matt. 5:44).

(17) Hatred (the quality of reacting against sin and sinners)

    a. Function

        This quality gives God an extreme dislike for and opposition toward sinners and their sins (Pss. 5:5; 11:5; Hos. 9:15; Mal. 1:2–3; Rom. 9:13). *Passively,* this hatred (Gk. *orge*) expresses itself as a hostile attitude toward sinners with a resolution to punish them (Rom. 1:18; John 3:36). *Actively,* this hatred (Gk. *thumos*) expresses itself as destructive judgment or punishment (Rev. 14:19; 15:1; 19:15).

    b. Comment

        This hatred is not the sinful, spiteful kind that humans naturally feel toward their enemies. Activated by the sin force, human hatred lacks justice and desires ill toward the offender rather than seeking his well-being. Moreover, we humans cannot justly determine the motivation of those who have hurt us or the circumstances that prompted this. Thus we are not allowed to avenge our wrongs (Rom. 12:17–21).

        Divine hatred is the stern, spontaneous reaction of God's holiness against sinners and their sins. While *holiness* emphasizes God's character as being separate from sin, *hatred* emphasizes His reaction to sin both emotionally and actively. Because of their guilt and depravity, He finds nothing in unsaved people that is acceptable to Him or that brings Him pleasure (Rom. 3:9–18). There is only that which is despicable to Him.

        Despite this hatred, God deliberately, graciously chose to love sinners and to provide for them the opportunity of salvation through Jesus. However, this sacrificial love for unrepentant sinners is not everlasting. When sinners fail to trust in God's Son and His atoning work (the greatest expression of divine love for humans), there remains for them only divine wrath (John 3:36). In all His hateful expressions, God is always just, dealing out to sinners their deserved punishment (Rom. 2:2–12).

        In our gospel ministry to sinners, we need to emphasize God's displeasure with them because of their sins before speaking of His gracious, sacrificial love for them. If we speak only of His love, this may be misunderstood as an indulgent sentiment that ignores their sins. While we are to love sinners graciously, as God does through the gospel, and compassionately, as He does through the blessings of common grace (Matt. 5:44–45), we must hate their sins (Rom. 12:9). Also, we must accept God's attitude toward sin and fear Him with wholesome reverence and respect (Heb. 12:28–29).

(18) Grace (the quality of exercising undeserved favor)

    a. Function

        This quality enables God to deal favorably with undeserving people according to His sovereign purpose (Gen. 6:8; Jonah 4:2; Eph. 2:8; Rom. 11:5; Heb. 2:9).

    b. Comment

        1) Grace is the only method by which God can save sinners (Gal. 2:16).

        Not recognizing unsaved people's merit, worth, or works, grace is the only method whereby God can deliver them from the penalty, ruin, and bondage of their sins (Eph. 2:8–9; see "The Principle Involved in Salvation" under Soteriology). The opposite principle of works, which requires God to deal with people as they deserve, is unsuitable, for sinners deserve death and hell (cp. Rom. 11:5–6; 6:23). Thus God cannot save them on the basis of their personal merit, work, or works (Eph. 2:9).

2) Grace maintains the salvation of saved people (Rom. 5:2).

Since it is by grace, salvation is wholly God's work, and the saved person is secure (Eph. 2:8; John 10:28–29). Consider the Corinthians' spiritual position in Christ (1 Cor. 1:4–9, 30), despite their spiritual lapses and carnal condition (1 Cor. 3:1–3).

3) By grace, God enables saved people to do His will (2 Cor. 1:12) and to endure their circumstances as they trust Him (2 Cor. 12:7–10; cp. chap. 4; Phil. 4:10–13).

Divine grace portrays God in action, doing for us what we cannot do for ourselves. With the help of this grace, we who are saved can be the kind of people He wants us to be and do the things He wants us to do (1 Cor. 15:10; 2 Cor. 1:12).

4) Grace responds to faith in God and His Word (cp. Eph. 2:8).[13]

Faith in God and His Word activates His grace in us for salvation, daily life, and ministry (Gal. 2:16, 20; Rom. 12:3, 6).

God's grace is more than sufficient for every demand of life (2 Cor. 9:8; 12:9–10). However, it responds only to faith in God and His promises. We have the choice of relying on God and His grace or upon ourselves and our meager human resources.

19. *Mercy (the quality of showing compassion)*

a. *Function*

This quality enables God to show a benevolent compassion toward the guilty and the distressed (Deut. 4:31).

b. *Comment*

1) In mercy, God shows compassion toward the guilty.

He does this by temporarily withholding the punishment that sinners deserve (Neh. 9:17; Jer. 33:23–26; Rom. 11:30–32; Eph. 2:4; Titus 3:5). However, God's mercy toward the wicked is not endless. In time He will deal out judgment to those who fail to respond positively to His general revelation in nature (Rom. 1:18–20) and to those who reject His special revelation of salvation in Christ (Rom. 2:8–9; John 3:36).

2) In mercy, God shows compassion toward those who suffer or who are in distress.

He grants them relief (Ps. 103:8–18; Isa. 49:13; Heb. 4:16; James 5:11).

Not only should we be grateful to God for His mercy to us but we should also show this mercy to others (Matt. 5:7; Col. 3:12). We can do what is pleasing to God only with the help of the Holy Spirit.

20. *Long-suffering (the quality of being patient)*

a. *Function*

This quality enables God to bear long with those who annoy or provoke Him (Rom. 15:5).

b. *Comment*

1) God is patient with His people (Ps. 86:14–17).

He is patient in that He puts up with their frailties, including their immaturity, dullness, ignorance, and obstinacy.

2) He is patient with the unsaved (Rom. 2:4; 9:22; 2 Peter 3:9).

Despite their sins against Him, He patiently gives them opportunity to respond to His general revelation and to seek Him. He also gives many the opportunity to hear the gospel. However, His patience with the unsaved is not endless. He will judge all who reject His general revelation and the gospel (Rev. 20:11–15).

We, too, are to be long-suffering toward others who try us and provoke us (Eph. 4:2). This forbearance is a fruit of the Holy Spirit as we yield to His control (Gal. 5:22).

(21) *Sovereignty (the quality of being supreme)*
    a. Function
       This quality gives God the highest position and authority.
    b. Comment
       1) God is supreme in position.
          He is above all persons, things, and places (Deut. 10:14; Isa. 40:15–17).
       2) God is supreme in authority.
          He commands all angels, humans, impersonal creatures, and things (1 Chron. 29:12; Pss. 47:2–3; 103:19; 119:91). Nothing exists that is not under His control (Job 1:15; 2:6).
       3) God is supreme in purpose.
          He will bring to pass all that He has decided to do (Isa. 14:24, 27; 46:11; Eph. 1:11).

It is our duty to recognize God's sovereignty over our lives and to submit daily to His will (Deut. 10:12–13; Rom. 12:1–2; 14:6–9; 2 Cor. 5:14–15; Eph. 5:10, 17). He also gives to some people positions of authority over such human institutions as civil government (Rom. 13:1–5), the local church (Heb. 13:7, 17), and the home (Eph. 5:22–23; 6:1), for which they are accountable to Him.

Again, observe that some of these divine qualities, to some extent, are transferable to God's people as they are reproduced in them by God the Holy Spirit (Gal. 5:22–23; Rom. 14:17; Eph. 5:9). These include holiness (1 Peter 1:15), righteousness (1 John 2:29), justice (James 2:1–9), goodness (3 John 11), faithfulness (1 Cor. 4:2), love (John 13:34–35; Matt. 5:44–45), hatred (Rom. 12:9), grace (Col. 4:6; 2 Cor. 6:1), mercy (Col. 3:12), longsuffering (Eph. 4:2), and authority (1 Cor. 12:28). To express these, we must submit ourselves to the Holy Spirit and rely on Him to reproduce these in us. Then it can be said that we are godly people, or a people like God in moral character and behavior (Matt. 5:16, 48; Eph. 5:1–17). On the other hand, the possession of these qualities does not mean that our human nature has been made divine and, thus, we are God. Produced in us by the Holy Spirit, they reflect a Christlikeness that belongs to our spiritual life, which is in the Lord Jesus (John 14:6; 15:4–5).

How wonderful our God is! Let us meditate upon these perfections and consider their many applications to our lives. Also, let us allow Him to fill us with the fullness of Himself and to express His light through us in this world's darkness (Eph. 5:1–21; Matt. 5:48). In our worship, we can praise God for these qualities of His nature and thank Him for all that He is doing for us (cp. Ps. 145).

HUMAN AND ANIMAL FEATURES ATTRIBUTED TO GOD

In the Bible, it is said that God has human forms (anthropomorphisms) and animal forms (zoomorphisms) and that He expresses human emotions (anthropopathisms), all of which are not attributable to His divine nature. Since God does not have parts as we do, the purpose of these figurative expressions is to reveal truth about Him in an impressive way to which we humans can relate. W. H. Griffith Thomas explained:

> In revealing Himself, God has to descend to our capacities and use language that can be understood. But this can never fully reveal Him since that which is finite could never explain the Infinite. So that God must necessarily speak of Himself as a Man, for so only could we comprehend anything about Him. Hence, both as to Person and actions, everything is spoken after the manner of men. But all these are only figures of speech, by which alone we can obtain any ideas of reality.[14]

We must keep in mind the purpose of God's self-revelation by these means lest we have distorted views of Him. On the other hand, having permanently taken to Himself a complete human nature, God the Son experiences all that His glorified, sinless humanity contributes to Him. In other words, the Second Person of the divine Trinity does have eyes, hands, mouth, and the like because He is man as well as God.

Human Features (anthropomorphisms)

This is any human physical part, action, or characteristic that is attributed to God. For example, God is said to have a soul (Isa. 1:14), eyes (Prov. 15:3), feet (Nah. 1:3), ears (Num. 11:18), hands (Amos 9:2), arms (Jer. 27:5), face (Num. 6:25), head (Ps. 60:7), and mouth (Jer. 9:20). It is also said that He remembered (Gen. 8:1), smelled (v. 21), saw (6:5), went down (11:5), and heard (21:17).

Human Feelings (anthropopathisms)

This is any human emotion that is attributed to God. God was said to be weary (Isa. 1:14) and jealous, which is usually regarded as an anthropopathism (Exod. 20:5; 34:14). Based on His relationship with His people, this jealousy means that He will not tolerate any compromise of His people's love for Him. He alone has exclusive claim to their devotion and is zealous to maintain the purity of this relation. Incidentally, God's love for us is not an anthropopathism. It is a quality of His divine nature.

Animal Features (zoomorphisms)

This is any animal part, action, or characteristic that is attributed to God. He is said to have feathers and wings (Ps. 91:4) and to roar like a lion (Hos. 11:10).

When you come across these graphic, figurative expressions in the Scriptures, consider what truths they convey about God. For example, when it is said that "the eyes of the LORD are in every place, beholding the evil and the good" (Prov. 15:3), one can visualize these divine "eyes" as being everywhere and beholding everything. This is a much more graphic, meaningful statement than to say that God is omniscient.

GOD'S UNITY AND TRIUNITY

Earlier, when we considered the divine attribute of unity, we noted God's singularity—that God is one God. It is also biblical teaching that God exists as three eternal, simultaneous Persons (1 John 5:7).[15] Regarding these truths, we can say that God is one in nature and three in Person. Let us look at this more closely.

The Unity of God's Essence

The singularity of God (His being one God) is taught in Deuteronomy 4:35, 39; 6:4; 1 Kings 8:60; 2 Kings 19:15; Psalm 86:10; Isaiah 45:5–6; Zechariah 14:9; Mark 12:28–29; John 17:3; Romans 3:30; Ephesians 4:6; and 1 Timothy 2:5.

God is one God because there is only one divine nature, or essence, which is undivided and indivisible. Although there are three Persons (personhoods) in the divine Trinity, They possess in common the one divine nature that makes Them one God.

The reason for the Old Testament's emphasis on the unity of God seems to be the fact of mankind's falling into idolatry after the Noachic Flood and their worshiping false gods and their images (Rom. 1:21–25). Even the nation of Israel fell into idolatry during their sojourn in Egypt (Josh. 24:14) and engaged in this sin at Mt. Sinai (Exod. 32:1–6) and in Canaan (Judg. 2:11–13, et al.; 2 Kings 17:7–23). Because of their role in God's salvation program, Israel needed to be reminded of God's unity while they lived among pagan nations that practiced idolatry. Israel's worship of the one, true God was a witness to His unity and was essential to their place in His program (Deut. 6:4–15; Isa. 43:10).

The Triunity of God's Personhoods

While unity emphasizes the oneness of God, triunity, or trinity, speaks of there being three Persons (personhoods), simultaneously possessing the one divine nature. We usually speak of this truth as the doctrine of the divine Trinity. The Trinity consists of three simultaneous, coexistent, eternal Persons—the Father, the Son, and the Holy Spirit (Matt. 28:19; 1 John 5:7). Let us examine this doctrine in greater detail.

1. *False views of the divine Trinity*

The early Christian thinkers of the post-New Testament Period did not have a clear conception of the doctrine of the Trinity. During the third and fourth centuries there arose heretical views that prodded the Church to define this doctrine. The chief false views of the Trinity follow:

a. *Sabellianism*

Sometimes called Modal Monarchianism, this view was taught by Sabellius, a teacher at Rome (c. 215). It held that God is a Monad (an ultimate unit of being) that expressed itself in three consecutive operational manifestations: the Father as divine essence, and the Son and the Spirit as its modes of self-expression. Thus, by a process of development, the Father projected Himself first as Son and then as Holy Spirit.[16]

Essentially, this view holds that the Persons of the Trinity are simply different, temporary (but not simultaneous) forms by which the Monad expressed itself. This false view is often unwittingly presented by this erroneous illustration of the Trinity: water as a solid (ice) becoming a liquid and then turning to steam.

Contrariwise, the Bible teaches that the Persons of the Trinity are distinct, eternal, coexistent Persons.

b. *Arianism*

This takes its name from Arius, a presbyter of Alexandria (4th Cent.), who held that there is only one God (God the Father), that the Son is a personal creature whom the Father formed out of nothing by command, and that the Spirit is an impersonal essence, unlike that of the Father. Later Arians regarded the Holy Spirit to be the noblest of the creatures produced by the Son at the Father's bidding.[17]

Contrariwise, the Bible teaches that the Son and the Holy Spirit, possessing the single divine essence with the Father, are each God and are equal to the Father in their essential qualities.

c. *Tritheism*

This holds that the Trinity consists of three Persons having their own separate divine nature. Thus, there are three Gods rather than one God.

Contrariwise, the Scriptures teach that there is only one God, existing as three distinct, eternal Persons, each of whom is God. Their possessing in common the one divine nature makes Them to be one God.

With these false views of the Trinity in mind, we must be on the alert for so-called Christian movements that are heretical in their teachings of the Trinity. The United Pentecostal church, for example, rejects the teaching of the Trinity as being separate Persons and holds that Jesus is at the same time the Father, the Son, and the Holy Spirit. This is a form of Sabellianism. The Jehovah's Witnesses deny the deity of the Lord Jesus Christ and the deity and personality of the Holy Spirit. This is Arianism. Any religious organization that denies the biblical teaching of the Trinity is not truly biblical or Christian. Let us now consider the biblical teaching of this doctrine.

2. The true doctrine of the divine Trinity

The biblical doctrine of the Trinity may be summarized as follows: There is one God; the Trinity consists of three Persons—the Father, the Son, and the Holy Spirit; the Father, the Son, and the Holy Spirit are distinct, coexistent, eternal Persons; and the Father, the Son, and the Holy Spirit are each wholly God.

a. The New Testament teaching of the Trinity

The New Testament gives us more details of this doctrine because it records the incarnation of God the Son and His relationship to God the Father. It also describes the various ministries of God the Holy Spirit as they relate to Jesus and to His people.

1) There is one God.

This is stated in 1 Corinthians 8:4; Galatians 3:20; 1 Timothy 2:5. It is also implied in Matthew 28:19, where the singular noun "Name" is used for the Trinity in the baptismal formula. Regarding this verse B. B. Warfield observed:

It does not say, "In the names (plural) of the Father and of the Son and of the Holy Ghost"; nor yet (what might be taken to be the equivalent to that) "In the name of the Father, and in the name of the Son, and in the name of the Holy Ghost," as if we had to deal with three separate Beings. Nor, on the other hand, does it say, "In the name of the Father, Son, and Holy Ghost," as if "the Father, Son, and Holy Ghost" might be taken as merely three designations of a single person. With stately impressiveness it asserts the unity of the three by combining them all within the bounds of the single Name; and then throws up into emphasis the distinctness of each by introducing them in turn by the repeated article . . . these three, the Father and the Son and the Holy Ghost, all unite in some profound sense in the common participation of the one Name.[18]

Jesus also said that He and His Father were one (John 10:30). Being Greek neuter gender, "one" means one thing, or one God. It is not masculine gender, or one person.

2) The Trinity consists of three Persons.

That the Trinity consists of three Persons is seen in Matthew 28:19 and 2 Corinthians 13:14. Here the word "God," occurring with the names of the other Persons of the Trinity, refers to the Father.

3) The Members of the Trinity are distinct, coexistent Persons.

This is seen in such passages as John 14:16–17, where Jesus speaks about asking the Father to send another Helper, who is the Holy Spirit. These words indicate that Jesus did not think of Himself as being the Father or the Holy Spirit. Including Himself, He refers to three Persons.

4) Each Member of the Trinity is wholly God.

The Father is God (John 6:27; Rom. 1:7; 1 Peter 1:2), the Son is God (John 1:1, 14; Rom. 9:5; Heb. 1:8; 1 John 5:20), and the Holy Spirit is God (1 Cor. 3:16; Acts 5:3–4). But these three Persons are not separate Gods, with individual divine natures. Their uniquely sharing the one divine nature, without dividing it, makes Them to be together one God, yet each Person to be wholly God.[19]

b. The Old Testament teaching of the Trinity

With reference to this, B. B. Warfield wrote:

The Old Testament may be likened to a chamber richly furnished but dimly lighted. The introduction of light brings into it nothing that was not in it before, but it brings into clearer view much of what is in it but was dimly or even not at all perceived before. The mystery of the Trinity is not revealed in the Old Testament, but the mystery of the Trinity underlies the Old Testament revelation, and here and there almost comes into view.[20]

    1) There is one God.
        This is stated in Deuteronomy 6:4 and implied in Isaiah 40:25; 45:5–6, 18, 22.
    2) The Trinity consists of three Persons.
        That the Trinity consists of more than two Persons is indicated by the plural noun "God" (Heb. *Elohim* in Gen. 1:1) and the plural pronoun "Us" (Gen. 1:26; 3:22; 11:7; Isa. 6:8). The three Persons of the Trinity are seen in Isaiah 48:16 and 61:1, with the Son (the Messiah) speaking in both passages (cp. Isa. 49:8–9 with Luke 4:16–21).
    3) The Members of the Trinity are distinct, coexistent Persons.
        These Persons are distinguished in various passages: "LORD," the Father, is distinguished from "Lord," the Son (Ps. 110:1); "The LORD" has a "Son" (Ps. 2:7, 12; cp. Prov. 30:4); the Holy "Spirit" is distinguished from "LORD" (Num. 27:18) and from "God" (Ps. 51:10–12); "God" the Son is distinguished from "God" the Father (cp. Ps. 45:6–7 with Heb. 1:8–9).
    4) Each Member of the Trinity is wholly God.
        The Father is called "LORD" (Heb. *Yahweh*), God's OT personal name (Ps. 110:1). The Father and the Son are each called "God" (cp. Ps. 45:6–7 with Heb. 1:8–9). The Son is called "Immanuel" (Isa. 7:14, meaning "God with us") and "Everlasting Father" (Isa. 9:6, meaning "Father of eternity"). As the speaker of the words of Jeremiah 31:33–34, quoted in Hebrews 10:15–17, the Holy Spirit is identified as the "LORD."
    This biblical evidence demonstrates the fact of the divine Trinity. Our God—the true and the living God—is one God, consisting of three simultaneous Persons: God the Father, God the Son, and God the Holy Spirit. We can readily grasp the truth that each Member of the Trinity is God and that each One is a Person. But it is incomprehensible how these three Persons possess the single divine nature in such a manner as to be one God, yet each One wholly God, without confounding the Persons or dividing the nature. This aspect of the doctrine has no analogy in nature and must be received by faith in God's Word.

3. The relations of the Persons within the divine Trinity

    We shall now try to understand those unfathomable, eternal processes that are involved in the internal, constitutional relationships of the Trinity. Let us first examine these relationships and then the subordinations that rise from them.

a. The relation of these Persons to each Other

    1) In Their constitution
        As the designations Father, Son, and Holy Spirit suggest, theologians have traditionally held that God the Son is begotten by God the Father and that God the Holy Spirit is breathed out, or exhaled, by the Father and, or through, the Son. They also have thought that these eternal, internal actions concern the whole person of the Son and of the Holy Spirit rather than only Their divine nature. They have also held that essence does not beget or spirate essence, but persons beget or spirate persons in the essence.[21]

    I prefer the view that *generation* relates only to the divine essence, or nature, of the Son and that *spiration* relates only to the divine essence, or nature, of the Holy Spirit and that these terms describe the manner by which the eternal Son and the eternal Holy Spirit, as persons, possess the one divine nature in common with the Father so that each One is God and that They still remain one God.

    The designations "Father" and "only begotten Son" indicate that the Father generates the Son (John 3:16; cp. 5:26; Ps. 2:7).[22] In our human experience generation is a single act initiating, as I believe, the divine creation of personhood and the natural propagation of human nature. However, with reference to God, generation is neither a single act in time nor the creation of someone or something. As I see it, by an eternal process the Father's generative action makes the divine nature common to Himself and to the Son. There is no creation of the Son's personhood or of a new divine nature. By this continuing process, the eternally existing divine nature is communicated to the Son in such a way that it remains undivided, yet wholly possessed by the Father and by the Son individually. By this eternal, perpetual generative action the Son is wholly God as the Father is wholly God (John 10:30).

Likewise, the divine nature, possessed in common by the Father and the Son, is communicated by Them to the Holy Spirit. This, too, is done in such a way that it remains undivided, yet wholly possessed by the Holy Spirit as well as by the Father and the Son. The designation "Spirit" means "breath" or "wind." This suggests that unlike the "begotten" Son, whose divine nature is generated by the Father, the Holy Spirit possesses the divine essence by an eternal act of spiration, or exhalation, by the Father through the Son.[23]

2) In Their activity

What did these divine Persons do from all eternity before Their creating the universe? The only thing that is revealed is Their having perpetual, intimate fellowship with each other (John 1:1, 18; 17:5).

b. *Their subordination of these Persons to each other*

The Scriptures show a subordination among the Persons of the divine Trinity. This subordination is represented by an arrangement of the names and activities of the Persons in a dependent series regarding Their order and work.

1) Their subordination in order

This is expressed by the arrangement of Their names (Matt. 28:19) and the internal relationships suggested by these names—the Father, the Son, and the Holy Spirit (cp. John 3:16). As we have seen, this subordination rises from the eternal, internal relationships that exist between these Persons. Being the Unbegotten One, the Father is first in order; being the only Begotten One, the Son is second; and proceeding from the Father through the Son, the Holy Spirit is third. Theologians call this subordination in order, position, or rank *ontological subordination,* for this concerns the Trinity's constitution, or essential makeup. This order of first, second, and third is not to be understood as representing qualitative differences between the Persons of the Trinity, for each One possesses the same divine essence, wholly and simultaneously, with the other two Persons. Consequently, They have equal qualities and powers.[24]

2) Their subordination in activity

There is also a subordination of the Persons of the Trinity in Their works, as expressed by Their external relation to and dealings with the universe. This is called *economical subordination* and is presented by the formula that everyone and everything outside the Trinity originate with (Gk. *ek*) the Father and are brought about through (Gk. *dia*) the Son by means of (Gk. *en*) the Holy Spirit (cp. 1 Cor. 8:6; 6:11). This subordination is manifest in the separate yet harmonious roles that these divine Persons have in Their relationships to people and things outside Themselves, as follows:

The Father is the *Originating Cause,* or the Personal Source, of the universe (1 Cor. 8:6; Rev. 4:11), divine revelation (Rev. 1:1), salvation (John 3:16–17), and Jesus' messianic, or human, works (John 5:17; 14:10).

The Son is the *Instrumental Cause,* or the Personal Agent, through whom the Father works to bring about these divine activities: the creation and maintenance of the universe (1 Cor. 8:6; John 1:3; Col. 1:16–17), divine revelation (Matt. 11:27; John 1:1; 16:12–15; Rev. 1:1), salvation (2 Cor. 5:19; Matt. 1:21; John 4:42), and His messianic, or human, works (John 5:17, 19; 6:38; 8:29; 14:10; 17:4).

The Holy Spirit is the *Dynamic Cause,* or the Personal Force, by whom the Father brings about these divine activities through the Son: the creation and maintenance of the universe (Gen. 1:2; Job 26:13; Ps. 104:30), divine revelation (John 16:12–15; Eph. 3:5; 2 Peter 1:21), salvation (John 3:6; 1 Cor. 6:11; Titus 3:5; 1 Peter 1:2), and Jesus' messianic, or human, works (Isa. 61:1; Acts 10:38).

In summary, all divine activities toward and dealing with the universe are done by the Father through the Son by means of the Holy Spirit.

One cannot reflect upon the nature and uniqueness of our God without being filled with awe and praise. We shall forever ponder these sacred mysteries and learn of these infinite divine Persons. Meanwhile, it is our privilege and joy, as saved people, to give ourselves daily to these divine Persons—to the Father as His children-sons, to the Lord Jesus as His slaves-friends, and to the Holy Spirit as His temples-dependents—to fellowship with Them, and to express our love for Them by our trust, obedience, and worship (Mark 12:30; John 14:15, 21, 23).

THE NAMES OF GOD

While we use proper names for labels of identification, in the Bible they serve additional roles. Biblical proper names are sometimes descriptive of people's character, as Nabal meaning "fool" (1 Sam. 25:25), and of people's appearance, as Esau meaning "red" (Gen. 25:25); commemorative of some event, as Ichabod meaning "inglorious" (1 Sam. 4:21); expressive of the faith or hope of parents, as Noah meaning "comfort" (Gen. 5:29); or a witness to prophecy, as Shearjashub meaning "a remnant shall return" (Isa. 7:3). Likewise, the names of God are a part of the self-revelation of His nature, character, and works.

THE KINDS

As we survey the biblical names of God, we must keep in mind the various kinds of designations that are used: *generic names,* representing kind of being; *functional names* (titles), representing work, office, or rank; and *personal names,* representing personal identification. Using "the man, President Abraham Lincoln" as an example, "man" is his generic name, "President" is his functional name, and "Abraham Lincoln" is his personal name.

GOD'S NAMES IN THE OLD TESTAMENT

God's Basic Hebrew Names

1. The generic name, Elohim (God)

This is the generic name of Deity and is translated in the KJV "God" (Gen. 1:1) or "gods" (Exod. 20:3). This plural form, *Elohim,* occurs about 2,500 times with reference to the true God. Its singular forms are *El, Eloah* (a poetic form often found in Job), and *Elah* (found in Ezra and Daniel).

With reference to the true God, *Elohim* is translated in the singular ("God"), and with few exceptions (cp. Gen. 3:5; Deut. 5:26) it imposes the singular on those parts of the sentence that are grammatically related to it. This shows that the plural form does not speak of more than one God.

Some believe that the plural form, *Elohim,* is the abstract plural of greatness, majesty, or rank, denoting God's unlimited greatness and power. We Trinitarians hold that it is a numerical plural, indicating the plurality of Persons within the divine Trinity, or Godhead. This plurality represents more than two Persons since *Elohim* has a Hebrew plural ending rather than a dual one *(Elohayim).*

Elohim derives from the Hebrew root word *el,* which means "strength" or "might" (cp. "power" in Gen. 31:29; Prov. 3:27). This generic name of Deity signifies "the putter forth of power."[25] The true God is the absolute Being to whom all power belongs (Gen. 1:1; 24:3; Ps. 91:2; Isa. 46:9).

2. *The functional name, Adonai (Lord)*

This is the primary OT title of God. Meaning "my lords" (Ps. 16:2), this title in KJV is translated "Lord" about 400 times with reference to God. *Adonai,* with its first singular pronominal suffix *(ai),* is the plural form of *Adon,* which means "lord" or "master" (12:4). Like *Elohim,* the plural form indicates the plurality of Persons within the divine Trinity. The significance of this title is seen in the following examples: lord or master of slaves (Gen. 24:9), of a wife (Gen. 18:12), of a people (1 Kings 22:17), of a country (Gen. 42:30), and of a household (Gen. 45:8). This title expresses a personal relationship of authority on the one hand and of allegiance and love on the other.[26] It was a title that a subordinate addressed to his superior.[27]

Adon means "the Lord as ruler" (Ps. 105:21) and *Baal* means "the Lord as possessor or owner"; thus God, "the Lord of all the earth" (Josh. 3:13), is the ruling Lord.[28] *Baal* was the title that the people of Canaan gave to their gods, with *Bel* as the supreme deity. For this reason, God never called Himself *Baal,* nor do the Scriptures show the Israelites often using this title for Him (cp. Hos. 2:16), although He is the owner of the universe (Pss. 24:1; 50:10–12).

With the meaning of *Adonai* in view, it is profitable to reflect upon its significance in Genesis 15:2, 8; Joshua 7:7; Judges 6:13, 15; Psalms 35:23; 110:1; 114:7; Isaiah 6:1, 8; and Malachi 1:6. Observe that *Adonai* refers to God the Son in Psalm 110:1 (cp. Matt. 22:41–46) and to God the Holy Spirit in Isaiah 48:16 (with "and" being an explanatory conjunction; "*Adonai Yahweh,* that is, His Spirit has sent me").

3. *The personal name, Yahweh or Jahveh (LORD)*

Being the OT personal name of God (Jer. 33:2), in the KJV it is translated "LORD" (Ps. 110:1), "Jehovah" (Ps. 83:18), and "God" when following "Lord" (*Adonai,* Gen. 15:2). "Jah" is an abbreviated form of *Yahweh* (Ps. 68:4). "LORD" occurs about 6,700 times in the Old Testament.

"LORD" is not a translation of the Hebrew word for God's personal name but an arbitrary substitute. In post-Old Testament times, *Yahweh* ceased to be pronounced aloud by Jews in the synagogue reading of the Scriptures and was replaced orally by the word *Adonai.*[29] Later, when the medieval Masoretes (Jewish scribes) added vowels to the consonants in the Hebrew text of the Scriptures, they added the vowel points of *Adonai* to the consonants YHWH (JHVH), God's personal name. This created the word YaHoWaH, or JeHoVaH. Scholars believe that *Yahweh,* or *Jahveh,* is nearer to the original pronunciation of YHWH, but this is not certain.

That *Yahweh* is the personal name of God is shown by the following: He says that it is His name (Isa. 42:8; Amos 5:8). It is not a title as are *Adon* (Ruler, Master) and *Baal* (Owner, Possessor). It never occurs with the genitive as "*Yahweh* of Israel," but as "*Yahweh,* God of Israel" (Josh. 24:2). Also, it never occurs as "the *Yahweh,*" "my *Yahweh,*" or "the living *Yahweh.*"

The name seems to come from the Hebrew root word "to be" (*hawah*) with a consonantal prefix *(Y)*. The meaning is indicated in Exodus 3:13–14, where in answer to Moses' question about His name, God reveals Himself as "I AM THAT I AM." The name was not a new revelation (Gen. 4:1; 14:22; 24:3; Job 12:9), but it was important to Israel that God renew its revelation and make known its meaning, which may have been lost during the nation's sojourn in Egypt (Ezek. 20:6–8; Josh. 24:14; cp. Exod. 6:2–3).

When *Yahweh* declares "I AM THAT I AM," He may be saying that He is the eternal, unchanging One. When He says that He is "I AM," He may be saying that He is ultimate Reality. The root word, translated "to be," suggests continuous, absolute, self-determining existence. The truth was vital to Israel that their God was the ultimate, continuing Reality and that He was with them to work on their behalf (Exod. 3:12, 17). Hence, as always, He is all that we need in our helplessness, trials, or adversities.

Yahweh is God's covenant name (see Gen. 15:1, 4, 18; Exod. 3:15–17; 20:1; 2 Sam. 7:4–16; Jer. 31:31–37). This name contained the pledge of all that He had promised to do for Israel and to be to them. Knowing Him in a personal, covenant relationship, they were to be His people, and He was to be their God. [30]

In addition to representing the divine Trinity (Deut. 6:4), *Yahweh* sometimes represents certain Persons of the Trinity: God the Father (Ps. 110:1; Isa. 48:16; 61:1), God the Son (Isa. 2:2–5; 33:21–22; 40:10; Jer. 23:6; cp. John 4:26; 8:24, 28; 13:9), and God the Holy Spirit (Isa. 48:16, "GOD" with "and" being an explanatory conjunction; Jer. 31:31–34 with Heb. 10:15–18).

God's Compound Hebrew Names

In addition to the basic Hebrew names of Deity, there are several OT compound forms that include the name of *El, Elohim,* or *Yahweh.* To understand their significance more fully, these names should be studied in their contexts, and a concordance should be used to locate other passages where they occur.

1. *The El forms*
   a. *El Shaddai*—"the almighty God" (Gen. 17:1)
      With *shad* possibly meaning "breast," *El Shaddai* suggests that God is the sufficient nourisher and comforter of His people.
   b. *El Olam*—"the everlasting God" (Gen. 21:33)
   c. *El Elyon*—"the most high God" (Gen. 14:18–20)
   d. *El Qodash*—"God, the holy One" (Josh. 24:19)
   e. *El Qanno*—"the jealous God" (Josh. 24:19)
   f. *El Elohe Israel*—"God, the God of Israel" (Gen. 33:20)
   g. *El Roi*—"the God who sees" (Gen. 16:13)
   h. *El Gadol waw Nora*—"the great and terrible God" (Deut. 7:21)
      The fear that God incites is terror in His enemies and reverence in His people.
   i. *El Chanun waw Rachum*—"the gracious and merciful God" (Jonah 4:2)
   j. *El Neeman*—"the faithful God" (Deut. 7:9)
   k. *El Chai*—"the living God" (Josh. 3:10)
2. *The Elohim forms*
   a. *Elohim Chayim*—"the living God" (Deut. 5:26)
   b. *Elohim Sabaoth*—"the God of hosts (armies)" (Amos 3:13)
3. *The Yahweh forms*
   a. *Yahweh Sabaoth*—"The LORD of hosts (armies)" (1 Sam. 17:45)
   b. *Yahweh Jireh*—"the LORD who sees" (Gen. 22:14)
      Therefore, He provides for His people.
   c. *Yahweh Rapha*—"the LORD who heals" (Exod. 15:26)

d. *Yahweh Nissi*—"the LORD, my banner" (Exod. 17:15)
A banner was a standard or flag around which people rallied.
e. *Yahweh Qadash*—"the LORD who sanctifies" (Lev. 20:8)
f. *Yahweh Rohi*—"the LORD, my shepherd" (Ps. 23:1)
g. *Yahweh Tsidkenu*—"the LORD our righteousness" (Jer. 23:6)
h. *Yahweh Shalom*—"the LORD (is) peace" (Judg. 6:24)
i. *Yahweh Shammah*—"the LORD (is) there" (Ezek. 48:35; cp. Zech. 8:22; 14:16–17)

Other Names

Other OT functional names of God are "Rock" (Deut. 32:4; Ps. 18:1), "Fortress" (2 Sam. 22:2; Ps. 18:1), "Maker" (Job 36:3), "King" (1 Sam. 12:12), "Redeemer" (Ps. 19:14; Isa. 43:14), "Savior" (2 Sam. 22:3; Isa. 43:3), "Judge" (Gen. 18:25), "Shield" and "Buckler" (Ps. 18:2; Gen. 15:1), "Strength" (1 Sam. 15:29), and "Portion" (Jer. 10:16).

With the context determining its meaning, "the Angel of the LORD" sometimes refers to God (Gen. 16:7–13; 21:17–18; 22:11–12; 31:11–13; Exod. 3:2–4; Judg. 6:11–16). This is probably a theophany of God the Son, who is the divine Revelator or Word (Matt. 11:27; John 1:1). In other passages "the Angel of the LORD" refers to a holy angel (2 Sam. 24:16; 2 Kings 19:35; Ps. 34:7).

GOD'S NAMES IN THE NEW TESTAMENT

The New Testament lacks the variety of the divine names that are found in the Old Testament. The full name of Deity is stated in the phrase, "in the name of the Father and of the Son and of the Holy Spirit" (Matt. 28:19). The functional names, or titles, of the individual Persons of the divine Trinity are given under Paterology, Christology, and Pneumatology.

The Generic Name, Theos (God)

Occurring more than one thousand times, this is "God" (Gk. *Theos*) as in Romans 1:1. When it occurs alone, "God" may refer to the divine Trinity when the context does not restrict the designation to a certain divine Person (James 1:13). In passages that also refer to the Son, "God" usually represents the Father (John 3:16; Rom. 1:8–9; 1 Cor. 1:3–4). However, in several passages "God" represents the Son (1 John 5:20; also see endnote 19) or the Holy Spirit (Acts 5:3–4; 1 Cor. 3:16), as determined by the context.

The Functional Name, Kurios (Lord)

Occurring about six hundred times, God's primary title is "Lord" (Gk. *Kurios*), as in Ephesians 4:5. In quotations from the Old Testament, "Lord" represents either *Yahweh* or *Adonai*, as determined by their original references (cp. Matt. 3:3 with Isa. 40:3). When it is used in other passages, "Lord" seems to have a meaning similar to *Adonai*, for its Greek root, meaning one "having power or authority," suggests this.[31] Also, the ancient translators of the Old Testament into Greek (the *Septuagint*) used *Kurios* for *Adonai*. Generally, this title refers to God the Son (Acts 2:36; Eph. 4:5; 1 Cor. 8:6), rarely to God the Father (Acts 4:24; Rev. 4:11; 11:15), and very rarely to God the Holy Spirit (2 Cor. 3:17; Heb. 10:15–16).

The Personal Name

There are no divine personal names revealed in the New Testament for the Persons of the divine Trinity. The titles "Father," "Son," and "Holy Spirit" are used as divine personal names. "Jesus" is God the Son's human personal name as man (Matt. 1:21; Luke 1:31).

THE DECREE OF GOD

In this area of our study, we probe beyond the limits of our understanding. Because of this, we must avoid hasty conclusions that present a distorted, unbiblical concept of God and of man. As much as possible, we must also avoid looking at this doctrine from only a human point of view. We must try to understand it from God's point of view as well. It is best to withhold final judgment until we have examined all this doctrine. Whatever our final judgment may be, the truth lies in what the Bible says about God and man, and it allows God to be God and man to be man.

ITS DEFINITION

God's decree is His plan by means of which He has determined all things that relate to the universe, including His own actions toward it and all that comes to pass in it and of it. In the Scriptures, God's decree, or plan, is represented by the words "counsel" (Isa. 46:10; Ps. 33:11; Acts 2:23; Eph. 1:11; Heb. 6:17), "purpose" (Isa. 14:24–27; Acts 4:28; Rom. 8:28; Eph. 1:11; 3:11), and (decretive) "will" (Eph. 1:1, 5, 9, 11), which is to be distinguished from His preceptive will, consisting of His commands. Note that the "decree" of Psalm 2:6–9 refers to God the Son's incarnation and messianic work (cp. Ps. 13:33; Matt. 3:17), not to His eternal generation.

ITS CHARACTERISTICS

God's Decree Is One (Eph. 1:11; 3:11)

That God's plan is one is indicated by the singular words, "purpose" and "counsel." W. G. T. Shedd wrote, "The Divine decree is formed in eternity, but executed in time. There are sequences in the execution, but not in the formation of God's eternal purpose. . . . For God there is no series of decrees, each separated from the others by an interval of time. God is omniscient, possessing the whole of His plans and purposes simultaneously." [32]

God's Decree Is Eternal (Eph. 3:11)

Although all the parts of God's plan come to pass in their divinely appointed time, the plan itself is eternal. From our time-conscious point of view, the decree was formulated before the foundation of the universe (2 Tim. 1:9; Rev. 13:8; Titus 1:2; Eph. 1:4); from God's point of view, it has always existed in His mind.

God's Decree Is Immutable (Heb. 6:17)

Being the product of the unchanging God, this plan is never changed or altered; it always remains the same (Ps. 33:11). His plan is never affected by mistake, ignorance, or inability on His part or by anything outside Himself like the forces of evil or the activities of angels or humans.

God's Decree Is Universal (Eph. 1:11; Rom. 11:36)

God's decree comprises everything that exists or comes to pass in the universe. This includes the decisions, actions, conditions, and circumstances of all angels and humans, whether good or evil (2 Chron. 10:15; 36:22). It also includes the actions, conditions, and circumstances of all living and nonliving things (Ps. 119:90–91). Moreover, God appoints for humans such things as "chance" events (Prov. 16:33; 1 Kings 22:34), the sphere of habitation (Acts 17:26), the direction of life (Prov. 16:9), and the duration of life (Job 14:5).

Furthermore, this plan includes all God's external actions relating to the universe like His creating it, sustaining it, governing it, and using it to accomplish His objectives (Rev. 4:11). God's decree does not determine divine internal matters like the essential qualities of the divine nature or the internal relationships of the divine Persons.

God's Decree Is Certain (Prov. 19:21; Isa. 46:10)

All that God has decreed will certainly come to pass without fail. Nothing can thwart His purpose (Prov. 21:30), for all that exists is determined by His decree. His decree renders certain the actions of all creatures and all created things, but God, as we shall see, does not produce all these actions or accept the responsibility of them, such as Jesus' crucifixion (Luke 22:22; Acts 2:23; 4:27–28).

God's Decree Is Absolute (Acts 4:27–28)

God has determined not only all that shall be but also how it shall come to pass. The fulfillment of His decree in all its particulars is not dependent upon anything that is not part of the decree itself. For instance, in planning Jesus' death, God determined the circumstances of His death (Acts 4:27–28) as well as its means (John 10:18). God leaves nothing to "chance" (this does not exist). He has determined every detail of every event that comes to pass in and during the existence of the universe.

God's Decree Is Free (Eph. 1:5, 9, 11)

God freely determined what His plan should be and what details it should include. He was not influenced by anyone or anything outside Himself. With nothing existing outside the divine Trinity, God decreed freely, voluntarily, according to His own pleasure and will (Ps. 135:6; Isa. 40:13, 14; Rom. 11:33–36). At that time, nothing had been made certain by any previous decree, so there was nothing to be foreseen that would influence the making of His plan.

God's Decree Is Hidden (Eph. 3:9–11)

Being hidden within Himself, as shown by the mystery of Gentiles' and Jews' being members of the same body, God's decree is secret except for that part that He has revealed in His Word and that which has come to pass (see Deut. 29:29; 1 Cor. 2:6–12; Rom. 16:25–26; Amos 3:7; John 15:15).

God's Decree Is Christocentric (Eph. 3:11)

God's decree centers on Christ Jesus in the sense that its composition (Eph. 1:4) and fulfillment are related to His divine activities as the Father's Agent (1 Cor. 8:6) and to His human, messianic works as the Father's Servant or Slave (John 6:38; Eph. 1:10; 2 Tim. 1:9; Rev. 1:8; cp. Isa. 42:1–7).

The foregoing qualities show that God's decree is not controlled by or synonymous with fate, which is a system of undetermined, impersonal causes and effects. God's decree is personal; fate would be impersonal. God's decree is wisely planned for specific ends; fate would be the action of chance, which would produce random, uncertain results. Because of God's decree, neither fate nor chance exists.

ITS RELATIONS

The fact of the divine decree raises inquiry about its relation to God and to His creatures.

The Decree's Relation to God

To His Foreknowledge

In our study of God's omniscience, we noted that His decree is the basis of His free knowledge, or foreknowledge, of all actual things (see "God's Attributes: Omniscience"). This view is supported by the following: the order of Romans 8:28–29 where God's "purpose" precedes His "foreknowledge"; the truth that His election is one of divine grace, not of foreseen human works or merit (Rom. 9:11; 11:5–6; 2 Tim. 1:9); the fact that "foreknowledge" is grammatically equated with His "counsel" in Acts 2:23 (see endnote 11); and God's absolute sovereignty (Isa. 46:10), which precludes any rival or equal that would influence His actions. The fact remains that nothing can be foreseen until it has been made certain by the divine decree. That which is not decreed remains in the realm of possibility, but it never becomes a reality or has existence.

To His Transitive Activities

With reference to His activities, God's decree concerns only His transitive acts—His works with reference to things outside Himself like the creation of the universe, His dealings with creation, and His atonement for sins. His decree does not pertain to His essential Being like His decreeing to be holy or to exist as three Persons. Also, it does not relate to immanent activities within the Trinity like the Father's decreeing to love the Son.

The Decree's Relation to the Activities of Creatures

Its Efficient Aspect

While God's decree makes certain the actions of all creatures, including angels and humans, these are not all brought to pass in the same manner. God brings some things, like the creation of the universe, to pass directly (Gen. 1:1). He brings other things to pass indirectly through intermediate agencies like natural law (Acts 14:17) or the activities of humans (Dan. 1:9; 1 Cor. 15:10). In either case, this is known as the *efficient aspect* of His decree, for which He assumes the responsibility of His action and receives the credit for what comes to pass.

Its Permissive Aspect

God allows other things to come to pass that are made certain by His decree but that He Himself does not bring to pass, directly or indirectly, and for which He does not assume the responsibility nor receive the credit. This is known as the *permissive aspect* of His decree. This aspect concerns the sinful actions of angels and humans and their inherent ruinous effects (cp. Rom. 9:22–23; see Appendix J: "The Order of God's Decree"). This is not to suggest that God passively allows evil to occur as though He could not prevent or control it. It means that He actively and freely chose evil to be a part of His decree and allowed it to express itself within divinely determined limits of time and activity that by it He might attain His purpose (cp. Jesus' crucifixion, Acts 2:23; Luke 22:22; see "The Decree of God: Its Objective" in this chapter). But He is not the efficient Cause, or Producer, of evil or of evil persons and their evil deeds.

ITS DISSIMILARITY

In our thinking about God's decree, we sometimes overlook the fact that His decree is not synonymous with the actions of personal creatures (angels and humans) or with His revealed desire for them. Let us look at this more closely.

71

The Decree Is Not Synonymous with the Actions of Personal Creatures

For instance, while the decree included Adam's sin and made it certain, this part of the decree was not the act itself. The decree did not produce the sin, nor is God guilty of this sin. He did not by decree command Adam to sin. God's decree is not addressed to mankind, and it is not to be regarded as law, imposing obligation on their will.[33]

The Decree Is Not Synonymous with God's Revealed Desires

As strange as it appears, God's decree is not identical to His revealed will for His personal creatures. Actually, being two different things, these truths are not contradictory. God's decree (His decretive will, Eph. 1:5, 9, 11) is His secret plan, while His commands (His preceptive will, Eph. 5:17; 1 Thess. 4:3) are His revealed desires for His personal creatures.

For example, His desire for His people is that they not sin (cp. 1 John 2:1), yet in our experience we often deviate from God's preceptive will. This deviation falls within the permissive aspect of the divine decree, but it is not God's preceptive will for us. Moreover, we are responsible for our sinning and for the divine parental correction that it incurs (Rev. 3:19). Again, God's revealed desire for the unsaved is that they might be saved (1 Tim. 2:4; 2 Peter 3:9), but His decree is that only they whom He has chosen will be saved (2 Thess. 2:13; Eph. 1:4–5). Whether elected or not, the unsaved person is responsible for his sinning and for his guilty and ruined condition (Luke 22:22; Rom. 1:18–32; 9:22–23).

In the light of this distinction between God's decree and His revealed preceptive will, it is our duty to be more concerned about His will for us than about His decree, which is hidden from us. Failure to recognize this distinction has led Arminian theologians, like Richard Watson, to reject the absolute free character of God's decree and to make it dependent upon events that He did not desire for His creatures and yet He foresaw would take place.[34]

ITS OBJECTIVE

The ultimate goal of God's decree is to bring glory to Himself (Isa. 42:8; 43:7; Rom. 9:17, 22; Eph. 1:3–6, 11–12; 3:21; Rev. 4:11). The glory of God consists of some manifestation of His Being, like His power (Ps. 19:1; John 2:11) and grace (Titus 2:11), and of the praise that this manifestation evokes from His creatures (Matt. 5:16; 9:8; Rev. 5:11–14).

Although this goal may appear to be one of prideful self-exaltation, which would be sinful in personal creatures, this is not true of God. It is the Creator's inherent right to exalt Himself and to receive from His creation all praise, for it is the creature's duty, whose very existence depends upon the Creator, to glorify his Maker. Actually, God has no equal, and there is no person or thing that can rightfully claim independent existence and, thus, equal praise. Our highest duty is to glorify the Creator in all that we do (1 Cor. 10:31; 6:20). This means that we are to live in a manner that will bring Him credit and praise. While sin in our lives makes us unlike Him and discredits Him, our obedience in His strength manifests His qualities and works in our lives and brings Him praise (Matt. 5:16, 48; cp. John 17:4). We exist for this purpose (Eph. 1:12).

ITS PROBLEMS

Surpassing the limits of our finite minds, the doctrine of God's decree poses two problems that we cannot wholly resolve.

The Problem of Man's Moral Freedom

At first sight it would appear that God's decree, which renders all things contained therein certain, denies to angels and humans their freedom of moral choice and the responsibility of their actions. It would also appear that people's actions are not free or, as the Arminians hold, they occur outside God's decree. But Jesus' crucifixion shows that, although God has decreed human's actions, people are still personally responsible for them as charged (Luke 22:22; Acts 2:23; 3:13–15; 4:27–28; 5:30; 10:39).

Our problem of understanding lies in our conception of freedom. We generally think of liberty as being absolute, unrestrained self-determination, but we personal creatures do not have such freedom (Jer. 10:23). Various factors affect our self-determination like the moral influences and training that govern our evaluations, our inner inclinations and motivations (cp. Paul's moral conditioning by the law, Rom. 7:7–9), our mental and physical states (cp. 2 Cor. 2:4; Gal. 4:13), our external environment (cp. the influences of people and weather), the forces of evil (Rom. 7:15–23; Eph. 6:11–13; Rom. 12:2), and those of God (Ezra 6:22; 7:27–28; Prov. 21:1; Dan. 1:9; John 6:44; Phil. 2:13; Rev. 17:17).

On the other hand, we are not mechanically determined or controlled like puppets or robots. As relatively free agents, we have the capability of choosing and starting action. It is in the realm of our consciousness that we freely choose our courses of action without any sense of divine necessity (1 Cor. 7:37).[35] Thus having moral awareness and the power of conscious self-determination, we are accountable for our actions (Rom. 14:12). But below the level of our awareness, God acts upon our wills in such a way that He accomplishes His purpose and preserves the integrity of our conscious freedom and responsibility. This is the heart of the problem, and it is beyond our resolution. Since God's absolute sovereignty and man's responsibility are both the teachings of Scripture, we must accept these humanly irresolvable truths by faith.

The Problem of God's Relation to Sin

It would appear that God's decree, which renders all things contained therein certain, makes Him to be the efficient Cause, or Producer, of sin. But this concept of God contradicts what He has revealed about His character (Ps. 92:15; James 1:13; 1 John 1:5) and capability (James 1:13; Titus 1:2). He is not sinful nor can He sin.

God knew the possibility of sin and for good reasons included it in His decree, but He Himself did not bring it to pass. Angels and humans did this. Being divinely given the ability to make moral choices, of necessity this gave these personal creatures the ability to make a wrong choice and, thus, to initiate sin in their lives. Lucifer chose to admire and to exalt Himself and his beauty rather than God. This wrong choice generated within him the sin force and led to sinful pride and ambition. He refused to remain in his God-given place (1 Tim. 3:6; Ezek. 28:13–17; John 8:44).

In His permissive decree, God chose to allow sin to come into existence, but He does not accept any responsibility for it. L. Berkhof explained:

> The decree merely makes God the author of free, moral beings, who are themselves the authors of sin. God decrees to sustain their free agency, to regulate the circumstances of their life, and to permit that free agency to exert itself in a multitude of acts, of which some are sinful. For good and holy reasons He renders these sinful acts certain, but He does not decree to work evil desires or choices efficiently in man. The decree respecting sin is not an efficient but a permissive decree, or a decree to permit in distinction from a decree to produce sin by divine efficiency.[36]

ITS PRACTICALITY

This doctrine has practical application to life, as A. H. Strong observed:

1. It inspires humility by its representation of God's unsearchable counsels and absolute sovereignty.
2. It teaches confidence in Him who has wisely ordered our birth, our death, our surroundings, even to the smallest particulars, and has made all things work together for the triumph of His kingdom and the good of those who love Him.
3. It shows the enemies of God that, as their sins have been foreseen and provided for in God's plan, so they can never, while remaining in their sins, hope to escape their decreed and threatened penalty.
4. It urges the sinner to avail himself of the appointed means of grace if he would be counted among the number of those for whom God has decreed salvation.[37]

OBSERVATIONS

One: In no way does this doctrine stand in the way of anyone who wants to be saved. All who trust in the Savior and His atoning work are promised salvation (John 1:12; 3:16; 6:37). In fact, all are commanded to receive Him (Acts 17:30).[38]

Two: In all our thoughts about God, we must grant Him the highest honor. We must beware of Satan's attempts to lead us to hold wrong concepts of God because of our lack of understanding (Rom. 3:4; 9:20; 11:33–36; cp. Gen. 3:1–5).

Three: We must be on the alert against human reasoning that would lead us to embrace conclusions that are not supported by the clear teaching of Scripture or that conflict with the Scriptures.

Four: We who are saved should give our attention to God's preceptive will for us rather than to what He has decreed. What He has decreed is His concern; what He desires for us should be our concern.

Five: God's sovereignty and man's freedom, with its responsibility, cannot be reconciled in our human thinking. To hold to one and to reject or diminish the other results in our having a distorted view of biblical truth. What we cannot understand by reason must be accepted by faith, for God has spoken, and His Word is true.

THE WORKS OF GOD

In this section we shall look at God's major transitive acts that relate to the present universe. The psalmist described God's works to be great, majestic, glorious, wondrous, faithful, and right (Ps. 111:2–4 BV). This contemplation led him to exclaim, "Holy and awe-inspiring is His Name" (v. 9). As we examine these works, may our hearts be filled with similar praise.

GOD'S CREATION OF THE UNIVERSE

True, reliable knowledge of God's creative work is only found in the Scriptures (Gen. 1–2) and is to be received by faith in the integrity of His Word (Heb. 11:3). Any opinion or theory that ignores this and that does not make divine Truth its premise is flawed speculation.

A Definition of God's Creative Work

Creation may be defined as the work of God in bringing all persons and things comprising the universe into existence. This did not include sin, which was generated later by some of His personal creatures.

A Scriptural Analysis of God's Creative Work

1. It was the joint work of the divine Trinity.

It was the work of the Father (1 Cor. 8:6), the Son (John 1:3; 1 Cor. 8:6; Col. 1:13–17), and the Holy Spirit (Gen. 1:2; Job 26:13; 33:4; Ps. 104:30; Isa. 40:12–13). While the work of creation is attributed to each Person of the Trinity, all things originated with the Father and came about through the Son and by the Holy Spirit (1 Cor. 8:6; John 1:3; Job 26:13). Thus the Father is the Originating Cause of the universe, the Son is its Instrumental Cause, and the Holy Spirit is its Dynamic Cause (see "The relations of the Persons within the divine Trinity" in this chapter).

2. It was the free act of God.

God was not compelled to create by some force or necessity outside Himself. He did this freely, according to the counsel of His decretive will (Eph. 1:11; Rev. 4:11).

3. It was done in two steps.

The first step was God's initial creative work. This was His creating the universe without using preexistent material, of which there was none (Gen. 1:1; Ps. 148:2–5; Heb. 11:3). This is described as *ex nihilo* creation, that is, "out of nothing" creation. Many people who ignore this biblical truth speculate that the universe consists of matter that is eternal, an emanation of the divine essence, or some phenomenal appearance of Deity.

The second step was God's subsequent creative work by which He prepared the earth for man's habitation (Gen. 1:3, 6, 9, 14). God also made Adam and Eve as well as vegetation and animal life (Gen. 1:11, 20, 24, 26–27; 2:7, 21–22). He used the existing created elements of water and soil to make their physical bodies. He imparted to these bodies physical life, which in animals and humans has its source in their soul and spirit (Gen. 1:20, 24; 2:7; 6:17; 7:21–22; Eccl. 3:19–20). Not having soul and spirit, plant life consists simply of certain chemical actions and reactions.

4. It gives the universe distinct, dependent existence.

This means that the universe is not God or a part of Him, but it was derived and is distinct from Him (Acts 17:24–25). While God is not in any way dependent upon the universe (John 5:26; Acts 17:25), the universe is wholly dependent upon Him for its existence (Heb. 1:3; Col. 1:17).

God's relation to the universe is transcendent and immanent. Being transcendent, He is separate from, above, and other than the universe. Being immanent, He is everywhere in, with, and throughout the universe; but He is not a part of it or limited by it. This truth indicates that the universe is neither a part of God nor independent of Him. While being distinct from Him, the universe and all therein are wholly dependent upon Him for their existence.

5. Its primary purpose is to glorify God.

God uses the universe to glorify Himself by manifesting His perfections through it (Ps. 19:1; Rom. 1:20), accomplishing His purpose for it (Rev. 4:11; Eph. 1:11–12), and evoking praise from His creatures by it (Ps. 148; Rev. 5:13; Rom. 11:33–36).

The Contents of God's Creative Work

This is all that was contained in the divinely created universe regarding its entity and place (Col. 1:16; Neh. 9:6; John 1:3). *Entity* refers to what He made—material and immaterial, animate and inanimate, personal and impersonal, visible and invisible. *Place* refers to where these persons and things exist. God created all persons and things in the heavens, on earth, and under (or within) the earth (Phil. 2:10; Rev. 5:13), which refers to hades, the current prison of some fallen angels and of all dead unsaved humans (see Addendum: "Sheol, Hades").

Did God create evil? In those instances where "evil" means adversity, He does bring this about by intermediate causes (Isa. 45:7; cp. Amos 3:6; Isa. 10:5–6). On the other hand, where "evil" means the sin force and its evil works through angels and humans, God is not the efficient Cause of these. Rebellious angels and humans were the generators of this evil force. Sin was not a part of the original creation (Gen. 1:31). It was produced by personal creatures, who were created sinless and who chose to rebel against their Creator.

The Biblical Account of God's Creative Work

1. Its record

The only reliable information that man has of God's creative activity is that which the Creator has been pleased to give in the Scriptures (cp. Gen. 1:1–2:25). Under divine inspiration, Moses accurately recorded this information for all future generations. Being God's Word, this revelation must be received by faith, regardless of scientific opinion, if we are to understand correctly the origin of the universe and of the planet on which we live (Heb. 11:3). The Lord Jesus Himself acknowledged the historicity and authenticity of the biblical account (Matt. 19:4–5). It is noteworthy that this account does not include any of the false ideas that were held in Moses' time.[39]

God's creative activity during the six days of creation week is indicated by His creative command "let," which does not allow a self-existent universe, independent creative agencies, or random chance start and development. His creative activity includes the following:

On the first day (Gen. 1:1–5), God created instantly by command the heavens and the earth, including time, space, matter, energy, and gravity (Ps. 33:6, 9). The heavens included the angels and the physical celestial bodies, with their environment (Neh. 9:6; Pss. 136:5–6; 146:6; Exod. 20:11; Rev. 14:7). The angels were present when God created the earth (Job 38:4–7). He also ordered a temporary light to illuminate the earth until the fourth day, when He caused sunlight to shine upon it (Gen. 1:17). He set in motion the diurnal rotation of the earth, which determines our days of twenty-four hours.

On the second day (Gen. 1:6–8), God created the earth's atmosphere ("firmament," meaning an expanse), which lay between the water on earth and the Noachic Flood water that was suspended above the earth in vapor form.[40]

On the third day (Gen. 1:9–13), God separated the sea and the land into individual masses and created vegetation "after its kind" (vv. 11–12).[41]

On the fourth day (Gen. 1:14–19), God directed the solar, lunar, and stellar bodies to give their light simultaneously upon the earth.[42] Verse 16 is a parenthetic flashback to the first day, when He created these bodies. On the fourth day He set them in place and caused their light to shine instantaneously upon the earth, although they were millions of light-years away. This fact negates all estimates of the universe's age by the distance of its furthest stars. God also gave these celestial bodies for seasons, days, years, and signs. He gave the stars names (Ps. 147:4; Isa. 40:26), apparently for the purpose of their silently reminding mankind of the coming Conqueror-Savior during the 2,500 years before Moses wrote Genesis (Rom. 10:16–18; Ps. 19:4).[43] Another way in which celestial bodies are divinely used for signs is to indicate impending prophetic events (Matt. 2:2; Luke 21:25).

On the fifth day (Gen. 1:20–23), God created animal marine life and flying creatures, which are described as "living souls" (KJV "living creatures").[44]

On the sixth day (Gen. 1:24–31), God created land animals, creeping forms of life, and man and woman. Humans are distinguished from animals by being made in the image of God. This image is that of similarity ("likeness"), not identicalness; it consists of personhood, not soul (see "Humans Are Complex Beings" under Anthropology). God also gave to newly created man certain duties to fulfill (see "The Dispensations of God" in this chapter).

That this divine creative activity was limited to six days is indicated in Genesis 2:1 and is declared in Exodus 20:11. On the seventh day (Gen. 2:1–3), God ceased or rested from His creative activity, not because of exhaustion (Isa. 40:28) but because of His having completed His creation work.

The second biblical account of Creation (Gen. 2:4–25) gives more details about the creation of Adam and Eve and their duties. Note that verse 19a is a flashback to 1:21–25. The information of this second account completes what is given in the first creation account (1:1–2:3). It also provides information that is essential to a right understanding of mankind's initial sin and moral fall, recorded in Genesis chapter 3.

2. Its interpretation

How should we interpret the creation account? Religious liberalism regards it as an unreliable redaction of earlier pagan traditions or a fallible statement of truth in the form of myth. Contrariwise, people who believe in the divine inspiration of Genesis interpret the account literally or accommodatively. Let us examine these methods more closely.

a. The literal interpretation of the creation account

This interpretation, which I support, understands the account to be a simple, straightforward statement of God's creative activity in normal language. This also holds that this activity occurred during the time of six twenty-four-hour days (Exod. 20:11).[45] It understands Genesis 1:1 to be a general declaration of God's creation of the heavens and the earth. What follows (vv. 2–31) is a detailed account of how God prepared the newly created, uninhabitable earth for man. It is noteworthy that verse two does not grammatically contain action, but, having three circumstantial clauses, it describes the earth's original condition. Grammatically, these descriptive clauses modify the main verb "said" in verse three.[46] Creating the earth a desolate mass, enveloped in darkness and covered with water, the Holy Spirit is seen hovering over the face of the waters, sustaining what had been done and waiting to carry out the remaining creative activity.

In reply to the protest that the description in verse two is one of an imperfect state, it may be said that creation was not "perfect" in the sense that it was finished until the end of the six days, but each step was perfect according to God's purpose.[47] The description of the earth as being "without form" (meaning "desolation" or "emptiness") and "void" (meaning "wasteness") "does not affirm that it was a confused mass, in the sense of being disordered or jumbled, but simply that it was not habitable, not ready for man. . . . All was well-ordered and precisely as God desired it to be."[48] Thus, although the earth was incomplete (not yet ready for man), it was perfect for God's immediate purpose and its condition was in keeping with the divine will.[49] Furthermore, the "darkness" of verse two is to be understood as literal darkness, for God had not yet commanded light to appear. It is not to be interpreted as a figurative expression for sin or its results. It is noteworthy that God Himself, being light, has eternally dwelt in the absence of any other kind of light (2 Chron. 6:1; Ps. 97:2). He created darkness as well as light for the benefit of the universe (Isa. 45:7; Ps. 104:19–20).

The literal interpretation of the creation account holds that God's creative activities are fiat in nature, that is, by divine command. When He said, "Let there be . . ." it was done immediately, uniquely, apart from natural law, and wholly by divine power (Ps. 33:6, 9). Being infinite in power, God did His creative work instantaneously. For example, if ten men can do a piece of work in one hundred days, then (disregarding logistics and the like) a hundred men could do the same work in ten days and a thousand could do the work in a day. Thus the use of infinite power requires no time at all.

b. Accommodative interpretations of the creation account

These interpretations are attempts to harmonize the biblical account of creation with scientific opinion about the universe. However, I believe that these should be rejected, for any attempt to harmonize God's inerrant account with changing scientific opinion not only requires an unnatural explanation of the creation record but also subjects God's true, authoritative Word to man's fallible reasoning. The thinking that underlies scientific opinion is governed by the limitations of the scientific method, which cannot deal with such questions as origins, and by the presuppositions of the scientist, which are often contrary to the teachings of the Scriptures. To my mind, it seems very unlikely that God would reveal such important truth of primary interest to all generations in a form that could not be correctly understood until modern times. Several accommodative interpretations of Genesis chapter 1 follow:

1) The Day-Age Theory

This holds that the days of Genesis chapter 1 were six periods of time that represented the ages of geological history and that the creative events were carried out by God through natural processes within nature over vast periods of time.[50]

2) The Progressive Creation Theory

This holds that on each day of geological history, God started the creative activity by command and brought it to completion through the processes of natural law.[51]

3) The Gap, or Reconstruction, Theory

While holding that the earth was prepared for man's habitation in six days, this theory believes that preceding this reconstruction, there was an interval of time during which a perfect earth suffered divine judgment and experienced geological upheaval.

Some believe that this gap was before Genesis 1:1.[52] This means that the initial creation (John 1:3; Col. 1:16; Heb. 11:3) and Satan's rebellion (Ezek. 28:12–15) took place before Genesis 1:1. According to this view, Genesis 1:1–2 describes a later refashioning of a judgment-ridden earth in preparation for man's creation and habitation.

Others believe that this gap followed Genesis 1:1. Popularized by *The Scofield Reference Bible,* a more commonly held view of the gap theory is that Genesis 1:1 refers to the original creation of the universe in perfect, finished form, with the earth under Lucifer's (Satan's name before his fall) supervision. But his revolt against God brought divine judgment upon the earth, resulting in the desolation described in verse two. After an unrecorded gap of geological ages, verse 3 marks the beginning of the earth's reconstruction for man.[53]

4) The Theistic Evolutionary Theory

This allegorizes the creation account as being a poetic expression of spiritual truth. This theory holds that God used an evolutionary process to create forms of life and to bring them to their present stage of development.

Accommodative interpretations of Genesis chapter 1 generally assume that modern understanding of geological data is correct, that God initially created the earth in finished form, that the revolt of Lucifer took place before Genesis 1:3, that the linking verb "was" means "became" (v. 2), that other biblical references describe the "chaos" of verse two as a divine judgment, and that death was the universal experience of creatures before man's fall. However, these assumptions are not necessarily biblical ones, for the following reasons: *One,* geological data may be the result of creative processes, the Noachic Flood, and other natural disturbances of the earth's crust.[54] *Two,* in the light of Genesis 1:31 and 26 with 9:2, it appears that Satan's revolt did not take place until after the creative week. After the Flood, man did not have the same authority over the earth that Adam had (cp. Heb. 2:8). I believe that when he sinned, Adam lost his worldwide authority to Satan (John

12:31). *Three,* grammatically, the translation "was" (Gen. 1:2), rather than "became," is the right one in this context.[55] *Four,* the contexts of Isaiah 24:1 and Jeremiah 4:23–26 show that these references speak of the prophetic future rather than of Genesis 1:2. *Five,* it appears that creatures with soul (Heb. *nephesh,* Gen. 1:20–21, 24; 2:7) did not die until man's sin and the divine "vanity" was imposed upon them (3:17–19, 21; 4:8; Rom. 5:12; 8:20–22). It is noteworthy that land animals and airborne creatures were herbivorous before man's fall (Gen. 1:29–30).

That the six days of the creation week were twenty-four-hour days is supported by the following considerations: *One,* this is the primary, ordinary meaning of "day" in the Bible. *Two,* the phrase "evening and morning" points to the diurnal rotation of the earth upon its axis.[56] *Three,* this view is supported by Exodus 20:9–11, where literal days are mentioned regarding the workweek and the Sabbath. *Four,* in biblical usage whenever the word "day" is preceded by a numerical adjective or occurs in plural form, it means literal days (cp. Gen. 7:10–12). *Five,* Adam was created on the sixth day, yet he was only 130 years old when Seth was born (5:3). *Six,* vegetation, created on the third day would need for their survival the warmth and light of the sun, reaching earth on the fourth day, and the pollination of insects, created on the fifth day. *Seven,* whenever the word "day" is used in the Bible for daytime or a period of more than twenty-four hours, it is indicated by the context (cp. 1:5; 2:4).

The Date of God's Creative Work

Many scientists believe that the earth is billions of years old.[57] This estimate is ultimately based on the principle of uniformitarianism, which is applied to the interpretation of geological data and to the evaluation of radioactive dating materials.[58] Since nothing can be verified historically before the Noahic Flood (2348 B.C.), all estimates of age beyond this are only guesses. The only reliable chronological record is given in the Bible, which points to an age of 5,995 years to sunset on September 19, 1996.[59]

The Antagonists of God's Creative Work

The antagonists of biblical revelation regarding the origin of the earth are scientism and its associate, evolutionism. *Scientism* is the philosophy that exalts the scientific method above God's Word and that says that, where this method does not apply, nothing exists. While the scientific method has legitimate application to material things, like their content and function, it is incapable of making any authoritative pronouncements about metaphysical matters like the origin of the universe. Such questions as origins, meaning, and purpose can be answered only by divine revelation (1 Cor. 2:9–10).

When unsaved people reject God's revelation of His creative activity, their alternative is to embrace the erroneous view that the universe is the product of impersonal chance. Having no explanation for the origin of matter, these people regard it to be eternal and to have arrived at its present form by random, chance, evolutionary processes.

Organic evolution has been defined as "the belief that existing animals and plants developed by a process of gradual, continuous change from previously existing forms."[60] Although many noncreationists now hold that these changes took place rapidly, all attribute this development to certain impersonal mechanics of change now observable in nature, namely, adaptation, mutation, and natural selection.

We who accept God's account of His creative activity in the Scriptures hold the view of *creationism*—the belief that various basic forms of life were created by God apart from any evolutionary process. God may have used built-in mechanics of change to bring about variety within definite boundaries, as determined by the original "kind" of plant or animal (Gen. 1:11–12, 21, 24–25). This may also account for the racial distinctions of mankind.

William J. Tinkle offers the view that living organisms were created heterozygous, that is, with mixed genes that produced more, but not higher, types.[61]

1. The evolutionary theory's opposition to the Scriptures

This opposition is expressed by the following comparisons:

One: Evolution attributes the present existence and form of the universe to impersonal chance—a view that is wholly mechanistic and materialistic. Contrariwise, the Scriptures reveal that the universe is the creation of the personal Creator God. Philosophically, the concept of theistic evolution is absurd, for it says that God worked together with chance in creating the universe.[62]

Two: Evolution holds that all present life arose from a few simple forms. Contrariwise, the Bible teaches that God created life "after its kind" (Gen. 1:1–12, 21, 24–25). This does not say that all creatures living today appear exactly as their original "kinds" were created since there was a development of variety within the limits of their orders. But this development is not to be regarded as evolutionary since higher types, or species, did not develop from lower ones.

Three: Evolution teaches that mankind is experiencing a moral improvement and that sins are traits of animal ancestry, which will gradually disappear with the continuation of people's development. Contrariwise, the Bible reveals that people are responsible creatures who have sinned against their Creator and have incurred to themselves dreadful penalties by their evil actions.

Four: Regarding the universe as a closed system (a vast machine that operates wholly on its own), evolution rejects the fact of the transcendent sovereign God who rules over the affairs of the universe. According to evolution, any god there may be is a part of the machine and consists of the same substance as the universe. Contrariwise, the Bible teaches that God is a Reality other than the universe and that He governs its affairs to achieve His own purpose.

2. The theory of evolution's opposition to natural law

Christian scholars and scientists point out that those natural processes that evolutionists believe account for evolutionary development really contradict several basic principles within the framework of which all natural processes must operate. These principles are the first and second laws of thermodynamics and biogenesis.

The first law of thermodynamics (the law of conservation) states that although energy or matter changes form, the total quantity is conserved; matter is neither created nor destroyed. This principle contradicts the evolutionary view of spontaneous creation of energy that accounts for increasing organization, integration, and development. The Bible supports this law of conservation (Gen. 2:1–3; Heb. 4:3–4, 10; 2 Peter 3:10).

The second law of thermodynamics (the law of deterioration) states that all physical systems, if left to themselves, tend to become less ordered and useful. While the total amount of energy in the universe remains the same, the amount available for work becomes less. Thus processes run down and things wear out or become disorganized. Any temporary increase in an order requires an input of energy from outside the system itself (cp. Heb. 1:3). This principle contradicts the evolutionary view that a perpetual increase of organization and development is taking place in the universe according to natural processes.[63] Psalm 102:25–27 teaches otherwise.

The theory of evolution also opposes the principle of biogenesis. This principle states that life derives only from life. This contradicts the evolutionary view that life spontaneously arose from inanimate material. With the teaching that the living Creator is the source of all life, the Bible supports the principle of biogenesis (Acts 17:24–25).

Although the theory of evolution contradicts these basic universal laws and rests upon the absurdity of random chance, brilliant people of the world prefer to accept this rather than the truth of the personal Creator. To accept the latter requires them to admit their creaturehood and their accountability to the Creator and their duty to honor and obey Him. Because they are in rebellion against God, unsaved people prefer Satan's lie above God's truth (cp. Rom. 1:18–25).

The Continuation of God's Creative Work

The present physical universe will continue until the close of Jesus' millennial kingdom. At that time God will dissolve the present universe, perhaps by reverting its mass to nonmolecular form (2 Peter 3:10–13; Rev. 20:11), and will create a new one that will continue forever (Rev. 21:1–3). Between the dissolution of the universe and the creation of a new one, there will take place the judgment of fallen angels and unsaved humans (20:11–15).

Meanwhile, during the present time the Lord is involved in a spiritual creative work. He is building His Church, which is called "one new man" (Matt. 16:18; Eph. 2:15). Also, all who trust in Jesus and His atoning work are made new creatures in Him (2 Cor. 5:17; Eph. 2:10).

GOD'S SOVEREIGN RULE

The Scriptures teach that God, as its Owner (Pss. 24:1; 50:12), exercises sovereign, absolute rule over the universe to do what He wills (1 Chron. 29:11–12; Ps. 103:19; Eph. 1:11). J. I. Packer observed,

> This view of God's relation to the world must be distinguished from (a) *pantheism,* which absorbs the world into God; (b) *deism,* which cuts it off from Him; (c) *dualism,* which divides control of it between God and another power; (d) *indeterminism,* which holds that it is under no control at all; (e) *determinism,* which posits a control of a kind that destroys man's moral responsibility; (f) the doctrine of *chance,* which denies the controlling power to be rational; and (g) the doctrine of *fate,* which denies it to be benevolent.[64]

The doctrine of God's sovereign rule is set forth in the biblical teaching of His preservation and providence.

His Preservation

Preservation concerns God's maintaining the existence of what He has made and His care of these things (Neh. 9:6; Col. 1:17; Heb. 1:3). He faithfully provides for the needs of the universe according to His purpose for these creatures and things. He cares for inanimate creation (Isa. 40:26), His creatures (Ps. 104:10–28), all people (Acts 14:17; 17:25, 28), and His elect people (Ps. 37:23–29; Isa. 41:10; Matt. 6:25–34; John 6:39; 10:28).

His Providence

Providence concerns God's directing everything to its divinely appointed goal. By His providence, God works out His decree for all actual things. This is seen in His fulfilling His sovereign purpose throughout the universe (Dan. 4:35) by His ruling all natural forces (Ps. 104; Job 38:4–38) and animals (Job 38:39–39:30; 40:15–41:34); by His controlling all angels (Job 1:12; 2:6; Ps. 103:20), nations (Dan. 4:25; Isa. 10:5–6; 2 Chron. 10:12–16), and individual persons (Isa. 44:28; Jer. 1:5; Prov. 16:9; 20:24; 21:1); and by His overruling people's misfortunes (Gen. 39:1–2, 21–23; 45:7). However, as we look at the truth of God's providence, several problems come into view.

1. The problem of the prosperity of the wicked

The psalmist was troubled by the prosperity of the wicked (Ps. 73:1–16). But when he went to God's temple, he learned that this prosperity was only temporary (v. 17a). He saw the disastrous end of the wicked (vv. 17b–19) and reflected on his own blessings (vv. 23–28). From the New Testament we learn that God is patient with the wicked, giving them opportunity to repent (Rom. 2:4; 2 Peter 3:9). However, the only prosperity they will ever enjoy is the blessings of common grace in this present life (cp. Matt. 1:20b; Acts 14:17 with Matt. 25:41, 46).

2. The problem of the suffering of godly people

God uses suffering for beneficial purposes (Prov. 3:11–12; Ps. 119:67, 71). He uses it to promote the practical sanctification and spiritual growth of His people (James 1:2–4), to correct them when they fail to deal with known sins in their lives (Rev. 3:19; 1 Cor. 11:30–32), to bring them into subordination to His will, to instruct them, and to cause them to be fruitful (Heb. 12:5–11). Despite Satan's doubts and lies, God has His people's spiritual well-being in view in all their suffering. We who are saved need to remember that our heavenly Father is more concerned about our spiritual state than our physical comfort. If necessary, He will deprive us of physical ease to promote our spiritual growth and well-being. Faithfully borne suffering glorifies God as well as bringing us personal blessing (Job 1:21; 42:1–6; John 9:1–3; James 1:2–4) and spiritual fruitfulness (John 15:2; Heb. 12:11; 2 Cor. 12:7–10).

Godly people also suffer from the world's hostility (John 15:18–20). Jesus declared that the world hates His people because of their severance from it and their association with Him. This hatred is largely impersonal and constitutional, due to the essential differ-·ences between unsaved and saved people and to the world's rebellion against God (cp. 2 Cor. 5:17; Phil. 1:29; 2 Tim. 3:12; 1 Peter 4:12–16; 1 John 3:13).

3. The problem of the suffering of undeserving people

This concerns the suffering of undeserving, helpless people, including infants and children. These suffer because they are a part of this sinful world. H. E. Guillebaud observed, "Hard as it is for the individual who suffers through another's wickedness, it is in the best interests of mankind that the ugliness of sin should not be hidden, and nothing does more to show it in its true light than the misery that it brings to the innocent. . . . A sinful world cannot be a world free of suffering." [65]

Suffering of all kinds is an inevitable result of sin's entrance into the human family. It will be acutely experienced by the unsaved forever (Matt. 25:46), but we who are saved will one day be forever delivered from it (1 Thess. 4:13–17; Rev. 21:3–5).

4. The problem of God's involvement in the actions of personal, accountable creatures

The Bible shows that God, according to His sovereign purpose, permits some sins (Ps. 81:12–13; 2 Thess. 2:7–12), prevents certain sins (Gen. 20:6; 1 Sam. 25:39), and limits certain evil actions (Job 1:12; 2:6; 2 Thess. 2:7). God not only allows unsaved people to do what they prefer (Rom. 9:22) but also prompts saved people to desire and to do His good pleasure (Phil. 2:13). This relation between God's sovereign influence upon personal creatures and their responsible actions is a *concurrence* (meaning a "running together," see Deut. 30:15–20; Prov. 16:9; 20:24; 21:1; Luke 22:22; Acts 2:23). James I. Packer again observed, "God's control is absolute, in the sense that men do only that which He has ordained that they should do; yet they are truly free agents, in the sense that their decisions are their own, and they are morally responsible for them (cp. Deut. 30:15ff.)."[66]

How God can control the actions of people and yet not deprive them of their freedom and responsibility is, indeed, a mystery that defies our understanding. But since this is the teaching of Scripture, we must be content to accept this truth by faith and to wait for the enlightenment that He will give us later (cp. 1 Cor. 13:11–12).

GOD'S SAVING WORK

Unquestionably, salvation is uniquely God's work (Isa. 45:22; Rom. 5:6; Eph. 2:8–9). While we shall examine this doctrine in greater detail later, it is fitting that we include it here with God's other works. To my mind, this is His greatest work, for it displays certain beneficent qualities of His nature, especially toward undeserving people, that no other work does. Because sinners were unable to deliver themselves from sin, God in His measureless grace was pleased to provide salvation. This saving work includes the following divine operations:

God's Choosing Whom He Would Save (2 Thess. 2:13)

This choice was not prompted by human works, worth, or merit (Rom. 9:11). It was solely by God's free will and pleasure (Eph. 1:9, 11; see "God's Part in the Application of Salvation" under Soteriology).

God's Atoning for Humanity's Sins (John 1:29)

Before He could save sinners, God's nature required Him to deal with their sins and to satisfy His holy demands against them. This involved the joint activity of the Trinity. The Father gave His Son to appease His wrath against sinful humanity (John 3:16; 1 John 4:9–10). In obedience to the Father, the Son gave His life to atone for humanity's sins by provisionally paying their debt (Matt. 20:28; John 10:18; Phil. 2:8; see "The Nature of Jesus' Atoning Work" under Christology). His atoning work was made effective by His resurrection (Rom. 1:4; 4:25). Finally, the Holy Spirit enabled the Lord Jesus, as man, to do all that His atoning work required (Heb. 9:14; Rom. 8:11).

God's Saving the Elect (2 Thess. 2:13; 1 Peter 1:2)

Drawn by divine action (John 6:37, 44), all who trust in Jesus and His atoning work receive the value of His sacrifice and experience God's saving work in their lives (John 3:16; 1:12–13). Being wholly God's work (Eph. 2:8–9), salvation manifests God's love, wisdom, power, and grace. This work includes God's choosing whom He would save; His delivering gospel believers from the ruin, debt, and bondage of their sins; His bringing them into a personal relationship with Himself; and His bestowing on them the riches of His grace. We who are saved shall never cease to praise Him for this gracious work in our lives.

GOD'S JUDGMENTS

As the Creator and Ruler of the universe, God is the Judge of all the earth (Gen. 18:25). In contrast to salvation, judicial judgment is His "strange work" (Isa. 28:21). Still, His holiness and justice, as well as the accountability of His personal creatures, require this (Rom. 14:12; 1 Peter 4:5). The apostle Paul described divine judicial judgment as being factual (Rom. 2:2), fair (v. 6), and impartial (v. 11).

The biblical concept of divine judgment generally represents any of three ideas, as determined by its scriptural context: *one,* God's assessment or trial of accountable personal creatures; *two,* His judicial sentence upon them; or *three,* the execution of His sentence. Several biblical periods of divine judgments, with some of their recorded aspects, follow:

During Time Past

These were divine judgments, not messianic ones.[67]
1. Adam and Eve: trial and sentence (Gen. 3:14–19); execution (vv. 23–24)
2. The world's destruction by the Noachic Flood: assessment (Gen. 6:5), sentence (v. 6–7), and execution (7:17–24)
3. Sodom and Gomorrah: assessment (Gen. 18:20–21; 19:13) and execution (19:13, 24–25)
4. The plagues on Egypt: assessment (Exod. 7:3–4, 22) and execution (7:20–12:30)
5. Judah's Babylonian captivity: assessment (2 Chron. 36:11–16) and execution (vv. 17–21)

In Jesus' Trial and Death

These were messianic judgments.
1. Satan and his world system: their trial and sentence (Gen. 3:15; John 12:31; 16:11)[68] Their execution will be in the future (Rev. 20).
2. Jesus' bearing the penalty of our sins: execution (Isa. 53:10; 1 John 2:2; 4:9–10)

In the Future

These will be messianic judgments.
1. Those of the Tribulation Age: execution (Rev. 6–18)
2. Jesus' return to earth and the Battle of Armageddon: execution (Rev. 19:11–21)
3. Earth dwellers who survive the Tribulation Age: trial, sentence, and execution, including Israel (Ezek. 20:33–38) and the Gentiles (Matt. 25:31–46)
4. All the unsaved people and fallen angels: trial, sentence, and execution (Rev. 20:11–15; 2 Peter 2:4; Matt. 8:29; 25:41). Unsaved people are already divinely condemned for their sins (John 3:18; Rom. 5:18). Their future trial concerns their answering to God for their wrongdoing and God's deciding the degree of punishment that they will receive in everlasting hell (Matt. 11:20–24).
5. The judgment of gospel believers (Rev. 22:12; 2 Cor. 5:10). This will not be a judicial one. It will be the Master's appraisal of the works of His servants for calculating their rewards. Saved people will never come into judicial judgment for their sins, for the Lord Jesus bore this for them on the cross (John 5:24; 1 Peter 2:24; Rom. 8:1, 31–34; Col. 2:13).

One cannot reflect upon the excellency of our God's person and works, in contrast to the false, ineffective gods of this world, and not be filled with gratitude and praise for His self-revelation. The true and living God deserves more loyalty from His people than that which the false gods of this world receive from their devotees (1 Thess. 1:9–10). To express this loyalty, let us learn more about His will for us, as given in the dispensation that He has given to us to observe, and do it with loving hearts.

THE DISPENSATIONS OF GOD

Throughout human history, God has given people certain responsibilities, or duties, which we call "dispensations." Our understanding of these dispensations gives us insight into God's will for mankind and for us who are saved.[69]

THEIR DEFINITION

The NT word "dispensation" basically means "a house rule" (Gk. *oikonomia*). In its biblical usage, the word may mean "management" of a household (Luke 16:2–4), "administration" or "stewardship" (1 Cor. 9:17; Eph. 3:2; Col. 1:25), an "arrangement" or "plan"

(Eph. 3:9), "fellowship" (1:10), or "training" (1 Tim. 1:4, KJV "edifying").[70] Paul spoke of his apostolic duties as a "dispensation," or stewardship, for the execution of which he was endued with divine grace (Eph. 3:1–2; cp. Rom. 12:3).

With this in view, I define a *dispensation,* as it relates to our present study, to be those duties that God assigns to mankind or to certain people for a period of time, for which they are accountable to Him.

Although a dispensation involves time, the emphasis should be placed on the duties that the dispensation imposes on its recipients. While God works through these dispensations to accomplish His purpose (cp. Eph. 1:10; 3:9), our primary concern in this study is with the duties that these dispensations require their recipients to observe. Excepting the first one, these dispensations should not be regarded as tests of obedience to the divine will. Rather, they are declarations of the divine will for the people to whom they are given and for which these people are accountable.

A *dispensationalist* is one who recognizes the biblical divine dispensations and the people to whom they are given. Also, *dispensationalism* is the interpretation and application of the Scriptures that recognizes the various dispensations and their features, the people to whom each dispensation is given, and the portion of the Bible that relates to the dispensation and its recipients.

THEIR DISTINCTION FROM THE AGES

We should distinguish between a dispensation and an age and not use these terms synonymously.[71] In the Bible the word *age* has several meanings relating to time. In addition to referring to a person's age (1 Chron. 23:3; John 9:21), the word *age* has two meanings that have dispensational significance. These meanings may be characterized by the words *dynamically* and *ethically.*

Dynamically, an age is a period of time that is characterized by some activity of God, man, or Satan. For instance, the period during which the Lord is building His Church is called the Church Age. According to the pretribulational rapture view, the period immediately starting after the rapture of the Church to the Lord's second coming to earth is called the Tribulation Age. This alludes to the many judgments that earth dwellers will experience during this time (Rev. 6–19). The period of 490 years during which God would deal with Israel—the 70 sevens ("weeks") of Daniel 9—is sometimes called the Jewish Age (cp. Matt. 24:3, KJV "world," lit. "age"). Also, our Lord's rule over the earth for one thousand years is called the Kingdom Age.

Ethically, an age is what the world is morally and philosophically at any moment of its history. For instance, when he writes, "Be not conformed to this age" (Rom. 12:2, KJV "world"), the apostle Paul is urging his saved readers not to adopt the sinful lifestyle and thinking of unsaved people.

An age may be concurrent with a dispensation. For instance, the Kingdom Age coincides with the Dispensation of our Lord's Earthly Rule. An age may also coincide with only part of a dispensation. For example, I believe that the Church Age and the Tribulation Age fall within the Dispensation of Grace. Finally, an age may extend beyond the limits of a dispensation. For example, the Jewish Age covers parts of the Dispensation of the Mosaic Law and the Dispensation of Grace.

THEIR AID IN BIBLE INTERPRETATION

The recognition and understanding of the dispensations are important to a right interpretation and application of the Bible, especially in the following ways:

One: This observes the distinctions between the divine dispensations and the divine covenants, together with the people to whom they belong. An example is the distinction between Israel and the Universal Church. Those who disregard this distinction regard Israel to be the Church of the Old Testament and the Church to be the Israel of the New Testament, with common spiritual blessings and functions. However, dispensationalists hold that each of these groups has its own particular duties, blessings, and functions. Having the Dispensation of Grace, the Church is not obligated to observe the Dispensation of the Law of Moses, nor does it fulfill the same function as Israel in God's program.

Two: This also allows a literal interpretation of the Bible, especially in the area of unfulfilled prophecy. The literal interpretation of Bible prophecy was demonstrated by the literal fulfillment of those OT prophecies that related to our Lord's first coming to earth. Nondispensationalists, for instance, usually believe that Israel, by their rejection of Christ, forfeited their future place in God's program and that all prophecies about the future of this nation are to be interpreted allegorically as pertaining to the Church.[72] On the other hand, dispensationalists hold that Israel has a definite place in God's future program, as the biblical prophecies indicate, and that the elect of this nation must experience the fulfillment of God's covenant promises to them as a function of His essential faithfulness.

Three: Many dispensationalists rightly hold that throughout human history there is only one method of salvation and that salvation brings basic, common blessings to all gospel believers, regardless of their time in history. These blessings are the forgiveness of sins and a personal relationship with God (Jer. 31:33–34; John 17:3). On the other hand, the redeemed peoples of the various dispensations appear to have different functions in God's program. For instance, Israel had a special covenant relationship with the LORD [Yahweh] as His wife (Exod. 19:5; Jer. 3:14, 20; Hos. 2). Although the nation broke this relationship by their idolatry (2 Kings 17:15–16; Jer. 31:32; chap. 3), this union will be reestablished with God when the Lord returns to earth for His millennial reign (Jer. 31:31; Hos. 2:7, 14, 16, 19–20). The elect remnant of Israel will enjoy the blessings of their special relation to God as His wife and as the foremost nation on earth (Jer. 3:14; Hos. 2:21–23; Zech. 8:23; Mic. 4:1–7; Isa. 59:20–60:22). On the other hand, the Church will function as Jesus' bride (Eph. 5:22–32; Rev. 19:7).[73] This indicates that she will have a special relation to the Lord Jesus above all other redeemed peoples. Unlike Israel, the Church will not be an earthly national entity but will have the Lord Jesus and His blessings for her inheritance (John 14:3; 1 Thess. 4:17; Eph. 1:11).

THEIR APPLICATION TO LIFE

One: We who are saved are responsible for observing the Dispensation of Grace, which consists of most commands of the New Testament. This portion of the Bible was given by the Lord Jesus for the direction of His people during His absence from earth (John 16:12–15; Eph. 4:21; Col. 3:16; Gal. 6:2; Rev. 1:1–2).

Two: While our Lord's teachings, recorded in the Gospels, were given during the Dispensation of Mosaic Law, they actually belong to the Dispensation of Grace, for the Lord was preparing His disciples for life and ministry in the Church Age, which began on the Day of Pentecost, ten days after our Lord's return to heaven. Examples of these teachings are given in the Sermon on the Mount (Matt. 5–7) and in the Upper Room Discourse (John 14–16).

Three: We must recognize that while it is all profitable to us, the Bible is not all about us (2 Tim. 3:16; Rom. 15:4; 1 Cor. 10:11). Most of the Old Testament (Exod. 19–Mal. 4) concerns God's dealing with Israel under the Dispensation of the Mosaic Law. Since the New Testament gives God's dispensation for His people today, we may follow the instructions of the Old Testament, like the Ten Commandments (Exod. 20:1–17), insofar as these directions reflect, or are in harmony with, those of the New Testament. For instance, we are not directed to observe the Sabbath or follow the Levitical sacrificial ritual. On the other hand, we read of the duty of fearing God (Ps. 34:9; Prov. 1:7; Eccl. 12:13), which is also commanded in the New Testament (Eph. 5:21; Heb. 12:28; 1 Peter 1:17; 2:17).

Four: Certain prophetic NT passages, like Matthew chapters 24–25 and Revelation chapters 6–18, do not directly apply to us who are living in the Church Age. These passages will be of special value to God's people who will be living in the Tribulation Age. On the other hand, such admonitions as our being ready and watching for Jesus' return are important for us to heed (Matt. 24:42, 44; cp. 1 Thess. 5:1–10).

Five: There are recorded in Acts certain events, experiences, and practices that belong to the transition period into the Dispensation of Grace and that are not normative for us today. These include waiting for the promise of the Father (Acts 1:14), the experience of the Pentecostal phenomena (2:1–4), the common holding of private property (v. 45), and praying for the gift of Holy Spirit (8:14–17). Today, gospel believers receive the Holy Spirit's indwelling, baptism, and anointing at salvation (see "The Holy Spirit's Ministry to Saved People: At the Time of Salvation" under Pneumatology). Because of this, it is unnecessary to seek these as additional works or blessings of grace.

ULTRADISPENSATIONALISM

I believe that some dispensationalists carry dispensationalism beyond the limits that are clearly indicated by the Scriptures. These people are *ultradispensationalists.* They hold that the Great Commission of Matthew 28:19–20 is exclusively Jewish; that although the "Jewish church" began on the Day of Pentecost (Acts 2), "the Gentile Church" began with Paul, either after his conversion (Acts 13:2) or after his arrival in Rome (Acts 28:28); that water baptism is not for the Church Age, and that Acts 2:38 sets forth a works kind of salvation.

These extreme views can be refuted by showing that the building of the Church began on Pentecost (Acts 1:5; 11:15), that water baptism was observed by the early church (Acts 18:8), that salvation is always by grace through faith in Jesus (Eph. 2:8), and that the Great Commission is self-perpetuating (Matt. 28:19–20). In Acts 2:38, the phrase "for the remission of sin" can also be read "because of the remission of sins." [74] Water baptism should follow salvation as a public testimony to one's salvational faith in Jesus and His atoning work (Acts 18:8).

THEIR DISTINCTION FROM THE DIVINE COVENANTS

We avoid confusion and misunderstanding when we clearly distinguish between God's dispensations and His covenants. While a dispensation represents the duties that God gives to certain people to fulfill, a covenant declares by promises what God will do for certain people. There are divine covenants within dispensational periods of time, but except for the Mosaic Law these covenantal promises are not an essential feature of any dispensation. The Mosaic Law functioned simultaneously as a dispensation and a covenant. As we shall see, the primary feature of a dispensation is the duties that God imposes upon certain people; that of a covenant is the promises that God makes to certain people.

THEIR NAMES

1. The Dispensation of Created Mankind (Gen. 1:28–29; 2:15–17)
2. The Dispensation of Fallen Mankind (Gen. 3:16–4:7)
3. The Dispensation of Governed Mankind (Gen. 9:1–7)

4. The Dispensation of the Patriarchs (Gen. 12:1; 17:1; 26:5; 31:3, 13; 35:1; 46:1–4)
5. The Dispensation of the Mosaic Law (Exod. 20:1–7; 21:1–23:19; Lev. 1–27; Num. 5–6, 9–10, 15, 18–19, 27–30)
6. The Dispensation of Grace (John 1:17; Matt. 28:19–20; Titus 2:11–12)
7. The Dispensation of Christ's Earthly Rule (Isa. 2:1–3)[75]

THEIR DESCRIPTION

In our study of the dispensations, we shall observe the following outline:

1. The recipients of the dispensation

These are the people to whom the dispensation is given. As we shall see, five dispensations are universal in that they are given to all people worldwide, one is given to a man and to certain members of his posterity, and one is given to a nation.

2. The duties of the dispensation

These express God's will for the recipients.

3. The recipients' response to the dispensation

The response is either obedience or disobedience. Each dispensation imposes upon its recipients the responsibility of fulfilling its duties.

4. God's reaction to people's response

He blesses the obedient and punishes the disobedient. We shall see that God's chosen people, when they are submissive to Him and rely on Him, are by divine grace sufficiently obedient to allow Him to fulfill His purpose for their lives.

5. The duration of the dispensation

This is the span of time during which the duties of a dispensation are in force.

6. God's use of the dispensation

According to their dispensation, God works through people's lives to carry out His purpose for them and for mankind. Since salvation is a primary divine activity in human history, we shall look at this aspect of God's use of the dispensations.

THEIR CONTENT

The Dispensation of Created Mankind (Gen. 1:28–29; 2:15–17)

1. The recipients of the dispensation

These were Adam and Eve. That they were historical persons is indicated in the New Testament (Matt. 19:4; Luke 3:38; Rom. 5:12; 1 Cor. 11:8–9; 15:45; 1 Tim. 2:13–14). God created Eve to help Adam meet the requirements of the dispensation as well as to minister to his personal needs (Gen. 1:28; 2:18; 1 Cor. 11:9).

2. The duties of the dispensation

a. To be fruitful and fill the earth (Gen. 1:28)

Man was to reproduce his kind and populate the earth. The KJV word *replenish* in the Hebrew text is "fill."

b. To subdue the earth and have dominion over the lower forms of life (Gen. 1:28)

This duty seems to apply particularly to the environment outside Eden. Subduing the earth meant that man was to control his environment so as to make the best use of it for his needs and God's glory. This subjugation included his learning about his environment through exploration and study, his wisely using earth's resources, and his domesticating animals to serve his needs. Observe that animals did not fear man before the Noachic Flood (Gen. 9:2). The fact that God gave man dominion "over all the earth" indicates that Satan had not yet rebelled against God and seized this world's authority from Adam, God's viceroy (see "The Fall of Lucifer" under Angelology).

c. To eat vegetables, grain, and fruit (Gen. 1:29)

Mankind, as well as animals (Gen. 1:30), was to eat vegetables, grain, and fruit. People were not divinely authorized to eat animal flesh until after the Noachic Flood (Gen. 9:3).

d. To dress the garden and keep it (Gen. 2:15)

The garden was man's first home. He was to work it and care for it. Being a lifelong activity, this work contributed to man's well-being, for it gave him opportunity to express his abilities and to provide for himself and his dependents. The woman's duty was to be her husband's loving companion and helper (Gen. 2:18).

e. Not to eat the fruit of the forbidden tree (Gen. 2:16–17)

There were two unique trees in the garden of Eden—*the tree of life* (Gen. 2:9; 3:24; Rev. 2:7; 22:2, 14), which would have enabled Adam and Eve to live forever in their natural state, and *the tree of the knowledge of good and evil,* which was divinely selected as a test for them. Because Adam and Eve could make moral choices, this test gave them opportunity to choose voluntarily God's domination and direction for their lives. By obeying Him, they would have gained an experiential knowledge of good and a theoretical knowledge of evil, and they would have entered a permanent state of holiness and righteousness. Although the couple knew God personally and had spiritual life, their disobedience would bring them guilt, with its experiential knowledge of evil, immediate spiritual death and ruin, and subsequent physical death.

Until their eating the forbidden fruit, the couple, by carrying out their duties, was acquiring a record of personal righteousness and holiness, which was subject to change. Their continued obedience, however, would have changed their mutable righteousness and holiness into permanent, unchanging form. It would also have given them a perception of evil like God's knowledge of it.

This test indicates that humans were created to be ruled as well as to rule (1 Cor. 11:3). To whatever controlling principle, or force, they would surrender themselves, that principle, whether God or sin, would direct their lives and use them for its expression (cp. Rom. 6:11–13, 16; Luke 6:45). With His prohibition, God declared what penalty disobedience would bring them (Gen. 2:17; Rom. 6:23).

3. The recipients' response to the dispensation

Both Adam and Eve chose to disobey God (Gen. 3:1–6). Eve's choice was preceded by satanic deception through a snake (Gen. 3:1; Rev. 12:9); Adam was not deceived (1 Tim. 2:14). Speaking through the snake, Satan misled Eve to think that her disobedience to God would satisfy her natural desires (Gen. 3:6).

4. God's reaction to people's response

God reacted to the couple's sinning with judgment (Gen. 3:7–19). The guilty pair immediately experienced the natural results of their sinning, including spiritual death, the total corruption of their personhood and human nature, the generation of the sin force, and their coming under its control. Furthermore, they were judicially examined by God (Gen. 3:9–13) and received penal sentences (Gen. 3:16–19). Eventually, they died physically (Gen. 5:5).

Despite the necessity of this judgment, God graciously provided salvation for Adam and Eve (Gen. 3:20–24). His sentence upon Satan, who had used the snake as a means to speak to Eve (v. 1; Rev. 12:9), contained the promise of the woman's Seed (the coming Conqueror-Savior), who ultimately would deliver the Devil a lethal blow and would gain power over death and sin (John 16:11; Col. 2:15; Heb. 2:14; Rom. 8:3; Rev. 20:1–3, 10). Adam's faith in this promise was manifest in his calling his wife "Eve," or "living" (Gen. 3:20). He believed that she would be the divine means not only of perpetuating the human race but also of providing, through her Seed, mankind's ultimate victory over Satan and death (Heb. 2:14–15). Eve's faith in the promise was indicated by her accepting her name and by her utterances at the births of Cain and Seth, which suggest that she believed that God had given her the promised Conqueror-Savior (Gen. 4:1, 25).

In response to the couple's faith in the promise of the Conqueror-Savior, God clothed them in garments of animal skins (Gen. 3:21). This was the first of many animal sacrifices that would be offered for the covering of human sins from God's sight and that would anticipate the sacrifice of God's Lamb for humanity's sins (John 1:29). The making of these garments required the death of innocent animals and the shedding and offering of their blood. By this action, God established the arrangement for the OT atonement of human sins (Lev. 17:11). Also, this portrayed the substitutionary character of Jesus' atoning death and the offering of His blood, by means of which He paid the debt of our sins (Matt. 20:28; Rom. 6:23; 5:8). The garments portrayed the righteousness that gospel believers receive at salvation and in which they stand before God (Rom. 3:22; 1 Cor. 1:30; 2 Cor. 5:21).

After providing these garments, God drove the saved couple from the garden in order that they might not eat from *the tree of life* and live forever in their unsaved bodies (Gen. 3:22–24). This was an act of divine mercy.

5. *The duration of the dispensation*

It continued from the time of Adam's and Eve's creation until their first sin and its divine judicial sentence. This was perhaps only a few days.

6. *God's use of the dispensation*

By this, God allowed Adam and Eve to choose their life-dominating moral force and spiritual allegiance, with their consequences. He used the opportunity, afforded by their disobedience, to announce in veiled language the Savior's coming and work, to demonstrate symbolically His method of atoning for human sins, and to begin saving those whom He had chosen to redeem. His clothing the couple with animal skins and evicting them from Eden set the stage for the outworking of His salvation program.

The Dispensation of Fallen Mankind (Gen. 3:16–4:7)

Although Adam and Eve believed God's salvational promise and were delivered from the judicial results of their sinning, all future generations of their descendants would experience the effects of their sinning.[76] They would be conceived as sinners, with wholly corrupted personhoods and human natures (Rom. 5:12–19).

1. *The recipients of the dispensation*

These were Adam, Eve, and their posterity.

2. *The duties of the dispensation*

Adam and Eve's banishment from Eden ended their care of the garden, but they still had other duties that belonged to the first dispensation. These were filling the earth with posterity, subduing it, and eating a vegetable, grain, and fruit diet. Moreover, by his sinning Adam lost his absolute dominion "over all the earth" (Gen. 1:26; Heb. 2:5–8) to the usurper Satan, who by this became the "prince of this world" (John 12:31; Matt. 4:8–9).[77] Also, a wife must continue to live in subjection to her husband (Gen. 3:16). This confirmed the principle of man's leadership in human society, which was established by the woman's creation as his helper (Gen. 2:18; cp. 1 Cor. 11:3, 7–9). The new dispensation brought mankind additional responsibilities:

a. *To eke out a living from the divinely cursed ground (Gen. 3:17–19)*

With the first sin of earth's noblest creatures, God placed a curse upon the ground and lower forms of life (Rom. 8:20–22; cp. Mark 11:12–14, 21). With this divine curse, nature became subject to disease and death, and it became hostile toward mankind. This made people's work toilsome and their lives hazardous. Both plants and animals developed defense mechanisms. Undomesticated animals became predators of other animals and of humans. The blight of disease and death settled upon all forms of animal and plant life. Insects became bothersome and destructive, and many forms of vegetation became inedible or toxic. Both bugs and weeds were unwelcome, tenacious squatters in fields and gardens. Disease and predators took their toll of humans and animals. People had to eat their meatless diet by the sweat of their brow until they died.

   b. To approach God by means of an animal sacrifice (Gen. 4:1–5)

This substitutionary sacrifice was in keeping with the divine arrangement for dealing with human sins, established in Genesis 3:21. When God clothed Adam and Eve with the skins of animals, He must have revealed to them the gospel of the coming Conqueror-Savior and His atoning sacrifice and have instructed them in the manner of approaching Deity by substitutionary animal sacrifice. Consequently, only by this animal sacrifice could the offerer's sins be covered from divine view and he or she be accepted by God (cp. Heb. 9:22; Lev. 17:11). Cain refused to offer the required sacrifice, and his was therefore rejected by God. However, Abel's sacrifice was divinely received, for he obeyed with faith (Heb. 11:4). His exercise of faith in God indicated the existence of God's revelation of His will in these matters. Abel believed God's word and followed His direction; Cain did not do this.

Although He did not receive Cain's vegetable offering, God graciously gave him the opportunity to make the acceptable sacrifice (Gen. 4:6–7). Had he done this, Cain's obedience would also have corrected his relationship with Abel as well as with God.[78]

   c. To do well (Gen. 4:6–7)

Doing "well," or good, is doing the will of God, which is given by special revelation (cp. Rom. 12:2; Heb. 13:21; James 4:17). Since there is no record of His giving to the Gentile world a written moral law like the Law of Moses (Rom. 5:13), it seems that God directed man to follow his own moral instincts, "the law written in their hearts" (Rom. 2:14–15). Being made in the divine image with a sense of morality, unsaved Gentiles instinctively possess moral values, make moral evaluations, engage in moral conduct, and make moral judgments of one another. It appears that these people who have no formal moral code from God are responsible for obeying this "law written in their heart" and that they will be divinely judged according to this law (Rom. 2:1–3; see "The Law and Sin: Pagans Without a Written Divine Law" under Hamartiology). Needless to say, sinners cannot keep laws of any kind in a way that pleases God (Rom. 3:9–20).

   3. The recipients' response to the dispensation

Most people, like Cain and his descendants, disobeyed God (Gen. 4:8, 16–24; 6:1–7, 11–12; 2 Peter 2:5; Jude 11). By the grace of God, some among the descendants of Seth obeyed the Lord (Gen. 5:6–32; 6:8). These were people who had faith in God (Heb. 11:4–7).

   4. God's reaction to people's response

God judged the disobedient of Noah's day by destroying all living flesh upon the earth except Noah and his sons and their wives (Gen. 6:13, 17; 7:21–23).[79] The rapid growth of human wickedness (Gen. 6:5) appears to have been accelerated by the invasion of evil angels (demons), who succeeded in corrupting the human race to the extent that the fulfillment of God's promise of the coming Conqueror-Savior (Gen. 3:15) was threatened. From Jude 6–7; 1 Peter 3:18–20; and 2 Peter 2:4, one learns that these angels "gave themselves over to fornication, going after another kind of flesh." Resulting from some kind of sexual relation between these evil angels and human women, there were born "fallen ones"

(Gen. 6:4, KJV "giants"), who came to be "mighty ones of old" and "men of renown."[80] The divine judgment that followed was a devastating, worldwide flood that prevailed for 150 days (Gen. 6:11–13, 17; 7:19–20, 24; 2 Peter 3:6). This occurred during A.M. 1656–1657, or 2348–2347 B.C.

God blessed the obedient, who by His grace believed His Word and did His will (Gen. 4:4; 5:24; 6:8–9, 13–22; Heb. 11:4–7). He accepted Abel's sacrifice, translated Enoch, and delivered Noah and his family from the Flood. Other godly people of this time died before the Flood occurred (cp. Gen. 5:27, 31). Methuselah, Noah's grandfather, died the year of the Flood; Lamech, Noah's father, died five years earlier (See Addendum: "The Genealogy from Adam to Abraham").

5. *The duration of the dispensation*

This dispensation continued from mankind's moral fall to the end of the Noachic Flood (Gen. 3:16–8:22), some 1,657 years, if the Fall occurred within the first year of man's creation.

6. *God's use of the dispensation*

Satan almost succeeded in corrupting the human race to the extent that the divine promise of the coming Conqueror-Savior (Gen. 3:15) could not have been fulfilled. But in His sovereignty and grace, God prevailed to preserve a godly nucleus by whom to repopulate the earth and to assure the lineage of His coming Son.

The Dispensation of Governed Mankind (Gen. 9:1–7)

Upon their leaving the ark and presenting burnt offerings (Gen. 8:15–20), Noah, his sons, and their wives received a new dispensation for the new start of the human race.

1. *The recipients of the dispensation*

Noah, his three sons, their wives, and their posterity (Gen. 9:1, 18).

2. *The duties of the dispensation*

The fact that God accepted Noah's offerings (Gen. 8:21), and later, Abraham's (Gen. 12:7), indicates that people were to continue approaching Him by animal sacrifices (cp. Gen. 3:21; 4:4). This duty continued until God's Lamb came and atoned for humanity's sin (Heb. 9:12–14; 12:24). Other requirements of the previous two dispensations remained in force, like subduing the earth, eking out a living from the cursed ground, the submission of the wife to her husband, and people's continuing to live by the law written in their hearts (Rom. 2:14–15). The new dispensation imposed the following additional duties upon mankind:

a. *To reproduce and fill the earth (Gen. 9:1)*

The previous world population had been destroyed by the Noachic Flood (Gen. 7:21–22). Now people were to fill the earth not only by reproducing their kind but also by scattering over the face of it (Gen. 11:4, 9).[81]

b. *To have dominion over the lower forms of life (Gen. 9:2)*

Although by his sinning he relinquished his world dominion to Satan, man still has the use of his environment, including animals, vegetation, and other lower forms of life. God has instituted human government as His agent (Rom. 13:1–6).

c. *To eat animal flesh in addition to a vegetarian diet (Gen. 9:3–4)*

With this permission for humans to eat flesh, God instilled in animals a fear of man (Gen. 9:2). Wild animals must now be hunted and taken by force. The only prohibition relating to eating flesh was the consumption of blood, perhaps for the following reasons: *One,* this may have been given because the body's animating principle, soul (Gen. 9:4, KJV "life"; Heb. *nephesh*), is associated with blood (Lev. 17:11). Thus the observation of this prohibition shows respect for physical life. *Two,* the shedding and offering of blood together with the death of an animal substitute was the OT means of making atonement for sin. And *three,* modern medical science shows that the blood is the carrier of most diseases that animals have in common with man.

d. To exercise capital punishment (Gen. 9:5–6)

While mankind had family and civil government before the Noachic Flood (cp. Gen. 4:17), there was no mandatory punishment by death for capital crimes. Up to this time, God reserved capital punishment to Himself (cp. Gen. 4:8–15). Now this new dispensation gave mankind the authority to take human life for homicide.[82] This would strengthen the government's hand in maintaining law and order (cp. Rom. 13:1–6). It would make government more efficient in protecting life, repressing violence, and deterring anarchy.

The stated reason for capital punishment was this: "For in the image of God made He man" (Gen. 9:6). To mutilate or to destroy humans, all of whom reflect the divine image, is to outrage the majesty of God. God considers personhood, the divine image in man that distinguishes him from animals, to be sacred. Thus, malicious manslaughter requires the death of the murderer. It is noteworthy that unsaved people, having the divine image, are still persons, not animals (James 3:9). In today's discussion about capital punishment, many people are overlooking the divine reason for it. While capital punishment may be a means of curbing crimes of violence (Rom. 13:4), its divinely intended purpose was to show respect for God by punishing those who disregard His image in the people whom they unlawfully kill. To disregard this image by lethally violating people is to insult God.

3. The recipients' response to the dispensation

Most people have disobeyed God. The earliest recorded action of human rebellion against God occurred about one hundred years after the Flood when people built a tower to make a name for themselves (Gen. 11:1–9). God considered this to be a sinful act of defiant self-will (Gen. 11:6–8). Also, idolatry, with its perverse worship and conduct, existed at this time and was carried throughout the earth with man's dispersion (Gen. 11:9; Rom. 1:21–25; Rev. 17:5). Today, in addition to worshiping false gods, unsaved people, who do not have God's Word, to some degree ignore capital punishment, abuse civil authority, eat blood, ignore God's general revelation, and violate the law written in their hearts. This universal disobedience will reach its climax in the blasphemous reign of Satan's human agent, the Beast out of the sea, during the last half of the coming Tribulation Age (Dan. 7:7–27; Rev. 13; 1–8; 2 Thess. 2:3–10).

By the grace of God a few people have obeyed Him. The Bible speaks of several Gentiles, who, living after the flood, had a right relation with God, such as Job (Job 1:1), Melchizedek (Gen. 14:18), and Jethro (Exod. 18:1–23). It seems that God revealed Himself directly to these people, as He did to Abraham (Acts 7:2–3; cp. Gen. 15:5–6) or that they believed the promise of the coming of the Conqueror-Savior, preserved in their traditions (Ps. 145:4–7), and displayed by the stellar constellations (Ps. 19:1–6; Rom. 10:18).[83] The dietary and judicial aspects of this dispensation are included in the Dispensation of Grace, which saved people observe today (cp. Acts 15:19–20; Rom. 13:1–4).

4. God's reaction to people's response

God immediately judged those who were involved in the rebellion at Babel by confounding their language and dispersing them over the earth (Gen. 11:5–9). In time, He sent them various woes, which arose out of their perverse worship and immorality (Rom. 1:21–32). At times, He exercised forbearance by not dealing with sinners severely before their cup of iniquity was full (Gen. 15:16; Rom. 2:4; 3:25). In the future, God will release the terrible judgments of the Tribulation Age upon wicked earth dwellers (Rev. 6–19).

God blessed those who were obedient to His will (cp. Job 1:1–3). This is not to say that this obedience was meritorious or wholly a human work, for people cannot obey God apart from His grace (Eph. 2:8–9; 1 Cor. 15:10; Gen. 6:8–9). Both Noah and Job were imperfect men (Gen. 9:20–23; Job 40:4; 42:6), yet they were people of faith and recipients of true righteousness (Heb. 11:7; Job 1:8; Ezek. 14:14; Gen. 6:9).[84]

5. The duration of the dispensation

Being universal in its extent and having never been annulled, I believe that this dispensation continues in force for those people who do not have the New Testament, which presents the Dispensation of Grace. Not having access to this dispensation, these people are responsible for the duties of the third dispensation, preserved by their traditions and written in their hearts. To be saved, however, people who today live under this dispensation must hear and believe the gospel of the Lord Jesus. God provides them with this opportunity as they respond favorably to His general revelation (cp. Acts 10; Rom. 1:19–20). This third dispensation, I believe, will continue for those who do not hear the gospel or have the New Testament until the Lord Jesus returns to earth, overthrows the present world order, and establishes His millennial earthly kingdom, with its own dispensation (Isa. 2:1–3; see Acts 15:20; Rom. 13:1–7).

6. God's use of the dispensation

By giving human government the power of capital punishment and by directing people to fill the earth, this dispensation preserved humanity from anarchy and extinction. Thus it assured the continuation of the Savior's lineage (Luke 3:23–36) and the fulfillment of God's program for mankind (2 Tim. 1:10; Titus 2:11).

The Dispensation of the Patriarchs (Gen. 12:1; 17:1; 26:5; 31:3, 13; 35:1; 46:1–4)

With the preceding universal dispensation still in force, God gave an additional one to Abraham and to selected members of his posterity—Isaac, Jacob, and his twelve sons (Gen. 35:22–26). These people are called "the patriarchs" (Acts 7:8; Heb. 7:4).

1. The recipients of the dispensation

Throughout the period of His dealing with the patriarchs, God gave direction to Abraham (Gen. 12:1), Isaac (Gen. 26:1–3), and Jacob (Gen. 31:11–13). Also, Jacob's posterity was to keep in touch with the Lord and obey Him, since He promised to be with them and make of them a great nation (Gen. 46:3–4). They were God's people (Exod. 3:7, 10).

2. The duties of the dispensation

This dispensation, which was given to Abraham in several divine revelations, includes the following duties:

a. To leave Ur and go to a land to which God would lead him (Gen. 12:1; 15:7; Neh. 9:7; Acts 7:2–3)

b. To walk before God and be perfect (Gen. 17:1)

This means that he was to live in touch with God and to be what he ought to be. The word *perfect* (Heb. *tom*) means "complete" or "whole." It refers to a spiritual person of faith like Jacob (Gen. 25:27, KJV "plain"; Heb. 11:21), despite his many faults, or like Job (Job 1:1, 8), in contrast to a carnal, profane person like Esau (Heb. 12:16).

c. To obey the Lord's commands (Gen. 18:19; 26:5)

These commands were additional to those that are preserved in the Genesis record. God also gave orders, which are recorded, to Isaac (Gen. 26:1–3) and to Jacob (Gen. 31:3, 11–13; 35:1; 46:1–4).

3. The recipients' response to the dispensation

Despite their temporary lapses (Gen. 16:2; 27:6–25) and unwise moves (Gen. 12:10; 20:1–18; 26:6–23), the patriarchs were men of faith (Gen. 15:6; Heb. 11:8–22) and obedience (Gen. 12:1–4; 18:19; 22:1–18; 26:5, 23–33). However, the descendants of Jacob almost lost their ancestral faith while in Egypt (Josh. 24:14; Exod. 32:1–6; Ezek. 20:6–8). This faith was activated by the ministry of Moses (Exod. 3:13–15; 4:29–31).

4. *God's reaction to people's response*

God brought judgment upon the disobedient. He disciplined the patriarchs when they stepped out of His will (cp. Gen. 20:1–18; 26:6–23). He also allowed their descendants to suffer slavery and hard labor in Egypt when they fell into idolatry (Exod. 1:8–14; Josh. 24:14).

God saved those who believed the promise of the coming Conqueror-Savior (Gen. 15:6; Gal. 3:8, 16) and blessed those who obeyed Him (Gen. 24:35; 26:12–14; 32:28; 47:27). In fulfillment of His promise to Abraham (Gen. 15:13–14), God also delivered Israel from Egyptian bondage (Exod. 3:7–10; 14:30; Deut. 7:7–8). However, this redemption was physical rather than spiritual (Exod. 14:10–14). Israel's deliverance from Egypt did not spiritually save them and bring them eternal life.

5. *The duration of the dispensation*

This dispensation extended from the call of Abram to leave Ur (Gen. 12:1) until Israel's reception of the Mosaic Law at Mt. Sinai in A.M. 2513 (Exod. 19:8).[85] This span of time was 430 years, plus the years between Abraham's call in Ur and his entrance into Canaan when he was seventy-five, in A.M. 2083 (Gen. 12:4–5). Israel's sojourn of 430 years (Exod. 12:40–41; Gal. 3:17) began with Abraham's entrance into Canaan.[86]

6. *God's use of the dispensation*

Through this dispensation, God maneuvered the patriarchs into a position where He could make them an elect nation, by which the Savior was to come (Gen. 12:3; 15:5; Gal. 3:8, 16; John 8:56; Matt. 1:1; Heb. 2:16).[87]

The Dispensation of the Mosaic Law (Exod. 20:1–7; 21:1–23:19; Lev. 1–27; Num. 5–6, 9–10, 15, 18–19, 27–30)

While the third dispensation continued in force over the earth, God gave one to the recently delivered Israelites from Egypt for forging them into a regulated, holy society.

1. *The recipients of the dispensation*

This was only the nation of Israel (Exod. 19:3; Neh. 9:13–14; Ps. 147:19–20)

2. *The duties of the dispensation*

a. *The law given at Mt. Sinai, consisting of moral laws (Exod. 20:1–17), civil laws (Exod. 21:1–23:13), and religious laws (Exod. 23:14–19; Lev. 1–27)*

b. *Additional regulations: see Numbers 5–6, 9–10, 15, 18–19, 27–30.*

The greatest of these 613 laws were Israel's loving God (Deut. 6:5) and loving their neighbor (Lev. 19:18; see Mark 12:28–34).

3. *The recipients' response to the dispensation*

No one but the Lord Jesus Christ kept all the Mosaic Law (Matt. 5:17; Heb. 7:26). Everyone else in Israel in some way violated it (Acts 7:53; 15:10; Jer. 31:32). There were several reasons for this failure: *One,* the people were sinners by nature (Rom. 3:9; 5:19). *Two,* the law did not provide divine enablement for its observance (Heb. 7:18–19). And *three,* being unable to correct man's sinful condition, the law could only condemn and slay its violators (Rom. 3:19–20; Gal. 3:10, 21). Being legal in character (Exod. 19:5–8; Lev. 26:3, 14), the law could not save sinners (Gal. 2:16).[88] It required God to deal with Israel as they deserved. Thus the nation repeatedly came under divine judgment such as foreign invasion and captivity in the eighth and seventh centuries B.C. (2 Chron. 36:15–16; Neh. 9:26–30) and in A.D. 70 (John 1:11; Matt. 23:37–39; Acts 7:51–52).

Rather than allowing the law to humble them and to lead them to Jesus as their Messiah-Savior (Gal. 3:19–24), Israel misused it. They made it a badge of pride, which distinguished them as being religiously superior to other nations (Rom. 9:4; Eph. 2:14–15), and they attempted to use it to establish their own righteousness before God (Rom. 9:30–10:5). Under the teachings of the rabbis, they displaced the Mosaic Law with the Tradition of the Elders, which became the major religious influence in their lives (Mark 7:1–13).[89] Consequently, the Judaism of the New Testament Period was largely based on this tradition and consisted of its application to daily life.

It is noteworthy that the saved people of Israel observed the commandments of the Mosaic Law (Luke 1:6; cp. Ps. 119:51, 55–56, 63). Although they were not sinless (Luke 1:18–20), they were sufficiently obedient to allow God to work out His will in and through their lives. While the law did not provide the divine enablement for its observance, these godly people were enabled by divine grace to do what was pleasing in God's sight, just as we are today (2 Cor. 1:12; Phil. 4:13). But lacking this grace, which accompanies salvation, unsaved Jews were not able to keep the Mosaic Law.

4. God's reaction to people's response

The Law of Moses carried its own penalties for the violations of its regulations. Some of these violations like Sabbath breaking, rebellion, and murder required the death of the offender (Num. 15:30–36; Lev. 24:17; see endnote 82). It seems that in the days of Israel's apostasy, the penalty of many violations was not carried out, although the nation superficially and inconsistently observed the Levitical ritual (cp. Isa. 1:1–23). Consequently, God repeatedly chastened them by the hands of Gentile nations. Eventually, He allowed the northern kingdom of Israel to be carried away captive into upper Mesopotamia and the southern kingdom (Judah and Benjamin) to be taken to Babylon (2 Kings 17:6–23; 2 Chron. 36:15–21; cp. Judg. 2:10–15). Finally, upon their rejecting Jesus as the Messiah, the Jews were dispersed again in A.D. 70 when the Romans took Jerusalem (Luke 19:41–44). Long before, Israel had been warned of the frightful results of their turning away from God (Lev. 26:14–39; Deut. 28:15–68).

Despite these events, God graciously dealt with lawbreakers when they turned to Him, confessed their sins, obeyed His voice, and fulfilled the suitable Levitical ritual (Deut. 4:30–31; 2 Sam. 12:13; Ps. 51:3, 16–17; Lev. 4–5). God was impelled to do this by His gracious promises of the Abrahamic covenant (Deut. 4:31; 2 Kings 13:23; cp. Mic. 7:19–20).

5. The duration of the dispensation

While the Mosaic Law as a covenant ceased with Jesus' death (Heb. 10:9, 16; 12:24), the law has continued as a dispensation from its reception at Mt. Sinai in 1491 B.C. until now for those who assume its obligations. Paul recognized that the Jews of his day were still under the law (1 Cor. 9:20; Gal. 4:4–5; 5:3). However, the commands of the Mosaic Law, except the moral requirements, are no longer binding on those Jews who have been born again and have become the recipients of the Dispensation of Grace.

To be a saved person and to assume the duties of the Mosaic Law is to fall from grace, with its liberty and requirements, and to place oneself under the principle of law-works (Gal. 5:3–4). While the Galatian gospel believers were salvationally secure in grace, their following the false legal teachings of Judaizers (proponents of keeping the Mosaic Law) caused them to try to live by the principle of works, or merit. One cannot be saved by grace and live a life pleasing to God by the works of self-effort. The grace of God that saved us is also available through faith to enable us to live godly lives (John 15:5; 1 Cor. 15:10; 2 Cor. 1:12; 12:7–10; Gal. 2:20; Phil. 4:13).

6. God's use of the dispensation

God used the Mosaic Law to show Israel their need for the coming Messiah-Savior (Gal. 3:19–24). Giving sin the character of legal offense against God (Rom. 3:20; 4:15; 5:13), the law revealed to Israel their sinfulness before Him.

God also used the law to make Israel a holy nation in the midst of Canaanite immorality, thus preserving the line by which the Savior was to come (Exod. 19:5–6; Deut. 7:6). While most Israelites did not directly benefit spiritually from the law because of their unsaved state and disobedience, those who were saved did. The law caused these people to cast themselves upon the sure mercies of God and to look for redemption in Jerusalem (cp. Dan. 9:1–19; Luke 1:46–55; 2:25, 38). In this manner, the law had a sanctifying spiritual influence on their lives (Exod. 19:6; Rom. 7:12–13). Such saved people as Zacharias and Elizabeth were divinely enabled to keep it (Luke 1:6; Ps. 119:51, 55–56, 63). Also, it was into this kind of a home that our Savior was born (Matt. 1:19; Luke 1:46–55; 2:21–24).

The Dispensation of Grace (John 1:17; Matt. 28:19–20; Titus 2:11–13)

We must not allow the designation of this dispensation to lead us to think that God's grace did not operate during the Old Testament period. The testimony of God's people throughout history indicates that they had God's special revelation, whether oral or written, for their faith (Luke 1:70) and His grace for their salvation and obedience (Gen. 6:8; Exod. 33:12; Heb. 11). But with the coming of the Savior, God's grace was fully manifested by Jesus' life, teachings, and works (John 1:14–17; 2 Tim. 1:9–10). The duties of this dispensation rest upon this grace, express this grace, and are fulfilled by it (1 Cor. 15:10; 2 Cor. 1:12). Meanwhile, it seems that the third dispensation (Governed Mankind) continues in force over those people who do not have the New Testament (there is no record of its being canceled) and that the Mosaic Law (as a dispensation) continues to exert its domination over those who attempt to keep it.

1. *The recipients of the dispensation*

These are unsaved people of accountable age and all saved people (Titus 2:11–12). All who hear the gospel have the duty of obeying it. All saved people who have the New Testament have the duty of obeying its commands that relate to Christian life and ministry.

2. *The duties of the dispensation*

This dispensation is more detailed in content than that of Governed Mankind. Being universal in its extent, there are two aspects of the Dispensation of Grace.

a. *The duty of unsaved people, who hear the gospel, is to obey it (Titus 2:11; Acts 17:30; 20:21; Rom. 1:5; 16:25–26; 1 Tim. 2:4; 2 Peter 3:9; 1 John 3:23; cp. Matt. 28:19).*

b. *The duty of saved people is to follow the teachings of God's grace (Matt. 28:20).*

These duties consist of the Lord's instructions (Titus 2:12; Eph. 4:20–21; Col. 3:16), or His law (Gal. 6:2; 1 Cor. 9:21; James 1:25). Those commands that He gave during His earthly ministry are recorded in the four Gospels; those that He gave through His servants after His return to heaven are recorded in the remainder of the New Testament (John 16:12–14; Acts 1:1–2; Rev. 1:1). It is noteworthy that the Lord's commands to His disciples (cp. Matt. 5–7), who lived under the Mosaic Law, apply to us today, for He anticipated their living under the Dispensation of Grace. God's moral standards are always the same, whether under grace or law.

Some of the 650 different commands in the New Testament for all saved people are these: abiding in Christ (John 15:4–5), being filled with the Holy Spirit (Eph. 5:18), loving others with Jesus' love (John 13:34), growing in the spiritual life (2 Peter 3:18), bearing witness to unsaved people (Acts 1:8), yielding self to God (Rom. 12:1–2), understanding and doing God's will (Eph. 5:17, 10), living a holy life (1 Peter 1:15), not sinning (1 John 2:1), giving Jesus and God's Word central place in the heart (Eph. 3:17; Col. 3:16), pleasing and glorifying God (2 Tim. 2:15; 1 Cor. 10:31), living a godly life (Titus 2:12), fearing God (1 Peter 2:17), and looking for the Lord's return (Matt. 24:42, 44; Titus 2:13). Unlike the Mosaic Law, God's grace provides strength by the Holy Spirit for carrying out these duties as we submit ourselves to Him (John 14:16–17, KJV *Comforter* means "Helper"; Gal. 5:25; 2 Cor. 1:12; 2 Peter 1:3).

3. The recipients' response to the dispensation

By God's grace, those among the unsaved who were divinely chosen for salvation are believing the gospel (John 6:37; Acts 13:48; 1 Cor. 1:26–29). Also, by God's grace, many saved people are walking in obedience to the Lord. While gospel believers do sin occasionally (1 Cor. 3:1–3), it is likely that those who profess to be saved and who are living sinful lives for an extended period without incurring divine corrective chastisement have never been born again (cp. 2 Cor. 13:5; Matt. 7:21–23; 1 John 2:3–4; Rev. 3:9).

4. God's reaction to people's response

Regarding the unsaved, God saves all who exercise salvational faith in Jesus and His atoning work (John 6:28–29, 47; Acts 16:31; Rom. 10:9–13), and He will banish to hell all who do not do this (John 3:18, 36; Matt. 7:21–23). On the other hand, God faithfully chastens His people who persist in disobedience (1 Cor. 11:31–32) and blesses those who walk in His fellowship (1 John 1:7; John 13:17).

5. The duration of this dispensation

Since there does not seem to be any special dispensation for the Tribulation Age, I believe that the Dispensation of Grace extends from the Day of Pentecost (Acts 2) unto Christ's second coming to earth (Rev. 19) at the end of the Tribulation Age.[90] Thus I believe that the Dispensation of Grace will be in force throughout the Church Age and the Tribulation Age, which follows.

This view is based on the following considerations: *One,* the unsaved will still have the duty, as today, of obeying the gospel. *Two,* many people will be saved during the forepart of the Tribulation Age (Rev. 7:9–17), and these will have the New Testament for their guidance. *Three,* there is no duty of the Dispensation of Grace that would not apply to Tribulation Age gospel believers and that they could not keep, for they will have the Holy Spirit, just as we do today.[91] *Four,* the Scriptures do not indicate that any special dispensation will be given for or during the Tribulation Age.

6. God's use of the dispensation

Having come to this world and returned to heaven, the Lord Jesus has two tasks during this dispensation. *One,* during the present Church Age He is building His Church quantitatively and qualitatively (see "The Formation of the Universal Christian Church" under Ecclesiology). And *two,* during the Tribulation Age He will prepare the elect of Israel and of the Gentiles, who will be on earth and will be saved during those days, for His second coming to earth and His millennial rule. These activities are a part of His messianic work, which He is doing as man in obedience to the Father.

The Dispensation of Christ's Earthly Rule (Isa. 2:1–3)

Climaxing God's dealings with earth dwellers, this dispensation will be the last that will be given to mankind.[92] Our Lord's earthly rule, with its righteous government and restored environment, will complete God's current program for humanity and will fulfill the universal longing for lasting peace and just government.

1. The recipients of the dispensation

These will be all those people who are on earth during the Lord's millennial rule (Ps. 72:8–11; Isa. 2:1–4; Zech. 14:9, 16–17).

2. The duties of the dispensation

During the Kingdom Age mankind will receive this dispensation directly from King

Jesus, perhaps by means of prophecy (Isa. 2:1–3; Joel 2:28). This dispensation will include the following requirements:

    a. That all people do the will of the King regarding their civilian lives (Isa. 2:1–3)

    b. That unsaved people believe the gospel (cp. Joel 2:32)

    People born in kingdom days will be sinners in need of salvation.

    c. That saved people follow the Lord's will for their spiritual lives

    Besides those that the Lord Jesus will give directly, this will include all of the suitable precepts that we find in the New Testament, or the Dispensation of Grace.[93]

  3. The recipients' response to the dispensation

    Disobedience to the King will be rare. Unsaved people will give external lip service (Ps. 66:3, margin: "yield feigned obedience"; Matt. 15:8) and the saved will give loving heart obedience (cp. Mark 12:30). Because there will be no temptation by Satan and his demon allies, and there will be no open sinning and moral pollution, as we have today, unsaved people will, for a time, externally observe the civilian laws of the kingdom. Many unsaved people will be on earth at the close of the Lord's rule (Rev. 20:7–9).

  4. God's reaction to people's response

    During His reign, the Lord will slay those unsaved people who openly violate His laws (Isa. 11:4; 65:20). The rest of the unsaved, who survive to the end, will be destroyed when they participate in Satan's revolt against the Lord (Rev. 20:7–9). Saved earth dwellers will live throughout the Kingdom Age and will enjoy the Lord's abundant blessings (Matt. 25:34; Ps. 72:7).

  5. The duration of the dispensation

    The Lord's earthly kingdom will continue for one thousand years after His second coming to earth (Rev. 20:1–7). Following His millennial rule, there will be the dissolution of the present universe (2 Peter 3:10–13) and the judgment of the unsaved (Rev. 20:11–15). After these events, the Lord Jesus' earthly kingdom will merge with the universal kingdom of the Father and will continue forever (Rev. 21:1–3; 1 Cor. 15:23–28; Luke 1:32–33). As man and Messiah, the Lord Jesus will always be subject to the Father's authority and will serve Him (1 Cor. 15:28; cp. John 6:38; 8:29).

  6. God's use of the dispensation

    Continuing His messianic work as the Father's Slave, the Lord Jesus will rule until He has achieved the divine objectives of His present messianic work. These objectives include His subjugation of all rebels against God (1 Cor. 15:25; Rev. 19:11–20:3, 7–15), His subjection of the earth and its creatures (Heb. 2:5–9; cp. Gen. 1:28), His restoration of the earth to its primeval state by lifting the divine curse on creation and by reconciling to God all things that were involuntarily affected by man's sin (Rom. 8:19–22; Col. 1:20; Acts 3:20–21; Eph. 1:10; Isa. 11:6–9; cp. Gen. 3:17), His completing the salvation of elect humans (Rom. 11:26–27; Joel 2:32; 2 Thess. 2:13), and His fulfilling the promises of His gracious covenants (Deut. 30:3–5; Jer. 31:31–34; Gen. 17:8; 2 Sam. 7:16).

THEIR DURATION

Created Mankind (a few days) • • • • •

Fallen Mankind (4004–2348 B.C.)   • • • • •

Governed Mankind (2347 B.C. onward)   • • • • • • • • • • • • • • • • • • •

The Patriarchs (before 1921 to 1491 B.C.)   • • • • •

The Mosaic Law (1491 B.C. onward)   • • • • • • • • • • •

Grace (A.D. 30 onward)   • • • • •

Christ's Earthly Rule (1,000 years)   • • • •

In our seeking God's will for us and our interpretation of the Scriptures, it is important that we gospel believers recognize these dispensational distinctions, the people to whom they are given, and the passages of Scripture that relate to them. While all the Scriptures are profitable to us (2 Tim. 3:16), they do not all express God's will for us (2 Tim. 2:15). Because of this, we should give special attention to the Dispensation of Grace, given in the New Testament, which God has given us to observe, and to those OT commands that are in harmony with these NT commands. Moreover, we should carry out these duties in the power of the Holy Spirit and for the glory of God. In addition to giving people duties, God has also made promises to them. Let us briefly look at these great divine covenant promises.

THE COVENANTS OF GOD

Throughout human history God has made great covenant promises that relate to His program for mankind. For a more accurate understanding of the Scriptures, it is important that we distinguish between a divine covenant and a divine dispensation. A covenant declares in the form of promises what God will do for people, but a dispensation states in the form of commands what He wants people to do. Although God may make one or more covenants during the time that a dispensation is in force, these are not necessarily a part of the dispensation's requirements. The single exception is the Law of Moses, which was both a dispensation and a covenant, with its dispensation being the condition of its covenant promises.

THEIR KINDS

There are two kinds of biblical covenants—those between men and those between God and man. Let us look at these.

Covenants Between Men

The most common form of human covenants in the Scriptures is the *bilateral covenant*. This is an agreement that is voluntarily made by two parties who commit themselves to the terms of the compact (cp. Gen. 31:44–55; 1 Sam. 18:3; 23:18; 1 Kings 5:12). The rarer form is the *unilateral covenant,* which is undertaken by one of two parties. This may be a disposition in the form of a law imposed by a superior party like a king (Ezek. 17:13–14), or it may be a declaration in the form of a will made by a testator (Heb. 9:16–17).

Covenants Between God and Man

These are solemn divine statements, made to certain people, of what God promises to do for them. Observe that divine covenants differ from human covenants in two ways: *One,* they are never the result of both parties' bargaining; *two,* God Himself is never subject to any condition that is made by man.

THEIR NAMES
1. The Noachic covenant (Gen. 9:8–17)
2. The Abrahamic covenant (Gen. 17:1–19; also 12:1–3; 13:14–17; 15:4–21; 22:15–18)
3. The Mosaic covenant (Exod. 19:1–8; Lev. 18:5)
4. The Palestinian covenant (Deut. 28:1–29:1; 30:1–10)
5. The Davidic covenant (2 Sam. 7:10–16)
6. The new covenant (Jer. 31:31–40)

THEIR DESCRIPTION

In our study of God's covenants, we shall observe the following features:

1. *The recipients of the covenant*
   These are the people with whom the covenant is made.
2. *The promises of the covenant*
   This is a statement of what God promises to do for its recipients.
3. *The obligations of the covenant*
   This is what the recipients must do, if anything, to experience the fulfillment of the covenant promises.
4. *The character of the covenant*
   This indicates whether the covenant is gracious or legal and is conditional or unconditional. "Gracious" or "legal" represents the principles of grace and law, which are methods of God's dealing with people.[94] "Conditional" or "unconditional" indicates whether or not the recipient must meet certain specified conditions to experience the fulfillment of the covenant promises.
5. *The duration of the covenant*
   This is the length of time during which the covenant is in force.
6. *The covenant sign or witness*
   This assures the recipients that the covenant is in force, and it reminds them of its promises.
7. *The importance of the covenant*
   While the dispensation defines God's will for its recipients, the covenant, by its promises, often defines His relationship with its recipients and the blessings of this relationship.

CONDITIONAL GRACIOUS COVENANTS

Although gracious in character, certain divine covenants impose certain obligations on their recipients for their experiencing the promised blessings. Nevertheless, the conditional character of these covenants does not conflict with the principle of grace or make these covenants legalistic, for God enables the believing recipients of gracious covenants to fulfill the covenant stipulations. God's gracious prompting and power enables these recipients to exercise faith in and obedience to Him (cp. Acts 11:18; 16:34; 2 Peter 1:1; Phil. 2:13, with reference to the new covenant). Because of this, the recipients' fulfillment of the gracious covenant condition is not a meritorious work that receives the promised blessings as a reward or pay. Their obedience by divine grace allows God to do what He has promised and brings Him all credit and all praise.

The one legal covenant is the Mosaic Law, which was given to Israel. God's fulfillment of the promises of this covenant was according to the principle of law, or works (Exod. 19:5). Unless they were saved people (see below), this legal covenant required the recipients to do their part without divine assistance. Because this was a two-party contract, the recipients, by their disobedience to the covenant obligations, broke the covenant and released God from His duty to fulfill His promises (Jer. 31:32; Lev. 26:14–16). However, in His sovereign mercy God continued to honor the broken covenant by recognizing Israel as His people until He replaced it with the new covenant (Exod. 33:19; Jer. 3:14; Rom. 9:15, 25–27). He did, however, extend mercy and forgiveness to the repentant people of Israel on the basis of the Abrahamic covenant (Mic. 7:18–20).

Being the work of God in man, the fulfillment of the gracious covenant's conditions cannot be regarded as a meritorious human work. Despite their conditional character, these gracious covenants are not legalistic. Their conditions do not represent man's meritorious work but God's gracious work in and through man in response to faith.

COVENANT THEOLOGY

Being the theology of the Reformed churches, the English Puritans, and the Scottish theologians, covenant theology views God's dealing with man as being covered by two covenants—the covenant of works and the covenant of grace, and it interprets the Bible accordingly. This theology holds that God made a covenant of works with unfallen Adam. By this covenant Adam was made the representative head of the race so that he could act for his descendants; he was temporarily put on probation so as to determine whether he would willingly subject himself to God's will; and he was promised eternal life if he should obey God. Upon Adam's disobedience and his making the covenant void, God made a covenant of grace for the purpose of saving the elect of fallen mankind.[95] Although this second covenant was offered right after man's fall, its details were not clearly stated until the giving of the Abrahamic covenant and thereafter. Covenant theology holds that all the OT covenants, including the Mosaic Law, are expressions and amplifications of the covenant of grace. Replacing ritual circumcision, water baptism is regarded as the sign and seal of the covenant of grace today, implementing and certifying one's entrance into the covenantal community.

Covenant theology holds that there is only one people of God. The people who were in covenantal relationship with Him during the Old Testament Period made up His Church then as well as those who are in covenantal relationship with Him today. Many covenantal theologians believe that the nation of Israel has no place in God's future prophetic program and that the prophecies about this nation, which must be interpreted allegorically, are being fulfilled in the Church today. Covenant theology understands the Bible as teaching one covenant of grace, one chosen people of God, one general resurrection and final judgment upon Christ's one return to earth.

A Dispensationalist's Response

Opposing covenant theology in favor of dispensationalism, I offer the following:

One: Distinguishing the various covenants from the dispensations, I see that God made special promises to Israel in the Abrahamic, Palestinian, Davidic, and new covenants that will still be fulfilled to this nation in the future (cp. Isa. 54:7–8; Rom. 3:3–4; Heb. 6:13–20). For instance, consider the promise of a land for Israel (Acts 7:4–5; Heb. 11:9 with Gen. 13:15–17; 15:18).

Two: While salvational blessings are essentially the same in every age (cp. Jer. 31:33–34), functional blessings differ among groups of redeemed peoples, like the Church being Jesus' bride (Eph. 5:32) and Israel's being Jehovah's wife (Hos. 2; see endnote 73).

Three: The apostle Paul distinguished between the Mosaic covenant, which held its recipients in bondage, and the new covenant, which liberates gospel believers (Gal. 4:19–31).

Four: Being a bilateral, legal covenant (Exod. 19:5–8; 24:3–8), the Mosaic Law was broken by Israel's disobedience and apostasy (Deut. 31:16; Jer. 3:6; 22:9; 31:31–32; Ezek. 44:7). Dealing with them as they deserved, God had to administer judgment rather than His promised blessings.

Five: Nowhere does the New Testament indicate that water baptism is the sign of the new covenant. Rather, following salvation, it is a witness to one's salvational faith (Acts 18:8). The cup of the Lord's Supper is the sign of the new covenant (Luke 22:20).

Six: Jesus' Universal Church could not have existed before His incarnation and exaltation. As a part of His messianic work, our Lord is building His Church upon the foundation of His Person, atoning work, and prophetic word (NT revelation), and by the baptism of the Holy Spirit (Matt. 16:18; Eph. 2:20; 1 Cor. 12:13, 27; Eph. 1:22–23; 2:20).

Seven: For saved Gentiles to be called "Abraham's seed" (Gal. 3:29) does not mean that all or only Gentiles are his seed (John 8:37; Rom. 9:6–8; Gal. 3:16). For Gentiles to be called "the children of Abraham" (Gal. 3:7) means that they are saved and are people of faith as he was a person of faith.[96]

Eight: For Gentiles to be grafted into the stock of Abraham does not necessarily replace Israel in God's program or shut the door to their restoration to His favor and blessing (Rom. 11:11–15, 26–27). Since salvation is of the Jews (John 4:22), and the covenant promises about the Messiah-Savior were given to Abraham and to his descendants through Jacob (Rom. 9:4), it was necessary for the Gentiles, who had no such hope (Eph. 2:12), to look to Jesus, the Seed of Abraham, and by faith to partake of the promised blessings in Him (Gal. 3:16, 14).

Nine: The apostle Paul's reference to saved Gentiles' being "the Israel of God" (Gal. 6:16) does not indicate that Israel's estrangement from God is permanent. God will restore this nation to Himself (Jer. 3:14; Hos. 2:7, 14, 16, 20, 23; 5:15–6:1; Isa. 54:4–5, 7–8) and will fulfill His gracious promises that He made to their fathers (Jer. 32:17–44; Ezek. 36:21–28). Meanwhile, all Jews who are saved during the present age are members of Jesus' Universal Church (Eph. 2:15; 3:6).

THEIR CONTENT

Many dispensationalists teach that God made two covenants with man before the first one that is definitely recorded in the Bible (Gen. 9:8–17).[97] These are the *Edenic covenant,* allegedly made with Adam before his initial sin (2:16–17), and the *Adamic covenant,* made after his fall (3:15–19). In my opinion, this view is conjectural, based upon alleged evidence that fails to distinguish between a covenant and a dispensation. The directive concerning the trees of which man might or might not eat (2:16–17) was a part of the dispensation that God gave to newly created mankind. Also, the veiled reference to the coming Seed, who would utterly defeat Satan (3:15), was a part of God's judicial sentence upon the Devil. This was addressed to Satan, not to man. These statements were not covenant promises.

I do not see any divine covenants recorded in Genesis before the Noachic covenant (9:8–17), which was anticipated in Genesis 6:18. When God clothed Adam and Eve in response to their salvational faith (3:21), He was not fulfilling a covenant promise as such, but He was honoring their faith in what this judicial sentence declared about the coming Conqueror-Savior, brief as it was. It is strange that such an important provision, if given with a covenant promise, was not recorded. Animal sacrifice was, however, a requirement given to mankind by the second dispensation, as the sacrifices of Abel and Noah show.[98]

The Noachic Covenant (Gen. 9:8–17; cp. 6:18)

1. *The recipients of the covenant*
   In A.M. 1657, God gave this covenant to Noah, his sons, and their posterity (Gen. 9:8–9). He also gave it to all the animals that were on the ark (vv. 10–12).
2. *The promise of the covenant*
   God promised never again to destroy all flesh with water (Gen. 9:11, 15).
3. *The obligations of the covenant*
   There are none since the covenant was made with animals as well as with mankind (Gen. 9:10).
4. *The character of the covenant*
   The covenant was gracious and unconditional, for it was also made with animals.

5. *The duration of the covenant*

The words "for perpetual generations" (Gen. 9:12) and "everlasting" (v. 16) indicate that the promise will be effective as long as the present earth continues (cp. 8:22). After our Lord's millennial rule, the earth will be destroyed, not by water but by the dissolution of its essential elements (2 Peter 3:10–13).

6. *The sign or witness of the covenant*

God gave the rainbow as His assurance to man that He would remember His promise (Gen. 9:13–17).

7. *The importance of the covenant*

In the light of what He has revealed for the future, God assured humans and animals that He would not end the present natural world order until He has accomplished His purpose for it. God's objectives for the present world order will be achieved by the Lord Jesus' messianic millennial rule (see "The Prophecy of the Messianic Millennial Kingdom" under Eschatology).

The Abrahamic Covenant (Gen. 17:1–19; also 12:1–3; 13:14–17; 15:4–21; 22:15–18)

1. *The recipients of the covenant*

Abraham and his posterity (Gen. 17:7) through Isaac (Gen. 17:19, 21; 26:1–4) and Jacob (Gen. 28:10–15; 35:9–12; 1 Chron. 16:15–18).

2. *The promises of the covenant*

These were given to Abraham by a series of divine revelations (Gen. 12:1–3, 7; 13:14–17; 15:1–7, 13–16; 17:1–21; 18:9–19; 21:12–13; 22:15–18; cp. 24:7).

a. *The promises relating to Abraham himself*

1) To bless Abraham and to make him a blessing (Gen. 12:2; 22:17)

God made Abraham rich (Gen. 13:2; 24:35) and a mighty prince in the eyes of the people of Canaan (23:6).

2) To give Abraham a noble, invincible, numerous posterity through Sarah (Gen. 12:2; 13:16; 15:5; 17:5–6; 22:17)

This promise refers to Abraham's natural posterity (John 8:37) by Sarah in the descendants of Isaac and his son Jacob (Gen. 21:1–3; 25:23).

3) To be the God of Abraham and of his posterity (Gen. 17:7)

Referring to Abraham and his posterity, Isaac and Jacob, this promise concerns their having a special relationship with God that was based on these covenant promises.

4) To bless them that bless Abraham and to curse him who curses Abraham (Gen. 12:3)

History has shown the fulfillment of this promise in God's blessing and cursing both nations and persons according to their treatment of Abraham's descendants.

b. *The promises relating to Israel*

1) To give Abraham and his posterity through Isaac and Jacob the land of Canaan and more for an everlasting possession (Gen. 13:15; 15:18–21; 17:8; 26:3; 28:13; 35:12)

The extent of the land that God promised to Abraham far exceeds that of the land of Canaan. It extends from the Nile River in Egypt to the Euphrates River in Mesopotamia (Gen. 15:18). Although Abraham never possessed the land in his lifetime, this promise was partially fulfilled in the days of Joshua (Josh. 21:43; cp. Gen. 17:8) and of Solomon (1 Kings 4:21). It will be completely fulfilled in the future when the Lord Jesus sets up His earthly kingdom and restores the elect people of Israel to their land (Deut. 30:1–5; Ezek. 34:11–13; 36:24, 28). Meanwhile, the Lord promised Abraham and other OT people of faith a heavenly city, where those who have died now reside until their resurrection and their possession of the promised land in the future millennial kingdom (Heb. 11:8–10, 13–16).

2) To deliver Israel from Egyptian bondage (Gen. 15:13–16)

Centuries later, in keeping with this promise, God delivered Israel from Egypt in A.M. 2513 (Exod. 6:5–8; Acts 7:17).[99]

c. *The promises relating to Jesus, the Messiah*

1) To give to Abraham a seed (Gen. 15:5; 22:17–18)

In this promise the word *seed* has multiple meanings, referring not only to Isaac and his posterity through Jacob but also to Christ Jesus (Gal. 3:8, 16; see endnote 96). Those who believed the promise of the coming "Seed" (Jesus) were saved through this (cp. Gen. 15:6; 12:3). This truth was the "John 3:16" of the precross period, that is, the time of human history before Jesus died.

2) To bring universal blessing to mankind through Abraham's seed (Gen. 12:3; 18:18; 22:18)

By this promise God alluded to Jesus and to the blessing that mankind would receive through His messianic work. This universal blessing is now being offered through the gospel, which speaks of our Lord's atoning work and the divine offer of salvation through faith in Him (Gal. 3:8, 13–14). This promise will be universally experienced in the blessings of our Lord's messianic rule over the earth during His millennial kingdom (Mic. 4:1–5). Many of these promises were repeated to Isaac (Gen. 26:3–4) and to Jacob (Gen. 28:10–15; Lev. 26:42).

3. *The obligations of the covenant*

Although the promises are fulfilled by divine grace, the actual realization of the personal promises required people's faith in and obedience to God (Gen. 17:9–10; 22:16–18; 26:3–5; Heb. 11:8–29). God's grace enabled these people to trust and obey Him.

4. *The character of the covenant*

This covenant is gracious. While the fulfillment of the promises relating to the patriarchs' personal lives was conditioned upon their obedience to God, those promises relating to Christ and to national Israel are unconditional, so far as this covenant is concerned. Having fulfilled His personal promises to Abraham, Isaac, and Jacob, delivered Israel from Egypt, and sent the Messiah-Redeemer, God will fulfill the remaining promises in His time as the prophetic Scriptures indicate.

5. *The duration of the covenant*

It is everlasting (Gen. 17:7; Ps. 105:8–10).

6. *The sign or witness of the covenant*

God's covenant with Abraham was solemnized by a ritual that He did and that He required Abraham to do. This was God's passing between sacrificial victims (Gen. 15:9–10, 17), which was a customary way of ratifying contracts (Jer. 34:18–19). The burning fire pot and the fiery torch indicated God's presence (Gen. 15:17). The covenant was also solemnized by the male recipient's submitting to circumcision (17:9–14).[100] By this rite the recipient identified himself with the covenant and was constantly reminded of its promises. The reception of the covenant sign in his body did not spiritually save the recipient, but it did prevent his being excluded from the temporal spiritual and material blessings that were enjoyed by the covenant community (v. 14).

In Romans 4:9–12, the apostle Paul argues that the determining factor of Abraham's righteous status before God was not his circumcision but his faith in God's justificatory promise (Gen. 15:6) before he was circumcised (17:26). His circumcision was a seal that authenticated and confirmed the genuineness of the righteous status that he had received by God's grace through faith in His promise. His circumcision did not create or enhance this status of righteousness, as the Jews of Jesus' day wrongly believed (John 8:33–44; Rom. 4:9) and as some Christian Jews believed later (Acts 15:1). It was a sign of this status only to those who truly possessed the divine gift of righteousness through faith in God's promise.

To my mind, there is no biblical basis for the covenantal concept that water baptism has replaced circumcision as the sign and seal of the covenant of grace. They who hold this view baptize infants in order, as they allege, to make them members of the covenantal community, as circumcision did among the descendants of Abraham in the precross era before Jesus died. Contrariwise, we who are saved were made members of the new covenantal community at salvation by the Holy Spirit, who by His baptism placed us into Christ Jesus (Gal. 3:26–28) and into the Lord's body, the Church (1 Cor. 12:13, 27; Eph. 1:22–23).

7. *The importance of the covenant*

With the promise of the coming Messiah-Seed, the covenant was the basis for the salvational faith of Abraham and his posterity, including those who lived under the Mosaic Law. Since it pointed to the coming Savior and His messianic work (Gal. 3:8, 13–16), the covenant promises of Genesis 12:3 and 15:5 gave something for these people to believe. These promises were a kind of OT "John 3:16" (cp. Luke 1:68–75; consider the apostle Paul's remarks in Gal. 3:8, 14, 16). People who lived beyond the reach of this revelation, given to Israel, still had whatever truth of the coming Conqueror-Savior that persisted in their traditions and the witness of the stellar constellations (Ps. 19:4; Rom. 10:18; see endnote 43). As time elapsed, however, these ancient traditions became more distorted and the pictorial message of the constellations was less clear. Certainly, by the first century the world was ready for the appearing of the Savior and for the universal proclamation of the gospel.

This covenant was the basis for God's gracious dealings with disobedient Israel in the past (Exod. 2:24–25; 6:1–8; Deut. 30:20; 2 Kings 13:23); it will also be this with repentant elect Israel when the Lord returns to earth (Lev. 26:40–45; Jer. 30:3; Ezek. 36:28; Mic. 7:18–20). Israel's present occupation of Palestine is not a fulfillment of this covenant, nor can any aggression on their part ever be justified by it. The Lord Jesus will restore the elect to their land, as promised by this covenant, when He comes to earth again.

The Mosaic Covenant (Exod. 19:1–8; 24:1–8, Lev. 18:5; 26:3–46)

1. *The recipients of the covenant*

The Mosaic Law was given to Moses on Mt. Sinai in A.M. 2513, fifty days after Israel's exodus from Egypt (Exod. 12:40–41; 13:3–4; 19:1, 11; Gal. 3:16–17; see endnote 99). This covenant was given only to the nation of Israel (Exod. 19:3; 2 Chron. 6:11; Ps. 147:19–20). It has never been given to any other people.

2. *The promises of this covenant*

a. *To make Israel a peculiar treasure for God's possession (Exod. 19:5)*

This means that they were to be God's special people above all other nations. Later, Israel was portrayed by this covenant as being God's wife (Isa. 54:5; Jer. 3:14; Hos. 2:7, 16).

b. *To make Israel a kingdom of priests, who would serve God (Exod. 19:6)*

The saved people of Israel served God by their being a witness to His existence and singularity, their being writers and guardians of the OT Scriptures, their worshiping Him, and their giving birth to Jesus the Messiah.

c. To make Israel a holy nation (Exod. 19:6)

The Mosaic Law made this group of recently delivered slaves a theocracy and gave them national organization and political identity. Moreover, it made them morally different and separate from their grossly immoral neighbors.

d. To give Israel spiritual life (Lev. 18:5; cp. Deut. 8:1; Neh. 9:29; Prov. 4:4; Ezek. 20:11, 13, 21; Rom. 10:5; Gal. 3:12)

Although it promised spiritual life (not salvation) to anyone who kept it (Matt. 19:16–17), the Mosaic Law could not save or give life to those who violated it (Gal. 3:21; Rom. 7:10). Since no one but Jesus fully kept the law (Matt. 5:17; Acts 15:10), no one ever received spiritual life from it. The law could not save or give spiritual life to sinners.[101] Only God in His grace can do this (cp. Luke 18:18–27).

e. To prosper Israel and to allow them to remain in the Promised Land (Lev. 26:3–12; cp. Deut. 5:33; 28:2–14)

The Mosaic Law required Israel's obedience for their remaining in the promised land (Lev. 26:3–13). Disobedience to God's law would bring them divine judgment, including eviction and dispersion (vv. 14–33)

3. *The obligations of the covenant*

Israel's obligation was to keep the Mosaic covenant by observing all that the Lord had commanded therein (Exod. 19:5–8; Lev. 26:3, 14–15). The Mosaic Law consisted of the following: the *commandments,* stating the moral laws (Exod. 20:1–17 with Deut. 6:5; Lev. 19:18; see Mark 12:28–31); the *judgments,* presenting the social laws (Exod. 21:1–23:19); the Levitical *ritual,* regulating Israel's approach unto God and prescribing the duties of the priests (Leviticus); and *additional regulations,* given in Numbers (chaps. 5–6, 9–10, 15, 18–19, 27–30).

4. *The character of the covenant*

The Mosaic covenant was legal in character. Because the Mosaic Law was both a divine dispensation and covenant, its conditions were expressed by its laws, or dispensational features. Being based on the principle of law-works, it provided no divine enablement for its observance and required God to deal with its recipients as they deserved (cp. Exod. 19:5; Lev. 18:5; 26:3–4; Rom. 9:31–32; Gal. 3:11–12, 21–22). If a person were able to fulfill the covenant obligations, then his works would require God to do what He promised, for his obedience would place God in his debt (Rom. 4:4). On the other hand, his failure to fulfill his obligations would break the covenant and incur divine punishment (Lev. 26:14–39; Gal. 3:10). God would then be no longer obligated to keep these conditional promises.

Being weak and sinful, the unsaved people of Israel broke the covenant continually during the time it was in force (Jer. 31:32; 11:7–10), even before they left Mt. Sinai (Exod. 32:1–10). Because it was unable to minister to their spiritual need, the Mosaic Law could not help these people. It could only condemn and slay them; it could not give them spiritual life (Rom. 7:9–10; Gal. 3:10). On the other hand, the saved people of Israel, like Zacharias and Elizabeth (Luke 1:6), were able to keep the law sufficiently to be used of God. They did this, as we who are saved do, by the divine grace that accompanies salvation (cp. 1 Cor. 15:10; 2 Cor. 1:12).

God graciously gave to Israel the Levitical ritual and offerings in order to provide a means of keeping them alive physically when they sinned and of maintaining the covenantal relationship. But no provision was made for deliberate sins (Num. 15:30–31) or for such capital crimes as Sabbath breaking (Exod. 35:2), murder (Exod. 21:12), idolatry (Exod. 22:20), and adultery (Lev. 20:10; see endnote 82). As always, Jews were spiritually saved by faith in the promise of the coming Messiah-Seed of Abraham (cp. Gen. 15:5–6;

Gal. 3:6–14), not by keeping the law or by observing its rituals. The Levitical offerings only covered certain sins and thereby kept the Israelites from suffering judicial death by the law; these offerings could not take away sins and their guilt before God (Heb. 9:9–10; 10:1–4). Undoubtedly, the offerings had greater meaning to godly Jews who were looking for the promised Messiah-Savior (Luke 2:25, 38).

5. The duration of the covenant

Despite Israel's repeated violations, this covenant continued in force from its being given on Mt. Sinai (Exod. 19:8; 24:7–8), throughout the remainder of the Old Testament Period (Mal. 4:4), and until Jesus' death (2 Cor. 3:6–14; Gal. 3:19; Eph. 2.14–16; Col. 2:14; Heb. 10:9). God replaced it with the new covenant, which was mediated by our Lord's death and resurrection (Luke 22:20; Heb. 7:18–22; 10:5–10). Although the Mosaic Law as a covenant ended with the mediation of the new covenant, it continues as a dispensation to all who strive to fulfill its duties (cp. the Jews of the apostle Paul's day). God no longer will honor its covenant promises.

6. The sign or witness of the covenant

Being a two-party covenant, the Mosaic Law was ratified by the people and by God. The people agreed to the covenant when they promised to obey its obligations (Exod. 19:8; 24:3, 7). Later, individual submission to the covenant was expressed by males' receiving ritual circumcision (Exod. 12:43–49; John 7:23; Acts 15:1, 5; 21:21; Gal. 5:2–3; see endnote 100) and by all the people's observing the Sabbath (Exod. 31:12–17; Ezek. 20:12). Ritual circumcision reminded its possessors of the promises of the Abrahamic and Mosaic covenants and of their duty to observe the requirements of Mosaic Law. Sabbath observance, which was for physical rest (Exod. 20:10) and worship (Lev. 23:3, "holy convocation"), was a token of continued obedience to the Mosaic Law. Responding to the people's acceptance and acting as God's agent, Moses ratified the covenant when he sprinkled the people with sacrificial blood (Exod. 24:3, 8).

7. The importance of the covenant

The Mosaic Law did not cancel or replace the Abrahamic covenant. It was given alongside the Abrahamic covenant to bring Israel into a nuptial relationship with God, to fulfill a disciplinary role in their lives, and to point them to Jesus, the Messiah, who was to come (Gal. 3:17–19).

The apostle Paul set forth the importance of the Mosaic covenant in Galatians 3:19–25. He declared that it served as a *teacher,* to establish and to reveal the character of sin as transgression (Gal. 3:19; cp. Rom. 3:20; 5:20; 7:7–13; 4:15); as a *jailer,* to confine the people to the awareness of their sins and of their need for the coming Messiah-Savior (Gal. 3:23; cp. 1 Tim. 1:9–10; Heb. 10:2–3); and as a *child-guardian,* to restrain the people until they entered the freedom of adult-sonship by salvational faith in Jesus and His atoning work (Gal. 3:24–25; cp. 4:1–5). The apostle also stated that the Mosaic Law, together with the prophets, bore witness to Jesus and His messianic work (Rom. 3:21; cp. the messianic OT prophecies and the symbolism of the Levitical offerings and the tabernacle).

While the Mosaic Law was spiritually ineffective in the lives of most Israelites, it was fruitful in the lives of saved people like David. They responded to its condemnatory and disciplinary work by casting themselves upon the grace of God, expressed in the Abrahamic covenant (2 Sam. 12:13; Lev. 20:10; Pss. 32; 51; cp. Lev. 26:40–42; Mic. 7:19–20).

God used the Mosaic Law in the hearts of the saved Israelites to create of them a holy nation (Exod. 19:6). Although the law itself could not save sinners or give them spiritual life, it did show the elect their need for God's grace and for trusting the promise of the coming Savior (see "The Abrahamic Covenant" in this chapter). Those who trusted the promise not only were saved but also were enabled by divine grace to observe the law's commandments. As we have seen, these saved people did not keep the law perfectly, but they were obedient to the extent that they could be used of God to accomplish His purposes for their lives and for the nation of Israel (cp. Luke 1:6, 27–28; Matt. 1:19). Receiving no help from the law to keep its commandments, unsaved Israelites violated it continually.

The Palestinian Covenant (Deut. 28:1–29:1; 30:1–10)

1. *The recipients of the covenant*

Just before the death of Moses in A.M. 2553, God made this covenant in Moab with the second generation of Israelites and their posterity (Deut. 28:14–15, 22–29), whose parents had come up out of Egypt and had died in the wilderness (29:1, 9).

2. *The promises of the covenant*

This covenant has two major parts: *One part* is a restatement of what God had promised under the Mosaic covenant in Leviticus 26:3–39 (Deut. 28:1–29:1). This was blessing for obedience (vv. 1–14) and judgment for disobedience (28:15–29:1). *The second part* is a list of new promises that Jesus will fulfill when He returns to earth to rule over His millennial kingdom (Rev. 19:11–16). This return will be in response to the Israelite remnant's turning to Him and obeying His voice (Deut. 30:1–10; cp. Lev. 26:40–45; Ezek. 36:16–38). Let us consider the gracious promises of the second part of this covenant.

a. *To restore Israel to their land (Deut. 30:3–5)*

In the event of Israel's removal from their land because of their breaking the Mosaic covenant, God promised to restore again those who would repent. A few Jews returned from Babylonian captivity to Palestine in the sixth century B.C. But the prophecy mainly concerns both Judah and the northern kingdom when Jesus returns to establish His earthly millennial kingdom (cp. Jer. 30:3–24; Ezek. 34:11–13; 36:24).

b. *To bless and multiply them (Deut. 30:5; cp. Jer. 23:3–4; Ezek. 37:26; Amos 9:11–15)*

The Lord Jesus will bless the repentant of Israel in an unprecedented way when He restores them to their land (see Appendix K: "Israel's Future as Described in Biblical Prophecy").

c. *To regenerate them (Deut. 30:6; cp. Ezek. 36:25–27; 37:14)*

For Israel to circumcise their hearts means for them to humble themselves, accept the punishment for their sins (Lev. 26:41), and renew their pledge of loyalty and obedience to God, including believing the gospel (Jer. 4:4; cp. Deut. 10:16; see Jer. 3:11–22). For God to circumcise the heart in response to Israel's fulfilling her part is a figurative expression for His removing the guilt of their sins and giving the people spiritual cleansing and renewal (Deut. 30:6; Col. 2:11; Heb. 9:26; cp. "The New Covenant" in this chapter). This results in their experiencing eternal life and loving God.

d. *To curse their enemies (Deut. 30:7; cp. Jer. 30:11, 16)*

God promised to deal with Israel's enemies in judgment for their persecuting His people (cp. Gen. 12:3). This will especially take place at the Battle of Armageddon (Rev. 19:11–21) and with Jesus' judging the nations to determine who are qualified among earth dwellers to enter His millennial kingdom (Matt. 25:31–46).

e. *To cause them to prosper (Deut. 30:9) both spiritually and materially (Ezek. 37:26–27; 34:11–31; 36:24–38; Isa. 35, 60)*

God will cause restored, repentant Israel to flourish during our Lord's millennial rule. At that time, they will again be the wife of the Lord (Isa. 54:5; Hos. 2:6–23), but this relationship will be based on the irrevocable new covenant. This means that, above all other earthly nations, Israel will enjoy a special relationship with God.

3. The obligations of this covenant

In the event of their disobedience and dispersion, it will be Israel's duty to return to the Lord (meaning to repent) and to obey His voice (Deut. 30:2, 8, 10). This will involve their repentance toward God and salvational faith in the Lord Jesus Christ (Acts 20:21; 2:38–39; 17:30; Rom. 16:25–26; John 6:28–29).[102] This was the message that John the Baptizer, the Lord Jesus, the apostle Peter, and the apostle Paul preached to Israel (Matt. 3:1–2; 4:17; Acts 2:38; 20:21). By the grace of God, the elect of Israel who are living in that day will do this (cp. Zech. 12:10; Joel 2:12–18; Jer. 32:27– 44; Ezek. 36:16–28; Acts 19:4). When they turn to Him, the Lord Jesus will return to earth, fulfill His covenantal promises to these people, and will rule over His millennial earthly kingdom (Deut. 30:2; Acts 3:19–21), including Israel (Luke 1:32–33; Zech. 14:8–9). These are the people whom the apostle Paul had in view in Romans 11:25–26.

4. The character of the covenant

The first major part of the Palestinian covenant is legal in character, for it restates a portion of the Mosaic Law (Deut. 28:1–29:1 with Lev. 26:3–39). Accordingly, God dealt with disobedient Israel as they deserved by dispersing them among the Gentiles.

The second major part is both gracious and conditional (Deut. 30:1–10). The elect of Israel will be graciously restored to their land and to God's blessing when they return to the Lord (repent) and receive Jesus as their Savior. God will not have forgotten the gracious promise that He made to Abraham regarding their land (Gen. 15:18; 17:8; Lev. 26:42; Deut. 30:20).

5. The duration of the covenant

The gracious promises of the Palestinian covenant will endure forever (Ezek. 37:25; cp. Jer. 32:37–39). Indeed, in that day God will make an everlasting covenant (the new covenant) with Israel that will assure them of the perpetual continuation of these blessings (Jer. 32:40).

6. The sign or witness of the covenant

Historically, this may have been the two stone piles that Israel erected upon crossing the Jordan River (Deut. 27:1–8; Josh. 4:1–9). Presently, it may be the survival of the people of Israel (cp. Jer. 31:35–37). Consider how God has preserved them through these many years while other nations, much greater than they, have perished. After many centuries, the political state of Israel was established in 1948 and continues to engage in the various political activities that will lead eventually to the fulfillment of God's future program for this nation. However, Israel's restoration to their land, according to the promises of the Abrahamic and Palestinian covenants, will not take place until Jesus returns to earth to establish His millennial kingdom (Deut. 30:3; Ezek. 36:23–28).

7. The importance of the covenant

In the event of their dispersion, this covenant promised Israel their restoration to their land and God's blessing them in the land. It also gave instruction regarding what they must do to experience this restoration.

The Davidic Covenant (2 Sam. 7:10–16)

1. The recipients of the covenant

During King David's reign over Judah and Israel (A.M. 2950–90), God made this covenant with him and his posterity through Solomon (2 Sam. 7:12–13, 16; cp. 1 Kings 1:29–30; 2:45–46; 9:1–9; 1 Chron. 28:5–7).

2. The promises of the covenant

Called "the sure mercies of David" (Isa. 55:3; Acts 13:34; cp. 2 Sam. 7:15), these promises are listed as follows:

110

a. To Israel God promised a permanent place of habitation as well as deliverance from their enemies (2 Sam. 7:10; cp. Deut. 30:2–5).

This concerned the future restoration of the elect remnant of Israel to their land, as promised by the Palestinian covenant (Deut. 30:2–5), when the Lord Jesus comes to rule over the earth. God also promised that they would never be dispersed again.

b. To David God promised a perpetual house (dynasty), kingdom, and throne (2 Sam. 7:16; cp. Ezek. 34:23–24; 37:24–25; Jer. 30:9).

This assured that David and his posterity through Solomon would be the ruling dynasty of Israel forever. During the nation's subsequent history, David's house under Solomon and Rehoboam ruled all Israel; from Rehoboam through Jehoiachin, it ruled the tribes of Judah and Benjamin (1 Kings 12:17, 21; 2 Kings 24:12).

The promise also assured that David's house would be the ruling dynasty in our Lord's millennial kingdom. David himself will rule Israel as the Lord's viceroy (Ezek. 34:23–24; 37:24–25: Jer. 30:9) while the Lord Jesus will rule the whole earth, including Israel (Luke 1:32–33; Acts 2:30; Pss. 2:8–9; 72:8; Isa. 9:6–7; Zech. 14:9–21; Rev. 19:11–16).

c. To David's Seed (Solomon and his lineage) God promised mercy and the establishment of his kingdom forever (2 Sam. 7:13–15; cp. Ps. 132:11, 17).

Of David's nineteen sons (1 Chron. 3:1–9), God selected Solomon to be the successor to Israel's throne. In contrast to the five dynasties that ruled the northern kingdom of Israel (1 Kings 12:20; 15:28; 16:16; 2 Kings 9:13–14; 15:17–20), there was but one ruling dynasty of Judah (cp. Gen. 49:10; 1 Kings 15:4). Later, a divine curse fell upon Solomon's line that thereafter prevented the members of this dynasty from occupying and prospering on David's throne (Jer. 36:30; 22:30), but they still transmitted the title to the throne (Matt. 1:12–16). Eventually, the title to David's throne was transmitted to the Lord Jesus through His legal (not actual) father, Joseph, a descendant of Solomon (Matt. 1:6–16, 20, 24). Our Lord's divine virgin conception and birth will allow Him to avoid the divine curse upon the royal line and to rule with God's favor. Because He has no male heirs and is alive forevermore, the Lord Jesus will possess the title to David's throne forever (Luke 1:31–33; see Acts 13:22–23, 32–39; Jer. 33:15; Rom. 1:3; 2 Tim. 2:8).

3. *The obligations of the covenant*

God promised that He would never terminate Solomon's dynasty as He did Saul's (2 Sam. 7:14–15; Ps. 89:30–37; 2 Chron. 7:17–20). Although there were no obligations for the fulfillment of this promise, obedience to God was required for any Davidic king to remain on the throne and to enjoy God's blessing (1 Kings 2:3–4; 9:4–9; Jer. 36:30; 22:30). Despite the divine removal of Davidic kings from rule, the title to David's throne continued to be transferred until it reached Joseph, "son of David," the legal father of Jesus (Matt. 1:20; see vv. 6–16).

4. *The character of the covenant*

The Davidic covenant is gracious and unconditional. There are no conditions for man to meet for the promises to be fulfilled. God will bring all this about in His time.

5. *The duration of the covenant*

Upon their future restoration to their land, Israel will never again be threatened with invasion or dispersion (2 Sam. 7:10). Having sworn by His holiness, God will never break this covenant (Ps. 89:33–37). It will continue forever (2 Sam. 7:16; 23:5; see Luke 1:32–33).

6. *The sign or witness of the covenant*

This appears to be the continuation of David's house and throne in his descendant, Immanuel, the virgin Mary's son, the Lord Jesus (Isa. 7:10–14; 9:6–7; Luke 1:30–33; Matt. 1:20–23; 2 Tim. 2:8; Rev. 3:7; 22:16).

7. The importance of the covenant

The Davidic covenant establishes the reality and legality of Jesus' future rule over Israel from David's throne (Luke 1:32–33). While this title gives the Lord Jesus the right to rule over Israel, it does not authorize Him to rule over the earth. His right to rule over the earth, which was given Him as an inheritance (John 3:35; 13:3), is by divine appointment (Ps. 2:6–9). His rule over both dominions will be messianic, that is, He will do this as man, as the Father's Slave and Viceroy (Isa. 2:1–4; 42:1–12; 61).

The New Covenant (Jer. 31:31–40)

1. The recipients of the covenant

These are all who are saved from sin through faith in Jesus and His atoning work (Luke 22:20; cp. 2 Cor. 3:6–18; Heb. 10:14–18; 12:24; 13:20). This includes all the saved of human history (cp. Heb. 11:39–40) as well as future elect Gentiles and the elect remnant of Israel in the day of their salvation and restoration to God (Isa. 59:20–21; Jer. 31:31; Ezek. 37:26–27).[103] There are not two new covenants, one for Israel and one for the Church, as some suppose. As the New Testament shows, the one new covenant, with its one Mediator (Heb. 8:6; 9:15; 12:24), applies to all who trust in Jesus as their Savior from sin.

2. The promises of the covenant

The promises of the new covenant were predicted in Jeremiah 31:31–40 and are repeated in Hebrews 8:6–13; 10:15–17. These promises concern salvation and its basic blessings as described in the New Testament, that portion of the Bible that deals with the new covenant. God promises:

a. To put His law in their inward parts (Jer. 31:33a)

Unlike Israel's breaking the Mosaic Law by their disobedience, the recipients of the new covenant will not do this because God's law will be in their hearts and in command of their lives. While saved people today obey God periodically by His gracious prompting and enablement (cp. Phil. 2:13), in their future glorified state they will actually have His Word in their hearts and will obey Him continuously. God's people will not have to carry Bibles, for His Word will forever exist in their memory as well as exert its influence on their lives. Meanwhile, being judicially forgiven of all their sins (Col. 2:13), people who are saved cannot make the covenant ineffective by their sinning (Rom. 8:31–34).

b. To be their God (Jer. 31:33b–34a)

To "know the LORD" refers to one's having a right relationship with God, brought about by divine forgiveness and the new birth (cp. John 17:3; 10:27; 1:12). This relationship with God also involves a right attitude toward Him—to fear God (Jer. 32:39–40; cp. Deut. 10:12–13; 1 Peter 1:17; 2:17). To fear God is to revere Him (Ps. 33:8), be in agreement with Him (Prov. 3:7; 8:13), obey Him (Prov. 14:2), trust His promises (Prov. 14:26), and accept His instructions (Prov. 1:7; 15:33).

c. To forgive their sins (Jer. 31: 34)

This means that the gospel believer's judicial debt of sin is canceled by the divine application of the value of Jesus' atoning work (cp. Eph. 1:7; Acts 10:43). The declaration, "I will remember their sins no more," refers to God's judicial memory. He will no longer hold these sins against His people. With this memory clause being parallel to the words, "I will forgive their iniquity," God's not remembering sin means the same as His forgiving sin, that is, releasing the sinner from the obligation to bear punishment for his or her sins.

Gospel believers experience the fulfillment of these three promises in reverse order: First, at salvation there is divine forgiveness of their sins and their being brought into a personal relationship with God. Finally, God's laws (His Word) will be permanently written in their hearts when their bodies will be delivered from mortality and sin upon the Lord's return (Phil. 3:20–21; 1 John 3:2).

3. The obligations of the covenant

To enter the bond of the covenant and to experience its promised blessings, one must exercise salvational faith in Jesus, the Mediator of the new covenant (Heb. 12:24; Acts 13:32–39). Observe that water baptism is not required for participation in the covenant. As a minister of the new covenant, the apostle Paul appealed to people only to exercise salvational faith in the Lord Jesus (Acts 20:21; 2 Cor. 3:6; 5:18–20).

4. The character of the covenant

The new covenant is gracious and conditional. It is gracious in that God offers salvation to undeserving people as a gift (Eph. 2:8–9); it is conditional in that obedience to the gospel is required to bring one into the bond of the covenant (Acts 13:32–39; Rom. 1:5). However, this obedience is not a meritorious effort of man. Salvational faith is graciously, divinely imparted to those whom God has chosen to save (Acts 3:16; 5:31; 11:18; 2 Peter 1:1).

5. The duration of the covenant

The relationship between God and His people according to this covenant will continue forever (Jer. 31:35–37). Unlike the Law of Moses, this gracious covenant is not a two-party contract that can be annulled by people's disobedience (v. 33). With all their sins being judicially forgiven (Col. 2:13), God's people cannot nullify the covenant by their sinning (see "The Permanence of Salvation" under Soteriology). However, their failure to deal with known sins in their lives will incur divine parental chastisement in this life (Rev. 3:19).

Because of the perpetual quality and effectiveness of these promises, this covenant is described as being "everlasting" (Isa. 61:8; Jer. 32:40; Heb. 13:20) and "a covenant of peace" (Ezek. 37:26). All who become the recipients of this covenant through trusting in Jesus as Savior are reconciled to God and justified forever (Rom. 5:9–10; 8:30–34). Are you in this covenant relationship with God?

6. The sign or witness of the covenant

The initial sign was that by which the covenant was divinely made effective—our Lord's shed blood together with His death and resurrection (Heb. 12:24; 13:20; Rom. 1:4; see "The Blood of Christ" under Christology). Today this sign is symbolically portrayed by the "cup" of the Lord's Supper (Luke 22:20; 1 Cor. 11:25–26), which reminds us of the Lord's atoning work—a central fact of our faith. In the future, this covenant sign will be displayed to all by the crucifixion marks in Jesus' body (John 20:24–28) and by the various memorial sacrifices that will be offered in the millennial temple (Ezek. 43, 45–46). Being commemorative rather than effective, these offerings will remind the Lord's people of His atoning work as His Supper does today.

7. The importance of the covenant

The importance of the covenant is manifest in its salvational promises. Being based on our Lord's atoning work, the new covenant fulfills and replaces the salvational aspect of the Abrahamic covenant, which foresaw the coming Seed and the blessings that Jesus would bring to all who trust in Him and His atoning work. But this covenant does not cancel or replace the promises of earlier covenants that promised other things, like Israel's title to the promised land, which are yet to be fulfilled. The new covenant did replace the covenantal aspect of the Mosaic Law (Heb. 8:6–13), which promised eternal life to those who kept it (Lev. 18:5; Matt. 19:16–17).

The new covenant will also be the basis of Israel's future restoration to God and of their nuptial relationship with Him (Jer. 31:31; Isa. 54:10; 61:8; Jer. 32:40; Ezek. 16:60; Rom. 11:26–27). In fact, all who exercise salvational faith in the Savior during the Church Age, Tribulation Age, and Kingdom Age will receive the promised blessings of the covenant. However, as we have seen, not all the recipients of this covenant have the same functional place in God's program. While the covenant's salvational blessings are the same for all gospel believers, these blessings are to be distinguished from the functional roles, with their particular blessings, that various groups of redeemed people will have. For example, while the Church and the future elect of Israel will have the same salvational blessings promised by the new covenant, they will have different functional roles during the earthly millennial kingdom. The Church will be Jesus' bride, and Israel will be God's wife.

Several Distinctions

Observe the following distinctions in your study of these covenants:

One: All these covenants relate to Israel (Rom. 9:4): the Noachic covenant was given to all mankind; the Abrahamic covenant gives Israel title to certain territory; the Mosaic covenant states the condition of their remaining in the Promised Land; the Palestinian covenant declares the conditions for their restoration to the land in the event of their dispersion; the Davidic covenant assures Israel of their permanent restoration to the Promised Land and the perpetuity of David's dynasty; and the new covenant promises salvation to all who trust in Jesus as their Savior from sin.

Two: The Abrahamic and new covenants are salvational covenants: The Abrahamic covenant, which spoke about the coming Seed and the blessing He would bring, was the salvational covenant of the Old Testament Period from Abraham's time onward. The new covenant, based on Jesus' atoning work, is the current, final salvational covenant, fulfilling and replacing the salvational aspects of the Abrahamic covenant.

Three: Only the Noachic and new covenants directly relate to Gentiles; the Abrahamic covenant does so indirectly.

In addition to these covenant promises, God has given many other promises in His Word, which give His people's faith in Him something to rest on (cp. Isa. 41:10; Rom. 8:28). It is important, however, that we claim only those promises that are given to us. While many OT promises concur with NT promises, others were given specifically to Israel (cp. Lev. 26:3–13) and do not apply to us today. Let us now consider how to cultivate our daily personal relationship with our covenant keeping God.

FELLOWSHIP WITH GOD

Having been born again, the gospel believer can have intimate fellowship with God (John 17:3), which is the greatest of all human experiences (Ps. 63:1–8; Phil. 3:7–10; 1 John 1:1–3). However, to have this, one must do one's part (James 4:8). The saved person's daily relationship with God is not one of passivity, where he or she does nothing but waits for God to do everything. There are things that we must do to fellowship with God and to develop this intimate relationship with Him. God will do His part as we do ours in His strength.[104]

What must we who are saved do to maintain and deepen our daily personal fellowship with the living God? Keep in mind that this does not concern our salvational relationship with God, which is divinely maintained and is unchanging. We cultivate this fellowship by observing certain principles of interpersonal relationships with God and by interacting with the Persons of the divine Trinity individually.

PRINCIPLES OF INTERPERSONAL RELATIONSHIPS

These principles relate to personal relationships with people who are our superiors. We shall consider these principles as they relate to our interaction with God, or with the Persons of the divine Trinity collectively. They also apply to our relations with the divine Persons individually.

Our Listening to God (Ps. 1:1–3)

Fellowship with others involves our listening attentively to what they say. God has given us His Word, the Bible, for our learning about Himself, ourselves, and His will for our lives (2 Tim. 3:16–17). Since He uses the Scriptures to address His people and to minister to their spiritual needs, God's Word works effectively in the lives of all who receive it (Ps. 1:1–3; 1 Thess. 2:13; see "The Maintenance of the Christian Life: The Bible" under Zoeology).

Our Talking to God (Phil. 4:6)

Fellowship with others requires our verbal interaction.[105] Through our great High Priest, the Lord Jesus, God has provided for His people direct access to Himself (Heb. 4:14–16). We can talk to Him about all that concerns us with the confidence that He invites us, loves us, knows us, listens to us, and is able to minister to our needs whatever these may be (see "The Maintenance of the Christian Life: Prayer" under Zoeology).

Our Pleasing God (2 Cor. 5:9)

Fellowship with others, especially with our superiors, requires us to please them by doing those things that they command us. God not only wants us to live holy, sinless lives but also to live righteous lives, which consist of our doing His will (1 Peter 1:15; 1 John 2:1, 3, 29; 3:7). This requires our learning His will and doing it in His way (Eph. 5:10, 17; Rom. 12:2; see Appendix F: "Learning and Doing God's Will").

Our Not Offending God (1 John 1:5–9)

Fellowship with others requires our avoiding that which is offensive to them and our dealing immediately with offenses when they occur. Sin not only offends God but also interrupts our fellowship with Him (1 John 1:5–7). To avoid sinning and to receive divine cleansing and forgiveness of sins, we must do the following:

One: Because of changes that were made in us at salvation, we do not have to sin anymore, despite the urges of the sin force within us, our ability to sin, and the temptations of Satan and the evil forces of the world. To avoid sinning, we must not yield to these temptations and, as much as possible, we must elude those people and things that tempt us. However, to do this successfully, we must be submissive to the Holy Spirit, resist temptation in His strength (James 4:7), and do God's will (the holy alternative) in His strength (Eph. 4:22–29; 5:17; Gal. 5:16).

Two: When we sin, we incur personal guilt and moral defilement. Although at salvation we received God's judicial acquittal of the guilt of all our sins and His judicial cleansing from their defilement (Col. 1:14; 2:13), we still need His parental cleansing and forgiveness of those filial sins that we now commit as His children. To receive this, we must inwardly repent of our sins (Rev. 2:5); confess our wrongdoing to God (1 John 1:9); make right our offenses to others, should others be involved (Matt. 5:23–24); and forgive repentant offenders (Matt. 6:14–15; Luke 17:3).

Our avoiding as much as possible those things that would tempt us and our dealing immediately with sin when it occurs will enhance our fellowship with God (2 Cor. 6:17–7:1;

James 4:8–10). He is absolutely holy and desires that we live holy, obedient lives (1 Thess. 4:1–5; 1 Peter 1:13–16; 1 John 1:5–7).

Our Loving God (Mark 12:28–30)

Fellowship with others best occurs in a relationship of friendship love where one is pleased with friends, grateful for them, and considerate of them. Because of who God is and what He does, we owe Him our love. In fact, the Lord Jesus regarded this as the foremost commandment of the Mosaic Law, and it remains our duty today (Mark 12:29–30; cp. John 21:15). As shown in the life of the Lord Jesus (John 14:31), we express our love for God by obedience to His will (Exod. 20:6; Deut. 30:20; John 14:15; 1 John 5:3, KJV "of " should be "for"; 2 John 6). When man's will conflicts with God's will, he must obey God (Acts 5:29). This exclusive love for God has a commitment like that of married love, which is not to be shared with anyone else or with anything (1 John 2:15, KJV should read "love for the Father"). We may love other people and things but not with the love that we owe to God. When we compromise this love by directing it to another object, we become a spiritual adulterer or adulteress (cp. James 4:4).

Our Respecting God (Deut. 10:12–13; Eccl. 12:13–14; 1 Peter 2:17)

Fellowship with others, especially our superiors, is built on respect for them. Likewise, we must show respect for God. This is described as "fearing" Him, which is the duty of all personal creatures to their Creator. In view of the world's disregard for God (Rom. 3:18), saved people should certainly give Him the honor and fear that are due Him as God (2 Cor. 7:1; 1 Peter 1:17; Heb. 12:28). This fear is not a terror or dread that is incompatible with love (1 John 4:18; 2 Tim. 1:7). On the other hand, it recognizes God's holy intolerance of sin and His paternal corrective chastening of those who neglect to deal with evil in their lives. Our fearing God is expressed by a profound reverence for God's Being and majesty (Ps. 33:8), an agreement with His attitude toward good and evil (Prov. 3:7; 8:13), confidence in His promises (14:26), acceptance of His instructions (1:7; 15:33), and obedience to His will (14:2). This fear not only prolongs our days (Prov. 10:27) but also equips us for life and service (Phil. 2:12; Heb. 12:28; 1 Peter 3:15) and assures us of reward in the coming appraisal because of its impact upon our behavior (Eccl. 12:14; 1 Cor. 3:13–15; 2 Cor. 5:9–10; Heb. 12:28–29). This fear of God is essential to our fellowship with Him.

By observing these principles of personal relationships, we engage in fellowship with God. By striving to follow these principles more fully and consistently, we improve this relationship in our daily experience (1 Thess. 4:1). Evaluate your relationship with God and give special attention to those areas that need strengthening or refining. God will help you to deal with these areas, as you rely on Him, and He will bless you for any improvement that you may make. The promise is this, "Draw nigh to God, and He will draw nigh to you" (James 4:8). Observe that we must make the first move in this relationship. Let us now focus on our relationship with the individual Persons of the divine Trinity.

INTERACTION WITH THE PERSONS OF THE DIVINE TRINITY

Fellowship with others calls for personal interaction. Lest we think of God as being a vague, impersonal entity, we should keep in mind that the Christian God consists of three divine Persons: the Father, the Son (Jesus), and the Holy Spirit. Because we humans are persons made in God's image, we who are saved can refine our personal relationship with these divine Persons individually as we would with any other person. Although we shall look at these interactions in greater detail later, here is a summary of them.

Our Interaction with God the Father as His Children-Sons

The concept of God the Father as being our Father is probably our most moving concept of Him, especially if we have or have had a loving human father.[106] However, He is the Father of only those people who have been born again through faith in Jesus and His atoning work (John 1:12).

The new birth admitted those of us who are saved into God's family as children (John 1:12–13; Gal. 3:26) and into His kingdom as citizens (John 3:3–5; Phil. 3:20). Immediately after our birth into God's family, we children received the position of adult sons by divine adoption (Rom. 8:15; Eph. 1:5). This position gives all God's children the same rights and privileges as well as the same obligations. Jesus often spoke about God the Father's being the Father of His people (Matt. 5:16, 45, 48; 6:1, 26, 32; 7:11; 13:43; 23:9). As His children-sons, we who are saved can have fellowship with the Father (1 John 1:3).

We can improve our relationship with the Father by praying to Him (Matt. 6:6, 9; John 16:23; 1 Peter 1:17), submitting to His parental dealings with us, trusting in Him and His Word (Mark 11:22), obeying His will (Matt. 7:21), following His example (Eph. 5:1; Matt. 5:48), receiving His gifts (Phil. 4:19; Matt. 7:7–11), seeking to glorify Him in all we do (1 Cor. 10:31), and worshiping Him (John 4:22–23).[107]

Our Interaction with God the Son (the Lord Jesus) as His Slaves-Friends

At salvation, we who have been born again were delivered from bondage to our former spiritual enemies (sin, Satan, and the world) and were made permanent slaves of the Lord Jesus, who purchased us with so great a price (Eph. 6:6; Matt. 20:28; Acts 20:28; Rom. 1:1; 14:8; 1 Cor. 6:20; 1 Peter 1:18–19). However, this relationship is not a burdensome bondage, for our Master knows what it is to live under the Father's yoke as His Slave (John 6:38; 8:28–29; Isa. 42:1–4). The Lord Jesus will help us with our load as we daily submit to His leadership (Matt. 11:28–30). In fact, we have been called into His fellowship (1 Cor. 1:9), for we are His friends as well as His slaves (John 15:15; cp. Matt. 12:47–50), and He loves us very much (John 13:1; 15:9; Gal. 2:20).

We experience the Lord's fellowship as we pray to Him (John 14:13), submit to His authority (Luke 6:46–49; Matt. 11:28–30) and vitality (John 15:4–5), have faith in Him (Gal. 2:20), follow His instructions (John 8:30–32) and example (Matt. 10:25; John 13:34–35; 1 Peter 2:21), participate in His sufferings (John 15:18–21; 1 Peter 2:20–21; Matt. 5:10–12, 38–42, 44–45), receive His gifts (John 14:13), live unto Him (2 Cor. 5:14–15), abide in Him (John 15:4–5), labor with Him in building His Church (Rom. 12:1–8; 1 Cor. 3:8–15), and worship Him (John 5:19–23). We express our friendship and love by obeying His commands (John 14:15; 15:14).

Our Interaction with God the Holy Spirit as His Temples-Dependents

We who have been born again received God the Holy Spirit at salvation as our permanent resident Helper (KJV "Comforter," or "Helper"; John 14:16–17; 1 John 3:24). Therefore, our bodies are His temples in which He dwells (1 Cor. 6:19), and we are His dependents who are in constant need of His help (Gal. 5:16; Eph. 5:18).

Since the Holy Spirit is a person like the other Persons of the divine Trinity, we can have fellowship with Him (2 Cor. 13:14; Phil. 2:1). We experience this relationship by submitting ourselves to His control (Eph. 5:18); following His leading (Rom. 8:14); trusting Him for His work in our lives (Acts 5:6) like helping us to do God's will (Acts 1:8; 6:5), to stand against our spiritual enemies (Gal. 5:16), and to teach us spiritual truth (1 John 2:27); not giving our bodies over to sin and harmful things (1 Cor. 6:18–20; 1 Thess. 4:3–7); and worshiping Him (Rev. 22:9). This fellowship also involves our talking to Him.

Our thinking about God becomes more real and personal when we interact with the Persons of the Trinity individually, according to our primary relationship with Them and our needs. As a child-son one can look to the heavenly Father, as a slave-friend one can look to the Lord Jesus, and as a temple-dependent one can look to the Holy Spirit. Observing these distinctions is not necessary for our approaching God. Yet being familiar concepts, these distinctions assist us in developing a more intimate relationship with the true God. Because this interaction is a unique, personal experience, each gospel believer will develop his own manner of fellowship with these divine Persons. They wait to respond to us.

It is, indeed, an unspeakable privilege to belong to the true, living God. As we attend to life's functions and duties, we must develop the habit of looking to the Persons of the Trinity for their fellowship, direction, and ministry. As we draw near to Them, They promise to draw near to us (James 4:8). They will fulfill Their part in this sacred, intimate interaction as we do ours. With each new day and each time that we sin, we must give ourselves anew to God. We must share with these divine Persons all that the day brings us, walk in Their fellowship, draw upon Their abundant resources, and enjoy Their gracious blessings. By this, we experience a growing intimacy with Them, gain a greater understanding of Them, and enjoy a greater experience of Their blessings (Ps. 144:15).

What has been your response to God's self-revelation by His Word? Have you entered a personal relationship with the true God by the new birth? Are you walking in the fellowship of these divine Persons today? Does your life radiate godliness and glorify God?

A Review of Theology Proper

1. How may we define God?
2. How do we know that God exists?
3. Give the four witnesses to God's existence by means of general revelation.
4. Briefly explain the four rational arguments for God's existence. In what circumstances may these arguments be useful?
5. Why do we not have to prove God's existence to unsaved people?
6. To what extent is God's witness to mankind clear?
7. Give and describe the various non-Christian views of God.
8. What is the Christian view of God called?
9. Describe the active and passive forms of God's revelation.
10. Why is it necessary that God reveal Himself to man?
11. What are the two kinds, or stages, of divine revelation?
12. Describe these stages and to whom they are given.
13. In what way is general revelation insufficient?
14. In what way is general revelation effective?
15. In what ways is special revelation sufficient?
16. In what ways is special revelation effective?
17. In what ways was special revelation given during the OT Period?
18. In what ways was special revelation given during the NT Period?
19. What was the unique manifestation of special revelation in the NT Period?
20. Why do we say that new special revelation is not being given today?
21. When will new special revelation be given again?
22. How does religious liberalism view special revelation?
23. What is God's primary constitution, or makeup?
24. What features show that God has personhood?
25. Of what substance does the divine nature consist?
26. What are the qualities of the divine nature called?

27. Which of these qualities are communicated to saved people? By what means are they communicated?
28. Describe God's qualities, or attributes. Give a blessing that each attribute is to us who are saved.
29. Explain God's transcendence and His immanence.
30. Give the three kinds of God's love. How does God's love differ from human love?
31. What is the greatest expression of divine love toward the world?
32. How does God's hatred differ from human hatred?
33. What two kinds of wrath does God's hatred express?
34. Explain and give an example of each of the following terms: anthropomorphism, anthropopathism, and zoomorphism.
35. Of what does the unity of God consist?
36. Why is the unity of God emphasized in the Old Testament?
37. Of what does the triunity (Trinity) of God consist?
38. Why is the triunity (Trinity) of God emphasized in the New Testament?
39. Give a four-statement summary of the biblical doctrine of the divine Trinity.
40. Explain the three false views of the Trinity.
41. What makes each of the three Persons of the Trinity to be God?
42. What makes the three Persons of the Trinity to be together one God?
43. Why do the three Persons of the Trinity have equal attributes?
44. Explain the relationships among the Persons of the Trinity with reference to the divine nature.
45. Explain the subordination that is manifest among the Persons of the Trinity with reference to Their internal relationships and to Their relationships to the universe.
46. Give the three basic kinds of names, or designations.
47. Give the three basic Hebrew names for God in the Old Testament, their meanings, and how they are expressed in the King James Version of the Bible.
48. Give the three kinds of names found in the New Testament for each Person of the divine Trinity.
49. What is the human personal name of God the Son? When did He receive this name?
50. What is God's decree? Give the biblical words that stand for His decree.
51. Give and explain the various qualities that characterize God's decree.
52. What actions of God are governed by His decree?
53. Explain the efficient and permissive aspects of God's decree.
54. What evidence shows that people are not mechanically determined by God's decree like parts of a machine?
55. For what aspect of His decree does God not assume responsibility?
56. State the difference between God's decree and His revealed will for mankind. With what should we be concerned?
57. What is the ultimate objective of God's decree?
58. How did sin have a place in God's decree?
59. What should our attitude be toward biblical doctrines that we do not understand?
60. Define God's act of creating the universe.
61. Give the two steps that were involved in God's creative work.
62. Describe the roles of the Persons of the Trinity in the creation of the universe.
63. Describe the events of the six days of God's creative activity.
64. What appears to be the purpose of accommodative interpretations of these six days of divine creative activity?
65. Describe the accommodative interpretations of Genesis chapter 1.

66. Why is it inadvisable to harmonize Scripture with scientific opinion?
67. What are scientism, organic evolution, chance, and fate?
68. List and explain the natural laws and the principle with which the theory of evolution conflicts.
69. What creative works is God doing today? In the future?
70. Describe God's acts of preservation and providence as these relate to the universe.
71. What problems arise when we look at God's providence? How are these resolved?
72. Define the terms *dispensation, dispensationalist, dispensationalism,* and *ultradispensationalism.*
73. Dispensationally, what two meanings does the word *age* have in the New Testament?
74. What is the difference between a divine dispensation and a divine covenant?
75. List the divine dispensations, their recipients, and their duties.
76. What dispensation are saved people to follow today?
77. Throughout history some people have, to a large degree, obeyed God. By what means did they do this?
78. Explain the difference between a legal-works covenant and a gracious covenant?
79. List the divine covenants, their recipients, and their promises.
80. What is covenant theology? Why do dispensationalists reject this?
81. What covenants relate especially to Israel? What do they promise these people?
82. Which dispensation was also a covenant?
83. What salvation covenant particularly applies to those of us who are saved today?
84. List the sign or witness of each covenant. What purposes do these signs serve?
85. In addition to creation, dispensation, covenants, and rule, give two other works of God.
86. Give the three theological meanings that the word *judgment* has in Scripture and give an example of each meaning.
87. What two primary things must we do to maintain and deepen our fellowship with God?
88. Give the six principles of interpersonal relationships that deepen our fellowship with God.
89. Into what personal relation has salvation brought us with each Person of the Trinity?
90. Give several ways by which we can interact with each Person of the Trinity and can deepen our fellowship with Him.
91. Did you have your devotional time with God today? Did you give yourself to Him?

Endnotes

1. The Bible often uses the singular personal pronouns "He" and "Him" and the possessive pronoun "His" for God, although the divine Trinity consists of three Persons—the Father, the Son, and the Holy Spirit (Gen. 1:10; 2:2; Ps. 150:1; Acts 17:24; Rom. 1:20; 1 Peter 5:6). The word *God* sometimes refers to God the Father when another Person of the Trinity is mentioned in the context (cp. Rom. 1:1–3, 8–9).

2. These first three arguments for God's existence are called *a posteriori arguments,* by which reasoning leads from particulars to principles. This kind of reasoning considers the facts and draws from them certain principles or conclusions. In contrast to this kind of argument, the ontological argument is called an *a priori argument,* which is based on principles that are recognized as being true apart from observation or experience. This kind of reasoning leads from principles to particulars. It argues from abstract, but necessary, ideas.

3. A. H. Strong, *Systematic Theology* (Philadelphia: American Baptist Publication Society, 1907), 87.

4. James I. Packer, "God Speaks to Man," in *Christian Foundations* (Philadelphia: The Westminster Press, 1965), 2:29.

5. Benjamin Breckinbridge Warfield, *The Inspiration and Authority of the Bible* (Philadelphia: The Presbyterian and Reformed Publishing Company, 1948), 75.
6. I do not believe that the personal inner impressions by which the Holy Spirit leads His people (Rom. 8:14) should be classified as special revelation that is to be followed by others. Even these inner urges or voices must be evaluated in the light of Scripture, for Satan, too, can impress God's people.
7. James I. Packer, *Fundamentalism and the Word of God* (London: Inter-Varsity Fellowship, 1958), 92. For a recent survey see D. A. Carson, *The Gagging of God* (Grand Rapids: Zondervan Publishing House, 1996).
8. I use the words *nature* and *essence* interchangeably.
9. W. G. T. Shedd, *Dogmatic Theology* (Grand Rapids: Zondervan Publishing House, 1969), 1:334.
10. We are accustomed to thinking of time as measured by our clocks. Our day of twenty-four hours is determined by the single rotation of the earth upon its axis; our year of 365 1/4 days is determined by the single revolution of the earth around the sun.
11. With "the counsel" being first in order in Acts 2:23, the Granville Sharp Greek rule applies as follows: "When the copulative *kai* ('and') connects two nouns of the same case, if the article *ho* ('the') or any of its cases precedes the first of the said nouns or participles and is not repeated before the second noun or participle, the latter always relates to the same person (or thing) that is expressed or described by the first noun or participle." Quoted from H. E. Dana and J. R. Mantey, *A Manual Grammar of the Greek New Testament* (New York: The Macmillan Company, 1941), 147. For other examples see Titus 2:13, "our great God and Savior"; 2 Peter 1:1, "the God and Savior"; 2:20, "the Lord and Savior"; and 3:2, "the Lord and Savior."
12. Shedd, *Dogmatic Theology*, 1:359.
13. See F. H. Barackman, "The Principle of Biblical Faith" in *Where Is Your Faith?* (Endicott, N.Y.: F. H. Barackman, 1994), 18f.
14. W. H. Griffith Thomas, *The Principles of Theology* (London: Church Book Room Press Ltd., 1963), 15.
15. Its being favorably quoted by Jerome, Augustine, Cyprian, and Tertullian.
16. J. N. D. Kelley, *Early Christian Doctrines* (New York: Harper & Row Publishers, 1960), 121f.
17. Ibid., 226–31, 255.
18. "Trinity," *The International Standard Bible Encyclopaedia* (1949), 5:3017.
19. With His conception by the Holy Spirit in the womb of the virgin Mary (Matt. 1:20–25; Luke 1:27–35), the eternally preexisting God the Son took upon Himself a sinless, complete human nature (body, soul, and spirit), divinely made of Mary's substance, and became a human being, with the human name "Jesus," meaning "the LORD is salvation." Having the two natures, the divine and the human, God the Son is now forever both God and man—the God-man, with the human name Jesus (1 John 5:20; 1 Tim. 2:5).
20. "Trinity," 5:3014.
21. See W. G. T. Shedd, *A History of Christian Doctrine* (New York: Charles Scribner & Co., 1867), 1:344.
22. It appears that the Father's words in Psalm 2:7 refer to the eternal generation of the Son, for this declaration concerning the Son was made in the day of God's decree, which itself is eternal (Eph. 3:11). The decree itself was not about the generation of the Son (an eternal, internal relationship that is not determined by the divine decree), but it concerns the incarnation and messianic work of God the Son, as shown by the context of Psalm 2:7 and by the apostle Paul in Acts 13:33 (cp. v. 22). The external relationships of the Persons of the divine Trinity to the universe and Their interpersonal relationships required by this are determined by divine decree. Thus the eternal generation of God the Son is not determined by divine decree, but His incarnation and messianic work as man are.
23. Since the third Synod of Toledo (589), the Western church has held that the Holy Spirit proceeds from the Father and the Son; the Eastern church continues holding the earlier view, from the Father through the Son (Shedd, *A History of Christian Doctrine*, 1:361). I prefer the view that this spiration is by the Father through the Son, rather than by the Father and the Son, to

avoid the suggestion that the Holy Spirit is generated by the Father as the Son is generated by Him. This would make the Holy Spirit a second Son.

24. Jesus' words, "The Father is greater than I" (John 14:28), refer to rank, not to constitution.

25. Herbert F. Stevenson, *The Titles of the Triune God* (London: Marshall, Morgan & Scott Ltd., 1955), 16.

26. Ibid., 25.

27. Edmond Jacob, *Theology of the Old Testament* (New York: Harper & Row Publishers, 1958), 59.

28. Ludwig Koehler, *Old Testament Theology* (London: Lutterworth Press, 1957), 30.

29. See J. Barton Payne, *The Theology of the Old Testament* (Grand Rapids: Zondervan Publishing House, 1962), 147.

30. Stevenson, *Titles of the Triune God,* 22.

31. G. Abbott-Smith, *A Manual Greek Lexicon of the New Testament* (Edinburgh: T. & T. Clark, 1937), 261.

32. Shedd, *Dogmatic Theology*, 1:395f.

33. L. Berkhof, *Systematic Theology* (London: The Banner of Truth Trust, 1941), 103.

34. Richard Watson, *Theological Institutes* (New York: Hunt & Eaton, 1889), 2:423–29.

35. Lewis Sperry Chafer, *Systematic Theology* (Dallas: Dallas Seminary Press, 1947), 1:240.

36. Berkhof, *Systematic Theology,* 108.

37. Strong, *Systematic Theology,* 1:368.

38. "Repent" is a figure of association (synecdoche) for salvational faith (cp. Acts 2:38; 26:20). See Appendix X: "Figures of Association: Synecdoche and Metonymy."

39. See "The Creation Epic," *Ancient Near Eastern Texts,* ed. James B. Pritchard (Princeton: Princeton University Press, 1955), 60ff.

40. See Joseph C. Dillow, *The Waters Above: Earth's Pre-Flood Vapor Canopy* (Chicago: Moody Press, 1961).

41. This implies that the various kinds of life, both flora and fauna (Gen. 1:21, 24–25), were so made that each would produce essentially the same as itself. Room was allowed within these "kinds" for the development of varieties.

42. With the sun's being on the equinoctial colure, this marked the beginning of the solar year, with the earth's revolving about the sun in 365 1/4 days. See J. B. Dimbleby, *All Past Time* (London: E. Nister, 1897), 10.

43. Although satanically distorted by astrology, this message is still being conveyed by the meaning of the ancient language names of the constellations and their major stars that belong to the zodiac, the circle of the visual heaven, which is divided into twelve parts. These star pictures were divinely named so that people might be constantly reminded of the promise of the coming Seed (Jesus), who would destroy Satan (Gen. 3:15), and of the hope of salvation through His atoning sacrifice, which was portrayed by the OT animal sacrifices (Gen. 3:21; 4:1–5; Heb. 11:4). The twelve constellation signs of the zodiac, with their decans (their satellite constellations), served to remind pre-Mosaic people of this message, which was orally preserved in their traditions for 2,500 years before the first written Scriptures were given. See E. W. Bullinger, *The Witness of the Stars,* and Joseph A. Seiss, *The Gospel in the Stars,* both reprinted by Kregel Publications.

44. Like the creation of man (Gen. 2:7), God made the bodies of animals from existing matter (water and soil) and animated their bodies by giving them soul and spirit. The Hebrew word *nephesh* translated "creature" in KJV (1:20, 21, 24) means "soul" (cp. Rev. 16:3). Animals also have a "spirit" or "breath" (Eccl. 3:21, Heb. *ruach*; cp. Gen. 7:15, 22; Ps. 104:25–29). Both soul and spirit animate the bodies of humans and animals (see "The Nature of Mankind" under Anthropology).

45. Some hold that the first three days were not twenty-four-hour days, for the sun did not shine upon the earth during this time. In reply, it can be said that a twenty-four-hour day is determined by the rotation of the earth upon its axis, which began on the first day as indicated by the reference to evening and morning (Gen. 1:5).

46. Edward J. Young. This may be paraphrased, "At the time when God said, 'Let there be light,'

the three-fold condition, recorded in verse two, already existed." See his *Studies in Genesis One* (Philadelphia: Presbyterian and Reformed Publishing Co., 1964), 8f.

47. Henry M. Morris, *Studies in the Bible and Science* (Philadelphia: Presbyterian and Reformed Publishing Co., 1966), 32.

48. Young, *Studies in Genesis One,* 13, 38.

49. Note that Isaiah 45:18 does not refer to Genesis 1:2 but to the fact that God did not fail to accomplish His purpose in providing inhabitants for the earth rather than leaving it empty.

50. See Walter J. Beasley, *Creation's Amazing Architect* (London: Marshall, Morgan & Scott, Ltd., 1955).

51. See Bernard Ramm, *The Christian View of Science and Scripture* (London: The Paternoster Press, 1955), 76–79.

52. Merrill F. Unger, "Rethinking the Genesis Account of Creation," *Bibliotheca Sacra*, vol. 115, no. 457 (1958), 28.

53. Rev. C. I. Scofield, ed., *The Scofield Reference Bible* (New York: Oxford University Press, 1917), 3.

54. John C. Whitcomb and Henry M. Morris, *The Genesis Flood* (Philadelphia: The Presbyterian and Reformed Publishing Co., 1962), chap. 6.

55. Weston W. Fields, *Unformed and Unfulfilled* (Phillipsburg, NJ: Presbyterian and Reformed Publishing Co., 1978), chap. 4.

56. A day of twenty-four hours is determined by the time consumed by a complete rotation of the earth, whether or not solar light reaches it.

57. Uniformitarianism is the theory that existing processes, observable in nature, have always operated essentially as they do now. While uniformity is manifest in nature, this theory ignores those divine interventions in the past that have interrupted or altered these processes to the extent that they cannot now be projected backward with accuracy over long periods of time.

58. See Fields, *Unformed and Unfulfilled,* 219f. for a review of radiocarbon dating and the assumptions upon which its accuracy rests.

59. See J. B. Dimbleby, *All Past Time* (London: E. Nister, 1897) and *The Historical Bible* (London: E. Nister, 1897). Mr. Dimbleby, who was Premier Chronologist to the British Chronological and Astronomical Association, London, has given us a Bible chronology that is based on the chronological statements of the Scriptures and that is supported by astronomical reckoning and data. He states that "there is no other book in the world than the Bible which contains scientific time" (*All Past Time*, 11). He demonstrates that "all biblical time is planetary motion, which shows marked harmony between the science of astronomy and the truths of revelation" (*The Historical Bible*, 2). Holding that the seven days of creative work were "natural days of 24 hours, he states that the first day was Sunday; the solar system was arranged on the fourth day, at the time of the autumnal equinox; the sun and the moon were set in their maximum positions, the point from which all the cycles of time proceed—a point where we find them all abreast on one line, a position which they can never resume again" (ibid., 4ff.). The A.M. (*anno mundi* meaning "in the year of the world") dates that are given in *Practical Christian Theology* are Dimbleby's. For B.C. dates, subtract A.M. dates from 4004; for A.D. dates, subtract 3999 from A.M. dates. Furthermore, the Bible gives a complete genealogy from Adam to Christ (Luke 3:23–38; see endnote 11 under Anthropology).

60. "Evolution," *The New Columbia Encyclopedia* (New York: Columbia University Press, the fourth edition, 1975), 908.

61. William J. Tinkle, *Heredity* (Grand Rapids: Zondervan Publishing House, 1970), 88–92.

62. Chance, or fate, is a system of random, undetermined impersonal causes and effects. This has no place in a universe over which God has sovereign control.

63. Henry M. Morris, *The Twilight of Evolution* (Grand Rapids: Baker Book House, 1963), chap. 2, and *Biblical Cosmology and Modern Science* (Grand Rapids: Baker Book House, 1970), chap. 8.

64. J. I. Packer, "Providence," *The New Bible Dictionary* (Leicester, England: Inter-Varsity Press, 1982), 990.

65. H. E. Guillebaud, *Some Moral Difficulties of the Bible* (London: Inter-Varsity Fellowship, 1949), 35. Believing that children who die before reaching moral accountability are saved at death, I (FHB) see something worse than their death. It would be their living, experiencing the rigors of this life, and in the end going to hell for not having received the Savior. On the other hand, I do not support abortion, which is murder, save in the rare case of saving the mother's life. In this instance, the mother's life is of more value than that of an undeveloped infant.

66. Packer, *The New Bible Dictionary,* 991.

67. When He said that the Father committed all judgment to Him (John 5:22), the Lord Jesus had in view those judgments that are related to His messianic work. Compare the reason for this authority being given in verse 27, "because He is the Son of Man"—a messianic title. Because of this, I do not consider the divine judgments of the Old Testament Period to be exclusively the work of God the Son, since they occurred before His incarnation and the beginning of His messianic work as man.

68. The justice of God's previous condemnation of Satan (Gen. 3:15) and of the world (John 3:18; Rom. 5:18) was confirmed by their sinful, abusive treatment of Jesus (Matt. 26:67; 27:26; 29–30, 35, 39–41; see "His Humiliation: The Work of Jesus While on the Cross" part 2, under Christology).

69. For an introduction to dispensationalism, see Charles C. Ryrie, *Dispensationalism Today* (Chicago: Moody Press, 1965), chaps. 2–3; also see Wesley R. Willis and John R. Master with Charles C. Ryrie as consulting editor, *Issues in Dispensationalism* (Chicago: Moody Press, 1994).

70. William F. Arndt and F. Wilbur Gingrich, *"oikonomia," Greek-English Lexicon of the New Testament* (Chicago: The Chicago University Press, 1957), 562.

71. Robert Cameron defined an age to be "a period of time, having a well defined beginning, and marked by certain moral and providential characteristics which distinguish it from all other periods of time" (*The Doctrine of the Ages*, 18). With "age" (Gk. *aion*) often translated "world" in KJV, the Bible speaks of God's creating the ages through Christ (Heb. 1:2; 11:3), His wisdom being ordained before the ages (1 Cor. 2:7), the mystery of Gentile and Jewish equality not revealed in previous ages (Eph. 3:5; Col. 1:26), Satan's being the god of the present age (2 Cor. 4:4) and his demon hosts as its rulers (Eph. 6:12), the present age's being evil (Gal. 1:4; Rom. 12:2), the end of the age (Matt. 13:39–40; 24:3; 28:20), the age to come (Matt. 12:32; Luke 20:34–35; Eph. 1:21), the end of the ages (1 Cor. 10:11; Heb. 9:26), and the ages to come (Eph. 2:7).

72. See Albertus Pieters, *The Seed of Abraham* (Grand Rapids: Wm. B. Eerdmans Publishing Co., 1950), 212ff.

73. Objectors ask, "Will not the marriage of the Church to Jesus be bigamous because of God's relation to Israel?" In reply, I hold that people's relationships with Jesus as man are not the same as their relationships with God, the collective Persons of the divine Trinity. For instance, His Apostles are never seen in the Bible as being God's Apostles (2 Cor. 1:1; 2 Peter 3:2; Jude 17) and His Church is never described as being God's Bride or Wife. She is "the Lamb's Wife," the wife of Jesus in His humanity (Rev. 21:9).

74. The preposition "for" (Gk. *eis*) sometimes indicates the basis of, or ground for, an action as "at" in Matthew 12:41, "because they repented at the preaching of Jonah."

75. Several of these names differ from those that are usually given, for, to my mind, they are more descriptive of their dispensation.

76. They were not delivered from the physical ruin that they received by their sinning. Because of their mortal bodies, they not only physically died but also transmitted to their offspring the sin force, inherent corruption, and death (see "The Kinds of Sin: Original Sin" under Hamartiology).

77. It is noteworthy that God did not restate man's dominion over the earth in the dispensation that He gave him after the Noachic Flood (Gen. 9:2 with 1:26).

78. This is true if the last clause of verse seven refers to his younger brother and "sin" means "a sin-offering."

79. J. C. Whitcomb and Henry M. Morris estimate that the world population at this time was over a billion people (*The Genesis Flood,* 26).

80. The nature of these fallen ones is not clear. Were they human clones possessed by demons?

Were they the heroes of ancient mythology? That angels are incapable of having sexual relations with women was said only of holy angels, who are in heaven (Matt. 22:30).

81. See John Pilkey, *Origin of the Nations* (San Diego: Master Book Publishers, 1984), 115ff., 130, 156, 163ff., 195ff., 202ff.

82. The Bible gives several exemptions from capital punishment: accidental manslaughter (Num. 35:11), killing in self-defense (Exod. 22:2; cp. Luke 14:31–32), and execution for the state (Rom. 13:4). In acting for the state, as in going to war, one must be convinced that the cause is just and in keeping with biblical principles. It is noteworthy that the Bible says nothing about the form that human government should take or the extent of its functions other than maintaining law and order by dispensing justice (Rom. 13:1–7). Under the Mosaic Law, the capital crimes were abuse of parents (Exod. 21:15, 17), kidnapping (v. 16), idolatry (22:20), Sabbath breaking (35:2), child sacrifice (Lev. 20:2–5), adultery (v. 10), sodomy (v. 13), bestiality (vv. 15–16), blasphemy (24:11–16), murder (Num. 35:16–18), false prophesying (Deut. 13:1–5), and rape (22:23–24).

83. See Bullinger, *The Witness of the Stars;* and Seiss, *The Gospel in the Stars*.

84. Noah's drunkenness (Gen. 9:20–21) may have been due to the acceleration of the fermentation process because of the change of the atmosphere and solar radiation, which caught him off guard (see John C. Dillow, *The Water Above: Earth's Pre-Flood Vapor Canopy*, 102ff.). Ham's wrongdoing seems to be his disrespectfully reporting his father's naked condition rather than covering him. Ham's punishment fell to his posterity, the Canaanites, who became a servile people.

85. Abraham entered Canaan in A.M. 2083 (1921 B.C.). The A.M. dates are from Dimbleby, *The Historical Bible*. To obtain B.C. dates, subtract A.M. dates from 4004.

86. Stephen's reference to four hundred years (Acts 7:6; Gen. 15:13) concerns the sojourn of Abraham's seed, starting with the weaning of Isaac and the casting out of Ishmael in A.M. 2113, thirty years after Abraham's entrance into Canaan (Gen. 21:5–12).

87. The Israelites entered Egypt in A.M. 2298 as the family of Jacob (Gen. 46:1) and came out 215 years later in A.M. 2513 as a nation.

88. Under the Mosaic Law salvation was not by law observance (Rom. 3:20; Gal. 2:16; 3:21–22) but by God's grace through faith in the promise of the coming Messiah-Savior (cp. Gen. 15:5–6; Gal. 3:8, 16; John 5:39–40; Luke 1:46–55; 2:25, 38; Isa. 49:1–6). The Levitical offerings did not save people spiritually, but they were a gracious provision that allowed unintentional lawbreakers, guilty of noncapital crimes, the continuation of physical life within the covenant community. Failure to keep the required ritual resulted in one's being cut off from Israel (Lev. 4, 5). Under the law, David should have died for his sins of adultery and murder (2 Sam. 11; 12:9; Lev. 20:10). But he repented, and God graciously spared his life (2 Sam. 12:1–14; Pss. 32; 51; Rom. 4:6–8).

89. Taught by the Pharisaic scribes, this oral tradition largely shaped NT Judaism. Beginning in the days of the Babylonian captivity, this tradition was developed by the Jewish scribes. It consisted of several ingredients: a restatement of the Mosaic Law, the application of the Mosaic Law to a new way of life like that belonging to an urban or commercial people (the Mosaic Law was suited to a pastoral people), man-made regulations to prevent violations of the Mosaic Law, and an extensive commentary on the Mosaic Law.

90. As it is today, the Law of Moses will be a dispensation during the Tribulation Age for those who assume its responsibilities (Matt. 24:20).

91. Some erroneously teach that the Holy Spirit will be removed from earth with the rapture of the Church. Second Thessalonians 2:7 concerns the removing of His present restraint on evil. Being God, the Holy Spirit is always everywhere present. He will be active in regenerating, teaching, and helping people at that time as He does today.

92. The "dispensation of the fullness of time" (Eph. 1:10) seems to refer to the Dispensation of Christ's Earthly Rule, which brings to a completion our Lord's messianic work relating to the present world order (cp. Col. 1:20; Heb. 2:5–9).

93. The Sermon on the Mount (Matt. 5–7) does not, as some suppose, present laws that apply exclusively to the millennial kingdom; it presents the characteristics and duties of the citizens of Christ's kingdom (saved people) who are now living on earth (Col. 1:13). The sermon deals with conditions that will not exist during kingdom days, like persecution, temptation, theft,

and false prophecy (Matt. 5:10–12; 6:13, 19; 7:15). Indeed, God's will shall be done on earth during those days (6:10).

94. These methods of God's dealing with people according to the principles of grace and law are contrasted as follows:

The grace method, involving a gift and responding to faith (Rom. 4:5; Eph. 2:8–9):	*The law or works method,* involving pay or debt and responding to meritorious works or worth (Rom. 4:4):
1. God deals favorably with undeserving people.	1. God deals with people in a way they deserve.
2. It does not recognize human merit, worth, or works. These do not contribute anything to the fulfillment of the promises.	2. It recognizes human merit, worth, or works. If possible, these would contribute to the fulfillment of the promises.
3. The fulfillment of the promises is wholly God's work and brings Him all the praise.	3. The fulfillment of the promises would be partly man's work, bringing him part of the praise.
4. Human obedience (by God's grace) to the covenant conditions allows God to fulfill the promises.	4. Human obedience (by self-effort) to the covenant conditions would compel God to fulfill the promises.
5. This is the only method that allows God to keep His promises to sinners or unworthy people.	5. This method bars sinners or unworthy people from God's promised blessings.

95. "The covenant of grace, established in history, is founded on still another covenant, the covenant of redemption, which is defined as the eternal pact between God the Father and God the Son concerning the salvation of mankind." —M. E. Osterhaven, *Evangelical Dictionary of Theology,* Walter A. Elwell, ed. (Grand Rapids: Baker Book House, 1984), 279.

96. The phrase, "the seed of Abraham," has four meanings in the Scriptures, as determined by its context: *one,* Abraham's natural descendants (John 8:37); *two,* his natural descendants who are saved people—the true Israel (Rom. 9:6–8); *three,* Gentiles who are saved people of faith (Gal. 3:29; cp. "children" in vv. 6–9, which means "children" or "sons" in character [not in descent]); people of faith as Abraham was a person of faith (cp. John 8:39); and *four,* the Lord Jesus Christ in His humanity (Gal. 3:16; cp. Heb. 2:16).

97. See *The Scofield Reference Bible* (1917), 5, 6, 9, and *The New Scofield Reference Bible* (1967), 5, 7.

98. Apparently, when He clothed Adam and Eve with the skins of animals, God established the OT means of atonement for human sins, which anticipated the coming Conqueror's atoning work (Gen. 3:21). This is verified by Abel's obedience in offering his animal sacrifice by faith, as directed by divine revelation (Heb. 11:4). Observe that faith must have God's word, whether spoken or written, upon which to rely.

99. Observe that the "400 years" (Gen. 15:13; Acts 7:6) refers to the span of time that started with the weaning of Isaac, thirty years after Abraham entered Canaan in A.M. 2083 (Gen. 21:5–12) and that included Israel's being in Egypt 215 years. The "430 years" (Exod. 12:40–41; Gal. 3:17) was this span of time, starting with Abraham's entrance into Canaan.

100. Apparently, females were related to the Abrahamic and Mosaic covenants by the circumcision of their covenantal fathers; otherwise by that of their husbands.

101. That the Mosaic Law was unable to help or save sinners (Rom. 7:10) was due not to any inherent defect (vv. 12–13) but to the sinfulness of the people who could not keep a perfect, moral law (8:7–8). Demanding complete obedience (Gal. 3:10), the law could not compensate for this weakness (Rom. 8:3). It could only condemn and slay (7:10–11; Gal. 3:10). It could not take away sin and give its violators spiritual life (Heb. 7:19; 9:9; 10:4).

102. Keep in mind that repentance often is a figure of association (synecdoche) to represent all that is involved in exercising salvational faith, which consists of assent to the facts of the gospel,

repentance (a change of mind and attitude), and trust in Jesus and His atoning work (see "The Sinner's Part in the Reception of Salvation" under Soteriology; also, see Appendix X: "Figures of Association: Synecdoche and Metonymy").

103. Being a salvation covenant, the new covenant has wide application through our Lord's atoning work. God has applied the value of this atoning work, by which this covenant was made effective, to all precross believers who looked for the coming Messiah-Savior (Rom. 3:25; Heb. 9:15; see "The Work of Jesus While on the Cross: Jesus Mediated the new covenant" under Christology), as well as to us gospel believers today (Heb. 9:14; 1 Peter 1:2). Thus these salvational promises are fulfilled to all who trust in Jesus and His atoning work .

104. A reminder that the Bible often uses the singular personal pronouns "He" and "Him" and possessive pronoun "His" for God, although the divine Trinity consists of three Persons—the Father, the Son, and the Holy Spirit. See endnote 1.

105. The theological basis for prayer is that we who are saved have access to God through Jesus' sacrificial mediation, which removed the barrier of our sins, and by means of the help of the Holy Spirit (Eph. 2:18; Heb. 10:19–22). The Lord did not confine His people's praying only to the Father in John 16:23–27. He simply stated that His disciples could themselves look to the Father for their needs as they had looked to Him (cp. Matt. 6:9–11). As we shall see, we can pray to the Lord Jesus and to the Holy Spirit.

106. This relationship is not the same as that between God the Father and God the Son, which is eternal and by which the Son inherently possesses the divine nature that makes Him to be God.

107. The Father's parental dealings with us include His removing from us those things that hinder our spiritual fruitfulness (John 15:3), His nourishing us by His Word (1 Peter 2:1–2; 2 Tim. 3:16–17), His disciplining us by trials (Heb. 12:5–12; James 1:2–4), and His correcting us (Rev. 3:19).

Paterology

4

PATEROLOGY
The Doctrine of God the Father

This doctrine is usually included with theology proper, but its importance requires our special attention. The following study is largely from New Testament passages that unquestionably refer to the First Person of the divine Trinity. This is not to suggest that the Father is not mentioned or alluded to in the Old Testament (see Isa. 63:16; Hos. 11:1; Prov. 30:4), but the designation *God* (Heb. *Elohim*) probably more often represents the divine Trinity collectively, as the plural form of the Hebrew word indicates. In the New Testament, the word *God* often represents the Father, especially in passages where references to God the Son occur as well (see Rom. 1:1–3, 8–9; 1 Cor. 1:9; 1 John 5–7).[1]

THE FATHER'S NATURE
This concerns who and what God the Father is.

HE IS A PERSON
That the Father is a person is indicated by His possessing features of personhood like self-awareness (John 4:23; Matt. 3:17), self-determination (John 6:38–39), moral awareness (Luke 10:21; Matt. 7:11), personal distinctiveness (John 14:16), and perpetuity (Rev. 4:9). Other features that many believe are qualities of personhood are intelligence (Matt. 6:8; Mark 13:32), emotion (1 John 4:9–10), and communication (Heb. 1:1–2; Matt. 3:17; John 12:28).

The Father also functions as a person. He speaks (Matt. 3:17; John 15:15), sees (Matt. 6:6), gives (John 14:16), works (John 5:17), blesses (Eph. 1:3), keeps (John 17:11), sends (John 20:21), promises (Luke 24:49), comforts (2 Cor. 1:3–4), directs (1 Thess. 3:11), chooses (Eph. 1:4), calls (1 Cor. 1:9), disciplines (Heb. 12:6–10), prunes (John 15:1–2), bears witness (John 5:37), saves (2 Tim. 1:9), and forgives (Matt. 6:14).

HE IS GOD
Possessing the divine nature in common with the other Persons of the Trinity, the Father is God. His deity is indicated by the following:

He Is Called God
See Romans 1:7; 1 Corinthians 1:3; Ephesians 4:6; Philippians 2:11; and 1 Thessalonians 3:13.

He Manifests Divine Attributes
These include life (John 6:57), self-existence (John 5:26), omnipotence (John 10:29), omniscience (Rom. 8:27; Matt. 6:8, 18), omnipresence (John 14:23; 16:32), sovereignty (Luke 10:21), wisdom (Rom. 16:27), holiness (John 17:11), perfection (Matt. 5:48),

righteousness (John 17:25), love (John 3:16), mercy (Luke 6:36), grace (Eph. 1:6), faithfulness (1 Cor. 1:9), and goodness (Matt. 6:25–30; Eph. 1:3).

He Does the Works of God

Being the Source of all created things, God the Father was active in the creation of the universe (1 Cor. 8:6; Rev. 4:9–11). He is also the source of all divine revelation (John 16:15; Rev. 1:1; 1 Cor. 2:9–10; Heb. 1:1–2). Initiating salvation (Eph. 1:4–5), He gave His Son for the atonement of human sins (John 3:16; 1 John 4:9–10) and raised Him from the dead (Gal. 1:1). He begets all who believe the gospel, making them His children, forgiving their sins, and giving them eternal life (1 Peter 1:3; Matt. 6:14). Finally, He is supreme over all things (Luke 10:21; Eph. 4:6) and is judge of all personal creatures (1 Peter 1:17; 2 Peter 2:4) through the Lord Jesus (John 5:22).

He Receives Supreme Honors

The Father receives worship (John 4:23; Eph. 3:14–21; Rev. 4:10) and adoration (Gal. 1:5; Phil. 2:11; 4:20; Rev. 1:6; 5:13). Moreover, the Lord Jesus honored the Father (John 8:49) by obeying Him (John 8:29; 6:38; 17:4) and glorifying Him in all that He did (John 12:28; 17:4).

These truths clearly show that the Father is God and is worthy of our worship, love, and obedience.

THE FATHER'S RELATIONSHIPS

TO THE OTHER PERSONS OF THE DIVINE TRINITY

Being God, the Father is equal to the other Persons of the Trinity in the powers and extent of His essential attributes, for these three Persons equally possess the same divine nature.[2] However, we observe the following distinctions regarding the Father's ontological relationships to the other Persons of the Trinity:[3]

The Father's Ontological Relationship to the Son and to the Holy Spirit

1. *To the Son*

The Father is the Generator, or Begetter, of the only Begotten Son (cp. John 3:16). He is generator by an eternal act, whereby He makes the one divine nature common to Himself and to the Son (cp. John 5:26). In this ongoing process there is no creation of the personhood of the Son or of new divine nature, nor is there a division of the existing divine nature. By this act of generation the eternally existing divine nature is communicated to the Son in such a way that it remains undivided, yet wholly possessed by the Father and by the Son, individually. Notice that Jesus' human nature (body, soul, and spirit), conceived in the virgin Mary, was generated by the Holy Spirit, not by the Father (Luke 1:35; Matt. 1:18, 20).

2. *To the Holy Spirit*

Scholars believe that the Father is the Spirator of the Holy Spirit, either through or with the Son.[4] By this eternal act of spiration (exhaling, not generating), the Father and the Son communicate the divine nature to the Holy Spirit in such a way that it remains undivided yet wholly possessed by the three Persons, individually. The Scriptures never say that the First Person is the father of the Holy Spirit, nor is the Holy Spirit begotten by the Father, else He would be another Son.

The Father's Ontological Ascendancy

As to order, or rank, the Father is first (Matt. 28:19). This does not imply that there are qualitative differences in attributes or substantive differences in the divine nature, possessed by the Persons of the Trinity, for each One has the same divine nature wholly and simultaneously with the other Persons. Nor does it imply that the Father first existed alone and then generated the other divine Persons. This order only concerns Their eternal essential, or constitutional, interpersonal relationship, with the unbegotten Father being first in rank.

TO THE UNIVERSE

The Father's relationship to the created universe is as follows:

The Father Is the Source of All Created Things (1 Cor. 8:6; Rev. 4:9–11)

While the Son is the creative Agent through whom all created persons and things came about (John 1:1–3), the Father is the creative Source from whom all these persons and things, excepting sin, initially proceeded. This does not mean that the universe is an emanation of the divine nature and thus is a part of God. Yet, the Father has a metaphysical relationship with all created persons and things, by which He gives and sustains their existence through the Son and by the Holy Spirit. In this sense, all human beings are described as the "offspring of God" (Acts 17:29).

The Father Is the Ruler over All Things (Luke 10:21)

All personal creatures (angels and humans) and all things are under the Father's sovereign authority (Matt. 11:25; Eph. 4:6). By His determinate and beneficent rule (Acts 17:24–28), the Father is carrying out the divine decree (Eph. 1:11). He will supremely rule over all things forever, with the Lord Jesus as His Viceroy, or Assistant (1 Cor. 15:24–28).

TO HIS PEOPLE

To Ancient Israel

Historically, Israel's relationship to God usually involved the Trinity collectively, as seen in the plural form of the divine names ("God" or *Elohim;* "Lord" or *Adonai*), which included the Father. The nation of Israel was identified collectively as God's son and firstborn (Exod. 4:22; Jer. 31:9; Hos. 11:1), by inference as His wife (Isa. 54:5; Jer. 3:14), and individually as His children (Deut. 14:1; Isa. 1:2). He was also their Father (Deut. 32:6; Isa. 63:16; 64:8; Jer. 3:4; 31:9). While the whole nation enjoyed certain divine blessings because of their special relation to God under the Mosaic covenant (Exod. 19:5; Deut. 7:6–11), their idolatry broke the covenant and prevented their experiencing all that God desired for them (Jer. 31:32; see chap. 3; Isa. 54). On the other hand, the few Israelites who were saved enjoyed a personal relationship with God (Pss. 103:1–5, 13; 89:20–26), as promised by the Abrahamic covenant (Gen. 17:8; 12:3).

To Saved People
1. The nature of this relationship

Today, each saved person, whether Jew or Gentile, has a personal relationship with God the Father as His child and son (John 1:12; Rom. 8:16, 14; Gal. 3:26). However, this relationship is not the same as that between God the Father and God the Son (cp. John 20:17). Because of this, the Lord Jesus never said "our Father," as though He and His disciples had a common relationship with the Father. There were two reasons for this: *One,* the relationship between the Father and the Son is an eternal one; and *two,* the Son, inherently having the divine nature, is essentially identical to the Father in His qualities and powers. In short, we who are saved are not God, nor shall we ever be God.

We who are saved are children of God in the sense that by the new birth God the Father has given us a new kind of life, called "eternal life" (John 1:12–13). But this life is not God's own self-existent life, for He does not essentially share with His personal creatures His divine nature or make their angelic or human nature divine.[5] God the Father is like a father to those of us who are saved because He has imparted to us our new spiritual life and gives us paternal care (see "Regeneration" under Soteriology). Immediately following the new birth through faith in Jesus and His atoning work, gospel believers are given, by divine adoption, the position of full-grown sons in God's family (Eph. 1:5; Gal. 4:1–7; see "Adoption" under Soteriology).

2. The beginning of this relationship

A saved person's relation with God comes about at salvation by the new birth, not by adoption (John 3:3–6). Upon faith in Jesus and His atoning work, the gospel believer receives divine cleansing from his sins, experiences the renewal of his personhood and his inner human nature (soul and spirit), receives the divine gift of spiritual life, and becomes a child of God (John 1:12–13; Rom. 6:23; Gal. 3:26).

At that time, God takes up His residence within the gospel believer (1 Cor. 6:19; John 14:23) and by this the saved person becomes a partaker of the divine nature (2 Peter 1:4). However, this does not mean, as we have said, that he becomes God. Although he becomes a new creature in Christ (Eph. 2:10; 2 Cor. 5:17), the saved person will forever be a human being, fashioned after the likeness of Jesus' glorified humanity (Rom. 8:29; Phil. 3:20–21; 1 John 3:2; 1 Cor. 15:45–49).

3. The blessings of this relationship

The concept and reality of God's being our heavenly Father is an indescribable blessing to us who are His children (Matt. 5:16, 45, 48; 6:1, 6, 8–9, 18, 32; 7:11): He cares for us (Matt. 6:25–33; 10:29–31), keeps us (John 17:11), gives us good things (Matt. 7:11; James 1:17), fellowships with us (1 John 1:3, 7), desires our spiritual maturity (Matt. 5:48), disciplines and trains us (Heb. 12:5–11), prunes us (John 15:1–3), makes us His heirs (Rom. 8:16–17), loves us (John 16:27), invites our prayers (John 16:23), speaks to us by His Word (Heb. 1:1–2), sees us (Matt. 6:6), knows us (Matt. 6:32; 2 Cor. 11:31), forgives us (Matt. 6:14), indwells us (John 14:23), sanctifies us (John 17:17; Jude 1), comforts us (2 Cor. 1:3–4), blesses us (Eph. 1:3; Matt. 6:31–34), judges us (1 Peter 1:17), commands us (2 John 4), and gives us a place in His house (John 14:2). How blessed it is to be His children!

4. The demands of this relationship

Our being children of this heavenly Father imposes upon us certain duties like obeying Him (1 Peter 1:14–15), submitting to His pruning (John 15:2–3) and discipline (Heb. 12:7, 9), sharing our cares with Him (1 Peter 5:6–7), glorifying Him in all that we do (1 Cor. 10:31), walking in His fellowship (1 John 1:5–7), dealing with our sins (Rev. 2:5; 1 John 1:9), serving Him (1 Thess. 1:9), worshiping Him (Eph. 1:3), imitating Him (Eph. 5:1; Matt. 5:48), praying to Him (Matt. 6:6, 9), trusting Him (Matt. 6:25–34), and loving Him with our total being (Mark 12:30). (See "Our Interaction with God the Father as His Children-Sons" in this chapter.)

Nowhere does the Bible teach the erroneous idea of God's universal fatherhood in the sense that He is the spiritual father of all people, saved and unsaved alike. The fallen human race is alienated from God by their sins (Eph. 2:1; 4:18). In their spiritual state, unsaved people are the products of Satan (John 8:44) and of sin (Rom. 1:21–32). They are characterized as being the children of disobedience and of divine wrath (Eph. 2:2–3).

THE FATHER'S WORKS

In other sections we have considered the Father's involvement in the creation of the universe (1 Cor. 8:6; Rev. 4:11), its government (Luke 10:21, "Lord of heaven and earth"), and in the giving of special revelation (Rev. 1:1).[6] Let us briefly consider two other activities of the Father.

IN THE SALVATION OF THE ELECT

While the Trinity is involved in this great work, it was the Father's role in eternity past to choose whom He would save (2 Thess. 2:13–14) and to predestinate them to adoption (Eph. 1:5) and to Christ-conformity (Rom. 8:29). In time, He gave His Son to atone for humanity's sins (John 3:16; 1 John 4:10). He is now drawing the elect to Himself (John 6:44), begetting gospel believers unto a living hope (1 Peter 1:3), calling them to His kingdom and glory (1 Thess. 2: 12), and keeping them safe (John 17:11–12). Finally, He will bring them home to glory (Heb. 2:10; cp. Phil. 3:20–21; Col. 3:4).

IN JESUS' MESSIANIC WORKS

At Jesus' water baptism, God the Father anointed Him with the Holy Spirit for the messianic, human work that He came to do as the Father's Slave (Ps. 45:7; Isa. 42:1; 61:1; John 1:32; 3:34; Phil. 2:7–8). Acting in the roles of prophet, high priest, and king, the Lord Jesus must attain certain objectives, given Him by the Father, during His first and second comings to earth and during the intervening time. With the power of the Holy Spirit (Acts 10:38), the Lord Jesus as man is achieving these goals by doing the Father's will (John 6:38; 8:28–29) and by speaking His words (John 12:49–50).

Jesus' messianic works are really the Father's works, for He is doing what the Father commanded Him to do and what He saw the Father do (John 5:36, 19).[7] Moreover, He is doing these works in an intimate association with the Father that allows the Father to do them through Him (John 14:9–11). Being done in the sphere of Jesus' humanity (John 5:17–36), these works glorify the Father (John 12:28; 17:4). When His messianic work for the present world order is completed, the Lord Jesus as man will remain in subjection to the Father so that God may be all in all forever (1 Cor. 15:20–28).

THE FATHER'S LOCATION

Being God, the Father is everywhere present in and throughout the universe. However, Jesus spoke about the Father's being in heaven (Matt. 5:16; 6:9, 14, 26, 32; 7:11, 21). Perhaps He was referring to the Father's being there so as to distinguish Him from our earthly fathers, or perhaps He was referring to a visible manifestation (theophany) of the Father that is seen by heavenly personal creatures (Rev. 4:2–3; 5:1).

Having only the divine nature, both the Father and the Holy Spirit are invisible to creatural eyes (Col. 1:15; 1 Tim. 1:17). However, in heaven the Father's presence is indicated by a visible manifestation, seated upon a throne (Rev. 4:2–3, 9; 5:1, 7, 13; Heb. 1:3; 12:2). The Father innately makes known His presence with His people on earth when they obey Him and walk in His fellowship (John 14:23; 1 John 1:7).

When the present universe is replaced by a new heaven and earth, God will live forever with His people on earth (Rev. 21:1, 3). Since the Father does not have a body as Jesus does, He will assume some visible form to indicate His presence.

THE FATHER'S NAMES

HIS GENERIC NAME

With generic names describing kind of being, the Father is called "God" in those OT passages that also refer to God the Son (Pss. 22:1; 45:2, 7; Isa. 42:5; 49:4–5). He is also called "God" in the New Testament (Rom. 1:9; 1 Cor. 8:6; Eph. 4:6), especially in those passages that also refer to Jesus (John 3:16; 2 Cor. 13:14; Phil. 2:9–11). Moreover, the Father is called "the Lord God Almighty" (Rev. 21:22).

HIS FUNCTIONAL NAMES

These refer to one's titles, representing one's functions or offices.

Several Old Testament Titles

We find references to the Father as "the Ancient of days" (Dan. 7:9, 13, 22); "the Lord," or *Adonai* (Isa. 48:16); "the Redeemer of Israel"; and their "Holy One" (Isa. 49:7).

Several New Testament Titles

These are "Father" with the definite article or an adjective (Matt. 5:48; Eph. 3:14; Rev. 1:6), "Lord" (Gk. *Despotes*) meaning absolute owner (Luke 2:29; Acts 4:24; Rev. 6:10), "Lord" (Gk. *Kurios*) meaning one supreme in authority and power (Matt. 11:25; Acts 4:29: Rev. 4:11; 11:17), "Vinedresser" (KJV) or "Husbandman" (John 15:1), and "Savior" (KJV) or "Deliverer" (1 Tim. 1:1).

HIS PERSONAL NAMES

A personal name is that which distinguishes one from others within a given order or class of beings.

In the Old Testament

The personal name for God in the Old Testament is "LORD" *(Yahweh),* or "Jehovah" (Jer. 33:2). That this was also the personal name of God the Father is seen in Psalms 2:7; 110:1; and Isaiah 48:16, "God"; 49:1, 5.

In the New Testament

As with the other Persons of the Trinity (the Son and the Holy Spirit), the title "Father" without the article or an adjective may also be in NT usage a divine personal name of the First Person of the Trinity (John 12:28; 17:1). Other than this, no personal name has been revealed for our heavenly Father. We find the OT personal name "LORD" in quotations like Matthew 22:44 or Psalm 110:1.

OUR INTERACTION WITH GOD THE FATHER AS HIS CHILDREN-SONS

We have seen that all who have trusted in Jesus and His atoning work for salvation have been born into God's family as His children (John 1:11–13) and by adoption have been given the position of His adult sons (Rom. 8:15; Gal. 4:5). This means that, as members of God's family, we who are saved have equal privileges and duties. Because of our filial relationship with the Father, we can have fellowship with Him (1 John 1:3, 7). We can improve our daily relationship with Him as His children-sons by engaging in the means of fellowship like those that follow:

OUR PRAYING TO HIM (MATT. 6:6, 9; JOHN 16:23; 1 PETER 1:17)

The theological basis for prayer is that we who are saved have access to God through Jesus' sacrificial mediation, which removed the barrier of our sins, and by means of the Holy Spirit (Eph. 2:18; Heb. 10:19–21). However, this basis for approaching God does not confine our praying to God the Father. It only describes how prayer is possible.[8] On this basis, we can address any Person of the Trinity, including the Father. We are to approach God by prayer with sincere heart, confidence, and cleansed of known sins

(Heb. 10:22). We deal with known sins in our lives by repentance and confession (Rev. 2:5; 1 John 1:9).

1. *We can pray about all that concerns us as His children-sons (1 Peter 5:7).*

This includes our understanding of His will for us (Matt. 6:10), our needs (vv. 25–34), our sins (v. 12), our spiritual and human enemies (6:13; 5:44), and our desires (7:7–11).

2. *We can pray with the confidence that:*
   a. *He is aware of all that relates to our lives (Matt. 6:8; 10:28–31).*
   b. *He promises to respond to our prayers (Matt. 7:7–11; 18:19; John 15:16).*
   c. *He loves us very much (John 16:27; 17:23; 1 John 4:10).*

What part of your life are you sharing with the Father in prayer? Do you talk to Him about everything that concerns you as His child-son?

OUR SUBMISSION TO HIM (HEB. 12:9)

God the Father is concerned about our spiritual growth and fruitfulness. He promotes this by removing that which hinders this development and fruitfulness and by fostering that which promotes them. Our duty is to submit ourselves to His parental dealings, which He uses to accomplish these things in our lives. These dealings, to which we are to submit ourselves, consist of His pruning us and His nurturing us.

The Father's Pruning Us

This pruning is the Father's removing from us those things, like sins and self-reliance, that hinder our bearing spiritual fruit.[9] He does this as we respond favorably to:

1. *His Word (John 15:1–3)*

Through the Scriptures He points to sins that we must deal with (2 Tim. 3:16; Heb. 4:12) and to sinful things that we must put away or avoid (Col. 3:8; 2 Cor. 6:17–7:1; 2 Tim. 2:22–23).

2. *His corrective chastisement (Rev. 3:19; cp. 1 Cor. 11:27–32)*

When we fail to heed His Word, we incur His corrective discipline, which serves to turn us toward Himself (Ps. 32:3–4; Ruth 1:20–21). This is usually more painful than our readily responding favorably to His Word.

The Father's Nourishing Us

By this nurturing process, the Father aims to promote the spiritual development of His people.[10] This growth is in the areas of Christian character (1 Thess. 3:12), faith (2 Thess. 1:3), knowledge (Col. 1:10), righteous activity or doing His will (2 Cor. 9:8), and grace or the utilization of divine power (2 Peter 3:18; cp. Phil. 4:13). We experience this growth as we yield to:

1. *His parental dealings with us (Heb. 12:5–13)*

Our heavenly Father sends us not only blessings but also trials to perfect us (James 1:2– 4). Rather than ignoring them or fainting because of them, He wants us to endure them with His help (Heb. 12:5–7; 1 Cor. 10:13; Heb. 2:18). His dealings with us lead us to be submissive to His authority, to live holy lives, and to be spiritually fruitful (Heb. 12:9–11).

2. *His instruction through the Word (1 Peter 2:1–2; 2 Tim. 3:16–17; Ps. 1:1–3)*

The Scriptures give us all that we need to know for our spiritual life and godliness. We must remember that our Father will not do for us what we can do for ourselves with His help. He gives us directions in His Word regarding how to achieve spiritual growth, to be victorious over temptation, to learn and do His will, and to work with the Lord Jesus in building His Church.

3. His ministry through other believers (Heb. 10:24–25)

Our Father ministers to us through others who love us with His love and who are concerned about our spiritual well-being (1 Thess. 5:11–15).

To receive benefit from these paternal ministries, we must give ourselves to them with the confidence that God is too wise to err and too loving to abuse us. This is an essential part of our daily fellowship with Him. If we stubbornly refuse to respond to His dealings with us, He will remove us prematurely from the earthly scene (John 15:2; Prov. 15:10; 29:1; 1 John 5:16; Heb. 12:9). Are you allowing the Father to cultivate your life to make it more fruitful? Thank Him for what He is lovingly, wisely doing in your life and give yourself anew to Him and to His dealings with you (Heb. 12:5–6; "chastening" refers to His parental dealings with us).

OUR FAITH IN HIM (MARK 11:22)

We respond positively to the Father by wholeheartedly trusting Him and His Word. This includes faith in His wisdom, love, faithfulness, concern for our well-being, and promises. He wants us to rely upon Him rather than on ourselves and our meager human resources. A common concern is our basic needs. We can trust our heavenly Father to give us direction and strength to provide for ourselves or to provide us with those necessary things that we cannot secure by ourselves. Addressing the problem of our worrying about the necessities of life (Matt. 6:25–34), the Lord Jesus spoke of:

The Futility of Worry (Matt. 6:25–32a, to "take thought" means to worry)

Worry is needless (vv. 25–26), useless (v. 27), and sinful (vv. 28–32a; Rom. 14:23).

The Remedy for Worry (Matt. 6:32b–34)

1. *Believe that the Father knows your needs (v. 32b; 10:29–31).*
2. *Evaluate your relation to Him (v 33a).*

Are you a citizen of His kingdom by the new birth (John 3:3–5) that He provides for His people?

3. *Do His will (v. 33b, "His righteousness").*

He provides for His obedient people.

4. *Believe His promise to provide for you (v. 33c; cp. Phil. 4:6–7; James 1:6–8).*
5. *Accept His admonition about the future (v. 34; cp. Deut. 33:25, 27a).*

We can appeal to God about every matter of concern in our lives (1 Peter 5:7), knowing that He is acquainted with every detail and wants what is best for us (Matt. 6:26–30; 7:11).

Are you sharing your needs with the Father, believing that He can and will help you? This reliance on the Father is essential to your fellowship with Him.

OUR OBEDIENCE TO HIM (MATT. 7:21)

Obedience is a distinguishing quality of God's family (Matt. 12:47–50; cp. 17:5; John 17:4). As His children-sons, we must give priority to His "righteousness" (His will) for our daily lives (Matt. 6:33; see Appendix F: "Learning and Doing God's Will"). When we obey the Father:

1. *We are assured of our membership in His kingdom (Matt. 7:21–23; cp. John 6:28–29).*
2. *We are aware of His love, presence (John 14:21, 23), and fellowship (1 John 1:5–7).*
3. *We receive His provisions (Matt. 6:33).*
4. *We are assured of weathering life's storms (Matt. 7:24–25).*
5. *We receive His rewards in this life (Matt. 6:1–18).*

These rewards include His compensating us for our giving to others in need (vv. 1– 4), His answering our prayers (vv. 5–15), and His fulfilling the purpose for our fasting (vv. 16–18).[11]

Observe that obedience is an expression of love for the Father (John 14:31). This is essential to fellowship with Him. Is this a priority in your life? Are you in His will today?

OUR IMITATING HIS EXAMPLE (EPH. 5:1; MATT. 5:48)

In Matthew 5:45, our being "children" or "sons" of God concerns our being godly, or like Him in character (v. 48). We are to be "perfect" like Him in the character of our moral conduct and attitudes as these are displayed by Jesus (cp. Eph. 5:1–2; John 14:8–11; cp. 1:14). For example, we are to be like the Father in compassionate love (Matt. 5:44–45; 1 John 3:16–18) and in holiness, or sinlessness (1 Peter 1:14–16; 1 John 2:1).

Our being like the Father pleases Him. Indeed, it makes this relation possible (1 John 1:5–7).

OUR RECEIVING HIS GIFTS (PHIL. 4:19)

The Father has much that He wants to give us.

The Kinds of Gifts

These gifts include divine resources (2 Peter 1:3), grace and peace (Rom. 1:7), hope (Rom. 15:13; 1 Peter 1:3), wisdom (James 1:5–7), daily necessities (Matt. 6:31–33), and the like.

The Extent of His Giving (Phil. 4:19, "according to His riches in glory")

His larder has infinite supply.

The Means by Which He Gives (Phil. 4:19, "by means of" or "in" Jesus; cp. Eph. 1:3)

The divine application of the value of Jesus' sacrifice to us removed the barrier of sin between us and God. Our position in Jesus opens the door to this rich bounty (Eph. 1:3). Indeed, we gospel believers are heirs of God and joint heirs with Jesus (Rom. 8:17; Heb. 1:2; John 3:35).

The Reception of His Gifts (Matt. 7:7–11; 2 Cor. 8:1–5)

The conditions for receiving His gifts are prayer, submission to God, faith in His ability and willingness to provide, and generosity toward others. This promise of God's gifts (Phil. 4:19) was given to the Macedonian gospel believers, who despite their material poverty were a generous people (2 Cor. 8:1–5). If we continue with unsupplied needs, the fault is ours (cp. James 4:2–3). Our willingness and preparedness to receive what He has for us promotes our fellowship with Him.

OUR GLORIFYING HIM (1 COR. 10:31)

The glory of God consists of any manifestation of His essential qualities like those which we see in Jesus (John 1:14) or in the heavens (Ps. 19:1). We glorify God by allowing Him to produce in and through us His fruit (John 15:1–5, 8) and by our doing His will in His way in everything (Matt. 5:16).

By these actions people see the Father's moral qualities and good works in our lives and give Him praise for who He is and what He does (Matt. 5:16). The Lord Jesus sought to glorify the Father in all that He did (John 12:28; 14:8–11; 17:4). We exist for this purpose (Eph. 1:12; 2:10). Our desire and effort to glorify God by our lives enhance our fellowship with Him.

OUR WORSHIPING HIM (JOHN 4:22–23)

Worship is giving God the gifts and honors that are due Him. Since the Father is looking for people who will do this, worship contributes to our fellowship with Him. Consider the manner of worshiping God and the essential ingredient of this worship.

The Manner of Worshiping the Father (John 4:24)

1. *In Spirit (Phil. 3:3)*
This is by the power and direction of the Holy Spirit (John 14:16–17; Eph. 5:18).
2. *In truth (Heb. 10:19–23; cp. 9:23–28)*
Unlike Judaism with its symbolism, true worship occurs in the sphere of spiritual reality and in accord with God's truth because of Jesus' completed atoning work. We have direct access to the Father through Jesus' mediating sacrifice (Heb. 4:14–16; 10:22).

The Essential Ingredient of Worshiping the Father (1 Peter 2:5)

Since worship is our giving God what is due Him, the essential ingredient is offering sacrifice (2 Sam. 24:24). Today, we offer spiritual sacrifices, or gifts, to God, including these:

1. *Ourselves (Ps. 100:3; Rom. 12:1)*
By this we acknowledge that, as His people, we are ready to be and to do all that He desires for us (Rom. 1:15–16).
2. *Our service (Ps. 100:2; Heb. 9:14; 13:16, 21; Matt. 5:16)*
This is our doing His will with love and recognition of His parental authority.
3. *Our thanksgiving (Ps. 100:4; Heb. 13:15; 1 Thess. 5:18)*
By this we express our gratitude for all that He is and does for us.
4. *Our praise (Ps. 100:1, 4; Heb. 13:15)*
This consists of our acknowledging and proclaiming His deity, qualities, and works (cp. Pss. 100:5; 103:1–2; 111:1–10; 2 Cor. 1:3; Eph. 1:3–14; James 3:9; 1 Peter 1:3–5; Rev. 5:9).
5. *Our giving to others who have need (Heb. 13:16; Phil. 4:18)*
This includes our giving to God's work and to His people, including His servants.

Again, worship consists of our freely giving God that which is due Him with joy and confidence (Pss. 100:1–2; 40:6–8). We can worship the Father at any time or in any place. This is essential to our fellowship with Him. What have you given Him today?

What kind of a relationship are you having with God the Father? If you have believed the gospel, do you really think of yourself as His child-son? Have you learned from the Gospels what Jesus taught about the Father? Do you show Him the love and respect that He deserves? Are you trusting Him with everything in your life? Are you wholeheartedly submissive to His dealings with you and to His will for you? Do you worship Him daily? Can you think of ways of improving your relationship with your heavenly Father? He will be pleased with any wholehearted effort that you give to this and will bless you for it (James 4:8).

How grateful we are for the truths that our heavenly Father has revealed about Himself and for the indescribable blessings that we enjoy as His children-sons. May we seek daily to honor Him in all things by our lives (John 8:29; Matt. 5:16), walk in His fellowship (John 14:23; 1 John 1:5–7), and look forward to living with Him in His house forever (John 14:2–3).

If you should not personally know the Father, you can become related to Him through trusting in Jesus and His atoning work for salvation from sin and receiving the new birth by the Holy Spirit (John 1:12–13; 3:3–5, 16; 17:3; see "The Sinner's Part in the Reception of Salvation" under Soteriology).

A Review of Paterology

1. Describe the Father's nature.
2. What features show that He has personhood?
3. What features indicate that He is God?
4. What is the Father's ontological relationships with the other Persons of the Trinity?
5. What is the Father's ontological ascendancy over the other Persons of the Trinity?
6. What is the Father's relationship to the universe?
7. What is the Father's relationship to Israel?
8. What is the Father's relationship to saved people: its nature, beginning, blessings, and demands?
9. How does the relation of God the Son to the Father differ from that of saved people to the Father?
10. Why is the idea of the universal fatherhood of God in error?
11. In what works relating to the universe is the Father involved?
12. How is the Father involved in our Lord's messianic works?
13. What is the Father's location?
14. If the Father is invisible, how does He appear to people in heaven?
15. What generic names are given for the Father in the Old and New Testaments?
16. What functional names do the Scriptures give for Him?
17. What are His personal names in the Old and New Testaments?
18. What can we do to improve our fellowship with the Father?
19. What truths encourage us to pray to the Father?
20. To what two kinds of divine parental dealings should we submit ourselves?
21. What is God's remedy for worry?
22. What blessing does our obedience to the Father bring us?
23. In what ways are we to imitate the Father?
24. What kinds of gifts does the Father give to His people?
25. To what kind of saved people does the Father promise to provide all their needs?
26. What does it mean to glorify the Father?
27. What does it mean to worship the Father?
28. What is the essential ingredient of this worship?
29. Are you a child of God? Did you give yourself to the Father today? Are you walking in His fellowship?

Endnotes

1. For the exceptions to this, see endnote 1 under Christology.
2. See "The relations of the Persons within the divine Trinity" under Theology Proper.
3. "Ontological" pertains to ontology (the theory of reality), in this case, to the Trinity's essential being, or makeup, relating to Their possessing the one divine nature.
4. John 20:22 symbolically portrays spiration; see Theology Proper, endnote 23.
5. Second Peter 1:4 may mean that our renewed human nature is the product of God's creative work (Eph. 2:10), that we received God's Seed (1 John 3:9) who may be the Lord Jesus Christ (John 14:6; 1 John 5:12), or that we received God into our being so that our bodies are His temples (1 Cor. 6:19; Col. 1:27; John 14:23). Partaking of the divine nature does not make us divine anymore than eating an apple makes us an apple.
6. Also see "The Father's Relationships: To the Universe" above and "The relations of the Persons within the divine Trinity" under Theology Proper.

7. These are the works that He is doing as man in obedience to the Father's will. See "The Messianic Works of Jesus" under Christology.
8. The Lord did not confine our praying to the Father in John 16:23–27. He simply stated that after His return to heaven, His disciples could themselves look to the Father for their needs as they had looked to Him while He had been with them (cp. Matt. 6:9–11).
9. This fruit consists of spiritual knowledge (2 Peter 1:8); Christian character (Gal. 4:19; 5:22–23); good works, or doing God's will (Col. 1:10); and Christian ministry (Rom. 1:13) to saved people (vv. 11–12) and to unsaved people (vv. 15–16).
10. See "The Growth of the Christian Life" under Zoeology.
11. Fasting is our disregarding our physical needs during some spiritual exercise, like communicating with God (cp. Matt. 4:2; 17:21; Acts 13:2).

Christology

5

CHRISTOLOGY
The Doctrine of the Lord Jesus Christ

We now focus our attention upon the Person and work of God the Son, the Lord Jesus Christ. Because of the importance of Jesus' messianic work, including His atoning sacrifice, and of the objective of the Holy Spirit to exalt Him (John 16:14), we find much information in the New Testament about our Lord's earthly life and ministry. Also, much of this is supported by the prophecies of the Old Testament. Starting with the divine declaration that Eve's Seed would crush Satan's head (Gen. 3:15), from time to time God revealed more about the coming Conqueror-Savior (Gen. 15:5; Isa. 42:1–7; 49:1–7; 52:13–53:12; John 5:39; 8:56; Gal. 3:8, 16). Consisting of OT prophecy and NT fulfillment and additional truth, this divine revelation has been preserved that sinners might believe in Jesus' deity and atoning work and that they might receive eternal life through faith in His name, which represents who He is and what He has done (John 20:30–31). As we who are saved study this truth, may our faith in Him be deepened, our commitment to Him be strengthened, and our esteem and love for Him be increased.

THE DEITY OF THE LORD JESUS CHRIST

The fact that the Lord Jesus Christ is God the Son is fundamental to biblical Christianity and to salvational faith in Him. As we shall see, only One who is God can be the Savior (Isa. 43:11). The Scriptures teach that Jesus Christ is God, the Second Person of the divine Trinity, and that all that can be said of God can be said of Him. The following biblical truths bear witness to this truth.

HIS DIVINE NAMES

God

The Lord Jesus is called "God," a generic name (Isa. 9:6; John 1:1, 18; 20:28; Rom. 9:5; 14:7–12; 1 Tim. 3:16; Titus 1:3; Heb. 1:8; 1 John 5:20).[1] He exists in "the form of God" (Phil. 2:6); He is "the image of the invisible God" (Col. 1:15); and He is "the express image of His (God's) Being" (Heb. 1:3, KJV "person").

Lord

A comparison of certain NT passages with their OT sources shows that Jesus is sometimes identified as "LORD" (*Yahweh* or *Jehovah*), the OT personal name of God, as in Luke 1:68 with Psalm 106:48; Luke 3:4–6 with Isaiah 40:3–4; 1 Corinthians 1:30 with Jeremiah 23:5–6; Revelation 1:7 with Zechariah 12:1, 10; Ephesians 4:8–10 with Psalm 68:4, 18; and Hebrews 1:10–12 with Psalm 102:12, 25–27.

He is also identified as "Lord" (*Adonai*), the primary OT title of God, as in Matthew 22:41–46 with Psalm 110:1; and John 12:37–42 with Isaiah 6:1.

The Word

As a spoken or written word expresses one's thoughts or feelings, so God the Son, as "the Word" (a title, John 1:1, 14; Rev. 19:13), has always manifested the invisible God and expressed His truth to man (Col. 1:15; 2:9; Matt. 11:27). Before His incarnation (His coming to earth and taking on Himself a sinless human nature), God the Son expressed certain qualities of God's nature by His creative work (John 1:1–3; cp. Ps. 19:1) as well as God's thoughts by the words of OT prophets and Scripture writers. With His incarnation, the Son manifested God the Father by His human words, attitudes, and actions; later He transmitted by the Holy Spirit the NT Scriptures to their writers (John 1:14, 18; 5:19; 12:49–50; 14:8–11; 16:12–13; Rev. 1:1). Only one who is God can fully reveal God (Matt. 11:27; Heb. 1:3; Col. 1:15; 2:9).

The Son of God

This title is used of angels (Job 1:6) and humans (Luke 3:38; Rom. 8:14; cp. Ps. 82:6), for they possess God's image, which is personhood (see Angelology and Anthropology). But when it is used of the Lord Jesus, this title expresses His eternal divine relationship to and equality with God the Father (John 5:18–26). Observe that He was the Son of God before His incarnation (Ps. 2:7; Gal. 4:4) and that the Holy Spirit was the father of His human nature (Matt. 1:20; Luke 1:35). The Jews regarded "Son of God" to be a title of Deity (John 5:17–18; 10:31–36). In biblical language, to be a son of someone or something is to have the character of that person or thing (cp. Matt. 5:45; John 17:12; Eph. 2:2–3). In the case of Jesus, He manifested the character of the Father, for He and the Father are one (John 10:30).[2] This emphasizes Their essential unity, Their having in common the single divine nature. Thus Jesus is the Son of God because He inherently possesses the divine nature by the Father's eternal generation (see "The relations of the Persons within the divine Trinity" under Theology Proper).

Closely related to the concept of Jesus' divine sonship are the following designations:

1. He is "the First Begotten."

This designation marks His priority in time or rank, as in the following examples:

a. He is prior to and ranks above all creation (Col. 1:15).

The self-consistency of the Scriptures requires us to regard "of creation" as a genitive of reference rather than a genitive of identification.[3] Thus God the Son is above all with reference to creation, not as a part of creation (cp. Col. 1:16–17).

b. He is Mary's firstborn son, being born before her other children (Matt. 1:25; Luke 2:7).

c. He is the first to rise physically from the dead, never to die again (Col. 1:18; Rev. 1:5).

d. As the Last Adam, He is the first member and leader of the new humanity, as its Pattern and Leader, whose human likeness all saved people will share (Rom. 8:29; 1 Cor. 15:47–49; 1 John 3:2).

It is the first of these examples that speaks of Jesus' deity, as the divine Creator (Col. 1:15). The remaining three examples relate to His humanity.

2. He is "the Only Begotten Son."

This designation (John 1:14, 18; 3:16, 18; 1 John 4:9) emphasizes the uniqueness of God the Son in His divine relation to God the Father. As the Father's only Son, the Second Person of the divine Trinity is the Only Begotten One in a sense that no one else is. Unlike creaturely sons of God, the Son's divine nature is being eternally generated by the Father, and by this He eternally possesses the divine nature in common with the Father (cp. Luke 7:12; 8:42; 9:38; Heb. 11:17).

HIS ETERNAL PREEXISTENCE

Several biblical passages speak of God the Son's existence before His incarnation (John 1:1, 14, 30; 6:33, 38; Gal. 4:4; Heb. 10:5). However, it is the fact of His eternal preexistence that underscores His deity. This is stated emphatically in Micah 5:2, "Whose goings forth have been from old, from everlasting," and it is implied in Isaiah 9:6 (Heb. "Father of eternity"); John 1:1; 17:5; Colossians 1:16–17; and Revelation 1:11.

HIS DIVINE ATTRIBUTES

We would expect that He, in Whom "dwells all the fullness of the Godhead bodily" (Col. 2:9), "Who being in the form of God thought it not robbery to be equal with God" (Phil. 2:6), "Who is the image of the invisible God" (Col. 1:15), and "Who is the express image of His [God's] Being" (Heb. 1:3, KJV "person"), possesses all the attributes of God. Some of these are eternality (Mic. 5:2; John 1:1; Rev. 1:11); omnipresence (Matt. 28:20; John 3:13; Col. 1:27); omnipotence (John 1:1–3; 1 Cor. 1:24; Heb. 1:3); omniscience (John 2:24–25; 6:64; Col. 2:3); truthfulness, or His being real (John 7:18; Rev. 3:14; 19:11) as well as the Truth (the revelation of God, John 1:14, 17; 14:6; Eph. 4:21); faithfulness (2 Thess. 3:3; Heb. 2:17; Rev. 19:11); righteousness (2 Tim. 4:8; Acts 3:14; 22:14; 1 John 2:1); goodness (Acts 10:38); holiness, or His transcending all things (Isa. 6:1–3; John 12:41) as well as being sinless and morally pure (1 John 3:3, 5; Heb. 7:26; Acts 3:14); love (John 13:1, 34; 15:9; Rev. 1:5); grace (2 Cor. 8:9; John 1:14); mercy (1 Tim. 1:12–16; Heb. 2:17); long-suffering (1 Peter 2:18–24; Rev. 1:9); and sovereignty (Mark 4:37–41).

There is also His immutability (Heb. 1:10–12; 13:8). Although by His incarnation God the Son assumed a complete human nature, His divine nature remained unchanged. This human nature was joined to His personhood, not to His divine nature (see "His Condescension: Jesus' Human Incarnation" in this chapter).

God the Son is alive (John 6:51), and He is self-existent (John 5:26; Col. 1:16–17). As the Instrumental Cause of all things, He is the conveyer of all life, both physical (John 1:3–4; 5:28–29) and spiritual (John 14:6; 11:25; 17:3; Col. 3:3; 1 John 5:11–12, 20). As man, He also has and experiences physical life and spiritual life, which is an intimate, human relationship with God the Father.

HIS DIVINE WORKS

The Trinitarian view of God sees the Persons of the divine Trinity as being active before time in formulating the divine decree, by which all events of the universe were chosen and rendered certain, and during time in executing its details. Being the Instrumental Cause of all things, the Son is involved in every aspect of God's total work relating to the universe.[4]

His Creating All Things

Acting with the other Persons of the Trinity, the Son was the Father's Agent, or Instrumental Cause, in bringing all created things, excepting sin, into existence (1 Cor. 8:6; John 1:3; Col. 1:16).

His Sustaining All Things

The Son not only "holds together" all things (Col. 1:17) but also is "upholding all things by the Word of His power" (Heb. 1:3).

His Revealing the Father

As the eternal Word, the Son revealed the Father (Matt. 11:27). He did this by His creative work (John 1:3; Rom. 1:19–20), His giving OT revelation (John 1:1, 18), and by His earthly life and His words (John 1:14; 14:8–11; Rev. 1:1).

His Forgiving Sins

Only God can forgive people their sins, since all sins are ultimately against Him who is sovereign over the universe. Jesus exercised the divine authority of forgiveness, which the Jews understood as belonging only to God (Luke 5:20–25). He demonstrated the reality of His having this authority by healing the man whom He had forgiven (see Luke 7:47–49).

His Giving Life

In addition to imparting physical life to His creation (John 1:3–4), the Lord Jesus also has the power to give spiritual life to those who trust in Him as their Savior (John 6:32–40). Moreover, He will raise all dead persons to physical life (John 5:21, 25).

His Exercising Judgment

Only God can justly exercise judgment and give people what they deserve for their lifetime behavior, for He knows their motivations and intentions as well as their overt actions (Rom. 2:2, 6, 11, 16). Knowing the hearts of all people (John 2:24–25), the Son of God will judge all people (John 5:22–23, 25–29): He will appraise His own people upon His return for the Church (2 Cor. 5:10; Rev. 22:12); He also will judge earth dwellers after His return to earth (Rev. 19:11–15; Matt. 25:31–46); furthermore, He will judge the unsaved, both angels and humans, after His millennial rule (Rev. 20:11–15; Acts 17:31).

His Authoring Salvation

Only One who is God could be the Instrumental "Cause" of salvation (Heb. 5:9; KJV "Author") because of the greatness of sin's ruin and power in human lives and of sinful mankind's indebtedness to God. The Lord Jesus is the only Savior from the guilt, ruin, and bondage of human sin (Matt. 1:21; Luke 2:11; Acts 4:12; 1 John 4:14).

His Expressing Divine Authority

Only One who is God could exercise such authority as that seen in Jesus' rebuking His enemies, like Satan (Matt. 4:10; 16:23; cp. Jude 8–9) and demons (Mark 1:24–26), and in His declaring additional or new moral laws (Matt. 5:28, 32, 34, 39, 44; 7:28–29; John 13:34–35).

HIS ASSERTIONS

Jesus made assertions that would have been blasphemous if they were untrue. On the other hand, only One who was God could have said these things without lying (cp. John 14:6).

He Affirmed His Equality to the Father

He asserted His equality to God the Father in receiving honor (John 5:23), in being the object of faith (John 14:1; 12:44), in His words and works (John 5:19; 12:49–50; 14:10, 24), and in His revelations (John 12:45; 14:9). When He said that the Father was greater than He (John 14:28), Jesus was referring to His humanity and to His messianic role of being the Father's Servant, or Slave (Phil. 2:7; John 6:38). In His deity, the Lord Jesus is equal to the Father in every way.

He Affirmed His Unique Relation to the Father

This is seen in His being the Father's Revelator (Matt. 11:27; John 12:45), His Imitator (John 5:17, 19–20), His Intimate (John 14:7–10, 20), and His Son (John 10:36). He also said that He and the Father were one (John 10:30). As we noted earlier, the Greek neuter predicate adjective "one" indicates oneness of purpose and nature rather than Their being the same Person. They are distinct, divine Persons but together one God.

He Affirmed His Ability to Satisfy People's Deepest Needs

Unlike the apostle Paul (2 Cor. 4:5), Jesus proclaimed Himself as the One who could provide for people's needs (see John 4:14; 6:35; 7:37–38; 10:9–10; Matt. 11:28–30).

He Affirmed His Ability to Give Eternal Life and Safety to His People

See John 6:37–40; 10:27–29.

HIS RECEIVING HONORS DUE TO GOD

The Lord Jesus receives worship (Matt. 8:2; 28:9, 17; John 5:23; 20:28; Phil. 2:9–11; Rev. 5:11–13). Neither the apostles nor holy angels allowed people to worship them (Acts 10:25–26; Rev. 22:8–9).

HIS WITNESSES

The testimony of competent witnesses is allowed in our courts as evidence. Various ones gave testimony to Jesus' deity, including God the Father (John 5:17–18, 31–39), John the Baptizer (1:34; 31), the apostle Nathanael, or Bartholomew (1:49), the apostle Peter (Matt. 16:16–17; John 6:69), the apostle John (John 20:30–31; 1 John 5:20), a Roman centurion (Mark 15:39), Satan (Matt. 4:3, 6), and demons (Mark 1:24).[5]

All these truths demonstrate clearly and conclusively that the Lord Jesus Christ is God the Son and that everything that can be asserted about God can be asserted about Him.

THE HUMANITY OF THE LORD JESUS CHRIST

This portion of our study is concerned with God the Son's taking upon Himself a complete, sinless human nature and becoming man, the God-man (1 Tim. 2:5), when He came to earth long ago (Gal. 4:4). We shall especially look at His condescension, humiliation, and exaltation.

HIS CONDESCENSION

The condescension of God the Son refers to His "stooping" to come to earth, to assume a human nature that was lower than that of His servants, the angels (Heb. 2:9), and to live among sinful people. In this section we shall look at His human incarnation, His human character, and His human activities.

Jesus' Human Incarnation

The word *incarnation* speaks of the initial action and following condition of taking on a human nature and being embodied in flesh (John 1:14). The incarnation of God the Son was His taking upon Himself a complete, sinless human nature (body, soul, and spirit), so that everything that can be asserted of sinless man can be asserted of Him. Several aspects of His incarnation follow:

1. *Jesus' self-emptying (the "kenosis")*

Having asserted Jesus' deity (Phil. 2:6), the apostle Paul declared that the Lord "emptied Himself" (Gk. v. 7), when He took upon Himself a slave's attributes and was made in men's likeness. What does His self-emptying mean?

147

a. An explanation of His self-emptying
   1) An unacceptable explanation
      This is the view that in His incarnation God the Son laid aside less essential attributes that belonged to His divine nature. My objections to this view are these: *First,* it is impossible to discard any manifest quality, or attribute, of an essence without changing its fundamental nature. *Second,* it is illogical to say that some attributes are more essential to deity than others since all the attributes of deity are possessed and determined by the divine essence. *Finally,* this view conflicts with the biblical teaching that the Son continues to be God during His incarnation (Col. 1:15–17; 1 John 5:20). To my mind, His divesting Himself as God of any divine attributes would make Him to be less than God.
   2) My understanding of His self-emptying
      When God the Son took upon Himself a complete, sinless human nature, there were certain qualities of His deity that He did not bring into His human experience.[6] These divine qualities remained with His divine nature and continued to express themselves in His divine experience and activity as God (Col. 1:17; Heb. 1:3). Thus our Lord's self-emptying concerns His excluding from His human experience certain divine qualities and powers that were not compatible with human nature and with God's will for Him as man. However, as God He still possesses all His divine qualities and powers.
b. Several observations about His self-emptying
      These observations are based on the view that with His incarnation God the Son now has two separate natures—one divine and the other human, and that He is now both wholly God and wholly man. This view also holds that the makeup of the Members of the divine Trinity constitutes individual, separate personhoods (Father, Son, and Holy Spirit) and a single divine nature, which is commonly possessed by Them and that makes Them each God and together one God. Thus, although the self-emptying concerned the Son's deity, it was not an occurrence within His divine nature or within His experience as God. It related wholly to His human experience as man.
      One: As man, the Lord Jesus continually expressed the glory of divine moral character throughout His earthly, human lifetime (John 1:14). However, only once did He humanly display His preincarnate glory before men (Matt. 17:2; cp. John 17:5). Only when He returned to heaven was this radiant glory given to His humanity when He was exalted to the highest majesty (Acts 9:3–4; 10:36; 26:13–14; Eph. 1:20–22; Phil. 2:9–11; Heb. 2:9). He will express this glory when He comes to earth again (Matt. 24:30; 2 Thess. 1:7–9).[7]
      Two: As man, the Lord Jesus did not exercise His inherent divine power in His human experience. Being the Messiah (one anointed with the Holy Spirit), He did, and is doing, all His human works by the power and direction of the Holy Spirit (Luke 4:1, 14, 18; Acts 10:38; cp. Isa. 11:1–5; 61:1).
      Three: As man, the Lord Jesus did not in His human experience manifest certain divine attributes like omnipresence (John 11:6–7) and omniscience (Mark 13:32; John 8:26, 28, 40), for these are not compatible with human nature. In His human experience Jesus was not physically able to be in more than one place at a time. Also, as man, He did not know everything that could be known (Mark 6:38). Although at times He seemed to be aware of what was going on beyond the range of His physical senses (John 1:48; 2:24–25; 11:14), this perception may have been given Him by the Holy Spirit (cp. Acts 5:3; 13:39). He developed in human knowledge as a child (Luke 2:40, 52) and had limited human knowledge as an adult (Mark 13:32; John 5:20). He received from the Father His knowledge of the spiritual truth that He taught (John 7:16; 8:26, 28; 12:49–50). His self-emptying was His denying Himself these divine powers in His human experience as man.
      Four: As man, the Lord Jesus did not work or exercise authority independently of the

Father, for He was the Father's Slave (cp. Phil. 2:7; Isa. 42:1–7; 49:1–6; 52:13–53:12; John 6:38; 8:28–29; 17:4). Being subordinate to the Father's authority (John 14:28), Jesus in His human experience never acted independently of the Father (John 8:28; 12:49; 14:9–10) or contrary to Him (John 8:29; 17:4).

Five: The authority that Jesus displayed over man, nature, illness, and demons (Mark 4:39, 41; Matt. 4:23–24), was the messianic authority that the Father gave Him over all things (John 3:35; Matt. 28:18). He also was given authority to raise the dead and to judge angels and humans (John 5:19–30; 11:40–44).

Six: In His human experience the Lord Jesus displayed divine moral attributes, which are compatible with humanity. These included holiness (John 8:46; 1 Peter 2:22), love (John 15:9; righteousness (8:29), mercy (Luke 18:31–43), holy hatred (Mark 3:5; cp. Matt. 23), grace, and truth (John 1:14). By the Holy Spirit, these qualities can be reproduced in and displayed by His people as well (Gal. 5:22–23).

Seven: Thus His self-emptying as God (Phil. 2:6–7) appears to be a figurative expression (an anthropomorphism), relating to His humanity and human experience. To relate it to His deity creates irresolvable problems. Certainly, as God He did not divest Himself of any qualities of His deity and thus ceased to be God. However, it can be said that when God the Son became man, in His humanity He was as man divested of the amoral qualities of deity that were incompatible with human nature, like omnipresence, omniscience, and omnipotence. Any similarity to or manifestation of these divine qualities in His human experience must be attributed to the Holy Spirit, who energized His life and ministry (Luke 4:1, 14; Acts 10:38). Having, as man, defeated death and Satan (Heb. 2:14) and having been exalted to the highest majesty (Phil. 2:9–11; Eph. 1:21; 1 Peter 3:22), Jesus is truly Lord of all in His humanity as He is in His deity (Acts 2:36; 10:36; Heb. 2:6–9).

Eight: Any consideration of the Lord Jesus Christ, as He is presented in the Scriptures after His incarnation, must distinguish between His attributes and functions as God and those as man. He does, however, express His moral attributes simultaneously in both realms of existence. Most references to Him in the New Testament relate to His human activity as the Messiah of OT prophecy. Being uniquely one person with two natures, He functions simultaneously both as God and as man. Because of its uniqueness, this truth cannot be understood; it must be accepted by faith in what the Scriptures say of Him.

2. *Jesus' conception and birth*
   a. *Its meaning*
        Ordinarily, human conception takes place when a sperm unites with an ovum. This union results in the beginning and development of human life. The unique feature of Jesus' birth is that it was the result of supernatural conception, not of human generation. Mary did not conceive by the agency of a man (Matt. 1:18, 25; Luke 1:34–35), with or without divine help (cp. Elizabeth, Luke 1:5–7, 24–25). Mary conceived by God the Holy Spirit, who fathered Jesus' humanity (Matt. 1:20; Luke 1:35). While His prenatal development within Mary and the subsequent birth event were natural processes (cp. Luke 1:57; 2:7), Jesus' conception was uniquely and radically different from all others. It was wholly of the Holy Spirit, who produced of Mary's substance a complete human nature, consisting of body, soul, and spirit (Matt. 26:12, 38; 27:50). Thus God the Holy Spirit was the father of Jesus' human nature.

This work of the Holy Spirit did not include the creation of Jesus' personhood, for this, together with His divine nature, existed from eternity (Mic. 5:2; Gal. 4:4; John 1:1; 8:42). With His incarnation God the Son did not acquire another personhood so that He would be a combination of two persons, one divine and the other human. Rather, He acquired another nature—a human nature, so that there were united in Him, the one Person, the nature of God and the nature of man. This acquisition made Him, who was God, also to be man—the God-man.

With this truth in view, we can understand why the angel described that which was begotten in Mary as being "that holy thing" (Luke 1:35).[8] The neuter gender indicates that, in Jesus' supernatural conception, Mary gave Him only His human nature, not His personhood and His divine nature. She bore a human male child, who was already God, the Second Person of the divine Trinity. She was not the mother of God.

b. Its importance

One: Our Lord's divine conception was necessary for His saving work (Matt. 1:21). Preserving His sinlessness, it qualified Him to make atonement for the sins of others (Heb. 2:9; 7:26–27). One who is a sinner can neither discharge himself from the debt of his sins nor deliver others from their obligation to God. The Lord's unique conception prevented His receiving from a human parent inherent corruption (Luke 1:35) and from the father the imputed guilt of Adam's initial sin (Rom. 5:12–19; Gen. 5:3; 1 Cor. 15:22). Being absolutely sinless (1 Peter 2:22; 1 John 3:5), Jesus was able to pay for others their dreadful debt of sin (Rom. 5:8; 1 Peter 2:24; Heb. 9:26; 1 John 2:2).

Two: The Lord's divine conception also made it possible for Him to rule one day from David's throne over Israel (Matt. 2:2; 2 Sam. 7:12–17; Luke 1:32–33). The title to David's throne was transmitted through Solomon and his posterity (1 Chron. 28:4–7; Matt. 1:1–16, 20). However, because of King Jehoiakim's sin of burning God's Word (Jer. 36), a divine judgment decreed that none of his posterity could sit or prosper on the throne (v. 30). This was repeated to his son, Jehoiachin (Coniah), the last Judean ruler of David's royal dynasty (22:30). By His virgin conception the Lord Jesus avoided this divine curse and received the title to David's throne from Joseph, His foster father. Jesus did not come under the divine judgment, for He was not Joseph's actual son. Still, being Joseph's eldest legal son, He inherited the title to David's throne.[9]

Three: Jesus' divine conception also established His Davidic ancestry. He was a true descendant of David through His mother, Mary, and her ancestor, Nathan, a son of David (Luke 3:23–31; 1 Chron. 3:5; Rom. 1:3; 2 Tim. 2:8). Luke gives Mary's lineage through her father, Heli (Luke 3:23).[10] Matthew gives Joseph's royal lineage through Solomon (Matt. 1:6–16) and shows Jesus' legal connection to Joseph through Mary (v. 16). Consequently, because of His legal connection with Joseph, the lineal heir to David's throne, and His blood relation to David through His mother, Mary (Luke 3:23–31), the Lord Jesus is the last dynastic heir to David's throne and the only one who can rule Israel with God's blessing (Luke 1:30–33).

Four: By His incarnation God the Son became the Last Adam. In this role He is the leader and pattern of the new humanity that God is creating of all saved people, who once were members of the old humanity with Adam as its leader and pattern (1 Cor. 15:22, 45–49; 2 Cor. 5:17; Eph. 2:10). This divine creative work in gospel believers is in fulfillment of the divine purpose to make a people in the image of God's Son, as this relates to His humanity (Rom. 8:29; Phil. 3:20–21; 1 John 3:2).

3. The fact of Jesus' humanity

We have seen that God the Son assumed a complete, sinless human nature within the virgin Mary. He will continue to possess His human nature forever as the God-man (1 Tim. 2:5; Rev. 1:18). Early heretics denied Jesus' humanity (1 John 4:3, see "False views about the hypostatic union" in this chapter), but the Scriptures show that it was, and is, real and unique.

a. Its reality

The fact of Jesus' humanity is shown by His prenatal development and birth, which were normal, natural processes (Luke 2:5–7; cp. 1:57). The Lord also had a complete human nature: a body (Matt. 26:12), soul (26:38), and spirit (27:50; John 11:33).[11] Jesus had a human appearance (John 4:9; 8:57; 10:33). He experienced normal human development in body, human knowledge (Luke 2:40, 52), and spiritual awareness (vv. 46–50). He manifested His spiritual awareness at the age of twelve, when He spoke of His personal relation to God the Father and of the necessity of His being about the "things" (KJV "business") of His Father. Being sinless, He did not experience moral development. However, He did develop socially (Luke 2:51–52), submitting Himself to the authority of His parents and advancing "in favor with God and man." This means that He pleased the Father (Matt. 3:17) and maintained people's admiration and respect.

The reality of Jesus' humanity is also seen in His living an ordinary human life in Nazareth, fulfilling His domestic, vocational, and religious duties (Matt. 13:55–56; Mark 6:3; Luke 4:16). Moreover, He experienced the sinless limitations of human nature like hunger (Matt. 21:18), sleep (8:24), weariness (John 4:6), and confinement to place (11:6–7). There is no indication that He was ever sick, which results from the inherent corruption of one's sinful physical nature. He experienced human emotions, including grief (Mark 3:5; John 11:35), love (John 11:36), agitation (12:27), astonishment (Mark 6:6; Luke 7:9), exultation (Luke 10:21), anger (Mark 3:5), trust (Luke 23:46), suffering (1 Peter 3:18), and compassion (Mark 9:36). He was tempted as we are yet was without sin (Heb. 4:15).[12] Finally, He died (Matt. 27:5; Heb. 2:9, 14–17). While physical death is a natural result of sin, this was not the direct cause of Jesus' death. Uniquely, He voluntarily laid down His life in obedience to the Father (John 10:17–18).

b. Its uniqueness

Before He died and arose again, Jesus had a complete human nature, as we do; yet, it differed qualitatively from ours in that it was perfect and sinless. Regarding the perfection of Jesus' human character, He fully displayed the moral qualities of God in His humanity (John 1:14).[13] W. H. Griffith Thomas wrote of Jesus:

He embraces all the good elements which mark other men. . . . He possesses all these in a higher degree than any one else, and with perfect balance and proportion. There is no weakness, no exaggeration or strain, no strong or weak points, as is the case with the rest of mankind. There are certain elements and traits of character which are not found elsewhere, such as absolute humility, entire unselfishness, whole-hearted willingness to forgive, and the most beautiful and perfect holiness.[14]

Regarding the sinlessness of Jesus' humanity, the Scriptures testify that He never sinned, nor was He a sinner (cp. Matt. 27:4; Luke 23:47; John 8:46; 19:4, 6; Acts 3:14; Rom. 8:3; 2 Cor. 5:21; 1 Peter 1:19; 2:22; 1 John 3:5; Heb. 4:15); therefore, He did not belong to the category of sinners (Heb. 7:26). There is no record that He ever confessed sin or sought forgiveness. Although Jesus submitted Himself to water baptism (Matt. 3:13–17), this rite was not indicative of His repenting of sin as it was with others (cp. Mark 1:4). His baptism was the occasion of His divine anointing with the Holy Spirit for His human, messianic work (Matt. 3:16; John 1:32).

We who are saved look forward to the time when our bodies will be delivered from mortality, inherent corruption, and the resident sin force at the Lord's return (Rom. 8:10, 23). Then we shall be made like Him in His humanity, with His kind of glorified body (1 John 3:2; Phil. 3:20–21; Rom. 8:29).

4. The union of Jesus' two natures

Now we consider the relation of Jesus' divine and human natures to each other and to His personhood. Keep in mind that *nature* is that essence, with its qualities and powers, that gives to the person possessing it his particular identity and character of being. *Personhood* is that unique, self-conscious, self-asserting, responsible subject who possesses a certain kind of nature and whose essential qualities and capabilities are determined by this nature.

a. The meaning of the hypostatic union of these two natures

From eternity, God the Son was a person who possessed the divine nature (the nature of God). As we have seen, at His incarnation God the Son took upon Himself a human nature, divinely made of Mary's substance. But He continued to have His divine nature and to be God. The union of these two natures (the divine and the human) in the one personhood is called "the hypostatic union." "Hypostatic" is from the NT Greek word *hupostasis,* which means "that which stands under." Theologically, the word *hupostasis* can relate to the divine nature and to the Son's personhood as follows:

1) Its relation to God's divine nature

Hupostasis as it relates to God's nature is found in Hebrews 1:3, "the exact impress of His nature."[15] God the Son bears the exact impress of the divine nature, for this nature is equally possessed by each Person (personhood) of the Trinity. Thus in Hebrews 1:3 *hupostasis* refers to the divine nature, which underlies the three Persons (personhoods) of the Trinity—the Father, the Son, and the Holy Spirit.

2) Its relation to the Son's personhood

Hupostasis as it relates to God the Son's personhood is a theological concept that sees His personhood as underlying His two natures, the divine and the human. Thus the doctrine of the hypostatic union of Jesus' two natures is their being united in His single personhood.

b. Features of the hypostatic union as it relates to Jesus

1) The divine and human natures are united in the one personhood.

The Lord Jesus is not two persons, one human and the other divine; but having one personhood, He is one Person. In His incarnation, God the Son did not assume a human person, but a human nature, divinely made of Mary's substance (Luke 1:35). Although His incarnation gave Him a human nature and made Him human, Jesus still possesses the divine nature, by which He is God. Thus He is a personal being with two natures, making Him to be the God-man.

2) The divine and human natures are inseparably united in His personhood, yet they are not mingled or confounded.

Our Lord's incarnation does not affect His divine nature in any way, for there is no interaction or exchange between the two natures; the properties of one nature never become the properties of the other. They are never mixed or combined so as to lose their distinctiveness or to form a third nature. On the other hand, these natures do not function independently of His personhood like separate persons. They continuously and simultaneously communicate their powers and qualities to His personhood without conflict so that He functions at the same time as God and as man.

When He was on earth, Jesus' personhood had complete control over the manifestations of His deity in the realm of His human experience (Matt. 17:1–2; John 18:5–6). Although He seldom displayed the visible qualities of His divine nature in His human experience, He still possessed this nature. When He expressed His deity by speaking the divine name "I AM" in Gethsemane (John 18:5–6), He was still a man, whom they bound and led away (vv. 12–13). When He humanly slept in a boat (Matt. 8:24), He was no less

God, upholding the universe by the Word of His power (Heb. 1:3). With this in view, we can better understand the apostle Paul's reference to God's blood (Acts 20:28). Although blood is not a part of the divine nature, it was an essential element of Jesus' unglorified human nature. Being God and man, God the Son purchased His Church with His own human blood, which represented His human atoning sacrifice (Eph. 5:25).

   c. *Problems of the hypostatic union of the two natures in Jesus*

   These problems are not inherent in the union itself, but belong to our understanding of this union.

   1) There is the problem of Jesus' limited knowledge (Matt. 27:34; Mark 13:32).

   Being God, the Lord Jesus knows all things (Col. 2:3), but as man His knowledge was limited to what the Father had revealed to Him (John 5:19–20; 8:26, 28, 40). Having the two natures, He has both divine knowledge and human knowledge, with the extent of each being determined by its respective nature. The mystery remains how a person can experience both unlimited and limited knowledge at the same time. It has been suggested that His divine knowledge existed below the level of His human consciousness. Because there were certain things that He was not given to know or teach as a man, He did not allow them to flow into His human consciousness.[16]

   2) There is the problem of His being tempted (Matt. 4:1–10).

   Let us seek answers to three questions:

First: Could Jesus have sinned? Unfallen human nature is capable of being involved with sinning as the sins of Adam and Eve show (Gen. 3:1–6). However, Jesus possessed the divine nature, which had an infinite moral influence on His personhood, making Him infinitely holy.[17] Jesus could not sin, for He was God as well as man.

Second: Were the Lord's temptations real? Yes, as much so as Adam's and Eve's temptations were real (Heb. 4:15; Matt. 4:1; Gen. 3:1–6). His and theirs were external temptations, for there was no evil force within them that these temptations could arouse or to which these temptations could appeal. However, the Lord Jesus never experienced the inner struggle of conflicting moral forces as people who have the sin force do (Rom. 7:14–23; Gal. 5:17). Having a sinless human nature, Jesus' commitment to the Father's will was absolutely unwavering (Matt. 4:1–10; Heb. 10:7; John 6:38). With this commitment Jesus' human will was supported by His divine will (cp. Matt. 26:39). Also, there was no need or lack within Him, to which temptation could successfully appeal. As His temptations in the wilderness demonstrate (Matt. 4:1–10), any amoral need, like for food, to which the tempter might appeal, was superseded by the greater need of pleasing the Father (cp. John 4:34). While Adam and Eve had to establish by choice which moral force (God or sin) would dominate their lives, Jesus had already made His choice to obey the Father when He came into the world (Heb. 10:7; John 6:38).

Third: If Jesus could not sin, why did Satan tempt Him? It is obvious that Satan thought that Jesus could sin and that he could conquer Him as he had Eve and Adam. But the Devil grossly underestimated his Opponent, who utterly defeated the adversary on every count. Keep in mind that the sin force causes all whom it dominates to think irrationally, that is, not in harmony with God's truth.

   3) There is the problem of Jesus' death (Rom. 5:8).

   How could One who was God die, especially when God cannot die and death naturally is a result of sin (James 1:14)? Jesus' death was entirely a human experience— He died as man. However, because He was God, it can be said that God the Son died, but this was not a divine experience. For like reason, the apostle Paul could speak of the blood of God (Acts 20:28).

   While He was upon the cross, Jesus experienced separation from the Father in spiritual death (Matt. 27:46). His words, "My God," indicate that this was a human experience. In His separation from the Father (for bearing the punishment of our sins, which is the experience of hell), there was no division of the divine nature, which each Person of the Trinity wholly possesses in common with the other Persons, else Jesus would have ceased being God. The separation was between the Father and the Son in their personal fellowship; it was not a division in their essential relationship.

In His physical death, Jesus did not die naturally from sin as we do. When our sins were laid on Him (1 Peter 2:24) and He was made sin (2 Cor. 5:21), He was identified with them only in a forensic (legal) manner for the purpose of atoning for them. But He Himself did not become a sinner nor was He subject to sin's debilitation so as to die from its natural physical effects. As man, He uniquely died by deliberately laying down His life in obedience to the Father and with His authority (John 10:18).

4) There is the problem of Jesus' being perfected, or completed (Heb. 2:10; 5:9).

How could one be God and be in need of completion? This need related to His human experience, not to His divine experience. Jesus did not need moral completion, for He had no moral flaw or lack (John 1:14; 1 Peter 2:22; 1 John 3:5); He needed functional perfection, or completion. There was something lacking in His human experience that He would need for His human, messianic work as Savior (Heb. 5:8–9) and High Priest (4:15). This need was supplied by His sufferings (Heb. 2:10; 5:8), at both the hands of men (Matt. 26:67; 27:26–30, 35) and at the hand of God the Father (Isa. 53:10).

The Lord's sufferings prepared Him to be a savior (Heb. 5:8). He experienced both spiritual death (Matt. 27:46; 1 Peter 2:24; 2 Cor. 5:21) and physical death (Luke 23:46) when He atoned for our sins. By this suffering He learned the meaning of obedience (Heb. 5:8), not because He was rebellious but because as God He had never been subordinate to authority before His incarnation as the Father's Slave. His greatest display of obedience was in His death (Phil. 2:8). His submission to death demonstrated His worthiness to be our Savior as well as effecting our redemption. This was in contrast to Adam's disobedience, which was his and our undoing. Jesus' obedience unto death qualified Him to be the Cause of salvation (Heb. 5:9, KJV "Author") as well as its Leader (Heb. 2:10, KJV "Captain"). Having willingly submitted to suffering as the sinner's substitute on the cross, He is now the Savior of all who obey the gospel (Acts 10:43; John 3:16).

The Lord's sufferings also prepared Him to be a compassionate high priest (Heb. 4:15). During His lifetime, Jesus suffered poverty (Luke 9:58), ridicule, and rejection (John 1:11; 8:48, 59). In His death, He suffered the humiliation and trauma of an unjust trial, scourging, and crucifixion (Matt. 26:57–27:35; Ps. 22:6–8, 17). By His sufferings, Jesus learned the meaning of pain, poverty, hunger, weariness, rejection, abuse, abandonment, humiliation, mockery, and false accusation. Because of these sufferings, He is sympathetic toward us who suffer in God's will (Heb. 4:14–16).[18] As our great High Priest, the Lord Jesus is able to sympathize with us and to provide us with grace for our needs (cp. 2 Cor. 12:9).

How did the Lord Jesus react to these perfective sufferings? He committed Himself to God (1 Peter 2:23), whom He feared (Heb. 5:7–9). This led Him to pray for deliverance out of (Gk. *ek*) death, and He was heard (cp. Ps. 22:1–21). He was delivered out of spiritual death by His restoration to the Father's fellowship (Luke 23:46; 1 Peter 3:18) and, later, out of physical death by His resurrection from the tomb (Rom. 1:4).

These explanations do not remove all the mystery that surrounds the union of the two natures in Jesus, but they may help our understanding.

d. False views about the hypostatic union

Since our Lord's incarnation, certain people have held wrong views about the hypostatic union. These false views have spawned erroneous teachings about Jesus, which in turn hinder people's salvational faith in Him. One cannot be saved and refuse to accept what the Bible teaches about Him regarding His deity and humanity (Rom. 10:9; 1 John 4:1–3).

1) There are those who assert Christ's deity but deny His humanity.

The Docetae (second century) denied the reality of His body (cp. 1 John 4:3). They held that Jesus was too divine to suffer agony and death and that He only appeared to do so. Some taught that the divine Christ came upon Jesus at His baptism and left Him at His death. *The Apollinarians* (fourth century) denied the completeness of Jesus' human nature. They held that He had a human body and soul but no human mind, or spirit. This was replaced by the divine Logos (the Word).

2) There are those who assert Jesus' humanity, but deny His deity.

The Ebionites (second century) denied Jesus' virgin birth, holding that He was the offspring of Mary and Joseph. *The Arians* (fourth century) held that the Son was a creature (the first created being), infinitely transcending all other creatures, with definite beginning and liability to change and sin.

3) There are those who deny the one personhood of Jesus.

The Nestorians (fifth century) denied that the two natures are united in the one personhood. They held that there are two personhoods.

4) There are those who deny the two natures of Jesus.

The Eutychians (fifth century) confused the two natures, making them one that was more divine than human. Sometimes this is called "Monophysitism." *The Monothelists* (seventh century) held that Jesus acted as one unitary energy with one will.

We need to be on the alert today for such false views concerning the natures of Jesus, especially as held by those who profess to be Christians or who are ignorant Christians.

Jesus' Human Character

1. Its description

While *personality* is the manifestation of one's personhood as affected by one's human nature, *character* is a description of a person's inner qualities as seen in his or her daily life. Some of Jesus' human inner qualities were His meekness and humility (Matt. 11:29), compassion (Matt. 9:3), obedience (John 8:29), love (John 13:1), industry (John 9:4; 17:4), patience (John 14:1–9), grace (2 Cor. 8:9), forgiveness (Luke 23:34), tenderness (John 8:3–11), firmness, courage (Luke 9:51), and holiness (Mark 1:24). We who are saved can exhibit these qualities by submitting ourselves to the Holy Spirit and looking to Him to reproduce them in us (Gal. 5:22–23).

2. Its importance

Our Lord's human character was very important to His work.

a. It showed that He was qualified to be our Savior (Heb. 7:26–27; cp. 1 John 3:5; 1 Peter 2:22).

b. It manifested the moral character of God the Father (John 1:14, 18; 14:9).

c. It exposed and rebuked wickedness (John 3:19–20; 15:22–24).

d. It set forth the ideal standard for His people to follow (Eph. 5:1–2; 1 Peter 2:21).

Observe that we who are saved must be concerned about our inner characters as well as our external physical activities of doing God's will, for our inner characters determine the quality of our actions (Luke 6:41–45).

Jesus' Human Activities

A purpose for our Lord's being man was that, being the Father's Slave and the Last Adam, He might carry out His human, messianic assignment in God's program for mankind (cp. Heb. 2:5–9, 16–17). A summary of these activities follows:

1. During His first coming to earth

The Lord Jesus presented Himself to Israel as the Messiah for their acceptance or rejection (Isa. 49:4–7; Luke 4:42–44; John 1:11). By allowing Himself to be crucified, He confirmed the divine sentence of condemnation against God's enemies (Rom. 8:2; John 12:31; 16:11). He also gave His life for the provisional atonement of humanity's sins (Matt. 20:28; see in this chapter, "The Nature of Jesus' Atoning Work") and arose in triumph over sin, death, and Satan (Rom. 8:3; Acts 2:24; Heb. 2:14; Rev. 1:18). Finally, He prepared His apostles for their ministry of establishing biblical Christianity in the world (Matt. 15:21–18:35; John 14–16; Acts 1:3).

2. During His physical absence from the earth

The Lord Jesus is now building His Church (Matt. 16:18), preparing a place for His people (John 14:2–3), and interceding for them at the Father's right hand (Rom. 8:34; Heb. 7:25).

During the Tribulation Age, He will prepare earth dwellers for His return to earth by universal gospel preaching (Matt. 24:14), by dealing with the elect of Israel and bringing them to repentance (Deut. 30:1–3), and by pouring out dreadful judgments upon the wicked (Rev. 6, 8–9, 12–13, 16)

3. During His second coming to earth

The Lord Jesus will destroy Israel's enemies (Rev. 19:11–21), evict Satan (Rev. 20:1–3), determine who among surviving earth dwellers should enter His earthly kingdom (Ezek. 20:33–38; Matt. 25:31–46), rule over the earth for one thousand years (Rev. 20:4), and finally judge the unsaved (vv. 11–15). This will complete His messianic assignment in His dealings with the present world order (1 Cor. 15:24–25). We shall examine details of these activities later.

HIS HUMILIATION

The humiliation of the Lord Jesus refers to the inexpressible shame and degradation that He experienced in His obedience to the Father unto death (Phil. 2:8). He suffered gross indignities at the hands of wicked men; He also was the Father's offering for humanity's sins. The indignities that He suffered at the hands of wicked men included their mocking Him, striking Him, spitting upon Him, scourging Him, and crucifying Him (Matt. 26:67; 27:26–35). Although they did not contribute to Jesus' atoning work, these abusive indignities revealed the true spiritual state and the just condemnation of all who were involved in these heinous crimes (Acts 4:27; Luke 2:34–35). Furthermore, when He gave His life in atonement for our sins, our Lord experienced indescribable humiliation by being made sin and by bearing our sins and their indescribable judgment.

Our Lord's atoning death and triumphant resurrection are the foundation of the Christian faith and message (1 Cor. 15:1–20). Since God's gracious provision of salvation rests upon these truths, it is important that we thoroughly understand their meaning, not only for our own edification but also for the edification of other gospel believers and for the clear presentation of the gospel to the unsaved.

Although the biblical word *atonement* is used only in the Old Testament for those animal sacrificial offerings that covered sins from divine view (Lev. 17:11; the single NT reference, Rom. 5:11, should be "reconciliation"), I use the word *atonement* in a theological sense to represent our Lord's dealing provisionally with humanity's sins by His sacrifice to satisfy the demands of divine justice and to establish a basis for harmony between God and gospel believers. This work had to be done before God could save sinners. In fulfillment of prophecy (Luke 24:25–26; Ps. 22:1–21; Isa. 52:13–53:12), God the Son came to earth for this purpose (1 John 3:5; 4:9–10; John 1:29; Matt. 20:28). The apostolic witness, given of the Holy Spirit and preserved in the New Testament (John 16:12–14; Acts 2:32), reveals the historicity and meaning of our Lord's atoning work. Let us look at this more closely.

False or Incomplete Theories of the Atonement

Throughout the present age, theologians have tried to explain the meaning of Jesus' death. Although the following theories do not correctly or sufficiently state what the Scriptures teach about the Atonement, our acquaintance with these views will help us to recognize them when we meet them and will also help us to understand better the biblical view.

1. *The Recapitulation Theory of Irenaeus, a bishop of Lyons, Gaul (second century)*

He believed that Jesus reversed the course of human life by repeating in Himself all its stages and experiences, including those of sinners. By His obedience, He compensated for Adam's disobedience and became the transforming agent of mankind.

This theory is incomplete, for it fails to state the basis of the Atonement other than the Lord's obedience.

2. *The Ransom Payment to Satan Theory of Origen, a teacher of Alexandria, Egypt (third century)*

He taught that Jesus' death was a ransom paid to Satan for the purpose of delivering humanity from his claim.

This theory is wrong, for it ignores the truth that the debt of sin was owed to God since it was His law that was violated (1 John 3:4).

3. *The Commercial Theory of Anselm, Archbishop of Canterbury, England (eleventh century)*

This holds that Jesus' death by way of satisfaction restored God's honor, which was violated by sin. Jesus also secured a merit that He Himself did not need and that is passed on to all who obey the gospel.

This view overlooks the truth that sin incurs a divine penalty that must be paid. God's holiness, rather than offended honor, demands this.

4. *The Moral Influence Theory of Peter Abelard, a French scholar (twelfth century)*

He believed that Jesus' death was not a ransom but a revelation of God's love that awakens a response in the sinner and delivers him from the power of sin.

This view fails to explain the substitutionary and propitiatory character of Jesus' death (Rom. 5:8; 1 John 2:2; 4:10).

5. *The Theory of Thomas Aquinas, an Italian Dominican theologian (thirteenth century)*

He held that the Atonement was not necessary and that God could have redeemed man without it. He also believed that Christ's total life contributed toward His atoning work.

This view makes the Atonement arbitrary. Actually, God cannot act contrary to His holiness and justice. Although Jesus' obedience and sinlessness were necessary qualifications of His saviorhood, salvation rests upon His obedience unto death (Phil. 2:8).

6. *The Acceptilation Theory of Duns Scotus, a Franciscan theologian (thirteenth century)*

Similarly to Aquinas, Scotus believed that the method of Atonement was entirely arbitrary (God could have chosen another person or way to atone for sin) and that there was no inherent necessity for rendering God satisfaction.

This view ignores the truth that the necessity for the Atonement lay in God's nature rather than only in His will.

7. *The Example Theory of Faustus Socinus, an Italian Unitarian (sixteenth century)*

He held that Jesus did not bear the exact, full penalty of the law since this would require Him to die as many deaths as there are sinners. He believed that forgiveness of sins is an act of pure mercy, based on man's repentance and obedience.

This theory ignores the connection between Jesus' death and the salvation of sinners (Matt. 20:28; 26:28). God could not save sinners without the debt of their sins being paid.

8. The Governmental Theory of Hugo Grotius, a Dutch jurist (seventeenth century)

He held that Jesus' death was symbolic, showing God's hatred of sin. This ignores that the Lord's death paid the debt of our sins.

9. The Mystical Theory of Edward Irving, a Scottish minister (nineteenth century)

Rejecting penal satisfaction, he associated the Atonement with Jesus' purifying human nature. He believed that Jesus assumed a corrupt, evil, human nature, purified this by His sufferings and obedience, and reunited it to God. People are saved by becoming partakers of Jesus' purified humanity by faith.

This ignores the need for a divine propitiation for sin (1 John 4:10).

10. The Vicarious Confession Theory of John McLeod Campbell, Scottish theologian (nineteenth century)

He believed that Jesus offered to God, on behalf of humanity, the repentance that was necessary to fulfill the condition of divine forgiveness. Jesus made this confession by His death, which showed His agreement with the Father's condemnation of sin.

There is no scriptural support for this theory.

The true view of our Lord's atoning work is Penal Substitutionary Atonement. Let us look at this in detail.

The Nature of Jesus' Atoning Work

1. An analysis

Atonement had to be made before God could deliver sinners from the guilt, debt, ruin, and bondage of their sins and could bring them into a right relation with Himself. This is expressed by the words of John 3:16: "For God so loved the world that He gave His only begotten Son, that whosoever believes on Him should not perish but have everlasting life." What does it mean for God to give His only begotten Son? Why must the sinner believe in the Savior to receive everlasting life? The answers to these questions are found in the biblical teaching of the Atonement. With "penal" referring to judicial punishment, the divine Atonement involved the principles of penal substitution and judicial satisfaction.

a. Our Lord's sacrifice was substitutionary (Rom. 5:8).

The idea of substitution is that Jesus died for sinners (Mark 10:45; 2 Cor. 5:14–15). With "for" (Gk. *huper*) meaning "on behalf of," this emphasizes the truth that Jesus took the place of sinners on the cross. As their substitute, "the Just One for the unjust ones," He bore the punishment of their sins (1 Peter 3:18). In Matthew 20:28, "for" (Gk. *anti*) means "instead of."

The question in saving sinners was this: How could God who was holy and just deal with sinners as they deserved and still deliver them from the punishment of their sins? Since the debt of sins had to be paid, a substitute had to be found if sinners were to be delivered from this obligation. Only God Himself was qualified to be this substitute. According to divine plan, God the Son came to earth, received a sinless human nature, submitted to crucifixion, and while on the cross, received the divine stroke for sinners as their substitute (Isa. 53:10). There was no other way of dealing effectively with humanity's sins so people could be saved. There is no other Savior-Substitute than Jesus (Acts 4:12; John 14:6).

b. Our Lord's death was satisfactory (1 Cor. 15:3).

With "for" (Gk. *huper*) meaning "concerning," this emphasizes the truth that Jesus' death related to humanity's sins and their penalty. The Scriptures teach that by His death Jesus satisfied God's demands against sinners, for His law required their death (Ezek.

18:20; Rom. 6:23).[19] By His death in their place, Jesus provisionally satisfied this requirement on their behalf.

There are two features of this satisfaction: Jesus' death was propitious and provisional.

1) Jesus' death for humanity's sins was propitious (1 John 2:2; 4:10).

A propitiation is a sacrifice that appeases or placates God's wrath.[20] God was angry with mankind, for all had broken His laws and offended His person. However, with unparalleled grace and love, God the Father gave His only Son to appease His wrath against sinners. As the divine propitiation for sins, the Lord Jesus received the punishment that was due sinners. By this sacrifice, God's wrath against sinners was appeased, and His demands were satisfied, but only in a provisional sense.

2) Jesus' death for humanity's sins was provisional (John 3:16, 18, 36).

By His atoning work the Lord Jesus secured a value that He did not need for Himself and that could be divinely applied to the account of others (2 Cor. 5:18–20). That His death was provisional means that the value, which His atoning work obtained, is not divinely applied to the sinner's account until he exercises salvational faith in the Savior (Acts 10:43). Thus the sinner's debt for his sins was not paid to God at the time Jesus died. If it were, then all for whom Jesus died would have been saved at that time. When He died, Jesus secured the value that God demanded of sinners and that is now offered to everyone through the gospel. This value is divinely applied when the sinner trusts in Jesus and His atoning work for his salvation. Until he receives the Savior, the sinner is still obligated to pay the debt of his sins, despite our Lord's atoning work. However, at the time he trusts in Jesus and His atoning work, the gospel believer receives the value of Jesus' sacrifice on his account, which is rendered "paid in full." This is the meaning of divine forgiveness (Eph. 1:7).

Now we can understand why unsaved people must place their trust in Jesus for their salvation. The Lord Jesus is the only qualified substitute. If sinners accept the Lord's atoning work by faith, God applies its value to their accounts; if sinners do not trust in the Savior as their substitute, then they themselves must bear the punishment of their sins (John 3:36). There is no other way to be delivered from this dreadful obligation (Acts 4:12; John 14:6). This truth must be given in gospel presentations.

2. Several observations

One: The means of the Atonement was determined by God's nature rather than only His will, that is, it was not subject to divine whim or option. While His gracious love motivated Him to find a way to deliver sinners from sin's guilt, debt, ruin, and bondage, God's holiness, righteousness, and justice determined what this way should be—by penal substitution and judicial satisfaction (Ezek. 18:20; John 3:16; Rom. 3:25–26). God always acts in agreement with His nature; He cannot deny Himself (2 Tim. 2:13). He had to deal with people's sins before He could set gospel believers free from their obligation and bestow on them the riches of His grace.

Two: The Lord Jesus not only bore our sins (1 Peter 2:24; Isa. 53:6) but was also made sin (2 Cor. 5:21). He was more than just an instrument for exposing our sins to divine wrath. Being made sin, He personally received and experienced the full measure of God's wrath against our sins (cp. Matt. 27:46; Ps. 22:6; Isa. 53:10).

Three: The Lord Jesus' atoning sufferings, which He experienced while on the cross, were penal. This means that they were judicial punishment from the Father's hand to satisfy the demands of His divine nature and law against our sins (cp. Isa. 53:10; Ezek. 18:4; Rom. 5:8).

Four: While on the cross, the Lord Jesus did not suffer from the natural results of sin, like disease. He bore sin's legal consequences.

Five: Our Lord's physical death was deliberate and voluntary. He did not die from natural causes like loss of blood or weakness. He was not a suicide, dying from self-infliction, nor was He killed. He uniquely, voluntarily laid down His life (John 10:18).

Six: Our Lord's atoning work was wholly confined to the time that He was on the cross (cp. Matt. 20:28; Col. 1:20; John 19:30). His sinless, obedient human life, which He had lived since His incarnation, demonstrated His worthiness to be the Savior, but this did not atone for our sins. His atoning work took place while He was on the cross during the hours of supernatural darkness, from noon to 3:00 P.M. (Matt. 27:45–46).

Seven: Jesus' enemies did not contribute to His atoning work, for only God could make atonement for humanity's sins. The pain and indignities of abuse, scourging, and crucifixion, which He suffered at the hands of wicked men, did not have atoning value. Their crucifying Jesus was humanity's greatest crime against God. This wicked act supported the justice of their divine condemnation (John 3:18, being "condemned already"). The Atonement does not rest on this crime.

Eight: Man's shedding Jesus' blood did not in itself make atonement anymore than it did in the Levitical animal sacrifices. The people who brought their sacrificial animals to the temple slew them by bloodshedding; the priests then took this shed blood and offered it upon the altar (Lev. 1:2–5). Representing the life of the substitute, sacrificial blood had to be offered upon the altar to have atoning value (Lev. 17:11). Jesus' blood was shed in volume by His enemies after He had died (John 19:34). Unlike the sacrificial animals that died by bloodshedding, Jesus Himself uniquely gave His life in death (John 10:18). He was not killed; He did not die from loss of blood or by self-infliction. The wages of sin that Jesus paid was His giving His life in death (Rom. 6:23). Jesus' work was done when He cried with a loud voice, "It is finished," and gave up His life (John 19:30). To fulfill the OT typology and to assure His death, it was necessary that His blood be shed, but this was not the cause of His death. It expressed the wicked intention of man to slay Him. Both God and man were active at Calvary: the One, exercising the greatest measure of grace and love; the other, manifesting the greatest expression of hatred and rebelliousness.

Nine: It was God the Father, not sinful men, who offered Jesus at Calvary for the atoning sacrifice (Isa. 53:10; John 3:16). Evil people crucified Jesus with the intention of destroying Him. Taking the symbol of man's hatred for Him and His Son, God the Father used the cross as an altar upon which He offered His Son for humanity's sins.

Ten: By His atoning work the Lord Jesus secured an atoning value for sinners that He Himself did not need and that could be divinely applied to others (2 Cor. 5:18–20). This value, which is sufficient for all people (1 John 2:2), is being presented to all through the gospel and is divinely applied to the elect when they favorably respond to the gospel by trusting in the Savior and His atoning work (Acts 10:43).

Eleven: It was necessary that the substitute be both God and man. Only One who was God could qualify morally for the Atonement and do its work; only one who was man could identify with the human race and could die (Heb. 2:14; Rom. 5:6; 2 Cor. 5:18; Ps. 3:8; cp. Job 9:32–33).

Twelve: The Atonement was the combined work of the Persons of the divine Trinity. The Father gave His only Son as an offering for sin (Isa. 53:10; 2 Cor. 5:19; John 3:16; 1 John 4:10); the Lord Jesus gave His life (Matt. 20:28; John 1:29; 10:17–18; 1 Peter 3:18) in the power of the Holy Spirit (Heb. 9:14). Likewise, our Lord's resurrection, which made His atoning work effective, was the operation of the Father (Gal. 1:1), the Son (John 10:18), and the Holy Spirit (Rom. 8:11).

Thirteen: We must distinguish between the Atonement and salvation, as expressed by the first and second halves of John 3:16. God could not save sinners until He had given His Son to atone for their sins. Upon his trust in the Savior and His atoning work, the gospel believer is delivered from the guilt, ruin, and bondage of his sins, is born into God's family, and becomes the recipient of God's gracious blessings.

The Validity of Substitutionary Atonement

Liberal theology and other forms of unbelief reject the biblical view of penal substitutionary atonement. Since this rejection concerns such a primary biblical doctrine, let us consider some of the objections of unbelief and the replies that H. E. Guillebaud so ably gave.

Objection One: It is wrong for a judge
to sentence an innocent man to die for a guilty person.

In reply, Mr. Guillebaud points out that the objector sees four distinct parties involved in this case besides the guilty criminal, let us say, a murderer.[21] These are the judge, the innocent substitute, the wronged party (the family of the murdered man and through them the whole community), and the king, representing the law of the land, to whom the judge is under oath to administer justice. It is observed that, if the innocent substitute could by his voluntary consent surrender his own rights, the judge's action would be a double outrage against the wronged party and the law that he had sworn to administer. He would be committing a crime against both of these by releasing the murderer and ordering the execution of an innocent person. However, in the teaching of substitutionary atonement, the case is different. Mr. Guillebaud wrote:

> There is the condemned criminal, the guilty sinner. But beside him there is only One, who is Judge, Wronged Party, King (or Law), and Substitute. God was not administering someone else's law, but His own, and the sin was not committed against someone else, but against Him; and above all He did not take someone else and accept him as a substitute for the condemned sinner, but He came Himself, took upon Himself the nature of the guilty ones, and bore the penalty of His own law. The Substitute who died on Calvary expressly declared Himself to be the Judge of the world. Instead, therefore, of a judge punishing an innocent third party in place of the criminal, we have a Triune Judge, One of whose Persons identified Himself with the nature of the criminal in all except his sin, then takes the sin itself upon Himself, and suffers the penalty of His own Law, which indeed has no existence independent of Him. Moreover, not only is there this identity between the Substitute and the Judge, but also in a mysterious sense between the Substitute and the criminal, when the latter becomes willing to accept the identification. Can this be termed immoral?[22]

One problem of unbelief is its refusal to accept the truth that Jesus was more than a man. He was and is the God-man. Were He only a guiltless man, His sacrifice for others would be immoral, for He did not deserve this death.[23]

Objection Two: How could a few hours of suffering
by the substitute be equivalent to everlasting hell for sinners?

This objection disregards the fact that quantity, bulk, length of time, and distance are conceptions that have little significance in the spiritual world in contrast to quality. Mr. Guillebaud wrote:

The reply to this objection is that the importance of the sacrifice of the Son of God is not measured by the duration in time of His sufferings, but by their quality, and above all by the quality of Him who suffered. . . . Quantity is a conception wholly out of place in considering the sufferings of the Savior: the very idea of balancing those sufferings in quantity against the doom of unsaved mankind is entirely alien to the Bible. . . . But if we think in terms of spiritual quality, surely it is not incredible that such sufferings endured by the Judge Himself should be adequate to "propitiate" His eternal justice and make it possible for Him righteously (and gladly) to forgive the sinner who truly turns to Him.[24]

L. S. Chafer observed that the value of the sacrifice is not discovered in the intensity of the Savior's anguish but in His dignity and infinite worth.[25]

Objection Three: Guilt cannot be transferred from one person to another.

This objection rests upon the misunderstanding that guilt is the same as the evil effects of sin upon one's life. Guilt really concerns one's obligation to God to pay the penalty that one's sins have incurred. At the cross our sins were judicially transferred to the Savior; and He bore their guilt, that is, the obligation to pay their judicial debt, which was death. He did not experience on the cross the natural results of sin, like disease. Mr. Guillebaud asked, "Is it incredible that He (God), under conditions that seem right in His eyes, can lift that responsibility from us and take it upon Himself in Christ?"[26]

We conclude this section of objections by quoting Mr. Guillebaud again: "If man needs to be saved, and if salvation is the work of God, surely, in the nature of things, it is from God that man must learn about it."[27] God, with His Word, is the final authority on the matter.

The Kinds of Death That Jesus Experienced

Since the wages of sin is death (Rom. 6:23; Gen. 2:17) and the divine arrangement for atoning for sin was death and the offering of life by sacrificial blood (Lev. 17:11), it was necessary for the Savior to die that He might atone for our sins (Matt. 20:28; Rom. 5:6, 8). When Adam and Eve sinned, they immediately died spiritually (Gen. 2:17) and later died physically (5:5). Moreover, the unsaved will forever experience the desolation of perpetual separation from God in hell (Rev. 20:15). Our Lord experienced these basic kinds of death when He was upon the cross.

1. Jesus experienced spiritual death and hell (Matt. 27:46).

During the three hours of darkness while He was on the cross (Matt. 27:45), our Lord bore humanity's sins (1 Peter 2:24; Isa. 53:6; 1 John 2:2) and was made sin (2 Cor. 5:21). The full fury of God's wrath fell upon Him and crushed Him (Isa. 53:10). As man, Jesus was separated from the Father's fellowship, as indicated by His cry, "My God, My God, why hast Thou forsaken Me?" (Matt. 27:46).[28] By this separation the Lord Jesus experienced spiritual death and hell, with its indescribable desolation, during those hours of darkness (cp. Ps. 22:1–6, 11–21; Heb. 5:7). The Father forsook Him, for His holy nature reacted against the Sin-bearer and His burden of humanity's sins (Hab. 1:13).

2. Jesus experienced physical death (Luke 23:46).

When He had exhausted God's wrath against our sins, Jesus was restored to fellowship with the Father. This is indicated by His addressing God, "Father" (Luke 23:46). Being made alive in His human spirit (1 Peter 3:18, Gk.), He cried out triumphantly, "It is finished" (John 19:30), commended His human spirit to the Father, and died physically (Luke 23:46).

The manner of our Lord's physical death was unique in that He deliberately laid down His life in obedience to the Father (John 10:18). Having borne the wrath of God against our sins, He voluntarily, decisively laid down His physical life. No one took it from Him, although His enemies were charged with His murder as this was their intention (Acts 2:23; 3:15; 5:30). Our Lord did not die from exhaustion (Luke 23:46), loss of blood (John 19:33–34), or a broken heart. Neither was His death suicide, for He did not take His life by self-affliction. But with authority from and in obedience to the Father (John 10:17–18), He uniquely, deliberately laid down His life by giving up His human spirit (Matt. 27:50; cp. James 2:26).

While it was necessary for the atonement, our Lord's physical death was not the dreadful experience of divine wrath as was His spiritual death. Being in complete fellowship with the Father, Jesus voluntarily laid down His physical life to gain power over death, Satan, and the realm of the dead (hades) by His resurrection (Acts 2:23–32; Heb. 2:14; Rev. 1:18). He aggressively invaded the realm over which Satan and sin held power (Heb. 2:14; 1 Cor. 15:56) and challenged them, as it were, to bind Him as they had bound the human race. But since they could not lay claim to Him (Acts 2:24), He broke their power forever. They could not hold Him, for He was personally sinless (1 John 3:5; John 14:30). As the Messiah, He now has authority over these evil forces (John 12:31; Rom. 8:3) and lethal powers (Rev. 1:18).

Our Lord's atoning work involved His spiritual and physical deaths and required His resurrection (Rom. 4:25). While His deaths satisfied the demands of divine holiness and justice, His resurrection made His atoning work effective and broke the power of the enemy that held mankind in its grip.

The Crucifixion of Jesus

Foreordained of God (Acts 4:27–28), our Lord's crucifixion was a fulfillment of prophecy (Zech. 12:10; 13:6; Ps. 22:16–17; Matt. 20:19; 26:2). Sparing us the painful details, the sacred record simply says, "They crucified Him" (Matt. 27:35). That which Jesus suffered at the hands of evil men in His trial and crucifixion did not contribute to His atoning work, but it did reveal the spiritual state and just condemnation of all who were involved in this heinous crime (Acts 4:27; Luke 2:35). As God was about to do His greatest work in making His Son an offering for humanity's sins, fallen angels and rebellious humanity were committing their greatest crime against Him (Matt. 27:26–44; Ps. 2:1–3). They subjected their Creator to a shameful, humiliating, painful execution with the intention of murdering Him (John 11:53; Acts 3:15; 5:30; 10:39; 13:28). Their heinous act revealed the gross depravity of their character and the malignant nature of sin (Acts 2:23; 3:15; 7:52).[29]

Death by crucifixion was the most shameful punishment that was inflicted in those times. To be crucified was to be identified with the lowest criminals. Roman law forbade the crucifixion of Roman citizens. The lowest term of reproach that a Roman could apply to another was "crucifer" or "crossbearer."[30]

Crucifixion was an agonizing experience, with the victim living from two to seven days. Torn flesh and infected wounds, taut muscles and swollen tissues, the unnatural position of the body, the heat of the sun and the cold of night, the bites of insects and the attacks of animals combined to make this a most excruciating experience.

The Jews regarded anyone who was crucified to be cursed of God (Deut. 21:23; Gal. 3:13); thus a crucified Savior was a stumbling block to them (1 Cor. 1:23). So great was the scandal of the cross to Gentiles that they considered the Christian teaching that gave to a crucified person a place in the divine Trinity and the role of Savior sheer madness (vv. 18, 23).

While the New Testament has preserved for us the indignities that were done to Jesus before His execution, Psalm 22:6–21 prophetically speaks of those sufferings that He experienced while upon the cross. His spiritual sufferings are expressed by His awful cry (v. 1). His mental suffering is indicated by His being despised (v. 6), mocked (vv. 7–8), and the object of immodest gaze (vv. 17–18), for crucified victims were naked. Jesus also suffered physically (vv. 12–18). But in faith He looked to the Lord for help (vv. 19–21). And when it seemed that He could no longer endure, God intervened. The Savior's atoning work was done; His human spirit revived; He sighed, "You have heard Me!" (v. 21). Then He cried, "It is finished" (John 19:30). His work ended when He gave up His human spirit, after He had borne the divine judgment of humanity's sins.

The Work of Jesus While on the Cross

1. Jesus atoned for human sins.

Just before He died physically, Jesus triumphantly cried out, "It is finished" (John 19:30). He died with the awareness that His atoning work was done. This work did not begin until He was upon the cross, and it was completed with His physical death. His resurrection made this work effective (1 Cor. 15:14–19; cp. Rom. 4:25). In our study of His atoning work, we must distinguish between the *Atonement* (that which He did on the cross) and *salvation* (the benefits of the Atonement that are divinely applied to the gospel believer).[31] Let us now look at what Jesus accomplished by His atoning work.

a. He judicially dealt with humanity's sins.

We gospel believers can say that the Lord Jesus dealt with our sins decisively by judicially paying their debt and putting them away from God's view (Heb. 9:26; Gal. 1:4; 1 John 3:5; 1 Cor. 15:3). As we noted earlier, dying for the world, He dealt with humanity's sins propitiously and provisionally. Let us review these concepts.

To understand His dealing with humanity's sins propitiously, we must ask this: How could God, who is holy and just, deal with sinners in a way that they deserve and yet satisfy His love by delivering them from sin's penalty and ruin? Motivated by gracious love, He sent His Son to be the propitiation for our sins and for those of the world (1 John 2:2; 4:10). Although He could not change His holy demands against sinners, God could perfectly and justly satisfy these demands on their behalf and by this could appease His wrath. Pagans seek to propitiate the anger of their deities by offering them gifts, but God Himself was propitious. He gave the necessary sacrifice that would satisfy His demands and placate His anger against mankind. The Lord Jesus dealt with humanity's sins propitiously when He received their punishment and provisionally satisfied God's holy demands against them.

The Lord Jesus also dealt with humanity's sins provisionally. This means that the value of His atoning work was obtained for all sinners by His death, but it is not divinely applied to them until they exercise faith in the Savior and His atoning work (Acts 10:43). Until they do this, unsaved people are obligated to pay the debt of their sins themselves, despite the Lord's sacrifice. Only when people believe the gospel does God apply to them the value of Jesus' atoning work. Then they receive His forgiveness and the salvational blessings of justification (Rom. 5:1, 9), redemption (Eph. 1:7), reconciliation (Col. 1:20–21), and regeneration (1 John 4:9; 5:11). We who are saved can look back to our Lord's atoning work and see that by this He obtained for us these benefits (cp. Heb. 9:12). But no one can claim these blessings before he trusts in the Savior and receives the value of Jesus' atoning work. If the sinner does not accept the Savior, he remains indebted to God for his sins as though Christ had not died.

b. He took away the sins of precross believers.

By His atoning work, the Lord Jesus put away the sins of those people who were saved during the ages before His death (Rom. 3:25; Heb. 9:15–17). While their sins had been covered by the blood of animal sacrifices (Gen. 3:21; Lev. 17:11), they had not been dealt with in a final, permanent way (Heb. 9:9; 10:4, 11; see 9:26). For this reason, these precross believers had not been perfected, received the promised inheritance, or gone to heaven when they died (cp. Heb. 11:8–16, 39–40). Instead, they went to "Abraham's Bosom," or "Paradise," in hades to await our Lord's atoning work and His victory over death, which would put away their sins and would release them from death's power (cp. Luke 16:22; 23:43; Gen. 25:8; 1 Kings 2:10; see Heb. 2:14–15; Col. 2:15; Heb. 12:22–23). Upon applying to them the value of His atoning work, the Lord took these disembodied precross believers with Him to heaven to await the time of their return with Him and the resurrection of their bodies (cp. Eph. 4:8).

c. He secured the basis of divine parental forgiveness.

Jesus' atoning work is the basis not only of divine judicial forgiveness of unsaved people (Col. 2:13) but also of divine parental forgiveness of saved people (1 John 1:9). When people believe the gospel, they receive God's judicial forgiveness of all their lifetime sins, which cancels their going to hell (John 3:16; Col. 2:13; Rev. 20:14). When saved persons deal with known sins in their lives, they receive God's parental forgiveness, which cancels divine corrective chastisement (Rev. 3:19; 1 Cor. 11:27–32). Since Jesus dealt with this family aspect of the sins of His people (1 John 1:7) as well as with their judicial aspect (Col. 1:14), our heavenly Father is able to grant those of us who are saved His parental forgiveness, which removes the threat or the ongoing experience of corrective chastisement. Apparently, we are automatically forgiven of filial sins in our Christian lives that are unknown to us (1 John 1:7). But when we learn of these sins or commit sin knowingly, then we must deal with them by repentance and confession to receive divine parental forgiveness (Rev. 2:5; 1 John 1:9; see "The Divine Forgiveness of Sins" under Hamartiology).

2. Jesus confirmed the condemnation of God's enemies.

In keeping with the demands of justice and orderly judicial procedure, an accused offender must be found guilty of an alleged crime before he or she can be sentenced to punishment. God had already handed down a sentence of condemnation against His enemies (cp. Gen. 3:15; John 3:18; Rom. 3:19; 5:18). But their guilt was fully established and clearly manifested by their wicked actions against the Lord Jesus during His trial and crucifixion. The gross injustice of the Jewish and Roman courts, the physical abuse associated with these trials, and their nailing Him to a cross with the intention of killing Him proved to be the greatest crime of fallen angels and sinful humans against their Creator (Matt. 26:57–27:44). These heinous actions were self-incriminating, exposing the guilt of their hatred and rebellion against God (John 3:20; Luke 2:35; 18:32–33; 22:2; Rom. 8:3). Their wicked actions against Jesus, prompted by Satan and sin, confirmed the justice of the divine verdict of their condemnation. Let us look more closely at this.

a. The condemnation of the sin force (Rom. 6:10; 8:3)

Directed by Satan (Luke 22:53), Jesus' enemies acted with the impelling energy of the inner sin force.[32] This was especially evident in Jesus' trials and crucifixion, when this evil force manifested its abhorrent, wicked character in the abusive, shameful actions against Him (cp. Mark 14:61–65; Luke 23:32–37; Acts 2:23). Thus these sinful actions were self-incriminating.

The Lord Jesus not only demonstrated and confirmed the justice of God's condemnation of the sin force by giving Himself to its abuses but He also broke its power of death

(Rom. 6:23) by His resurrection (James 1:15; Acts 2:24; 1 Cor. 15:56–57). He now can liberate gospel believers from sin's claims (Rom. 6:6–7, 16–22; 8:2–4) and can grant them occasions of victory over its urges in their lives as they submit themselves to Him (Gal. 5:16; Rom. 6:1–13). Although the inherent power of this evil force presently remains undiminished, it ceases to exist in the lives of God's people with their death, and it will cease with the change in the bodies of the living at Jesus' return (Rom. 8:10–11, 23). It will also come to an end in the universe with the death of the last unsaved person (Rev. 20:9).[33]

b. *The condemnation of fallen angels (John 12:31; 16:11; Matt. 25:41)*

The Scriptures imply that this world's ruler, Satan, (John 12:31), tried to keep Jesus from going to the cross (Matt. 4:8–10; 16:21–23; cp. 26:36–39). This was because of the ancient, divine sentence against him (Gen. 3:15). When he failed to defeat Jesus during His lifetime, the Devil and his demons did all within their power to make Jesus' trial and crucifixion as odious and painful as possible (John 13:27; Luke 22:53; Matt. 26:57–27:44; cp. Ps. 22:12–21). This revealed their guilt before God.

Because He confirmed the justice of God's condemnation against Satan and broke his power by His death and resurrection (Heb. 2:14; Rev. 1:18), the Lord Jesus now sets gospel believers free from Satan's authority (Col. 1:13; Acts 26:18) and gives those who submit to Him occasions of victory over satanic temptations (James 4:7). When He returns to rule, the Lord Jesus as the Last Adam will evict the Devil and his evil angels from earth (Rev. 19:11–16; 20:1–3). At the close of His millennial earthly rule, the Lord Jesus will banish Satan and his angels to hell forever (Rev. 20:7–10; Matt. 25:41).

c. *The condemnation of the world (John 12:31)*

In the Scriptures, the word *world* has various meanings as determined by the context.[34] Here it refers to the world-system of unsaved mankind. This system is headed by Satan (John 12:31), its works are evil (7:7), and its philosophy is deceptive and vain (Col. 2:8). The world's representative peoples (Acts 4:27)—their religion (Institutional Judaism), government (Roman Imperialism), and culture (Greek Hellenism)—united to crucify the Lord Jesus. By this crime these people revealed their guilt and the gross wickedness of the world order of which they were a part.

Upon His confirming the divine sentence against the world order, the Lord Jesus now delivers gospel believers from its membership and authority (John 15:19; Gal. 6:14).[35] He can give them occasions of victory over its evil influences as they give themselves to His will for their lives (Rom. 12:2; 1 John 2:15–17; Matt. 6:19–24; Col. 3:1–3), and one day He will deliver them physically out of it (1 Thess. 4:17; cp. Gal. 1:4). Moreover, as the Last Adam and the Viceroy of God the Father, the Lord Jesus will replace the present world order with a new one when He returns and sets up His kingdom on earth (Heb. 2:5–9; Dan. 2:44–45; Matt. 13:41–42, 49–50; 25:31–46; Rev. 11:15–18; 19:11–21; Isa. 2:1–5; 11:1–9).

3. *Jesus mediated the new covenant.*

Representing both God and man (1 Tim. 2:5–6), the Lord Jesus was God's sacrifice for sinful humanity (John 1:29; 3:16). As the Mediator of the new covenant (Heb. 8:6; 9:15; 12:24), He made this covenant effective by His atoning sacrifice (Heb. 9:11–28) and His resurrection (Heb. 1:3; 10:12–18). Unlike the Mosaic covenant, which could only condemn its violators (Gal. 2:16; 3:10–11; Heb. 7:19; 9:9), the new covenant, with its salvational promises (Jer. 31:31–34), provides the promissory basis for the salvation of sinners.[36] The salvational promises of the new covenant (forgiveness of sins and a personal relationship with God), as presented in the gospel, are fulfilled for all who trust in Jesus as their Savior from sin (cp. Heb. 9:14; 10:14; 2 Cor. 3:6; Rom. 1:1–4). This covenant is explained in detail in the new covenant (New Testament) section of the Bible, and it is celebrated by those who observe the Lord's Supper (Luke 22:20).

At this time the Lord Jesus also brought an end to the Mosaic covenant that God had made with Israel (Exod. 19:3–6; 2 Cor. 3:6–14; Gal. 3:25; Eph. 2:14–16; Col. 2:14; Heb. 7:18–19; 10:9). While the Mosaic Law continues as a dispensation for those who submit themselves to it (Acts 15:21; 21:21), its covenantal promises (Exod. 19:5–6; Lev. 18:5), annulled by Israel's idolatry (Deut. 31:16; Jer. 31:32), are no longer honored by God.

4. Jesus laid the basis for the reconciliation of all things.

By His atoning work, the Lord Jesus laid the ground for the reconciliation to God of all impersonal creatures and things that were involuntarily affected by the divine curse at the time of man's first sin (Gen. 3:17–18; Rom. 8:19–22; see Col. 1:20). The apostle Paul is not speaking about everyone's being saved (he is careful not to refer to things under the earth, cp. Phil. 2:10), for this would contradict the doctrine of the everlasting punishment of the unsaved (Matt. 25:46; John 3:36).[37] The apostle anticipates the time when the Lord Jesus will return to establish His earthly, millennial kingdom. Then He will lift the divine curse that rests upon creation and will restore earth to its primeval, pristine state (Rom. 8:19–23; Eph. 1:10; Acts 3:21; cp. Isa. 11:6–9; chap. 35; Amos 9:13; Ps. 8). This reconciliation may also provide the basis for the eventual resurrection of all human bodies since they, at death, return to soil (Gen. 3:17–19; John 5:28–29). In some way, the Lord's atoning work allows God to withdraw His judicial action upon impersonal nature and to bring about this universal reconciliation. The whole creation waits for this glorious deliverance (Rom. 8:19–21).

5. Jesus purchased the whole human race.

By His sacrifice, the Lord Jesus purchased all mankind, both the unsaved (2 Peter 2:1; cp. Rom. 14:9; Heb. 10:29; Matt. 13:44; cp. Exod. 13:12, 15) and the saved (1 Cor. 6:20; 7:23). By this purchase, He as man became the owner of mankind, to do with as He pleases in keeping with the divine plan. Consequently, as the Messiah, the Lord Jesus is truly Lord of all (Acts 2:36; 10:36) by costly purchase as well as by divine gift (John 3:35; Matt. 28:18; Ps. 2:8). Also, being God, He is sovereign over the universe as its Creator (John 1:3; Ps. 24:1).

When He returns to earth again, the Lord Jesus, as the Last Adam, will evict the usurper Satan, will take charge of earth as its lawful Owner, and will rule over His subjects as God the Father's Viceroy (Rev. 19:11–20:4; Ps. 2:6–9). Moreover, He, to whom all people are accountable (John 5:22), will judge mankind to determine who are qualified to enter His millennial kingdom (Matt. 13:41–42, 49–50; 25:31–46) and, later, will judge those who will be cast into the lake of fire (Rev. 20:11–15). He will appraise the lives of His people when He comes again (Rev. 22:12).

The Extent of Jesus' Atoning Work

1. The meaning of "extent"

In His dealing with human sins on the cross, did Jesus atone for the sins of all mankind or for those of the elect alone? W. G. T. Shedd observed that the word *extent* has two meanings in usage: *passively*, it means value like the extent of one's property; *actively*, it speaks of the act of extending.[38]

a. Passively

The word *extent* passively refers to the Atonement's value, which Jesus secured by His sacrifice, and which is sufficient to satisfy God's judicial demands against the sins of all mankind.

b. Actively

The word *extent* actively refers to the divine application of the Atonement's value to those who believe the gospel.

Thus, in its passive sense, the Atonement, being for all mankind, is unlimited (sufficient for all); in its active sense, it is limited to the gospel believing elect (efficient to the elect). Although the Lord Jesus died for all mankind, the salvational benefits of His atoning work are experienced only by gospel believers and by those who die before having developed moral awareness and accountability (see "The Salvation of Infants" under Soteriology).

2. *A summary of the extent of the Atonement*

The following propositions set forth my understanding of this doctrine:

One: Jesus died for all mankind (Heb. 2:9; 1 John 2:2; 2 Cor. 5:14–15; John 3:16–17; 1 Tim. 2:1–6); thus He is the Savior of the world (1 John 4:14; John 1:29; 1 Tim. 4:10).

Two: Jesus' death seems to include a wider purpose than only the salvation of the elect. It also provided a value for the nonelect to reject, to the added condemnation of those who hear the gospel (John 3:18; 2 Peter 2:1). While it is God's intention to save the elect when they believe, it seems also to be His intention by Jesus' atoning work to make the gospel's universal appeal real and true (John 3:16; Acts 17:30; 20:21; Col. 1:23). We can take the word of reconciliation to everyone in the world with the assurance that Jesus provisionally died for them (2 Cor. 5:18–20; 1 John 2:2). God does have something to say to the nonelect through the gospel. They are not relieved of their duty to receive the Savior by a limited Atonement. Because the Lord Jesus died for the nonelect, they can never say that they could not have been saved if they had chosen to receive Him. On the other hand, if He did not die for them, how can they be guilty of rejecting a value that does not exist for them?

Three: Although universal in its extent, the Lord's atoning work was provisional in the sense that the benefits derived from it are not received and possessed until one exercises salvational faith in the Savior (Acts 16:31; 10:43). While the Lord Jesus atoned for the sins of the whole world by bearing their punishment, God applies the value of this sacrifice only when the sinner receives the Savior. There is no transference of the atoning value of Jesus' sacrifice before one believes the gospel. Until the unsaved persons trust in the Savior, this value remains with God, and the sinners themselves are obligated to pay the debt of their sins. Their going to hell for their sins is not a second payment, for the value of Jesus' atoning work was never divinely put to their accounts. If they fail to receive the Savior, the sinners themselves must pay the debt of their sins as though Jesus had not died, for their guilt and the debt of their sins remain with them.

Four: We must distinguish between Jesus' atoning work (His dealing with humanity's sins) and salvation (the benefits derived from the Atonement). People receive salvation when they exercise salvational faith in Jesus rather than when He died on the cross. Salvational faith precedes personal reception of the components of salvation, including redemption, justification, reconciliation, regeneration, and sanctification (Acts 10:43; 16:31). The value of the Atonement, with its salvational blessings, is not divinely applied until the sinner believes the gospel.

Five: A distinction must be recognized between God's unrevealed decree, or purpose, and His revealed will, or desire, for sinners. His revealed will for all people is that they believe the gospel and be saved (2 Peter 3:9; 1 Tim. 2:4). This is indicated by the universality of the gospel's statement and appeal and of the provision that God has made in Jesus (John 3:15–16; Acts 17:30). But God's secret decree is to save only those whom He has chosen (2 Thess. 2:13; Acts 13:48). Our duty is to give the gospel to everyone (Luke 24:47, Gk. "to all nations") and leave it with God to save whom He will.

Six: Since Jesus died for the whole world and secured, thereby, a value that is now offered by the gospel for everyone to receive or reject, we can present the gospel to everyone with the assurance that God will save all who exercise salvational faith in Jesus. The "whosoever" of the gospel appeal is to be taken literally, for God, who cannot lie, means what He says. When speaking about the word and ministry of reconciliation (see "Reconciliation" under Soteriology), the apostle Paul observed that God did not reckon to unsaved people their sins and send them to hell (2 Cor. 5:18–20). Rather, He laid them on Jesus for the purpose of provisionally reconciling the world unto Himself. Consequently, anyone in the world can be reconciled to God by receiving the message of reconciliation. Because of this, we can beseech people everywhere to be reconciled to God. Those who fail to hear or to receive this message will go to hell. As we present the gospel everywhere, God will work according to His sovereign purpose in the hearts of all who hear it (Luke 24:47; Mark 16:15; Acts 18:9–11).

Seven: In summary, it can be said that the Lord's atoning work was unlimited in its value, for He died for all people. However, in the divine application of this value, His atoning work is limited to those who believe the gospel. Jesus did not actually pay the debt of humanity's sins while He was on the cross. By His death, He secured a value that is now offered through the gospel and that is divinely applied to all who trust the Savior for their salvation at the time they believe the gospel. Those who do not receive the Savior must themselves forever pay in hell the debt of their sins.

The Blood of Christ

Jesus' *blood* is a common topic in the New Testament. In its biblical usage, it has both literal and figurative meanings. Literally, it is that which flowed from His body in Gethsemane (Luke 22:44) and after His death (John 19:34). Figuratively, His "blood" represents His atoning work. Let us examine this topic further.

1. Its necessity

The shedding of blood and its being offered on an altar (Lev. 17:11), a ritual representing life given in death, was God's arrangement for atoning for people's sins.[39] He ordained this when He clothed sinful Adam and Eve (Gen. 3:21); He honored this when He accepted Abel's offering (Gen. 4:4; Heb. 11:4); and He stated this in the Mosaic Law (Lev. 17:11; Heb. 9:22). Although these animal blood sacrifices could not take away sins (Heb. 10:4, 11) or purge the conscience of guilt (Heb. 9:9; 10:1–3), they pointed to the coming Lamb of God who, by His sacrifice, would provisionally take away the sins of the world (John 1:29; Heb. 9:14, 23–26; 10:5; 1 John 3:5; see in this chapter, "The Nature of Jesus' Atoning Work").

2. Its purpose

Since the wages of sin is death (Gen. 2:17; Rom. 6:23), it may be that God required bloodshedding for two reasons: *One,* for making certain that the sacrificial victim had died. The shedding of our Lord's blood after His death assured His physical death (John 19:34). Were it not for this precaution, some might argue that He did not really die and thus His atoning work was not completed. *Two,* being the vehicle of the soul, which has the animating force of the body, the blood was the material means by which intangible life could be offered in sacrifice on an altar (Lev. 17:11).[40] The sacrifice's life, which was resident in its blood, could be offered only as this blood was shed, caught in a basin, and poured out at the base of or sprinkled upon the altar, as the offering required (Lev. 4:7).

3. Its significance

Throughout the Bible, the shedding of blood is a symbol of violent death.[41] Jacob understood this when he saw Joseph's gory coat (Gen. 37:33). A murderer was said to have upon him the blood of the person whom he killed (2 Sam. 1:16; cp. Matt. 27:24–25). Stephen's death was described as his blood being shed (Acts 22:20). When murder provoked vengeance, the one who retaliated was an avenger of blood (Num. 35:19). If death was the result of a person's own folly, his blood was said to be upon his own head (Josh. 2:19).

With the exception of two references to bloodshedding (Luke 22:44; John 19:34), of five references to blood's being used as a sign of violent death (Matt. 27:4, 6, 24–25; Acts 5:28), and of one reference to blood as a part of His unglorified human nature (Heb. 2:14), all the remaining thirty-three NT "blood" references are to Jesus' blood[42] and are to be understood as having figurative meaning for His atoning work (cp. Rom. 5:9).[43]

As we have seen, the atonement process required the ritual of shedding blood and offering it on an altar (Lev. 17:11; Heb. 9:22). Bloodshedding was also the means by which the sacrificial animal died (Lev. 1:5). In the case of Jesus, the shedding of His blood did not bring about His death (John 10:18), but it did assure His death and the fulfillment the OT typology as seen in the animal sacrifices. Jesus' bloodshedding was by man; its being offered in atonement was by God the Father, who by this was propitiated (Rom. 3:25).[44]

An example of Jesus' blood's being interpreted figuratively is the words, "The blood of Jesus Christ, His Son, cleanses us from all sin" (1 John 1:7). The apostle John is not speaking about the physical application of Jesus' blood. Rather, he is speaking about the divine application of the value of Jesus' atoning work, which was accomplished by His substitutionary death and the offering of His blood (cp. John 6:53–56).

4. *Its divine application*

The importance of our Lord's blood, as figuratively representing His atoning sacrifice, is seen in its divine application to gospel believers at their salvation and during their Christian lifetime.

a. *At salvation*

Upon trusting in Jesus as Savior and receiving the divine application of the value of Jesus' atoning work, as represented by His "blood," the gospel believer is judicially forgiven of all his or her sins (Eph. 1:7; Rev. 1:5), cleansed of sin's defilement (Heb. 9:14), redeemed (Eph. 1:7; 1 Peter 1:19), purchased (Acts 20:28), given spiritual life (John 6:53), reconciled to God (Col. 1:20), sanctified (Heb. 13:12), made near to God (Eph. 2:13), and made a recipient of the salvational promises of the new covenant, which Jesus mediated by His atoning sacrifice ("blood," Luke 22:20; 1 Cor. 11:25; Heb. 12:24; 13:20; 1 Peter 1:2).

b. *During our Christian lifetime*

Because of Jesus' "blood," or atoning sacrifice, we who are saved have an approach unto God (Heb. 10:19), and we experience divine parental forgiveness (1 John 1:7, 9), spiritual renewal (John 6:54–56), fellowship with Jesus and His people (1 Cor. 10:16), and victory over our spiritual enemies (Rev. 12:11).

We thank God for the blood of His Son and for what it means. However, let us avoid thinking of His literal blood as being divinely applied to our spiritual needs or using the word *blood* as a magical means by which we can effectively command and dispel our spiritual adversaries. At salvation we were delivered from the authority of our spiritual enemies by our Lord's blood (atoning work), and now we can experience daily victory through His blood by acknowledging His purchasing us, submitting to His authority, resisting in His name, and doing His will in His strength (James 4:7; Gal. 5:16).

The Atonement and Physical Healing

1. *The question*

Does our Lord's atonement provide for physical healing today?[45] Some believe that as we can trust Jesus for salvation so we can trust Him for physical healing with the confidence that He will always heal a sick body. This belief is based on the erroneous view that our Lord made atonement for our diseases as well as for our sins and that our bodies are now redeemed. If true, then a gospel believer should never be sick. Should one suffer from some disease or illness, so the theory goes, it is because one has failed to appropriate fully the benefits of the Atonement through faith, or is guilty of some personal sin, for which sickness is a divine judgment. This theory holds that it is always God's will to heal, at least until one reaches seventy years (Ps. 90:10), if one deals with one's sins and believes in Jesus' atoning work. Advocates of this view look to Isaiah 53:4–5 and James 5:14–15 for their support.

2. *The answer*

One: I believe that this theory, as given above, is unbiblical, for Isaiah 53:4–5 represents a double prophetic outlook: *(a),* this prophecy refers to our Lord's healing sick people during His ministry to Israel before and apart from His atoning work (cp. v. 4 with Matt. 8:17). And *(b),* this prophecy refers to the atonement of sin (cp. v. 5 with 1 Peter 2:24). Observe that the words "with His stripes we are healed" refer to spiritual healing (Pss. 41:4; 103:3; 147:3).

Two: Another reason for rejecting this theory is that, while He was on the cross, Jesus bore the judicial penalty of our sins, which is death. He did not bear the natural consequences, such as disease (Rom. 6:23; 5:8). In this regard, A. J. McClain wrote,

> Sickness is not sin; it is rather the result of sin. We punish men for sinning, but not for getting sick. . . . Christ died for our sins, not for our diseases. He was made sin for us; He was not made disease for us. Christ never forgave disease; He forgave sin and healed diseases. Death is the divine penalty for sin, not for disease. Therefore, the death of Christ as our Substitute was penal, not pathological.[46]

Three: James 5:14–15, which directs sick people to call for the elders of the church for their anointing and prayers, does not guarantee recovery. It gives the ritual of committing the sick person to God for healing according to the divine will. God gives the prayer of faith when it is His intention to heal. Should He not give this assurance of divine healing, then one must pray that God's will be done.

Four: The theory that healing is in the Atonement and our bodies are now redeemed conflicts with the biblical portrayal of them as still being unredeemed and mortal, or subject to death (Rom. 8:10–11, 23). Since redemption concerns the total person, we who are saved will experience the redemption of the body (its deliverance from inherent corruption, sin, and death) when Jesus comes for His Church (Rom. 8:11; Phil. 3:20–21; Rom. 13:11; 1 Cor. 15:50–57).

Five: If we can be healed at any time by exercising faith, it is strange that the apostle Paul did not receive healing in answer to his prayers (2 Cor. 12:7–10). He also advised Timothy to take medication for his infirmities (1 Tim. 5:23).

Six: This theory ignores the fact that sickness serves divine purposes for the Lord's people. It may be for divine parental chastisement (1 Cor. 11:30–32), spiritual productivity (2 Cor. 12:9–10), or solely the glory of God (John 9:3).

HIS EXALTATION

The Lord Jesus anticipated His being glorified as man (John 7:39; 12:16; 13:31; 17:5). With His death's ending His humiliation, there were no more indignities done to Him or to His body. Ordinarily, the bodies of crucified persons were left on their crosses as an impressive warning against crime, or they were cast unto a refuse dump. But God overruled all this by leading Joseph of Arimathea to remove Jesus' body from the cross and to place it in his new, unused tomb (Luke 23:50–53).

Theologically, the burial of Jesus' body was proof of His death and a prerequisite to His resurrection. Upon His death Jesus' personhood and immaterial human nature (soul and spirit) went directly to the Paradise region of hades to await the time of His resurrection (Matt. 12:40; Luke 23:43; Acts 2:31; Rom. 10:7; see Addendum: "Sheol, Hades"). While there, Jesus made an announcement of undisclosed content to the imprisoned fallen angels who had sinned in the days of Noah (1 Peter 3:19–20; Gen. 6:1–13).[47] Meanwhile, His sinless, entombed body, unlike that of His friend Lazarus (John 11:39), did not deteriorate (Acts 2:27; 13:37).

Having completed the divine purpose for His condescension and humiliation, our Lord as man was exalted to the supreme majesty by the Father (Phil. 2:9–11; cp. Heb. 2:9). This exaltation was a partial reversal of His condescension (He still remained a man), with the restoration of His radiant preincarnate glory (John 17:1, 5; Matt. 17:1–2; Acts 26:13). Moreover, as man He was exalted above all personal creatures and things (Eph. 1:20–22; Phil. 2:9–11; 1 Peter 3:22; cp. Heb. 2:9, 16). Being delivered from the humiliation of His death by the burial and resurrection of His body, Jesus is now released from the limitations of an unglorified body and will forever possess His resurrected body with its new life and powers (Rom. 8:11; John 20:26; cp. 1 Cor. 15:42–49). However, being the Father's anointed Slave, He will as man remain in subjection to God the Father forever (1 Cor. 15:28).

Our Lord's exaltation includes His resurrection, ascension, enthronement, and second coming to earth. Let us look at these components.

Jesus' Resurrection from the Dead

The Lord Jesus predicted His resurrection (Matt. 16:21; 17:9, 23; 20:19; John 2:19; 10:18; cp. Isa. 53:10–11).

1. A description of His resurrection

Jesus' resurrection consisted of the reunion of His personhood and the immaterial parts of His human nature with His body, which was changed and made alive by the Holy Spirit (Rom. 8:11), and His physically rising from the grave, never to die again (Luke 24:5–6; Acts 2:24, 32; 26:23; Rev. 1:18).

2. Several features of His resurrection

a. It was a divine resurrection.

While Jesus' resurrection was a human experience, it came about by the combined activity of the divine Trinity (Gal. 1:1; John 2:19; 10:18; Rom. 8:11).

b. It was a physical resurrection (Luke 24:36–40; 1 Cor. 15:3–4).

The burial of our Lord's body shows the reality of His physical death and resurrection, for only the bodies of the dead are buried, not their personhood, soul, and spirit. Again, resurrection consists of the body's being changed and made alive for the eternal state and the reunion of one's personhood, soul, and spirit with one's body. Jesus demonstrated that His resurrection was physical by showing His disciples His hands and feet (Luke 24:39; 1 John 1:1), by eating before them (Luke 24:41–43) and with them (Acts 10:41), and by "many infallible proofs" (Acts 1:3).[48]

c. It was a unique resurrection (1 Cor. 15:23; Rev. 1:18).

The Lord Jesus was the first to be restored to physical life with a reconstituted physical body, never to die again (Acts 26:23; Rom. 6:9; Rev. 1:18). Others had been restored to natural life (2 Kings 4:32–37; Mark 5:35–43), but these restorations were only reanimations. These people died again, for Satan, who had the power of death, had not yet been conquered (Heb. 2:14). As a kind of "first fruits" (1 Cor. 15:23), Jesus' resurrection was the first unto everlasting physical duration, and it was the pledge of the resurrection of His people.

3. The importance of Jesus' resurrection

Together with His atoning sacrifice, our Lord's resurrection is the keystone of the Christian faith. Consider the following:

a. Its importance to Himself

One: Jesus' resurrection was the seal of the Father's satisfaction with His life and atoning work (Acts 2:22–24). If this were not true, He would not have risen from the dead.

Two: Jesus' resurrection was the mark of His divine Sonship (Rom. 1:4) and his human messiahship (Acts 2:36). It was His greatest messianic sign to Israel (John 2:18–21; cp. Matt. 12:38–40).

Three: Jesus' resurrection reconstituted His body for everlasting existence (Acts 2:31; cp. 1 Cor. 15:44–45). Vitalized by the Holy Spirit (Rom. 8:11; 1 Cor. 15:45), His resurrected body was prepared for the laws and conditions of life in heaven and in the eternal state. For instance, His resurrected body manifested powers that it did not have before His death, like the ability to appear and disappear at will (Luke 24:15–16) and to enter closed rooms without difficulty (Luke 24:36; John 20:19). With His resurrection, Jesus will forever possess His complete human nature and be the God-man (1 Tim. 2:5).

Four: Jesus' resurrection made possible His future messianic work, like His building the Church and His millennial earthly rule (Matt. 16:18; Rev. 19:11–16).

b. Its importance to His people

One: Jesus' resurrection gave value and force to His atoning work on the cross (1 Cor. 15:14–20). It was the essential complement to His atoning death. If He had not risen, then His death would be of no value in saving sinners, and the gospel would be ineffective. A savior still dead cannot save. But He did rise, and by this He activated all that He died to achieve, including the new covenant (cp. Heb. 8:6–13; 13:20). For instance, His death laid the basis for justification by dealing with humanity's sins, and His resurrection made it actual for all who believe the gospel (Rom. 4:25; cp. 1 Peter 3:21).

Two: Jesus' resurrection made it possible for Him to give His people new spiritual life and power, by which they can live and serve with Him (John 14:19–20; Rom. 6:4; 8:2; Gal. 2:20; Eph. 1:18–20; Phil. 4:13).

Three: Jesus' resurrection gave His people a living hope (1 Peter 1:3, 13; Titus 2:13), which includes the expectation of His imminent return for His Church and the blessed events that are associated with His coming (cp. 1 Thess. 4:13–17; 1 Peter 1:3–5; Titus 1:2; see "The Prophecy of Jesus' Return for His Church" under Eschatology).

Four: Jesus' resurrection guaranteed the resurrection of His people (see "The Resurrection of Mankind" under Anthropology).[49] This is because His resurrection was the first fruits of all resurrections (1 Cor. 15:20–23), and the resurrecting Holy Spirit now indwells His people (Rom. 8:11). Earlier resurrections were reanimations of bodies, which in time died again.

Five: Jesus' resurrection made possible His present work on behalf of His people. This includes His building the Church (Matt. 16:18), His preparing a home for His people (John 14:2–3), His interceding for them (Heb. 7:25), His teaching them (Eph. 4:20–21), and His ruling over them (Col. 1:13).

Six: Jesus' resurrected body is the prototype for the changed bodies of His people (Phil. 3:21; Rom. 8:11). The bodies of the Lord's people will be delivered from their inherent corruption and mortality and will be changed to His kind of glorified, incorruptible body (1 Cor. 15:42–53). Like His resurrection, this change will prepare them physically for the eternal state (see "The Resurrection of Mankind" under Anthropology).

c. Its importance to His enemies

One: Jesus' resurrection gave Him final victory over His enemies, both human and angelic. The world crucified Him with the intention of removing Him forever from their midst (Ps. 2:1–3; Acts 2:23), but God raised Him up (Acts 2:24; 5:30) and gave Him the power to destroy those who destroy the earth (Rev. 11:15–18; 19:11–21; Ps. 2:4–12; Col. 2:12, 15). Before Jesus' resurrection, Satan had the power of death (Heb. 2:14) in that he inflicted death (Job 1:12–19), and he ruled the sphere in which the unsaved abide (Acts 26:18; 1 John 5:19). By His unique physical death, Jesus aggressively invaded death's domain; by His resurrection, He broke death's power, including Satan's grip on mankind, and became the Warden of death and hades (Acts 2:24; Heb. 2:14; Rev. 1:18). Although Satan continues to hold the unsaved in death's power and by divine permission can still inflict death on rebellious gospel believers (1 Cor. 5:5), this is only temporary, for the Lord will restore all people to physical life (John 5:28–29). Upon His return for the Church and His second coming to rule, He will deliver His people from physical death (1 Cor. 15:51–57; 1 Thess. 4:16; Rev. 20:4, 6). After His millennial earthly rule, He will raise the unsaved to their judgment and final doom (1 Cor. 15:25–26; Rev. 20:10, 13–15).

Two: By His defeating the power of death by His resurrection, our Lord also conquered the power of sin, the impersonal producer of death (Rom. 8:3, 6, 10, 13, "flesh" is the sin force; 1 Cor. 15:54–57). This victory is now realized in the lives of His people, who, accounting themselves to be dead to sin and alive unto God, give themselves to God, obey Him, and express His spiritual life in their behavior (Rom. 6:1–13; Gal. 5:16, 22–23, 25; 6:7–8). They will forever be divested of the resident sin force when their bodies are delivered from hereditary corruption and are made like Jesus' body of glory (1 Cor. 15:50–57; Phil. 3:20–21).

Three: The Lord's resurrection guarantees the resurrection and judgment of the unsaved (John 5:28–29; Acts 17:31). Their judgment is certain, for the Judge is alive and Satan, their leader, has been judged (John 16:11) and will eventually be cast into hell (Rev. 20:10). The apostle Paul preached this truth to pagans (Acts 17:18, 31).

d. Its importance to His new world order

Our Lord's resurrection will allow Him to fulfill the divine predictions about the new world order that He will establish when He returns and rules over the earth (Ps. 2:6–9; Matt. 19:28; Acts 3:19–21; cp. Isa. 11:1–9; Rev. 11:15; 19:11–16, 19). Satan seized dominion over the earth from Adam by leading him through Eve to sin (Gen. 1:26; 3:1–6; John 16:11; Heb. 2:5–9). Having broken the Devil's power (John 12:31; Heb. 2:14; Col. 2:15), the Lord Jesus will cast out the adversary when He returns to rule over the earth (Rev. 19:11–16; 20:1–3).

e. Its importance to salvational faith

Belief in our Lord's resurrection is an essential part of salvational faith (Rom. 10:9), for His rising again made His atoning work effective. The apostle Paul argued that if Christ did not rise, then gospel preaching and faith would be empty, or without content (1 Cor. 15:14–15, KJV "vain," Gk. *kenon*), and ineffective (vv. 16–19, KJV "vain," Gk. *mataia*). Because of the futility of faith in a savior still dead, they who have trusted in Jesus would still be in their sins (v. 17) and those who have died in Christ would have perished (v. 18). There would be no savior from sin if Jesus did not rise from the dead. But since He did rise from the dead, the gospel is true and the Atonement, of which it speaks, is effective toward all who trust in the living Savior and His atoning sacrifice (v. 20). The apostles' preaching emphasized the Lord's resurrection as well as His atoning death (Acts 2:24–33; 3:15; 4:33; 5:30; 10:40–41; 13:30; 17:3, 18, 31; 28:31). No one who rejects the truth of Jesus' physical resurrection is saved, for a savior still dead is no savior at all.

Jesus' Ascension into Heaven

1. A description of His ascension

Forty days after His resurrection the Lord Jesus as man departed physically and visibly from the earth and was immediately received into heaven (Mark 16:19–20; Luke 24:50–53; Acts 1:6–12; 1 Tim. 3:16).

2. Several features of His ascension

One: Like His resurrection, the Lord's ascension was a human experience that transferred His human residence from earth to heaven (Heb.1:3; 4:14–15). However, as God, He is everywhere present on earth as well as throughout the universe (Matt. 28:20; John 3:13).

Two: Jesus' ascension was not merely a physical disappearance or a changed physical state but an actual physical passing from earth to heaven, where He was received by the Father (Acts 1:9; see v. 11; 2:33; 3:21; 7:55–56; Rom. 8:34; Eph. 1:20; Phil. 3:20; 1 Thess. 1:10; 4:16; 1 Tim. 3:16; Heb. 8:1; 9:24; 10:12; 12:2; Rev. 5:5–12; 19:11).

Three: He ascended forty days after His resurrection (Acts 1:3–9). Some teach that He also ascended to heaven and returned to earth on His resurrection day, as implied in John 20:17 and Hebrews 9:6–12. Support for this view is the typology of the high priest's entering the Holy of Holies on Atonement Day and his sprinkling the sacrificial blood upon the mercy seat (Lev. 16:14). It is argued that, in a similar way, Jesus went to heaven and presented the blood of His sacrifice before the Father.

If this were true, how could He say that His work was finished while He was still on the cross (John 19:30)? We read that He entered into the Holy Place (heaven) "through" or "by way of " His blood, representing His atoning work, not "with" it (Heb. 9:12, Gk. *dia*). The cross was the altar where God the Father poured out His wrath upon His Son, the Sin-bearer (Isa. 53:10; Matt. 27:46). I believe that His shed blood went into the ground. The Lord's words to Mary Magdalene (John 20:17) can be translated, "Stop clinging to Me." Her spontaneous action was improper and stood in contrast to that of the other women who worshiped at Jesus' feet (Matt. 28:9). In His exalted state, the Lord no longer has the same relation with His people as He did when He was with them during His earthly ministry (cp. John 14:20).[50]

3. The importance of Jesus' ascension

One: It marked the end of His first advent and earthly mission (John 17:4). He had accomplished all that He came to do.

Two: It made possible His present messianic, human work in heaven. This includes His building the Church through His people on earth (Matt. 16:18; 1 Cor. 6:15; 12:27; Eph. 4:11–12), His governing the Church (Eph. 1:22), His preparing a place for His people (John 14:2), His being their intercessor and advocate (Heb. 7:25; 1 John 2:1), and His communicating His spiritual life to His people through the indwelling Holy Spirit (John 14:6; Col. 3:4; Rom. 8:2; see "The Nature of the Christian Life" under Zoeology).

Three: It allowed the localized Christ as man to become universal in the lives and ministries of His people (John 14:20). He does this through a union with His people that is effected by the baptism with and indwelling of the Holy Spirit (Gal. 3:27; John 14:16–18). Because the bodies of His people on earth are His members through which He works (1 Cor. 6:15), the Lord Jesus as man can build His Church on earth while He Himself is seated at the Father's right hand in heaven.

Four: It allows the Holy Spirit to perform His work during this age (John 16:7). This includes the giving of NT revelation (John 16:12–13) as well as convicting, regenerating, baptizing, anointing, and indwelling gospel believers (John 3:3–6; 16:8–11; Acts 1:5, 8; John 14:16; 16:13).

Jesus' Enthronement at the Father's Right Hand

1. A description of His enthronement

Upon His return to heaven, the Lord Jesus as man was given the position of highest rank at the Father's right hand, far above all created beings and things and their authorities (Acts 2:33; Heb. 1:3; 2:9; Rom. 14:9).

2. Features of His enthronement

One: This exalted position concerns Jesus as man, not as God. When He took upon Himself the nature of man, God the Son in His humanity assumed a position lower than His servants, the holy angels (Heb. 2:9, 16 with 6–7). With His enthronement at the Father's right hand, the Lord Jesus was exalted to the highest position, far above all angelic and human beings and their authorities (Eph. 1:20–22; Col. 2:10; 1 Peter 3:22). With this exaltation, Jesus was elevated in His humanity to be Lord of all (Acts 2:36; 10:36; Phil. 2:9–11).

Two: Although He is so exalted, the Lord Jesus as man remains the Father's Slave forever, in keeping with His continuing office as the Messiah (1 Cor. 15:28).

3. The importance of His enthronement

One: Jesus' enthronement marked the completion of His glorification as man. This glorification consists of His continuing *moral glory* (John 1:14), His resurrection *physical glory* (Phil. 3:21; Acts 26:13), and His *achievement glory*. This last glory includes His being the Mediator of the new covenant (Heb. 12:24), the Redeemer of God's people (Rev. 5:5–10), the Builder of the Church (Matt. 16:18), and the Warden of death and hades (Rev. 1:18). In addition to these glories He also has a *positional glory* since He occupies the place of supreme authority, far above all created persons, creatures, and things (Eph. 1:20–22; Phil. 2:9–11; 1 Peter 3:22). In His humanity, He is now "Lord of all" (Acts 10:36) and is worthy of the highest honor (John 5:23; Phil. 2:10–11; Rev. 5:8–14).

Two: The Church, the Lord's bride, will share in these glories (John 17:22, 24; Eph. 2:6), including the achievement glory of working with Him in building His Church (cp. Phil. 3:20–21; Eph. 2:6; 5:27; 1 Thess. 2: 19–20; 2 Thess. 1:11–12). However, He alone will receive the honors that are due Him for His salvational work and His universal authority over all persons and things, including the Church (Eph. 4:15; 5:23–24).

Jesus' Second Coming to Earth

Unlike His first coming to earth, the Lord Jesus' second coming and earthly, millennial rule, marking the final phase of His exaltation, will be with power and great glory (Matt. 24:30; 26:64; 2 Thess. 1:7–10; Rev. 19:11–16). As the earth was the scene of His great humiliation so will it be that of His triumphant exaltation. Being the Last Adam, He will come as "the Lion of the Tribe of Judah" (Rev. 5:5) and as "the King of kings and Lord of lords" (19:16) to destroy His enemies and to rule over His people. He will achieve what the first Adam failed to do (Heb. 2:5–9) and will carry out the divine covenantal promises to His people (Rev. 19:11–20:3; see Gen. 12:3; Deut. 30:3–5; 2 Sam. 7:16; Ezek. 36; Rom. 11:26–27). His house will be exalted above all others (Isa. 2:2), and His rule will be without parallel in human history (Isa. 11:1–9). All this, as well as the other aspects of His exaltation, will glorify God the Father (Phil. 2:11; John 12:28; 13:31; 17:1).

THE MESSIANIC WORK OF JESUS

Our understanding of Jesus' life and work as man rests upon our grasping the meaning of His being the Messiah, or the Christ. As we examine this truth, let us look to the Holy Spirit to illuminate and to bless our hearts.

HIS BEING THE MESSIAH

As an official title of Jesus (Matt. 1:1; Luke 2:11), the word *Christ* (Gk.), or *Messiah* (Heb.), means "Anointed One." This points to the OT practice of anointing with oil prophets (1 Kings 19:16), priests (Exod. 29:7; Lev. 8:12), and kings (1 Sam. 9:21–10:1). This action represented God's consecration of a person or thing to His service (Exod. 28:41; 40:9–15; Lev. 8:10–12).

The Occasion of Jesus' Anointing

God the Father anointed Jesus with the Holy Spirit (Acts 4:27) when, at the age of thirty, He was baptized (immersed in water) by John the Baptizer (Matt. 3:13–17). Upon Jesus' baptism, the invisible Holy Spirit descended upon Him in the visible form of a dove (v. 16). By this theophany John recognized that Jesus was the Messiah of OT prophecy (John 1:29–34; cp. Isa. 42:1–7; 61:1–2). Jesus' submission to baptism and His praying (Luke 3:21) represented His complete surrender to this anointing by the Holy Spirit and to all that it meant. God the Father responded to this event by expressing His satisfaction with Jesus (Matt. 3:17), whom He had chosen to be the Anointed One (Isa. 42:1; 1 Peter 2:4). His words imply that He was pleased with Jesus' earthly life up to this time and with the Lord's first act of obedience relating to His messiahship. Our Lord's baptism marked the end of His secular life as a carpenter, or woodworker (Mark 6:3), and the beginning of the spiritual work that He came to do as the Father's Anointed One.

The Medium of Jesus' Anointing

Unlike those who were previously anointed, Jesus gave Himself not to anointing oil but to baptismal water, another symbol of the Holy Spirit (John 7:37–39). The mass of water in which He was immersed (Matt. 3:16) portrayed the unlimited fullness of the Holy Spirit, which He then received and by which He would carry out His messianic functions (John 3:34; Acts 10:38). Thus the Father was the Anointer of Jesus (Isa. 61:1; Acts 4:27); Jesus was the Anointed One; and the Holy Spirit was the Anointing Agent, in whose power Jesus would forever carry out all His messianic functions as man.

The Meaning of Jesus' Anointing

We learn the meaning of Jesus' anointing from Samuel's anointing David to be the king of Israel (1 Sam. 16:1, 13). This divine anointing signified two things:

1. The divine appointment to an office or work (1 Sam. 16:1)

David's anointing indicated his divine appointment as king of Israel. We also see this meaning of appointment to office in the anointing of the priests of Israel, who by this rite were consecrated to their priestly service (Exod. 28:4; 40:9–15; Lev. 8:10–12).

In Jesus' case, He was appointed to the office of being the Father's Servant, or Slave (Isa. 42:1; 52:13; 53:11; Phil. 2:7–8). This was for the purpose of His carrying out the Father's will during the unending course of His human life and ministry (Isa. 49:1–10; 61:1–2; John 6:38; 8:28–29). As the Father's Slave, He does all His messianic works in union with the Father (John 14:8–11) with identical mind and purpose (John 10:30, Gk. "one thing" not "one person").

When He came into the world, Jesus had already been divinely consecrated to His messianic mission (John 10:36) and had committed Himself to this work (Heb. 10:5–7). Also, as a child He was aware of His messianic mission (Luke 2:49). However, the events that accompanied His baptism marked His divine anointing and the beginning of His messianic work (Matt. 3:16–17).

2. *The reception of the Holy Spirit for His help with this work (1 Sam. 16:13)*

Upon his being anointed with oil, David received the Holy Spirit, who enabled him to fulfill the duties of his office as king of Israel (v. 13). After his sin with Bathsheba, David prayed that he would not lose this anointing as Saul had lost his (Ps. 51:11; 1 Sam. 16:14).

With His baptism, Jesus permanently received the Holy Spirit (John 1:32), who would forever empower Him for His messianic works as the Father's Slave (Isa. 42:1–7; 61:1–2; Luke 4:1, 14; Matt. 12:28; Acts 10:38). Although Jesus is still God and equal to the Father and to the Holy Spirit in every way, in His humanity the Lord will forever be subordinate to the Father's will and will function as the Father's Slave (John 14:28; 1 Cor. 15:28). He will also forever carry out all His messianic duties in the Holy Spirit's power (John 3:34). His divine works, like upholding the universe (Heb. 1:3; Col. 1:17), are not messianic in nature.

HIS WORK AS THE MESSIAH

Jesus began His messianic career as the Father's Slave after His baptism and anointing. Because His humanity will continue forever, Jesus' messianic career will continue forever (Ps. 110:4; Luke 1:33). The nature of His messianic works is indicated by the functions of those people who were anointed in OT times—the prophet (1 Kings 19:16), the high priest (Exod. 29:7), and the king (1 Sam. 10:1). The details of these messianic works are given in OT prophecy like Isaiah 2:1–5; 11; 42:1–7; 49:1–12; 50:4–9; 52:13–53:12; and 61:1–3.

In His messianic office as the Father's anointed Slave, the Lord Jesus is carrying out the Father's will in the roles of prophet, high priest, and king. Although the Lord has other messianic functions, like those of Savior and Intercessor (Matt. 1:21; Heb. 7:25), these appear to relate to His continuous primary roles of prophet, high priest, and king.

The great prophetic statement of a goal of His messianic commission is given in Isaiah 49:5–6, namely, to restore Israel to God (vv. 5–6a) and to be a light to the Gentiles (v. 6b), all being accomplished in the salvation of these peoples (Isa. 46:13; 49:6; 62:11; cp. Matt. 1:21; Luke 1:69–79; 2:28–30). However, to achieve this, He must first die for their sins (Isa. 52:13–53:12) and evangelize them with the gospel (Isa. 52:6–7; Rom. 10:4–15). Keep in mind that these messianic works relate specifically to His human ministry, which He carries out in the power of the Holy Spirit (Matt. 12:28; Luke 4:1, 14; Acts 10:38).

The Functions of Jesus' Messianic Office

1. *Jesus' functions as prophet (Deut. 18:18; John 7:40; Heb. 1:1–2)*

A prophet was God's spokesman. Under the control of the Holy Spirit, he spoke or wrote God's words (2 Sam. 23:2; 2 Peter 1:21). As the Prophet foreseen by Moses, Jesus speaks the words of God the Father (Deut. 18:15, 18; John 12:49–50).

One: During His first coming to earth, Jesus spoke the Father's words in His teaching and preaching ministries (John 3:34; 7:16–18; 8:28; 12:49–50; 14:10, 24).

Two: During His absence from earth, Jesus gave his servants the divine revelation that He received from the Father and that they wrote under divine inspiration as the NT Scriptures (John 16:12–15; Rev. 1:1–2).

Three: During His second coming to earth, Jesus will give whatever additional divine revelation needed by the citizens of His millennial kingdom (Isa. 2:1–3; Joel 2:28) besides the written Scriptures that we now have (1 Peter 1:25).

2. *Jesus' functions as high priest (Ps. 110:4; Heb. 4:14; 5:5–6)*

During OT times the high priests of Israel were mediators between God and His people. They taught the people God's Law (Deut. 33:8–10), offered sacrifices like those on the Day of Atonement (Lev. 16:3–16), and made intercessory prayers for God's people (Exod. 28:29–30; 1 Sam. 12:23).

One: During His first coming, Jesus taught the people and His disciples (Matt. 5:1–2; Mark 1:21–22; Luke 19:47), prayed for His people (Luke 22:31–32; John 17:9–24), gave Himself for humanity's sins (Matt. 20:28; Heb. 9:14), and mediated the new covenant (Heb. 8:6–13; 12:24).[51]

Two: During His absence from earth, Jesus is saving all who trust in Him (John 6:33, 35), teaching His people through the Scriptures (Eph. 4:20–21) and by the Holy Spirit (1 John 2:27), providing access to God for His people (Heb. 4:14–16; 10:19–22), praying for them (7:25; Rom. 8:34), and representing them as their Advocate (1 John 2:1). Also, during the present age He is building His Church both quantitatively and qualitatively (Matt. 16:18; Acts 16:5) and is preparing a place for her (John 14:2).

Three: During His second coming to earth, Jesus will continue His priestly work throughout His millennial rule (Ps. 110:4; Zech. 6:12–13; Heb. 5:6; 7:24–25).

3. *Jesus' functions as king (Isa. 9:6–7; Luke 1:32–33; Matt. 2:1–11)*

With the executive, legislative, and judicial branches of government united in Him, Jesus' regal functions are to judge (John 5:22) and to rule (Rev. 19:15).

One: During His first coming to earth, Jesus did not exercise political authority (John 3:17; 18:36–37). However, having received the title to all things (John 3:35; 13:3), He did as man exercise authority over nature (Mark 4:41) and fallen angels (demons and Satan; Mark 1:23–26; Matt. 4:10–11). He also commanded men to follow Him (Mark 1:17).

Two: During His absence from the earth, as the Head of the Church, He is the king of gospel believers (Eph. 4:15–16; 5:23), their judge (2 Tim. 4:7–8), and their deliverer from their spiritual enemies, including sin and its effects (Matt. 1:21; Col. 1:13; John 15:19). As man He has been exalted over all things, including angels and humans (Matt. 28:20; 1 Peter 3:22; Eph. 1:20–23; 1 Tim. 6:14–15; see in this chapter, "His Exaltation").

Three: During His second coming to earth, He will as the Last Adam evict Satan, destroy His enemies, appraise the lives of all earth dwellers, and rule as absolute Sovereign over Israel and the earth as the viceroy of God the Father (Heb. 2:5–9; John 5:21–29; Rev. 19:11–20:4; 22:12; Matt. 25:31–46; Ps. 72:8–11; Jer. 23:5; Zech. 14:9; see "The Prophecy of Jesus' Second Coming to Earth" and "The Prophecy of the Messianic Millennial Kingdom" under Eschatology).

Several Observations

One: All of Jesus' human works are messianic, done in the power of the Holy Spirit (Acts 10:38). His divine works as God are not messianic works.

Two: All of Jesus' messianic works are done in such a way that allows the Father to do them through Him (John 5:17; 12:49–50; 14:10–11). Jesus never acts independently of the Father (5:19, 30; 8:28).

Three: There are two aspects of our Lord's messianic work as the savior, or deliverer, of His people (Luke 2:11): *(a),* His priestly work of offering Himself as the atoning sacrifice for their sins (Isa. 53:5, 10; Matt. 1:21; Heb. 7:27) and of applying its value to gospel believers at their salvation (Heb. 9:14; Col. 1:14); and *(b),* His regal work of being His people's Lord (1 Cor. 6:20; Rom. 14:8–9) and of delivering them from their spiritual enemies, including the power of sin and death (Isa. 61:1–3; Rom. 6:17–22; 13:14; Col. 1:13; James 4:7; Heb. 2:15; Rev. 1:18; 1 Cor. 15:57).

Four: Being humanly alive forever (1 Cor. 15:20), the Lord Jesus will always have messianic duties to fulfill in future programs that the Father will have for Him throughout eternity (cp. Eph. 2:7; Ps. 110:4; Luke 1:33). Like today, we who are His purchased slaves (1 Cor. 6:20; Rom. 14:8) will assist Him in these programs (Heb. 9:14; 1 Cor. 3:9; Rom. 6:15–22).

Five: In all His messianic works, it is our Lord's supreme purpose to glorify the Father (John 12:28; 17:4; see "The Prophecy of the Messianic Millennial Kingdom: The Objectives of the Messianic Kingdom" under Eschatology).

We who are saved were anointed by God at salvation (2 Cor. 1:21). At that time we received the Holy Spirit, who now indwells us (2 Tim. 1:14; 1 John 3:24) as our Helper (John 14:16–17). By this anointing, we were appointed to be the Lord's slaves-friends (John 15:16; Rom. 14:8–9; 1 Cor. 4:1). It is remarkable that we have the same Source of power that Jesus has to guide us and to enable us to do the Lord's will. It is important to keep in mind that as the Lord Jesus allowed the Father to do work through Him so we must allow Jesus to work through us by abiding in Him (John 15:4–5; see "The Fruitfulness of the Christian Life" under Zoeology). It is also important that we learn what His will for us is and do it wholeheartedly to the glory of God (Eph. 2:17; Col. 3:23; 1 Cor. 10:31; see Appendix F: "Learning and Doing God's Will"). Our Lord is our Example as well as our Master in our serving with Him in His work (1 Peter 1:21; Matt. 10:24–25a).

We who are saved do not have to seek the Holy Spirit's anointing, which is erroneously regarded as His baptism or a special work of grace, for we were anointed at salvation (2 Cor. 1:21–22). The Holy Spirit, however, does wait to help us as we submit ourselves to His filling (Eph. 5:18). This filling is not our receiving more of the Holy Spirit but our cooperating with Him in such a way that allows Him to help us to be and to do all that God requires of us who are saved (see "The Holy Spirit's Ministry to Saved People: Throughout the Gospel Believer's Lifetime" under Pneumatology).

THE NAMES OF THE LORD JESUS CHRIST

HIS GENERIC NAMES

Generic names describe one's kind of being. The Lord Jesus is God and man.

God

Having the divine nature, He is called "God" in the Old Testament (Isa. 9:6; 7:14; Ps. 45:6–7) and in the New Testament (Rom. 9:5; 1 Tim. 3:16; Heb. 1:8; 1 John 5:20).

Man

With His incarnation and receiving a human nature, He is called "man" (Acts 17:31; Rom. 5:15; 1 Tim. 2:5). This was predicted in Isaiah 53:3.

Having the divine and the human natures, He is at once both God and man—the God-man.

HIS FUNCTIONAL NAMES

These are titles that relate to His offices and works.

His Old Testament Titles

1. *Those relating to His deity*

"Lord," meaning "My Master" (*Adonai*, Ps. 110:1; cp. Matt. 22:41–45), "Son" (Ps. 2:7), and "Father of eternity" (Isa. 9:6, KJV "Everlasting Father")

2. *Those prophetically relating to His humanity*

"The Branch" (Isa. 11:1; Jer. 33:15), "Counselor" (Isa. 9:6), "Immanuel" (7:14), "King" (Ps. 2:6), "Messiah the Prince" (Dan. 9:25), "Messiah" (v. 26), "Priest" (Ps. 110:4), "Prince of peace" (Isa. 9:6), "the Prophet" (Deut. 18:15, 18), "Redeemer" (Isa. 59:20), "the Seed" (Gen. 3:15; 15:5), "Servant of the LORD" (Isa. 42:1), "Son of man" (Dan. 7:13), "the Stone" (Ps. 118:22), and "Wonderful" (Isa. 9:6)

His New Testament Titles

1. Those relating to His deity

"Lord" (Gk. *Kurios* in Matt. 4:7; Luke 2:11; Rev. 19:6), "Son" (Matt. 3:17; Gal. 4:4), "the Son of God" (Matt. 26:63–65; John 20:31; cp. 5:17–18; 10:33, 36), and "the Word" (John 1:1–3, 14)[52]

2. Those relating to His humanity

"Apostle and High Priest" (Heb. 3:1), "the Beloved" (Eph. 1:6), "the Bread from heaven" (John 6:32), "Christ" meaning "Anointed One" (John 20:31; Acts 2:36), "the Door" (John 10:9), "the Faithful Witness," "the First Begotten of the dead," "the Prince of the kings of the earth" (Rev. 1:5), "the Good Shepherd" (John 10:11), "Judge" (Acts 10:42), "the Image of the invisible God" (Col. 1:15), "the King of kings and the Lord of lords" (Rev. 19:16), "the Lamb of God" (John 1:29), "the Last Adam" (1 Cor. 15:45), "the Light of the world" (John 8:12), "the Lion of the Tribe of Judah" (Rev. 5:5), "Lord" *(Kurios)* referring to His being a master (often in the Gospels: Matt. 8:25; Luke 5:8; John 6:68) or to His human supremacy in authority and power after His return to heaven (Acts 2:36; 10:36; see endnote 52), "Lord" (Gk. *Despotes*) referring to His absolute ownership (2 Peter 2:1; Jude 4), "Master" meaning "Teacher" (Matt. 8:19), "the Resurrection and the Life" (John 11:25), "the Rock" (Matt. 16:18), "Savior" meaning "Deliverer" (Luke 2:11; Phil. 3:20), "the Second Man" (1 Cor. 15:47), "the Son of Man" speaking of His identification with mankind (Mark 10:45), "the True Vine" (John 15:1), "the Way, the Truth, and the Life" (14:6)

HIS PERSONAL NAMES

A personal name is that which distinguishes one from others within a given order or class of beings.

Before His Incarnation

The personal name for God in the Old Testament is "LORD" (*Yahweh*, or Jehovah; Jer. 33:2). This name is attributed to God the Son as in Psalm 2:11–12; Isaiah 2:2–5; 40:3, 10, "God"; and Jeremiah 23:6.

Since His Incarnation

1. His divine personal name

He is called "Lord" in 1 Corinthians 15:47 and in Luke 2:11, which seems to be a reference to the OT divine personal name "LORD," or *Yahweh* (also see Matt. 3:3 with Isa. 40:3). As with the other Persons of the divine Trinity (the Father and the Holy Spirit), the title "Son" in NT usage sometimes is used as a divine personal name, especially when it occurs alone (1 Cor. 15:28; Gal. 4:4, 6; 1 Thess. 1:10). He identified Himself as "I Am" (John 18:4–6).

2. His human personal name

His human personal name is "Jesus," meaning "the LORD *[Yahweh]* is salvation" (Matt. 1:21; Luke 1:31; 2:21).

His full human name is "the Lord Jesus Christ" (1 Thess. 1:1), "Jesus Christ our Lord" (Rom. 5:21), or "Christ Jesus our Lord" (1 Cor. 15:31). While "Jesus" is His human personal name and "Christ" is a human title that speaks of His being the "Anointed One," "Lord" (Gk. *Kurios*) is the human title of His supreme authority over all people and things (Acts 2:36; 10:36; Matt. 28:18).

OUR INTERACTION WITH THE LORD
JESUS CHRIST AS HIS SLAVES-FRIENDS

We who have been born again were at salvation delivered from bondage to our former spiritual enemies (sin, Satan, and the world) and were made permanent slaves of the Lord Jesus, who purchased us with so great a price (1 Cor. 7:22; Eph. 6:6; Matt. 20:28; Acts 20:28; Rom. 1:1; 14:8; 1 Cor. 6:20; 1 Peter 1:18–19). However, this relationship is not a burdensome bondage, for our Master knows what it means to live under the Father's yoke (John 6:38; 8:28–29). Being the Father's Slave (Isa. 42:1–4), He is ready to help us with our load as we daily submit to His leadership (Matt. 11:28–30). In fact, we have been called unto His fellowship (1 Cor. 1:9), for we are His friends as well as His slaves (John 15:15; cp. Matt. 12:47–50), and He loves us very much (John 13:1; 15:9; Gal. 2:20). We experience and cultivate the Lord's fellowship as we do the following:

OUR PRAYING TO HIM (JOHN 14:13)

Our talking to Jesus is necessary for fellowship with Him (Acts 7:59; 1 Cor. 1:2; 2 Cor. 12:8; 2 Tim. 2:22).

We Can Talk to Him About Anything.

We can speak to Him about everything that concerns us as His slaves-friends, like His will for us, our working with Him in building the Church, those evil forces that would hinder us, and our personal needs or desires (Heb. 4:14–16; 12:2; 13:5–6).

We Must Fulfill Certain Conditions.

To receive what we ask for, we must fulfill certain conditions.

One: We must ask in His name (John 14:13). Since His name represents who He is and what He does, to ask in His name is to ask according to His interests, or work, in this world (Matt. 16:18) and in keeping with His objective, which is to glorify the Father (John 12:28).

Two: We must ask according to His will for us (1 John 5:14–15).

Three: We must abide in Him (John 15:7). Our abiding in Him (see below) and having His Word abiding in us and directing our lives (Col. 3:16; Ps. 1:1–3) allow Him to shape our requests and to give us what we ask (Ps. 37:4).

Fellowship with the Lord Jesus requires our talking to Him as well as our allowing Him to talk to us through the Scriptures. Did you talk with Him today about His will for you as His slave-friend?

OUR MINISTERING TO HIS NEEDS (EPH. 1:23)

As Eve completed Adam by satisfying his need for a loving companion and helper (Gen. 2:18–22), so the Lord's people fulfill Him by satisfying His human need for love, fellowship, and help in accomplishing His messianic work in this world. Although the Church, as His wife, will completely fulfill this role in her glorified state, as members of His espoused bride (2 Cor. 11:2) we can now minister to the Lord Jesus as His loving helpers and companions in the following ways:

One, by expressing our love and friendship for Jesus by wholehearted obedience to His will and by walking in His fellowship (John 14:15, 21; cp. 15:14; 1 Cor. 1:9; Luke 17:7–10).

Two, by giving ourselves and our bodies daily to Jesus for His service in this world (Rom. 12:1). We must think of ourselves as Jesus' body on earth (1 Cor. 6:15; Eph. 1:22–23). This concerns our allowing Him to use us in His work of building the Church quantitatively and qualitatively by our being His evangelistic ambassadors to the world (2 Cor. 5:18–20), ministers to His people (Heb. 10:24), and fruitbearers (John 15:1–5).

Three, by keeping ourselves pure for Jesus (2 Cor. 11:1–3; 6:17; 2 Tim. 2:21–22). We do this by resisting sin when we are tempted (James 4:7; Rom. 6:11–13), dealing with it when it occurs (Rev. 2:5; 1 John 1:9), avoiding evil people and influences (2 Cor. 6:17–7:1), and giving ourselves to Him for His use (cp. Rom. 13:14; see chap. 6).

Four, by seeking to fulfill Jesus' overall objective (John 12:28; 17:4; 1 Cor. 10:31). This is to glorify the Father by allowing the Lord to use us and to express Himself through us in all that we do (Matt. 5:16).

Five, by contributing to Jesus' glory. We exalt Him by submitting to His authority and will (cp. 1 Cor. 11:3, 7–9; Gen. 2:18).

Our doing these things pleases the Lord and allows Him to use us in His great work. Are you fulfilling His needs? This is necessary for our fellowship with Him.

OUR ABIDING IN HIS LOVE (JOHN 15:9–10)

This is not our maintaining His love for us but our being in the place where we are aware of His great love for us and of His presence with us (John 14:21, 23). This place is that of obedience to His will for us. That He ever loves us (John 13:1; Rev. 1:5) and is always with us (Matt. 28:20) are our greatest supports for life in this world (Ps. 16:8). Our obedience to Him allows Him to make us aware of these blessings and to minister to us and our needs by them (1 John 1:7). Are you aware of these blessings today? This is essential to your fellowship with Him.

OUR FAITH IN HIM (GAL. 2:20)

To fulfill our duties as the Lord's slaves, we must trust Him completely with our lives and work. This requires our wholehearted reliance on the following truths:

1. Jesus' universal authority (Matt. 28:18)

He has all authority in heaven and on earth (Phil. 2:9–11). We recognize His authority by wholehearted obedience to His will (Eph. 5:17; John 13:17). He has full right to command our lives.

2. Jesus' presence with us (Matt. 28:20)

As God, Jesus is everywhere present. But faith in His promise makes us aware of His presence with us in a personal way, wherein we can walk in His fellowship (Ps. 16:8).

3. Jesus' competence to lead us (John 8:12; 10:27)

The Lord proved this ability to His disciples (Luke 5:1–10). The NT record of His capability is sufficient for our faith in this truth and for our reliance upon His direction (Matt. 17:5; John 17:4).

4. Jesus' love for us (John 13:1; 15:9; Rev. 1:5; cp. Gal. 2:20)

Amazingly, He loves us to the extent that the Father loves Him. This assures us of His loving care and guidance as our Great Shepherd (John 10:14, 27–28).

5. Jesus' faithfulness to us
This is seen in His:
   a. Helping us (Phil. 4:13)
   b. Praying for us (Heb. 4:14–16; 7:25)
   c. Representing us before the Father (1 John 2:1; Rev. 12:10; Rom. 8:31–39)
   d. Sustaining us (John 10:28; 2 Cor. 12:9)
   e. Answering our prayers (John 14:13)
   f. Producing fruit in us (John 15:14–15)
   g. Returning for us (John 14:1–3; Titus 2:13; 1 John 3:1–3; Rev. 22:12; cp. Matt. 24:42–51)

This reliance upon the Lord Jesus is summarized in Hebrews 12:2 as our "looking unto

Jesus, the Leader [KJV 'Author'] and Completer [KJV 'Finisher'] of our faith." When we look only at ourselves or our circumstances, we are doomed to defeat and despair. As long as we look to Jesus, we are "strengthened with might by His Spirit in the inner man" (Eph. 3:16). We cannot look to ourselves and to Him at the same time.

OUR PARTICIPATING IN HIS SUFFERINGS (JOHN 15:18–21)

Our fellowship with Him involves our willingness to suffer, or to be persecuted, for His sake in this world (Phil. 1:29; 3:10; 1 Peter 2:20–21; 1 John 3:13). Because of the world's hatred for the Lord Jesus (they crucified Him), we who are His slaves cannot expect better treatment from them. The more openly we follow the Lord Jesus, the more unsaved people will persecute us. But He helps us to respond well and to fulfill His purpose for this suffering in our lives.

1. *How are we to respond to this suffering for His sake?*

We are not to respond with retaliation (Matt. 5:38–42; Rom. 12:17–21) but with rejoicing (Matt. 5:10–12; 1 Peter 4:12–16), expressing God's compassionate love for our enemies (Matt. 5:43–45) and praise to God (1 Peter 4:16).

2. *Why does Jesus allow us to suffer for His sake?*
   a. *That we might display godliness (Matt. 5:44–45)*
   b. *That Jesus might be manifested in us (2 Cor. 4:10–12)*
   c. *That we might become more spiritually mature (James 1:2–4)*
   d. *That this trial of faith might bring us future glory and reward at Jesus' return (1 Peter 1:7; 4:13; Matt. 5:12)*

How are unsaved people treating you? We must avoid that behavior that brings us deserved reproach because of our evildoing (1 Peter 4:14–16). Willingness to suffer for Jesus' sake is necessary for fellowship with Him (Phil. 1:25–30; 3:10).

OUR RECEIVING HIS GIFTS (JOHN 14:13)

The Lord will provide us with all that we need as we look to Him for this. He has given to us the Holy Spirit at salvation (Rom. 8:9), whose gifts include His peace (John 14:27), grace (2 Cor. 12:9; Heb. 4:16), joy (John 15:11), strength (Phil. 4:13), help (Heb. 13:5– 6), satisfying our needs (John 6:35; 7:37–39), and NT instructions (John 15:15; 16:12–14). Our use of His gifts and our gratitude for them enhance our fellowship with Him.

OUR WORSHIPING HIM (JOHN 5:19–23)

Although He ever seeks to glorify the Father (John 12:28; 17:4), the Lord Jesus deserves to be honored as our Savior and Lord as well as our God (John 20:28; cp. 5:19–23). He is worthy of such spiritual sacrifices as our commitment, obedience, thanksgiving, and praise for all that He is and for all that He does.

The Lord Jesus is "the Wonderful Counselor, the Mighty God, the Father of Eternity, the Prince of Peace" (Isa. 9:6). He has been highly exalted in His humanity far above every authority and name that is named, not only in this age but also in that which is to come (Phil. 2:9; Eph. 1:21). He is greater than the prophets (Heb. 1:1–3), the angels (Heb. 1:4–14; 2:5–18), Moses (Heb. 3:1–6a), and the Aaronic priests (Heb. 5:1–10; 7:1–10:18). He is "Alpha and Omega" (Rev. 1:8; 22:13), "the Lion of the Tribe of Judah and the Root of David" (Rev. 5:5), the judicial "Lamb" (Rev. 5:6–10), "the King of kings and the Lord of lords" (Rev. 19:16). He is God's "dear Son . . . the Image of the invisible God" (Col. 1:13, 15). "By Him all things were created . . . and by Him all things consist" (Col. 1:16–17). He is "the Head . . . of the church" and the One in whom "all the fullness (of Deity) dwells" (Col. 1:18–19). This truth impels us to worship Him. This enriches our fellowship with Him.

OUR SUBMISSION TO HIM (LUKE 6:46– 49)

Having bought us with His atoning blood (1 Peter 1:18–19), the Lord is our Master (Col. 4:1; 1 Cor. 7:22), Head or Leader (Eph. 5:23; cp. Heb. 2:10), and King (Col. 1:13; 1 Tim. 6:14–15). Thus, it is our duty to be submissive to Him (Eph. 3:17; 5:24; John 13:13–17). Daily, we must yield ourselves to His authority and vitality. What does this mean?

Our Being Submissive to His Authority (Matt. 11:28–30; Eph. 3:17; cp. 1 Peter 3:15)

Our Lord has supreme authority over the universe, including us who are saved (Matt. 28:18; John 3:35; Acts 2:36; 10:36; Phil. 2:9–11; 1 Peter 3:22). With the heart as the fountain of one's daily activities (Prov. 4:23), that which occupies it commands one's life (Luke 6:45). Needless to say, as His slaves, we must daily give the Lord our hearts or the control of our lives (Prov. 23:26; Eph. 3:17).[53] When we trustingly, wholeheartedly yield ourselves to the Lord's supervision, we cease struggling to meet life's demands and problems with our insufficient human knowledge and resources. Then we experience the rest that faith in Him brings (Matt. 11:28–30; Heb. 4:9–11) and the help that His infinite resources provide (2 Peter 1:3). We find that with His support and direction, we can bear the burden of life's load. His "yoke" for us is kindly to wear, for it agrees with us as new creatures in Him; and His "burden" is light (Matt. 11:28–30), for He gives us the strength to do His will. Did you wholeheartedly give yourself to Jesus today? Is He now in command of your life? Are you ready to do His bidding?

Our Being Submissive to His Vitality (John 15:1, 4–5)

By these words the Lord explained the relationship that allows Him to live in and work through the lives of His people in building His Church (John 14:12; Acts 14:26–27; Matt. 16:18).[54] As the vine supports, nourishes, and produces fruit in its connected branches, so the Lord, as the spiritual life of His people (Gal. 2:20; Phil. 1:23; Col. 3:4), does these things for all who abide in Him. This relationship allows Him to work in and through us to produce the fruit of godly character, good works, loving service, and spiritual knowledge (Gal. 5:22–23; Col. 1:10; Rom. 1:13; 2 Peter 1:8). This relationship of abiding in Him requires the following:

One: Our submission to Jesus' authority and leadership (Matt. 11:29)

Two: Our obedience to Jesus' will in the Holy Spirit's power (Matt. 11:29; Phil. 4:13)

Three: Our reliance upon Jesus to do His part as we do ours (John 15:4; Gal. 2:20)

Four: Our communication with Jesus (1 Cor. 1:9) by allowing Him to speak to us through the Scriptures (Col. 3:16) and by our praying to Him about everything that concerns our spiritual fruitfulness and His will for our lives (1 Thess. 5:17)

Five: Our following His example of Christian character and behavior (1 John 2:6)

When we abide in the Lord Jesus in this way, we allow Him to abide in us in the full productivity of His life and power to produce His fruit in our lives (John 15:4–5). Apart from Him we cannot do anything of which He can approve; we can only sin (v. 5b; Rom. 14:23). The apostle Paul likened this submission to Jesus to putting on a garment (Rom. 13:14). Can you think of any parallels here? Are you living in touch with Him today? Is His fruit seen in your life? This submission to His authority and vitality is essential to our fellowship with Him.

OUR FOLLOWING HIM (JOHN 8:12)

We who are the Lord's slaves-friends are also to be His disciples, or pupils (Matt. 10:24–25a; John 8:31; 15:8; see "The Discipleship of the Christian Life" under Zoeology). Discipleship requires us to follow Jesus as we learn from Him.

The Nature of Our Following Jesus

1. *We are to follow His teachings and commands (John 8:30–32).*
   See "The Dispensation of Grace" under Theology Proper.
2. *We are to follow His example (Matt. 10:25; John 13:34–35; 1 Peter 2:21).*

Since "eternal life" is the Lord's spiritual life as man (John 14:6), it is fitting that we look to Him as our model for Christian life and ministry (Eph. 5:1–2; 1 Cor. 11:1). Christlikeness is the true expression of eternal life in the daily lives of His people (see Rom. 13:14; Gal. 4:19).

The Reasons for Our Following Jesus

1. *For serving in His present work of building the Church (John 14:12; 1 Cor. 3:9)*
2. *For being aware of His love and presence (John 14:21, 23)*
3. *For receiving His blessings (John 13:17)*
4. *For pleasing Him and giving Him a good account of our lives (2 Cor. 5:9–10; 1 Cor. 3:6–15)*

Being necessary for discipleship, our following the Lord Jesus is essentially "living unto Him" (2 Cor. 5:14–15; Col. 3:23). This is to make Him, including His concerns and desires for us, the primary preoccupation of life (Col. 3:1–2; Rom. 12:2). Our lives are to be inclined toward Him, not toward ourselves or anything or anyone in this world (cp. Luke 14:26, 33; Heb. 12:2; Col. 3:1–2). Are you truly one of His disciples? This is essential for our fellowship with Him.

OUR COMMITMENT TO HIM (MARK 8:34–38)

It is our duty as His slaves to acknowledge His claim to us and to commit ourselves to Him daily for His service (1 Cor. 3:9). Like many things, serving the Lord requires our wholehearted commitment and endeavor (Col. 3:23; Rom. 12:1). His people must decide between spending their one lifetime for Him or for this world, which is passing away (1 John 2:15–17). We cannot serve two masters (Matt. 6:24). The question is this: Where are you placing your lifetime investment? In Jesus or in the world?

The Lifetime That Is Invested in Jesus' Interests (Mark 8:34, 35b)

1. *The nature of this investment (v. 34)*
   We invest our lives profitably by losing them for Jesus' sake. We do this as follows:
   a. *By denying ourselves the mastery of sin (1 John 2:1; 1 Cor. 15:34; James 4:7)*
      Having been set free from bondage to our spiritual enemies, including sin, we can now, in God's strength, refuse to give ourselves to their demands and control.
   b. *By taking up Jesus' cross and giving Him mastery of our life (Rom. 6:1–4, 11–13)*
      The "cross" speaks of our death with Jesus. Having died to sin and being alive to God, it is urgent and right that we now give ourselves to the Lord and His will for us daily (Rom. 12:1–2).
   c. *By following Jesus (Mark 1:17; Matt. 11:28–30; Col. 3:1–4)*
      Our duty is to follow the Lord's instructions and direction as these are given in the Scriptures (Rom. 12:2; Eph. 5:17; John 13:17; see Appendix F: "Learning and Doing God's Will").
2. *The earnings of this investment (v. 35b)*
   When He reviews the works of our Christian lifetime at the coming appraisal, the Lord will return to us with dividends what we invested of our lives in His interests and work (2 Cor. 5:10; 1 Cor. 15:58; 2 Tim. 4:7–8; see "The Prophecy of Jesus' Appraisal of His Church" under Eschatology).

The Lifetime That Is Invested in This World (Mark 8:35a, 36–38)

1. The nature of this investment (vv. 36–37)

We invest our lives unprofitably by keeping them to ourselves and for the things of this world. Such a life is sinful, for it is energized and directed by the inner sin force and is lived apart from God (Rom. 14:23; John 15:5, "nothing" that He can approve).

2. The earnings of this investment (vv. 35a–38)

All that we invest in self and in the world apart from God will bring us loss (1 John 2:15–17; 1 Cor. 3:15). What does it profit a person to gain the whole world and lose his life (KJV "soul"), or lose what his life would have brought him had he given it over to Jesus and His will?

What investment are you making of your life? What is your commitment to the Lord? The wise person will seek to give his remaining time in this world to that which will count for eternity and will glorify God (2 Cor. 5:9–10, 14–15). We must make this commitment each day. Whenever we neglect to do this, the inner sin force takes command of our lives and uses us for its evil expressions (cp. Luke 6:45; Prov. 4:23; 23:26; Eph. 3:17). It was our Lord's delight to do the Father's will (John 4:34; 6:38; 8:28–29). He said, "If you know these things, happy are you if you do them" (John 13:17).

What kind of a relationship are you having with the Lord Jesus? Do you really regard Him to be your Lord as well as your Savior? Do you stand with those who sincerely say, "Behold, your servants are ready to do whatever my lord the king shall choose" (2 Sam. 15:15)? Are you His friend (John 15:14)?

What a wonderful, loving Savior and Lord we have! May we increasingly live unto Him and allow Him to work and to manifest His character through our lives so that others may be attracted to His light and life for the glory of God.

A Review of Christology

1. What does the deity of Jesus mean?
2. What basic truths bear witness to His deity?
3. What does His being "the Word" mean?
4. What do "First Begotten" and "Only Begotten Son" mean?
5. What is the meaning of His eternal preexistence?
6. Why does God the Son have the same attributes as God the Father?
7. What works of the Son bear witness to His deity?
8. What divine honors may be given to Jesus?
9. What assertions did Jesus make that speak of His deity?
10. Give the names of several people who bore witness to Jesus' deity.
11. What does the humanity of Jesus mean?
12. What does the condescension of God the Son emphasize?
13. What is the meaning of His incarnation?
14. What is the basic idea of His self-emptying?
15. Why would it be erroneous to say that in His self-emptying Jesus laid aside some of His divine attributes?
16. Who fathered Jesus' human nature? Who fathers His divine nature?
17. Of what parts does our Lord's human nature consist?
18. How was His human nature different from ours?
19. Why was Mary not the mother of God? Of what was she the mother?
20. What was the importance of Jesus' virgin conception and birth as these related to His saviorhood? Kingship?

21. Explain the doctrine of the hypostatic union of the two natures in Jesus. What is the hypostasis of this union?
22. How could the Lord Jesus have limited knowledge and yet at the same time have unlimited knowledge?
23. Why could Jesus not sin? Were His temptations real?
24. Give several ways that show the importance of Jesus' unique human character.
25. How long did, or will, Jesus possess His human nature?
26. What is the meaning of Jesus' humiliation?
27. What is the theological idea of atonement as generally used in this work?
28. Why did atonement have to be made before God could save people from their sins?
29. Jesus' atoning work was substitutionary and satisfactory. What do these terms mean?
30. What is the meaning of propitious and provisional with reference to the Atonement?
31. What is the value that Jesus secured for all people by His atoning work and that is now offered through the gospel?
32. Since Jesus died for everyone, why will not everyone be saved?
33. Why could God not take a perfect human being from among men to be our substitute?
34. What two kinds of death did Jesus experience on the cross? Which of these was associated with divine wrath?
35. What was unique about His physical death?
36. Why was the crucifixion of Jesus man's greatest crime again God?
37. What five things did Jesus accomplish while He was on the cross?
38. By His death Jesus confirmed the divine condemnation of God's enemies. What or who were these enemies?
39. How is this confirmation of the guilt of these enemies helpful to us who are saved?
40. What is the new covenant that Jesus mediated by His death?
41. Explain how our Lord's atoning work is unlimited and how it is limited.
42. What is the figurative meaning of the "blood of Christ"?
43. Give several blessings that saved people have because of Jesus' blood in its figurative sense.
44. In establishing the Atonement, why did God include the shedding and offering of blood when the wages of sin was death?
45. Some say that we can be healed physically through faith in Jesus just as we are saved through faith in Him. Why is this view in error?
46. What is the theological importance of Jesus' burial?
47. Give the four steps in Jesus' exaltation.
48. Define each of these steps and describe their importance. How does each of these steps benefit those of us who are saved?
49. How did Jesus' resurrection differ from those people who were earlier restored to life?
50. How many days after His resurrection did Jesus ascend to heaven? Was this a divine or a human experience for Him?
51. What outstanding event did He experience in His humanity upon His return to heaven?
52. What did anointing with oil in OT times signify?
53. What did this anointing medium represent?
54. When was Jesus anointed? What was the physical anointing medium? To what office was He appointed? How long will He continue in this office?
55. What roles is He now fulfilling in this office as the Anointed One?
56. Explain His activities in carrying out these roles: when He was here, during His present absence, and when He comes to earth again.
57. What are Jesus' generic names?

58. Give some of His functional names, or titles, in the Old Testament: those relating to His deity and those that are predicted of His humanity.

59. Give several of His divine titles in the New Testament. Give several human titles.

60. What was Jesus' divine personal name before His incarnation?

61. What is His divine personal name since His incarnation? His human personal name?

62. What is the meaning of the designation, "the Lord Jesus Christ"?

63. Give several ways by which we can interact with the Lord Jesus and thus improve our fellowship with Him as His slaves-friends.

64. Is your trust in Jesus and His atoning work for your salvation?

65. Are you living in reliance on and in obedience to Him today?

66. Are you looking for His imminent return? ◄!►

67. Have you committed yourself to Him as His slave?

68. Are you occupied with His affairs in this world?

69. How does a person show himself friendly toward the Lord Jesus?

Endnotes

1. According to the Granville Sharp rule, the Greek text also identifies Jesus to be God in Eph. 5:5, "the Christ and God"; 2 Thess. 1:12, "our God and Lord Jesus Christ"; 1 Tim. 5:21, "the God and Christ Jesus"; Titus 2:13, "the great God and our Savior"; 2 Peter 1:1, "our God and Savior Jesus Christ"; and v. 2, "the God and Jesus our Lord." This rule of Greek grammar is as follows: "When the copulative *kai* ('and') connects two nouns of the same case, if the article *ho* ('the') or any of its cases precedes the first of the said nouns or participles and is not repeated before the second noun or participle, the latter always relates to the same person that is expressed or described by the first noun or participle, i.e., it denotes a further description of the first-named person"—from H. E. Dana and J. R. Mantey, *A Manual Grammar of the Greek New Testament* (New York: The Macmillan Company, 1941), 147.

2. The Greek neuter predicate adjective (one) indicates one thing, like one nature or purpose rather than one person.

3. This is the principle that there is in the Bible perfect agreement among the parts that comprise the whole revelation of truth. Because the whole biblical revelation of a specific teaching exceeds that which any single passage gives, we should seek to understand what all the Bible says about the doctrine or topic.

4. Observe that Jesus' doing miracles during His earthly ministry is not listed as proof of His deity. As man, He did (and does) all His messianic works by the power of the Holy Spirit (Acts 10:38) as did His apostles (Heb. 2:3–4). Satan, too, can do miracles (2 Thess. 2:9; Rev. 13:13–14). Nevertheless, we should expect Jesus, who is God as well as man, to do wonders.

5. The Greek *if* here views the condition as fulfilled or as a fact, reading, "since You are the Son of God."

6. One physical exception was the single instance of His manifesting His divine, preincarnate glory (Matt. 17:1–2). His human moral character always exhibited His divine moral qualities (John 1:14).

7. Matthew 17:1–2 records our Lord's transfiguration, by which He manifested the radiance of that glory that He had before His incarnation and that He received upon His return to heaven (John 17:5; Acts 26:13; Rev. 1:13–16). He did not cease manifesting this glory as God. However, in His earthly humanity He did not manifest this glory before His ascension and exaltation at the Father's right hand (Phil. 2:9–11; Heb. 1:3).

8. Also, see Matthew 1:20, "that [thing]." The Greek neuter article *to* is translated as a demonstrative pronoun.

9. The Lord Jesus as man will also rule over the earth (Ps. 2:6–9; Heb. 2:5–9). As the Last Adam, He will return to earth, will evict the usurper Satan, and will rule over the world from Jerusalem (Heb. 2:5–9; Zech. 8:3; 14:17; Rev. 19:11–16; 20:1–3). He will do this justly, for He

defeated Satan by His resurrection, received the title to earth by divine inheritance, and will rule the world by divine appointment (Heb. 2:14; Matt. 28:18; John 3:35; Ps. 2:6–9).

10. Luke 3:23 should read, "And Jesus began to be about thirty years of age, being (as it was popularly supposed, the son of Joseph) the (grand)son of Heli (Mary's father)."

11. Observe that the human spirit is not the same as God's divine nature, which is spirit (John 4:24).

12. All of Jesus' temptations were wholly external. Unlike us, He had no inner sin force that would urge Him to sin or that could be aroused by external temptation (1 John 3:5).

13. Hebrews 2:10 and 5:9 assert that Jesus was made perfect, or completed, by His sufferings. The completion that He needed was the fulfillment of a lack that He had rather than a correction of a moral flaw. He had to learn the meaning of suffering and obedience by experience so that He could be a merciful High Priest (Heb. 4:14–16) and an effective Savior (Heb. 2:10; 5:9; Phil. 2:8). See "Problems of the hypostatic union of the two natures in Jesus" in this chapter.

14. W. H. Griffith Thomas, *Christianity Is Christ* (London: Longmans, Green and Co., 1909), 12.

15. In KJV this word is translated "person"; however, it would be more accurate to translate it "nature" since "person" may refer to one's total being, including personhood.

16. Stafford Wright, *What Is Man?* (London: The Paternoster Press, 1955), 185f.

17. Keep in mind that it is one's personhood that sins, not just one's nature. Having the ability to make moral choices, it is one's personhood ("I") that chooses to sin and thus does sin, for which one is responsible.

18. Observe that the Lord is not sympathetic toward His people in their sinning. When we deal with our sinning by repentance and confession (Rev. 2:5; 1 John 1:9), God forgives us, but this does not eliminate the undesirable results of our wrongdoing.

19. This penal death includes both physical death and the "second death," or the spiritual death that unsaved people will experience perpetually in hell (Rev. 20:14). See in this chapter, "The Kinds of Death That Jesus Experienced."

20. God's wrath, or anger, is not simply the reaction of uncontrollable emotions but the judicial reaction of His holy nature in its opposition against sin and sinners (see "God's Attributes: Hatred" under Theology Proper). God's holiness, justice, and righteousness demand that sin's punishment be borne by sinners, that divine justice be satisfied, and that divine law be upheld.

21. H. E. Guillebaud, *Why the Cross?* (London: InterVarsity Fellowship, 1954), 146–63.

22. Ibid., 147f.

23. This point needs to be made to the Jehovah's Witnesses, who deny Jesus' deity but mentally accept His atoning work.

24. Guillebaud, *Why the Cross?* 160f.

25. L. S. Chafer, *Systematic Theology* (Dallas: Dallas Seminary Press, 1947), 3:68.

26. Ibid., 163.

27. Ibid., 180.

28. Observe that there was no division of the divine nature during these hours. It was a separation of Persons in their intimate fellowship.

29. Acts 3:17 does not acquit these religious and civil rulers of their guilt as the passages, cited above, show. However, blinded by Satan and governed by sin, these rulers did not really know Jesus' true identity or the prophecies of His death on a cross (Acts 13:27; 1 Cor. 2:8). The Lord's prayer of forgiveness (Luke 23:34) concerned the soldiers who crucified Him, not the rulers, as the cited passages show.

30. See William Wood Seymour, *The Cross in Tradition, History and Art* (New York: The Knickerbocker Press, 1898), part I, chap. III.

31. See W. G. T. Shedd, *Dogmatic Theology* (Grand Rapids: Zondervan Publishing House, 1967), 2:469.

32. The sin force is that inner law, or force, that energizes and impels angels and humans to sin (Rom. 7:23, 25; 8:2). It is more accurate to think of it as a force than as a nature, since it is not an essential part of angelic or human composition. The Lord Jesus, who possesses a perfect, complete human nature, never had this evil force.

33. Not being a part of original creation, the sin force became an alien, nonessential force within

angels and humans when they chose to disobey God, and it is still confined to them. Because of Adam's sin, impersonal creation came under a divine curse (Gen. 3:17–19; Rom. 8:20–21), which will be lifted when the Lord sets up His millennial kingdom (Isa. 11:1–9). Since the sin force is resident in the body's flesh, it perishes with the body's death and dissolution (Rom. 7:17–21). In my opinion, the resurrected bodies of unsaved people will not have the sin force. Also, Satan and his angels will be divested of this evil force. I do not think of hell as a place where fallen personal creatures will continue to exist in sin's grip and to express their hostility toward God. Although they will continue forever in conscious suffering and desolation, all unsaved beings will bow to Jesus and acclaim Him to be Lord (Phil. 2:11; cp. Luke 16:24–28). Sin had a beginning; when it has served the divine purpose, it will end. It will cease to exist when its product, death, is abolished (1 Cor. 15:25–26).

34. The word *world* (Gk. *kosmos*) can mean, according to its context, the sum total of all that was created (John 17:5), the earth (9:5), mankind (3:16; 12:19), or the world system, embracing the total society, culture, and philosophy of unsaved mankind.

35. Saved people are still subject to the world's political authority (Rom. 13:1–7; 1 Peter 2:13–17) insofar as its demands do not conflict with God's will for His people (Acts 5:29).

36. This is seen in the ministry of the apostle Paul and his associates, who were ministers of the new covenant (2 Cor. 2:14–3:6), and in the future salvation of the elect remnant of Israel (Jer. 31:31–34; cp. Ezek. 36:25–29). See "The Covenants of God: The New Covenant" under Theology Proper.

37. "Under the earth" refers to hades, where unsaved people go upon death (Ps. 63:9; Isa. 14:9) and where many fallen angels are imprisoned (cp. Luke 16:22–23; 1 Peter 3:18–20; 2 Peter 2:4; Rev. 20:13; see Addendum: "Sheol, Hades"). There is no opportunity for these to be saved. When He went to hades upon His death (Matt. 12:40; Rom. 10:7), Jesus made a proclamation to these imprisoned angels, perhaps of His impending resurrection and victory over death and Satan, but He did not evangelize them (1 Peter 3:19).

38. Shedd, *Dogmatic Theology*, 2:464.

39. Note that the word *shedding* in Heb. 9:22 is a figure of association—a synecdoche (see Appendix X: "Figures of Association: Synecdoche and Metonymy") and is to be understood as including the offering of the shed blood as well (Lev. 17:11).

40. See Franz Delitzsch, *A System of Biblical Psychology* (Grand Rapids: Baker Book House, 1966), 281ff.

41. See A. M. Stibbs, *The Meaning of the Word 'Blood' in Scripture* (London: The Tyndale Press, 1954), 9f., 16–19; also, Leon Morris, *The Apostolic Preaching of the Cross* (London: The Tyndale Press, 1955), chap. III.

42. Matthew 26:28; Mark 14:24; Luke 22:20; John 6:53–56; Acts 20:28; Romans 3:25; 5:9; 1 Corinthians 10:16; 11:25, 27; Ephesians 1:7; 2:13; Colossians 1:14, 20; Hebrews 9:12, 14; 10:19, 29; 13:12, 20; 1 Peter 1:2, 19; 1 John 1:7; 5:6, 8; Revelation 1:5; 5:9; 7:14; 12:11.

43. In those references where it has figurative meaning, the word *blood*, like *death* (Rom. 5:10), is a figure of association (synecdoche) for the atonement (see Appendix X: "Figures of Association: Synecdoche and Metonymy").

44. Some hold that Jesus took His blood to heaven and offered it to God there (Heb. 9:12). I prefer the view that the cross on which Jesus died was the altar where God the Father offered His Son, and the Son gave His life in atonement for humanity's sins. The Greek preposition *dia* with the genitive denotes "manner" (F. Blass and A. Debrunner; R. W. Funk, trans., *A Greek Grammar of the New Testament and Other Early Christian Literature* [University of Chicago Press, 1961], 119). Thus "by way of His own blood," or by way of His atoning sacrifice, He (eventually) entered heaven.

45. See Appendix S: "Physical Healing."

46. A. J. McClain, *Was Christ Punished for our Diseases?* (Winona Lake, Ind.: The Brethren Missionary Herald Co., n.d.), 7f.

47. Perhaps the Lord declared His impending victory over Satan, which would occur with His physical resurrection.

48. As the apostle Paul shows (1 Cor. 15:42–49), our bodies are suited to live on earth but must be

changed to survive off the earth, like in heaven. Although Jesus' body had no inherent corruption, it, too, needed to be changed for the eternal state. See "The Resurrection of Mankind" under Anthropology.

49. The word *first* in "the first resurrection" (Rev. 20:5–6) concerns the kind of resurrection event rather than the number of resurrection events (cp. John 5:28–29). *The first kind of resurrection* is that of saved people (Rev. 20:5–6; John 5:28–29), which includes three resurrection events: *one,* that of the dead Church believers (1 Thess. 4:13); *two,* that of the OT or precross believers (Luke 13:28; Gen. 17:8; 28:13; Heb. 11:13; Dan. 12:2–3; Ezek. 34:23–24); and *three,* that of the Tribulation Age martyrs (Rev. 20:4; cp. 6:9–11; 7:9–17; 12:17; 13:7, 15; 15:2). *The second kind of resurrection* will be that of unsaved people after our Lord's millennial rule (Rev. 20:5a, 12–13; cp. John 5:28–29).

50. See John F. Walvoord, *Jesus Christ Our Lord* (Chicago: Moody Press, 1969), 220f.

51. As a priest-king, the Lord Jesus belongs to the priestly order of Melchizedek, which was greater in honor and tenure than that of the Aaronic priesthood (Heb. 7). Jesus' priestly work follows that of the OT Aaronic order.

52. *Kurios* is one who has power, or authority (G. Abbott-Smith, *A Manual Greek Lexicon of the New Testament* [Edinburgh: T. & T. Clark, 1954], 261). After Jesus' return to heaven, most NT references to "Lord" (Gk. *Kurios*) outside of the Gospels seem to refer to His human lordship over all (Acts 2:36; 10:36; Rom. 14:9; 1 Cor. 2:8; Phil. 2:11; cp. Acts 5:14; 10:48; Rom. 12:11; 14:8; 2 Cor. 5:8 etc.). In the Gospels, "Lord" was sometimes used as a term of respect for Jesus in direct address (Matt. 8:2, 6, 8; John 4:11, KJV "sir"; 6:68). However, Luke and the apostle John seem to use this title with Jesus' exaltation in mind (Luke 7:13; 10:1; 11:39; John 20:20). Thomas recognized Jesus as being his Lord and God (John 20:28).

53. Note that the inner sin force takes possession of our hearts upon every opportunity and without invitation. The Lord possesses our hearts only with our invitation and submission to Him. When we fail to do this, sin immediately occupies this control center and uses us for its evil expressions. When we yield ourselves to the Lord, resist the urges of the sin force, and do the Lord's will in His strength, then we do not sin but do that which pleases the Lord.

54. See "The Fruitfulness of the Christian Life" under Zoeology.

Pneumatology

6

PNEUMATOLOGY
The Doctrine of God the Holy Spirit

With the growing emphasis on the work of God the Holy Spirit and the spreading influence of the charismatic movement, it is urgent for the Lord's people to understand what the Bible teaches about this wonderful Person and His activities. It is Satan's strategy to deceive the unwary by part-truth doctrine and counterfeit experience, which are widely accepted as being of God. A careful study of the Bible's teaching about the Holy Spirit and His ministries will help us to avoid error and will show us who are saved how to cooperate with Him so that He can do His work in and through our lives.

THE NATURE OF THE HOLY SPIRIT

This concerns who and what He is. He is a person and He is God.

HE IS A PERSON

Unitarians, false cultists, and company deny the personhood (sometimes called "personality") of the Holy Spirit, but the Bible teaches otherwise. The Holy Spirit's having personhood, or being a person, is shown by the following biblical propositions:

- **The Holy Spirit possesses certain features of personhood.**

These are self-awareness (Acts 13:2, personal pronouns "me," "I"), self-determination (1 Cor. 12:11), individuality (John 14:26), moral awareness (Acts 5:3; Rom. 1:4; Gal. 5:16–17), and perpetuity (Heb. 9:14). Other qualities that are attributed to personal beings are found in Him, like intelligence (1 Cor. 2:10–12), emotion (Rom. 15:30; Eph. 4:30), and will (Acts 13:2, 4).

- **The Holy Spirit does work that only persons can do.**

These include teaching (John 14:26), reproving (16:8), interceding (Rom. 8:26), leading (Rom. 8:14), calling (Rev. 22:17), and witnessing (Rom. 8:16).

- **The Holy Spirit's responses to human actions and needs indicate His having personhood.**

These include His grieving over sin (Eph. 4:30), giving satisfaction (John 7:37–39), helping (John 14:16), and imparting power (Gal. 5:16; Acts 1:8; Eph. 1:19).

- **Certain things may be done to the Holy Spirit which point to His being a person.**

These are His being obeyed (Acts 10:19–21), lied to (5:3), resisted (7:51), blasphemed (Matt. 12:31), and insulted (Heb. 10:29).

- **Both apostle John and apostle Paul used masculine pronouns for Him.**

A masculine demonstrative pronoun occurs in John 15:26, KJV "he," Gk. "that one"; 16:13–14; a masculine relative pronoun is used in Ephesians 1:14, KJV "which," Gk. "who"; and the masculine personal pronoun is used in John 16:7, "him."[1]

- **The Holy Spirit's relation to other persons indicates His having personhood.**

His relation to people like the Lord Jesus (John 16:14) and gospel believers (Acts 15:28; 16:6–7) shows that He is a person.

These evidences of personhood show that the Holy Spirit is more than an impersonal influence or force. In all of our thoughts about Him and our relationships with Him, we should regard Him to be a personal being as we are personal beings.

HE IS GOD

The Holy Spirit is a person who possesses the divine nature, which makes Him to be God.[2] Like His personhood, the deity of the Holy Spirit is also widely denied today. That He is God is shown by the following biblical facts:

- **The Holy Spirit has divine names.**

The apostle Peter referred to the Holy Spirit as being God (Acts 5:3–4). The apostle Paul wrote of Him as "the Spirit of our God" (1 Cor. 6:11), "the Lord is the Spirit," and "the Spirit of the Lord" (2 Cor. 3:17–18). His indwelling His people, whose bodies are called "the temple of God," also indicates that He is God (1 Cor. 3:16). For His identification with the divine personal name "LORD" (KJV), see Jeremiah 31:31–34 with Hebrews 10:15–18; Judges 15:14 with 16:20; and with the generic name "God," see Matthew 12:28 with Luke 11:20.

- **The Holy Spirit has the attributes of God.**

These are life (Rom. 8:2; John 3:5–6), eternality (Heb. 9:14), omnipresence (Ps. 139:7; 1 Cor. 6:19), omnipotence (Job 33:4; Ps. 104:30; Gen. 1:2), omniscience (1 Cor. 2:10–11; John 16:13), truthfulness (John 14:17; 15:26; 16:13; 1 John 2:27; 5:6), holiness (Rom. 1:4), righteousness (Rom. 8:4), grace (Heb. 10:29), love (Rom. 15:30; 5:5), and sovereignty (1 Cor. 12:11; Acts 10:19–20).

- **The Holy Spirit does the works of God.**

The Holy Spirit was active in the creation of the universe (Gen. 1:2; Ps. 33:6; Job 26:13); He inspired the prophets (2 Peter 1:21); He brought about the conception of Jesus' sinless human nature (Luke 1:35); and He produces the new birth of gospel believers (John 3:3–8).

- **The Holy Spirit is listed with the other Persons of the divine Trinity.**

See Matthew 28:19 and 1 John 5:17.

These biblical evidences point to the fact that the Holy Spirit is God in every respect as the Father and the Son are each God.

THE HOLY SPIRIT'S RELATION TO THE OTHER PERSONS OF THE DIVINE TRINITY

The Holy Spirit is equal to the other Persons of the Trinity in the extent of His powers and attributes since the three Persons commonly possess the single, divine nature, which makes Them to be God. However, the subordination of the Holy Spirit to the Father and the Son is as follows:

HIS SUBORDINATION IN RANK

This is that ontological subordination that concerns the internal relationship of the divine Persons (see "The relations of the Persons within the divine Trinity" under Theology Proper). In the communication of the divine nature, God the Father breathes out, or exhales, the divine nature through the Son to the Holy Spirit, who thus is third in order (Matt. 28:19).[3]

HIS SUBORDINATION IN ACTIVITY

This is that economical subordination which is related to the external or transitive works of the Persons of the Trinity. The Holy Spirit is the Dynamic Cause, by whom the Son carries out that which is initiated by the Father, as determined by the divine decree. This is seen in the divine works of creation (Job 26:13; Ps. 33:6; Gen. 1:2) and of giving oral and written divine revelation (John 16:12–15; 2 Peter 1:21; Rev. 1:1).

THE NAMES OF THE HOLY SPIRIT

THOSE NAMES ASSERTING HIS DEITY

The Holy Spirit is identified as "God" in both Testaments (Gen. 1:2; 1 Cor. 3:16). In the Old Testament He is seen as "the Lord God" (Isa. 48:16, *Adonai Yahweh*).[4] The apostle Paul identified the Holy Spirit as "the Lord" (2 Cor. 3:17–18). The titles "Holy Spirit," "the Spirit of God," and "the Spirit of the Lord" are used as personal names in certain contexts (cp. John 14:26).

THOSE NAMES INDICATING HIS RELATIONSHIP TO THE FATHER AND TO THE SON

To the Father

These are "Spirit of God" (Matt. 3:16), "Spirit of our God" (1 Cor. 6:11), "Spirit of the Lord" (Isa. 59:19), "Spirit of the Lord God" (61:1), "Spirit of your Father" (Matt. 10:20) and "Spirit of the living God" (2 Cor. 3:3).

To the Son

These are "Spirit of Him" (Rom. 8:9), "Spirit of Jesus Christ" (Phil. 1:19), and "Spirit of His Son" (Gal. 4:6). These are not references to Jesus' human spirit, as in Mark 2:8; 8:12; Luke 23:46; 1 Peter 3:18, nor do they imply that there is more than one divine Spirit (cp. 1 Cor. 12:11, 13; Eph. 4:4). They refer to the Third Person of the divine Trinity. These designations may derive from the fact that Jesus' messianic works are wrought in the Holy Spirit's power (Acts 10:38) and that Jesus' spiritual life is conveyed to His people by the Holy Spirit, who regenerates and sanctifies them (John 14:6; 3:6; Titus 3:5; Rom. 8:2).

THOSE NAMES DESCRIBING HIS ATTRIBUTES

These are "Holy Spirit" (Luke 11:13), "One Spirit" (Eph. 4:4), "Eternal Spirit" (Heb. 9:14), "Spirit of glory and of God" (1 Peter 4:14), "Spirit of life" (Rom. 8:2), "Spirit of holiness" (1:4), "Spirit of wisdom and revelation" (Eph. 1:17), "Spirit of truth" (John 14:17), and "Spirit of grace" (Heb. 10:29).

THOSE NAMES DESCRIBING HIS WORKS

These are "Spirit of adoption" (Rom. 8:15), "Spirit of faith" (2 Cor. 4:13), "Helper" (KJV "Comforter"; John 14:16), and "the Anointing" (1 John 2:27). Isaiah 11:2 indicates several ministries of the Holy Spirit to the Lord Jesus during His earthly, millennial, messianic reign. The Holy Spirit will give to Him wisdom, understanding, counsel, might, knowledge, and the fear of the Lord.

SYMBOLS AND THEOPHANIES OF THE HOLY SPIRIT

SEVERAL SYMBOLS

Biblical symbols are things that represent something or someone else (Rev. 11:4). Several biblical symbols of the Holy Spirit are oil (1 Sam. 16:13; Heb. 1:9), an earnest (2 Cor. 1:22; Eph. 1:14), a seal (Eph. 1:13; 4:30), and water (John 3:5; 4:14; 7:38–39).[5]

SEVERAL THEOPHANIES

A theophany is an appearance of God in some temporary, visible form. Several theophanies of the Holy Spirit are a dove (Matt. 3:16; John 1:32), wind, and fire (Acts 2:2–4). Perhaps the phrase, "the seven Spirits" (Rev. 4:5), indicates the Holy Spirit's simultaneous presence and work in each of the seven churches in the Roman province of Asia (2:7, 11, 17, 29; 3:6, 13, 22).

THE WORK OF THE HOLY SPIRIT

It is supremely important to understand the works of the Holy Spirit, especially those that relate to the present time. The following study surveys His work in eternity past as well as during mankind's past, present, and future.

HIS WORK IN ETERNITY PAST

Together with the other Persons of the Trinity, the Holy Spirit was active in formulating the divine decree, or plan (cp. Gen. 1:26; Acts 2:23; 4:28; Eph. 1:11). This means that He is involved in the total work of God, not only in devising the decree but also in administering it. This administration of what God has planned concerns the Trinity's activity in creation, preservation, providence, revelation, and salvation.

HIS WORK DURING THE OLD TESTAMENT PERIOD

Keep in mind the roles that the Persons of the divine Trinity have concerning their dealings with the universe: God the Father is the Originating Cause of all things (1 Cor. 8:6), God the Son is the Instrumental Cause of all things (v. 6), and God the Holy Spirit is the Dynamic Cause of all things (cp. 1 Cor. 6:11). In all these transitive actions of the Trinity, God the Father works through God the Son by the power of God the Holy Spirit.

Regarding Creation

That the Holy Spirit was active with the other Persons of the Trinity in the work of creating the universe is stated in the Scriptures (Gen. 1:2; Job 26:13; 33:4; Pss. 33:6; 104:29–30; Isa. 40:12–14). This is also implied in the name "God," which in Hebrew is usually plural (Elohim), and the personal pronoun "Us," which point to the plurality of these divine Persons (Gen. 1:1, 26).

Regarding Divine Revelation

The Holy Spirit enabled certain people to receive God's special revelation and to convey it orally or to record it verbally without error or omission as the very Word of God. This work of the Holy Spirit upon these people is called "divine inspiration" (see 2 Peter 1:21; 2 Sam. 23:1–2; Mic. 3:8; Acts 1:16; 28:25; 1 Cor. 2:13; Heb. 10:15; see "Divine Inspiration" under Bibliology).

Regarding Humans

The Holy Spirit came upon people, or anointed them, for the purpose of enabling them for a specific ministry (Judg. 13:25; 14:6, 19; 15:14; 16:20; 1 Sam. 16:13).[6] He also filled certain people for a special work (Exod. 31:3; 35:31). He even entered some people, but He did not remain in them permanently (Ezek. 2:2; 3:24).

Although He did not indwell people permanently, as He does today, the Holy Spirit was with His people (John 14:17; cp. Ps. 139:7–10; Dan. 4:8–9, 18; 5:11–12). He was with them to do many of the things that He does for His people today, like giving them understanding (Neh. 9:20), wisdom (Exod. 31:1–6), administrative ability (Num. 11:16–17; Deut. 34:9; 1 Sam. 16:13), physical strength (Judg. 14:19), and the ability to do miracles (2 Kings 2:9–15). He enabled them to walk with God and to serve Him. After his sin with Bathsheba, David feared losing his anointing to rule over Israel, as Saul had lost his (Ps. 51:11; cp. 1 Sam. 16:13–14).

HIS WORK DURING GOD THE SON'S INCARNATION

Keep in mind that the Holy Spirit inspired the prophets (2 Peter 1:21), who spoke of the events of Jesus' first and second comings to earth (cp. Isa. 7:14; chaps. 53; 11), and the gospel writers, who recorded the events of Jesus' life and ministry (John 16:12–14). With the first coming of God the Son into the world, the person and work of the Holy Spirit were brought into view to a greater degree than ever before. The Holy Spirit had, and will forever have, a very important part in the life and ministry of Jesus the Messiah as man.

The Holy Spirit's Activity in Jesus' Conception

The conception of Jesus' human nature came about by the action of the Holy Spirit rather than by the agency of a man (Matt. 1:20; Luke 1:35). He made of Mary's substance a complete, sinless human nature that was immediately received by God the Son. By this reception God the Son became a human being. He is now forever the God-man.

The Holy Spirit's Activity During Jesus' Private Life

Although it is not revealed what Jesus' relationship to the Holy Spirit was throughout His private life in Nazareth, the fact that God's grace was upon Him implies that His life was influenced by this divine Person (Luke 2:40). We know that Jesus was aware of His mission on earth (Luke 2:49; Heb. 10:5–7) and that He pleased the Father during these years (Matt. 3:17).

The Holy Spirit's Activity in Jesus' Ministry

During His ministry, the Lord Jesus was filled with and led by the Holy Spirit (Luke 4:16–21). He received the anointing of the Holy Spirit at His baptism (Luke 3:21–22; John 1:32; 3:34). This means that as the Father's Slave Jesus received the Holy Spirit's enablement for the messianic work that the Father had commissioned Him to do. This event also marked the beginning of Jesus' human, messianic ministry. All of Jesus' messianic activities, like His teaching and doing miracles, were by the Holy Spirit's power (Acts 10:38; Isa. 42:1; 61:1; cp. Matt. 12:28; Luke 4:1, 14). The Holy Spirit will forever enable Jesus as man to do the Father's will (Isa. 11:1–5).

The Holy Spirit's Activity in Jesus' Death

The Holy Spirit strengthened Jesus for His priestly work of offering Himself in sacrifice for humanity's sins (Heb. 9:14). He enabled Jesus to endure the abuses that were inflicted by wicked men (Matt. 26:67; 27:26–35) and the judgment of our sins that He received from the Father's hand (Matt. 27:46; Isa. 53:5–10).

The Holy Spirit's Activity in Jesus' Resurrection

In cooperation with the Father (Gal. 1:1) and the Son (John 10:18), the Holy Spirit participated in bringing about Jesus' physical resurrection from the dead (Rom. 8:11; cp. Eph. 1:19–20). He provided the new life force that made Jesus' dead body alive and that will animate the changed bodies of His people (cp. 1 Cor. 15:44, "a spiritual body"). He also changed Jesus' body, which had been created to live on earth, so that it could exist forever in the eternal state (1 Cor. 15:45; see "The Resurrection of Mankind" under Anthropology).

The Holy Spirit's Activity in Jesus' Ascension and Enthronement

By the Holy Spirit's power, Jesus as man physically ascended into heaven and sat down at the Father's right hand (Eph. 1:19–22). There, the Lord Jesus continues His messianic work as our great High Priest (Heb. 4:14–16) and waits until the Father makes His enemies His footstool at His second coming to earth (1:12; 10:12–13; Rev. 19:15).

The Holy Spirit's Activity in Jesus' Building the Church

Although as man He is in heaven, the Lord Jesus is building His Church on earth through the Holy Spirit (Matt. 3:11; 16:18; Acts 1:5), who transmits to His people Jesus' spiritual life and power (cp. John 14:20). This power connection between the Lord and His people is formed by the baptism and indwelling works of the Holy Spirit, which results in their being in Jesus and His being in them (Gal. 3:27; 1 Cor. 6:19; Col. 1:27). The Holy Spirit's baptism also places gospel believers into Jesus' mystical body to form the Universal Church, which now serves as His body on earth (1 Cor. 12:13, 27; Eph. 1:22–23).

The Holy Spirit's Activity in Jesus' Work During the Tribulation Age

During the Tribulation Age the Lord Jesus will engage in those events that will prepare earth dwellers for His second coming to earth (Rev. 5–16). These events include His evangelizing earth dwellers by the preaching of the 144,000 evangelists (chap. 7), His pouring out judgments on wicked earth dwellers (chaps. 6, 8–10, 16), and His dealing with the elect remnant of Israel to bring them to repentance and to faith in Himself (chap. 12; Hos. 3:4–5; 5:14–6:3). Jesus will do all this as man by the power of the Holy Spirit (cp. Isa. 59:19; 61:1–2).

The Holy Spirit's Activity During Jesus' Earthly Rule

The Lord Jesus will continue His messianic work during His millennial, earthly kingdom by the Holy Spirit's power (Isa. 11:2–5; 42:1–4). In fact, the Holy Spirit will continue to energize the Lord Jesus for His messianic works throughout all eternity (1 Cor. 15:28; Luke 1:33).

HIS WORK DURING THE CHURCH AGE

The Holy Spirit is currently active on earth in restraining evil, ministering to the unsaved, and working in the lives of His people.

The Holy Spirit's Restraint on Lawlessness

This is implied in 2 Thessalonians 2:7, "For the mystery of iniquity does already work, only He who now restrains [KJV "lets"] will restrain until He be taken out of the way." A *mystery* is a sacred secret, or a hidden divine truth, that is now revealed to the Lord's servants as part of the NT revelation (see Appendix O: "The Divine Mysteries of the New Testament"). *Iniquity* is lawlessness—that indwelling evil force that asserts itself against

God and that violates His laws (cp. 1 John 3:4; Rom. 8:7). The manifestation of lawlessness in this world is not a secret, for it is seen in every part of sinful human society (cp. Matt. 7:21–23; 23:28). The "mystery of lawlessness," unknown to the world but revealed to God's people, is the fact that the guiding genius of this world's lawlessness is Satan and that it will reach a climax in the career of his human agent, the Beast out of the sea, during the second half of the Tribulation Age (2 Thess. 2:3–12; Rev. 13).

Although the Holy Spirit is not named in 2 Thessalonians 2:7, the interpretation that identifies the pronoun "he" as referring to Him, in my opinion, best fits the context. He alone is capable of holding Satan and sin in check until God's time for their full, unbridled activity and expression. When the Lord's present work of building His Church is completed and He removes her from the earth, then the Holy Spirit will relax His restraint upon lawlessness and will allow the Beast ("the lawless one") to pursue his prophetic career under Satan's direction (2 Thess. 2:8–10; Rev. 13:1–9). The Holy Spirit's relaxation of restraint, described as His being "taken out of the way," does not mean that He will be removed from the earth. Being God, the Holy Spirit is always omnipresent; also, God's program and His people will need the Holy Spirit's continued ministry in this world. It means that He will allow lawlessness to run its full course, without divine restraint.

In restraining evil today, the Holy Spirit uses the lives of godly people (Matt. 5:13), human government (Rom. 13:1–4), people's innate sense of morality (2:14–15), and the influence of the Scriptures (John 17:17) as well as the direct application of His own sovereign power. It is this restraint that will be removed from earth during the Tribulation Age. Social conditions will be so wicked in those days that good social influences will be absent or ineffective (Matt. 24:10, 12).

The Holy Spirit's Presalvational Ministry to Unsaved People

The Holy Spirit ministers evangelistically to unsaved people by showing them their spiritual need for salvation, testifying to Jesus' atoning sacrifice, appealing to them to trust in the Savior and, in the case of the elect, imparting to them salvational faith in Jesus. ✓ This presalvational ministry of the Holy Spirit to the elect may be described as a kind of presalvational "sanctification," or their being set apart unto the gospel (1 Peter 1:2; 2 Thess. 2:13; cp. Rom. 15:16).

1. *The Holy Spirit's ministry of conviction*

The Lord Jesus' description of this work is given in John 16:8–11.

   a. Its meaning

The verb *reprove* (John 16:8; Gk. *elenkei*) may also be translated "convince," "convict," or "rebuke." It bears the connotation of bringing something to light, exposing, setting forth, or of pointing out something (John 3:20). The reproving work of the Holy Spirit is His showing the unsaved person his or her spiritual need for salvation from sin.

   b. Its necessity

The need for this convicting ministry is that unsaved people are spiritually blind to the essential facts of the gospel (2 Cor. 4:3–4). Also, being spiritually dead, they are naturally unreceptive to divine things, spiritual values, and biblical truth (Eph. 4:17–19; cp. Rom. 3:11, 18; 1:21–23). Finally, they are totally depraved (Rom. 3:10–12), which means that sin has adversely affected their total person. In their natural state unsaved people by themselves have neither the desire nor the ability to move toward God (cp. John 5:40; 6:44; Rom. 1:18; 3:10–12).

   c. Its content

The Holy Spirit convicts sinners of sin, righteousness, and judgment (John 16:8–11).

1) "Sin" is the unsaved person's problem before God (John 16:9).

The Holy Spirit shows unsaved people their sinfulness before God. Because of their unbelief toward the Savior, they are still in their sins, both original and actual, which brings them divine condemnation (Rom. 5:18; 3:9–20; John 8:24, 34; 3:18).

2) "Righteousness" concerns the unsaved person's lack before God (John 16:10).

The Holy Spirit shows unsaved people their lack of righteousness—the quality and condition of life that God requires of His personal creatures (Rom. 3:10) and that is exemplified by Jesus (Matt. 3:17; John 3:19; 1 John 2:29). The sinner has nothing wherewith he can commend himself to God (Rom. 3:10–23). Even his religion, whatever it may be, is insufficient to provide him with the required righteousness. The Savior's returning to the Father points to the success of His atoning work and to the availability of God's gift of righteousness in Him, which is now offered to all through the gospel (Rom. 3:21–24; 5:1; 1 Cor. 1:30).

3) "Judgment" points to the unsaved person's accountability to God (John 16:11).

Possessing moral awareness and self-determination, people must answer to God for their actions (cp. Acts 24:25; Heb. 9:27; Matt. 12:36–37). Being already divinely condemned and having a judge who is alive forevermore, the sinners' judicial accounting is inescapable and their doom is certain (Rom. 5:18; John 3:18; Acts 7:31). Also, because his condemnation was confirmed by our Lord's crucifixion and his power was broken by Jesus' resurrection, the Devil's execution is sure (Rev. 20:10; 1 John 2:17). All who remain on Satan's side are serving a lost cause and will share their leader's doom (Matt. 25:41, 46; Rev. 20:15).

When we present the gospel to unsaved people, we can cooperate with the Holy Spirit by emphasizing these truths, which He uses to show them their spiritual condition and need.

2. The Holy Spirit's witness to Jesus

The Holy Spirit also points to the Lord Jesus as the only one who can provide for unsaved people's spiritual need (cp. John 15:26; Acts 4:12). Because of His atoning work, only the Lord Jesus can deliver people from the guilt, ruin, and bondage of their sins, provide them with true righteousness, and save them from divine judgment.

In our gospel presentation we can cooperate with the Holy Spirit by speaking to unsaved people about Jesus' atoning death in their place and His triumph over death by resurrection (1 Cor. 1:23–24; 2:1–5; 15:1–3). This explanation of His atoning sacrifice gives the reason for their trusting in Him as their Savior from sin. He is the only One who can deliver them from their sins and their dreadful effects (John 3:16; 6:35; 14:6; Acts 4:12). This is "the preaching of the cross" (1 Cor. 1:18).

3. The Holy Spirit's urging people to believe in the gospel

This ministry of the Holy Spirit is evident in the appeals of the gospel and of its messengers to unsaved people to trust in Jesus and His atoning work (Acts 10:43; 16:31; 17:30; 20:21; 26:20, 28; cp. 1 Cor. 2:4; Heb. 3:7–8). Gospel presentation involves more than declaration of truth; it also includes exhortation for a positive response to this truth (Acts 2:40; 28:23). We must gently urge people to accept God's offer, for it is "the day of salvation," and they may never have another opportunity (2 Cor. 6:2). But we must be careful not to coerce them.[7] If they are gospel rejecters, we must let them be (Matt. 7:6; Acts 13:45–46).[8]

4. The Holy Spirit's imparting repentance and faith

Left to themselves, sinners would never receive the Savior, although they may be aware of their spiritual need and of Jesus' atoning sacrifice. Because of their complete depravity and inability, they neither desire nor are able to take the initiative to move toward God (John 5:40; 6:44; Rom. 3:11). However, in keeping with the divine sovereign purpose, the Holy Spirit gives the elect the disposition of heart to repent (Acts 5:31; 11:18) and to trust in the Savior and His atoning work (2 Peter 1:1; Acts 3:16).

Calvinists identify this influence of the Holy Spirit that results in the salvation of the elect as *efficacious grace,* or *irresistible grace,* which cannot be resisted successfully. Wesleyans, who are Arminian in their theology, hold the doctrine of *prevenient grace.* This states that God has already bestowed His grace upon all people, that this grace sets aside the guilt of original sin and creates in unsaved people the beginning of spiritual life, which leads on to further life if they respond to it, and that this grace can be successfully resisted unto one's damnation. Thus, according to the Arminian view that sees man's will as free, the sinner has the final say about his salvation. This Arminian view sees salvation, then, as a two-party contract, "a covenant of personal relationship with God," which is entered voluntarily and which can be annulled by sinning.[9] In keeping with the biblical concept that salvation is wholly God's work, I prefer the Calvinistic view.

Although unsaved people are incapable of trusting in the Savior by themselves, God still makes a genuine appeal through the gospel for them to do so. Because the Lord Jesus died for all mankind (1 John 2:2), anyone can be saved who trusts in Him for their salvation. Moreover, the gospel messengers' duty is to minister to all the world (Mark 16:15; Luke 24:47). They have no way of recognizing those whom God has chosen to save before they receive or reject the Savior.

The Holy Spirit's Ministry to Saved People

The Holy Spirit has a key role in saved people's lives, not only at the time of their salvation but also throughout their Christian lifetime and ministry. As you consider this, ask Him to give you an understanding of these truths and to help you make any needed adjustments in your life so that He can do for you what He longs to do.

At the Time of Salvation

When we who are saved trusted in the Lord Jesus as our Savior, we immediately received several simultaneous works of the Holy Spirit. Let us look at these divine operations.

1. *The Holy Spirit regenerated us (Titus 3:5; cp. John 3:3–8).*
   a. *Definition*
     Regeneration is the act of God the Holy Spirit whereby, in response to salvational faith, He cleanses and renews the gospel believers' inner beings and imparts to them spiritual life.[10]
   b. *Observations*
   One: Like the other parts of salvation, regeneration is an act of the divine Trinity (John 1:13)—the Father (1 Peter 1:3), the Son (John 10:28), and the Holy Spirit (Gal. 5:25; John 3:3–7).

   Two: The renewing work of regeneration is preceded by cleansing or the removal from gospel believers the guilt and defilement of their sins (Titus 3:5; 1 Cor. 6:11; Heb. 9:14).

   Three: Contrary to the teaching of Calvinistic theology, which holds that regeneration precedes the exercise of salvational faith, I prefer the view that regeneration follows this faith (John 6:53–57).[11] Being God's gift, salvational faith, which is itself dynamic, imparts to the elect person the ability to believe the gospel. While it is true that unsaved people are totally depraved and are naturally unwilling and unable to receive the Savior, those elected to salvation are divinely given salvational repentance and faith so that they can and will trust in the Savior (2 Peter 1:1; Acts 3:16; 11:18). However, this gift of salvational faith is not to be regarded as the gift of spiritual life. To my mind, unsaved people are not made spiritually alive before they believe the gospel (cp. John 1:12; Acts 16:31); they are made spiritually alive immediately upon trusting in the Savior (John 6:53).

Four: Although it requires a human response to the gospel (John 3:36; Acts 17:30), regeneration takes place apart from human means (John 1:13). It immediately follows the divine impartation of salvational repentance and faith (Acts 3:16; 5:31; 11:18; 20:21).

Five: Regeneration occurs instantly in response to salvational faith, whereas the presalvational work of the Holy Spirit may cover a period of time, often many years (cp. John 1:13; 3:3, 5, 7).

Six: Regeneration itself is imperceptible in that it is not a sensuous, human experience. The Christian experience of blissful feelings and good works proceeds from the inward renewal and the new life that are produced by this instantaneous, regenerative act of God (Acts 16:33–34).

Seven: Before imparting spiritual life to the gospel believer, the Holy Spirit first renews (Titus 3:5), not replaces, his inner being (personhood, soul, and spirit), which had been ruined and defiled by sin (Eccl. 9:3; Jer. 17:9; Mark 7:20–23; Eph. 4:17–19; cp. Luke 5:37–38). By recreating his inner being in righteousness and holiness (Eph. 4:24), this divine renewal gives the gospel believer the capability to understand spiritual truth, to express godly emotions, to have right attitudes, and to make right moral decisions. Thus the gospel believer is inwardly renovated (Acts 15:9; 1 Peter 1:9, 22; Heb. 10:39), and he is made a new creature in Christ (Eph. 2:10; 2 Cor. 5:17; Col. 3:10). Although the body still has the sin force and is mortal, or subject to death (Rom. 7:17–18; 8:10), one can anticipate its future deliverance from sin and death (Rom. 8:11, 23; Phil. 3:20–21). Despite the fact that their saved inner beings are still susceptible to the sin force, resident in the body's flesh, saved people can now yield their total beings to the Holy Spirit and allow Him to use them as holy instruments of righteousness (Rom. 6:11–13, 17–22).

Eight: The everlasting life, which the Holy Spirit imparts to gospel believers by regeneration, is more than the perpetuation of life's present experience in this world. It is a new kind of life, which is the spiritual life that the Lord Jesus has in His humanity and that He gives to gospel believers (John 14:6; Col. 3:4; 1 John 5:11–12). Derived from an intimate relationship with God (John 17:3), this new life brings gospel believers a new power (Phil. 4:13; John 14:6), a new rule of conduct (Gal. 6:2; 2 Tim. 3:16–17), a new life objective (1 Cor. 10:31), a new knowledge (1 Cor. 2:12), a new association (1 Cor. 1:9; 1 John 1:3), a new character (Gal. 5:22–23), new resources (Heb. 13:5–6; John 7:37–39; 2 Peter 1:3), a new desire and activity (Phil. 2:13), a new life direction (Eph. 2:10; 5:17), new interests (Col. 3:1), a new citizenship (Phil. 3:20), a new expectancy (Titus 2:13), and a new destination (John 14:2–3).

Nine: By regeneration gospel believers are born into God's family as His children (John 1:12; Eph. 2:19; 5:1) and are made members of His kingdom as citizens (John 3:3; Col. 1:13).[12] Immediately following their entrance into God's family by the new birth, gospel believers are given, by divine adoption, the position of adult-sons in His family (Eph. 1:5; see "The Components of Salvation: Adoption" under Soteriology).

Ten: The gospel believer's new life (eternal life) is Jesus' human spiritual life, not His divine life (John 14:6).[13] The Holy Spirit communicates to us this new life to the extent that Jesus and His life are now in all who are saved (John 14:20; Col. 1:27; Heb. 3:14; 1 John 5:12). As we keep in touch with Jesus by abiding in Him, we allow Him to produce His fruit in us and to express Himself through us as Christlikeness (John 15:1–5). Though we shall never become God, we gospel believers are members of a new human race, of which Jesus, the Last Adam, is the Leader and Pattern (1 Cor. 15:22; 2 Cor. 5:17; Rom. 8:29) and in which we, with Him, are brothers (Rom. 8:29; Heb. 2:11).

2. *The Holy Spirit baptized us.*

a. *Definition*

There are two aspects of the Holy Spirit's baptizing work. Keep in mind that *baptism* (Gk. *baptisma*) means an immersion or placement into something.

One: There is His baptizing gospel believers into Christ (Gal. 3:27–28). This aspect of the Holy Spirit's baptizing work emphasizes His bringing gospel believers into a spiritual position in Jesus and into a spiritual union with Jesus and with all other believers who are in Him. This baptism into Jesus (Gal. 3:27) is the basis for gospel believers' positional blessings "in Him" (Eph. 1:3, 7, 11; 2:6, 10; Col. 2:10–13; 1 Cor. 1:2, 30) and their positional unity with Him and with one another in Him (John 17:21; Gal. 3:28; 1 Cor. 10:17).

Two: There is His baptizing gospel believers into the Universal Church (1 Cor. 12:13). This aspect of His baptizing work emphasizes His bringing Church Age gospel believers into the Lord's mystical body, the Universal Church (1 Cor. 12:27; Eph. 1:22–23; Gal. 3:27). This baptism unites all Church Age gospel believers to form an organism, of which Jesus is the life and head (Eph. 1:22; 4:14–15; 5:23; Col. 1:18; 3:4). Although as man Jesus has a physical body in heaven, yet by means of the Holy Spirit He lives in and works through His people on earth to build His Church (John 14:20; 15:1–5; 1 Cor. 6:15; Rom. 12:1–5; see "The Holy Spirit indwelt us" in this chapter).

b. *Several observations about His baptizing work*

One: In His saying that His method of baptizing with the Holy Spirit corresponded to John's baptizing with water (Acts 1:5; cp. Matt. 3:11; Mark 1:8; Luke 3:16; John 1:33), Jesus announced His baptizing placement of His people "into" [Gk. *en*] the Holy Spirit (Acts 1:5). This occurred first on the Day of Pentecost (2:1–4). Today, it occurs at salvation (1 Cor. 12:13; Gal. 3:27).[14]

Two: The aspects of this baptism are instantaneous and nonexperiential, occurring beyond the range of our sensation and feeling.[15]

Three: This baptism occurs once for all to all gospel believers at the time of their salvation (1 Cor. 12:13; Gal. 3:27). There is no NT command for people to seek this baptism or to receive it.

Four: The initial baptism with the Holy Spirit took place on the Day of Pentecost, ten days after Jesus' ascension to heaven. This is shown by the Lord's prediction (Acts 1:5) and by the apostle Peter's interpretation of the Pentecostal phenomenal events as indicating that the baptism by the Holy Spirit had occurred (Acts 11:15–16 with 2:1–4). While some hold that all gospel believers, living at this time, received the Holy Spirit's baptism, it is more likely that only the 120 believers who were gathered in an upper room in Jerusalem received this initial baptism (Acts 1:12–15). Apparently, gospel believers in other places did not receive this baptism until they were contacted by the Lord's apostles (cp. Acts 19:2–6). Today, this baptism takes place immediately at salvation (Gal. 3:26–28; 2 Cor. 5:17; Eph. 2:10). We are never commanded to seek this baptism as a "second work of grace." Furthermore, we are never commanded to seek the Pentecostal signs of this event since we now have the NT Scriptures that provide us with the teaching that gospel believers are baptized with the Holy Spirit at salvation.

Five: It appears that OT saved people were also baptized into Christ (not into His body, the Church) after the completion of His atoning work (perhaps before His ascension, for He is the redemption and righteousness of all His people [1 Cor. 1:30; cp. 15:22; 2 Cor. 5:17; Eph. 2:10; see Appendix D: "The Ones Who Are in Christ"]).

Six: The baptism with the Holy Spirit must be distinguished from His filling gospel believers to energize and direct them (Eph. 5:18). Being distinct, separate works, this baptism occurs once for all at salvation, whereas His filling takes place repeatedly throughout the believer's lifetime (cp. Acts 1:5 with 2:4; 4:8, 31). The people who were baptized with the Holy Spirit on the Day of Pentecost were also filled with Him (Acts 1:8; 2:4).

Seven: We must distinguish between the baptism with the Holy Spirit into Christ (Gal. 3:27; Rom. 6:3) and ritual baptism into water in the name of the Lord (Acts 2:38; 8:16; 10:48; 19:5). The only relation that water baptism (immersion) has to the Holy Spirit's baptism is that this ritual is a symbolic reenactment of the gospel believer's participation in Jesus' death, burial, and resurrection by virtue of his spiritual union with Him. The saved person is to accept the fact of his being dead to sin and his being alive to God and to conduct himself accordingly (cp. Rom. 6:1–13; Eph. 2:5–6).

3. *The Holy Spirit indwelt us (John 14:16–17; Rom. 8:9, 11; cp. Titus 3:5–6).*

    a. *Definition*

        The indwelling of the Holy Spirit is His taking up His residence within the gospel believer's body and His abiding in him forever.

    b. *Observations*

One: Being instantaneous and nonexperiential, this action occurs once for all at salvation (Rom. 8:9; Acts 5:32; 19:2). However, the Lord Jesus gave the Holy Spirit to His disciples as their indwelling Helper on the evening following His resurrection (John 14:17; 20:22).

Two: This action results in our having the Holy Spirit as God's promised gift (John 14:16–17; Rom. 5:5; 1 Cor. 2:12; 12:13; 2 Cor. 5:5; Gal. 3:2; 4:6; 1 John 3:24; 4:13). This reception of the Holy Spirit must be distinguished from His baptizing and anointing the Lord's disciples on the Day of Pentecost (Acts 1:5, 8; 2:4). This anointing with power for service was the result of their being brought into union with Jesus (John 14:20). Today, the indwelling, baptism, and anointing of the Holy Spirit are simultaneous events, occurring at salvation (cp. Acts 10:44–47; 11:15–16; 19:1–6).[16]

Three: It is impossible to be saved and not have the Holy Spirit (Rom. 8:9; Jude 19).

Four: The Holy Spirit indwells His people forever (John 14:16). By this emphasis the Lord assured His disciples that the Holy Spirit would never leave them, as He Himself was about to do (John 13:33).

Five: While He did not permanently indwell precross saved people (Ezek. 2:2; 3:24), the Holy Spirit was with them to perform all the ministries that He does for us today (cp. John 14:17; Luke 2:25–27).

Six: The bodies of the Lord's people are the sanctuaries of the Holy Spirit (1 Cor. 6:19, Gk. *naos,* the inner shrine of a temple where God abides). Observe that the Holy Spirit lives within the gospel believer's body, whereas the sin force is resident within the cells of the body's flesh (Rom. 7:18–20). Thus the Holy Spirit is not a part of our physical body as the sin force now is.

Seven: Besides the Holy Spirit, God the Father and God the Son indwell gospel believers (1 John 4:12–13; Col. 1:27). Keep in mind that being God, these divine Persons are everywhere present.

Eight: The Holy Spirit's indwelling seems to be complementary to His baptizing work. In keeping with Jesus' prediction, "I in you and you in Me" (John 14:20), the Holy Spirit's baptism placed us into Jesus and His indwelling brought Jesus into us (Col. 1:27; 1 John 5:12). By this twofold work, the Holy Spirit becomes the spiritual connection between the Lord Jesus and His people, by Whom there is transmitted to each of His people Jesus' power and vitality. This seems to be the only purpose for the Holy Spirit's indwelling us, for He does not have to be in us to minister to us, as the lives of precross saved people show. However, as we shall see, we must abide in Jesus to receive the practical vitality and benefits of this spiritual lifeline. Our abiding in Jesus closes this circuit and allows His vitality to energize us and His life to be manifest in us.

Nine: The Holy Spirit's presence is the divine seal that secures us until the redemption of our bodies (Eph. 4:30) and that is the pledge and foretaste of our future blessings in Christ Jesus (2 Cor. 5:5; Eph. 1:14 "earnest" means a down payment given as a pledge that the balance will be paid).

4. *The Holy Spirit sealed us (Eph. 1:13; 4:30; 2 Cor. 1:22).*

   a. Definition

   The sealing of the Holy Spirit is the work of God the Father, who sets the Holy Spirit as a seal upon each gospel believer to preserve him until the redemption of his body, which completes his salvation.

   b. Observations

   One: A seal is a device with a design that can impart an impression on a soft substance like clay or wax. It may also be the substance that has received this impression.

   Two: In the Bible a seal signifies several things: a completed transaction (Jer. 32:9–10), security (Matt. 27:66), ownership (2 Tim. 2:19), approval (John 6:27), authenticity (1 Cor. 9:2), and intimate dearness (Song 8:6). The primary significance of the Holy Spirit's sealing seems to be security (Eph. 1:13–14; 4:30), which anticipates the completion of our salvation experience with the redemption of our bodies from their inherent corruption, sin, and death (Rom. 8:23, 10–11). This will take place when the Lord Jesus returns for His Church (Phil. 3:20–21). Meanwhile, none of His people will be lost during their lifetime on earth (John 17:11–12), for they are preserved by this divine Seal. Although the primary significance of this sealing is security, it also conveys the other truths that are listed above. Consider how these truths relate to us who are saved.

   Three: This sealing occurs at salvation (Eph. 1:13 should read, "When you believed, you were sealed with that Holy Spirit of promise").

5. *The Holy Spirit anointed us (2 Cor. 1:21–22; 1 John 2:20, 27).*

   a. Definition

   The anointing of the Holy Spirit signifies our being divinely appointed to be Jesus' servants, or slaves, and our receiving the Holy Spirit for His helping us to do the Lord's will.

   b. Observations

   One: This anointing is by God the Father (2 Cor. 1:21), who uses the Holy Spirit as His means of anointing (cp. 1 Sam. 16:13; Isa. 61:1; Luke 3:21–22; 4:16–21).

   Two: As in the cases of David and Jesus, this anointing relates to service or ministry. It signifies the divine appointment of a person to an office, or work, and the divine enablement for this work (1 Sam. 16:1, 13; Isa. 42:1; Phil. 2:7; John 6:38; Acts 10:38). We who are saved are Jesus' slaves, for He bought us with His atoning sacrifice (Matt. 6:24; 1 Cor. 6:19–20; Rom. 1:1; 6:22; 14:8–9; 1 Peter 1:18–19). From the moment of our salvation, we have been given His commission and power to do His will (Matt. 28:19–20; Eph. 5:17; Phil. 4:13; 1 Thess. 1:10; Heb. 9:14). It is urgent that we learn what our Lord's will is for our Christian life and ministry and that we serve with Him in His great work of building the Church.[17]

   Three: By their receiving the Holy Spirit, the early Church was initially anointed with Him for service on the Day of Pentecost (Acts 1:8). Today this anointing takes place at the gospel believer's salvation (2 Cor. 1:21–22). We are not commanded to seek or ask for it. This anointing of the Holy Spirit should not be equated with His filling us, which occurs repeatedly throughout our Christian lifetime as we give ourselves to Him (Eph. 5:18).

   These works of the Holy Spirit at salvation are instantaneous, permanent, and involuntary. They never need to be sought for or repeated. We were also filled with the Holy Spirit at salvation, but this is not an abiding spiritual reality. We need His filling repeatedly.

Throughout the Gospel Believer's Lifetime

Since the Holy Spirit is the gospel believer's Helper (John 14:16–17), it is of utmost importance that we who are saved understand His ministry to His people so that we might cooperate with Him and allow Him to do all that He desires in and through our lives.

1. The need for His help

We saved people soon learn that the Christian life demands of us far more than what our human resources can provide. God requires us to manifest our Lord's moral character (Eph. 5:1–2), understand His truth (Col. 1:9), do good works or His will (Eph. 2:10; Heb. 13:21), resist powerful spiritual enemies (1 Peter 2:11; Eph. 6:12), engage in His service (2 Cor. 5:20), and worship Him (John 4:24). In short, we are to live a life of Christlikeness—the expression of Jesus' living in and working through His people (Gal. 2:20; Phil. 1:21; Col. 3:4).

How, then, can we do this? By means of the complete, abundant resources that God has given us (2 Peter 1:3). These include His Word (2 Tim. 3:15–17), grace (2 Cor. 12:9), faith (2 Peter 1:1; Gal. 2:20), prayer (John 14:13), the means of divine forgiveness and cleansing from sin (2 Cor. 7:1; Rev. 2:5; 1 John 1:9; 2 Tim. 2:21), the ministries of other saved people (Heb. 10:24–25), and the ministries of our divine Helper, who communicates to us the life and power of the Lord Jesus. The Holy Spirit is ready to help us to be and to do all that God requires of us.

2. The sufficiency of His help

The sufficiency of the Holy Spirit's help (2 Peter 1:3; 2 Cor. 3:5) is seen in His being able to reproduce in us our Lord's character (Gal. 5:22–23), teach us God's truth (1 Cor. 2:9–12; 1 John 2:27), enable us to do God's will (Rom. 8:4; Phil. 2:13; cp. 4:13), give us victory over our spiritual enemies (Gal. 5:16), energize and lead us in a fruitful Christian ministry (Acts 1:8; 15:4; Rom. 8:14), and help us to render acceptable worship (Phil. 3:3). He will do these things for us as we follow the instructions of His Word, rely on Him to do so, and seek by this to glorify God (1 Cor. 6:19–20). Thus it is consistent with our new life in Christ that we live by means of the Holy Spirit, who imparted to us this new life (Gal. 5:25).

3. The ways in which He helps us

As we examine the various ministries of the Holy Spirit that relate to the Christian life, we should keep in mind that His praying for us, convicting us of sin, and witnessing to us are wholly unconditional and involuntary on our part. Other ministries like His teaching us, guiding us, and sanctifying us occur with our favorable response to Him and His Word. Still other ministries are wholly conditional and voluntary on our part, like His filling us and enabling us to use our spiritual gifts in special ministry.

The Holy Spirit Prays for Us (Rom. 8:26–27)

This is not His unscrambling our prayers. The Holy Spirit actually prays within us with inaudible, inexpressible sighs. While this takes place below our level of awareness, from time to time it may rise to our consciousness as the yearnings of our human spirit. This intercession is effective, for the Father knows the mind of the Holy Spirit, who always prays according to the divine will (v. 27). He also enables us to pray effectively (Jude 20).

The Holy Spirit Convicts Us of Our Sins (1 John 3:20)

Since He convicts the unsaved of their sins (John 16:8–11), we can assume that the Holy Spirit shows us our sins as well. He points to known sins in our lives by our automatic moral monitor—the conscience ("heart," see Appendix B: "The Conscience") or by the reproof of others (Acts 5:3). He also shows us through the Scriptures those sins in our lives that are unknown to us or that we have forgotten (cp. Ps. 139:23–24). To receive divine forgiveness and to avoid divine parental chastisement (Rev. 3:19), we must deal with these sins immediately by repentance and confession (Rev. 2:5; 1 John 1:9).

The Holy Spirit Bears Witness to Us (Rom. 8:16)

The Holy Spirit bears witness to our human spirit of our relationship to God.[18] By this witness He makes meaningful to us the promises and declarations of God's Word that certify this relationship (cp. 1 John 5:6–12). He also gives us the inclination to call God "Father" (Rom. 8:15; Gal. 4:6).

The Holy Spirit Teaches Us (1 John 2:27)

Sometimes called "divine illumination," this is the Holy Spirit's giving His people an understanding of divine truth (John 14:26; 1 Cor. 2:7–12). He also gives His people discernment to distinguish between spiritual truth and error (cp. 1 John 4:1–6). We who are saved are not left to the mercy of human teachers for this understanding, for we, too, are taught by the Holy Spirit (1 John 2:27; cp. Acts 17:11). Nevertheless, we can profit from what the Holy Spirit has taught others. Apart from this divine ministry, it is impossible for anyone to understand the spiritual teachings of God's Word (1 Cor. 2:11–12, 14; 2 Cor. 4:3–4). Whenever we approach the Scriptures, our prayer to the Holy Spirit should be, "Open Thou my eyes that I may behold wondrous things out of Thy law" (Ps. 119:18; also 36:9).

The Holy Spirit Guides Us (Rom. 8:14)

The verb "led" probably means management as well as showing the way (cp. v. 5, KJV "after" means "according to"). As we look to Him for direction, the Holy Spirit shows us and leads us in the will of God (cp. Acts 16:6–10). He renews our mind in order that we may recognize and approve God's will for us (Rom. 12:2; Eph. 5:10, 17; 1 Thess. 5:21–22).

The Holy Spirit leads us by various means:

One: He uses the Scriptures, which by their commands, guiding principles, and examples, indicate what is God's will for us (Ps. 119:11, 105; 2 Tim. 3:16–17; Rom. 15:4; 1 Cor. 10:11; see Appendix F: "Learning and Doing God's Will").

Two: He leads us by inward impressions or urges (Isa. 30:21; Luke 2:27). However, we must discover the source of any urge by the teachings of Scripture before we give ourselves to it, for our spiritual enemies tempt us. We also must seek divine confirmation of the inner urge by prayer.

Three: He guides us through our circumstances, including people (Acts 11:24–26; 17:13–14; Prov. 21:1) and events (Gal. 4:13 with Acts 13:14).

As we give ourselves to the leadership of the Holy Spirit and look to Him for direction, we receive His guidance (Prov. 3:5–6). He will never lead us contrary to the Scriptures.

The Holy Spirit Sanctifies Us (1 Cor. 6:11; 2 Cor. 3:18)

To be sanctified is to be set apart from sin unto God for His manifestation and use. This occurs not only positionally at salvation (1 Cor. 1:2; 6:11) but also practically throughout the Christian life as one yields oneself to God and does His will (Rom. 6:11–23; 2 Cor. 3:18). God who is holy must have a people who are holy in their daily behavior (1 Peter 1:15–16; 1 Thess. 4:3, 7; 1 John 2:1). This requires them to avoid sinning and to do what is right in His sight (Rom. 6:16–22; see "The Components of Salvation: Nearness to God" under Soteriology).

To become holy in behavior is to be increasingly like the Lord Jesus. It is to move away from the old, sinful lifestyle that we had when we were unsaved, to conform to the will of God, and to display the moral qualities of Jesus (Eph. 4:17–5:20; Gal. 5:22–23). To experience this, we must separate ourselves from attitudes and behavior that are unlike Jesus (2 Cor. 6:14–7:1) and give ourselves to that which expresses Him (Eph. 5:1–2; Col. 3:8–14). The Holy Spirit brings this sanctification about as we respond to His prompting, instruction, and discipline (John 15:3; 17:17; Heb. 12:10; Rev. 2:7; cp. Rom. 6:11–13; 18–22; 8:2–4; Gal. 5:16, 22–25; Eph. 5:9).

The Holy Spirit Fills Us (Eph. 5:18)

This does not concern our receiving more of the Holy Spirit, for, being a person, He wholly resides in us who are saved and cannot be consumed. To be filled with the Holy Spirit is to be under His control or influence. This control is not absolute in the sense that we are passive and our personal faculties cease to function. It is to cooperate with Him in a way that allows Him to do His part as we do our part (cp. Acts 2:4; 4:8, 31; 6:3, 5, 8–11; 11:24; 13:52; contra 5:3). This cooperation with the Holy Spirit allows Him to energize us and to do, through us, all that He desires. While His filling is an intermittent experience, we should seek to be under His control more often and for longer periods of time (Eph. 5:18, "be filled" is in the Greek present tense of continuous action). What must we do, then, to be filled with the Holy Spirit and to remain filled with Him?

1. Our becoming filled with the Holy Spirit

To be filled with the Holy Spirit requires our adjusting ourselves to His presence and our cooperating with Him. This allows Him to do His part as our Helper. We do this by the following steps:

One: We must deal with known, personal sins, for these grieve the Holy Spirit (Eph. 4:30). When we become aware of sins in our lives, we must repent and confess these sins to God (Rev. 2:5; 1 John 1:9). Repentance, or a change of mind or attitude, is necessary, for a by-product of sinning is our justifying or excusing our wrongdoings. With repentance we regret and accept the responsibility of our wrongdoings and deal with them. We then must confess our sins to God with the confidence that He will forgive us as He promises. Keep in mind that confession without repentance is futile, for God knows the heart (1 Kings 8:39). In the case of those sins that involved other people, we must make right our wrongdoing and seek the forgiveness of those whom we have offended (Matt. 5:23–24). We must also forgive those who have offended us and have repented and made right their wrongdoing (Matt. 6:14–15; Luke 17:3; see Appendix W: "The Saved Person's Forgiveness of Others"). When we neglect to deal with known sins, we cause the Holy Spirit grief, which makes us very unhappy (Ps. 32:3–4).

Two: We must yield ourselves to the Holy Spirit's direction and power (1 Thess. 5:19; cp. Rom. 6:11–13). To "quench" the Holy Spirit is not to extinguish Him as one puts out a fire, for He permanently indwells us (John 14:16). It is to stifle Him or to hinder His activity in our lives by refusing to cooperate with Him. We do this when we resist Him or give ourselves to sin. We can correct this by dealing with our rebellious attitude and by giving ourselves to the Holy Spirit for His direction and enablement. We yield to His control by heart decision and prayer. The prophet Isaiah said "Here am I" (Isa. 6:8).

Three: We must rely on the Holy Spirit to do His part, as we do ours in Christian life and ministry (Acts 6:5). Since we cannot see or feel Him, we must rest on the promise that He will help us (John 7:37–39). Giving faith something to believe, our Lord's invitation is extended to all who thirst, that is, who have an inner desire rising from some spiritual need.[19] All who have spiritual thirst are invited to go to Jesus and drink (v. 37). We go to Him by prayer; we drink when, exercising faith in His promise, we receive from Him what we desire (v. 38). In response to this faith and expectation, the Lord provides for our thirst through the activity of the Holy Spirit, who resides within our inner being (KJV "belly"). The powerful energy by which the Holy Spirit ministers to our needs is vividly described as "rivers of living water." This powerful torrent, which is more than adequate for any need, flows from within us and abundantly satisfies our spiritual thirsts.

When we cooperate with Him in this manner, we allow the Holy Spirit to fill us. His filling, or controlling us, does not stop or replace our use of volitional, mental, or physical functions, for we are to be fully active (Rom. 12:2; 1 Cor. 14:15).[20] But as we act, we must rely on Him and the Scriptures in every circumstance for the enablement and direction that we need to do God's will. Also, His filling is not registered by our physical senses, but it is indicated outwardly by Christlikeness and inwardly by such fruits of the Holy Spirit as peace, joy, patience, and self-control (Gal. 4:19; 5:22–23). L. L. Legters wrote, "There is an evidence to you when you are filled with the Holy Spirit. . . . [It] is that Jesus becomes everything to you. You see Him. You are occupied with Him. You are fully satisfied with Jesus. He becomes real."[21]

We experience variation in the frequency and scope of the Holy Spirit's filling or control. The first is determined by the frequency of our surrender to Him and of our reliance on Him. The scope of His filling us is determined by the extent to which we give ourselves to Him. Although we may consciously give ourselves wholly to Him, there may be sinful attitudes or activities in our lives that we are not aware of because of our spiritual immaturity or ignorance. We do not knowingly sin as long as we remain yielded and obedient to the Holy Spirit (Gal. 5:16), but we may unknowingly sin at this time because of our lack of understanding. For instance, new gospel believers may not understand that they should be ✓ baptized after receiving Jesus as their Savior (Matt. 28:19; Acts 8:12; 18:8). This neglect would not prevent them being filled with the Holy Spirit until they learned their duty from the Scriptures. If they refuse to obey God in this matter, then they are living in disobedience, which is sinful in God's sight. Or they may be ingesting material that, unknown to them, is harmful to their bodies, the temples of the Holy Spirit (1 Cor. 6:19–20). But when the Holy Spirit makes them aware of this abuse, then it becomes a known sin that must be dealt with. We cannot be responsible for what we do not know, but we can be responsible ✓ for not learning what we should know. *LAW ?*

As saved people, our power of choice is always free; our control by the Holy Spirit or by the sin force is not absolute.[22] When we are under the Holy Spirit's control, we can still choose at any time to give ourselves over to the sin force and to its demands. At that moment, we cease to be under the control of the Holy Spirit and come under the control of the inner sin force. In like manner, when we are under sin's control, we can give ourselves over to the control of the Holy Spirit and do what is right in God's sight. In either case, we have liberty to yield ourselves (our hearts) to either controlling principle, God or sin, that would dominate our lives. During their conscious periods, saved people are never without the influence of one or the other of these forces upon their lives, as determined by their choice or by their neglect to give themselves to God. God does not take command of us without our invitation; the sin force takes command at every opportunity without invitation. Because of this, saved people are responsible to God for all their conscious actions (2 Cor. 5:10). Thus we should give ourselves each morning to God and throughout the day as new demands and needs arise in our lives.

2. *Our remaining filled with the Holy Spirit*

God not only wants us to be filled with the Holy Spirit but also to remain filled with Him (Eph. 5:18, "be filled" is in the present tense of continuous action). Keenly desiring to manage our lives (James 4:5), the Holy Spirit will continue to fill us as long as:

One, we are adjusted to Him. We experience His control as long as we immediately deal with those sins that He makes known to us (1 John 1:7, 9), give ourselves to Him whenever we consciously have need of His ministry (John 7:37–38; James 4:7), and exercise practical faith in Him (Gal. 5:25), sharing with Him all that concerns us and depending upon His direction and enablement.

Two, we follow His leading and obey His commands (Rom. 6:16–22; 8:14). When we refuse to cooperate with Him, we come under the control of sin and walk in spiritual darkness (1 John 1:5–7).

Three, we trust Him to do His part (Gal. 2:20; 5:16). The Holy Spirit will fill us as long as we rely on Him to help us.

Four, we give ourselves to those things that He uses to sanctify our lives like Bible reading (Ps. 1:1–3), prayer (James 4:8–10), worship (Ps. 34:1–3; 1 Thess. 5:17–18), Christian fellowship (Heb. 10:24–25), and submission to divine discipline (Heb. 12:5–12; James 1:2–4).

Five, we avoid what is evil (2 Tim. 2:19–22; 1 Peter 2:11). Our remaining filled requires us to avoid those things that are morally unlike Jesus, lead us to sin, hinder our spiritual lives, and compromise our Christian testimony (2 Cor. 6:14–7:1; Col. 3:8; Gal. 6:7–8; Heb. 12:1).

We lose His filling the moment we knowingly disobey God or yield ourselves to temptation. But we do not lose the Holy Spirit, for He remains with us forever. When we sin, we must deal with this by repentance and confession and must seek His filling again.

To be filled with the Holy Spirit is like closing an electric circuit that supplies power to an electrical appliance. The appliance will operate as long as the circuit is closed. In like manner, the Holy Spirit will control us as long as we are submissive to Him, follow His direction, rely on Him, and give ourselves to those things that He uses to make us more like Jesus. Such a relationship with the Holy Spirit is, indeed, a very intimate one. We can turn over our needs to Him and reaffirm our trust in Him at all times, for He is always with us as our Helper (John 14:16–17; Phil. 2:1; 2 Cor. 13:14).

Someone has given us a timely reminder: "We are warned to remember that there is no separate Gospel of the Spirit. Not for a moment are we to advance, as it were, from the Lord Jesus Christ to a higher or deeper region, ruled by the Holy Spirit." I would add that we should be suspicious of any movement or ministry that exalts the Holy Spirit above the Lord Jesus, for it is the Holy Spirit's purpose to bear witness to Jesus and to exalt Him (John 15:26; 16:14–15).

HIS RELATION TO SPIRITUAL GIFTS

As the Lord's slaves-friends, we who are saved have been left on earth for a while that we might labor with Him in the building of His Church (John 15:16; 1 Cor. 3:9).[23] The Lord is doing this work through His people by a general ministry that belongs to all saved people alike, which includes prayer (1 Thess. 5:25), giving (Gal. 6:6), Christian living (Eph. 4:1; 5:1–18), and sharing the gospel with others (Acts 1:8; 11:19–21). The Lord is also using a special ministry that differs among saved people and that is carried out by their exercising their spiritual gifts, with or apart from their natural abilities (Rom. 12:3–8). Every saved person has one or more spiritual gifts that enable him or her to serve with the Lord in this special ministry (1 Cor. 12:1–11). Needless to say, it is very important that we learn what our special ministry is and begin this work by the direction and power of the Holy Spirit. Let us consider what the Scriptures teach about spiritual gifts, how we can learn what our gifts are, and how to use them effectively for God's glory.

A Definition

"Spiritual gifts" (Gk. *charisma*, "grace gifts") are various measures of divine grace, or power, by which the Lord Jesus through the Holy Spirit enables His people to perform special ministries in His work of building the Church (1 Cor. 12:1–11; Rom. 12:3, 6; 1 Peter 4:11).

Several Observations

The Scriptures teach the following truths about spiritual gifts and their ministries:

One: As in other divine undertakings, Christian ministry in building the Church involves the activity of the divine Trinity (1 Cor. 12:4–6): the Holy Spirit is the Dynamic Cause in the distribution and exercise of spiritual gifts (vv. 4, 11), the Lord Jesus is the Instrumental Cause in carrying out the various operations through His people by the Holy Spirit (v. 5; Matt. 16:18), and the Father is the Originating Cause in initiating and bringing about the divine purpose for these operations (1 Cor. 12:7; 8:6).

Two: These spiritual gifts are measured operations of divine grace (Eph. 4:7; Rom. 12:3, 6; 1 Peter 3:10–11). This grace represents God's power in action (cp. 1 Cor. 15:10; 2 Cor. 1:12; 12:9). The various measures of this grace determine the kinds of special work that Jesus does through His people by the Holy Spirit (cp. Rom. 12:4–6; cp. 12:3; 15:16). The apostle Paul likens the Lord's people, with their various gifts and ministries, to the organs of the body, with their particular functions (12:6–8; 1 Cor. 12:12–31).

Three: These spiritual gifts are various manifestations of the Holy Spirit's working in His people (1 Cor. 12:7, 11); therefore, we must be filled with the Holy Spirit to exercise them effectively (Acts 4:8). To attempt to do these ministries apart from Him is futile and sinful (John 15:5; Rom. 14:23).

Four: These spiritual gifts are allotted by God (1 Cor. 12:11a, 28; Eph. 4:7–8) to all gospel believers at their salvation (1 Cor. 12:7, 12b; 1 Peter 4:10). No spiritual gift is possessed by all gospel believers; no believer has all the gifts. As Head of the Church, only the Lord Jesus has all the spiritual gifts and this to an unlimited degree (John 3:34).

Five: These spiritual gifts are activated by suitable measures of faith, which may be described as ministerial faith (Rom. 12:3).[24] Our reliance upon the Holy Spirit allows Him to empower us for and to direct us in these special ministries.

Six: These spiritual gifts are God-given abilities (1 Peter 4:11). Unlike our natural abilities, which are natural powers belonging to human nature, spiritual gifts are superhuman abilities that operate within the format of human environment and activity. Natural abilities may be used in special ministries in conjunction with spiritual gifts like those of helps, exhortation, and administration.

Seven: The exercise of spiritual gifts is concurrent with human activity. However, keep in mind that they cannot be truly exercised apart from the enablement of the Holy Spirit. Again, to go through the physical motions of a spiritual gift without His direction and energy is sinful.

Eight: These spiritual gifts are given to us for ministry to other people (1 Peter 4:10; 1 Cor. 12:7), not for our own benefit. We are blessed, however, when we exercise our gifts in God's will and way.

Nine: The exercise of spiritual gifts by the Holy Spirit's power glorifies God (1 Peter 4:11). Our use of these gifts under divine direction is stewardship, for which we are accountable to God (v. 10; cp. Rom. 14:12; 2 Cor. 5:9–10).

Ten: These gifts must be exercised in conjunction with Christian love (1 Cor. 13:1–3). The presence of this love in our lives indicates that we are filled with the Holy Spirit (Gal. 5:22), whose control is essential to the exercise of these gifts. This love also provides the proper attitude and motivation with which we can effectively minister to others (1 Cor. 13:4–7; Rom. 13:8–10; Gal. 5:13–16). Other essential qualities that should accompany the exercise of spiritual gifts are sincerity, diligence, and cheerfulness (Rom. 12:8).

Eleven: As we shall see, certain spiritual gifts ceased when there was no further need for them.[25] Also, God has enabled His people to use certain spiritual gifts, like prophecy, in OT times (1 Sam. 10:10). He will likewise do so in the future (Rev. 11:3; Joel 2:28–29). Our survey concerns those spiritual gifts that are given in the Scriptures, especially those that the Lord is using today in building His Church through His people.

The Recognition of Your Spiritual Gifts

To learn what spiritual gift or gifts you may have, consider the following procedure:

One: Give yourself wholeheartedly to the Lord with the willingness to do whatever special ministry that He has for you.

Two: Ask the Lord to show you what your gift or gifts are.

Three: Become acquainted with the nineteen NT spiritual gifts (Rom. 12:6–8; 1 Cor. 12:8–11, 28–30; Eph. 4:11, offices indicating gifts; 1 Peter 4:11), as given in the following survey.

Four: Ask the Lord to give you a desire for the work for which you are gifted and a burden for the people to whom you are to minister with your gift or gifts.

Five: As the Lord leads and gives you opportunity, for a short time try the various kinds of ministries in which you are interested and for which you may be gifted.

Six: Evaluate the results of these trial runs and seek the judgment of godly people regarding this ministry. Were you comfortable with your ministry? Were others blessed by it?

Seven: Seek those gifts that are most needed where you are or for the people whom the Lord has laid on your heart (1 Cor. 12:31).

Eight: Since your spiritual gift may involve the use of some natural ability, evaluate your natural abilities—like verbal comprehension, reasoning ability, physical skills, mechanical skills, and musical ability—and the opportunities that you have to use these abilities in ministry in conjunction with the exercise of some spiritual gift like helps, exhortation, or evangelism.

As you discover your gift or gifts, you will know what special ministry the Lord has for you in working with Him in building His Church.

A Survey of the NT Spiritual Gifts VS. ABILITIES

There are nineteen spiritual gifts cited in the New Testament. I do not believe that there are others. Let us look at the gifts that are operating today and those that are now inactive.

1. *The eleven spiritual gifts that are operating today*
   a. *The spiritual gifts relating to Bible ministry*
      1) The gift of evangelism (Eph. 4:11)
         (a) Description
             This office indicates the gift of evangelism, which enables a person to present the gospel clearly and effectively to unsaved people.
         (b) Application
             We must distinguish between exercising this gift in evangelizing and the duty of witnessing. All gospel believers are to be witnesses in the sense that they should tell what Jesus did in saving them and what He will do for others who trust in Him and His atoning work (Acts 1:8; cp. Mark 5:19). However, as the Lord's distinction between sowing

and reaping indicates (John 4:35–38), not all believers have the gift of evangelism. Witnessing is largely sowing the gospel seed; evangelizing includes reaping the gospel harvest as well as sowing this seed.

Formally, this means being a full-time evangelist at home or abroad. Informally, this means engaging in various church evangelistic outreach ministries, like home visitation, jail services, and hospital calling.

2) The gift of pastoral care (Eph. 4:8, 11)

(a) Description

This office indicates the gift of pastoral care, which enables a person to look after the spiritual needs of the Lord's people like those who constitute a local church. This care includes ministering to people's spiritual lacks and difficulties, promoting their spiritual growth, directing their united worship, preparing them for Christian service, and being an example to them. Keep in mind that God uses His Word to minister to people's spiritual needs (2 Tim. 3:16–17; 4:2).

(b) Application

This gift enables men to do formal pastoral work (see "The Administration of a Local Christian Church" under Ecclesiology).[26] This gift may be used informally by men or women to provide spiritual care for special groups of people within or outside the local church. In many cultures only women can give pastoral care to other women and to children.

3) The gift of exhortation (Rom. 12:8)

(a) Description

Represented by a verb (Gk. *parakaleo*), which means to admonish, encourage, comfort, or cheer, this gift enables a person to urge others to do God's will (Acts 2:40), to encourage the discouraged and fainthearted (1 Thess. 5:14), or to comfort the afflicted and bereaved (2 Cor. 1:3–7).

(b) Application

This gift is needed for practical applications in teaching God's truth (1 Tim. 6:2; Acts 20:2), evangelizing unsaved people (Acts 2:40), preaching to gospel believers (2 Tim. 4:2), speaking to people about their sins (2 Tim. 4:2), encouraging people in distress (Acts 27:22; 1 Thess. 5:14), directing people (2 Thess. 3:12), and exercising pastoral care (Titus 2:15).

Although one may not have this gift for a ministry of exhortation, one still has the duty to exhort others when the need arises (1 Thess. 4:18; 5:11, "comfort"; Heb. 3:13; 10:24–25). In exercising this gift, one should use God's Word (cp. 2 Tim. 4:2). This allows God to do His work in the hearts of people, and it gives one's exhortation divine authority. We who are saved must be willing to receive exhortation as well as to give it (Heb. 13:22).

4) The gift of teaching (Rom. 12:7; 1 Cor. 12:28)

(a) Description   DiscipLESHip

This gift enables one to explain God's truth clearly and effectively.

(b) Application

The Lord Jesus has given teachers to the Church to equip His people for ministry and to promote their spiritual growth (Eph. 4:11–12; Acts 18:11). Teaching God's Word allows the Holy Spirit to give people an understanding of spiritual truth (1 Cor. 2:12; Eph. 1:18), which is essential to bringing about their salvation and spiritual growth (Acts 16:14–15; Rom. 10:17; 1 Thess. 2:13; 2 Tim. 3:15–17). On the other hand, God's people are not at the mercy of teachers, for they, too, have the Holy Spirit to teach them (1 John 2:27) and the duty of verifying from the Scriptures all that is taught them (Acts 17:11).

This gift should be distinguished from the natural ability of teaching. The gift of teaching enables one to grasp and to convey to others the meaning of God's Word, which differs radically from other kinds of knowledge (1 Cor. 2:9–12). Women who have the gift of teaching should, whenever possible, avoid positions where they are required to exercise biblical teaching authority over men (1 Tim. 2:12; Titus 2:3–4). All teachers of biblical truth, whether in Sunday school or in seminary, must have this gift.

  5) The gift of the utterance of knowledge (1 Cor. 12:8)
    (a) Description
      It appears that this gift enables a person to understand, formulate, and state Bible doctrine in an organized way. This is suggested by the parallelism in 1 Corinthians 14:6, where prophecy and doctrine are presented as outward expressions of their internal counterparts—revelation and knowledge.
    (b) Application
      We should distinguish between teaching Bible truth and organizing this truth. The person with this gift can recognize, sort out, and put together in systematic order the teachings of Scripture. Not having this ability, many teachers of biblical truth must use teaching materials that are prepared for them.

  6) The gift of the utterance of wisdom (1 Cor. 12:8)
    (a) Description
      Since in the Bible *wisdom* sometimes refers to the practical use of knowledge (Eccl. 2:13–14; cp. Col. 4:5; James 1:5), it appears that this gift enables a person to discern the spiritual needs of others and to apply God's truth to their lives in suitable, practical ways (Acts 6:3).
    (b) Application
      People like Christian counselors who have this gift can relate God's truth to the everyday spiritual needs of God's people.

  b. *The spiritual gift relating to administering the Lord's work*
  1) The gift of administration (Rom. 12:8; 1 Cor. 12:28)
    (a) Description
      This gift enables a person to serve in a leadership position in the Lord's work, whether by making organizational and operational policies or by implementing them.
    (b) Application
      This gift is needed by church and parachurch administrative officers, including pastors (Heb. 13:7, 17, "rule" means to lead). The management know-how of the secular world does not itself qualify one to administer the Lord's affairs, for His work involves spiritual principles, methods, and goals that are not found in secular management (cp. Matt. 16:18; 2 Cor. 3:1–6; 1 Cor. 2:1–7; 10:31; see 2 Tim. 2). On the other hand, there are helpful applications of the world's administrative knowledge to the Lord's work, like organizational structure, operational procedures, and data procurement and preservation. The apostle Paul was careful not to misuse his administrative authority by abusing people (2 Cor. 1:23–24; 10:8; 12:19; 13:10).

  c. *The spiritual gifts relating to practical forms of Christian service*
  1) The gift of giving (Rom. 12:8)
    (a) Description
      This gift enables one to give in an extraordinary way of temporal things, like money or goods, to the Lord's work and to the needs of others, as unto Him (cp. Matt. 25:40).
    (b) Application
      This ministry, as well as ordinary giving, is needed for the support of the poor (Luke 12:33; Rom. 12:13; 1 John 3:17) and of the Lord's work (Gal. 6:6). The

generosity of the poor Macedonian churches may illustrate this gift (2 Cor. 8:1–5, 10–15). Despite their poverty, God's grace enabled these people to give liberally, sacrificially, and joyfully to support the apostle Paul in Corinth and in Rome (2 Cor. 9:1–7; cp. Phil. 4:10–20).

2) The gift of service (Rom. 12:7, KJV "ministry"; 1 Peter 4:11, KJV "minister")

(a) Description

This gift enables a person to function in the local church office of deacon or to serve people's temporal needs in some other capacity (2 Tim. 1:18). The word "ministry" is also used to represent one's spiritual service, like that of the apostle Paul (2 Cor. 3:3; 4:1; 5:18).

(b) Application

A related word *deacon* (Gk. *diakonos*) is used for an officer in a local church (Phil. 1:1; see "The Administration of a Local Christian Church" under Ecclesiology). Because of the wide usage range of the word *ministry* and its related terms, this gift apparently enables both men and women (Rom. 16:1–2) to serve the temporal needs of others (Acts 19:22; 1 Cor. 16:15; 2 Cor. 9:1; Eph. 6:21; Col. 1:7; 4:7; 2 Tim. 1:18; Heb. 6:10). It appears that this gift also covers the use of those natural abilities that are suitable to this ministry.

3) The gift of helps (1 Cor. 12:28)

(a) Description

This gift enables a person to render some form of support or assistance to another or to others in their ministries.

(b) Application

While the gift of service enables one to minister to the temporal needs of others, the gift of helps empowers one to assist another in his or her ministry. Covering the use of suitable natural abilities, this gift has a wide range of application. From the NT use of the word "helps" and its cognates, this gift includes assisting others in their ministries (Luke 5:7; 10:40; see Acts 19:22; Rom. 16:3–4, 21) and helping people to resolve their problems in ministry (Phil. 4:2–3). Exercising this gift in assisting others in ministry may include the use of natural skills in singing, instrumental music, secretarial work, church and property maintenance, and the like.

4) The gift of showing mercy (Rom. 12:8)

(a) Description

This gift enables a person to minister compassionately to the needs of others who are experiencing some kind of a crisis situation or personal distress.

(b) Application

This gift has a broad range of applications, especially in the form of emergency, medical, nursing, and social services (see Matt. 9:27; 15:22; 17:15; 18:33). While all believers are to seek to alleviate the distress of others (1 John 3:16–18), they who have this gift do so as their special ministry. The exercise of this gift also includes praying for these distressed people and ministering to their spiritual needs as one has opportunity and ability.

2. *The eight spiritual gifts that are not operating today*

Along with these eleven gifts that we have just reviewed, the eight remaining spiritual gifts were also active in the early churches before the New Testament was completed and widely distributed. However, these eight spiritual gifts are not needed today, for the New Testament now fulfills their purposes or functions.

a. *The gift relating to apostolic authority and activities*

1) The gift of apostleship (1 Cor. 12:28; Eph. 4:11; Rom. 12:3)

(a) Description

This gift enabled the twelve apostles to speak with Jesus' authority and to fulfill their commission as the Lord's authorized representatives in this world (Mark 3:13–19). The apostle Paul also had this gift (Acts 26:15–18; Rom. 1:1).[27]

The commission of the Lord's apostles was to introduce Christianity to the world after His return to heaven (John 20:21; Matt. 28:19–20). They did this by preaching the gospel and teaching Jesus' doctrines (Matt. 28:19–20; Acts 8:25; 15:35; Rom. 1:1–6; Eph. 4:20–21) to Jews (Acts 2:14–40; 9:20) and to Gentiles (Acts 10; Rom. 15:15–19), by bearing witness to Jesus' death and resurrection (Luke 24:46–48; Acts 1:8; 2:32; 3:14–15; 5:29–32), by planting and supervising the first Christian local churches (Acts 8:14; 14:26–27; 15:35–41; 18:23; Rom. 15:18–19; 2 Cor. 11:28; Titus 1:5; Rev. 1:4), and by giving the official account of Jesus' earthly life and ministry (John 15:27; 20:30–31; 21:24–25; Luke 1:2; 2 Peter 1:16; Acts 10:34–43).

(b) Application

This gift, with its alleged apostolic succession, is not needed today, for the New Testament, having Jesus' inherent authority, gives His teachings and supervision for His people. The title "apostle," meaning "one who is sent with a commission to fulfill," may apply to people who are sent out to preach the gospel (cp. Barnabas in Acts 14:14). But these people do not have the gift of apostleship and its inherent apostolic authority.

  b. *The gifts relating to giving divine revelation*
    1) The gift of prophecy (Rom. 12:6; 1 Cor. 12:28; cp. chap. 14; 1 Peter 4:11)
      (a) Description

This gift enabled a person under divine inspiration to speak or to write God's words (Deut. 18:18; Heb. 1:1; 2 Peter 1:21).

      (b) Application

Before the NT Scriptures were written and widely distributed, God made known His will and direction to the local churches through people with this prophetic gift (Acts 13:1–2; cp. Eph. 2:20). However, today there is no need for prophecy since the New Testament gives us all the divine revelation that we need for Christian life and ministry at this time (2 Tim. 3:16–17; cp. Rev. 22:18–19).

This gift must not be equated with preaching God's Word. *Preaching* is based on the natural ability of oral communication plus the spiritual gifts of exhortation and teaching and/or evangelism. The preacher does not speak God's Word except when he reads or quotes the Scriptures. He interprets God's Word, applies this truth to the spiritual needs of his listeners, and exhorts his hearers to respond suitably to what he is saying. *Prophesying* was actually speaking or writing God's words (Deut. 18:18). First Corinthians 14:3 describes how God used His Word, given through NT prophets, to minister to the spiritual needs of His people.

    2) The gift of discerning spirits (1 Cor. 12:10)
      (a) Description

This gift enabled one to perceive immediately whether or not a person who supposedly was exercising the gift of prophecy was speaking by the inspiration of the Holy Spirit.

      (b) Application

With prophecies being regularly given in church meetings and with many false prophets around giving their demonic messages, there was need for an immediate discernment between true and false revelations (1 John 4:1–3). Because of this, every congregation had at least two people with this gift for the positive recognition of the source of the prophecy, whether it was of the Holy Spirit or of a demon (Acts 13:1; Deut. 19:15). Having the Scriptures by which we can evaluate all alleged prophecies or messages from God, we do not need this gift today (cp. 1 John 4:1–3). We should distinguish between this gift and spiritual discernment or insight, which all who are taught in the Scriptures have for evaluating the spiritual character of people or situations.

c. *The spiritual gifts that served as proofs and/or signs*

As *proofs*, the gifts of healings and miracles bore witness to the divine commission of God's servants and to His working through them (Heb. 2:4). As *signs*, the gift of tongues conveyed special meaning to skeptical Jews, both unsaved and saved (cp. Matt. 12:38–39; 1 Cor. 1:22). In certain situations, this gift was also proof of the gospel believer's baptism and anointing by the Holy Spirit (see below).

1) The gift of healings (1 Cor. 12:9, 28, 30; Gk. plural)

(a) Description

This gift enabled one to impart, without therapeutic means, immediate healing to the sick.

(b) Application

This gift did not prohibit or replace the use of medical means in treating illness (1 Tim. 5:23). It was not exercised in every case of illness (2 Tim. 4:20), nor was it God's intention to heal all illnesses (2 Cor. 12:7–10). Since many illnesses were caused by demons, this gift apparently included the ability to cast out these evil spirits (Mark 3:14–15; 16:17; cp. 1:34; 3:15). The exercise of this gift served as proof to certify the Lord's apostles' divine commission (Heb. 2:4; cp. Acts 3:1–16; 4:29–30; 5:12–16; 28:8–10). Undoubtedly, God does heal some people miraculously today, and He heals others in response to the prayer of faith (James 5:13–16), with or apart from therapeutic means. Moreover, history shows that God does expel demons in answer to prayer. But I doubt that the spiritual gift of healing now exists that brings about instant, permanent cures on demand (see Appendix S: "Physical Healing").

2) The gift of miracles (1 Cor. 12:10, 29)

(a) Description

This gift enabled one to perform superhuman works in the physical realm, apart from and contrary to natural law.

(b) Application

Miraculous works, performed by the exercise of this gift, included raising the dead, showing immunity to venom (Acts 9:37–42; 28:1–6), and doing other wonders (5:12). The exercise of this gift served as proof to certify the apostles' divine commission (Mark 16:17–20; Heb. 2:4). God does miracles today, but these incidents do not require the possession and exercise of this gift.

3) The gift of tongues (1 Cor. 12:10, 30)

(a) Description

This gift enabled one to express one's inner feelings of praise to God by unique, nonrational utterances (see Appendix A: "The Nature of Speaking in Tongues"). The gift of tongues was not speaking in a foreign language unknown to the speaker but known to others.

(b) Application

The gift of tongues served several purposes:

As *proof*, speaking in tongues bore witness to the fact that the gospel believers in Jerusalem on the Day of Pentecost had received the Holy Spirit's baptism and anointing, which Jesus had predicted (Acts 1:5, 8). Since these spiritual realities could not be detected by the physical senses, God used hearing wind, seeing fire, and speaking in tongues to indicate to His waiting people that these predicted divine operations had taken place (Acts 2:1–4). Tongues speaking was also a proof of these divine works in the house of Cornelius, the first Gentile to be saved (Acts 10:44–46; 11:15–18) and among the

Ephesian disciples of John the Baptizer, who had not yet received the indwelling of the Holy Spirit (19:1–7). We do not need this kind of proof today, for the New Testament teaches that these works of the Holy Spirit take place at salvation. Hence it does not command us to seek them (Gal. 3:26–28; 1 Cor. 12:13; 2 Cor. 1:21–22; 1 John 2:20, 27).

As a sign, speaking in tongues conveyed special meaning to skeptical, or unbelieving, people (1 Cor. 14:22), especially Jews (1:22; Matt. 12:38–39). Tongues speaking on Pentecost was a sign to unsaved Jews that Jesus was the Messiah and Lord (Acts 2:4–6, 29–36). Tongues speaking in the Corinthian church, which met next to a Jewish synagogue (Acts 18:7), very likely was a sign to these unsaved Jews that God blesses all who trust in Jesus as the Messiah and Savior (Acts 18:3–11; 1 Cor. 1:4–9). Also, tongues speaking was a sign to saved Jews that gospel believing Gentiles also had received the blessings of salvation (Acts 10:23–24, 34–45). Finally, tongues speaking was a sign to precross saved Jews, like certain disciples of John the Baptizer who had not heard of Jesus' death and resurrection, that the apostolic message of Jesus' completed atoning work and resurrection was true (Acts 19:1–7). Today, salvational changes in the lives of gospel believers are sufficient evidence for skeptics.

As a means of edification, speaking in tongues blessed the speaker and, when interpreted, the congregation (1 Cor. 14:4–5). However, prophecy was more edifying, for it better ministered to people's spiritual needs by communicating God's Word and by doing this in the language of the congregation. Keep in mind that tongues speaking expressed only praise; it did not communicate divine revelation (vv. 1–33).

Not to be equated with the NT spiritual gift of tongues, today's alleged "tongues speaking" is a religious phenomenon, which at best rises from religious ecstasy or intense excitement. Other historical expressions of religious ecstasy have been jumping, shaking, barking, rolling, swooning, and, more recently, laughing. Biblical Christianity is a rational religion that is based on God's Word. True Christian emotion rises from an understanding of God's truth, not from irrational, emotional experiences that are open to demonic deception and influence. Because of this, the Lord's people must be wary of seeking spiritual satisfaction through some unusual experience rather than from an understanding of truth gained by the study of God's Word (John 6:35, 63; Col. 3:16a; Pss. 1:1–3; 119:97–105). All spiritual satisfaction and growth must be rooted in God's Word, by which He ministers to our spiritual needs and prepares us for every good work (1 Peter 2:2; 2 Tim. 3:16–17).

4) The gift of interpreting tongues (1 Cor. 12:10, 30)

(a) Description

This gift enabled one to understand and explain to the congregation the meaning of what was spontaneously uttered by people who were speaking in tongues.

(b) Application

This gift was necessary if the congregation was to be edified by the praise expressed by tongues speaking and if the speaker did not interpret what he had uttered (1 Cor. 14:5, 13–19, 27–28). The person who felt constrained to speak in tongues was to remain quiet if no interpreter was present (v. 28).

5) The gift of faith (1 Cor. 12:9)

(a) Description

This faith allowed God to do miracles through people who had this gift (1 Cor. 13:2).

(b) Application

It is associated with the doing of miracles (Matt. 17:20; Luke 17:6; Acts 6:8).

The Use of Spiritual Gifts and Native (Natural) Abilities

As we shall see, spiritual gifts and natural abilities are used by the Lord in the special ministry related to building His Church (see "The Formation of the Universal Christian Church" under Ecclesiology and "The Ministry of Working with God" under Zoeology).

One: The foregoing nineteen spiritual gifts of the Holy Spirit are all that are given in the New Testament. I do not believe that there are other spiritual gifts beside these, for the Scriptures provide us with the means to evaluate all spiritual activities and experiences so that we might discern what is of God and what is of Satan. Those that may appear to be extrabiblical gifts are, to my mind, natural abilities that are used in association with certain spiritual gifts like helps, service, or showing mercy.

Two: The Christian local church, together with the community that it serves, provides the arena of Christian ministry for most saved people. Therefore, it is important for saved people to learn what their special ministries are and look for opportunities to use them in their local churches or in the areas where they live. Many opportunities for ministry are also to be found on mission fields in other areas.

Three: We must distinguish between spiritual gifts and inherent abilities with which people are born. These abilities include verbal comprehension, reasoning, physical skills, manual dexterity, mechanical skills, space visualization, mathematical ability, clerical ability, linguistic ability, creative ability, artistic ability, dramatic ability, speaking ability, musical ability—both instrumental and vocal—writing ability, persuasive ability, leadership ability, teaching ability, culinary ability, organizational ability, and the like. In my opinion, the Lord uses these abilities in His work, in association with certain spiritual gifts, as indicated above in the survey of spiritual gifts. Among the many ministries in local churches and parachurch organizations (schools, hospitals, publishing, mission agencies, and youth camps) that require people with these innate abilities, there are secretarial work, financial work, ushering, hospitality, maintenance and repair, transporting, library work, various musical ministries, grounds keeping, cooking, interior decorating, translation work, literature publication and supply, auditing, custodial work, publicity, and reporting.

Four: When you learn what your spiritual gift or natural ability is, seek opportunities to exercise it where you are until God leads you forth to some other place of service (Acts 11:25–26; 13:1–4). If your gift or ability is not needed where you are, you may ask God for that which will meet the need, when there is no one else available (1 Cor. 12:31), or you may seek some other place where your gift or ability is required.

Five: Some spiritual gifts, which are required for special kinds of Christian service, are exercised in a format that requires special training. As you seek His direction, God will show you where you should receive this training as you consider the institutions that provide this instruction.

Six: Whatever your spiritual gifts and natural abilities may be, never attempt to use them apart from the Holy Spirit and without right attitudes (Rom. 12:6–8; 1 Cor. 13:1–3; Gal. 5:13, 22–23). Always seek to use them for the glory of God (1 Cor. 10:31). Also, do not allow them to remain inactive in your life (2 Cor. 6:1; 1 Peter 4:10–11).

Seven: The reception of spiritual gifts by the laying on of apostolic hands (1 Tim. 4:14; 2 Tim. 1:6) apparently, like speaking in tongues, was a sensuous, physical experience that indicated the activity or presence of nonsensuous spiritual realities. But this was not always done (Acts 10:44–48). With our having the New Testament, which gives us the truth of the Holy Spirit's ministry, including His gifts, we do not need the laying on of hands today to indicate the presence of certain gifts in our lives. Sometimes this is done in ordination

221

services as a symbolic act of identification and fellowship with the candidate in his gospel ministry (13:3).

HIS MINISTRY IN THE ACTS OF THE APOSTLES

Any study about the Holy Spirit must recognize that the book of Acts covers an important transition period in sacred history. It bridges the gap between the Gospels, which deal primarily with the messianic earthly ministry of the Lord Jesus, and the Epistles, which deal with Christian doctrine, life, and service.

While the book of Acts is a vital link in the transition from life under the Dispensation of the Mosaic Law to life under the new Dispensation of Grace, certain events of this transitional period are not normative for Christians today. These include waiting for the baptism and the anointing of the Holy Spirit (Acts 1:4–5, 8), experiencing the Pentecostal phenomena (2:1–4), the common holding of private property (vv. 44–45), and praying for the gift of the Holy Spirit (8:14–17). Today, we receive the Holy Spirit's baptism, anointing, and indwelling at salvation. Since we have the teachings of the New Testament that assure us of these truths, it is not necessary for us to pray for these blessings of grace or to experience their evidential phenomena, like speaking in tongues.

Although the Universal Christian Church and the Church Age began on the Day of Pentecost, ten days after Jesus' return to heaven, a number of years passed before the permanent pattern and character of the new age were established. For this reason, we should be cautious in seeking for or adopting a work of the Holy Spirit that was characteristic of those early days.

Roy L. Aldrich offers helpful observations regarding the transition problem of Acts:

1. A transition period was necessary to overcome the natural psychological resistance to change. It took a special revelation to Peter to convince him of the universality of Christianity.

2. A special period of preaching the gospel first to the Jew was necessary to confirm the promises made to the fathers. The "no difference" pattern of ministry developed gradually after the conversion of Cornelius. It should be remembered that in Acts the gospel was preached exclusively to the Jew first for about seven years (Acts 11:19). No one would argue for such a program today.

3. The signs and wonders can be partially explained as God's method of dealing with Israel. That these public miracles were intended to be temporary is proved simply by the historical fact that they were temporary—Pentecostalism to the contrary.

4. The signs and miracles were also apostolic in the broader sense to attest the authority of the messengers and their message for the new age. There was no personal apostolic succession. The appearance of the New Testament gave permanent inspired form to apostolic doctrine.

5. A transition period was necessary to reach all living believers with the new message and its accompanying Pentecostal experience. The inspired historical record indicates that only 120 believers were baptized by the Spirit at His initial coming. The Church began with this small nucleus out of thousands of living saints. The others were subsequently united to the Church by the baptism of the Spirit when they were contacted by the apostles or their associates. Thus Acts 19:1–7 (the incident about the disciples of John) is a sample of the common experience of believers who passed from one dispensation to the other without immediately hearing the Pentecostal message. Those who were saved after Pentecost received the Spirit at the time of faith. The one exception in the case of the Samaritans has been noted and explained.[28]

Paul's experience was not an exception, for it is distinctly stated that what he received in the house of Ananias was a filling of the Spirit (Acts 9:17). In the transition period there was an interval between regeneration and the baptism of the Spirit only for the Samaritans and for the living saints who passed into the new age without immediately hearing of Pentecost. For all others since Pentecost, regeneration and Spirit baptism are simultaneous (1 Cor. 12:13).[29]

HIS PART IN THE PRODUCTION OF THE NEW TESTAMENT

The New Testament revelation had its source in God the Father (Rev. 1:1–2; John 12:49–50; 14:10; 16:15), was given through the Lord Jesus (John 16:12–15; Eph. 4:20–21; Heb. 1:1–2; Rev. 1:1–2) and, like the OT canonical books, was inspired in its production and content by the Holy Spirit (2 Peter 1:21; 2 Tim. 3:16). This means that the Holy Spirit so controlled the NT writers that, without setting aside the human factor, He enabled them to receive the divine revelation and to record it verbally without error or omission, as the very Word of God. This work of the Holy Spirit was predicted by Jesus (John 16:12–15), asserted by the apostles (1 Cor. 2:9–13; 2 Peter 1:16–21; 3:2, 15; Rev. 1:1–2, 10–11), and testified to by the Holy Spirit Himself (Rev. 2:7; 14:13).

HIS WORK DURING THE PROPHETIC FUTURE

During the Tribulation Age

After the Universal Church has been completed and removed to heaven, the Holy Spirit will continue His work on earth as He does today, except for His baptizing people into the Church (1 Cor. 12:13, 27).[30]

During the Tribulation Age He will withdraw His restraint upon the forces of evil in this world (cp. 2 Thess. 2:7–8). Yet, at the same time, He will continue His work of saving the elect (Matt. 24:13–14; Rev. 7:9–14; 14:3–4) and of helping them in their spiritual lives and ministries (Matt. 10:16–23; 25:34–40; cp. Rev. 7:3–4; 12:13–14, 17).

During the Kingdom Age

During the Lord's earthly millennial kingdom, the Holy Spirit will continue His salvational work (Ezek. 11:19; 36:26; 37:9–10; Zech. 12:10) and will minister to the needs of His people (Isa. 30:21; 59:21). He will also enable Jesus for His messianic work (Isa. 11:2–3; 42:1–7) and will make known the Lord's will for His subjects by prophecy (Isa. 2:3; Joel 2:28–29). Meanwhile, He will continue to indwell His people (John 14:16), doing for them all that is required.

During Eternity to Come

The Holy Spirit will forever energize the Lord Jesus for His messianic work as prophet, high priest, and king, for the Lord's kingdom will continue forever after it unites with that of the Father (1 Cor. 15:24–28; Isa. 9:7; Luke 1:33). What new messianic programs the Father has for Him have not been revealed. Also, the Holy Spirit will continue to indwell all saved people forever as their Helper (John 14:16). He will enable them, as He does today, to minister with the Lord Jesus in His messianic works and will continue to animate their changed bodies. He will also continue to give them understanding of the unending revelation of the infinite God (1 Cor. 2:11–12).

NEED HELP IN ETERNITY?

OUR INTERACTION WITH GOD THE HOLY SPIRIT
AS HIS TEMPLES-DEPENDENTS

We have seen that all gospel believers received God the Holy Spirit at salvation as their permanent resident Helper (John 14:16–17, 26; 15:26; 16:7; 1 John 3:24, KJV "Comforter" means "Helper"). Therefore, their bodies are His temples in which He dwells (1 Cor. 6:19), and they are His dependents who are in constant need of His help (Eph. 5:18). Since the Holy Spirit is a person like the other Members of the divine Trinity, we who are saved can have intimate fellowship with Him (2 Cor. 13:14). We have considered the various ways in which He helps us as we look to Him to do so. Now let us consider the various ways by which we can enhance our relationship with Him as His temples-dependents.

OUR PRAYING TO HIM (PHIL. 2:1)

Our talking to the Holy Spirit is essential to this fellowship (2 Cor. 13:14). Since He is a person and our indwelling Helper, we can talk to Him about everything that concerns our needs for His ministries in our lives. You will recall that these ministries include His leading us (Rom. 8:14), His teaching us divine truth (1 John 2:27; 1 Cor. 2:9–12), His sanctifying us (2 Cor. 3:18), and His filling us for Christian life and service (Eph. 5:18).

Have you talked to the Holy Spirit today about your spiritual needs, duties, and the demands of life? Prayer is essential to our fellowship with Him.

OUR FAITH IN HIM (ACTS 6:5)

We must rely on the Holy Spirit to do His part as our indwelling Helper. This is illustrated by walking, which the apostle Paul uses as a metaphor for one's complete trust in the Holy Spirit (Gal. 5:16). As we rely upon our legs to carry and move us, so we must rely upon the Holy Spirit to help us in our being Christlike, resisting temptation, overcoming sin, doing God's will, serving with Jesus, and worshiping God worthily. We rely on Him by decision, submission, and trust—by deciding to do so, giving ourselves to Him, and depending on Him to do His part as we do ours. We cannot be or do acceptably what God requires of us without His help. Needless to say, when we are not trusting Him, we are sinning. Then we must deal with this by repentance and confession and give ourselves anew to Him.

Upon what are you relying for your life today? Are you depending upon yourself and your human resources or upon the Holy Spirit and His ministries? Did you give yourself to Him today with the confidence that He can be trusted to do His work in your life? This dependence on Him is essential to fellowship with Him.

OUR OBEDIENCE TO HIM (ROM. 8:14)

Since one of His ministries is to direct us, it is imperative that we follow His leading in our lives, whether His will is made known to us by the Scriptures or by other means (Acts 16:6–7). The Holy Spirit speaks to us as we read the Scriptures by impressing us with certain phrases or words. He also leads us by inner impressions or by outward circumstances and people. This obedience to His prompting is essential to fellowship with Him.

OUR CARING FOR OUR BODIES (1 COR. 6:12–20)

Since our bodies are His temples, it is important to avoid abusing and misusing them. We have the duty of caring for them, properly feeding them, and doing all that is required to maintain our physical health and strength. The Holy Spirit is pleased when we do not unnecessarily weaken our physical stamina, which directly affects our mental and physical capabilities, and when we use our bodies for holy purposes.

OUR WORSHIPING HIM (REV. 22:9)

Although He seeks to exalt the Lord Jesus (John 16:14), the Holy Spirit is worthy of our worship as well, for He is God (1 Cor. 3:16). We should respect His authority, give ourselves to His direction, praise Him for His person and works, and express to Him our gratitude for His love, faithfulness, and all that He does for us.

Did you thank the Holy Spirit today for His faithfulness, love, and ministries in your life? Can you adoringly and wholeheartedly give yourself to Him in gratitude for His abundant mercies and for His ministries in your life today (Rom. 12:1–2)?

What kind of a relationship are you having with the indwelling Holy Spirit? Are you honoring Him by allowing Him to fill His temple and to express His fruit and works through your life? Did you give yourself anew to Him this morning and ask Him to enable you to do and be all that God desires for you today? Are you sharing your daily activities with Him as your closest friend? He is pleased when you do this. It enhances your fellowship with Him.

We are grateful for the person and ministry of the indwelling Holy Spirit. It is urgent and fitting that we learn about all that He wants to do for us and that we cultivate an intimate relationship with Him. Then we can experience in our lives all that He lives within us to do, to the glory of the Father and the Lord Jesus.

A Review of Pneumatology

1. Give six reasons for believing that the Holy Spirit is a person. *P. 195-6*
2. Give four reasons for believing that He is God. *P. 196*
3. Why does the Holy Spirit have attributes that are equal to those belonging to the other Persons of the divine Trinity? *P. 197*
4. In what ways is the Holy Spirit subordinate to the other Persons of the divine Trinity? *197*
5. Give the generic, functional, and personal names of the Holy Spirit in the Old and New Testaments. *197*
6. Give four symbols found in the Scriptures that represent the Holy Spirit. *198*
7. What theophany of the Holy Spirit was manifest at Jesus' baptism? What theophanies were manifest on the Day of Pentecost? *198*
8. What role did the Holy Spirit have in the transitive actions of the divine Trinity in creating the universe and in giving divine revelation?
9. In what ways did the Holy Spirit help people during the Old Testament Period?
10. Briefly explain the Holy Spirit's activity in the following aspects of God the Son's incarnation: His conception, private life, messianic work, death, and resurrection, as well as in His building the Church today and His coming earthly rule. *199*
11. How long will the Holy Spirit continue to empower the Lord Jesus for His messianic works?
12. Why do many believe that the Holy Spirit is the Restrainer of 2 Thessalonians 2:7?
13. When this restraint upon evil is removed, why is it theologically incorrect to say that the Holy Spirit will be removed from the earth? *OMNIPRESENT*
14. Give four things that the Holy Spirit does to bring people to salvational faith in Jesus.
15. What does it mean for the Holy Spirit to convict people? *208*
16. Give and explain the three things of which the Holy Spirit convicts unsaved people to show them their need of salvation. *f 208*

209   17. Of what does the Holy Spirit bear witness to Jesus in His dealing with unsaved people?

18. Why are unsaved people not able and willing to place their trust in Jesus for salvation apart from the Holy Spirit's presalvational ministry?

19. Give the meanings of *irresistible grace* and *prevenient grace*.

20. Give and explain the five things that the Holy Spirit does for the gospel believer at salvation.

21. What parts of the gospel believer does the Holy Spirit renew by regeneration?

22. What kind of life does the Holy Spirit impart at salvation?

23. List several features of this new life that He imparts to the gospel believer.

24. According to the author's view, does regeneration precede or follow salvational faith?

25. How can people who are spiritually dead respond to the gospel without their being made spiritually alive first?

26. Into what family and kingdom have regenerated people entered?

27. Give the two aspects of the baptism of the Holy Spirit. Which of these is essential for membership in the Lord's Universal Church?

28. When did the first baptism of the Holy Spirit occur? When does it occur in our lives now?

29. How do we know whether or not we have been baptized with the Holy Spirit if we are not to seek the signs of this event?

30. Which of these two aspects of the Holy Spirit's baptism will continue to occur in those who believe the gospel during the Tribulation Age and Kingdom Age?

31. How long will the Holy Spirit indwell gospel believers?

32. Explain the meaning of John 14:20b, "You in Me and I in you." By what actions of the Holy Spirit are we gospel believers in Jesus, and He is in us?

33. What does the sealing work of the Holy Spirit mean? Why is this work important to the present state of our salvation?

34. What does the anointing work of the Holy Spirit mean?

35. What is the basic function of the Holy Spirit in the life of the saved person?

36. What other ministries does He perform in our lives?

37. By what means does the Holy Spirit guide us?

38. What does the sanctifying work of the Holy Spirit mean? How can we cooperate with Him in this?

39. What does it mean to be filled with the Holy Spirit?

40. What must we do to become filled? To remain filled?

41. What immediately ends our experience of the Holy Spirit's filling? How can we recover His filling?

42. Give a definition of spiritual gifts. What are natural abilities?

43. What is the relation of spiritual gifts to the Lord's work of building the Church?

44. How can one recognize one's spiritual gift or gifts?

45. What twelve spiritual gifts are operating today? Describe these gifts.

46. Which gifts are useful in ministering God's Word? In administering the Lord's work? In doing practical forms of service?

47. What spiritual gifts may cover the use of natural abilities in the Lord's work?

48. Which gifts should a pastor of a church have? A Sunday school teacher? An evangelist? A counselor? A youth worker?

49. What seven gifts are not operating today? Describe these gifts. Why are they not needed today?

50. Why should we be cautious in seeking to experience all that is recorded of the Holy Spirit's activities in the book of Acts?

51. What was the Holy Spirit's role in the production of the New Testament?
52. What will be the work of the Holy Spirit during the Tribulation Age? The Kingdom Age? Eternity?
53. How can we who are saved improve our daily relationship with the Holy Spirit?
54. What does it mean to be a temple-dependent of the Holy Spirit?
55. Is it proper to talk to the Holy Spirit? Give a reason for your answer.
56. What does it mean to "walk in the Spirit"?
57. What kind of a personal relationship are you now having with the Holy Spirit? Is He filling you daily?

Endnotes

1. This is contrary to normal Greek New Testament usage, which gives the word *spirit* neuter gender. Observe that in KJV "ghost" is often used for "spirit."
2. Observe that the Holy Spirit must be distinguished from the divine nature, which is spirit (John 4:24). These two "spirits" are not the same thing. The OT Hebrew words for "spirit" with reference to the Holy Spirit are *ruach* (Gen. 1:2; Isa. 40:7), from a verb meaning "to breathe out through the nose with violence," and *neshamah,* for ordinary breathing (Job 32:8, "inspiration"; Isa. 30:33). —Norman N. Snaith, *Distinctive Ideas of the Old Testament* (London: The Epworth Press, 1960), 143ff. The NT Greek *pneuma* means "wind" or "breath"— G. Abbott-Smith, *A Manual Lexicon of the Greek New Testament,* 367.
3. This was the view of the Eastern church. In 539 at the Synod of Toledo, the Western church asserted that He proceeds from the Father and the Son (W. G. T. Shedd, *A History of Christian Doctrine* [New York: Charles Scribner & Co., 1867], 1:361). To my mind, direct procession from the Father suggests the generation of sonship, which is not a biblical concept of the Holy Spirit. There is only one God the Son.
4. The conjunction "and" in Isaiah 48:16 may be explanatory, reading, "The Lord GOD, *even* His Spirit, has sent me."
5. Observe that an earnest (Eph. 1:14) is a token or a pledge, like a down payment on a purchase, which assures that the balance will be paid. A seal (v. 13) is a device with a design that can impart an impression on a soft substance like clay or wax. It also designates the substance that has received the impression. As we shall see, a seal may indicate authority, ownership, security, or a finished transaction.
6. There is a question about the meaning of Genesis 6:3, "The LORD said, 'My Spirit shall not always strive with men.'" Some believe that this refers to the Holy Spirit's striving with men to restrain them from their evil ways (cp. 2 Thess. 2:6–7). —H. C. Leupold, *Exposition of Genesis* (Grand Rapids: Baker Book House, 1953), 256. Others think that "spirit" refers to the "breath of life by which men are animated" and which "shall not always be powerful (KJV 'strive') in men." —Franz Delitzsch, *A New Commentary on Genesis* (Edinburgh: T. & T. Clark, 1899), 1:227.
7. The Arminian view that unsaved people have free will and are themselves capable of trusting in the Savior leads to coercive forms of evangelistic appeals. Having presented the gospel and urged people to receive it, we must leave it with God to draw these people to Himself according to His purpose (John 6:44).
8. Observe that in their response to the gospel, enlightened nonelect people may go to the point of recognizing their spiritual need, knowing what Jesus did about it, and understanding the gospel's offer. But if they reject this and refuse to go on to true repentance and trust in Jesus and His atoning work for their salvation, they will never again be brought to this point of gospel decision (Heb. 6:4–8; 10:26, 29–31).
9. See Charles W. Carter, general editor, *A Contemporary Wesleyan Theology* (Grand Rapids: Francis Asbury Press, 1983), 1:498.
10. See "The Components of Salvation: Regeneration" under Soteriology.
11. "Regeneration is the cause of conversion. The Holy Spirit acts in regeneration, and as a consequence the human spirit acts in conversion. . . . The converting activity of the regenerate soul

moves in two principal directions: (a) Faith, which is the converting or turning the soul to Christ as the Redeemer from sin; (b) Repentance, which is the converting or turning of the soul to God as the supreme good." —W. G. T. Shedd, *Dogmatic Theology*, 2:509; also see L. Berkhof, *Systematic Theology*, 468ff., 483ff.

12. Observe that the born-again person is God's product (Eph. 2:10), not His offspring in the sense that he has received the divine nature and has become God.

13. Second Peter 1:4 seems to mean that we are partakers of the divine nature (God's nature) in the sense that we have received God the Holy Spirit who indwells us (cp. v. 3, "God's divine Power"; Acts 10:38; Rom. 15:13, 19; also Acts 5:32; 1 John 3:24). We do not ourselves become God in this manner anymore than we become apples by partaking of them. If "nature" here refers to our human nature, then it is divine in the sense that it has been divinely renewed (Acts 1:9; Titus 3:5), though still human, and is now capable of expressing God's moral qualities like His love and holiness (Matt. 5:44–48; 1 Peter 1:15–16) by the Holy Spirit (Gal. 5:22–23; Rom. 14:17).

14. I belive that the Greek preposition *en* (Acts 1:5, "with") has the locative meaning "in" or "into." by Jesus' baptizing His people "into the Holy Spirit" at salvation, they are brought into a spiritual union with the Holy Spirit, who is the divine connection between them and Jesus. By this connection saved people are spiritually in Jesus and He is in them (John 14:20; 2 Cor. 5:17) and by this they receive His spiritual life and power (Col. 3;4; Phil. 4:13). Those, whom Jesus baptized into the Holy Spirit on the Day of Pentecost (Acts 1:5), had been saved earlier, but they had not yet received the Holy Spirit, as Jesus had predicted, until this day (John 14:16–17; 16:13). Gospel believers now receive Him at salvation (Rom. 5:5; 8:9).

15. With the initial baptism of the Holy Spirit on the Day of Pentecost, ten days after Jesus' return to heaven, God gave sensuous signs to indicate that what Jesus had predicted had occurred (Acts 1:5; 2:1–4). Having the teachings of the New Testament, we do not need these signs today.

16. The irregular events of Acts 8:14–17 may refer to the Samaritan gospel believers' receiving the Holy Spirit's baptism and/or His anointing rather than His person, or indwelling. See endnote 30.

17. See "His Relation to Spiritual Gifts" in this chapter; Appendix F: "Learning and Doing God's Will," and "The Ministries of the Christian Life: The Ministry of Working With God" under Zoeology.

18. The human spirit is the dynamic source of our human understanding (cp. Eph. 4:23). See "Humans Are Complex Beings: The Immaterial Parts of Human Nature" under Anthropology.

19. Our new life in Jesus has spiritual desires for holiness, righteousness, understanding, growth, courage and the like. See Appendix U: "Our Inward Desires."

20. See "His Deceptions: Satan Uses the Deception of Passivity" under Angelology.

21. L. L. Legters, *The Simplicity of the Spirit-Filled Life* (Philadelphia: Pioneer Mission Agency, 1939), 48–50.

22. Passages like Romans 6:12–13, 16 indicate that we who are saved always have the liberty to choose what moral force—God or sin—will control our lives. This special liberty is unaffected by the spiritual force that is presently dominating us. Hence, we are to use this liberty rightly and resolutely (Gal. 5:1, 13) and for the purpose of obeying or serving God (1 Peter 2:16).

23. The Lord Jesus is building His Universal Church on earth during the present Church Age (Matt. 16:18). He is doing this quantitatively by saving gospel believers and adding them to the Church (Acts 16:5b) and qualitatively by developing the spiritual lives of His people (v. 5a; Eph. 4:11–15). Because He is doing this work as man from heaven, the Lord Jesus is using the Scriptures, the Holy Spirit, and His people who are on earth.

24. See Floyd H. Barackman, "The Kinds of Biblical Faith: C. Biblical Ministerial Faith," pt. 2 of *Where Is Your Faith?* (Endicott, NY: F. H. Barackman, 1994).

25. First Corinthians 13:8 should not be used as proof that certain gifts like tongues have ceased. Using the gifts of prophecy, tongues, and knowledge as examples, the apostle seems to say that certain spiritual gifts, in contrast to Christian love, are transitory. They exist only as long as they are needed. He indicates what this need is by referring to what is partial which, to my mind, is the present, earthly spiritual experience of the Lord's people. Certain gifts minister to

their spiritual growth in their present incomplete state. In the future, these gifts will no longer be needed for this purpose, for these people will have entered the fullness of spiritual life (Titus 1:2; cp. 1 Cor. 3:11–12).

26. See Floyd H. Barackman, "The Kinds of Biblical Faith: B. Biblical Practical Faith," pt. 2 of *Where Is Your Faith?*

27. Matthias was appointed to take the place of Judas Iscariot, who had betrayed Jesus and committed suicide (Acts 1:15–26). The ministry of the twelve apostles was primarily to the Jews (Gal. 2:7–9); the apostle Paul's ministry was primarily to the Gentiles (Rom. 11:13; 15:15–16).

28. Dr. Aldrich's explanation of the experience of the Samaritans is this: "Peter and John ministered the Spirit to them sometime subsequent to their initial faith in Christ (Acts 8:14–17). The reason for this exception is not stated, probably because it is so obvious. The traditional conflict between the Jews and the Samaritans, about which people possessed the truth, had to be settled in accord with the Lord's dictum, 'Salvation is of the Jews' (John 4.22). The ministration of the Spirit by the official leaders from Jerusalem was necessary to avoid a destructive schism in the apostolic church" (p. 240).

29. Roy L. Aldrich, "Transition Problems in Acts," *Bibliotheca Sacra*, vol. 114, no. 455 (1957), 241f.

30. The Holy Spirit will baptize into Jesus these postchurch gospel believers, including those who will be saved during the millennial kingdom. These people will be made new creatures in Jesus (2 Cor. 5:17), will partake of His positional blessings (1 Cor. 1:30), and will be part of the new human race that God is creating in Jesus of all saved former members of the old human race in Adam (1 Cor. 15:22, 49; Gal. 3:27–28; Eph. 2:15–16).

Angelology

7

ANGELOLOGY
The Doctrine of Angels

That there are other created personal beings in the universe besides humans arouses our curiosity and alarm. Who are these creatures, and what is their intention? Are they friendly or hostile? Will they do us good or harm? The Scriptures reveal that these personal creatures are angels, both holy and evil, who live beyond the range of our sensuous means of detection and who are active in our lives. Let us consider what God's Word reveals about them.[1]

THE ORIGIN OF ANGELS

Angels are divinely created personal beings (Col. 1:16–17; cp. Ezek. 28:15). As part of the initial creation of the universe (Gen. 1:1), angels were created before the earth, perhaps before any material thing (Job 38:4–7). Like all else, angels were created by God and for His glory (Col. 1:16; Rev. 5:11–13). They were all created as holy angels. They never had preexistence as something or someone else and then became angels.

THE NATURE OF ANGELS

Angels are personal beings with an angelic nature.

THEY ARE PERSONAL BEINGS

That they have personhood, which makes them to be personal beings, is indicated by their manifesting personal features like self-awareness (Luke 1:19), self-determination (Isa. 14:12–14), moral awareness (Matt. 13:41), and perpetuity (25:41), as well as intelligence (Ezek. 28:12; Rev. 22:16; Eph. 3:10), emotion (Job 38:7; Luke 15:10; Rev. 12:12), desire (1 Peter 1:12), and accountability (1 Cor. 6:3; 2 Peter 2:4).[2] Also, like humans (Luke 3:38) they are called "sons of God" (Job 1:6; 2:1; 38:7; cp. Ps. 89:6), for having personhood they possess the divine image and are God's creation.

THEY HAVE AN ANGELIC NATURE

Unlike humans with human nature (body, soul, and spirit), angels have an immaterial nature (Luke 24:37–39), which makes them "spirits" (Heb. 1:7, 14). However, we must not think of their spirit nature as being the same as God's uncreated divine nature, which is spirit (John 4:24), or as our created human spirit, which is a part of our human nature (1 Cor. 2:11).

The unique spirit nature of angels (Heb. 1:14) has some kind of bodily organization or form (Luke 24:4; Dan. 10:5–6; cp. Gen. 18:2, 22; 19:1, 8; Jude 7), is indestructible (Dan. 3:25), is normally invisible to our sight (Ps. 34:7; cp. 2 Kings 6:15–17), and does not die (Luke 20:36). Sometimes, when appearing to humans, their faces radiate like lightning, and their clothes are dazzling, white as snow (Matt. 28:3; Judg. 13:6; Luke 24:4). Their flying may indicate that they have wings (Dan. 9:21; Rev. 14:6) as do the angelic orders of cherubim and seraphim (Ezek. 1:5–8; Isa. 6:2, 6). Whatever it may be, this angelic nature makes these personal creatures angels.

SEVERAL FACTS ABOUT ANGELS

1. They are many in number (Dan. 7:10; Luke 8:30; Heb. 12:22; Rev. 5:11).
2. They belong to a higher creature order than we humans in our present state (Ps. 8:4–5; Heb. 2:6–7).[3] Thus, they have superhuman strength and ability (Gen. 19:11; 2 Kings 19:35; Ps. 103:20; Matt. 28:2; Acts 5:18–23; 12:5–11; 2 Peter 2:11) and are not confined to earth (Matt. 22:30). However, they do not have infinite power, for they do not have God's divine nature.
3. Normally, angels are invisible to our present sight (cp. Num. 22:22–31; 2 Kings 6:17; Ps. 34:7). They have the ability to appear and disappear at will (cp. Acts 12:7, 10).
4. They are masculine (Dan. 9:21; Mark 16:5; Luke 24:4; Rev. 10:1–3). However, there is no biblical evidence for their having the capability to reproduce themselves (Matt. 22:30). Still, being masculine, evil angels are capable of having some kind of sexual union with female humans (Gen. 6:4; Jude 6–7).
5. They speak (Matt. 28:5–7; Acts 12:7) and sing (Job 38:7).
6. Having limited knowledge (Matt. 24:36), they are capable of learning about God's infinite wisdom and grace, as seen in His salvation work and in His program for the Church and for other saved people of mankind (Eph. 3:10; 1 Peter 1:12).
7. Being indestructible, they will exist forever (Luke 20:35–36)—the holy angels with God (Heb. 12:22–23) and the evil angels separated from God in hell (Matt. 25:41, 46).
8. They are irredeemable (Matt. 25:41). There is no evidence that Jesus' atoning work, which was for mankind, extended to fallen, sinful angels. In fact, hell was prepared for them (v. 41). The angels who were divinely elected to remain holy have no need for redemption (1 Tim. 5:21).

THE NAMES OF ANGELS

Their generic name is "spirit," which describes the nature that makes them angels (Heb. 1:7, 14). Most of their other designations are titles that express their functions. The most common title is "angel," meaning "messenger" (Luke 1:11–19). The only angels in the Bible whose personal names are revealed are Michael, meaning "Who is like God" (Dan. 10:13, 21; 12:1; Jude 9; Rev. 12:7); Gabriel, meaning "Mighty one of God" (Dan. 8:16; 9:21; Luke 1:19, 26); and Lucifer, meaning "Light-bearer" (Isa. 14:12), which was Satan's name before his moral fall, or initial sin. Although it is now used as a personal name, "Satan" is a title meaning "adversary." Michael and Gabriel are holy angels.

THE KINDS OF ANGELS

While all angels seem to have the same essential components—personhood and angelic nature—they are distinguished by their moral character. There are holy angels (Matt. 25:31; Luke 9:26) and evil angels (Matt. 25:41). Like Adam and Eve, angels apparently were given a probationary period to decide whom or what they would serve. The majority chose to serve God; others rebelled against Him.

Within each group there is a hierarchy of rank, with Michael as the leader of the holy angels (Jude 9) and Satan as the leader of fallen angels (Matt. 25:41). In Ephesians 1:21 and Colossians 1:16, these ranks are indicated by the words (KJV) *principality* or rule, *power* or authority, *dominion* or lordship, *might* or power, and *thrones* or kingly powers.

THE HOLY ANGELS

Their Functional Orders

These holy angels have specific designations according to their functions, or roles, in God's government and service.

1. The cherubim (Ps. 99:1) or the living creatures (Ezek. 10:15, 20)

The biblical references to the cherubim and the living creatures indicate that they belong to the same order of angelic beings. The cherubim are portrayed as belonging to the highest order of these celestial beings (Gen. 3:24; Exod. 25:17–22). They are closely associated with God's throne (Ps. 99:1; 2 Kings 19:15; Ezek. 28:14). They are also called "living creatures" (Ezek. 10:15, 20), who form a platform-vehicle for God's throne (1:4–28; chap. 10). They probably are the "beasts" (KJV), or "living creatures" (Rev. 4:6–8; 5:8, 14), who are active in the worship of God and in divine judgment (6:1, 3, 5, 7).

2. The seraphim (Isa. 6:2–7)

Hovering near God's throne, these angels proclaim the glory and holiness of God. A seraph, meaning "fiery one," was an agent in Isaiah's purification for his ministry to Judah (vv. 5–7).

3. The twenty-four elders (Rev. 4:4)

While many people believe that these angelic beings are redeemed humans who represent the saved peoples of the Old and New Testament periods, I prefer the view that they are an order of angelic beings.[4] They appear to hold some kind of administrative position in God's government, for they sit on thrones and wear crowns (Rev. 4:4, 10; 5:8).[5] Moreover, they serve in a priestly capacity, engaging in worship (4:10; 11:16–17) and presenting prayers (5:8; cp. 6:9–10; 8:3–5). They also engage in prophetic activity, perceiving God's purpose for creation (4:11), recognizing Jesus' atoning work (5:5, 9), and anticipating the future blessings of the Tribulation Age martyrs (7:13–17) and of Jesus' messianic millennial reign (11:16–18).

4. The angel of the LORD

This designation at times refers to a theophany of God (Gen. 16:7–13; Judg. 6:12–14) and at other times to a holy angel (2 Sam. 24:16). One can determine the identity by the context in which the designation occurs.

5. Ordinary angels

With "angel" meaning "messenger," these are active in serving God. Sometimes they are described as a "host," meaning "army" or "company" (Ps. 148:2; Luke 2:13). Their leader, Michael the archangel (Rev. 12:7–8; Jude 9), is also the defender of Israel (Dan. 10:21; 12:1).

Their Various Ministries

In obedience to God, holy angels perform a variety of services. The following is a list belonging to ordinary angels:

1. They render worship (Rev. 5:11–12).
2. They deliver divine messages to people (Luke 1:11, 26–27) and convey divine revelation to God's servants (Acts 7:53; Rev. 1:1).
3. They inflict divine judgments (2 Kings 19:35; see Rev. 8–9, 15–16).
4. They influence the human leaders of earthly government (Dan. 10:12–11:1).
5. They war against the forces of evil (Dan. 10:12–13, 20; Rev. 12:7–9).
6. They care for children (Matt. 18:10) and for God's people (Gen. 19:1–22; 1 Kings 19:5–8; Dan. 6:22; Acts 5:19–20; 12:7; Heb. 1:14; Pss. 34:7; 91:11–12; cp. their caring for Jesus, Matt. 4:11; Luke 22:43).

7. They do miracles (Acts 12:7, 10).
8. They observe people (1 Cor. 4:9; 11:10).
9. They bear dead humans to their destinations (Luke 16:22).

Observe that holy angels do not receive worship (Rev. 22:8–9). There is no biblical command for us to pray to angels. All our prayers are to be addressed to God collectively or to the Persons of the divine Trinity individually (see "Fellowship with God" under Theology Proper).

THE EVIL ANGELS

These are the angels who followed Satan in his rebellion against God shortly after creation week (Gen. 1:31; cp. Rev. 12:4, 7–9). They have an organizational structure (Eph. 6:12), with Satan as their leader (Matt. 12:24–26; 25:41). Loyal to Satan, these angels actively oppose God and His people and seek to influence world affairs (Dan. 10:13; John 14:30). The common biblical designations for these evil angels are "demons" (KJV "devils") and "spirits" (Matt. 8:16), including ones who are "unclean" (10:1), "evil" (Luke 7:21), "wicked" (11:26), "seducing" (1 Tim. 4:1), and "foul" (Mark 9:25).[6] Many of these fallen angels are free to follow their master, Satan. Others are imprisoned. [7]

Those Who Are Free

Displaying personal features (Mark 5:8–12) and superhuman strength (9:18; Acts 19:16), these evil spirits do Satan's bidding in the following ways:
1. They cause humans to have certain physical, emotional, and mental disorders (Matt. 12:22; Luke 13:11; Mark 5:1–7) and inspire self-destruction (Mark 9:17–22).
2. They teach false doctrine (1 Tim. 4:1) and inspire false prophets (1 John 4:1, 3).
3. They incite wickedness (Matt. 12:42–45) and hinder spiritual activity (1 Thess. 2:18).
4. They influence human political leaders (Dan. 10:12–11:1).
5. They tempt and lead people astray in their spiritual lives (1 Thess. 3:5).
6. They blind people to truth (2 Cor. 4:3–4) and project evil thoughts into people's minds (Matt. 16:22–23).
7. They snatch God's truth from unsaved people's hearts (Luke 8:12).
8. They do miracles (Matt. 12:22–24; 2 Thess. 2:7–9; Rev. 13:13–14; 16:13–14).
9. They invade and possess certain humans (Luke 8:26–36) and influence others (Acts 5:3).[7]

Those Who Are Permanently Bound

These are the fallen angels who corrupted humanity before the Noachic Flood (Gen. 6:1–13). They "came in unto the daughters of men, and they [these daughters] bare" offspring (vv. 2, 4). Jude supports this record when he compares the sin of Sodom and Gomorrah to that of these angels: "Even as Sodom and Gomorrah and the cities about them, in like manner *to these* [angels] [Gk. text addition], giving themselves over to fornication and going after strange flesh" (v. 7). "Strange flesh" means flesh of another or different kind. Like the homosexuals of Sodom and Gomorrah (Gen. 18:20; 19:5), these angels had departed from the appointed course of nature and did that which was unnatural. In this case, they committed fornication with female humans—a people of different flesh or nature. The result of this perverse activity was the birth of unnatural offspring (6:4), who are described as "fallen ones" (the meaning of Heb. *Nephilim* for KJV "giants"), emphasizing their depraved sinful state; "mighty ones," emphasizing their demonic superhuman strength and powers; and "men of renown," who were celebrated for their mighty exploits, which were retold in popular legends that were preserved in the mythology of ancient nations (cp. Rom. 1:21–23). The enormity of this demonic action is seen in God's destroying all flesh with water (Gen. 6:12–13) and in His permanently imprisoning these wicked angels in *Tartaros,* a region in hades (2 Peter 2:4–5, KJV "hell"; Jude 6) to await their final judgment of being cast into the lake of fire.[8]

Those Who Are Temporarily Bound

It is very likely that the "locusts" of Revelation 9:1–10 are evil spirits, who are now confined to the "bottomless pit."[9] Being the executioners of the Fifth Trumpet Judgment in the Tribulation Age, these evil spirits will be released for the purpose of tormenting earth dwellers for five months. Their king, named "Destroyer" (Heb. *Abaddon,* Gk. *Apollyon*) is probably a holy angel, who has charge of the Abyss in hades.

In Revelation 9:14, we read of four angels who are bound at the Euphrates River. When they are loosed for the sixth Trumpet Judgment, these evil angels will lead an army of 200 million supernatural, demonic horsemen to destroy a third of the earth's population at a designated hour (vv. 15–19).

THE MORAL FALL OF SOME ANGELS

God created all angels good (Gen. 1:31; Ezek. 28:14–15). Since they possessed personhood, with the ability to make moral decisions, they were given the choice of remaining loyal to their Creator and serving Him forever or of rebelling against Him and serving sin.

THE FALL OF LUCIFER

Satan was created a holy angel of highest rank, who was described as "the anointed cherub" (Ezek. 28:13–14), and whose original name was "Lucifer," meaning "Light-bearer" of divine glory (Isa. 14:12).[10] Moreover, he was "full of wisdom" and "perfect" in all his ways until he sinned (Ezek. 28:13, 15). He was stationed in heaven, which was described as "Eden the Garden of God" or "the Mountain of God" (vv. 13, 16), apparently located next to God's throne (cp. 1:26).

Being a creature with personhood, Lucifer had the capability of making moral choices and of worshiping his Creator. But, struck by his inherent beauty and dazzling dress, he chose to exalt and worship himself (Ezek. 28:13, 17). This wrong choice and action generated within him the sin force and pride, which, thereafter, totally energized and governed him (1 Tim. 3:6). It also led God to cast him out of heaven (Ezek. 28:16). Satan then set out on an irrational course to seize for himself God's position and authority (cp. Isa. 14:12–14).[11]

It appears that Lucifer initially sinned after creation week (Gen. 1:31) and before man's moral fall (3:1–6). When, through Eve, he induced Adam to sin, Satan seized man's authority over the earth (1:26) and became the "prince of this world" (John 12:31; 14:30; 16:11; cp. Heb. 2:5–8) and the ruler of unsaved earth dwellers (Acts 26:18; Col. 1:13; 1 John 5:19, KJV "in wickedness" means "in the wicked one").

THE FALL OF OTHER ANGELS

Apparently responding to Satan's example and persuasion, as many as a third of the angelic host chose to revolt against God and to follow the Devil (Rev. 12:4). Their wrong choice and action engendered within them the sin force and brought them spiritual death and ruin, as their designations "evil spirits" and "unclean spirits" indicate. It also brought them under Satan's authority (Matt. 12:24; 25:41).

THE ETERNAL FUTURE OF ANGELS

Like humans, angels are accountable to God for their conduct and will exist forever (1 Cor. 6:3; Luke 20:36).

THE FUTURE OF HOLY ANGELS

COULD NOT NOW CHOOSE TO FOLLOW SATAN?

Being chosen by God to remain unfallen (1 Tim. 5:21), the holy angels will worship and serve their Creator forever (cp. Heb. 12:22–23; Rev. 5:11–12; 21:12). This truth indicates that the probationary period, during which angels decided whom they would serve, is past and that holy angels can never sin. There is no need for a future judgment for them.

THE FUTURE OF EVIL ANGELS

Eventually, these fallen angels will be judged (1 Cor. 6:3; 2 Peter 2:4) and will be cast into the lake of fire (hell), where they, with Satan, will suffer torment forever (Matt. 25:41; Rev. 20:10). They are aware of the doom that awaits them (Matt. 8:29; Mark 5:7; Luke 8:28).

Nowhere do the Scriptures teach that salvation has been provided for evil angels who sinned, despite their greater knowledge of God and His glory. Colossians 1:20 seems to refer only to that which was involuntarily affected by man's sin. The apostle Paul does not refer to those in hades under the earth, the region of dead unsaved humans and imprisoned fallen angels (see Addendum: "Sheol, Hades").

SATAN

While it is urgent for us to learn what God has revealed about His archenemy, Satan, we must be careful not to give the adversary honors that belong only to God. Moreover, we must take care not to allow an unhealthy curiosity about the Devil and his works to involve us with literature and practices that open our hearts to satanic deceptions and dangerous influences. God has revealed in His Word all that we need to know about the Devil. It is safe and wise to be contented with this information. On the other hand, it is very important for us to learn the information that God has given us about this enemy.

HIS NAMES

In his morally fallen state, the archenemy of God has several titles: "Satan," meaning "adversary," is generally used as his personal name (Job 1:10; Matt. 4:10). His most common title is "the Devil," meaning "the slanderer" (Matt. 4:1; cp. Rev. 12:10). Other titles are "dragon" (Rev. 12:9; 20:2), "the original snake" (12:9, KJV "old serpent"; cp. Gen. 3:15), "the tempter" (Matt. 4:3), "the prince of this world" (John 12:31), "the father of lies" (8:44), "the prince of demons" (Matt. 12:24), and "the god of this age" (2 Cor. 4:4, KJV "world"). The Pharisees called Satan "Beelzebub," meaning "lord of flies," which represents that which is vile and loathsome (Matt. 12:24–26).

HIS NATURE

Although many people deny his personhood and regard him as only an evil force, the Scriptures reveal what Satan is. As our study of the nature of angels revealed, we see that Satan is a person with an angelic nature.

He Is a Person

Satan's personhood is indicated by his self-awareness (Matt. 4:9), self-expression (Isa. 14:13–14), moral awareness (Matt. 4:1), perpetuity (Rev. 20:10), as well as his craftiness (Eph. 6:11; 2 Cor. 2:11) and emotions (Rev. 12:12).

He Is an Angel

Since he was created to be "the anointed cherub" (Ezek. 28:13–14), Satan still has an angelic nature, with superhuman qualities and powers. However, like all fallen angels his sinning brought him spiritual ruin, bondage, and spiritual death. This means that his angelic nature lost its pristine beauty and wisdom and was inclined toward sin, that he became wholly energized and dominated by the sin force, and that he no longer has a personal relationship with God. Like all created beings, he is finite and is subject to God's supreme authority (Job 1:12; Rev. 12:9–12).

HIS CHARACTER

Having a totally depraved angelic nature and being wholly governed by the sin force, Satan is wicked (John 17:15), murderous (8:44), deceptive (Rev. 12:9; John 8:44), proud (1 Tim. 3:6), powerful (Job 1:12–19; 2:7; 2 Thess. 2:9), insolent (Matt. 4:9), cunning (2 Cor. 2:11; Eph. 6:11), persevering (Luke 4:13), and insane, being obsessed with the absurd idea that he can defeat and unseat God (Isa. 14:12–14). For deceptive purposes, he lies (John 8:44) and is able to transform himself into an "angel of light" when this is to his advantage (2 Cor. 11:14).

HIS ACTIVITIES

In addition to ruling the world of unsaved earth dwellers (John 12:31; 14:30; 16:11) and opposing God and His people (1 Peter 5:8), the primary activity of Satan seems to be to thwart God's judicial sentence against him—his utter defeat by the woman's Seed, or Jesus, the Conqueror-Savior (Gen. 3:15, KJV "bruise" means "crush"). We can trace his effort against God's sentence throughout human history.

After Receiving God's Sentence

First, Satan tried to stop the incarnation of God the Son, as foretold by the OT prophetic Scriptures. He attempted to destroy the human line of decent into which his Conqueror would be born. The Devil led Cain to slay Abel (Gen. 4:8) but Eve bore Seth (v. 25). The Devil brought destruction to the human race by unprecedented corruption (6:1–13), but God preserved Noah and his family (6:8–8:19).[12] Satan influenced the post-flood world to turn to idolatry (Rom. 1:21–25), but God appeared unto Abram in Ur, saved him, led him to sojourn in Canaan (Acts 7:2–4; Gen. 12:1–4), and promised that he would be the father of the messianic line into which Jesus would be born (Gen. 15:5–6; Gal. 3:16). The adversary had the Israelites enslaved in Egypt and their male infants slain (Exod. 1:7–22), but God raised up Moses to deliver them from their house of bondage (Exod. 3:9–10). Satan led Israel into idolatry and other gross sins, which finally brought Judah and David's house into Babylonian captivity (2 Kings 24–25; Isa. 1:1–9), but God used the Persian conqueror of Babylon, Cyrus, to allow Jews to return to Jerusalem (2 Chron. 36:22–23). Although Satan had induced Judah's King Jehoiakim to burn God's word, and by this to incur the divine judgment that blocked any of his posterity from ruling on David's throne (Jer. 36:30; also 22:30), God circumvented this curse by Jesus' virgin conception and Mary's marriage to Joseph, heir to David's throne (Matt. 1:20, 16). Later, as we shall see, the Devil unsuccessfully plotted against Jesus' life (Matt. 2:1–16) and sought to divert Him from the work that He came to earth to do (Matt. 4:1–10; Luke 4:28–29).

Today

Satan is doing all he can, within the limits of God's permissive decree, to oppose saved people and to hinder the Lord's work of building the Church (Eph. 6:10–12). It irks the

Devil to see his former subjects serving the Lord Jesus and bearing witness to the gospel and its truth. Untiringly, Satan seeks to stop this and to render their lives ineffective (1 Peter 5:8–9). But the Lord is faithful in protecting His people from the evil one (2 Thess. 3:3; 1 Cor. 10:13).

The Devil has also persecuted the Jews throughout the present age. During Adolf Hitler's control of Germany (1933–45), 6 million European Jews were systematically slaughtered. Satan also opposed the formation of the state of Israel in 1948 and afterward incited her Muslim foes to make several attempts to overrun the nation. He is now opposing Israel's efforts to establish peace with her Muslim neighbors, but this accord will succeed (Dan. 9:27; Ezek. 38:8, 11, 14). *TEMPORARY ONLY*

In the Future

In the middle of the coming Tribulation Age, Satan and his angels will be confined to earth (Rev. 12:7–10; cp. Isa. 14:12–17). Realizing that his time is short, the Devil will again attempt to destroy Israel (Rev. 12:13–17; Jer. 30:6–7), for he knows that the Lord Jesus will not return until the elect remnant of Israel repents and turns to the Savior (Deut. 30:2–3). Satan will attempt to do this through his human agent, "the Beast out of the sea," by whom he will rule the earth and will persecute God's people (Rev. 13:1–8; Dan. 7:21, 25). But Satan will not succeed in this endeavor, for God will preserve His elect people (Rev. 12:14–16) and will bring them to repentance (Hos. 3:4–5; 5:14–6:3). The Lord Jesus will return to earth in power and great glory (Matt. 24:29–30; Rev. 19:11–16). The Devil's human confederates will be destroyed in the Battle of Armageddon (Rev. 19:11–21), and he himself and his evil angels will be cast into the Abyss for a thousand years (20:1–3). *WHY?*

At the close of the Lord's millennial rule over the earth, the Devil will be released from the Abyss to lead a final revolt of unsaved earth dwellers against King Jesus at Jerusalem (Rev. 20:7–9). But the human rebels will be killed by divine fire and Satan will be cast into the lake of fire (v. 10), where he and his allies will remain forever (Matt. 25:41, 46).

HIS DEFEAT BY JESUS

With His incarnation, the Lord Jesus came to earth as the Last Adam (1 Cor. 15:45), with the title to everything, including this world (Matt. 11:27; John 3:35; 13:3; Heb. 1:2; Ps. 2:6–7). However, He could not claim His inheritance until He had defeated Satan in the arena where the first Adam had lost his authority to the Devil. Also, before He could evict the usurper, the Lord Jesus had to bring the adversary to justice (John 16:11) by confirming the justice of the divine sentence against him. He also had to defeat the adversary's personal attacks against Him and break his power of death by His own death and resurrection. Needless to say, the Devil did everything he could to destroy Jesus.

Satan's Defeat at Jesus' First Coming

At His first coming, the Lord Jesus broke Satan's lethal power. By His obedience to the Father, Jesus defeated Satan during His preministry years in Nazareth (Matt. 3:17). At the beginning of His messianic work, the Lord Jesus was victorious over Satan's temptations to abandon His mission (4:1–10). He also defeated Satan throughout His public ministry when the adversary approached Him through His enemies who sought His life (Luke 4:28–29; John 7:30, 44; 8:40–44, 59; 10:31, 39; Matt. 22) and through the sentimental urges of His friends to avoid the cross (Matt. 16:22–23). When Satan tried to kill Jesus in Gethsemane (Matt. 26:36–39), the Lord declared His commitment to the Father's will and was divinely preserved (Luke 22:42–43).[13]

The Lord was victorious over the adversary in His trials and at the cross. Committing Himself to the Father and His will (Matt. 26:42–44; 1 Peter 2:23), the Lord Jesus submitted Himself to the abuses of His enemies (John 18:4–11; Matt. 26:51–68; 27:26–31). He did not sinfully respond with hostile acts and retaliatory threats (Matt. 26:63–64; 1 Peter 2:22–23). He also gave Himself to crucifixion (Luke 23:33–34), the most humiliating of all executions. These anguishing experiences revealed the hatred of Satan and of unsaved people against God and the Lord Jesus (John 3:17–20). What Satan and the world did to Jesus was self-incriminating. It confirmed the justice of their divine condemnation (John 12:31; 16:11).

The Lord Jesus decisively defeated Satan by breaking his lethal power. Uniquely laying down His life in death (John 10:18), Jesus invaded the Devil's domain, yielded to death's power, and snapped the bond of death and Satan by His resurrection (Heb. 2:14–15; Col. 2:14–15). Death could not hold Jesus, for it had no claim to Him (Acts 2:22–24) because of His sinlessness (Rom. 6:23; 1 Peter 2:22; 1 John 3:5). Today, the risen Lord Jesus has authority over death and hades, the place where dead unsaved people and imprisoned evil angels are detained (Rev. 1:18), as well as over all angels, both holy and evil (Eph. 1:20–21; 1 Peter 3:22).

Satan's Defeat at Jesus' Second Coming

At His second coming, the Lord Jesus will break Satan's earthly political power. Because of His previous victories over Satan and His subsequent exaltation, together with the repentance of the elect remnant of Israel at the close of the Tribulation Age (Deut. 30:2–3), the Lord Jesus will triumphantly return to earth as King of kings and Lord of lords (Rev. 19:11–16). He will deal with His human enemies in the Battle of Armageddon (vv. 17–21) and will confine Satan and his demons to hades (20:1–3). The Lord will then establish a new political world order, based on the inheritance and mandate that He received from the Father (Ps. 2:8–9; John 3:35). The Lord's worldwide reign will continue for one thousand years (Rev. 20:1–7; cp. Pss. 2:7–9; 72:8–11; Matt. 11:27; 28:18). As the Father's anointed Slave and the Last Adam, He will do what the first Adam failed to do—subdue and rule earth for God's glory (Heb. 2:5–9).

As we have seen, the millennial kingdom will close with Satan's release from hades and his leading earth dwellers in a final revolt against King Jesus (Rev. 20:2–9). These rebels will be consumed, and Satan will be crushed and cast into the lake of fire where he will remain forever (v. 10; Matt. 25:41). Through the Lord Jesus, the chosen Anointed One (Isa. 42:1–4), God the Father will have gloriously triumphed, not only in putting away the enemy forever but also in accomplishing the divine purpose for the Devil's existence and his wicked deeds (Rom. 9:22; Rev. 11:15–18). We who are saved can look forward to this triumphant event (Rom. 16:20). God will also accomplish His purpose, too, for man's rule over the earth in the administration of the Lord Jesus—the Last Adam, the Second Man (1 Cor. 15:45, 47).

HIS DEFEAT IN THE LIVES OF SAVED PEOPLE

Although he has been defeated by the Lord Jesus in every contest thus far, the Devil is still very active in his warfare against his former earthly subjects, the Lord's people (Col. 1:13). However, we who are saved can have occasions of victory over this adversary as we prepare for the conflict and take those steps that lead us to victory. I say "occasions of victory," for if we fail to do our part, we shall be temporarily defeated by the adversary. God can only give us victory in our skirmishes with the Devil as we look to Him to help us (James 4:7). Happily, these defeats do not determine the outcome of the campaign, although they do sully our testimony and hinder our spiritual progress. One day, when He completes the Church, the Lord will remove His people from the scene of this spiritual warfare (Gal. 1:4; 1 Thess. 4:13–18). To experience victory over this enemy, we must prepare for his attacks and take those steps that lead to victory when he does attack. Also, we must always be on the alert for his next strike.

Our Preparation Before Satan Attacks

To be victorious, we must do certain things to prepare ourselves before the enemy launches his attack against us.

1. We must learn about the Devil from God's Word (2 Tim. 3:16–17).

We must not be ignorant of his devices or designs (2 Cor. 2:11). The enemy takes advantage of our spiritual immaturity and ignorance (Eph. 4:11–15). The Bible gives us all the information that God would have us to know about this adversary.

2. We must constantly strengthen ourselves in the Lord (Eph. 6:10).

We can meet the enemy in the Lord's strength only as we daily read the Bible (Ps. 119:11, 130; Col. 3:6; 1 Peter 2:1–2), live by faith in God (Gal. 2:20; 1 Peter 5:8–9), and obey Him (Rom. 12:2). Because of this, the enemy seeks to disrupt our daily fellowship with the Lord.

3. We must put on the whole armor of God (Eph. 6:11–18).

This armor, which we are to put on daily, consists of spiritual realities that are found in Jesus and that manifest Him in our lives (cp. Rom. 13:11–14). Since these qualities are reproduced in us by the Holy Spirit, we put them on by giving ourselves to Him (Eph. 5:18) or to the Lord Jesus (Rom. 13:14) and by relying on Him to help us be what this armor represents (Gal. 2:20; cp. John 7:37–39; Phil. 4:13).

Beginning this section with a command to "put on the whole armor of God" (Eph. 6:11), with its goal of withstanding Satan (vv. 11, 13, "that") and its reason, "for we do not wrestle against flesh and blood" (humans) but powerful evil spirits (v. 12), the apostle Paul lists the parts of the armor that we are to put on (vv. 14–17). He compares these spiritual qualities to the battle gear of a Roman soldier.

a. The belt of truth (Eph. 6:14; cp. John 14:6)

While "truth" may refer to God's Word (John 17:17), which we are to read, understand, and apply, here it more likely refers to truthfulness and honesty in daily life. The enemy, who is a liar (John 8:44) and a deceiver (Rev. 12:9), wants us to be dishonest and deceitful. With this belt on, we are truthful in our word and honest in our conduct.

The soldier's belt was a broad leather one, covering the lower part of his body and reaching down to the middle of his thighs. It held his gear in place.

b. The coat of righteousness (Eph. 6:14; cp. Phil. 1:11)

Righteousness is a state of being or doing right. We became righteous when we were saved (Rom. 5:1; 1 Cor. 1:30). Now it is our duty to do what is right in God's sight or His will (Eph. 2:10; Rom. 12:2; 1 Tim. 6:11). Satan wants us to disobey God. When we have this coat on, we do God's will (see Appendix F: "Learning and Doing God's Will").

The soldier's coat of mail consisted of two parts: one covering his chest and stomach, the other his back. This was usually made of leather, plated with metal. It protected the body from wounding blows.

c. The sandals of preparation (Eph. 6:15; cp. 2 Cor. 5:20)

These sandals represent willingness of heart (Rom. 1:14–16) and promptness of action (Acts 16:30–31) to share the gospel with unsaved people when the opportunity arises. Satan wants us to remain silent. But we do not need to be ashamed of the gospel, for it is true and effective (Rom. 1:16–17). When we put on these sandals, we are prepared to bear witness to the good news of God's offer of salvation through faith in Jesus and His atoning work.

The soldier's sandals were heavy, hobnailed ones that protected his feet from road bruises.

  d. *The shield of faith (Eph. 6:16; cp. Gal. 2:20)*

This refers to biblical practical faith, which rests upon God and His promises.[14] Satan shoots at us flaming arrows of fear, bitterness, doubt, and the like at us. But by faith in such promises as Isaiah 41:10; Romans 8:28; and Hebrews 10:23, we can quench these arrows and experience peace, praise, and confidence in God's Word. Satan wants us to rely upon ourselves and our ineffective human resources rather than upon God, His Word, and His all-sufficient resources. When we use this shield by relying on God's promises, we quench the flaming arrows of the adversary and allow God to do what He says.

The apostle speaks of the large Roman shield, which was semicylindrical and measured four-by-two-and-a-half feet. It was made of boards, covered with coarse cloth under an outer layer of rawhide. The arrows were tipped with pitch and were set on fire before they were discharged.

  e. *The helmet of salvation (Eph. 6:17; cp. Heb. 13:6)*

Our Lord wants us to know the biblical teaching of the plan, components, and assurance of salvation (see "The Assurance of Salvation" under Soteriology). He also wants us to experience His deliverance over our spiritual enemies in daily life and His vitality in our daily behavior. Moreover, He wants us to be assured of our salvation if we have trusted in Jesus as our Savior from sin (1 John 5:13). Satan wants us to be ignorant of these things so that we remain in doubt of our salvation and continue in bondage to sin's power.

The Roman helmet was made of leather or metal. Protecting vulnerable parts of the body, the helmet covered the head, brows, cheeks, and neck.

  f. *The sword of the Spirit (Eph. 6:17; cp. John 1:14)*

This is the Word of God, wielded in the power of the Holy Spirit. To use God's Word effectively against the enemy, we must learn its content, obey its commands, and depend upon the Holy Spirit to teach us its truths and to help us apply these to our spiritual needs. Since the Scriptures give us God's complete instructions for our spiritual lives (2 Tim. 3:16–17), Satan wants us to ignore them and to follow his evil suggestions or the world's misguided advice to satisfy our spiritual needs or to solve our spiritual problems (2 Cor. 10:1–5; Col. 2:8). We must respond to the adversary as Jesus did—with the Word of God in the power of the Holy Spirit (Matt. 4:1–10).

The Roman sword was a short, two-edged pointed one that the soldier carried as a sidearm and used in close combat.

Like putting on a garment, we put these pieces on as a unit when we give ourselves daily to the Lord Jesus (Rom. 13:14). However, when the enemy assails us in these various areas of our spiritual lives, we can submit ourselves to the Lord, appropriate the piece of armor that we need, and use it to ward off the Devil's attack. Study Jesus' use of the Scriptures in Matthew 4:1–10.

  4. *We must pray constantly for ourselves and others (Eph. 6:18a).*

By prayer, we not only ask God for things and share with Him all that concerns us but we also focus our attention on God and the sufficient resources that He has provided for us (Heb. 12:2; 2 Peter 1:3; cp. Matt. 6:9–10).[15] Satan seeks to disrupt our praying or cause us to neglect it.

  5. *We must be alert for the enemy (Eph. 6:18b).*

The enemy is ever searching for unwary prey (1 Peter 5:8). By his "roaring," he deceitfully conveys the idea that he, like a sated animal, is harmless; but this is not true.

We know that the adversary is near when he raises doubts about God and suggests behavior that is not in keeping with God's will for us, when he has us hurry in making some important decision without our seeking God's will, when he gets us worked up about some issue, when he seeks to inflate us with pride, when he casts over us unfounded fear or depression, and when in our thinking he pushes things to an extreme so that they are out of balance with other related matters.

By our following these suggestions daily, we prepare ourselves for battle with this powerful enemy before he attacks us. Are you ready for him?

Our Response When Satan Attacks

If we have prepared ourselves to meet the enemy, then we shall experience victory when he strikes by taking the following steps:

1. Remembering that God will give us victory as we look to Him (1 Cor. 10:13; Heb. 2:18)

Since He defeated Satan during the course of His earthly life, the Lord can now defeat the enemy through us as we allow Him (Phil. 4:13). But we must believe that He will do this (1 Peter 5:8–9; Gal. 2:20).

2. Immediately giving ourselves to God for victory (James 4:7)

As we give ourselves to the Lord Jesus or to the Holy Spirit and believe that He will help us as He promises, we allow Him to confront the enemy through us (Phil. 4:13). By this submission, He takes command of our hearts and lives for as long as we trust and obey Him (Eph. 3:17; Luke 6:45).

3. Resisting Satan's attack by relying on the Lord and by saying no to the Devil (James 4:7; 1 Peter 5:8–9)

We cannot, however, firmly say no to the Devil until first we have said yes to Jesus. Only in the Lord's strength can we successfully resist the enemy and refuse to submit to his evil suggestions and his relentless assaults. If the attack comes through a human person, we can rebuke him (Matt. 16:23) or leave his presence (Gen. 39:12). If it comes in the form of an evil thought, we can turn it over to Jesus and think on right things (2 Cor. 10:5; Phil. 4:8).

4. Remembering and relying on God's promise of victory (James 4:7)

This reliance on God allows Him to put the enemy to flight as He promises.

5. Remembering and doing God's will as it relates to our circumstances (Eph. 5:17)

When we are faced with doing wrong, we must remember to do what is right for the situation. Jesus did this when He quoted Scripture to the enemy (Matt. 4:4, 7, 10). This Scripture stated God's will for Jesus. By quoting it, the Lord also declared to Satan what He would do. God's will for us is revealed in the Scriptures by precepts (commands) and guiding principles, which we may apply to any circumstance of life (see Appendix F: "Learning and Doing God's Will"). When we are confronted with the temptation to sin, we must think of its holy alternative and do this in reliance on God (Eph. 4:25–32).

Victory is assured if we follow the course that leads to it. Defeat is certain if the enemy finds us unprepared and unwilling to follow the steps given in God's Word.

Our Remaining Alert for the Next Attack

The enemy will not leave us for long (Luke 4:13). The fact that we are attacked by him does not make us blameworthy, nor is it to be feared, for the indwelling Holy Spirit is our Helper. Although we are aware of Satan's craftiness and power, we should consider his attacks as opportunities to defeat him in Jesus' name and power. As with other trials of faith, each experience of victory through faith in God and obedience to His Word strengthens our faith and spiritual life (James 1:1–3).

242

HIS STRATEGY

That Satan has a strategy is indicated by the words *wiles* (Eph. 6:11) and *devices* (2 Cor. 2:11). His *wiles* are his methods of procedure that he follows to achieve his goals; his *devices* are his designs, plans, or plots against his prey. His strategy against the Lord's people is shown by the kinds, manner, and timing of his approaches. Let us look at these.

The Kinds of Approach

Because he is not present everywhere, Satan usually approaches the Lord's people through his demon allies, although he is named as the tempter in the Scriptures (James 4:7; 1 Peter 5:8).[16]

1. Satan tempts us.

He seeks to gain our consent to his proposals that would lead us to act contrary to God's will for us (1 Thess. 3:5). Keep in mind that we should not equate being tempted with sinning; yielding to the temptation results in sinning. Henry Drummond wrote, "It is only when a man sees temptation coming and goes out to meet it, welcomes it, plays with it, and invites it to be his guest that it passes from temptation into sin."[17]

2. Satan assaults us.

With this approach Satan attempts to injure or harass us without our consent. His assaults against the Lord's people include their experiencing various losses (Job 1:14–19), unfounded criticism (Job 4:7–8), physical illness (Job 2:7; Luke 13:11, 16; 2 Cor. 12:7), hindrance to spiritual endeavor (1 Thess. 2:18), violence (Acts 7:57–58), mental obsession and torment (1 Sam. 16:14), and inner evil influence (Acts 5:3). However, all these are done within limits that are determined by God (Job 1:12; 2:6; 1 Cor. 10:13).

The Manner of Approach

Genesis 3:1–6 reveals much about the procedure that Satan follows when he seeks to secure our consent to his evil proposals. We must ever keep in mind that the Devil is a cunning deceiver (1 Tim. 4:10) and a habitual liar (John 8:44).

1. He approaches people in disguise (Gen. 3:1).

Being the archdeceiver, he aims at making things appear differently from what they really are. While he uniquely spoke to Eve through a snake (Gen. 3:1; cp. Rev. 12:9), Satan often approaches us through other people (Matt. 16:21–23; Job 2:9; 2 Cor. 11:13–15) or speaks directly to our hearts, or minds, without identifying himself (Acts 5:3; 2 Cor. 10:5).

2. He seeks to undermine people's trust in God (Gen. 3:1–5).

He attacks our faith in God, the means of our defense against him (Eph. 6:16; 1 Peter 5:9). Our exercise of faith in God and His promises allows Him to confront the enemy through us, to minister to our needs, and to enable us to do His will. When Satan diverts our faith to some object other than God, then we are rendered powerless and defenseless. The Devil's words to Eve indicate several ways by which he undermines our faith in God for help. Satan does this:

a. By asking a question that raises doubt about God's goodness or love (v. 1)

"You shall not eat of every tree of the garden?" This question implied that God was unduly strict or stingy.

b. By speaking a lie that raises doubt about God's integrity (v. 4)

"You shall not surely die." This lie suggests that God did not mean what He said and that He was trying to intimidate man.

c. By making an insinuation that raises doubt about God's motives (v. 5)

"For God does know that in the day that you eat of it your eyes will be opened and you will be like God, knowing good and evil." The Devil suggested by this that God was keeping something good from man, namely, that one can be like God in knowledge by exercising independent choice.[18] This, of course, is what brought about Lucifer's moral fall.

3. *He often appeals to people's innate desires or needs (Gen. 3:6).*

Satan appeals to physical needs as in Jesus (Matt. 4:3), to sympathetic feelings as in Peter (Matt. 16:21–23; cp. Acts 21:12–13), and to religious devotion as in the Israelites (Exod. 32:4–6; 2 Kings 16:10–13; 17:8–12). When he succeeded in turning Eve's attention away from God, Satan then appealed to her natural physical, aesthetic, and intellectual desires, which were in themselves sinless. He offered her the satisfaction of these desires in a way that was contrary to God's will for her. Eve's initial mistake was to talk with the Devil, for he convincingly gave her reasons for following his evil suggestions.

The Time of Approach

While the Devil may attack anytime, he will do so when it is most suitable for his purposes and when we are least expecting it. For example, he may approach us when we are in the wake of a great spiritual experience (Matt. 3:16; 4:1–2), when we are at the beginning of some spiritual endeavor (v. 17), when we are physically weak or mentally exhausted (v. 2), or when we are alone (v. 1). We can expect Satan to challenge our commitments to the Lord as he challenged Jesus' commitments to the Father's will throughout His ministry (vv. 1–11; 16:21–23). We must always be alert for the adversary (1 Peter 5:8), for he generally attacks us unexpectedly (Matt. 16:21–23).

HIS DECEPTIONS

Satan is a master deceiver, who misleads people by his disguises, maneuvers, and lies (Rev. 12:9; 2 Cor. 11:3, 14). We who are saved are vulnerable to his deceptions when we are ignorant of spiritual truth or are not walking in God's fellowship. Only by learning God's truth about the Devil and God's will for us and by walking in God's fellowship can we avoid being deceived by the Devil's lies (cp. John 8:32). Let us look at this more closely.

Satan Uses the Deception of Teachers

While the Lord has given to the Church people who are gifted teachers (Eph. 4:11–12), we must always be alert for false teachers and deceived teachers (1 Tim. 4:1–3; Matt. 7:15–20). *False teachers* are unsaved people who teach satanic lies for biblical doctrines. They take texts of Scripture out of their contexts to support their false doctrines. *Deceived teachers* are saved people who unknowingly teach things that are contrary to essential biblical truth. Every gospel believer must examine all religious instruction in the light of what the Bible says about these subjects (Acts 17:11). Moreover, we must look at the character of these teachers, the results of their ministry, and what truths they regularly omit from their teachings as well as what they say (Matt. 7:15–20).

By their false teachings, deceiving evil spirits aim at weakening the authority of the Scriptures in the minds of people by distorting biblical truth with the erroneous thinking of ungodly men. In many cases, they succeed in replacing God's truth altogether with demonic doctrines (cp. Mark 7:5–13). False teachers and their doctrines will increase in the closing days of this age (1 Tim. 4:1).

Satan Uses the Deception of Appearance

Eve was deceived, in part, by the appearance of her situation (Gen. 3:6). Being the master of deception (Rev. 12:9), Satan can make things, including himself, appear to be something other than what they really are (2 Cor. 11:14). Some hold that God will not allow His people to be deceived, but the Lord Jesus urged his disciples to be alert for this very thing (Mark 13:5–6; 1 John 4:1). Regarding his spiritual life, the apostle Paul refused to live solely by the appearance of things as he humanly saw them (2 Cor. 5:7; cp. chap. 4). His living by faith indicated that he trusted in God and His Word to direct him and to help him evaluate situations correctly, regardless of how things might appear (Prov. 3:5–6). Those who are spiritual, or filled with the Holy Spirit, will "investigate" all things in the light of God's Word (1 Cor. 2:15, KJV "judges").

Satan Uses the Deception of Passivity

Being the opposite of activity, passivity is a false view of faith that would have a person quench all personal actions of mind, judgment, reason, and will, as well as other forms of activity, and to wait passively for God to move him or her.

> The powers of darkness would make man a machine, a tool, an automation; the God of holiness and love desires to make him free, intelligent sovereign in his own sphere—a thinking, rational, renewed creation, created after His own image (Eph. 4:24). Therefore, God never says to any faculty of man, 'Be thou idle.' . . . God requires cooperation with His Spirit and the full use of every faculty of the whole man. . . . Passivity must not be confused with quietness, or the 'meek and quiet spirit.' . . . Quietness of spirit, of heart, of mind, of manner of voice and expression may be coexistent with the most effective activity in the will of God (1 Thess. 4:11).[19]

Several statements which express this dangerous passivity are these:

"Christ lives in me; therefore, I do not live at all."
"God works in me; therefore, I need only surrender and obey as He moves me."
"God wills instead of me; therefore, I must not use my will or make any decisions."
"God has commanded that we not judge; therefore, I must not use my judgment."
"Since I have the mind of Christ, I must not have any mind of my own."
"God speaks to me, so I must not think or reason but only do what He tells me."
"Since I must wait on God, I cannot act until He moves me."
"Since I am crucified with Christ, I must be dead, or inactive, in my feelings, thinking, and the like."[20]

This passive, unguided, mindless attitude opens the door to all kinds of demonic influences. Actually, God requires our activity of intelligence, will, and body so that we may employ His spiritual resources in our daily experience (Rom. 12:1–2; Eph. 5:17, 10; 2 Peter 1:3; see endnote 15). God wants us to learn what these resources are and to use them with an active faith that believes that God will do His part as we do ours (James 4:8). Never for a moment are we to cease thinking, evaluating, deciding, resisting evil, or trusting and obeying God. But in all this, we must be certain that we are walking in God's fellowship by obeying His commands and following His instructions as given in His Word (cp. Rom. 6:11–13; Col. 3:1–17; 1 John 1:5–7).

Satan Uses the Deception of Instant Solution or Perfection

Many gospel believers are looking for a quick, one-experience, permanent fix—that dramatic happening that will cure them of all ills, deliver them from their sinful appetites and habits, electrify their spirit, propel them into instant material prosperity and spiritual perfection. This is a satanic illusion. Spiritual development and holiness are not achieved by some overwhelming experience as we wait on God to act dynamically upon us. This expectation opens the door to satanic intrusion and deception.

There is something for us to do besides sitting idly by if we are to experience what God desires for us. Our new life in Jesus is subject to step-by-step spiritual growth and development (1 Peter 2:1–2; 2 Peter 3:18). This growth is in spiritual character as expressed by the fruit of the Holy Spirit (1 Thess. 3:12; Gal. 5:22–23), in the use of practical faith and divine grace (2 Thess. 1:3; 2 Peter 3:18), in securing spiritual knowledge (Col. 1:10), and in doing God's will (2 Cor. 9:8). God has given us complete instructions in His Word regarding what we are to do to experience this growth as well as to be victorious over our spiritual enemies. This growth comes about over time as we deal with known sins in our lives, submit to God's control, study the Scriptures, and apply biblical truth to our lives (1 Peter 2:1–2).

We must keep in mind that biblical Christianity is a religion based on revealed biblical truth, which is to be believed and studied. True Christian action, emotion, motivation, and change are based on our understanding of this truth, our acting upon this truth, and our having a relationship with God that springs from this truth. They are not based on spontaneous, indescribable mystical experiences that have no biblical authorization and which are open to the deceptions of evil forces. God assures us that, as we draw near to Him with true humility and clean hearts, He will draw near to us (James 4:8–10).

Needless to say, our adversary the Devil seeks to hinder our studying the Scriptures and our following its teachings in our lives. He also seeks to confuse us and to mislead us by the false teachings of others. But as we look to the Holy Spirit to teach and help us, we can understand God's truth, do His will, and live for His glory.

DEMONIC POSSESSION

With the increase of overt demon activity in our day, we must distinguish between demonic influence (Acts 5:3) and demonic possession (Luke 8:26–36).[21] *Demonic influence* means for a person to be subjected to or affected by a demon, but not possessed by one. The affected person retains his self-determination and personality. *Demonic possession,* or demonization, means for a person to be invaded by one or more demons and to some degree be under demonic control. This control will vary in power and influence as well as in expression of moral depravity and wickedness according to the power and depravity of the demon. In severe cases, the subject has no self-determination and expresses the personality of the demon.

Bible scholars are not agreed as to the possibility of saved people's being demon possessed. Many do not think that this is possible, for the Holy Spirit indwells all who are saved (1 Cor. 6:19). But this view fails to consider that the Holy Spirit, being God, is everywhere present and that saved people have the same inner sin force that dominates the personalities and activities of demons. However, we believe that demons cannot invade a person without his permission or his giving himself to those things that make this entrance possible.

Rev. John L. Nevius, a Presbyterian missionary to China for forty years, summarized his observations of demon-possessed subjects.[22] Excerpts of this summary follow:

One: The supposed demoniac at the time of "possession" passes into an abnormal state, the character of which varies indefinitely, being marked by depression and melancholy or vacancy and stupidity . . . or he becomes ecstatic or ferocious and malignant.

Two: During the transition from normal to abnormal state, the subject is often thrown into paroxysms, more or less violent, during which he sometimes falls on the ground senseless or foams at the mouth, presenting symptoms similar to those of epilepsy or hysteria.

Three: The duration of the abnormal state varies from a few minutes to several days. The attacks are sometimes mild and sometimes violent.

Four: The violence of the paroxysms is increased if the subject struggles; when he yields himself to them, the violence abates or ceases.

Five: The most striking characteristic of these cases is that the subject manifests another personality, which is entirely different from that which really belongs to him.

Six: Many demon-possessed persons express knowledge that cannot be accounted for in ordinary ways. They often appear to know Jesus and express fear of Him. They sometimes converse in foreign languages, of which they normally are ignorant.

Seven: The subject's moral character is often changed.

Merrill F. Unger recognized degrees of demonic possession.[23] Because demons vary greatly in power and depravity, their influences will vary. There are milder forms of possession, involving false doctrine, pornography, and occultism.[24] There are also moderate forms, including sinning "scandalously and recklessly."[25] Finally, there are extreme forms, with a new personality (Mark 5:7),[26] superhuman strength (Mark 5:3–4), aversion to God (James 2:10), and clairvoyance or discernment of things not naturally discernible to the senses (Mark 5:6–7).[27]

Do we who are saved have the power today to command Satan and demons and to cast them out of possessed persons? While the Lord Jesus, seventy of His disciples, and His apostles had this power (Matt. 4:24; 10:5–8; Luke 10:17; Acts 16:18; cp. Mark 16:17), I do not know of any NT instruction for us to do this today. However, we are able to pray for the possessed person's deliverance (Matt. 17:19–21; John 14:13).

We thank God for the victory that our Lord gained over Satan and for that which we can experience through our Savior and the Holy Spirit (2 Cor. 10:4; Phil. 4:13; John 14:15, KJV "Comforter"). Needless to say, we must ever be on the alert for Satan. We must avoid any literature, pictures, films, devices, rituals, and people that would open our hearts to satanic deception, influence, and control. Daily, we must give ourselves to the Lord and to the Holy Spirit, so that They are in control of our hearts, minds, and lives (Rom. 8:5; Gal. 5:16; Eph. 3:17; 5:18). The Scriptures give us all the information that we need to know about the Devil and his allies, but we must learn what this is. As gospel believers, we have the expectation of the apostle Paul, who declared that the Lord would deliver him from every evil work and would preserve him unto His heavenly kingdom (2 Tim. 4:18; cp. Gal. 1:4). We look forward to the time when we shall be removed to heaven and no longer have to contend with the Devil.

We thank God, too, for the ministry of His holy angels in our lives. Although it is not given to us to know our guardian angels personally or to ask them for help (they are God's servants to carry out His will), we are grateful for their ministry in our lives. We must always look to God for whatever assistance that we may need (Heb. 4:16). He will graciously respond in the way that is best for us in our situations, whether by direct intervention or through some agency like the ministry of angels or humans.

A Review of Angelology

1. Where did angels come from?
2. Describe the nature (makeup) of angels.

3. How do we know that angels have personhood?
4. What is the basic description of angelic nature?
5. Why are angels called "sons of God"?
6. Why does their having a spirit kind of nature not make them God?
7. How are angels greater than humans? How are they less than God?
8. What is the generic name of angels?
9. What is the meaning of *angel?*
10. What moral kinds of angels are there?
11. What are the functional orders of holy angels?
12. What are some of the duties of ordinary holy angels?
13. Who is the angelic leader of holy angels?
14. What three kinds of evil angels are there relating to freedom and bondage?
15. What is a common biblical designation for free, evil angels?
16. What are some of the activities of free, evil angels?
17. Why are some evil angels permanently imprisoned?
18. Describe how Lucifer sinned or fell morally.
19. How did other angels sin or fall?
20. What is the future of holy angels? Of evil angels?
21. Give several biblical names of Satan.
22. What does the word *Satan* mean? The *Devil?* Which is used as his personal name?
23. What evidence is there that Satan has personhood and thus is a personal creature?
24. Describe the character of the Devil.
25. Describe Satan's primary activity throughout his career. Why is this?
26. Describe Jesus' defeat of Satan at the Lord's first and second comings.
27. When will the Devil be cast into the lake of fire?
28. What must we do to prepare for the Devil's attacks against us?
29. What is the armor of God? How do we put this on?
30. What does each part of this armor represent in the Christian life?
31. How can we detect the Devil's presence?
32. What are the steps to victory when the Devil attacks us?
33. Why does the Devil flee when we face him in reliance on God?
34. Describe two kinds of Satan's approach to a Christian.
35. When does temptation become sinful to us?
36. What can we learn about the manner of Satan's approach by his tempting Eve?
37. At what times does Satan seem to prefer to attack us?
38. How can these attacks be beneficial to us?
39. What kinds of deception does Satan use?
40. What does the deception of passivity mean and why is this dangerous?
41. People today are looking for instant and permanent solutions for their spiritual problems. Why is this not possible? How can this expectation be spiritually dangerous?
42. What spiritual resources do gospel believers have to deal with their problems?
43. Distinguish between demonic influence and demon possession.
44. How can we have victory over demonic harassment?
45. How can we avoid much demonic activity in our lives?
46. Should we try to communicate with our guardian angel? Give a reason for your answer.
47. What can we learn about worship from that of holy angels as portrayed in the Scriptures? (See Rev. 4–5.)
48. Did you put on the armor today? Do you know how to put it on?

Endnotes

1. For an excellent study of angels, see C. Fred Dickason, *Angels: Elect and Evil* (Chicago: Moody Press, 1995).

2. Possessed by all created personal beings (angels and humans), personhood (the divine image) is that self-conscious personal entity, described as "I" or "me," which is to be distinguished from the essential nature, whether angelic or human, that one has (cp. Job 7:11). If a person has an angelic nature, this makes him tan angelic being; if he has a human nature, this makes him a human being.

3. In His becoming man, the Lord Jesus for a little while was lower than the angels (Heb. 2:9). But with His exaltation, He was as man elevated above them in glory, position, and order (Eph. 1:20–23; Phil. 2:9; 1 Peter 3:22). As members of the new humanity (2 Cor. 5:17), we who are saved will share in this exalted position and order in our glorified state (Eph. 2:6; 1 John 3:2).

4. See Rev. 5:9–10 in *The Greek New Testament*, ed. Kurt Aland, Matthew Black, Bruce M. Metzger, and Allen Wikgren. This Greek text translates the KJV "us" and "we" as "them" and "they." These elders are not speaking of their own redemption.

5. "Crown" (Gk. *stephanos*), a victor's garland, was often worn by people of authority (Rev. 6:2).

6. "Devils" in the KJV means "demons." There is only one Devil, who is Satan (Rev. 12:9; 20:2). Some scholars hold that demons, or evil spirits, are something other than angels because of the distinction made in Acts 23:9 between spirit and angel. However, "or" could be an explanatory conjunction, "a spirit, *that is*, an angel," further identifying the spirit. In this case, the reference is to a holy angel rather than to an evil one.

7. Distinguish between demonic influence and demonic possession. See "Demonic Possession" in this chapter.

8. When He died, the Lord Jesus went to hades, or paradise (Matt. 12:40; Luke 23:43). While there, He made an announcement to these imprisoned evil angels (1 Peter 3:19–20). Among other things, He very likely declared the hopelessness of their situation because of His imminent triumph over their leader Satan by His impending resurrection and because of the certainty of their everlasting judgment (Heb. 2:14–15; 1 Peter 3:22; Rev. 1:18; cp. Acts 17:31).

9. This is "the pit of the Abyss," a lower region in hades where some evil angels are confined (cp. Luke 8:31, "deep") and where Satan will be confined during the Lord's millennial reign (Rev. 20:1, 3; cp. Rom. 10:7).

10. Both Ezekiel 28:11–17 and Isaiah 14:12–15 look beyond the human political rulers of Tyre and of Babylon to Satan, the ruler of this world (John 12:31). These prophecies anticipate the time when Satan and his demon allies will be cast into the Abyss at the beginning of our Lord's millennial, earthly reign (Rev. 20:1–3).

11. I prefer the view that the event described by Isa. 14:12 is Satan's being confined to earth in the middle of the Tribulation Age (Rev. 12:7–12). He is not presently confined to earth as other passages indicate (Job 1:6; Eph. 2:2).

12. That these "sons of God" were angels is indicated by the usage of "sons of God" in the OT Scriptures (Job 1:6; 2:1; 38:7; Dan. 3:25) and by the information given in 1 Peter 3:19–20; 2 Peter 2:4–5; and Jude 6–7.

13. When He prayed that this first "cup" might pass (v. 42; Matt. 26:39), the Lord was speaking not of the events of the next day but of what was happening to Him in the garden at this time (Matt. 26:37–38). "If" here introduces a Greek fulfilled condition. It was possible and the Father was willing for this "cup" and "hour" of imminent death to pass, as the Lord's words indicated, "Since You are willing to remove this cup from Me" (Luke 22:42). The Father answered this prayer by sending an angel to strengthen Jesus (v. 43). It was not His plan for Jesus to die in Gethsemane.

14. See Floyd H. Barackman, *Where Is Your Faith,* "Biblical Practical Faith."

15. These divine resources include the Bible (2 Tim. 3:15–17), the Holy Spirit (John 14:16–17), divine grace (2 Cor. 12:9; Heb. 4:14–16), faith (2 Peter 1:1; Gal. 2:20), prayer (John 14:13), the means of divine forgiveness and cleansing from sin (2 Cor. 7:1; Rev. 2:5; 1 John 1:9), and the ministries of other saved people (Heb. 10:24–25).

16. Here the designation "the devil" is metonymy, or a figure of association, where the agent

stands for the instrument or, in this case, Satan represents his demon associates (see Appendix X: "Figures of Association: Synecdoche and Metonymy").

17. Quoted by James Strahan, *Hebrew Ideals in Genesis* (Grand Rapids: Kregel Publications, n.d.), 289. This is a fine book on the lives of the patriarchs in Genesis 12–50.
18. Others are attracted to the idea of being like God in power, authority, glory, or as the object of worship.
19. Mrs. Penn-Lewis and Evan Roberts, *War on the Saints* (Leicester: The "Overcomer" Book Room, 1922), 71.
20. Adapted from Mrs. Penn-Lewis and Evan Roberts, *War on the Saints,* 66.
21. Filling the heart means controlling or influencing the mind or life (cp. Rom. 8:5–8; Eph. 5:18; see Luke 6:45).
22. John F. Nevius, *Demon Possession and Allied Themes* (Chicago: Fleming H. Revell Co., 1893), 143ff.
23. Merrill F. Unger, *What Demons Can Do To Saints* (Chicago: Moody Press, 1977), 99ff. Also, see his *Demons in the World Today* (Wheaton, Ill.: Tyndale House, 1971).
24. Unger, *What Demons Can Do To Saints*, 106ff.
25. Ibid., 112.
26. Ibid., 121ff., 129ff.
27. See the writings of Kurt E. Koch (Grand Rapids: Kregel Publications); and David Powlison, *Power Encounters* (Grand Rapids: Baker Book House, 1995).

Anthropology

8

ANTHROPOLOGY
The Doctrine of Man

The Bible gives us exclusive, reliable information not only about God but also about ourselves. Ignoring this revelation, modern scientific opinion regards man to be a higher kind of animal that has evolved to its present form over many years. But the facts of man's origin, nature, and destination cannot be known apart from what God has revealed in His Word. Any opinion that is not grounded on and governed by this revelation will be conjectural and faulty. As human beings, we should seek to learn what the Creator has revealed about mankind. As saved people, we should accept this revelation as absolute truth and base our understanding on it.

THE ORIGIN OF MANKIND

ITS MANNER

The first man and woman were created by the direct, personal act of God,[1] apart from any evolutionary process (Gen. 1:27; 2:7, 21–22; 5:1–2; 6:6; Ps. 100:3; Eccl. 7:29; Matt. 19:4).[2] This creative work was the joint action of the Persons of the divine Trinity (Gen. 1:26, "Us") in fulfillment of Their earlier determination, as expressed by Their decree (Eph. 1:11).

Regarding the two accounts of mankind's creation, the second one (Gen. 2:7–25) completes the first (1:26–29). The first account presents man's creation as it relates to the events of the creative week and to his commission to govern the earth as God's viceroy. The second account presents man's creation as it relates to his personal interaction with God, his Creator, and as this relates to woman, who was created to be man's loving companion and helper.

The Creation of Adam (Gen. 2:7)

Following a two-step process that He used in the creation of animals (Gen. 1:24; 2:19; cp. 1:20; 7:21–22), God directly created man in this way:

One: He formed Adam's body from existing material—"dust" (Heb. *'aphar*), "the dry, fine crumbs of earth" (cp. Gen. 3:19; Job 4:19; Ps. 103:14; Eccl. 3:20; 12:7).[3] "Adam" means "red arable soil."[4]

Two: God breathed into Adam's nostrils "the breath of lives" (Heb.), with the result that man "became a living soul," or a living creature (cp. Gen. 1:20–21, 24; 2:19). It appears that God did several things in this second step of man's creation. First, He animated man's body by imparting a human spirit (Gen. 6:17; 7:21–22; cp. Ps. 104:29; Zech. 12:1) and soul (Gen. 35:18; 1 Kings 17:21–22). Then He imparted the divine image (Gen. 1:26), which I believe is personhood.[5] Finally, He gave man spiritual life (cp. 2:17), by which he had a conscious, personal relationship with God (Luke 3:38; cp. John 17:3).

Upon the completion of this creative process, "man became a living soul." While other passages, as we shall see, show that man has a soul as a separate component of his makeup, this clause seems to emphasize his becoming a living creature.[6]

The Creation of Eve (Gen. 2:18–25; 1 Cor. 11:8–12)

1. The manner of her creation

Following a two-step process, God created Eve on the same day that He created Adam (Gen. 1:27; 5:1–2, "man" in v. 1 is generic, including woman):

One: God made Eve's body from Adam's rib (Gen. 2:21–22). Creating her body from living tissue, God did not have to impart to her the physical life-giving sources of soul and spirit as He did to Adam.

Two: God imparted to Eve the divine image (her unique personhood, Gen. 5:1–2; 9:6) and spiritual life (2:17). By this creative process, Eve became a living human being, with the same essential parts as Adam—personhood and human nature, consisting of body, soul, and spirit (cp. 5:1–2; 7:21–22).

2. The purpose for her creation

God created Eve for Adam so that she might fulfill certain needs in his life (1 Cor. 11:9; Gen. 2:18–25).

a. For his social needs

Being lonely (Gen. 2:18), the first man needed a companion like himself, yet differing, with whom he could have a loving, intimate relationship and by whom he would be completed.

b. For his functional needs

He also needed a helper with whom he could share the service of God and the labors of life and with whom he could reproduce his kind (Gen. 1:28; 2:15). The phrase, "a help meet for him" (2:18 KJV), literally reads, "a helper corresponding [or suited] to him."

Eve was her husband's divinely appointed loving companion and helper.

3. The event of her creation

Adam became aware of his need for a companion and helper when he named the animals and birds of his area (Gen. 2:19–20). He observed that each creature had its mate, yet he did not find any among them that suited him physically, intellectually, and emotionally. But God met his need. Placing him in a deep sleep, He took one of Adam's ribs, made of it Eve, and presented her to him (vv. 21–25). Indeed, it was love at first sight! Why did God make Eve from a rib? Perhaps, being near his heart, it was to remind Adam of the affection that he should have for his wife.

That God made Eve for Adam was for the woman's and the man's humiliation and glory (1 Cor. 11:7–9, 11–12). "It is humbling to the woman to know that she was created for the man, but it is for her glory to know that she alone can complete him. Likewise, it is humbling to the man to know that he is incomplete without a woman, but it is to his glory to know that the woman was created for him."[7]

ITS TIME

The Bible states that God created man on the sixth day of creation week (Gen. 1:24–31), but there are differences of opinion among scholars about how long ago this was. Bible chronologists James Usher, Martin Anstey, Philip Mauro, Richard Niessen, and Eugene W. Faulstitch offer the dates 4004, 4124, 4025, 4174, and 4001 B.C., respectively.[8] To my mind, the most accurate calculation was made by J. B. Dimbleby who gave us a Bible chronology from 0 A.M. (*Anno Mundi*, "in the year of the world") forward that is based on the chronological statements of the Scriptures and that is supported by astronomical reckoning and data.[9] His date of man's creation is 4004 B.C.

Some believe that more time was needed for man's dispersion over the earth and for accommodation to scientific opinion about man than a face-value computation of Bible chronology allows.[10] Therefore, they assume the possibility of gaps in the Genesis genealogical records (Gen. 5, 10–11) or hold that the names listed in these records represent the first ancestor of a clan or family. However, these arbitrary interpretations of the genealogical records create problems. They open the door to all kinds of conjecture regarding the antiquity of man and assume that the Bible does not present an unbroken line of descent from Adam to Christ (Luke 3:23–38).[11] Actually, as the forenamed chronologists show, the Bible does give a complete chronology from Adam to Christ, with sufficient detail to compute accurately the span in years. We should keep in mind that there are no absolute means of verification of any date earlier than 3500 B.C., the beginning of recorded history. Despite people's opinions to the contrary, I prefer the witness of Bible chronology.

Regarding the discovery of Pleistocene hominid fossils, the question remains whether any of these were human. Some believe that these hominids were pre-Adamic races of creatures that resembled man but that they were not made in God's image. However, the Bible nowhere hints at pre-Adamic races nor does the creation week, as I understand it, allow for their existence.[12] All remains of true humans must be the descendants of Adam. Without doubt, some races of human beings became extinct, particularly with the Noachic Flood.

Although early mankind may have made extensive use of stone implements, this does not necessarily mean that they were ignorant savages. People with stone-age culture today show us otherwise. Also, we must distinguish between civilization (an advanced state of cultural and technical development) and spirituality (a state of having a relationship with God). Though early mankind may have had a less complex culture, yet by divine grace some were able to please God and walk in His fellowship (Gen. 2:15; 4:4; 5:24; 6:9). History has repeatedly demonstrated that a complex civilization, which represents people's attempts to get along without God, is a hindrance to true spirituality (cp. Gen. 4:16–24; Luke 16:15; 1 John 2:15–17; Rev. 17, 18). The civilization that is built on the unbiblical beliefs and values of unsaved people cannot provide for their spiritual needs or resolve the social problems that these needs generate.

THE NATURE OF MANKIND

Having examined what the Scriptures reveal about mankind's origin, let us look more closely to see what humans and their makeup are.

HUMANS ARE CREATURES

Unfallen Humans

In their unfallen moral state, Adam and Eve were products of God, divinely made by direct creation (Gen. 1:26–27).

Sinful Humans

While they remain human creatures and are God's property (Ps. 24:1), unsaved people are Satan's product (John 8:44), for their present fallen, sinful condition (physical, psychological, and spiritual) is the result of his deceptive activity (Gen. 3:1–6; Eph. 2:2; John 8:44).

Saved Humans

Having been recreated by God, saved people are His workmanship in Christ Jesus (Eph. 2:10; 2 Cor. 5:17). But this divine work will not be completed until the Lord returns and changes their unsaved bodies (Phil. 3:20–21; 1 Cor. 15:50–57). In their changed state, saved people will forever be like Jesus in His glorified humanity (1 John 3:2). Observe, however, that saved people will never become God; they will always be His human personal creatures.

HUMANS BEAR THE IMAGE OF GOD

Adam and Eve were deliberately made in God's image (Gen. 1:26–27; 5:1).[13] However, there are various opinions regarding what this image in humans is. For instance, many believe that it is an entity that gives people reason, emotion, and will (cp. Isa. 1:18; John 3:16; Eph. 1:11). However, these features, to a lesser degree, are manifest in higher forms of animal life as well as in man. Let us examine this.

The Distinction of This Image

While both "image" and "likeness" express correspondence to God, "likeness" indicates that this correspondence is one of similarity, not identicalness. That the image of God in humans is not one of identical correspondence is supported by the fact that this image was created while God Himself is uncreated. Also, it is very likely that God's image has unrevealed features that the divine image in people does not have. Keep in mind that this divine image in humans is not essentially their having God's divine nature. This would make them to be God. To my mind, it means that humans have a created feature, apart from their propagated human nature, that is like something that belongs to God's makeup and distinguishes them from lower creatures. This correspondence gives humans a sacredness, dignity, and value that animals do not have (Gen. 9:6; James 3:9; cp. 2 Peter 2:12).

The Identity of This Image

I believe that the divine image in humans is personhood—the unique, personal entity that at conception is created by God (Mal. 2:10) and that is immediately and forever joined to one's propagated human nature (body, soul, and spirit). It is the "I" or "me" as being distinct from one's body, soul, and spirit, which are components of one's human nature. Job said, "Therefore, I will not refrain *my mouth*, I will speak in the anguish of *my spirit*, I will complain in the bitterness of *my soul*" (Job 7:11, italics mine; cp. Isa. 26:9). Since the possession must have a possessor, I identify this possessor as personhood.[14] It appears that angels also have this image since they express the characteristics of personal creatures and, like humans, are called "sons of God" (Job 1:6; 38:7; Luke 3:38; cp. 20:36).[15] Thus, man and angels are like God in that, having personhood, they are persons. This corresponds to the true God, who consists of three Persons—the Father, the Son, and the Holy Spirit, with each One having His own personhood. However, humans and angels, with their particular natures, are human and angelic persons, unlike the Persons of the divine Trinity who possess the single divine nature and are God.

We should not confuse the divine image in man (personhood) with the image of the Lord Jesus Christ, after which we who are saved are being made by God (Eph. 4:24; Col. 3:10; Rom. 8:29). In His humanity, the Lord Jesus is the leader and pattern of a new human race, of which we who are saved are members (1 Cor. 15:22, 45–49; 2 Cor. 5:17; Heb. 2:11). By His sanctifying work in our lives, the Holy Spirit is reproducing in us the moral qualities of the Lord Jesus as we submit to His Word and to His dealings with us (2 Cor. 3:18; Heb. 12:10; John 17:17; 2 Tim. 3:16–17). When He comes again, the Lord will deliver our unsaved, mortal bodies from inherent corruption and will make them like His resurrected body of glory (Rom. 8:23; Phil. 3:20–21; 1 Cor. 15:45–53). Then we shall be fully like Him in human nature (1 John 3:2; See Appendix V: "The Human Body-Grid").

The Duration of This Image

While humans were created in God's image or with personhoods, do unsaved people have this image? The Scriptures show that they do (Gen. 9:6; James 3:9). People's sinning did not cause them to cease being persons, although it radically affected their entire being (personhood and human nature).[16] Moreover, all humans, both saved and unsaved, will forever possess their personhoods and forever experience either God's blessing or His judgment, according to their spiritual relationships with Him (Matt. 25:46).

HUMANS EXIST AS MALE AND FEMALE (GEN. 1:27; 5:2; CP. MATT. 19:4)

God created man and woman, with their peculiar distinctions and drives, in order that they might complete one another and together fulfill His purpose for their existence in this world (Gen. 1:26; 2:18, 21–25). The Bible never suggests that these distinctions and drives are in themselves evil or base, although the human natures of unsaved men and women are wholly corrupted by sin. Being given of God, these distinctions between men and women can be completely expressed and fulfilled in the marriage state and in the social order that God has established for humans.

The Institution of Marriage

Marriage is a formal, legal commitment before God to an exclusive love between a man and a woman. Its sanctity rests upon its being instituted by God and its bond being effected by Him, not by sexual union (Gen. 2:22–25; Matt. 19:4–6). Although marriage is given to the human race, it is God's will that gospel believers marry only saved people (2 Cor. 6:14; 1 Cor. 7:39). On the other hand, in the case of unsaved people, when a spouse becomes saved, the union with the unsaved spouse is still sacred in God's sight (1 Cor. 7:12–14). The marriage bond can only be broken by abandonment, adultery, or death (1 Cor. 7:15; Matt. 19:9; Rom. 7:2).

God forbids premarital and extramarital sexual relations (Eph. 5:3–5; 1 Thess. 4:3, 7; 1 Cor. 6:15–18).[17] The reasons for this prohibition may be that these illicit relations portray a spiritual union (the marriage bond) that really does not exist; thus, they perpetrate a lie, which God hates (Prov. 6:16–17). Also, adultery violates one's pledge of exclusive love to one's spouse and severs the marriage bond (Matt. 19:6).

Despite ecclesiastical Christian teaching influenced by pagan Greek philosophy about the body and sexuality, the marriage state, being instituted by God (Gen. 2:24), is as holy and good in His sight as the single state (cp. 1 Cor. 7:14; Heb. 13:4).[18] However, in certain situations, like persecution or the demands of certain ministries, marriage may not be as suitable as singleness (cp. 1 Cor. 7:26–35).

In addition to perpetuating the race and providing a home for offspring, the purpose of marriage is to provide a couple with the opportunity to experience that completeness that is achieved by sexual union, reciprocal love, and mutual trust and sharing. In marriage, a man and a woman are brought together into a unique oneness of life, by means of which both find completion in each other (Gen. 2:24). This oneness is expressed by the words *one flesh*. Within the marriage state, the husband and his wife are united to the extent that former natural ties are severed, and a new tie is made by God (Matt. 19:5–6). The sexual relation is a physical symbol and expression of this union. Moreover, the sexual function is not merely the means of continuing the race. It is the deepest symbol of personal understanding and love. It expresses the meaning and quality of the relationship between a husband and his wife. It expresses the depth of communion, where one surrenders oneself to and for the other. Thus the self-giving, loving sexual relation in marriage is not something that is evil and shameful, but holy, pleasurable, and purposeful. It promotes the growth of mutual understanding and love.

The union between a saved husband and saved wife portrays the relationship between the Lord Jesus and His Church (Eph. 5:22–32). Being espoused to Jesus at salvation (2 Cor. 11:2), we who are saved have the duties of remaining faithful to Him (James 4:4; 2 Cor. 6:17–7:1) and of completing Him as Eve did Adam (Eph. 1:22–23). This female role includes our being His loving companion-friend (1 Cor. 1:9; John 15:4–5, 14) and subordinate helper (John 15:14–16; 1 Cor. 3:8; cp. Eph. 5:22–33). In the future, we who comprise His Church shall live with Him forever as His wife (Rev. 19:7–8).

The Social Order of Leadership

Contrary to the world's view, God has established what the human social order should be. He has given the leadership of human society to men (Gen. 1:28; 1 Cor. 11:3). This is not to say that women are inferior to men spiritually, mentally, or skillfully (Gal. 3:28), but from the beginning God has given women the position of social subordination as man's helper (Gen. 2:18; 1 Cor. 11:9). When Eve abandoned this position and assumed that of leadership, she brought sin to her husband and through him to the human race (Gen. 3:1–6). With this sin, she also brought upon her female descendants sinful men's cruel despotism and lustful exploitation. A divine punishment for her sin was the continuation of her subordination to man (v. 16).

The subordination that women are to express to men is not in the nature of bondage or to the extent of disobeying God's commands, which supersede those of man (Col. 3:18; Acts 5:29). It is a voluntary subordination that puts the interests and goals of the man, for whom she was created as helper, above herself, and that exalts the man (1 Cor. 11:7–9).

The apostle Paul gave God's social order for mankind in 1 Corinthians 11:2–16, where he points out that the woman was made of and for the man (vv. 8–9).[19] Elsewhere, he affirms man's leadership in the home (Eph. 5:22–23; Col. 3:18), the local church (1 Cor. 14:34; 1 Tim. 2:11–12), and civil government (Rom. 13:4). On the other hand, with his leadership position in the home, the husband has the responsibility of loving his wife as himself and as the Lord loves the Church (Eph. 5:25, 28, 33; Col. 3:19). This makes it much easier for a wife to fulfill her role as companion and helper (Gen. 2:18), to be submissive to her husband's leadership (Eph. 5:22; Col. 3:18), and to love him (Titus 2:4). When God's social order is honored, it brings His blessing. When it is ignored, it incurs trouble and unhappiness.

HUMANS ARE COMPLEX BEINGS

Their makeup consists of personhood and human nature. Having personhoods, humans are like God; having bodies, souls, and spirits, they are like animals.[20] Let us look at these parts more closely.

Humans Have Personhoods

Unlike animals, humans are personal beings, for they have personhoods, which, I believe, are the image of God in people (Gen. 1:26–27). What is personhood and its qualities?

1. *A description of personhood*
Personhood is that basic, personal entity that we sometimes call "self" and that is

identified by the personal pronouns "I" and "me." [21] This entity—the image of God in man that makes us people or persons—provides the capability within our human existence for personal self-awareness, responsible moral self-determination, and unique self-expression.

By *self-awareness,* I mean that because of his personhood a person is aware of himself and his distinction from other people and from things. By *responsible moral self-determination,* I mean that because of his personhood a person, when he sufficiently develops, has moral awareness, can make moral choices, and is responsible for his actions. By *unique self-expression,* I mean that because of his personhood his existence and functions are unique personal activities and experiences rather than the mechanical processes of impersonal automation or instinct as with animals.

2. *Personhood's distinction from human nature*

Job's distinction between his personhood ("I") and his human nature—body ("mouth"), spirit, and soul (Job 7:11)—indicates that personhood is something other than human nature (cp. Isa. 26:9;).[22] While body, soul, and spirit are the essential parts of human nature, personhood is an entity in humans that is other than human nature or a part thereof.

As I see it, personhood is that unique, personal entity that, at one's conception, is created by God (cp. Mal. 2:10) and that is immediately and permanently joined to one's human nature.[23] Personhood could hardly be propagated, for being derived from and consisting of the personhoods of the parents, it would not be unique or distinct from their personhoods. On the other hand, human nature, consisting of body, soul, and spirit, is produced by and transmitted from the parents to their child by propagation at conception. Possessing the genetic code of one's ancestors and the effects of original sin (Gen. 5:3; Ps. 51:5), the propagated human nature qualifies one's personhood and makes one to be the kind of person that one is, generically and morally—a human being and a sinner.[24]

I believe theologians make a mistake when they equate personhood with the soul. While it sometimes represents the total person (Gen. 46:26; Acts 27:37), the soul should not be equated with personhood.[25] To do so is to create theological confusion. For example, this would make Jesus, having a human soul (Matt. 26:38), two persons. He is one person with two natures—the divine and the human, which make Him the God-man.

3. *The qualities of personhood*

While the propagated human nature imparts human qualities to personhood and makes one to be human, it appears that personhood itself has inherent qualities that it imparts to and expresses with one's human nature. Not found in nonpersonal forms of life like animals, these qualities of personhood correspond to features in God's personhood. These qualities include conscious individuality, responsible morality, and enduring existence.

a. *Conscious individuality*

Conscious individuality refers to that peculiarity of being, not of character, which distinguishes man from other beings of his kind.[26] For example, in the case of identical twins who have very similar human natures, they still are distinct persons. Thus, each human being is uniquely distinct from all other humans, not only in personality (the expression of personhood as affected by human nature) but also in personhood itself. Moreover, one is aware of one's distinctiveness from other persons and things.

Individuality is also seen in the divine Trinity. While possessing the one divine nature, the Members of the Trinity have separate personhoods, which makes Them distinct Persons—the Father, the Son, and the Holy Spirit. Having the one divine nature, these Persons are equal in Their divine qualities and powers (John 14:16; Matt. 28:19). The Lord Jesus perceived Himself as being someone other than the Father and the Holy Spirit (John 14:16–17).

b. Responsible morality

It appears that personhood gives to human beings the essence and the awareness of morality as well as the awareness of God (cp. Rom. 2:14–15). This quality imparts to humans the ability to engage in moral behavior, for which they are responsible to God and to man (Rom. 2:6, 16; 13:1–5). It also enables them to recognize and to distinguish between good and evil, right and wrong, and to make moral evaluations and moral decisions or choices. Furthermore, because of their personhoods humans have an innate awareness of God's existence and of their accountability to Him. This motivates them to worship what they consider to be God.[27]

God also has morality. This is seen in His recognition of good and evil (Gen. 3:22; Prov. 15:3) and in His judging mankind (Acts 17:31).

c. Enduring existence

This is one's continuing forever. Having personhoods, all humans will survive death and will exist forever—the saved with God and the unsaved apart from Him in hell (Matt. 25:46). It is personhood that gives perpetuity to human nature, for personhood will require the continuing function of human nature for one's afterlife, human experiences. On the other hand, not having personhoods, animals have no need for the perpetuation of their natures. There is no biblical evidence that they survive death.

God also has perpetuity (Ps. 102:12). The Persons of the divine Trinity continue forever.

Because of their having personhoods, all humans, despite of sin, have a nobility that earthly animals and things do not have. Because of this, God requires the death sentence for capital crimes against mankind (Gen. 9:5–6). Furthermore, being persons, all who are restored to God's fellowship by salvation can interact with the Persons of the divine Trinity (Eph. 2:13; see "Fellowship with God" under Theology Proper).

Humans Have a Human Nature

In addition to personhoods, humans have a nature that makes them human persons.

1. Its description

Human nature is that propagated essence, with its qualities and powers, that is at conception united to our divinely created personhoods and that interacts with it, making us human persons, physically, rationally, emotionally, and volitionally. Wholly transmitted to us by our parents, our human nature consists of a human body, soul, and spirit. However, in its unsaved natural state, human nature from its conception bears Adam's image (Gen. 5:3; 1 Cor. 15:49, see endnote 13) and the effects of man's original sin (Rom. 5:12).28

When we think of human nature, we must distinguish it from the divine nature of God and from the angelic nature of angels. All personal beings have their own kinds of nature that makes them what they are.

2. Its essential parts

Human nature consists of material and immaterial parts. Obviously, the material part is the physical body, but the immaterial parts (soul and spirit) are not clearly defined in the Scriptures. To the Hebrews, the various parts of man's nature were not considered to be contrasting elements, as in pagan thought, but differing aspects of one, vital personality. They regarded the immaterial parts as being almost physical and the physical parts as having psychological functions so that whatever activity people engage in the predominant aspect represents the whole person (cp. Gen. 2:7; Ps. 51:8).29 Nevertheless, the Scriptures still identify the parts of human nature, with their distinctive functions.

a. The material part of human nature—the body

1) Its substance

The body was originally made from dust of the ground (Gen. 2:7; 3:19). Because of this, it needs elements that are found in soil for its sustenance. We ingest these elements through food, both vegetation and flesh. What a variety God has provided for us! When it dies, the body returns to dust until its resurrection (Gen. 3:19; John 5:28–29). Although the body in its natural state has such a lowly origin and ending, medical science is still learning about its inherent wonders, for which David long ago praised God (Ps. 139:14).

While the apostle Paul distinguished between human flesh and animal flesh (1 Cor. 15:39), both are animated by the same means. Living bodies of flesh are presently animated by the soul (Gen. 35:18; Matt. 26:38; Luke 12:20) and the spirit (Gen. 7:22; Ps. 104:29; Luke 8:55; 23:46; James 2:26). When its condition no longer allows these animating forces to function, they depart and the body dies and returns to dust. Physical life, now transmitted by the propagated human spirit and soul, returns to God who imparted it to man in the beginning (Gen. 2:7; Eccl. 12:7; Job 34:14–15).

2) Its condition

(a) Presently

Programmed with the genetic code of our parents and ancestors, our bodies give us our personality characteristics. Also, as we have seen, our bodies in their present state are made alive by the soul and spirit (Gen. 35:18; James 2:26), but they are physically sustained by our ingesting nourishing food and breathing air. Furthermore, since Eve's and Adam's first sin, human bodies have been inherently corrupt and mortal (Rom. 8:10; 1 Cor. 15:53; see Addendum, "Human Physical Mortality"). This means that, being affected by sin with defective genes and immune systems, these bodies are subjected to aging, weakness, degeneration, disease, and finally death (cp. 1 Cor. 15:42–44). Moreover, the sin force resides in the body's cells and energizes the body as well as the other parts of human nature for its evil expressions (Rom. 3:9; 7:17–18, 23; Gal. 5:19–21). However, as we shall see, we who are saved should no longer give our bodies over to the demands of this inner sin force, for our relation to this force has been changed. We have died to it and are now alive unto God (see Rom. 6; see "The Gospel Believer and Sin: The Believer's Relation to Original Sin" under Hamartiology).

(b) In the future

The bodies of saved people will be delivered from their inherent corruption when the Lord Jesus returns to receive His Church (Phil. 3:20–21) and comes again to establish His millennial kingdom (Dan. 12:2–3; Luke 13:28–29; Rev. 20:4). At these times, He will instantly recreate the bodies of His people to prepare them for the eternal state. He will raise the disintegrated bodies of dead saved people to incorruptibility, never to die again; He will change the bodies of living saved people to immortality, never to face death (1 Cor. 15:50–53; see below, "The Resurrection of Mankind"). Presently, our bodies are subject to the laws and conditions that govern physical life in this world. But when they are changed, these bodies will be prepared for life off the planet and for the eternal state (1 Cor. 15:50–55; 1 Thess. 4:16–17; Rev. 21–22).

These changes will be substantive, not ethereal as certain cults teach (cp. Luke 24:39). Being animated and energized by the Holy Spirit, these changed bodies will differ from our present ones in their qualities, powers, and animating principle (1 Cor. 15:35–44; Rom. 8:11). Because of this, the apostle Paul wrote of the changed body as being "spiritual" rather than "natural" (Gk. "soulish," 1 Cor. 15:44–50). "Spiritual" and "soulish" seem to refer to the principles by which the body is animated: presently the body is made alive by the human soul-spirit ("soulish"); in the future it will be made alive by the Holy Spirit ("spiritual").

Being made like the glorified body of the Lord Jesus in its essential construction (Phil. 3:20–21), our changed bodies will allow us to experience all that God has for us in the eternal state and to express Jesus' human intellectual, emotional, and volitional qualities (see Appendix V: "The Human Body-Grid"). Having His kind of body, we shall truly be like Him (1 John 3:2). Presently, in their unsaved state, our bodies are like that of fallen Adam and those of our intermediate ancestors. They now express the qualities of Adam's sinful state and the genetic features of our ancestors. But all this will be changed when Jesus returns.

3) Its functions

The body is our mechanical means of perception, expression, and reproduction in this world. Also, as we have seen, it is the instrument of the principle or moral force, whether God or sin, that presently dominates our lives (Luke 6:45; Rom. 6:12–13; 8:5). The sin force wholly dominates the lives of unsaved people and uses their total human natures for its evil expressions (John 8:34; Rom. 3:9; 6:16; Gal. 5:19–21; Eph. 2:2–3; 1 John 3:8). However, sin's domination over the lives of gospel believers was broken when we were saved. As God sees it, at that time we died to the sin force and were made alive to Him and His authority (Rom. 6:1–10). Thus, we are to regard our bodies as broken tools that have been rendered useless to sin (v. 6) and as remade tools that are instruments of God and righteousness (v. 13). Having been acquitted of sin's claim to us (v. 7), we can now respond to God's claim and give ourselves to Him and His will for us (vv. 11–13; 12:1). Nevertheless, because this evil force is not dead, it seizes every opportunity to take control of our lives.

Despite the body's present corruption, the gospel believer should possess it in sanctification and honor (1 Thess. 4:4), for by the power of God it can now serve holy purposes, including the following (1 Cor. 6:12–20):

One: The gospel believer's body is an earthly member of Christ (v. 15). The Lord's people are the means through which He works to build His Church. He uses them and their bodies in this ministry (Rom. 12:1–2; John 15:4–5; Acts 14:27).

Two: The gospel believer's body is the earthly temple of the Holy Spirit (1 Cor. 6:19; John 14:17). For this reason, one must respect one's body and care for it as the place where Holy Spirit resides.

Three: The gospel believer's body is the only means he has by which to express himself and to glorify God in this world (1 Cor. 6:20; 10:31). He cannot express himself or function apart from his body (see Appendix V: "The Human Body-Grid").

4) Its care

Because of these truths, we should never abuse the body or regard it as our enemy, as pagan philosophy and practice do. Rather, we should daily care for our body, nourish it, discipline it, yield it to God for His holy purposes, and use it for His glory (Rom. 6:16, 19; 12:1–2; 13:14; Eph. 5:28–29; 1 Cor. 9:26–27; 1 Thess. 4:3–7).

Since our physical condition directly affects the quality of our life and ministry, it is important that we maintain our physical well-being (Mark 6:31; Luke 8:55; Acts 27:33–35). It is sinful to disregard the laws and means of physical health, like proper food and sufficient rest, unless circumstances force us to do so. Traditional religious self-mortification, with its physical self-affliction, comes from pagan thought, which considers the body to be inherently evil and a threat to the soul.[30] While there are times when spiritual duty or some crisis transcends our physical needs (Matt. 4:1–4; Acts 13:2–3), ordinarily we should maintain our physical well-being. A body that is racked with pain or bound by weakness is a handicap to one's efficiency in thought and action. On the other hand, when God in His wisdom sends physical affliction, we can look to Him for the grace that we need to rise above this and do His will (2 Cor. 12:7–10).

5) Its designation "flesh"

While we do not have difficulty in understanding the word *body*, the biblical meaning of "flesh" is more complicated. The word *flesh* (Heb. *basar,* Gk. *sarx*) has different meanings, as determined by its biblical usage and context. These are as follows:

One, the physical structure of humans and animals (Exod. 29:14; Dan. 1:15; Luke 24:39; Rom. 7:18; 8:3, third occurrence of "flesh"; 1 Cor. 5:5; 2 Cor. 10:3, first occurrence of "flesh"). Having been made to live on earth, our bodies in their present state are described as "flesh and blood" (1 Cor. 15:50; note that this phrase is a synecdoche for man in Eph. 6:12).

Two, living humans and animals (Gen. 6:17; 7:15–16; Acts 2:17).

Three, representing what is human in nature (John 1:14; Rom. 8:3, first and second occurrences of "flesh"; Heb. 2:14). This is in contrast to what is divine (Matt. 16:17) and what is angelic (Eph. 6:12).

Four, one's relatives, ancestors, or posterity (Gen. 29:14; Acts 2:30; Rom. 1:3; 9:3).

Five, human frailty and temporariness (Ps. 78:39; Isa. 40:6; Rom. 6:19).

Six, people's responsiveness to God (Ezek. 36:26). This is in contrast to "stone," which represents their obstinacy to God.

Seven, Jesus' atoning work (John 6:53–56; Eph. 2:15). "Flesh" represents our Lord's physical death, which was involved in the atonement (Rom. 5:8, 10).

Eight, a person's total being (2 Cor. 7:5; Heb. 9:13).

Nine, human nature dominated by the sin force (John 8:15; Rom. 8:3, first occurrence of "flesh"; Gal. 6:12; Eph. 2:3, second occurrence of "flesh"). In this usage, the emphasis is on the human nature of unsaved people, which is solely dominated by the sin force.

Ten, the sin force dominating a person's human nature (Rom. 7:5; 8:1, 4–5, 8–9, 12–13; 13:14; 2 Cor. 1:17; 10:2, 3, second occurrence of "flesh"; 11:18; Gal. 3:3; 5:13, 16–17, 19, 24; 6:8; Eph. 2:3, first occurrence of "flesh"; Col. 2:23; 2 Peter 2:10, 18; Jude 23). In this usage, the emphasis is on the sin force, sometimes in contrast to the Holy Spirit (Rom. 8:9, 13; Gal. 3:3; 5:16–17) or to Jesus (Rom. 13:14).

When we come upon the word *flesh* in the Bible, we should consider which one of these meanings best fits the passage and its context.

b. The immaterial parts of human nature—the soul and spirit

What soul and spirit are is not clear. Although the Bible uses designations that indicate that they are distinct, simultaneous entities (1 Thess. 5:23; Heb. 4:12), soul and spirit may refer to the same thing, for they have similar functions (Isa. 26:9; 57:16; Luke 1:46–47). Their separate designations, "soul" and "spirit," may come from the ways in which the single immaterial entity of human nature is related to the body: its relation to the body in association with blood being "soul" (Lev. 17:11, 14, KJV "life" is *nephesh,* soul) and its relation to the body in association with breath being "spirit" (Isa. 42:5; Gen. 7:22, Heb. "the breath of the spirit of life").

However this may be, soul and spirit seem to provide personhood with the dynamics, or forces, of intelligence, emotions, and will, and to give the body the ability to express these human activities insofar as it allows. Thus, soul and spirit seem to be the dynamic source of these functions in contrast to body, which is the mechanism for expressing these functions. Also, soul and spirit impart to the earthly body physical life. To facilitate our study, I have sorted the biblical terms for these immaterial parts of human nature into two groups—those that have their own names and those that are represented by bodily parts.

1) Parts having their own name
(a) The human soul

The Bible reveals that humans have a soul as a part of their human nature

(Ps. 3:2; Luke 1:46). When He created man, God imparted to him soul (and spirit) with the result that Adam became a living soul (Gen. 2:7) or a living creature (cp. Gen. 1:20–24).

The soul's relation to the body is in its association with the body's blood.[31] Blood itself is not the soul, but it is the container or vehicle of the soul (Lev. 17:11, 14; Deut. 12:23, KJV "life" should read "soul").[32] Soul resides with the blood and conveys life to the cells of the body. Soul also imparts to the body the necessary ability for the physical activity of reasoning, expressing emotions, and making decisions. However, if the body is impaired, then these activities are restricted or distorted. The soul survives death (Rev. 6:9), for it is needed by personhood in the afterlife to continue to provide the human dynamics of the intelligence, the emotions, and the will.

The functions of soul, as given in the Old Testament (Heb. *nephesh*, occurring about 750 times) and in the New Testament (Gk. *psyche*, occurring about one hundred times), are similar.

One, the human soul represents human beings (Gen. 46:22–27; Acts 27:) and one's total self (Ps. 120:6; Luke 12:19). Here "soul" is a synecdoche, a figure of association, by which a part represents the whole person (see Appendix X: "Figures of Association: Synecdoche and Metonymy").

Two, the soul represents the physical life force of the body (Gen. 35:18; Job 2:4, 6; 1 Kings 17:21–22; 19:10; Jonah 4:3, KJV "life"; John 10:11, 15, 17; Acts 20:10).

Three, it is the dynamic source of the intellect in thinking (Gen. 23:8, KJV "mind"; Prov. 23:7, KJV "heart") and knowing (Ps. 139:14; Prov. 24:14). Compare Acts 14:22; 15:24.[33]

Four, it is the dynamic source of the emotions like distress (Gen. 42:21; Job 30:16; Ps. 6:3; John 12:27; Mark 14:34), sorrow (Job 30:16), desire (Ps. 42:2; Rev. 18:14), joy (Ps. 35:9; Matt. 12:18), and love (Song 1:7; Mark 12:30).

Five, it is the dynamic source of the will (Ps. 27:12 "will"; 41:2, "will"; Acts 4:32).

When we come across "soul" in the Scriptures, we must determine what meaning it has according to these biblical functions listed above and the context in which the word occurs.

(b) The human spirit

Human beings also have spirit as a part of their immaterial human nature (Gen. 41:8; Eccl. 3:21; 2 Tim. 4:22; often translated "ghost" in KJV, as in John 19:30). This human spirit must be distinguished from angelic spirits (holy ones, Heb. 1:14, and evil ones, Matt. 8:16), from God the Holy Spirit (Gal. 5:16), and from the substance of which God's divine nature consists (John 4:24).

The spirit's relation to the body appears to be in its association with the body's breath (Gen. 7:21–22, Heb. "the breath of the spirit of life"; Isa. 42:5). This is not to say that spirit itself is breath anymore than soul itself is blood. However, one's breath in some way must relate to one's spirit and allow one's spirit to act upon the body. Like soul, spirit is the means by which physical life is imparted to the body. Spirit also supplies the dynamics for intelligence, emotion, and will. Together with the soul, the spirit survives death (Heb. 12:23), for it, too, is needed by personhood in the afterlife to provide the dynamics for intelligence, emotion, and will.

The functions of "spirit" in the Old Testament (Heb. *ruach*, occurring about eighty times) and in the New Testament (Gk. *pneuma*, occurring about fifty-five times) are similar:

One, the human spirit represents, though rarely, human beings (1 Cor. 5:5; 2 Tim. 4:22; Heb. 12:9, 23) and one's total self (2 Cor. 7:13).

Two, it represents the physical life force of our present body (KJV "breath" in Gen. 6:17; 7:15, 22; Job 27:3; Ps. 104:29; Isa. 2:22; 42:5; Luke 8:55; James 2:26).

Three, it is the dynamic source of the intellect, as demonstrated in our like thinking (Eph. 4:23; Col. 2:5), understanding (Job 20:3; 1 Cor. 2:11), and perceiving (Mark 2:8).

Four, it is the dynamic source of the emotions like distress (Job 7:11; John 13:21), grief (Gen. 26:35 "mind"; Exod. 6:9), joy (Luke 10:21), and anger (Judg. 8:3 "anger"); and of such dispositions (2 Cor. 12:18) such as meekness (1 Cor. 4:21), humility (Ps. 34:18; Matt. 5:3), fervor (Rom. 12:11), faith (2 Cor. 4:13), patience, pride (Eccl. 7:8; Prov. 14:29), and impatience (Exod. 6:9).

Five, it is the dynamic source of the will (Exod. 35:21).

Again, when we come across "spirit" in the Scriptures, we must determine what kind of spirit it is (divine, angelic, or human) and what meaning it has according to these biblical functions listed above and the context in which the word occurs.

2) Parts represented by bodily organs

In biblical times people often attributed the meanings or functions of soul and spirit to various organs of the body. The following are found in the Bible:

(a) Heart

The word *heart* is the most comprehensive biblical term for the nonphysical parts and their functions in humans. It is used to represent the soul (Acts 4:32), spirit (Exod. 35:21), mind (1 Chron. 28:9), conscience (1 John 3:20) as well as one's total inner being (Rom. 10:10). Of the many occurrences of this word in the Bible, very few literally mean the physical organ (2 Sam. 18:14; 2 Kings 9:24; Ps. 45:5).

In the Old Testament the word *heart* (Heb. *leb*, 598 times; *lebab*, 252 times) has various functions or meanings: the dynamic source of physical energy and life (Ps. 22:14; Isa. 1:5); the dynamic source of the emotions (Exod. 4:14; Judg. 18:20; 2 Kings 6:11; Ps. 61:2) and desire (Prov. 6:25); the dynamic source of one's disposition or mood (Exod. 4:21; 2 Sam. 17:10; 1 Kings 8:23; 11:3; 12:27; Ezek. 21:7); the dynamic source of the will (2 Sam. 7:27; 2 Kings 12:4); the dynamic source of reasoning (Gen. 6:5), perception (Deut. 29:4), and understanding (1 Kings 3:9; Prov. 28:26); self (Gen. 17:17; 1 Kings 8:47, "themselves"; Eccl. 2:1); and the conscience (1 Sam. 24:5; 2 Sam. 24:10).

In the New Testament, the word *heart* (Gk. *kardia,* occurring about 155 times) has functions or meanings similar to its OT usage: the dynamic source of physical life and energy (James 5:5); the dynamic source of the emotions (John 14:1; 16:6; Acts 2:26; 2 Cor. 2:4); the dynamic source of the will (Acts 11:23; 2 Cor. 9:7) and desires (Rom. 10:1); the disposition (Matt. 11:29; 13:15; 1 Peter 1:22); the dynamic source of reasoning (Luke 12:45) and the mind (Acts 7:23; 1 Cor. 2:9); the self (Matt. 15:6; Rom. 6:17; 10:10; James 1:26), and the conscience (1 John 3:20–21).

In many passages, *heart* represents the control center of a person's life (Prov. 4:23; Matt. 6:21; 12:35; Mark 7:21–23; Luke 6:45). Although the heart itself has no active moral qualities, whatever moral force (whether God, Satan, or sin) occupies it (Prov. 23:26; Acts 5:3; Heb. 3:12) or whatever object becomes its focus of life (Luke 12:15–34) governs the life and expresses itself in one's behavior. Being inherently corrupted, *the hearts of unsaved people* are inclined toward sin (Jer. 17:9; 18:12). On the other hand, being purified by the Lord's atoning sacrifice, *the hearts of saved people* are inclined toward righteousness (Acts 15:9; 2 Tim. 2:22; Heb. 10:22; 1 Peter 1:22). Thus, from the heart springs forth both good and evil conduct, as determined by the moral force (God, Satan, or sin) or earthly object which acts upon it (Ps. 119:11; Luke 6:45; 12:34; Acts 5:3; Rom. 5:5; Col. 3:15–16; Eph. 3:17; Rev. 17:17). Needless to say, we must give God our hearts daily and each time that we sin so that He commands our lives (Prov. 23:26; Eph. 3:17). In Mark 7:21–23, the Lord has in view the heart that is dominated by the sin force (cp. Jer. 17:5, 9; Matt. 12:34–35; Gal. 5:19–21).

The Holy Spirit's being given to our heart (2 Cor. 1:22; Gal. 4:6) simply means that He was given to us at salvation and now indwells us (1 John 3:24; John 14:16–17). God's being the searcher of hearts (1 Sam. 16:7; 1 Chron. 28:9; 2 Chron. 6:30; Ps. 44:21; Jer. 17:10) indicates that He knows all about us, especially our inner thoughts, purposes, motivations, desires, and feelings (Rom. 8:27). His trying our hearts means that He examines our inner life, looking for that which He can approve (1 Thess. 2:4). To believe with the heart is to exercise salvational faith with our total inner being—our reasoning, emotions, and will as well as our personhood (Rom. 6:17; 10:10; cp. Matt. 15:8). Again, to act with the heart means to act with our whole being (Col. 3:23; Mark 12:30; Matt. 15:8). Observe that there is nothing in Scripture about receiving Jesus into the heart for salvation. To be saved from the guilt, ruin, and bondage of sin, we must with our hearts place our trust in Jesus and His atoning work (Rom. 10:10; John 1:12). On the other hand, people can be saved and not have Jesus in their hearts (Eph. 3:17), although they do have Jesus in their lives (1 John 5:12).

(b) Belly

In addition to its physical meaning (Judg. 3:21–22; Jer. 1:5), the word *belly* (KJV; Heb. *beten*, belly or womb) in the Old Testament represents the dynamic source of the emotions (Job 20:20; Ps. 31:9) and thoughts (Job 15:35), and also can represent one's self (15:2).

In the New Testament, the word (Gk. *koilia*) stands for one's inner being (John 7:38) or self (Rom. 16:18). Generally, it refers to the physical organ (Luke 15:16; 1 Cor. 6:13).

(c) Bowels

Sometimes this refers to the physical organ (2 Chron. 21:18; Acts 1:18), but more often it has psychical or spiritual functions.

In the Old Testament, the bowels (Heb. *mehgim*) represents the dynamic source of the emotions (Isa. 16:11; Jer. 31:20; Song 5:4; Lam. 1:20).

In the New Testament, the word (Gk. *splagchna*) represents the dynamic source of the emotions (2 Cor. 6:12; Phil. 1:8; 2:1; Col. 3:12; Philem. 7) and the self (vv. 12, 20).

(d) Reins or kidneys

In the Old Testament, *reins* (Heb. *kelayoth*) refers to the dynamic source of the emotions (Prov. 23:16), the mind (Ps. 16:7), the inner self with its thoughts, purposes, and motivations (Pss. 7:9; 26:2; Jer. 11:20; 12:2; 20:12), and the conscience (Ps. 73:21).

In the New Testament, the word (Gk. *nephros*) occurs only as the inner self with its thoughts, purposes, and motivations (Rev. 2:23).

(e) Bones

Only in the Old Testament do the bones (Heb. *estem*) function as the dynamic source of the emotions (Ps. 51:8; Prov. 12:4; 15:30; 16:24; Isa. 66:14; Jer. 20:9; Lam. 1:13; Hab. 3:16). Usually, they keep their physical meaning (Gen. 50:25).

In the New Testament, they (Gk. *osteon*) have only physical meaning (John 19:36; Luke 24:39).

c. *Several observations about soul and spirit*

One: Soul and spirit depart from the body at death (Gen. 35:18; James 2:26). However, the personhood of the deceased still retains these parts of his immaterial human nature and continues to be made human by them (Luke 16:19–25; Heb. 12:23; Rev. 6:9–11). The physical life energy, which soul and spirit impart to the body, returns to God at death (Eccl. 12:7; Job 34:14–15). Ecclesiastes 3:21 indicates that the destination of humans and animals differs. Actually, animals, not having personhoods, cease to exist upon death. However, like humans their physical life ("spirit") returns to God. Vegetation does not have soul/spirit physical life as humans and animals do. Their "life" seems to consist only of chemical processes and reactions.

Two: The dynamic source of spiritual life within the saved person is not the human spirit or soul but the Holy Spirit, who transmits to us the spiritual life of Jesus in His humanity (John 14:6; Rom. 8:2, 9–10; 1 John 5:12). "Spirit" in Romans 8:10 probably refers to the human spirit, which is made spiritually alive by regeneration, a component of salvation.

Three: At first glance, it may appear that the conscience is another separate part of our immaterial human nature (Acts 23:1). But this is not the case. The conscience is a part of our memory bank, located in the brain, with its input of innate morality from personhood and of external moral values from moral law and instruction.[34]

Four: The apostle Paul speaks of the soul and spirit of the gospel believer as the "inner man" (Rom. 7:22; 2 Cor. 4:16; Eph. 3:16). This is in contrast to the "new man," which a born again person is as a new creature in Christ (Eph. 4:24).[35]

Five: The gospel believer's soul and spirit, together with his personhood, is the part of his human makeup that is now saved (1 Peter 1:9, 22; Rom. 8:10, with "spirit" referring to the human spirit).[36] This, together with his saved personhood, makes the gospel believer a new creature in Christ (2 Cor. 5:17; Eph. 2:10). The body, which is unsaved, has yet to be delivered from inherent corruption, mortality, and the resident sin force (Rom. 8:10;7:18).[37] Nevertheless, the body of the saved person is no longer the proper instrument of sin but of righteousness (Rom. 6:1–13).

Six: That both soul and spirit are saved when we receive the Savior is indicated by the following truths: By the *renewed human spirit* we worship God (Luke 1:47; John 4:23; 1 Cor. 14:14–16; Phil. 3:3), serve Him (Rom. 1:9), and know Him (Eph. 4:23; Rom. 8:16). Also, by the *renewed human soul* we worship God (Luke 1:46), love Him (Mark 12:30), thirst after Him (Ps. 42:2), follow after Him (63:8), bless Him (103:2; 146:1), wait for Him (130:5), obey Him (119:129), and enjoy spiritual prosperity (3 John 2). Salvational faith results in the saving of the soul (Heb. 10:39). The believer's spirit "is life" in contrast to his body, which is still mortal and subject to death (Rom. 8:10).

Seven: As long as the gospel believer's soul and spirit are exposed to the urges of the sin force within and of evil influences without, these parts are just as susceptible to the influences of evil as they are to that of the Holy Spirit. When we yield our total self to the Holy Spirit, however, we can think holy thoughts, have right attitudes, feel proper emotions, make God-honoring resolutions, do those things that please Him, and resist evil (Rom. 8:4; James 4:7). On the other hand, when we yield to the sin force within or to temptation without, this results in our having evil thoughts, emotions, attitudes, purposes, and our doing evil acts, all of which are contrary to our renewed soul and spirit. Consequently, this makes us very unhappy. The soul and spirit are temporarily defiled by our sinning and have need of cleansing (2 Cor. 7:1; Rev. 2:5; 1 John 1:9). But our sinning does not radically and permanently affect them as did the first couple's sins, for we who are saved have been forever delivered from sin's dreadful judicial effects through our Lord's sacrifice (Rom. 8:1, 31–34).

Eight: The human soul and spirit survive death (Rev. 6:9; Heb. 12:23) and continue to make their indigenous personhoods human. However, they will not provide the changed body with physical life, as they do now, for the Holy Spirit will do this (Rom. 8:11). But they will continue to provide their possessors with the dynamics of intelligence, emotion, and will. As we have seen, all physical life energy returns to God upon death (Eccl. 12:7).

Nine: Representing Himself and His life, the Lord Jesus gave His human soul (Matt. 20:28; John 10: 11, 15, 17; 1 John 3:16, "life") and His human spirit (Luke 23:46) in atonement for our sins. In His separation from the Father during the hours of darkness on the cross, Jesus humanly experienced spiritual death in His soul and spirit, which were alienated from the Father by humanity's sins (Matt. 27:46).[38] Then, when His human spirit (and soul) was revived, and He was restored to the Father's fellowship, Jesus gave up His soul and spirit in physical death (1 Peter 3:18; John 19:30).

Ten: It appears that the soul and spirit of all unsaved people are alike, and those of all saved people are alike (Ps. 33:15). The personality differences between humans, whether among unsaved or among saved people, are due to differences in their bodies, determined by their genetic history, bodily chemistry, and physical state (see Appendix V: "The Human Body-Grid"). Also, because of the changes that salvation brings to their immaterial beings, saved persons differ from unsaved persons, not in their essential humanness but in their deliverance from the ruin and bondage of sin and their beings new creatures in Christ, created unto good works (2 Cor. 5:17; Eph. 2:10; 5:8; 1 Peter 1:22; Rom. 6:11–13).

Again, observe that the biblical view of man is synthetic (this sees man as a whole) as expressed in Hebrew thought rather than analytic (this sees man in parts) as expressed in some ancient Greek thinking (see next paragraph).[39] This means that the Scriptures usually portray man as a unity, which is seen in the several aspects of one, vital human personality, not as a combination of contrasting elements. Behind each aspect of human nature (body, soul, and spirit) is the whole person. For example, the mind is not seen as an isolated faculty, but as man knowing, understanding, and judging. Man is described as a living soul, not simply one who has a soul. Moreover, man's personhood is inseparably and forever united to his human nature. He will never be divested of his human nature, except of his body during the interim between its death and resurrection. Because of this union and wholeness of being, whatever our human nature experiences or expresses, our personhood experiences or expresses. One does not function without the other. However, in responsible moral actions, it is man's personhood that is credited with doing what is right or wrong, not his human nature. All divine moral directives are addressed to his personhood (to him, her, or me), not to his nature. As human persons, we ourselves experience thought, action, speech, weariness, rejoicing, pain, physical and psychical desires, and death. But all this is in unison with our human nature, which gives us the ability to experience these things.

The Orphic Greek Mysteries and Plato held that the body and soul were antagonistic toward each other. They taught that the body, being material, was inherently evil, corrupting and imprisoning the soul.[40] But the Bible doe not present this antagonism. Our enemy is not the body or even self, but the sin force that is resident within the body's cells (Rom. 7:17–18, 23). While unsaved people are wholly corrupted by original sin, their salvation brings to their total being, excepting their bodies, deliverance from sin's ruin and bondage and renewal by God's power (Rom. 8:10–11; 1 Cor. 6:1; Eph. 4:22–24; Phil. 3:20–21; 1 Thess. 5:23; James 1:21). As we who are saved yield ourselves to the Holy Spirit and to Jesus daily, our total being becomes in His hand an instrument of righteousness, which He uses for the glory of God (Acts 14:27; Rom. 6:11–13, 19; 12:1; 13:14). Did you give your heart to Jesus today (Eph. 3:17)?

Traditional Views About the Makeup of Humans

Throughout the Christian era, scholars have presented various views regarding people's essential parts and the origin of their souls. However, much of this, to my mind, is unscriptural, for they have equated personhood with the soul. The Bible teaches that personhood, as a separate entity, is to be distinguished from the soul and spirit. The possession must have a possessor (Job 7:11, "my mouth . . . soul . . . spirit"). This is I, or personhood.

1. About people's parts

While all agree that humans consist of material and immaterial parts, not all concur on the divisions of theses immaterial parts and their functions. Let us look at these views.

a. Trichotomy

Proposing that a human person consists of body, soul, and spirit, this theory was held by the earlier Greek church Fathers, and for some time it was the prevailing view of the Eastern church. Today many trichotomists explain people's threefold construction as follows: The *body* is the means by which people attain world or sense consciousness and by which they make contact with their physical environment. The *soul* is the means by which they attain self-consciousness and self-expression in their relation with other humans. And the *spirit* is the means by which they attain God consciousness. This view equates personhood with soul and regards the spirits of unsaved people as not functioning since these people are spiritually dead toward God and divine things.

As our study has shown, this explanation of the functions of people's essential parts is not in accord with the biblical teaching of human nature. It also ignores that the total being of unsaved people, including their spirits, is active, but not toward God (see endnote 28). Furthermore, it fails to see personhood as a separate part of people's makeup.

b. Dichotomy

From the first, this view prevailed in the West, being held by Tertullian (c. 160–225) and Augustine (354–430). It says that a human person consists of body and soul, with the soul representing the higher or spiritual element in man. Personhood and spirit are regarded as aspects of the soul.

I prefer the view that a person's makeup consists of personhood and human nature; that human nature consists of body, soul, and spirit; and that the immaterial part of human nature consists of soul and spirit, which having similar functions may be a single entity (Heb. 4:12). In 1 Thessalonians 5:23, the apostle Paul seems to emphasize that our whole being is preserved until the coming of Jesus (cp. Deut. 6:5; 2 Kings 23:25).

2. About people's souls

Philosophers and theologians have given considerable attention to the origin of the soul, which they equate with personhood. They have proposed the following theories:

a. The Theory of Preexistence

This holds that all human souls were created simultaneously as angels at the beginning of time before the creation of matter and man.[41] However, because of their apostasy, fallen angels were given human bodies as punishment and are confined to earth until their restoration to their former angelic state. The leading proponent of this theory was Origen (185– c. 254). This theory has been universally rejected by the Church.

b. The Theory of Creationism

This holds that the body alone is propagated, whereas the soul is directly created by God and is placed in the body at birth.[42] This theory was dominant in the Eastern church and became so in the Western church during the Middle Ages. It continues in the Roman Catholic and Eastern Orthodox churches today. Appeal is made to Ecclesiastes 12:7; Zechariah 12:1; Isaiah 42:5; 57:16; Hebrews 12:9 to support this theory. It is more consistent with the popular view that relates the soul to people's higher nature and the body to their lower nature.

My objections to this theory follow: It makes God the creator of sinful souls (Prov. 21:10). It ignores the fact that God is indirectly the creator of body as well as of the soul (Ps. 139:13–14; Jer. 1:5). It does not account for posterity being in the loins of their ancestors (Heb. 7:4–10). Also, the Bible does not say that the soul and body are higher and lower parts, respectively, of human nature as the pagan Greek philosopher Plato taught.[43]

c. The Theory of Traducianism

With its designation coming from the Latin verb *traduco*, meaning "to lead, bring across or over," this theory holds that the soul was created at the time of man's creation

(Gen. 2:7) and is transmitted and individualized by propagation.[44] This was the view of the early Western church, being first stated by Tertullian and established by Augustine. During the Middle Ages, creationism prevailed over traducianism. The revival of Augustinian anthropology during the Reformation led to the appearance of traducianism in Lutheran and Calvinistic teachings. Today, advocates of creationism and traducianism are found among Protestant scholars.

Advocates of traducianism point out that Adam begot a son in his own likeness (Gen. 5:3) and that descendants are said to be in the loins of their ancestors (Gen. 46:26; Heb. 7:4–10). This theory best explains the inherent corruption of fallen human nature and mankind's participation in Adam's initial sin (Rom. 5:12–19; 1 Cor. 15:22).

The principle objection to this theory is that it implies a division of substance. How can the immaterial soul be propagated in this way? W. G. T. Shedd replies:

> When it is said that that which is divisible is material, divisibility by man is meant. It is the separation of something that is visible, extended and ponderable, by means of material instruments. But there is another kind of divisibility that is effected by the Creator, by means of a law of propagation established for this purpose. God can divide and distribute a primary substance that is not visible, extended and ponderable, and yet real, by a method wholly different from that by which man divides a piece of clay into two portions.[45]

Observe that these theories of the origin of the soul do not deal with personhood as a separate element of human makeup. They assume that the soul is one's personal entity or self. It is more in accord with the Scriptures to regard personhood as being distinct from human nature (body, soul, and spirit, cp. Job 7:11; Isa. 26:9). I prefer the view that soul together with spirit and body are propagated by the parents and that personhood is at human conception directly created by God. At the moment of conception, the newly created personhood is immediately and permanently joined to one's propagated human nature. Upon this union, one's personhood assumes all the qualities of sinful human nature and by this is made human and sinful. In turn, personhood communicates to human nature the qualities of conscious individuality, morality, and perpetuity. This view allows God to be the Creator of unique personal individuals, who were created morally neutral and who were corrupted by their fallen, propagated human nature, derived ultimately from Adam and Eve. This also explains how descendants were in the loins of their ancestors by means of their human natures. Since our human nature qualifies our personhood and makes us everything that our nature represents, in effect people were in the loins of their ancestors because their human natures were involved in the lives of their forefathers. The solidarity of the human race rests upon people's having commonly derived human natures, not in their having a common personhood (Acts 17:2; 1 Cor. 15:45, 47, 49; see Appendix C: "The Relation Between Personhood and the Soul").

MANKIND IS BOTH UNITED AND DIVERSE

The Unity of Mankind

Despite mankind's multiple racial distinctions, speech communities, and political states, there is only one human race. All human beings have sprung from a common ancestry and thus form a unity. God uses the words *man* and *Adam* to speak collectively of Adam and Eve (Gen. 1:26–27; 5:2). Moreover, the whole human race descended from this couple

(Acts 17:26; Gen. 3:20; chaps. 4–5) and later from Noah and his three sons and their wives after the Flood, which destroyed all mankind but eight people (Gen. 9:1, 19; chap. 10). The apostle Paul described Adam as "the first man" (1 Cor. 15:45, 47). He also spoke of the solidarity of the human race with and in Adam when mankind participated in his first sin and inherited its woeful results (1 Cor. 15:22; Rom. 5:12–19).

The Diversity of Mankind

Biblical history reveals that God destroyed the earth's population with a flood of universal extent (Gen. 7:17–24). It has been conservatively estimated that after eighteen generations, with only one previous generation still living, the world population at the time of the Noachic Flood was over 1,030 million people.[46] If the remains of prehistoric manlike creatures are truly human, they may indicate a diversity of preflood races, similar to what exists today.

Racial distinctions developed further after the Flood. Different languages began with the confounding of people's original universal language and their dispersion over the earth (Gen. 11:7–9). This diversity was completed with their being confined to their divinely allocated areas of habitation (Gen. 10:32; Deut. 32:8; Acts 17:26).

Evolutionists account for racial distinctions as being the result of certain mechanics of change, such as mutation, adaptation, selection, and isolation.[47] It is believed that racial distinctions did not express themselves in man until the isolation of groups, which resulted in intermarriage, the strengthening of the gene pools, and the triggering of the forces of adaptation and selection.

Some creationists hold a similar view, believing that racial differences rapidly came about after the Flood within small, isolated populations that were acted upon by the forces of natural selection, mutation (to a lesser extent), and genetic drift.[48] Others believe that God created man with mixed genes.[49] This gave man latent possibilities that were later expressed in various types of human beings.

Creationist John Pilkey points out that Noah and his three sons could not be the key to race origin because the three sons shared the racial character of their father. He believes that racial distinctions were embodied in the four wives who were divinely selected for this purpose from four antediluvian stocks, including a red matriarch, a yellow matriarch, a black matriarch, and a white matriarch. He believes that these primary racial types, which already existed before the Flood, came about by the genetic potential of Adam and Eve. He also holds that the racial diversities within each color group after the Flood derived from a process of eugenic polygamy within Noah's immediate family.[50]

While mutations can cause changes, this does not appear to be the principal method of adding variety to living things, for mutant individuals lack vigor and most die out in natural selection. Most varieties probably came about by the regrouping of the genes. These changes are not "evolutionary," for they create variety within the species not higher types.

There is no factual basis for the theory that the racial characteristics of black people are the result of the curse that Noah placed on his grandson, Canaan (Gen. 9:25). The descendants of Canaan were never black. The prophetic curse was that the Canaanites would become a servile race (vv. 25–26). This was realized in the conquest of Palestine by the Hebrews, Philistines, and Arameans. Later, the Greeks and the Romans subjugated the great Phoenician colonies. People who are some color other than ruddy (*Adam* means "red soil") are so because of God-given mechanics of change not because of some curse.

THE WORK OF MANKIND

ITS ORIGIN

When He created Adam and placed him in the garden, God gave man work to do (Gen. 2:15). This work extended beyond his caring for the garden. Man also was to subdue the earth, making it subservient to his will (1:28). God also created and appointed Eve to be Adam's helper (2:18). However, with the couple's sinning their work became wearisome, sorrowful toil (3:17–19). From the divinely cursed ground they were to eke out their living and eat its produce.

ITS BENEFITS

Despite this hardship, work still contributes to people's good (Eccl. 2:24). It gives them opportunity to express their ability and creativity, to provide for their livelihood and that of their dependents, and to achieve certain goals that minister to the general well-being of mankind.

From its beginning, Christianity has condemned idleness (1 Thess. 4:11; 2 Thess. 3:10–12). The Lord taught the principle that the laborer is worthy of his hire (Luke 10:7). Legitimate work, suited to one's abilities and temperament, not only is personally satisfying and healthful but also is a means by which one can bring blessing to others (1 Tim. 5:8; 6:17–19; Eph. 4:28).

ITS DUTIES

In his instructions to Christian slaves regarding their work (Eph. 6:5–8), the apostle Paul presents principles, or duties, that apply to Christian employees as follows:

One, to carry out the will of those for whom we work (Eph. 6:5–6; Col. 3:22; 1 Peter 2:18). A person who hires himself out for employment commits himself to the will of the employer.

Two, to have goodwill toward the employer (Eph. 6:7). The success of his business determines the benefits that the employees receive.

Three, to hold a right attitude toward God, who is our real Employer in our work (Col. 3:22; Eph. 6:5–6). This attitude includes fear, with singleness of heart to please Him. If our work requires us to choose between God's will and man's will, we must obey God (Acts 5:29).

Four, to do our work as unto the Lord, not just for men (Eph. 6:5–7; Col. 3:23).

Five, to anticipate a reward from God for our work as well as a paycheck from our employer (Eph. 6:8; Col. 3:24–25). Work rightly done will bring double pay (1 Cor. 15:58; 10:31; 2 Cor. 5:9–10).

The apostle also gave instructions to Christian masters or employers (Eph. 6:9; Col. 4:1).

ITS SANCTITY

Since secular work makes up the larger part of life for most saved people, we should look at this more closely. Ordinarily, to give it spiritual significance, the Lord's people think of their secular occupation in one of several ways. Some think of it as an opportunity to share the gospel with unsaved people whom they contact on the job. Others think of it as a means of providing for their material needs while they serve the Lord in their local church or elsewhere. Still others consider it as a way of securing money to finance the Lord's work in their local church or elsewhere.

While these are valid views, I believe that the saved person should also regard his secular work, when done in God's will and way, as a ministry unto the Lord. The apostle

Paul exhorted Christian slaves, "Be obedient . . . as unto Christ" (Eph. 6:5); "as the servants of Christ, doing the will of God from the heart" (v. 6); "with good will doing service as to the Lord" (v. 7). Actually, the saved person's total life should be regarded as a service to God (Rom. 12:1–2; 2 Cor. 5:15). As we abide in the Lord, we allow Him to express Himself in all we do (John 15:4–5). While we pursue our secular employment, we can allow Him to minister through us to others according to His sovereign purpose. On the other hand, there is still need for people to enter full-time gospel ministry, which provides for their livelihood.

THE REPRODUCTION OF MANKIND

Unlike angels, humans have the power to reproduce their kind. Needless to say, this places upon us a great responsibility. Both God and humans take part in this awesome event, which begins with conception.[51]

GOD'S PART IN HUMAN REPRODUCTION

God gives or withholds the fruit of the womb according to His sovereign purpose (Gen. 16:2; 30:2; 1 Sam. 1:5–6, 19–20; Job 1:21; Luke 1:24–25). The view that one's personhood is directly created by God and one's human nature is propagated by human parents points to human reproduction as being something more than the operation of a natural law (see Appendix C: "The Relation Between Personhood and Soul"). Every conception involves God as well as humans.

MANKIND'S PART IN HUMAN REPRODUCTION

Although it is God's right to give and take life, this does not relieve people of their responsibility in the exercise of their procreative powers. Because of this, many people believe that any interference with natural processes is an interference with the providence of God and is therefore sinful, regardless of the motivation. Actually, man's subjugation of the earth and dominion over it require him to interfere with the processes of nature so that his environment may serve higher purposes (Gen. 1:28; 3:17–19).

The Bible does not provide specific guidance for family planning in the present dispensation.[52] The Scriptures leave the matter of birth limitation and family planning to the individual conscience and to the motivation of NT principles that govern Christian conduct (see Appendix F: "Learning and Doing God's Will"). Married, saved people need to develop the concept of responsible parenthood, which takes into consideration the physical, emotional, spiritual, and economical conditions of the home.[53]

Although both God and humans take part in reproduction, this occurs in such a way as not to rob God of His sovereignty and humans of their responsibility. God allows people to do what they will, but they must bear the consequences of their actions. The Lord is pleased when His people seek His guidance for their lives and seek to glorify Him in all they do.

THE DEATH OF MANKIND

Death is a phenomenon that affects the whole human race (Rom. 5:12). A universal enemy (1 Cor. 15:26), death snatches away our loved ones and friends, often suddenly and without permission, and in time it ends our lives in this world as well. What are we to think of this powerful force? Where did it come from? Does it have a master? Can it ever be conquered? Will it ever cease to exist? Let us examine what the Bible reveals about death and about the victory that the Lord Jesus has gained over it for Himself and for His people.

ITS ORIGIN

Like sin, death was not a part of God's original creation (Gen. 1:31). As a product (James 1:15) and penalty of sin (Rom. 6:23), death entered the human race by Eve's and Adam's initial transgression (Gen. 2:17; 3:19; Rom. 5:12). Consequently, it has affected all mankind as an inevitable experience of life in this world (Gen. 5; Pss. 90:9–10; 103:15–16; Eccl. 3:19; 9:2–3; Heb. 9:27). Still, Enoch and Elijah escaped physical death (Gen. 5:24; 2 Kings 2:11). Also, gospel believers who will be living at the time of the Church's Rapture (1 Thess. 4:17) will not experience it.[54] Death is a universal enemy (1 Cor. 15:25–26), feared by the unsaved (Heb. 2:14–15) but not to be feared by those who are saved (vv. 14–15; Rev. 1:17–18).

Apparently, there was no death among animals before Eve and Adam sinned and God placed a judicial curse upon nature (Gen. 3:17; Rom. 8:20–21).[55] Newly created humans and land animals were to eat only plants, grain, and fruit. They were not to eat flesh (Gen. 1:29–30).

ITS DESCRIPTION

Death may be described in the light of biblical teaching and according to its effects in those who experience it.

The Biblical Kinds of Death

The Scriptures indicate three kinds of death for humans: spiritual death, physical death, and everlasting death. Let us consider these, with their events and subsequent states, or conditions.

1. *Spiritual death*

Spiritual death primarily relates to a person's spiritual condition and to his personal relationship with God. Among humans, it was the *event* of Eve's and Adam's being wholly corrupted (ruined and defiled) by their initial sinning (Gen. 2:17; 3:7) and of their being severed from their personal relationship with God (3:8).

By this event, the couple entered the *state* of spiritual death, in which they experienced the continuation of these results (Gen. 3:7–10). Their sinning not only cut them off from fellowship with God but also continued to alienate them from Him. This was manifested by their attempting to hide from God (because of their awakened conscience, with its guilty feelings and its awareness of spiritual inadequacy), by their effort to compensate for their inadequacies by their clothing themselves, and by their attempting to shift the blame of their sinful action (vv. 9–13).

While the first couple entered the state of spiritual death by their initial sinning, their posterity, including us, would be conceived in this state because of Adam's sin (Rom. 5:12, 19). From the moment of conception, all unsaved people exist in the state of spiritual death (Eph. 2:1; 4:18), for all humans, excepting Jesus, have participated in Adam's sin and have incurred its guilt and penalty of death. Being alienated from God by Adam's sin and their personal sins, they are naturally unresponsive to divine things (Rom. 3:11, 18). Incidentally, although they have spiritual life, gospel believers who live under the control of the inner sin force express spiritual death by their behavior, the product of this evil power (Rom. 8:6; Gal. 6:7–8; 5:16–26), and are denied God's fellowship and blessing as long as they continue to refuse to deal with their sins (1 John 1:5–7).

2. *Physical death*

Years later, Adam and Eve also experienced physical death as a part of God's judicial sentence for their sinning (Gen. 3:19; 5:5).[56] This is the *event* of one's personhood and one's immaterial human natures (soul-spirit) leaving the body and one's body ceasing to

274

live (James 2:26; Gen. 35:18). The body dies when its condition does not allow soul-spirit to continue its life-giving function (Gen. 35:18; 1 Kings 17:21–22).

By this event, one's dead body enters the *state* of corruptibility, or destruction (1 Cor. 15:50, 53). Physical death triggers the forces of decay that reduce the body to dust (Gen. 3:19; Ps. 124:15; 1 Cor. 15:50, 53). Because of sin, all humans on earth have mortal bodies and will, in time, experience physical death (Heb. 9:27).

While death is due to human sin, God also imposed physical death upon animals and vegetation as part of a general curse to make life more difficult for man (Gen. 3:17–19). The apostle Paul speaks of this general curse, with its universal physical death, as "the bondage of corruption" (Rom. 8:20–23; Heb. 2:14–15). Animals can experience physical death (Gen. 7:21–22; Eccl. 3:19–21), because they have the same vulnerability and physical life force (soul-spirit) as humans (Gen. 1:20–21, "creatures"; 7:22; Eccl. 3:21).[57]

3. Everlasting death

In the future, the divine judicial punishment for sin that unsaved people will experience will be everlasting spiritual death, or "the second death" (Rev. 20:14). This everlasting death is the *event* of their being cast into the hell, or the lake of fire (v. 15). By this event, they will enter the everlasting *state* of unrelieved suffering and absolute isolation from God (Matt. 25:46; 2 Thess. 1:9; Rev. 14:10–11).

The Meanings of Death   6.

Death assumes many meanings according to its various effects on those who experience it.

1. A separation

With each kind of death, a person experiences a separation: with spiritual death, a separation from a personal relation with God (Eph. 4:17–19); with physical death, a separation from his body (James 2:26); and with everlasting death, an everlasting separation from God (2 Thess. 1:9).

2. A punishment

Death in its various forms is the divine judicial punishment, or retribution, meted out to unsaved people for Adam's and their sins (Gen. 2:17; 3:19; Rom. 5:12; 6:23; Ezek. 18:4, 20; Rev. 20:14–15; cp. Gen. 6:11–13). God also uses untimely physical death in His parental punishment of saved people who persist in disobeying Him (Prov. 15:10; John 15:2; 1 Cor. 5:1–5; 11:29–32; Heb. 12:9).

3. An enemy

Like sin, physical death is an enemy, for it interrupts natural life processes and holds people in a bondage from which they cannot deliver themselves (1 Cor. 15:26; Heb. 2:15). However, for those of us who are saved, death is no longer an enemy to be feared, for the Lord Jesus has conquered it and now controls its power in the lives of His people (Heb. 2:14–15; Rev. 1:18).

4. An exit

Physical death is the way by which most people, whether unsaved or saved, leave this world (cp. Luke 16:22; Phil. 1:19–24). However, a few have avoided it (Gen. 5:24; Heb. 11:5; 2 Kings 2:11), and others will when the Lord returns (1 Thess. 4:13–17).

5. An incomplete existence

Although death for humans is never an annihilation or a state of nonexistence (Matt. 8:22; 25:46), it causes one to experience a state of incompleteness. The person who dies physically is left without his earthly body, which is his means of personal expression and of receiving external impressions (see Appendix V: "The Human Body-Grid"). However, upon dying all humans, whether in heaven or in hades, are joined to temporary intermediate bodies until the resurrection of their own bodies (Luke 16:22–24; Rev. 6:9–11, "souls" is a synecdoche for people; 7:9; 14:1–5; see Appendix X: "Figures of Association: Synecdoche and Metonymy"). Without these temporary bodies, these people would have no means of experiencing their new environment, receiving communication, or transmitting their thoughts, feelings, and desires.

Because they are spiritually dead, unsaved people fail to experience all that God desires for mankind, like His fellowship and spiritual blessings (cp. 1 Cor. 1:21; Eph. 2:12 with 1:3). This is also true of believers who are living under the power of the sin force (Rom. 8:6; 1 John 1:5–7).

ITS MASTERS

Who has control of this powerful lethal force?

God

Being sovereign over all things, God has absolute authority over death (Deut. 32:39; 1 Sam. 2:6; 1 Chron. 29:12; Job 1:21; Pss. 68:20; 103:19). As the Creator and Giver of life, He can take life and not be guilty of murder.

Satan

Satan is a murderer (John 8:44), for he brought death to mankind, which was not his creation. He presently has limited power to inflict physical death (John 8:44; Heb. 2:14; Job 1:12–19; 1 Cor. 5:5). But this is not in an absolute sense so as to inflict it on whom he pleases, for he can do this only with God's permission (1 Cor. 5:5; Job 1:12–19). Satan also rules the sphere of spiritual death, in which unsaved people now abide (Acts 26:18; Col. 1:13; 1 John 5:19). However, he is not the ruler of hades (Rev. 9:1–2), where unsaved people go when they die (Luke 16:22–23). Neither will Satan be the ruler of the lake of fire, the everlasting destination of all unsaved humans and evil angels (Rev. 20:10, 15; Matt. 25:41).

The Lord Jesus

By His physical death, the Lord Jesus as man invaded Satan's realm of authority (Heb. 2:14); by His resurrection, He broke Satan's lethal power and became the warden of death and hades (Rev. 1:18). Being sinless, Jesus was not subject to death's claim (Acts 2:22–24; 1 Peter 2:22; 1 John 3:5). He voluntarily gave Himself to death and broke its power by rising again (John 10:17–18; 1 John 3:8). As God, He has always had authority over Satan (Matt. 4:10–11) and death (John 11:27, 43–44).

The Lord Jesus is the only Savior who can deliver people from the penalty, ruin, and bondage of their sins, including death (Matt. 1:21; Acts 4:12). As the Messiah, He now has absolute power over this enemy and will resurrect the bodies of all humans who die (John 5:25, 28–29). With His resurrecting all unsaved people after His millennial kingdom, physical death will be abolished forever (Rev. 20:11–12; 1 Cor. 15:24–26, 54–57).

THE DESTINATIONS OF PEOPLE UPON DEATH

Whether unsaved or saved, people are transported upon death to their destination by angels (cp. Luke 16:22). Where are they taken?

The Destination of Unsaved People

Upon death, all unsaved people are taken to hades (OT sheol) and are confined there until the resurrection of their bodies and their judgment (Luke 16:23; John 5:28–29;

Rev. 20:13).[58] That they have bodily parts and experience torment during their stay in hades (Luke 16:19–31) indicates that they possess intermediate bodies for expressing themselves and receiving impressions until their reunion with their own resurrected bodies (vv. 23–24). After their resurrection and judgment, the unsaved are cast into the lake of fire (Rev. 20:11–15).

The Destination of Saved People

1. Before Jesus' resurrection

Before Jesus' resurrection, all saved people who died were taken to a place of bliss in hades (OT sheol; Ps. 16:10, KJV hell). This was also known as "paradise," or "Abraham's Bosom" (Luke 16:19–31; 23:43).

2. Since Jesus' resurrection

Since the Lord's resurrection, paradise has been removed to heaven (2 Cor. 12:2, 4). At death all gospel believers are immediately taken to heaven to be with the Lord Jesus (2 Cor. 5:6, 8; Phil. 1:21–26; Rev. 14:1–5).

SEVERAL OBSERVATIONS ABOUT DEATH

One: The death of gospel believers is sometimes called "sleep" (1 Cor. 15:51; 1 Thess. 4:15, 17). Because of this, some hold that dead people are asleep during the interval between their death and resurrection. But the Bible does not support this interpretation of these passages (cp. Luke 16:22–23; Phil. 1:23; Rev. 6:9–10). Besides references to sleep, the concept of death as sleep seems to come from the appearance of the body in death and the temporariness of this state (cp. John 11:11–14). However, the Scriptures indicate that all who are dead are in a state of consciousness and are aware of their surroundings, whether in hades or in heaven (Luke 16:19–32; Rev. 7:9–17; 1 Peter 3:19).

Two: There is no scriptural indication that the dead are able to view earthly events or to contact earthly people, save the single case of the prophet-priest Samuel, whom God used to pronounce a judicial sentence on King Saul of Israel (1 Sam. 28:1–20).

Three: A person may hasten his death by suicide (1 Sam. 31:4–5) or by defiant sinning (1 Cor. 11:30; 1 John 5:16). But this would only be effective according to God's permissive, decretive will. It is not one's right to take one's own life; it is one's duty to give it to God and with His help and direction to live for His glory (Rom. 12:1–2; 1 Cor. 10:31).

Four: When we who are saved come to die, there will be no need to fear death, for the Lord Jesus, who controls it, will lead us safely through this unique experience to receive us to Himself (Ps. 23:4). Apparently, angels carry dead persons to their destinations (Luke 16:22).

Five: We who are saved should not be looking for death but for the Lord's return for His Church (Titus 2:13; 1 Thess. 5:1–11). Meanwhile, we should be occupied with His work of building the Church until He comes (Luke 19:13; 2 Cor. 5:9–10; Col. 3:1–17).[59] Our times are in His hands (Ps. 31:15). As long as we walk in obedience to Him, we are immortal until our work is done. We need to redeem the time, making each day count for the Lord Jesus by abiding in Him and doing His will (John 15:4–5; Eph. 5:8–17; cp. 2 Tim. 4:6–8).

THE RESURRECTION OF MANKIND

As they are destined to die (Heb. 9:27; Gen. 3:19), all humans are also destined to be resurrected from the dead (John 5:28–29). This reversal of God's judicial sentence of physical death was made possible by several events that relate to the Lord Jesus. *One,* this was made possible by His atoning work, by which He reconciled to Himself all things involuntarily affected by man's sin (Col. 1:20). This seems to includes the future deliverance of the bodies of all people, whether unsaved or saved, from the grip of physical death. *Two,* this was made possible by the Lord's resurrection, by which He became the master over death (Rev. 1:18; Heb. 2:14–15). He was the first person to rise from the dead, never to die again (Acts 26:23; 1 Cor. 15:23). While others had been raised from the dead before Jesus' resurrection, these were only reanimations or restorations to mortal physical life. They were to experience death again (2 Kings 4:18–37; John 11:43–44).[60] Because of His victory over death by His resurrection (Rev. 1:18), the Lord Jesus now has the authority and power to raise all dead humans (1 Cor. 15:20–23).[61] And *three,* this was made possible by His divine appointment to be the judge of mankind (John 5:22–29). As the Messiah and Lord of all, Jesus will raise all humans from the dead in their appointed times and will judge them (vv. 28–29; Acts 24:15).[62]

THE RESURRECTION OF SAVED PEOPLE

This resurrection is called "the resurrection of the righteous" (Luke 14:14, KJV "just") and "the resurrection of life" (John 5:29).

The Time of Their Resurrection

Not all the saved people of human history will be raised at the same time.
1. *The resurrection of Church saved people (1 Thess. 4:13–17)*
Bringing these people with Him (v. 14), the Lord Jesus will raise their bodies from the dead at His return for the Church at the end of the present age.
2. *The resurrection of all other saved peoples*
After He comes to earth again to set up His millennial kingdom, the Lord will raise the bodies of all saved people who died before His resurrection and of all Tribulation Age martyrs (Rev. 20:4–6; Matt. 8:11; Dan. 12:2–3; Ezek. 34:23–24). He will do this at the beginning of His millennial kingdom (see the Prophetic Chart under Eschatology).

The Event of Their Resurrection

Like that of Jesus, the personhoods and immaterial human nature (souls-spirits) of these saved people will be reunited with their resurrected bodies, which will be recreated and made alive by the Holy Spirit (Rom. 8:11). Then they will rise bodily from the dead, never to die again. In the case of those who are alive at the Lord's return, their bodies will immediately be changed without dying (1 Thess. 4:17; 1 Cor. 15:51–52). Thus the bodies of all saved people will be changed for the eternal state (cp. 2 Cor. 5:1–5).

The Change of Their Resurrected Bodies

The bodies of saved people must be changed, for they cannot physically enter God's eternal kingdom in their present condition, which is only suited for living on earth (1 Cor. 15:50–57). Thus, the bodies of those who have died will be changed from corruptibility to incorruptibility, from decay and dissolution to the state of permanent restoration. The bodies of those who are alive at the Lord's return will be changed from mortality to immortality, from the prospect of death to the state of deathlessness. In both cases, these changed bodies will be the same in nature, for they will be made like unto our Lord's glorified resurrected body (Phil. 3:20–21).

But what will these changed bodies be like? The apostle Paul answers this question in 1 Corinthians 15:35–49. After indicating that the changed body will be made of the physical elements of the present body (vv. 35–41), the apostle contrasts the body in its future changed state with its present condition (vv. 42–49).

1. *The contrast of their qualities (1 Cor. 15:42–43)*
   The present mortal body is sown:
   "In corruption" with gradual disorganization and decay
   "In dishonor" with disagreeable ills, functions, and conditions
   "In weakness" with chronic limitations and deficiencies[63]

   The future changed body is raised:
   "In incorruption" with endless life
   "In glory" with flawless beauty, dignity, and grace
   "In power," with new vigor, capacities, and capabilities

2. *The contrast of their animating forces (1 Cor. 15:44)*
   The internal parts of human nature are soul and spirit, which from their similar functions appear to be a single entity. A function of the soul-spirit is to animate, or to make alive, the present body (James 2:26; Gen. 35:18). The apostle describes our present body as being a soulish (KJV "natural") body, that is, made alive by the soul-spirit (cp. Gen. 2:7) and our future changed body as being a "spiritual" body, that is, one that will be made alive by the Holy Spirit (Rom. 8:11). He is not speaking here about an ethereal, vaporous body.

3. *The contrast of their models (1 Cor. 15:45–49)*
   Our bodies in their present condition are like Adam's body after he had sinned; our bodies in their changed condition will be like Jesus' resurrected body, prepared to live forever in the eternal state. The apostle contrasts the heads, or leaders, of the two kinds of humanity (v. 22) and their human natures, particularly their bodies.

The First Man, Adam, of the Earth

v. 45: He was a living soul, or creature.
v. 46: His soulish ("natural") body was the first kind that humans now have.[64]
v. 47: Adam, who was earthly in origin, had a body that was prepared to live on earth.
vv. 48–49: He was the image of the earthly, especially of unsaved people and the unsaved aspects of human nature.

The Second Man, Jesus, from Heaven

v. 45: He is a life-giving spirit.[65]
v. 46: His spiritual (resurrected) body will be the second kind they will have.[66]
v. 47: Jesus, who was heavenly in origin, has a body that was prepared by resurrection to live in heaven.
v. 48–49: He is the image of the heavenly—of saved people and the saved aspects of human nature (Rom. 8:29; Phil. 3:21; 1 John 3:2; cp. 2 Cor. 5:17).[67]

Because our changed bodies will be like Jesus' resurrected, glorified body, we shall fully express Christlikeness in our thinking, emotions, and will (1 John 3:2; see Appendix V: "The Human Body-Grid"). We shall also have new capacities for the wonders that eternity will reveal and new capabilities for the new existence that the eternal state will require (cp. John 20:19; Luke 24:51). The abiding presence of the Holy Spirit assures us of these changes and His continuing help (2 Cor. 5:5; John 14:16–17).

The apostle Paul concludes that, since our bodies in their present condition as "flesh and blood" (1 Cor. 15:50) cannot "inherit," or exist, in God's kingdom (heaven, 2 Tim. 4:18), they will be prepared for the eternal state at the last trumpet sound (1 Cor. 15:51–53).[68] As trumpets were used in biblical times for signals (cp. Num. 10:1–10), trumpet blasts will signal the changes in the bodies of the Lord's people when He comes for His Church (1 Thess. 4:16).

THE RESURRECTION OF UNSAVED PEOPLE

This resurrection is called the resurrection of "the unrighteous" (Acts 24:15, KJV "unjust") and "the resurrection of judgment" (John 5:29, KJV "damnation"). Despite their physical resurrection, the unsaved will remain in the grip of spiritual death and will suffer divine judgment for their sins forever (Matt. 25:46).

The Time of Their Resurrection

The Lord Jesus will raise all the unsaved dead after His millennial earthly rule and the following dissolution of the universe (Rev. 20:11–15; see the chart, "The Prophetic Future," on page 552).

The Event of Their Resurrection

The personhoods and immaterial human natures (soul-spirit) of unsaved people will be removed from hades and will be reunited with their recreated, reanimated bodies.

The Change of Their Resurrection Bodies

Since these people will exist forever in an unearthly environment, it appears that their resurrected bodies will be similar in nature to those of resurrected saved people. These bodies, I believe, will be physical, animated by the Holy Spirit, and reorganized without the sin force.[69]

From this study, we have seen that we humans are complex, noble beings, made in the image of God. Because of this, we should treat ourselves and others with respect (Mark 12:31). The ungodly idea that sees man as a higher form of animal undermines his dignity and encourages the inhumanity of selfish exploitation, cruel domination, and senseless violence. People behave according to what they believe they are.

By God's grace, let those of us who are saved strive to be all that He has made us to be as new creatures in Jesus. Ever keep in mind that we who are saved are the Lord's members on earth (1 Cor. 6:15) through whom He works in this world in building His Church (Matt. 16:18; 1 Cor. 3:6–9; Acts 14:27). Let us daily give ourselves into His hand (Rom. 12:1–2), walk in His fellowship (1 John 1:5–7), and do His bidding in the Holy Spirit's power (Eph. 5:18). Then we shall fulfill the purpose for which we were saved and recreated by His grace, which is to glorify Him (Eph. 2:8–10; 1:12).

A Review of Anthropology

1. Why is the biblical record of man's creation more accurate and acceptable than man's scientific opinions?
2. Describe the two-step process of Adam's creation.
3. What did God do in the second step besides imparting to man's body physical life or soul and spirit?
4. What does it mean when it says that man became "a living soul" (Gen. 2:7)?
5. How do we know from Genesis 2:7 that pre-Adamic races of humans did not exist?
6. What was the process in God's creating Eve?
7. What did God not do in creating Eve that He did in creating Adam? Why did He use Adam's rib rather than his foot?

8. What were the two purposes for God's creating Eve?
9. When did God create Eve?
10. Distinguish between civilization and spirituality.
11. What is the image of God in man? What human beings have this image?
12. What leads us to think that angels have this image, too?
13. Distinguish between the image of God in humans and the image of Jesus in gospel believers.
14. What is marriage?
15. Give three purposes for marriage.
16. Why does God forbid premarital and extramarital sexual relations?
17. What spiritual relationship does marriage portray?
18. What is God's social order for mankind?
19. To what areas of human life does the Bible show that this social order applies?
20. What is the purpose and extent of woman's subordination to man? What is the husband's duty to his wife?
21. What is man's essential makeup or constitution?
22. What is personhood?
23. How do Job's words in Job 7:11 indicate that personhood exists?
24. What qualities does personhood have and contribute to our humanity? Explain these qualities.
25. What is human nature? What are its three parts?
26. What is the present condition of the bodies of all living humans?
27. When will the gospel believer's body be saved or changed?
28. What appears to be the primary functions of the body of living humans?
29. In addition to these, what are the holy functions of the saved person's body?
30. Although the saved person's body is still corrupt and mortal, why is it no longer the proper instrument of sin?
31. Why is it important to care for the body?
32. Give the ten meanings of *flesh* in the Scriptures.
33. What two parts make up the immaterial part of our human nature?
34. What reason is there to believe that these parts may be one entity?
35. How is the soul related to the body? How is the spirit related to the body?
36. Give the five basic functions of soul and spirit.
37. What is the dynamic source of spiritual life in the believer?
38. What part of the gospel believer is now saved?
39. What does it mean to say that soul and spirit are saved?
40. What part of human nature survives death? Why?
41. What is the most comprehensive biblical term for the inner part of man?
42. What is the conscience?
43. To what part of our being does the conscience belong?
44. What other faculty of moral judgment do we have beside the conscience? (See Appendix B: "The Conscience.")
45. Which of these two faculties is stronger than the other?
46. Why is it sinful to act contrary to one's conscience?
47. How can we reprogram the conscience?
48. What does it mean to have a "seared" conscience?
49. What does it mean to do something with heart or heartily?
50. In what circumstances are people's hearts evil? When is the believer's heart evil? Pure?

51. What are the theories of dichotomy and trichotomy?
52. Give the theological theories for the origin of the soul (personhood).
53. What is the writer's theory?
54. What part of our makeup is created by God? What part is propagated?
55. What accounts for the unity of the human race? Its diversity?
56. How does work contribute to man's good?
57. In what ways may secular work have spiritual significance?
58. In human reproduction there is a concurrence of divine and human activities. What are these activities?
59. Why is it not wrong to interfere with natural processes? When is it wrong to do so?
60. Give the three biblical kinds of death.
61. Give the functional meanings of death.
62. How are God, Satan, and Jesus related to physical death?
63. Why can God take life and not be a murderer?
64. How did Jesus break Satan's power over death?
65. Where do unsaved people go when they die? Where do saved people go?
66. What biblical evidence is there against soul-sleep?
67. Why should a person not commit suicide?
68. Describe what happens to the body when it is resurrected.
69. When will saved people be resurrected?
70. When will unsaved people be resurrected?
71. Describe the resurrection body in contrast to the present body.
72. What comfort do we have when saved love ones and friends die?
73. Did you give your body and self to the Lord today?

Endnotes

1. The verb *created* (Gen. 1:27, Heb. *bara*) does not mean to create something out of nothing, as Genesis 1:20–21 shows, but to create something new. It is joined with *made* (Heb. *asah*) in Genesis 2:3. See Franz Delitzsch, *A New Commentary on Genesis* (Edinburgh: T. & T. Clark, 1899), 1:74.
2. These theoretical evolutionary processes are *naturalistic evolution,* man's being made solely by immanent processes of nature; *deistic evolution,* God's beginning the creative process and leaving it to natural processes to complete it; and *theistic evolution,* God's beginning the creative process and continuing to work through natural processes. See Millard J. Erickson, *Christian Theology* (Grand Rapids: Baker Book House, 1984), 2:478ff.
3. Ludwig Koehler and Walter Baumgartner, "'aphar," *Lexicon in Veteris Testamenti Libros* (Leiden: E. J. Brill, 1953), 723.
4. Ibid., "adam," 13.
5. See "Humans Are Complex Beings" in this chapter; also Appendix C: "The Relation Between Personhood and Soul."
6. That man became a living creature by God's creative breath refutes any theory that he had been another kind of creature before this divine act which, it is said, made him human.
7. Dwight Hervey Small, *Design for Christian Marriage* (Westwood, N.J.: Fleming H. Revell Co., 1959), 32.
8. Thomas Hartwell Horne, *An Introduction to the Critical Study and Knowledge of the Holy Scriptures* (Boston: Littell & Gay, 1868), 2:556; Martin Anstey, *Chronology of the Old Testament* (Grand Rapids: Kregel Publications, 1973), 149; Philip Mauro, *The Chronology of the Bible* (Boston: Hamilton Bros., 1922), 22; Richard Niessen, *Creation Research Society Quarterly,* vol. 19, June 1982, 60ff.; Eugene W. Faulstitch, *It's About Time* (Spencer, Iowa: Chronology-History Research Institute), January 1987, 11; March 1987, 13.
9. The conclusions of Mr. Dimbleby, Premier Chronologist to the British Chronological and

Astronomical Association, London, are given in his *All Past Time* (London: E. Nister, 1897) and *The Historical Bible* (London: E. Nister, 1897). Holding that the seven days of creation week were twenty-four-hour days, Mr. Dimbleby believed that man was created on Friday, September 25, 0 A.M., or 4004 B.C. The solar system was arranged on Wednesday, the fourth day of creation week, at the time of the autumnal equinox, September 23 of the solar year (*All Past Time*, p. 10). This day marks the astronomical beginning of the years of the Bible. Creation itself took place on the first day, which was Sunday. See Addenda for "The Genealogy from Adam to Abraham."

10. Incidentally, if people migrated three miles a day, in ten years they would travel 10,000 miles, the length of North and South America.

11. There is the problem of Cainan in Jesus' genealogy through Mary (Luke 3:36). Although listed in the Greek translation *(LXX)* of Gen. 11:12, his name is not found in the Hebrew text; he may never have existed at all.

12. The fact that man at his creation became a living soul, or creature, precludes any prior existence (Gen. 2:7; 1:27).

13. Distinguish between the following biblical "images": The *image of God*, which is the personhood that all humans have (Gen. 1:26–27; 9:6; James 3:9); *the image of Adam*, with which humans are born and that all unsaved people have—a sin-ruined human nature (Gen. 5:3; 1 Cor. 15:49); and *the image of Christ* (of His humanity), which is the renewed inner human nature (soul-spirit) that all saved people have (Rom. 8:29; 1 Cor. 15:47, 49; see Titus 3:5; Acts 15:9; 1 Peter 1:22). This image of Christ will be completed in gospel believers when He changes their bodies at His return (Phil. 3:20–21). Then they will be wholly like Him in His humanity (1 John 3:2). Incidentally, God the Son in His deity is "the express image" of the Father's divine nature or deity (Heb. 1:3, KJV "person").

14. See Franz Delitzsch, *A System of Biblical Psychology* (Grand Rapids: Baker Book House, reprinted 1966), 179–81. "The most internal nature of man is his Ego, which is distinct from spirit, soul, and body." Professor Delitzsch often used the word "personality" for personhood.

15. Ibid., 78f.

16. Observe that we humans are "people" or "persons," not "individuals." The modern widespread use of "individuals" as a noun for persons, to my mind, is depersonalizing.

17. The Scriptures also forbid homosexuality and treat it as an abhorrent sin (Lev. 18:22; 20:13; Rom. 1:26–27; 1 Cor. 6:9; 1 Tim. 1:9–10).

18. The Lord Jesus supported the biblical teaching about marriage (Matt. 19:3–6) and further expressed His approval of it by attending and contributing to a wedding feast (John 2:1–11).

19. In 1 Cor. 11:2–16, the apostle gives what may be called, "The Principle of Social Leadership." An outline follows: *I.* The Principle Stated (3). *II.* The Principle Violated (4–10): *A.* Examples (4–5); *B.* Offenses (6–10): *1.* To the rule of consistency (6); *2.* To the divine purpose (7–9); *3.* To angels (10). *III.* The Principle Established (11–12). *IV.* The Principle Vindicated (13–16): *A.* By a sense of propriety (13); *B.* By an understanding of nature (14–15); *C.* By an awareness of common church practice (16).

20. That animals have soul and spirit is not commonly recognized. In Gen. 1:20–21, 24, the word "creature" (KJV) is a translation of the Hebrew word *nephesh* or soul. That they have a spirit is indicated in Gen. 7:21–22 and in Eccl. 3:19, 21. The soul and spirit of animals provide their bodies with physical life as well as with elementary intelligence, emotion, and nonmoral self-determination.

21. Like the word *person, self* may represent one's total being or inner being, including soul and spirit, rather than only personhood.

22. See Delitzsch, *A System of Biblical Psychology,* 179–81.

23. That personhood exists from conception is indicated by Exod. 21:22–25, where retribution was meted out to the offender in the case of the injury or death of the unborn child as in the case of other humans (Deut. 19:21).

24. See "Original Sin" under Hamartiology. The single exception is the sinless human nature of Jesus, which was fathered by God the Holy Spirit (Matt. 1:20; Luke 1:35).

25. See Appendix C: "The Relation Between Personhood and Soul"; also Delitzsch, *A System of*

Biblical Psychology, 181; Ludwig Koehler, *Old Testament Theology* (London: Lutterworth Press, 1953), 144, "The soul is not the I."

26. See Delitzsch, *A System of Biblical Psychology,* 180.

27. See D. A. Carson, *The Gagging of God* (Grand Rapids: Zondervan Publishing House, 1996), 209ff.

28. Unsaved people have a complete, functioning human nature. However, this is wholly corrupted and is dead toward (naturally unresponsive to) God and the things of God. For their hearts, representing their inner human nature (soul-spirit), see Mark 7:21–22; Jeremiah 17:9; Ecclesiastes 9:3; for their soul, see 1 Peter 1:22; Proverbs 21:10; for their spirit, see Proverbs 16:2, 18; 25:28; Psalm 78:8; and for their bodies, see Romans 8:10; 1 Corinthians 15:50. Also see Ephesians 2:2–3; 4:17–19; Romans 1:18–32; 3:9–18.

29. W. David Stacey, *The Pauline View of Man* (London: Macmillan & Co. Ltd., 1956), 85.

30. See Stacey, *The Pauline View of Man,* 73f.

31. See Delitzsch, *A System of Biblical Psychology,* 281ff.; Koehler, *Old Testament Theology,* 145.

32. It is in this sense that we must understand the prohibition of Gen. 9:4 and Deut. 12:23. The eating of blood was forbidden, "because it contained the life or soul, and this was the property of God," Stacey, *The Pauline View of Man,* 86.

33. Special Greek words are used for the intellect and its functions in the New Testament. These include *nous,* with the ideas of making moral judgments (Rom. 7:23, 25; 12:2), understanding truth (1 Cor. 14:14, 19; Phil. 4:7; Rev. 13:18), a frame of mind (1 Cor. 1:10; 2 Thess. 2:2) and thinking (Rom. 14:5); and *dianoia* with the ideas of the organ of thought or understanding (Mark 12:30; Eph. 2:3; 4:18) and a kind of thinking or disposition (Col. 1:21; 1 Peter 1:13).

34. See Appendix B: "The Conscience." There is no special Hebrew word for the conscience in the Old Testament. It is represented by the words "heart" (1 Sam. 24:5), "spirit" (Prov. 20:27), and "reins" (Ps. 73:21). In the New Testament, it is usually represented by its own word "conscience" (Gk. *suneidesis*; see Acts 23:1; Rom. 2:15; 9:1; 1 Cor. 8:7; Heb. 10:22) and sometimes by "heart" (Acts 2:37; 7:54; 1 John 3:20–21).

35. Observe that the "old man" is what we were in Adam when we were unsaved (1 Cor. 15:22); the "new man" is what we are now in Jesus (2 Cor. 5:17). This "putting off" and "putting on" took place at salvation, as indicated by the aorist tense of these verbs in the Greek text (Col. 3:9–10; Eph. 4:22–23). Because of this truth, we are to put off sins (Col. 3:8–9) and put on Christlike qualities (vv. 12–17) in daily behavior, not to become new persons, but because we are new people in Him. This is one of our strongest motivations for Christian living.

36. What does it mean for the soul and spirit to be saved? First, they are, at salvation, delivered from inherent corruption, with its bent toward sinning (1 Peter 1:22) and from spiritual death (Rom. 8:10). Second, being divinely renewed (not replaced, Titus 3:5), they are created in righteousness and holiness (Col. 3:10; Eph. 4:24) and are given spiritual life. Being made righteous and holy, the gospel believer's soul and spirit have a bent toward pleasing God. Also, being divinely renewed, they give him or her the capability to understand spiritual truth and to think right thoughts, to express right emotions like God's love, and to make right decisions in harmony with God's will.

37. In 1 Corinthians 5:5, the apostle seems to have in view the final salvation of the sinning saved person, whom he represents by the word "spirit" (a synecdoche for the whole person; see Appendix X: "Figures of Association: Synecdoche and Metonymy"), as the purpose for the disciplinary destruction (death) of his or her body (cp. 11:30, 32).

38. There was no essential separation between the Father and the Son by division of the divine nature. His repeated words, "My God" are words of His humanity.

39. Stacey, *The Pauline View of Man,* 85.

40. Ibid., 62ff., 73.

41. W. G. T. Shedd, *A History of Christian Doctrine* (New York: Charles Scribner Co., 1868), 2:4ff.

42. Ibid., 10ff.

43. Stacey, *The Pauline View of Man,* 73.

44. See Shedd, *A History of Christian Doctrine,* 2:13ff.

45. Shedd, *Dogmatic Theology,* 2:83.

46. John C. Whitcomb and Henry M. Morris, *The Genesis Flood* (Philadelphia: Presbyterian and Reformed Publishing Co., 1961), 25f.

47. *What Is Race?* (Paris: United Nations Educational, Scientific and Cultural Organization, 1952), 11–36.

48. R. Daniel Shaw, "Fossil Man," in *A Symposium on Creation III*, ed. Donald W. Patton (Grand Rapids: Baker Book House, 1971), 132–34.

49. William J. Tinkle, *Heredity*, 85–99.

50. John Pilkey, *The Origin of the Nations* (San Diego: Master Book Publishers, 1984), 11–16.

51. The existence of humans as persons begins with conception not birth (Ps. 51:5; Gen. 5:3; Jer. 1:5; Ps. 139:13–15; Luke 1:41–44; cp. Exod. 21:22–25).

52. The case of Onan is entirely irrelevant (Gen. 38:6–10). He incurred the Lord's displeasure by his disobeying his father's command and his brother's desire, thus refusing to perpetuate the family line, in this case, the messianic line. Later, this levirate custom became a law in Israel (Deut. 25:5–10).

53. See Dwight H. Small, *Design for Christian Marriage*, 101, and M. O. Vincent, "Moral Considerations in Contraception," in *Birth Control and the Christian*, ed. Walter O. Spitzer and Carlyle L. Saylor (Wheaton: Tyndale House Publishers, 1969), 248–53.

54. This will also be true of those living, saved people who enter the Lord's millennial kingdom (Matt. 25:34, 46).

55. Not having soul-spirit, plants do not have the same kind of physical life or experience the same physical death process as humans and animals do. Their "life" consists of the divinely designed dynamics of certain chemical actions and reactions. Their "death" is a cessation of these inherent chemical processes.

56. Medical science recognizes several kinds of physical death, including *clinical death*, in which the respiration and heartbeat stops; *brain death*, in which the functions controlling consciousness and the nervous system, heart, and lungs cease; *biological death*, which consists of the permanent end of bodily life; and *cellular death*, which is the final termination of all life processes in the body. Theologically, physical death occurs when the soul and spirit leave the body, or when the body is so traumatized that it does not allow them to continue to impart life to it.

57. Animals have a similar nature to that of humans, consisting of body, soul, and spirit (Gen. 1:20; 7:15, 22; Eccl. 3:21). However, not having personhoods (the image of God), there is nothing in animals to survive death. As with man's life, animals' physical life-giving force, related to soul-spirit, returns to God (Eccl. 12:7).

58. The KJV translation "hell" for *sheol* (Deut. 32:22) and *hades* (Matt. 11:23) is confusing. In this study, I use "hell" (Gk. *sehenna*) for the lake of fire, the final abode of the unsaved. See Addendum: "Sheol, Hades."

59. See "The Ministries of the Christian Life: The Ministry of Working with God" under Zoeology.

60. Those people who had been dead and who appeared bodily in Jerusalem were resurrected after Jesus had risen from the dead (Matt. 27:51–53).

61. See "His Exaltation: Jesus' Resurrection from the Dead" under Christology.

62. See Revelation 20:5–6. The "first resurrection" refers to that of saved people, which consists of several resurrection events before His millennial reign. After the Lord's millennial reign and the dissolution of the universe, all unsaved people will be raised in "the second resurrection" (vv. 6, 12), which is a single event.

63. The word *sown* seems to refer to the whole course of our present, earthly physical life.

64. This is a body that is animated by soul-spirit, which gives it a physical life that is suitable for living on earth.

65. Unlike Adam, who could propagate only physical life, Jesus gives spiritual life to all who trust Him and His atoning work for their salvation (John 6:33, 47) and will raise their bodies from their graves (5:25). Jesus does all these messianic works by the power of the Holy Spirit (Rom. 8:2; 2 Cor. 3:6; Acts 10:38; Isa. 11:1–5).

66. This is a resurrected body that is animated by the Holy Spirit, who will give us a new kind of physical life that is suitable for living forever in the eternal state.

67. The image into which we are being made (Rom. 8:29) is that of Jesus' humanity, not His deity. We shall never be God or gods. Man was made in the likeness of God's image in that we were given personhoods, not divine natures. We who are saved are partakers of the divine nature (2 Peter 1:4) in that we possess God, the indwelling Holy Spirit (1 John 3:24). The gospel believer's soul-spirit, often represented by "heart," was divinely cleansed and renewed at his salvation (1 Peter 1:22; Rom. 8:10; Titus 3:5; cp. Acts 15:9).

68. "Flesh and blood" describes the "soulish" body (vv. 44, 46 "natural"), that is animated by the soul-spirit and whose blood and breath are the conveyers of this source of physical life (Lev. 17:11; Gen. 7:22).

69. Since the sin force is an alien part of the body (Rom. 7:18) as well as of the universe (Gen. 1:31), I do not believe that it will exist in the resurrected bodies of unsaved people or in the eternal state. That death will be abolished suggests that its parent, sin, will also be abolished (1 Cor. 15:26, 54). I believe that Revelation 22:11, 15 describes the continuing character of the unsaved, as determined by their earthly lifetime, not their continuing sinful actions.

Hamartiology

9

HAMARTIOLOGY
The Doctrine of Sin

Contrary to popular opinion, the Bible teaches that humans are not what God created them to be, for they are sinners. Adam's and Eve's disobedience to God brought about ruinous change in their total being and generated within them the sin force. These cataclysmic results also extend to all their posterity. Therefore, it is urgent that we understand the dynamics of sin and God's provision for our experiencing deliverance from its disastrous effects and victory over its tenacious evil power.

THE NATURE OF SIN

The Scriptures teach that sin is an impersonal, temporal, evil force that is confined to fallen angels and all earthly humans and that expresses itself through their natures. Thus, there are two aspects of sin: sin as an evil force or energy, and sins as the evil expressions of this energy in the wicked activities of fallen angels and earthly humans.

SIN AS A FORCE

Its Description

This aspect of sin, as portrayed in the Bible, is an evil force or law that impels angels (Satan and demons) and humans to sin (Rom. 7:23; 8:2).[1] It is the root of which sins, the evil expressions of this force in the behavior of humans and angels, are the fruit (cp. Gal. 5:19–21, "flesh" represents this sin force).[2] In the New Testament, this evil force is represented by the singular word *sin* in passages that are not speaking of some particular expression of sin or actual sin.[3] In James 1:14, this evil force is represented by the word *lusts,* or the inner evil desires, by which it induces people to sin. *Lust* here is a metonymy for the sin force (cp. Rom. 6:12; 13:14; Gal. 5:16, 24; 1 Peter 2:11).[4]

Its Distinction

It is important that we distinguish between the sin force and personhood with its nature, whether angelic or human. Although this evil force is resident in humans within the cells of our mortal bodies (Rom. 7:17–18, 23, 25; 8:2), it must not be equated with self or human nature. Being self-generated by rebellious angels and humans, this evil energy was never an essential part of newly created angels and humans. Like batteries energizing a flashlight, the sin force induces and energizes one's personhood and one's nature, whether angelic or human, to produce sinful actions, words, thoughts, motives, emotions, intentions, and attitudes. That personhood and its nature are sin's passive instruments (cp. Rom. 6:13) is shown by the apostle Paul's declaration, "It is no more I that do it but sin that dwells in me" (Rom. 7:17, 20). Our enemy is neither our personhood nor our human nature but the sin force that would dominate and use our total person for its evil expressions.

Its Distribution

The sin force is possessed by everyone on earth, both unsaved people and saved people. Being resident in the body's cells, it perishes with the body's death.

1. In unsaved people

The sin force completely dominates the lives of unsaved people to the extent that they are ever its slaves (Rom. 3:9–12; John 8:34). Despite the relatively good things that they do, their whole bent of life is toward sinning, and the total output of their lives consists only of sins in God's sight (Rom. 3:10, 12; cp. 14:23). Because divinely acceptable behavior consists of right motivation and godly moral energy as well as action (Luke 6:45), unsaved people have neither the will nor the ability to do what is right before God.

2. In saved people

Every saved person on earth still has the sin force within his bodily flesh (Rom. 7:18; 6:11–13; 1 John 1:8). This accounts for those inner evil urges that we feel (James 1:14, "lust"; Rom. 13:14; Gal. 5:24), our ability to sin (1 John 2:1), and God's exhortations against our sinning (Rom. 6:12; Col. 3:8; 1 John 2:1). However, because of the radical changes that salvation has made in our personhood and immaterial human nature, we no longer sin continuously as unsaved people do (1 John 2:29; 3:4–10, observe the present tense). We now commit acts of sin and acts of righteousness, according to the dominating moral force, God or sin, that is in command of our hearts (Luke 6:45, see "The immaterial parts of human nature—heart" under Anthropology).

As we shall see, it is natural for unsaved people to sin, for their human nature, which is wholly corrupted by original sin, has a bent toward sinning and is wholly dominated by the sin force (Rom. 8:7–8). On the other hand, saved people sin contrary to their human nature, for this (excepting the body) has been renewed by divine regeneration and is now bent toward doing righteousness or God's will (Col. 3:9–10; Eph. 4:24; Rom. 6:18–19, 22). Having a new resident governing moral force (the Holy Spirit) within us, we who are saved must necessarily yield our total being to God as an instrument of righteousness in His hand (Rom. 6:11–13).[5] However, as long as we have the sin force, we shall be susceptible to its urges and its temporary domination and shall have need of daily victory over its demands.

SIN AS AN EXPRESSION

As we have observed, specific sins of word, action, thought, will, emotion, attitude, intent, and motive are the fruit of the sin force as it energizes and uses our personhoods and human natures for its evil expressions. Without an instrument of expression, this evil force could not manifest itself by these evil works. We are like musical instruments that are being played, as it were, by God or by sin. When we yield to God's control and obey Him, He expresses through us the harmonious music of spiritual life and the beauty of holiness; when sin has control of us, it expresses by our evil behavior the discordant noise of sinful activity, moral depravity, and spiritual death (Rom. 8:6; Gal. 6:7–8; Mark 7:21–23). We shall look at this more closely when we consider the topic of actual sins.

THE CHARACTER OF SIN

The character of sin is revealed by divine revelation and is determined by its contrast with the character of God. Sin is not only unlike God in its character but it is also opposed to Him in its action (1 John 1:5; Ps. 51:4; Gen. 39:9; Isa. 59:2; Rom. 8:7). It is active rather than dormant. We see the character of sin in the following biblical terms that are used for its designations.

IN THE OLD TESTAMENT

"Sin" (Deut. 19:15; Heb. *hatta:* to fail, miss; *hattah,* failure). Sin is recognized as a failure or a clear violation of a given command or prohibition.

"Iniquity" (2 Sam. 22:24; Heb. *awon:* acting crookedly). Sin is an action that is not straight or right. It originates with wrong intention.

"Transgression" (Mic. 1:5; Heb. *pesha:* rebellion, revolt). Sin is a revolt of the human will against the divine will.

"Trespass" (Lev. 5:15; Heb. *maal:* faithlessness). Sin is acting contrary to one's duty.

"Unrighteousness" (Lev. 19:15; Heb. *awel*: unrighteousness). Sin is wrongdoing, acting against God's will.

"Evil" (Gen. 2:9; Heb. *raw:* bad, evil). This word has a wide range of applications including the concepts of disaster (Gen. 44:34), illness (Deut. 7:15; cp. 28:47) and that which is unpleasant (Gen. 28:8). It is used with ethical meaning in Genesis 2:9; Deuteronomy 1:39; 2 Samuel 14:17; 1 Kings 3:9; and Psalm 34:14.[6]

IN THE NEW TESTAMENT

"Sin" (John 1:29; Gk. *hamartia:* missing a mark or goal, failure to attain an end). Sin is to miss the moral standard that is fixed by God (Rom. 3:23).

"Disobedience" (Rom. 5:19; Gk. *parakoe:* failing to hear, hearing amiss). Sin is a failure to hear God, which results in disobedience.

"Iniquity" (Matt. 7:23; Gk. *anomia:* lawlessness). Sin is to act contrary to law.

"Transgression" (1 Tim. 2:14; Gk. *parabasis:* overstepping). Sin is a violation of law.

"Trespass," "offense" (Matt. 6:14–15; Rom. 5:15–18, 20; Gk. *paraptoma:* falling behind, lapse, or deviation). Sin is a deviation from truth or righteousness.

"Unrighteousness" (Rom. 1:18; Gk. *adikia:* unrighteousness). Sin is doing wrong, acting against God's will.[7]

OBSERVATIONS ABOUT SIN

One: Being a unique force, sin is positive, absolute evil, not a lesser degree of goodness (Gen. 2:9; cp. 1 John 1:5–6).

Two: Sin is not only unlike God in its character, but it also is actively opposed to Him and His will (Gen. 39:9; Isa. 42:24; John 3:20; Rom. 8:7; 1 John 1:5; 3:4).

Three: Being an energy rather than a generic nature, sin was not part of original creation (Gen. 1:31). It was an alien, unnatural force, produced by rebellious angels and humans.

Four: The sin force always produces or expresses death, both spiritual and eventually physical (James 1:14–15; Gen. 2:17; Gal. 6:7–8). It can never impart life.

Five: Having a definite beginning, the sin force will cease to exist in humans when all mortal bodies die or are changed (Luke 16:22–28; cp. Job 3:17; Phil. 2:10–11). When death is abolished by the resurrection of all humans (1 Cor. 15:26, 54), its parent, the sin force, will also be abolished. Apparently, fallen angels are deprived of the sin force at the time of their judgment (cp. Rev. 20:1–10). I do not believe that unsaved humans will sin in hell, although they will forever pay the penalty of sinning during their former earthly lifetime (Matt. 25:46; cp. Phil. 2:10–11; 1 Cor. 15:25–26). It appears that their resurrection bodies, which will be reconstituted for the eternal state, will not have the sin force. I understand Revelation 22:11, 15 to describe the continuing character of the unsaved, as determined by their earthly lifetime, not their continuing actions in their eternal state.

Six: That actual sins have qualitative differences is seen in the variation of punishments they incur (Matt. 11:20–24; 23:14; Mark 3:28–29; John 19:11). These differences seem to be determined by the amount of spiritual knowledge against which one sins as well as the intrinsic evil character of the sin itself (cp. murder *v.* lying).

Seven: Actual sin occurs with the decision to do wrong as well as in the action that follows. When we decide to do wrong, we are guilty of evil intention. Although we may not be physically able to carry out our sinful purposes, we are still guilty, for with our decisions to do wrong we committed these sins in our minds (cp. Matt. 5:27–28).

THE ORIGIN OF SIN

Contrary to philosophical dualism that sees good and evil as eternal principles, the Scriptures reveal that sin had a definite beginning. Let us see what the Bible says about this and sin's relation to God and His personal creatures.

ITS RELATION TO GOD

God Included Sin in His Decree

With only limited understanding of this profound doctrine, we have observed that God's decree includes everything that comes to pass in the universe, whether good or evil (Rom. 11:36; cp. Acts 2:23; 3:18, 4:27–28). Evil belongs to the permissive aspect of God's decree. This means that, while He actively chose sin to be a part of His decree and thus made it certain, God was not compelled to accept sin as a foreseen evil, nor does He Himself bring it to pass or assume responsibility for it (see "The Decree of God" under Theology Proper).

God Did Not Create Sin

The Scriptures do not suggest that sin was a part of the original creation, which God saw to be "very good" (Gen. 1:31). However, when He created angels and humans with the ability to make moral choices, this gave them the ability to sin. They had the free choice of obeying their Creator or rebelling against Him.

Nevertheless, we cannot credit God with being the author (efficient cause) of sin, for this would attribute to Him a quality that contradicts His self-revelation (2 Tim. 2:13). With reference to character, He is unlike sin (1 John 1:5; Ps. 92:15; Hab. 1:13); with reference to ability, He cannot sin (James 1:13; Titus 1:2). God cannot be or act contrary to what He is.

God's Reasons for Choosing Sin

At least two reasons may be offered for God's choosing to include sin in His plan for the present universe.

One: The capability of doing evil was the necessary alternative to doing good. There could be no true moral choice if doing good was the only option that personal creatures had. Being free moral agents with self-determination, angels and humans were allowed to choose the ruling moral force—God or sin—that would govern their lives. They had the ability and were given the opportunity to make this choice between what was right and what was wrong.

Two: Sin's existence was a way for God to manifest certain qualities of His nature. These divine qualities were His holiness that makes Him to be wholly unlike sin and without sin (1 John 1:5), His holy wrath and judicial power as manifested by His displeasure with sinners and His judgment of them (Rom. 9:17, 22), His righteousness and justice as exercised in His judgments (2:5), and His mercy and grace as displayed in salvation (Eph. 2:4, 7). His mercy and grace could only be displayed in His dealings with sinful personal creatures who deserved His judicial wrath. The glories of God's character radiate more brightly against the dark backdrop of sin. His glories stand in striking contrast to sin and are enhanced by it.

ITS RELATION TO PERSONAL CREATURES

We must not think of the sin force as being like a radioactive cloud that floats about the universe and pollutes everything with its fallout. Actually, this evil force exists and functions in a closed system. This means that it is confined to fallen angels and to earthly humans, with whom it originated. Despite all appearances, I do no think that it resides in impersonal creation, like vegetation and animals, and causes evil behavior. The depredation, disease, degeneration, and death that these impersonal forms of life express and experience are from a divine curse that God placed on them when man sinned (Gen. 3:17; Rom. 8:20–22; cp. Matt. 21:18–19). When He sets up His earthly, millennial kingdom, the Lord Jesus will lift this curse and will restore the earth to its pristine state (Isa. 11:1–9). How God implemented this curse is not clear. Perhaps it was by genetic alteration.

Sin and Angels

As we have seen, the angel Lucifer (Satan) was the first personal creature to sin (Ezek. 28:11–19). Being the anointed cherub, he was created perfect in all of his ways. However, in response to his beauty, Lucifer misused his God-given power of moral choice by choosing to admire and exalt himself rather than God (Ezek. 28:15, 17). This wrong choice produced within him the sin force, which has dominated him ever since. This sinful act of self-exaltation also led to pride and to his irrational ambition to take God's place over the universe (1 Tim. 3:6; Isa. 4:13–14).

Following Lucifer's example and persuasion, other angels chose to revolt against God and give their allegiance to the Devil (Matt. 25:41; Rev. 12:4, 7–9). As in the case of humans, it appears that angels were given a probationary period to choose whom they would follow. Many angels chose to follow Satan rather than God (cp. Rev. 12:4).

Observe that in the case of angels as well as humans, their initial sin occurred with their decision to do wrong as well as in the action that followed. Their revolt against God was the outcome of their wrong choice.

Sin and Humans

1. Man's probation (Gen. 2:17)

God's prohibition against human's eating the fruit of the tree of the knowledge of good and evil was a test that their moral self-determination required and that stimulated their free choice as moral beings. It required Adam and Eve to choose the ruling moral force (the authority of God or of the power of sin) that would govern their lives. This test gave the couple opportunity to choose God's direction for their lives and to enter a permanent state of righteousness and holiness. By obeying their Creator during this period, they would have expressed their love for Him by choosing Him as their life manager, passing from a state of changeable righteousness and holiness to an unalterable righteous and holy state, and receiving a divine understanding of good and evil. Meanwhile, God warned Adam of what would take place if he should disobey this prohibition (v. 17b).

2. Man's disobedience (Gen. 3:1–6)

This is the only literature of antiquity that explains how the human race became sinful. Liberal theologians regard this record as a fable or myth that is to be interpreted allegorically. However, there is a great difference between this record of man's fall and well-known fables: the record of man's moral fall has no moral attached to it; the passage is not poetry but prose; the historicity of the event is underscored by the apostle Paul's reference to it (Rom. 5:12–19; 1 Tim. 2:13–14); and God's curse upon the snake indicates that it was more than a symbol of evil.[8] Being a historical event, Eve's and Adam's fall probably occurred very soon after their creation, perhaps within a few days, certainly before a child was conceived.

a. Eve's sin (Gen. 3:1–6a)

Like that of fallen angels, Eve's sin of disobedience was self-produced, not contracted like some disease. Rather than obeying God, she chose to satisfy her natural desires for food, beauty, and wisdom in a way that was contrary to God's will (cp. 1 John 2:16). Her wrong choice produced within her the sin force, which immediately took charge of her life.

Eve was led to make this choice by Satan's deceptive strategy (2 Cor. 11:3; 1 Tim. 2:14). First, the Devil attracted her attention by speaking through the snake (Gen. 3:1). Then, he undermined her confidence in God. He did this by discrediting God's goodness with a question (v. 1), "Yea, has God said, 'You shall not eat of every tree of the garden?'" ("Fruit was made to be eaten, but God will not let you eat it.") He also did this by discrediting God's integrity with a lie (v. 4), "You shall not surely die." ("This prohibition is only a threat; God does not mean what He says.") Finally, he did this by discrediting God's intention with a suggestion (v. 5), "For God does know that in the day you eat thereof, then your eyes shall be opened and you shall be as God, knowing good and evil." ("God is selfish; He does not want you to be like Him.") Satan then used this part-truth to motivate her and lead her to sin.

Stripped of her spiritual defense and motivated by the hint that she could be like God, Eve sought to satisfy her natural desires by taking the forbidden fruit and eating it in disobedience to God's command. But she was deceived, for she did not experience the benefits that Satan suggested that the fruit would give (1 Tim. 2:14). Moreover, she immediately received the divine judgment of her wrongdoing. God meant what He had said!

Several possibilities may be given for Satan's approaching Eve before Adam. First, being subordinate to her husband and dependent upon him, she may have been more susceptible to the Devil's strategy. Also, since she had not received the prohibition directly from God (when it was given, she had not yet been created), she may have been more vulnerable to satanic argument and doubt. Finally, being Adam's wife and helper, she was the most effective agent in leading her husband to sin.

b. Adam's sin (Gen. 3:6b)

Adam was not deceived by his wife (1 Tim. 2:14). With full knowledge of the consequences, he deliberately chose to accept Eve's offer (Gen. 3:6) rather than to follow God's command (2:16–17). His sin was outright disobedience (Rom. 5:19). It produced within him the sin force, which immediately dominated his life.

Eve's sinning had made a difficult choice for her husband. Would he express his love for his wife by following her direction? Or would he express his love for God by following His command? Rather than leaving the problem of his fallen wife to God (cp. Luke 1:38) and expressing greater love for Him, Adam accepted the fruit and ate it.

As in the case of fallen angels, the initial sins of Eve and Adam began with a wrong choice and this, in turn, produced within them the sin force. Unlike angels, humans propagate their kind. Both Adam and Eve transmitted the corrupting, ruinous results of their initial sin to their posterity (Gen. 5:3; Rom. 5:12–19; 1 Cor. 15:21–22). This means that, unlike Adam and Eve who were created without sin, all their descendants, except Jesus, are conceived as sinners and receive from their parents wholly corrupted human natures that have the sin force.

THE RESULTS OF MAN'S SIN

Satan's rebellion against God apparently led to the fall of a third of the angelic host (Rev. 12:4). He also deceived Eve and encouraged her to sin. In turn, Eve persuaded Adam to eat the forbidden fruit. This chain of events introduced sin, with its devastating results, into the human race (Rom. 5:12).

THE EFFECTS OF EVE'S AND ADAM'S DISOBEDIENCE UPON THEMSELVES

There were immediate as well as later effects of Eve's and Adam's disobedience upon themselves.

The Immediate Effects

The immediate effects were the spontaneous, inherent results of their sinning.[9] Choosing to disobey God, they immediately became sinners and began to experience a different kind of existence characterized by spiritual death, degeneration, defilement, guilt, and fear (Gen. 3:7–10).

1. Spiritually

In their unfallen state, the couple possessed spiritual life, for they had a personal relationship with God (cp. John 17:3). With their newly created lives organized about their Creator, they enjoyed His fellowship and blessing and began to carry out their stewardship. But the moment they sinned, Eve and Adam died spiritually (Gen. 2:17). Their conscious, personal relationship with God ceased, for their sin separated them from Him (cp. 3:8).

2. Naturally

Their sinning brought ruinous changes to their newly created human natures. While they remained human beings, this degeneration was devastating. Their human natures became sinful, being inclined toward sin, energized by sin, and made the instruments of sin. Their sinning immediately produced within them the sin force, which became the ruling moral energy of their lives (Rom. 3:9; 6:17).

3. Morally

Upon sinning, they immediately were morally polluted and filled with guilt, as manifest by their sense of nakedness before God and their hiding from Him (Gen. 3:7–8; cp. 2:25). Their eyes were opened to an experiential understanding of sin, their consciences were violated, and their hearts were filled with the awareness of sin's defilement and guilt.[10] Their sense of nakedness and feeling of fear were symptoms of their awareness of having transgressed God's command. Therefore, they attempted to alleviate their defiled, guilty feelings by dealing with the symptoms of their wrongdoing. They tried to cover their nakedness and hide from God, but God cannot be satisfied in this way.

The Later Effects

These effects were the judicial results of their sinning. It was inevitable that the sinful pair would be confronted by their Creator and be required to give an account of their disobedience (Gen. 3:9–13). Despite their efforts to shift the blame to others, God found them guilty and sentenced them to punishment.

1. God's sentence upon Eve (Gen. 3:16)

God's sentence upon Eve was especially severe because, leaving her role as Adam's helper, she was instrumental in his sinning (Gen. 2:18; 3:6). The divine sentence included not only the increase of the pain and distress that are peculiar to women and of the frequency of conception but also the continuation of woman's subjection to the will and domination of man. Eve was already subordinate to her husband as his helper (Gen. 2:18;

1 Cor. 11:9), but now she was placed in permanent subjection to him. She would not be free to attain her desire (will) without his permission, for he would rule over her. Whereas this social subordination brings women shameful, cruel exploitation and oppression by evil men, it brings blessing to the saved couple who are motivated by obedience to God and by love for each other (Eph. 5:21–33; 1 Cor. 11:7; Titus 2:4).

  2. *God's sentence upon Adam (Gen. 3:17–19)*

  Although God addressed Adam, it appears that His words apply to both men and women. For mankind's sake, God cursed the ground so that the soil would be less productive and that it would bear such nuisances as thorns and thistles.[11] Thus, their work became sorrowful toil. They were required to eke out a living from the field, with sweat and pain, all the days of their lives. History bears continual witness to people's struggle to overcome this sentence, but the curse remains, and their work is still toil. It appears that God did not want them to become too attached to this world. He wanted them to anticipate something better beyond this world that they would ultimately receive through salvation.

  Another part of this sentence is that God imposed upon people's bodies judicial mortality, that made them subject to the corruptibility of disease, deterioration, and death (Gen. 3:19; 5:5; Rom. 6:23; 8:11; 1 Cor. 15:42, 50–53; see "The Death of Mankind" under Anthropology and the Addendum: "Human Physical Mortality").

  By ejecting the couple from the garden and barring them from it (Gen. 3:22–24), God dramatically asserted that He would not allow humans to live on earth forever in their sinful state. They must prepare for death and what lies beyond it. To insure this, He mercifully prohibited the couple's access to the tree of life, which would have given them perpetual physical life in their unredeemed bodies in a divinely cursed environment.

THE EFFECT ON THE SNAKE (GEN. 3:14)

  God cursed the snake above all animals. If it appears strange that God should curse an impersonal creature for being Satan's tool (cp. Rev. 12:9; 20:2), the Scriptures reveal that it is a part of God's order for animals to be punished for any harm they may inflict upon mankind (Gen. 9:5; Exod. 21:28–32). Possibly this is because animals exist for people's benefit.

  God also decreed that the snake should crawl on his belly and eat dust, the latter being figurative language. These actions are signs of defeat or degradation (Lev. 11:42; Ps. 72:9; Isa. 49:23; Mic. 7:17). This judicial sentence upon the snake will continue throughout the Lord's earthly kingdom as a perpetual reminder of the involvement of its kind in man's initial sin (Isa. 65:25).

THE EFFECT ON SATAN (GEN. 3:15)

  Since it was Satan who tempted Eve through the snake (Rev. 12:9; 20:2), God pronounced a severe sentence on the Devil. Speaking words that went beyond the snake to Satan, God placed a state of hostility between Satan and Eve that would be perpetuated between their seeds.

The Meaning of Seed

  This reference to "seed" has two meanings. *One,* if we think of *seed* as meaning "spiritual product" rather than "natural offspring," then the *seed* of *Satan* would be fallen angels (demons) and unsaved humans (John 8:44; Matt. 25:41). Also, *the seed of Eve* would be saved humans, redeemed through the atoning work of her descendant, the Lord Jesus Christ (Isa. 53:10). Satan and the world, of which he is prince, hate the Lord Jesus and His people (John 15:18–21). And *two,* in a prophetic sense, *the seed of the woman* was a veiled reference to Jesus, the son of the virgin Mary (Isa. 7:14; Matt. 1:20–23; Luke 1:31). In this case, the woman represented the nation of Israel, through which God the Son entered the human family (Rom. 1:3; Rev. 12:4).

The Sentence on Satan

God's sentence declared that the woman's seed would crush (KJV "bruise") Satan's head. This is a mortal blow, which speaks of the Devil's final defeat at the hand of the Conqueror-Savior, the Lord Jesus. That the Devil has taken this sentence seriously is seen in his attempt throughout human history to thwart its fulfillment (see "Satan: His Activities" under Angelology). Our Lord broke Satan's power of death by His death and resurrection (Heb. 2:14), and He will smash the Devil's world authority and its political structure when He returns to establish His messianic, millennial kingdom (Rev. 19:11–20:3; see "His Defeat by Jesus" under Angelology).

THE EFFECT ON THE HUMAN RACE

Eve's and Adam's sinning completely affected themselves and all their posterity. We shall look at this when we consider original sin in the following section.

THE KINDS OF SIN

Theologians distinguish between original sin and actual sins. Original sin refers to Adam's and Eve's first sin and its effects upon themselves and their posterity. Actual sins refer to the sins that people commit during their experience on earth.

ORIGINAL SIN

Its Components

Original sin refers to Adam's and Eve's first sin and its effects upon themselves and their posterity (Gen. 3:6).[12] Notice that their subsequent sins did not affect their descendants in the same way as their first one. To my mind, original sin has both humanly propagated components that are related to Adam and Eve and a divinely imputed judicial component that is related only to Adam.

1. *The humanly propagated components of original sin*

These parts, which follow, appear to be derived from both Adam and Eve, since they imparted their germinal cells to their offspring at their conception.

a. *A corrupted human nature*

1) Its meaning

By their initial sinning, Adam and Eve corrupted and ruined their human natures (body, soul, and spirit) for doing righteousness and made them instruments of the sin force, with an inclination toward sinning.[13] It was this kind of a human nature that they transmitted to their offspring. Out of this corrupted inner nature, dominated by sin, flows all kinds of defiling moral sewage like evil thoughts, actions, words, attitudes, and the like (Mark 7:20–23), which express spiritual death (Rom. 8:6; Gal. 6:8).[14] Also, because of the ruinous effect of sin, the body experiences degeneration, disease, and eventually physical death (Gen. 3:19). Thus spiritual death, as it relates to human nature, is the sinful behavioral expression of this corrupted nature. This corrupted human nature also produces physical death.

Since sin totally corrupted the human natures of Adam and Eve, each of their children and their posterity (except Jesus) have received from them a corrupted human nature (Gen. 5:3; 6:5; Job 14:4; Ps. 51:5; Eccl. 9:3; Jer. 17:9; Rom. 1:21–32; 3:9–18; 5:12). The human natures of unsaved people can only function as the tool of sin in expressing actual sins or unrighteousness and, thereby, spiritual death (cp. Rom. 6:12–13, 19). Their soul and spirit, represented by the word *heart,* are deceitful and desperately wicked (Jer. 17:9).

2) Its extent

This corruption of nature is often called total depravity and total inability. *Total depravity* means that this inherent corruption extends to every part of the unsaved person's makeup—his personhood and his human nature (body, soul, and spirit). It affects his thinking (Gen. 6:5; 8:21; Rom. 1:21–23; 3:11; 8:5–8; 1 Cor. 2:14; Eph. 4:17–18), his emotions and attitudes (John 3:19–20; Rom. 1:24–32; 3:18; Eph. 4:18), his will (John 5:40; 8:44; Eph. 2:2–3), and his body (Rom. 8:10; 1 Cor. 15:50). Jesus alluded to this when He spoke about the spiritual character of unsaved people's hearts (Matt. 12:33–35; Mark 7:15–23). Total depravity does not mean that an unsaved person is as evil in his conduct as he can be, for common grace (God's restraining, beneficent influence on mankind) and people's innate sense of morality (Rom. 2:14–15) prevent this (cp. 2 Thess. 2:7–8; Acts 14:17). On the other hand, there is no part of the unsaved person's being that has escaped the corruption and ruin of original sin (Rom. 3:12). He possesses this corruption from his conception (Ps. 51:5).

Total inability means that, of himself, the unsaved person neither desires nor is able to do God's will (John 3:19–20; 5:40; 6:44; 8:44; Rom. 8:7–8). Prompted by common grace and his innate sense of morality (Rom. 2:14–15), he can do relatively good things that are in accord with the ethical standards of fallen man, but he cannot, of himself, do absolute good (the will of God done in His way), nor does he desire this (3:12, 18). The unsaved person's relatively good deeds have no merit in God's sight, for they are sinful (Eph. 2:8–9; Rom. 8:7; 14:23; Heb. 11:6).

While the personhood and human nature of unsaved people are wholly corrupted by sin and are sinful, actual sins are produced by the sin force that is resident in the physical part of human nature and that uses the total person as its means of expressing evil.

b. *The sin force*

Adam's and Eve's sinning also produced within their flesh the sin force, or evil energy, that would dominate them and their posterity throughout their unsaved, earthly lives (Rom. 3:9; 6:17, 20). This evil force, which apparently is transmitted by the germinal cells, completely energizes and dominates the lives of unsaved people to the extent that all that they do is sinful in God's sight (Rom. 3:9–19; 1 John 3:8, 10).

The Scriptures reveal that the sin force is resident within the (cells of the) body's flesh (Rom. 7:17–23; cp. Eph. 2:3) and exerts its evil influence upon one's total being (Rom. 3:9; 6:13). Unlike a disease that is contracted at an early age, the sin force is transmitted by propagation, together with a person's human nature, and it remains with him until his body's dissolution in death. Because it will not be revived in the changed or resurrection body (cp. 1 Cor. 15:50), I believe that this force will be wholly eradicated in humans with the resurrection of all the dead (John 5:28–29; 1 Cor. 15:25–26), and its evil works will perish with the dissolution of the universe (2 Peter 3:10, 13; 1 John 2:17). Moreover, it appears that people in hell neither will have this sin force, nor will they sin (cp. Phil. 2:10–11).[15]

2. *The divinely imputed component of original sin*

a. *Its description*

Being the judicial result of man's sinning, this is imputed guilt, with its penalty of death.

1) Imputed guilt

Adam's sin incurred for himself and his posterity the guilt of his sin (Rom. 5:12–21; 1 Cor. 15:22). This guilt included a sense of moral defilement as well as the divine sentence of condemnation (Gen. 3:7–8; Rom. 5:16; see "The Divine Reaction to Sin" in this chapter).[16] This means that his violated conscience gave him a sense of being morally unclean, and his sinning contaminated his record as well as his human nature before God. God found him guilty of sinning and sentenced him to punishment.

Since this first sin involved Adam's posterity, it also brought them its guilt (Rom. 5:12; 3:23). When the apostle Paul writes that all have sinned, he seems to be speaking about the involvement of the human race with Adam's first sin. This implication was not one of voluntary transgression within the life experience of each member of humanity. It was an involuntary participation that came from humanity's corporate union with Adam by their propagated human natures. Because of this union, God judicially imputed to, or reckoned to the account of, each member of the human race the guilt of Adam's first offense as his or her own sin. This imputation was seen in God's condemning the whole race (Rom. 5:18). Unlike the preceding features of original sin, which are propagated, the guilt of Adam's sin is divinely, directly imposed upon each member of the race as a legal sentence (for other kinds of divine imputations, see endnote 23 under Soteriology).

2) Its penalty, death

Not only was death a natural product of the sin-ruined human nature, it was also a divine sentence for the violation of God's command. Eve's and Adam's sinning brought them the judicial penalty of immediate spiritual death, or separation from God (Gen. 2:17), and eventual physical death, or separation from their bodies (3:19). Dying spiritually, they ceased being active toward God and became responsive to the sin force that was produced within them by their disobedience. Being deprived of access to the tree of life (vv. 22–24), they were destined to certain physical death because of the corruption of their bodies (see Addendum: "Human Physical Mortality"). Consequently, because of their participation in Adam's first sin and its guilt, all their posterity are conceived in a state of spiritual death (Eph. 2:1) and are destined to die physically (Rom. 5:12). From the moment of conception, all unsaved humans are spiritually alienated from God and are naturally unresponsive to His things (Eph. 2:1–3; 4:17–19).

b. Its relation to the human race

Some object to this imputation on the basis that people are not accountable for the sins of others (cp. Ezek. 18:19–20). But this overlooks the fact that people are not as independent of Adam as they may think. Everyone has participated in Adam's sin (Rom. 5:12) because of their physical union with him (Acts 17:26; 1 Cor. 15:22).[17]

It is not agreed among those who hold the divine imputation of Adam's sin to his posterity how God's justice is vindicated in this act. The chief theories are federalism and realism. *Federalism* is the theory that Adam was divinely appointed by covenant to act for the human race; therefore, when he sinned, he involved the race representatively, but not actually. But I see no biblical evidence for Adam's acting as an agent for the race. *Realism* is the theory that all humans, having germinal existence in Adam, actually cosinned with him. Although we were not present in our personhoods, our human natures existed in him and participated in the act. Since a person's nature qualifies his personhood, we virtually sinned with Adam. Keep in mind that the unifying element of the race is not personhood but human nature. Consequently, his sin and its guilt are reckoned by God to all of Adam's posterity. The realism theory seems to be more in accord with Scripture (cp. Heb. 7:9–10). This is like one's toe being involved in a murder although it did not pull the trigger. Despite the toe's disclaimer, it does not escape the guilt of the murder and its punishment, for it was part of the same body as the trigger finger.

Some teach that our Lord's atoning work removed from the whole human race the guilt of original sin and that people are now guilty only of actual sins. If this were true, why are all people, including infants and imbeciles who have not committed actual sins, still condemned in God's sight (John 3:18; Rom. 5:18) and are subject to death (vv. 12, 14, 17)?

    c. A comparison of the two Adams
        1) Their identity
        The apostle Paul shows that there are two Adams: the First Adam, who was the first man whom God created, and the Last Adam, "the Second Man who is the Lord [Jesus] from heaven" (1 Cor. 15:45, 47).
        2) Their positions (1 Cor. 15:22)
        The apostle implies that these two Adams hold unique, identical positions relating to two groups of human beings, of which the human race consists—they who are in Adam and they who are in Jesus (v. 22).[18] Because of their union to the particular head or leader, of their group, these people share the action and character of the Adam who leads their group (cp. vv. 45–49; Rom. 5:12–19).

They who are in the First Adam are his natural posterity, or all unsaved people. These people share Adam's kind of human nature, which is soulish (KJV "natural") and earthly (1 Cor. 15:44–49; cp. John 3:6) and which became corrupted and dominated by sin (Rom. 1:21–32; 3:9–18; Eph. 2:1–3).[19] They also share the guilt of his disobedience and the results of his first sin (Rom. 5:12, 18–19; see the following section, "Their actions").

All saved people are in Christ Jesus. These are divinely redeemed, recreated, and placed in Him at salvation (Eph. 2:10; 2 Cor. 5:17; Gal. 3:27–28). They were severed from Adam and removed from his group and were joined to Jesus and brought into His group, where all things are new (2 Cor. 5:17). This is the new human race of which the Lord Jesus is the Head and Pattern (2 Cor. 5:17; Eph. 4:15; Rom. 8:29). Being in Christ, gospel believers have the Lord's kind of immaterial human nature, with the prospect of having His kind of body. They also share in Jesus' righteous actions. (Rom. 5:15–19, see below).

        3) Their actions (Rom. 5:12–19)
        In a complex passage, the apostle Paul contrasts the moral actions of Adam and Jesus and their results:

Adam's Action and Its Results

One: Adam's action was against God's will. It was a "sin" (v. 12), "transgression" (v. 14), "offense" (vv. 15, 17–18), and "disobedience" (v. 19). His wrongdoing involved his posterity in this sin and its penalty, death (vv. 12, 14, 17; cp. 6:23). While the apostle seems to be speaking primarily of physical death, his words also allow for spiritual death (v. 15).

Two: Adam's sin also incurred for himself and all in him the divine sentence of condemnation (vv. 16, 18). Both he and his posterity in him were found guilty of this first sin and were sentenced to punishment. Adam's sin also resulted in his becoming a sinner and the human race in him being constituted sinners (v. 19). All unsaved people are conceived as sinners, are under divine condemnation, and are ruled by death as well as sin (3:9; 6:17).

Jesus' Action and Its Results

One: Jesus' action was in harmony with God's will. This act of obedience, supported by a lifetime of compliance to the Father's will (John 17:4), was His submission to crucifixion and His giving His life for sin's atonement (Phil. 2:8). The apostle declares that Jesus' action was an exercise of divine "grace" (Rom. 5:15), "a righteous deed" (v. 18, KJV "righteousness"), and "obedience" (v. 19).

Two: Because of Jesus' obedience, all who are in Him have God's gift of righteousness (Rom. 5:15, 17) and are thereby made righteous (v. 19; 2 Cor. 5:21; 1 Cor. 1:30). Thus, God's sentence regarding all who are saved is justification—He divinely acquits them of condemnation and declares them to be righteous in His sight (vv. 16, 18). This sentence also results in their having life (spiritual life now and future deliverance from physical death) and their reigning in life through the Lord Jesus (vv. 17–18).[20]

d. *The principle of solidarity*

The question remains: How are these Adams and their people united so that these people are involved in the action of their particular head, or leader, and its results (1 Cor. 15:22)?

The First Adam's posterity, consisting of all unsaved people, are united to him physically, for they received from him their human natures. Although they were not personally present when Adam sinned, their human natures, germinally existing in his body, were active in his sinning (cp. Heb. 7:9).

The Lord Jesus and His people are united spiritually, for at salvation saved people are placed in Him by the Holy Spirit (John 14:20; Gal. 3:27–28). Being in Him and one with Him (1 Cor. 6:17), they now share in His obedience and righteousness as well as in His death and resurrection (Rom. 6:3–4; 2 Cor. 5:21).

Historical Views on Original Sin

The doctrines of sin and grace did not seriously engage the attention of the Church until the beginning of the fifth century.[21] While the Church universally rejected the view of Pelagius, the Eastern branch accepted the doctrine of inherited corruption and the Western branch also accepted the doctrine of imputed guilt. Gradually, however, the Western church embraced the Semi-Pelagianism, endorsed by the Council of Trent. Following Augustine, the Reformers Luther and Calvin supported the doctrine of inherited corruption and imputed guilt, while Zwingli leaned toward the Semi-Pelagian position. After Protestantism became established, the old antagonism between these doctrines revived in the Calvinist-Arminian controversy and continues to this day. During the latter part of the eighteenth century, liberal elements among American Calvinists (John Taylor, Jonathan Mayhew, Samuel Webster, and Charles Chauncey) voiced their objection to imputed guilt. Today only a few Protestants accept this biblical doctrine.

1. *The view of Pelagius (c. 354–420, a British monk)*

He held that man, being unaffected by Adam's sin, is morally well. Like newly created Adam, each person determines his moral state by his own actions.

2. *The view of Augustine (354–430, Bishop of Hippo, North Africa)*

In keeping with the teachings of the Scriptures, he regarded man as being morally and spiritually dead. Believing in man's total depravity, he asserted that the human race was wholly affected by Adam's sin and that the guilt of his sin was divinely imputed to each person.

3. *The view of the Semi-Pelagians*

This view arose in certain French churches in the fifth century. They held that humankind, being greatly weakened physically and morally by Adam's sin, is spiritually sick, but not dead or totally depraved. Although man needs the assistance of divine grace to attain salvation and to produce holiness, yet his freedom of will and natural power to do good were not lost by the fall. There is sufficient power in the will to set in motion the beginning of salvation, but not enough to complete it. They held that water baptism removes imputed sin and its guilt.

4. *The view of Roman Catholicism*

This was formulated at the Council of Trent (1545–63). This view regards man as being imperfect at his creation because of the inherent antagonism that existed between his body and soul. To correct this, God added to man a gift of righteousness so that his body might be kept in subjection to his soul. When man fell, he lost this righteousness and reverted to his former state of conflict. The effect of Adam's sin upon the race is their experiencing this conflict between the body and the soul. This state of unrestrained physical desires provides fuel for sin and weakens the will, but it is not one of sin and guilt. Baptism, so they believe, removes the guilt of Adam's sin.

5. The view of the Reformers

Both Martin Luther (1483–1546) and John Calvin (1509–64) followed Augustine in their views of hereditary corruption and imputed sin and its guilt. On the other hand, Huldrych Zwingli (1484–1531) held that Adam's sin was not truly sin for his posterity, for they had not committed a crime against law. According to his view, the race's sin in Adam should be regarded as the disease of self-love and the condition of bondage. There was no imputation of sin and its guilt.

6. The view of the Arminians

a. The earlier view

This represents the view of James (Jacobus) Arminius (1560–1609) and later of John Wesley (1703–91).[22] They held that original sin involved man in guilt and exposed him to divine wrath. However, this guilt was removed by the Atonement, which made it possible for all people to cooperate with God through the Holy Spirit. While Arminius believed that the ability that enables man to cooperate flows from God's justice, Wesley believed that it was conferred by prevenient (going before) grace. By this gift of grace, all are released from the guilt of Adam's sin and have created in them the beginnings of life, which will lead them on to further life if they respond favorably to it. This grace gives to everyone the power to choose the good and incentive to follow the good.[23] Despite this, people can resist this grace and be lost, for they make the final decision about salvation.

b. The later view

This view was held by the Remonstrants, led by the Simon Episcopius (1583–1643), who protested the extreme Calvinistic doctrine of predestination. They held that original sin did not include imputed guilt with its punishment and that inherited depravity affected the body and the intelligence, but not the will. Man's will is competent of itself to cooperate with the assistance of the Holy Spirit in the keeping of God's law.

Observe that the earlier Arminianism accepted the view that inherited depravity is of the nature of sin, while the later Arminianism denied this. The earlier view held that man is totally depraved and cannot cooperate with God apart from grace; the later view held that the fall did not affect man's will. While the errors of the later view are obvious, the belief of the earlier view, which holds that the imputed guilt of all men is removed by Christ's atoning work and that all men are given the grace that releases the will from depravity and that gives it power to choose the good, is unscriptural.

7. The view of religious liberals

Prior to 1750, the New England Puritans held the doctrine of original sin as given in the Westminster Confession of Faith, which speaks of hereditary corruption and imputed guilt (Articles VI, IX). However, with the infiltration of the rationalism of the European Enlightenment into New England, this doctrine was modified under the label of the New School Theory among Congregationalists and Presbyterians. This theory denied the doctrine of imputed guilt.

With the publication of the Darwinian theory of evolution, there developed within the New England School of Calvinism a theology that discounted the idea of original sin altogether. This school of thought viewed man as emerging from lower forms of life and, at some moment in his development, becoming aware of a conflict between his lower and higher natures. The concept of sin became that of inherited disabilities, which are not sinful in themselves and which are capable of moral improvement.

World War I shattered the optimism of this theology of moral and social progress. In its place there was revived in liberalism a false view of original sin that interpreted the fall as a myth rather than a literal fact. It understood the fall to illuminate the psychological situation in which man encounters temptation and becomes a victim of sin.[24]

Despite the unpopularity of original sin, the biblical view, as I understand it, is that all members of the human race (with the exception of Jesus) receive by propagation a totally corrupted human nature and the sin force. Humans also have divinely imputed to them Adam's sin, with its guilt and its penalty, death. Because of this, all unsaved people are sinners by nature and are guilty by divine imputation.

ACTUAL SINS

Actual sins are the sins that people, energized by the sin force, commit during their lifetime on earth. These include sinful actions, decisions, words, thoughts, attitudes, emotions, motivations, and desires.

Their Causes

Actual sins result from people's yielding to the demands of the inner sin force or to the external temptations of Satan and of the evil influences of the world. Let us look at these sources more closely.

1. The sin force

This internal cause of actual sin is the evil, impersonal force, or law, that is resident in the flesh of our bodies and that impels us to sin (Rom. 7:17, 23; 3:9). While unsaved people have a totally corrupted human nature and we who are saved still have a corrupted body, it is the sin force within the flesh of these bodies that actively causes humans to sin. The corrupted condition of unsaved people's human nature gives them an inclination to sin, but the sin force energizes all people, whether unsaved or saved, to commit sins.

Living continuously under sin's domination, unsaved people commit sins all the time (Eph. 2:3; Rom. 3:9). As we shall see, we who are saved no longer have to give in to sin's demands. In fact, we are not to sin at all (Rom. 6:1–13; 1 John 2:1). Nevertheless, we do sin occasionally.

2. Satan and his demon host

An external cause of actual sin is Satan and his demon confederates (fallen angels), who tempt humans to sin (Luke 4:2; 1 Cor. 7:5). By their temptations, these evil angels seek to gain people's consent to their proposals that would lead them to act contrary to God's will. Cunningly, Satan and his demons plot and execute strategies and devices against their prey to lead them into sin (Eph. 6:11; 2 Cor. 2:11; 1 Peter 5:8; see "His Defeat in the Lives of Saved People" under Angelology). It is not sinful to be tempted; it is sinful to yield to temptation and to act contrary to God's will.

3. The world

This external cause of actual sin is the world system of unsaved people who, hating God, have arrogant attitudes, engage in immoral behavior, and hold humanistic, vain philosophies (Rom. 3:9–18; Eph. 4:17–19; Col. 2:8). This system is headed by Satan (John 16:11), its works are evil (7:7), it is condemned by God (12:31; 1 John 2:17), and it fails to satisfy man's spiritual need (1 Cor. 1:21).

Since we who are saved are no longer a part of this world system (John 15:19; Col. 1:13), we are continually threatened by its hostility (John 15:18) and evil influences (Rom. 12:2; 1 John 2:15–16). It solicits us to satisfy our physical, emotional, mental, and spiritual needs in ways that are contrary to God's will for us. The apostle John describes these solicitations as "the lust of the flesh, the lust of the eyes, and the pride of life" (1 John 2:16; see Appendix U: "Our Inward Desires"). When we who are saved yield ourselves to this influence and seek to satisfy our needs in these ways, we express the world's sinful lusts and pride. But having died to the world (Gal. 6:14), we should follow a different lifestyle than this (Rom. 12: 2; Ps. 1:1–3). In keeping with our new life and creaturehood in Christ (2 Cor. 5:17), it is fitting that we focus our lives on things above and express the moral qualities of the Lord Jesus (Col. 3:1–17; Eph. 5:1–20; 1 Peter 1:21; 2 Peter 1:3–8).

While the sin force, Satan, and the world are closely allied in their assaults against us, the sin force supplies us with the energy to sin as well as urging us to sin, and the world and the Devil externally solicit our will to yield to their sinful suggestions. In any case, we are responsible for our sinning, for it is we who sin, not just our human natures. Also, we would not sin if we would give ourselves to God and refuse to submit to temptation and to allow sin to use us for its wicked expressions (James 4:7; Rom. 6:11–13; 12:2; Acts 5:3). We who are saved can do what is right by giving ourselves to Jesus or to the Holy Spirit and by allowing God to use us as an instrument of righteousness (Rom. 6:16–19; Gal. 5:16).

We gospel believers have a unique liberty, by which we can choose the dominating force, whether God or sin, that would use us for its expression, regardless of what moral force currently occupies our heart (see endnote 40). This choice, which unsaved people do not have, is an aspect of Christian freedom that belongs to all saved people alike (Gal. 5:13; 1 Peter 2:16). It is important that we use this liberty rightly.

Their Occurrence

How do actual sins occur? The operation of sin and its start are the same in all people, whether saved or unsaved. Let us look at these.

1. The act of sinning

James 1:14–15 describes how sinning occurs. Using metaphors that relate to physical reproduction, the steps in sinning are these:

a. Seduction ("tempted, drawn away . . . and enticed"; cp. Gal. 5:16–17, "lust" or "desire")

This is the temptation or urge to sin, whether from the sin force within or from Satan and the world without. This evil urge appeals to us to do its sinful bidding.

b. Submission (cp. Rom. 6:13a, 19)

This is our giving ourselves to this temptation, either voluntarily by decision or involuntarily by compulsion. The sin force does not wait, as God does, for an invitation to take control of our hearts and lives.

c. Conception ("when lust has conceived"; cp. Matt. 5:27–28)

Sin is conceived, or initially occurs, in the "heart," or mind. Thus we are guilty of committing the sin, when we decide to do it, even before we carry it out in action.

d. Birth ("it brings forth sin"; cp. Gal. 5:19–21, "flesh" is a metonymy for the sin force; see Appendix X: "Figures of Association: Synecdoche and Metonymy")

This is the sinful action of the person who yields to the control of the sin force.

e. Death ("when it is finished, it brings forth death"; cp. Rom. 6:21; 8:2, 6a).

A result of sinning is one's expressing spiritual death (Gal. 6:7–8) and eventually experiencing physical death. Although saved people have spiritual life, they still express spiritual death by their sinful behavior when the sin force is in control of their hearts (Rom. 8:6a). Moreover, they express spiritual life, or Christlikeness, by their holy behavior when the Holy Spirit is in control of their hearts (v. 6b). Our sinning also shortens our physical life (Heb. 12:9).

2. *The start of sinning*

How does the act of sinning, as described above, begin? There is involuntary sinning and voluntary sinning.

  a. Involuntary sinning

    This is our sinning without doing so deliberately.

    1) Compulsive sinning

      We often sin despite our determination not to (cp. Rom. 7:15, 19). This involuntary sinning occurs when we fail to take the necessary action to avoid wrongdoing, for the sin force is always waiting to assert itself. In this case, the failure is due either to our ignorance of the way to successful resistance to the urges of our spiritual enemies or to our neglect of taking the action that leads to this victory (James 4:7). We shall always be overpowered by our spiritual enemies when we attempt to resist them in our own strength, for they are much stronger than what we by ourselves can withstand.

    2) Ignorant sinning

      We also sin unknowingly when we have not yet learned that certain actions are sinful in God's sight (see below, "Their Variety: Regarding awareness").

  b. Voluntary sinning

    Much of our sinning is the result of our deliberate decision and submission to the urges of the sin force within or to the temptations of Satan or of the world's evil influences without. Upon our submission, we are energized and led by the inner sin force to do what is wrong in God's sight. Immediately following our decision, we commit the sin in our hearts, or minds (cp. Matt. 5:27–28). Thus, we are guilty of committing the sin even before we physically carry it out. On the other hand, our carrying out this intention may lead to greater sinning and more serious consequences, both in substance and in extent.

Their Variety

Since the entire human nature is susceptible to the influence of the sin force, the human nature's parts and functions may be used by this evil force to express various actual sins like sinful actions (Eph. 4:28), thoughts (Matt. 5:28), emotions (Eph. 4:26), attitudes (v. 31), motivations (Acts 5:3–4), desires (Col. 3:5), and words (Eph. 4:31); also see Mark 7:21–22; Romans 1:29–31; Galatians 5:19–21. In addition to these evil expressions, there are other classifications of actual sins, like the following:

1. *Regarding awareness*

There are known sins (Rom. 7:7–8) and unknown sins (5:13), or sins of ignorance (Heb. 9:7).

2. *Regarding activity*

There are sins of action and sins of inaction and omission, or neglect (James 4:17).

3. *Regarding intent*

There are deliberate sins, or sins of rebellion (Isa. 1:20), and compulsory sins because of force of habit or overwhelming circumstances (Rom. 7:15–20).

4. *Regarding ethical standards*

There are violations of God's laws (Rom. 5:14; 7:7–8), man's laws (13:4), and one's own moral training, or the dictates of one's conscience (14:14, 20; see Appendix B: "The Conscience").

5. *Regarding offense*

There are sins against other people (1 Cor. 8:12) and against one's self (Matt. 5:30; 1 Cor. 6:18; 2 Peter 2:7–8; 2 Cor. 7:1). Observe that all sins are against God (Gen. 39:9; Ps. 51:4; 1 Cor. 8:12) and that everything that is done independently of Him is sinful (Rom. 14:23).[25] This sin of independence is the most common sin of saved people.

THE DIVINE REACTION TO SIN

God's stern, inflexible reaction to sin rises from the holiness of His nature (Hab. 1:12–13) and His hatred of evil (Prov. 6:16–19) and of sinners (Ps. 11:5).[26] Thus, His justice compels Him to deal with sin and sinners as they deserve. This includes His condemning sinners and punishing them.

GOD CONDEMNS SINNERS

Condemnation is the judicial sentence that declares, after examination and affirmation of wrongdoing, that one is guilty of an alleged crime and is subject to punishment. God has condemned the whole human race for Adam's original sin (Rom. 5:12, 18) and also those of moral accountability for actual sins (John 3:18; Rom. 3:9–19). On the other hand, He judicially acquits gospel believers of this condemnation and justifies them (Rom. 5:1). This means that He makes them righteous in Jesus and declares them to be right in His sight (8:33–34; 2 Cor. 5:21).

The Meaning of Guilt

Guilt is the fact or condition of one's having committed a crime. It is also the convicted person's obligation to satisfy justice by bearing the punishment of his or her offense.

We must distinguish between being guilty and having guilty feelings. Guilty feelings do not always indicate real guilt. The gospel believer's experience of guilty feelings after having been saved or dealing with sins may arise from Satan or from a wrongly programmed conscience (see Appendix B: "The Conscience"). The divine forgiveness of sins, whether judicial or parental, includes the removal of guilt as well as cleansing from moral defilement (Heb. 9:14; 1 John 1:7). Real guilt is determined and dealt with by divine process, not by one's feelings.

The Incurrence of Guilt

God has imputed to, or reckoned to the account of, all members of the human race (except Jesus) the guilt of Adam's first sin, because by their human nature they cosinned with him (Rom. 5:18). On the other hand, people do not inherit the guilt of the wrongdoing of others (Deut. 24:16; 2 Chron. 25:3–4; Ezek. 18:20), although they often suffer the natural results of these people's sins (Exod. 20:5).

All who have sufficiently developed in human nature to have moral awareness and self-determination at some time in their lives are guilty of the actual sins they knowingly commit (Lev. 5:1–4; Rom. 3:19; cp. Jonah 4:11). On the other hand, I believe that people who die in infancy or who have always been mentally disabled do not have this guilt. Also, their guilt of original sin is covered by Jesus' atoning work (1 John 2:2; see "The Salvation of Infants" under Soteriology).

GOD PUNISHES SINNERS

The Meaning of This Punishment

Divine punishment is the active expression of God's anger toward sinners and sins in the form of judgment (Rom. 2:5–6, see "The Works of God: God's Judgments" under Theology Proper). Sometimes this punishment is viewed as a penalty that one must pay for breaking God's law.

God's anger is the judicial reaction of His holiness against sinners and their sins. *Passively,* this divine wrath expresses itself as a hostile attitude toward sinners (Rom. 1:18; John 3:36). *Actively,* it expresses itself as destructive judgment (Ps. 5:5–6; Rev. 14:19; 15:1; 19:15).

The Kinds of Punishments

Human beings experience several kinds of punishment for wrongdoing.

1. Natural punishments

These include economic, emotional, or physical problems, including death, resulting from the violation of economic, psychological, or physical laws (Eccl. 4:5; 10:18; Prov. 5:22; 23:1–3).

2. Societal punishments

These include fines, imprisonment, restitution, and death, incurred by violating man's laws (Rom. 13:2–4).

3. Divine punishments

The violation of God's law incurs His retribution upon the unsaved and His corrective chastisement of the saved. In both cases, sinning shortens physical life (Rom. 6:23; James 1:15).

a. Divine retribution

This is God's punitive dealings with the unsaved. They proceed from His holiness and give sinners what they deserve. Divine retribution is not remedial, that is, it does not have for its purpose the sinner's restoration and well-being. This is not to say that others cannot profit from visitations of divine retribution on sinners (cp. Josh. 2:9–13), but these are not given to improve the condition of the ones on whom they fall. The wicked are cut off without remedy (Prov. 29:1). On the other hand, God sometimes uses the natural consequences of sin to draw unsaved people to Himself (Luke 18:35–43). Divine retribution assumes the form of severe woes in this life (Rom. 1:22–32) and of hell (the lake of fire) in the eternal state (Matt. 25:46). It exhibits God's judicial power and His holy character (Rom. 2:5; 9:17, 22; Heb. 12:18–29).

b. Divine corrective chastisement

Being a part of His parental dealings with His children (Heb. 12:3–16), corrective chastisement is God's punitive action toward saved people who disobey Him. Proceeding from His holiness, it is tempered by His love (Rev. 3:19) and is remedial in purpose (Heb. 12:11). It intends to restore the wayward to the place of God's fellowship and blessing and to preserve them from divine condemnation (1 Cor. 11:31–32). When His people are unresponsive to His corrective chastisement and set themselves against it, God prematurely removes them from earth to heaven (John 15:2a; Heb. 12:9). They are no longer useful to Him in this world.

THE DIVINE FORGIVENESS OF SINS

In His marvelous, loving grace, God has acquitted all gospel believes of divine condemnation and has forgiven them their sins. As we shall see, this acquittal is related to justification and this forgiveness to redemption. Both are benefits of our Lord's atoning work.

THE DIVINE ACQUITTAL OF CONDEMNATION

Gospel believers were divinely justified when we trusted in the Savior for salvation (Rom. 5:1, 9). This means that dropping His verdict of condemnation against us, God made and declared us to be righteous. Since then, we are no longer judicially guilty before Him as sinners (Heb. 9:14; 10:22; Rom. 5:16–20). Because of this, we should not allow Satan to torment us with guilty feelings about our forgiven sins. Rather, we should rest on the truth of our justification through the Lord Jesus (Rom. 5:1, 9, see "The Components of Salvation: Justification" under Soteriology). Yet, as a part of His present work in our lives, the Holy Spirit convicts us of present sins that we need to deal with by repentance and confession (cp. Rev. 2:5; 3:19; 1 John 3:20; 1:9).

THE DIVINE FORGIVENESS OF SINS

Forgiveness concerns the release from an obligation or the cancellation of a debt (Matt. 18:23–27; Luke 7:41–42). In divine forgiveness of sins, God releases repentant sinners from the obligation of bearing the punishment or paying the debt of their sins. God is able to do this on the basis of Jesus' atoning work (Eph. 1:7; 1 John 1:7b), which secured for sinners a redemptive value sufficient to pay off their sin debt (1 Peter 2:24; 3:18; Rom. 5:8). In response to their fulfilling the requirements of forgiveness, God applies to repentant sinners the value of Jesus' atoning work and cancels the indebtedness incurred by their sinning. Let us look at God's judicial forgiveness of unsaved people and His parental forgiveness of saved people.

Divine Judicial Forgiveness of Unsaved People

1. Its description

This kind of forgiveness relates to the court and sees God as a judge and the unsaved sinner as a criminal. When they believe the gospel, unsaved people are judicially forgiven by God of all their sins—past, present, and future (Acts 10:43; Eph. 1:7; Col. 2;13). By this action, they are forever released from the punishment of divine retribution for original sin and for all their actual sins (John 5:24).

Since we who are saved have taken refuge in the Lord Jesus and His atoning work, any charge that may be brought against us now concerns Him (Rom. 8:31–34). Being in Christ, we are personally beyond the reach of any charge that may be made against us before God (Rev. 12:10).

2. Its reception

The requirement for sinners' receiving divine judicial forgiveness is their believing the gospel. This is to give assent to the facts of the gospel, to repent, and to trust in Jesus and His atoning work for deliverance from the guilt, debt, ruin, and bondage of their sins (Acts 10:43; see "The Sinner's Part in the Reception of Salvation" under Soteriology).

Divine Parental Forgiveness of the Child of God

1. Its description

This kind of forgiveness relates to the family and sees God as a father and the saved sinning person as an offending child. God readily forgives His children of the known (filial) sins that they judge, or deal with, by repentance and confession (1 Cor. 11:31; Rev. 2:5; 1 John 1:9). By this forgiveness, the saved person is released from the ongoing punishment of corrective chastisement or the threat of this action. If he deals with his sins immediately when they occur, he will be spared corrective chastisement; if he deals with his sins while he is in the throes of corrective chastisement, his punishment will cease. While divine forgiveness of any kind cancels the punishment for sins, it does not erase the consequences of wrongdoing in one's life or in the lives of others.

In His dealings with those of us who are saved, God first speaks to us about the things in our lives that displease Him (filial sins) and gives us the opportunity to deal with them. But if we are unresponsive to His voice, He disciplines us (Rev. 3:19). When we deal with our sins the moment we become aware of them, we continue in God's fellowship (1 John 1:7). The sins of which we are not aware are automatically cleansed away by the blood of Jesus (representing the value of His atoning work), else imperfect people could not walk in fellowship with an infinitely holy God (vv. 5–7). As we adjust ourselves to Him by dealing with known sins and by doing His will, we walk in God's fellowship in the light where He is. If we fail to do this, we walk in darkness alone, apart from His fellowship and blessing.

2. *Its reception*

What must we do to receive divine parental forgiveness? Remembering that the Lord's atoning work is sufficient for cleansing us from our filial sins (those we commit as saved people), we must repent, or have a change of mind and attitude (Rev. 2:5, 16, 22; 3:3, 19), confess our sins to God (1 John 1:9), make right our wrongdoing to others whom we have offended (Matt. 5:23–24), and be forgiving toward others who have repented and made right their wrongdoing toward us (Matt. 6:12, 14–15; Luke 17:3; see Appendix W: "The Saved Person's Forgiveness of Others"). Then God immediately applies to us the value of our Lord's atoning work and forgives us as He promises (1 John 1:9). Observe that all filial sins are forgivable.

With this distinction between judicial and parental forgiveness in view, we can understand how a saved person who dies with known sin in his life is still justified and is taken to heaven. When he was saved, he was judicially forgiven of all the sins that he had committed and that he would commit throughout the remainder of his lifetime (Col. 2:13). Therefore, he will never again be condemned by God or be obligated for the judicial debt of his sins. On the other hand, because he is responsible for his actions, he will give an accounting of his unrepentant wrongdoing to the Lord Jesus in the coming appraisal (cp. 1 John 2:28; 2 Cor. 5:10). Parental forgiveness is needed during the course of a gospel believer's life on earth for his fellowship with God, but this is not required for his going to heaven.

We should ever be grateful to God for the fact of divine forgiveness. Of all people who seek divine forgiveness, only the child of God can know beyond doubt that he has been judicially forgiven of his sins. Blessed be the Lord Jesus who was willing to pay this awful debt on our behalf (Matt. 20:28; Eph. 1:3–7)! By this payment, He purchased us to be His slaves (Rom. 14:8–9; 1 Cor. 7:22). Let us daily own Him as our Master and seek to learn and do His will for God's glory (Matt. 11:28–30; Rom. 12:1–2). Also, let us immediately deal with any sin that we commit so that our fellowship with Him remains uninterrupted (1 John 1:7, 9). Better still, let us not sin at all (1 John 2:1)!

THE GOSPEL BELIEVER AND SIN

Although it seems contrary to our experience, we who are saved are no longer related to sin as we once were. It is very important for us to learn what God has revealed about this to avoid unnecessary misery and irreparable loss and to live holy and victorious lives.[27]

THE BELIEVER'S RELATION TO ORIGINAL SIN

To better understand the gospel believer's relation to original sin, we must first look at his or her new relation to the Lord Jesus, which undergirds His truth.

The Believer's Relation to the Lord Jesus Christ

The apostle Paul declared that, for gospel believers, the old things have passed away and everything is now new (2 Cor. 5:17). At salvation, we gospel believers were severed from Adam and his group, together with the effects of this relationship, and were joined to Jesus and His group (1 Cor. 15:22; 2 Cor. 5:17; Gal. 3:27–28), the new human race of which the Lord is the Head and Pattern (Eph. 4:15; Rom. 8:29; see Appendix D: "The Ones Who Are in Christ"). Being in Christ, we have everything new, including our sharing the Lord's kind of immaterial human nature and the prospect of having His kind of body (Phil. 3:20–21), His obedience unto death and the blessed results of this obedience (Rom. 5:17–19), and His death and resurrection (6:3–4). This new relation with the Lord Jesus means that we are no longer related to original sin as we once were.

The Believer's Changed Relation to Original Sin

We have seen that unsaved people have an active relation to original sin and its effects. They have a corrupted personhood and human nature, are dominated by the inner sin force, are spiritually dead, and are morally defiled and guilty before God. But with their salvation people's relationship to original sin is dramatically changed.

1. *Gospel believers are divinely forgiven of imputed sin and its guilt.*

We can say that Adam's initial sin and its guilt are no longer divinely imputed to those of us who are saved for two reasons: *One,* we have been divinely, judicially forgiven of all sins, both original and actual (Eph. 1:7; Col. 2:13); and *two,* we have been justified by God (Rom. 5:1, 9; 8:30, 33; Titus 3:7). We could not be righteous now in God's sight (justified) if we were still guilty of original sin. In fact, we cannot now be successfully charged with or condemned judicially for any sin because of the atoning work and intercession of our Substitute, the Lord Jesus (Rom. 8:34; Heb. 7:25).

Although most of Christendom believes that water baptism removes imputed sin and its guilt, this is not the teaching of Scripture. These are forever taken away by the divine application of the value of our Lord's atoning sacrifice in response to a gospel believer's faith in Jesus as his or her Savior (Rom. 3:21–25; Eph. 1:7; Heb. 9:26; Rev. 1:5).

2. *Gospel believers are inwardly delivered from inherent corruption.*

a. *Their personhoods, souls, and spirits*

The gospel believer's personhood and immaterial part of his human nature are delivered from the corruption of original sin (Acts 15:9; Eph. 5:25–26; Titus 2:14) and are renewed (3:5).[28] The apostle Paul referred to this when he stated that (at salvation) we put off the "old man" (what we were in Adam when we were unsaved) and that we put on the "new man" (what we are in Jesus as new creatures), "which after God was created in righteousness and true holiness" (Col. 3:9–10; Eph. 4:22–24). The apostle also spoke of our being renewed in the spirit of our mind (Eph. 4:23) and of people's calling on the Lord out of a pure heart (2 Tim. 2:22). Moreover, he declared that "the (human) spirit is life" (Rom. 8:10). The apostle Peter spoke about our soul's being purified in obedience to the gospel (1 Peter 1:22) and its being saved (v. 9; cp. Heb. 10:39).

With the deliverance of our personhoods, souls, and spirits from hereditary corruption, we who are saved now have the capability to understand spiritual truth, to express holy emotions, and to make right moral decisions. Because of this, we can now worship and serve God with our spirits and souls (Phil. 3:3; Rom. 1:9; cp. 1 Cor. 14:15) as did Mary the mother of Jesus (Luke 1:46–47; cp. Ps. 103:1–2).[29]

Although our personhoods, souls, and spirits are delivered from hereditary corruption, they are still susceptible to the influences of our spiritual enemies. The apostle Peter wrote about "fleshly lusts, which war against the soul" (1 Peter 2:11) and about Lot's righteous soul being tortured (KJV "vexed") by what he saw and heard in Sodom (2 Peter 2:8). Both the Scriptures and experience show us that our personhoods and the saved immaterial part of human nature can come under the temporary domination of the sin force, Satan, and the world and can be used as their instrument of evil expression (Gal. 5:19–21; Eph. 4:25–31; 1 Peter 2:11; 1 John 2:15; Acts 5:3). But this does not mean that our personhoods and immaterial nature are in themselves inherently evil or corrupted, although they are still susceptible to these evil influences.

b. *Their bodies*

Being unredeemed, the gospel believer's body has resident in its flesh the sin force, hereditary corruption, and mortality—the forces of sin, deterioration, and death. Because of this, we who are saved still suffer physical weakness, sickness, aging, and death, and feel the urges of the sin force (1 Cor. 11:30; 15:53; Rom. 7:17–18; 8:10–11; 1 Tim. 5:23). But despite their inherent corruption, our bodies do not functionally have the same relation to sin as they did have, for we do not have the same relation to sin that we had in our unsaved state (Rom. 6:11). Thus, being dead to sin, we should regard the body as being rendered powerless to sin, like a broken tool of unrighteousness (vv. 6–8, 11–13).[30] It is now a member of Christ and a temple of the Holy Spirit (1 Cor. 6:15, 19–20). God uses the bodies of His people as tools of righteousness, or right doing, when they yield them to His control and do His will (Rom. 6:13, 19). These bodies will remain in their corrupt condition until they are changed at the Lord's coming (Rom. 8:11; Phil. 3:20–21; 1 Cor. 15:50–53).

It is our duty to yield our personhoods and total human nature to the control of the indwelling Holy Spirit (Rom. 12:1) and to allow Him to produce His holy fruit in our lives (Gal. 5:16, 22–23).[31] He can keep our spiritual enemies in check as well as help us to do what is pleasing in God's sight (Gal. 5:16; James 4:7; Rom. 8:2–4).

3. *Gospel believers are made spiritually alive.*

With his renewal (Titus 3:5), the gospel believer's personhood and immaterial human nature received eternal life and he or she was made spiritually alive (John 3:16; 6:47; Eph. 2:1; see "The Components of Salvation: Regeneration" under Soteriology). This new life springs out of a new, personal relationship with God (John 17:3) that gospel believers enter when they are born into God's family (John 1:12), and they become citizens of His kingdom (3:3–6; Col. 1:13). Being the spiritual life of the Lord Jesus in His humanity (John 14:6; 1 John 5:12), this new life is communicated to God's people by the Holy Spirit (Rom. 8:2; Gal. 5:25).[32] It provides the dynamics for their interacting with God and for their displaying Christlikeness in daily life (see "Making Moral Behavioral Changes in the Christian Life" under Zoeology).

4. *Gospel believers are no longer slaves of the sin force.*

Since our unredeemed bodies still possess the sin force, we saved people have this evil energy to contend with throughout our earthly lives. This is indicated by the teachings of Scripture (Rom. 6–7; 1 John 1:8), God's appeals against His people's sinning (1 John 2:1; Col. 3:8), and various biblical case histories (1 Cor. 3:1–3; Eph. 4:28–31). Although we are still able to sin, we no longer have to give in to sin's demands because of the radical changes in our relation to this evil force when we were saved. We died to the sin force and were delivered from its authority. We are now alive unto God and are the property of the Lord Jesus, being subject to His authority (Rom. 14:8–9; 1 Cor. 6:20; Matt. 11:28–30).

a. *We died to the sin force (Rom. 6:1–14).*

The apostle Paul argued that if grace superabounds where sin abounds (5:20), then the logical inference would be to keep on living in sin's grip (6:1). But the apostle recoiled from this conclusion (v. 2). How can people who have died to the sin force continue to live under its domination? In explaining this answer, God wants us to:

1) Know certain truth (vv. 3–10)

Because of our baptism (placement) into Jesus at salvation (Gal. 3:27), as God sees it, we died with Him; thus we died to the sin force (vv. 3, 6; 1 Peter 2:24). We also were buried with Him (Rom. 6:4a; Gal. 3:27). Finally, we arose with Him; thus, we are alive unto God (Rom. 6:4b–5, "if" means "since," a fulfilled condition.)

This truth affects us in two ways: *One,* we do not have to sin (Rom. 6:6–7), for we are like a broken tool to the sin force (v. 6), and we have been freed of its claim on us (v. 7). This means that we have been divinely acquitted of sin's claim on us and of the divine penalty that our sinning incurred. Just as a corpse does not respond to external stimuli or greet people at the mortuary door, so we, having died to this evil force, must ignore its demands ("lusts"), despite its urging us to sin.[33] Also, *two,* we are now alive to God to do His will (8–10). Upon asserting the principle that we have died unto sin (KJV "if" means "since") and are now alive unto God (v. 8; Gal. 2:20), the apostle sees an analogy of this truth with our Lord's physical experience of death and resurrection (Rom. 6:5, 9–10). As Jesus' resurrection severed death's grip on Him, so our death with Him has severed our relation to the sin force and our resurrection with Him has made us alive unto God. Now we can "walk in newness of life" (v. 4).

2) Act upon it (vv. 11–13)

Considering our being dead to sin and being alive to God to be true (v. 11), we must respond to this truth by decision and action in a suitable way (vv. 12–13). This is to stop giving ourselves to the demands of the sin force and to start giving ourselves to God as His tools of right doing. We have liberty to make this decision and to act upon it at anytime (1 Peter 2:16; Gal. 5:13). The Holy Spirit will help us as we look to Him to do so (Gal. 5:16).

b. *We were delivered from sin's authority (Rom. 8:1–9).*

Having referred to this fact in Romans 6:7, 22, the apostle Paul addressed it more fully in 8:1–9. While God the Father delivered us at salvation from the guilt and penalty of sin and declared us to be righteous in His sight (v. 1a), He also delivered us from the tenacious authority of the sin force (6:7). Having stated this deliverance from sin's authority (8:2, "law" means an operational force), the apostle now presents the divine basis of this deliverance (v. 3), its experience in the saved person's life (vv. 4–8), and its reality (v. 9).[34]

1) Its basis (v. 3)

The basis of this deliverance is the fact that the sin force was effectively judged at the cross. Jesus' abusive, illegal, undeserved trial and crucifixion demonstrated God's justice in condemning the evil force that energized His enemies; Jesus' resurrection broke Satan's and sin's power of death (Acts 2:24; 1 Cor. 15:56; Heb. 2:14). On this ground, the Lord is now able by the Holy Spirit to deliver gospel believers initially from sin's authority at salvation and daily from its dominating power as they give Him command of their lives (John 8:36; Rom. 12:1–2; 13:14).

2) Its experience (vv. 4–8)

God's purposes for His action against this evil force is that His people might experience deliverance from its domination and express righteous behavior in their doing the divine will (Rom. 8:4) and that they might have a spiritual mind-set in daily life (vv. 5–8; KJV "after" means "under the dominion of "). Let us look more closely as the latter.

The new birth brought us a new mind-set (Eph. 4:23; Rom. 12:2; Titus 3:5); therefore, with the aid of the Holy Spirit, we can understand God's truth and make decisions in harmony with this truth. We maintain this new mind-set by daily giving ourselves to the Holy Spirit and by following His direction, evaluation, and reasoning in the light of His Word (cp. Prov. 4:23; Ps. 119:105; Col. 3:16). In Romans 8:5–6, the apostle states that people who are dominated by the sin force are "carnally minded," with minds that are directed by this evil force and that are set on evil things. Those who are dominated by the Holy Spirit are "spiritually minded," with minds that are directed by God and His Word and that are set on holy things.

The apostle then contrasts these mind-sets (vv. 6–8), which he describes as "the mind of the flesh" and "the mind of the Spirit." People who have *the mind of the flesh* (the "carnal mind"), which is governed by the sin force, *one,* express spiritual death (v. 6; cp. Gal. 6:8). Like unsaved people (Rom. 1:21–22; 1 Cor. 2:14; Eph. 4:17–18), saved people with this mind-set do not think God's thoughts or understand spiritual truth. *Two,* they are hostile toward God, for this evil force is rebellious toward Him and His will (Rom. 8:7). People with this mind-set refuse to obey God. And *three,* they cannot please God

(v. 8; 14:23). Directed by sin, the carnal gospel believers do not and cannot do what is acceptable to God.

People who have *the mind of the (Holy) Spirit* (the "spiritual mind"), which is governed by God, *one,* express spiritual life and experience God's peace as well as the other fruits of the Holy Spirit (Rom. 8:6; Gal. 5:22–23; 6:8). *Two,* they interact with God. This mind-set understands and is responsive to God's Word and is submissive to His will (1 Cor. 2:9–16; Rom. 6:16, 18). And *three,* they alone can please God (1 Cor. 2:10–12; Heb. 11:6).

3) Its reality (v. 9)

The apostle then declares the fact of this deliverance from sin's authority (Rom. 8:9; "in" refers to the positional sphere of authority). Being "in Christ" (2 Cor. 5:17; Eph. 2:10), saved people are in the sphere of His authority, the realm of spiritual life (Rom. 6:18, 22; Col. 1:13). Being in sin (represented by being "in the flesh"), unsaved people exist in the sphere of the sin force's authority (Rom. 3:9; Gal. 3:22), the realm of spiritual death and of Satan (Heb. 2:14; Acts 26:18; Eph. 2:1–3). Although they are in Christ, saved people can temporarily give themselves over to sin and its authority.

Being in Christ, we who are saved are no longer positionally "in the flesh," the sphere of sin's authority (Rom. 8:9a). Our victory over the daily demands and influence of the sin force rests on our not being any longer under its authority as we were when we were unsaved (Eph. 4:22–24; Rom. 6:1–4, 6–7). Having died to the sin force, we have been set free from its authority (Rom. 6:1–3, 6–7).

We who are saved are now positionally "in the Spirit" as well as in Christ, the sphere of God's authority (Rom. 8:9b). Being alive to God and having the Holy Spirit (1 John 3:24), we are now under His dominion and have access to His help (John 14:16–17). Any temporary power that sin might have over us can immediately be broken by our decision to yield to God, our submission to the Holy Spirit, and our resisting sin in His strength (Rom. 6:11–13; James 4:7). Also, with His help we can obey God and be all that He desires. If anyone does not have the Holy Spirit ("the Spirit of Christ"), he is not saved (Rom. 8:9c; cp. 1 John 3:24).

Salvation has radically altered our relation to original sin. We have been forgiven of imputed sin with its guilt. Our personhoods and the immaterial parts of our human nature have been delivered from hereditary corruption and have been made righteous for holy purposes, although they are still susceptible to the evil influences of our spiritual enemies. We have spiritual life whereby we can obey God and have fellowship with Him. Finally, we have a new Master, the Lord Jesus Christ, who Himself is the Father's Slave. Since we have died to the sin force and are alive unto God, it is now our duty to quit submitting ourselves to sin's evil demands and to yield ourselves to the will of our new Master for His use and glory.

THE BELIEVER'S RELATION TO ACTUAL SIN

Although we who are saved are able to sin and do sin, as we have seen, we no longer have to sin. In fact, God does not want us to sin at all (1 Cor. 15:34; 1 John 2:1). He wants us to do righteous acts, or His will (1 John 2:3; 3:7, see Appendix F: "Learning and Doing God's Will"). We cannot sin continuously over an extended period of time, as we once did, because of our having new creaturehood with renewed personhood and immaterial human nature (2 Cor. 5:17; Eph. 4:22–24), our having Jesus who cannot sin (1 John 5:12; 3:9, "God's Seed"), our having innate desire to obey God (Phil. 2:13), our having the ability not to sin (1 John 3:6; Gal. 5:16), and our having been set free from sin's claim to us (Rom. 6:6–7).[35] The apostle John argues that if a person sins continuously, or all the time, he is not saved (1 John 3:4–10). Actual sins are inconsistent with and contrary to the new life that we have in Jesus. Having put off what we once were (the old man) and having put on what we are now in Jesus (the new man), it is fitting that we allow Him to express Himself in and through our lives (Col. 3:1–17). It is God's desire that we put off actual sins by ceasing to commit them (v. 8) and that we cleanse ourselves from their defilement and guilt by repentance and confession (2 Cor. 7:1; Rev. 2:5; 1 John 1:9). We pay a high price when we neglect these.

Our Paying the Toll of Sinning

While our conscious sinning does not require those of us who are saved to pay the divine judicial penalty of sin, it does take a spiritual toll and incurs natural penalties.

1. Our sinning interrupts our fellowship with God (1 John 1:6–7; cp. Isa. 59:2).

To fellowship with God is to live in conscious touch with Him by sharing with Him all that concerns us, drawing from Him all that we need, communicating with Him by prayer and the reading of His Word, participating with Him in His work, living according to His will, and resting on His promises. Our sinning interrupts this fellowship by turning our hearts away from God and bringing us His displeasure (Ps. 66:18).

We can have fellowship with God only as we walk in the light, as He is in the light (1 John 1:5–7). This requires us to adjust to His holy character (Matt. 5:48; 1 Peter 1:15–16), to be responsive to His Word (Pss. 1:1–2; 119:11), and to do what He desires for us (Rom. 12:1–2; Eph. 5:17). It is possible for imperfect people to have fellowship with God because of the means of cleansing and enablement that He has provided for us. When God's Word or our conscience points to some sin in our lives, we must immediately repent and confess it to God (Rev. 2:5; 1 John 1:9). Moreover, we must give ourselves to the Holy Spirit and depend upon Him to enable us to do those things that are pleasing to Him (Gal. 5:16). When we neglect these things, our fellowship with God ceases until we have dealt with our sins and have given ourselves anew to Him and His will (James 4:8–10). If we sin unknowingly and God does not reveal this sin to us, then the value of our Lord's atoning work is automatically applied to us for our cleansing (1 John 1:7). However, it is of utmost importance that we immediately deal with known sins when we become aware of them, for neglecting this will interrupt our fellowship with God.

2. Our sinning hinders our receiving help from the Holy Spirit (1 Thess. 5:19).

Our conscious sinning stifles the Holy Spirit's enablement and production in our lives, which are necessary for our being and doing all that God requires (Gal. 5:16, 22–23, 25). Furthermore, our conscious sinning causes us to be very unhappy, for it grieves the Holy Spirit (Eph. 4:30; cp. Ps. 32:3–4; Matt. 26:75), violates our consciences (Ps. 32:3–4; 1 John 3:20), and defiles our personhoods and inner human nature (2 Cor. 7:1). This is a high price to pay when we consider that it is through the Holy Spirit's work that we experience all the expressions and blessings of the new life in Jesus (Rom. 8:4–9).

3. Our sinning arrests our spiritual growth (1 Peter 2:1–2).

It is God's command that we grow in our spiritual lives, for our new life in Christ has this capability and need as our physical life does (2 Peter 3:18). This growth occurs in the areas of Christian character (1 Thess. 3:12), spiritual knowledge (Col. 1:10), practical faith (2 Thess. 1:3), spiritual activity (2 Cor. 9:8), and grace (2 Peter 3:18). The purpose of this growth is that we might increasingly become like Jesus (Rom. 8:29; 2 Cor. 3:18). However, sin, which is unlike Him, arrests this growth. The apostle Paul rebuked the Corinthian believers for acting like unsaved people (1 Cor. 3:1–3) and described them as being "carnal" (ones living under the domination of the sin force) and "babes" (infants in spiritual maturity). The apostle Peter admonished his readers to lay aside sin and to desire God's Word that they might grow (1 Peter 2:1–2). God wants us to be spiritually mature and strong (Eph. 4:14–15; 6:10). Sin retards and weakens us.

4. *Our sinning brings us God's corrective chastisement (1 Cor. 11:28–32).*

When we fail to deal with known sins in our lives, we incur God's corrective discipline (Rev. 3:19). In chastening His people, God deals with them so as to remove what hinders their fruitfulness, to supply what is lacking, to correct what He disapproves of, and to help them walk in His way (John 15:2; Heb. 12:1–15). Not all adversity that we experience is the result of unjudged sins (James 1:2–4), but this must be our first consideration when it strikes us (cp. Ruth 1:20–21). If we promptly deal with the sin that we are aware of or that is made known to us, then we avoid God's corrective action (Rev. 3:19; 1 Cor. 11:31). We can avoid many difficulties in life by dealing promptly with that which displeases Him.

5. *Our sinning incurs the loss of reward (2 Cor. 5:10; 1 Cor. 3:13–15).*[36]

Since we who are saved are the Lord's slaves and have the responsibility of doing His will, we must give an account to Him of our behavior during our Christian lifetimes in this world (Rom. 14:12). All that we have done in keeping with His will and in His strength will bring us His approval and reward. But all else will bring us His reprimand and loss (2 Cor. 5:10; Col. 3:24–25). We must ever keep in mind that we can live pleasing to the Lord only as we share our lives with Him and allow Him to do His part as we do ours (John 15:4–5; Rom. 14:23). This appraisal is not a judicial judgment that concerns salvation; it is the Master's evaluation of the lives of His servants. He will require His people to give an account of the actions of their Christian lifetimes that they might receive suitable rewards for their activities on earth.

6. *Our sinning energizes us to manifest spiritual death (Gal. 6:7–8).*

During every conscious moment, we who are saved are manifesting by our behavior either spiritual life or spiritual death. This is determined by the moral force (God or sin) that is dominating and energizing us. If we yield ourselves to the Holy Spirit, we allow Him to manifest through us spiritual life by righteous works, words, and attitudes (Rom. 6:22; 8:6). In this way, we reflect Christlikeness. On the other hand, when we give ourselves to the sin force, we allow it to use us as an instrument of unrighteousness, and we manifest spiritual death by sinful works, words, and attitudes (James 1:15; Rom. 6:21; 8:6). This does not mean that we have lost eternal life; it means that we manifest this new life in Jesus only as we abide in Him and do His will (John 15:4–5). There is no neutrality in the spiritual experience of gospel believers (Gal. 6:7–8), for they are either expressing spiritual life or death, according to the moral force that now commands their hearts (Luke 6:45). What commands your heart today?

Our Receiving Divine Forgiveness and Cleansing

When gospel believers sin it does not change their human natures, as it did Adam's and Eve's, but it does temporarily defile them (2 Cor. 7:1). Sin that we unknowingly commit is automatically forgiven and cleansed away by the divine application of Jesus' blood (the value of His atoning work, 1 John 1:7). But when we knowingly sin or when the Holy Spirit shows us that some action is sinful, we must then immediately deal with this as sin and by this allow God to cleanse us from its defilement and guilt (2 Cor. 7:1; 1 Cor. 11:31). Let us consider the procedure for cleansing and the assurance of being forgiven.

1. *The procedure for receiving divine parental forgiveness and cleansing from sin*

Although we who are saved are not able of ourselves to remove sin's defilement and guilt, God has provided the means by which we can do this. The cleansing agent is Jesus' blood (1 John 1:7), which represents the value of His atoning work by which He dealt with this sin on the cross (see "His Humiliation: The Work of Jesus While on the Cross" under Christology). Let us consider what we who are saved must do to receive divine parental forgiveness and cleansing.

a. We must repent of the sin (Rev. 2:5).

Repentance is a change of mind and attitude toward the sin that we committed; it is to see it as God does (cp. Matt. 21:29). This is necessary, for sinning leads one to make excuse for one's wrongdoing, to blame someone else for it, or to ignore it. The repentant person accepts the responsibility of his or her wrong action, regrets the sin, and repudiates it (2 Cor. 7:10; Prov. 28:13).

b. We must confess the sin to God (1 John 1:9).

This is to acknowledge to God our sin, calling it what He says it is and not attempting to make it something less than what it is. Observe that there cannot be true outward confession if this was not preceded by inward repentance, for God searches the heart (Ps. 139: 23–24; Rom. 8:27).

c. We must make right our offenses (Matt. 5:23–24).

If by our sinning we have wronged another person, we must confess this to him or her and do whatever is necessary to make right our wrongdoing. If the offended person sustained injury and/or property damage or loss, then we must make restitution for this (Luke 19:8; cp. Exod. 21:30–36; Prov. 6:30–31). On the other hand, if our sinning against someone was wholly in our mind, and we did not express these thoughts to the person or to anyone else, then this is a private matter between God and us. We have no obligation to report this sinful thought to the person whom we had in mind or to anyone else.

d. We must have a forgiving spirit toward repentant offenders (Matt. 6:12, 14–15; Luke 17:3).

When we are offended, we must immediately give ourselves to God for His help and direction in our having right attitudes toward the offender and in our dealing with the matter in a biblical way (Eph. 5:18; Gal. 6:1; Matt. 5:44). If we have been wronged by saved people, we must have a forgiving attitude toward them only when they repent and make right their wrongdoing (Luke 17:3). God will not forgive us the sins that we confess to Him as long as we have an unforgiving attitude toward an offender who has repented and has made right his wrongdoing. However, until they do this, we must not ignore the offense and pretend that it never happened. On the other hand, we must not retaliate against unrepentant offenders (Rom. 12:19–21) or harbor ill-will toward them (Matt. 5:44; 1 Cor. 13:5). If the offender does not come to us to make things right, then we must go to him or her with God's love and seek this person's restoration to God's fellowship and to ours (Gal. 6:1; see Appendix W: "The Saved Person's Forgiveness of Others"). When unsaved people offend us, we cannot expect them to make this right (John 15:18–21; 1 John 3:13). We anticipate hostility from unsaved people because of their rebellion against God.

2. The assurance of divine forgiveness and cleansing

Upon taking these steps, God immediately applies to us the value of Jesus' sacrifice and forgives and cleanses us as He promises (1 John 1:9; cp. v. 7). Observe that we do not have to ask God to forgive us our sins, for He has promised to do this when we fulfill the conditions of repentant confession. God is not only faithful to forgive us but is also righteous (KJV "just") to do this because of our Lord's sacrifice, which dealt with these sins (1 Peter 2:24).

While all sins that we may commit are forgivable, this truth does not give us freedom to sin as we please. As we noted earlier, we cannot sin without experiencing great loss in our lives. Moreover, the natural consequences of sinning continue, despite God's forgiving us and removing our guilt. Moreover, our sinning brings us the loss of time and energy that could have been used in doing God's will and the loss of any reward that obedience to God would have earned us (2 Cor. 5:10; Col. 3:24–25).

Upon our receiving divine forgiveness and cleansing, the pending threat or the action of corrective chastisement is canceled, and our fellowship with God is restored. The way is then open for us to "perfect holiness in the fear of God" (2 Cor. 7:1). We bring about this practical holiness in our lives by yielding ourselves to God and by doing His will in the power of the Holy Spirit (see Appendix E: "Righteousness and Holiness").

Are there any known sins in your life that remain unforgiven, because you have neglected to deal with them? How are things between you and other people? Is there anything in your relationships that needs to be corrected? As long as you neglect to deal with known sin in your life, you are living in spiritual darkness, deprived of God's blessing and power (1 John 1:5–9).

Our Victory over Sinning

We sin when we yield ourselves to the demands of the inner sin force (James 1:14–15).[37] But since we have been delivered from its authority and do not have to yield to these demands, we can experience occasions of victory over this enemy. I speak of "occasions of victory," for there is no permanent victory over our spiritual enemies in the sense that we are no longer the objects of their assaults. As long as we are in this world, we are susceptible to their attacks and influences. How, then, can we experience victory over these enemies when they attack us? We have considered what our response should be to Satan and his forces (see "Our Response When Satan Attacks" under Angelology). Let us look now at those steps that we should take to be victorious over the urges of the sin force within us. The apostle Paul gave us directions in Romans chapter 6. Although we have considered the forepart of this passage earlier ("The Believer's Relation to Original Sin"), let us look at it again with God's provision of victory in mind. We can experience this victory by knowing certain truths and by acting upon them in obedience to God.

1. *God wants us to know certain truths (Rom. 6:1–10).*
   a. *He wants us to know that we died to the sin force and its demands (vv. 2–3, 6–7).*[38]

   In God's thinking, at salvation we became participants in the Lord's death. This took place by our being joined to Him by the baptism of the Holy Spirit (Gal. 3:27). By this union, we came to share in His death and died to the sin force and its claim on us. Setting us free from sin's claim, this death rendered us and our human nature ineffective as the lawful instruments of sin (Rom. 6:6–7).

   b. *God wants us to know that we are alive unto Him (vv. 4–5, 10).*

   In God's thinking, we also participated in the Lord's resurrection. As our sharing in His death was effective in severing our bondage and service to the sin force, so our sharing in His resurrection enables us to experience our new life in Him and to fulfill our duty of obeying God (2 Cor. 5:14–15). Consequently, we do not have to submit to the demands of the sin force and to sin, for we have died to sin and have been set free from its claim (vv. 6–7). We are now alive unto God to do His will (vv. 8–10).

2. *God wants us to reckon these truths to be so (Rom. 6:11).*

   Giving us stimulus and direction for action, this reckoning means to consider the facts that God wants us to know are true and to respond to them in a suitable manner. Having died to sin, we are to refuse to give in to its demands, for it is unnatural to respond to it in a favorable way. Being alive unto God, we are to respond to Him with submission and obedience.[39] It is our privilege to give Him the place in our lives that sin once held and seeks to recover.

3. *God wants us to take suitable action (Rom. 6:12–14).*
   a. *Quit yielding to sin (vv. 12–13a).*

   In the light of our being dead to sin and alive unto God, we are to quit yielding ourselves to the demands of the sin force and allowing it to rule us. Yielding to sin allows this evil force to use us as a tool of unrighteousness for its evil purposes. This is not suitable for us whose lawful Master and Life is the Lord Jesus (14:8; Col. 3:4).

b. *Yield self to God* (v. 13b–14).

God wants us to yield ourselves to Him (Rom. 6:13b), for we are under His grace, with its new position and resources (v. 14; Eph. 1:3–7; 2:7). As ones who are alive from spiritual death and sinful bondage, it is our duty and privilege to give God our personhood and human nature (body, soul, and spirit) as tools of right doing for His use in this world. When we fail to do this, we cannot avoid sin's taking command of us and causing us to sin, for it is stronger than we are alone. However, regardless of sin's grip on us, we are always free to yield ourselves immediately to God and to serve Him.[40]

4. *God wants us to practice the holy alternative to sinning* (Rom. 6:15–23).

In answering the question, "Shall we continue to sin?" the apostle points out that we are slaves of that which we obey (vv. 15–16), as our history of bondage to sin shows (vv. 17–18). Our duty, therefore, is to be slaves of righteousness (our doing God's will; v. 19). When we look at the results of serving sin (vv. 20–21) and of serving God (v. 22), it is not difficult to determine what is the right choice.

Upon our yielding ourselves to God, it is our duty then to obey Him and to do His will (righteousness) in the energy of the Holy Spirit (Gal. 5:16, 25). Our doing this results in our expressing holiness, or sinlessness, and eternal life, or Christlikeness (Rom. 6:19, 22). In this way, we develop holy habits, and we replace sinful ones. Whatever our spiritual enemies would have us do, there is the holy alternative of God's will that we are to do in its place (Col. 3:8–17). It is important that we know what this is (2 Cor. 5:9; Eph. 5:17; cp. 4:25–5:5, 15–18).[41]

In Romans 8:12–13, the apostle Paul states that we who are saved have no obligation to the sin force (vv. 12–13a). In fact, for one to "live under the domination of (KJV "after") the sin force" ("flesh") leads to death. Our sinning expresses spiritual death and hastens physical death (6:23; Gal. 6:7–8). On the other hand, we owe God everything (Rom. 8:13b; 2 Cor. 5:14–15). If we put to death ("mortify") the deeds of the body, which are produced by the resident sin force (Rom. 8:13b; Col. 3:5), by reckoning ourselves to be dead to sin and by submitting ourselves to God (see endnote 39), we shall express spiritual life and shall prolong our physical life (Gal. 6:7–8). As we do, we express righteousness by doing God's will and holiness by not sinning.

When we become aware of the urges of the sin force within us or of temptation from without, we can experience immediate victory by yielding ourselves to God, resisting the temptation in His strength, and with His help doing His will (James 4:7; Phil. 4:13). When we do this, we allow the Holy Spirit to hold the sin force in abeyance and to enable us to do what is right in God's sight (Gal. 5:16; 1 John 3:6). In this way, sinful habits are unwound and holy ones are formed. As we have seen, whenever we sin we must repent and confess this sin to God and give ourselves anew to His control. Keep in mind that there is no way in this life to divest ourselves of this evil force and its demands. Like Satan and the world, this enemy is always present to tempt us and to take control of us when we are not submissive to God.

Observe again that no matter how strong sin's grip may be, it can immediately be broken by the decision and action of giving ourselves to God. But with this submission to God, there must also be faith that the Holy Spirit will provide the power and direction for our doing God's will (cp. John 7:37–39; Gal. 5:16).

We thank God for this marvelous truth—our being dead to sin and alive to Him. We no longer have to sin; we can now do what is right in His sight. Just as we once were slaves of sin, ever ready to do its bidding, so now are we the Lord's slaves to do His bidding (2 Cor.

5:14–15). Let us daily give ourselves to Him as His instruments of righteousness and seek to glorify God in all we do (1 Cor. 10:31; 6:20; Phil. 1:11).

THE LAW AND SIN

A characterization of sin is that it is a transgression of divine law (1 John 3:4). If people are to be made aware of sin as transgression and be convicted of violating law, they must possess God's stated law (Rom. 3:20). Where there is no law, this guilt cannot be incurred (4:15; 5:13). On the other hand, people without a written divine law are guilty of actual sins on grounds other than transgressing divinely revealed law. Let us consider those who have no written law and those who do.

PAGANS WITHOUT A WRITTEN DIVINE LAW

The apostle Paul points out that pagans, who do not have divinely revealed law like the Law of Moses or Christ's Law (see below), instinctively do things that are prescribed by moral law (Rom. 2:14–15). This is because, being made in the image of God, they possess innate morality, which gives them the ability to distinguish between good and bad, to make moral evaluations and decisions, and to engage in moral activities for which they are responsible to God and to man (vv. 6, 16; 13:1–5). This innate morality is seen in their having consciences and in their community relationships. Although pagans do not have a written divine law, they are guilty of actual sins, based on their violating their consciences and the laws of their communities, which reflect the "law written in their hearts."

Being responsible moral creatures, pagans have the obligation to respond favorably to God's self-revelation in nature and to fulfill basic duties that personal creatures owe the Creator, like gratitude and worship (Rom. 1:18–23). They also have certain civil obligations to each other, which they violate (cp. vv. 29–32; 2 Tim. 3:2–3; Titus 3:3).

When the apostle preached to pagans, he did not use written divine law, like the Mosaic Law, to bring them under the conviction of sin (Acts 14:6–18; 17:15–34; 24:25). Rather, he reminded them of their creaturehood (17:24–26, 28–29) and their guilt of dishonoring God by neglecting to seek after Him (v. 27) and by regarding Him to be less than what He reveals Himself to be in nature (vv. 24–25, 29). Being a messenger of the gospel, he also declared their duty to seek the Lord (v. 27), to repent (v. 30, a synecdoche for salvational faith in Jesus; see Appendix X: "Figures of Association: Synedoche and Metonymy"; cp. v. 18), and to prepare for coming judgment (v. 31). As the experience of Cornelius shows, when people who do not have God's Word seek the true God, He will respond by communicating the gospel to them, whether by missionary, printed page, or other means (Acts 10).

PEOPLE AND THE TEN COMMANDMENTS

While the Mosaic Law was given to Israel as a dispensation, its moral precepts, like the Ten Commandments, may be used universally to bring people under the conviction of sin. Being absolute and timeless, God's moral laws transcend dispensational boundaries. They apply to people of every age everywhere.[42] This is also true of the two greatest laws of the Mosaic Dispensation—our loving God (Deut. 6:5; by our obedience, John 14:15, 21, 23) and our loving our neighbors as ourselves (Lev. 19:18; see Mark 12:19–31; Rom. 13:9; Gal. 5:14; James 2:8; 1 John 5:3).[43]

Having been a rabbi, the apostle Paul was keenly aware of the Mosaic Law in his early Christian life (Rom. 7:7–14). The law made him conscious of the activity of the sin force within him, but it could not deliver him from sin's domination (vv. 15–24). He was to

319

learn that only God can do this by His grace in response to one's submission to and reliance on the Holy Spirit (7:25–8:4; Gal. 2:20; 5:16, 25).

GOSPEL BELIEVERS AND CHRIST'S LAW

We who are saved are under Christ's Law (Cor. 9:21; Gal. 6:2), which consists of the precepts and guiding principles that are given throughout the New Testament (cp. James 1:25, "the law of liberty").[44] We manifest the fullest expression of this law when we allow the Lord's love to work in our hearts and to govern our relations with others (John 13:34–35; Rom. 5:5; 13:8–10; Gal. 6:2; 1 John 3: 16–23; 1 Cor. 13:4–7).

The Old Testament is profitable to the saved person (see "The Old Testament: Its Value" under Bibliology). But we should remember that, although all the Bible is profitable to us who are saved (2 Tim. 3:16), not all of it relates to us. Most of the Old Testament concerns God's law for Israel and His dealings with this nation under the Mosaic Law. Since the Lord's commands for His people today are given in the New Testament, we should follow only those OT directions that reflect, or are in harmony with, these NT commands. For instance, we are not obligated to observe the Mosaic dietary laws or the Levitical rituals (Mark 7:14–19; Rom. 14:2, 14; Heb. 10:1–22), but we are required to fear God (Eccl. 12:13; 1 Peter 2:17).

For the Lord's people, all human laws are subordinate to His law (Acts 5:29). This does not mean that we should disregard man-made laws (Rom. 13:1–8; 1 Peter 2:13–15), but we recognize that in dying with Christ, we have died to man's laws and customs to the extent that we must give God's law priority above all others that conflict with it (Rom. 7:1–6). The apostle Paul sought to accommodate himself to man's sinless customs so as to win unsaved people to Christ (2 Cor. 9:19–23) and to live conscientiously as a Roman citizen (Acts 23:1). Yet, he was ever mindful of his being "in-lawed to Christ" (1 Cor. 9:21). When we know the "good" action that is prescribed by our Lord's law and fail to do it, we sin (James 4:17). But as we look to Him, we can obey Him in His strength (Phil. 1:11; 4:13). To obey God in His way is to do righteousness, which is an evidence of our salvation (1 John 2:29) and a means by which to glorify Him (Matt. 5:16).

A SUMMARY: THE OPERATION OF SINFUL AND RIGHTEOUS ACTIONS

THE SOURCES OF THESE ACTIONS

Sinful action (disobeying God) has its source in the impersonal, resident sin force that uses us for its evil expressions (Rom. 7:17; Mark 7:20–23; Gal. 5:19–21).

Righteous action (obeying God) has its source in the personal indwelling Holy Spirit, who enables us to please God (John 14:16–17; Rom. 8:4; Gal. 5:16; 22–23).

THE STEPS LEADING TO THESE ACTIONS

The steps leading to our sinning (James 1:14–15):
1. The sin force's *seduction*, urging us to sin (Gal. 5:16–17)
2. Our *submission* to this sinful urge (Rom. 6:13a, 19), resulting in our minds' being controlled by sin (8:5)
3. The *conception* of sin in our hearts or minds (Prov. 23:7; Matt. 5:27–28)
4. The *birth* of sin, expressed in our actions and/or attitudes (Luke 6:45; Rom. 6:19; Gal. 5:19–21)
5. The expression of spiritual *death* by our sinning (Rom. 6:21; 8:6; Gal. 6:8). This leads to earlier physical death (Rom. 8:13)

The steps leading to our doing right:
1. God's *appeal*, urging us to obey Him (Rom. 12:2; Eph. 6:6)
2. Our *submission* to Him and His appeal (Rom. 6:13b), resulting in our minds' being controlled by God (Rom. 8:5)
3. The *conception* of right doing in our hearts or minds (Prov. 23:7)
4. The *birth* of right doing, expressed in our actions and/or attitudes (Luke 6:45; Rom. 6:19; 14:17)
5. The expression of spiritual *life* by our doing God's will (Rom. 6:22; 8:6; Gal. 6:8) This leads to longer physical life (Rom. 8:13).

MOTIVATING REASONS FOR NOT DOING WRONG AND FOR DOING RIGHT

(Moral action usually begins with a decision; motivation incites us to make this decision to act as we do.)

For not sinning
1. This is commanded (1 John 2:1).
2. We are dead to sin (Rom. 6:1–3, 11).
3. We are set free from sin's authority (Rom. 6:17; 8:2).
4. We owe sin nothing (Rom. 8:12).
5. Sinning discredits God (Prov. 28:7).
6. Sinning breaks our fellowship with God (1 John 1:5–6).
7. Sinning brings us misery (Prov. 13:15).
8. Sinning causes us to die sooner physically (Rom. 8:13).
9. This brings us loss of reward (1 Cor. 3:15).

For doing right
1. This is commanded (John 14:15).
2. We are alive unto God (Rom. 6:4, 11).
3. We are under God's authority (Rom. 6:18, 22).
4. We owe God everything (2 Cor. 5:14–15).
5. This glorifies God (Matt. 5:16).
6. This maintains our fellowship with God (1 John 1:7).
7. This brings us God's blessings (Luke 11:28).
8. We live longer physically (Rom. 8:13).
9. This brings us gainful reward (1 Cor. 3:14).

Our study of sin has shown us its enslaving and destructive force in the lives of personal creatures who chose to disobey God and of those who are conceived with hereditary corruption. But having been graciously delivered from sin's ruin, bondage, and guilt, we who are saved can now have divine parental forgiveness and cleansing and have decisive victory over actual sins in our daily lives. We also anticipate the time when the Lord will deliver us from this present evil world and will make our mortal bodies like unto His body of glory.

When did you knowingly sin last? What did you do about it? Have you dealt with this by repentance and confession? Are you remembering that you have died to sin and are alive unto God? Did you give your heart to God today? Are you His instrument of righteousness today through whom the Lord can manifest spiritual life and can minister to the needs of others?

A Review of Hamartiology

1. What are the two aspects of the nature of sin?
2. Explain what the sin force is.
3. To what part of human nature is the sin force most closely related?
4. How do we know that the gospel believer still has the sin force?
5. What determines the evil character of sin? Give several basic characteristics of sin.
6. How do we know that God did not create sin?
7. Why did God include sin in His decree?
8. How did sin begin in angels and humans?
9. Why did God create these personal creatures with the ability to commit their first sin?
10. How was Adam's first sin like Eve's sin? How was his sinning different from hers?
11. What were the immediate effects of their first sin?
12. What punishments did God mete out to Eve, the snake, Satan, and Adam?
13. In His judgment on Satan, what did God declare would take place?
14. Why did God banish Adam and Eve from the Garden of Eden?
15. What is original sin? What are its effects upon the human race?
16. What are the two kinds of human races and their heads that now exist?
17. What does the corruption of human nature mean?
18. What is total depravity? Total inability?
19. What evil force was produced within Eve and Adam when they sinned?
20. What death did Eve and Adam experience when they sinned? Describe this death.
21. What are the two theories as to how the guilt of Adam's initial sin was imputed to the human race? Which theory is preferred by the author?
22. Distinguish between the Pelagian, Semi-Pelagian, and Augustinian views on man's depravity. What are the views of the Wesleyans and Calvinists?
23. What are actual sins?
24. What are the causes of actual sins?
25. Describe how the act of sinning occurs.
26. How does sin start involuntarily? Voluntarily?
27. What varieties of sin are there?
28. What is the meaning of divine condemnation? Guilt? Divine punishment?
29. What two kinds of punishment does God mete out to people who sin? To what people is each of these punishments given?
30. Which kind of punishment is remedial and what does this mean?
31. What is the basic idea of forgiveness?
32. What kind of forgiveness does God offer to unsaved people? To saved people?
33. What must one do to receive divine judicial forgiveness? To receive divine parental forgiveness?
34. What is the gospel believer's present relation to the Lord Jesus? 309
35. Explain the gospel believer's relation to each effect, or part, of original sin. *310*
36. Why do gospel believers not have to sin anymore? How can they not sin? What must they do when they are tempted to sin?
37. Why can a gospel believer not sin continuously, as he did before he was saved? *314*
38. What price does a gospel believer pay for sinning? *314*
39. What must saved people do to receive cleansing from sins? 315
40. Describe the Christian's forgiveness of others. *316*
41. What steps must we take to experience victory over sin in our daily lives? 317
42. Although pagans do not have God's written law, by what law do they live? Of what sins may they be convicted? 319

43. Why may the presentation of the Ten Commandments bring people under the con- *319* viction of sin, although they do not live under the Mosaic Law?
44. What law has highest jurisdiction over saved people today? Where do we find this law in the Scriptures? What must we do to keep this law? *320*
45. Summarize the sources of sinful and righteous actions and the steps leading to these actions. *320*
46. What motivating reasons do we have for not doing wrong and for doing right? *321*
47. When did you knowingly sin last? What did you do about it?
48. Did you give God your heart today?

Endnotes

1. While this aspect of sin is commonly called "the sin nature," it is more accurate to speak of it as "the sin force" for the following reasons: *One,* it is called a law (Rom. 7:23, 25; 8:2); *two,* not being created by God, it was not a part of original creation (Gen. 1:31); *three,* it is not an essential part of human nature as those of Adam and Jesus show; and *four,* it must be distinguished from sinful human nature. Contrariwise, I understand "nature" theologically to be the created essence, or substance, that determines the generic kind of being, like human nature or angelic nature. Mankind, whether saved or unsaved, has only human nature. In its unredeemed state, the human nature is sinful and corrupted. All humans on earth have within their bodily flesh the sin force, which would use them and their human natures as its instruments of expression. See A. T. Robertson, *Word Pictures in the New Testament,* 6:208, 1 John 1:8; and W. F. Arndt & F. W. Gingrich, *A Greek-English Lexicon of the New Testament, nomos,* 542.
2. Observe that in the New Testament *flesh* often means the sin force, dominating one's human nature and personhood (see Rom. 7:5; 8:1, 4, 5, 8–9, 12–13; 13:14; 2 Cor. 1:17; 10:2–3, second occurrence of *flesh;* 11:18; Gal. 3:3; 5:13, 16–17, 19, 24; 6:8; Eph. 2:3, first occurrence of *flesh;* Col. 2:23; 2 Peter 2:10, 18; and Jude 23).
3. See John 8:84; Rom. 3:9; 5:20–21; 6:1, 2, 6–7, 10–14, 16–18, 20, 22; 7:14, 17, 20, 23, 25; 8:2–3; Gal. 3:22; and 1 John 1:8.
4. A metonymy is a figure of association, in this case, an effect representing its cause; see Appendix X: "Figures of Association: Synecdoche and Metonymy."
5. This is our personhood and human nature, with our actions, words, thoughts, will, emotions, motivations, attitudes, and intentions.
6. See Ludwig Koehler, *Old Testament Theology,* 169–71.
7. See Kenneth S. Wuest, *Studies in the Vocabulary of the Greek New Testament* (Grand Rapids: Wm. B. Eerdmans Publishing Co., 1945), 95–100.
8. Edward J. Young, *Genesis Three* (London: The Banner of Truth Trust, 1966), 10–14.
9. I believe that at this time Adam lost his world authority to Satan. This is indicated by God's sentence upon Satan (Gen. 3:15), by the fact that man's authority over the earth was not mentioned in the dispensation given to Noah after the flood (Gen. 9:2 with 1:26–28), by Jesus' not contesting the truth of the Devil's offer to give Him the kingdoms of earth (Matt. 4:4:8–9), by Jesus' declaration that Satan is the prince of this world (John 12:31; 14:30; 16:11), and by the writer of the epistle to the Hebrews, asserting "You have put all things in subjection under his (man's) feet. . . . But now we see not yet all things under him (2:8)." When He comes again to establish His earthly messianic kingdom, the Lord Jesus, who broke Satan's lethal power by His resurrection (v. 14; KJV "destroy" means to render powerless), will expel the usurper from earth and will confine him to the Abyss (Rev. 20:1–3). He will rule the earth by divine mandate (Ps. 2:6–9; John 3:35).
10. This understanding of evil was intensified by their concurrent understanding of good, which came from their awareness of morality, inherent to their personhood (Rom. 2:14–15).
11. When God cursed the ground, it seems that He also cursed all of impersonal creation, at least relating to earth (Rom. 8:20–21). This accounts for the disease, ferocity, depredation, decay, and death that we see in animal life and vegetation. As He has imposed this curse, God also

can and will remove it for Jesus' millennial, earthly kingdom (Isa. 11:6–9; chap. 35; Hos. 2:18; Amos 9:13). Besides making man's work laborious and his life hazardous, this divine curse was necessary for man (God's highest earthly creature) to retain his superiority over his environment after his fall (Gen. 9:2).

12. The only one who did not partake of the effects of original sin was the Lord Jesus in His incarnation (1 John 3:5). His divine conception within the virgin Mary, without a human father, avoided His receiving imputed sin and its guilt (Luke 1:35; Matt. 1:20). Also, in forming Jesus' human nature, the Holy Spirit prevented any transmission of inherent corruption from Mary. Perhaps He did this by correcting or excluding any defective genes and by keeping out harmful microorganisms and the sin force, which normally would have been transmitted.

13. As the parable of the wineskins demonstrates (Luke 5:37), the ones that burst perished, or were ruined, in the sense that they no longer could serve their original purpose. Likewise, sin so ruined Adam and Eve that they could no longer, because of their altered, sinful state, be and do that for which they were created for God's glory. Also, see endnote 15.

14. Note the distinction between the expression of spiritual death in behavior and the experience of spiritual death in one's relation to God. The former is that which is conveyed by the sin force through sinful human behavior, even that of saved people (Gal. 6:8; Rom. 8:6); the latter is the state of unsaved people's being spiritually separated from God (Eph. 2:1; cp. 4:18).

15. Two effects of original sin—the corruption of human nature and the sin force—together are sometimes called "hereditary corruption." Note that Adam and Eve, by their sinning, corrupted their personhoods. However, the personhoods of their posterity, being divinely created without sin at conception, are corrupted the moment that they are joined to the newly conceived corrupted human natures.

16. This sense of moral defilement, resulting from acting contrary to the conscience and from deserving divine punishment for sinning, is indicated by the divine cleansing of the conscience (Heb. 9:14; 10:2–4) and by divine forgiveness (cancellation of sin's punishment) when the value of our Lord's atoning work is divinely applied to the repentant sinner, whether unsaved (Acts 15:9; 1 Cor. 6:11; Eph. 5:26; 1 Peter 1:22) or saved (1 John 1:7, 9). God regards anyone who is holy, or without sin, as being "clean" and anyone who is not holy, or with sin, as being "unclean" (Lev. 10:10). This divine cleansing also purges the saved person's personhood, soul, and spirit of any moral contamination that may have been received by sinning (2 Cor. 7:1).

17. Still, as we shall see, no one will go to hell solely because of Adam's sin. In my opinion, infants and mentally disabled people who die before they are personally accountable for their actions are covered by the Lord's atoning work. People who go to hell are guilty not only of original sin but also of those actual sins that they committed during their accountable lifetime in this world (see "The Salvation of Infants" under Soteriology).

18. See "The Resurrection of Mankind" under Anthropology.

19. "Soulish" implies not sinfulness but the manner in which the body is presently animated, or made alive (see "Humans Are Complex Beings: The human soul" under Anthropology). "Spiritual" implies that the changed body (Phil. 3:20–21) will be animated by the Holy Spirit (Rom. 8:11). See "The Resurrection of Mankind" under Anthropology.

20. This is in contrast to the unsaved who are enslaved to spiritual death and physical death (Eph. 2:1; Heb. 2:14–15).

21. See W. G. T. Shedd, *History of Christian Doctrine* (New York: Charles Scribner & Co., 1868), 2:50–186.

22. H. Orton Wiley, *Christian Theology* (Kansas City: Beacon Hill Press, n.d.), 2:108, 136ff.

23. See Leo G. Cox, "Prevenient Grace—A Wesleyan View," *Journal of the Evangelical Theological Society* (1969), 143–49.

24. See H. Sheldon Smith, *Changing Conceptions of Original Sin* (New York: Charles Scribner's Sons, 1955), chap. 9.

25. For "The Unforgivable Sin" and "The Sin unto Death," see the Addenda.

26. God's holy hatred, with its expressions of anger and judgment, is not an evil attitude that expresses itself periodically by outbursts of uncontrollable emotion. It is the judicial reaction

of His holy nature in its opposition against sin and sinners. God's holiness, justice, and righteousness demand that sin's penalty be paid, that divine justice be satisfied, and that divine law be upheld. See "God's Attributes" under Theology Proper.

27. See Floyd H. Barackman, *Victors, Not Victims* (Grand Rapids: Kregel Publications, 1993).

28. Our immaterial natures were corrupted by their being propagated by our human parents, whether saved or unsaved, because of their unsaved bodies; our divinely created personhoods were corrupted by their union with the corrupted human natures at the moment of conception. Furthermore, with its salvation, our immaterial human natures are never made divine (2 Peter 1:4), which would make us to be God. To partake of the divine nature does not necessarily make us divine anymore than ingesting an apple makes us an apple. By receiving the Holy Spirit at salvation, it can be said that we partook of the divine nature (cp. 1 Cor. 10:18).

29. In 1 Cor. 5:5, the apostle Paul was not necessarily suggesting that the saved person's spirit is not now saved. The discipline, which he directed the church to administer, is remedial to the extent that the sinning person will remain saved and experience the final aspect of his salvation when Jesus comes (cp. Rom. 13:11; 1 Cor. 11:32).

30. This is what the apostle Paul had in view when he commanded that we mortify (put to death) our members (bodies) that are upon the earth (Col. 3:5). We do this by reckoning ourselves, including our bodies, to be dead to sin and alive unto God and by giving ourselves to God for His use and direction (Rom. 6:11–13; 12:1–2).

31. "Body" here is a synecdoche for the total person; cp. James 4:7; see Appendix X: "Figures of Association: Synecdoche and Metonymy."

32. The gift of "eternal life" is not God's own divine life, which belongs exclusively to His divine nature and by which He has self-existence. "Eternal life" or "everlasting life" is Jesus' spiritual life, by which He as man has a spiritual relationship and fellowship with the Father. When we receive Jesus' physical life at His return, His image will be completed in us (Rom. 8:29; 1 Cor. 15:49).

33. Observe that, although we have died to sin, the sin force itself is not dead nor can we slay it. Some refer to Galatians 5:24 as supporting the idea that "the flesh," or the sin force, with its passions and desires, has been put to death in the believer and that he must consider it to be inactive. Since other passages clearly state that we who are saved died to this evil force (Rom. 6:1–2, 11) and that this force is still active in us (7:19–20), the passage in question must be understood with these truths in view. As God sees it, our participation in Jesus' death, which condemned sin (8:3), broke the power of the sin force in our lives to the extent that we can regard it as having been crucified. What we were in Adam, dominated by sin's power, died (6:6). Thus, through death with Jesus, we were set free from this force (vv. 7, 17–18, 22). While the sin force is as active as ever, in God's sight its power is broken in our lives since we died to it. Now we must consider this to be true and respond only to God and His demands.

34. Note that the second half of Romans 8:1 does not occur in many Greek manuscripts.

35. See 1 John 3:8–9. The present tense of these verbs indicates continuous action. See Barackman, *Victors, Not Victims*, 44–48.

36. See "The Prophecy of Jesus' Appraisal of His Church" under Eschatology.

37. We also sin when we yield ourselves to the temptations of our external enemies—Satan and the world. Our victory over these enemies is achieved by the same procedure as that given here for victory over the sin force (see James 4:7).

38. We also died to the world and its leader, Satan (Gal. 6:14; Col. 2:20). Review "The Believer's Relation to Original Sin" above.

39. This helps us understand Romans 8:13, to "mortify (put to death) the deeds of the body." Counting ourselves, including our body, to be dead to the sin force, we avoid being used by sin for its sinful expressions by giving ourselves to God and allowing Him to use us and our bodies for righteous deeds and Christlikeness.

40. Observe that our yielding to God's control does not render us unable to give ourselves to the sin force when we decide to do so. While we are under the influence of the moral force that possesses our heart, at any time we have the liberty to give ourselves to the opposite force and

its influence. We are warned, however, against misusing this liberty, which has been given to us for loving others and serving God (Gal. 5:13; 1 Peter 2:16), by yielding ourselves to the demands of sin.

41. See Appendix F: "Learning and Doing God's Will"; Appendix E: "Righteousness and Holiness."

42. Observe that nine of the Ten Commandments are covered by the present Dispensation of Grace (1 John 5:21; Eph. 6:2–3; 1 Thess. 4:3–5; Eph. 4:28; Col. 3:5, 9). The single exception is Sabbath-keeping, which is nowhere commanded in the New Testament for us today. With our freedom in Christ, we may regard any day or every day as "unto the Lord" (Rom. 14:5–7).

43. Proper self-love consists of self-respect, based on a sense of self-worth (2 Cor. 5:17; Phil. 3:20; John 17:6, 9) and self-care (Eph. 5:29). If we do not have these for ourselves, we shall not have respect or care for others. See Appendix Z: "Our Loving God and Others."

44. See "The Dispensation of Grace" under Theology Proper; and Appendix F: "Learning and Doing God's Will."

Soteriology

10

SOTERIOLOGY
The Doctrine of Salvation

The apostle Paul exhorted the Ephesian gospel believers to put on the helmet of salvation as a part of their armor against Satan (Eph. 6:17). This helmet seems to represent an essential knowledge of salvation and its delivering power in daily life. Because of our familiarity with the gospel, it is easy for those of us who are saved to treat this doctrine lightly. However, it is urgent that we learn all that God has revealed about it for our personal blessing and for the benefit of others. Having been given the ministry of reconciliation to a lost world, it behooves us as the Lord's ambassadors to learn all we can about God's work of reconciliation (2 Cor. 5:18–20). A fuller understanding of salvation's need, benefits, provision, application, and components will help us to be more efficient witnesses to unsaved people (Acts 1:8) and will give us a greater appreciation for all that God has so graciously done for us (Ps. 68:19).

THE NATURE OF SALVATION

ITS BIBLICAL DESCRIPTION
Essentially, salvation is a deliverance. To save is to rescue or to deliver someone from calamity, loss, or destruction. In the Bible, the word has both secular and spiritual meanings.

Its Secular Meaning
Secular salvation is a deliverance from some natural or physical danger or affliction (Exod. 14:30; Ps. 34:6; Matt. 14:30; Acts 27:42–44).

Its Spiritual Meaning
Spiritual salvation is deliverance from the ruin, guilt, and debt of our sins as well as from bondage to our spiritual enemies and their works in our lives. These spiritual enemies are the sin force, Satan, and the world of unsaved people (Eph. 2:1–10).

ITS THEOLOGICAL DESCRIPTION
Theologically, salvation is a blanket term for all that takes place spiritually in people when they trust in the Lord Jesus as their Savior from sin. A theological description of salvation is this: Salvation is the gracious work of God whereby He delivers gospel believing sinners from the guilt, penalty, and ruin of their sins and from bondage to their spiritual enemies and their works; brings them into a right, vital relationship with Himself; and bestows upon them the abundant benefits of His grace.

THE CHRONOLOGICAL ASPECTS OF SALVATION

Timewise, a gospel believer experiences several phases of salvation: past, present, and future.

IN THE PAST

This was the time when the gospel believer trusted in Jesus and His atoning work for his salvation (2 Tim. 1:9). He was immediately and forever delivered from divine condemnation (Rom. 5:1), divine retribution (v. 9), hereditary corruption of personhood, soul, and spirit (Acts 15:9; 1 Peter 1:22), and bondage to his spiritual enemies—the sin force (Rom. 6:6–7), Satan (Acts 26:18), and the world (John 15:19).

DURING THE PRESENT

This is the saved person's lifetime since his salvation, when he experiences occasions of deliverance (James 1:21) from the urges and domination of the sin force, the temptations of Satan, and the evil allurements of the world (Gal. 5:16; James 1:27; 4:7). Moreover, with the help of the Holy Spirit he also expresses the reality and qualities of his new life in Christ (Phil. 2:12–13; Gal. 5:25) as he submits to the Lord's authority and obeys His Word (Pss. 1:1–3; 119:11).

IN THE FUTURE

The saved person anticipates the future deliverance of his body (Rom. 13:11) from hereditary corruption and the resident sin force (Phil. 3:20–21) as well as his physical removal from this world to heaven when Jesus returns for His Church (Gal. 1:4; 1 Thess. 4:13–17).

THE NEED FOR SALVATION

People's need for salvation is marked by the lack of necessary spiritual realities in their lives as well as the presence of undesirable ones. Before one can be saved, one must be made aware that one is a sinner (a breaker of God's laws) and has spiritual needs (cp. John 4:15–19; 6:34–36; 16:7–11). While sinners may feel more pressing needs, like physical or material ones, their primary needs concern their sins and their deliverance from guilt, penalty, ruin, and bondage. Keep in mind that Jesus came to be the Savior from sin (Matt. 1:21; 1 John 3:5). Only when the matter of sin is divinely settled in the lives of sinners can they receive God's blessings and His help for other needs that they may have. In their natural, unsaved condition before God, all people are as follows:

1. *They are sinners by constitution (Rom. 5:19) and by practice (Eph. 2:3; Rom. 1:21–32; 3:9–18; Titus 3:3).*

They are conceived as sinners with original sin and in time commit actual sins. They sin by breaking God's laws (1 John 3:4) and by failing to attain His moral standard for His personal creatures (Rom. 3:10, 23).

2. *They are slaves of sin (John 8:34; Rom. 3:9; 6:16–17).*

Their lives are wholly dominated by the sin force as well as by Satan (Acts 26:18; 1 John 5:19, "in the wicked one") and by the world, of which they are a part (John 15:19). See Ephesians 2:1–3.

3. *They are condemned by God (John 3:18).*

They have already been found guilty by God and have been sentenced to hell for their sins (Rom. 3:9–19; 5:18). Their future judgment concerns their accountability for their lifetime behavior and the degree of punishment that they deserve (Rev. 20:11–15; Matt. 11:22).

4. *They are indebted to God for their sins (Gen. 2:17; Ezek. 18:4; Rom. 6:23).*

They are obligated to bear the punishment of their sins. They can never pay off this debt of everlasting hell and gain their release (Matt. 25:46).

5. *They are enemies of God (Rom. 5:10).*

Because of their sinful state, they are hostile and rebellious toward Him (John 3:20; Rom. 3:12, 18; 8:7), and God is angry with them (John 3:36; Rom. 1:18).

6. *They are lost or ruined (Luke 19:10; Rom. 3:9–18; 2 Cor. 4:3).*

They are not lost to God's view, but they are wholly, ruinously affected by sin and have a natural bent toward sinning.

7. *They are spiritually dead toward God and divine things (Eph. 2:1; 4:18; Rom. 1:21–23; 3:11; 1 Cor. 2:9, 14).*

They are naturally unresponsive to the things of God. On the other hand, they are very responsive, or alive, to sin, Satan, and the world (Eph. 2:2–3).

8. *They are the spiritual children of Satan (John 8:44) and a part of the world-system that is evil in God's sight (John 3:16; 7:7; 15:19; Rom. 3:19; Eph. 2:2).*

Thus they are in bondage to these evil forces (see above) and will suffer their fate (Matt. 25:41; 1 John 2:17).

9. *They are helpless to correct their spiritual condition or to provide for their spiritual needs (Rom. 5:6; Eph. 2:8–9).*

They need a rescuer; they need the Lord Jesus—the only Savior!

Observe that this is the spiritual condition of all humans who are not saved. This description and the Lord's instruction to evangelize the unsaved (Luke 24:47) indicate that all humans need to be delivered from the guilt, penalty, ruin, and bondage of their sins. Having the continual witness of divine general revelation, they who have not heard the gospel have the duty of seeking the Creator and fulfilling their basic duties to Him (Rom. 1:19–20; Acts 17:23–29) as well as obeying the law written in their hearts (Rom. 2:14–15). Moreover, they who respond favorably to God's witness in creation and who want to know more about Him will in time be given the gospel, which informs them how they can personally know God and be rightly related to Him (cp. Acts 10:1–43). This gospel ministry is the work of worldwide evangelical missions.

THE BENEFITS OF SALVATION

Salvation immediately brings radical changes in the gospel believer's nature and behavior as well as in his or her relationship to God. Although we shall consider these more thoroughly later, here is a list of these benefits.

1. *Saved people are no longer sinners but saints or holy persons (1 Cor. 1:2; 6:11).*

They no longer belong to the category of sinner, although they still sin. Set apart in Christ, they are holy or sanctified people.

2. *Saved people are no longer slaves of the sin force, Satan, and the world but are now slaves of the Lord Jesus and righteousness (Rom. 6:16–19; 14:8; 1 Cor. 7:22).*

Their duty is to live unto the Lord Jesus and to do His will (2 Cor. 5:14–15).

3. *Saved people are no longer divinely condemned but are now justified (Rom. 5:1, 9, 18).*

They have been acquitted of condemnation and have been made righteous in Jesus and have been declared so by God (Rom. 8:30–34; 2 Cor. 5:21).

4. *Saved people are no longer indebted to God for their sins but are now judicially forgiven of all their sins (Acts 10:43; Eph. 1:7; Col. 2:13).*

They are forever released from the divine judicial punishment, or retribution, of all their sins—past, present, and future.

5. *Saved people are no longer enemies of God but are now His friends (Rom. 5:10; Col. 1:21).*

The war is over! God's anger has been placated by the Lord's atoning sacrifice (1 John 4:10). Now His people must express loving friendship by their obedience to Him (John 15:14).

6. *Saved people are no longer spiritually ruined but are now new creatures in Christ (2 Cor. 5:17).*

Their personhoods and inner human natures have been renewed, with a bent toward doing God's will and with the capability of understanding spiritual truth, making right decisions, and expressing holy emotions (Eph. 2:10; 4:24; 1 Peter 1:22).

7. *Saved people are no longer spiritually dead but are now alive toward God (John 5:24; Eph. 2:1).*

Having eternal life, they each now have a personal relationship with God and are responsive to divine things (Eph. 2:13; 5:1–2).

8. *Saved people are no longer the spiritual children of Satan and a part of this world-system but are now children of God and citizens of His kingdom (John 1:12; 3:3, 5; Col. 1:134).*

Being free to serve God (Gal. 5:1, 13), they are now responsible to God's authority and are the objects of His blessings and care (cp. Matt. 6:24–33; 7:7–11).

9. *Saved people are no longer helpless but now have the indwelling Holy Spirit as their Helper (John 14:16–17) and the spiritual life of Jesus for their vitality (Phil. 4:13).*

This divine Helper (KJV "Comforter") and the vigor of our Lord's spiritual life enable them to be and to do all that God requires of them (Gal. 5:16, 22–23; 2:20).

We who are saved have cause to thank God daily for the radical changes that He has brought about in our lives. These gracious benefits are manifest in our lives when we walk in God's fellowship and live in His will and power with the help of the Holy Spirit.

THE PROVISION OF SALVATION

This explains why God sacrificially gave His only begotten Son for the salvation of sinners (unsaved people) and why they must trust in Jesus and His atoning work to be saved (John 3:16). Since sinners cannot deliver themselves from their spiritual plight and there is no other deliverer, God has graciously provided His Son to be their Savior (Matt. 1:21; John 14:6; Acts 4:12; 1 John 4:9–10). To help us understand this divine provision, let us consider the following question and its answer.

THE QUESTION

How can God, who is holy and just, rightly deliver sinners from the divine retribution that they deserve and bring them into a right relationship with Himself? His holiness moves Him to oppose and condemn sinners and their sins; His justice requires Him to deal with sinners as they deserve. Contrary to the view of sentimentalists, God cannot in love override His holiness and ignore His justice (cp. Luke 19:41–44). How, then, can God rightly justify sinners who deserve hell?

THE ANSWER

While He could not change His holy demands against sinners, God Himself, as their substitute, could satisfy these demands on their behalf. With deliberate, measureless love and grace (Rom. 9:15; Eph. 2:4–6), God the Father gave His Son as a sacrifice for humanity's sins (Isa. 53:10; John 1:29; 3:16; 1 John 4:9–10), and God the Son gave His life to pay provisionally the debt of these sins (Matt. 20:28; 1 Cor. 15:3–4; 1 Peter 2:24;

Rom. 5:8; Heb. 9:26; 1 John 2:2). Jesus' atoning work required His bearing these sins and His being made sin (1 Peter 2:24; 2 Cor. 5:21), His experiencing spiritual death and the divine offering of His blood (Matt. 27:46; Heb. 9:22; 1 Peter 1:18–19), and His dying physically and rising from the dead (Heb. 2:14; 1 Cor. 15:54–55). On the basis of this substitutionary sacrifice, God can now freely and justly save everyone who trusts in the Savior and His atoning work (John 3:16, 18, 36; Rom. 3:21–26).

The apostle Paul described the answer to this question by using the word *cross* and the gospel declaration of the Atonement by the phrase, "the preaching of the cross" (1 Cor. 1:18, 22–23; 2:1–2). This is what people must believe about Jesus to be saved—that He, as the Son of God, is the only living Savior from sin and the only way to God (Acts 4:12; John 14:6; 20:31; Rom. 10:9–10; review "The Nature of Jesus' Atoning Work" under Christology).

THE APPLICATION AND RECEPTION OF SALVATION

This concerns the divine and human activities that are involved in sinners receiving salvation from their sins. These two activities are described as "sanctification by the [Holy] Spirit and [the sinner's] belief in the truth" (2 Thess. 2:13) and as his "obedience [to the gospel] and the sprinkling of the blood of Jesus" (1 Peter 1:2). This sprinkling of blood is the divine application of the Atonement's value to the gospel believer. Let us look at God's part and the sinner's part in the application and reception of salvation.

GOD'S PART IN THE APPLICATION OF SALVATION

Although the sinner has something to do to be saved (John 6:28–29; Rom. 10:9–10), salvation is wholly God's work in all who respond favorably to the gospel (Eph. 2:8–9). God's part in the application of salvation is given in Romans 8:28–30.

God's Salvational Actions Before the Beginning of Time

1. *God elected those whom He would save (Rom. 8:28b; Eph. 1:4; 2 Thess. 2:13).*
Note that those "who are the called according to His purpose" are the elect, whom God has chosen to save according to His decree.[1]
    a. *Definitions*
       1) God's election
       Divine election is the sovereign act of God whereby He freely chose certain human beings for salvation.
       2) God's preterition ✓✓
       Divine preterition is God's passing by those whom He did not choose to save and His allowing them to perish.
    I prefer the term *preterition* for God's action toward the nonelect rather than *election,* for the latter involves God's sovereign action in fulfilling the purpose of His choice while *preterition* does not involve this divine action. While God is active in bringing about the salvation of those whom He has chosen to save, He is not active in bringing about the unsaved state of those whom He did not choose to save. Their unsaved condition and retribution are due to their own wrong choices and sinning (cp. Rom. 9:22–23). Thus, preterition avoids the false concept that God causes the nonelect to be unsaved in the same sense that He causes the elect to be saved (see Appendix J: "The Order of God's Decree").
    b. *Features of divine election*
       1) God's election was sovereign.
       This means that He freely chose whom He would save according to His good pleasure (Eph. 1:9, 11). He was not prompted or influenced by people's works, merit, or worth, none of which existed at the time of this choice (cp. Rom. 9:11, 15–16).[2]

2) God's election was gracious.

It was an act of undeserved favor toward people who would be sinners (Rom. 11:5).

3) God's election was eternal.

It was a part of His eternal plan (Eph. 1:4).

4) God's election was in Christ.

All of God's purpose for the elect, as well as for everything not voluntarily affected by sin (cp. Eph. 1:10; Col. 1:20), is in Christ Jesus (Eph. 3:11), including their being made alive in Jesus (1 Cor. 15:22), their blessings (Eph. 1:3), and their election (1:4). As God's Agent in carrying out the efficient aspect of the divine plan (1 Cor. 8:6), the Lord Jesus encompasses the whole program of God, as it relates to the salvation and the destiny of the elect. All the worth, which His people have, is because of Him (1:30; 2 Cor. 5:17; Eph. 2:10).

   c. Objections to divine election

     1) "His choosing only some to be saved was not fair."

God's choice was not unfair, for all people, being sinners, deserved hell. Had they deserved heaven and were not chosen, then such discrimination would have been unjust. Moreover, the Creator, who is absolutely just, has the right to do whatever He pleases with His creatures (Rom. 9:14–24). Because His pleasure is always in harmony with His nature, His choice was sovereign, gracious, and just.

     2) "If He chose some to be saved, then He also elected the remainder to be lost."

This view is called the "decree of reprobation." God's selecting some to be saved inevitably left the rest to suffer for their sins. However, His passing by the nonelect did not necessitate, or bring about, their perdition, although His decree made it certain. While divine election is an efficient cause in the salvation of the elect, preterition is not an efficient cause in the perdition of the nonelect. God simply decided to leave the nonelect alone to their self-chosen sins and their consequences.[3] Seeing this distinction in Romans 9:22–23, the apostle Paul declared that God prepared "the vessels of mercy" (the elect) unto glory, but he did not say that God fitted "the vessels of wrath" (the nonelect) unto destruction. Sinners fit themselves for divine judgment by their sinning.

     3) "Divine election concerns only service."

This statement ignores 2 Thessalonians 2:13; Ephesians 1:4; and Romans 11:5–6. The principle and character of divine election remains the same, regardless of its application (cp. Rom. 9).

  2. God predestinated those whom He would save (Rom. 8:29; Eph. 1:5, 11–12).

   a. Definition

Predestination is the sovereign act of God whereby He determined beforehand what He would do with those whom He elected to salvation.[4]

   b. Features of predestination

Keep in mind that, in its narrow sense, salvation refers to deliverance from sin. Upon choosing whom He would save, God then decided beforehand what He would do with these chosen people when He delivered them from their sins.[5]

     1) He predestinated them to adoption (Eph. 1:5).

This determined what these elect people would be. While the new birth makes gospel believers God's children by bringing them into His family, adoption gives these children the status of adult-sons within God's family. This means that all saved people equally have all the privileges and duties that belong to this position.

     2) He predestinated them to conformity to Christ (Rom. 8:29).

This determined what kind of adult-sons these elect people would be. God decided that saved people should be like His Son, Jesus (Heb. 2:10–12). While gospel believers shall never share in our Lord's deity, they are being made in the image of His glorified humanity (2 Cor. 3:18). This is because He is the Head and Pattern of the new humanity, of which Christians are a part (1 Cor. 15:22, 45–49). God will bring this conformity to completion at the Lord's return, when our bodies will be made like His body of glory (1 Cor. 15:50–53; Phil. 3:20–21; 1 John 3:2; see Appendix V: "The Human Body-Grid"). This image also includes His moral likeness (Eph. 1:4; 5:27; 1 Cor. 1:8).

3) He predestinated them unto the praise of His glory (Eph. 1:11–12).

This determined what the ultimate purpose for the existence of saved people would be. The glory of God consists of some manifestation of His divine qualities (Ps. 19:1; John 2:11; 17:4). We glorify God when we allow Him to manifest His character in us and to do His works through us (Phil. 1:20; 4:13) and when we give Him praise (Rom. 11:33–36; Matt. 5:16). Also, by our salvation we glorify God in a way that angels can never do. We who are saved will forever be the supreme manifestation of His grace, for He gave His Son for our salvation and gave us an incalculable inheritance in Him (cp. Eph. 1:11–12; 2:7; John 3:16). God decided that our very existence should glorify Him, and He also decided how this should be done (Eph. 1:18, 23; 2:7, 10; 3:10).

God's Salvational Actions During the Lifetime of the Elect

1. God calls (Rom. 8:30; Acts 2:39; 1 Tim. 6:12).[6]

    a. Definition

    This is the act of God whereby He commands sinners through the gospel to receive His gift of salvation in Jesus.[7]

    b. Features of divine calling

    Calvinists recognize two kinds of divine calls to salvation: a general call and a special call. The general call is that which God extends through the gospel to the nonelect (Matt. 22:14; cp. 11:28; Mark 16:15; Isa. 45:22). This call does not result in their salvation. The special call is that which God extends through the gospel to the elect and which results in their salvation (1 Cor. 1:2, 9, 24; Rom. 8:28, 30; 1 Thess. 2:12). This is sometimes identified as God's effectual call.

    This special call to the elect appears to be more than a command to receive the Savior. It embraces the whole presalvational work of God in bringing them to exercise salvational faith in Jesus, including the following divine activities: One, God sweeps away satanic blindness (2 Cor. 4:3–6) and gives understanding of the gospel (Acts 8:30; 16:14; 2 Cor. 4:6). Two, He convicts the elect of their sins (John 16:8–11). And three, imparting repentance (Acts 5:31; 11:18; 2 Tim. 2:25) and faith (2 Peter 1:1; Acts 3:16), He draws the elect person to Himself (John 6:37, 44). Since this divine activity occurs below the level of human awareness, the person's desire and decision to receive the Savior are, in effect, his or her own.

    Steps one and two apply also to the nonelect as a part of God's general call. Hebrews 6:4–6 portrays one who, being at the threshold of salvational faith, is warned not to fall away from trusting in Jesus and His atoning work. Should the person fall away from doing this, he or she would never be restored to this place again. On the other hand, the good works of people who are saved bear witness to their salvational faith and to the fact of their salvation (vv. 9–10; James 2:14–26).[8]

    Holding that sinners must be made spiritually alive before they can believe the gospel, Calvinists speak of this presalvational work as "regeneration" and the experience of salvation as "conversion." However, the Scriptures show that the impartation of spiritual life follows faith in Christ (John 1:12; 3:16, 36; 6:53). God can give salvational faith to one who is spiritually dead as readily as He can make inanimate stones cry out (Luke 19:40). The divine gift of salvational faith itself has the inherent force to enable its recipients to trust in the Savior just as the gift of life enables them to live.

    c. Questions about divine calling

       1) "Is God's general call genuine and sincere?"

        Regardless what His secret decree may be, God's revealed desire for all people is that they be saved (1 Tim. 2:4; 2 Peter 3:9). Thus, He sincerely extends to the nonelect the general call to salvation through the gospel, which He knows will be refused. On the other hand, anyone who wants to be saved may respond to the call and be saved (John 3:16; Acts 10:43; 17.30). Because of the universal and provisional qualities of the Lord's atoning work, there is something substantive for the nonelect to believe or to reject (1 John 2:2; 2 Cor. 5:19).

       2) "Is God's special call irresistible?"

        God's calling does not consciously coerce people's will. It works within their hearts, below their awareness. God's special call to salvation is irresistible, not in the sense that it is never resisted, but in the sense it is never resisted successfully. On the other hand, the truth of God's general call makes it the duty of all people to believe the gospel when they hear it (Luke 13:3; Acts 20:21).

    2. God justifies (Rom. 8:30).

    Upon exercising salvational faith in Jesus and His atoning work, the believer experiences God's saving work, of which justification is a part. Doing all that He promises through the gospel, God delivers gospel believers from the guilt, penalty, ruin, and bondage of their sins and imparts to them spiritual life. Later, we shall consider justification as a component of salvation.

God's Salvational Action in the Future

    The apostle Paul wrote that those whom God justified He also glorified (Rom. 8:30). Being already accomplished in God's mind, glorification speaks of the completion of the salvational experience of gospel believers (v. 23; 13:11). This will take place when God delivers their bodies from mortality (corruptibility, if dead), inherent corruption, and the resident sin force, and He changes them for the future state (1 Cor. 15:50–53). This will take place when Jesus returns for His Church (Phil. 3:20–21; 1 Thess. 4:13–17) and later for other redeemed people when He returns to earth to establish His millennial kingdom (Rev. 20:4–6; Matt. 8:11).

    Observe that these divine activities show that salvation is wholly God's work from start to finish (Luke 18:24–27). Sinners cannot make it, earn it, or buy it (Eph. 2:8–10). Because of their total depravity (Rom. 3:10–12), inability (John 6:44), and unwillingness (5:40), sinners, left to themselves, would never seek God (Rom. 3:11). Thus, God receives all the credit for their salvation (1 Cor. 1:26–31). We who are saved readily give Him praise and thanksgiving for what He has done for us.

THE SINNER'S PART IN THE RECEPTION OF SALVATION

    Although salvation is wholly the work of God, there is something that a person must do to be saved from sin and its woeful effects (Matt. 7:21; John 6:28–29; 20:30–31). He or she must believe the gospel, or the good news of salvation in Jesus (Mark 16:15; Acts 14:7, 21; Rom. 1:15–16; 1 Cor. 15:1–2; Eph. 1:13; 2 Thess. 1:8; 1 Peter 4:17). This exercise of faith in the gospel should not be regarded as a meritorious work for which God gives salvation as a reward or pay. Rather, it is the personal reception of God's gracious offer of His forgiveness of sins and of His gift of spiritual life in Christ Jesus. Furthermore, the gospel believer cannot receive any credit for believing the gospel, for salvational faith is God's gift, even when this faith seems to be one's own (2 Peter 1:1; Acts 3:16; 11:18). Let us look more closely at this salvational faith in the gospel, especially its parts, its use, and God's response to it. Needless to say, it is urgent that we understand this truth so that we can more clearly present the gospel to others as well as have greater knowledge concerning it ourselves.

The Parts of Salvational Faith

What does it mean to believe the gospel, to receive Jesus as Savior, or to exercise salvational faith in Him and His atoning work? It is more than asking Jesus to come into one's heart to go to heaven. This salvational belief consists of several ingredients—repentance, assent, and trust.

1. *Repentance (Luke 13:3; Acts 20:21; 26:20)*

This does not mean a change of life as though a Christian must reform before he trusts in the Savior.[9] Repentance is a change of mind and attitude toward God and the things of which the gospel speaks (cp. Matt. 21:29). The sinner normally is hostile toward God, indifferent toward divine things, and exalts himself above God (John 3:20; Rom. 3:11–12, 18; 1 Cor. 2:14). Also, he seeks to justify his wrongdoing or makes excuses for it. But when he repents, he manifests this by such attitudinal "works" as humbling himself before God, submitting to His authority, and repudiating his sins (Acts 26:20; Prov. 28:13). The awareness of the holiness of God and the enormity of his sins give the repentant sinner sorrow of heart, from which true repentance rises (2 Cor. 7:10). This change of mind and attitude is brought about by God (Acts 5:31; 11:18; 2 Tim. 2:25). Without it, there is no salvation (Luke 13:3). A repentant sinner is not smiling when he is believing the gospel. Joy comes as a result of his salvation.

2. *Assent to the facts of the gospel (Acts 16:14, 32; 1 Cor. 15:1–4)*

These facts are what the gospel says about people's spiritual need (see "The Need for Salvation" in this chapter), God's gracious provision of salvation in Christ (see "The Provision of Salvation" in this chapter), and what the sinner must do to be saved. To give assent to these facts is to acknowledge their truthfulness. Rather than being a nonrational leap into some undefined experience, salvational faith embraces what God says in His Word about the sinner's need for salvation and its divine provision, based on Jesus' atoning death and resurrection (Rom. 10:8, 17; 2 Tim. 3:15; 4:2, 5; 1 Peter 1:23, 25). The presentation of these facts should be accompanied with explanation so that they may be meaningful to unsaved people who are ignorant of these truths (Acts 8:30–35; 17:2–3).

3. *Trust in the Lord Jesus and His atoning work (John 1:12; Gal. 2:16)*

This is indicated by the phrase "believe on His name" (John 1:12), which is to trust in who Jesus is and what He has done. Being more than a general faith in God or in Jesus, this is a sinner's specifically placing his complete trust in Jesus and His atoning work for the purpose of receiving God's deliverance from sin and His gift of spiritual life.

Because of widespread faulty or incomplete instruction, many people miss salvation at this point. They direct their faith to some physical, invitational action like saying a prayer, raising a hand, or walking an aisle rather than to Jesus and His sacrifice for their salvation. He alone is the living Savior from sin; one must place one's trust in Him for this purpose (Acts 4:12). Many people are not confronted with the fact that their sins are the primary issue between them and God. While other problems may seem greater, salvation concerns deliverance from the guilt, penalty, ruin, and bondage of their sins and their being brought into a right relationship with God, whom they have offended. It does not concern the state of their finances, health, social relationships, and the like. The salvational faith that sinners must exercise to be saved consists of these three ingredients. If any of these is missing, then they do not experience salvation.

The Exercise of Salvational Faith

How does a person believe the gospel? Consider what the apostle Paul wrote about this in Romans 10:10. There are inward and outward aspects of this exercise of salvational faith.

1. *Inwardly*
    There is decision of will and enactment of faith.
    a. *Decision*
        He must decide to believe in Jesus and His atoning work for his salvation. This decision is an act of the will in response to God's appeal through the gospel (Acts 16:31; 17:30).
    b. *Enactment*
        The gospel believer then enacts his decision by believing the gospel. He does this by carrying out the three ingredients of salvational faith: assent to the facts of the gospel, repentance, and trust in Jesus and His atoning work (Rom. 10:10a). This hearty response involves the total self, including the will and the mind. God is aware of this heart-trust in His Son and His atoning work and responds as He has promised (1 Chron. 28:9; 1 John 3:20).
2. *Outwardly*
    Having decided to believe the gospel and having done this, then he should express his faith in Jesus to God by prayer, confessing his sinful state and expressing his trust in Jesus as his Savior (Rom. 10:10b, 13; cp. Matt. 12:34). While God immediately responds to the inner exercise of faith, the outward verbal confession, which expresses the inner, intangible faith, is important to the gospel believer. It defines and fixes for future reference the specific action and time of his trust in the Savior for salvation.

God's Response to Salvational Faith

God immediately responds to salvational faith (Rom. 10:13) with the following:

One: He applies to the gospel believer the value of Jesus' atoning work and cancels the judicial guilt and debt of all his sins—past, present, and future (Acts 10:43; Eph. 1:7; Col. 1:13).

Two: He inwardly cleanses and renews the gospel believer's personhood, soul, and spirit (Titus 3:5) and gives him spiritual life (John 3:16). This imparts the capacity for Christlikeness and the capability to express this in daily behavior.

Three: Placing the gospel believer in Christ, God makes him a new creature in Christ (2 Cor. 5:17; Eph. 2:10). He also puts Jesus' righteousness on his account and makes him righteous in Christ (Rom. 4:22–25; 1 Cor. 1:30; 2 Cor. 5:21).

Four: He admits the gospel believer into His family and His kingdom (John 1:12; 3:5).

Five: He bestows upon the gospel believer the wealth and resources of His grace (Eph. 1:3; 2 Peter 1:3).

Six: He gives the gospel believer the Holy Spirit as the divine pledge of his spiritual inheritance and as his permanent, indwelling Helper (Eph. 1:14; John 14:15–17; 1 John 3:24).[10]

Observations About Salvational Faith and Evangelism

One: Continual refusal to receive the Savior results in hardening his heart toward the gospel (Acts 19:8–9). There seems to be a point in the life of the gospel hearer when he makes a final decision to accept or to reject the gospel. If he decisively rejects it, then he will never again be brought to this point of salvational faith in Jesus (Heb. 6:4–6).

Two: So called "evangelistic" preaching or teaching does not convey the gospel when it does not proclaim "the cross" (1 Cor. 1:18) that speaks of our Lord's atoning work, when it does not speak of sin as being people's greatest problem before God (Rom. 3:23), when it does not demand repentance or a change of attitude toward God and sin (Acts 17:30; 20:21), and when it speaks sentimentally of God's now loving sinners (John 3:16; 1 John 4:10) and fails to speak of His holy anger toward those who reject the Savior (John 3:36; Heb. 10:26–31).[11] Such deficient preaching produces in its hearers a defective or misdirected faith and a false hope. It makes unreal "conversions," with the result that people think that they have been saved and are not. Despite their initial, short-lived enthusiasm (Matt. 13:20–21), the profession of these "converts" is not supported by their works (James 2:26; Matt. 3:8; Eph. 2:20; 1 John 2:3). Are you really trusting in Jesus and His atoning sacrifice for your salvation from sin?

Three: While not all saved people have the spiritual gift of evangelism, all have the duty to bear witness to the gospel and to God's saving work in their lives (Acts 1:8; Mark 16:15; Luke 24:47; see "His Relation to Spiritual Gifts: The gift of evangelism" under Pneumatology). Consequently, we who are saved should be ready to share the gospel with others as the Holy Spirit impresses us. To do this effectively, however, we must know what people must do to be saved, be able to explain this clearly to them, rely on the Holy Spirit to lead in this witness, leave the saving work and its results with Him, and with His help live the kind of life that supports the verbal gospel witness that we seek to give.

Additions to Salvational Faith

Despite the Bible's teaching that we are saved by God's grace through faith (Eph. 2:8), "plus nothing, minus nothing," many people insist that there is more to do than to believe the gospel. Consider the following additions:

1. *"One must submit to water baptism."*
    a. *Its aspects*
       There are two aspects to the view that water baptism is necessary for salvation:
       1) Baptism is the instrument of salvation.
          This holds that baptism, imparting divine grace, is the instrument by which the Holy Spirit produces regeneration.[12] In the case of infants, baptism washes away original sin and imparts faith (Lutheran), is the beginning of new life in Christ (Anglican High church), or is the grace of adoption (Roman Catholic). In the case of adults, baptism also washes away actual sins.
          Contrariwise, I believe that the death of Jesus, along with the divine offering of His blood, is an adequate basis for divine forgiveness and cleansing (Col. 2:13; Heb. 9:14, 26; 1 John 1:7; Rev. 1:5). The grace of God in salvation responds to faith in the Savior, not to water baptism (Eph. 2:8; cp. Acts 16:31). The new birth, adoption, and placement into the Lord's Church immediately follow personal, salvational faith in the Savior (John 1:12–13; Gal. 4:6; 1 Cor. 12:13, 27; Eph. 1:22–23).
       2) Baptism completes salvation.
          This holds that water baptism, following repentance and faith, completes the salvational process (Disciples of Christ). The moment that the gospel believer is immersed, he is saved.
          Contrariwise, I believe that the gospel believer is saved the moment he exercises salvational faith in Jesus (Acts 16:31; John 3:16). Water baptism should follow salvation as a formal, public witness to faith in the Savior (Acts 18:8; Matt. 28:19–20).

b. Its biblical support

The few New Testament passages that appear to support the view that water baptism is needed for salvation have alternate translations or explanations, as follows:

Acts 2:38: "Repent and be baptized every one of you in the name of Jesus Christ for the remission of sins." "Repent" is a figure of association (synecdoche) for exercising salvational faith (cp. Acts 17:30). "For the remission of sins" can be read in the Greek text "because of the remission of sins" (cp. Matt. 12:41, KJV "at"). The remission of sins is not a result of baptism but the basis for baptism. The gospel believer's baptism is the occasion of his formal public witness to his faith in Christ and to the truth that his sins were forgiven when he trusted in the Savior (Acts 10:43).

Acts 22:16: "Arise and be baptized, and wash away your sins, calling on the name of the Lord." "Calling" (Gk. aorist middle participle, "having called") indicates that Saul (Paul) called upon the Lord as an expression of his salvational faith (Rom. 10:9–10, 13) before he was baptized. "The use of 'wash away thy sins,' in Acts 22:16, in connection with 'baptize,' cannot be properly insisted on as teaching baptismal salvation since the Oriental symbolism often put the symbol to the forefront in descriptions when, as a matter of fact, the experience preceded the symbol in order of time. We know, in fact, that this was the case here, for Saul not only was already converted but had received the Holy Spirit before his baptism (Acts 9:17f.)."[13]

John 3:5: "Except a man be born of water and of the Spirit, he cannot enter into the kingdom of God." From the context we know that entrance into God's kingdom is by the new birth, which is effected by the Holy Spirit (vv. 6–8). While some believe that water is a metaphor for physical birth (1:13) or for the Scriptures (Eph. 5:26), I prefer the view that it represents the Holy Spirit (John 7:37–39; Titus 3:5) as the context shows. The word *and*, joining *water* and *the Spirit,* may be understood as being an explanatory conjunction, which causes the passage to read, "Except a man is born of water, namely, the Spirit, he cannot enter the kingdom of God."

I Peter 3:21: "The like figure whereunto even baptism does also now save us, not the putting away of the filth of the flesh, but the answer of a good conscience toward God by the resurrection of Jesus Christ." *Baptism* is in apposition with *figure* (the counterpart of reality). Peter is careful to explain that he is not teaching baptismal regeneration (baptism is the instrument of salvation), for he says, "not the putting away of the filth of the flesh." Baptism is "the answer of a good conscience toward God," that is, it is our response to an inquiry regarding our conscience that we have done what God requires for salvation, which was made effective by Jesus' resurrection (Rom. 4:25).[14]

Mark 16:16: "He that believes and is baptized shall be saved, but he that believes not shall be damned." Although baptism, according to this verse, seems to be necessary for salvation, failure to be baptized is not stated as a cause for being damned. If baptism were really necessary for salvation, the word would be repeated here.

2. "One must submit to the Lordship of Christ."

This view holds that salvational faith must also include the confession that Jesus is one's Lord (cp. Rom. 10:9; Matt. 11:28–30). Certainly, the sinner who rebelliously asserted his independence of God must surrender this when he trusts in the Savior. However, his confession of Jesus as Lord is actually involved in his repentance, which is a change of mind and attitude toward God and Jesus. Although we may in our gospel presentation speak of Jesus as being the Lord of all who receive Him, we must not emphasize this fact to the point that it eclipses or replaces the truth of His saviorhood. People can only be saved as they trust Jesus to be their Savior from sin; they are not saved by only confessing Him as Lord (Matt. 1:21; John 8:24; Acts 10:43). With his salvational faith, the repentant gospel believer has the disposition to accept everything the Bible says about Jesus, including His lordship, although at the time he may not understand what all this means.

While trusting in Jesus for salvation is the first step of discipleship (cp. John 6:64–66), people's meaningful commitment to Jesus' lordship really follows salvation as they gain an understanding of the Lord's claim to their lives by His redemptive sacrifice (1 Cor. 6:20), even as the apostle Paul came to this conclusion early in his Christian life (2 Cor. 5:14–15). Moreover, this commitment to Jesus' lordship must be made daily if they are to walk in the Holy Spirit's power and direction rather than live under sin's domination (Rom. 12:1–2; 13:14; Eph. 3:17).[15]

3. *"One must do good works as well as believe in Jesus to gain final salvation."*

These people hold that salvation is a two-party contract that is entered by faith and maintained by good works. If one willfully sins and fails to repent, one breaks the contract and forfeits salvation. Only by faithfully doing good works can one hope to achieve the final salvation of one's soul in glory.[16]

This view is a faith-plus-works kind of salvation that is contrary to the teaching of Scripture (Eph. 2:8–9; Gal. 2:16). "Good works" (doing God's will) are an important evidence that one is saved, for they bear outward witness to one's inner salvational faith (James 2:14–20; 1 John 2:3–5). But they are never a condition of or make a contribution to salvation, initially or finally. The two-party contract concept (synergistic view, see below) of salvation is not, in my opinion, a biblical one, as we shall see. People are saved initially and forever through faith in the Lord Jesus and His atoning work. No contributory or meritorious human works of any kind are involved in securing or maintaining salvation. All is of God. Even one's salvational faith is God's gift (Acts 3:16; 11:18) and is maintained by Jesus' prayers (Luke 22:32; Heb. 7:25).

Household Salvation

Some understand the apostle Paul's words, "Believe on the Lord Jesus Christ and you will be saved and your house" (Acts 16:31, KJV) to teach that, if parents believe the gospel, this guarantees that their children will be saved. The biblical teaching is that all unsaved people must themselves trust in the Lord Jesus for salvation (John 3:16). The apostle also gave God's word to the jailer's household, who themselves believed (Acts 16:32). Humanly speaking, children who are raised in a Christian household are more likely to be saved, because of the teaching and example that they receive, than those who do not have this privilege.

Again, salvation is wholly God's gracious work, which is received only through faith in the Lord Jesus and His atoning work. It is not a two-party works contract as was the covenant of the Mosaic Law (Exod. 19:5, 8; 24:3, 7; Gal. 2:16).

SCHOLASTIC OPINIONS ABOUT THE RECEPTION OF SALVATION

Scholars have been divided about the extent to which human will plays in the exercise of salvational faith. Some like Augustine and Calvin hold a *monergistic view*—that the unsaved person, being totally depraved, does not effectively cooperate in his salvation by believing the gospel. These scholars regard salvation to be wholly God's work, including His gift of salvational faith. On the contrary, the Arminians hold a *synergistic view*—that salvation is a joint work of God and man. This means, that assisted by divine grace, the sinner can effectively cooperate with God in his salvation. The Wesleyan Arminians believe that grace releases the human will from bondage to sin so that the sinner, with his freed will, can accept or reject the Savior. Thus, according to this view, people have the final say about their salvation; moreover, they are able to fail in their perseverance of faith and lose their salvation.

341

Calvin

I prefer the concept of monergistic salvation. Although sinners must believe the gospel to be saved, as indicated by the appeals of the Lord's apostles (Acts 2:38–40; 16:31; 17:30), yet they cannot receive credit for this, for all of salvation (including salvational faith) is wholly God's work. In the reception of salvation, sinners do cooperate with God in the sense that they must believe the gospel, or trust in the Savior (Acts 16:31; John 1:12). But this response does not contribute anything to salvation by completing it, adding to it, effecting it, or meriting it. The sinner does not even make the final decision to be saved. Left to himself, he would neither desire salvation nor respond to the gospel (Rom. 3:11; John 3:19–20; 5:40; 6:44). When the elect person is effectually called of God, he freely responds by trusting in the Savior. But his decision to accept the Savior is not one of absolute freedom or independent cooperation. It is the conscious, personal response that is prompted and carried out by the sovereign, inward activity of God below the level of human awareness. The elect person's obedience to the gospel is initiated and completed by the divine impartation of salvational faith.

THE PRINCIPLE INVOLVED IN SALVATION

There are only two principles that relate to the way that God deals with people—grace and law. Throughout human history, God has saved people by His grace (Eph. 2:8–9; Ps. 103:10–12; Gen. 6:8; 15:5–6; Rom. 4:1–5,16; 11:5–6). According to this principle, God deals favorably with sinful people in a way they do not deserve. The only other principle by which God can deal with people is law, or works. This principle requires Him to deal with people in a way that they do deserve. Since sinners deserve death and hell, they cannot be delivered from this penalty by this works principle (Rom. 3:20; 8:3; Gal. 2:16; 3:10–12; Heb. 7:18–19). Their spiritual blindness is evident in that all their religions teach that people are saved by their works, the very principle that bars them from acceptance with God. No one can ever be saved from his sins apart from God's grace. Regardless of how good a person may be, one sin will bring him or her divine condemnation and hell. The fact is that "all have sinned and come short of God's glory" (Rom. 3:23).

The principles of grace and law are opposite in their manner of operation and their results (Rom. 11:6; 4:4–5). Observe the following contrasts between them:

THE PRINCIPLE OF GRACE OR GIFT

This responds to faith: Ephesians 2:8–9; Galatians 2:16; Romans 1:17; 4:16.
1. This allows God to deal favorably with people in a way they do not deserve.
2. This is the only way sinners can be saved from sin.
3. This does not recognize human merit, works, or worth as causing, earning, or contributing to salvation.
4. The human response of faith allows God to work graciously as He promises.
5. Salvation is wholly God's work; He receives all the credit and praise for it.
6. Being solely God's work, salvation by this method cannot fail.
7. This is the only principle by which sinners can be saved.

THE PRINCIPLE OF LAW OR WORKS

This responds to works, merit, or worth: Exodus 19:5; 24:3, 7; Galatians 3:12.
1. This causes God to deal with people in a way they do deserve.
2. This bars sinners from salvation.
3. This would recognize human merit, works, or worth as causing, earning, or contributing to salvation.
4. The human response of meritorious works would compel God to fulfill His obligation.

5. Salvation would be a cooperative endeavor of God and man; thus both would receive credit and praise.
6. Relying on man's doing his part, salvation by this method would never be certain.
7. There can be no salvation by this principle.

The gracious principle of divine dealing with unsaved people only relates to salvation. Apart from this, God deals with them according to their works, or as they deserve. God follows the meritorious principle of works when He deals with unsaved people in judgment. They justly receive what they deserve—full, everlasting punishment for their sins.

Observe that the principle of grace also applies to living the Christian life and to doing Christian ministry (1 Cor. 15:10; 2 Cor. 1:12). This means that we must look to the Lord by faith in His promises for the divine enablement and direction we need to please Him (Gal. 2:20). We cannot please Him by works done in our own strength (John 15:5; Phil. 4:13).

THE ASSURANCE OF SALVATION

It is God's desire that His people know that they are saved (1 John 5:13a). Satan uses unfounded doubt to cause us inner unrest and to hinder our spiritual development and ministry. On the other hand, we should not take our salvation for granted without valid evidence of its reality in our lives (2 Cor. 13:5). The assurance of salvation rests upon two lines of evidence. These are the witness of the Holy Spirit and the signs of new life.

THE WITNESS OF THE HOLY SPIRIT (1 JOHN 5:6, 10)

The Holy Spirit indwells every saved person (1 John 3:24; 4:13; Rom. 8:9). One of His ministries is to bear witness to the saved person's relation to God as a child (Rom. 8:16) and as a son (Gal. 4:6). The agency that He uses for this witness is God's Word (1 John 5:9–13a). Using the promises and declarations of Scripture that relate to salvation, He impresses these upon our human spirit, the dynamic source of our understanding, and makes them meaningful to us. These declarations and promises certify that we have been born again and now have eternal life if we have fulfilled the condition of exercising salvational faith in the Savior (2 Tim. 3:15; 1 John 5:13a).

THE SIGNS OF NEW LIFE (1 JOHN 5:11–12)

Upon our receiving the Savior, we are made new creatures in Him, possessing a new kind of life and experiencing the spiritual renewal of our personhoods and inner human natures (John 1:12; 2 Cor. 5:17; Col. 3:9–10). It is impossible to have this new life and to experience this change within ourselves without manifesting these spiritual realities in daily behavior (cp. Acts 16:33–34). Although this manifestation may vary and, at times, be eclipsed by sinning, nevertheless the signs of this new life will be expressed intermittently in the lives of all who have it. Let us consider several of these signs.

The Sign of Fellowship with God and His People (1 John 1:3)

Being members of God's family, saved people have an affinity for Him and His people. They desire and enjoy spiritual fellowship with one another, for they share a common spiritual life and interests. On the contrary, being rebels, unsaved people oppose God and hate His people (John 3:20; 15:19; Rom. 3:11, 18).

The Sign of Obedience to God (1 John 2:3, 29)

Obedience to God and doing righteousness concern our doing God's will in His strength (Phil. 1:11; 4:13; Rom. 8:4). Saved people have an innate desire to obey God (Phil. 2:13), although, at times, they feel the rebellious urges of the inner sin force and yield themselves to it. Our response to the command of the gospel is the beginning of a life of obedience to our new master, the Lord Jesus (2 Cor. 5:15). Our doing God's will is evidence of salvational faith in the Savior (James 2:14–16). On the contrary, unsaved people never willingly obey God, nor can they do what is right in His sight (Rom. 3:10, 12; 8:7–8; Eph. 2:2; 1 John 3:10).

The Sign of Love for God's People (1 ©John 3:14)

This is Christ's love reproduced in our hearts by the Holy Spirit (Rom. 5:5; Gal. 5:22). It is manifested by our desire and effort to minister to the needs of others, including their spiritual needs, even at personal cost (1 John 3:16–18). This expression of divine love is also a mark of true discipleship (John 13:34–35). On the contrary, unsaved people do not love God's people in this way (15:17–19), nor do they love God, which requires their obeying Him (3:20; 14:15).

The Sign of Confessing Christ Jesus (1 John 4:15)

This confession is our agreement with and our declaration of the NT teachings about the Lord Jesus. Saved people readily receive God's witness about His Son and willingly confess their belief in this truth to others (1 John 5:6, 9–10). On the other hand, nonelect people reject the witness that God has given of His Son (1 John 4:1–3).

Other Signs

In addition to these signs, there is the saved people's concern for the salvation of the unsaved and for the spiritual growth of God's people, which is a practical expression of His love (Rom. 10:1; 1 Thess. 1:8). Also, saved people can no longer knowingly sin comfortably or derive real pleasure from it, for sinning is no longer compatible with their renewed personhoods and inner human natures (Col. 3 8–14), and it also grieves the indwelling Holy Spirit (Eph. 4:29–30). While one's sinning may temporarily conceal some of these signs, one will incur God's corrective chastisement if one should fail to deal with one's sins by repentance and confession (Rev. 3:19). This, too, is a sign of one's relationship to God (Heb. 12:6; 1 Cor. 11:28–32).

A saved person can be assured of his relationship to God (cp. 1 John 1:7; 2:3; 3:14; 5:11–13). If he is not certain of his salvation, he should review the steps of receiving salvation, make a definite decision to trust in the Lord Jesus and His atoning work for his salvation, enact his decision, and express this trust to God by prayer (see "The Sinner's Part in the Reception of Salvation" above). Having definitely trusted in the Savior, he then can be assured of his salvation by the promises of Scripture, such as Romans 10:13 and John 1:12.

THE PERMANENCE OF SALVATION

Can someone who is truly saved involuntarily or voluntarily lose his salvation? I believe that the Scriptures teach that the saved person is forever safely kept, regardless of what he may do or experience. Let us look at this permanence as it relates to God and gospel believers.

THIS PERMANENCE AS IT RELATES TO GOD

Consider the following propositions:

God Wills to Keep His people.

This is the will of the Father (John 6:39–40) and of the Son (17:11–12, 24), whose petitions have never been denied by the Father. The Lord Jesus declared that He had safely kept His apostles and that none was lost, except Judas, the son of perdition. The Scriptures show that the betrayer had never been saved (6:70–71; 13:10–11).

God Is Able to Keep His People

Sometimes people are not able to carry out their purposes, but this is not a problem to the omnipotent God. He is able to fulfill His purpose for us and to finish His work in us (2 Tim. 1:12; Jude 24; John 10:28–29; Phil. 1:8). There is no power or creature that can hinder Him or cause Him to fail (Isa. 46:10). Since salvation is wholly His gracious work from start to finish, human failure of saved people does not render void the new covenant or jeopardize their salvation (cp. Rom. 3:3–4; Jer. 31:31–37).

God Is Free to Keep His People

Since the judicial debt of all our sins—past, present, and future—has been paid by our Lord's atoning work, we who are saved can never again incur divine condemnation by sinning (Rom. 8:1a, 32–34). Any charge that may be brought against us now falls on our Substitute, the Lord Jesus, who justly, fully paid our debt. Being justified by God and reconciled to Him, we are forever saved by Jesus' ongoing life (Rom. 5:9–10) and intercession for us (8:31–34; Heb. 7:25).

God Has Provided for the Safekeeping of His People

Their safekeeping is secured by the following provisions:

1. *The Lord's advocacy for us (1 John 2:1)*

The Lord Jesus, our righteous Advocate, pleads our case before the Father when we are accused by Satan of some sin (Rev. 12:10). Our Lord neither begs the Father to be lenient with us nor makes excuse for us. Instead, He presents the value of His sacrifice as just grounds for Satan's accusation being thrown out of court (Rom. 8:31–34). Our Lord's advocacy, however, does not make it easier for us to sin; it is revealed so that we do not sin (1 John 2:1). It is not easy to sin when we know that this is an open matter in heaven and requires this special ministry of Jesus our Lord.

2. *Christ's intercession for us (Heb. 7:25)*

While the Lord's intercession includes His advocacy and His praying for us, it is more than this. As our great High Priest, He is our official representative before the Father. He looks after all that concerns our well-being while we are here on earth (Heb. 4:14–16; John 17:9–24; Luke 22:31–32). Because of this, He is able to keep us secure forever.

3. *The Father's corrective dealings with us (1 Cor. 11:31–32)*

God the Father faithfully deals with His sinning people who fail to heed the warnings and appeals of His Word (Rev. 3:19).[17] This parental, corrective chastisement indicates that we are His children and that we shall not be condemned with the world (Heb. 12:6; 1 Cor. 11:32). To be condemned with the world would be to share the guilt and penalty of their sins. But this is impossible for those of us who are saved, for we are justified on the basis of Jesus' atoning work (Rom. 8:31–34; 5:1). God does not chasten those who are not His people. He deals out to them His retribution, or judicial punishment.

4. *The Holy Spirit's presence as a seal (Eph. 4:30)*

God the Holy Spirit is the divine seal that preserves us until the completion of our salvation. For us who are alive, this will be the redemption of our bodies from inherent corruption, the sin force, and mortality; for those who are dead, it will be from corruptibility (Rom. 8:23, 10–11). Ordinarily, any operation or process is vulnerable until it is completed. But in this case, the Holy Spirit keeps us secure until God's salvation work is finished in us.

God Promises to Keep His People

God's offer of eternal life through the gospel is based on the promises of the new covenant, which Jesus mediated by His death and resurrection (cp. Heb. 8:6–12; Jer. 31:31–34; Luke 22:20). Being gracious in character, this covenant is everlasting (Jer. 31:35–37; Heb. 13:20; Rom. 4:25). Unlike the covenant of the Mosaic Law, which Israel broke by its disobedience, the new covenant cannot be annulled by human failure. By this gracious covenant, God promises its recipients everlasting life and security (cp. John 10:28–29).

THIS PERMANENCE AS IT RELATES TO GOSPEL BELIEVERS

The permanence of salvation rests not only upon God but also upon the gospel believer's continuance or perseverance in salvational faith (1 Peter 1:5). However, this continuance of salvational faith is not solely a human achievement, for its source is in God (2 Peter 1:1), and it is sustained by the prayers of the Lord Jesus (Luke 22:31–32; Heb. 7:25). While he may not always exercise practical faith, the believer is never without salvational faith. It is noteworthy that the Lord never accused His disciples of having no faith (Matt. 6:30; 8:26; 14:31; 16:8), except on one occasion when He was speaking about their practical faith (Mark 4:40).

This truth distinguishes between those who profess to be saved and those who are really saved. The professing person will not continue indefinitely in his false professed faith (Matt. 13:20–22); the professing person will persevere until the final aspect of his salvation rests upon Jesus' return for him (24:13; cp. John 14:2–3).

This principle is confirmed by several passages, which at first glance seem to teach the possibility of losing salvation. From Colossians 1:21–23, the inference may be drawn, "If we do not continue in the faith, we shall be lost." Actually, we have not been saved if we do not continue in the faith. The past fact of our being reconciled to God (v. 21, Gk. aorist tense) will be manifest by our continuing in the faith (v. 23). Again, from Hebrews 3:6 the inference may be drawn, "If we do not hold fast, then we shall cease to be Christ's house and shall be lost." But the verse does not say this. It says that, if there is no perseverance of faith in the future, we are not now Christ's house. Our failure to meet the future condition is due to our not experiencing the past conclusion (cp. v. 14).

OBJECTIONS TO THIS PERMANENCE

1. *"This doctrine grants gospel believers a license to do what they please while guaranteeing their perpetual salvation."*

While we gospel believers can do as we please, this doctrine does not give us permission to sin. It is God's will that we not sin (1 John 2:1). God has counterbalanced this doctrine with those of divine punitive chastisement (1 Cor. 11:30–32) and unprofitable reward (2 Cor. 5:10; 1 Cor. 3:15; Col. 3:25). We are accountable to God the Father and to Jesus our Master for our conduct. Anyone who sins with insensitivity and abandon may never have been saved (2 Cor. 13:5; cp. Phil. 2:13; 1 John 3:8–9).

2. *"Some passages indicate that we can lose salvation."*

John 15:2, 6: In this allegory the Lord is speaking not about salvation but of the relation that His people must have with Him to be spiritually fruitful. Verse two may refer to premature physical death due to divine punitive chastisement (1 Cor. 11:30; Prov. 15:10; Heb. 12:9). Verse six may concern the believer's works being appraised by the Lord and the unacceptable ones being burned, or rejected (1 Cor. 3:15; cp. John 15:16).

Hebrews 6:4–12: The writer distinguishes between the readers who are saved (vv. 9–12, "you") and others who, experiencing the presalvational work of the Holy Spirit, are at the threshold of salvation (vv. 4–8, "they"). He warns the latter against rejecting Christ and returning to Judaism.

1 John 3:6–10: The present tense of these verbs points to the general character of life that unsaved people have rather than to particular acts of sin.[18] Having been set free from bondage to the sin force (Rom. 6:1, 6–7), the gospel believer no longer continually sins as he once did when he was unsaved. He now commits only acts of sin (1 John 2:1). It is impossible for the saved person to be in character what he was in his unsaved state, for he is a new creature in Christ (2 Cor. 5:17), possessing God's Seed (1 John 3:9, probably Jesus and His spiritual life) and having a renewed inner nature (Col. 3:9–10; Eph. 4:22–24).[19] While the gospel believer is capable of sinning and does, this is not in accord with his renewed state (Col. 3:1–17). He no longer sins all the time as unsaved people do.

OBSERVATIONS

One: There is a concurrence of God's sovereign action and gospel believers' perseverance in salvational faith for their safekeeping (1 Peter 1:5; Luke 22:32). Despite satanically implanted doubts, this persistent awareness of salvational faith in the Savior shows that they are saved. The lack of this trust indicates that they were never saved. We should never take our salvation for granted. The apostle Paul exhorted his readers to examine themselves to see if they were in the faith (2 Cor. 13:5). Tragically, the salvational faith of many people rests upon the words of men or some physical response to a gospel invitation rather than on God's Word and the Savior (cp. 1 Cor. 2:1–5).

Two: Again, salvational faith should be distinguished from practical faith, which we are to exercise in the Lord for matters of daily life (Prov. 3:5–6; Matt. 17:19–20; Mark 11:22; 1 Tim. 6:17). Because it is God's gift and is supported by the Lord's intercession, salvational faith is always consistent, but practical faith varies from day to day in strength and expression (Matt. 6:30; 15:28; Mark 4:40; Rom. 4:20).[20]

THE DIVINE GOALS OF SALVATION

Whatever God's objectives for saving the elect may be, they apparently include His creating a new human race who will serve Him and who will bring Him glory.

TO CREATE A NEW HUMAN RACE

This creative work is not the creation of a new order of personal creatures but the renewal of humans who were formerly members of Adam's race and who were ruined by his sin. It involves the recreation of the gospel believer's personhood and human nature, not the replacement of his or her essential parts (Eph. 4:22–24; 1 Peter 1:22).

God was pleased to create Adam and Eve in His image with a holiness and a righteousness that were subject to change. But their sin brought them and their posterity total ruin and divine condemnation (Rom. 3:9–18; 5:12–19; 1 Cor. 15:22). Today, with chosen members of the old human race, God is creating a new human race in Christ Jesus (2 Cor. 5:17). The Holy Spirit is doing this by His ministries of regeneration (John 3:6; Titus 3:5) and baptism into Christ (2 Cor. 5;17; Eph. 2:10; Gal. 3:27).

In addition to possessing the image of God (personhood), the members of this new race bear in their human natures Jesus' human image (Col. 3:10; Rom. 8:29; 2 Cor. 3:18; 1 John 3:2), for He is the Head and Pattern of this new humanity (1 Cor. 15:22, 45–49; Eph. 4:15). With our personhood and inner human nature (soul and spirit) now delivered from sin's ruin, this renewal will be completed when our bodies are changed at the Lord's return (1 Cor. 15:50–53; Phil. 3:20–21).

TO CREATE A PEOPLE THAT WOULD SERVE HIM (2)

That all personal creatures were created to serve the Creator is universally recognized (Pss. 2:11; 100:1–2; Matt. 4:10). But because they had moral self-determination, they were given the opportunity to choose whom they would serve—God or sin. The biblical record shows that many angels and the first human couple chose to serve sin. Thus, a divine goal of salvation is to deliver elect humans from the servitude of sin so that they might serve the living God (Luke 1:74–75; Heb. 9:14). Being the purchased slaves of the Lord Jesus (1 Cor. 6:20; Rom. 14:8), we who are saved now have the obligation and innate desire to serve Him rather than our former spiritual masters (Rom. 6:15–22; 1 Peter 2:16, 24; Rom. 12:1–2; Phil. 2:13).

TO CREATE A PEOPLE THAT WOULD GLORIFY HIM (3)

God is glorified by manifesting certain qualities of Himself by His works (Ps. 19:1). Recognizing His works in the realm of nature, His creatures give Him praise for His power and wisdom (Pss. 145–148). But, He will forever be glorified by the members of the new humanity, for these saved people will ever manifest the exceeding riches of His love, grace, and mercy that He exercised in their salvation (Eph. 1:12; 2:4–7; Rom. 9:23). These glorious, divine qualities could only be expressed toward undeserving sinners (1 Tim. 1:12–17). God's saving those whom He has chosen displays His grace and wisdom to the holy angels (1 Peter 1:10–12; Eph. 3:10). They, as well as we, shall give Him endless praise for redeeming people from every nation (cp. Rev. 5:8–14). Since we exist for His glory (Eph. 1:12), we who are saved should seek now to bring God praise in all that we do (1 Cor. 10:31; Matt. 5:16; cp. John 17:4).

THE COMPONENTS OF SALVATION

The word *salvation* is generally used as a blanket term for all that occurs to persons at the moment they trust in Jesus as their Savior. The components of salvation are the various parts or aspects of it that gospel believers receive when they are saved. These aspects are part of the overall blessings that salvation provides (Eph. 1:3; 2:7; see "The Benefits of Salvation" in this chapter). The more we understand these components, the more meaningful salvation will be to us who are saved, and the more cause we shall have to rejoice in them and be grateful to God for them. Let us rely on the Holy Spirit to give us understanding of these precious truths. While all these components occur simultaneously at the moment one trusts in the Savior, they have a logical order as follows:

REDEMPTION (ROM. 3:24; 1 COR. 1:30; EPH. 1:7; HEB. 9:12)

Its Definition

Redemption is the act of God whereby, on the basis of Jesus' ransom payment, He releases the gospel believer from bondage to his evil spiritual masters and from the penalty of his sins and brings him into bondage to the Lord Jesus, his Benefactor.

Its Necessity

The need of unsaved people for redemption is manifested by their being in bondage to their spiritual masters and by their being in debt to God for their sins.

1. Their bondage to their spiritual masters

Unsaved people are in bondage to sin, Satan, and the world system with its various influences and religious laws. They are slaves of the sin force, which dominates their total being (Eph. 2:3), and of actual habitual sins (John 8:34). They also are in bondage to

Satan, for they live under his authority (Acts 26:18; Col. 1:13) and are continually subject to his evil influences upon their lives (Eph. 2:2). Furthermore, they are in bondage to the world system and its culture, of which they are a part (John 15:19). The apostle Paul stated that the unsaved live "according to the course of this age" (Eph. 2:2; KJV "world"). During their lifetime on earth, they live under the domination of the world's philosophy, fads, moods, and works, all of which are evil in God's sight (John 7:7). They also are in bondage to the world's religious laws and ethical principles, which are part of their culture (Acts 15:10; Rom. 2:14–15; 7:1–6; Gal. 4:1–10).

2. *Their indebtedness to God for their sins*

Unsaved people are guilty before God of original sin (Rom. 5:16, 18) and of their actual sins (3:9–19). The divine penalty for sin is everlasting punishment in hell (Rev. 20:12–15; Matt. 25:46). This debt is such that no sinner can ever discharge him-or herself from this obligation by any means, including meritorious works and pay (Matt. 25:41; John 3:36).

3. *Its Basis*

Redemption is essentially concerned with a release that is secured by the payment of a ransom. In ancient times, people were often released from slavery or prison by ransom payments (Exod. 6:6; Ps. 107:2). A man, who because of poverty sold himself to another, could redeem himself or could be redeemed by a relative (Lev. 25:47– 49).

God's requirements for the kinsman (relative) redeemer were these: He must be related to the person who needed redemption (Lev. 25:47–9; cp. Ruth 3:12–13), he must be able and willing to redeem this person (cp. Ruth 4:4–6), and he must be personally free of the calamity that had befallen his unfortunate relative. In meeting these requirements, God the Son became identified with mankind by His incarnation (Heb. 2:9, 14, 16; 10:5–7); He was able and willing to give His life as a ransom to pay provisionally the debt of humanity's sins (John 10:11, 18; Matt. 20:28); also, being sinless, He was personally free of sin and its debt (1 Peter 2:22; 2 Cor. 5:21; 1 John 3:3, 5; cp. Acts 2:24).

In their unsaved state, people cannot deliver themselves or others from the bondage and debt of sin. But, by His death and atoning work, the Lord Jesus confirmed the justice of the divine sentence against humanity's evil spiritual masters (Rom. 8:3; John 12:31; 16:11) and secured a value that could pay the woeful debt of mankind's sins (Rom. 5:8; 6:23; Matt. 20:28). On the basis of this atoning work, God is now able to apply the value of our Lord's atoning sacrifice to all who believe the gospel and to deliver them from this bondage and indebtedness forever (Eph. 1:7; Heb. 9:12).

4. *Its Blessings*

Upon trusting in the Lord Jesus as our Savior or Redeemer, we gospel believers received the following redemptive blessings:

1. *We were released from the judicial debt of all our sins.*

Upon the basis of our Lord's atoning work and resurrection, God forgave, or canceled, the judicial debt, or punishment, of all our sins, both original and actual—past, present, and future (Eph. 1:7; Col. 2:13; Rev. 1:5). Never again shall we incur divine condemnation and spiritual death and face the prospect of everlasting separation from God in hell (John 5:24; Rom. 8:1a). We are now justified by the highest court—by God Himself (Rom. 8:33).

2. *We were released from bondage to our evil spiritual masters.*

The Scriptures teach that we who are saved have been set free from bondage to the sin force (Rom. 6:7, 18), Satan's authority (Acts 26:18; Col. 1:13), and the world system of unsaved mankind (John 15:19), with its ethical and religious regulations (Rom. 7:1–10; Gal. 3:13; 4:3–5; Col. 2:8–23). In God's thinking, because we participated in Jesus' death and died to these former masters (Rom. 6:2–3; Gal. 6:14), we do not have to give in to sin's demands, yield to Satan's temptations, conform to the world's evil ideas, or obey those laws and customs that clearly conflict with God's will for us (Acts 5:29).[21] Redemption has delivered us from these dominating forces (John 8:36).

3. Our personhoods and immaterial human natures were delivered from hereditary corruption.

As we have observed elsewhere, we not only were delivered from the guilt of original sin but also from its impact upon our personhoods and immaterial human natures (souls and spirits; see "The Believer's Relation to Original Sin" under Hamartiology). Although they are still susceptible to the urges of the sin force, these parts of our makeup are no longer inherently corrupted and inclined toward sin. They have been released from inherent corruption and sin's domination (Acts 15:9; Titus 2:14; 1 Peter 1:22). Also, being renewed, they are the instruments of righteousness (1 Peter 1:9, 22; Rom. 6:13; 8:10; Eph. 4:24, this should read "did put on"). While our body is still inherently corrupt, it, too, can be an instrument of righteousness when we give it to God (Rom. 6:11–13; 12:1–2).

4. We were released for holy purposes.

Our redemption is the basis of our Christian liberty (John 8:36). We have been set free from bondage to our former spiritual masters that we might serve God (1 Peter 2:16), express His love to others (Gal. 5:13), and grow in Christlikeness (2 Cor. 3:17–18). This freedom is not exemption from external authority, but it is the liberty to give ourselves to God for those holy purposes for which He has set us free.

We experience this new freedom when we yield ourselves to the limitations that are imposed upon us by the Scriptures (1 Cor. 9:21; James 1:23–25) and by the Holy Spirit (2 Cor. 3:17; Rom. 8:14; Gal. 5:16). As we yield to God's direction, we allow Him to express Himself in and through our lives by holy character and good works (Phil. 1:11, 21; Gal. 2:20; John 15:4–5).

We can misuse this liberty by giving ourselves to the sin force for its evil expressions (Rom. 13:14; Gal. 5:13). Then we temporarily come under the domination of our former evil masters. Observe that at no time do we lose this liberty of self-surrender to the moral force, God or sin, that would dominate us. We continue to have this liberty of moral decision and submission, regardless of the force that is dominating our lives. Thus, when we are walking in sin, we can at any time yield ourselves to God and in His strength do His will; or, when we are walking with God, we can give ourselves over to the demands of our spiritual enemies. Being completely dominated by these evil forces, unsaved people do not have this freedom to choose what moral force will govern their lives.

Although we often yield to the demands of our former evil masters, this is unnatural and wrong, for we have died to them, and they no longer have lawful claim to us (Rom. 6:1–7). Purchased by His sacrifice, we are now the Lord's property (1 Cor. 6:19–20; Matt. 20:28). It is our duty and privilege to yield ourselves constantly to His authority as we formerly did to sin's demands (2 Cor. 5:14–15). When we do, we exercise our freedom in the right way and with holy, satisfying results.

JUSTIFICATION (ROM. 3:24; 4:25; 5:1, 9, 18; 8:30; 1 COR. 6:11)

Its Definition

Justification is the judicial act of God whereby He acquits the gospel believer of the divine verdict of condemnation and declares him to be righteous, for He has made him so.

Its Necessity

The need of unsaved people for justification is seen in their condemnation by God and their lack of acceptable righteousness.

1. The unsaved person stands condemned before God (John 3:18).

To be condemned is to be found guilty of a crime and sentenced to punishment. God has already found unsaved people guilty of original sin (Rom. 5:16, 18) and of actual sins (3:9–19) and has passed sentence on them (John 3:18, 36; Matt. 7:13–14). In the case of those who hear the gospel, this condemnation is increased if they should refuse to receive the Savior (Matt. 11:20–24).

2. The unsaved person is without acceptable righteousness (Rom. 3:10).

Righteousness means the condition of being right in God's sight or the act of doing right. Unsaved people fall short of the righteousness that God requires of His personal creatures (Rom. 3:23). In their rebellion against Him, they substitute their own ethical standard and conduct for what He requires of them. But this self-righteousness is not acceptable to Him (Isa. 64:6). He declares that no one is righteous in His sight without His gift of righteousness (Rom. 3:10, 22; 1 Cor. 1:30).

Its Basis

We who are saved were graciously justified by Jesus' blood, that is, by His atoning work (Titus 3:7; Rom. 5:9).[22] In our unsaved state, we could neither deliver ourselves from divine condemnation nor attain the righteousness that God required of us. But in His gracious love (John 3:16; Titus 3:4), God provided the way whereby He could be just (or righteous) and still justify undeserving sinners (Rom. 3:24–26). By His atoning work, the Lord Jesus dealt with our sins and paid their awful debt (5:8; Heb. 9:26).

Upon our faith in Jesus and His atoning work, God applied to our account the value of this sacrifice, acquitted us of condemnation, made us righteous in Jesus, and declared us to be righteous in His sight (Rom. 5:16–17). While His death atoned for our sins, the Lord's resurrection made this work effective for our justification (4:25). Like all other aspects of salvation, justification is a gracious divine work (3:24; Titus 3:7).

Its Blessings

Justification brought the following blessings to us when we trusted in Jesus:

1. We were forever acquitted of the sentence of condemnation (Rom. 8:1a, 33–34).

This is more than a pardon, which implies that we are still guilty of a crime although we are exempted from its punishment. We shall never again come under divine judicial wrath (5:9; cp. 1 Thess. 1:10; 5:9), for we have peace with God (Rom. 5:1). Having judicially forgiven us of all our sins—past, present, and future, He no longer sees us guilty of any sin (Col. 2:13).

2. We were declared righteous in God's sight.

God could declare us to be righteous for two reasons: *One,* He gave us this righteousness (Rom. 3:22; Phil. 3:9). This righteousness was imputed to us (Rom. 4:1–4, 20–24), that is, it was judicially credited to our account in the place of our sins.[23] And *two,* God has made us righteous in Christ (2 Cor. 5:21; cp. Rom. 5:19; 1 Cor. 1:30). [24] This essential righteousness is now a quality of our divinely renewed personhoods and inner human natures (Eph. 4:24; cp. 1 Peter 1:22; Acts 15:9).

The righteousness that God gives His people consists of Jesus' perfect obedience to the Father, even unto death (Rom. 5:19; Phil. 2:8; John 8:29). Since our Lord's messianic works were done in conjunction with the Father (John 14:10), this righteousness is the Father's as well (Rom. 3:22). Thus, justification is not only the divine declaration that gospel believers are righteous but also the divine imputation of this righteousness, which makes them to be righteous. How blessed is this truth!

3. *We are able to do righteousness (1 Peter 2:24; 1 John 2:29; 3:7).*

Being righteous (not sinless), we are now able to do what is right in God's sight, or His will, by the power of Christ through the Holy Spirit (Phil. 1:11; 4:13; Rom. 14:17). This requires our abiding in the Lord, relying on the Holy Spirit, and obeying His Word. This allows this righteousness to be expressed in our behavior (John 15:4–5; Rom. 14:17; 2 Tim. 3:16; see Appendix E: "Righteousness and Holiness").

4. *We are assured of future glorification and inheritance (Rom. 8:30; Titus 3:7).*

Guaranteeing the permanence of our salvation (Rom. 8:31–34), justification assures us of the completion of our salvation experience with the deliverance of our bodies from mortality and inherent corruption (vv. 23, 30), our participation in our Lord's glory (John 17:22; Col. 3:4; Rom. 8:18), and our reception of our inheritance (Rom. 8:17; Eph. 1:11; 1 Peter 1:3–4). We shall share in that which the Father has given to the Lord Jesus (John 3:35).

3. RECONCILIATION (COL. 1:20–21; ROM. 5:10–11, KJV "ATONEMENT")

Its Definition

Reconciliation is the act of God whereby He does away with the hostility between the gospel believer and Himself and establishes peace.

Its Necessity

The need of unsaved people for reconciliation is manifested by the state of hostility that exists between God and them because of their sins (Rom. 5:10; Col. 1:21).

1. *The sinner is rebellious toward God.*

Rejecting the Creator's claim to them, sinners violate God's laws with indifference and defiance (Rom. 1:18; 3:11–12, 18). Moreover, they hate the searching, penetrating light of divine revelation that is brought to bear on them. This exposes their sinfulness (John 3:20) and reminds them of their accountability (Matt. 12:36–37).

2. *God is angry toward the sinner.*

God's holiness and justice strongly react against unsaved people to the extent that He hates them (Pss. 5:5; 11:5; Hos. 9:15; Mal. 1:3; Rom. 9:13) and their sins (Prov. 6:16–19) and that He is angry with them (Rom. 1:18; John 3:36; see "God's Attributes: Hatred" under Theology Proper). Unlike sinful humans, however, God's holy hatred and anger do not lead Him to act irrationally and maliciously, but they move Him to punish people justly for their sinfulness (Rom. 2:1–11).[25] That God should freely choose to love sinners and provide salvation through His Son is an expression of infinite grace (1 John 4:10; 2:2).

Its Basis

In their unsaved state, the sinners have neither the desire nor the means to remove the hostility that exists between God and themselves. Only God could do this by dealing with the cause of this hostility (their sins) and by provisionally putting it away by our Lord's sacrifice (Col. 1:20; John 1:29; Heb. 9:26; see "The Nature of Jesus' Atoning Work" under Christology). Motivated by infinite love and grace, God did this by sending His Son to be a propitiation for humanity's sins (1 John 2:2; 4:10; cp. John 1:29).[26]

While pagans seek to propitiate (appease) the anger of their deities by offering them gifts, God Himself was propitious. He graciously provided the necessary sacrifice for appeasing His own wrath against sinners when He gave His Son to atone for their sins.

Bearing their sins and being made sin (Isa. 53:5–6; 2 Cor. 5:21), Jesus bore the full stroke of God's anger in their place (Isa. 53:10; Matt. 27:45–46).

Because of our Lord's sacrifice, God's demands against sinners are satisfied when they trust in Jesus, their substitute (John 1:29; Heb. 9:26; Rom. 3:25). Thus, by His sacrifice Jesus made peace for gospel believers by removing the aggravating thorn of contention (sin) between them and God (Col. 1:20–21).[27] That God was completely satisfied by His Son's sacrifice was demonstrated by His raising Him from the dead (Acts 2:22–24; Rom. 4:25). On the basis of this propitious, atoning work, God is now able to reconcile to Himself all who trust in the Savior.

Its Blessings

Salvation brings the following blessings of reconciliation to all who trust in the Savior:

1. *We have peace with God (Col. 1:20–21; Rom. 5:1, 10).*

Praise God! The war is over! We now enjoy a harmonious relation with God as well as personal well-being. With Christ Jesus as our propitiation (1 John 2:2), we shall never again be exposed to God's judicial wrath (John 5:24; Rom. 5:9; 8:1, 31–34; 1 Thess. 1:10; 5:9). With the confidence of children, we can approach God with reverent boldness (Heb. 4:16; Eph. 2:18), even with confession of our sins (1 John 1:9), without fearing divine hostile reaction. While unjudged sins may temporarily eclipse our inner peace (Gal. 5:22) and bring us God's corrective chastisement (1 Cor. 11:32), our reconciliation with Him remains steadfast forever (Rom. 5:10–11). Observe that this truth does not grant us immunity to man's wrath (2 Tim. 5:10–11; John 15:18–21; 1 Peter 4:12–19; 1 John 3:11–13).

2. *We have peace with others who are reconciled to God (Eph. 2:14–19).*

Throughout their history, a state of hostility has existed between Jews and Gentiles because of the Law of Moses. Having the law, Jews felt superior to the Gentiles. Also, the Gentiles regarded the Jews as religious bigots. By His death, the Lord Jesus removed the cause of this hostility (the partition wall that separated them) and atoned for their sins, including those that were expressed by their bitter attitudes toward each other. "The partition" was the Law of Moses; the "wall" was the things of the law that kept Jews and Gentiles apart. These things included ritual circumcision, restricted diet, Sabbath-keeping, and certain religious ceremonies.

The Lord Jesus brought the Law of Moses to an end, as a viable covenant, and mediated the new covenant. By this covenant, saved Jews and saved Gentiles are brought peacefully together in Him and have a common relation to God (Gal. 3:26–28). By their reconciliation to God, people who were traditional enemies are reconciled to each other. This is God's solution to the ethnic unrest that permeates this world. Also, when their hearts are filled with the Holy Spirit, God's people experience this peace in their church and social relationships (Eph. 4:2–3).

3. *We have God's peace (Isa. 26:3–4; John 16:33; 2 Thess. 3:16).*

This peace is a garrison to our hearts in the midst of life's trials and adversities (Phil. 4:6–7). Since it is a fruit of the Holy Spirit (Rom. 14:17; Gal. 5:22), we experience this peace only as we are rightly adjusted to Him and are trusting in God's promises. Unjudged known sins bar this peace from our hearts and cause us unrest and unhappiness (1 Cor. 3:3). Heart peace is restored when we deal with these sins by repentance and confession (Rev. 2:5; 1 John 1:9) and yield ourselves anew to God (Prov. 23:26; Eph. 5:18).

4. *We can anticipate God's reconciling all things to Himself (Col. 1:20; Acts 3:21; Eph. 1:10).*

This concerns those things that were involuntarily affected by God's curse upon creation when man morally fell (Gen. 3:17; Rom. 8:19–23). These verses do not teach universalism, or the idea that everyone eventually will be saved. In his listing that which is reconciled to God (Col. 1:20), the apostle Paul omits those who are under the earth in hades, the detention center of the unsaved dead. When He comes again to establish His earthly kingdom, the Lord Jesus will lift this curse and will restore creation to its primeval state (Isa. 11:6–9; Pss. 8; 98).

5. *We have been given the ministry of reconciliation (2 Cor. 5:18–20; Matt. 5:9).*

Since the Lord regards those of us who are saved as His ambassadors to this world and has given us the message of reconciliation, we have the duty of sharing the good news with others so they, too, can be reconciled to God through faith in Jesus and His atoning work. This ministry, determined by our gifts and calling, ranges from formal gospel proclamation to informal personal witness to Jesus' saving work in our lives. It is a privilege to be colaborers with the Lord and to possess such an effective message (1 Cor. 3:9; Rom. 1:16; see "The Formation of the Universal Christian Church" under Ecclesiology). Are you faithfully representing Him and His message of peace to a troubled world?

4. REGENERATION (TITUS 3:5)

While this word is used in Titus 3:5, the truth is taught in John 1:12–13; 3:3–7; 1 Peter 1:3, 23.

Its Definition

Regeneration is the act of God whereby He cleanses gospel believers of the defilement of sin, renews their personhoods and the immaterial parts of their human natures (soul-spirits), and imparts to them spiritual life.

Its Timing

Calvinistic and Lutheran theologians regard regeneration as including the presalvational work of God in the sinner's heart as well as its completion in conversion. I prefer the view that regeneration consists of the inward renewal and impartation of spiritual life immediately following salvational faith in Christ (John 1:12–13; 3:16; 6:53). Though totally depraved, the sinner does not have to be regenerated to believe the gospel since salvational faith is God's gift and has within itself the power to enable people to trust in Jesus (2 Peter 1:1; Acts 3:16). Any inclination of the heart toward God is a part of the Holy Spirit's presalvational work in drawing people to God (John 6:44).

Its Means

Immediately following his salvational faith in Jesus (John 1:12; 6:53), the gospel believer is regenerated by the Holy Spirit (John 3:5–8; Titus 3:5), who works through God's Word (1 Peter 1:23; Rom. 10:17).[28]

Its Necessity

Besides their inherent defilement and ruin, unsaved people's need for regeneration is indicated by their being spiritually dead and members of Satan's kingdom.

1. *They are spiritually dead.*

Being spiritually dead, unsaved people exist in a state of alienation from God (Eph. 2:1; 4:18) and are a spiritual ruin (Luke 19:10, "lost"; 1 Cor. 1:18, "perish"; Rom. 3:12). This means that they are so affected by sin that they are naturally unresponsive to God and to divine things and are responsive only to sin and their evil spiritual masters (Eph. 2:1–3).

2. *They are members of Satan's kingdom.*

Affected by original sin, unsaved people are Satan's product and have his moral character (John 8:44; Eph. 2:2–3). Being a part of the world system of which Satan is leader, they live under his authority (John 16:11; 1 John 5:19; Acts 26:18). However religious they may be, they are not members of God's kingdom before they are born again (Matt. 7:21–23; John 3:3–7).

Its Basis

The Lord's atoning sacrifice provided the basis for the divine removal of those sins that had separated gospel believers from God and for the divine cleansing of their inner being from moral defilement (John 3:16; 1 John 4:9; cp. John 6:53–54). This divine cleansing, together with divine inner renewal, were necessary for the reception of spiritual life and entrance to God's family and kingdom (Titus 3:5).

Its Blessings

By divine regeneration, we gospel believers were inwardly cleansed and renewed, received a new kind of life, and were brought into a new relation with God.

1. We were inwardly cleansed and renewed.

Observe that gospel believers must be inwardly prepared for the reception of eternal life (cp. Luke 5:38; putting new wine in new wineskins). This preparation involved God's cleansing us from the defilement of sin by applying to us the value of the Lord's sacrifice (Titus 2:14; 3:5; see Acts 15:9; 1 Peter 1:22; Eph. 5:25–27). It also involved His renewing our personhoods (2 Cor. 5:17) and our immaterial human natures (Titus 3:5), which He recreated in righteousness and holiness (Eph. 4:24; cp. 2:10; 2 Cor. 5:17). This inner cleansing and renewal gave us the capacity and capability to experience and to express our new life in Christ intellectually, emotionally, and volitionally as well as behaviorally (see Appendix E: "Righteousness and Holiness").

2. We received a new kind of life.

Divine regeneration also imparted to us gospel believers a new life (John 3:16), which makes us responsive to God and to divine things (Rom. 8:10, "spirit" is the human spirit). In contrast to physical life, this new life is called "eternal life" or "everlasting life" (John 3:15–16) and, in this study, "spiritual life." This new life is something more than living forever, which all people will do. It is Jesus' spiritual life, which He possesses as man (John 14:6; Col. 3:4; 1 John 5:12) and which He gives to gospel believers by the Holy Spirit (John 6:27; 10:28; Rom. 8:2).

Several features that this new life conveys to saved people are a new spiritual power (Gal. 5:25; John 14:16), a new rule of conduct (Gal. 6:2),[29] a new spiritual knowledge (1 Cor. 2:9–12), a new association (1 John 1:3; 1 Cor. 1:9), a new life purpose (Matt. 6:33; 1 Cor. 10:31), new spiritual resources (Heb. 13:5–6; 2 Peter 1:3),[30] new desires and activities (Phil. 2:13), a new spiritual character (Gal. 5:22–23), a new heavenly citizenship (Phil. 3:20; Col. 1:13), a new expectation (Titus 2:13), and a new destination (John 14:2–3; 2 Cor. 5:8). Thus, having eternal life is more than living forever. It is to have a radically new kind of life, which we can daily experience as we live in fellowship with the Persons of the divine Trinity (1 John 1:7; John 8:12; Rom. 8:4–5; see "Fellowship with God" under Theology Proper). We express this new life in our behavior as we abide in Jesus (John 15:4–5) and are filled with the Holy Spirit; otherwise, we sin and express spiritual death (Gal. 6:7–8; Rom. 8:4–6).

3. We were brought into a new relation with God.

The Lord Jesus spoke about eternal life as springing from a personal relationship with God, whereby gospel believers intimately know the Persons of the divine Trinity (John 17:3; cp. 1 John 2:3–6). Two aspects of this relationship follow:

a. Regenerated gospel believers are members of God's family.

By the new birth, a person becomes a child of God (John 1:12–13), and God the Father becomes his heavenly Father (20:17; 2 Thess. 2:16; Matt. 6:8–9).[31] But this does not mean that the regenerated person becomes God. His partaking of the divine nature (2 Peter 1:4) is not to partake of it in a way that makes his human nature divine or that replaces his human nature with a divine one.[32] God is his Father in the sense that He imparted to him a spiritual life that is in Jesus; He did not impart to him His own inherent, self-existent divine life.

We gospel believers possess several blessings that spring from this relationship with God.

1) We know God (John 17:3).

Our inward renewal and new life in Jesus gave us the capability and the opportunity to know God in a personal way. This intimate knowledge, which is capable of growth (2 Peter 3:18), is cultivated by our study of God's Word and by our experiencing God's dealings with His people (2 Tim. 3:16–17; Heb. 12:5–11; cp. Job 42:5).

2) We have fellowship with God (1 John 1:3, 7).

This is a child-parent relationship. When we consider all that this relationship with God involves, we find it to be the highest experience in the Christian life. This includes our sharing our lives with Him and all that they contain, our drawing from Him all that we need, our talking to Him in prayer and our listening to Him as we read His Word, our trusting Him and His promises in every situation, our participating with Him in His work on earth, and our living in complete agreement with His revealed will (see "Fellowship with God" under Theology Proper). To fellowship with God, we must daily live where He is—in the light of His holiness (1 John 1:5–7) and of His Word (Ps. 119:105).

3) We are subject to God's parental discipline (Heb. 12:5–7).

The heavenly Father deals with His people, not only to correct them (1 Cor. 11:32) but also to lead them to submit to His authority (Heb. 12:9), to produce in them His practical holiness (v. 10), and to make them more spiritually productive (v. 11; cp. John 15:2). He does this with infinite love and wisdom. Therefore, we who are saved should not faint because of His dealings with us or ignore them (Heb. 12:5), but we should endure them patiently (v. 7) that we might receive the benefits that He has for us.

4) We are the objects of God's loving care (Matt. 6:31–33; 10:29–31).

The heavenly Father lovingly cares for us every moment that we are on earth. Although powerful evil forces are arrayed against us, a multitude of details engage our attention and tax our human resources, and much else escapes our notice, yet God is ever aware of our needs and ministers to us continuously. He has provided for all that we need for our pilgrimage through this world and for our achieving all that He desires for us (2 Peter 1:1–4, see endnote 30). We must be careful, however, not to think of Him as our servant, who responds to our every whim (James 4:3). He is our God, whom we worship and serve forever. As we humbly draw near to Him, He draws near to us (James 4:8–10), and, as we delight ourselves in Him, He satisfies our hearts' desires (Ps. 37:4).

5) We are God's heirs (Rom. 8:17).

In the Scriptures, an inheritance is something that is given to another for his possession (cp. Ezek. 44:28; Luke 12:13; 15:12). Today the Lord Jesus is the inheritance of His people (Eph. 1:11). In Him we have wisdom, righteousness, sanctification, redemption (1 Cor. 1:30), peace (Eph. 2:14), grace (2 Cor. 12:9), spiritual life (Col. 3:4), help (Heb. 13:5–6), satisfaction (John 6:35), and untold blessings (Eph. 1:3).

In the future, we shall share in our Lord's earthly inheritance when He returns to take possession of it (John 3:35; Rom. 8:17; Heb. 1:2; Matt. 11:27; Ps. 2:8–9). Meanwhile, another portion of this future inheritance is reserved for us in heaven. This seems to consist of the untold blessings that God has prepared for His people there (1 Peter 1:4–5; Heb. 10:34; John 14:1–3). The profusion of this future inheritance is indicated by the present, blessed ministries of the Holy Spirit, which represent only the first installment of all that awaits us (Eph. 1:14).

　　b. Regenerated gospel believers are citizens of God's kingdom.
　　　1) Its place

　　　As a newborn person automatically becomes a citizen of the country to which his parents belong, so likewise by the new birth the child of God becomes a subject, or citizen, of God's kingdom, of which the Lord Jesus is Viceroy. The new birth is the only means by which unsaved people can enter this kingdom (John 3:2–7; Matt. 7:21).

While "the kingdom of God" has various meanings in the Scriptures (see Appendix R: "The Kingdom of God"), here it is the realm where God's authority is acknowledged and obeyed. Its citizenship extends to everyone in heaven and to all those on earth who are rightly related to Him.

Presently, this kingdom, of which the Lord Jesus is Viceroy (Col. 1:13), is located in heaven (Phil. 3:20; 2 Tim. 4:18) as a spiritual, invisible, nonpolitical entity. But when the Lord returns to earth, His kingdom will become visible, geographical, and political. He will expel Satan and his demon allies, will assume command of the earth, and will rule for one thousand years (Rev. 19:11–20:3).

　　　2) Its blessings

　　　As subjects of God's kingdom, we who are saved enjoy many blessings. Among these, we have unrestricted access to our Sovereign (Eph. 2:18; 1 Thess. 4:17), we enjoy His loving direction and care (Prov. 3:5–6; 1 Peter 5:7), and we anticipate the benefits of His millennial, earthly rule and His rule with the Father throughout eternity (2 Peter 1:11; 1 Cor. 15:24–28). Also, we have the duty of submitting to His authority in everything (2 Cor. 5:14–15; Matt. 7:24–25). Furthermore, as His ambassadors, we have the privilege of representing Him to the world and proclaiming everywhere His message of reconciliation (2 Cor. 5:18–20).

ᛋ. ADOPTION (ROM. 8:15, 23; GAL. 4:5; EPH. 1:5)

Its Definition

Adoption (Gk. *huiothesia*) means "placing as a son." In biblical usage, it is a twofold action of God in the life experience of each gospel believer.

　1. At salvation (Eph. 1:5) SIMULTANEOUSLY
　　Immediately following his regeneration and birth into God's family, the gospel believer is given the position of an adult-son. Thus, all gospel believers are sons of God (Gal. 3:26, KJV "children" (Gk. *huioi*) is "sons"; Rom. 9:26; 1 Thess. 5:5; Heb. 2:10; 12:5).

　2. In the future (Rom. 8:23)
　　God will deliver the gospel believer's body from inherent corruption and will make it like unto the Lord's body of glory (Phil. 3:20–21). This will complete the transformation of his or her human nature, making it suitable for this adult-son position and all that this entails.

Observe again that we do not enter God's family by means of adoption; we enter by the new birth (John 1:12–13, KJV "sons" should read "children").

Its Necessity

The gospel believer's need for adoption is seen in his initial position in God's family as a newborn child and in the present condition of his body. Without adoption, he would still have the status of a child, who would require strict, detailed supervision and discipline and who would be vulnerable to those hurtful forces (KJV "elements") of the world that would take advantage of his minority (Gal. 4:1–7). Also, without adoption his body would remain under the power of inherent corruption and mortality (Rom. 8:10).

Its Basis

The basis of adoption is redemption (Gal. 4:5), by which the Lord Jesus has delivered, by purchase, all gospel believers from bondage to such world forces as its vain philosophy and religious laws, including the Mosaic Law (cp. Rom. 7:1–6). He will also deliver their bodies from inherent corruption (8:23).

Its Blessings

1. Its present spiritual blessings

The present blessings of adoption relate to our position in God's family. By adoption, we who are saved have been given the privileges and duties of adult-sons as members of God's family, regardless of our spiritual age or rate of spiritual growth. This means that all gospel believers have the same obligation to obey the law of Christ (as given in the New Testament), which expresses His will for their lives. Moreover, since adoption eliminates our spiritual childhood and adolescence, we are not restricted in the use of our privileges or in the fulfillment of our duties. Within the sphere of their understanding of spiritual truth, all gospel believers have the same rights and privileges to enjoy as well as the same obligations to fulfill. Among these privileges we have immediate access to God (Eph. 2:18; Heb. 4:16), partnership with the Father and the Lord Jesus in the building of the Church (1 Cor. 3:9; John 15:1–5), and the liberty of free decision and action relating to behavioral matters that are not specifically dealt with in the Scriptures (Rom. 14:1–8; see Appendix F: "Learning and Doing God's Will").

The indwelling Holy Spirit is called "the Spirit of adoption" (Gal. 4:6; Rom. 8:15). By His activity, we are made aware through the Scriptures of our position in God's family, instinctively address God as our Father, make use of our spiritual privileges and rights, and fulfill our duties. Without His enablement, we either misuse or do not use the privileges and duties of adult-sonship.

2. Its future physical blessings

In addition to having the position of adoption, we who are saved will also have a body that will be suited to adult-sonship. This anticipates the time when we shall experience the completion of salvation with the redemption of our body from corruption, the sin force, and death (Rom. 8:23). Our adoption assures us that, being made like Jesus' glorified humanity, we shall be forever physically prepared for the full experience and blessing of all that this adult-sonship will involve throughout eternity (1 John 3:2; 1 Cor. 15:50–57).

Despite our position as adult-sons, our present experience on earth is like that of children because of our unsaved bodies. Due to the demands of the resident sin-force and the great restrictions that our unredeemed bodies place on us, we now need God's help in dealing with temptation and His care and supervision while we are here in this evil world. However, with the redemptive change of our bodies, these sinful demands and physical restrictions will be removed and we shall fully experience all that God has for us as His children (see Appendix V: "The Human Body-Grid").

6· NEARNESS TO GOD (EPH. 2:10–13)

Its Definition

This is the divine act whereby the gospel believer is brought near to God in Christ Jesus.

Its Necessity

The need of unsaved Gentiles for this aspect of salvation is dramatically stated by the apostle Paul in Ephesians 2:12.[33]

One: We Gentiles were without Christ. We had no relation to Him who is the only way to God, the personification of absolute Truth, and the essence of spiritual Life (John 14:6).

Two: We were shut out from the commonwealth of Israel. Being Gentiles, we had no share in the blessings that belonged to God's ancient, chosen people (Rom. 9:4–5).

Three: We were foreigners to God's covenant promises to Israel, like those relating to their being His people (Exod. 19:5), of their land (Gen. 13:15; 15:18–21; Deut. 30:1–5) and their king (2 Sam. 7:10–16).

Four: We had no hope or expectation of divine blessing in or beyond this life (1 Thess. 4:13).

Five: We were destitute of God (1 Cor. 1:21; Eph. 4:18). This is life's most tragic experience. G. G. Findlay wrote, "To be without God in this world is to be in the wilderness without a guide, on a stormy ocean without harbor or pilot, in sickness without medicine or physician, to be hungry without bread, weary without rest and dying with no light of life. It is to be an orphaned child, wandering in an empty, ruined house."[34]

Its Basis   *WHAT ABOUT SAVAGES*

In our unsaved state, we had neither the desire nor the ability to draw near to God. Our being made near is wholly God's work, as follows:

1. *This was made possible by Jesus' sacrifice (Eph. 2:13, "by the blood of Christ").*

His atoning work removed our sins, which separated us from God (Heb. 9:26). Removing the alienating cause, Jesus cleared the way to bring us near to God.

2. *This was made real by our baptism into Christ (Eph. 2:13, "in Christ Jesus").*

The Holy Spirit's baptism placed us into Jesus (Gal. 3:27; cp. Eph. 2:10; 2 Cor. 5:17; John 14:20). United spiritually to Jesus, we are as near to the Father as He is (Col. 3:3). No angel has such a close, exalted position as this (Eph. 1:3; 2:5–6).

Its Blessings

Our being made near to God in Christ forms the basis of two important doctrines, which in turn point to the blessings of this position. These doctrines are the gospel believer's standing and state and his or her sanctification.

1. *The gospel believer's standing and state*
   a. *His standing*
      1) Its description
         This refers to the gospel believer's spiritual position in Christ before God (Eph. 1:1). We received this position at salvation by God's creative work (2 Cor. 5:17–18; Eph. 2:10), namely, by the baptism of the Holy Spirit, which placed us into Jesus (Gal. 3:27).
      2) Its blessings
         This position grants those of us who are saved the blessings of sharing in what Jesus as man has done, in what He has, and in what He is.

One: In sharing in what He has done, we participate in His obedience, death, and resurrection (Rom. 5:16–19), which results in our being divinely accepted (Eph. 1:6), righteous before God (1 Cor. 1:30), secure (Col. 3:3; cp. John 10:28–29), and dead to sin and alive to God (Rom. 6:1–4).

Two: In sharing in what Jesus has, we have His spiritual life (Rom. 8:2; Col. 1:4) and are made wealthy as joint-heirs (Eph. 1:3, 11; Rom. 8:17; John 3:35; Heb. 1:2).

Three: In sharing in what He is, we are complete in Him (Col. 2:10), being made in His human image morally (2 Cor. 3:18) and in the future physically (Phil. 3:20–21; 1 John 3:2). This will fulfill the divine purpose of creating a new human race in the image of Jesus, the Last Adam, who by His incarnation and exaltation became the firstborn in time and rank among many "brothers" made like Him (1 Cor. 15:22, 45–49; Rom. 8:29; Heb. 2:11).

The blessings of this position are radically different from that which we had in Adam when we were unsaved (2 Cor. 5:17; Rom. 5:15–19; 1 Cor. 15:22). Then we shared Adam's corrupted human nature, his sin, his divine condemnation, and his death.

b. Their state

1) Its description

This refers to the spiritual condition of the gospel believer's daily life.

2) Its variation

We find that our spiritual state, or condition, is imperfect and changing because of our spiritual immaturity and ignorance, the opposition of our spiritual enemies, and our failure to apply consistently the spiritual resources that we have in God for a fruitful, victorious life (see endnote 30). It is God's desire that we increasingly live up to our standing in Jesus (Eph. 4:1; Col. 3:1–17). To this end, God deals with us (John 15:2; Heb. 12:5–13) and teaches us (2 Tim. 3:16–17; Eph. 4:11–15). The wise person studies God's Word, submits himself to these divine dealings, and seeks to be all that God desires for Him.

The truth of our standing and state answers the question of how we can be sanctified in Christ and still be carnal in daily life (cp. 1 Cor. 1:2–9; 6:11 with 3:1–4).[35] Professing gospel believers should not tolerate carnality in their lives, for those who are living constantly in sin may not be saved at all (2 Cor. 13:5). If they are saved, they will be denied God's blessings and will incur divine corrective chastisement when they persist in their sinning (Rev. 3:19) and do not deal with it by repentance, confession, and submission to God (2:5; 1 John 1:9; James 4:7; Rom. 12:1–2).

2. The gospel believer's sanctification

In Scripture usage, divine sanctification may be either an action or a state (condition) as determined by the context. As *an action,* sanctification is the activity of God whereby He sets His people apart unto Himself for His manifestation and use (cp. Eph. 5:26). As *a state,* it is the condition of being set apart that results from this divine action (cp. Eph. 5:27; 1 Cor. 1:2). Therefore, the basic ideas of sanctification are the action of setting apart and having been set apart (Lev. 20:26).

Several Bible words (translated from the same root words in the Hebrew and Greek texts) that relate to sanctification are: the verbs *sanctify* and *hallow;* the nouns *saint, sanctification, holiness,* and *Holy One;* and the adjectives *hallowed* and *holy.*

The concept of sanctification was held by pagans in their setting apart people and things for their deities (cp. 1 Kings 14:24, "sodomites" or "temple prostitutes"). In the Scriptures, we find God's sanctifying people, days, places, and things (Gen. 2:3; Exod. 29:44; 19:23); man's sanctifying himself, God, and things (1 Peter 3:15; Exod. 19:22; John 17:19; 1 Tim. 4:5); and a thing sanctifying other things (Matt. 23:19).

In addition to the sanctification that relates to the presalvational work of the Holy Spirit in gospel believers (2 Thess. 2:13; 1 Peter 1:2; cp. Heb. 6:4–6; 10:29), there are three aspects of divine sanctification that relate to us who are now saved.[36] These are positional, practical, and final sanctification.

a. Positional sanctification

1) Its meaning

This concerns our having been set apart unto God in Christ (1 Cor. 1:2). It is related to our position, or standing, in the Lord Jesus (1:30; 6:11).

2) Several observations

One: It takes place at salvation, with the result that we are in a permanent state of sanctification (1 Cor. 6:11), with Jesus as our sanctification (1:30).

Two: It is the instantaneous work of God the Father (Eph. 2:10), based on Jesus' death (Heb. 13:12), wrought by the Holy Spirit (1 Peter 1:2; 1 Cor. 6:11; cp. Gal. 3:27), in response to salvational faith (Acts 26:18).

Three: It belongs to every saved person alike, regardless of his or her condition of daily life (1 Cor. 6:11; cp. 3:1–4).

Four: Being perfect and complete for every gospel believer, this positional sanctification will continue forever (Heb. 10:10).

Five: This makes every saved person a "saint," or a "holy one" (1 Cor. 1:2; Phil. 1:1; Col. 1:2).

b. *Practical sanctification*

1) Its meaning

This concerns the spiritual condition of our daily lives (1 Peter 1:15).[37] Since He is holy, God wants His people increasingly to express holiness (moral perfection, or sinlessness) in their daily lives (Matt. 5:48; 1 John 2:1). We express this holiness when we separate ourselves from that which is morally unlike God (Col. 3:8; 2 Cor. 6:14–7:1), yield ourselves to Him (Rom. 6:11–13), and do His will (Eph. 6:6; Rom. 6:19, 22; 12:1–2; see Appendix E: "Righteousness and Holiness"). Our positional sanctification, or sainthood, in the Lord Jesus should motivate us to live holy, sinless lives (Eph. 4:1; 5:8; Col. 3:1–14). We should be holy in daily life, for we are holy in Jesus.

2) Several observations

One: Being closely related to spiritual growth, practical sanctification takes place throughout the gospel believer's spiritual lifetime. We never reach the place where we have no further need for holiness more often and for longer periods of time.

Two: It involves our separation from sinful practices, people, and things (2 Cor. 6:14–7:1; 1 Thess. 4:3, 7) as well as our dedication to God and our doing His will (Rom. 6:19, 22; 12:2; 1 Peter 1:14–15).[38]

Three: It is a process that involves an increase in the frequency and duration of those times that we are expressing holiness. This takes place not only as we live in obedience to God but also as we favorably respond to those divine activities that allow God to effect holiness in our daily life. These activities are His giving us victory over temptations of our spiritual enemies (Rom. 6:11–13, 22; James 4:7), His making us more like Jesus in character and works (2 Cor. 3:18; Rom. 8:2–4), His using His Word to influence and direct our lives (John 17:17; 15:3; 2 Tim. 3:16–17), and His parental dealings with each of us (Heb. 12:10; Rev. 3:19). As we respond favorably to these divine ministries, we advance in our practical sanctification.

Four: Its progress varies among saved people and within the lifetime of each believer. In this way, some people are more holy in their conduct than others; also, we are more holy at one time than another. This variation in holiness is not one of degree but of frequency and duration. Being an absolute, holiness itself does not express itself in varying degrees. Practical holiness is something that we are to express more often and for longer periods of time in daily life (2 Cor. 7:1).

Five: By this process, we are more frequently saintly in character and conduct for longer periods of time (1 Thess. 4:1–7; Rom. 6:19, 22). Actually, we are more like Jesus, who is our spiritual life and our sanctification (2 Cor. 3:18; Gal. 4:19; Col. 3:4; 1 Cor. 1:30).

Six: Negatively, practical holiness is sinlessness; positively, it is godliness (1 Peter

1:15). Practical righteousness concerns our doing God's will, which results in holiness and which expresses spiritual life (Rom. 6:19, 22; see Appendix E: "Righteousness and Holiness").

3) Note the following comparisons:

Positional Sanctification:
It relates to our standing in Christ.
It occurs at our salvation.
It is God's instantaneous work.
It is complete and absolute.
It is the same for every saved person.
It makes each saved person a saint.

Practical Sanctification:
It relates to our condition of daily life.
It occurs throughout our lifetime.
It is God's progressive work.
It is incomplete and relative.
It varies with each saved person.
It makes each saved person saintly.

c. Final sanctification

We who are saved shall experience this aspect of sanctification when the Lord returns for His Church. Then our bodies will be delivered from inherent corruption and will be made like our Lord's glorified body (Phil. 3:20–21). By this, we shall be brought into complete conformity to His character and humanity (1 John 3:2). From then on, we shall be as holy in our condition as we are in our position (1 Cor. 1:8; Eph. 1:4; 5:26–27; 1 Thess. 5:23; Jude 24).

Again, we should keep in mind the distinction between the atonement that Jesus accomplished on the cross and the benefits of this work that are granted to the gospel believer when he trusts in the Savior for salvation. The components of salvation, which we have just reviewed, are the gracious benefits of our Lord's atoning work. We who are saved can look back to the cross and say that He obtained for us eternal redemption (Heb. 9:12), justification (Rom. 5:9, 19), reconciliation (v. 10; Col. 1:20), life (1 Peter 3:24; 1 John 4:9–10), and sanctification (Heb. 10:10). However, these benefits are not divinely given until a person believes the gospel. The Lord's atoning work, with its benefits, is provisional in the sense that it does not become effective in one's life until one trusts in the Savior. Should anyone not do so, that person must pay the woeful debt of his sins himself, as though the Lord Jesus had not died. Is your trust in Jesus and His atoning work for your salvation? Are you certain of this? If so, praise Him for all that He has done for you. If not, settle this now by decisively trusting in the Savior and His atoning work.

THE DUTIES OF SALVATION

In our study of salvation, we have examined several of its parts—redemption, justification, reconciliation, regeneration, adoption, and our being made near to God. These salvational blessings are absolute in the sense that they belong to every gospel believer alike. But how do they relate to daily life? For many professed gospel believers, salvation is simply a ticket to heaven. As we have seen, it is much more than this. God intends that salvation should make an impact upon the daily lives of His people, not only in the changes it brings about but also in the duties it imposes on them. Let us look again at the components of salvation for the duties they place on those of us who are saved.

REDEMPTION

Having been divinely forgiven of all our sins (Eph. 1:7), we should now be forgiving toward others who have wronged us (Eph. 4:32; Matt. 6:14–15; 18:21–35) when they have repented and made right their wrongdoing (Luke 17:3; see Appendix W: "The Saved Person's Forgiveness of Others"). Harboring ill feelings, holding resentment, and seeking revenge have no proper place in the saved person's heart (1 Cor. 13:5; Rom. 12:17–21).

Also, having been freed from enslavement to the sin force, Satan, and the world (Titus 2:13), it is our duty daily to yield ourselves gladly to our new Master, the Lord Jesus, and to serve Him wholeheartedly as His purchased slaves (Rom. 6:11–13; 12:1–2; 14:8; James 4:7; 1 John 2:15). He alone has lawful, absolute claim to our lives (1 Cor. 6:19–20; 2 Cor. 5:14–15).

JUSTIFICATION

Since God has dropped all charges against us (Rom. 8:33–34), we should no longer feel guilty about those sins that we committed in the past or about those that we repentantly confess to Him now (Heb. 9:14). Satan often brings these sins to mind and tries to make us feel guilt ridden. This, in turn, makes us feel unfit for Christian life and ministry. However, God wants us to claim the fact of divine forgiveness and consequently of our being guiltless in His sight. On the other hand, we should experience the guilt of those sins that we knowingly commit now until we deal with them in the way that God prescribes in His Word (Rev. 2:5; 1 John 1:9).

God also expects those who are righteous in Christ (1 Cor. 1:30) to live righteous lives by doing right things, or His will in His way (Phil. 1:11; 2 Tim. 2:22; 3:16–17; Heb. 13:21; Rom. 6:13, 19; 12:1–2; 1 John 2:29). We find in His Word and in the leading of the Holy Spirit all the direction that we need for pleasing Him in this world (see Appendix F: "Learning and Doing God's Will").

RECONCILIATION

Being God's friends, we should show ourselves friendly by loving obedience to His will (John 15:14; 14:15). Furthermore, we should live peaceably with other gospel believers (Eph. 4:3, 31–32; 1 Thess. 5:13) as well as with the unsaved "in all godliness and honesty" (1 Tim. 2:2). We experience this peace when we are filled with the Holy Spirit and live in His power (Gal. 5:22, 16). Being at peace with God, we are His peacemakers to this world (Matt. 5:9). We have the ministry and message of reconciliation for those who are His enemies (2 Cor. 5:18–20).

REGENERATION

Our new life in Christ should be seen in our attitudes and character (Gal. 5:22–23), our doing God's will (Phil. 2:13; Eph. 5:17), our understanding of spiritual truth (1 Cor. 2:10–12), our fellowship with God and His people (1 Cor. 1:9; 1 John 1:3), our intention to please God (1 Cor. 5:9; 1 John 3:22), and our activity in the work of our Lord (Col. 3:1–3). It is our duty to cultivate these areas of our new life (2 Peter 3:18) as the commands of Scripture and the example of godly people indicate. We experience these things as we submit to the Lord Jesus and to the Holy Spirit, search out His Word, appropriate by faith what we need, and do what He commands (Phil. 4:13; John 7:38–39; Gal. 2:20; John 13:17).

Also, being members of God's family and subjects of His kingdom (John 1:12; Col. 1:13), we have the duty of reverencing Him and respecting His authority (1 Peter 2:17; 1:17), learning His truth (Eph. 5:17; Ps. 1:1–3), walking in His will and fellowship (1 John 1:5–7), yielding to His parental dealings (Heb. 12:1–15), and relying on His provision and care (1 Peter 5:7; Matt. 6:8, 25–34). However, He will not be our servant; He will not do for us what we can do for ourselves with His help (cp. James 4:8).[39]

ADOPTION

Having the position of adult-sons in God's family, we must determine what His will is for our lives and ministries while we are here in this world (see Appendix F: "Learning and Doing God's Will"). Being accountable people, we must take charge of our lives, make right decisions, obey God, and accept the responsibility of our actions (Rom. 14:12; 2 Cor. 5:10). Unlike parents of immature children, God does not do all our thinking for us or give us specific written orders for the details of each day. With our renewed minds and spiritual resources, including the Scriptures and the Holy Spirit, we can determine what His will is for us in every situation (Rom. 12:2; 8:14; 14:1–8; Ps. 119:105). Moreover, we have the liberty, as well as the duty, to use all our spiritual resources in carrying out His will for His glory (1 Cor. 10:31; see endnote 30). It is our duty as adult-sons to cultivate our spiritual growth so that we are not subject to false doctrine or sinful habits but are strong in our Lord's grace and fruitful in every good work (2 Peter 3:18; Eph. 4:14–15; 2 Tim. 2:1; Col. 1:10).

NEARNESS TO GOD

Because of our positional sanctification in Christ, it is our duty to live holy lives (1 Peter 1:15). This means that, increasingly, we must set ourselves apart from that which is unlike Jesus (Col. 3:8; 2 Thess. 3:14–15; Rom. 6:17–18; 2 Cor. 6:14–7:1; 1 John 2:15) and give ourselves to Him for His manifestation and use in this world (2 Cor. 5:15; Rom. 12:1–2; Col. 3:1–3; John 15:1–5).

God has provided all that we need for holy living (2 Peter 1:3), but to derive help from these resources we must use them. He has given us prayer (John 14:13), His Word (Ps. 1:1–3; Col. 3:16; Luke 8:18), the Holy Spirit (John 14:16–17; Eph. 5:18) and His fruit (Gal. 5:22–23; 1 Peter 1:5–7), faith (Gal. 2:20), His parental dealings (Heb. 12:7–14; James 1:2–4), and the ministry of others who love us (1 Cor. 14:26; Heb. 10:24).

Living a holy life is necessary for our pleasing God (1 John 3:22; 2 Cor. 5:9–10), serving Him (2 Tim. 2:19–22), glorifying Him (Matt. 5:16; 1 Cor. 10:31), and receiving His blessings (1 John 1:7; John 14:21, 23). God motivates us to live a holy life by His choosing us to be holy (Eph. 1:4), making us holy in Christ (1 Cor. 1:2), commanding us to be holy (1 Thess. 4:7; 1 Peter 1:15), and giving us the expectation of Jesus' imminent return and of our accountability to Him (1 John 3:2–3; 2 Cor. 5:9–10). There is no way out—holy people must live holy lives.

Our daily fulfilling these duties of salvation requires our resolute decision and hearty commitment to God and His will by prayer (Isa. 6:8). Did you give yourself to your Redeemer, the Lord Jesus, for His direction and use today (Rom. 12:1–2; Eph. 3:17)?

THE METHOD OF SALVATION IN OTHER AGES

How were people saved during the precross period before Jesus died? How will they be saved during the coming Tribulation Age and the Kingdom Age? While much information is lacking, the Scriptures give sufficient detail to answer these questions. The principle may be stated, however, that in every age of human history, God saves people in the same way—by His grace through their salvational faith in the divine revelation about Jesus, the Savior-Redeemer (Eph. 2:8).

DURING THE PAST PRECROSS PERIOD

This looks back to that span of time from the creation of man to Jesus' death. Both Adam and Eve believed God's promise of the coming Seed, who would eventually destroy Satan (Gen. 3:15). Adam's faith is indicated by his naming his wife "Eve," which means "Life" or "Living," as she would be the means of perpetuating the human race and of her Seed's ultimate victory over Satan and death (3:20). Eve's faith is seen in her accepting her name and in her words upon the births of her sons, Cain and Seth (4:1, 25). In response to their faith in this divine revelation, God clothed the couple with the skins of animals (3:21). By this action, He established the process of atoning for sins by the death and the offering of the blood of an innocent substitute (cp. Lev. 17:11).

By faith, Abel offered a more excellent sacrifice than that of Cain (Gen. 4:4; Heb. 11:4). By His acceptance of this gift, God bore witness to Abel's righteousness. The reference to Abel's faith presupposes a divine revelation to which his faith responded. This revelation, given when God clothed Adam and Eve (Gen. 3:20), concerned the right approach to Him through animal sacrifices (cp. 8:20), which pointed to the coming Conqueror-Savior (3:15). As always, Abel's righteousness was the divine gift of righteousness that accompanies salvation (cp. 15:6; Rom. 3:22).

Other people of faith who believed God's salvational revelation were Enoch (Gen. 5:22; Heb. 11:5–6), Noah (Gen. 6:8; Heb. 11:7), and Abraham (Gen. 15:5–6). Abraham's faith in the coming Seed (Savior) was divinely credited to him for righteousness. It appears that he had earlier believed the salvational revelation (Gen. 12:3; Gal. 3:8–9) and had rejoiced in the truth of the coming Savior (John 8:56; Gal. 3:16). How much detail was known about the Redeemer before written divine revelation was given mankind is not certain. It probably was more than the Old Testament record indicates (John 8:56; Heb. 11:10, 13, 14).[40] In any case, it was sufficient for salvational faith in Him.

With the written OT revelation, many details were given for faith in the coming Savior and His work, like His birth—including His race (Gen. 15:5), tribe (49:10), family (2 Sam. 7:12–13; cp. 2 Tim. 2:8), place (Mic. 5:2), and time (Dan. 9:25)—and His messianic work and atoning sacrifice (Isa. 49:6–7; 52:13–53:12; Zech. 9:9). In Luke's gospel, we see that Zacharias and Elizabeth (1:6, 41–45, 68–79), the virgin Mary (vv. 46–55), Simeon (2:25–32), and Anna (vv. 36–38) were believers in the coming Savior. Both Zacharias and Mary also refer to the Abrahamic covenant (vv. 55, 72–73), which may be regarded as the "John 3:16" of the Old Testament (see Gen. 12:3; 15:5; Gal. 3:8–9, 16; cp. Mic. 7:18–20).

These precross believers possessed the same basic salvational blessings that we enjoy today. These included the presence of the Holy Spirit (Ps. 51:11; John 14:17), forgiveness of sins (2 Sam. 12.13; Ps. 32:1), righteousness (Gen. 15:6), redemption (Isa. 29:22), faith (Heb. 11), joy (Ps. 51:12), the fear of God (89:7; Job 1:1), grace to please God (Gen. 6:8; 17:1; 26:5; cp. Luke 1:6), and fellowship with God (Gen. 5:22; 6:9; Deut. 34:10; Ps. 16:8–11).

During their lifetimes of faith, these precross gospel believers anticipated the fulfillment of God's promises (Heb. 11:8–10, 13–16). These promises concerned Jesus' first coming, His atoning work (Acts 13:23, 32–34; 26:6, 22–23; Gal. 3:16–19; Eph. 3:6), and their receiving an everlasting inheritance, which is a city (Heb. 9:15; 10:34–36; 11:13–16; cp. Rev. 21:10ff.). Although they did not go to heaven at death (Gen. 25:8; Ps. 16:10), they went to Paradise in hades (cp. Luke 16:22; 23:43) to await the Lord's atoning work and resurrection, which would put away their sins and release them from death's power (Heb. 9:15–17; 2:14). Apparently, they were removed to heaven upon our Lord's ascension (Eph. 4:8).

365

DURING THE COMING TRIBULATION AGE

During the first half of the Tribulation Age, there will be an intensive evangelistic ministry throughout the earth by 144,000 born-again Israelites, who will be saved immediately after the rapture of the Church (Rev. 7:1–8; 12:17; 14:3–4). Apparently immunized against the divine judgments of this age, they will preach the Gospel of the Kingdom with unprecedented results (Matt. 24:14; Rev. 7:9, 14). This gospel will be the same as that which we proclaim today, with additional emphasis on the Lord's imminent return to establish His earthly kingdom and the need to prepare for this event (Acts 20:24–25; cp. Matt. 24:42– 44).

What does the Lord Jesus mean when He says, "But he that shall endure unto the end, the same will be saved" (Matt. 24:13)? He certainly was not suggesting the possibility of these people's losing their salvation or of their being saved by good works. The Scriptures reveal that Satan will require gospel believers to deny their faith in Christ or to accept death during the beginning of the second half of the Tribulation Age (Rev. 13:7–8, 15; Mark 13:9–13). Those who remain faithful to Jesus "unto the end" (until their death or until the Lord's second coming) will experience the final phase of their salvation (Rom. 13:11), either by their resurrection if they are martyred (Rev. 20:4) or by their deliverance from their enemies if they survive until Jesus comes (19:15). All who deny their professed faith in Christ and who embrace the Beast (Satan's human agent) will, by this, indicate that they were never saved and will commit an unforgivable sin (14:9–11; 13:8). All who reject this gospel ministry during the forepart of the Tribulation Age will believe Satan's lie, will support and follow the Beast during the second half of this age, and will finally perish (2 Thess. 2:8–12; Rev. 19:11–21).

DURING THE MILLENNIAL KINGDOM AGE

From such passages as Matthew 7:21–23; 25:31–46, we infer that only saved people will be allowed to enter the Lord's earthly kingdom when He establishes it. However, during His millennial rule, the earth will be repopulated by saved earth dwellers who survived the Tribulation Age and who entered the kingdom in their unredeemed bodies. Born with inherent corruption, the children of these people will need to be saved as children do today. These people will have unprecedented opportunity and encouragement to trust Jesus for salvation, for "the earth shall be full of the knowledge of the LORD as the waters cover the sea" (Isa. 11:9). As always, salvation will be by grace through faith in Jesus and His atoning work, according to the terms of the new covenant (Jer. 31:31–34; Deut. 30:6; 36:24–38; John 3:16). But in spite of this, there will be many unsaved people on earth at the close of the thousand years (Rev. 20:7–9).

Since God can only save sinners by the principle of grace, we can assert that people in every age are saved in the same way—by God's grace through their salvational faith in the divine revelation about the Savior. The precross gospel believers looked forward to Jesus' coming and His atoning work; the postcross gospel believers look back to His coming and work. All the saved of every age have the same, basic salvational blessings—divine forgiveness of their sins, a personal relationship with God, and the gift of eternal life (Jer. 31:33–34), but not all will have the same functional blessings in ministry.[41]

THE SALVATION OF INFANTS

Contrary to a large segment of Christendom who believe that unbaptized infants who die perish, I believe that all infants who die before they are able to make responsible, moral decisions are saved upon death.[42] Although the Bible does not clearly state the destination of infants who die, the following inferences may be drawn:

One: All people, including infants, are divinely condemned and are unsaved because of their participation in Adam's initial sin (Rom. 5:12, 18–19; 1 Cor. 15:22).

Two: The Lord Jesus died for everyone, including infants who die (Heb. 2:9; 1 John 2:2; 4:14; John 1:29; 3:16–17; 1 Tim. 4:10). By this sacrifice, He secured the basis of the divine forgiveness of everyone in the human race.

Three: God is not willing that anyone, including infants, should perish (2 Peter 3:9; 1 Tim. 2:4; Matt. 18:14). Whereas all humans who fail to respond to God's general revelation are without excuse (Rom. 1:18–20), it seems that infants, being intellectually undeveloped and incapable of making moral decisions (Deut. 1:39; Jonah 4:11; Rom. 9:11), are exempt from this responsibility until they develop moral awareness and self-determination.

Four: Since salvation is wholly God's work, it is reasonable to assume that He saves all infants who die before their reaching the state of moral awareness and self-determination, which results in personal accountability. Applying to them the value of Christ's atoning work, God graciously saves them at death (cp. Mark 1:18–21; 3:9; John 3:18).

Five: While people are guilty of Adam's initial sin, they do not go to hell solely because of this. They are condemned for their actual sins as well (Rom. 1:18–21; 3:9–19; John 3:18). Infants who die have not yet committed actual sins.

In summary, it appears that infants who die, although born unsaved because of original sin, are saved upon death by God's applying to them the value of the Lord's atoning work. Being infinitely righteous and just, God always acts in conformity to His nature (Gen. 18:25). From these propositions, I infer that infants who die before the awakening of moral consciousness and accountability are part of the elect whom God has chosen to save.[43]

We can never reflect upon salvation without thanking God for such a wonderful Savior and provision for our deliverance from the guilt, penalty, ruin, and bondage of our sins. All is of His grace. There was nothing in us that meritoriously prompted this divine work. All is of God and to His glory. After serious reflection on these things, the apostle Paul reached the settled conclusion that he owed to the Lord Jesus his life (2 Cor. 5:14–15) and to others the gospel message (Rom. 1:14–16). We who are saved have this debt as well. Like the lepers of old who, in a time of famine, stumbled across the spoils of the Syrians, we do not do well to hold our peace in a day of salvation's good news (2 Kings 7:9). Incumbent upon us all who are saved is our continual witness to others of salvation in the Lord Jesus (Acts 1:8). We must be prepared not only to explain our spiritual experience to others (1 Peter 3:15) but also to share with them the gospel message, which they must believe to be saved (Acts 11:19–20). We must support our witness by a consistent holy life that reflects the reality of what we are saying to our unsaved friends. A witness that is rooted in God's Word, watered with prayer and love, and energized by the Holy Spirit will be fruitful and will glorify God. What message are you and your life conveying to others today?

A Review of Soteriology

1. What is the basic idea of salvation? *329*
2. Give its secular meaning and its biblical meaning. *329*
3. Give a theological description of salvation. *329*
4. Give the three aspects of salvation with reference to time. *330*
5. List the needs that unsaved people have for salvation. *330-1*
6. List the corresponding benefits that salvation brings to gospel believers. *331-2*
7. Explain the terms *condemned, spiritually dead,* and *lost.*
8. What question about divine justice confronted God when He thought about saving sinners? *332*

367

9. What was the answer to this question? *332*
10. What is "the preaching of the cross"? *?*
11. Give God's part in the application of salvation: before time, during the lifetime of the elect, and in the future. *333-335*
12. How does preterition differ from reprobation? *333*
13. To what did God predestinate those whom He elected? *334*
14. Distinguish between God's general and special calls to salvation. *335*
15. What divine activities make up His special call? *335*
16. In what way is God's special call to salvation irresistible? *336*
17. In what way is the gospel more than an invitation?
18. What must the sinner do to be saved? *337*
19. If there is something for the sinner to do to be saved, why is his salvation not of works?
20. Give and explain the parts of salvational faith. *337*
21. By what inward and outward actions does the gospel believer exercise salvational faith?
22. What does God immediately do in response to salvational faith?
23. What are two erroneous views regarding the place of water baptism in salvation?
24. What is the biblical purpose of water baptism?
25. What place does one's confession of the lordship of Christ have in salvational faith?
26. What is household salvation? Why is this in error?
27. What does monergistic salvation mean? Synergistic salvation? Which is biblical?
28. By what principle of dealing does God save people?
29. Why can He not save sinners by the principle of meritorious works?
30. What two primary lines of evidence provide the assurance of salvation?
31. List the signs of new life that indicate that a person is saved.
32. What might temporarily eclipse these signs of new life in one's experience?
33. Explain the difference between the assurance of salvation and the permanence of salvation.
34. What does God do to give permanence to our salvation?
35. What provisions has He made for this permanence?
36. What is our part in maintaining our salvation?
37. Explain how we are able to persevere in salvational faith.
38. How has God counterbalanced the doctrine of eternal security so that people do not think of this as giving them freedom to sin?
39. Explain the difference between salvational faith and practical faith.
40. Which of these two faiths is constant, or remains the same? Which fluctuates, or comes and goes?
41. What are the three ultimate goals for God's saving people?
42. List and define the six components of salvation.
43. What is the need for these components? What blessings do they bring a saved person?
44. What is Christian freedom, or liberty? What purposes does it serve in one's life?
45. Distinguish between the gospel believer's standing and state.
46. How did the Corinthian gospel believers illustrate the truth of one's standing and state?
47. What is the basic idea of sanctification, or holiness?
48. Describe the three aspects of the believer's sanctification.
49. What does it mean to live a holy life? How can we do this?
50. What activities of God contribute to our practical holiness?
51. What salvational duties rest upon those of us who are saved?
52. How were people saved during the precross period?

53. By what means were people reminded of the promise of the coming Conqueror-Savior during the centuries before the incarnation of God the Son?

366 54. How will people be saved during the Tribulation Age? The Kingdom Age?

367 55. Why is a person unsaved at the time of his or her conception?

367 56. Give reasons for believing that people who die in infancy or before the time of their moral awareness and accountability are saved at death.

57. Are you wholly and solely trusting in Jesus and His atoning work for your salvation? Should you have any questions or doubts about your salvation, review again "The Sinner's Part in the Reception of Salvation" and "The Assurance of Salvation."

58. What is your spiritual duty to unsaved people as a saved person?

Endnotes

1. Compare Romans 8:28. "Purpose" is God's decree or plan. I prefer the view that election logically follows God's decree to create humans and to permit their fall. See Appendix: J: "The Order of God's Decree."

2. That God's election was determined by His foresight of what people would do is a misunderstanding of 1 Peter 1:2. Here, "foreknowledge" is equated with and preceded by His "determinate counsel" in Acts 2:23. This means that God's foreknowledge is based upon His counsel, decree, or plan. His plan is not based on His foresight (see "God's Attributes: Omniscience" under Theology Proper).

3. See W. G. T. Shedd, *Dogmatic Theology* (Grand Rapids: Zondervan Publishing House, 1969), 1:444ff.; and A. H. Strong, *Systematic Theology* (Philadelphia: American Baptist Publication Society, 1907), 789.

4. Observe that Reformed theology holds that predestination covers election and reprobation. To my mind, it is more biblical to regard predestination as a distinct, separate act of God, in addition to election and preterition.

5. With reference to the nonelect, the biblical record relates predestination only to their hostile actions toward Jesus (Acts 4:27–28; cp. 13:27–29). These actions were divinely predestinated, for the Lord's death and its circumstances were determined by God (2:23) and were predicted by OT prophecy (cp. Ps. 22:6–21; Isa. 52:13–53:12). Still, these people were responsible for their heinous crimes (Luke 22:22; Acts 3:14–15).

6. Beside the initial call to salvation, there are other divine calls, including those to discipleship (Mark 1:17), fellowship (1 Cor. 1:9), holiness (1 Thess. 4:7), and service (2 Tim. 1:9). The calls to glory (2 Thess. 2:14; 1 Peter 5:10) and to God's kingdom (1 Thess. 2:12) relate to salvation. In 1 Cor. 7:20–24, "calling" probably refers to the social position that we have when we are "called" to salvation.

7. That people are commanded by the gospel to receive the Savior is indicated in John 3:36; Acts 5:32; 17:30; Romans 1:5; 16:26; 2 Thessalonians 1:8; and 1 Peter 1:22; 4:17.

8. These "good works" always refer to our doing God's will in His way (Heb. 13:21). See Appendix F: "Learning and Doing God's Will."

9. Being a part of salvational faith, *repentance* and its verb form *repent* often occur as figures of association (synecdoche) for salvational faith (Luke 24:47; Acts 2:38; 3:19; 5:31; 11:18; 17:30; 26:20; 2 Peter 3:9). See Appendix X: "Figures of Association: Synecdoche and Metonymy."

10. For other salvational blessings, see "The Benefits of Salvation" and "The Components of Salvation" in this chapter.

11. God's unsurpassing love for sinners was shown in His giving His Son to be their Savior (John 3:16). He still shows them compassionate love in providing the sunshine and the rain to bring them to repentance (Matt. 5:44–45; Rom. 2:4). The false idea that God loves sinners with friendship love misleads them to think that this love will somehow override His justice and will find a way to spare them His judgment. This human sentimentalism misrepresents God's holy attitude toward sinners, whom He hates and will cast into everlasting fire (Ps. 11:5; Hos. 9:15; Rom. 9:13). All who reject God's love, expressed in the giving of His Son to be their Savior, have left to them only His wrath (John 3:36; Heb. 10:26–31; 2 Thess. 1:7–9).

12. In the Reformed tradition, baptism, being a substitute for circumcision, makes one a member of the covenant community. This regenerates the person, but his or her conversion to salvation through personal faith in Christ occurs later.

13. A. T. Robertson, *Epochs in the Life of Paul* (New York: Charles Scribner's Sons, 1930), 55.

14. See Kenneth S. Wuest, *First Peter in the Greek New Testament* (Grand Rapids: Wm. B. Eerdmans Publishing Co., 1942), 109.

15. "Lord Jesus" (Rom. 10:9) is a common designation, as seen in Acts 1:21; 7:59; 8:16; 9:29; 19:5, 10, 13, 17; 20:35; 1 Cor. 6:11; 11:23. The Greek aorist tense of Rom. 12:1 does not necessarily indicate a once-for-all commitment to the Lord Jesus. Here, it may describe the action of commitment in its entirety (see Dana & Mantey, *A Manual Grammar of the Greek New Testament,* 196, a. The Constative Aorist), but it does not prohibit its being repeated at a later time.

16. See R. Larry Shelton, "Initial Salvation" in *Contemporary Wesleyan Theology* (Grand Rapids: Francis Asbury Press, 1983), 1:497f.

17. There are also other purposes for God's parental dealings with us like our instruction, maturation, productivity, and sanctification (Job 42:5; Heb. 12:5–11; James 1:2–4).

18. See F. H. Barackman, *Victors, Not Victims,* 44ff.

19. We "put off" the old man and "put on" the new man by divine action at salvation.

20. See F. H. Barackman, "The Quantities and Qualities of Practical Faith," *Where Is Your Faith?* (Barackman, 1996).

21. See "The Gospel Believer and Sin" and "The Law and Sin" under Hamartiology.

22. His atoning work is often represented in Scriptures by His "blood" (see "His Humiliation: The Blood of Christ" under Christology).

23. Being a legal concept, imputation is God's reckoning or putting something to a person's account (cp. Philem. 18). The Scriptures teach the divine imputation of Adam's first sin to all his posterity (Rom. 5:12–19), the imputation of humanity's sins to Christ while He was on the cross (2 Cor. 5:19, 21), and the imputation of Jesus' righteousness to gospel believers (Rom. 4:1–6, 20–24).

24. See John Murray, *The Epistle to the Romans* (Grand Rapids: Wm. B. Eerdmans Publishing Co., 1959), 1:349f. (Appendix A).

25. Many people are unwilling to accept the fact of God's wrath, for it does not square with their sentimental humanistic concept of His love. Being the stern reaction of His holiness against sinners and their sins, God's wrath, today, generally assumes the form of a strong, settled opposition against them (John 3:36; Rom. 1:18). But in the future, it will take the form of angry heat poured out in terrible judgments (Rev. 14:10–11; 15:1; 19:15). In His gracious love, God provided the sacrifice that could satisfy His holy demands against sinners and opened the way for Him to save all who believe the gospel (1 John 4:9–10).

26. A propitiation is the turning away of divine wrath by an appeasing sacrifice. The divine propitiation for humanity's sins was Jesus' atoning sacrifice, which could appease the demands of God's holiness and justice against sinners and turn away His wrath from them. However, this propitiation is effective only in the case of those who trust in the Savior. They who do not do this will forever suffer divine wrath and retribution for their sins.

27. Keep in mind that the Lord's atoning work was provisional in the sense that the value He secured for everyone is now offered by the gospel and is divinely applied only when sinners trust in Jesus for their salvation (2 Cor. 5:18–20).

28. Observe that in evangelism it is important to present the gospel as it is given in the Scriptures and to rely on the Holy Spirit to work according to the divine purpose. We must refrain from attempting to do the Holy Spirit's work when making gospel appeals. The Arminian view that sees the sinner as having a free will and as making the final choice in salvation may lead people to use harmful coercion in their evangelistic appeals. Needless to say, such means are counterproductive. We must leave it to the Holy Spirit to do that inner work that only He can do in drawing people to Himself.

29. This consists of most of the commands that are given in the New Testament. See "The Dispensations of God: The Dispensation of Grace" under Theology Proper.

30. These spiritual resources include God's Word (2 Tim. 3:15–17), the Holy Spirit (John 14:15–17), faith (2 Peter 1:1; Gal. 2:20), prayer (John 14:13), the means of forgiveness and cleansing from sin (2 Cor. 7:1; Rev. 2:5; 1 John 1:9; 2 Tim. 2:21), grace (1 Cor. 15:10; 2 Cor. 1:12; 12:8–10), and the support and ministries of other gospel believers (John 13:34–35; 2 Cor. 1:11; Phil. 4:10–20; Heb. 10:24–25).

31. Observe that one does not become a member of God's family by adoption. See "The Duties of Salvation: Adoption" in this chapter.

32. Second Peter 1:4 may mean that our renewed human nature is the product of God's creative work (Eph. 2:10), that we received God's Seed—the Lord Jesus Christ (1 John 3:9; cp. John 14:6; 1 John 5:12), or that we received God into our being so that our bodies are His temples (1 Cor. 6:19; Col. 1:27; John 14:23).

33. While Israel nationally had a special relation with God, based on the covenant of the Mosaic Law (Exod. 19:3–6; Rom. 9:4–5), they severed this relationship by violating the covenant, which was a two-party, works contract (Jer. 31:31; Hos. 1:9). In the future, God will restore His relationship to the elect remnant of Israel when they agree to the gracious new covenant (Jer. 31:31–34), which promises them salvation and everlasting relationship with Him. Meanwhile, individual saved Jews today are brought near to God in Christ, are made members of the Lord's Church, and enjoy a personal relationship with God, as promised by the new covenant (Eph. 2:14–18; Gal. 5:27–28; Heb. 8:6–13).

34. G. G. Findlay, *The Expositor's Bible: The Epistle to the Ephesians* (New York: Hodder & Stoughton, n.d.), 126.

35. "Carnal" describes a person who is living under the dominion of the inner sin force. God wants those of us who are saved to be "spiritual" (1 Cor. 2:15), that is, ones who are living under the control of the Holy Spirit (Eph. 5:18; Gal. 5:16).

36. See "The Holy Spirit's Presalvational Ministry to Unsaved People" under Pneumatology.

37. See "The Duties of Salvation: Nearness to God" in this chapter; also Appendix E: "Righteousness and Holiness."

38. See "The Victories of the Christian Life" and "The Separation and Dedication of the Christian Life" under Zoeology.

39. For further suggestions regarding our engaging in a relationship with God, see "Fellowship with God" under Theology Proper as well as the closing sections of Paterology, Christology, and Pneumatology.

40. That people were saved during OT times outside of the messianic line and outside of Israel is evident in the lives of Job (Job 1:1; 14:14), Melchizedek (Gen. 14:18), and Jethro (Exod. 3:1). During some 2,500 years before the first written Scriptures, the good news of the coming Conqueror-Savior was preserved in human traditions (Ps. 145:4–7) and was portrayed by the constellations, which God set in the heavens for "signs" (Gen. 1:14) and to which He gave names (Ps. 147:4; Isa. 40:26; see Rom. 10:16–18; Ps. 19:4). The longevity of life helped to preserve the accuracy of these traditions; between Adam and Abraham there were 1,078 years. Adam was a contemporary with Methuselah for 243 years; Methuselah lived 98 years during Shem's lifetime; Shem was a contemporary of Abraham for 150 years. There were five generations between Abraham and Moses, covering some 425 years (see the Addendum: "The Genealogy from Adam to Abraham"). Also, see Don Richardson, *Eternity in Their Hearts* (Ventura, Calif.: Regal Books, 1981); E. W. Bullinger, *The Witness of the Stars* (Grand Rapids: Kregel Publications, 1893, 1987); J. A. Seiss, *The Gospel in the Stars* (Grand Rapids: Kregel Publications, 1882, 1972); and C. H. Kang and Ethel R. Nelson, *The Discovery of Genesis: How the Truths of Genesis Were Found Hidden in the Chinese Language* (St. Louis: Concordia Publishing House, 1979).

41. See "Covenant Theology" and "The New Covenant" under Theology Proper; "The Universal Christian Church: Its Functions" under Ecclesiology.

42. This truth also applies to mentally deficient people of any age who were never able to make responsible moral decisions during their lifetimes.

43. Regarding the salvation of those who never heard the gospel, see "The Final State of the Unsaved" under Eschatology.

Zoeology

11

ZOEOLOGY
The Doctrine of the Christian Life

In this section, we shall focus on the Christian life, the daily expression of the new spiritual life that gospel believers receive at salvation. We shall consider its nature and those elements that are essential to its growth, fruitfulness, and ministry. May the Holy Spirit not only give us understanding of these truths but also enable us to experience them in daily life to the end that our spiritual vitality might abound in Christlikeness and good works to God's glory.[1]

THE NATURE OF THE CHRISTIAN LIFE

The authentic Christian life is something more than following a routine that engages in Christian activities. Many unsaved people, who profess to be Christians, do this. It is to live and express spiritual life—the new kind of life that gospel believers receive at salvation (John 3:36).

In contrast to physical life, this new life is spiritual in nature and is called in the Scriptures "eternal life" or "everlasting life" (John 3:15–16).[2] This spiritual life is not God's essential divine life, for our human nature has not been made divine or replaced with a divine nature. It is a life that God the Father gives to gospel believers and that expresses their personal relationship with Him (John 17:3). It also is Jesus' spiritual life, which belongs to His humanity and by which He experiences fellowship with the Father (14:6; Col. 3:4; cp. John 4:34; 6:38; 8:28–29; 12:28; 14:31; 17:4). Thus, to have the Lord Jesus is to possess this life (1 John 5:11–12). To allow Him to express Himself in and through us is to experience and to manifest this new life, which is Christlikeness (Gal. 2:20; 4:19; Phil. 1:21; 1 John 2:29; see "The Goal of Spiritual Growth" in this chapter). Our possessing His spiritual life is a part of our being made in the image of His humanity (Rom. 8:29; 2 Cor. 3:18). In the future, we shall have His kind of physical life as well (Rom. 8:11; Phil. 3:20–21).

In this study, we must keep in mind that, while gospel believers have spiritual life by the new birth, they do not always express this new life in their daily behavior. Because this new life is communicated to us by the indwelling Holy Spirit (Rom. 8:2), it is essential that we maintain a good relationship with this resident Helper. The purpose of this study is to learn how to express this new life in our behavior to the glory of God.

THE EXPERIENCE OF THE CHRISTIAN LIFE

Having this new life, the Holy Spirit, and renewed personhoods, souls, and spirits, saved people have the necessary equipment and capability to experience and express this new life in their daily behavior. Being a personal interaction with God and the things of God, Christian experience rests upon our personal relationship with God, is brought about by the activity of the Holy Spirit in our lives, and is understood and directed by the teachings of Scripture.[3] Unlike mysticism, which seeks contact with God by immediate intuition apart from His Word, Christian experience conforms to and is understood by the Bible's teachings about this subject. Some aspects of Christian experience follow:

1. *An awareness of a personal relationship with God*

As God's people, we are aware of this when we are filled with the Holy Spirit and walk in obedience to Him (John 14:21–23; cp. 1 John 1:5–7; Rom. 8:16).

2. *A growing knowledge of God and spiritual truth*

This knowledge is gained from the Scriptures and from God's dealings with us, as we understand them in the light of His Word (John 17:3; Col. 1:10; Eph. 1:17–19; cp. Job 42:5–6).

3. *The assurance of divine forgiveness*

Only the saved person knows that his or her sins are divinely forgiven. This assurance is based on the promises of God's Word (Col. 2:13; 1 John 1:9) and is verified by our fellowship with Him (1 John 1:5–7).

4. *The various ministries of the Holy Spirit, our Helper*

These include His convicting, teaching, guiding, sanctifying, and enabling us (1 John 5:3.20; 1 Cor. 2:12; Rom. 8:14; Rom. 8:2, 4; Eph. 5:18; see "The Holy Spirit's Ministry: Throughout the Gospel Believer's Lifetime" under Pneumatology). He also produces His fruit in our lives (Gal. 5:22–23; Rom. 14:17).

5. *Love for God and for others*

Our love for God springs from an affection that is expressed by our obedience to His Word (John 14:15, 21, 23). Our expressing God's love for others (1 John 4:7) is our seeking to minister to their needs, including spiritual ones, under the direction and enablement of the Holy Spirit (Gal. 5:22; 1 John 3:16–18). This compassionate love even extends to enemies (Matt. 5:43–47).

6. *A dissatisfaction with sin*

Sinning no longer brings us the pleasure that it once did, for it violates our conscience (1 John 3:20), grieves the indwelling Holy Spirit (Eph. 4:30), and is opposed to our renewed personhoods and natures (cp. 4:24; cp. Rom. 7:21–25). These negative reactions cause us to be unhappy with sinning.

7. *The blessing and satisfaction of obeying God*

Obedience to God allows Him to reveal Himself to us and bless us (John 14:21, 23; 13:17; Ps. 1:1–3).

8. *Answers to prayer*

In keeping with His many promises, God answers our prayers in His time and way when we meet His conditions (Jer. 33:3; John 14:13; 15:7; 1 John 5:14–15).

9. *The fulfillment of God's promises*

Our faith in God's promises (2 Peter 1:4) allows Him to do for us what He says that He will do (cp. Heb. 13:5–6).

10. *Occasions of victory over our spiritual enemies*

To yield to God, to resist the sin force's urges, Satan's temptations, or the world's evil influences in His strength, and to do God's will with His power are blessed experiences (Gal. 5:16; Phil. 4:13; James 4:7; Ps. 34:8).

11. *Involvement in the Lord's work of building the Church*

As His fellow workmen (1 Cor. 3:9), it is a rewarding experience to be active in the Lord's ministry of building His Church quantitatively and qualitatively and to allow Him to do this work through our lives (John 15:4–5; Rom. 12:1–2; cp. Acts 14:27).

12. *Christian fellowship*

Our fellowship with God and with others of like faith in the love and unity of the Holy Spirit is blessed (1 John 1:3–4).

13. Divine parental discipline

God continually deals with us to nurture our spiritual growth (John 15:1–3; Heb. 12:1–11; James 1:2–4) and to correct us (Rev. 3:19). Although sometimes painful, these divine parental dealings bring blessing (Job 42:5; Ruth 1:20–21).

Christian experience is not an illusion but a reality when it is of God. However, all religious experiences must be tested by the Scriptures to see if they are satanic deceptions or spiritual realities. We cannot go astray as long as we are yielded to God, follow His Word, and seek to glorify Him in all that we do.

THE GROWTH OF THE CHRISTIAN LIFE

Our experience and expression of spiritual life has the capacity for growth; therefore, we have the duty of cultivating this development (2 Peter 3:18; 1 Peter 2:1–2). When he rebuked the Corinthian believers for their carnality (living under the domination of the sin force), the apostle Paul described them as "babes" (1 Cor. 3:1–3). They were remaining infants in their spiritual development, for their sinning had blighted their spiritual lives and had retarded their spiritual growth (cp. Gal. 6:8; 1 Peter 2:1–2). The writer to the Hebrews chided his readers for their unresponsiveness because of their spiritual immaturity (Heb. 5:11–14). These instances point to the fact that at any particular time in our life experience, we are either progressing or regressing in our spiritual development, for there is no standing still. Let us look at this more closely.

A DESCRIPTION OF SPIRITUAL GROWTH

Like all growth, spiritual growth is a progressive increase or development in certain areas of our spiritual life and its experience. These areas include spiritual character as expressed by the fruit of the Holy Spirit (1 Thess. 3:12), the use of divine grace (2 Peter 3:18; cp. Phil. 4:13), practical faith in God and His promises (2 Thess. 1:3; cp. Luke 17:5–6), spiritual knowledge of God and of those things that relate to Him (Col. 1:10; 2 Peter 3:18), spiritual activity within God's will (2 Cor. 9:8; cp. Heb. 13:21; James 4:17), and appreciation for the Lord Jesus (John 3:30; cp. Phil. 1:21).

THE NATURE OF SPIRITUAL GROWTH

Since spiritual growth consists of the joint activity of the Holy Spirit and the saved person, it has both absolute and relative aspects. The growth experience of spiritual behavior is absolute, for we are either doing or being or are not doing or being what God desires. Behavioral growth consists of our doing God's will more often and for longer periods of time. For instance, our growing in love and patience means that we express these virtues, which God produces in us, more often and for longer periods of time; our growing in faith means that we are exercising faith in God more often and for longer periods of time; and our growing in grace is our making use of God's grace more often and for longer periods of time. Being absolutes, these divine productions in us do not admit degrees.

On the other hand, the growth experience of understanding spiritual truth and appreciation for the Lord Jesus is relative, for it is subject to correction, refinement, and expansion. As we add God's absolute truth to our fund of spiritual knowledge and our understanding of the Lord Jesus, we gain greater insight and appreciation of divine things. For example, the biblical truth of Jesus' deity is absolute, but our understanding of this truth is relative, being subject to development as we learn more about it from the Scriptures and as we correct our faulty understanding of it. Thus, as we learn more about the person and work of the Lord Jesus, we can honor and adore Him with greater understanding and appreciation.

THE GOAL OF SPIRITUAL GROWTH

The goal is to become increasingly like God (Matt. 5:48, perfect means "mature") and the Lord Jesus, who is our spiritual life (Eph. 4:11–16; 1 John 2:6). Because we are pre-destinated to Christlikeness (Rom. 8:29), this is brought about in us by the activity of the Holy Spirit in our lives (2 Cor. 3:18). It will be completed when our bodies are made like unto Jesus' body of glory at His coming for His Church (1 John 3:2; Phil. 3:20–21). Mean-while, we should become more like Jesus in our character (Eph. 5:25; 1 John 3:16–18) and in our actions (John 8:29; 1 John 2:29; see "Making Moral Behavioral Changes in the Christian Life" in this chapter).

THE MEANS OF SPIRITUAL GROWTH

How can we cooperate with the Holy Spirit to express spiritual life and experience its growth in our lives? There is a similarity between the means of spiritual growth and natu-ral growth. These means include eating, exercising, resting, and submitting to authority and instruction.

One: As the natural life requires regular nourishment, so the spiritual life requires the nourishment of God's Word (1 Peter 2:1–2; John 6:63; 2 Tim. 3:16–17; Ps. 1:1–3).

Two: As the natural life needs exercise, so the spiritual life needs the activity of obedi-ence to God's will in Christian life and ministry (1 John 2:5).

Three: As the natural life calls for rest, so the spiritual life requires faith in God and His Word. This is a reliance on God to do His part as we do ours in His strength (Gal. 2:20; 5:25; Rom. 1:17).

Four: As the natural life is fostered by parental care and discipline, so our spiritual growth is fostered by our submitting to God's care, authority, and discipline, lovingly heeding His instructions and patiently bearing His dealings with us (Rom. 12:1–2; 13:14; Eph. 5:17; Heb. 12:1–11; James 1:2–4).

When we faithfully appropriate these means of growth, we experience spiritual devel-opment. When we neglect these means, we come under the control of the sin force and allow it to produce its evil works in our lives (Gal. 5:19–21). If it is allowed to continue, this carnality not only will hinder our spiritual growth but will also cause retrogression in our spiritual experience (1 Peter 2:1–2; 1 Cor. 3:1–3). In fact, whenever sin is controlling us, we express spiritual death (Gal. 6:8; Rom. 8:6). On the other hand, the more we yield ourselves to the Holy Spirit and grow spiritually, the more we become like the Lord Jesus and manifest Him in our lives (Rom. 6:16–22; 8:4–6; 1 John 2:3–6).

Since the experience of spiritual life has an infinite capacity for growth, we should never be satisfied with our present spiritual condition. It is God's desire that we keep on growing throughout our Christian lifetime (2 Peter 3:18, present tense). Although we shall never attain absolute spiritual maturity in this world, we can be relatively mature for our spiritual age as we give ourselves daily to those means that God uses to bring this about in our lives. What progress are you seeing in your spiritual life?

THE MAINTENANCE OF THE CHRISTIAN LIFE

God has given us everything that we need for maintaining our spiritual life and for our pleasing and glorifying Him (2 Peter 1:3). These provisions include the Bible, faith, prayer, the means of cleansing from sin, the ministries of other believers, grace, and the Holy Spirit. However, to receive benefit from these resources, we must apply them to ourselves. Let us see how we can profitably use these provisions.

THE BIBLE

The Bible's value cannot be overstated. Consisting of the Old and New Testaments, it is God's complete written revelation to mankind. Thus it is a *library* for our understanding of God and the things of God (1 Cor. 2:9–13), *food* for our spiritual nourishment (1 Peter 2:2), a *lamp* for our guidance (Ps. 119:105), a *weapon* against our spiritual enemies (Eph. 6:17), and *equipment* for our every good work, or doing God's will (2 Tim. 3:17).

More and more, I am impressed with the fact that God uses the Scriptures to minister to the spiritual needs of His people. The apostle Paul not only exhorted Timothy to preach the Word (2 Tim. 4:2) but also declared that the Scriptures are profitable (3:16–17) for doctrine (teaching us what we should know), reproof (pointing to what is wrong in our lives), correction (showing us how we should deal with this wrong), and instruction in righteousness (teaching us what is God's will and how we should do it). Being God's Word, biblical truth effectively works in all who believe it and obey it (Heb. 1:1–2; 4:12; 1 Thess. 2:13). It is essential to our spiritual well-being and fruitfulness and to our pleasing God that we learn what He says and apply this to our daily lives.[4]

How to Read the Bible for Personal Profit

A person can read the Scriptures and receive little or nothing from them. To avoid this, the following procedure can be helpful in making your devotional reading more rewarding:

One: Pray, asking God to help you understand His message for you (Ps. 119:18).

Two: Read a Scripture passage, such as a chapter, straight through so as to get an overview of it.

Three: Reread the passage, studying it so as to discover and understand its teachings and instructions. As time allows, look up marginal references, consult a dictionary for unfamiliar words, and learn the meaning of difficult verses from commentaries.

Four: Reread the passage with your personal needs or desires in mind.

Five: Select some word, phrase, or clause that stands out or impresses you. God speaks to us through the Scriptures in this way.

Six: Think how this impressive part of the passage relates to your life or need.

Seven: Pray again, thanking God for speaking to you, asking Him to help you to apply this truth to your life, and giving yourself anew to Him that His will be done.

Do not leave the Word until God has given you something to think about. Look to the Holy Spirit to minister to your heart through the Word, not only as you read it but throughout the day as you recall it. There is no adequate substitute for daily reading of the Scriptures (John 6:63; Matt. 4:4). Avoid allowing devotional literature to take the place of this Bible reading and meditation.[5]

How to Understand the Scriptures

The following suggestions will help you to understand God's Word better:

1. *Follow the customary usage of language.*

Take the words of the Bible to mean what they say except where figures of speech like simile and metaphor are given. Learn the biblical usage of words and recognize the main ideas of the passage, as given by independent clauses. Also, recognize the relationships of independent and dependent clauses to one another by their introductory clause conjunctions.

2. *Understand the passage in the light of the context.*

The context of a passage or of its parts is that which precedes it and which follows it. Disregarding chapter and verse divisions, discover the main topic of the passage, who is speaking, who is being addressed, what are the antecedents of pronouns, and what are the historical and geographical settings. Also, from the background learn the writer's or book's theme, purpose, and plan.

   3. *Interpret Scripture by Scripture.*

   The Bible often gives its own explanation of words and phrases. With the aid of Bible marginal references or a concordance, see how primary words and phrases are used elsewhere in the Scriptures and what light this casts upon their meaning.

   4. *Recognize dispensational distinctions.*

   While all Scripture is profitable (2 Tim. 3:16), recognize that God has given specific commands to certain peoples throughout history. Historically, His will for Israel was expressed by the Mosaic Law. His will for us today is stated in those instructions given in the New Testament and those OT commands that agree with these. Keep in mind the people who are being addressed in the biblical portion that you are reading, especially as this relates to the personal application of God's commands and promises (see "The Dispensations of God" under Theology Proper).

   5. *Recognize the progress and unity of God's written revelation.*

   No single passage of Scripture gives a complete statement of any topic. Because of this, seek to understand what the Bible teaches on this topic. A wrong understanding of a doctrine often rises from an exaggerated or a partial understanding of a biblical truth. You should remember the principle of the self-consistency of the Scriptures, which says that there is in the Bible perfect agreement between the parts that comprise the whole revelation of a particular truth. Also, you should interpret obscure passages by what is clearly taught elsewhere in the Bible.

   6. *Seek to discover what a passage is really saying.*

   Try to be as objective as possible when seeking to understand the Scriptures. Distinguish between what a passage means and what truth it may illustrate, like the parable of the good Samaritan (Luke 10:30–35). The purpose of the parable was to show the lawyer who his neighbor was, although it illustrates salvation. On the other hand, the historical fulfillment of biblical prophecy, if it is recorded in the Scriptures, may clarify certain ambiguous features of it (Matt. 1:18–23).

   7. *Seek the enlightenment of the Holy Spirit.*

   He is your Teacher of divine truth (1 John 2:27; 1 Cor. 2:9–15). As you look to Him, He not only will direct you in your study but also will give you an understanding of the biblical truth that you need for your life and ministry. Remember the prayer of Psalm 119:18, "Open Thou my eyes that I may behold wondrous things out of Thy law."

   8. *Use reliable reference tools.*

   Use study aids that are written by doctrinally sound people and that are faithful to the teachings of God's Word. These can be identified by the reputation of the writer and of the publisher and by the content of the reference work. Consider what the reference book says about the Bible, God, the Lord Jesus, the Holy Spirit, and salvation. Does this agree with what the Bible teaches about these themes?[6]

How to Relate the Scriptures to Daily Life

God has given us His Word for more than satisfying our academic curiosity (Deut. 29:29). For the Word to do its sanctifying work in our lives, however, we must allow it to dwell in us richly (Col. 3:16), teaching us God's will, revealing our spiritual needs and God's infinite resources, alerting us to our spiritual enemies, and revealing to us our incomparable God. The following suggestions will help you to give God's Word its proper place in your daily life.[7]

Q 9

1. *Use the Bible in your fellowship with God.*

Regard the Scriptures as the means by which He will speak to you—enlightening, convicting, assuring, instructing, rebuking, restraining, warning, commanding, strengthening, encouraging, comforting, directing, and blessing you (Ps. 19:7–11).

2. *Regard the Bible's treasures as being inexhaustible.*

You can expect God to use it daily to give you fresh insight and suitable provision for your spiritual needs. You need to be reminded of familiar biblical truth as well as taught new biblical truth (John 6:35).

3. *Look for truth that will relate to your spiritual needs.*

Whether your needs are due to problems, adversities, temptations, failures, ignorance, duties, desires, weaknesses, or sins, the Scriptures are able to minister to these, for they are God's Word to you (2 Cor. 2:16; 3:5; 12:9; John 6:63) and are profitable for "teaching, reproof, correction, and instruction in righteousness [right doing]" (2 Tim. 3:16).

4. *Be a doer of the Word and not a hearer only.*

Looking to God for enablement, strive to be positively responsive to the Scriptures (James 1:21–25; cp. Luke 8:18). As you read in those sections that apply to gospel believers today and you come upon a warning, heed it; a failure or sin, confess it; a promise, claim it; an instruction, receive it; a command, obey it; a rebuke, accept it; or a blessing, give thanks for it.[8]

5. *Seek to build up a fund of systematic doctrinal knowledge.*

When you learn new biblical truth, relate it to what you already know about this topic. In this way, you will accumulate a fund of knowledge about the various biblical themes. Aim to understand thoroughly what the Bible teaches about key doctrines, and share this truth with others.

6. *Prepare to give a biblical answer for your faith.*

Learn from the Bible what saved people should believe and why they should believe it (1 Peter 3:15). Be able to appeal to the Scriptures for your assertions of spiritual truth when you are questioned by others (Acts 17:11).

7. *Seek to work out a practical ethical code.*

Only God's Word provides the absolute standard for the behavior that pleases Him. The Scriptures will show you what is right and wrong, good and evil, true and false. They give divine precepts and guiding principles, by which you can evaluate the moral decisions and situations that confront you and by which you can learn God's will regarding these things (Ps. 119:105, 9–11; see Appendix F: "Learning and Doing God's Will").

8. *Recognize the need for returning daily to the Scriptures.*

Your need for all that the Bible offers never ends (Ps. 1:1–3). There is always more to learn, there is always the duty of walking in God's will, and there is always the need to discern Satan's deceptions and lies (2 Tim. 2:15; 3:16–17; Eph. 5:17; 6:16). God uses the Scriptures daily to direct our steps (Ps. 119:105) and to nourish our spiritual lives (1:1–3; Deut. 8:3).

We thank God for His Word. May we increasingly give it a larger place in our lives and look to it daily for spiritual guidance and understanding (Ps. 1:1–3; Luke 11:27–28).

PRAYER

Prayer is an amazing provision for the Christian life. It may be defined as our communicating with God by word, thought, or a heavenward glance (Mark 6:41; 7:34). When we reflect upon the nature and works of God and the fact that we can talk to Him about everything (1 Peter 5:7; Phil. 4:6) at anytime (1 Thess. 5:17), this provokes within us humility and awe. Yet, His many appeals encourage us to pray. He is pleased when we come often to Him with childlike simplicity and confidence. Although He knows what our needs are before we pray, He invites us to come boldly before His throne of grace for His help (Matt. 6:32; Heb. 4:16).

The Forms of Prayer

Our prayers may assume any form of communication like thanksgiving (2 Cor. 2:14), praise (Acts 2:47), confession of sin (Ps. 51:1–4), petition (Rom. 1:9–10), intercession (Eph. 6:18–20), expression of reliance (2 Chron. 14:11), holy argument (Exod. 32:11–13), questions (Ps. 10:1), complaint (Jonah 4:1–3), fellowship (Luke 6:12; 1 John 1:7), submission (Isa. 6:8), and expression of salvational faith (Rom. 10:13). Actually, we can talk with God about all that is on our hearts and all that concerns us, including our work, problems, desires, disappointments, duties, fears, pleasures, affections, weaknesses, afflictions, and sins. We can be candid with God, for He knows all about us (Ps. 139:1–6, 23–24; Matt. 6:8).

The Addressees of Prayer

We gospel believers may talk to all or any Person of the divine Trinity according to our desire or need. As children-sons we may address the Father, as slaves-friends we may talk to the Lord Jesus our Master, or as temples-dependents we may speak to the Holy Spirit our resident Helper. We also can address the Trinity collectively as God.

Ephesians 2:18 gives us the theological basis for prayer, stating that we have approach to God through the mediating sacrifice and intercession of Jesus and by the Holy Spirit. Misunderstanding Jesus' words in John 16:23–27, some believe that all prayers should be directed to God the Father. As I see it, the Lord was saying to His disciples, who had not been looking to the Father for their needs, that they were now able to pray to the Father themselves in His name. This was important, for the Lord was about to leave them physically and to return to heaven. Jesus' name represents His atoning work, which removed those sins that separated us from God (Eph. 2:18; Heb. 10:19–22). It also represents His interests, with which we should be concerned in this world (John 14:13). Other Scripture passages indicate that we can pray to Jesus (Acts 7:59; 1 Cor. 1:2, 9; 2 Cor. 12:8; 2 Tim. 2:22; 1 John 1:3) and to the Holy Spirit (2 Cor. 13:14; Phil. 2:1) as well as to the Father (1 Peter 1:17).

Several Rules of Prayer

There are no rules for posture, time, length, or place. These are determined by the direction of the Holy Spirit, custom, and circumstances. On the other hand, as in all spiritual exercises, we must depend on the Holy Spirit to give us enablement and direction for our praying (Rom. 8:14; Jude 20), and we must be morally clean (Ps. 66:18; Prov. 15:29; Heb. 10:22). Also, there are certain conditions that we must meet if we are to receive answers to our petitions. As we consider these conditions, observe the promises that accompany them and that encourage our faith.

1. We must *ask in Jesus' name* (John 14:13–14).

This is more than appending His name to our prayers. Representing His person and work, His name stands for what He is and does. To pray in His name is to pray according to His interests (Matt. 16:18), His will (1 John 5:14–15), and His objective to glorify the Father (John 12:28; 17:4). The glory of God should be the supreme motivation for our asking Him for things. When we fail to do this and seek only the satisfaction of our desires, we ask amiss (James 4:3). God will never be our servant to minister to our whims, however worthy they may be. We are ever His servants, who exist for doing His will and living for His glory (Eph. 1:12).

2. *We must ask definite requests (James 4:2).*

But is this necessary, since God knows everything (Matt. 6:8)? Our making definite petitions shows our recognition of our need, our dependency upon God, and our faith in His ability and willingness to answer our petitions (cp. Eph. 3:20; Mark 10:47–51).

3. *We must abide in Jesus (John 15:7).*

This concerns our daily relationship with Jesus. To abide in Him is to keep in touch with Him by self-surrender, obedience, faith, and communication. As we do, we allow Him to abide in us in the fullness of His spiritual life. As we allow His Word to abide in our hearts and to direct us (Col. 3:16; Ps. 119:11), we give Him control. Then we may ask what we desire with the confidence that God will grant our requests. He can do this without contradicting Himself or injuring us, for our desires are surrendered to His will and are shaped by His indwelling Word (cp. Col. 3:16; 1 John 3:22; Ps. 37:4).

4. *We must believe that God will answer as He promises (Matt. 21:22; Mark 11:22–24).*

God encourages us to pray by promising to answer our prayers. This promises provides an object for our faith; it gives us something to believe. While we believe that He means what He says (Titus 1:2) and is able to do what He promises (Eph. 3:20), can we believe that He will do this for us? His promises assure us that He will. Also, He has no favorites, for He is no respecter of persons (Rom. 2:11). Let us not limit God to what we think is possible for Him to do. Since He is able to do exceedingly abundantly above all that we ask or think, let us ask Him for great things that will magnify His name (Eph. 3:20; cp. Matt. 9:28–29).

5. *We must ask persistently (Luke 11:5–10).*

Jesus' parable and the verbs He uses (present imperatives) indicate the need for our continuing to pray about a matter until we receive our request or are shown that we are asking amiss. This kind of praying is similar to our placing an order with a catalog merchandising house and our daily looking for its arrival. The condition of persistent praying is for our benefit. Persistent praying expresses our confidence that God will answer, it prepares our hearts for the answer, and it gives God time to work with other people to bring about the answer. It also brings us the blessing of waiting on God in His fellowship, and it allows us to evaluate our requests and to make sure that they are in keeping with His will and for His glory. Sometimes, He requires us to present cause for His granting our requests (cp. Exod. 32:9–14).

Needless to say, petitions make up a large part of our praying. However, we must make certain that we meet God's conditions if we are to receive favorable replies to our requests. God is ready to do far more than what we ask of Him. Let us look to Him to do great things for us and for others for the glory of His name.

Several Reasons for Unanswered Prayer

There are times when God does not answer or delays answering our petitions. This may be due to one or more of the following reasons:

1. *Our failure to meet the conditions of His prayer promises*
   See the above section.
2. *Our not allowing Him to answer in His time and way*

Regarding God's time, we may not be ready for the answers, others for whom we are praying may not be ready, or perhaps the details that are involved in the answer have not yet been worked out. Regarding God's way of answering our prayers, this may be in a manner that we did not anticipate or do not recognize (cp. Rom. 15:30–32; Acts 27–28; Phil. 1:12–13).

3. *Our faulty relations with God (Ps. 66:18) or with others (Prov. 21:13; 1 Peter 3:1, 7)*

Faulty relations with others especially concern those that are not governed by God's love (John 13:34; 1 John 3:16–23; 1 Cor. 13:4–7). These are sinful in His sight.

4. *Our having improper motivation for prayer (James 4:3)*

To ask for something so as "to consume it upon our lust" (KJV) refers to our praying according to our own desires rather then God's will for us (cp. Eph. 5:10; 1 John 5:14–15; Matt. 26:39). In everything, we should pray that God's will be done (Matt. 6:10; 26:39) and that He be glorified (1 Cor. 10:31; John 14:13).

5. *Our experiencing satanic hindrance (Dan. 10:12–13)*

Powerful evil forces are working against us to hinder every aspect of our spiritual lives. This passage in Daniel reveals the struggle between holy and evil angels to exert their influences on nations and people. However, all is controlled by God to fulfill His purposes.

6. *Our asking for that which is not for our good (Matt. 7:11)*

God will only give us good things that are in keeping with His will for us (Rom. 12:2) and that contribute to our spiritual well-being (James 1:17; 1 Tim. 6:17; 1 John 5:14–15).

We must never be contented with unanswered prayer. God would have us examine our prayers, looking for possible reasons for their not being answered, and to make whatever adjustments that may be necessary. We are speaking here not of negative answers to prayer but of God's not answering at all.

Since it is an essential ingredient of fellowship with God, prayer is very important to our life. A. J. Gordon once said, "You can do more than pray after you have prayed, but you can never do more than pray until you have prayed." Are you a regular prayer? Are you receiving answers to your prayers? Your reply to these questions will determine what you need to do.

PRACTICAL FAITH

Practical faith is that trust in God and His Word that we who are saved are to exercise during the course of daily living (Gal. 2:20; 2 Cor. 5:7).[9] Because of God's demands, the possibility of unbelief, the threat of our spiritual enemies, and the requirements of daily life, we must strive to rely on God and His Word constantly, for without this we shall fail to be and to do what He requires of us (Heb. 4:11; 11:6). Our reliance on God and His Word is an essential act of obedience (Mark 11:22), which is an expression of our love for Him (John 14:15) and the key to personal happiness (Ps. 34:8; Prov. 16:20). Let us briefly look at the employment of practical faith.

The Mechanics of Exercising This Faith

The employment of practical faith begins with our being aware of a need that we have and our deciding to trust God to provide for this. This decision is our positive response to God's appeal to rely upon Him (Prov. 3:5; Mark 11:22). Then we enact our decision by trusting in God to work on our behalf or on behalf of others according to the promises of His Word.

The Aspects of This Trust

We express trust in God in the following ways:

1. *Giving ourselves to God (Ps. 37:5)*

As a person with appendicitis must entrust himself to the surgeon for the removal of the infected organ, so we must entrust ourselves to the Father, the Lord Jesus, or the Holy Spirit to receive His help and blessing.

2. *Believing in God's promises (Acts 27:25)*

God has given us in His Word "exceeding great and precious promises" relating to every need that we may have in this world (2 Peter 1:4). These divine promises assure us of what God will do in response to our faith in Him. Our believing these promises makes them effective in our lives. Therefore, we must learn what these promises are and apply the ones that are suitable to our specific needs. For examples, in times of distress, see Isaiah 41:10; when needing guidance, see Proverbs 3:5–6.

3. *Trusting in God's instructions (Prov. 3:5–6)*

This trust relates to our wholeheartedly accepting the teachings of God's Word and obeying His will for us. We are to do this with the confidence that God is all-wise and that His will is good for us, being suited to our new life in Jesus and perfect for us (Rom. 12:2).

4. *Accepting God's self-disclosures (John 20:27)*

God continually reveals Himself to His people not only by the Scriptures but also by life's experiences (Job 42:5; Ps. 72:23–28). As we learn more about the true God, we must believe this glorious truth and trust Him accordingly.

5. *Looking to God for the future (Ps. 31:14–15)*

The exercise of faith includes our trusting God for the future, both earthly and heavenly, for "our times" are in His hands (cp. 1 Peter 1:3, 7–9, 13; Heb. 11:1). Thus, we have no reason to worry, for as we do our part in praying and trusting God (Phil. 4:6), He will do His part in providing for our needs or in showing us how we can provide for ourselves with His help (Matt. 6:25–34).

Practical faith is our daily human link to God. Unsaved people trust in themselves and their human resources, but we who are saved are privileged to trust in the Creator and Sustainer of the universe. They who rely on Him shall never have cause to be ashamed because of His unfaithfulness or inability (Rom. 10:33). On the other hand, everything that we do independently of Him is sinful in His sight (14:23).

THE MEANS OF CLEANSING FROM SINS

Every gospel believer is painfully aware that he still sins. This occurs when we give ourselves over to the inner urges of the sin force or to the external temptations of Satan and the world and allow them to use us for sinful behavior (James 1:14–15; Rom. 7:15–23). However, God has graciously provided for our cleansing, which is so necessary for our fellowship and service with Him (1 John 1:5–7; 2 Tim. 2:21).[10]

The means of cleansing is the Lord's "blood" (1 John 1:7), which speaks of His atoning work by which He secured for us the basis of God's judicial forgiveness and His parental forgiveness of our sins. When we learn about our sins or knowingly commit them, we have the duty of dealing with them (2 Cor. 7:1), or judging them (1 Cor. 11:31), by repentance (Rev. 2:5; Prov. 28:13) and confession to God (1 John 1:9). We must also have a forgiving attitude toward those who have wronged us (Matt. 6:12, 14–15), when they have repented and corrected their wrongdoing (Luke 17:3). Finally, we must seek the forgiveness of others whom we have wronged (Matt. 5:23–24; see Appendix W: "The Saved Person's Forgiveness of Others"). When we deal with our sins in this way, God immediately applies to us the value of Jesus' atoning sacrifice, releases us from sin's guilt, and cleanses us from its defilement (1 John 1:9).

It is urgent that we deal with our known sins promptly so that our fellowship with God is not long interrupted, and we do not incur His corrective chastisement. Unjudged, known sins are the most common cause for His people's lack of spiritual power and fruit in their lives. While there is no sin that we can commit that is not forgivable (1 John 1:7, 9), we must remember that our wrongdoing will enter the Lord's calculation of our reward (2 Cor. 5:10; Col. 3:24–25). If these sins have been dealt with, and we have received God's parental forgiveness, there still will be the loss of time, energy, and opportunity, which were wasted on sinning, that cannot be recovered and used gainfully.

Can you remember when last you knowingly sinned? What did you do about it? If you failed to deal with it by repentance and confession, this sin stands between you and God's fellowship and blessing.

THE MINISTRIES OF OTHER GOSPEL BELIEVERS

Fellow members of our local church, as well as saved people among our acquaintances, can exert a great influence for good on our lives when we are receptive to this. Some of the ways in which they can help us and we, in turn, can help others are these: expressing Christian love (1 John 3:16–18; 1 Cor. 13:4–7); being an example (1 Tim. 4:12; 1 Cor. 11:1; Phil. 3:17; 4:9); praying (2 Cor. 1:11; Eph. 6:18–19); giving encouragement and reproof (1 Thess. 5:14; Heb. 10:24; Gal. 6:1); exercising spiritual gifts like pastoral care, teaching, and showing mercy (1 Cor. 14:26; Eph. 4:12–16); and giving bodily or material assistance (1 Cor. 16:1; Gal. 6:10; Phil. 4:15–16).

Are you allowing others to minister to you? Are you willing to learn from others who, in their spiritual growth, may not be as far along as you? Ask the Lord to replace any arrogance that you may have with humility. Thank God for the people in your local church and for their various ministries to your life. Do not neglect allowing them this opportunity (Heb. 10:14–15). Also, minister to the needs of others as you have opportunity and means.

GRACE AND THE HOLY SPIRIT

Divine grace portrays God in action, doing for us what we cannot do for ourselves. With the help of this grace, generated by the activity of the Holy Spirit, we can be the kind of people He wants us to be and do the things He wants us to do (1 Cor. 15:10; 2 Cor. 1:12). Also, by God's grace we can make the best of our circumstances (2 Cor. 12:8–10).

Implementing this grace, the Holy Spirit stands ready to enable us to do and to be all that God requires of our lives, like expressing Christian character (Gal. 5:22–23; Eph. 5:9), doing God's will (Phil. 2:13), waging victorious warfare against our spiritual enemies (Gal. 5:16), performing Christian service (Acts 1:8; 1 Cor. 15:10), and rendering to God acceptable worship (Phil. 3:3; John 4:24). In fact, we can do these things only by the vitality of Jesus' spiritual life, which is conveyed to us by the Holy Spirit (Phil. 4:13; Heb. 13:21; John 15:5).

To obtain the Holy Spirit's help, we must receive His filling, which allows Him to work in our lives (Eph. 5:18).[11] Our surrender to His control does not make us passive instruments in His hand. We must still exhibit right attitudes, fulfill our commitments, and attend to our duties. But we must do these things in union with the Holy Spirit by looking to Him to direct and to help us do them in a way that will glorify God. Whenever we fail to do this, we sin (Rom. 14:23; Gal. 5:16). Then we must repent, confess our sin to the Lord, and yield ourselves anew to our divine Helper. Since the Holy Spirit is a person, we can talk to Him about all that concerns us and can express our dependence upon Him for His help (2 Cor. 13:14).[12]

These divine provisions will help us only as we make use of them. Let us daily employ them and allow God to work through them to make us the kind of people that He wants us to be and to help us to do what He wants us to do. He will do His part through these provisions as we do our part in appropriating them to our lives (James 4:8–10).

THE FRUITFULNESS OF THE CHRISTIAN LIFE

When we received the Lord as our Savior, we were brought into a complete spiritual life union with Him by the Holy Spirit's baptism and indwelling (John 14:20; cp. Gal. 3:27; John 14:16–17). A result of this union is our bringing forth spiritual fruit unto God (Rom. 7:4). To this end, we were chosen and appointed (John 15:16). Other Scripture passages reveal that the fruit we are to bear consists of Christian character (Gal. 5:22–23), good works (doing God's will, Col. 1:10; Phil. 1:11), knowledge of Jesus (2 Peter 1:8), and Christian ministry (Rom. 1:13) toward the unsaved (vv. 15–16) and the saved (vv. 11–12). This fruit represents the whole expression and productivity of the Lord Jesus in the gospel believer's spiritual life (cp. Gal. 4:19; 2:20). The Lord's allegory in John 15:1–6 teaches that the production of this fruit comes about by the cooperative work of the vine, the branch, and the vinedresser.

THE VINE'S PART   *Jesus*

The vine does everything in the production of the fruit as long as the branch remains in living union with it. The vine bears the branch, nourishes it, and produces fruit in it.

In like manner, the Lord Jesus produces in His people the fruit that God the Father requires of their lives. As the dispenser of spiritual life, the Lord is the spiritual vitality of His people (John 14:6; Col. 3:4; 1 John 5:11–12). He also produces the practical expressions of this life in the daily experiences of His people (Gal. 2:20; Phil. 1:21). In other words, a true Christian is one who has Christ; Christian living is the Lord Jesus' expressing Himself through the lives of His people.

THE BRANCH'S PART   *Believer*

The branch's part in fruitbearing is to abide in, or to keep in touch with, the vine (John 15:4–5). This allows the vine to produce its fruit in and through the branch.

Likewise, we gospel believers must keep in practical touch with the Lord (v. 4) if we are to be fruitful (v. 5). This fruitbearing circuit was set up at salvation by the Holy Spirit's baptism and indwelling (cp. 14:20). However, we close this vital circuit in daily life and allow it to produce in us Jesus' fruit by our abiding in Him. This permits Him to abide in us in the full productivity of His life and power as He promises. He says, "Abide in Me and I [will abide] in you. . . . He who abides in Me and I [abide] in Him, the same brings forth much fruit" (15:4–5). We abide in the Lord when we surrender ourselves to His leadership, obey His will, exercise practical faith in Him, communicate with Him, and follow His example.

Our Surrendering to Jesus' Leadership (Matt. 11:29)

This is to acknowledge His claim to us and to submit to His authority and leadership in our lives (2 Cor. 5:15; Rom. 12:1–2). It is to take His yoke upon us and to regard Him as the senior member of this partnership. The Lord's claim to us is based on His being our Creator (John 1:3), Possessor (17:9; 3:35), and Redeemer (1 Cor. 6:20; 1 Peter 1:18–19). In short, because He owns us, He has the sole right to manage our lives. We exist for the glory of His praise (Eph. 1:12; John 17:10).

We give ourselves to Him by decision and prayer (cp. Isa. 6:8). It is urgent that we do this daily (Eph. 3:17; Rom. 12:1). When we fail to do so, we come under the dominion of the sin force within us and produce the sinful "works of the flesh" (Gal. 5:19–21).

Our Obeying Jesus (Matt. 11:29; 1 John 3:24)

Having given ourselves to His management, it is then our duty to learn from Him his will and to do it in the Holy Spirit's power.[13] To obey Him is to please Him in all that we do (1 John 3:22; Eph. 5:10, 17; 2 Cor. 5:9).

The Lord encouraged His people to follow His direction by describing Himself as be-ing "meek and lowly in heart" (Matt. 11:29). As the Father's slave, he knows what it is to live under a yoke (John 6:38). By the constraint of love, the Lord governs those who yield themselves to Him (2 Cor. 5:14). He said that His yoke is "easy" (kindly to wear) and His burden is "light" (in weight, Matt. 11:30). Both "yoke" and "burden" represent His will for us. Being suited to our new spiritual life and renewed human nature, His will is easy, or kindly to wear, in that it is perfect for us (Rom. 12:2). His will is also light, for He has given us a wonderful Helper, the indwelling Holy Spirit (John 14:16–17), and an inner desire to obey Him (Phil. 2:13). Contrary to Satan's lies, God's will for us is not burden-some or oppressive but perfect for us (1 John 5:3; Rom. 12:2).

Our Exercising Faith in Jesus (Gal. 2:20)

This refers to practical faith (see above), by which we share everything with Him (1 Peter 5:7) and depend upon Him in everything (Prov. 3:5–6). This kind of faith does not eliminate personal activity or responsibility, for God will not do for us what we can do for ourselves with His help. We must still learn God's will, make right decisions, use our spiritual resources, attend to duty, make preparation, engage in action, wage battle, secure a livelihood, and bear adversity. But in all these, we must look to the Lord for direction and help so that we might please Him. To function independently of Him is to sin and fail (Rom. 14:23; John 15:5b; cp. 8:28).

The life of practical faith is one in which we share everything with the Lord—our duties, work, problems, recreation, ministry, aspirations, and fears—and we rely on Him to help us to deal with these things in a way that would glorify God. Whatever need we may have, we can look to Him to satisfy this or to give us the grace to deal with it (John 7:37–38; 2 Cor. 12:8–10).

Our Communicating with Jesus (1 Cor. 1:9)

Since Jesus is our senior partner, He wants us to talk to Him about everything (1 Thess. 5:17). This is necessary if we are to share everything with Him. He also wants us to read His Word and to heed what He says (Col. 3:16). This, too, is necessary if we are to know His will and use rightly the resources that He provides.

Our Following Jesus' Example (1 John 2:6)

Being our spiritual life, the Lord Jesus is our model of Christian character and behav-ior. Avid sports fans have their athletes whom they admire and follow. Certainly, we who are saved should be following the Lord's example of obedience (John 6:38), love (13:1; 14:31), trust (1 Peter 2:23), prayer (Mark 1:35), compassion (Matt. 9:36), determination (Luke 9:51), holiness (1 Peter 2:22), truthfulness (John 16:7), faithfulness (17:4), and self-sacrifice (Matt. 20:28).[14]

When we abide in the Lord in this manner, we allow Him to abide in us in the full productivity of His life and power. Apart from Him we are not able to do anything that pleases Him or that will count for eternity (John 15:5b). When He appraises our lives (2 Cor. 5:10), He will be looking for those things that we shared with Him and that we allowed Him to do through us. He will reward us favorably only for that activity in which He had a part (Eph. 6:8; Heb. 13:21; cp. Gal. 2:20; Phil. 1:21). The wise person will daily abide in the Lord. What is your relationship with Him? Are you living in touch with Him today?

THE VINEDRESSER'S PART $\;$ *God*

The vinedresser's work is to cultivate the branches so that they bear more fruit. Here Jesus describes God the Father as the Vinedresser (KJV "Husbandman"), who prunes the fruitful branches and removes the unfruitful ones (John 15:2–3).

The Father Prunes Fruitful Gospel Believers (John 15:2b–3)

The purpose of this pruning is to remove from our lives all that obstructs the production of spiritual fruit, like sinful practices, ignorance, and self-reliance. He does this by His Word and corrective discipline.

1. *The Father prunes us by His Word (John 15:3).*

When we expose our hearts to God's Word and respond favorably to what He says, we allow the Father to remove from us that which is undesirable in His sight and to sanctify us (cp. 2 Tim. 3:16–17; Ps. 119:9–11; John 17:17). This is His painless method of pruning.

2. *The Father prunes us by corrective discipline (Rev. 3:19).*

When we fail to heed His Word, we incur the Father's corrective discipline until we obey what He says. This is His painful method of pruning. We can avoid much trouble by obeying God's Word and by responding favorably to His dealings with us.

With unerring wisdom our Father removes only what is hindering our bearing spiritual fruit. Nothing essential to our spiritual well-being is lost. We must ever keep in mind that God is more concerned with our fruitfulness than with our creaturely comforts and prosperity. In addition to pruning His children, the Father make them more fruitful by nourishing them with His Word and by applying to them constructive parental discipline (1 Peter 2:2; Heb. 12:5–11).[15]

The Father Removes Unfruitful Gospel Believers (John 15:2a, 6)

Keep in mind that the Lord is not speaking about salvation. If one fails to meet the conditions of fruitfulness and remains unresponsive to God's corrective discipline to the point of hating it, then one is prematurely removed from earth and is taken to heaven (v. 2), for such a person is a hindrance to the Lord's work on earth. To hate the Father's reproof and His corrective chastisement is to persist defiantly in sinning, which leads to certain physical death (1 John 5:16; Prov. 15:10; Heb. 12:9), for by this defiant attitude one renders oneself useless to God in this world.

With these truths in view, I understand that the branch's being "cast forth" is a reference to the physical death of the insubordinate gospel believer, its being "withered" (dried up) is his no longer having opportunity to bear fruit in this lifetime, and its being "cast into the fire and burned" is his sinful works being consumed in the coming appraisal (1 Cor. 3:13–15; 2 Cor. 5:10). It is our Lord's desire that our works survive this appraisal and that we receive a full reward (John 15:16; 2 John 8).

Our Father is concerned about the amount of fruit that we bear, for "much fruit" glorifies Him (John 15:8). This reference to quantity suggests that He wants us to be spiritually fruitful throughout our Christian lifetime. Observe that there are no degrees of the quality of fruitfulness since this fruit has only one standard that is acceptable to the Father—the expression of Jesus' spiritual life and righteousness, or Christlikeness (cp. John 15:5; Phil. 1:11).

By this allegory, the Lord Jesus described the nature of Christian life and ministry. It is His living and working through His people who are on earth even as the Father lived and worked through Him (John 5:19; 8:28–30; 10:38; 12:49–50; 14:8–11). We produce the fruit of Christlikeness as we abide in Him and submit to the Father's pruning and nourishing actions. When we fail to abide in the Lord, we produce the evil "works of the flesh" (Gal. 5:19–21), which express spiritual death (6:8; Rom. 8:5–6).

What kind of fruit is your life producing? You daily have the choice of producing either the fruit of spiritual life, or Christlikeness, by abiding in Jesus or the stench of spiritual death by allowing sin to use you for its evil expressions (Gal. 6:8; Rom. 8:6).

THE VICTORIES OF THE CHRISTIAN LIFE

Although we deal with this subject elsewhere, let us briefly look at spiritual victory here as it relates to daily life.[16] Evil temptation is the solicitation for us to act contrary to God's will. This comes from the sin force within or from Satan and the world of unsaved people without. Because we who are saved have been delivered from bondage to these evil forces (Rom. 6:17; Acts 26:18; John 15:19), we do not have to heed their sinful proposals anymore. In fact, in God's sight we have died to these evil forces and are now alive unto Him (Rom. 6:1–13; Gal. 2:20). How, then, are we to respond to these temptations?

WE MUST NOT YIELD TO TEMPTATION (JAMES 4:7)

Regardless of its source, we can be victorious over temptations to sin by decision and by doing the following:

1. *We must immediately submit ourselves to God (James 4:7).*

This gives Him command of our hearts and allows Him to give us strength to resist the temptation (Rom. 13:14; Gal. 5:16).

2. *We must resist the temptation in God's strength (James 4:7).*

Relying on God for help, we resist temptation by refusing its proposal or by leaving the scene of temptation (Phil. 4:13; cp. Gen. 39:12).

3. *We must then do the holy alternative to sinning, which is our doing God's will (Eph. 4:25–32).*

It is urgent that we learn God's will for us for daily life and how to do it in His way (see Appendix F: "Learning and Doing God's Will").

WE MUST AVOID THOSE THINGS AND PEOPLE THAT ARE TEMPTING (2 COR. 6:17–18)

We can avoid much temptation by staying away from those places, things, and people where temptation lurks. There are places where we should not go, pictures that we should not see, literature that we should not read, and people with whom we should not associate because of the temptations that these generate. As much as possible, we must keep ourselves from every form of evil (1 Thess. 5:22) and follow that which is good, which is God's will for us (v. 15; cp. Eph. 5:10).

WE MUST DEAL WITH SIN IMMEDIATELY WHEN IT OCCURS (2 COR. 7:1)

Our yielding to temptation results in our sinning (James 1:14–15), in our losing fellowship with God (1 John 1:5–6) and, in time, in our incurring God's corrective discipline (Rev. 3:19). Therefore, we must immediately deal with our sinning by repentance (Rev. 2:5) and confession to God (1 John 1:9) and by making right any wrongs that we did to others (Matt. 5:23–24). Upon our taking these steps, God at once forgives and cleanses us, as He promises (1 John 1:9). Faith in His promise assures us of His having forgiven and cleansed us. Then, we must give ourselves anew to God so that He occupies our hearts and directs our lives (Prov. 23:26; Eph. 3:17; Luke 6:45).

Since no victory over our spiritual enemies is permanent in this life, it is best to think of these defeats as occasions of victory (Luke 4:13). The enemy attacks us daily, so he must be defeated daily. How are you scoring in these conflicts?

THE SEPARATION AND DEDICATION OF THE CHRISTIAN LIFE

Practical sanctification essentially concerns our doing God's will, or "good works" and "righteousness," rather than sinning (Rom. 6:15–22; 1 Peter 1:13–16; Matt. 5:16). Although we sin from time to time, we can experience periods of conscious sinlessness in our daily lives. We initiate and express holiness by separating ourselves from that which is morally unlike God and by setting ourselves apart unto Him and His will for His manifestation and use in this world (2 Cor. 6:14–7:1).

OUR SEPARATION

We learn from the New Testament that we who are saved are to separate ourselves from sin, sinning gospel believers, false religious teachers, and worldliness.

We Are to Separate Ourselves from Personal Sin (Col. 3:8;1 Tim. 5:22; 6:11)

This is achieved by cleansing ourselves from sin's defilement (2 Cor. 7:1; cp. Rev. 2:5; 1 John 1:9), by refusing to submit to sin's demands (Rom. 6:11–13; see above), and by avoiding sinful practices (Eph. 5:11; Col. 3:5–6; 1 Thess. 4:3–7; 5:22; 2 Tim. 2:22; 1 Peter 2:11–12).

We Are to Separate Ourselves from Sinning Saved People (Matt. 18:15–17; 2 Thess. 3:14–15) DISCUSS

We are to separate ourselves from gospel believers who knowingly and unrepentantly sin in violation of some clear biblical precept (1 Cor. 5:9–11). As with church corrective discipline (see "The Discipline of the Local Christian Church" under Ecclesiology), we have the duty of praying for sinning saved people (1 John 5:16) and of speaking to them about their wrongdoing (Matt. 18:15; Gal. 6:1). If this fails to secure favorable results, then we should have no association with them (2 Thess. 3:6, 14). Yet, we are not to count them as enemies but continue to seek their restoration to the fellowship of God and His people (v. 15).[17] Needless to say, it is very important to receive them again into the Christian fellowship when they are repentant (2 Cor. 2:5–11).

We Are to Separate Ourselves from False Religious Teachers (Rom. 16:17–18; 1 Tim. 6:3–5; 2 Tim. 3:1–5; Titus 3:9–11; 2 John 10–11)

These false teachers are people who reject the primary doctrines of the Christian faith as given in the Scriptures, such as the Bible's being God's Word, God's being a divine Trinity, the deity and humanity of the Lord Jesus, His atoning work and His physical resurrection, and the personality and deity of the Holy Spirit. Like the Pharisees of old, false teachers lay aside, reject, and make void God's Word by their "philosophy and vain deceit" (Mark 7:5–13; Col. 2:8). What should be our reaction these people?

1. *We must identify false teachers (Rom. 16:17).*

We can spot them by their evil behavior and treacherous ministry (Matt. 7:15–20; Titus 1:16; 2 Peter 2). We discover them by evaluating what they say (and sometimes by what they do not say) about the Bible, God, the Lord Jesus, the Holy Spirit, and salvation. The Lord Jesus taught that the nature of a tree determines the kind of fruit it bears. Despite their veneer of piety and respectability, false religious teachers, like their leader Satan, live unholy lives (2 Peter 2:1–3, 10–22), use deceptive methods and masquerades (v. 3;

2 Cor. 11:13–15), serve selfish interests (Phil. 3:19), and cause dissension and offenses (lit. "snares") among the Lord's people (Rom. 16:17). Contrariwise, the marks of a true servant of Jesus are sound doctrine, a fruitful ministry, and a holy lifestyle (Matt. 7:17).

2. *We must avoid false teachers (Rom. 16:17c; 1 Tim. 6:5).*

JW ↓ When we recognize false teachers, we are to turn away from them (2 Tim. 3:5). When they appear in our churches and start sowing their heretical seed, they must be rejected and ejected (Titus 3:9–11). When they come to our homes, they are not to be welcomed (2 John 7–11). To befriend them and to encourage their ministries is to share in their evil deeds. *BRIAN McLAREN*

When these false teachers appear in a local church and have the majority support of the church's members, then the only option that spiritual, discerning members have is to sever their relationship with the church and to unite with another where God's Word is honored and taught in its purity. However, if these false teachers have the support of only a minority of members within a church, then they and their confederates should be ejected by the vote and action of the orthodox majority.

3. *We must warn others against false teachers (Acts 20:28–31).*

It is our duty to warn others of the doctrine and activity of false teachers. However, we are not to search them out and destroy them (Matt. 13:24–30). The Lord will deal with these people judicially in His time.

We Are to Separate Ourselves from the World (1 John 2:15)

The word *world* (Gk. *kosmos*) has various meanings in the New Testament. As determined by its context, *world* can mean the sum total of all that was created (John 17:5), the earth (9:5), mankind (3:16; 12:19), or the world system, embracing the total society, activity, culture, and philosophy of unsaved mankind. At this point of our study, we are concerned with this last meaning.

The world system is headed by Satan (John 12:31; 14:30; 16:11), its works are evil (7:7), it is condemned by God (12:31; 1 John 2:17), and it fails to meet man's spiritual needs (1 Cor. 1:21). Since we who are saved are no longer a part of this world system (John 15:19; Col. 1:13), we are continually threatened by its hostility (John 15:18) and its evil influence (1 John 2:16). Although we cannot placate its hostility and remain loyal to Jesus (James 4:4), we can be alert for and avoid its evil influences, which would lead us into a state of worldliness. We do this by our separation from the world. Let us look at this more closely.

1. *Our separation from the people of the world*

a. *What this is not.*

God does not direct us to isolate ourselves from unsaved people. For most of His people, this would be impossible (1 Cor. 5:9–11). Furthermore, this isolation would block our ministry to the unsaved (John 17:18; Mark 16:15; Acts 1:8; 2 Cor. 5:18–20). On the contrary, our Lord freely mingled with these people—entering their homes, eating at their tables, and listening to their problems (Luke 7:36; 11:37; 14:1; cp. Matt. 9:9–10). Although He was known as their friend (Matt. 11:19), He did not participate in their sins or approve of their wrongdoing (Heb. 7:26; 1 Peter 2:22). We, too, must make contact with unsaved people, be friendly toward them, and win their confidence if we are to gain their hearing of the gospel. Obviously, this has risks; but we are safe as long as we look to the Lord Jesus, remain submissive to Him, and follow His direction in these contacts.

b. *What this is.*

God does command us to avoid any association with the unsaved that would compromise our commitment to the Lord and hinder our doing His will (2 Cor. 6:14–17).

The apostle Paul did not describe the problem at Corinth that his readers were to avoid since this was known to them. Possibly he was referring to their commitment to certain false teachers or, more likely, to pagan clubs or trade guilds that required their members to participate in idolatrous practices. Whatever the situation, the apostle stated the principle that we who are saved are not to link ourselves with unbelievers in any association, like a business partnership or marriage, from which we cannot readily excuse ourselves or that would require us to violate God's will for us.[18]

We also are not to associate with people who would lead us to sin (1 Cor. 15:33, KJV "communications" means "associations") or to participate in their sinning (Eph. 5:11). The "blessed" person of Psalm 1:1–2 does not follow the moral advice of the wicked or conform to their evil lifestyle or make them his close associates; but his delight is in the law of the LORD and in His law does he meditate day and night.

2. *Our separation from the things of the world*

As long as we are on earth, we cannot isolate ourselves from the things of the world. We must use its products, attend its institutions, participate in its industries and arts, and be subject to its government. Many things of the world are not evil in themselves, but they may be used in wrong ways. The apostle Paul taught that we are not to be dominated by the world's amoral, permissible things (1 Cor. 6:12) or to use them to their utmost extent (7:31, "as not abusing it"). He seems to say that we are not to extract all that we can from these things to the extent that we allow them to mean everything to us, that we live for them, and that we prize them above God (cp. Matt. 6:19–24), for this is not profitable (1 Cor. 6:12; 10:23, KJV "expedient") and opens the door to idolatry (Col. 3:5; Luke 12:13–34). In other words, we are not to regard these things or live for them as unsaved people do (Matt. 6:32; Col. 3:1–3). To allow anything of this world to compete with our love for God, to weaken our spiritual life, or to hinder our doing God's will is to use it in an evil way. On the other hand, we should consider the permissible things of the world as commodities that God allows us to have and to use as He directs, for His interests and glory and for our well-being and that of others.

Anything of this world that we cannot share with God and use for His glory is prohibited. In fact, having died to the world and its things (Gal. 6:14), we must now be wholly committed only to God (2:20). We cannot serve Him and wealth simultaneously (Matt. 6:24).

3. *Our separation from worldliness*

Worldliness is a state of life that results from an improper relation to or attitude toward the world and its things. The worldly saved person is one who is dominated by the thinking and practices of the world (Rom. 12:2; KJV *world* is "age," the world's current philosophy and practices). He is also one who loves something of this world with the exclusive love that he owes to God (1 John 2:15, Gk. "love *for* the Father"; Matt. 6:24; 10:37). Since this latter form of worldliness is less known, let us look at it more closely.

There are many kinds of love that we can properly express, like patriotic love for country, married love for a spouse, instinctive filial love for parents and parental love for children, friendship love, Christian love for others, love for things, and self-love.[19] However, we are never to share with these people and things the special affection that we owe to God (1 John 2:15; cp. John 14:31). The Lord Jesus expressed this special affection for the Father by obeying Him (John 14:31), delighting in Him, (4:34), trusting Him (Matt. 27:43), and honoring Him (John 8:49). Like love for a spouse, this love for God is an exclusive love that we are to give to God above all other persons or things.

When we share with other people or things the love that we owe to God, or we love these more than we love God, we commit spiritual adultery (James 4:4) and open our lives to world domination (Rom. 12:2). Thus the worldly saved person has misdirected love, which he owes to God, and he is characterized by the fads, opinions, attitudes, goals, and interests of the world. Contrariwise, the godly gospel believer reckons himself to be dead toward the world system and its things and alive unto the Lord Jesus and His interests (Gal. 2:20; 6:14; Col. 2:20–3:17; 6:14; Matt. 6:33; Gal. 6:14). While he is still concerned about the needs of unsaved people and must use the world's commodities, the person who loves and pleases God is not dominated by these things as the unsaved person and the worldly gospel believer are (James 1:27).

Whether we are poor or wealthy, we are constantly threatened by the world's evil influences and by worldliness. Do you love God above all else? How lightly are you sitting on your material possessions? If the Lord should direct you to give away what you have or to sell what you have and give the proceeds to the needy, how would you respond? Only by giving can we preserve what we have for eternity (Luke 12:13–34; Mark 8:35).

OUR DEDICATION

To separate ourselves from unholy things is not enough. Separation alone forms a vacuum that draws into one's life such unholy attitudes and actions as pride, frustration, and faultfinding. With our separation there must also be commitment to God (Rom. 6:11–13; 12:1–2). This involves our giving ourselves to the Lord Jesus and our living unto Him (2 Cor. 5:15). This, in turn, allows Him to express Himself in and through our lives (Gal. 2:20).

Having received the Lord Jesus as Savior, we have a duty as gospel believers to dedicate ourselves entirely to the Lord and His work in this world (Rom. 12:1; cp. Isa. 6:8). We do this by heart decision and prayer.[20] The apostle Paul described this commitment as follows:

The Act of Commitment (Rom. 12:1)

1. *Its nature (What is it?)*

We are to present our body, or self, to God. We make this commitment by heart decision and by enacting this decision by prayer (Isa. 6:8) and obedience (Luke 6:46).

2. *Its qualities (What is it like?)*

It is like offering a sacrifice to God—the act of giving Him something that is costly to us (2 Sam. 24:24). It is to give God our self—our most valuable, personal possession. The apostle described this offering as being:

a. *A living sacrifice*

At salvation, we died to our former spiritual masters and were made alive unto God and to the Lord Jesus, our new Master (Gal. 2:20; Rom. 6:2–4). We must accept this truth and be as responsive to God as we were responsive to sin, Satan, and the world (Rom. 6:11–13).

b. *A holy sacrifice*

By this commitment, we set ourselves apart from sin unto God and express our purpose to be God's instrument of righteousness rather than sin's tool of evil works (Rom. 6:12–13; 2 Tim. 2:19–21).

c. *An acceptable sacrifice*

This commitment is pleasing to God (cp. 2 Cor. 5:9–10; 1 John 3:22). It allows Him to energize, direct, and use us to do His will and, by this, to glorify Himself (Luke 6:45; Matt. 5:16; Eph. 2:8–10).

3. *Its rationale (Why do it at all?)*

It is the reasonable thing to do. That serving the Lord is reasonable may have at least three meanings:

One. This may mean that it is a *rational* service in that it requires us to follow the Lord's direction and teachings, as given in the Scriptures, rather than our hunches and guesses (Matt. 11:28–29; 2 Tim. 3:16–17; Eph. 6:6; Col. 3:16).

Two. It may mean that it is an *obligatory* service. Our giving ourselves to God is the reasonable thing to do since the Lord Jesus willingly gave Himself for us (Matt. 20:28; 2 Cor. 5:14–15).

Three. It may mean that it is a *sensible* service in that it is better to be an instrument of righteousness for the glory of God and for the good of self and others than an instrument of unrighteousness to God's discredit and to the harm of self and others (Rom. 6:11–13; Gal. 5:19–23).

4. *Its purpose (What is it for?)*

This commitment is for the purpose of serving God (see "The Ministries of the Christian Life" in this chapter). One cannot and does not serve the Lord without this commitment. Tragically, without it one continues to serve one's former evil spiritual masters.

5. *Its motivations (What prompts it?)*

The apostle begged his readers to make this commitment. This was urgent because of the threat of their spiritual enemies (1 Peter 5:8), the importance of the Lord's work (Eph. 5:25–27), and the accountability of His people (2 Cor. 5:10). The apostle also appealed to those divine mercies by which God withheld His punishment for their sins. For this, they owed Him (and we owe Him) everything (vv. 14–15).

The Demands of This Commitment (Rom. 12:2)

When we give ourselves to the Lord, we express a willingness to comply with His instructions and demands (Matt. 11:29b). Consider two of these demands.

1. *That we stop conforming to the world (2a)*

Our commitment to God requires that we stop following the world's evil lifestyle and its godless kind of thinking and attitudes. To conform to the world is to assume a lifestyle that is not in agreement with what we are as God's people (Eph. 2:10) and that does not express Christlikeness or eternal life (Eph. 5:1–18; Col. 3:8–17; Gal. 6:7–8).

2. *That we constantly conform to God's will (2b)*

Transform means outwardly expressing an inner reality. Having Jesus, we must allow Him to manifest Himself in our attitudes, character, and actions (Gal. 2:20; 4:19). We do this by daily giving ourselves to Him and by following the biblical moral lifestyle that portrays Him (Rom. 13:14; Eph. 5:1–18; Col. 3:1–14; Matt. 5:48). This requires us to learn God's will and to do it willingly in the power of the Holy Spirit for God's glory (see Appendix F: "Learning and Doing God's Will").

Christian life and service demands our commitment to God and His will, not only initially but also daily. We also must yield anew to Him whenever we give in to the temptations of our spiritual enemies. Only the Lord Jesus has the absolute right to control us. He who sustains and controls the universe can do a better job of managing our lives than we can. This daily commitment allows God to bless us and use us as a blessing to others. To neglect this commitment makes us vulnerable to our spiritual enemies.

Have you given your life to the Lord? Did you give Him your heart today? Whatever occupies your heart controls your life (Luke 6:45; Eph. 3:17). The Lord will take command only by invitation; sin takes over at every opportunity without invitation.

THE DISCIPLESHIP OF THE CHRISTIAN LIFE

After He saves us, the Lord Jesus begins to show us the need for discipleship, which is essential to Christian life and ministry (cp. Mark 1:16–18). A disciple is a follower, a pupil, or a learner. True disciples are pupils who heed their teacher's instructions, apply them to their lives, and pass them on to others. Their supreme goal is to become like their teacher (Matt. 10:24–25). True disciples of Jesus not only receive His teachings and walk in His fellowship but also pass on His teachings to others and seek to forward His interests in this world. Discipleship is a spiritual discipline that is to continue throughout the lives of all gospel believers. It is required for Christian life and ministry. Let us consider what the Lord teaches about the requirements, kinds, and evidences of discipleship.

THE REQUIREMENTS OF DISCIPLESHIP (LUKE 14:25–35)

How many people there are who think that getting saved from sin is simply a means of going to heaven when they die. They go about their lives as though they belonged to themselves and feel no obligation to the Lord Jesus and His work in this world. Needless to say, salvation brings to the gospel believer new responsibilities to the Lord, who is the Master and God of His people as well as their Savior. To trust in the Savior for salvation is to assume the obligations of being the Lord's disciple. However, many are never told what this means and what its cost is. Because His ministry attracted many superficial followers, the Lord Jesus warned them of the cost of discipleship, as expressed in its requirements. He addressed this cost by showing them the nature of, need for, and the commitment to these requirements.

The Nature of the Requirements for Discipleship (Luke 14:26–27, 33)

One cannot be a disciple of Jesus without paying the cost. This cost is the requirement of discipleship. Consider what this cost is.

1. *Our forsaking all for Christ (Luke 14:26, 33)*

To forsake all is to set aside or to leave behind everything that would keep us from giving Jesus first place in our lives (cp. Matt. 6:24).

a. *It is to place the Lord Jesus above our possessions (Luke 14:33).*

We must prize Him above all that we have. Considering our possessions as a trust from Him, we must use them or dispose of them as He directs (Luke 12:33).

b. *It is to place the Lord Jesus above all other persons (Luke 14:26a).*

Jesus uses the word *hate* as a hyperbole (figure of exaggeration), for our hating others is contrary to the principle of Christian love (Matt. 5:44; Mark 12:31; John 15:12). We are not to love others less than what we do, but we are to love Jesus more with that exclusive love that we owe to God alone (Matt. 10:37; see "Our separation from worldliness" in this chapter). This means that when the claims of others conflict with those of God for us, we must always yield to His will for us (cp. John 2:4; Acts 5:29; Luke 1:38).

c. *It is to place the Lord Jesus above ourselves (Luke 14:26b).*

There is a proper self-love, which is concerned about one's worth and well-being (Matt. 22:39; Rom. 12:3; Eph. 5:28–29; see endnote 22). However, we are to love the Lord Jesus more than we love ourselves to the extent that we are willing to give up anything to do His will such as our personal comfort, plans, financial security, social status, pleasure, and even life itself (Rom. 12:1).

2. *Our taking up the cross (Luke 14:27a)*

Some understand cross-bearing to mean shouldering some heavy burden like a chronic ailment or some annoying adversity. But in the New Testament the cross is an instrument of humiliation and death. The only cross that concerns discipleship is that on which the Lord died and which today stands as a symbol of His humiliation, suffering, and atoning work.

a. *This cross-bearing is related to the denial of self (Luke 9:23).*

This is not a denial of self-existence. If "himself" is an accusative of reference and alludes to the person, then the Lord appears to be speaking about our denying (with reference to one's self) the usurpation of our spiritual enemies over our lives. Not explaining what He meant by this, He left it to later NT revelation to make this known (Rom. 6; 1 Peter 2:24). Neither sin, Satan, nor the world has any lawful claim to those of us who are saved since we are no longer under their authority (Rom. 6:14; Col. 1:13; Gal. 6:14). It is not right for us to give ourselves to them for their evil uses.

b. This cross-bearing takes place when we act upon the truth of Romans 6:1–13.

To bear the cross is to reckon that we died to our former spiritual masters and are now alive unto God. This means that discipleship requires that we refuse to submit to our former evil masters and that we yield ourselves to the Lord Jesus, our new lawful Master (Gal. 2:20; Rom. 13:14). We cannot serve Him and sin at the same time (Matt. 6:24).

3. Our following the Lord Jesus (Luke 14:27b)

Having forsaken all and having taken up His cross in denying ourselves the usurpation of sin, there remains our following the Lord's leadership. Following the Lord Jesus is essentially the same as abiding in Him (John 15:4–5; cp. 8:12). To follow Him we must yield ourselves to Him, obey Him, exercise faith in Him, communicate with Him as well as follow His example. This makes it possible for Him to teach us and to use us in His work in this world. If there are those who have any doubts about the Lord's competency to lead well, they should consider how the Lord demonstrated this to His disciples in Luke 5:4–11. Surely, He who directs the stars in their courses is able to direct our lives in a manner that accomplishes God's purposes and that brings us our greatest good.

The Need for the Requirements of Discipleship *(Luke 14:28–32, 34–35)*

The Lord gave His followers three parables that showed the need for their fulfilling the requirements of discipleship, or paying its cost.

One: The Lord pointed to the possibility of being ridiculed by the world for not completing the requirements of discipleship (Luke 14:28–30). To be saved is to be committed to a new way of life, with its new responsibilities to the Lord. Unsaved people consider those who profess to be Christians and who do not live as such as being hypocrites and fakes.

Two. The Lord also pointed to the folly of making a superficial commitment to discipleship without counting its cost (Luke 14:31–32). Many professed gospel believers have eagerly received the Savior as a ticket to heaven without being aware of the cost of living for and serving with the Lord. While salvation is God's free gift, it demands the total life commitment of the saved person. Upon being saved, a person becomes the property and slave of the Lord Jesus and is obligated to fulfill the requirements of this relationship. Too many people think of salvation as God's gift, to be received without any obligation or accountability in return.

Three. The Lord pointed out the undesirable results of not fulfilling the requirements of discipleship (Luke 14:34–35). Again, He was not speaking of salvation but of the coming appraisal when He will require His slaves to give an account of their activities in this world. Like the branches that are burned (John 15:6), all that is done apart from Jesus (Luke 14:5b) will be rejected and will fail to bring profitable reward. Having lost its spiritual saltiness by being apart from Jesus (Matt. 5:13), the carnal believer's sinful lifestyle will be rejected in the appraisal (John 15:6); yet, the believer will be saved "so as by fire" (1 Cor. 3:15).

Our Commitment to the Requirements of Discipleship *(Mark 8:34–38)*

Having stated the nature of these requirements for discipleship, or its cost (v. 34), the Lord then challenged His followers to consider the value of making their life commitment to Him. His people have only one lifetime to spend in this world. They must decide between spending this for Him who continues forever or for this world that is passing away (Rev. 1:18; 1 John 2:15–17). We cannot simultaneously serve two masters who are opposite to each other (Matt. 6:24). The question is this: Where are you making your lifetime investment? In Jesus or in the world?

1. *The lifetime that is invested in Jesus and His work in this world (Mark 8:35b)*
   a. *The nature of this investment (v. 34)*
   See "The Nature of the Requirements for Discipleship" above.
   b. *The earnings of this investment (v. 35b)*
   The life that is given over (lost) to Jesus and His gospel will be saved. When He appraises the works of the life that was invested in Him and His work, the Lord will return this life with the eternal dividends of profitable reward (2 Cor. 5:10; 1 Cor. 15:58; 2 Tim. 4:7–8).[21]

2. *The lifetime that is invested in this world (Mark 8:35a, 36–38)*
   a. *The nature of this investment (vv. 36–37)*
   We invest our lives unprofitably by keeping them to ourselves and for the things of this world. Such a life is a poor investment, for it is spent on what is transitory and sinful.
   b. *The earnings of this investment (v. 35a)*
   All that we spend on self and on the world apart from God will be consumed and will bring us loss (1 John 2:15–17; 1 Cor. 3:15; John 15:5).

The Lord challenged the logic of those who blindly believed that investing in this world is more profitable than in Him and His interests (Mark 8:36–37). What does it profit a person to gain the whole world and to lose it all in the end? All will be left at death (Luke 12:15–21). There is nothing in this world that is worth losing one's lifetime for. We owe everything to the Lord Jesus.

It would be folly for an investor to back an irreversible failing business. The wise investor seeks to place his capital in that which will bring him the greatest return. What investment are you making of your one Christian lifetime? What is your commitment to the Lord? Are you willing to make a full commitment to the Lord and to His work today? The wise person will seek to spend his remaining time in this world for that which will count for eternity and which will glorify God (2 Cor. 5:9–10, 14–15). Observe that we must make this commitment of discipleship to the Lord Jesus each day. Whenever we neglect to do this, the sin force within and Satan and the world without take command of our lives and use us for their evil purposes (cp. Luke 6:45; Prov. 4:23; 23:26; Eph. 3:17). The Lord Jesus is our example of making the right life investment (Heb. 10:7; John 4:34; 6:38; 8:28–29; 17:4).

THE KINDS OF DISCIPLES (JOHN 6:60–71)

Among the many people who followed Jesus, there were three kinds of disciples.

Nominal Disciples (John 6:60–66)

These were disciples in name only. They represented the majority among Jesus' followers. Lacking right motivation and, in many cases, salvation, they were attracted to Jesus by curiosity or by the possibility of receiving certain temporal benefits, like a free meal. These people were the ones whom Jesus challenged with receiving Him for salvation (John 6:48–58) and with following Him by setting forth the cost of discipleship (Luke 14:25–35). Full-time nominal disciples are not willing to pay the price of true discipleship (John 6:60, 66), but those who choose to do so demonstrate by this that they are saved and real disciples.

396

Real Disciples (John 6:67–69)

These are saved people who have proper motivation. Convinced that Jesus has the words of eternal life and is the Messiah, the Holy One of God, they realize that they cannot live without Him. They resolutely follow the Lord, regardless of the personal cost (John 11:16).

False Disciples (John 6:70–71)

While nominal disciples either become real disciples or eventually fade away and quit following when the demands are too great, unsaved false disciples remain and act like true ones. Judas Iscariot continued with the Lord's apostles as an impostor who was so influenced by Satan that he was called a devil. The Lord knows who are false disciples and will one day reject them (Matt. 7:21–23).

At this moment, all gospel believers are, in practice, either nominal or real disciples. Perhaps it would be more accurate to describe many of these people part-time disciples, whether nominal or real. May it be our purpose to become increasingly full-time, real disciples of the Lord Jesus Christ.

THE EVIDENCES OF DISCIPLESHIP

How can people know that they are true disciples or how can they identify others who are true disciples of the Lord Jesus? Real disciples are saved people who express several distinguishing features like the following:

They Are Gospel Believers Who Abide in God's Word (John 8:31).

They give close attention to the Scriptures and carefully ponder them (Col. 3:16; Pss. 1:1–3; 119:11). Rather than going away and forgetting what they have read or heard, they seek to understand God's Word and apply it to their lives (James 1:21–25).

They Are Gospel Believers Who Bear the Lord's Spiritual Fruit in Their Lives (John 15:8).

As they keep in touch with Him, the Lord abides in them in the fullness of His vitality (vv. 4–5) and produces in them the fruit of Christian character, conduct, and ministry (Gal. 5:22–23; Col. 1:10; Rom. 1:13). He who is the spiritual life of His people (John 14:6) expresses this life in and through those who are truly His disciples (Gal. 2:20; 4:19; Phil. 1:21).

They Are Gospel Believers Who Exercise His Love Toward Others (John 13:34–35).

Under the Mosaic Law, God's people were to love one another as they loved themselves (Lev. 19:18); we are to do this today (Gal. 5:13–15).[22] But this kind of love was limited to one's "neighbor" or to those with whom one was at peace. According to the present dispensation, it is our duty to love others with Christ's love—a love that is concerned with the well-being of our enemies as well as our friends (Matt. 5:44; cp. John 3:16). It is noteworthy that this love does not require us to like people, as human friendship love demands (God did not like us when we were sinners), but it does require us to be concerned about the spiritual and material well-being of others (1 John 3:16–20). We can exercise this compassionate love only as we are filled with the Holy Spirit and as He reproduces this love in our hearts (Gal. 5:22; Rom. 5:5).

It is noteworthy that the Lord Jesus made this love, not orthodox belief, the badge of Christian discipleship (John 13:34–35). While orthodox belief is important to those of us who are saved, the world cannot distinguish between true and false doctrine. But it does readily recognize the expressions of Christian love because of its uniqueness and practical applications. It is tragic that many churches that are orthodox in their doctrine do not convey a positive testimony of true discipleship to their communities because of the lack of this love for one another among their constituents.

The scarcity of teaching about discipleship may account for much of the carnality that we see among professed gospel believers and of their lack of involvement in the Lord's work. Without the commitment and motivation of discipleship, people are not willing to sacrifice their comforts and conveniences to serve the Lord sacrificially in undesirable, difficult places. It is noteworthy that our Lord called men to follow Him before He sent them out to special ministry (Mark 1:16–17; 3:13–14; 6:7–13). What kind of a disciple are you? Who or what are you following day by day? Is the Lord Jesus and His will for you first in your life? Perhaps your life is due for a reevaluation, for needed adjustments, or for radical changes.

MAKING MORAL BEHAVIORAL CHANGES IN THE CHRISTIAN LIFE

Earlier, we saw that the Christian life is capable of growth and change. Moreover, it is our duty to "perfect holiness in the fear of God" (2 Cor. 7:1). These changes concern not only our life direction but also our daily lifestyle—its words, thoughts, attitudes, motivations, and actions. We who are saved should seek to conform to what the Lord wants us to be and to do (Rom. 12:2; Col. 3:1–2). Increasingly, our lives should be involved in His work in this world, and daily we should be expressing Christlikeness by our behavior (Gal. 2:20, 4:19; Eph. 5:1–2; 1 Peter 2:21). The New Testament reveals how these changes are made; the Holy Spirit is ready to help us with this. To experience these changes, we must take the initiative by accepting the responsibility of our conduct, by understanding the basis for these changes, by keeping in view the goal of these changes, and by taking those steps that allow God to bring these about in our lives.

OUR ACCEPTING THE RESPONSIBILITY FOR THESE CHANGES

Our responsibility to God for our behavior is indicated by His commands to us (Eph. 4:29–32; James 4:17) and by our accounting for our behavior at the coming appraisal (2 Cor. 5:10). We must keep in mind that God will not do for us that which we can do for ourselves with His help (James 4:8). Since He has given us all the resources (2 Peter 1:3; see "The Maintenance of the Christian Life" above) and the instructions (2 Tim. 3:16–17) that we need for making these changes and doing His will, it is our duty to learn what these are and to follow them. These changes are not made by our pushing magic buttons or by solely waiting on God. They are made by disciplined obedience to God's directions and by faith in His doing His part as we do ours.

OUR BEING MOTIVATED FOR THESE CHANGES

God uses spiritual realities that took place in us at salvation to motivate us for making these changes. Here are several truths.

Our New Position in Jesus (2 Cor. 5:17)

By the baptism of the Holy Spirit (Gal. 3:27), we were removed from our position in Adam, with all of its negative associations, and were placed into Jesus where all is new (1 Cor. 15:22). With this new standing before God, we are divinely accepted and blessed in Him (Eph. 1:3–7) and have new spiritual life, resources, and relationships (1 Cor. 1:30; 2 Peter 1:3; Gal. 3:28). These truths should motivate us to make positive, holy changes in our lives.

Our Changed Personhood and Inner Human Nature (Eph. 4:24; Col. 3:9–10)

At salvation, we were made new creatures in Christ (2 Cor. 5:17). Our personhoods and inner human natures (souls and spirits) were recreated in righteousness and holiness after the image of the Lord Jesus (Rom. 8:29). In fact, we were recreated for good works, or the doing of God's will (Eph. 2:10). When we were made new creatures in Christ at salvation, we put off the old man (self), or what we were in Adam (1 Cor. 15:22), and put on the new man (self), or what we are now in Jesus (2 Cor. 5:17).[23] What does this mean?

1. *We did put off the old self, or the old man (Col. 3:9; cp. Eph. 4:22).*

The old self was what we were in Adam, sharing his corrupt kind of human nature, being guilty of his initial sin, and practicing the sinful lifestyle that characterizes his unsaved posterity. But at salvation all this was put off. Our relationship to Adam was severed and the old, unholy spiritual realities that we had in him were divinely removed from us (2 Cor. 5:17–18; Rom. 5:15–19). Although our bodies are still unsaved, they are properly the instruments of Christ and of His righteousness (1 Cor. 6:15; Rom. 6:13, 18–19).

2. *We did put on the new self, or the new man (Col. 3:10; cp. Eph. 4:24).*

The new self is what we are now in Christ, where all "things" (spiritual realities) are new (2 Cor. 5:17). In God's sight, we now have Jesus' kind of inner human nature (Rom. 8:29), righteousness (1 Cor. 1:30), and spiritual life (1 John 5:12). With these possessions we now have the human capacity and divine capability by the Holy Spirit to express Christlikeness in our behavior and to engage effectively in the Lord's work (2 Peter 1:3; 1 Cor. 3:9).

These spiritual realities provide us with the strongest motivation for changing our lifestyle and for serving the Lord in compliance with God's will for us. Having at salvation put off the old self and having put on the new self, it is now fitting that we quit sinning and that we live pleasing to God (Eph. 4:17–31; Col. 3:8–17). As new people in Jesus, we are now dead to sin and alive to God (Rom. 6:11–13, 18, 22). This truth points to the principle that underlies this change of behavior—we should conduct ourselves as pleasing to God, because we are His people, not to become His people. We should be Christlike in our behavior and engage in His work, because we are new creatures in Him, not for the purpose of becoming new creatures in Him.

OUR MAKING THESE CHANGES

Notice that God's commands are directed to our will, not to our feelings. He does not say, "Do this if you feel like it." We are to walk worthy of our calling (Eph. 4:1) and to be imitators of God morally as He is seen in Jesus' life (5:1–2). Let us look at the dynamics for these changes and the steps leading to these changes.

The Spiritual Dynamics for This Change

We who are saved possess everything that we need for spiritual life and godliness in this world (2 Peter 1:3). These resources include a renewed inner human nature with its new bent toward God and holy desires (Eph. 4:23; 1 Peter 2:22; Phil. 2:13), faith in God (2 Peter 1:1), the direction of the Scriptures (2 Tim. 3:16–17), the grace of God (2 Cor. 1:12), and the help of the Holy Spirit (John 14:16–17). How are we to utilize these resources?

The Steps Leading to This Change

One: We must decide to make a change and give ourselves to God for this purpose (Rom. 12:1–2). All positive moral action begins with personal decision and submission to God.

Two: We must pray for determination, strength, and direction for this change (1 John 5:14–15) and trust God to help us with it (Gal. 2:20).

Three: We must learn from the Scriptures what sinful conduct we are to put off from our behavior (cp. Col. 3:5–10; Eph. 4:25–31; Rom. 13:12). We put this off by dealing with sins by repentance (Rev. 2:5) and confession (1 John 1:9) and by refusing to give ourselves to the sin force's demands (Rom. 6:11–13; James 4:7).

Four: We must learn from the Scriptures what holy behavior we are to put on in the place of sinful behavior (Col. 3:12–17; Eph. 4:25–5:2; Rom. 13:12b–13). This holy behavior is God's will for us as taught in the Scriptures (Eph. 5:17; see Appendix F: "Learning and Doing God's Will"). Sometimes, it is necessary to restructure our lives to make way for these changes, like adding, eliminating, or rearranging certain details and circumstances so that it is more difficult for us to sin and easier to do God's will.

Five: Relying on the Holy Spirit for His help and direction, we must then do God's will—this holy alternative to sinning (2 Tim. 2:22; Eph. 5:8–18; John 13:17).

Six: As we continue doing God's will in this manner, our new behavior will become a holy habit. While there may be an occasional relapse, we need not despair. As we deal with our sin by repentance and confession and give ourselves anew to God, we can, with His strength, continue on for longer periods of time doing His will.

OUR FOCUS ON THE GOAL OF THESE CHANGES

The goal of these changes is to become more like the Lord Jesus (Eph. 4:11–16; 1 John 2:6). As we have seen, we achieve this by allowing the Lord to express His moral qualities in our behavior (Gal. 2:20; 2 Cor. 4:11). This is brought about in our lives by the sanctifying work of the Holy Spirit (2 Cor. 3:17–18). He communicates to us the spiritual vitality and qualities of the Lord Jesus (these are called "light" in Eph. 5:8–18) when we allow Him to do so (cp. Rom. 8:2–6; Gal. 5:22–23). Our Lord's likeness is then manifest in our character and action.

The Expression of Christlikeness in Spiritual Character

Jesus is manifested in our lives by the fruit of the Holy Spirit (Gal. 5:22–23). This fruit consists of qualities that we find in Jesus, like His love (John 13:1; Eph. 5:25), joy (John 15:11; Heb. 12:2), peace (John 14:27), long-suffering (John 18:11; Matt. 26:39, 42), gentleness or kindness (John 5:6–9), goodness (Heb. 7:26), faithfulness (John 17:4), meekness (Matt. 11:29), and self-control (1 Peter 2:23). When we give ourselves to the Lord Jesus, we express these character qualities in our behavior and disposition.

The Exercise of Christlikeness in Spiritual Action

Jesus is also seen in our lives by our actions. Because He is righteous (1 John 2:1), holy (Heb. 7:26), and loving (Eph. 5:25), the Lord Jesus is seen in us when we express these qualities in our behavior (1 Cor. 15:34; 1 Peter 1:16; John 13:34). It is obvious that we cannot of ourselves generate these qualities. But the Holy Spirit will reproduce them in our lives as we depend on Him to do so. Let us look at these action qualities.

1. Righteousness

This righteousness is the quality of being or doing right (1 John 2:29). Jesus is righteous in that He always does what is right, which is His doing the Father's will (John 6:38; 17:4). We who are saved are positionally righteous in Him (1 Cor. 1:30). At salvation God justified us, or declared us to be righteous (Rom. 5:1), for He gave us Jesus' righteousness (Rom. 3:22) and made us righteous in Him (2 Cor. 5:21). Consequently, He wants us to do right things by doing His will in reliance upon the Holy Spirit for help and direction (Rom. 8:4; 2 Tim. 2:22; 1 Peter 2:24; 1 John 2:29). This behavior is called practical righteousness.

2. *Holiness*

This holiness is the quality of being morally pure or not sinning. Jesus is holy in the sense that in Him was no sin (1 John 3:5), that He did no sin (1 Peter 2:22), and that He did not belong to the class of sinners (Heb. 7:26). At salvation, we were made holy in Christ (1 Cor. 1:2, 30). God now appeals to us to be holy in every aspect of our lives (1 Peter 1:15–16; 1 Thess. 4:3). This means that He wants us to separate ourselves from that which is sinful in His sight, like unholy alliances and morally unclean practices (2 Cor. 6:14–7:1); to consider ourselves to be holy vessels for His use in this world (2 Tim. 2:21; Acts 9:15); and not to sin at all (1 John 2:1). This kind of behavior is called practical holiness, or sanctification.

3. *Love*

This love has two objects: God and others.[24]

a. *Our love for God (Mark 12:29–30)*

Jesus expressed His love for God the Father by His obedience to the Father (John 4:31), delight in the Father (4:34), trust in the Father (Luke 23:46; Matt. 27:43), and seeking to honor the Father by His behavior (John 8:49; 12:28). Those who love God do these things as well (14:15, 21, 23).

b. *Our love for others (John 13:34)*

We are to love others, including our enemies (Matt. 5:44), with Jesus' love. This is a compassionate love that moves us to minister to their needs, even at personal sacrifice (1 John 3:16–18; 1 Cor. 13:4–7). The Lord does not ask us to like people, or to take pleasure in them, as does friendship love. He asks us to be concerned about their needs and to seek to minister to these needs. Needless to say, we can do this only through the power of the Holy Spirit (Gal. 5:22).

Our becoming Christlike is like putting on a garment (Rom. 13:14). When we put on a coat, we give ourselves to it, with the result that others see the coat on us. In like manner, by yielding ourselves to Jesus, we allow Him to exhibit Himself and to live His life through us.

We who are saved can become Christlike immediately by decision and by following these steps. We can stop sinful practices and replace them with holy ones that reflect Jesus in our lives. However, for this to occur, we must decide to do this and give ourselves to God. We can be and do everything that He demands of us by the help and direction of the Holy Spirit (John 14:16–17) and of the Lord Jesus (Phil. 4:13; Matt. 11:28–30). Occasionally, we look away from the Lord to self or to others and fail. But being creatures of habit, we can with perseverance and time develop habits of holy lifestyle and ministry. The decision is with you and me; God has already decided what He wants us to do, has given all the resources that we need for doing it, and has given all the instructions that we need in His Word.

THE MINISTRIES OF THE CHRISTIAN LIFE

Resting upon the principle of giving (Matt. 10:8), Christian service, or ministry, is our response as gospel believers to all that God has done for us and has given us in the Lord Jesus (Rom. 12:1–2; 2 Cor. 5:14–15; 1 Thess. 1:9). This ministry has both vertical and horizontal dimensions. Vertically, it is our worshiping God; horizontally, it is our laboring with the Lord Jesus in His work of building His Church. Let us examine these.

THE MINISTRY OF WORSHIPING GOD

The English word *worship* comes from "worthship," meaning the condition of deserving, or being held in, esteem or honor. Thus, worship refers to the act of paying honor or ascribing worth to one who deserves this. We who have been saved have the privilege of worshiping the true and living God, who is worthy of the highest honors (1 Thess. 1:9; Ps. 45:11). Our worship of the divine Trinity can be directed collectively to God or individually to the Father, to the Son, or to the Holy Spirit.

The Nature of Worship

Worship consists of giving God that which is due Him (Ps. 29:2). Before Jesus died, worship involved offering to God animal sacrifices and grain offerings (Gen. 8:20; 12:8; Lev. 1–5), which were often costly gifts (2 Sam. 24:24). In our worship today, we are to offer to God spiritual sacrifices (1 Peter 2:5). As seen in Psalm 100, these spiritual sacrifices include our:

1. *Giving God ourselves (Ps. 100:3b; Rom. 12:1)*
   By this we acknowledge that we are His product or His people to be and to do all that He desires for us (Eph. 2:10; 2 Cor. 5:17).
2. *Giving God our service (Ps. 100:2a; Matt. 4:10; Rom. 12:2; 1 Thess. 1:9)*
   Our doing His will with love and with recognition of His authority honors Him (cp. Matt. 5:16; Heb. 13:16, "good works"). Not all who serve worship whom or what they serve; but all who worship serve whom or what they worship (Matt. 4:10).
3. *Giving God our thanksgiving (Ps. 100:4; Heb. 13:15; 1 Thess. 5:18)*
   This consists of our expressing our gratitude for all that God is and all He does for us.
4. *Giving God our praise (Ps. 100:4; Heb. 13:15)*
   This consists of our declaring God's deity, qualities, and works (cp. Ps. 100:5; 2 Cor. 1:3; Eph. 1:3–14; James 3:9; 1 Peter 1:3–5; Rev. 5:9).
5. *Giving to others in God's name (Heb. 13:16; Matt. 25:34–40)*
   To give to the needs of others in His name is to give as He directs and for His glory (Rom. 12:13). This would also involve giving to one's local church to provide for its needs, including the support of its pastor and its missions program (Phil. 4:18).

We worship God when we offer to Him these spiritual sacrifices, either formally in a worship service or informally during the course of daily life.

The Attitudes of Worship

Worship not only involves the action of giving but also the attitudes with which we give, like the following:

1. *Joy and gladness (Ps. 100:1–2)*
   Worship is not to be regarded as a burdensome, doleful exercise. True worship is a joyful experience, for it proceeds from reflection upon God and the blessings of our relation to Him (cp. 2 Cor. 9:7).
2. *Wholeheartedness (Ps. 100:2; Col. 3:23)*
   Acceptable worship cannot be a thoughtless, mechanical ritual without heart, for this would be hypocritical (Matt. 15:7–8). Worship with "true heart" (Heb. 10:22) involves one's total being, and it is to be done with sincerity (cp. Matt. 15:7–8).
3. *Faith (Ps. 100:4; Heb. 10:19, 22)*
   Underlying worship is the confidence that we have access to God, as He teaches in His Word, and that He will respond favorably to the sacrifices that we offer Him when we do this as He requires.
4. *Fear (Pss. 5:7; 22:23)*
   This is the respect, honor, and reverence that we are to show Him (Deut. 10:12; see "Fellowship with God: Our Respecting God" under Theology Proper).

It is impossible to worship God without these attitudes. When we are filled with the

Holy Spirit, He conveys to us all these attitudes, which we see portrayed in the Lord Jesus (John 4:34; Heb. 5:7; 10:7; 1 Peter 2:23).

The Means of Worship   *947*

The Lord Jesus said that worship was to be "in Spirit and in truth" (John 4:24).

1. Worship must be "in Spirit."

This means that our worship must be by the power and direction of the Holy Spirit, our resident Helper (Phil. 3:3; John 14:16–17). This requires our being filled with the Holy Spirit (Eph. 5:18) or our cooperating with Him in such a way that allows Him to help us as we do God's will in our worship.

2. Worship must be "in Truth."

"Truth" conveys the ideas of reality and accuracy.

a. True worship concerns reality.

The worship of Judaism, with its Levitical ritual and sacrifices, was largely symbolic (Heb. 8:5; 9:9–10; 10:1–4). Because of Jesus' atoning work (Heb. 8:6; 9:11–14; 10:11–14, see vv. 19–25), true worship occurs in the sphere of spiritual reality, wherein we have direct access to God through Jesus (Eph. 2:18; Heb. 10:21–22) as we are energized by the Holy Spirit (Phil. 3:3). The only symbols that remain with Christianity are the ordinances of water baptism and the Lord's Supper.[25] The outward accessories of worship, like architecture, liturgy, and music should be regarded as aids to worship, not substitutes for worship.

b. True worship concerns accuracy.

The Samaritans worshiped in ignorance (John 4:22). Their worship was a mixture of the elements of paganism and of the Mosaic Law (2 Kings 17:24–41). True worship is in accord with the teachings and instructions of God's Word, which is truth (John 17:17).

The Preparation for Worship   *948*

As with any spiritual exercise, worship of the true God, whether in a worship service or at the beginning of a day, requires heart preparation. This includes examining our lives for any known sin that needs to be dealt with by repentance and confession (1 John 1:5–7; Pss. 29:2; 15; Heb. 10:22) and our giving ourselves to the Holy Spirit for His help and direction (Eph. 5:18). It is also fitting to thank God for the opportunity to worship Him, the true God, with the confidence that He will receive our spiritual sacrifices (Rom. 12:1; Heb. 12:15) and will be honored by them (1 Thess. 5:18).

What a privilege it is to belong to the true and living God and to worship Him. Let us seek to make our worship more meaningful and to give it a larger place in our lives. He is pleased when we do this (John 4:23).

THE MINISTRY OF WORKING WITH GOD   *949*

The apostle Paul states that we who are saved are laborers together with God (1 Cor. 3:9). This working with God concerns our laboring with the Lord Jesus as His slaves-friends in the building of His Church (cp. 1 Cor. 6:19–20; Rom. 6:16–18; 14:8; Gal. 1:10; Col. 3:24; 1 Peter 2:16; see "The Formation of the Universal Christian Church" under Ecclesiology). Upon saving us, the Lord has left us here so that we might serve with Him in this work.

The Nature of This Work   *950*

1. Its character

On the eve of His death, Jesus declared that His disciples would do what He did and greater works than these (John 14:12). Besides His atoning work, which was exclusively

His to do, the Lord Jesus also presented Himself to Israel as the Messiah of OT prophecy for their reception or rejection (cp. Isa. 49:1–6; Matt. 9:35; 15:24; Luke 4:43–44). He did this, not by public proclamation but by fulfillment of what OT prophecy declared that the Messiah would do, including performing miracles (cp. Luke 4:18–19). These miracles testified to His messianic office and divine commission (Isa. 61:1; Acts 10:38).

These miraculous signs also attended the ministry of His apostles as a confirmation of their divine commission (2 Cor. 12:12; Heb. 2:4). We do not have to do these things today, for our commission is given in the New Testament (Matt. 28:19–20; Acts 1:8), and it is confirmed by the results of the ministry of God's Word (Rom. 1:16).

The Lord also said that His disciples would do "greater works than these" because of His returning to the Father. These "greater works," being "greater" in kind than the physical miracles that He had wrought, refer to His present work of building His Church. His giving people spiritual life and sight is greater than their physical counterparts. He predicted His building the Church several months before He died (Matt. 16:18); several weeks later He began this construction on the Day of Pentecost, ten days after His return to heaven (Acts 2:41, 47). His building the Church is one of His messianic works that He is doing as man, seated at the Father's right hand.

2. *Its kinds*

The Lord is building His Church quantitatively and qualitatively. He is doing this work quantitatively by saving gospel believers and by uniting them to the Church by means of the Holy Spirit's baptism (Acts 2:47; 16:5b; 1 Cor. 12:13, 27; Eph. 1:22–23). He also is building the Church qualitatively by developing the spiritual lives of saved people (Acts 16:5a; 1 Cor. 14:26; Eph. 4:14–16).

3. *Its means*

Since He is doing this from heaven, the Lord is using means to build the Church. These means are the Scriptures (2 Tim. 3:15–17), the Holy Spirit (John 3:6; 1 Cor. 12:13, 27), and His people who are on earth (1 Cor. 3:5–10; Acts 15:4).[26]

The Ministries of This Work

The Lord has given to the Church pastors and teachers for the purpose of equipping the Lord's people for the work of building the Church (Eph. 4:11–12). This work, or service, consists of two kinds of ministries by which the Lord is building His Church through His people.

1. *The ministry of general service*

This ministry belongs to every gospel believer alike. It includes prayer (John 14:13; Eph. 8:18; Rom. 10:1), living a consistent Christian life (1 Peter 1:15; 2 Tim. 2:21; 2 Cor. 3:2), ordinary giving (Eph. 4:28; Phil. 4:14–17), and gospel witnessing (Acts 1:8; 11:19–20). Although the gospel believer may be a child, he or she can be taught to do these things and to serve the Lord in these ways.

2. *The ministry of special service*

This special ministry is determined by one's spiritual gifts and natural abilities (see "The Work of the Holy Spirit: His Relation to Spiritual Gifts" under Pneumatology). This ministry is one that each gospel believer has, yet which differs from that of others. God has created us in Christ Jesus for good works that He prepared beforehand so that we might walk in them (Eph. 2:10). The apostle Paul would have his Christian readers reflect soberly on themselves regarding the measures of faith and grace that God had given them in the form of spiritual gifts (Rom. 12:3–8; Eph. 4:7; 1 Cor. 12:1–11). As the human body has many organs and each organ has its own function, so Christ's mystical body, the Church, consists of many people, each of whom has his own function in the building of the Church

(Rom. 12:4–5; 1 Cor. 12:12–30). It is important that each of us knows what his function is and allows the Lord to use him in his special way (see "The Work of the Holy Spirit: His Relation to Spiritual Gifts" under Pneumatology).

The Calls to This Work

While the Lord sometimes calls people in an unusual way to extraordinary service (cp. Exod. 3; Acts 26:13–18), this is not the usual experience of most people. His calling us to *general ministry* simply consists of His appeals through the Scriptures for us to do the things of which this ministry consists, like our praying (Eph. 6:18–19), witnessing (Acts 1:8), and living a Christian life (Rom. 12).

His calling us to *special ministry* is His showing us what this ministry is and to whom it is to be done (Isa. 6:8–9a). Although the Lord's call to special service is unique for each of us, it appears to have the following common ingredients by which we may recognize it: one, our having an inner desire, with right motives, for a specific ministry (1 Tim. 3:1; Phil. 2:13; 1 Cor. 10:31); two, our learning what our spiritual gifts and natural abilities are; three, our seeing the need for the ministry that we desire and our having a growing burden for the work; four, our trying out the ministry of our interest and evaluating the results; and five, our having a growing conviction that a certain work is what the Lord would have us do. The Lord will show us what our special work is, as we look to Him and are willing to do His will, whatever this may be (Prov. 3:5–6). His giving us this understanding is His calling.

What, then, is Christian service? It is our cooperating with the Lord in such a way that allows Him to use us in the building of His Church quantitatively and qualitatively (Acts 14:27; 15:4). This cooperation involves our abiding in Him (John 15:4–5) and our exercising our spiritual gifts and natural abilities according to His will and power in the salvation of unsaved people and edification of His people (Rom. 15:15–16; 1 Cor. 14:26).

The Place of This Work

Until the Lord leads us elsewhere, we should seek to do our special ministry where we are (cp. Paul, Acts 9:30; 11:22–26). The local church is the arena of Christian ministry for most saved people (see "The Use of Spiritual Gifts and Natural Abilities" under Pneumatology). If the Lord should want us to serve in another place, He will make this known to us. Wherever we are, we must be on the alert for opportunities to serve Him and not allow our gifts to become dormant (Eph. 5:16; 2 Cor. 2:12; 6:1). Whatever ministry we undertake, we must remember that we cannot do anything apart from the Lord Jesus (John 15:4–5; Phil. 4:13) or the Holy Spirit (John 14:16–17). Also, we should keep in mind the primary purpose for Christian ministry, which is to do all for the glory of God (1 Cor. 10:31).

The Proper Attitudes Toward This Work

A fruitful ministry requires us to serve the Lord humbly (Acts 20:19), wholeheartedly (Col. 3:23), reliantly (John 15:5; Gal. 2:20), dynamically (Eph. 5:18; Acts 6:5, 8), obediently (Col. 3:22), reverently (Heb. 12:28), joyfully (Ps. 100:2), prayerfully (1 Thess. 5:17), thankfully (v. 18), expectantly (Isa. 55:11), and lovingly (1 Cor. 13:1–3).

The Lord has left us here for a while that we might serve with Him in this great work. Are you carrying out your general and special ministries? Many people expect the pastor to do all the work of a local church, but this is more than he can do in addition to his own duties (see "The Administration of a Local Christian Church" under Ecclesiology). It is important for each of us to learn what our special ministry is and to look for occasions to use this in our local church or wherever the Lord may send us. We should also remember the great spiritual need that is beyond the walls of our local church in the community and throughout the earth.

LAW AND THE CHRISTIAN LIFE

In the Bible, the word "law" has various meanings as determined by its context. These meanings are the Pentateuch (Luke 24:44), the Old Testament (John 12:34; 15:25), the Mosaic Law (Matt. 22:36), the Ten Commandments (Rom. 7:7), innate moral law or instinct (2:12–15), the Levitical ceremonial law (Heb. 8:4; 9:22), a moral force (Rom. 7:23,25; 8:2), law in general (7:1–2), civil law (1 Cor. 6:1, 6), a principle of divine dealings with men (Rom. 3:27), a principle of life experience (7:21), and the Law of Christ, or His teachings given in the New Testament (Gal. 6:2). What obligations do the Lord's people have to moral, religious, and civil laws?

OUR OBLIGATION TO MORAL LAW *killing Tribes*

Being made in God's image (James 3:9), pagans who do not have the Scriptures have an innate sense of morality, which is "the law written in their hearts" (Rom. 2:14–15). This innate law is reflected by their consciences and their community ordinances and is expressed by their moral evaluations and judgments. Their duty is to live by this innate law.[27]

We who have the Scriptures have the duty of fulfilling the moral requirements that are taught therein (Ps. 119:105). Although God's revealed moral laws, as given in the different dispensations, are not identical in their statement, they are similar in their substance, for underlying them is His unchanging righteousness. For example, the Ten Commandments were given to the nation of Israel (Exod. 20:1–17), but with the exception of Sabbath observance, they are all restated in the teachings of grace for those of us who live in the present dispensation (Matt. 6:24; 1 John 5:21; James 5:12; Eph. 6:1–2; 1 John 3:11–15; 1 Thess. 4:3–7; Eph. 4:28–29; Col. 3:5; Rom. 13:8–10).[28]

The apostle Paul considered himself to be under law to Christ (1 Cor. 9:21). We gospel believers, too, are subject to Christ's Law, which is expressed in the New Testament by about 650 commands, given to all saved people (Gal. 6:2; 1 John 3 23). The fullest expression of this law is our exercising the Lord's love in our relations with other people, whether saved or unsaved (John 13:34–35; 15:12; Col. 3:14; 1 John 3:16–18; Matt. 5:44). This compassionate love supersedes all other moral laws regarding our relations with other people (Rom. 13:8–10; cp. 1 Cor. 13:4–7).

OUR OBLIGATION TO RELIGIOUS LAW

The Jews lived under the Mosaic Law, which prescribed not only their civil life but also their religious duties (Exod. 23:14–19; Lev. 1–27). Other religions of man also have their laws and obligations that their devotees are to fulfill. How does one's salvation effect one's observance of religious law?

The apostle Paul taught the principle that we died to all religious laws when we were saved (Rom. 7:1–6, the religious ritual of the Mosaic Law). Sharing in Jesus' death and resurrection, we were released from bondage to these laws and became obligated to observe Christ's Law, as given in the commands of the New Testament. Being neither legalistic nor antinomian, the apostle respected all laws and accommodated himself to them whenever possible so as to win others to Christ (1 Cor. 9:19–23). But never did he forget that he was under a higher law—Christ's Law, to which he gave priority in his life (v. 21).

406

OUR OBLIGATION TO CIVIL LAW

Our heavenly citizenship does not lessen our duty to earthly government (Phil. 3:20; Rom. 13:1–7; 1 Peter 2:11–17). The duties of both realms simultaneously rest upon all who are saved, with duty to God's authority having priority over duty to man's authority (cp. Acts 4:19–20; 5:29). Let us consider the answer to several questions.

Why Are We Responsible to Civil Government?

First, because civil government has been instituted by God and serves His purpose in human affairs (Rom. 13:1–4), God uses government to prevent anarchy in this sinful world and to carry out His program for humanity. Government fulfills its function in two ways; *(a)* it carries the sword (v. 4), with the right to protect life, to curb evil, and to thwart injustice (1 Peter 2:14); and *(b)* it promotes good (Rom. 13:3–4) by allowing people to live together in a peaceable, orderly way. The apostle wrote of civil authority as being "the ordinance of God" (Rom. 13:2) and of the civil official as being "the minister of God" (v. 4; cp. 1 Peter 2:14). Long ago, God spoke of Nebuchadnezzar the Babylonian as His "servant" (Jer. 25:9), the Assyrians as His "rod" (Isa. 10:5), and Cyrus the Persian as His "shepherd" and "anointed one" (Isa. 44:28; 45:1). This is not to say that God approves of everything that civil officials do, but they are His agents, who are accountable to Him for their actions and who are used by Him to accomplish, in part, His purpose for mankind (cp. Dan. 4).

Second, the rights and privileges that we derive from government require our supporting civil authority. The apostle Paul testified that he lived "as a citizen" in all good conscience before God (Acts 23:1, Gk.). At the same time, he was mindful of his civil rights when he appealed his case to Caesar's court (25:10–11). The government that provides services, protection, and regulation for an orderly community also requires its subjects to live as law-abiding citizens.

Third, our Christian testimony to the world requires our being law-abiding citizens insofar as this does not conflict with our doing God's will (1 Peter 2:11–15; cp. Acts 5:28–29).[29]

Of What Does This Responsibility to Civil Government Consist?

1. We are to honor government officials (1 Peter 2:17).

To honor government officials is to evaluate their offices and their discharges of duty and to give them suitable respect. If we cannot respect the official as a man, we still must respect his office as God's agent. *MAN INTERPRETS*

2. We are to obey government (Rom. 13:1; Titus 3:1; 1 Peter 2:13–14).

Since government is God's institution and agency, no one is exempted from obeying it insofar as this obedience does not conflict with God's will, which is clearly stated in the Scriptures (Acts 5:29; Dan. 3:1–18; 6:10). Scriptural motivations for our obeying government are wrath's sake—penalties for violations of law (Rom. 13:2, 4), conscience's sake (v. 5), and the Lord's sake (1 Peter 2:13). Good citizenship contributes to a better government and to our gospel witness.

3. We are to support government by paying taxes (Rom. 13:6–7; cp. Matt. 22:17–21).

Taxes are the price we pay for governmental services.

4. We are to serve government in the will of God (Titus 3:1).

Gospel believers often are called upon to serve their government in some civil or military capacity. This is proper as long as this service and the government support people's basic human rights, like justice, self-preservation, and deliverance from oppression and that they honor worthy national alliances and commitments.

5. *We are to pray for government officials (1 Tim. 2:1–3).*

We are to pray and give thanks for them, for they are God's servants, divinely used to carry out, in part, His purposes for mankind. Our prayers result in better government and a peaceable way of life.

HEALTH PLAN - ABORTION FUNDS - HOW DO WE

To What Extent Are We Subject to Civil Laws? *PROTEST*

Q59

We who are saved must obey government intelligently, not blindly. When the will of the state clearly conflicts with God's will, as revealed in His Word, then the gospel believer must obey God (Acts 4:19; 5:29; see Dan. 3; 6:10).

Although the Christian, as a citizen, may make full use of his rights under the law (Acts 16:37; 22:25), he must also be prepared to accept the denial of these rights, as our Lord did during His trials before Jewish and Roman courts (26:57–27:35). C. B. Eavey wrote, "Opposition to one in lawful authority should not be made for the purpose of securing one's personal rights, but only in defense of the right. Often it may be the Christian's right to give up his rights. Never is a Christian justified in attacking the lawful right which belongs to a ruler or a government."[30] On the other hand, our Lord stood in defense of right when He questioned the motivation of His abusers (John 18:22–23). Dr. Eavey added,

> If and when a ruler becomes so corrupt as to be unable to adhere at all to the principle of true right and eternal justice, the Christian may find it necessary to resist his authority even to the extent of revolting against it and becoming a party to the establishment of another government. However, until it is clearly evident that a ruler or a government is unfaithful to its charge, it is the duty of the Christian to render allegiance to the existing authority, though it be guilty of much that is wrong.[31]

We who are privileged to live in a nation that has democracy should thank God daily for our leaders and for the freedoms that we enjoy as citizens. For those of us who live in lands that do not offer its citizens these freedoms, we must keep in mind that God in His sovereignty has placed us here to share His blessings with those around us. In any case, we who are saved are the salt of the earth as well as the light of the world (Matt. 5:13–16). We can look to God to use us to make our nation a better one as well as to make those around us better people.

It is obvious that the Scriptures, especially the New Testament, have much to say about the Christian life and its divine provisions. It is urgent that we learn this truth and apply it to our daily lives and, when we have opportunity, teach this to others. We are grateful for that incomparable Helper, the Holy Spirit, who teaches us this truth and enables us to incorporate it into our lives, as we trust and obey Him. As we have seen, the goal of the Christian life is Christlikeness in our attitudes and behavior. This is manifested when we are filled with the fruit of the Holy Spirit (Gal. 5:22–23), and when we are righteous and holy in our behavior (1 John 2:29; 1 Peter 1:15). Have you assessed your life recently? Are you truly saved? Are you walking in the light with God? Are you involved with the Lord's work in this world? Are you following Him as a real disciple? Always keep in mind that His return is near; then, He will appraise our Christian lives. The apostle Paul lived with this prospect in view (2 Cor. 5:9–10; 2 Tim. 4:5–8).

A Review of Zoeology

1. What is spiritual life? How do we receive this?
2. Define Christian experience. What are several features of Christian experience?

3. By what means should we test the genuineness of our religious experience
4. What is Christian growth?
5. In what areas of our spiritual life does this growth take place?
6. What is the goal of Christian growth? By what four means does this occur?
7. What has God given us for the maintenance of our Christian life?
8. What must we do to make Bible reading profitable?
9. Give eight rules that help us to understand the Bible. *P. 376,7*
10. Give eight ways in which we can relate the Scriptures to daily life. *378, 9*
11. What is prayer? Give several kinds of prayer.
12. Why is it proper to talk to Jesus and to the Holy Spirit?
13. What rules must we follow in prayers of petition?
14. What reasons may be given for unanswered prayer?
15. What is practical faith in God? Give several aspects of this trust.
16. What must we do to receive divine forgiveness and cleansing?
17. How can other gospel believers be helpful to us?
18. How does God's grace and the Holy Spirit relate to our daily lives?
19. What must we do to allow the Holy Spirit to help us?
20. What fruit are we to bear in our lives? *P. 385*
21. Who actually produces this fruit?
22. What does it mean to abide in Jesus?
23. By what means does the Father cause us to be more fruitful?
24. What must we do to experience occasions of victory over our spiritual enemies?
25. What is practical holiness? Practical righteousness?
26. From what are we to separate ourselves?
27. How can we separate ourselves from sin?
28. How can we recognize false religious teachers?
29. What should our relation to unsaved people be?
30. What should our relation to the things of the world be?
31. What is worldliness?
32. How can we avoid worldliness?
33. Why is it necessary to practice personal dedication as well as separation?
34. What features does dedication to God have according to Romans 12:1?
35. How often should we dedicate ourselves to God?
36. In addition to dedication, what must we do (Rom. 12:2)?
37. What does it mean to be a disciple of Jesus?
38. What are the requirements of discipleship?
39. What kinds of disciples are there? What are the evidences of true disciples?
40. What two reasons are given for our being responsible for making changes in our spiritual lives?
41. What motivations has God given us for this change? *39 B*
42. What steps will bring about this change in our lives?
43. What is the goal for making these changes?
44. What is the basic function in worship?
45. What spiritual sacrifices can we offer to God?
46. Give several attitudes that are necessary for worship. *402*
47. What does it mean to worship God "in Spirit"? "In truth"? *403*
48. What must one do to prepare for worship? *403*
49. What is Jesus constructing on earth during this age? *403*
50. What two kind of ministries is He using to build His Church? *403-4*

51. Which ministry is the same for all saved people? Describe this ministry.
52. Upon what does one's special ministry rest?
53. What are spiritual gifts and natural abilities? Do you know your spiritual gift or gifts?
54. What is the Lord's call to general ministry? To special ministry? *404*
55. Where should we first seek to do the special ministry that He has given us? *405*
56. As believers, what is our duty to moral law? *406*
57. What is our duty to religious law? *406*
58. What is our duty to civil law and to rulers? Describe these responsibilities.
59. Whose law has priority over all others? *God's P. 408*
60. Are you a growing, fruitful Christian? Are you living a holy life? Did you give yourself to Jesus today?

Endnotes

1. The prominence and importance given to the new kind of life that gospel believers receive at salvation require a separate theological category and treatment. The Greek word *zoe,* meaning "life," which is associated with "everlasting life" or "eternal life" some thirty-eight times (KJV) in the New Testament (cp. John 3:16, 36; 10:28; Acts 13:48; Rom. 6:22; 1 Tim. 1:16; Titus 1:2; 1 John 5:11, 13) is the basis for the name of this category.
2. For the nature and features of this new life, see "The Components of Salvation: Regeneration" under Soteriology.
3. See "Interaction with the Persons of the Divine Trinity" under Theology Proper.
4. See Appendix Y: "The Kinds of English Bibles."
5. For a fine devotional Bible study guide, I recommend Alan M. Stibbs, gen. ed., *Search the Scriptures* (Downers Grove, Ill.: InterVarsity Press, 1967).
6. See F. H. Barackman, *How to Interpret the Bible* (Grand Rapids: Kregel Publications, 1991) and Roy B. Zuck, *Basic Bible Interpretation* (Wheaton, Ill: Scripture Press Publications, 1991). David L. Cooper's "Golden Rule of Interpretation" follows: "When the plain sense of Scripture makes common sense, seek no other sense; therefore, take every word at its primary, ordinary, usual, literal meaning unless the facts of the immediate context, studied in the light of related passages and axiomatic and fundamental truths, indicate clearly otherwise."—*What Men Must Believe* (Los Angeles: Biblical Research Society, 1943), 63.
7. See Alan M. Stibbs, *Understanding God's Word* (London: The Inter-Varsity Fellowship, 1961), 58–64.
8. See "The Dispensation of Grace" under Theology Proper.
9. See F. H. Barackman, "The Kinds of Biblical Faith," pt. 2 of *Where Is Your Faith?*
10. See "The Believer's Relation to Actual Sin: Our Receiving Divine Forgiveness and Cleansing" under Hamartiology.
11. See "His Work During the Church Age: The Holy Spirit Fills Us" under Pneumatology.
12. See "Our Interaction with God the Holy Spirit as His Temples-Dependents" under Pneumatology.
13. See Appendix F: "Learning and Doing God's Will." In Matthew 11:29 KJV, "of Me" should read "from Me."
14. See "The Discipleship of the Christian Life" in this chapter.
15. See "Our Interaction with God the Father as His Children-Sons: Our Submission to Him" under Paterology.
16. See "Satan: His Defeat in the Lives of Saved People" under Angelology and "The Believer's Relation to Actual Sin" under Hamartiology.
17. Regarding 2 Thess. 3:14–15, note the command, "have no company with him"; the purpose, "that he may be ashamed"; and the extent, "yet count him not as an enemy but admonish him as a brother."
18. In 1 Cor. 7:1–17, the apostle Paul deals with the situation of a saved person's having an unsaved spouse.

19. See endnote 22 and Appendix Z: "Our Loving God and Others."
20. See the Lord's statement on the value of this commitment (Mark 8:34–38) under "The Discipleship of the Christian Life" in this chapter.
21. See "The Prophecy of Jesus' Appraisal of His Church" under Eschatology.
22. This proper self-love is one of self-respect (Rom. 12:3), based on the esteem that one has for oneself as a child of God (John 1:12), a new creature in Christ (2 Cor. 5:17), and the Father's gift to His Son (John 17:6). It is also one of self-care (Eph. 5:28–29), that provides for one's spiritual and physical needs.
23. The theological context of this action indicates that this took place at salvation rather than its being something that we are to do now. See "The Believer's Relation to Original Sin" under Hamartiology.
24. See Appendix Z: "Our Loving God and Others."
25. The cross was not regarded as a Christian symbol until the second century (Tertullian).
26. Observe that Christian ministry consists of what God does with us, not what we do for Him (Acts 14:27). Actually, we cannot do anything for God apart from the strength and direction that the Holy Spirit provides. Moreover, any effort to do so apart from God is fruitless and sinful (John 15:5; Rom. 14:23). For more on Christian ministry, see "The Formation of the Universal Christian Church" under Ecclesiology and "The Work of the Holy Spirit: His Relation to Spiritual Gifts" under Pneumatology.
27. See "The Dispensations of God: The Dispensation of Governed Mankind" under Theology Proper.
28. We must recognize that, although all of the Bible is profitable to us, it is not all about those of us who are saved. Most of the Old Testament concerns God's dealings with Israel under the Mosaic Law. Since the New Testament gives the Lord's commands for His people today (the Dispensation of Grace), we should follow OT instructions insofar as they reflect, or are in harmony with, those of the New Testament. That the church at Troas met on the first day of the week to "break bread" (Acts 20:7) indicates a practice, at least among Gentile churches. Sunday is a more fitting time for Christians to gather for worship and fellowship than Saturday (the Sabbath) since the Lord arose on the first day of the week (Matt. 28:1; John 20:1), and the Church was born on the Day of Pentecost (Acts 2:1), which was a Sunday. Nowhere in the New Testament are we commanded to observe the Sabbath (Rom. 14:5–6).
29. Observe the reason for Jesus' allowing Peter to pay the temple tax for both of them although the Lord was greater than the temple (Matt. 17:24–27; 12:6), "Lest we give them offense," asserting the principle that it is better to set aside personal rights in sacrificial love than to cause others to stumble by our bad example of attitude and behavior (see Rom. 14; 1 Cor. 8).
30. C. B. Eavey, *Practical Christian Ethics* (Grand Rapids: Zondervan Publishing House, 1959), 200.
31. Ibid.

Ecclesiology

12

ECCLESIOLOGY
The Doctrine of the Christian Church

Our being called unto the fellowship not only of God but also of other gospel believers is a blessing of salvation (1 Cor. 1:9; 1 John 1:3). The doctrine of the Christian Church reminds us that we who are saved are not isolated bits of humanity scattered about the world. Being spiritually united to all saved contemporaries, we belong to a great human fellowship that exceeds national and denominational boundaries, that has a special relation to the Lord Jesus, and that engages in worship, edification, ministries of compassionate love, and evangelism. In this section, we shall examine the universal and local aspects of the Christian Church.

THE MEANING OF *CHURCH*

The New Testament word "church" (Gk. *ekklesia*, a "called out" assembly of people) has secular, ethnic, or religious meaning, depending upon its context. Its *secular meaning* concerns a public assembly of people (Acts 19:32, 39, 41); with *ethnic meaning* it twice refers to Israel (Acts 7:38; Heb. 2:12); and with *religious meaning* it refers to groups of Christians: *one*, a local congregation of professing gospel believers (Acts 8:1; 14:27; 1 Cor. 1:2); *two*, the totality of gospel believers in a region (Acts 9:31, Gk. "church"; Phil. 3:6); and *three*, our Lord's Universal Christian Church, which is His mystical body (Eph. 1:22–23) and bride (2 Cor. 11:2). Notice that the NT word *church* never refers to a building. Our study concerns the universal and local aspects of the Christian Church.

THE UNIVERSAL CHRISTIAN CHURCH

A distinction between the Lord's Universal Christian Church and a local Christian church is seen in their memberships. The Universal Church consists only of saved people, who are involuntarily joined to Jesus at salvation by the Holy Spirit, while a local church is a voluntary society of professing gospel believers, including those who may never have been born again (cp. Rev. 2:14–15).

A DEFINITION OF THE UNIVERSAL CHRISTIAN CHURCH

The true Universal Christian Church consists of all who have been saved during the present Church Age and who have been joined by the Holy Spirit's baptism to the Lord Jesus and to one another in Him to form a mystical body, of which He is the Head and the Life, and to be His espoused bride.

THE ORIGIN OF THE UNIVERSAL CHRISTIAN CHURCH

Its Announcement

The Lord's Universal Church was not a subject of Old Testament prophecy (cp. Eph. 3:1–6).[1] This truth was kept secret until the Lord Jesus openly declared His purpose to build His Church (Matt. 16:18; cp. John 10:16; Eph. 3:3–6). His use of the future tense ("I will build") indicates that this construction had not yet begun. He declared that He Himself would be the Church's builder and foundation (cp. 1 Peter 2:3–6; 1 Cor. 3:11). Referring to the Church as His possession, He asserted that the gates of hades would not prevail against it.[2] Still, He did not say what the Church would be or when its construction would begin. This was left to later divine revelation (Acts 1:5; Eph. 3:6; cp. 1 Cor. 12:13, 27; Eph. 1:22–23). Veiled references to the Church's construction were made by John the Baptizer, when He spoke of Jesus' baptizing with the Holy Spirit (Matt. 3:11), and by Jesus, when He spoke about uniting two folds of sheep to form one fold (John 10:16). These folds are those Jews and Gentiles who are saved during the Church Age (1 Cor. 12:13; Eph. 3:6).

Its Fulfillment

Since the Lord's announcement pointed to the future, the construction of the Universal Church began at a point between His prediction of His disciples' being baptized with the Holy Spirit (Acts 1:5), an action essential to the Church's construction (1 Cor. 12:13, 27), and the first occurrence of the word "church" in Acts (2:47, KJV). It appears that this construction began on the Day of Pentecost, ten days after our Lord's ascension into heaven. This view is supported by three lines of evidence.

1. *The empirical evidence*

This evidence for the Holy Spirit's starting this special work of building the Church was the Pentecostal phenomena (Acts 2:1–4), which consisted of wind, fire, and speaking in tongues.[3] These phenomena, which could be detected by the senses, bore witness to the nonsensuous reality of the Holy Spirit's activity in the Church's construction (cp. Deut. 19:15). Incidentally, we do not need this kind of evidence today for the Holy Spirit's activity, for we have the teachings of the New Testament, which are more certain than empirical evidence (2 Peter 1:16–19).

2. *The testimony of the apostle Peter*

The apostle Peter referred to the events of Pentecost as "the beginning" (Acts 11:15–16) and spoke of the occasion of the predicted baptism with the Holy Spirit, which is essential to the Church's construction, as being on that day (1:5; 11:16; cp. 1 Cor. 12:13, 27).

3. *The inherent nature of the Church's construction*

Since its construction is by the baptizing work of the Holy Spirit (1 Cor. 12:13, 27; Eph. 1:22–23), the Church could not have existed before the Lord Jesus' exaltation and the subsequent coming of the Holy Spirit for this work (John 14:20; 16:7; Acts 1:5). There is no indication that the Holy Spirit baptized anyone during the OT period. His baptizing work must not be equated with His anointing people (cp. 1 Sam. 16:13; see "The Holy Spirit's Ministry to Saved People: At the Time of Salvation" under Pneumatology).

THE FORMATION OF THE UNIVERSAL CHRISTIAN CHURCH

The Lord's building His Church is a part of His messianic human work during the present age. This means that as man He is carrying out this aspect of the Father's will from heaven in the power of the Holy Spirit.

The Manner of the Church's Construction

The Lord is building His Church quantitatively through evangelism by saving sinners and qualitatively by ministering to saved people (cp. Acts 16:5).

1. *The Lord is building the Church quantitatively (Acts 16:5b).*

This means that He is doing this work by saving all who exercise salvational faith in

Him and His atoning work and by bringing them into union with Himself and with all others in Him to form the Church (cp. Acts 2:47).

2. *The Lord is building the Church qualitatively (Acts 16:5a).*

This refers to His developing the spiritual lives of His people who belong to His Church (Acts 9:31; 15:41; 20:32; 1 Cor. 14:26; 2 Cor. 12:19; Eph. 4:11–15; see "The Growth of the Christian Life" under Zoeology).

The Means of the Church's Construction

Since He is doing this work as a man, seated at the right hand of the Father in heaven, the Lord Jesus is using several means to save those who are guilty of and ruined by sin and to cultivate the spiritual growth of His people.

1. *Jesus is using the Scriptures to build His Church.*

He is especially using the NT Scriptures, since they contain His dispensation, or will, for His people today as well as the gospel, which they are to give to the world.

a. *In saving gospel believers (2 Tim. 3:15; 1 Peter 1:23)*

b. *In maturing the spiritual lives of saved people (2 Tim. 3:16–17; 1 Peter 2:1–2)*

It is important that we use God's Word when ministering to the spiritual needs of others (2 Tim. 4:2; Acts 8:4; 11:1; 16:32).

2. *Jesus is using the Holy Spirit to build His Church.*

a. *In saving gospel believers*

The Holy Spirit regenerates gospel believers (Titus 3:5; John 3:3–6), baptizes them into the "body," or the Church (1 Cor. 12:13, 27; Eph. 1:22–23; Col. 1:18, 24), and unites them with one another in Jesus (1 Cor. 10:17; cp. 12:12–27). This mystical "body" (the Church) must be distinguished from Jesus' physical body, which He has as man in heaven.

b. *In maturing the spiritual lives of saved people (2 Cor. 3:18)*

The Holy Spirit sanctifies the Lord's people by making them increasingly more like Jesus in character. He conveys to them Jesus' spiritual life and power and produces in them His character as they live under His influence and do God's will (Rom. 8:2, 4; Gal. 5:22–23; Eph. 5:17–18).

3. *Jesus is using His people who are on earth to build His Church.*

Because we who are saved are spiritually united to Jesus (John 14:20) by the Holy Spirit's baptism and indwelling presence, our bodies serve as the Lord's members through which He works on earth, individually (1 Cor. 6:15) and collectively (12:27).[4] This work is greater in nature than that which He did when He presented His messianic claims to Israel by physical miracles (John 14:12; cp. Matt. 4:23; John 10:24–25; Acts 2:22).

a. *In saving gospel believers*

He uses the biblical gospel ministry and witness of His people (Acts 1:8; Rom. 1:15).

b. *In maturing the spiritual lives of His people*

Among other things, He uses His people's prayers (2 Cor. 1:11), temporal gifts (Phil. 4:14–16), exercise of spiritual gifts and natural abilities (1 Cor. 14:26; 1 Peter 4:10), urgings (Gal. 6:1; Heb. 10:24), reproof (2 Tim. 4:2), example (1 Tim. 4:12), and expressions of Christian love (John 13:34; 1 Cor. 13:4–7).

Christian service is our cooperating with the Lord in such a way that, by doing His will in His strength or in the Holy Spirit's power, we allow Him to work through us in building the Church quantitatively and qualitatively (John 15:1, 4–5; 1 Cor. 15:10). This requires our abiding in Him by our submission, obedience, reliance, and communication (John 15:1–5; cp. Phil. 4:13; see "The Fruitfulness of the Christian Life" under Zoeology). Observe that

Christian service is not our doing something for Jesus but His doing something with us in His great work of building His Church (Acts 14:27; 15:4).

The Ministries of the Church's Construction

A duty of pastors and teachers is to equip the Lord's people for the ministry of building the Church (Eph. 4:11–12). The Lord is building His Church quantitatively and qualitatively through His people by two kinds of ministries. These are general and special ministries.

1. The Lord is using a general ministry to build His Church.

This is a ministry that belongs to all saved people alike. This general ministry includes praying (1 Thess. 5:25), giving (Gal. 6:6), Christian living (Eph. 4:1; 5:1–2), and sharing the gospel with others (Acts 1:8; 11:19–21). These activities are effective as we are submissive to the Holy Spirit, rely on Him to help us, and do His will. Anyone who is saved can learn how to do these things in a way that is suitable to his or her age and spiritual development and can serve the Lord. The biblical commands to do these things is His calling us to this general ministry.

2. The Lord is using a special ministry to build His Church.

This is a ministry that differs among saved people and that is carried out by their exercising their spiritual gifts and natural abilities in building the Church (Rom. 12:3–8). It is very important that we who are saved learn what our special ministry is, based on our spiritual gifts, and do it by the direction and power of the Holy Spirit.[5] The call to special ministry comes with the recognition of our spiritual gifts and of the people who have need for our particular ministry.

The Divine Provisions for the Church's Construction

The Lord has provided those of us who are saved with sufficient resources for our part in this work (2 Peter 1:3). These include God's Word (2 Tim. 3:15–17), the Holy Spirit (John 14:15–17), faith (2 Peter 1:1; Gal. 2:20), prayer (John 14:13), grace (1 Cor. 15:10; 2 Cor. 1:12; 12:8–10), the means of divine forgiveness and cleansing from sin (2 Cor. 7:1; Rev. 2:5; 1 John 1:9; 2 Tim. 2:21), and the ministry, love, and support of other gospel believers (John 13:34–35; 2 Cor. 1:11; Phil. 4:10–20; Heb. 10:24–25).[6] However, to receive benefit from these resources, we must give ourselves to them and use them. Our reliance solely upon ourselves and our human resources results in our sinning and failure (John 15:5; Rom. 14:23; Phil. 4:13).

The Extent of the Church's Construction

From the nature of salvation and the renewal that it brings (Eph. 2:8–10; 2 Cor. 5:17), it appears that all saved people are baptized with the Holy Spirit into Christ so as to participate in His character and works and to form the new humanity, of which He is the Head (Gal. 3:27–28; 1 Cor. 1:30; 15:22; see Appendix D: "The Ones Who Are in Christ"). Thus, the dead precross saved people were brought into Jesus upon the completion of His atoning work and resurrection (cp. Heb. 9:14–15).[7] Gospel believers of the present Church Age as well as those of the coming Tribulation Age and Kingdom Age experience this union with Jesus at their salvation. The Scriptures teach that the salvational blessings—personal relationship with God and the divine forgiveness of sins—are the same for all gospel believers of all ages, according to the promises of the new covenant (Heb. 8:6–13).

Although all the saved of all ages will be in Christ, I believe that only the gospel believers of the present Church Age are baptized into His mystical body by the Holy Spirit to form the Universal Church (1 Cor. 12:13, 27). The peculiar feature of Christ's Church is

416

not its union with Him, but the union of its members to form His mystical body, which the apostle Paul described the Church to be (Rom. 12:4–5; 1 Cor. 10:16–17; Eph. 1:22–23; Col. 1:18, 24). While union with Jesus is essential for one's justification and sanctification (1 Cor. 1:30), union with one another in Jesus to form the Church is not essential to one's salvation.

According to this view, I understand the Universal Church to be that company of saved people who by the baptism of the Holy Spirit are joined together with Jesus and with one another in Him to form His mystical body, of which He is the Head and Life.[8] The Church's formation continues from the Day of Pentecost, ten days after Jesus' ascension into heaven, until its rapture at the Lord's return for His people (1 Thess. 4:13–17). The Church consists only of those who are saved during this time, together with those gospel believers who were alive on earth at the Church's commencement.

THE FUNCTIONS OF THE UNIVERSAL CHRISTIAN CHURCH

Whereas all the redeemed of humanity have common salvational blessings, promised by the new covenant (Heb. 8:6–13), and positional blessings in Christ (Eph. 1:3; 1 Cor. 1:30), not all have the same functional blessings, as determined by their place in God's program. For example, in the past the nation of Israel bore witness to the unity of God and gave birth to the Messiah-Savior. In the coming millennial kingdom, Israel, as the foremost nation on earth, will be the wife of Yahweh (Hos. 2:16–23; Mal. 3:12; Zech. 8:23). But the Church has other functions that make her distinctive.[9]

The Church's Function as Jesus' Mystical Body

The Church serves as Jesus' mystical body on earth (1 Cor. 12:13, 27; Eph. 1:22–23; Col. 1:18, 24). Although as man He is seated at the Father's right hand in heaven, the Lord is using His people on earth to build His Church. The bodies of gospel believers are individually the Lord's members (1 Cor. 6:15); collectively, they are His Universal Church (12:27). As our bodies are the means by which we express ourselves, so the Church on earth is the means by which the Lord Jesus ministers in this present world (Gal. 2:20; Rom. 12:3–8; Acts 14:27; 15:4; 1 Cor. 15:10; Phil. 4:13). Daily we should give ourselves to Him so that He might use us in this work of building His Church (Rom. 12:1–2). It is important to learn what our gift or gifts are and what our place is in this work (see "The Work of the Holy Spirit: His Relation to Spiritual Gifts" under Pneumatology).

The Church's Function as Jesus' Bride

The Church is also Jesus' espoused bride (2 Cor. 11:2; Eph. 5:22–33), who will live with Him forever as His wife (Rev. 19:7–9; 1 Thess. 4:17). This means that all who comprise His Church will have a special spiritual relationship with Him that is analogous to that between a husband and his wife.

1. *The stages of this nuptial relationship*
   These are portrayed by those of who married in biblical times.
   a. *The betrothal*
      This was the act of the father or guardian in giving the maiden, with her consent (Gen. 24:58), to her future husband. Being done before witnesses, this was legally binding (cp. Deut. 20:7). It could not be broken except by divorce (Matt. 1:18–19). The betrothal was usually accompanied by a payment to the bride's father (Gen. 34:12).

The Church is the Father's gift to His Son (John 17:24). This also involved the cost of our Lord's giving His life as a ransom (Matt. 20:28; Eph. 5:25). The contract was sealed in our life experience when we gave our consent by trusting in Jesus as our Savior (2 Cor. 11:2).

417

b. The preparation

This was a period during which the bride and groom prepared themselves for the wedding (Rev. 19:7; Heb. 10:12–13). The groom set the date and sent his bride gifts to remind her of his love.

We should be expressing our love for Jesus and preparing for His return by Bible study, obedience to His will, and the maintenance of our moral purity (2 Cor. 6:14–7:1; 11:2–3; James 4:4; 1 John 2:15; Rom. 6:11–13). During our Christian lifetime, He has given us such loving gifts as His Word (Col. 3:16), the Holy Spirit (John 14:16–17), grace (2 Cor. 12:8–10), and the expectation of His return (Titus 2:13).

c. The wedding

When the time of marriage arrived, the bridegroom escorted his bride from her home, where her parents had pronounced a blessing, to his own residence (Gen. 24:60; Matt. 25:6, 10). There was no formal ceremony as there is today.

The Lord Jesus Himself will escort the Church to heaven (1 Thess. 4:16–17). After His appraising the lives of His people (2 Cor. 5:10), He will receive the Church as His wife before He returns to earth to establish His kingdom (Rev. 19:7).

d. The marriage feast

Continuing a week or more, the marriage festivities included feasting and competitive games (Gen. 29:22; John 2:2). The guests were seated at the table according to rank (Luke 14:8–9) and wore suitable clothing (Matt. 22:11).

Our Lord's wedding feast will take place on earth after His return with His bride and the establishment of His authority over the earth (Rev. 19:9, 11–16). At that time, all the saved dead of other ages will be resurrected and will join earth dwellers in the wedding festivities (cp. John 3:29; Rev. 20:4; Matt. 8:11; Dan. 12:2–3).

2. *The glories of this relationship*

Surpassing our comprehension, the Scriptures indicate what they are now and what they will be in heaven.

a. The Church is Jesus' fullness (Eph. 1:22–23).

As Eve completed Adam as his wife, by being his loving companion, helper, and friend (Gen. 2:18; 3:16; 1 Cor. 11:3, 7, 9) so the Church completes the Lord Jesus, the glorified Last Adam (1 Cor. 15:45), in these ways.

1) The Church's present relationship with Jesus

Although we are not with Jesus to see Him, we can have a relationship with Him as His companions, helpers, and friends, for we have His spiritual life. As His *companions,* we can communicate with Him by Bible reading and prayer (Col. 3:16; 1 Thess. 5:17); as His *helpers,* we can work with Him in building His Church (Rom. 12:1–8; 1 Cor. 3:9); and as His *friends,* we can express our love for Him by our obedience to Him (John 14:15, 21, 23; 15:14) and by our abiding in Him (15:1–5).

2) The Church's future relationship with Jesus

In her glorified state in heaven, the Church will complete His joy (Jude 24) and will satisfy His love (Eph. 5:25–27). We can imagine the eagerness with which the Lord Jesus looks forward to receiving the Church to Himself as His bride. Read again the Song of Solomon, which symbolically portrays this loving relationship between the Lord and His people through that between Solomon and his wife, the Shulammite (1:9–2:17; 4:1–5:1, 9–16; 7:6–8:4).[10]

b. The Church is blessed beyond measure (Eph. 1:3).

Already blessed with every spiritual blessing in Christ Jesus, the Church has more blessings awaiting her in her glorified state.

One: She will partake of the Lord's fabulous inheritance (Rom. 8:17). Being joint-heirs with Him, we shall share in all that was given Him by the Father (Heb. 1:2;1 Cor. 3:21–23).

Two: The Church will also share the glory of His exalted humanity (John 17:22, 24). This glory consists of His changed body (cp. 1 Cor. 15:49; Phil. 3:20–21), His holiness (Eph. 5:27), and His exalted position at the Father's right hand, far above all created persons and things (Eph. 1:20–22; 2:4–6).

Three: The Church will forever enjoy His love and fellowship (John 14:3; 17:24; 1 Thess. 4:18).

It is important that we who are saved remain faithful to the Lord during our pilgrimage in this world (James 4:4) and be occupied with His affairs (cp. Luke 19:13; Col. 3:1–4; Rom. 12:1–2). Our spiritual enemies would have us compromise our affection for Him (1 John 2:15) and be busy with that which is not His will for us (Matt. 6:24; Eph. 5:17). Being members of His espoused (engaged) bride, we must daily give ourselves to Him (Rom. 13:14), keep ourselves pure for Him by living holy lives, (2 Cor. 11:2–3; 1 Peter 1:13–16), express our love for Him by obeying Him (John 14:15), give attention to His Word and His affairs (Ps. 1:1–3; Col. 3:1–17), walk in His fellowship (1 Cor. 1:9; Gal. 2:20), abide in Him (John 15:4–5), and serve with Him in building the Church (1 Cor. 3:9; John 15:4–5). What kind of a relationship are you having with the Lord Jesus?

THE DISTINCTIVENESS OF THE UNIVERSAL CHRISTIAN CHURCH

Since the Church is a particular group of redeemed people who serve as Jesus' mystical body and espoused bride, I believe that we should distinguish her from other groups of redeemed peoples, living outside the Church Age. This distinction does not lie in the salvational and positional blessings that all the redeemed possess alike, such as redemption, justification, and regeneration. Rather, as we have seen, it is manifested in the distinctive function that each group has in God's program and in the particular blessings that attend this function.

The Church Is Distinct from Israel

Some hold that Israel and the Church are the same people of God, with Israel's being the church of the old covenant period and the Church's being the Israel of the new covenant era.[11] Some also hold that there is no prophetic future for the nation of Israel because of their rejection of Jesus; therefore, all that was prophesied about the future of this nation is now being fulfilled in the Church.[12] I prefer the view that sees true Israel and the Church as separate entities, being two groups of redeemed people who have their own special function and place in God's program. This view is supported by the following considerations:

1. Regarding the past

The Universal Church could not have existed during OT times for the following reasons:

One: The Church did not exist until after Jesus' declaration of His intention to build her (Matt. 18:18).

Two: The Church's construction is a messianic work that began after Jesus' return to heaven (1 Cor. 12:13, 27; Eph. 1:22–23).

Three: The Church is being built upon the teachings of the Lord's apostles and NT prophets, with Jesus Himself being the Chief Cornerstone (Eph. 2:20).

Four: The Church is related to Jesus as man, not as God (John 17:22, 24; 14:20; Rev. 19:7).

Five: There is no biblical evidence for the primary feature of the Church's construction, the baptism by the Holy Spirit (1 Cor. 12:13, 27), as having occurred in human history before the Day of Pentecost, ten days after Jesus' return to heaven (Luke 3:15–16; Acts 1:5).

Saved Jews During Church Age Not Part of Universal Church?

2. Regarding the present

While saved Jews and saved Gentiles during the present age belong to the Church (Eph. 3:6) and are one in Christ (Gal. 3:28), the Church has not replaced the Jews or Israel.

One: The apostle Paul distinguished between the Church and the Jews (1 Cor. 10:32).

Two: The apostle called gospel believers "the children of Abraham" and his "seed" (Gal. 3:6–7, 29), but this does not necessarily mean that we who are Gentiles are the patriarch's actual posterity. For someone to be the "child" or "son" of someone or something often meant that he possessed the characteristics of this person or thing (John 10:39, 44; Eph. 2:2–3). Whether Jews or Gentiles, saved people are characterized as being people of faith (cp. Acts 5:14; Eph. 1:1). Being an outstanding example of faith (Rom. 4:13–21), Abraham may be regarded as the head of a class of persons who are characterized by this kind of faith (Gal. 3:7, 9).

Three: When the apostle used the phrase, "Israel of God" (Gal. 6:16), he probably was referring to saved Jews, in contrast to the saved Gentiles to whom he was writing (cp. Gal. 3:14; Acts 13:46–48). Even his reference to his Gentile readers as "the circumcision" (Phil. 3:3) does not necessarily mean that God considers them to be Jews since elsewhere he uses circumcision as a symbol for the inner operation of the Holy Spirit upon the heart of the gospel believer at salvation (Rom. 2:28–29; Col. 2:11–13, Christ's "circumcision" was His putting off His body at death).

3. Regarding the future

One: Referring to himself as an example, the apostle Paul argues in Romans chapter 11 that God has not thrust away Israel but in the future will restore a remnant of the nation to Himself (vv. 1–6, 11–12, 25–27). This foresees the time when Jesus will return to earth, will gather Israel from among the nations, and will judge them, sifting out the apostates and saving those who trust in Him as Savior (Jer. 31:31–34; Deut. 30:3–8; Ezek. 11:17–21; 20:33–44; 36:24–30; 37:21–27). Although Israel is both the enemy and the beloved of God today (Rom. 11:28), they will not remain His enemy forever. As God is now showing mercy to Gentiles, so He will show mercy to the elect of Israel in the future by saving them from their sins (vv. 26–27, 30–31).

Two: When he quoted from the prophecy of Amos to relate God's intention of saving Gentiles (Acts 15:13–18; Amos 9:11–12), James seemed unwittingly to be used of the Holy Spirit to speak also of Jesus' future restoration of the house of David, of which Gentiles are not a part, when He establishes His earthly kingdom (cp. Ezek. 37:19–28).

Three: In contrast to the Church's future function as the wife of Jesus, saved Israel, as the wife of Yahweh, will be foremost among the nations on earth during the millennial kingdom (Hos. 2:7, 13–23; 3:1–5).[13] Furthermore, Israel's inheritance will be earthly, for they will possess the land that was promised them by the Abrahamic covenant (Gen. 15:18; Deut. 30:5; Jer. 16:14–15; 24:6–7). Like the Levites of old (Num. 18:20), the Church's inheritance is the Lord Jesus Himself and all that has been given Him (Eph. 1:11; Rom. 8:17; Heb. 1:2). Unlike Israel, the Church will not have a national entity or territorial possession on earth.

The Church Is Distinct from the Redeemed Gentiles of Other Ages

Nowhere do the Scriptures teach that the saved Gentiles of other ages are members of Christ's mystical body, the Church. While, in my opinion, the saved of all the ages will be brought into Christ (1 Cor. 15:22; Eph. 1:10; see Appendix D: "The Ones Who Are in Christ"), this is not the same as their being brought into His mystical body, which is essential to their membership in His Universal Church (1 Cor. 12:13, 27). While the Church will have a special relation to the Lord Jesus as His wife, the saved Gentiles who survive the Tribulation Age, for instance, will repopulate the earth and will comprise the nations that will exist on earth (together with Israel) during the millennial kingdom (Zech. 14:16; Matt. 25:31–34).

The Church Is Distinct from Christ's Kingdom

Gospel believers who belong to Christ's Universal Church are also a part of His kingdom (Col. 1:13; cp. John 3:3–7; Acts 20:25; 28:31), but the kingdom includes other saved people as well. Our Lord's earthly kingdom will embrace all redeemed humans, including the OT believers (Luke 13:28–29), the born again Tribulation Age martyrs (Rev. 20:4) and survivors (Matt. 25:31–46) as well as the elect remnant of Israel (Ezek. 36) and the Church Age gospel believers (1 Thess. 4:17). Presently, the Church is a part of Christ's kingdom, which now is invisible, nonpolitical, and nongeographical. In the future, she will be a part of His earthly kingdom, not in the sense that she will be a political entity like Israel or the Gentile nations, but in the sense that she will be Jesus' wife and subject to His authority.

It is, indeed, a privilege for those of us who are saved to be members of the Universal Church. Let us daily remember our present function as the Lord's earthly body and espoused, prospective bride. Let us give ourselves to Him daily for the ministry that He has for us as His coworkers. Also, let us keep ourselves pure of moral pollution, walk in His fellowship, abide in Him, express our love for Him by our obedience to His will, and look constantly for His return.

THE LOCAL CHRISTIAN CHURCH

With the beginning of the Lord's Universal Church on the Day of Pentecost, the Lord's disciples in Jerusalem (Acts 1:4, 14) became its first local manifestation in the form of a visible assembly of gospel believers (2:41–47). Supervised by the Lord's apostles, these gospel believers met regularly to hear their teachings, to fellowship with one another, to worship God, to participate in the Lord's Supper, and to pray. When the need arose, they adopted more organization (6:1–6). With the faithful gospel witness of their members, other assemblies were established (8:4, 40; 9:19). Pastors were appointed to supervise those that were beyond the reach of the apostles' personal ministry (20:17; Titus 1:5). Initiating a chain reaction that continues to the present, churches were planted in Palestine (Acts 9:31), Antioch, the capital of Syria (11:19–21), Rome (Rom. 16:5), and throughout the Roman Empire (Acts 15:41; 16:1–5, 12; 17:1; 18:1; 19:1; Rom. 15:19).

A DESCRIPTION OF A LOCAL CHRISTIAN CHURCH

From the New Testament we learn that a local Christian church is:

1. In content

A company of baptized gospel believers, belonging to a certain place, who profess faith in Jesus and His atoning work for their salvation from sin (Acts 2:41, 47; 11:20–26; 18:8–11);

2. In organization

Who are in agreement in doctrine, policy, and practice (Acts 2:46; Eph. 4:1–6) and who are organized with NT church officers—pastor(s) and deacons (Phil. 1:1);

3. In practice

Who, recognizing the Lord's presence (Matt. 18:20), assemble regularly to worship God (Acts 2:47; 13:2), participate in the Lord's Supper (2:42; 20:7; 1 Cor. 11:23–26), fellowship together in the study of God's Word and in prayer (Acts 2:42; 4:23–31), teach new converts (Matt. 28:20; Acts 16:5; 18:11), exercise their spiritual gifts for the edification of one another (Acts 9:31;13:1; 1 Cor. 12:1–31; 14:23–26), do good works (Acts 11:27–30; Gal. 6:10; Rev. 2:5), and exercise corrective discipline when this is needed (Matt. 18:15–20; 1 Cor. 5:4–5);

  4. *In mission*

  Who bear witness to the gospel at home (1 Thess. 1:8) and abroad (Acts 8:4; Phil. 4:10–18);

  5. *In expectation*

  And who are looking for the imminent return of Jesus (1 Thess. 1:10; Phil. 3:20; Titus 2:13; 1 Peter 1:3–4; 1 John 3:2–3) and their translation to heaven (1 Thess. 4:13–17).

THE MEMBERSHIP OF A LOCAL CHRISTIAN CHURCH

Of what people does a local Christian church consist and what are the advantages of local church membership?

The Constituency of a Local Christian Church

A local Christian church consists of people who profess salvational faith in Jesus and His atoning work, who are organized according to NT principles, and who are obedient to the Lord's ordinances (Eph. 1:1; 1 Cor. 6:11; Acts 2:41–42; 11:20–26; 18:8–11; Matt. 28:19–20). To my mind, parachurch organizations, like Christian schools, camps, study groups, and mission agencies, do not constitute local churches, for this is not the declared purpose for their existence and organization. Therefore, it would not be fitting, in my view, for the constituencies of these groups, like a home Bible-study gathering or a summer Bible camp, to observe the local church ordinances of baptism and the Lord's Supper apart from the supervision of a local church.

Without doubt, there are unsaved church members who have a defective salvational faith. But these are known to the Lord (Rev. 2:13–15), and He does not regard them to be His people (Matt. 7:21–23; cp. John 10:27). In these days of deepening religious confusion and apostasy, there are in Christendom many local churches that are not truly Christian, despite their name, for they do not have regenerated congregations, preach and teach God's Word, manifest the qualities of a biblical local church, and confess the Christian faith as this is given in the New Testament.

Did the early local churches have formal memberships? There is no NT record of gospel believers uniting with a local church. But there is evidence that they were formally a part of their churches, for they elected their own officers and delegates (Acts 6:3, 5; 11:29–30; 15:2–3, 22; 2 Cor. 8:19) and were subject to excommunication (1 Cor. 5:13).

The Advantages of Local Christian Church Membership

Except for unusual circumstances, people who profess to be saved should belong to a Bible believing and teaching local Christian church. Consider the following advantages:

One, their being a real part of the local church and, if it has congregational government, their participating in its direction. Membership allows one to speak and to vote on the policies and matters pertaining to the church.

Two, their having opportunity to exercise their spiritual gifts. Many churches do not allow people to teach or to hold key offices without their being members.

Three, their having accountability for their belief and conduct. All gospel believers need to be accountable to someone for these things.

Four, their sharing the support of the local church and its ministries. It is hardly equitable for people to benefit from the ministry of a local church for an extended time and not be involved fully in its support.

Five, their being identified to others regarding their doctrinal position and practice. By their membership outsiders know who these church members are religiously and what to expect of them.

Six, their receiving the loving care and support of fellow members. While we are to do good unto all people, we have a special duty to those with whom we are associated in the local church.

Seven, their meeting the requirement of many Christian organizations, with which they may seek association and opportunity for ministry.

Eight, their being members is expected by unsaved people. Lack of membership may be a hindrance to their gospel testimony.

A saved person in this hostile world without church membership is like a ship without a home port. He or she is, indeed, alone and vulnerable to the assaults of spiritual adversaries.

THE ADMINISTRATION OF A LOCAL CHRISTIAN CHURCH

The Lord Jesus is the supreme Head, or Leader, of both the Universal Church and the biblical local church (Eph. 4:15; 5:23; 1 Peter 5:4; cp. Rev. 2–3). Whenever His people gather in His name, the Lord is present (Matt. 18:20). The New Testament, given by the Lord Jesus, is the supreme authority of His people's faith and practice (28:20; John 16:12–15; Eph. 2:20;[14] 4:20–21; Col. 3:16; Rev. 1:1–2; 2:7). Let us look more closely at the officers and government (polity) of the local church.

Its Officers

At first the Lord supervised the local churches through His apostles and their representatives (Acts 6:1–6; 8:14; 15:36; 16:4; Gal. 2:7–10; 1 Tim. 1:3; Titus 1:5). This continued until the New Testament, which preserves His teachings and directives, was completed and distributed among the churches. Because of this, there was no need for apostolic succession; indeed, there is no biblical support for its existence today.

The New Testament describes two local church offices: the pastorate and the diaconate (Phil. 1:1). Our civil government also requires trustees for church corporations.

1. The pastorate

Under the Lord Jesus the general care and oversight of the local church belongs to spiritually gifted men who are divinely called to this office (Eph. 4:11; 2 Tim. 1:9, 11; Rom. 1:1; 1 Cor. 1:1) and who are spiritually qualified for their work (1 Tim. 3:1–7; Titus 1:6–9).[15] The men who are leaders of local churches are described in the New Testament by three titles: "elder," "bishop," and "pastor." That these titles refer to the same office is indicated by their being used interchangeably in Acts 20:17, 28; Titus 1:5, 7; and 1 Peter 5:1–2 (the KJV verb "feed" means to shepherd or tend). Let us consider the emphases that these titles bring to the pastorate, its duties, and its authority.

a. The pastor's titles

1) Elder (Acts 20:17; Gk. *presbuteros*)

Originally, this was one who was aged and, therefore, experienced. This title emphasizes the spiritual maturity and wisdom that a pastor should have for his pastoral work (cp. 1 Tim. 3:6; Titus 1:9). The word occurs in Acts 11:30; 14:23; 15:2, 4, 6, 22–23; 16:4; 21:17–18; 1 Timothy 5:17; Titus 1:5; James 5:14; and 1 Peter 5:1.

2) Bishop (Phil. 1:1; Gk. *episkopos*)

This is one who is an overseer, or superintendent. This title emphasizes the responsibility of presiding over the affairs of the church (Acts 20:28; 1 Tim. 3:2, cp. vv. 4–5; Titus 1:7; 1 Peter 2:25). The office (Gk. *episkope*) is mentioned in 1 Timothy 3:1. The verb form (Gk. *episkopeo*) occurs in 1 Peter 5:2.

3) Pastor, or shepherd (Eph. 4:11; Gk. *poimen*)

This is one who shepherds, or tends, the flock. This title emphasizes the duty of caring for the spiritual needs of the Lord's people as a shepherd cares for his sheep. See the verb form (Gk. *poimaino,* to tend) in John 21:16, "feed"; Acts 20:28, "feed"; 1 Peter 5:2, "feed"; Revelation 2:27, "rule"; 7:17, "feed"; 19:15, "rule." Also, see the verb to "rule" (Gk. *hegeomai,* to lead, go before) in Hebrews 13:7, 17, 24.

Likewise, the Lord Jesus is the Shepherd (John 10:11; Heb. 13:20; 1 Peter 2:25; 5:4) and Overseer (1 Peter 2:25) of His people.

It appears that the early churches often had more than one pastor (Acts 20:17; Phil. 1:1; cp. Titus 1:5). Perhaps this was due to the spiritual demands of their congregations and/or the pastors having to work for a living. Generally, the pastors of today's churches are fully financially supported. Larger churches have a number of pastors such as a pastor of youth, a pastor of visitation, and the like, who serve under the direction of the senior pastor. This is sometimes described as "plurality of elders." This is to be distinguished from "elder rule," which Presbyterian churches have, where the "ruling elders" (the Session) are given the responsibility of the total oversight and direction of the local church.

  b. *The pastor's duties*

In the pursuit of his ministerial responsibilities, the pastor has duties toward the saved and unsaved peoples of his congregation as well as to himself.

  1) His duties to saved people

Based on the gift of pastoral care (Eph. 4:11), this part of pastoral work concerns the pastor's ministry to the saved people of his congregation. This work involves teaching them biblical truth about Christian life and ministry as well as the great doctrines of the Christian faith and applying this truth to the lives of his people (1 Tim. 4:11; 6:2; 2 Tim. 2:2, 24).

Using God's Word where it applies, the pastor's duties are leading the people (Heb. 13:7, 17, 24); warning the wayward; pointing out their sins; exhorting them to do what is right (2 Tim. 4:2); caring for his people's spiritual needs (Matt. 20:24–28; Acts 20:28); being an example to them (1 Peter 5:3; 1 Tim. 4:12); protecting them from false teachers without, and ambitious persons within, the church (Acts 20:28–30); equipping them for Christian ministry in their local church (Eph. 4:11–12); and praying for them (Acts 6:4).

  2) His duties to unsaved people

Although he may not have the gift of evangelism, a pastor still has the duty of presenting the gospel to the unsaved, both publicly and privately (2 Tim. 4:5; Matt. 28:19–20). He must also conduct himself in a manner that is above reproach before the people of his community (2 Cor. 6:3–4a).

  3) His duties to himself

The pastor cannot fulfill the duties of his office effectively without maintaining and cultivating his own spiritual life (1 Tim. 4:12–16; Eph. 6:10). His constantly giving to others requires his replenishing his own spiritual store and vitality (Ps. 1:1–3; Mark 3:14; 1 Tim. 4:16). Being a primary target of Satan, it is imperative that he constantly wear the armor of God (Eph. 6:13–18) by daily putting on Jesus (Rom. 13:14) and strengthening himself in the power of the Lord (Phil. 4:13; Eph. 5:18). Moreover, he has the duty of cultivating those personal qualities that are required for his ministry (1 Tim. 3:2–4; Titus 1:6–9; Gal. 5:22–23).

  c. *The pastor's authority*

This is granted him by the teachings of the New Testament (1 Tim. 5:17; Heb. 13:7, 17, 24) and the constitution of the local church. However, in using this authority, he must avoid exercising autocratic dominion over his people (1 Peter 5:3; cp. Matt. 20:25–28).

The pastor must use his authority only for the edification of the Lord's people, not for their destruction or for self-serving purposes (2 Cor. 1:23–24; 10:8; 12:19; 13:10).

2. *The diaconate*

This refers to the office of deacon. The word *deacon* (Gk. *diakonos*) means "servant," "attendant," or "minister." While the noun does not occur in Acts, the verb form occurs in the record of the formation of this office (Acts 6:1–6; "serve" in v. 2). The apostle Paul speaks of the spiritual gift of ministry (Rom. 12:7) and gives the qualifications for this office (1 Tim. 3:8–13).

Although many churches have deacons who assist pastors in their spiritual oversight of the church, to my mind it would be more accurate to call these deacons elders, or pastors. The need leading to the formation of the office (Acts 6:1–6) and the absence of the ability to teach in the requirements for deacons (1 Tim. 3:8–13, contra v. 2) indicate that the duties of deacons in the early church were more temporal. While pastors ministered to the spiritual needs of the local church, the deacons dealt with people's physical and material needs. This was especially important at a time when there were no secular welfare agencies to care for the poor and needy. Apparently, women also served in this office to minister to the needs of females in their local churches (Rom. 16:1–2).

3. *Trustees*

Today, in addition to pastors and deacons we have the office of trustees. This office is required by the state to represent the local church in legal and financial matters.

Its Government (Polity)

Although the early churches were under the supervision of the Lord's apostles and the leadership of pastors, or elders, there was considerable congregational democracy. This is seen in their election of officers and delegates (Acts 6:3, 5; 11:29–30; 15:2–3, 22; 2 Cor. 8:19) and their exercise of corrective discipline (Matt. 18.17; 1 Cor. 5:4–5, 7, 13).

Today, church government differs widely throughout Christendom. The basic forms and their examples are these:

1. *Congregational (Baptist)*

In congregational polity, officers are chosen by the church membership and act in their name, but the authority still remains with the people.

2. *Republican (Presbyterian)*

In republican polity, the church's authority is constitutionally delegated to its elected officials (the session), who function as a ruling committee.

3. *Episcopal (Methodist)*

In episcopal polity, the authority of the church resides in regional bishops.

4. *Oligarchic (Eastern Orthodox)*

In oligarchic polity, there is a federation of self-governing churches, each with its own patriarch, like those of Constantinople and Jerusalem.

5. *Monarchical (Roman Catholic)*

In monarchical polity, all authority resides in the pope at Rome, whom Roman Catholics believe is God's vice-regent.

THE ORDINANCES OF THE LOCAL CHRISTIAN CHURCH

While the Roman Catholic and Eastern Orthodox churches practice seven sacred rites, called "sacraments," the New Testament gives only two rites that gospel believers are commanded to observe.[16] These are water baptism and the Lord's Supper (Matt. 28:19–20; Luke 22:19–20; 1 Cor. 11:23–26). The "sacraments" are regarded by their observers to be visible signs of invisible divine grace and channels through which divine grace flows from the church to its constituents as salvation and blessing. Many Protestants prefer to call water baptism and the Lord's Supper "ordinances," for gospel believers are commanded by the Lord to observe these. They do not believe that these rites minister saving grace to their participants. These two rites, however, bear witness to God's grace as manifested in the Atonement and in the lives of those who receive the Savior. Let us consider these ordinances.

The Ordinance of Water Baptism

In Matthew 28:19–20 the Lord commissioned His people to do three things: to make disciples of all people through gospel presentation, to baptize gospel believers, and to teach them to observe the instructions that He gave His apostles, now preserved in the New Testament. This commission and the practice of the early churches (Acts 2:41; 8:38; 10:46–47; 18:8) show that water baptism is an ordinance that is binding on all gospel believers who are physically able to comply. It involves obedience to the Lord's command.

1. *The NT kinds of baptism*

Of the various baptisms that are mentioned in the New Testament, only the baptism with the Holy Spirit and water baptism should be of immediate concern to the Lord's people. The involuntary baptism with the Holy Spirit, which places the gospel believer into Christ and into His mystical body, the Church, occurs at salvation. Water baptism is to be voluntarily received after salvation as a witness to one's salvational faith in Christ and to one's spiritual union with Him. Other baptisms of which the New Testament speaks are these:

a. *The baptism unto Moses (1 Cor. 10:2)*

This refers to Israel's recognition of Moses' divine commission and to their submission to his leadership in bringing them out of Egypt (Exod. 14:21–22, 31).

b. *The baptism of Jesus (Matt. 3:13–17)*

This symbolic act represented His obediently giving Himself to the anointing of the Holy Spirit, whereby He received the Holy Spirit and all the gifts and powers that His messianic work required (Luke 3:22; John 1:32–33; 3:34; Acts 10:38; cp. Isa. 61:1; Luke 4:16–19).

c. *The baptism of the cross (Mark 10:32–39)*

This refers to the intense suffering that Jesus was to experience on the cross, when He would be made sin (2 Cor. 5:21), and His soul would be divinely offered for our sins (cp. Luke 12:50; Matt. 26:42; Isa. 53:10). In Mark 10:39, the Lord seems to be referring to His people's receiving the value of His atoning work through faith in His sacrifice (John 6:53) and of their participating with Him in His death and resurrection, which is the basis for their being dead to sin and alive unto God (cp. Rom. 6:1–11).

d. *The baptism of ceremonial washings (Heb. 6:2; 9:10)*

These were rites, required by the Mosaic Law, for external purification and sanctification (cp. Exod. 29:4; 30:19–21; 40:12; Lev. 14:8–9; 16:4, 24; 17:15–16; 22:6; Num. 19:7–21; Deut. 21:6; 23:11).

e. *The baptism of fire (Matt. 3:10–12)*

This seems to relate to Jesus' future messianic judgments upon His enemies, especially the apostates of Israel, when He sets up His millennial, earthly kingdom (Ezek. 20:33–38; Mal. 3:1–3; 4:1–3).

f. *The baptism because of repentance*

This was practiced by John the Baptizer (Matt. 3:1–2, 11) and by Jesus' disciples (Matt. 4:17; John 4:1–2).[17] Although similar in mode and purpose to that practiced by later Christians, this baptism had particular meaning for Israel. The immediate establishment of the messianic kingdom depended upon Israel's repentance and return to the Lord (Deut.

30:2–3; Hos. 5:10–6:3; 14:1–2). Both John and Jesus called Israel to repentance and faith in the Messiah and to their public confession of this response by water baptism (cp. Acts 19:4). This message anticipated the Messiah's imminent appearance and the work that He would do.

g. The baptism for the dead (1 Cor. 15:29)

This isolated instance has been subjected to many interpretations. Since "for" (Gk. *huper*) may also mean "account of" or "because of," this verse seems to refer to people who were saved and baptized because of the witness of gospel believers who by then were dead.

2. The candidates for water baptism

Contrary to the teachings of Roman Catholicism, Anglicanism, and Lutheranism, all of which advocate infant baptism, I believe that the only proper candidates for water baptism are people who have trusted in Jesus and His atoning work for salvation from sin and who, thereby, have been born again (Acts 2:38, 41; 18:8). The erroneous notion that water baptism effects or completes salvation does not agree with NT teaching. The blood of Jesus, representing His atoning sacrifice, cleanses us from all sins (1 John 1:7; Eph. 1:7; Heb. 9:14; Rev. 1:5). Baptism cannot do this.

Furthermore, there is no biblical evidence that water baptism replaced ritual circumcision as a sign of the covenant of grace, as reformed, covenantal theologians insist. They hold that infant baptism is equivalent to OT ritual circumcision and that it is the means by which an infant becomes a member of the covenantal community and a recipient of its blessings. Actually, the sign of the new covenant is the cup of the Lord's Supper (Luke 22:20; Heb. 13:20). People become members of the new covenant Christian community by trusting in Jesus' atoning sacrifice, by which He mediated the new covenant (Heb. 8:6; 12:24; 13:20–21). Baptism is necessary for obedience to God, one's public witness to salvational faith, and membership in a local church.

3. The meaning of water baptism

Contrary to the view of most of Christendom which believes that baptism washes away sins and works salvational grace in one's life, I believe that it only bears witness to certain spiritual realities that God has wrought in the gospel believer's life and to those to which he aspires. Baptism is "the answer of a good conscience toward God" (1 Peter 3:21). By his water baptism, the gospel believer bears witness to the following:

a. To his salvational faith in Christ (Acts 18:8).

Water baptism provides the opportunity for a saved person to confess formally and publicly his salvational faith in the Savior and His atoning work.

b. To his union with Christ (Rom. 6:1–4).

Water baptism is the outward, visible, symbolic portrayal of the results of his baptism with the Holy Spirit into Jesus (Gal. 3:27; Rom. 6:1–4; Col. 2:10–13, 20; 3:1). Because of his union with Christ and his position in Him, the gospel believer participates in the Lord's death, burial, and resurrection. By his immersion in baptismal water and his emersion from it, he demonstrates his spiritual union and participation with the Lord in these events. But his baptism does not bring about these events.

c. To his desire to obey Christ (Matt. 28:19–20).

The gospel believer's observance of the ordinance of water baptism expresses his obedience to and love for his new master, the Lord Jesus. To be aware of this ordinance and its duty and not to submit to it, except in case of physical disability or lack of opportunity, is to sin against the Lord. This refusal disqualifies a person from partaking of the Lord's Supper, and it incurs divine chastisement (1 Cor. 11:29–30). By his submission to baptism, the gospel believer expresses his desire to obey the Lord in everything.

d. To his intention to follow Christ (Rom. 6:4).

The believer's baptism should mark his final break with his old lifestyle and the start of his new lifestyle as Jesus' disciple. Although he will experience spiritual lapses from time to time, with his baptism he has started on the path of holiness. Incidentally, a person needs to be baptized only once after he has been saved, not every time he sins or wishes to make a new commitment to the Lord Jesus.

e. To his cleansing from sin (Acts 22:16).

While baptism does not wash away sin, it does portray the gospel believer's judicial cleansing from sin's defilement and guilt by the divine application of the value of Jesus' atoning work (Eph. 1:7). This judicial cleansing from sin at salvation is final, once-for-all and complete, never needing to be repeated (Col. 2:13; Heb. 9:14; 10:10, 12, Rom. 8:31–34).

If the gospel believer has this understanding of water baptism, he will have greater appreciation for this rite when he submits himself to it or when he recalls this experience.

4. The mode of water baptism

There are various opinions about how water baptism should be administered. The most common forms are *affusion,* or pouring water on the candidate's head;[18] *aspersion,* or sprinkling water on one's head or face;[19] and *immersion,* or dipping the candidate completely in water. The last form has been practiced since the birth of the Christian Church.

There are several reasons for my believing that immersion is the proper, biblical mode of baptism.

a. The meaning of the word baptize

Coming from the Greek word *baptizo,* it means to dip or immerse. In non-Christian literature the word was used for dipping, plunging, or sinking.[20]

A. T. Robertson wrote, "It may be remarked that no Baptist has written a lexicon of the Greek language, and yet the standard lexicons . . . uniformly give the meaning of *baptizo* as dip, immerse. They do not give pour or sprinkle. The presumption is therefore in favor of dip in the NT."[21] Johannes Warns adds, "The Greek language has distinct words for 'sprinkle' and 'immerse.'"[22] In English versions of the New Testament, the Greek *baptizo* is not translated but is transliterated. To have translated the world would have shown that the practices of pouring and sprinkling are neither apostolic nor biblical.

Immersion was the prevalent mode until the Council of Trent (1545), when the Roman Catholic Church abandoned the practice. The Reformer John Calvin wrote, "It is evident that the term 'baptize' means to immerse and that this was the form used by the primitive church."[23] Nevertheless, he believed that sprinkling was as effective as immersion.

b. The practice of the New Testament church

The only description of water baptism in Acts is Philip's baptizing the Ethiopian official (8:38–39). They both entered the water, where Philip baptized the Ethiopian, and they came up out of the water. Although predating the church, John the Baptizer also baptized by immersion (John 3:23; Mark 1:5–10).

c. The portrayal of the results of the Holy Spirit's baptism

Immersion is the symbolic enactment of the gospel believer's participation in Christ's death, burial, and resurrection, resulting from his union with Jesus by the baptism with the Holy Spirit (Gal. 3:27; Rom. 6:3–4). While cleansing from sin and the outpouring of the Holy Spirit, symbolically portrayed by aspersion and affusion, are important to the Christian life, these do not present the basis of every spiritual blessing that we have in Christ (Eph. 1:3). Immersion alone portrays our union with the Lord.

Incidentally, to be baptized "into Jesus Christ" (Rom. 6:3), "into Christ" (Gal. 3:27) or, "into one body" (1 Cor. 12:13) represents the baptism of the Holy Spirit. However, baptism "in the name of the Lord Jesus" (Acts 8:16; 19:5) or "in the name of the Lord" (10:48) represents water baptism. To be baptized in "Jesus' name" probably is a synecdoche (a part representing the whole) for the baptismal formula, "in the Name of the Father, and of the Son, and of the Holy Spirit" (Matt. 28:19). Keep in mind that the word *name* represents a person and his work.

The early church departed from the practice of immersion when the false teaching arose in the second century that alleged that baptism washes away sins. This error led to the false conclusion that all people, including infants, needed to be baptized if they were to be saved. Thus, modes other than immersion were used if the candidates were infants or infirm.

The Ordinance of the Lord's Supper

The Lord Jesus instituted this rite on the eve of His death when He ate the Passover meal (Seder) with His apostles (Matt. 26:26–29; Mark 14:22–25; Luke 22:14–20; 1 Cor. 11:23–25). That the Lord's people are to observe this rite today is indicated by the commands that the Lord gave regarding eating and drinking when He instituted this memorial.

1. *The symbolism of the Lord's Supper*

The Lord Jesus clearly stated that "the [unleavened] bread" was His body and "the cup" was the blood of the new covenant, which was shed for His people (Luke 22:19–20; cp. Heb. 9:12–15; 13:20).[24] However, there is no universal agreement about the relation of the bread and the cup to His body and blood.

According to the Roman Catholic view, the bread and cup are changed by priestly consecration into the very body and blood of Jesus. Also, this consecration is a new offering of Christ's sacrifice. This view is called "transubstantiation."

The Lutheran view holds that the bread and cup remain what they were, but the communicant consumes the actual body and blood of Christ "in, with, and under" these elements. This view is called "consubstantiation."

With other Christians, I prefer the view that the bread and cup are and remain symbols of the Lord's broken body and shed blood (1 Cor. 11:24–25). This view is supported by the fact that when He instituted this rite, the Lord was physically present with His apostles, and His blood had not yet been shed. Also, the linking verb "is" can be used with symbols as well as with actual things, as demonstrated by Galatians 4:22–26 and John 6:55. In fact, the Lord said that the cup was the new covenant in His blood (Luke 22:20). Representing the means by which the new covenant was mediated, or made effective, the cup was a symbol of our Lord's atoning work (John 10:18; Eph. 1:7; Rom. 5:8–9). The bread was a symbol of our Lord's body, or His incarnation, which made possible His dying for our sins (Heb. 2:14; 10:10). Thus the Lord's Supper, with its symbolism, is a witness to and a reminder of His incarnation and His atoning sacrifice, which are the basis of the gospel believer's relationship to God.

2. *The prerequisites for participating in the Lord's Supper*

Some churches practice "closed communion," in which only the members are allowed to participate. Those who practice "open communion" believe that the Lord's table is open to all of His people, even if they are not members of the church in which the rite is held. However, certain requirements must be fulfilled before one participates in the Lord's Supper.

a. *Salvation and baptism*

Since the Lord gave this ordinance to His people (Matt. 26:26), it is obvious that one must be saved and be baptized (unless this is prevented by disability or lack of opportunity) to qualify for participation in the Lord's Supper. Able, saved people who refuse water baptism are unqualified for the Lord's Supper by their disobedience.

b. Heart preparation

A prerequisite that is often ignored is heart preparation. The apostle Paul rebuked the Corinthian believers for their observance of this rite in an unworthy manner (1 Cor. 11:22–34). Because of unrepented selfish actions that they had committed during a common meal before the Lord's Supper, these people were guilty of insulting the Lord (vv. 20–22, 27). They were partaking of the elements of the rite without considering their meaning and value. This brought upon them the Lord's punitive chastisement of weakness, sickness, and, in some cases, death (vv. 28–32). With this in view, heart preparation requires our self-examination and adjustment and our having the attitudes of commitment and expectation.

1) Self-examination and adjustment (1 Cor. 11:28)

This refers to our assessing our spiritual state by asking ourselves questions like these: Am I saved? Is there any known sin in my life that I have not dealt with? What should I be doing that I am neglecting? What place does God and His will have in my life? Have I wronged others or do I hold ill-feelings toward anyone? Upon completing this assessment, we must make whatever correction is necessary, like repenting and confessing any sins that are known to us (Rev. 2:5; 1 John 1:9) as well as righting any wrongs that we have done to others (Matt. 5:23–24).

2) Committal and expectation (Matt. 11:28–30)

Since the Lord purchased us by His redeeming sacrifice, it is fitting that at this time we submit ourselves anew to the Lord's authority (2 Cor. 5:14–15) and look to Him to impress upon us the truths that are suitable for the occasion and to bless us.

3. *The worthy observance of the Lord's Supper*

This requires our blessed meditation and joyful worship.

a. Blessed meditation (1 Cor. 11:24–25)

As we participate in the Lord's Supper, we should think about the meaning of its symbolism as a memorial, a proclamation, and a fellowship.

1) As a memorial (1 Cor. 11:24–25, "in remembrance of Me")

The bread and cup remind us of the Lord's coming into the world and His atoning work, upon which our salvation and our relationship to God rests (Rom. 5:9; Eph. 1:7; John 6:53).

2) As a proclamation (1 Cor. 11:26)

This rite declares the central truth of our faith. By this, we say that we have received the Savior and have found Him to be the true Redeemer and Lord. Having experienced its salvational benefits, we assert by this rite that our Lord's sacrifice is effective.

3) As a fellowship (1 Cor. 10:16–17)

This rite provides the Lord's people with the opportunity to fellowship with Him and with one another. As the "one loaf," He is the spiritual life and nourishment of His people (John 6:35, 55–57, 63); and as the "one body," we who are saved bear witness to our having partaken of Him and to our being one together in Him (1 Cor. 12:13).

b. Joyful worship (Acts 2:46–47)

We cannot approach the Lord's table and reflect upon its meaning without gratitude and joy. Here we are brought face to face with the God of grace and with the highest expression of His love, manifested in our Lord's atoning work (2 Cor. 8:9). When we consider what He has done for us, we are motivated to renew our commitment of self and of loving obedience to Him and to praise and thank Him for all that He is, has done, and does (2 Cor. 5:14–15).

We thank God for this reminder of our Lord's sacrifice and for the periodic opportunity to celebrate all that this rite represents. May it always be a blessed time.

THE DISCIPLINE OF THE LOCAL CHRISTIAN CHURCH

Although corrective church discipline of sinning members is always difficult, failure to administer it never resolves its need. Those churches that neglect this will become carnal, powerless, and short on God's blessing.

Its Value

Corrective discipline, administered with proper spirit and purpose, is good for those who commit offenses (Gal. 6:1). Hopefully, it will lead to shame, repentance, and restoration (2 Thess. 3:14; Gal. 6:1). To ignore someone's sin is to confirm that person in it.

Corrective discipline is also good for the church. Disciplinary action, taken toward sinning members, will deter the corrupting influence of sin in the church (1 Cor. 5:6–7). A holy church is powerful (Acts 5:1–16); a corrupt one is paralyzed (1 Cor. 3:1–4; 15:34). Prompt corrective action is also a warning to potential offenders (1 Tim. 5:20; Eccl. 8:11).

Its Duty

The church is obligated to discipline its wayward members, for this is commanded by the Lord (Matt. 18:15–22) and the apostle Paul (1 Cor. 5:1–13; 2 Thess. 3:6, 14–15).

Its Procedure

Needless to say, it is important that it be fully established that a person has really sinned or has violated the church's covenant or the articles of faith and practice, to which he or she agreed when becoming a member. If he is guilty and remains unrepentant, then the Scriptures give the following directions for dealing with the matter:

1. *Prayer must be offered for the offender (1 John 5:16).*

Those who are aware of any problems should pray the offender will deal with his or her sins, gain victory over them, and make right any wrongdoings. Also, the church body should pray that the offender will respond favorably to counsel if this should be needed. If the church body discerns that the offender is committing sins that will irrevocably lead to the divine judgment of premature physical death, then prayers should not be said, for this will not help the offender (1 John 5:16b; cp. Prov. 15:10; Heb. 12:9).

2. *One must meet with the offender alone (Matt. 18:15).*

One should meet with the offender alone. One should confront the offender with his or her sin for the purpose of restoration. Notice the spiritual qualifications for this ministry: spirituality (our being filled with the Holy Spirit), meekness (our human spirit being softened with love and clothed with humility), alertness (our watching lest we fall into temptation), and a knowledge of the Word (Gal. 6:1; 2 Tim. 4:2). If the offender responds favorably and makes right the wrongdoing, then the matter is settled. If the offender should reject this counsel, then one or two must go again (Matt. 18:18) and repeat the effort to restore him or her. If this fails, then the offender's rebellious attitude will be attested by those who visited him or her.

3. *If the offender is unrepentant, then the matter must be reported to the church (Matt. 18:17).*

At this point the pastor should be informed of the situation so that he, with members of the official board, may speak to any sinning members in an effort to restore them. If this fails, then the matter must be presented to the membership or its official representatives, and the following steps should be taken:

a. *Remove the offender's name from the church's membership (1 Cor. 5:13).*
He or she is no longer qualified for this association.

431

  b. *Have no more fellowship with the offender (2 Thess. 3:6, 14; 1 Cor. 5:2, 7, 9–12, 13b).*

Still, church members must continue to have contact with the offender so he or she can be ministered to and restored (see endnote 17 under Zoeology).

  c. *Do not count an offender as an enemy (2 Thess. 3:15).*

The church must continue to seek his or her restoration by admonition and prayer.

  d. *Forgive and reinstate the offender to membership upon his or her repentance (2 Cor. 2:7–11).*

Needless to say, it is very important that the church not hold against offenders wrongdoings that they have dealt with. Like our Lord, we are to be forgiving when they repent (Eph. 4:32; Luke 17:3). The blood of Jesus, representing His atoning sacrifice, does cleanse His people from all sins when they deal with these by repentance and confession (Rev. 2:6; 1 John 1:9). To their shame, churches too often either ignore their fallen members or refuse to forgive, reinstate, and love them when they repent (see Appendix W: "The Saved Person's Forgiveness of Others").

As you review your church membership, is there anyone who has need of your restorative ministry? Reflect on Galatians 6:1 and 1 Corinthians 13:4–7 before you approach this person.

THE ECUMENICAL MOVEMENT AND LIBERALISM

The word "ecumenical" (from Gk. *oikoumene,* meaning "inhabited earth") means "worldwide." This movement has striven to reverse the fragmentation of Christendom that came about with the Protestant Reformation. It has sought a visible, organizational unity of all of Christendom under one head for the fulfillment of Jesus' prayer, "that they all may be one" (John 17:21) and for the legislation of righteousness throughout the earth.

The movement began in England with the formation of the Evangelical Alliance (1846) for the purpose of promoting Christian union and religious liberty. This was followed by The World Student Christian Federation (1895) and the First International Missionary Conference (Edinburgh, 1910). Theological differences soon divided the spirit of these international conferences. Religious liberalism made inroads; Quakers, Unitarians, and mainstream Protestants met to consider economic, social, and industrial problems as well as spiritual matters. These earlier conferences consisted of prominent church leaders and theologians.

In 1948, a merger of the World Conference on Faith and Order (1927, 1937) and the Universal Christian Council for Life and Work (1925, 1937) resulted in the formation of the World Council of Churches, the first international council of Christian churches. Meeting in Amsterdam, this council consisted of 351 delegates representing 147 denominations of Protestant, Anglican, Eastern Orthodox, and Old Catholic confessions from forty-four countries and represented about 150 million professed Christians. This council has characterized the ecumenical movement as one that is willing to sacrifice doctrine and conviction for the sake of unity.

Originally, the leadership of the World Council of Churches was dominated by Protestant liberalism. But since 1961, with the admission of the Russian Orthodox church and its satellite churches, it has broken away from its Protestant mooring and its western heritage and is swinging toward the Catholic orbit. A keen observer reported that in policy and practice the WCC has (1) disowned an authoritative Bible, (2) rejected the idea that man is lost in sin and can only be saved by accepting and obeying the Christian gospel, (3) repudiated the fundamentals of the Christian faith in favor of an inalienable religious intuition comparable to that faith, and (4) accepted the establishment of God's kingdom (a redeemed society) as the mission of the church. It proposes that the church should be freed from the obligation of preaching a distinctive gospel for the conversion of individual souls so that it can cooperate with all agencies, both sacred and secular, for social improvement and the building of a better world.[25] It should also be pointed out that the Council has never recognized the threat of Marxist Communism to Christianity and has politically supported Third World leftist movements.

There is no indication in the Scriptures that this ecumenical movement is of the Lord. Jesus was not praying in John 17:11, 21, 23 for the organizational, ritualistic unity of His people, as ecumenism holds. He was praying for the inner, spiritual unity of His people, which transcends personal individuality and its expression in denominational distinctives and preferences. The unity for which Jesus prayed (v. 21) does not find its reality in any device of man but in God and in the union of His people with Himself (14:9–10, 20; 1 Cor. 10:17; 12:13, 27). This union is being effected by the baptism of the Holy Spirit (Gal. 3:27–28), which occurs at salvation. Its reality is expressed in the Universal Church, which the Lord is building during this age (Matt. 16:18). True gospel believers cannot have spiritual fellowship with religious apostates and teachers of error, who deny the divine authority of the Scriptures and who impose upon God's Word their humanistic philosophy (Rom. 16:17–18; Titus 3:9–11; 2 John 10–11).

During this century, three forms of liberal Protestant theology have collapsed: One, earlier modernism, with its pantheistic emphasis on God's immanence in the world and its denial of the supernatural and miraculous; two, neoorthodoxy, with its emphasis on God's transcendence and its view of divine revelation as being an unexplainable experience with God rather than written Scripture; and three, demythologizing theology, which saw the supernatural events of Scripture as being given in otherworldly language that needed to be existentially interpreted in terms of this world. Today, the trend of liberalism is toward a postmodernism that holds that determining objective truth is impossible and a religious pluralism that sees a common thread of divine authority in all religions.[26]

Among conservative Protestants, people are increasingly being attracted to the charismatic movement with its excesses; emphasis is being given to religious experience rather than biblical doctrine because of a lack of doctrinal teaching and biblical exposition; there is a growth of adherents to covenant theology, with the effort of some to Christianize world government and to establish the millennial kingdom; there is a decline of adherents to dispensationalism, with its doomsday (Tribulation Age) outlook; there is a greater effort in applying the gospel to social, economic, and political matters; there is an increasingly deficient evangelism that omits the preaching of the Cross, that is, the Lord's atoning work that dealt with humanity's sins; and there is excessive emphasis on God's love for sinners (His friendship love no less!).[27]

* * *

The Lord's Church, with its universal and local aspects, is indeed a unique institution. The Universal Church is a living organism, with the Lord Jesus as its Head and Life. The local Christian church is a regional organization, comprising professing gospel believers, who despite different personalities, origins, and vocations, agree in doctrine and purpose to worship and serve the true God and His Son, the Lord Jesus Christ. It is our duty as saved people to belong to, support, and be active in a local church, especially one that honors God's Word and the Lord's teachings and authority, that promotes His work in this world, and that provides the opportunity for exercising our spiritual gifts and the Christian fellowship that we need for our spiritual lives.

A Review of Ecclesiology *CALLED OUT*

1. What is the basic idea of the Greek word for "church"? *ASSEMBLy*
2. Define the Lord's Universal Christian Church *SAVED DURING PRESENT*
414 3. Where does the first direct reference to the Universal Church occur in the Scriptures?
'' 4. In His prediction about the Church (Matt. 16:18), what did Jesus say and what did He not say?
'' 5. At what time did the Universal Church begin?
'' 6. What three facts support this view?
414-5 7. In what two ways is the Lord constructing the Universal Church?
415 8. By what three means is the Lord constructing the Universal Church?
9. Why is He using these means?
415 10. In addition to regeneration, by what means is the Holy Spirit doing His part in this construction?
416 11. Of all the redeemed of the ages, what saved people belong to the Universal Church?
12. Describe the two aspects of the baptism of, or with, the Holy Spirit.
417 13. What are the functions of the Universal Church?
417-8 14. Give the time of the following events: the Universal Church's espousal (betrothal), preparation, marriage to Jesus, and wedding feast.
418 15. In what ways is the Universal Church the Lord's fullness?
418 16. In what ways is the Universal Church blessed beyond measure?
419 17. How is the Universal Church distinct from Israel?
421 18. How is the Universal Church distinct from Christ's kingdom?
19. When and where was the first local Christian church established?
20. Describe the local church in its content, organization, practice, mission, and hope.
21. What kind of people should make up the membership of a local church?
22. Give reasons for being a member of a local church.
23. Who is the supreme Head of a local church?
24. What NT offices should be found in a local church?
25. Describe the functions of these offices.
425 26. What church office is required by civil law today? Why? *TRUSTEES*
425 27. Describe the kinds of church government (polity) that exist today.
425 28. Give the two ordinances, or rites, that Jesus has given to the local church.
425-6 29. Why is it better to call these rites "ordinances" rather than "sacraments"?
426 30. To what spiritual truths do these ordinances bear witness?
426 31. Of the several kinds of baptism mentioned in the New Testament, which two directly relate to gospel believers today?
427 32. According to the New Testament, who are the proper candidates for water baptism?
427 33. What should water baptism signify to these people?
428 34. What three modes of water baptism are practiced today?
428 35. Which of these modes is the biblical mode?
36. For what reasons do some denominations baptize infants?
37. In the light of these practices, why should infants not be baptized?
38. What is the relation of water baptism to a person's salvation?
429 39. What is the symbolism of the Lord's Supper?
429 40. Give the three interpretations of the "bread" and "cup." Which one is the biblical interpretation?
429-30 41. Describe the two prerequisites for the observance of the Lord's Supper.
430 42. On what three meanings of its symbolism should we meditate during the Lord's Supper?

43. Why is the Lord displeased when we partake of His Supper with known sin in our lives? What should we do about this?
44. Describe the worthy observance of the Lord's Supper. *431*
45. What is the value of church discipline? *REDEEM MEMBER, KEEP CHURCH HOLY*
46. What procedure should be followed in administering this discipline?
47. What is the primary purpose of this procedure?
48. What is the ecumenical movement? What is its purpose? *432? REVERSE FRAGMENTATION*
49. What is the trend in religious liberalism today? *TRUTH NOT POSSIBLE, ALL*
50. What are the trends among conservative Protestants today? *433 RELIGIONS GOOD*
51. In what way is the Lord achieving the unity of His people today? *FRIENDSHIP LOVE vs.* *P433 EXPERIENCE COVENANT THEOLOGY EMPHASIZE GOD'S LOVE*

SACRIFICAL LOVE

Endnotes

1. The prophecy of Joel 2:28–32, cited by the apostle Peter (Acts 2:16–21), concerns the outpouring of the Holy Spirit, not the formation of the Church. The apostle Paul wrote of Gentiles and Jews, who are saved during this age, as having equal status and blessing in Christ (Gal. 3:28; Eph. 1:3) as well as their being members of the same body, His Church (Eph. 1:22–23). This truth was a mystery (Eph. 3:3–9), unknown during OT times (see Appendix O: "The Divine Mysteries of the New Testament").

2. While the phrase, "the gates of hades" (often interpreted "the forces of death") may imply that the Church would not be permanently bound by death (cp. 1 Cor. 15:20–23, 51–57), it seems better to interpret the words to mean that the members of the Lord's Church, upon dying, would not go to hades, as did all saved people before the Church Age. Later divine revelation shows that members of the Universal Church go immediately to be with Jesus in heaven (Phil. 1:21, 23; 2 Cor. 5:6, 8). Contrary to the experience of precross believers, the Church saints will never come under hades's authority, for they do not go there when they die (see Addendum: "Sheol, Hades").

3. See "His Relation to Spiritual Gifts: The gift of tongues" under Pneumatology and Appendix A: "The Nature of Speaking in Tongues."

4. See "The Ministries of the Christian Life: The Ministry of Working with God" under Zoeology.

5. See "The Work of the Holy Spirit: His Relation to Spiritual Gifts" under Pneumatology.

6. This is both practical faith and ministerial faith. See F. H. Barackman, "The Kinds of Biblical Faith," pt. 2 of *Where Is Your Faith?*

7. These are the saved people of human history who lived and died before Jesus died and rose again.

8. "Head" is a metaphor for the Lord's authority and supervision of His people; "life" refers to the Lord's human spiritual life ("eternal life") that His people receive with their regeneration at salvation.

9. Observe that despite the faults of Christendom—earthly Christianity in all it forms—the Universal Christian Church is the most powerful institution on earth. Protected by the Father's name (John 17:11) and energized by the Holy Spirit (14:16–17), the Church is God's shrine on earth (Eph. 2:19–22), the salt of the earth (Matt. 5:13), the light of the world (vv. 14–16), and God's ambassador to the world (2 Cor. 5:20), and will finally triumph over her enemies (Rom. 16:20). The Church's gospel message is the power of God unto salvation (Rom. 1:16). She is a united entity in Christ, despite her denominational differences (Gal. 3:28). In spite of the forces of evil arrayed against His people, the Lord's construction of His Church is on schedule and will be completed in His time without delay or derailment.

10. Observe that Solomon refers to his wife as "my love" and the Shulammite calls him "my beloved."

11. See Appendix Q: "A Contrast Between the Church and Israel."

12. See Albertus Pieters, *The Seed of Abraham* (Grand Rapids: Wm. B. Eerdmans Publishing Co., 1950), 121ff.

13. To be the wife of someone is to have an exclusive, intimate relationship with this person. As in OT times, Israel above all other nations will have a special relationship with God during the

millennial Kingdom Age (Exod. 19:5; Deut. 7:6; 14:2; Jer. 3:14; 31:22). Also, the Church above all other redeemed peoples will have a special relationship with Jesus (John 14:3; 1 Thess. 4:17).

14. These "prophets" were NT prophets, through whom divine revelation was given to local churches before the writing and distribution of the NT Scriptures (Acts 11:27; 13:1; 15:32; 1 Cor. 14:29). See "His Relation to Spiritual Gifts: The gift of prophecy" under Pneumatology.

15. That women are forbidden to be pastors of churches rests on their divinely assigned subordinate position as men's helpers (Gen. 1:26–28; 2:18; 3:16; 1 Cor. 11:9). This principle does not deny women a ministry in the church, like prayer and the exercise of their natural abilities and spiritual gifts (1 Cor. 11:5), especially to children and other women, but they are forbidden to exert the authority of a Bible instructor over men (1 Tim. 2:12).

16. These sacraments are baptism, the Lord's Supper, confirmation, penance, extreme unction, order, and matrimony,

17. "Unto" (Gk. *eis*) in Matthew 3:11 and "for" in Acts 2:38 should be translated "because of " or "at," as in Matthew 12:41, for one's repentance and reception of divine forgiveness are the basis of one's baptism, not its result. In keeping with Ephesians 2:8–9; Acts 16:31; John 1:12; 3:16; and 1 Corinthians 15:1–2, we should regard baptism as a witness to these spiritual realities rather than as the means of bringing them about.

18. Affusion was mentioned in *The Didache,* written about 150. "Baptism," in *Schaff-Herzog Encyclopaedia of Religious Knowledge* (New York: Funk and Wagnalls Company, 1891), 1:201.

19. Aspersion was reported in 251 but was not commonly practiced until the thirteenth century and, then, only in the West.

20. H. G. Liddell and R. Scott, *A Greek-English Lexicon* (London: Oxford University Press, 1940), 305.

21. "Baptism" in *The International Standard Bible Encyclopaedia* (1949), 386.

22. Johannes Warns, *Baptism* (London: The Paternoster Press, 1957), 52.

23. John Calvin, *Institutes of the Christian Religion* (Grand Rapids: Wm. B. Eerdmans Publishing Co., 1961), 2:524.

24. "Cup" is a metonymy for its content, which was "the fruit of the vine" (Matt. 26:29). See Appendix X: "Figures of Association: Synecdoche and Metonymy."

25. James DeForest Murch, "Where Is the Ecumenical Movement Headed?" *Moody Monthly*, November 1969, 26–29.

26. For the current picture of liberal Protestantism with its postmodernism and pluralism, see D. A. Carson, *The Gagging of God: Christianity Confronts Pluralism* (Grand Rapids: Zondervan Publishing House, 1996).

27. This emphasis on God's friendship love rather than His undeserved sacrificial love (John 3:16) conveys to sinners the false idea that God will ignore their sins and hostility against Him and will receive them in heaven as they are. This sentimentalism not only misrepresents God's love, expressed in His giving His Son, but also ignores His holy wrath against sinners for their sins, for which they need salvation. If sinners reject the Lord Jesus and His sacrifice, then there only remains for them God's everlasting hell (v. 36). In all gospel presentations, unsaved people must be warned of their destiny (Matt. 25:46; Acts 17:30–31).

Eschatology

13

ESCHATOLOGY
The Doctrine of Future Prophetic Events

In this section, we shall consider those events of God's program that are still in the future and that are the themes of unfulfilled biblical prophecy. The Bible is the only literature on earth that reveals with certainty the future of mankind (cp. Isa. 46:9–10). Hidden from the world's understanding (1 Cor. 2:6–8), this divine revelation is given to God's people for the purpose of motivating their obedience and stimulating their hope (Deut. 29:29; Rom. 15:4; 1 Peter 1:3; John 15:14–15). It may be helpful to refer to the chart, "The Prophetic Future," on page 552.

INTRODUCTION

METHODS OF INTERPRETING PROPHECY

One's understanding of biblical prophecy will be determined by the method of interpretation that one follows.[1] Here are two methods that are most widely used.

The *Allegorical Method*

This method subjectively regards the words of prophecy to have other, hidden meanings than what they say. In my opinion, there are several faults with this method. Disregarding the common usage of words, it allows unlimited speculation. Also, the minds of interpreters, influenced by their theological biases, become the basic authority rather than the Scriptures. Finally, there is no objective way to test the conclusions of the interpreters. Because of these faults, I prefer the literal method.

The Literal Method

This method allows each word of prophecy the meaning that it ordinarily has in biblical usage. As objectively as possible, it seeks to interpret the prophecy literally. It also recognizes figurative expressions and seeks to understand the truth that these convey. This method sees the Bible as a single, coherent revelation. It bases interpretation on fact and allows the self-consistency of the Scriptures to control it.[2] A precedent was established for this method of interpreting prophecy by the literal fulfillment of many prophecies about Israel (e.g. Lev. 26:33; Deut. 28:64–67) and about God the Son's first coming to earth (e.g. Matt. 1:22–23). In the following studies, I follow this method of interpretation.

I heard Dr. John F. Walvoord say that the study of unfulfilled prophecy is like putting a jigsaw picture together without first seeing the picture. The interpretation that fits the pieces together easily, with the least problems, and in keeping with the general teaching of Scripture, is the one that should be seriously considered. This is likely to be the most accurate interpretation of the prophecy.

REASONS FOR STUDYING PROPHECY

As complex as it is, the study of unfulfilled prophecy is rewarding to all who strive to understand its meaning (2 Tim. 3:16–17), for prophecy is a major part of the Holy Scriptures. The biblical prophecies reveal truths that God wants His people to know and that He uses to incite them to holy living and ministry (Deut. 29:29; Rom. 13:11–12; James 5:7–9; 2 Peter 3:11; 1 John 3:2–3). Reflection upon biblical prophecy has enlightened, challenged, and inspired hope in the hearts of God's people throughout history (cp. Gen. 3:15, 20; Jude 14; Gen. 15:5–6; Heb. 11:10; Dan. 9:2; Luke 2:25; Rev. 22:20). Let us have an ear to hear what the Holy Spirit says to us through the prophecies of His Word. They speak of God's future program for mankind and of our place in it.[3]

THE PROPHECY OF JESUS' RETURN FOR HIS CHURCH

We have seen that during the present age the Lord is building His Church. When He has completed this work, He will return to the earth's atmosphere and will receive the Church, His bride, to Himself. This truth is taught in 1 Thessalonians 4:13–18 and 2 Thessalonians 2:1. It is implied in John 14:3; Acts 1:11; 1 Corinthians 1:7; 16:22, "Maranatha" means "our Lord comes"; Philippians 3:20; 1 Thessalonians 1:10; 2:19; 3:13; 2 Timothy 4:1, 8; Titus 2:13; James 5:7–8; 1 Peter 1:7; 5:4; 1 John 2:28; 3:2; and Revelation 22:7, 12, 20. However, many, if not all, of these passages may also refer to Jesus' second coming to earth. They will fuel this anticipation in the hearts of gospel believers who will be living

during the Tribulation Age. Keep in mind that the Lord's return for His Church is not His second coming to earth or a part thereof, which takes place just before He establishes His millennial earthly kingdom.[4]

THE DETAILS OF JESUS' RETURN FOR HIS CHURCH

These are given in 1 Thessalonians 4:13–18.

Jesus' Descent from Heaven (v. 16a)

The Lord Jesus will come from heaven personally, descending to the earth's atmosphere (v. 17) and bringing with Him the Church people who previously had died and had gone to be with Him (v. 14; cp. Phil. 1:23; 2 Cor. 5:6, 8). These will return to earth so that they might be united with their resurrected bodies (1 Thess. 4:16).

Jesus' Command (vv. 16b–17a)

The Lord's shout will be a word of command (John 11:43; cp. Acts 8:38; 25:23) that will raise the dead bodies of Church people (John 5:28–29).[5] This shout will be with a commanding voice like that of an archangel—authoritative and loud (Jude 9; Rev. 10:1–3). The trumpet blasts[6] will signal the change that will transform the bodies of His people— those of the dead from corruptibility to incorruptibility and those of the living from mortality to immortality (1 Cor. 15:50–53).[7] All this will occur with eye-twinkling speed (vv. 51–52).

Jesus' Reception of the Church (v. 17b)

Upon changing the bodies of His people, the Lord Jesus will rapture them from the earth to meet Him in the air.[8] Then He will escort them quickly and safely through Satan's domain to heaven (cp. Eph. 2:2). There He will present them as a glorified Church (Eph. 5:25–27; Jude 24), marry them (Rev. 19:7–8), and will live with them forever (1 Thess. 4:17; 5:10).

THE BLESSED EVENTS ASSOCIATED WITH JESUS' RETURN FOR HIS CHURCH

The Lord's return for His Church and the events that are related to the Church's removal to heaven comprise the gospel believer's "hope," or expectation. Because of the blessing of these events, this hope is described as being "blessed" (Titus 2:13). It is also a "living" hope (1 Peter 1:3), for the Object of our hope, the Lord Jesus, is forever alive (1 Tim. 1:1; Rev. 1:18). Being an expectation, this hope rests upon God's true, certain Word (John 17:17; Titus 1:2). As we look at various NT passages that speak of this hope, let us consider these blessed events as they relate to their participants.

Their Experiencing the Transformation of Their Bodies (1 Thess. 4:13, 16–17).

This physical transformation will complete the work of salvation in the lives of the Lord's people (Rom. 8:23; 13:11; Phil. 3:20–21). Presently, the bodies of the dead are in a state of corruptibility (the disorganization and decay of death) and the bodies of the living are in a state of mortality (destined to die and return to dust). These bodies must be changed to incorruptibility and immortality (1 Cor. 15:53).

While it is not difficult to understand the need that the bodies of the dead have for this change, we may not be as aware of the need that we who are alive have. Our bodies presently possess the sin force, inherent corruption, and certain limitations, as determined by their constitution (Rom. 7:18–20; 8:10; Ps. 103:13–16). Moreover, the body's animating life force is the soul (and spirit) (1 Cor. 15:44, KJV "natural" means "soulish"), which is associated with the blood (Lev. 17:11, KJV "life" means "soul"). While the body in its present form and state is suited to life on earth, it must be changed for the future that God has prepared for His people (1 Cor. 15:50; 1 Thess. 4:17). The changed bodies of the living will have the same qualities and constitution as the resurrected bodies of those who were dead. The bodies of both living and dead will be changed and will be made like the resurrected, glorified body of the Lord Jesus Christ (Luke 24:36–43; Phil. 3:21; 1 John 3:2; see Appendix V: "The Human Body-Grid"). Meanwhile, we who are saved wait with mute and sometimes audible groaning for this glorious change (Rom. 8:23).

Their Seeing and Sharing in the Lord Jesus' Glory (Rom. 5:2).

Essentially, the glory of God is the visible radiance of His divine perfections, fully and equally manifested by each Person of the divine Trinity (cp. John 17:5). But we who are saved shall never possess this divine glory, for our human nature will never be divine. It is God's purpose to make us after the nature of our Lord's humanity (Rom. 8:29). It was our Lord's prayer, however, that His people see and participate in His glory, which is the glory of His exalted humanity (John 17:22, 24). As the Last Adam, the glorified Head and Pattern of the new humanity, He will share His exalted human glory with the members of the redeemed community (Heb. 2:9–13; cp. Rom. 8:18–19, 29; 1 Cor. 15:49; Phil. 3:20–21; Col. 1:27; 3:4; 1 Thess. 2:12; 2 Thess. 2:14; 2 Tim. 2:10; 1 Peter 5:10).

As a wife shares the glory of her husband, so the Church will share the glory of the Lord Jesus in its following manifestations: the glory of His resurrected, changed body (1 Cor. 15:43; Phil. 3:20–21), His moral glory (John 1:14; Eph. 5:27), the glory of His exalted position far above all creatures (Heb. 2:9; Eph. 1:20–21; 2:6), the glory of being colaborers in His messianic work of building the Church (1 Thess. 2:19–20; cp. 1 Cor. 3:9; 6:15), and the visible radiant glory of light (Acts 9:3; cp. Col. 3:4; Eph. 5:8; Rom. 8:29). While the Lord's people now bear His reproach in this evil world, their anticipation of future inheritance and glory brings them unspeakable joy (1 Peter 1:8).

Their Receiving Their Inheritance (1 Peter 1:3–6).

In the Bible, an inheritance was something that was given to another for his or her possession (cp. Luke 15:12). God's people are His possession (Eph. 1:18); their inheritance is the Lord Jesus (v. 11). Let us consider the present and future aspects of this inheritance.

Today, the Lord Jesus Himself is our possession (cp. Eph. 1:11; 1 John 5:12; Col. 1:27). Because of this, we have unlimited resources and blessings in Him (John 6:35; 1 Cor. 1:30; Eph. 1:3; 2 Cor. 12:9; Heb. 13:5–6; 2 Peter 1:3).

As to the future, our inheritance will consist of those spiritual realities and blessings that He has prepared and reserved for us in heaven (1 Peter 1:4; cp. John 14:2; 1 Cor. 2:9). The apostle Peter described this inheritance as being incorruptible (indestructible), undefiled (unstained by sin), unfading, and reserved for us. Moreover, we are being divinely kept for this inheritance (1 Peter 1:5). Furthermore, we shall share in the Lord's earthly inheritance when He returns to rule (Heb. 1:2; Ps. 2:8–9; Matt. 11:27; John 3:35; Rom. 8:17).

The riches of this future inheritance are indicated by the presence and ministries of the Holy Spirit in our lives (Eph. 1:14), which are only the first installment of all that we shall experience. Having the Lord Jesus and all that He has prepared for us makes us rich, indeed!

Their Seeing the Fruit of Their Earthly Lives and Ministries (1 Thess. 2:19).

This anticipates the time when the Lord, having completed His work of building the Church, will appraise the lives of His people. Then He will make known to them all that He was pleased to do through their lives (cp. 1 Cor. 3:5–13).

This truth should encourage us in our serving with the Lord, for our labor is not in vain in Him (1 Cor. 15:58). It should also motivate us to allow Him to do His work through us for God's glory (John 15:4–5, 8; Eph. 3:20; cp. 2 Tim. 4:7–8).

Their Entering Eternal Life (Titus 1:2; 3:7).

The Scriptures teach that all who are trusting in the Lord Jesus for their salvation now have eternal life (John 1:12; 1 John 5:11–12). But because our bodies are still unsaved, we cannot now experience all that this new life in Jesus offers. When the Lord changes our bodies, we shall fully enter the experience of all that this spiritual life means. With our changed bodies, we shall fully perceive and utilize all that God has for us and shall completely express our new life in Christ without the eclipses of sin and the smudges of imperfection. With bodies like that of Jesus, we shall be like Him in our thinking, will, and emotion (Rom. 8:29; 1 John 3:2; see Appendix V: "The Human Body-Grid").

These wonderful aspects of our expectation in the Lord Jesus have no equal in this world. Daily, we should anticipate these blessings as Caleb thought of his inheritance while traveling through the Sinai wilderness (Josh. 14:6–13). This will lighten burdens, sweep away discouragement, and add spice to our daily routine. As we embrace this truth, the God of all hope will fill us with all joy and peace so that we might overflow with hope by the power of the Holy Spirit (Rom. 15:13).

THE TIME OF JESUS' RETURN FOR HIS CHURCH

The exact time of the Lord's return for His Church has not been revealed. All who believe in His literal thousand-year reign on earth hold that He will return to this world before He begins this rule. Also, many hold that, immediately before His millennial rule begins, there will be a time of great worldwide tribulation, known as the Tribulation Age.

However, there are differences of opinion about the time of His return for His Church, as this relates to the Tribulation Age.[9] Let us consider these views.

The Partial Rapture View

This holds that only spiritual gospel believers, who are watching and waiting for Christ's return, will be raptured before the Tribulation Age begins. Those who are not ready (carnal gospel believers) will be left to go through part or all of the Tribulation Age, with its "purifying fires." These people will be raptured individually when they are ready or just before Jesus returns to establish His earthly kingdom. This view is based on an interpretation of Matthew 24:13; Luke 21:36; Philippians 3:20; 2 Timothy 4:8; and Hebrews 9:28.

Objections to this view include these: *One,* it conditions the privilege of participating in the Rapture, including the glorification of the body, on meritorious works, contrary to the whole scheme of salvation (cp. Eph. 2:8; Rom. 13:11). *Two,* it ignores the fact of Jesus' atoning work as having delivered gospel believers at the time of their salvation from divine judicial condemnation of all their sins—past, present, and future—and to prepare them for eternity (cp. Rom. 5:1; Col. 2:13; and Rom. 8:30–34). *Three,* it violates the concept of the unity of the Church (John 17:21–22). And *four,* it overlooks the final sanctification of gospel believers when they are presented faultless before the presence of God's glory (Jude 24; Eph. 5:26–27).

First Thessalonians 4:13–17 does not suggest this theory. Matthew 24:13 and Luke 21:36 occur in contexts that speak about the Tribulation Age. The words *be counted worthy* literally mean "be strong," "be able," or "prevail," without any suggestion of merit.

The Posttribulation Rapture View

This holds that the Lord will return and will remove His Church from the earth at the end of the Tribulation Age, just before or as a part of His second coming to earth. There are three views of this posttribulation event: *One,* the Tribulation Age is now past and the Rapture and the second coming of Jesus may occur at any time. *Two,* the Church is now in the Tribulation Age and the Rapture and the Lord's second coming are still future. And *three,* the Tribulation Age is still future, with the Rapture and the Lord's second coming at its close. Posttribulation rapturists base their view on an interpretation of Matthew 13:24–30, the use of "coming" (Gk. *parousia* meaning a "kingly visit") in 1 Thessalonians 4:15 and Matthew 24:3, and the anticipation of "tribulation" in 1 Thessalonians 3:3–4 and Acts 14:22.

Objections to this view are these: *One,* its ignoring the possibility of another interpretation of Matthew 13:24–30 that understands the "wheat" to represent postrapture saved people who will be on earth during tribulation days; *two,* its disregarding *parousia* as an ordinary word for "coming" (1 Cor. 16:17; 2 Cor. 7:6) and "presence" (2 Cor. 10:10); *three,* the failure of some to distinguish between the Church's suffering from man's hostility and from God's wrath (Phil. 1:29; 2 Tim. 3:12; contra 1 Thess. 1:10; 5:9); and *four,* its overlooking the absence of a resurrection event in Revelation 19:11–21 like that in 1 Thessalonians 4:16. The precross dead saved people and Tribulation Age martyrs will be resurrected for the millennial kingdom, but this appears to be later, before Revelation 20:4. If the Rapture were to take place at the end of the Tribulation Age, there would be no "sheep" for the Lord to separate from the "goats" in His judgment of Tribulation Age survivors (Matt. 25:31–46).

The Midtribulation Rapture View

This holds that the Church will be raptured in the middle of the Tribulation Age, before the final three and a half years. Believing that her people will not be exposed to God's wrath, this position holds that the Church will be translated before the outpouring of the bowls of

God's wrath (Rev. 16:1–12, KJV "vials"). It sees the Rapture as occurring with the "last trump" of 1 Corinthians 15:52, which is the seventh Trumpet Judgment of Revelation 11:15.

There are two objections to this view. *One*, it overlooks the word "filled" in Revelation 15:1 (meaning "completed" or "finished"), which indicates that all the divine judgments of this age, including those introduced by the breaking of seals and the blowing of trumpets, are expressions of divine wrath. We read. "For by them [the Bowl Judgments] is completed the wrath of God." *Two*, this view disregards the fact that trumpets, as in the past, will signal various events in the future (cp. Matt. 24:31; Num. 10:1–10; see endnote 6). The "last trump" (1 Cor. 15:52) may represent the last of a series of trumpet blasts that signal a series of events, which are involved in the resurrection of dead bodies and the transformation of living ones (cp. 1 Thess. 4:16–17).

The Pre-Wrath Rapture View

This more recent view places the Church's rapture in the third quarter of the Tribulation Age, or the "seventieth week" of Daniel 9.[10] It holds that the Rapture will take place after the great tribulation against the Jews (Matt. 24:15–22) and before the time of divine wrath against Gentile earth dwellers. This tribulation against Israel will start in the middle of the Tribulation Age, with the Antichrist's violation of the peace accord (Dan. 9:27; 2 Thess. 2:3–4). This period of Jewish trouble will be immediately followed by the Day of the Lord, a time of God's wrath on earth dwellers. This time of divine wrath will be introduced by the seventh Seal Judgment and will include the Trumpet Judgments (Rev. 8:1ff.). It is just before these judgments that the Lord will rapture the Church (Matt. 24:27).

My objections to this view are these: *One*, this view ignores the fact that the whole Tribulation Age is a time of divine wrath on earth dwellers, for all of the judgments of the Tribulation Age are expressions of God's wrath (Rev. 15:1). *Two*, the sixth Seal Judgment is a visual preview of the divine wrath that will be expressed by the Bowl Judgments (chap. 16) in reply to the martyrs' call in the fifth Seal Judgment for divine vengeance (6:8–17). *Three*, the seventh Seal Judgment will introduce the Trumpet Judgment series (chaps. 8–9), all of which will occur in the first half of the Tribulation Age, excepting the seventh Trumpet Judgment, which relates to Satan's earthly activities during the second half of the Tribulation Age (11:14; 12:7–12). Note that because of their severity, Trumpet Judgments five through seven are called "woes" (8:13; 9:12; 11:14; 12:12). And *four*, all the seven seals, with their judgments, are broken in the first half of the Tribulation Age.

The Pretribulation Rapture View

This holds that the Church in its entirety will be raptured before the beginning of the prophetic career of Satan's human agent, the Beast out of the sea (2 Thess. 2:1–8) and the beginning of the "seventieth week" of Daniel 9. I prefer this view for the following reasons:

1. *The Church appears to be unrelated to the Tribulation Age.*

If the Church were on earth at this time, it seems that there would be some direct reference to it. None is found between Revelation 4:1 and 19:7. It is significant that the Church is unrelated to the divine purpose, ministry, and people of this period.

a. *The Church is unrelated to the divine purpose for the Tribulation Age.*

A divine purpose for the Tribulation Age is to prepare earth dwellers for the Lord's second coming to earth and His millennial rule. This preparation will include His worldwide evangelistic mission through the ministry of the 144,000 Israelite evangelists, His dealing with Israel so as to bring about the repentance of the elect Jewish remnant, and His pouring out divine wrath upon wicked Gentiles. The Church does not need this special preparation before her rapture.

b. The Church is unrelated to the ministries of the Tribulation Age.

There will be two successive divine ministries during the Tribulation Age. During the first half of the Tribulation Age, there will be the ministry of the 144,000 saved Israelite evangelists, who will preach the gospel of the kingdom throughout the world with unprecedented results (Matt. 24:14; Rev. 7). These will be martyred at the beginning of the second half of the Tribulation Age by Satan through his human agent, the Beast out of the sea, who will prohibit all gospel proclamation (Rev. 12:17; 14:1–5).

During the second half of the Tribulation Age, there will be the ministry of God's two witnesses (Rev. 11:3–14). Although he will prohibit any proclamation of the gospel, the Beast out of the sea will not be able to silence these two men. Endowed with divine power, they will bear witness to the fact of God's existence in the midst of worldwide atheism. Also, being prophets, they will cry out against the unprecedented sin and blasphemy of those days. Moreover, they will declare that the world upheavals and distresses are visitations of divine wrath. At the end of this period, they will be killed, will be resurrected, and will ascend into heaven. If the Church is on earth during this time, why does God use these special forces rather than the Church?

c. The Church is unrelated to the gospel believers of the Tribulation Age.

Several groups of saved people belong to the Tribulation Age: the 144,000 evangelists (Rev. 7:1–8; 14:1–5), the earlier martyrs of the forepart of the Tribulation Age (6:9–11) and the later martyrs killed during the second half of the Tribulation Age (7:9–17; 13:7, 15; 15:2), the elect Jewish remnant (12:13–14), and a few saved Gentiles, who will survive this age (Matt. 25:31–34). But nowhere is there any indication that the Church will be on earth during this time.

2. An interval of time will be needed between the Church's rapture and her return to earth with the Lord Jesus.

Because only the saved will enter Christ's earthly kingdom, the Tribulation Age will be needed for the formation of a nucleus of saved people who will repopulate the millennial earth (Matt. 25:34).[11] Saved survivors of the Tribulation Age will enter the kingdom with unsaved bodies, which will be capable of reproducing children and of transmitting inherent corruption to their offspring. If the Church were raptured just before the Lord's second coming, these survivors would be changed and raptured.

3. The Lord's return for His Church is imminent.

His return may occur at any time. This truth is indicated by the present tense of "look" (Phil. 3:20), "to wait" (1 Thess. 1:10), and "looking" (Titus 2:13). The present tense speaks of the continuous expectancy that we should have toward the Lord's coming. Also, if she were to pass through part or all of the Tribulation Age, the Church would be aware of the time of the Lord's return because of the many details that have been revealed about this age. This knowledge would diminish the concept of imminency. On the other hand, those gospel believers who will be living on earth during tribulation days will look forward to the Lord's return to deal with their enemies and to establish His earthly kingdom (Matt. 24:42, 44). The truth of His second coming will encourage them to endure steadfastly unto death or unto His return (v. 13). However, they will not have this sense of imminency until the very end of the Tribulation Age.

In view of the above evidence, I firmly believe that the Lord Jesus will remove His Church from earth before the Tribulation Age begins. There is no prophecy that must be fulfilled before this glorious event. Prophetic events, like the building of the Jewish temple at Jerusalem, may come to pass, but these are not prerequisites to His coming. Many signs will attend His second coming to earth, but no sign, save the trumpet blast, will signal His return for His Church. Indeed, He may come today!

445

THE PRACTICAL VALUE OF THIS EXPECTANCY

The truth of our Lord's imminent return for His Church makes a great impact on the lives of all His people who believe it. It comforts them in bereavement (1 Thess. 4:18); it engenders patience in them in adversity (James 5:7–11; Rom. 8:18); it deters them from sinning (1 John 3:2–3; cp. Matt. 24:48–49) and spiritual lethargy (Rom. 13:11; 1 Thess. 5:6–7); and it incites them to diligence (Luke 19:12–13), abiding in Jesus (1 John 2:28) and love for Him and His return (2 Tim. 4:8).

We can profit from the Lord's appeal to the Tribulation Age saved people to be watchful and ready (Matt. 24:42–44). To be watchful is to keep awake or be alert. God has wisely withheld the time of the Lord's return so that we might constantly be on the lookout for Him and always be occupied with our spiritual duties (cp. vv. 48–50).

To be ready is to be prepared for His return. Of what does this preparedness consist? The answer is what we would do if we knew that the Lord was coming one month from today. Some of this preparation might include making sure that we are saved, putting our spiritual life in order, giving more time to prayer and Scripture meditation, witnessing to unsaved friends and relatives, making right any sins in our lives and wrongdoing to others, and seeking the Lord's will for the remainder of our time on earth. Would you be prepared if He were to come today?

THE PROPHECY OF JESUS' APPRAISAL OF HIS CHURCH

We who are saved are subject to three divine judgments: *One, as sinners we were judged* at the cross in the person of our beloved Substitute, the Lord Jesus (Rom. 5:8; 1 Peter 2:24; 2 Cor. 5:21). Because of His sacrifice, we were divinely acquitted of all charges and were justified, never again to be divinely condemned because of our sins (John 5:24; Rom. 5:9–10; 8:1, 30–34). *Two,* as God's children we are now subject to His parental corrective chastisement when we fail to deal with known filial sins in our lives (Rev. 3:19; 1 Cor. 11:26–32). And *three,* as the Lord's slaves we shall answer to Him for our behavior during our Christian lifetime (2 Cor. 5:9–10; Col. 3:24–25; 1 Cor. 3:8–15; 2 John 8). Having purchased us by His sacrifice (1 Cor. 6:19–20; 1 Peter 1:18–19), the Lord has left us here for a while that we might work with Him in the building of His Church. For this reason, we are obligated to do His bidding and are accountable to Him for our behavior (Rom. 14:7–12). However, many saved people do not seem to be aware of their present responsibility and of their future accountability to the Lord Jesus. Having received the Savior, they suppose that they have no further obligation to Him than to wait for their removal to heaven. For these, the coming appraisal will be a startling event. Let us look at this closely.

THE REASONS FOR THIS APPRAISAL

Observe that this judgment in no way relates to our salvation or eternal destination. These issues were settled when we trusted in the Savior for salvation (John 3:36; 5:24). The reasons for this appraisal of the Lord's people are these:

That Each Saved Person May Give an Account of His Behavior (Rom. 14:8, 12)

This means that we shall be required to explain the reasons for all our conscious earthly behavior since the time of our salvation (Luke 19:12–15). Because it is our duty to do the Lord's will and to carry out His commission for our lives in working with Him in building the Church (2 Cor. 5:9–10, 14–15; Matt. 28:19), we are answerable to Him for the use of our bodies, time, energy, abilities, opportunities, material goods, spiritual possessions, and the like.

That Each Saved Person May Receive His Proper Reward (1 Cor. 3:8; 2 Cor. 5:10)

By this appraisal, the Lord will evaluate everything that we did during our Christian lifetime and will determine what reward, or pay, we should receive. It is His desire that we receive a full reward (John 15:16; 2 John 8, KJV should read "you receive a full reward").

THE DETAILS OF THIS APPRAISAL

Its Time

The appraisal of the Church will take place after its translation to heaven, before she prepares herself for her marriage to the Lord Jesus (Rev. 22:12; 19:7). His people's present work will end with the completion of the Church's construction. Although our active participation ends with death, there are elements of our ministries that continue to make their impact on the lives of others, like a shared gospel witness or a Bible lesson. We shall be pleasantly surprised to see what the Lord did with those parts of our lives that were yielded to Him (1 Thess. 2:19–20).

Its Place

The appraisal will take place in heaven before "the judgment seat of Christ" (2 Cor. 5:10). In the Scriptures, this "judgment seat" is seen as a judicial bench where court decisions were made (Matt. 27:19; Acts 18:16). However, this appraisal should not be regarded as a judicial examination that will bring upon us divine condemnation for our sins. The atoning work of the Lord has adequately taken care of this for all who are trusting Him for their salvation (Rom. 8:1, 30–34). But we shall still answer for the total output of our Christian lifetime while we were on earth, for we are responsible for our actions.

Its Examiner

Various references to this appraisal reveal that the examiner will be our Master, the Lord Jesus (Rom. 14:7–12). The apostle John described our Lord's judicial appearance in Revelation 1:13–16, with each feature symbolically portraying some aspect of His judicial bearing. His clothing marked His dignity and honor; His white hair reflected the wisdom and equity of His judgments; His fiery eyes, penetrating and searching out all things, showed His assessing all things in the light of divine holiness; His glowing feet indicated His readiness to trample upon all that He will not approve; His roaring voice assured that His word will be final; His hand indicated His sovereign control over all people; His mouth, projecting a sword, declared God's Word, the criterion of what is good and right; finally, His brilliant face radiated the unveiled glory of God.

Although the apostle fainted at the sight, he was assured that he had nothing to fear (Rev. 1:17–18). Elsewhere, John declared that they who abide in Jesus will have boldness in His presence, but the rest will shrink from Him in shame (1 John 2:28).

Its Regulatory Principles

In appraising the lives of His people, the Lord will adhere to those divine principles that He follows in all His judicial evaluations and decisions (Rom. 2:1–16).

One: His judgments are according to truth (v. 2). They are factual and are in keeping with the moral standards of God's Word.

Two: His judgments are according to people's deeds (v. 6). They are in keeping with what people deserve (v. 6).

Three. His judgments are without respect of persons (v. 11). They are impartial, for He does not give preferential treatment.

These principles assure that the Lord will deal with each person fairly and will give him his due reward (1 Cor. 3:8).

A DESCRIPTION OF THIS APPRAISAL

The apostle Paul warned the many teachers, who were busy at Corinth, to take heed how they built upon the foundation that he had laid during his pioneer gospel work there (1 Cor. 3:8–12). He then gave three descriptive features of this appraisal (vv. 13–15):

Everyone's Work Will Be Made Visible (1 Cor. 3:13a)

Every conscious personal activity of our Christian lifetime will be revealed to us for the purpose of review, accounting, and evaluation. We shall have to give our reasons for doing what we did. Since this will be a personal matter, I believe that it will be a private review, carried on simultaneously with all who are being appraised (cp. Luke 24:34).

Everyone's Work Will Be Tried by Fire (1 Cor. 3:13b)

Fueled by divine holiness (Heb. 12:25–29), our Lord's fiery gaze will examine and evaluate these works for the purpose of approving those that meet His standards (Rev. 1:14; Heb. 4:12–13; 12:29).[12] The Lord will examine and evaluate all our actions, words, thoughts, emotions, attitudes, motivations, and intentions (2 Cor. 5:10; Col. 3:25; Rev. 22:12). The phrase "of what sort it is" indicates that He will be concerned with quality. The works that He will approve are represented by materials that withstand fire like precious metals and gems (1 Cor. 3:12). All else will be rejected and consumed like wood, hay, and stubble.

What kind of works will He approve? Only those in which He had a part (John 15:5)— that were in keeping with His will and that were done in His strength (Eph. 6:8; Heb. 13:21; 1 Cor. 15:10; Phil. 1:11, 21; 4:13). All that were done independently of Him will be rejected, regardless of their appearance and results, for they represent nothing more than what unsaved people can do and they are sinful in God's sight (Rom. 14:23; Heb. 11:6; John 15:5b).

Everyone's Work Will Receive Its Proper Reward (1 Cor. 3:8, 14–15)

That which pleases the Lord will bring us gain; that of which He disapproves will bring us loss. Keep in mind that the purpose of this appraisal is to reward us as His slaves; it is not to punish us judicially for our sinful works. However, being accountable people, we must answer to the Lord Jesus for the use of all that He committed to our trust while we were here on earth (cp. Luke 19:11–15).

THE OUTCOMES OF THIS APPRAISAL

The Lord's appraisal of our lives will bring us both gain and loss (2 Cor. 5:10). Let us look at the nature of these rewards and consider their calculation.

The Nature of These Rewards

The nature of these rewards, or wages, is illustrated by the Lord's parable about a lord and his three slaves (Matt. 25:14–30).[13]

1. *The profitable rewards (1 Cor. 3:14; cp. Matt. 25:20–23)*

Our works that survive the appraisal will bring us wages of gain, which is a part of our inheritance (Col. 3:24). The parable illustrates three kinds of profitable rewards.

a. The Lord's commendation (Matt. 25:21, 23)

In the parable, the lord declared that two of his slaves, who used their trust satisfactorily, were "good" and "faithful" and that their tasks were "well done" (cp. 1 Cor. 4:5; 1 Peter 1:7). These words indicate our Lord's recognition of those people who faithfully had done what was good in His sight, that is, His will (Rom. 12:2; Heb. 13:21). In His messages to the seven churches of Asia Minor (Rev. 2–3), the Lord used several metaphors that express and memorialize this commendation.[14]

1) The garland (Rev. 2:10, KJV "crown")

When he portrayed the Christian life as a race (1 Cor. 9:24–25), the apostle Paul alluded to the Isthmian Games that were held near Corinth every two years in a grove of spruce trees, sacred to Poseidon, the Greek god of the sea. Comparable to our Olympic gold medal, the prize was a garland, or wreath, of spruce. This represented the highest pinnacle of human achievement and happiness. It brought the winner the highest honors and the most coveted distinction a Greek could acquire.[15]

Unlike that of the Greek athlete, the gospel believer's garland will be an imperishable one (1 Cor. 9:25). It will represent our Lord's lasting recognition and commendation of His people's good works. The Scriptures describe several kinds of garlands: for soul-winners, a crown of rejoicing (1 Thess. 2:19); for obedient life-completers, a crown of righteousness (2 Tim. 4:8); for humble servers, a crown of glory (1 Peter 5:4); and for enduring sufferers, a crown of life (James 1:12; Rev. 2:10). Our receiving our crowns and wearing them will reflect an honor greater than anything that this world confers.[16]

2) The engraved white stone (Rev. 2:17)

Similar to our trophy cup, this tablet of white stone was engraved with the victor's name, and it certified his victory. The Lord will personalize His honoring obedient people by giving them new names, engraved upon trophy pieces.

3) The white garment (Rev. 3:5)

While the victorious Greeks were often clad in purple, overcoming gospel believers will clad themselves in white garments, whose fabric will consist of their righteous deeds (Rev. 19:8, KJV "righteousness" should be "righteousnesses" or "righteous deeds"). We are now weaving our garments by doing the Lord's will in His strength (1 John 2:29; Phil. 1:11; John 15:1–5). Careless, unrepentant gospel believers who are living in sin will have defiled garments (Rev. 3:4; cp. 18; 16:15). These garments will portray the overall kind of Christian life that we lived while on earth.

At the time of this appraisal, our Lord's commendation will be far more important to us than anything in our present life that would lead us to neglect pleasing Him (2 Cor. 5:9–10). What is your present priority in life? Are you running to win the Lord's commendation?

b. The Lord's granting greater responsibility (Matt. 25:21, 23)

In the parable, the lord of the slaves increased the duties of the faithful ones when he said, "I will make you ruler over many things." This portrays the reward of administrative positions in our Lord's earthly millennial kingdom, which will be filled by His people, regardless of the historical age in which they lived (Rev. 2:26–27; 2 Tim. 2:12; Luke 19:12–19; Rev. 20:4). The extent of one's authority will be determined by the amount of profitable reward that one receives.

We should remember more often the principle that faithfulness in small duties prepares us for greater responsibilities (Luke 16:10). Are you faithfully fulfilling your present duties, regardless of how small they may be? All that the Lord gives us to do, regardless of its quantity, is important. It must be done reliantly and heartily as unto Him (Gal. 2:20; Phil. 4:13; Col. 3:23–24).

c. The Lord's allowing intimate fellowship with Himself (Matt. 25:21, 23)

In the parable, the lord invited his faithful slaves to participate in the celebration of his return when he said, "Enter thou into the joy of your lord." The promises to the overcomer, like their eating "hidden manna," being given the "Morning Star," receiving Jesus' "new name," and sitting "with Him," suggest a reward that denotes some degree of intimate fellowship with the Lord (Rev. 2:17, 28; 3:12, 21). This view is supported by the degrees of fellowship that the Lord's disciples had with Him during His earthly ministry. That of John was the most intimate (John 21:20); then that of Peter, James, and John (Matt. 17:1); next that of the twelve apostles collectively (Mark 3:14); then that of the seventy disciples (Luke 10:1); and finally that of the distant crowd (7:11).

If, during this lifetime, we are developing a capacity for our future relationship with Jesus (cp. 2 Cor. 4:17), will not the saved person who now habitually abides in Him have a greater spiritual capacity and desire for the Lord's fellowship in the future than he who seldom walks in the Lord's fellowship during his earthly Christian lifetime? This reward is not a loss of heaven or happiness (1 Cor. 3:15). It means that careless people will be happy with less, because of their smaller capacity to receive all that the Lord has for them. This is like a person with little art education touring an art gallery. How much he loses in his appreciation and interpretation of what he sees! However, for those of us who are still alive on earth, it is not too late to do something about our daily relationship with the Lord Jesus (1 Cor. 1:9; John 15:4–5; Col. 3:16; Matt. 11:28–39).

The fact of gainful rewards manifests God's boundless grace. Amazingly, He not only enables obedient believers to do His will, but He also rewards them for it. This should encourage us to seek to please Him daily, as the apostle Paul did (1 Cor. 9:26–27; 2 Cor. 5:9–10; 2 Tim. 4:7–8; cp. 1 Cor. 15:58), and to live for His glory (1 Cor. 10:31).

2. The unprofitable rewards (1 Cor. 3:15; cp. Matt. 25:24–30)

The works that do not meet the Lord's approval will bring us unprofitable results, or wages. This return will be not only the loss of potential, favorable rewards that we could have had but also the gain of undesirable results.[17] Being forgiven, the filial sins that we commit and judge by repentance and confession (Rev. 2:5; 1 John 1:9) will not receive the Lord's censure. But our sinning brings us the irrecoverable loss of time, effort, and opportunity, which could have been used more profitably. Focusing on the slave who did his own will, Jesus' parable illustrates three kinds of unprofitable results (Matt. 25:24–30).

a. Reprimand (Matt. 25:26, 30)

In the parable, the lord reproved his slave for his being "wicked," "slothful," and "unprofitable." This means that, for failing to invest his lord's money profitably, the slave was wrong, lazy, and useless. This is a vivid description of the saved person who is carnal, or living in sin. He is doing wrong, is neglecting God's will, and is of no use to the Lord in this world. If he does not shape up, he will be prematurely removed from earth (John 15:2).

The Lord Jesus will express His disapproval of our unacceptable works (Rev. 2:4, 14, 20), which represent the unprofitable use of our time, energy, and possessions, and which make us sinful, fruitless, and ineffective.[18] Observe that the Lord has just claim to all that our lives can produce as well as to life itself (cp. Matt. 25:18, 25, 27). His reprimand will bring us shame (1 John 2:28) and grief (Heb. 13:17). But this will not affect our salvation (1 Cor. 3:15) or our positional sanctification in Jesus (1:2, 30).

b. Loss of responsibility (Matt. 25:28–29)

The lord had the unfaithful slave's talent taken from him. Manifesting our irresponsibility, our evil works will bring us loss of administrative duties or a lower office in the coming millennial kingdom (cp. Rev. 2:26–27).

c. Loss of intimate fellowship with Him (Matt. 25:30)

The unfaithful slave was not disowned, but he was not allowed to attend the celebration of his master's return. This portrays the loss of intimate fellowship with Jesus that more faithful people will enjoy. Our sinning results in our neglecting to walk in the Lord's fellowship, which, in turn, will limit our future capacity for fellowship with Him (Rev. 2:17; 2 Cor. 4:17; John 12:26).

It is urgent that we visualize the impact of these losses and allow this to motivate us to please the Lord Jesus in everything. The apostle Paul's reference to rejection in 1 Corinthians 9:27 refers to failure in winning profitable rewards, not to salvation.

The Calculation of These Rewards

Having done both good and evil during our Christian lifetime, we shall receive our Lord's commendation for our good works and His reprimand for our unjudged evil works. We shall also be given a suitable position of administration in His earthly kingdom and shall have some capacity for intimate fellowship with Him. The amount of these rewards will be determined by our use of that which God has allotted us for life and ministry in this world. While each of us has the potential for receiving a full profitable reward for his Christian lifetime, this seems unlikely because of inherent sin in our lives. On the other hand, we can earn full rewards for specific undertakings and activities over a period of time. In any case, as the apostle Paul shows, we should always strive to please the Lord in all that we do (2 Cor. 5:9–10), by dealing with our sins and by learning and doing His will (7:1; 6:1). We shall experience mixed emotions at this appraisal. We shall feel regret and shame for that which the Lord will disapprove; we shall rejoice over that which He will approve in our lives.

We cannot now calculate what our reward will be, for we do not see the total picture of our lives and their influence on others (1 Cor. 4:1–5). Only the Lord, who is aware of everything, can do this (Rom. 14:1–13). Now is the time to start living with this appraisal in view (2 Cor. 5:9–10, 14–15). Observe that church leaders and teachers will be especially accountable to the Lord for their ministries (Heb. 13:17; James 3:1).

Several Observations

One: We shall not lose any rewards that we actually have gained (2 John 8, some Gk. MSS give "you" for the first and third "we"). The loss will be of those potential rewards that we could have earned had we been faithful.

Two: While all believers will receive the same kind of rewards, they will not receive the same amount (1 Cor. 3:8). Moreover, as the Lord's parable in Matthew 20:1–16 illustrates, the length of Christian life does not bear on the amount of reward. What counts is our faithfulness to the Lord during the time that He allows us on earth after we are saved.

Three: We can earn more reward, or pay, by being more obedient to the Lord today and hereafter.

Four: We can lessen the Lord's reprimand by faithfully dealing with our sins by repentance and confession (Rev. 2:5; 1 John 1:9). However, our sinning, though forgiven, still leaves vacant, unprofitable gaps in our lives that would have been filled with profitable use of our possessions, time, energy, and ability had we obeyed God.

Five: The size of our consignment from the Lord is determined by our capability to carry it out for the glory of God (Matt. 25:15). This means that each gospel believer differs from others in capacities, capabilities, opportunities, circumstances, understanding, and the like, all of which are divinely determined (Eph. 2:10). While spiritual duties, as described in the New Testament, are the same for all, and God's spiritual resources are available to all, each believer has his or her own life to live and work to do, as granted by the Lord (cp. Eph. 3:1–8; 2 Peter 1:12–14). As with trial, the Lord does not give us more responsibility than we can handle in His strength (1 Cor. 10:13).

Six: What shall be our feelings at the results of the appraisal? At first we shall experience shame and grief because of what the Lord did not approve (1 John 2:28; Heb. 13:17), but then we shall rejoice in what He did approve. The Scriptures indicate that we shall experience all the happiness and blessing that our capacity will allow (Rev. 21:4–5). Still, it appears that our record of wrongdoing will remain, as in the cases of Peter and Demas (John 18:27; 2 Tim. 4:10; cp. 1 Peter 1:23).

Seven: Other passages show that the Lord will also appraise the lives of His people who lived in other ages (Dan. 12:2–3, 13). He will do this when He returns and establishes His earthly kingdom (Isa. 40:10; Rev. 22:12; cp. Matt. 25:14–19).

THE CRITERIA OF THIS APPRAISAL

By what standards will the Lord appraise our works to determine what pleases Him? He will evaluate our works by the following criteria, given in question form:

Were the Works Done in Keeping with God's Will for Us?

It is our duty to learn and to do what is pleasing to the Lord (Eph. 5:8–10, 17; Rom. 12:2; 2 Cor. 5:9; 1 Thess. 5:21–22; 2 Tim. 2:15) with complete loyalty and dependability (1 Cor. 4:1–2; cp. Luke 16:1–13). His will is expressed by those commands and teachings that are given in the New Testament (see Appendix F: "Learning and Doing God's Will").

Were the Works Done in Association with Jesus?

We cannot do anything that is acceptable unless we act in union with Jesus, who is our spiritual life (John 15:4–5; Col. 3:4). Apart from Him, we cannot be satisfactorily spiritually productive (Gal. 2:20; Phil. 1:11; 4:13; Heb. 13:21). Everything done apart from the Lord and the spiritual resources that He has given us is sinful, for it is done in the energy of the inner sin force (2 Peter 1:3; Rom. 14:23; cp. 13:14; Gal. 5:19–21).

Were the Works Done Heartily As unto the Lord?

This means our doing His will with our total being (Col. 3:23–24), not in a halfhearted, reluctant way (Eccl. 9:10; Rom. 12:11; cp. Matt. 15:8).

Were the Works Done unto the Glory of God?

This should be the goal of all our behavior (1 Cor. 15:10), for we exist for this purpose (Eph. 1:12). Our living pleasing to God allows Him to manifest Himself in and through our lives and to bring Himself praise (Matt. 5:16; 2 Cor. 3:5; Jer. 9:23–24).

The Lord Jesus Himself lived by these criteria when He was here on earth: He did the Father's will (John 6:38; 8:29), acted in association with the Father (8:28; 14:10), and did everything heartily and resolutely as unto the Father (4:34; Luke 9:51) and for the Father's glory (John 12:28; 17:4). With His help, we can do this, too (Phil. 4:13).

THE MOTIVATION PROMPTED BY THIS APPRAISAL

Motivation provides us with drive for action. The prospect of this coming appraisal is a legitimate motivation for godly living. The Lord Jesus, James, and the apostles Peter and John refer to this appraisal (Rev. 2:7, 10, 17; 3:5, 12, 21; 22:12; James 1:12; 1 Peter 1:7; 5:4; 2 John 8). Also, this appraisal was a strong motivating factor in the life and ministry

452

of Paul (1 Cor. 9:24–27; 2 Cor. 5:9–10; cp. Rom. 14:7–13). A top priority of the apostle's life was to please the Lord by learning and doing His will (1 Cor. 9:25–27) and doing this in God's way (2 Cor. 1:12; Gal. 2:20). Having lived with these criteria in mind, Paul knew what was in store for him (2 Tim. 4:7–8). Those who love Jesus love His appearing (cp. John 14:15) and anticipate an abundant entrance into His everlasting kingdom (1 Peter 1:3–9; 2 Peter 1:4–11).

The truth of the coming appraisal points to the seriousness of our present life in this world. Our Lord is concerned with the spiritual quality of our lives and expects us to give attention to this as well (Luke 19:12–13). Anticipating this appraisal, we should strive daily to please Him in everything. God's grace in salvation does not cancel our personal responsibility but intensifies it, for this grace has provided us with everything that we need for living holy, productive lives in this world (2 Cor. 9:8; 2 Peter 1:2–4). What kind of an investment are you making of your life (Mark 8:34–38)?

THE PROPHECY OF THE TRIBULATION AGE

When the Lord has accomplished His present purpose of building His Church and has removed this company to heaven, He then will prepare earth dwellers for His second coming and the establishment of His earthly millennial kingdom.[19] The period of time between the Lord's return for His Church and His second coming to earth to rule is usually called "the Tribulation Age" or "the Tribulation Period," for the Scriptures describe this as a time of unprecedented, worldwide trouble (Jer. 30:7; Matt. 24:21–22, 29). As we shall see, the unsaved will suffer from intense divine judgments, Israel will be severely persecuted, and saved Gentiles will suffer martyrdom. The entire period of some seven years will be a time of unrest, strife, violence, wickedness, and anguish, especially during the closing three and a half years. This seven-year period is that part of the Day of the Lord when God will judge His earthly enemies and will establish a new world order with the Lord Jesus as Ruler.[20]

GOD'S PURPOSE FOR THE TRIBULATION AGE

The purpose is to prepare earth dwellers for Jesus' second coming to earth and the establishment of His earthly millennial kingdom. This preparation will include the following events, which will be examined in greater detail later.

The Worldwide Ministry of the Gospel of the Kingdom (Matt. 24:14)

There will be an intensive evangelistic ministry during the first half of the Tribulation Age (Matt. 24:14; Rev. 7). This will give people everywhere the opportunity to be saved and to prepare for the Lord's earthly kingdom.

The Bringing of the Elect of Israel to Repentance (Hos. 5:14–6:3)

This is necessary for the Lord's return to earth (Deut. 30:1–3; Joel 2:12–32) and the fulfillment of God's covenant promises to these people (Mic. 7:18–20). These promises include their salvation (Rom. 9–11; Jer. 31:31–34), their restoration to Palestine (Deut. 30:1–10; Ezek. 36:16–38; 37:15–28), with David as their king (2 Sam. 7:16; Ezek. 34:23–24; 37:24–25).[21]

The Visitation of God's Wrath upon Wicked Gentiles (Isa. 13:9–13; 26:21)

In the past, God used Gentiles to chasten disobedient Israel (2 Kings 17:5–18; Isa. 10:5–18). But when these nations were satanically motivated with hatred and credited their victories to their pagan deities, they, too, incurred God's wrath and became subject to His judgments. During the Tribulation Age, God is going to use the nations' intense persecution of Jews, under the leadership of Satan, to bring the elect remnant of Israel to repentance. Then He will pour out the woeful expressions of His wrath upon these Gentiles for their abusive treatment of Israel and for their unprecedented wickedness (Isa. 13:11; Ezek. 38:16–39:7; Zech. 12:9; Rev. 6:1–17; 8:7–13:18; 16:1–21; 19:11–20:3).

THE DURATION OF THE TRIBULATION AGE

Q24   According to the pretribulational rapture view, which I hold, the Tribulation Age will extend from the Church's rapture to and including the Battle of Armageddon, which immediately follows the Lord's second coming to earth. This age consists of both unknown and known quantities of time.

An unknown quantity of time exists between the Church's rapture and the Beast's confirmation of a peace treaty with Israel. According to 2 Thessalonians 2:3, I understand the revelation of the Beast out of the sea (Satan's earthly human agent) to be the beginning of his biblical prophetic career. According to Daniel 7:23–24, he will begin to fulfill biblical prophecy by gaining the leadership of a Middle East ten-nation federation. At this time he will confirm an existing treaty that assures Israel's living at peace with her Arab or Muslim neighbors. How much time these events will take is not revealed.

The known quantity of time is indicated by the "seventieth week" of Daniel 9:24–27, which begins with the Beast's confirmation of this peace treaty with Israel and will span seven years (see Appendix G: "An Analysis of Daniel 9:24–27"). Thus the Tribulation Age will continue a little more than seven years.

THE MINISTRIES DURING THE TRIBULATION AGE

There are two ministries during this age: the ministry of the 144,000 evangelists and that of the two witnesses.

Q25   *The Ministry of the 144,000 Evangelists During the First Half of the Tribulation Age*

1. The message

This will be the gospel of the kingdom (Matt. 24:14). It will be the same gospel message that is preached today (Acts 20:25; 28:31), with additional emphasis on the Lord's imminent return to establish His earthly kingdom and the need to prepare for this event (Matt. 24:42–44). Keep in mind that salvation is always by God's grace through faith in Jesus and His atoning work (Eph. 2:8–9; John 3:16) and that entrance into God's kingdom is by the new birth (John 3:3, 5). People will be saved during the Tribulation Age in the same way that they are now.

The Lord did not contradict the grace principle of salvation when He declared the need for gospel believers to endure to the end (Matt. 24:13). He seemed to say that all who are truly saved will remain faithful to Him unto their death or unto His second coming, when they will be delivered from their enemies. All who abandon their professed faith in Christ, that they might avoid persecution and martyrdom, will show by this that they were never really saved. True gospel believers persevere in their salvational faith, regardless of their circumstances, for this is maintained by the Lord Jesus (1 Peter 1:5; cp. Luke 22:31–32; Heb. 7:25).

2. The messengers

This worldwide gospel ministry will be led by 144,000 saved Israelites (Rev. 7:4–8), who have the (gospel) testimony of Jesus (12:17). Regarding their spiritual state, they are

WHO WITNESSES TO THEM ? SEE P.444-BOTTOM

described as being "redeemed" and "the firstfruits unto God," that is, the first to be saved during the Tribulation Age (14:4; cp. Rom. 16:5; 1 Cor. 16:15). If they had been saved earlier, they would have been raptured with the Church. They also are morally upright (Rev. 14:4), being "virgins," that is, not defiled by the gross moral and religious impurity of this time (9:20–21). Being God's slaves, they are sealed to indicate their divine owner-ship and to immunize them against the divine judgments of the age (7:1–3; 14:1; cp. 2 Tim. 2:19; Matt. 27:66). But with the rise to world power of Satan's human agent, the Beast out of the sea, in the middle of the "seventieth week," these evangelists will be the first to be martyred at his hand (Rev. 12:17; 13:7; 14:1–3). There will be no further need for their ministry, for all earth dwellers will be required to follow the Beast or be slain. Those who choose to follow the Beast will, by this, commit an unforgivable sin and will place themselves beyond any hope of salvation (2 Thess. 2:8–12; Rev. 14:9–11).

3. *The gospel harvest*

Although it is not explicitly stated, the fact that Revelation 7:9–17 so closely fol-lows the description of the 144,000 evangelists (vv. 1–8) suggests that the passage is speaking about the people who will respond favorably to this evangelistic ministry. They are described as being "a great multitude," who acclaim that salvation is by their God (v. 10, "by" of instrumental agency rather than "to") and who "are coming out of the great tribu-lation" (vv. 13–14, Gk.). Their wearing white robes indicates that they are overcomers (3:5), apparently the later martyrs of the second half of the Tribulation Age (6:10–11; cp. 12:11; 13:7, 15; 15:2; 20:4). Very few saved people will escape the Beast's worldwide purge. But those who do will enter the millennial kingdom in their unsaved bodies and will repopulate the earth (Jer. 30:19–20; Ezek. 47:22). Meanwhile, the martyrs will enjoy unearthly blessings in God's presence in heaven (Rev. 7:15–17).

All who reject the gospel ministry during the first half of the Tribulation Age will come under the divine judgment of believing Satan's lie during the second half (2 Thess. 2:11–12). Many students of prophecy believe that the apostle Paul was speaking about people who reject the gospel during the present Church Age and who, entering the Tribu-lation Age, will not be able to trust in Jesus for salvation at that time. But this interpre-tation of the passage ignores the context. The apostle was writing about the career of the Beast when, with the Devil's authority, he rules over the earth during the second half of the Tribulation Age (vv. 4–10). Those who reject the gospel ministry of the 144,000 evangelists will come under God's judgment (vv. 11–12). They will be led to believe "the lie," propagated by the Beast's lieutenant, the False Prophet (Rev. 13:11–17). Those who receive the Beast and his false doctrine will forfeit any further opportunity to be saved (2 Thess. 2:12; Rev. 14:8–11).

The Ministry of the Two Witnesses During the Second Half of the Tribulation Age Q26

The Beast will not allow any gospel ministry during the three and a half years of his worldwide rule (cp. Rev. 12:17; 13:5–6). But God will not be without a witness to Him-self. He will appoint two humans who, divinely sustained and gifted, will bear witness to His existence and judicial activity during this time of unprecedented blasphemy and wickedness (11:1–3).

1. *The identity of the two witnesses*

The Scriptures symbolically represent these witnesses as "olive trees" and "lampstands" (Rev. 11:4). These metaphors may emphasize that their ministry is of the Holy Spirit and convey God's revelation in a dark place. Their standing before God points to their being His servants (cp. Zech. 4:14; 1 Kings 17:1). The fact that they die (Rev. 11:7)

WHY IF All HAVE By Now ACCEPTED
OR REJECTED CHRIST?

indicates that they are human, but what their names are is not revealed. Some have suggested Enoch and Elijah, for they never died (Gen. 5:24; 2 Kings 2:11).

2. *The ministry of the two witnesses*

These men are witnesses and prophets (Rev. 11:3). *As God's witnesses* they will constantly testify to His existence and to man's duty to honor Him. This will be especially suitable at this time, for the Beast will try to remove every evidence of God's existence from the earth (Dan. 7:25; Rev. 13:5–6). *As God's prophets* these men will convey God's message to the world at a time when the Scriptures will be banned. Presumably, they will cry out against the gross blasphemies and wickedness of the day and will identify the frightful adversities, suffered by earth dwellers, as visitations of divine wrath. Perhaps, they will also warn the world of Christ's imminent return.

Q27 These men will not preach the gospel, since everyone will have responded to the evangelistic ministry of the 144,000 evangelists and to Satan's lie (Rev. 13:5–7; 2 Thess. 2:11–12). Those who embrace this lie (the Beast and his image) will, by this, commit an unforgivable sin and will forfeit all possibility of being saved (2 Thess. 2:9–10; Rev. 14:9–11).[22]

Energized with the Holy Spirit, these men will exercise superhuman powers that will be shown by their self-preservation (Rev. 11:5), their doing miracles (v. 6), and their effective ministry (v. 10). When their work is done, God will allow them to be slain by the Beast (v. 7). Then, after three and a half days, they will be resurrected and will be translated to heaven (vv. 11–12). The ministry of these men will continue for three and a half years, or during the second half of the Tribulation Age, during the time that Satan's human agent will have world authority (v. 3; 13:5).

THE GOSPEL BELIEVERS OF THE TRIBULATION AGE ✓ *JEWS ONLY?*

As we noted earlier, many people will respond favorably to the preaching of the 144,000 evangelists and will be saved (Rev. 7:9–14). Baptized by the Holy Spirit into Christ (Gal. 3:27), not into His mystical body, the Church, they will partake of His righteousness, sanctification, and redemption (1 Cor. 1:30); hence, they are called "the righteous" (Matt. 25:37), "saints," or "holy ones" (Rev. 13:7), and "redeemed" (5:9). Having the Holy Spirit, they will remain loyal to Jesus unto death (12:11). Moreover, they will have the Bible for their instruction and direction (cp. v. 17; Matt. 24). Since there is no indication of any new revelation being given during this time, it appears that these gospel believers will live under the Dispensation of Grace, given in the New Testament. Their salvational faith in Jesus will be manifested by their good works, or doing God's will (Matt. 25:34–40; cp. James 2:18, 26).

THE DIVINE JUDGMENTS OF THE TRIBULATION AGE

Q28 The Lord will send upon wicked earth dwellers three series of unprecedented judgments during this age. This will be for their gross sins, their defiance of God, and their persecution of His people, both Israel and saved Gentiles (Isa. 13:11; 26:20–21). With all of these judgments being expressions of divine wrath (Rev. 15:1), they will bring unprecedented suffering to wicked mankind (cp. Matt. 24:21–22).[23] The first two series, save the seventh Trumpet Judgment, occur during the first half of the Tribulation Age; the seventh Trumpet Judgment and the Bowls of Wrath take place during the second half of this age. How long these judgments continue is not always clear. The record of these judgments is introduced by the apostle John's seeing God's judgment throne set up (Rev. 4:2) and the Lord Jesus installed as judge (5:2–7).

THE FIRST SERIES, *Released by Unrolling a Scroll and Breaking Its Seals (Rev. 6:1–17; 8:1)*

Seal One (6:1–2): The rider on a white horse

Taking place at the start of the Tribulation Age, this judgment seems to refer to the beginning of the Beast's prophetic political career, when by military conquest he will gain control of a Middle East ten-nation federation (Dan. 7:7–8, 24; 8:9; 11:21–35). This will upset the political-military equilibrium of the Middle East.

Seal Two (6:3–4): The rider on a red horse

This represents the conflict that will be triggered by the Beast's political conquest. See verse 8 for the magnitude of this war.

Seal Three (6:5–6): The rider on a black horse

This represents the famine that results from this conflict.

Seal Four (6:7–8): The rider on a green (KJV "pale") horse

This represents the death that this war will inflict by arms, disease, famine, and animals and/or insects, with "death" claiming the body and "hades" claiming the soul and personhood. Death will exert itself over a fourth of the earth (Matt. 24:6–7).

Seal Five (6:9–11): The early martyrs

This is a vision of the godly people who will be slain for Jesus' sake in the first half of the Tribulation Age (cp. Matt. 24:9–10). Standing before God's heavenly throne, they call for divine vengeance on their enemies. They are told to rest until the remainder of God's people are martyred, apparently during the second half of this age (Rev. 13:7, 15).

Seal Six (6:12–17): A vision of the time of their vengeance

God grants the martyrs' request with a preview of the events that are portrayed by this Seal Judgment. These revealed events will come to pass immediately before Jesus' second coming to earth (see Rev. 16:18–20; Matt. 24:29–30; Hag. 2:6–7). The Lord will avenge His people upon His return (Rev. 11:18; Zech. 14:1–3; Dan. 7:26–27).[24]

Seal Seven (8:1): The silence in heaven

This is a calm before the storm of the next series of judgments that will visit the earth.

THE SECOND SERIES, *Released by Blowing Trumpets (Rev. 8:2–9:21; 11:14–13:18)*

Trumpets were used in Bible times for signaling (Num. 10:1–10; cp. Matt. 24:31; 1 Thess. 4:16; 1 Cor. 15:57).

Introduction to this series of judgments (Rev. 8:2–6)

Following the Seal Judgments, the first six Trumpet Judgments will take place on earth in the first half of this age. The first four Trumpet Judgments affect a third of the earth, perhaps focusing on the Middle East. Being interpreted literally, we see that they affect various elements in nature and the people who are dependent upon them. The last three Trumpet Judgments are "woes," affecting the entire earth.

Trumpet One (8:7): Storm, destroying vegetation

This will destroy timber, fuel, and food.

Trumpet Two (8:8–9): Volcanic eruption, turning the sea to blood

Trumpet Three (8:10–11): Meteorite collision, contaminating fresh water

Trumpet Four (8:12): Curtailment of celestial light

Trumpet Five, or the First Woe (9:1–12): Torment of humans[25]

This woe will be inflicted by demons who are released from the Abyss (vv. 1–3). Having supernatural appearance (vv. 7–10), these demons will torture unsaved humans for five months (vv. 4–5, 10). People will seek death but will not be able to die (v. 6).

Trumpet Six, or *the Second Woe (9:13–21):* Slaughter of humans

This woe will be inflicted by 200 million demons who will be led by four fallen angels (vv. 14–15) and who have an unearthly appearance (v. 17). They will slay a third of mankind (vv. 15, 18). The first half of the Tribulation Age is hardly a peaceful time, as some teach, for the fourth Seal Judgment and the sixth Trumpet Judgment together will destroy half of the world population. Note the indifference of earth dwellers (9:20–21).[26]

Trumpet Seven, or *the Third Woe (Rev. 11:14–13:18):* Satan's world rule

There is first an introduction to this judgment (Rev. 11:15–12:17): *one,* heaven's anticipation (11:15–19) and, *two,* the heavenly signs (12:1–17) of the woman, Israel (vv. 1–2), and of the dragon, Satan (vv. 3–17). The seventh Trumpet Judgment (13:1–18) consists of Satan's activities upon his confinement to earth (chap. 12) during the second half of the Tribulation Age (11:14; 12:12). Revelation 13 gives the political entity, the Middle East ten-nation federation (vv. 1–2; Dan. 7:7, 23–24), and the men through whom Satan will rule over the earth—the Beast out of the sea (Rev. 13:3–10) and his deputy, the False Prophet (vv. 11–18).[27]

THE THIRD SERIES, *Released by Pouring Out Bowls of Divine Wrath (Rev. 16)*

This last series of judgments, described as bowls (KJV "vials") of God's wrath, will occur near the end of the Tribulation Age. These will be released by angels pouring out their contents on all who received the mark of the Beast (16:2b).

Introduction to this series of judgments (Rev. 15:1–8): (a) the martyrs' song (vv. 1–4) and (b) the preparation for these judgments (vv. 5–8).

Bowl One (16:2): Foul, painful ulcers (cp. Exod. 9:10)

Bowl Two (16:3): Coagulation of sea water

Bowl Three (16:4–7): Turning fresh water to blood (cp. Exod. 7:20)

Bowl Four (16:8–9): Increase in solar radiation

Bowl Five (16:10–11): Supernatural darkness (cp. Exod. 10:22)

Bowl Six (16:12–16): Drying up of the Euphrates River (cp. Exod. 14:21–22)

This is to prepare the way for the kings of the East. Their aim will be to attack the Beast (Dan. 11:44). But with Jesus' unexpected return, they will all end up in Palestine at the Battle of Armageddon (Zech. 12:2–3, 9; Rev. 19:17–21).

Bowl Seven (16:17–21): Earthquake and hail (cp. Exod. 9:23)

This judgment will include a great earthquake that splits "the great city" of Babylon, levels the cities of the nations (16:19; cp. 17:16–17; 18:8–10), and moves the islands and mountains (16:20). Also, there will be devastating hailstones, weighing 110 pounds each. Taking place immediately before the Lord Jesus' second coming to earth (Matt. 24:29–30; Rev. 19:11–16), this judgment will avenge the early martyrs of the fifth Seal Judgment, as shown in the sixth Seal Judgment (Rev. 6:9–17).[28]

So great will be the devastation of these judgments that, unless these days are shortened, no human life would survive (Matt. 24:21–22).[29] Still, as destructive and painful as these judgments will be, the wicked will not repent of their evil works (Rev. 9:20–21; 16:21). Their giving God glory (11:13) only indicates their acknowledgment that these judgments are from Him.

THE BEAST'S CAREER DURING THE TRIBULATION AGE

As I see it, the most prominent earthly human of the Tribulation Age will be Satan's agent, "the Beast," or "the Beast out of the sea" (Rev. 13:1–8), who is often called "the Antichrist" (1 John 2:18).[30] Other biblical designations for this person are "the Wicked One" (2 Thess. 2:8), "the Son of Lawlessness," "the Son of Perdition" (v. 3), "the Little

Horn" (Dan. 7:8; 8:9), "a King" (8:23), "the Prince" (9:26), "the Desolator" (one who causes horror) (Dan. 9:27), "the King of the North" (11:21–45), "the Abomination of Desolation" (Matt. 24:15), and "Gog" (Ezek. 38:2–3; 39:1). He is depicted by the king of Babylon (Jer. 25:12; cp. chaps. 50–51) and by the Assyrian (Isa. 10:5). For this study, see the chart, "The Prophetic Future," on page 552.

Q33   IS BARACKMAN TIMING THE RAPTURE?

The Beast's Activities During First Half of the Tribulation Age

It is very likely that this man is now alive, but we have no way of knowing who he is at this time. He cannot be recognized until he begins his prophetic political career (Dan. 7:23–24), after the rapture of the Church (2 Thess. 2:1–4). I understand the apostle's words "falling away" (v. 3, also meaning "departure") to refer to the Church's rapture (v. 1) rather than to a general, indecisive departure from orthodox doctrine. Paul seems to have in mind particular events that will mark the simultaneous beginning of the Day of the Lord and of the Tribulation Age. These events are the rapture of the Church and the revelation of the Beast, with his starting to fulfill the prophetic aspects of his career.

1. *The Beast's place of origin (Dan. 8:8–9)*

This prophecy concerns the future (vv. 17, 23a). The Beast (the Little Horn) will come from Babylonia, which once was in the northeastern quarter of Alexander the Great's empire, which fell to Seleucus. Today, this area is Iraq (see Appendix I: "Babylon").

2. *The Beast's political entity and his activities (Dan. 7:7–11, 19–28)*

Four kings, or kingdoms, will arise together in the Mediterranean basin (Dan. 7:3, 17, 23). In their description (vv. 4–7, 12), attention is given to the fourth beast, as follows:

a. *The Beast's political entity (Dan. 7:7, 19, 23–24a; Rev. 13:1–2)*

This will probably be a federation of ten Middle East Arab and/or Muslim states.

b. *The Beast's political activities (Dan. 7:8, 24b)*

By subduing three kings of the ten-nation federation, the Beast will gain control of the federation (Dan. 7:8, 24; 11:21–30a) and will become one of its seven successive leaders during the first half of the Tribulation Age (cp. Rev. 17:9–11). The Beast will then confirm Israel's peace treaty for seven years (Dan. 9:27; 11:30b; cp. Isa. 28:14–29; Ezek. 38:8). This confirmation will mark the beginning of the "seventieth week," or the final segment of the Jewish Age of 490 years (Dan. 9:24, 27; see Appendix G: "An Analysis of Daniel 9:24–27"). The Beast's political rise (7:8a, 24b; Rev. 17:17) will trigger international war (Rev. 6:1–8; see the first four Seal Judgments). He will be an unusual person with penetrating eyes and persuasive speech (Dan. 7:8b, see below).

3. *The Beast's death*

At some time during the first half of the Tribulation Age, the Beast will be killed "by a sword" (Rev. 13:3, 14, KJV "wounded to death" literally means "slain" as in v. 8; 5:6). Upon his assassination, he will descend to hades (the Bottomless Pit or the Abyss) to await his resurrection (17:8, 10–11). Meanwhile, the king (one of the "heads") of a member state of the federation will become leader. The "horns" are the individual rulers of the member states, or kingdoms, of the federation (vv. 9–12; Dan. 7:7, 24).

The Beast's Activities During Second Half of the Tribulation Age *Q29*

Near the middle of the Tribulation Age, Satan, "the god of this age" (2 Cor. 4:4) and "the prince of this world" (John 12:31), will be confined to the earth (Rev. 12:7–13). Angry and aware that his time is short, the Devil will try to exterminate the Jews and all who confess the name of Jesus and will seek to erase God's name from the earth. Furthermore, he will secure for himself the open worship of mankind, lead the world in unprecedented blasphemy and wickedness, and make a final stand against the Lord Jesus. To do these things, he will need a human agent through whom to work. This agent will be the Beast out of the sea, who formerly was a leader of the ten-nation federation during the first half of the Tribulation Age and who was killed.

1. The Beast's resurrection and world authority

Q30

After Satan's confinement to earth in the middle of the Tribulation Age, the Beast will be resurrected from hades. This apparently will be done by the Lord Jesus.[31] That the Beast will be raised to life (Rev. 13:3b, 12, 14, "became alive") is indicated in Revelation 17:8, 11 and in his being cast alive into the lake of fire after the Battle of Armageddon (Rev. 19:20; cp. Heb. 9:27). Satan will then do the following:

One, install the divinely resurrected Beast as the eighth and final leader of the ten-nation federation (Rev. 17:8–11, 13; 13:4–5; 11:7).

Two, give the Beast and his political base worldwide authority (Rev. 13:1–4; Dan. 7:7, 19–25) for forty-two months (Rev. 13:5; Dan. 7:25). Babylon, not Rome, will be Satan's and the Beast's capital of the world (Rev. 17:5, 18; cp. Jer. 50–51; see Appendix I: "Babylon"). Revelation 17–18 describes the city's character (17:1–6), its relation to the Beast (vv. 7–15), and its destruction (vv. 16–18), with the reactions of earth dwellers (18:1–19) and heaven dwellers (18:20–19:6).

2. The Beast's description

    a. *His having fierce looking face (Dan. 8:23; 7:20)*
    b. *His being blasphemous (Dan. 11:36; Rev. 13:5)*
    c. *His understanding the occult (Dan. 8:23) and worshiping Satan (11:37–39)*
    d. *His having superhuman powers (Dan. 8:24; 11:36–38; Rev. 13:4)*
    e. *His using deception to attain his goals (Dan. 8:25; 2 Thess. 2:9)*
    f. *His exalting himself and Satan (Dan. 8:25; 11:36–38; Rev. 13:4–8)*

3. The Beast's satanic activities (Rev. 13:4–7)

Being used by Satan to carry out the Devil's goals on earth during the second half of the Tribulation Age, the Beast will:

One, rule the earth for three and a half years (Dan. 7:25; Rev. 13:4–8).

Two, abolish all organized religion and promote the worship of Satan and himself (2 Thess. 2:4, 10–12; Rev. 13:4, 8). He will do this with the aid of his deputy, the False Prophet (Rev. 13:11–18, see below).

Three, speak great blasphemies against God and His institutions (Rev. 13:5–6; Dan. 7:25; 11:36).

Four, persecute God's people, both Christians and Jews (Rev. 13:7a, 15; 12:17; 11:7; Dan. 7:21; 8:24). Having agreed to Israel's peace treaty at the beginning of his prophetic political career (Dan. 9:27a), the Beast will be resurrected and will break this after Satan's eviction to the earth in the middle of the Tribulation Age (Rev. 12:7–17; Dan. 9:27b). The Beast will destroy the Jewish temple (Dan. 8:11–14) and will tread Jerusalem underfoot for forty-two months during the second half of the Tribulation Age (Rev. 11:2a). Because of Israel's sins (Lev. 26:14–39), including breaking their covenant relationship with God (Jer. 31:32; chap. 3; Hos. 2), the Lord will allow Satan to persecute the Jews through the Beast (Rev. 12:13–17; Zech. 13:8; 14:1–2; Joel 2:1–11; Matt. 24:21–22). However, the elect Jewish remnant (Rom. 11:5; Isa. 1:9) will be divinely preserved (Isa. 26:20; Rev. 12:14–16), will repent of their sins (Joel 2:12–20; Hos. 5:14–6:3; Deut. 30:1–3), and will eventually be restored to God (Ezek. 36:24–38). But those who follow the Beast will perish (Isa. 28:14–15; Ezek. 11:21; Rev. 14:9–11).

4. The Beast's deputy, the False Prophet (Rev. 13:11–18)

Although, at the beginning of his career, the Beast out of the sea will be closely associated with organized religion (Rev. 17:1–3), this will not continue. When he is resur-

BEAST   *P31*

rected and receives his worldwide authority, the Beast will be led by Satan to abolish all religion and to proclaim the Devil and himself as the sole objects of worship (cp. 2 Thess. 2:4). The False Prophet will help him with this.

The False Prophet, "the beast out of the earth" (Rev. 13:11–18; 16:13), will act as the Beast's minister of religion (13:11–15) and of economics (vv. 16–18). Also, endued with satanic power, the False Prophet will carry out the wishes of the Beast. Doing miracles, he will deceive the unsaved and will secure their allegiance for the Beast (vv. 4, 8, 14–15; 2 Thess. 10–12). He also will control the world's market and economy by requiring everyone to receive the mark of the Beast, without which they will not be able to buy and sell (Rev. 13:16–17).

The False Prophet seems to be a man whom Jesus will also raise from the dead, for he, too, will be cast alive into the lake of fire (Rev. 19:20; 20:10). Some think that this will be Judas Iscariot, the betrayer of Jesus (John 6:70; 13:27; 17:12).

5. The Beast's defeat

Near the end of the Beast's forty-two-month rule, God will bring about a revolt against his worldwide authority (Rev. 17:16–17). Babylon will be destroyed by her supporters (18:8), and uprisings in the north and in the east will trouble the Beast (Dan. 11:40–44; Rev. 16:12). The "King of the South" (Egypt) will attack the Beast (the King of the North). Insane with fury and frustration, the Beast will react by invading Palestine, with the armies of the rebellious nations at his heels (Dan. 11:45).

At this time, the elect remnant of Israel will repent and will turn to the Lord Jesus (Joel 2:12–20). The Lord will respond by His second coming to earth and arriving at Jerusalem (Deut. 30:1–3; Zech. 14:1–4; Rev. 19:11–16). Uniting under the Beast's leadership, the armies of earth will attack the Lord and will be utterly defeated (Rev. 19:19–21; 17:14). The Beast and the False Prophet will be cast alive into the lake of fire (2 Thess. 2:8; Rev. 19:19–20; Dan. 7:26; 8:25; 9:27; 11:45); their armies will be destroyed (Rev. 19:21; 14:19–20; Zech. 12:3–4; 14:12–15); and Satan and his demon allies will be confined to the Abyss in hades (Rev. 20:1–3).

ISRAEL AND HER ELECT REMNANT DURING THE TRIBULATION AGE

Her Covenantal Relation to God

Israel's major place in future events was determined by her past relation to God.

1. God's choosing them to be His special earthly people (Deut. 7:6–8; Exod. 19:5)

By the Mosaic covenant, God made certain promises to Israel (Exod. 19:5–6; Lev. 18:5), including their being His exclusive people, as He says, "You shall be a peculiar treasure unto Me above all people." Because the Mosaic covenant was a two-party working contract, both Israel and God had to fulfill their parts for these covenantal promises to be fulfilled or to remain fulfilled. Agreeing to this contract (19:8; 24:3, 7), the nation entered this relationship with God as His special covenant people.

2. The breach of this covenantal relationship

There was no doubt that God would fulfill His part of this contract (Judg. 2:1). However, Israel failed to fulfill their part by their insistent, adulterous relationships with the pagan gods of their neighbors (Jer. 3; Ezek. 20:1–32) and thereby broke the covenant (Jer. 31:32).[32] God first dealt with the northern ten tribes of Israel for forsaking their covenant relationship (Hos. 2:1–5; 4:12–13) by putting them away "by a bill of divorce" (Jer. 3:8). He gave them over to the Assyrians, who removed them from their land during 734–722 B.C. (2 Kings 17:18; cp. Deut. 28:64). Likewise, He later sent Judah and Benjamin into Babylonian captivity during 605–582 B.C. (2 Kings 17:19; 24–25), for they also "played the harlot" by

their idolatry (Jer. 3:8–10). Finally, they were dispersed by the Romans in A.D. 70 for rejecting Jesus and delivering Him to crucifixion (John 1:11; Matt. 23:23–39).

3. God's giving them great covenantal promises

Because, from time to time, God made gracious covenantal promises to Israel, it is
necessary that He fulfill these for His name's sake, or for the sake of His integrity (Ezek.
36:21–22; Num. 23:19). However, He cannot do this as long as the nation remains in
unbelief and in opposition against Him. A purpose for the Tribulation Age is to turn a part
of this nation, the elect remnant, to God so that He can keep His Word to them.

The primary gracious promises of God's covenants that He must fulfill to these people
are these: In the Abrahamic covenant, God promised Israel's existence and a land for an
everlasting possession (Gen. 15:5, 18); in the Palestinian covenant, He promised that when
Israel returned to Him, He would come and would restore them to this land and bless them
(Deut. 30:1–5); in the Davidic covenant, He promised Israel an everlasting king of David's
house (2 Sam. 7:13–16) and the permanent, peaceful possession of their land (v. 10); and
in the new covenant, He promised Israel forgiveness and restoration to a permanent relationship with Him as His wife (Jer. 31:33–34; cp. Hos. 2–3; Isa. 54). The Lord Jesus
mediated this salvational covenant by His atoning sacrifice so that it is now effective for
all who trust in Him as their Savior from sin (Heb. 8:6; 12:24).

God's Dealings with Israel During the Tribulation Age

After the Lord has completed His present work of building His Church, He will give
His attention to the restoration of the elect remnant of Israel to Himself and to the fulfillment of His covenant promises to them (Acts 15:13–18).[33] Although Israel dealt treacherously with God, "as a wife treacherously departs from her husband" (Jer. 3:20), through
His prophets God implored the nation to return to Him, saying, "For I am married to you;
and I will take you one of a city and two of a family and I will bring you to Zion" (v. 14).
To compel their return to Him, God will afflict them by the rod of the nations (30:1–7). He
will do this by Satan's human agent, the Beast, during the second half of the Tribulation
Age. Let us briefly consider the Beast's dealings with these people.

1. The Beast's agreement with Israel's peace treaty with her neighbors (Dan. 9:27a)

As we have seen, he does this at the beginning of his prophetic political career when
he becomes the leader of the ten-nation federation. This agreement will mark the beginning of the "seventieth week" of Daniel 9, or the last seven years of the Jewish Age of 490
years (vv. 24–27).[34]

2. The Beast's breaking this agreement (Dan. 9:27b)

This violation will occur after Satan's confinement to earth in the middle of the
Tribulation Age (Rev. 12:7–17). Because of their sins (Lev. 26:14–39), including breaking
their covenant relationship with God (Jer. 31:32; chap. 3) and rejecting His Son (John
1:11; Acts 3:12–15), Israel will be persecuted by Satan's human agent, the Beast (Rev.
12:13–17; 13:7; Zech. 13:8; Matt. 23:34–39; 24:21–22).

One: The Beast will break the pact by a military assault against Jerusalem (Dan. 9:27;
cp. v. 26; Luke 21:20; Ezek. 38:8–16a). This will mark the beginning of unprecedented
Jewish persecution, known as "the time of Jacob's trouble" (Jer. 30:7).

Two: The Beast will invade the Jewish temple sanctuary and will proclaim himself the
object of worship (Matt. 24:15; 2 Thess. 2:3–4).

Three: Stopping the daily sacrifice, the Beast will erect an image of himself in the
temple and will require the Jews to worship him and his image (Dan. 8:11; 9:27; 11:31; cp.
12:11; Rev. 13:14–15).

Four: The Beast will then destroy the temple (Dan. 8:11–14) and will make Jerusalem desolate (Dan. 9:9–26b; Matt. 23:38–24:2), trampling the city under foot for three and a half years, or forty-two months, during the last half of the Tribulation Age (Luke 21:20; Rev. 11:2).

Five: The Beast will slay many Jews and will lead others away captive (Dan. 11:31–34; Isa. 1:9; Jer. 30:7; Zech. 13:8; Matt. 24:21; Luke 21:21–24).

Six: Motivated by intense anger and frustration, because of the rebellion of nations in the north and east, the Beast will attack Jerusalem again at the end of the Tribulation Age (Dan. 11:44–45; Zech. 12:1–9; 14:1–3; Isa. 29:1–8; Ezek. 38:16b, 18; 39:2). This will lead to the Jewish remnant's repentance, the Lord's return to earth, and the Battle of Armageddon (Deut. 30:2–3; Ezek. 38:18–39:7; Rev. 19:11–21).

3. God's preservation of the elect remnant of Israel

God has chosen among the physical descendants of Jacob a remnant, or part, who are the true spiritual Israel (Rom. 9:6–13, 27; 11:1–5). Today, elect Jews who are saved are a part of the Church (Eph. 3:6; 1 Cor. 12:13). During the Tribulation Age, the remnant of Israel, which will be a small part of the total world population of Jews (Isa. 1:9), will comprise two small groups of Jews: a few homeland Jews (Matt. 24:16–22) and some Jews who are dispersed throughout the world (Isa. 11:10–12; Jer. 23:31; 31:7–8). Although the 144,000 Israelite evangelists will be martyred (Rev. 12:17; 14:1–3), the Jewish remnant will be divinely preserved from Satan's wrath and will be alive when the Lord Jesus returns to earth (12:13–16; Matt. 24:22, 31).

The Lord Jesus spoke of God's care of this remnant during this period as follows:

One: The Lord gave two signs that will signal the Beast's breaking his agreement with Israel and the time for the remnant to flee from Palestine. These signs will be the Beast's attack against Jerusalem (Luke 21:20–24) and his desecration of the Jewish temple (Matt. 24:15; see "The Beast's breaking this agreement" above).

Two: The Lord gave instructions for the homeland remnant to flee when these signs occur (Matt. 24:16–22; Luke 21:21–24). The Scriptures indicate that the Lord will provide them with shelter and staples beyond the reach of their enemies (Rev. 12:14–16; Isa. 16:4; 26:20).

Three: The Lord also instructed the remnant to ignore any rumor of His coming (Matt. 24:23–28). The "flood" (Rev. 12:15) may be Satan's use of his false prophets to spread untrue reports of Christ's return so as to lure the remnant from their hiding places. Jesus declared that His coming would be so spectacular that no announcements of His arrival would be necessary, for His coming would be known by everyone (Matt. 24:27; Rev. 1:7).

4. The repentance of the elect remnant of Israel

Although a judicial blindness rests upon Israel today because of their persistent unbelief (Matt. 13:13–15; John 12:37–41; Rom. 11:25; 2 Cor. 3:6–18), God will lift this blindness from the hearts of the elect remnant, will give them the Spirit of repentance, and will save them from their sins and their enemies (Rom. 11; Isa. 1:9; 10:20–22; 11:11–18; Jer. 23:3–4; Joel 2:12–18; Zech. 12:10). "In their affliction they will seek Me [God] early, saying, 'Come let us return unto the LORD, for He has torn and He will heal us'" (Hos. 5:15–6:1). "She [Israel] shall follow after her lovers, but she shall not overtake them. . . . Then she shall say, 'I will go and return to my first husband, for then was it better with me than now'" (2:7). God said, "I will allure her and bring her into the wilderness and speak comfortably unto her" (v. 14). "'And it shall be in that day,' says the LORD, 'that you shall call Me Ishi (my Husband)'" (v. 16). He also said, "I will betroth you unto Me in faithfulness and you shall know the LORD" (v. 20). "And I will say to them which were not My people, 'You are My people'; and they shall say, 'You are my God.'" (v. 23). [35] This repentance will allow the Lord to return to earth, to deliver His people from their enemies and restore them to their land, and to establish His earthly kingdom (Deut. 30:1–5; Zech. 13:8–14:5).

Q39
Current Events That Relate to Israel in the Tribulation Age

1. The establishment of the State of Israel on May 14, 1948

Ezekiel saw Israel reassembled without spiritual life (Ezek. 37:1–8). The formation of the State of Israel was necessary for the fulfillment of prophecy, especially that relating to the Tribulation Age. In 1995, about 4.4 million Jews lived in Israel; about 8.5 million Jews lived outside of Israel with 5.6 million in the United States, 530,000 in France, 410,000 in Russia, 350,000 in Canada, and 300,000 in the United Kingdom. Two million Jews were religious, or belonged to a synagogue, 6 million were ethnic, 4 million had some cultural tie, and 1 million followed Jewish law but were otherwise secular. Large numbers are returning to Israel yearly. The two great transfers of Jews in our time are from Arab countries and from the Soviet Union. However, Israel is still alienated from God.

2. The peace treaty between Israel and her Arab and/or Muslim neighbors

Again, Ezekiel saw Israel living in unwalled villages, which indicated their living in peace among their Middle East neighbors (Ezek. 38:8, 11, 14). That a peace accord is imperative to Israel's future is indicated by the fact that the 4.4 million Jews in Israel are surrounded by 130 million Muslims.

The first to agree to a treaty of peace with Israel was Egypt in 1979. However, of greater consequence was the breakthrough between Israel and the Palestinian Liberation Movement, beginning in 1993, which eventually allowed the Palestinian Arabs self-government. This was followed by Jordan and Morocco in 1994. Despite satanic efforts to block the peace process and even to destroy it, this agreement will be reached by Israel with others of her neighbors in God's time. It is to this treaty that the Beast will agree at the beginning of his prophetic political career (Dan. 9:27).

3. The preparation for the rebuilding of the Jewish temple in Jerusalem

The Jewish temple must be in place by the middle of the Tribulation Age (Dan. 8:11, 13; Matt. 24:15; 2 Thess. 2:4). Presently, everything is ready for constructing a temple, installing a priesthood, and resuming the Levitical offerings (Hos. 3:4–5). The Temple Mount Faithful (nine thousand members), a movement led by Gershon Salomon, is ready to lay a four-ton foundation stone for the third temple. However, the temple site at Jerusalem is now under Arab control. It remains unknown how Israel will gain permission to build on the site, which now has the Arab's Haram-al-sharif (a mosque) and the Dome of the Rock, the third most sacred spot in Islam. From this site, Muhammad was supposed to have been translated to heaven for three days.

Certainly, God has not cast away His people but has a glorious future planned for them. However, to prepare Israel for this future, they must be subjected to His corrective discipline so that they will turn their hearts to Him. In these momentous times, we should be praying for the peace of Jerusalem and for the Jews' change of heart that will lead them to say, "Blessed is He [the Messiah] who comes in the Name of the Lord" (Ps. 122:6; Matt. 23:39).

THE PROPHECY OF JESUS' SECOND COMING TO EARTH

The Lord Jesus' second coming, often called His second advent, is His returning to earth again and staying here as He did almost two thousand years ago. Let us consider several features relating to this important event.

JESUS' RETURN FOR HIS CHURCH AND HIS SECOND COMING CONTRASTED

We must distinguish between our Lord's return for His Church and His second coming to earth. His return for the Church is not an advent to earth or a part of His second coming. Consider the following contrasts between these events:

One: His return for His Church is called "the Rapture," for the Church will be caught away (1 Thess. 4:17). His second coming is called "the revelation," for at that time He will reveal Himself to the world (2 Thess. 1:7; 1 Peter 1:13).

Two: When He returns for His Church, He will come to the earth's atmosphere (1 Thess. 4:17). In His second coming, He will arrive at the Mount of Olives, east of Jerusalem (Zech. 14:4).   Q 40

Three: He will return *for* His Church (2 Thess. 2:1). In His second coming He will come *with* His Church (1 Thess. 4:17).

Four: His return for the Church will occur quickly and secretly (1 Cor. 15:51; Rev. 22:12). His second coming to earth will take place suddenly, openly, and spectacularly (Matt. 24:27; Rev. 1:7).

Five: The Church's rapture will be signaled by trumpet blasts (1 Thess. 4;16; 1 Cor. 15:52) while the Lord's second coming will be attended with convulsions in nature and distress of nations (Matt. 24:29–30; Luke 21:25–27).

SEVERAL FACTS ABOUT JESUS' SECOND COMING TO EARTH

Its Time (Matt. 24:29–30)

The Lord's second coming to earth will occur at the close of the Tribulation Age. The Battle of Armageddon, which immediately follows His return, will be the final event of this age.

Its Attending Phenomena (Matt. 24:29)

The heavens and the earth will be shaken and men's hearts will be seized with fear (Rev. 6:12–17; 16:20; Luke 21:25–26). Celestial bodies will not give their light, meteorites will fall to the earth, and the sky will be swept away like the rolling up of a scroll.

Its Manner (Matt. 24:30)

The Lord Jesus will come personally (Matt. 24:30), bodily (Rev. 19:11–16), openly (Matt. 24:27; Rev. 1:7), powerfully (2 Thess. 1:7; Rev. 19:14–15), and gloriously (Matt. 24:30; Mark 8:38; 2 Thess. 1:10; Rev. 19:16). The world has not seen Him since He hung upon the cross. His coming with power and glory will send shock waves throughout mankind (Rev. 1:7).

The Lord will have a striking appearance (Rev. 19:11–16). His fiery eyes of penetrating omniscience and holiness (Col. 1:19), His crowns of universal authority (Matt. 28:18), His bloody garments of conquest (Isa. 63:1–6; Rev. 19:15), His verbal sword of judicial destructiveness (2 Thess. 2:8; Heb. 4:12; John 12:48; Rev. 1:16), and His radiant glory (Matt. 24:30) will combine to terrify His enemies and overpower all opposition against Him (Rev. 6:16–17).

Its Company (Rev. 19:14)   Q 40

There will come with the Lord Jesus his holy angels (2 Thess. 1:7; Matt. 24:31), His bride (the Church) (John 14:3; 1 Thess. 4:17b; Col. 3:4), and the disembodied precross saved people and saved Tribulation Age martyrs, who will be reunited with their changed bodies upon their resurrection (cp. Luke 13:28–29; Rev. 20:4).

THE PURPOSE OF JESUS' SECOND COMING TO EARTH

Upon His second coming to earth, the Lord Jesus will complete the messianic work that He was commissioned by God the Father to do (cp. Rev. 11:15–18). This work will include:

One, His dealing with His longtime enemy, Satan (Gen. 3:15), and with those demonic and human allies of Satan who oppose Him (Rev. 19:17–20:3; Matt. 25:41).

Two, His delivering His people from their enemies (Dan. 12:2–3; Zech. 14:3; Rom. 11:26) and His blessing them (Ezek. 36:24–30; Matt. 25:34).

Three, His establishing, as the Last Adam, the earthly millennial kingdom of prophecy and ruling for a thousand years for God's glory, until every enemy, including death, is wholly subdued (Heb. 2:5–9; Rev. 19:15; 1 Cor. 15:25).

All that He achieved during His first advent, especially by His death, resurrection, and subsequent exaltation, will be the basis of His work during His second advent to earth (cp. Heb. 2:14; 9:28; Col. 1:20).

THE EVENTS RELATED TO JESUS' SECOND COMING TO EARTH

Upon our Lord's return to earth, the following events will take place:

The Battle of Armageddon

The word *Armageddon* (Rev. 16:16) is from the Hebrew words *Har* (mount) and *Magedon.* The meaning of *Magedon* is uncertain, although some identify it with the site of Megiddo in Galilee. Upon the Lord's return to earth, the military might of the Beast and of the nations will unite against their common Foe and will attack the Lord at Jerusalem (Zech. 12:1–3; 14:4; Dan. 8:25; Zeph. 3:8; cp. Rev. 16:13–16). But their effort will fail, for they will fall by the Lord's word and will be destroyed (2 Thess. 2:8; Rev. 19:19–20; Zech. 12:1–4; 14:3, 12–15; Ezek. 39:3–7; Isa. 34:1–8).

The carnage of this battle is described as being like a harvest of grapes that are trodden in a winepress (Rev. 14:17–20). Blood will flow the length of Palestine, some 180 miles, to the depth of a horse's bridle, four to five feet. It is also described as "the supper of the great God," to which vultures will be invited to devour the carrion (19:17–18; Luke 17:34–37; Isa. 34:2–3; Ezek. 39:17–20). This battle will end all resistance to the Lord's establishing His authority over the earth. Not only will His human enemies be destroyed but also Satan and his demon allies will be confined to the abyss (hades) for one thousand years (Rev. 20:1–3; Isa. 24:21–22; 14:9–17).

Since the Lord will come to the Mount of Olives, east of Jerusalem, and will tread upon His enemies outside the city (Zech. 14:4; Rev. 14:20), it appears that this conflict will extend throughout Palestine, with Jerusalem as its focal point.

The Judgment of the Tribulation Age Survivors

After the Battle of Armageddon and the destruction of the world's military power, the Lord will send forth His angels to bring to Him all people who are still alive on earth (Matt. 24:31; Jer. 16:16–17). The purpose of this gathering is to determine who among surviving earth dwellers are qualified to enter His millennial kingdom. Only people who are born again will qualify (Matt. 7:13–14, 21–23; John 3:1–7; 6:29). To make this determination, He will judge both surviving Jews and Gentiles.

1. *His judgment of the Jews*

When He has gathered the surviving Jews together (Isa. 11:11–12; 27:12–13), the Lord will pass judgment on them (Ezek. 20:33–38; Mal. 3:1–6, 17–18). Those who are repentant and receive Christ as their Savior—the elect remnant (Hos. 5:15–6:3; Joel 2:12–18; Zech. 13:9; Ezek. 36:24–26)—will receive the blessings of the new covenant (Jer. 31:31–34) and will be restored to their promised land (Deut. 30:1–10; Isa. 10:20–30; 11:10–16; 43:1–13; Jer. 23:1–8; Ezek. 34:11–31; 36:16–38; 37:20–28; 39:23–29; see below). The apostate Jews who had embraced the Beast will be destroyed (Ezek. 11:21; 20:38; cp. Luke 19:27).

2. His Judgment of the Gentiles

The Lord's judgment of the Gentile survivors will be personal and individual, not national as the word "nations" suggests (Matt. 25:31–46). Again, the purpose of this is to determine who are qualified to enter His earthly kingdom (vv. 32–33). The "sheep," representing "the righteous," or saved people, will be qualified to enter. The "goats," representing "the cursed," or unsaved people, will not be qualified (vv. 37, 41).

What is it that will qualify one for entrance to the Lord's kingdom? A casual reading of Matthew 25:35–40 might lead one to believe that entrance is by good works, but this interpretation is contrary to the salvational principle of grace (Eph. 2:8–9; Titus 3:5; see "The Principle Involved in Salvation" under Soteriology). The works to which the Lord referred, indicate the presence of salvational faith (James 2:14–26; 1 John 2:29). As the Lord declared to Nicodemus, only born-again people qualify to enter His kingdom (John 3:3, 5). The salvation of these "sheep" will be manifested during the Tribulation Age by their treatment of the Lord's "brothers," that is, people who belong to Him (Matt. 12:49–50; Heb. 2:10–11). Only saved people will have the desire, love, and courage to give aid to those who suffer from their enemies for Christ's sake. The unsaved will not have this love (Matt. 24:10, 12).

The "sheep" will be invited to enter the kingdom, which has been prepared for them (Matt. 25:34). On the other hand, the "goats" will be banished from the Lord's presence (v. 41) and will die (cp. Rev. 19:21; Luke 19:27), to await their resurrection and final judgment (Matt. 25:41, 46). Those earth dwellers who are saved will enter the kingdom in their unredeemed bodies so that they might repopulate the earth. The children who are born to these people during kingdom days will have the inherent corruption of original sin and will need to be saved.

The Resurrection of Precross and Tribulation Age Gospel Believers

Since the precross believers and Tribulation Age martyrs are members of the Lord's kingdom (cp. Luke 13:28–29; 23:42–43; Matt. 8:11; Rev. 20:4; cp. Ezek. 34:23–24), they must be raised from the dead to share in His rule (cp. Rev. 20:4–5; Dan. 12:2–3,13; Isa. 26:19; John 5:28–29). These will have a part in the first (kind of) resurrection—that of saved people (Rev. 20:5–6).[36]

The Appraisal of These Gospel Believers

The Lord will not only determine who are qualified to enter His earthly kingdom but will also appraise the works of His people so that He can reward them. He will appraise and reward His people who survive the Tribulation Age (Matt. 16:27) as well as the precross gospel believers and the Tribulation Age martyrs, all of whom He will raise from the dead to enter His earthly kingdom (Rev. 22:12; Luke 14:14). These rewards will be the same as those given to Church believers, including positions of authority in the kingdom (Matt. 25:14–30; see "The Prophecy of Jesus' Appraisal of His Church" above).

The Marriage Supper of the Lamb

In Bible times, the wedding ceremony was very simple, but the wedding feast that followed involved several days of happy festivities. While the marriage of the Lord Jesus and His bride will take place in heaven (Rev. 19:7–8), the festivities celebrating this occasion will be on earth, after the Lord returns with His Church (v. 9). All the redeemed of human history, other than those of the Church Age, will be the invited guests (cp. John 3:29). Being on earth in their bodies, they will be able to participate in this celebration, which will include the consumption of food (Matt. 8:11; Luke 22:16).

The Restoration of the Elect Remnant of Israel

1. The basis of this restoration

The basis of this restoration to a renewed relationship with God will be the new covenant that God will establish with those people who turn to Him (Jer. 31:31–40; cp. Deut. 30:1–6). God states, "I will make a new covenant with the house of Israel and with the house of Judah . . . I will put My law in their inward parts . . . and I will be their God and they shall be My people. . . . for I will forgive their iniquity" (Jer. 31:31–34). "'My kindness shall not depart from you, neither shall the covenant of My peace [the new covenant] be removed,' says the LORD who has mercy on you" (Isa. 54:10). Despite Israel's breaking their first covenant relationship (Exod. 19:5) and God's temporarily putting her away (Jer. 3:8), He will forgive all who repent and trust in the Savior and will renew His nuptial relationship with them on the basis of the gracious, everlasting new covenant (Ezek. 34:11–31; 36:16–38).[37]

2. The outcome of this restoration

In addition to their being divinely forgiven and restored to their previous relationship with God, the repentant elect remnant of Israel will be restored to their land, will receive the fulfillment of God's covenantal blessings, and will be abundantly blessed of God (Deut. 30:1–10; Ezek. 20:33–43; 34:11–31; 36:16–38; 37:20–28; 39:23–29; Zeph. 3:11–20; Zech. 8:23; 12:10–13:1, 7–9). As the wife of Yahweh, Israel will be the leading state among the nations (cp. Hos. 2:7, 14–23; 3:1–5; Isa. 54; 60:1–3; 62:1–5; Zeph. 3:20), with Jerusalem as the world's capital (Hos. 3:3; Isa. 60; Mal. 3:16–17).

Having by His death and resurrection broken Satan's power, the Lord Jesus is presently waiting for the time when He can return again and take the command of earth, which Adam lost to Satan by his wrong choice (Heb. 2:5–9; 10:12–13). Let us consider Jesus' earthly millennial reign.

THE PROPHECY OF THE MESSIANIC MILLENNIAL KINGDOM

Any consideration of this kingdom[38] must distinguish between God's universal kingdom and the Lord Jesus' messianic mediatorial kingdom, the topic of our study.[39] God's universal kingdom, which is everlasting (Pss. 10:116; 74:12; Jer. 10:10), embraces all the things that are determined by His decree (Ps. 103:19; 1 Chron. 29:11–12; Eph. 1:11). While being a part of the Father's universal kingdom, Jesus' mediatorial kingdom is His rule as the Father's Viceroy, to bring God's enemies into subjection to His authority and to accomplish other divine objectives, which we shall later consider.

This rule was briefly realized in Adam before his fall (Gen. 1:26, 28; Heb. 2:5–8) and was later foreshadowed in the regional reigns of Saul, David, and Solomon over Israel (1 Sam. 9:16; 16:1, 12–13; 2 Sam. 7:8, 12–13; 1 Kings 1:13, 46–48; 1 Chron. 22:9–10). But God's revealed objectives for these reigns were not achieved because of the disobedience of Israel's leaders and their subjects (1 Sam. 15:22–23; 1 Kings 11:4; 12:19–20, 25–30; 14:21–24). Therefore, God spoke through His prophets about a time in the future when this kingdom would be established and governed by a perfect Ruler, and His laws would be written on the hearts of His subjects (Pss. 2:6–9; chap. 72; Isa. 9:6–7; 11:1–5; Dan. 2:44; Zech. 14:9–19; Jer. 31:33).

God the Son came to earth, received a human nature, and was anointed as man to be the Father's Servant, or Slave, for the purpose of achieving the divine objectives for the mediatorial kingdom (Isa. 42:1–7; 49:1–9; 52:13–53:12; 61:1–2; John 6:38; 8:28–29; Phil. 2:7–8). During His first advent, the Lord Jesus presented Himself to Israel for their acceptance or rejection. By His death and resurrection, He broke Satan's power over mankind (Heb. 2:14–15; John 16:11); and by His subsequent exaltation (Phil. 2:9–11), He laid the foundation of his future messianic work, including His mediatorial earthly kingdom. Take note that the Lord Jesus will rule over the earth by right of divine inheritance (Ps. 2:6–9; John 3:35), and He will rule over Israel by right of His human relation to David and His legal relation to Joseph, heir to David's throne (Luke 1:31–33; Matt. 1:16; see "Jesus' conception and birth" under Christology). Let us look more closely at His kingdom.

THE ASPECTS OF THE MESSIANIC KINGDOM   *Q45   Q46*

Presently, *in its visible form,* the Lord's messianic kingdom is nominally represented on earth by Christendom, which comprises all that bears the name of Christ in this world (Matt. 13, "the kingdom of heaven"). *In its real form,* the Lord's messianic kingdom presently is spiritual, nongeographical, and nonpolitical, embracing all who are saved, whether living or dead (Col. 1:13); see Appendix R: "The Kingdom of God."

In the future, the Lord's messianic kingdom in its real form will be political and earthly, embracing at that time the world's total population. Still, as we shall see, it will have spiritual qualities as well as physical features.

THE DURATION OF THE MESSIANIC KINGDOM   *Q45*

Upon His establishing His earthly kingdom at His second coming, the Lord's reign will continue for a thousand years (Rev. 20:1–7). When it has ended, His messianic kingdom will merge with the Father's universal kingdom (1 Cor. 15:24–28; Luke 1:33), and the Father and the Lord Jesus will rule forever. However, the Lord Jesus as man, being forever in subjection to the Father, will rule with the Father as His Subordinate, or the Father's Viceroy (1 Cor. 15:28).

THE OBJECTIVES OF THE MESSIANIC KINGDOM   *Q 47*

The Lord Jesus will complete the following objectives by His mediatorial rule:

The Dominion of the Earth and Its Creatures (Heb. 2:5–9)

The Lord Jesus will accomplish what Adam failed to do (Gen. 1:26, 28; Ps. 8; Heb. 2:5–9). He will rule the earth in a manner that will accomplish the divine objectives for His rule, will reflect God's wise beneficent authority, and will glorify the Father (cp. John 12:28; 17:4).

The Salvation of the Elect (John 6:37; 14:6; cp. Isa. 45:5–25)   ②

The final group of elect humans, born during kingdom days, will be saved (Isa. 49:6). Also, all the redeemed of mankind will experience the blessings of our Lord's earthly rule.

The Subjugation of All Rebels Against God (1 Cor. 15:25; Phil. 3:21)   ③

When He establishes His messianic kingdom, the Lord Jesus will cast Satan and his demon allies into the Abyss (Rev. 20:1–3) and will judge earth dwellers to determine who are qualified to enter His kingdom (Matt. 25:31–46). Unsaved people will not be allowed to enter the kingdom. Unsaved subjects, born during kingdom days, will be dealt with at the end of His rule (Rev. 20:7–9). Finally, being related to the unredeemed body, death and the sin force will be abolished with the physical change of saved earth dwellers to immortality and the resurrection of the saved and unsaved dead to incorruptibility (1 Cor. 15:25–26; James 1:15; Rev. 20:12–14).

4. The Restoration of the Earth to Its Primeval State (Col. 1:20)

When the Lord establishes His earthly kingdom, He will lift the divine curse upon nature that God imposed with man's fall (Gen. 3:17–19; Rom. 8:19–23; Isa. 11:6–9), will cleanse earth of its pollution, and will restore it to its original fertility and beauty (Isa. 35).

5. The Fulfillment of the Divine Covenant Promises (Num. 23:19)

As we have seen, most of these gracious covenantal promises were made to Israel (Rom. 9:4), including a land (Gen. 15:18; 17:8), their restoration to their land (Deut. 30:3–5), and their being governed by David's house (2 Sam. 7:16; Luke 1:31–33), never to be dispersed again (2 Sam. 7:10). God also promised to bring universal blessing through Abraham's Seed, the Lord Jesus, which earth dwellers will experience by His benefi- cent rule (Gen. 12:3; 18:18; 22:18). Finally, the true, saved Israel as well as saved Gentiles will enjoy the salvational blessings of the new covenant (Jer. 31:31–34; Heb. 12:24; 8:6).

It is noteworthy that the supreme goal of all that our Lord does in His messianic works is to glorify the Father (John 12:28; 14:13; 17:4; Phil. 2:8–11). This should be our goal as well in all that we do (1 Cor. 10:31).

THE CITIZENS OF THE MESSIANIC KINGDOM

When He sets up His worldwide kingdom, the Lord Jesus will allow only saved people to enter (cp. Matt. 7:21–23; 25:31–46; John 3:3, 5; Heb. 8:11). These people will include the risen, glorified gospel believers of other ages as well as the saved earth dwellers who survive the Tribulation Age. These survivors will enter the kingdom in their unredeemed bodies and will repopulate the earth (Ezek. 36:10–11; 47:22; Jer. 30:18–20; Isa. 65:20–25). Because of their having inherent corruption, children born to these people in kingdom days will need to be born again when they develop to the age of accountability. The decep- tive and rebellious character of sin will be revealed by the fact that many people will not trust in Jesus as their Savior for their salvation (Rev. 20:8–9).

THE ADMINISTRATION OF THE MESSIANIC KINGDOM

The Lord Jesus Christ will be the sovereign ruler of the millennial kingdom (Rev. 19:15–16; Isa. 9:6–7). His authority will be worldwide (Ps. 72:8–11; Zech. 14:9–19; Matt. 11:27; 28:18), with the seat of His government at Jerusalem (Isa. 24:23; 2:3; Zech. 14:16– 17; Matt. 5:35).

The Lord's administration will include David as the king of Israel (Ezek. 34:23–24; 37:24–25; Jer. 30:9), the twelve apostles (with Matthias replacing Judas Iscariot, Acts 1:15–26) as rulers of the individual tribes of Israel (Matt. 19:28), the apostle Paul as gov- ernor of the Gentile nations (Rom. 15:15–16), and the gospel believers of all ages holding lesser administrative positions as rewards (Rev. 2:26–27; 20:4; cp. Matt. 25:21; see "The Prophecy of Jesus' Appraisal of His Church" above). Apparently, angels will not have civil authority over earth dwellers.

The character of our Lord's rule will be unique to human history (Isa. 11:1–5). Possess- ing the Holy Spirit without measure (John 3:34), the Lord Jesus will not need human counselors or advisers. He will rule with wisdom, fairness, faithfulness, and severity, for the Holy Spirit, as now, will empower Him for all His messianic works (Isa. 61:1–2). Rebellion against the King will be dealt with directly and unsparingly (Isa. 65:20; cp. Matt. 5:29–30).

470

Q 50

THE BLESSINGS OF THE MESSIANIC KINGDOM

Our sinful, stressful world has long dreamed of an earthly utopia, but it has never been able to bring it about. However, "the zeal of the LORD" will achieve what sinful people cannot do (Isa. 9:6–7).

Its Spiritual Blessings

All who enter the Lord's earthly kingdom at its inception will be saved people, who will enjoy the things that accompany salvation (Jer. 31:31–34; Ezek. 36:26–28). The Holy Spirit will be poured out upon everyone (Joel 2:28–29), bringing them the blessings of His manifold ministry. At the start, everyone will "know" the Lord with that knowledge that springs from a personal relationship with God (Jer. 31:33–34; John 17:3). In time, however, people will be born, and these will be unsaved.

Its Ethical Blessings

With Satan and his demon allies confined to hades, there will be no outward temptation or cultural moral pollution on earth (Rev. 20:1–3). Yet, having the sin force, earth dwellers with unredeemed bodies will sin. Salvation through faith in Jesus will be available to the unsaved, and the means of cleansing from sin will be at hand for the saved (2:5; 1 John 1:9; cp. the sin-offerings of Ezek. 43:19–27).[40] The Word of the Lord will go forth from Jerusalem (perhaps by prophecy) throughout all the earth (Isa. 2:3; cp. Joel 2:28). It will be the standard of all moral judgments and values. It will be taught to children as well as to adults (Isa. 2:3; 54:13). Saved people will be motivated and enabled to obey the Lord (Ezek. 36:27; Jer. 31:33). Also, they will have keen moral discernment (Isa. 32:4–5: Mal. 3:18).

Its Social Blessings

All warfare will be permanently abolished (Ps. 46:9; Isa. 2:4; Mic. 4:3–4). Absolute social justice will prevail everywhere (Ps. 72:4, 12–13; Isa. 11:4). The helpless and the hopeless will be rejuvenated (Isa. 35:5–6), and all will be tenderly cared for (40:11; 42:1–4; Zech. 8:1–8). With the divine curse of Babel removed, there will be one universal language (Zeph. 3:9; cp. Gen. 11:1–9).

Its Political Blessings

Although Israel, the wife of the LORD (Yahweh), will be exalted above all other nations (Ps. 47; Isa. 60), the Gentiles will also be richly blessed (Rom. 11:11–12; Mic. 4:1–7). The King not only will make wise, impartial political decisions that will contribute to the good of all mankind but He will also be able to carry these through (Isa. 2:3–4; 11:2–5; Jer. 23:5–6). Nations will live together in perpetual peace and will enjoy unprecedented prosperity as long as they honor the King (Zech. 14:16–18).

Its Physical Blessings   _LIVE A 1000 YEARS?_

Everyone will enjoy health and long life, with saved people living throughout the millennium (Isa. 33:24; 35:5–6; 65:22). While earth dwellers will experience the natural events of procreation, birth, and development, they will not die unless they are incorrigible sinners, who refuse to submit to the King's authority (11:4; 65:20; Jer. 31:30). All unsaved people who are still alive at the end of the millennium will die in the final revolt (Rev. 20:7–9). Apparently, the hazards and diseases of our present human experience will not exist during kingdom days (Ezek. 34:23–31; Ps. 91:10–12; Isa. 11:9; 65:23–25).

With the Edenic curse lifted, desolate areas will be reclaimed and inhabited (Isa. 61:4), animals will be at peace with each other and with man (11:6–8; Hos. 2:18; Ezek. 34:25), and the land will be more productive (Isa. 32:13–15; 35:1–2; Ezek. 34:29; 36:4–11, 29–30; Amos 9:13). Thus, the drudgery of toil will be removed (cp. Gen. 3:17–19). There will be more rainfall and new water supplies in desert areas (Joel 2:23; Isa. 32:15; 35:6–7). Natural light will also be increased (Isa. 30:26; 60:19–20). The topography of Palestine (and possibly the whole earth) will be changed, with the Dead Sea's being fed and made to support life by a river flowing from Jerusalem (Zech. 14:10; Ezek. 47:1, 8–12; the "sea" of v. 8 is the Dead Sea; the "sea" of v. 10 is the Mediterranean).

THE WORSHIP DURING THE MESSIANIC KINGDOM

People will worship the Lord everywhere (Mal. 1:11), but formal worship will be observed in Jerusalem, the city of the King (Zech. 6:12–13; 14:16–17; Jer. 33:15–18).[41] The worship services at the temple will include offerings and feasts, similar to those of the Mosaic ritual (Jer. 33:18; Ezek. 43:18–27; 45:21; 46:4). Like the Lord's Supper, these offerings and feasts appear to have commemorative and symbolic significance, celebrating the various aspects of our Lord's atoning work and its benefits to the worshiper. They will remind worshipers of this redemptive work and of their duty to appropriate its value to their needs (cp. 1 Cor. 11:24–26; 2 Cor. 7:1; 1 John 1:9). There will be a priesthood, with the Lord Jesus as the High Priest (Heb. 5:5–6; Zech. 6:13). People who neglect the formal worship of the Lord at Jerusalem will be visited with divine chastisement (Zech. 14:16–19).

THE END OF THE MESSIANIC KINGDOM

Satan's Revolt

The Lord's one-thousand-year rule will close with a worldwide revolt, led by Satan upon his release from the Abyss (Rev. 20:7–10). As we have seen, people will be born during these kingdom years who will not trust in Jesus as their Savior from sin. At the close of this time, God will release Satan and his demons from the Abyss and will use them to sift out the unsaved people who are still alive on earth. Led by Satan, they will attack Jerusalem, where they will be slain with divine fire from heaven, and Satan will be cast into the lake of fire.

The reference to "Gog and [his people] Magog" (Rev. 20:8) seems to be speaking of the unsaved earth dwellers who participate in this final revolt. In my opinion, these names have no relation to the prophecy of Ezekiel chapters 38–39. They are used to describe those millennial rebels, who have the same evil force and character as the Beast (Gog) and his confederates, who invaded Palestine many years earlier in the middle and again at the end of the Tribulation Age (Dan. 9:26; 11:40–45).

This revolt will forever demonstrate two truths: One, the fact that unsaved people are incurably evil and are incapable of correcting their fallen spiritual state. Despite perfect government and temptation-free environment, they still need to be born again. Their depravity will be manifested in their revolting against the Lord, despite His just and beneficent government. Without the new birth, people remain sinners and outside of God's spiritual kingdom. Their inherent sinful disposition and character are the same as that of their spiritual father, Satan (John 8:44; Eph. 2:1–3). Two, this revolt will also demonstrate that God's calling to salvation is effectual in the sense that without it no one would be saved. Unsaved people do not naturally have the inclination and will to trust in Jesus and His atoning work for their salvation (John 5:40; 3:20; Rom. 3:11).

472

The Dissolution of the Universe

Immediately following this revolt and its judgment, God will bring about the dissolution of the present universe (2 Peter 3:10–13; Matt. 24:35; Rev. 20:11; 21:1). That this is a dissolution rather than a purging is indicated by the words "shall pass away" (2 Peter 3:10) and "were passed away" (Rev. 21:1) and by "melt," or "be dissolved" (2 Peter 3:10–12, literally, "be loosed" or "broken up"). Apparently, the present universe will revert to formless energy, with which God will make new heavens and a new earth (2 Peter 3:13; Rev. 21:1). Keep in mind that the sin force is not an inherent part of the present universe. It is presently confined to fallen angels and human earth dwellers.

With this dissolution in view, the apostle Peter urges his readers to live holy, godly lives, "looking and striving for the coming of the Day of God" with its "new heavens and new earth, wherein dwells righteousness" (2 Peter 3:11–13).

THE PROPHECY OF THE RESURRECTION AND THE JUDGMENT OF THE UNSAVED

The resurrection and judgment of unsaved humans will be the last part of our Lord's messianic work relating to the present universal order (Rev. 20:11–15; cp. 1 Cor. 15:25–26; John 5:28–29). This will also include His judging fallen angels, or demons (Jude 6; 1 Cor. 6:3; 2 Peter 2:4). Let us look at this judgment more closely.

THE SCENE OF THIS JUDGMENT (REV. 20:11)

With the heavens and the earth gone (Matt. 24:35; 2 Peter 3:10–13), we see a "Great White Throne," reflecting God's awesome majesty and consuming holiness. The occupant will be the Lord Jesus Christ, the judge of the universe (John 5:22; Acts 10:42; 17:31).

THE SUBJECTS OF THIS JUDGMENT (REV. 20:12–13)

They are called "the dead," although they have been resurrected (John 5:28; Acts 10:42; Rev. 20:5a). These are the unsaved who, being in their sins, are still spiritually dead toward God (Eph. 2:1; 4:18). Their personhoods and the immaterial parts of their human natures have been removed from hades and have been reunited with their resurrected bodies, which had been given up by the sea and the grave ("death" in Rev. 20:13). Regardless of their station in their former earthly life, they stand alike before the Lord with no place to hide.

The nature of the resurrected body of unsaved humans probably will be similar to that of saved people (Matt. 25:46, see "The Resurrection of Mankind" under Anthropology). Reorganized without the sin force and inherent corruption, these bodies with their occupants will be prepared to live forever in the lake of fire.

THE INQUIRY OF THIS JUDGMENT (REV. 20:12–13)

It will not be the purpose of this judgment to determine unsaved people's spiritual state and destination. These were settled during their earthly lifetime (John 3:36). However, having self-determination and moral awareness, all unsaved people will answer to the Lord for their behavior and will receive their just dues (Rom. 2:6).

The unsaved will be judged by the contents of books, of which there are three kinds (Rev. 20:12): one, those that have an accurate complete record of the total life behavior of these people; two, the Scriptures, which set forth the principles of divine judgments (Rom. 2:2, 6, 11), the absolute standard of moral behavior (3:20), people's basic duties to their Creator (Rom. 1:18–21; Acts 17:24–29), and the way of salvation (vv. 30–31; John 20:31; 2 Tim. 3:15); and three, "the Book of Life," which is the register of all who are saved (Rev. 20:15; Phil. 4:3; Rev. 3:5; 13:8; 17:8; 21:27; 22:19).[42]

With the record of their works opened before them, the unsaved will answer for the total output of their accountable lives—their deeds (Rom. 2:6), words (Matt. 12:36–37), thoughts (1 Chron. 28:9; Heb. 4:12), secrets (Rom. 2:16), motives (Heb. 4:12), omissions (James 4:17), attitudes (Eph. 5:3–6), and response to God's self-revelation (Rom. 1:18) by His works (vv. 19–20) and words (John 3:18; 5:45–47;12:48). Very likely, their memory will confirm the record as being true.

THE SENTENCE OF THIS JUDGMENT (REV. 20:12–15)

Since the sentence will be according to people's works (Rev. 20:12–13), each person will receive what is due him. Although all will share the same destination and doom (Matt. 25:41, 46), like people assigned to the same prison, yet there will be degrees in the severity of punishment according to the measures of guilt (10:15; 11:21–24; Luke 12:47–48; Rom. 2:5–6). This measure of guilt will be determined by the amount of light, or knowledge, a person has had of God's truth (2 Peter 2:21) and by the wickedness of his or her sin (Mark 14:21). While none will be guiltless (Rom. 1:18–20; 3:19), some will have sinned against greater light than others and some will have been more wicked than others. Thoroughly knowing all people and their life circumstances, the Judge will pronounce a just sentence upon each person (John 2:25; Rev. 19:11; Gen. 18:25).

Each one whose name is not written in the Book of Life will be cast into the lake of fire, which is called "the second death" (Rev. 20:14–15). People's first death ends their careers on earth, with the separation of their personhoods and immaterial human natures from their bodies (James 2:26). By this "second death," the unsaved will enter the everlasting state of absolute separation from God in unrelieved suffering and terrifying isolation (Matt. 25:46; 2 Thess. 1:9; Rev. 14:10–11).

The statement that "death and hades" (KJV "hell") will be cast into the lake of fire (Rev. 20:14) indicates that they will no longer be needed. "Death" represents physical death and the grave, the receptacle of dead bodies, while "hades" represents the receptacle of unsaved people's personhoods and immaterial human natures upon their physical death.[43] When the unsaved are resurrected, these receptacles will be discarded, and the last enemy, physical death, will have been forever destroyed (1 Cor. 15:25–26). Confined to the body (Rom. 7:17–18), the sin force within people ceases upon their physical death. Neither sin nor its fruit, physical death, will enter the eternal state.

THE PROPHECY OF PEOPLE'S FINAL, ETERNAL STATES

The Day of the LORD will end with the passing away of the present universe and the judging of the unsaved. This will be followed by the Day of God, which will continue forever (2 Peter 3:12; cp. 1 Cor. 15:28).[44] The eternal state, or people's everlasting existence, will begin with the creation of a new universe and its order (2 Peter 3:13; Rev. 21:1). Two aspects of the eternal state are the subjects of prophecy: the final state of the saved and that of the unsaved (Matt. 25:46). Let us look at these more closely.

THE FINAL STATE OF THE SAVED

Their Habitation

The saved will dwell with God forever on a newly created sealess earth (Rev. 21:1, 3). Their residence will be the New Jerusalem, which will descend from heaven to the new earth (vv. 2, 9, 10). Throughout human history, God's people have anticipated this city, which would give them a permanent, secure home (cp. Heb. 11:10, 13–16; 13:14; Rev. 3:12; John 14:1–3).

The apostle John described this city as being in the form of a cube (Rev. 21:16), with sides 1,380 miles long. It is made of pure gold (v. 18), surrounded by a jasper wall 216 feet high (v. 17). This wall rests upon twelve foundations, which are colorfully arrayed with precious stones (vv. 14, 19–20). The wall has twelve entrances, three on a side and each with a pearl gate (vv. 12–13, 21). Each gate is attended by an angel and has written above it the name of a tribe of Israel (v. 12). In the middle of the city, there is a wide central square (KJV "street") of pure gold (v. 21), through which runs the river of the Water of Life (22:1–2). This river flows from the throne of God to water the Tree of Life, which straddles it. Fed by the Water of Life, the Tree of Life will perpetuate forever the lives of all who eat of it (cp. Gen. 2:9; 3:22; Rev. 2:7). This city will have no temple building or external light (Rev. 21:22–23; 22:5), for God the Father and the Lord Jesus are its Temple and Light. The unholy (the unsaved) will never be allowed to enter its open gates (21:25–27), and there will be no night or curse there (v. 25; 22:3; Gen. 3:17).

Their Experience

If the presence of the Holy Spirit and the blessings of His ministries in our lives are a foretaste of our future (Eph. 1:14), what wonderful things God has prepared for His people (1 Cor. 2:9, 1 Peter 1:4)! The Scriptures reveal that saved people will have unrestricted fellowship with God (Rev. 21:3); that everything will be new (vv. 4–5); and that there will be absolute security (Heb. 12:28), greater knowledge (1 Cor. 13:12), rest from present trials and labors (Heb. 4:9; Rev. 21:4), endless pleasure (Ps. 16:11), loving companionship (John 14:3; 1 Thess. 4:17), the satisfaction of every desire (Rev. 21:6), and ceaseless worship (5:11–14).

This does not mean that eternity will be like a long church service. The phrase "the ages to come" (Eph. 2:7) suggests that the Lord and His people will be involved in new programs, or work projects, which have not yet been revealed. Having Jesus' kind of human nature, His people will be wholly occupied with His interests, will experience His emotions, will have His understanding and skills, and will be in perfect agreement with His decisions (see Appendix V: "The Human Body-Grid"). Also, the word "ages" indicates time. Being creatures, we shall always experience the time that is associated with the succession of events.

RECOGNIZE LOVED ONES ?

THE FINAL STATE OF THE UNSAVED

Their Habitation

After their judgment, the unsaved will be cast into the lake of fire (Rev. 20:15), or hell (Matt. 10:28; 23:33), a place originally prepared for Satan and his angels (demons) (25:41). Hell is described as a place of fire (Mark 9:43; Rev. 20:15), darkness (2 Peter 2:17; Jude 13), worms (Mark 9:48), and the awareness of God's absence (Matt. 7:23; 2 Thess. 1:9; cp. Matt. 27:46). Since the Beast, the False Prophet, and Satan will be cast into the lake of fire before the dissolution of the present universe (Rev. 19:20, 20:10; 2 Peter 3:10), hell must have existed before this event and will be divinely preserved from this universal dissolution.

Their Experience

The unsaved in hell will experience various kinds of mental and sensuous torments, including unfulfilled desires, loneliness, hopelessness, and restlessness. There will be conscious suffering and torment (Rev. 14:10–11; Rom. 2:8–9), crying and gnashing of teeth (Matt. 13:42), stark loneliness (2 Thess. 1:9), shame and contempt (Dan. 12:2), utter ruin (Matt. 10:28), and the terror of endless darkness (Jude 13).[45] There appears to be no social communication with others in hell. There will only be the terrible experience of God's perpetual wrath (Rev. 14:10–11; Rom. 9:22) and the sense of His utter abandonment (Matt. 7:23). *PHYSICAL SUFFERING ?*

Their Duration

Being condemned as sinners (Rom. 5:12, 19; John 3:18), the punishment of all unsaved people will endure forever (Matt. 25:46; 2 Thess. 1:9; Rev. 14:9–11). Their destruction (literally "ruin" as in 2 Thess. 1:9; Matt. 7:13; see endnote 45) will not be a loss of essential existence but of meaningful or purposeful existence, as in the cases of torn wineskins (Luke 5:37), lost coins (Acts 8:20), and used ointment (Matt. 26:7–8, "waste"). Their personal ruin, together with their punishment, will continue forever (John 3:16, 18; Matt. 25:46).

A growing number of evangelicals are embracing unbiblical, sentimental views about the eternal future of unsaved people, like the following: *One,* that unsaved people will be saved by believing what divine revelation that they have although this is not the gospel; *two,* that unsaved people, especially those who have never heard the gospel, will after death have opportunity to trust in Jesus as their Savior; and *three,* that the impenitent will experience annihilation and extinction rather than everlasting suffering.[46]

These human sentiments do not express God's sense of justice. God's redemptive love for the world was infinitely expressed by His giving His Son as a sacrifice for mankind's sins (John 3:16; 1 John 2:2; 4:9–10). For God arbitrarily to release responsible sinners from their penal obligation without their trusting in the Savior and His sacrifice is to violate justice, insult the Savior, and invalidate His atoning work. There is no biblical evidence that any morally responsible person will be saved after death (see "The Salvation of Infants" under Soteriology). Death ends a person's opportunity for acting upon the divine revelation about salvation. Beyond this life, there is only eternal judgment for the unsaved (Heb. 9:27). Now is the day of salvation, hence the urgency of evangelism (2 Cor. 6:2). *THOSE WHO HAVE NOT HEARD?*

RELEVANT QUESTIONS

One cannot reflect upon these final states without facing several questions.

How Is the Eternal Destiny of the Lost Compatible with God's Love?

God's attributes have their own areas of expression; therefore, His love cannot override His holiness and justice, which require the unsaved to pay the debt of their sins (cp. Luke 19:41–44). God the Father's gracious love was expressed to an infinite degree in His giving His Son for humanity's sins (John 3:16). All who reject this love must bear His wrath (v. 36). Keep in mind that this was not divine friendship love.

Will the Unsaved Eventually Be Annihilated?

No, they will experience everlasting existence and conscious suffering (Matt. 25:46; Rev. 14:11).

Will the Unsaved Eventually Be Saved?

No (Matt. 25:46). When he wrote about the reconciliation of all things unto God (Col. 1:20), the apostle Paul did not refer to the unsaved who are now under (within) the earth in hades.

How Can We Who Are Saved Be Happy When We Know That Our Unsaved Relatives and Friends Are Suffering in Hell?

Since we shall be like the Lord Jesus (1 John 3:2), we shall regard these people as He does. Our natural ties with these people will be severed (Rev. 21:4). We shall understand the enormity of their sins and shall accept God's justice in His punishing them as He does.

Will People Who Never Heard About Jesus Go to Hell?

Yes, for having and rejecting the continual witness of divine general revelation, they are without excuse (Rom. 1:18–20). Unsaved people are already condemned for their sins (5:18; 3:9–19; John 3:18). If people who have never heard the gospel would respond favorably to God's general revelation in nature and seek Him, in time they would be contacted with the gospel as was Cornelius, so they could be saved (see Acts 10). This is God's use of evangelical missions.

Do People Go to Hell Because of Adam's Initial Sin?

I believe not. While all people are condemned because of his sin (Rom. 5:18), it is my view that they who die before having moral awareness and the ability to respond to the gospel have divinely applied to them at death the value of Jesus' atoning work and are thereby saved (cp. Matt. 18:14; see "The Salvation of Infants" under Soteriology). People go to hell because of their actual sins, one of which is their rejecting God's self-revelation (Rom. 1:18–20). Anyone who desires in his or her lifetime to be saved may trust in the Savior and His atoning work, for He died for all mankind (John 3:16; 1 John 2:2).

Will People Continue to Sin in Hell?

I believe not. While the penalty of their sins will continue forever (Matt. 25:46), sin itself, as a force and as an action, seems to cease in humans with the death of the body, in whose flesh it is resident (Rom. 7:17–18). There is no evidence in the Scriptures that indicates that humans continue sinning after death. The changed attitude and concern of the rich man in hades is a striking example (Luke 16:27–30). People who are in hell will be wholly submissive to Jesus' authority (Phil. 2:11) and will accept the justice of their punishment (cp. Luke 23:41). Without the influence of external or internal temptation, they will never again rebel against God. The description of the lost in Revelation 21:8, 27 seems to refer to their moral character during their previous earthly lifetime, which will be on their record forever. This does not necessarily mean that they will continue to do these things forever. I do not see sin as an everlasting force, or principle. It had a definite beginning, and it will have a decisive ending.*

Needless to say, nothing can now be known of the eternal state apart from that which God has revealed in the Scriptures. He has given us all the information that we need to know at this time. The reality of these things so supersedes our present experience that more revelation would be of little value to us now. On the other hand, God has revealed enough to show the unsaved their need to receive the Savior and to motivate those of us who are saved to walk in His fellowship until He calls us to glory (Deut. 29:29; John 15:14–16).

If you should not be an authentic, born-again Christian, then it is urgent that you obey God's command to believe the gospel. This belief is more than an intellectual assent to facts about Jesus. It is decisively to trust in Jesus as your Savior from sin and to receive, by faith, God's forgiveness and gift of new life (1 John 3:23; John 20:31; see "The Sinner's Part in the Reception of Salvation" under Soteriology).

The Lord Jesus Himself declared the necessity of our being born again (John 3:7). In the context of His words, we find that there are two things that keep people out of heaven—their inability to go there of themselves (vv. 3–6) and their liability to God for their sins (vv. 9–12). Our natural birth equips us for life on earth, but it does not prepare us for life in heaven. We cannot physically leave earth and survive without some kind of earthly life-support system. By the new birth, God renews our personhoods and human natures (and eventually our bodies) so that His people can live with Him in heaven. Furthermore, in our natural state all humans are sinners and owe God the debt, or penalty, of our sins, which is death and hell (Rom. 6:23). There is no way that anyone can discharge himself from this obligation and live (Matt. 25:46).

In His great love and grace, God the Father sent His Son to earth to be our Savior (John 3:14–16). The Son took upon Himself a sinless human nature, allowed wicked people to crucify Him, and bore our sins while on the cross (1 Peter 2:24). Being made sin, He died for us, and His shed blood was divinely offered (2 Cor. 5:21; Rom. 5:8). His resurrection manifested His effectiveness in provisionally dealing with our sins and placating God's wrath against us (Rom. 1:4; 4:25; Acts 4:10–12). On the basis of His atoning work, God is now able to save all who places their trust in Jesus and His sacrifice for their deliverance from sin's guilt, penalty, ruin, and bondage.

We cannot reflect upon the everlasting destination of the unsaved without being motivated to share the gospel with our sin-ruined loved ones and acquaintances, to say nothing of strangers and the unknown masses beyond our doors and land. The apostle Paul was burdened for the unsaved and sought to persuade them with the gospel (2 Cor. 5:11; Rom. 1:13–16; 10:1). If we saw a child in the path of an oncoming vehicle, would we not, if at all possible, try to save that child from harm's way? May God give us the heart of our Savior, who came to seek and to save that which was ruined by sin (Luke 19:10), even at the cost of indescribable suffering and life itself! May we see the world with His eyes and weep over the unsaved with His tears (Luke 19:41). May we no longer be ashamed of the gospel, which is God's power unto salvation, but courageously, courteously, and joyfully share the good news with those around us and, if God so leads, in the vast regions beyond our narrow horizon. May we walk so close to the Savior that others will see Him in our attitudes, words, and actions and will desire to have His love, strength, joy, and peace in their lives.

Dear Christian reader, your days are numbered; at best, the time is short; the Lord is at the door. Give your heart to Him today, set your mind on things above, and be occupied with Him and His affairs in this world until He comes.

A Review of Eschatology

1. What are the two primary methods of interpreting prophecy?
2. Which method does the author prefer? Why?
3. What are several practical reasons for studying prophecy?
4. Why is it better to speak of Jesus' coming for the Church as His return rather than as His second coming?
5. Where are most NT details given of His return for the Church?
6. Where will the Church meet the Lord upon His return?
7. What blessed events will the saved experience when the Lord returns for the Church?

441 8. Describe the qualities and constitution of the gospel believer's changed body.

11 9. What features of Christ's glory will saved people share?

442 10. What inheritance will they receive? What inheritance do they now have?

442 11. What does it mean to enter eternal life?

12. Briefly explain the various views regarding the time of the Church's rapture as this relates to the Tribulation Age.

13. Why does the author prefer the pretribulation rapture view?

14. What impact should the prospect of the Lord's imminent return have on us?

15. Why must gospel believers appear before the judgment seat of Christ?

16. Where and when will this appraisal take place?

17. What will the Lord examine in our lives? What regulatory principles will He follow?

18. What description does the apostle Paul give of this appraisal in 1 Corinthians 3:13–15?

19. What do the profitable rewards appear to be? The unprofitable rewards?

20. How does our sinning affect our receiving profitable rewards even though we deal with these sins by repentance and confession?

21. What criteria will the Lord follow in this appraisal? How can this be helpful to us now? *452*

22. What is God's purpose for the Tribulation Age? *453*

23. By what three events will the Lord achieve this purpose? *453*

24. When does the "seventieth week" of Daniel 9 begin? What brings it to an end? *454*

25. When will the 144,000 Jewish evangelists minister? What is their message? *454*

26. When do God's two witnesses minister? What is the purpose of their ministry? *455*

27. Why do the two witnesses not preach the gospel during their ministry? *456*

28. Give the three series of divine judgments that will be released during the Tribulation *456* Age. When will these judgments occur? Which are expressions of divine wrath? *456* *All*

29. When will Satan be confined to the earth? *459*

30. What two humans will Satan use to carry out his earthly actions during the last half of the Tribulation Age? *460, 461* BEAST, FALSE PROPHET

31. Under Satan's direction who will be the world political leader? The religious leader?

32. What appears to be unusual about these two men? *460, 1* BOTH RESSURECTED FROM DEAD

33. Describe the career of the Beast out of the sea during the first half of the Tribulation Age. P.*459*

34. When will the Beast out of the sea confirm a peace treaty with Israel? Break this treaty? *459*

35. What Jews will Satan first slay after his confinement to earth?

36. Why does Satan not succeed in destroying the elect Jewish remnant?

37. What part does the False Prophet have in Satan's program during the second half of the Tribulation Age? What earth dwellers will refuse to comply with his orders?

38. What event will bring the Lord back to earth to deal with Israel's enemies? *464*

39. What current events relating to Israel today show the closeness of the Tribulation Age? *465*

40. To what place does Jesus come when He returns to earth? Who comes with Him?

41. What people are involved in the Battle of Armageddon? *466*

42. Who will win this battle? What will be unusual about this battle? *466*

43. What judgment will Jesus hold after this battle? What will be the purpose of this judgment? *466, 7*

44. What will the Lord do with the repentant remnant of Israel? *466*

45. Describe God the Father's universal kingdom and the Lord's messianic mediatorial kingdom. How long will each of these kingdoms last? *469*

FOREVER   1000 YRS.

MARRIAGE SUPPER OF THE LAMB

46. Describe the Lord's kingdom in its present form and in its future form. *469*
47. Give the five objectives for the Lord's earthly messianic rule. *469, 470*
48. What kind of people will the citizen's of Jesus' kingdom be? *470*
49. Give the administrative organization of the millennial earthly kingdom. *470*
50. Describe the blessings of the millennial kingdom. Describe worship in kingdom days. *471*
51. Why will people, born in kingdom days, need to be saved?
52. How will the Lord's messianic kingdom end? *472 REVOLT*
53. What will Satan's revolt demonstrate about people's need for salvation?
54. What will happen to Satan? *473*
55. When does the present universe come to an end? How will it end?
56. How will Jesus' rule be extended forever?
57. What is the purpose of the Great White Throne Judgment?
58. What is hades? What is the lake of fire? *474*
59. What will be the final habitation and experience of the saved?
60. What will be the final habitation and experience of the unsaved?
61. Why does the author think that people will not sin in hell?
62. How long will the existence of the saved and the unsaved continue?
63. What will be the experience of unsaved people throughout eternity?
64. How was God's love expressed for unsaved people?
65. How can a loving God allow unsaved people to suffer forever? *476*
66. What is your everlasting destination? Are you saved?
67. Are you warning others of this judgment? Are you working with Jesus in building His Church?

Endnotes

1. See F. H. Barackman, *How to Interpret the Bible* (Grand Rapids: Kregel Publications, 1991), 79ff.; Paul Lee Tan, *The Interpretation of Prophecy* (Winona Lake: BMH Books, Inc., 1974), and J. Dwight Pentecost, *Things to Come* (Grand Rapids: Zondervan Publishing House, 1965), 1–63.
2. This holds that there is perfect agreement in the Scriptures among the parts that comprise the whole revelation of divine truth. Because the whole revelation of a specific doctrine exceeds that which any single passage gives, we should seek to understand what all the Bible says about this teaching.
3. See the chart, "The Prophetic Future," on page 552.
4. I prefer to use the phrase, "the second coming," to refer to the Lord's second advent to earth, not to His coming for His Church. By His second coming, He will return to earth and remain for a while as He did long ago with His first coming. I also do not think of the Lord's return for His Church and His second coming to earth as two aspects of one event since these are separate events. The description of His second coming as having two parts belongs to the posttribulation rapture view.
5. Does the phrase, "the dead in Christ," include the Old Testament saved people who are now with the Lord (v. 16; see Appendix D: "The Ones Who Are in Christ")? Since these people are not part of the Church, it is more likely that they will be raised with the Tribulation Age martyrs when the Lord returns to set up His earthly kingdom.
6. According to Numbers 10:1–10, trumpets were used in Israel to call the people for assembly (vv. 1–4), for breaking camp and travel (vv. 5–6), for alarm (v. 9), and for the observance of religious events (v. 10).
7. See "The Resurrection of Saved People" under Anthropology.
8. The word *rapture* is from the Latin *rapere* meaning to seize, catch up, take away by force (Acts 8:39).
9. During the past century, adherents to the partial rapture view are R. Garret, G. H. Lang, D. M.

Patton, and J. A. Seiss; to the posttribulation view, R. H. Gundry, G. E. Ladd, J. B. Payne, and A. Reese; to the midtribulation view, J. O. Buswell, Jr., N. B. Harrison, and H. J. Ockenga; and the pretribulation view, J. D. Pentecost, C. C. Ryrie, G. B. Stanton, and J. F. Walvoord.

10. Marvin Rosenthal, *The Pre-Wrath Rapture of the Church* (Nashville: Thomas Nelson Publishers, 1990). For a refutation, see Paul S. Karleen, *The Pre-Wrath Rapture of the Church: Is It Biblical?* (Langhorne, Pa.: BF Press, 1991).

11. See John F. Walvoord, *The Rapture Question* (Grand Rapids: Zondervan Publishing House, 1964), 92ff.

12. This is testing for the purpose of approving (Gk. *dokimazo*). See Luke 14:19; 2 Corinthians 8:8; Galatians 6:4; 1 Thessalonians 2:4; 5:21; and 1 Peter 1:7.

13. The talents that were entrusted to these slaves were huge sums of money, which they were to use in a way that would bring their master a profitable return. A talent was worth about six thousand days, or twenty years, of wages for a common laborer. The Lord Jesus has given us the priceless "talents" of life, time, strength, opportunity, natural abilities, spiritual gifts, spiritual and material resources, and the like to be used as He directs for God's glory.

14. In Revelation chapters 2 and 3, the word "overcomer" has in view the Greek athlete who has won the contest. Contextually, this overcomer refers to the gospel believer who hears and comprehends what the Lord says by the Holy Spirit through the Scriptures and who obediently responds to His message. By the Lord's strength, the spiritual overcomer rises above the spiritual declension around him and keeps the Lord's works (does His will) unto the end (Rev. 2:6). The Lord's promises to the overcomer reveal much about the nature of rewards.

15. Harry Thurston Peck, ed., *Harper's Dictionary of Classical Literature and Antiquities* (New York: American Book Company, 1896), 159.

16. Unlike in competitive sports, all can win garlands in the race of the Christian life (1 Cor. 9:24). We are not contending against one another but against our spiritual enemies, which would use us for their evil expressions. Exercising holy self-control by yielding to God's control, the apostle Paul ran to win (1 Cor. 9:25–27; cp. Gal. 5:16, 21–22).

17. These do not include the judicial penalty of sin, which is hell and which Jesus bore for us.

18. All that is done apart from Jesus is unacceptable to Him, for it is sinful in His sight (John 15:5b; Rom. 14:23). Indeed, it is impossible for anyone to live the spiritual life without Him who is this life! See John 14:6; Galatians 2:20; and Colossians 3:4.

19. See the chart, "The Prophetic Future," on page 552; Appendix L: "An Outline of the Prophetic Chapters of Daniel"; and Appendix M: "An Outline of the Book of Revelation."

20. The Day of the Lord extends from the Church's rapture to and including the Great White Throne Judgment of the unsaved, which follows the Lord's millennial reign. For references to the Day of the Lord, see Isaiah 2:12; 13:6, 9; 34:8; Jeremiah 46:10; Lamentations 2:22; Ezek. 7:19; 13:5; 30:3; Joel 1:15; 2:1, 31; 3:14; Amos 5:18, 20; Obadiah 15; Zephaniah 1:7, 14, 18; 2:2–3; Zechariah 14:1; Malachi 4:5; 1 Thessalonians 5:2; 2 Thessalonians 2:2, Greek; 2 Peter 3:10.

21. As we shall see, the Lord Jesus will be ruler over Israel (Luke 1:31–33), with David as His viceroy. Jesus will also be ruler over all the earth (Ps. 2:6–9; Isa. 11:1–9).

22. The angelic proclamation of "the everlasting gospel" (Rev. 14:6–7) is an appeal to earth dwellers to fear God and worship Him, rather than the Beast and his image (13:15), for the time of God's judgment has come (cp. 11:15–18).

23. "For by them [the Bowl Judgments] the wrath of God is completed, or finished." This implies that the earlier Seal and Trumpet Judgments were expressions of divine wrath as well. God's wrath, or anger, is the stern judicial reaction of His holiness against sinners and their sins. Today, this is His hostile attitude (Gk. *orge*) toward the sinner (John 3:18; Rom. 1:18); in the future, it will take the form of His anger poured out (Gk. *thumos*) in terrible judgments (Rev. 14:10–11, 19; 15:1; 16:19; 19:15).

24. After this Seal Judgment there follows the first of four interludes, which occur in Revelation. These interludes, which provide additional information, are pauses in the progress of these visions. This first interlude (Rev. 7:1–17) concerns the evangelistic ministry of the 144,000 (7:1–8; cp. 14:4; 12:27) and the results of their labors (7:9–17).

25. Described as "woes," Trumpet Judgments five through seven appear to be divine judicial infliction through fallen angels (demons) upon wicked mankind. In His divine sovereignty, God controls all creatures and things (cp. Job 1–2).

26. The record of these six Trumpet Judgments is followed by the second interlude (Rev. 10:1–11:14), consisting of three visions: a mighty angel who declares that there will be no more delay in the remainder of God's program for this age (chap. 10); the Jewish temple in Jerusalem (11:1–2) and who will be qualified to worship there; and God's two witnesses, who will minister during the second half of the Tribulation Age (11:3–14). In an atheistic society, they will bear witness to the true God and to these judgments as being from Him.

27. The third interlude (Rev. 14:1–20) follows, consisting of a vision of the 144,000 dead evangelists in heaven (vv. 1–5), three angelic proclamations (vv. 6–13), and the two divine penal harvests (vv. 14–20).

28. This series of judgments will be followed by the fourth interlude (Rev. 17:1–19:10), consisting of the destruction of Babylon (17:1–18:8), the reaction of earth dwellers to Babylon's fall (18:9–19), the celebration in heaven (18:20–19:6), the marriage of the Lamb (19:7–9), and the reaction of the apostle John (v. 10).

29. This may mean their being confined to God's prophetic timetable rather than running their natural courses.

30. In Revelation 13:1–2; 17:3, 7, 16, "the beast" represents the ten-nation federation, which will have Satan's worldwide authority during the second half of the Tribulation Age (Dan. 7:7, 23; Rev. 13:2, cp. 5). Satan's human agent, "the Beast out of the sea," will become the leader of this political federation at the beginning of his prophetic career (Rev. 13:3–4; Dan. 7:24). Other references to this man are given in Rev. 13:12, 14–15, 17–18; 11:7; 14:9, 11; 15:2; 16:2, 10, 13; 17:8, 11–13, 17; 19:19–20; 20:4, 10. Also, see Dan. 7:24–26; 8:9–11, 23–25; 9:26–27; 11:21–45; Ezek. 38:1–39:4. For a fascinating study of this man see G. H. Lang, *The Histories and Prophecies of Daniel* (London: The Paternoster Press, 1950), chaps. II, VII–IX, XI. Also see his *The Revelation of Jesus Christ* (London: Oliphants Ltd., 1945), chap. IX. Mr. Lang is a partial-rapturist.

31. Only the Lord Jesus, who alone has conquered death, has been given the authority to raise the dead (John 5:26–29; Rev. 1:18). He will not have to return to earth to do this. Apparently, He will do this from heaven, where He sits at the Father's right hand.

32. In addition to their worshiping the golden calf (Exod. 32), Israel engaged in idolatrous practices during other periods of their history: first, during the wilderness journey (Deut. 4:1–4; 31:20), for which the original generation died in the wilderness; then after the death of Joshua (Judg. 2, et al.); and also during their later history, as indicated above, for which they were carried into captivity.

33. Only the repentant, elect remnant of Israelites will be restored to God (Rom. 9:27; 11:5). "All Israel" (11: 26) is a figure of association (a synecdoche: the whole representing a part) for the Jewish remnant. See Appendix K for a list of biblical prophecies about Israel.

34. Four hundred eighty-three years of this 490-year period started with the decree of the Persian ruler Artaxerxes I to restore Jerusalem (either the city, Neh. 2, or the temple, Ezra 7) and ended with Jesus' ministry and death (see Appendix G: "An Analysis of Daniel 9:24–27"). The remaining seven years have yet to be fulfilled.

35. "Not my people" in the sense of their breaking the Mosaic covenant and denouncing their covenant relation with God.

36. The "first resurrection" refers to those saved people, which will consist of several resurrection events before Jesus' millennial reign. After the Lord's millennial reign and the dissolution of the universe, all unsaved people will be raised in "the second resurrection," which will be a single event.

37. This new covenant is "an everlasting covenant" in Isaiah 55:3; 61:8; Jeremiah 32:40 (cp. 31:35–37); Ezekiel 16:60; 37:26; "a perpetual covenant" in Jeremiah 50:5; and "a covenant of peace" in Isaiah 54:10; Ezekiel 34:25; 37:26. See Appendix K: "Israel's Future as Described in Biblical Prophecy" for other prophetic passages relating to Israel.

38. See Appendix R: "The Kingdom of God."

39. See Alva J. McClain, *The Greatness of the Kingdom* (Grand Rapids: Zondervan Publishing House, 1959), chaps. IV–V. Dr. McClain proposes that the mediatorial kingdom (the rule of God over the earth through a human agent) has existed since Adam. I prefer the view that the mediatorial kingdom has not existed since Adam's fall when his earthly authority was seized by Satan, the present prince of this world (Heb. 2:5–8; John 12:31; 14:30; 16:11). Being synonymous with Jesus' messianic earthly rule, the mediatorial kingdom will be reestablished after the Lord's second coming to earth. As the Last Adam and the Father's Viceroy, He will rule earth for one thousand years for the glory of God.

40. These millennial offerings do not necessarily indicate a return to the Mosaic Levitical ritual. Probably, they will symbolically portray our Lord's atoning work and the need for people's seeking the divine application of the value of His sacrifice for cleansing from sin, whether by salvational faith in Jesus or by filial repentance and confession.

41. The prophet Ezekiel seems to give details of the millennial temple (Ezek. 40–43), the sanctuary ministry (chaps. 44–46), the River of Life (47:1–12), the boundaries of the Israel's land (vv. 13–21), and the portions of the Israelite tribes (chaps. 47–48).

42. In the case of those people who never had access to God's Word, it appears that they will be judged by "the law written in their hearts" (Rom. 2:14–15), which is an essential part of their inherent morality, belonging to their personhoods.

43. It is regrettable that the KJV translates the Greek word *hades* "hell." Hades is the place where unsaved people go, upon their physical death, to await their resurrection, judgment, and final doom (see Addendum: "Sheol, Hades"). The English word *hell* should be exclusively used for the lake of fire, the final doom of the unsaved, as in the passages where it stands for the Greek word *Gehenna* (Matt. 5:22, 29–30; 10:28; 18:9; 23:15, 33; Mark 9:43, 45, 47; Luke 12:5; James 3:6). Gehenna, a synonym for hell, was the Valley of Hinnom, south of Jerusalem, where refuse was burned. Jesus used this place name as a symbol of hell, the lake of fire.

44. I prefer the view that the Day of God should not be equated with the Day of the Lord. The KJV "wherein" is rendered by the ASV "by reason of which" (2 Peter 3:12), suggesting the purpose for the dissolution of the universe, which is to make way for the Day of God.

45. Matthew 10:28, "destroy"; John 3:16, "perish"; and 2 Peter 3:7, "perdition" are from Greek *apollumi*, meaning "ruin," which does not mean to annihilate, that is, to cease to exist, as the present ruined state of unsaved people shows (Luke 19:10, KJV "lost") and the parable of the wineskins demonstrates (Luke 5:37). Even the death of the prophets (Luke 13:33) did not annihilate them because of their immortality. It does mean that these people or things are so altered that they cease to experience or fulfill their original divine purpose or function. God did not create people in their sin-ruined condition; this was the result of their sinning. They will experience this state of ruin forever in isolation from Him (Matt. 25:46). The wineskins of the parable continued to exist after they could no longer fulfill their original purpose.

46. John Sanders, *No Other Name* (Grand Rapids: Wm. B. Eerdmans Publishing Co., 1992); Clark H. Pinnock, *A Wideness in God's Mercy: The Finality of Jesus Christ in a World of Religions* (Grand Rapids: Zondervan Publishing House, 1992). These sentimental views are refuted by Ronald H. Nash, *Is Jesus the Only Savior?* (Grand Rapids: Zondervan Publishing House, 1994) and D. A. Carson, *The Gagging of God: Christianity Confronts Pluralism* (Grand Rapids: Zondervan Publishing House, 1996), 285–313.

Appendixes, Chart, and Addenda

APPENDIXES

APPENDIX A

The Nature of Speaking in Tongues

The widespread practice of alleged tongues speaking today requires us to examine more closely what the Scriptures teach about this subject. I understand that the gift of speaking in tongues was a special, nonrational utterance that was unique to each possessor. Also, I believe that the exercise of this gift is no longer needed today, for the New Testament replaces its function as proofs and signs. Let us look at several aspects of this spiritual gift.[1]

ITS NATURE

What was the gift of speaking in tongues?

ITS FORM

Bible students are not agreed on what this utterance was. Some hold that it was a foreign language, unknown to the speaker but known to others. Others hold that it was an ecstatic utterance, which had no grammatical structure. Still others hold that it was a foreign language in Acts (chaps. 2, 10, 19) and an ecstatic utterance in 1 Corinthians (chaps. 12, 14). I prefer the view that in every New Testament instance tongues speaking was an ecstatic utterance, unique to the one who had the gift. I believe that the following observations support this view.

One: A foreign language does not necessarily have a greater capability for expressing one's thoughts or feelings than one's own language.

Two: The gift of tongues appears to have been a nonrational, ecstatic utterance of a divinely driven human spirit (1 Cor. 14:2, 14–16). It was the speaker's expression of how he felt in his human spirit rather than his explanation of what he felt. Thus, his speaking was not a rational statement. It may be compared to a person's response to being pricked with a pin. He does not reason how he will react to this, but he spontaneously expresses his feelings, and usually he does so emphatically.

Three: The words *other* (Acts 2:4, Gk. *heterais*) and *new* (Mark 16:17, Gk. *kainais*) indicate an utterance that is different from other forms of speech and that is new in nature.

Four: The tongues that were spoken by the Lord's disciples on the Day of Pentecost were addressed to God and to themselves before the crowd had gathered (Acts 2:4).

Five: That each person heard the disciples speak in his or her own dialect (Acts 2:6, 8, 11) may have resulted from a miracle of hearing, similar to the gift of the interpretation of tongues. The Scriptures do not say that the disciples actually spoke in these languages.

Six: The use of foreign languages to communicate with the people was unnecessary as the apostle Peter's following address, presumably in Greek, shows (Acts 2:14ff.). Greek was the universal language of the eastern Mediterranean world.

Seven: The charge of intoxication indicates that the disciples spoke with ecstatic utterances (Acts 2:13–15). Apparently, the mockers were not miraculously hearing the disciples' words in their own dialects (vv. 6–8).

Eight: Being novel, ecstatic utterance would better serve as a sign to skeptical people (1 Cor. 14:22).

Nine: The plural number of the word *tongues* (Acts 2:4; 10:46; 19:6; 1 Cor. 12:28, 30; 14:5–6, 18, 22–23) indicates that the utterance was unique to each speaker and that no utterance was the same for all speakers. This view is supported by the words *kind* and *diversities* (1 Cor. 12;10, 28, Gk. *gene*), which indicate varied manifestations of this gift.

Ten: That tongues required interpretation (1 Cor. 12:30; 14:5, 13, 27, Gk. *diermneuo*) rather than translation (Gk. *methermneuo*) indicates an ecstatic utterance that had no grammatical construction. The primary emphasis of interpretation is making clear the meaning of something (Luke 24:27, "expounded"; John 1:38) while the emphasis of translation is turning a literary work or statement from one language into another (Gk. *methermneuo*, see Matt. 1:23; Mark 5:41; 15:22, 34; John 1:41–42; Acts 4:36; 13:8).

ITS CONTENT

To my mind, speaking in tongues was a form of ecstatic prayer (1 Cor. 14:2, 14, 28), expressing praise (Acts 2:11, KJV "works" is "things"; 10:46) and thanksgiving to God (1 Cor. 14:16–17). Because tongues did not communicate divine revelation, the apostle Paul exalted prophecy, which did, for it better edified the Church (vv. 1–5, 19) and had something to say to unbelieving persons (vv. 23–25).

ITS DURATION

It is debated among the Lord's people whether or not the gift of tongues has ceased and, if it has ceased, when this occurred. Since the value and duration of spiritual gifts during this age are determined by their usefulness in the building of the Lord's Church, I believe that the gifts of tongues, the interpretation of tongues, prophecy, miracles, the discernment of spirits, and apostleship ceased with the completion and distribution of the New Testament. This portion of the Bible, which is more certain than sights and sounds (2 Peter 1:16–21), now fulfills the divine purposes for these gifts.[2] Moreover, praise in divine worship can be adequately expressed in one's own language.

Some people appeal to 1 Corinthians 13:8 for proof that speaking in tongues has ceased. The apostle Paul did not clearly say here when this cessation would occur. He seemed to imply that all spiritual gifts, represented by tongues, prophecy, and knowledge, will cease when they are no longer needed. He underscored this point by contrasting our present spiritual experience, which is partial, with our future glorified state, which will be complete (vv. 9–10). He illustrated this contrast between the partial and the complete by referring to a child's speech and comprehension (v. 11) and to one's imperfect reflection in a first-century mirror (v. 12).

ITS PRACTICE

Although the apostle Paul valued prophecy more than speaking in tongues (1 Cor. 14:1–5, 23–25), he did not prohibit the exercise of tongues (v. 27), for as we have seen, it served God's purposes at that time. However, he did regulate its practice.

One: Tongues were to be spoken in the assembly only if an interpreter was present (vv. 13, 28).

Two: The one speaking in tongues could be his own interpreter (v. 5).

Three: Only two or three, taking turns, were to speak in tongues (v. 27). Apparently, this allowed other spiritual gifts to be exercised during the service (v. 26).

Four: Except for their prophesying or praying, women were to remain silent in the churches (11:5; 14:34; cp. 1 Tim. 2:11–12).

Five: All things were to be done "decently" (becomingly, properly) and "in order," with a view to edifying the Lord's people (1 Cor. 14:40, 26).

SEVERAL OBSERVATIONS

One: While tongues could be spoken to one's self (1 Cor. 14:28), like all spiritual gifts its use was for the edification of the Church, not for self-edification (vv. 5, 26).

Two: Like all spiritual gifts, speaking in tongues could be restrained if there was no need in the service for this ministry (1 Cor. 14:28, 32).

Three: We should never make any spiritual gift a test of a person's spirituality, for no one spiritual gift is the common possession of all gospel believers (1 Cor. 12:8–10, 14–25; Rom. 12:4–6).

Four: No radical action that divides or confuses the Lord's people should be allowed in the church service (1 Cor. 14:28–33, 40). The peace, unity, and edification of the Lord's people are more important than the exercise of some spiritual gift that disrupts this condition (vv. 26; Eph. 4:3). If people feel constrained to exercise some spiritual gift that is not acceptable to or needed by a congregation, then they should seek out a church where this will be received, or in the case of an obsolete gift, they should stop practicing it altogether.

Five: While rejecting the practice of tongues speaking in church services, some believe that it is permissible to do this in an informal gathering or during private devotions. While one may do as one pleases during private spiritual exercises, any so-called tongues speaking, to my mind, should not be regarded as exercising the gift of tongues. It should be regarded as a religious phenomenon like swooning, shaking, rolling, laughing, barking, and other unusual behavior that sometimes occurs in seizures of religious fervor.

Six: Spiritual gifts are effective and beneficial only as one does them in the power of the Holy Spirit (1 Cor. 13:1–4; Gal. 5:13, 22, 25). One may try to do them apart from Him, but this neither edifies others nor glorifies God. Such self-serving activities are used by Satan to deceive and confuse the unwary and to inflate the actor with pride.

Seven: The apostle exhorted his Christian readers to seek the gifts that most edify the congregation (1 Cor. 12:31; 14:1–5, 39). The desirability of a spiritual gift should be determined by its usefulness and the spiritual need of others rather than by its display.

Eight: Believers must be wary of seeking spiritual satisfaction through unusual experiences like tongues speaking (see observation five above). We must always look to the Lord Jesus and His Word for the satisfaction of our spiritual needs and for progress in our spiritual life (John 6:35; 7:37–39; 10:9). Satan can provide us with an experience that counterfeits what we are seeking (Matt. 7:21–23; 24:24; cp. 2 Cor. 11:13–15). Contrariwise, the Holy Spirit ministers to us in ways that exalt the Lord Jesus, that are in harmony with the Scriptures, and that minister to our spiritual needs (John 16:12–14; 2 Tim. 3:16–17; Rom. 8:6).

Nine: The apostolic laying on of hands was a significant act by the official representatives of Christ, whereby on some occasions the Holy Spirit was communicated to recipients of the gospel (Acts 8:14–17; 19:6) and at other times spiritual gifts were imparted or ignited (2 Tim. 1:6). However, this was not always done (Acts 10:44–48), nor is it necessary today since the New Testament teaches us about the Holy Spirit's activities at salvation and His ministries in the Christian life. Again, like tongues this was a physical action that indicated the presence or occurrence of spiritual realities. In Acts 13:3 and 1 Timothy 4:14, the laying on of hands was an act of identification, by which members of a local church expressed their fellowship with these people in their gospel ministries.

APPENDIX B

The Conscience

THE CONSCIENCE AND THE MIND

We humans possess two faculties of moral awareness and evaluation—the conscience and the mind. The *conscience* seems to be a part of one's memory bank, with its input of innate morality from one's personhood and of acquired moral values that are received from moral laws and instruction. According to its programmed input, the conscience immediately, involuntarily, and automatically recognizes the moral character of a proposed action and alerts its possessor (1 Cor. 8:7, 10; 10:27–28; 1 John 3:20–21, "heart"). With our *minds,* we can deliberately evaluate a proposed action in the light of a moral standard and can decide what course we should follow (Rom. 12:2).

Since the mind is capable of making deliberate moral evaluations, what need is there for a conscience? The conscience appears to be a monitor that automatically warns us of an impending temptation or a sin-threatening situation. It alerts the mind to evaluate deliberately the situation before we enter it or continue with it. The conscience is a protective warning device that helps us shun personal sinning in an evil world. The accuracy of the conscience's detection role is determined by the degree that its programmed moral instructions harmonize with God's biblical commands for His people today.

THE FUNCTION OF THE CONSCIENCE

Several views about the function of the conscience follow.

IT IS A JUDGE

This sees the conscience as a judge that deliberately determines what is morally right or wrong. But this view gives the conscience the function of the mind, with its more objective moral assessment and deliberation. The conscience automatically functions according to its subjective moral input, or programming.

IT IS A DIVINE VOICE

This sees the conscience as the voice of God. This is true only when the conscience has been programmed with God's Word and relays this truth by its warnings.

IT IS A PROGRAMMED MONITOR

As the preferred view, this sees the conscience as being programmed for its function by moral instruction and conditioning (1 Cor. 8:4, 7, 10; cp. Rom. 14:14). The conscience automatically plays back this moral input, alerting its possessor in threatening or questionable moral situations.

THE REPROGRAMMING OF THE CONSCIENCE

Overriding the conscience for good or bad, the mind can reprogram it. A part of the saved person's spiritual growth is his reprogramming his conscience as he learns right moral values and behavior from God's Word (see Rom. 14). For instance, because of his religious training, an Orthodox Jew believes that it is wrong for him to eat pork (Lev. 11:7–8) or food that had been offered to idols (Exod. 20:3–5; 32:6; 1 Cor. 10:18). On the other hand, a saved Jew may eat pork or meat that came from pagan temples, for he is no longer under the dietary restrictions of the Mosaic Law (Mark 7:19b; Acts 10:12–15; Rom. 14:14, 20; 1 Cor. 6:12; 8:8; 10:25–26; 1 Tim. 4:4; Titus 1:15), and he knows that pagan gods do not exist (1 Cor. 8; 14:18–33). However, he cannot do this without qualms of conscience until he has learned from the Scriptures that this is permissible, and his conscience has been reprogrammed thereby.

Our reprogramming the conscience by the Scriptures brings this moral warning system more into harmony with God's will for us. It is essential that, by biblical study, we delete from our consciences those earlier moral instructions that are contrary to, or are not in harmony with, God's will for us and that we enter those moral instructions that are taught in His Word.

THE ABUSES OF THE CONSCIENCE

TO IGNORE OUR CONSCIENCES

When we act contrary to our consciences, we sin, whether the action of which we were warned is inherently sinful or not (Rom. 14:14, 22–23). Acting contrary to the conscience is sinful in attitude and procedure, for by doing this we act defiantly and independently of the moral monitor that God has given us humans. In turn, this sinful action defiles the conscience (1 Cor. 8:7).

TO INFLUENCE OTHERS TO IGNORE THEIR CONSCIENCES

To influence another by example or persuasion to act contrary to his conscience is to wound it and to sin against him and God (1 Cor. 8:4–13; 10:23–32; Rom. 14:13–21). The fact that gospel believers have different programmed consciences creates a situation that may easily become the scene of carnal division and strife (1 Cor. 3:3). The presence in our local churches of people with "strong" consciences, which are reprogrammed with more information from God's Word, and people with "weak" consciences, with less biblical information, creates a tension that is favorable to sinful disputation (Rom. 14:13–23; 1 Cor. 8). It is the duty of "strong" conscience people to accommodate lovingly their behavior to the opinions of the "weak," lest these be led to act contrary to their consciences and sin. Being filled with the Holy Spirit and acting in God's love, the stronger conscience person will avoid being a stumbling block to his weaker conscience brother and will follow a peaceful course (Rom. 14:19). Yet the stronger person should seek to liberate his weaker brother from unbiblical cultural bondage by instructing him of his freedom in Christ and of the teachings of God's Word (cp. 6:7; 7:4; 8:2). Hopefully, this will reprogram and strengthen the weaker brother's conscience. To avoid wrangling, both the strong and the weak must be filled with the Holy Spirit and allow the mind and love of the Lord Jesus to govern their relations (Eph. 4:2–3).

THE KINDS OF CONSCIENCES

THE CONSCIENCE OF SAVED PEOPLE

While the saved person has only one conscience, it can assume various qualities like the following:

1. A cleansed conscience (Heb. 9:8–14)

The Mosaic Law could never perfect the conscience of one who offered its prescribed offerings, for this ritual never took away sins (Heb. 10:4, 11). Thus, the conscience of the law observer was never free of guilt (Heb. 9:9; 10:4). However, the saved person has a judicially purged, or saved, conscience because of Jesus' effective work of redemption (9:11–14, 26) and the assurance of God's Word regarding divine forgiveness (Acts 10:43).

2. A defiled or evil conscience (1 Cor. 8:7; Heb. 10:22)

By sinning, the conscience of a saved person becomes defiled and evil (1 Cor. 8:7; Rom. 14:14, 23). However, God will cleanse it and render it holy when the person deals with his sin by repentance and confession and walks in obedience to God (2 Cor. 7:1; cp. Rev. 2:5; 1 John 1:9; Rom. 6:19).

3. A good or pure conscience (Acts 23:1; 24:16; 2 Tim. 1:3)

This conscience supports a person's behavior and motives for actions, especially when it is programmed with the commands and moral values of God's Word and when his behavior is in harmony with these.

4. A weak conscience (1 Cor. 8:12)

This is a conscience that remains largely programmed with moral ideas and values that are not taught in the New Testament as being God's will for His people today (cp. Rom. 14). This kind of a conscience is detrimental to the behavior that God requires of His people, for it inaccurately reads their moral situations. On the other hand, it can be said that a conscience that is largely programmed with God's moral values and commands is a strong one, making its possessor spiritually strong (cp. 15:1).

5. A witnessing conscience (Rom. 9:1; 2 Cor. 1:12; cp. 4:2)

The apostle Paul's conscience supported his assertion of having sorrow for a people who sought his life (Rom. 9:1) and of his behavior as being by God's grace (2 Cor. 1:12). Thus, the conscience determines the sincerity of one's assertions.

What kind of a conscience do you have? The apostle Paul said that he lived in all good conscious before God (Acts 23:1). Can you say this?

THE CONSCIENCE OF UNSAVED PEOPLE

The conscience of the unsaved person is programmed by the innate morality of his personhood (Rom. 2:14–15) as well as by his moral training and conditioning. Consequently, his conscience monitors his moral actions as does that of the saved person. However, much of the moral input of the consciences of unsaved people is faulty, for it consists of the unbiblical moral values of the world (Eph. 2:2–3; 4:17–19).

The unsaved conscience can be seared (1 Tim. 4:2) in the sense that the person rationalizes, or justifies, certain wrong actions to the point that his conscience no longer bears witness against his wrongdoing. It is doubtful that this can be true of a saved person, for he still has the convicting work and witness of the Holy Spirit through His Word. Upon being confronted with their sins, unsaved people (Acts 2:37; 5:33; 7:54) as well as saved people (1 John 3:20) may be pricked in their consciences.

APPENDIX C

The Relation Between Personhood and Soul

While the soul often represents human beings (Gen. 46:22–27) and one's own being (Ps. 42:5–6), it should not be equated with personhood (self, I) alone, as those traditional theologians who were influenced by Greek philosophy have done, for the Scriptures distinguish between these parts of our being (Job 7:11; Ps. 131:2; Isa. 26:9).

THE ARGUMENT FOR THIS DISTINCTION

One: The human soul is a part of human nature, which is wholly propagated by human parents. I suggest that personhood—that unique personal entity (self, I) that is God's image in humans and that distinguishes them from lower creatures—is at the moment of conception created by God and is permanently united to the propagated human nature (Mal. 2:10; cp. Ps. 139:13–15). With this union, a person's human nature qualifies his or her personhood to make that person a human being. In turn, personhood gives to human nature conscious selfhood, moral awareness, and perpetuity.

Two: This distinction between personhood and nature is seen in the constitution of the divine Trinity, which consists of three distinct Persons—the Father, the Son, and the Holy Spirit. Each of these Persons has an individual, unique personhood, which must not be equated with the divine nature. However, Their possessing the one divine nature makes Them divine Persons yet one God.

Three: This distinction is also shown by our Lord's incarnation. In this case, an eternal, divine Person received a complete human nature (body, soul, and spirit), divinely made of Mary's substance. This resulted in His having two natures—one divine and one human, not His being two persons. In our case, our personhoods' being directly created by God accounts for our unique individuality and morality, and their union with our human natures account for our human personalities, by which we express the qualities and powers of our human natures.

Four: This view, I believe, accounts for the various functions of the soul and spirit, as taught in the Scriptures, such as providing the dynamics for intelligence, emotions, and will. Our personalities do not exist independently of these parts of human nature, but they are the result of their acting upon our personhoods. Because of the union of our personhoods with our human natures, we are human beings who express and experience all the features of human personality like reasoning, feeling emotions, and making moral choices.

Five: Since the unsaved person's propagated human nature is wholly affected by inherent corruption, his sinful human nature adversely qualifies his created personhood and makes him in his natural state a fallen, corrupted human being (Ps. 51:5). Adam's image in his posterity consists of the corrupted, propagated human nature, with which everyone is born (Gen. 5:3; 1 Cor. 15:49).[3] Salvation renews one's personhood and immaterial human nature to the extent that one is made a new creature in Christ (2 Cor. 5:17) with His image (Eph. 4:24; Col. 3:10; 2 Cor. 3:18; Rom. 8:29).

Six: This view, which sees personhood and human nature as distinct, inseparable entities, allows God to be the Creator of unique personhoods, who at their creation are morally and qualitatively neutral (Ps. 139:14–15; Jer. 1:5; Mal. 2:10). The personhood receives its humanity and corruption from its propagated, inherently corrupted, human nature. Since human nature is wholly propagated, this accounts for those hereditary characteristics that offspring receive from their parents and ancestors, as well as the inherent corruption they receive from original sin. This explains why the soul and spirit are portrayed in the Scriptures as expressing the functions of human personality (Pss. 42:5–6; 139:14; Gen. 42:21; Job 7:11). When they contribute their human powers to one's personhood, the soul and spirit give one the human ability to think, express verbal concepts, make decisions, feel and show emotion, and select motivations and direction.

OBJECTIONS TO THIS DISTINCTION

1. *"God has ceased His creative work" (Gen. 2:2).*

While this is true of material things, it does not apply to the immaterial realm (Eph. 2:10). God is now creating people anew in Christ Jesus (2 Cor. 5:17).

2. *"Christ's incarnation was a unique event, involving an eternal divine Person."*

True, but it still demonstrates the distinction between personhood and human nature. God the Son received a human nature, which He did not have before His incarnation.

3. *"The descendants are said to be in the loins of their ancestors" (Heb. 7:5, 9–10; 1 Cor. 15:22).*

Since a person's human nature qualifies his personhood to make him human, in effect, people are in the loins of their ancestors, for their human natures were involved in all that their ancestors were and did. The solidarity of the human race rests upon people's having commonly derived human natures, not upon their having a common personhood or their being the same person (Acts 17:26; 1 Cor. 15:45, 47, 49).

4. *"God would not unite a newly created personhood with a corrupted human nature."*

It should be remembered that God's procedure for creating man was established before man's fall. The newly created personhood has no features that are destroyed by its union with fallen human nature, although it is adversely affected by this nature. Unsaved people are as much persons as saved people are (James 3:9). The features of selfhood—conscious individuality, moral awareness, and perpetuity—continue in fallen man. If it is God's procedure to create personhood and to unite this to one's propagated human nature, then any impropriety of this would be due to Adam's sinning, which corrupted his entire being, both personhood and nature. It would not be due to the procedure that God established before man's fall.

To my mind, it is wrong to equate personhood with the soul, as traditional theologians have done. This leads to confusion and irresolvable problems. I believe the view that I have presented better relates to the Scriptures, to the functions of the soul and spirit, to the solidarity of the human race, and to the doctrine of personal beings, whether God, angels, or man. All are persons, with their own kind of nature that makes them to be what they are.

APPENDIX D

The Ones Who Are in Christ

Distinguishing between the Holy Spirit's baptizing gospel believers into Christ (Gal. 3:27) and His baptizing them into the mystical body of Christ, the Universal Church (1 Cor. 12:13), it seems to be the teaching of Scripture that all the saved people of human history are baptized into Christ. This conclusion is based on the following considerations:

One: Since salvation is only in and through Jesus and His sacrifice (Acts 4:12; 1 Thess. 5:9; 1 Tim. 2:5–6; Heb. 5:9), it follows that all saved people must be baptized into Him to partake of the spiritual blessings that are in Him (1 Cor. 1:30; Eph. 1:3) and to be made complete in Him (Col. 2:10). If there is any righteousness or redemption apart from the Lord Jesus that God accepts, then our Lord's atoning work was not necessary. The Scriptures show that the method of salvation is the same in every age. It is always by God's grace through faith in the divine revelation of the Savior and His atoning work, whether promised (Gen. 3:15, 21; 15:5–6; Heb. 11:41) or fulfilled (John 3:16). To be accepted by God, one must partake of the Lord's redemption and righteousness—that which He accomplished efficaciously and that He was morally (Rom. 5:1, 9–10, 19; 2 Cor. 5:21).

Two: It appears that all the saved of every age must now be in Jesus to be members of the new humanity, of which He is the Head and Pattern (1 Cor. 15:22, 45–49; Rom. 8:29). God sees each member of the human race as being either in Adam or Christ—the unsaved in Adam and the saved in Christ. In striking contrast to those who are in Adam, all the saved share Jesus' kind of human nature, His obedience unto death (the ultimate manifestation of divinely acceptable human righteousness), and His human spiritual life, which is eternal (Rom. 5:17–19). No third group or kind of human being is indicated in the Scriptures.

Three: The regenerative aspect of salvation requires that we be in Christ, for this involves the deliverance of our personhoods and immaterial human natures from inherent corruption (Titus 3:5; 1 Peter 1:22), our being created in righteousness and true holiness (Col. 3:10; Eph. 4:24) infused with spiritual life (Rom. 8:10; Eph. 2:1). With Christ as our life (Col. 3:4), these realities spring from our being created in Him (Eph. 2:10) and our being new creatures in Him (2 Cor. 5:17).

Four: While precross gospel believers (those of human history who lived and died before Jesus died) received divinely imputed righteousness (Gen. 15:6) and enjoyed a personal relationship with God (17:1), they did not go to heaven when they died (25:8; cp. Luke 16:22) or receive the promised inheritance (Heb. 11:13–16). These realities were not possible before our Lord's incarnation, atoning work, death, resurrection, and return to heaven (Heb. 9:15). Only then could He bring His people into union with Himself and impart to them the blessings of the new covenant. Probably the precross saints who had died were united to Him at the time of His return to heaven when they were taken with Him (Eph. 4:8). With this union, He became their righteousness and redemption (1 Cor. 1:30), fulfilling what previously had been extended to them, as it were, on credit (Rom. 3:25; Heb. 9:15–17).

Five: One of God's objectives is to bring together for Himself all things in Christ (Eph. 1:10; cp. Col. 1:20). Whatever this means, it seems to include the redeemed of all the ages (John 17:20–22; Gal. 3:27–28) as well as the things that were involuntarily affected by God's curse on nature (Gen. 3:17–19; Rom. 8:19–22).

Six: Again, to be in Christ does not necessarily mean to be in His mystical body, the Church, for these are distinct concepts, realities, and activities of the Holy Spirit. The baptism into Christ (Gal. 3:27) is a distinct work from the baptism into His body (1 Cor. 12:13, 17; Col. 1:18). While Church Age gospel believers (those saved during this age) experience both aspects of the Holy Spirit's baptism, all other saved peoples of human history—the precross gospel believers and those of the Tribulation Age and Kingdom Age—are only baptized into Him and partake of the positional blessings that are in Him.

There is no evidence, that I am aware of, that they are members of the Lord's Church.

APPENDIX E

Righteousness and Holiness

Righteousness and holiness are moral qualities that belong to God and that He desires for the lives of His people. He commands, "Awake to righteousness and sin not" (1 Cor. 15:34); and "Be you holy, for I am holy" (1 Peter 1:16). While we who are saved are righteous and holy in Christ (1 Cor. 1:30), we also are to be righteous and holy in daily behavior (1 Peter 2:24; 1:15). It is obvious that we cannot of ourselves generate these qualities. But the Holy Spirit will reproduce them in our lives as we depend on Him to do so and as we do God's will with His help. But what does it mean to be righteous and holy in daily life?

1. *Righteousness*

"Righteousness" is the quality of being or doing right. God is righteous in that He always does what is right in keeping with His divine nature and laws (Ps. 145:7, 17). We who are saved are positionally righteous in Christ (1 Cor. 1:30). At salvation, God justified us, or declared us to be righteous (Rom. 5:1), for He gave us Jesus' righteousness (3:22) and made us righteous in Him (2 Cor. 5:21). Consequently, He wants us to do right things, or His will, in reliance upon the Holy Spirit for help and direction (2 Tim. 2:22; 1 Peter 2:24; 1 John 2:29). This behavior is practical righteousness.

2. *Holiness*

"Holiness" is the quality of being morally pure. God is holy in the sense that He is set apart from sin (1 John 1:5–7). This means that there is no sin in Him and that He does not sin; He is morally pure (Hab. 1:12–13; 1 John 1:5). For this reason, it is His will that His people be holy, too (1 Peter 1:15–16; 1 Thess. 4:3).

Positionally, we are sanctified, or made holy, in Christ (1 Cor. 1:2, 30). This took place at salvation when, by the Holy Spirit, we were brought into spiritual union with Jesus (6:11). Because we are holy in Christ and, therefore, called "saints" (holy ones), God appeals to us to be holy in every aspect of our lives (1 Peter 1:15). This means that He wants us to separate ourselves from that which is sinful in His sight, like unholy alliances and morally unclean practices (2 Cor. 6:14–7:1), and consider ourselves to be holy vessels for His use in this world (2 Tim. 2:21; Acts 9:15). This kind of sinless behavior is practical holiness, or sanctification.

With these descriptions in view, notice that righteousness, or obedience to God's will, precedes holiness, or sinlessness (Rom. 6:19). While holiness emphasizes our being sinless in our behavior, righteousness stresses our being obedient to God's commands. When we are obeying God, we are not sinning.

Although we do not live righteous and holy lives all the time, since we still are capable of sinning and are tempted to sin, we can express intermittent righteousness and holiness by our daily behavior. This means that we can live for periods of time in obedience to God's will without sinning. With the help of the Holy Spirit, we can resist the temptations of our spiritual enemies, and we can do God's will. The choice is ours. As long as we choose to give ourselves to Jesus and do His will in His strength, we express His righteousness, or obedience (Rom. 6:13, 19), and holiness, or sinlessness (v. 22). We grow in righteousness and holiness by being obedient to the Lord, and can remain sinless more often or for longer periods of time.

Our God, the true and the living God, has called us to righteousness (1 Cor. 15:34) and to holiness (1 Thess. 4:7). He wants us to be morally perfect, as He is (Matt. 5:48). Thus, righteous, holy behavior is essential for our pleasing God, exhibiting Christlikeness (Eph.

5:1–14), serving God (Rom. 12:1–2; 2 Tim. 2:19–22), experiencing His fellowship and blessing (1 John 1:5–9; 2 Cor. 6:17–18), and bringing praise to Him (Matt. 5:16).

APPENDIX F

Learning and Doing God's Will

Our obedience to God is not merely the fulfillment of duty; it is the means of our experiencing personal happiness (John 13:17), our pleasing God (1 John 3:22), and our expressing our love for Him (John 14:15, 21, 23). Simply telling God that we love Him may be only an expression of sentimentalism or wishful thinking. God searches our hearts and lives as well as listening to our words for true expressions of our affection for Him. Despite Satan's lies to the contrary, obedience to God is not grievous (1 John 5:3) but good for us, suitable to our renewed personhoods and human natures, and perfect for us (Rom. 12:2). Although we have an inner desire to obey God (Phil. 2:13), we experience resistance to God's will from the inner sin force (Rom. 7:15–18; 8:7) and from Satan and the world without (1 Peter 2:11; 5:8). Our obedience to God requires that we learn His will for us in everything, and that we do it in His way and time. It is noteworthy that God's commands and appeals are directed to our will, not to our emotions. He never relieves us of our duty, because we do not feel like doing it or do not want to do it. God's will for His people today is found in the commands and appeals of the New Testament (the Dispensation of Grace) and in those of the Old Testament that are in harmony with these NT commands. Certainly, it is God's desire that we learn and do His will for us (Col. 1:9; Eph. 5:17). Let us first consider how to learn God's will for us and then how we are to do His will.

OUR LEARNING GOD'S WILL FOR US

This requires our preparing our hearts and our using spiritual discernment.

HEART PREPARATION

Discovering God's will for us requires heart preparation (2 Chron. 19:3) as follows:

One: We must be wholly yielded to God (Prov. 23:26; Eph. 5:18; Rom. 12:1). God teaches us only as we are submissive to the Holy Spirit, our Teacher, and are properly motivated to obey and glorify Him (Prov. 3:5–6; 1 Cor. 10:31).

Two: We must be willing to do His will, whatever this may be (Rom. 12:2). This requires our confidence in the truth that God's will is best for us.

Three: We must deal with any known sin in our lives (Rev. 2:5; 1 John 1:9). He does not heed us when we are displeasing Him (Ps. 66:18).

Four: We must ask God to show us His will (James 4:2). We can do this with the confidence that He desires to make known His will for us (Col. 1:9; 1 John 5:14–15).

SPIRITUAL DISCERNMENT

Having prepared our hearts for learning God's will for us, we can depend on the Holy Spirit to show us what this is (Rom. 8:14). There are four kinds of divine will for those of us who are saved that we need to learn about: God's preceptive will, His selective will, His commitment will, and His practical will.

GOD'S WILL AND HIS COMMANDS

This concerns God's will for us as described or commanded in the Scriptures. The saved person should give special attention to the New Testament, since this portion of the Bible sets forth the Lord's will, or dispensation, for His people during the present time. While all the Bible is profitable for us (2 Tim. 3:16–17), it is not all directed to us (2:15). For example, we are not obligated to follow the sacrificial ritual of the Mosaic Law, like offering animal sacrifices or worshiping at the temple in Jerusalem. On the other hand, we should observe the moral directions that we find in the Old Testament, for God's moral requirements are unchanging (cp. Eccl. 12:13; Prov. 4:23; for Exod. 20:1–17 see 1 John 5:21; Eph. 6:1–3; 1 Thess. 4:3–4; Eph. 4:28; Col. 3:5, 9; for Deut. 6:5; Lev. 19:18 see Matt. 12:28–31; Rom. 13:9; also John 13:34; see Appendix Z: "Our Loving God and Others").

There are about 650 commands, or precepts, given in the New Testament to all saved people. For example, one of these is our expressing Christian love toward others by ministering to their needs with a caring heart (John 13:34–35; 1 John 3:16–18). Others are given by the Lord Jesus in His addresses to His disciples, like His Sermon on the Mount (Matt. 5–7) and His Upper Room Discourse (John 14–16), and by the writers of Acts and the Epistles.

GOD'S WILL AND MATTERS NOT DEALT WITH IN THE BIBLE

God has not given us specific direction for every matter of daily conduct. He has left it to us to discern the rightness of those things that are not specifically dealt with in the Scriptures. To assist us in this evaluation, He has given us guiding questions that we can apply to these matters. As we apply these questions to questionable practices and situations, we can discern God's will for us in these things. These guiding questions follow in three primary behavioral applications:

1. *Those questions that relate the questionable behavior to God*
   a. *Will this action glorify God (1 Cor. 10:31)?*
      To glorify God is to bring Him praise by allowing Him to express His moral character in us and to do His work through us (Phil. 1:11; 1 Peter 4:1; Matt. 5:16).
   b. *Can I do this by faith in God (Gal. 2:20)?*
      Practical faith in God consists of our sharing our activities with Him and our relying on Him for help and direction in doing His will. To have doubt about the rightness of the action or to act independently of God is to sin (Rom. 14:23; Heb. 11:6).
   c. *Can I do this in the Lord's name (Col. 3:17)?*
      This is to act in keeping with His present work, interests, and pleasure (cp. vv. 1–3). Our giving thanks is our recognition of His faithfulness in helping us and in working through us to achieve His purpose in this world.

2. *Those questions that relate the questionable behavior to other people*
   These questions are expressions of Christ's love that is to govern all our associations and relationships with other people, whether they are saved or unsaved (John 13:34–35; Rom. 13:8–10; Gal. 5:13; 1 John 3:23; Matt. 5:44). This love must be distinguished from friendship love, which consists of our liking people who please us some way. Our having Christ's love gives us a concern for the needs of others, whom we may not like, and motivates us to help them, even at personal cost (1 John 3:16–18).
   a. *Will this action cause others to stumble (1 Cor. 8:9, 13; 10:32)?*
      To cause another to stumble is to throw an obstacle in his way that will hinder him spiritually. This obstacle may be a wrong action that leads him to sin, or it may be a

lawful action that encourages him to act against his conscience and, thus, to sin (1 Cor. 8:10–12; see Appendix B: "The Conscience"). We also must maintain to the unsaved a consistent gospel witness that is supported by a holy life (1 Peter 2:12).

In our associations with others, we must respect their opinions and prejudices and accommodate ourselves to their beliefs in matters of moral indifference (1 Cor. 9:19–23; 10:24–29).[4] This does not mean that we should become helpless victims of the opinions of others, for we can show them that gospel believers have died to social customs and prejudices (Rom. 7:1–6) and are obligated to follow the Lord (1 Cor. 9:21). Also, when we cannot agree with their notions, rather than pretending to concur, we should explain why we believe as we do. Still, when we are with them, we must accommodate ourselves to their peculiar views in matters of moral indifference like kinds of food and forms of modest dress. In doctrinal matters, we must remain loyal to our convictions; however, we must be open to new insights of truth that we can learn from others (cp. Acts 18:24–26).

    b. Will this action promote the well-being of others (1 Cor. 8:1; 14:26)?

When our Lord's love possesses our hearts, it prompts us to seek the well-being and edification of others in all that we do (1 Cor. 13:4–7; 9:19–23; 10:23–33; Rom. 13:10).

    3. *Those questions that relate the questionable behavior to ourselves*

    a. What effect will this action have on my body and mind (1 Cor. 6:13–15, 18–20)?

We must avoid doing those things that would injure the body or mind. Although it is still unredeemed, the saved person's body is holy, for it is the Lord's member on earth (1 Cor. 6:15), the Holy Spirit's temple (v. 19), his means of glorifying God in this world (v. 20), and when submitted to God, an instrument of righteousness (Rom. 6:13). Therefore, we must respect the body's integrity and function by avoiding those things that would harm or violate its well-being and sanctity (cp. 1 Thess. 4:3–7; 1 Cor. 6:18).

We must also avoid that which would enslave the body or mind (1 Cor. 6:12; Rom. 6:12). Since the Lord Jesus alone is our absolute Master, He has the sole right to use our bodies and minds as He pleases. It is our duty to yield them daily to Him and to His Word for His use and expression through us (Rom. 12:1; Eph. 3:17; Col. 3:16). It is sinful to yield them to anything that would lead us to use them in ways that are contrary to His will for us (Rom. 6:11–13; 8:5–8; Gal. 6:8; Col. 3:5–8; Acts 5:3).

    b. What effect will this action have on my spiritual life (1 Peter 2:1–2; 2 Peter 3:17–18)?

In reply, we may ask questions like these: Will this action decrease my love for God (1 John 2:15)? Will this disrupt my fellowship with Him (1:5–7)? Will it dull my appetite for His Word, prayer, worship, the fellowship of godly people, and Christian ministry (1 Peter 2:1–2)? Does it conflict with my conscience (Rom. 14:5, 23)? Will my doing this tarnish my Christian life and testimony (1 Tim. 4:12; 2 Tim. 2:22)?

When we prayerfully evaluate questionable behavior in the light of these questions, we can readily discern God's will for us. For example, should gospel believers use tobacco products? Knowing the addictive nature of nicotine and the harm it does to the body, believers will readily conclude from the above questions that it is a sinful behavior. Furthermore, since gambling is an effort to gain from the loss of others, it is not good stewardship nor an expression of Christian love. This love moves us to help others at personal sacrifice rather than to fleece them for personal gain (1 John 3:16–18). God's preceptive will for us is absolute. It must always be obeyed.

GOD'S WILL AND INDIVIDUAL CHOICE

This concerns God's will for us in our choice of allowable options, as in the selection of a spouse or in the purchase of a car. I believe that God has a preferred option for us in this matter and that He will show us this as we seek His will. When Abraham sent his servant back to Mesopotamia to find a bride for Isaac, God led him to Rebekah, the daughter of Bethuel, Abraham's brother (Gen. 24). Having prepared our hearts, we can learn God's selective will as follows:

WE MUST CONSIDER THE OPTIONS THAT ARE OPEN TO US AND SELECT THE MOST SUITABLE ONE

We do this by carefully considering all the facts that we can obtain and by selecting the option that seems to be most suitable to our needs, interests, health, financial state, purpose, or circumstances. We then must tabulate the advantages and disadvantages of this option and decide whether or not it is best for us. If it appears to be the most suitable option for us, then we proceed to the next step.

WE MUST EVALUATE THIS SELECTED OPTION IN THE LIGHT OF GOD'S INDICATORS

These indicators are as follows:

1. The teachings of Scripture

The option under consideration must agree with the Scriptures in the sense that it does not conflict with God's preceptive will for us or create in us unholy attitudes like pride.

2. The impressions of the Holy Spirit

The Holy Spirit leads by inner urges or impressions. However, we must determine the source of these urges since the sin force and Satan can produce these as well. These urges are tested by biblical teaching and prayer. If the impressions are of God, they will become stronger as we look to Him in prayer.

3. Our circumstances

Since God controls all circumstances, is it possible to pursue this option at this time?

WE MUST PRAY ABOUT THIS SELECTED OPTION

If this selected option passes the evaluation of these indicators, then we must regard this as our primary choice and pray about it. If, with prayer, our conviction deepens that this selected option is right, and we have inward peace, then we can conclude that this is the Lord's will for us. If we do not have inward peace about this selection or if new information casts doubt on its suitability, then we should select another option and evaluate it as we did the first one. We should continue this procedure until we come to the option about which we have inward peace and assurance that it is the Lord's choice for us. We should also thank the Lord for His direction.

WE MUST CARRY OUT THE APPROVED SELECTED OPTION

If we have concluded that this option is the Lord's will for us, then we must do it in His way (see below).

We should avoid considering more than one option at a time, for this can be confusing and misleading. If we should impulsively choose a wrong option and act upon it, we must deal with this as a sin, with repentance and confession, and seek God's direction as to how to resolve the results of this sinful choice. Having done this, if we find that the wrong selection is irresolvable, we must believe that God has forgiven us of our wrong action and will help us to live with its results until they change. In some instances, we may have to live with the consequences of impulsive, sinful actions for many years. Even then, the Lord's grace will help us to live with these consequences and will teach us profitable lessons by them. For instance, John Mark left Paul and Barnabas during their first missionary journey (Acts 13:13; 15:36–40). Later, he overcame the stigma of being a quitter and became useful again for the ministry (2 Tim. 4:11). Unlike God's preceptive will, God often has a "second best" selective will for us.

GOD'S WILL AND PREVIOUS COMMITMENTS

This consists of our fulfilling previous commitments, promises, or obligations (Eccl. 5:4–5; 2 Cor. 8:10–11). If we entered these agreements with the conviction that they were God's will for us, then we must abide by them. For instance, if a person works for an employer or is enrolled in a course of study, he does not normally need to ask God whether or not he should go to work or to class. Unless God allows hindering circumstances to intervene, we should fulfill these agreements. On the other hand, if these agreements were made impulsively, then we must deal with these decisions as being sinful and with God's help honorably divest ourselves of them as soon as it is possible to do so.

GOD'S WILL AND COMMON SENSE

Much of daily life consists of our following sanctified common sense. "Common sense" is our seeing things in their natural relationships and our exercising sound judgment about them. This means that, having asked the Holy Spirit for direction, we should do what appears to be the most reasonable thing in our circumstances. For instance, we can assume that God would have us to wear warm outdoor clothing in cold weather if this is at hand. Also, when Joseph, Mary, and baby Jesus returned from Egypt to Bethlehem, they were warned of God not to remain in Judea because of the rule of Archelaus, the son of Herod the Great (Matt. 2:19–23). Joseph then did the sensible thing. He took his family to Nazareth, from whence he and Mary had first come. There they would be with relatives and friends, and Joseph could resume his carpenter's trade.

God's practical will requires us to accommodate ourselves to things over which we have no control. Since God controls all things (Pss. 103:19; 119:90–91), we can do this with the confidence that He is working out that which is best for us and which will glorify Him. When we are assured that God is leading us by our circumstances, we must rely on the Holy Spirit to open seemingly closed doors and to give us special wisdom for the situation. He did this for Paul during his second missionary journey when the apostle tried to preach the gospel in the Roman provinces of Asia and Bithynia (Acts 16:6–13). By divinely controlled circumstances and specific direction, Paul was led on to Philippi, Macedonia, where he began his fruitful European ministry.

These four kinds of God's will show us what He wants us to do in every part of our lives. Since we have been saved to walk in "good works" (Eph. 2:10), which consists of our doing God's will (Heb. 13:21), it is important that we look to God for direction in everything that concerns us (see addenda, "God's Will Regarding Human Government," p. 557).

OUR DOING GOD'S WILL

ITS OPERATION

Conscious moral action involves evaluation, decision, and enactment. Evaluation consists of our looking critically at a proposed action to see what it is and assessing its worth in the light of our moral standard, God's Word. Based on this evaluation, we must then decide whether or not we should do it. Finally, we enact the decision. This first takes place in our hearts (minds) and then in outward behavior (cp. Matt. 5:28). Needless to say, when we are confronted with God's demands, it is always our duty to obey Him by suitable decision and behavior.

ITS MANNER

The manner in which we do God's will is essential to our pleasing Him. If we have not been obeying God, then we must first deal with this sin of disobedience by repentance and confession (Rev. 2:5; 1 John 1:9).

Obedience to God's will requires, *one,* thanksgiving for God's showing us His will (1 Thess. 5:18); *two,* believing that God's will is best for us (Rom. 12:2); *three,* deciding to do God's will (Josh. 24:15); *four,* submitting to God for His direction and strength in carrying out His will (Eph. 5:18; Phil. 4:13; John 15:4–5); *five,* relying on God to do His part as we do our part in obeying Him (Gal. 2:20; 5:16); *six,* having right motivation for doing His will (1 Cor. 10:31; cp. 2 Cor. 5:9–21); *seven,* obeying Him wholeheartedly and enthusiastically (Col. 3:23); *eight,* being alert for Satan's efforts to divert us from doing God's will (1 Peter 5:8; cp. Matt. 4:10); and *nine,* acting in God's time for carrying out His will (cp. John 2:4; 7:6, 30). In knowing God's time for our doing His will, we may have to follow the procedure of learning His selective will, especially in those things that do not require immediate action.

Occasionally, God does not show us all His will at once. Rather, He reveals it in parts as we obey Him in what He has already made known to us (cp. Acts 8:26–27). He has so designed the Christian life that His people must continually look to Him for direction (Prov. 3:5–6; Heb. 12:2) and rely on Him for help (Phil. 4:13; John 14:16–17). This is required for our walking in His fellowship.

Are you willingly and intelligently doing God's will today? It is the key to your fellowship with Him and your receiving and enjoying His blessings (1 John 1:5–7; John 13:17). Being the Father's Slave, the Lord Jesus is your Model (John 6:38; 8:29; 17:4).

APPENDIX G

An Analysis of Daniel 9:24–27

THE PEOPLE AND THE PLACE THAT THE MESSAGE CONCERNS (v. 24)

These are Daniel's people, the Jews, and his city, Jerusalem.

THE THINGS THAT GOD WILL ACCOMPLISH (v. 24)

These things will take place at the close of the "seventieth week," or of the Tribulation Age.

GOD WILL DEAL WITH THE SINS OF THE ELECT REMNANT OF ISRAEL

One: "To finish the transgression and to make an end of sin." God will bring to an end their sinful condition and action (cp. Jer. 3; 31:32; Matt. 13:15; 23:37).

Two: "To make reconciliation [atonement] for iniquity." Applying to them the value of Jesus' atoning work, God will deliver them from sin's guilt, penalty, ruin, and bondage and will bring them into a right relationship with Himself (Rom. 11:26–27; Ezek. 36:25–27).

GOD WILL "BRING IN EVERLASTING RIGHTEOUSNESS."

This probably refers to Jesus' millennial, earthly rule, which will be characterized by righteousness, or justice (Jer. 33:14–16; Isa. 11:4–5).

GOD WILL "SEAL UP [COMPLETE] THE VISION AND PROPHECY."

All will be fulfilled regarding the Jews and Jerusalem in God's appointed time (cp. 12:4; see Appendix K: "Israel's Future as Described in Biblical Prophecy").

GOD WILL "ANOINT THE MOST HOLY [HOLY OF HOLIES]."

This seems to be the dedication of the millennial temple, which will mark the beginning of our Lord's priestly rule over the earth (cp. Exod. 40:9–11; Dan. 8:13–14; Zech. 6:12–13).

THE TIME SPAN OF THE CONTENT OF THIS MESSAGE:

"Seventy weeks" (Heb. *week* means "seven") represent 490 units of time. From the context (Dan. 9:2) these units appear to be years, with 490 years in view. These 490 years are divided by the prophecy into two parts, 483 years and seven years, with an undisclosed interval between them.

THE FIRST PART: "SEVEN WEEKS" AND "SIXTY-TWO WEEKS," OR 483 YEARS

This period of 483 years lies between the beginning of the fulfillment of this prophecy and the death of Jesus (Dan. 9:25–26a). Why this first part of "69 weeks" (483 years) is divided into two periods (v. 25; "seven weeks" [49 years] and "62 weeks" [434 years]) is not clear. Not including the periods of interruptions, perhaps it took 49 years of work to complete the restoration of Jerusalem's walls and buildings. The starting date of this period of "69 weeks" was 445 B.C., when Nehemiah rebuilt the walls (v. 25; Neh. 2:1–8, 17–18) in the twentieth year of the Persian ruler Artaxerxes I Longimanus.[5]

The "69 weeks," or 483 years, came to an end just before Jesus' death (Dan. 9:26a). Being born in 5 or 4 B.C., before the death of King Herod the Great in 4 B.C. (Matt. 2:1), Jesus began His ministry about the age of thirty (Luke 3:21–23) and died several years later. A calculation of this period of 483 years, based on *lunar years* of 354 days each, would end it in A.D. 23; if based on solar years of 365¼ days each, it would end in A.D. 38. However, if this period is based on prophetic years of 360 days each, this would bring this period of 483 years to a close in A.D. 31, about the time of Jesus' death.[6] Note that several biblical passages speak of a prophetic year as being 1,260 days (Rev. 11:3; 12:6), "42 months" (11:2; 13:5) or to "time, times, and a half a time," which represents three-and-a-half periods of 360 days each (12:14 with v. 6; Dan. 7:25; 12:7; cp. vv. 11–12; 8:14).

THE UNDISCLOSED INTERVAL BETWEEN THE TWO PARTS

In my opinion, there is an undisclosed interval between the phrases "but not for Himself" and "the people of the prince" (Dan. 9:26), which represents the Church Age. That this interval of time exists is implied by the separate part of one "week" (seven years) and by the words "the end" and "the consummation" (vv. 26–27), which often relate to events that are associated with the Lord's second coming to earth (cp. 8:19; 11:27, 35, 40; 12:4, 9, 13; Matt. 24:3, 6, 13–14).

THE SECOND PART: "ONE WEEK," OR SEVEN YEARS

This part is described in Daniel 9:26 as follows: "And the city and the holy place shall the people of a coming prince [chief, leader] destroy; and it shall be with a flood, and unto the end there shall be war, determined desolations." Although most futuristic commentators believe that this refers to the destruction of Jerusalem by the Roman general Titus in A.D. 70, the context does not require this interpretation, which introduces a part of the Church Age into the prophecy. In my opinion, this prophecy is a reference to the future fall of Jerusalem to Satan's human agent, the Beast, when in the middle of the "seventieth week," he will violate Israel's peace treaty (Luke 21:20–24; Matt. 23:38–24:2, 15–21; Rev. 11:2; Dan. 8:11–14).

I believe that Daniel 9:27 is an explanation of events that will lead to the fall of Jerusalem in the middle of the "seventieth week" as described in verse 26b. If "and" is interpreted as an explanatory conjunction, then verse 27 may be translated this way: "That is [by way of explanation], he [the Beast] shall make strong a covenant with many [Israel] for one [period of] seven [years]; and at the half of seven [years] he will cause the [temple] sacrifice and meal offering to cease even upon a wing of abominations [detested things], desolating even unto complete destruction; and that which is [divinely] determined shall be poured forth upon the Desolator [the Beast]."

This verse gives us important details about the Beast and his relation to Israel. His confirmation of the peace treaty with Israel will mark the beginning of the "seventieth week." He will break this pact in the middle of the seven-year period by invading Jerusalem, stopping the temple daily sacrifice, desecrating the temple, and then destroying the temple and the city (Matt. 24:15; 2 Thess. 2:4; Rev. 13:5–7). But three and a half years later, that which has been divinely determined will be poured out upon the Desolator (the Beast, Rev. 19:19–20; Dan. 2:44; 7:26; 8:25; 11:45). Incidentally, we should not assume that the Beast is a Roman simply because the Romans took Jerusalem in A.D. 70.

APPENDIX H

An Analysis of Ezekiel 38 and 39

Many interpreters of these chapters expect Russia to invade Palestine in fulfillment of this prophecy. The view that these chapters speak of Russia is based on the similarity between the place names "Meshech" and Moscow, "Tubal" and Tobolsk, and "Rosh" (*Septuagint* translation for "chief" in Ezek. 38:2) and Russia. Moreover, this view is supported by Russia's chronic hostility toward Israel and by the invading army's coming from the north (Ezek. 38:15; 39:2).

While Russia, indeed, may invade Palestine to strike against Israel, this would not necessarily be in fulfillment of this prophecy. It is known from ancient cuneiform texts that Meshech (ancient Mishku) and Tubal (ancient Tabal) were located in central and eastern Anatolia (modern Turkey).[7] It is noteworthy that the man (the Beast), whom Gog prophetically represents, was the subject of several prophets earlier than Ezekiel (Ezek. 38:17; cp. Isa. 10:5–34; Jer. 25:12; Joel 1:1–2:11; Mic. 5:3–15; Zeph. 1:1–2:3). This is not true of Russia or its leaders.

These chapters look ahead to the time when God will deal with the nation of Israel by the hand of wicked Gentiles (Ezek. 38:8, 16) and will restore His people permanently to their land (39:23–29). The prophecy will be fulfilled at a time when Israel will dwell safely in their land (38:8, 14, 16) before their final restoration by the Lord Jesus (39:22–29). Apparently, their safety will rest on an international peace agreement, especially with her Arab and/or Muslim neighbors. "In the latter years" the Beast, Satan's human agent (Dan. 9:27), will confirm this peace treaty at the beginning of his prophetic political career when he becomes leader of a Middle East ten-nation federation (7:7–8, 19–27; see "The Prophecy of the Tribulation Age: The Beast's Career During the Tribulation Age" under Eschatology).

Rather than speaking of Russia, which like the United States is not a subject of biblical prophecy, Magog, with their leader Gog, more likely represents the prophetic Middle East ten-nation federation and its leader, the Beast, through whom Satan will rule the earth during the second half of the Tribulation Age (Dan. 7:7–8, 19–27; 8:9–12, 23–25; 11:21–45; Rev. 13:1–10; 17:8–11).

These chapters appear to enlarge upon Ezekiel 37:28 by describing the time and manner by which the Lord will make Himself known to the nations as the One who sanctifies (the remnant of) Israel and restores them permanently to their own land (vv. 20–27). Moreover, these chapters are a preface to the millennial kingdom scene of chapters 40–48 (cp. 43:7; 48:35).

My understanding of these chapters follows in outline form:

GOD'S DECLARATION OF HIS DEALINGS WITH GOG (Ezek. 38:1–7)

God declares His opposition to Gog and his people Magog and reveals what He will do with them. He will turn Gog and his confederates back and will bring them against Israel a second time (so implied in v. 4). Gog's confederates are probably members of the ten-nation federation, which he leads (vv. 5–6). This federation will consists of nations of the Mediterranean area (Dan. 7:2, with the federation described in vv. 7, 19; Rev. 13:1–2). In His sovereignty, God will bring Gog and his confederates against Israel twice and then on to the Battle of Armageddon (Zeph. 3:8; Zech. 12:1–3; 14:1–2).

THE DETAILS OF GOD'S DEALING WITH GOG (Ezek. 38:8–39:20)

Representing the enemy of God's people (cp. Rev. 20:8), Gog is Satan's human agent, the Beast out of the sea, through whom Satan will rule the earth with wickedness and cruelty during the last half of the Tribulation Age (Rev. 13:1–8).

THE BEAST'S FIRST INVASION OF ISRAEL (EZEK. 38:8–16a)

Taking place in the middle of the Tribulation Age, this military invasion will violate the Beast's peace agreement with Israel (see Dan. 9:27; Luke 21:20–24; Matt. 24:15–21).

1. The time and target of the invasion (38:8)

This will take place "against the mountains of Israel" right after Satan's confinement to earth and his resurrecting the Beast to be his human agent, through whom he will govern the earth (Rev. 12:7–13; 13:3–5).

2. The Beast's assault against Israel (38:8–9, 14–16a)

3. The Beast's motivation for his assault (38:10–12)

4. International protest against this invasion (38:13)

Upon this invasion, the Beast will trample Jerusalem underfoot for the remaining three and a half years of the Tribulation Age (Rev. 11:1–2). At this time, the Jewish temple will be razed, Jerusalem will be destroyed, and the people will be killed or dispersed (Matt. 24:1–3, 15–26; Luke 21:20–24).

THE BEAST'S SECOND INVASION OF ISRAEL (EZEK. 38:16b–39:20)

Politically frustrated and supernaturally influenced, the Beast will attack what remains of Jerusalem at the close of his three-and-a-half-years world rule (Dan. 11:44b–45; Rev. 16:13–16). This will lead to the Jewish remnant's repentance (Joel 2:1–20), the Lord's return to earth (Deut. 30:1–3; Zech. 4:1–3), and the Battle of Armageddon, wherein the Beast and his confederates will be utterly defeated (Rev. 19:11–21). The battle itself will extend throughout Palestine, with Jerusalem as its focal point (14:20; Zech. 12:1–3).

1. *The beast's second assault against Jerusalem (38:16b–17; 39:1–2)*
This will occur at the close of the Tribulation Age.

2. *God's judgment upon the Beast and his confederates (38:18–39:7)*
This judgment will include various expressions of divine wrath (Ezek. 38:18–19a; cp. Luke 21:22; Rev. 14:14–20; 16:17–21; 19:15) like a convulsion of the land (Ezek. 38:19b–20; cp. Rev. 6:12–17; 16:18) and a battle in which the Beast's soldiers will irrationally fight against one another, and God will discharge lethal volleys of disease, rain, hail, fire, and brimstone (Ezek. 38:21–23; cp. Zech. 12:4; 14:12–15; Rev. 16:21). These weapons of divine wrath will devastate the enemy on the battlefield (Ezek. 39:1–5) and at home (v. 6).

3. *The following cleanup (39:8–20)*
The debris and carnage of battle will be so great that it will take seven years to burn the litter (vv. 9–10) and seven months to bury the remains of the dead (vv. 11–16), whose flesh will be devoured by scavenger birds and animals (vv. 17–20; cp. Luke 17:37; Rev. 19:17–18, 21).

THE OUTCOMES OF GOD'S DEALINGS WITH GOG (Ezek. 39:2–29)

GOD WILL BE GLORIFIED (EZEK. 39:21; 38:23)

He will be exalted in the eyes of surviving nations by His woeful expressions of holy wrath (cp. Rom. 2:8–9; 9:22). He will also be known universally as the LORD *(Yahweh),* the Holy One in Israel (Ezek. 39:7).

THE ELECT REMNANT OF ISRAEL WILL BE BLESSED (EZEK. 39:22–29)

1. *They will know that the Lord is their God (39:22, 28).*
This means that they will not only know that the Lord is their God but that they will also be brought into a right relation with Him according to the promises of the new covenant (Ezek. 36:24–29; Jer. 31:31–40; cp. John 17:3).

2. *They will be restored permanently to their land (39:23–28).*
See Genesis 17:8; Deuteronomy 30:1–5; Ezekiel 11:17–20; 20:33–44; 34:11–31; 36:6–38; 37:12–14, 21–28.

3. *They will be anointed with the Holy Spirit (39:29).*
They will receive Him and the blessings of His many ministries (36:20–27).

APPENDIX I

Babylon

PROPHETIC BABYLON

While many commentators hold that prophetic Babylon is Rome (Rev. 17–18), I prefer the view that it is the Iraqi city of Babylon, which is currently being restored, or one that will be built near this ancient site. After the Noachic flood, false religion was organized under the leadership of Nimrod, the builder of the first kingdom of Babylon (Gen. 10:8, 10; cp.

Rom. 1:21–23).[8] With the dispersion of the people, its doctrines were spread over the earth. Today, they are perpetuated by all the religions of the world, including unbiblical forms of Christianity. In the future, they will be united in the worship of the Beast and his image (Rev. 13:8, 15; 17:2; 18:3; Dan. 7:25), with the result that Satan will be honored (Rev. 13:4), the nations will be deceived (13:13–14; 18:23), and God will be blasphemed (13:5; 17:3; Dan. 7:25).

ITS IDENTITY

Although portrayed as a woman (Rev. 17:3– 4, 9, 18), Babylon is identified as being a city (v. 18; 18:10, 16, 18–19, 21). I believe that Babylon must be rebuilt, for the prophecies of its career and destruction must be fulfilled. For instance, it was prophesied that its destruction would take place in the Day of the Lord (Isa. 13:1, 6, 9; cp. Jer. 51:6), suddenly and completely (Jer. 50:26; 51:8, 25, 37), making it a desolation forever (50:13, 39–40; 51:26, 62; Isa. 13:19–20). Also, this would be at the time when Israel returns to the Lord (Jer. 50:4–7).

Ancient Babylon never experienced these events. When he took the city in 539 B.C., Cyrus the Great restored it and made it the provincial capital of Babylonia. The city continued to flourish until 293 B.C., when the Greek general Seleucus built Seleucia, some forty miles north of Babylon. The rubble of Babylon was used for the construction of many buildings (cp. Jer. 51:26). In 275 B.C., Antiochus ordered the remaining civilian population of Babylon to be removed to Seleucia. A hundred years later, Antiochus IV placed a Greek colony in Babylon, which flourished for a time. Early in the second century B.C., the city was destroyed by the Parthians. In the first century A.D., merchants from Palmyra colonized the site. The Roman emperor Trajan wintered there (116) during his campaign against the Parthians. Thus, history shows that the area was not deserted forever. Until recently, men pitched their tents among its ruins (cp. Isa. 13:19–20). The city is currently being restored.

ITS CAREER

According to prophecy, Babylon will be Satan's and the Beast's world capital during the last half of the Tribulation Age (Rev. 13:5). Supported by the Beast's political structure (17:1–3; cp. 13:1–2), the city will be the administrative (v. 15; cp. Dan. 2:31–35), commercial (Rev. 18:3, 9–19), and religious (17:4–5; 13:11–17) center of earth.

ITS DESTRUCTION

It appears that this will be brought about by the individual leaders of the nations that make up the Beast's political entity (Rev. 17:16–17). Impelled by God, they will destroy the city in "one hour" (18:10, 17, 19), utterly burning it with fire and making it desolate (vv. 8, 18–19; 16:19). This will fulfill the ancient prophecies of the city's destruction (Isa. 13; Jer. 50–51).

AN ANALYSIS OF REVELATION 17 AND 18

THE CITY'S DESCRIPTION (REV. 17:1–6)

The "whore" is the city of Babylon (v. 18). She is seen *politically,* supported by the Beast's political entity, the ten-nation federation (v. 1–3); *commercially,* arrayed in costly garments and jewels (v. 4; see 18:12–14); *religiously,* holding the cup of her doctrinal and ritual abominations and filthiness with the label as the mother of these (17:4–5); and *morally,* drunk with the blood of the Lord's people whom she slew (v. 6; see 6:9; 12:17; 13:7, 15; 16:5–6).

THE CITY'S RELATION TO THE BEAST (REV. 17:7–15)

In verses 3 and 7, "the beast" is the political entity (ten-nation federation; cp. "many waters," vv. 1, 15; 13:1–2) of the Beast (Satan's human agent) of verses 8–11. "The seven heads," or "the seven mountains upon which the woman sits" (17:9), are the "seven kings" (v. 10), or the successive leaders of the ten-nation federation, which later becomes the political entity of the Beast. "The ten horns" (vv. 12, 16; Dan. 7:24) are the ten kings or governors of the individual nations of the federation. "The waters" (Rev. 17:1, 15) are the people of earth, over whom the Beast and his national federation rule during the last half of the Tribulation Age (13:7; 17:18; 18:3).

At the time John saw the vision, these ten kings, whose nations make up the federation, had not yet received their authority and kingdoms (Rev. 17:12), but they will have these when the Beast begins his prophetic career (Dan. 7:7–8, 19–27). These kings will give their authority to the Beast, when he is divinely restored to life, and will acclaim him as their leader at the beginning of the second half of the Tribulation Age (Rev. 17:13; cp. 13:3–7). Having been a leader of the federation before his death (cp. 13:3; 17:10; Dan. 7:24), the Beast upon his resurrection will become the eighth and last leader of the federation (Rev. 17:11), when Satan gives it worldwide political power, with Babylon as its capital (Dan. 7:23; Rev. 13:2–5).

THE CITY'S DESTRUCTION (REV. 17:16–19:6)

1. The destruction event (17:16–17)

Unwittingly motivated by God, the ten rulers of the ten nations that comprise the federation will destroy Babylon. This will be an act of rebellion against the Beast, the federation's satanic leader, who at this time will be in or near Palestine (Dan. 11:44–45; Rev. 18:8, 18–19).

2. The proclamation of the city's fall (18:1–8)

This includes an announcement (vv. 1–3), an order for God's people to leave the city, perhaps given earlier in the middle of the "seventieth week" (vv. 4–5), and a command for its judgment (vv. 6–8).[9]

3. The universal reaction (18:9–20; 19:1–6)

There will be reaction from earth dwellers everywhere: rulers (18:9–10), merchants (vv. 11–16), and their transporters (vv. 17–19). There will also be a rejoicing in heaven (18:20; 19:1–6).

4. Its permanence (18:21–24)

See Isaiah 13:19–20; Jeremiah 50:39; 51:62.

APPENDIX J

The Order of God's Decree

In their thinking about God's decree as it concerns man's creation, fall, election, and salvation, theologians have attempted to put these parts in a logical order that shows their relation to one another. The names of these proposed orders are based on the word *lapsarian* (from Latin, *lapsus,* meaning "fall"), which relates these orders to man's initial sin, or fall. The primary orders are supralapsarianism, infralapsarianism, and sublapsarianism.

SUPRALAPSARIANISM

With *supra* being Latin for "before," this term places God's decree to elect and to reprobate before man's fall. Held by high Calvinists, this view follows this order:

1. *To elect some people to salvation and to reprobate (foreordain, appoint beforehand) the remainder to perdition (their paying the penalty of their sins). This is called double predestination.*[10]
2. *To create the people who are elected and reprobated*
3. *To permit their fall*
4. *To justify the elect and to condemn the nonelect*

The main objection to this order is that election and reprobation concern nonentities since they precede the decree to create.

INFRALAPSARIANISM

With *infra* being Latin for "after," this term places God's decree to elect and to reprobate after man's fall. Held by moderate Calvinists, this view follows this order:

1. *To create man*
2. *To permit man's fall*
3. *To elect some people to salvation. This is called single predestination, for it does not hold that God reprobates the lost to perdition.*
4. *To leave the remainder (nonelect) to their sins and their punishment. This is called preterition.*

To my mind, this order is more logical than that of supralapsarianism.

The Arminian view is largely infralapsarian, with the distinction that God's election and preterition are based on divinely foreseen faith or unbelief, as the case may be. They consider these to be divine judicial (not sovereign) acts in the nature of reward and punishment.

SUBLAPSARIANISM

L. S. Chafer prefers this view. With *sub* being Latin for "below," this term places God's decree to provide salvation between steps 2 and 3 in the infralapsarian order.[11]

1. *To create man*
2. *To permit man's fall*
3. *To provide salvation*
4. *To elect some people to salvation*
5. *To leave the remainder (nonelect) to their sins and their punishment*

W. G. T. Shedd observes that unlike the decree of reprobation, the decree of preterition (God's passing by the nonelect) does not necessitate, or bring about, perdition, although it makes it certain. It is a permissive act, not an efficient one, on the part of God. He decides to do nothing in the case of the nonelect sinner. Leaving him alone, God allows him his own self-determination and voluntary inclination. This permission is not causation. The nonelect sinner is condemned and ruined, not because God did not elect him but because he sinned and came short of God's glory. While election is the efficient cause of salvation, preterition is not the efficient cause of perdition. It only makes perdition certain to those who have fitted themselves for destruction (Rom. 9:22).[12] By contrast, the decree of reprobation, as held by many Calvinists, is efficient, necessitating perdition. I believe that the concept of preterition is more biblical than that of reprobation.

APPENDIX K
Israel's Future As Described in Biblical Prophecy

Genesis
Their land: 15:18; their future: chap. 49

Leviticus
Their dispersion: 26:27–39; their restoration: 26:40–45

Numbers
Their blessings: 24:15–19

Deuteronomy
Their dispersion: 4:27–28; 28:15–68; their restoration: 4:29–31; 30:1–10

2 Samuel
Their restoration: 7:10

Psalms
Their restoration: 53:6; 69:35–36; their messianic kingdom blessings: chaps. 67, 72

Isaiah
The remnant: 1:9; their restoration: 10:20–22; 11:11–16; 14:1–3; 26:1–19; 27:12–13; 29:17–24; 30:15–26; 32:15–20; 35:1–10; 41:14–20; 43:5–9; 49:5–26; 51:11; 52:8–12; 54:1–17; 59:20–21; 60:1–22; 62:1–12; 65:9–10, 19–25; 66:10–14; their messianic kingdom blessings: 2:1–22; 4:1–5; 11:1–9; 51:3; 65:17–25

Jeremiah
Their restoration: 3:14–18; 16:14–21; 23:3–8; 24:6–7; 30:3–9, 17, 22; 31:8–16; 32:37–44; 46:27–28; 50:19–20; their return to the Lord: 3:12–14, 22–4:9; the remnant: 15:11, 19–21

Ezekiel
Their dispersion: 33:23–29; their judgment: 11:21; 20:37–38; 34:17–22; their restoration: 11:17–20; 16:60–63; 17:22–24; 20:33–44; 28:25–26; 34:11–31; 36:6–38; 37:12–14, 21–28; 39:25–29

Daniel
The Jewish Age: 9:24–27; their relation to the Beast: 8:11–14; 9:27; 11:31–35; 12:11

Hosea
Their judgment: 1:4–6, 9; 9:11–12; 13:7–8, 15–16; their return to the Lord: 3:4–5; 5:14–6:3; 14:1–2; their restoration: 1:10–11; 2:14–23; 11:9–11; 13:9–10, 14; 14:4–8

Joel
Their judgment: 1:4–20; 2:1–11; their restoration: 2:12–3:1, 17–21

Amos
Their judgment: 9:1–10; their restoration: 9:11–15

Obadiah
Their messianic kingdom blessings: 1:17–21

Micah
Their restoration: 2:12–13; 5:3; 7:7–20; their messianic kingdom blessings: 4:1–8

Zephaniah
The remnant: 3:12–13; their restoration: 3:14–20

Zechariah

Their restoration: 8:1–8, 11–14, 23; 10:1–12; 12:10–13:1, 8–9; their messianic kingdom blessings: 2:8–13; 14:9–11, 16–21

Malachi

Their judgment: 3:1–5; the remnant: 3:16–18; 4:2–3

Matthew

The remnant: 24:9–31 (cp. Mark 13:11–27; Luke 17:20–32; 21:12–28); their judgment: 25:14–30

Romans

The remnant: 11:25–36

Revelation

The remnant: chap. 12

APPENDIX L

An Outline of the Prophetic Chapters of Daniel

CHAPTER TWO: NEBUCHADNEZZAR'S DREAM OF THE IMAGE AND ITS INTERPRETATION

This gives the place where the Beast's government will be located.
A. The dream (2:31–35)
B. Its interpretation (2:36–45)
    1. Of the image (2:37–43)
        a. The head of gold: Babylon under Nebuchadnezzar (2:37–38)
        b. The breast and arms of silver: Persia (2:39; cp. 5:28)
        c. The belly and thighs of brass: Greece (2:39; cp. 8:21)
        d. The legs of iron; feet of iron and clay: The later historical and the future prophetic empires (2:40–43)
          1) The legs of iron: the later historical empire (2:40)[13]
          2) The feet of iron and clay: the future Beast's empire (2:41–43; 7:23–25; 8:23–24) [4][14]
    2. Of the Stone (2:44–45) [6]
    The Lord Jesus will defeat the Beast and will establish His own kingdom (Rev. 19:11–21).

CHAPTER SEVEN: THE VISION OF THE FOUR WILD BEASTS

This gives the political environment of the Beast and his government.
A. The vision (7:1–14)
B. Its interpretation (7:15–27)
    1. Of the four kingdoms or federations of nations (7:2–7, 17) [2]
    These arise simultaneously (vv. 3, 12) in the Mediterranean area (cp. Ezek. 47:15, 19–20).
    2. Of the fourth kingdom, the empire of the Beast (7:7, 19–25)
        a. Its structure at the time of the Beast's political appearance (7:7–8, 24) [2]

1) It will be a ten-nation federation (7:7, 24; Rev. 13:1).
2) The Beast will begin his career by subduing three of these nations (7:8, 24).
b. Its character at the time of the Beast's world supremacy (7:7, 23, 25) [4]
1) It will be worldwide in its extent (7:7, 23; Rev. 13:1–7).
2) It will continue for three and a half years (7:25; Rev. 13:5).
c. Its termination at Jesus' second coming (7:9–14, 26–27) [6]
1) The setting up of God's judgment throne (7:9–11; Rev. 4)
2) The investiture of the Son of God (7:13–14; Rev. 5)
3) The destruction of the Beast's kingdom and the establishment of Jesus' worldwide authority (7:11, 14b, 26–27; 2:44–45; Rev. 19:11–21)

CHAPTER EIGHT: THE VISION OF THE RAM AND HE-GOAT

This shows that the Beast will rise in the site of Alexander's ancient empire.
A. The vision (8:2–14)
B. Its interpretation (8:15–24)
1. Of the ram and the he-goat (8:3–8, 15–22)
a. The ram represents the kings of Media and Persia (8:3–4, 20).
The great horn is Cyrus the Great, who conquered the Babylonians and forged the Persian Empire.
b. The he-goat represents Alexander the Great of Greece (8:5–7, 21–22).
He conquered Persia and left his realm to his four generals. Babylonia went to Seleucus.
2. Of the little horn, the future Beast who will lead the ten-nation federation (8:9–12, 23–25)
a. Rising in Babylonia, the Beast's political achievements (8:9, 23; cp. 17, 19)
1) His early exploits (8:9; see 7:8, 24) [2]
2) His later exploits as the final head of the ten-nation federation (8:23; cp. 7:23, the federation) [4]
b. His character and anti-God exploits (8:10–14, 23–25; 7:25; Rev. 13:3–8) [4]
c. His end (8:13–14, 25b; 7:11, 26; 2:35; Rev. 19:19–21) [5–6]

CHAPTER NINE: THE VISION OF THE "SEVENTY WEEKS"

This gives the time and the duration of the Beast's rule.
A. Daniel's prayer (9:1–19)
B. God's response (9:20–27)
1. The circumstances (9:20–23)
2. The message (9:24–27)
a. The people whom the message concerns: the Jews and Jerusalem (9:24a)
b. The things that God will accomplish by 490 years (9:24b)
1) To end the Jews' transgressions and their sins [6]
2) To save them on the basis of Jesus' atoning work (Ezek. 36:25–26) [6]
3) To bring in everlasting righteousness with Jesus' earthly rule (Jer. 33:14–15; Isa. 11:4–5) [6]
4) To fulfill the themes of these prophecies (Dan. 12:4) [1–6]
5) To anoint the temple's Holy of Holies (Dan. 8:13–14; Zech. 6:12–13) [6]
This will mark the beginning of our Lord's priestly one-thousand-year rule.
c. The time span of this message (9:24a, 25–27)
1) The first part of 483 years (9:25–26a)

From the rebuilding of Jerusalem (Ezra 7:1–6; Neh. 2:1–11) to Jesus' ministry. The parenthetical Church Age lies between these two parts: ". . . himself" (Church Age) "and the people of the prince . . ."

    2) The second part of seven years (9:26b–27) [2–4]
From the Beast's agreement with the peace accord to his defeat by Jesus. After three and a half years, the Beast will break this treaty by attacking Jerusalem and desecrating the temple. [3]

CHAPTERS TEN THROUGH TWELVE: THE VISION OF THE TIME OF THE END

A. The angelic struggle for the control of the nations (10:1–11:1)
    1. Daniel's praying (10:1–4)
    2. The angelic messenger and his struggle (10:5–14)
    3. Daniel's reaction (10:15–19)
    4. The angel's parting words (10:20–11:1)
B. The activities of the Beast, Satan's human agent (11:2–45)
    1. Beyond Daniel's time: the kings of Persia and Alexander of Greece (11:2–4)
    2. Beyond our time (11:5–45) [1]
    The future Middle Eastern political events that will lead to the rise of the Beast (the third "King of the North") in the "latter days" (Dan. 10:14; 11:6, 35)
       a. The conflict between the North and the South (11:5–20) [1]
       b. The beginning of the Beast's prophetic career as the third "King of the North" (11:21–30a) [1–2]
       c. The Beast's dealings with the Jews (11:30b–35) [3–4]
       d. The Beast's satanic world supremacy (11:36–39) [4]
       e. The closing events of the Beast's career and Armageddon (11:40–45) [5–6]
C. God's dealings with Israel (12:1–3, 5–12)
    1. He promises to deliver the elect remnant (12:1). [6]
    2. He promises the remnant resurrection and glory (12:2–3). [6]
    3. He declares the duration of these events (12:5–7, 11–12).
       a. Three and a half years (12:5–7) [4]
       b. Plus thirty days and forty-five more days (12:11–12) [6]
       For His judging the nations and establishing the millennial kingdom
D. God's final words to Daniel (12:4, 13)
    1. He is to seal the book (12:4).
    The prophecy will not be understood until the time of the end.
    2. He must go his way (unto death) until his resurrection and appraisal (12:13).

APPENDIX M

An Outline of the Book of Revelation

A. Introduction (1:1–8)
    1. The source and theme of this book (1:1–2)
    2. The promise to the reader and hearer (1:3)
    3. The apostle John's greeting (1:4–8)

B. "The things which you have seen" (1:9–20)
   The vision of Jesus among the lampstands
C. "The things which are" (2:1–3:22)
   Jesus' letters to the seven churches of the Roman Province of Asia
   1. At Ephesus (2:1–7)
   2. At Smyrna (2:8–11)
   3. At Pergamos (2:12–17)
   4. At Thyatira (2:18–29)
   5. At Sardis (3:1–6)
   6. At Philadelphia (3:7–13)
   7. At Laodicea (3:14–22)
D. "The things which shall be" (4:1–22:5)
   Visions of the future
   1. The visions of the Tribulation Age judgments (4:1–19:10)
      a. The Seal Judgments (4:1–8:1)
         1) Introduction (4:1–5:14)
            a) The judgment throne of God (4:1–11) [1] (see endnote 13)
            b) The investiture of the Lamb Jesus (5:1–14) [1]
         2) The judgments (6:1–8:1)
            a) The rider on the white horse (6:1–2) [1–2]
               The rise and political conquests of the Beast
            b) The rider on the red horse (6:3–4) [2]
               International war, rising from first seal judgment
            c) The rider on the black horse (6:5–6) [2]
            d) The rider on the pale horse (6:7–8) [2]
               Bringing death to one-fourth of the world population
            e) The vision of the first Tribulation Age martyrs (6:9–11) [2]
            f) The vision of their divine vengeance (6:12–17) [2]
               This vengeance will be fulfilled in 16:18–20 [5].
               The first interlude (7:1–17)[15]
                  One: The vision of the 144,000 evangelists (7:1–8) [2]
                  Two: The vision of the great multitude of believers (7:9–17) [4]
                  This is the result of the ministry of the 144,000.
            g) Silence in heaven (8:1)
               A pause before the next series of judgments
      b. The Trumpet Judgments (8:2–13:18)
         1) Introduction (8:2–6)
         2) The judgments (8:7–13:18)
            a) Hail, lightning, bloody shower (8:7) [2]
            b) Volcanic eruption, affecting seas (8:8–9) [2]
            c) Meteorite, poisoning of fresh water (8:10–11) [2]
            d) Natural light decreased (8:12) [2]
            e) *The first woe:* people tormented by demons (9:1–12) [2]
            f) *The second woe:* demons slay a third of mankind (9:13–21) [2]
               The second interlude (10:1–11:14)
                  One: The vision of the mighty angel (10:1–11) [3]
                  Two: The vision of the temple in Jerusalem (11:1–2) [3–4]
                  Three: The vision of God's two witnesses (11:3–14) [4]
            g) *The third woe:* Satan's rule over the earth (11:15–13:18) [4–5]

(1) Heaven's anticipation (11:15–19) [3]
(2) Heavenly signs (12:1–12): Christ (1–2) [1] and Satan (3–12) [3]
(3) Satan's persecution of Israel (12:13–17) [4]
(4) Satan's rule over the earth (13:1–18)
   His superstate (13:1–2) and supermen (13:3–18) [4]
   The third interlude (14:1–20)
      One: The vision of the 144,000 in heaven with Jesus (14:1–5) [early 4]
      Two: The vision of the angelic proclamations (14:6–20)
         1. Giving God's final appeal (14:6–7) [early 4]
         2. Announcing the fall of Babylon (14:8) [5]
         3. Warning against worshiping the Beast (14:9–20) [5]
c. The Bowl Judgments (15:1–19:10)
   1) Introduction (15:1–8)
   2) The judgments (16:1–21)
      a) A foul, painful ulcer afflicting earth dwellers (16:2) [5]
      b) The seas becoming blood (16:3) [5]
      c) Freshwater becoming blood (16:4–7) [5]
      d) Increase in solar radiation and heat (16:8–9) [5]
      e) Terrifying, supernatural darkness (16:10–11) [5]
      f) Gathering of the nations for Armageddon (16:12–16) [5]
      g) A great earthquake and hail (16:17–21) [5]
         The fourth interlude (17:1–19:10)
            One: The judgment of Babylon (17:1–18) [5]
            Two: The reaction of earth dwellers (18:1–19) [5]
            Three: The rejoicing in heaven (18:20–19:6) [5]
            Four: The marriage of the Lamb in heaven (19:7–10) [5]
2. The vision of Jesus' second coming and millennial kingdom (19:11–20:6)
   a. His second coming to earth and the Battle of Armageddon (19:11–21) [6]
   b. The eviction and binding of Satan (20:1–3) [6]
   c. The earthly, millennial, messianic kingdom (20:4–6) [6]
3. The visions of the final judgments (20:7–15)
   a. The final overthrow of Satan (20:7–10) [6]
   b. The judgment of the unsaved (20:11–15) [6]
4. The vision of the eternal states (21:1–22:5)
   a. The eternal state of the saved (21:1–7) [6]
   b. The eternal state of the unsaved (21:8) [6]
   c. The eternal state of the saved (continued, 21:9–22:5) [6]
E. Conclusion (22:6–21)
   1. The truthfulness of the prophecy (22:6)
   2. The declaration of Jesus' imminent return (22:7)
   3. John's reaction (22:8–10)
   4. Jesus' closing statement (22:11–20)
   5. John's benediction (22:21)

APPENDIX N

Giving

Although the love of money is a root of all evil (1 Tim. 6:10), money or other means of exchange holds a very important place in the Lord's work. Giving money or goods is a unique spiritual exercise in the gospel believer's life, service, and worship (Rom. 12:8; 2 Cor. 8:1–5; 9:7; Gal. 6:6; Phil. 4:14–18; 1 Tim. 6:17–18; 1 John 3:17–18). Let us consider what God says about this.

THE LORD'S ADVICE TO TREASURE SEEKERS (Luke 12:13–37)

Our materialistic and affluent age ever tempts us to have an improper attitude toward material possessions (cp. 1 Tim. 6:8–10; 1 John 2:15). When He was requested to settle a disputed inheritance, Jesus gave a timely response to the appellant and to His own disciples.

HE WARNED AGAINST OUR LAYING UP TREASURES ON EARTH (LUKE 12:15–21)

Other passages teach that we should provide for our dependents (2 Cor. 12:14; 1 Tim. 5:8), the needy (Eph. 4:28; Gal. 6:10), the Lord's work (Phil. 4:14), and our personal needs (Acts 18:3; 2 Thess. 3:7–13). But there are several objections to our laying up for ourselves treasures on earth.

1. *It opens the door to covetousness (v. 15a).*

Covetousness is a dissatisfaction with what we have and an eager, greedy desire for more. This is a form of idolatry (Col. 3:5).

2. *It does not constitute life (v. 15b).*

We humans are not only physical beings but also spiritual ones, with a capacity for spiritual life and fellowship with God. Consequently, material things do not completely satisfy us, for they do not minister to our spiritual needs (Matt. 4:4). Only the Lord Jesus can do this (John 6:35).

3. *It does not bestow eternal benefits (vv. 16–21).*

This farmer was a shrewd, successful businessman, but God said that he was foolish, for He lived for time and not for eternity. He was not rich toward God, for he had left God out of his life and did not consider his possessions as a trust from Him. Thus he did not seek divine guidance for the use and disposal of his property. Our Lord does not condemn thrift and the possession of earthly goods, but He does warn against our having a covetous attitude toward them, our giving them God's place in our lives, and our using them in a wrong way.

HE EXHORTED HIS PEOPLE TO LAY UP TREASURE IN HEAVEN (LUKE 12:22–37)

How can we do this?

1. *By trusting His loving care rather than uncertain riches (vv. 22–30).*

Since life does not consist of the abundance of one's material possessions (Luke 12:15), we do not have to worry about these things. We must not make them the primary object of our trust or concern (v. 22). This does not excuse us from the duty of providing for ourselves and our dependents (2 Thess. 3:10; 1 Tim. 5:8). Ordinarily, we must earn our own livelihood, manage our income, live within our means, and look to the Lord for direction and help in these things (Luke 12:22–30).

2. *By seeking the things of God's kingdom (v. 31a).*

Unlike the unsaved (v. 30), we are to seek those things that concern God's kingdom and interests (v. 31; Col. 3:1–2). He has not left us here to pursue selfish, materialistic ambitions; we are here to serve with Him in building His Church. Although much of our time is spent in securing a living, we can regard this as a service to the Lord as well as an opportunity to minister unto others (Col. 3:22–24; Acts 1:8; see "The Work of Mankind" under Anthropology). As we place the Lord's interests first in our lives, we can depend upon Him to help us to provide for our needs and those of our dependents.

3. By disposing of our possessions as He directs (vv. 31b–33).

Since we are God's stewards (1 Peter 4:10), all that we have is from Him and belongs to Him (1 Cor. 4:7; Ps. 24:1). We should use our possessions as He directs and for His glory (1 Cor. 10:31). We must not prize these things and live for them (Luke 12:34; cp. 1 Cor. 6:12; 7:31).[16] When we have right attitudes toward our possessions, we can trust the Lord to provide for us when we cannot provide for ourselves (Luke 12:31b–32; Matt. 6:25–33). All who anticipate the Lord's imminent return sit lightly on their possessions (Luke 12:35–37) and look forward to the dividends that their heavenly investment will bring them (v. 42–43; cp. Mark 8:34–37; 2 Cor. 5:9–10).

PRINCIPLES THAT SHOULD GOVERN OUR GIVING

The New Testament presents several principles that guide us in our giving in a manner that pleases God. They recognize the distinction between the Dispensation of the Mosaic Law and the Dispensation of Grace, under which we live today. These principles are stated in the answers to the following questions:

WHO SHOULD GIVE TO THE LORD AND HIS WORK?

Only saved people, for the admonitions and instructions about giving are addressed to His people. Giving in God's way is a spiritual exercise, for which unsaved people have neither desire nor ability. Contrariwise, the gifts of Cornelius, a Gentile with no Levitical sacrifice, were a memorial before God (Acts 10:2–41). It is likely that his giving was in response to the manifestation of the true God by general revelation and was his way of honoring God, whom he was seeking. Saved people should give to the Lord and His work, for, in addition to being motivated by gratitude and love, by the promise of reward, and by the urgency of need, the gospel believer will also be impelled by his relationship to God as follows:

1. Each gospel believer is a steward of God (1 Peter 4:10).

In biblical times, a steward was the chief servant of a household, who had the responsibility of administering his master's possessions (Luke 16:1). Being God's stewards (1 Cor. 4:1), we have the duty of using the things that He has entrusted to us for His glory. These things include our lives, bodies, energy, time, skills, and material possessions. We are to discharge this stewardship—*blamelessly*, according to His will (Titus 1:7); *faithfully*, with His purpose and interests in view (Luke 12:42); *wisely*, according to His direction (v. 42); and *efficiently*, by means of His strength and for His profit (v. 43)—until Jesus returns (Luke 19:13).

2. Each gospel believer is a priest unto God (1 Peter 2:5).[17]

Since there is no hierarchy within God's family, all believers have equal priestly rank and privilege. Through the Lord Jesus, all have direct access to God (Heb. 10:19–22; Eph. 2:18). Moreover, our allegiance is to the Lord Jesus, our great High Priest (Heb. 4:14). In addition to worship and prayer, we have the priestly function of offering to God spiritual sacrifices. Although they do not contribute to our salvation, these sacrifices are an expression of worship and a means of exalting God. They include our offering our bodies to God (Rom. 12:1), our giving Him praise and thanksgiving (Heb. 13:15), our fruitful witness (Rom. 15:16), our offering our lives in death (Phil. 2:17), and our sharing with others our possessions (Heb. 13:16; Phil. 4:18).

   3. *Each gospel believer is a partner with the Lord Jesus in His work (1 Cor. 3:9).*

   In this fellowship of building the Church, we share in His interests, possessions, and activities as members of His earthly body (1 Cor. 12:13, 27). This includes the activity of giving (Rom. 12:8).

BY WHAT MEANS ARE WE TO GIVE?

   All spiritual exercises, including giving, must be by means of God's grace (2 Cor. 8:1–7; cp. 1 Cor. 15:10). The Macedonian gospel believers' giving was not prompted by sentimentality, natural generosity, or the nuisance of surplus wealth. It was divine grace that motivated and enabled them to give, despite the obstacles of persecution (Phil. 1:28–30; 1 Thess. 1:6; 2:14) and poverty (2 Cor. 8:2). They gave sacrificially (v. 2) beyond their natural ability (v. 3a) and voluntarily without external pressure (vv. 3b–4). Their submission and obedience to the Lord (v. 5) allowed God's grace to operate in their giving (cp. vv. 1, 9) as well as in providing for their needs (Phil. 4:19).

HOW MUCH SHOULD WE GIVE?

   1. *The basis for this determination is not the Mosaic Law (Rom. 6:14; Gal. 5:18).*

   The law directed Israel to give several tithes (a tithe is 10 percent) of their gross income to the Lord. *One tithe* of herds and crops was given annually to the Levites (Lev. 27:30–34; Num. 18:21); *a second tithe* of herds and crops was brought annually to the worship center, or temple, during the sacred festivals (Deut. 14:22–26); and *a third tithe* was given every three years for the support of local Levites, strangers, widows, and orphans (vv. 28–29; 26:12–14). In addition to these tithes, the law also required the people to offer various sacrifices throughout the year (Lev. 1–7). Tithes were given to God before the Mosaic Law, but these appear to be voluntary in nature, expressing to God both gratitude (Gen. 14:20) and devotion (28:22).

   2. *The basis for this determination is Christ's law (1 Cor. 16:1–2; 2 Cor. 8–9).*

   Since giving today is by the grace of God, and the gospel believer is God's steward, then we must look to God for what and to whom we are to give. Under grace, giving is not simply a mathematical calculation, the payment of a debt, or an impulsive response to an appeal. The Lord has so designed our giving that we must assess what He has given us, seek His direction, learn His will, and look to Him for the needed grace to give as His responsible stewards. Under grace, giving is a spiritual exercise that rises from fellowship with the Lord Jesus. It is a source of rich spiritual blessing and a means of spiritual growth.

   Under grace, no percentage is stipulated for giving. We must learn the amount directly from God as He makes known to us His will. Each believer must determine this amount for himself (2 Cor. 9:7a), when he reviews God's material provisions and blessings in his life (8:11–12; 1 Cor. 16:2). Incidentally, the apostle Paul distinguished between ordinary giving and sacrificial giving (2 Cor. 8:11–15). *Ordinary giving* is from that which is in excess of what we need for ourselves; *sacrificial giving* is from that which we need for ourselves (cp. the Macedonians, vv. 1–5). God does not command us to give sacrificially (the apostle spoke of a principle of equality in vv. 12–15), but God is pleased when we follow His leading in giving this way (Mark 12:41–44).

WHAT IS THE RECOMPENSE OF GIVING?

   A universal spiritual law decrees that a person will reap as he sows (2 Cor. 9:6). By this law, God gives both inducement and warning. He promises the generous giver that he will reap bountifully now (cp. Phil. 4:19) and in the future (cp. Luke 12:33; 2 Cor. 5:10), for He will not be a debtor to anyone (cp. Prov. 3:9–10; 11:25). He also warns that the miserly giver will reap sparingly (cp. v. 24b). He will suffer material lack as well as spiritual impoverishment.

TO WHOM OR TO WHAT SHOULD WE GIVE?

1. The Mosaic Law method

Sometimes called "storehouse tithing," this requires people to bring all their tithes and offerings to their local church and to allow the church to determine how these gifts should be used or distributed. This method is based on God's appeal to Israel when the Jews were withholding their tithes that supported the temple priests and their operation (Mal. 3:7–12; cp. Deut. 14:22–26). While this appeal may offer us a spiritual lesson, it is not binding on us, since we are not under the Mosaic Law.

2. The grace method

The order we should follow today is given in 1 Corinthians 16:2. The apostle Paul wrote, "Upon the first day of the week, let every one of you lay at the side of himself, storing up whatever he may be prospered in, that there be no gatherings when I come." This verse provides several details about giving under grace.

a. The place of giving

We should keep in mind that the local church building does not have exactly the same function as did the temple in Jerusalem. The temple was the place where God dwelt among His people. Because of this, the people brought their gifts and offered their sacrifices there. God does not dwell in a church building today, for the bodies of His people are His temples (1 Cor. 6:19). Moreover, He is present with His people wherever two or three are gathered in Jesus' name (Matt. 18:20).

Rather than depositing gifts in a church, the gospel believer is directed to accumulate their gifts "at the side of himself" in a private fund at home. This is to be held in reserve for the Lord until some need arises and divine direction is given for its use. At the suitable time and occasion, each household is to give from their fund whatever they believe that the Lord would have them do. When the collection was being received for the Jerusalem gospel believers (1 Cor. 16:1, 3), the united action in support of this program was a church action, yet it allowed each one to give from his private fund as he was led of the Lord.

b. The day of giving

This is the first day of the week (1 Cor. 16:2). While there may have been some practical reason for this, the Lord's Day (Sunday) is a fitting time to review His blessings, to worship Him with gratitude, and to lay by in store as He directs. It is also a time in which we have opportunity to give to the needs of the local church and its programs.

c. The needs for giving

During the first century, gospel believers gave to support of their local church (Gal. 6:6; 1 Tim. 5:17–18; 1 Cor. 9:4–14), missionaries (Phil. 1:3–5; 4:14–18), and needy people (Gal. 6:10; Eph. 4:28). In our giving to people or causes that we do not know, we must exercise caution by asking such questions as these: Is there really a need? Will the money be used wisely? Can we assist in a better way than by giving money? Is the person or work truly Christian? Is the organization doctrinally and financially sound? Does it do what it was established to do? Does it publish regular accounts of its financial receipts and disbursements, or are these records available for public inspection? As we seek God's direction regarding what and where we are to give, we must base our decisions on facts rather than on impulses, feelings, or appeals.

HOW SHOULD WE GIVE?

While man looks on the outward appearance, God looks on the heart. He evaluates people's actions by assessing their motivations. If our giving is to please God, we must be motivated by right attitudes like the following:

1. *Love (2 Cor. 8:8, 24)*

This prompts us to give obediently (John 14:21) and sacrificially (1 John 3:16–18) as the need requires.

2. *Willingness and eagerness (2 Cor. 8:8–12; 9:2; cp. 1 Chron. 29:9)*

3. *Generosity (2 Cor. 9:6; 8:2–5)*

4. *Resoluteness (2 Cor. 9:7)*

This means that our giving is to be with personal conviction regarding the Lord's will in the matter.

5. *Cheerfulness (2 Cor. 9:7)*

We should not mourn over that with which we must part, for God promises to give us something better (Luke 12:32–33; Heb. 10:24). Also, we are not to give of necessity under the pressure of external coercion. Rather, we are to respond to God's inner restraint of love. We are to give cheerfully with the joy of the Holy Spirit (2 Cor. 9:2; Acts 20:35; Gal. 5:22).

6. *Confidence (2 Cor. 9:8)*

This is faith in the sufficiency of God's grace to enable us to abound in every good work. Practical faith activates this divine grace in our lives (Gal. 2:20). Keep in mind that the divine grace of giving is the enabling activity of the Holy Spirit; therefore, we must be filled with Him if we are to give in a manner that pleases God (Eph. 5:18).

THE PATTERN OF GIVING

As the Lord Jesus is our pattern, or model, of the Christian life (John 14:6; Matt. 10:24–25; Gal. 2:20; 4:19; Eph. 5:1; 1 Peter 2:21), so He is the pattern for our giving (2 Cor. 8:9). When we submit ourselves to the Holy Spirit and follow His directions, we allow the Lord to give through us in His characteristic way. What are the qualities of the Lord's giving, as seen in 2 Corinthians 8:9?

1. *His giving was gracious.*

The Lord Jesus was motivated by divine grace when He gave Himself for us (2 Cor. 8:9). We did not deserve the least benefits of His atoning work.

2. *His giving was sacrificial.*

Giving Himself for us, the Lord Jesus gave His all (Matt. 20:28). Laying aside His visible glory, He came to earth, received a nature lower than that of His servants the angels, and became beggarly poor (Luke 9:58). Furthermore, He gave His life as a ransom for us (Matt. 20:28).

3. *His giving was beneficial.*

We who are saved are indeed rich, for we possess every spiritual blessing in the Lord Jesus (Rev. 2:9; Eph. 1:3). With the apostle Paul we say, "Thanks be to God for His inexpressible Gift" (2 Cor. 9:15).

In like manner, if our giving is to please God, it, too, must have these qualities. This means that, as we are led, we must be willing to give to others, even undeserving people, at personal cost with a view to ministering to their needs (1 John 3:16–18). These qualities manifest Christlikeness.

As God's stewards we should be looking forward to the Day of Christ when the Lord Jesus will escort His Church to heaven. Then we shall experience the redemption of our bodies (Phil. 1:6; 3:20–21; Rom. 8:23), be presented faultless before God's presence (Eph. 1:4; 5:27; Col. 1:22; Jude 24), see what He did with our lives in His program of building the Church (Phil. 2:16; 2 Cor. 1:14), and be rewarded for our obedience to Him in our stewardship (2 Cor. 5:9–10; cp. Luke 19:12–19). Until this day, we should be living suitable lives that glorify God (Luke 19:13; Phil. 1:10–11).[18]

APPENDIX O

The Divine Mysteries of the New Testament

These mysteries are "sacred secrets," or divine truths, that had not been revealed in previous ages but that have been made known to the Lord's people by the New Testament (cp. Eph. 3:1–5, 9; Rom. 16:25). A list of these mysteries follows.

THE MYSTERIES OF THE KINGDOM (Matt. 13:11; Mark 4:11; Luke 8:10)

Given in parabolic form, these mysteries describe the present state and course of Jesus' kingdom in this world, which is generally described as "Christendom" (earthly Christianity in all its forms), during His physical absence from earth. In Matthew 13:5–53, these mysteries include the kinds of responses to the gospel (the sower and the soils, vv. 3–9); the Lord's present policy regarding His enemies (the wheat and the weeds, vv. 24–30); the phenomenal growth of Christendom (the mustard seed, vv. 31–32); the false teaching, hypocrisy, and bad politics found in Christendom (the leaven, v. 33); the present status of the elect remnant of Israel (the hidden treasure, v. 44); the redemption of true gospel believers and a hint of the Church (the valuable pearl, vv. 45–46); and the Lord's judgment of earth dwellers when He returns and sets up His millennial kingdom (the dragnet, vv. 47–50).

THE MYSTERY OF ISRAEL'S BLINDNESS (Rom. 11:25)

Although this divine judicial blindness, or hardening of heart to spiritual truth, was a subject of prophecy (Isa. 6:9–10; cp. Matt. 13:10–17), the mystery concerns its extent ("in part") and its duration ("until the fullness of the Gentiles be come in"). An exception is the deliverance of elect Jews from this blindness during the present Church Age (Rom. 11:5–6). In the middle of the Tribulation Age, if not earlier, God will remove this blindness from the elect remnant of Israel; will enable them to understand the gospel and His Word, like Matthew chapter 24; and will eventually bring them to repentance and faith in the Lord Jesus by the intense persecution, waged by Satan through his human agent, the Beast (Rev. 12:3–6; 13:5–7; cp. Deut. 30:1–3; Joel 2; Matt. 24:15–34). At this time, "all Israel shall be saved," that is, they will be delivered from their enemies as well as from their sins (Rom. 11:26; Zech. 14:3–9; Ezek. 36:25–29). "All Israel" is a figure of association (synecdoche, where the whole represents a part) for the elect Jewish remnant (see Appendix X).

Some understand "the fullness of the Gentiles" as referring to the opportunity Gentiles now have to receive the Savior and to become a part of the Church (Acts 15:14; Rom. 15:8–24). To my mind, it more likely refers to their final opportunity to be saved through the ministry of the 144,000 evangelists during the first half of the Tribulation Age (Matt. 24:14; 2 Thess. 2:10–12; Rev. 7).

THE MYSTERY OF THE GOSPEL (Rom. 16:25; Eph. 6:19; cp. Col. 4:3)

Hidden from times eternal, yet contained in the Old Testament (Rom. 1:1–2; chap. 10; Gal. 3:8, 16; Acts 17:1–3; Luke 24:25–27; John 5:39), the gospel was not fully expressed or understood until Jesus' incarnation, earthly ministry, and atoning work (John 1:17, 17; 2 Tim. 1:8–10); the writing of the New Testament (John 16:12–15; 20:30–31; Mark 1:1; Luke 1:1–4); and the teaching ministry of the Holy Spirit (John 14:26; 1 Cor. 2:9–12; 1 John 2:27; cp. Luke 24:44–45). Only in the light of this additional divine revelation and illumination can people fully understand the Savior, the events, and the message of the gospel that was anticipated in the OT prophecies.

THE MYSTERY OF GOD'S WISDOM (1 Cor. 2:6–8)

In this context, "wisdom" is God's special revelation that He gave to His people in the form of the written Scriptures (Eph. 1:17; cp. Prov. 2:6; chap. 8; Eccl. 12:9–11). While the meaning of this revelation is hidden from the world, the Holy Spirit gives God's people an understanding of this truth (1 Cor. 2:9–14; 1 John 2:27; cp. Deut. 29:29).

THE MYSTERY OF THE CHANGED BODY (1 Cor. 15:51)

The resurrection of humans was a subject of OT prophecy (Job 19:23–27; Dan. 12:2). The mystery seems to concern the nature of changed bodies—those of dead people from corruptibility to incorruptibility and those of living people from mortality to immortality at the Lord's return (1 Cor. 15:52–53). See verses 42–50 for a description of the changed body (also see "The Resurrection of Mankind" under Anthropology).

THE MYSTERY OF GOD'S DECRETIVE WILL (Eph. 1:9)

God's decretive will is His decree, or plan, which is secret until it is divinely revealed or it comes to pass. In this context, His "will," or decree, appears to be that which relates to the future, as explained in verse 10. This anticipates the reconciliation and union in Christ of all things in the heavens and on earth that have been involuntarily affected by God's curse in His reaction to man's sin (cp. Rom. 8:19–23). Based on the Lord's atoning work (Col. 1:20; see Christology) and having been prophetically revealed, this reconciliation will be achieved in His millennial earthly kingdom (Acts 3:19–21; Rom. 8:19–22; Isa. 11:6–9). Besides dealing with His enemies (Rev. 19:11–16; 1 Cor. 15:25), the Lord's restoration of universal harmony in nature and among earth dwellers will be His climactic messianic work relating to the present world order (cp. Isa. 11:1–9; 2:4; chap. 35).

THE MYSTERY OF GENTILES AND JEWS BELONGING TO THE SAME BODY (Eph. 3:3, 9)

Speaking of Gentiles and Jews who are saved during this Church Age, this mystery (Eph. 3:1–6) reveals their having equal status and blessing in Christ (1 Cor. 12:13; Eph. 1:3) as well as their being members of the same body, His Church (Eph. 1:22–23). The Old Testament anticipated God's blessing for Gentiles (Gen. 12:3) but not their equal status with Jews. The Lord Jesus also alluded to this union (John 10:16). This "fellowship" (Eph. 3:9, meaning "arrangement" in Gk.) of saved Jews and Gentiles in Christ reveals to angels the manifold wisdom of God (Eph. 3:10).

THE MYSTERY OF THE UNION BETWEEN JESUS AND HIS PEOPLE (Col. 1:26–27)

This truth was stated by the Lord Jesus (John 14:20; 17:21–23, 26) and was illustrated by the apostle Paul when he wrote of the Church's being the Lord's earthly mystical body

(Eph. 1:22–23; 1 Cor. 6:15). This truth consists of the Lord's being spiritually united to His people by the Holy Spirit's baptism (Gal. 3:27) and His indwelling (John 14:16–18). Because of this union, the Lord, as His people's spiritual life (Col. 3:4), lives and works through them on earth to build His Church (John 15:1–5). Unknown in OT times, this union was not possible before our Lord's incarnation and exaltation.

THE MYSTERY OF GOD AND CHRIST (Col. 2:2–3)

This seems to refer to the relationship between the Father and the Son, "in Whom are hidden all the treasures of wisdom and knowledge," especially with reference to Jesus' human messianic work. As the Messiah, He is the Father's Agent (Slave), through Whom the Father does this work (John 8:26–28; 14:9–11). The Old Testament anticipated the Messiah's being the Father's "Servant" and foresaw His work (Isa. 9:6–7; 42:1–7; 49:1–7; 52:13–53:12; Ps. 110:1), but it did not reveal the Father's involvement in Jesus' messianic work. This truth was made known by the Lord Jesus and by NT revelation (cp. Matt. 22:41–46; John 1:14; 5:18–23, 30, 36; 6:38; 8:28–29; 12:49–50; 14:9–11; Phil. 2:5–7; Heb. 10:7; see "The Messianic Work of Jesus: His Work as the Messiah" under Christology).

THE MYSTERY OF INIQUITY (2 Thess. 2:7)

This speaks of the lawlessness that is widespread throughout the world. Unknown to the world, the guiding mind of this lawlessness is Satan (Eph. 2:2), and its energy source is the sin force that dominates Satan and the lives of all unsaved people on earth (Rom. 3:9; 8:7–8). Lawlessness, especially against God, will reach its climax in the worldwide rule of the Beast, Satan's human agent, during the second half of the Tribulation Age (Rev. 13:5–8; 2 Thess. 2:3–10).

THE MYSTERY OF THE FAITH (1 Tim. 3:9);
THE MYSTERY OF CHRIST (Eph. 3:4)

If the phrase "the faith" refers to the body of Truth that God has given through Christ by divine revelation (Jude 3; Rev. 1:1), then this mystery refers to the New Testament, which contains doctrines and truths that have never been revealed before, like those taught by the apostle Paul (Eph. 3:4). Deacons, as well as other church officers, are to be loyal believers of this portion of the Bible and followers of its teachings.

THE MYSTERY OF GODLINESS (1 Tim. 3:16)

This mystery seems to refer to that character of life that, although puzzling to the world, effectively bears witness to the essential elements of the Lord's first advent (cp. 1 Tim. 3:1–15). When filled with the Holy Spirit, the gospel believer's life manifests the reality of the gospel and of all that is associated with it, including the person and work of the Lord Jesus, who is our Life and the Captain and Author of our salvation (cp. Rom. 1:16; 13:12–14; 2 Cor. 2:14–16; Gal. 2:20; 4:19; Phil. 1:21; 4:19; Heb. 2:10; 5:9).

THE MYSTERY OF THE SEVEN STARS AND LAMPSTANDS (Rev. 1:20)

This concerns the Lord's relation to the seven churches of the Roman Province of Asia and their messengers, to whom these messages were addressed.[19] The context indicates that the Lord Jesus is present with His people and appraises their actions (Rev. 2:1–2; Matt. 18:20). The Old Testament anticipated the Lord's return to earth and rule (Deut. 30:3; Zech. 14:3–4; Isa. 11:1–10; 40:10), but it did not foresee His present activity during the Church Age of building His Church and supervising His local churches through the NT Scriptures (Matt. 16:18; John 16:12–15; Eph. 2:20; 4:20–21; Rev. 1:1).

THE MYSTERY OF GOD (Rev. 10:7)

This seems to refer to the remainder of God's program for the second half of the Tribulation Age and the establishment of the millennial, earthly kingdom (Rev. 12–19, cp. 11:15–18). Not anticipated by the world, these divinely scheduled events will with the seventh Trumpet Judgment proceed without further delay (10:6–7). This judgment will introduce the third woe, which represents Satan's confinement to earth and his activities through the Beast during this period (11:15–13:18). The Tribulation Age will end with the Lord's return to earth and His triumph over His enemies (Rev. 19:11–20:3).

THE MYSTERY OF BABYLON (Rev. 17:5)

Under Satan, ancient Babylon conceived and fostered false doctrine, idolatry, and abominable rituals that persist to this day (Gen. 11:1–9; cp. Rom. 1:21–25). I believe that the city will be rebuilt to be the world center of religion, administration, and commerce during the Beast's satanic rule over the earth in Tribulation Age days (Rev. 17–18; see Appendix I: "Babylon"). The mystery appears to relate to the world's ignorance of the satanic nature of the religion that this city has propagated throughout its history and of the role it will have in the future.

We who are saved are stewards of "the mysteries of God" (1 Cor. 4:1). Essentially, this consists of the new doctrines and truths that are revealed in the New Testament, including those that concern us and our work in this world (cp. "The Mysteries of the Kingdom" above; Matt. 13:1–30). It is our duty to understand them and to respond to them accordingly (cp. Matt. 13:51–52).

APPENDIX P

Baptist Distinctions

While, historically, Baptists have been General (Arminian) and Particular (Calvinistic) in their doctrinal persuasion, they have all agreed on certain propositions that have made them distinctive from other denominations. Some of these are gleaned from Edward T. Hiscox, *The New Directory for Baptist Churches.*[20]

THE ABSOLUTE AUTHORITY OF THE BIBLE
IN MATTERS OF FAITH AND CONDUCT

"The Bible is a Divine Revelation given of God to men, and is a complete and infallible guide and standard of authority in all matters of religion and morals; what it teaches is to be believed; whatever it commands is to be obeyed; whatever it commends is to be accepted as both right and useful; whatever it condemns is to be avoided as both wrong and harmful; but what it neither commands nor teaches is not to be imposed on the conscience as of religious obligation" (p. 11).

THE LOCAL CHURCH, CONSISTING OF SAVED, IMMERSED MEMBERS

"Baptists assert that the only proper subjects for baptism are regenerated persons; those who have exercised and professed a saving faith in Christ, and are living orderly Christian lives" (p. 16).

"What class of persons should be admitted as members of the fellowship of Christian churches? Baptists say that godly persons, baptized on a profession of faith, are the only proper and suitable persons. That all others should be denied admission, and if already within the Church, should be cast out. Consequently, to receive unconverted persons, whether infants or adults, destroys the spiritual character of the body, and forms an unholy alliance with the world, instead of maintaining a broad and distinctive separation between them" (p. 17).

SEPARATION BETWEEN CHURCH AND STATE

"Civil governments, rulers, and magistrates are to be respected, and all temporal matters, not contrary to conscience and the Word of God, to be obeyed; but they have no jurisdiction in spiritual concerns, and have no right of dictation to, of control over, or of interference with, matters of religion; but are bound to protect all good citizens in the peaceable employment of their religious rights and privileges" (p. 12).

"No organic union of church or State should be tolerated, but entire separation maintained: the church should neither ask for, nor accept of, support from civil authority, since to do so would imply the right of civil dictation and control. The support of religion belongs to those who profess it" (pp. 12f.).

THE AUTONOMY OF THE LOCAL CHURCH

"Baptists assert that each particular local church is self-governing, and independent of all other churches, and of all persons and bodies of men whatever, as to the administration of its own affairs; that it is of right, and should be, free from any other human authority, whether civil or ecclesiastical and that this is the New Testament idea of church government" (pp. 17f.).

THE LIBERTY OF CONSCIENCE, OR SOUL LIBERTY

"Every man by nature possesses the right of private judgment in the interpretation of the Scriptures, and in all religious concerns; it is his privilege to read and explain the Bible for himself, without direction from, or dependence on, anyone, being responsible to God alone for his use of the sacred truth" (pp. 11f.).

"Every man has the right to hold such religious opinions as he believes the Bible teaches, without harm or hindrance from anyone on that account, so long as he does not intrude upon, or interfere with, the rights of others by so doing" (p. 12).

"All men have the right, not only to believe, but also to profess and openly declare, whatever religious opinions they may entertain, providing they be not contrary to common morality, and do no injustice to others" (p. 12).

"All men possess the common right to worship God according to the teachings of the Scriptures, as they understand them, without hindrance or molestation, so long as they do not injure or interfere with the rights of others by so doing" (p. 12).

OTHER DISTINCTIONS

Other distinctions that are often given are these:
1. The two officers of the local church—pastors and deacons
2. The two ordinances—water baptism and the Lord's Supper
3. The priesthood of all gospel believers
    This asserts the ability and right of all saved people to worship God without the help of any intermediary other than the Lord Jesus Christ (1 Tim. 2:5).[21]

APPENDIX Q

A Contrast Between the Church and Israel

Covenant theology considers the Church to be the seed of Abraham under the new covenant. Many subscribers to this theology hold that "all the prophecies concerning Israel not yet fulfilled and still to be fulfilled must be fulfilled in her (the Church), leaving nothing at all of either promise or prophecy for those who are merely descendants of Abraham after the flesh."[22] While the apostle Paul identified gospel believers as "the children of Abraham" and "his seed" (Gal. 3:6–7, 29), this does not necessarily mean that saved Gentiles are the patriarch's actual posterity. Whether Jews or Gentiles, the apostle characterized saved people, who are people of faith (cp. Eph. 1:1), as belonging to a class of persons with Abraham as their exemplar (Gal. 3:9). In this case, to be a child of someone is to be like him in some way (cp. Matt. 5:45). Consider the following contrasts between the Church and Israel:

THEIR CONSTITUENCIES

The Church consists of all saved people from the Day of Pentecost after Jesus' return to heaven until His return to receive her to Himself (Acts 2; 1 Thess. 4:13–17).

Historically, Israel has consisted of the descendants of Jacob. In the future, the prophetic, true Israel will consist of the elect remnant of these descendants, who will be saved at Jesus' second coming to earth (Rom. 9; Deut. 30:1–10; Ezek. 36:16–38).

THEIR DIVINE COVENANT RELATIONSHIPS

The Church is related to God by the new birth (John 1:12–13), based on the new covenant that Jesus mediated by His atoning death (Heb. 8:6; 12:24; 1 Cor. 11:25).

Israel was related to God by the Mosaic covenant (Exod. 19:5), which they broke (Jer. 31:32) by their idolatry (Jer. 3; Hos. 2:1–5; 4:12–13). The elect remnant of Israel will be restored to God, as promised by the new covenant (Jer. 31:31–40; Ezek. 36:21–38).

THEIR NUPTIAL RELATIONSHIPS TO GOD

Being espoused to Jesus (2 Cor. 11:2), all who compose the Church corporately constitute His bride (Eph. 5:23–32).

Having been God's wife (Jer. 3:14), Israel will be restored to this relationship in the coming earthly kingdom (Isa. 54:1–8; Hos. 2:6–7, 14–23).

THEIR INHERITANCES

That of the Church is Jesus and His universal wealth (Eph. 1:3, 11; Rom. 8:17; Heb. 1:2).

That of Israel is the land God promised to Abraham, Isaac, and Jacob (Gen. 15:18; 35:12; Deut. 30:5; Jer. 16:14–15) and its rejuvenation (Isa. 35).

THEIR HISTORIES

The Church could not have existed in OT times because of the time and nature of her formation. Her formation did not begin until after Jesus' return to heaven (Matt. 16:18; Acts 1:5; Acts 2; 11:15). She is being formed by the Holy Spirit's baptism, a Church Age work (Acts 1:5; 1 Cor. 12:13, 27; Eph. 1:22–23) and is built upon the teachings of the Lord's apostles and the NT prophets, now recorded in the New Testament, with Jesus as her chief cornerstone (Eph. 2:20).

Israel was a nation from their departure out of Egypt and their receiving the Mosaic Law, c. 1491 B.C. (Exod. 19:1–6) until their final dispersion by the Romans in A.D. 70. She was revived as a nation on May 14, 1948. The divinely elected remnant of her people will be saved at Jesus' second coming to earth and will continue forever (Jer. 31:36; Amos 9:11–15; Ezek. 37:19–28). See Romans 11:1–6, 11–12, 15–17, 26–27, 30–31.[23]

THEIR PLACES IN JESUS' MILLENNIAL KINGDOM

The Church is presently a part of our Lord's nonpolitical, spiritual kingdom (Col. 1:13). As His wife, she will also have a nonnational place in His earthly, millennial kingdom, with Church members and other saved people ruling with Him (Rev. 2:26–27).

Israel will be the foremost nation in our Lord's earthly, millennial kingdom (Ps. 47; Isa. 55:5; chap. 60; Zech. 8:23; Mal. 3:12). Jerusalem will be the capital of Jesus' world government (Isa. 24:23; Zech. 14:16–17; Matt. 5:35).

APPENDIX R

The Kingdom of God

Ordinarily, a kingdom must have a government, territory, and people who are subject to a king. In the Scriptures, the concept of God's kingdom has various meanings, as determined by its use in a passage and its context.

IN THE OLD TESTAMENT

1. *God's universal kingdom*
   This embraces all persons, creatures, and things (Ps. 103:19; cp. 2 Chron. 20:6).
2. *God's mediatorial kingdom*
   This is God's rule over the earth through a human agent, or viceroy.
   a. *Through Adam (Gen. 1:26, 28; cp. Heb. 2:5–8)*
   When he sinned, Adam lost this authority to Satan (John 12:31; 14:30; 16:11).
   b. *Through the Lord Jesus*
   This is the predicted messianic millennial kingdom of the Lord Jesus (Ps. 2:6–9; chap. 72; Isa. 9:6–7; 11:1–5; Dan. 2:44; Zech. 14:9–19). This kingdom will be earthly, visible, geographical, and political.

IN THE NEW TESTAMENT

1. *Christ's physical presence (Luke 17:21, "within" can also be read "among")*
   Jesus' words (vv. 20–21) may mean that the millennial kingdom of prophecy was not to come at that time, with the manifestations and in the manner that the unsaved Jews expected. It was already among them in the presence and messianic works of the King during His first advent (cp. 10:9; 11:20).
2. *The Jews of Jesus' day with their corrupted Judaism (Matt. 12:12; Luke 13:18–21)*
3. *Christendom, or earthly Christianity (Matt. 13, "kingdom of heaven")*
   This is what represents Christ in the world today during His absence from earth. It includes all professing Christians, both real and false, and their institutions.

4. *Christ's true spiritual kingdom today (Col. 1:13)*

Being invisible and nonpolitical, this kingdom includes all people who are saved. This is entered by the new birth (John 3:3–7; cp. Mark 12:34).

5. *Heaven (2 Tim. 4:18; cp Phil. 3:20)*

6. *God's mediatorial kingdom*

This is the Lord Jesus' worldwide, messianic kingdom of prophecy, over which He will rule for one thousand years as God's Viceroy (Matt. 3:2; 6:10; 2 Tim. 4:1; Heb. 2:5–9; Rev. 11:15; 19:11–16; 20:4, 6).

7. *The eternal state of the saved (1 Cor. 15:50)*

The apostle Paul declared that our bodies, animated by the soul (with the blood; Lev. 17:11), cannot now enter the eternal state without being changed (vv. 51–53, see vv. 42–49).

8. *God's future universal kingdom (1 Cor. 15:24–28)*

When the Lord Jesus has achieved the objectives of His millennial, earthly rule, then His earthly mediatorial kingdom will merge with the Father's universal kingdom. They will jointly rule forever, with the Lord Jesus' ever being subject to the Father as His Slave and Viceroy.

APPENDIX S

Physical Healing

With the growing healing phenomenon of the charismatic movement, I offer the following view, which considers the gift of healings as being inactive today.[24]

MIRACULOUS HEALING

Henry W. Frost has made the following observation:

> When a saint (gospel believer) is sick, he has three possible courses divinely set before him: first, he may seek healing through a physician and his treatment; second, without a physician and his ministry, but through rest and change of scene and occupation; or third, without a physician and without rest and change and through God alone. It is to be recognized that all of the three kinds of healing referred to are divine healings, that God alone being the Creator, maintainer and healer of the body. It is further recognized that the last named kind of healing—which is properly miraculous healing—is no more divine than the two healings first named, all being of God and all manifesting Him, the only difference being miraculous healing more fully demonstrates the divine presence and power.
>
> Miraculous healing may be tested and discovered by applying to each supposed case the New Testament conditions of such where the healings were always immediate, complete, and final. If these conditions do not pertain to a given case of healing, then it is divine healing, but it is not miraculous.
>
> In seeking for healing, the saint is to have regard to the nature of the disease with which he is afflicted. If this is entirely within the scope of man's ability to give aid, it—apart from special guidance to the contrary—would be unlawful to

set aside what God has graciously provided, and hence, recourse is to be had to a physician. . . . If it does not call for medical assistance, rest and change will be sufficient. . . . If it is of such a nature that means of any sort and all sorts are valueless, then God may be appealed to in the hope and confidence that He may do what man and natural processes have failed to do and cannot do. In all three of these methods, prayer and faith are to be exercised, as, whether means are or are not used, it is God alone who heals. . . .

God, judging from the Scriptures and experience, may possibly put forth miraculous power and heal apart from means under the following circumstances: first, when from the beginning the disease is of such a nature as to make all known means valueless; second, when it is impossible—as sometimes occurs on the mission field—to secure medical aid; third, when medical men have attempted to bring healing to pass and have failed to do so; fourth, where a servant of God has a divinely appointed task set before him which some ailment hinders his fulfilling, where this task must immediately be performed and where there is neither time nor opportunity to have recourse to usual means; fifth, where a missionary is laboring in unevangelized parts and the Bible, because uncirculated and unknown, cannot be appealed to, and where a miracle is needed to prove God's existence and the missionary's divine appointment; and lastly, where God indicates, whether at home or abroad, there is need of giving a new demonstration of His presence and power in proof that He is the living and loving Father in heaven.

The saint is to remember, in all of the foregoing conditions, that God is the judge as to whether or not He will display Himself and His power by a miraculous act, and also when, where, how, and with whom this will be done; and he is to keep constantly in mind that God is just as faithful and loving when He does not so display Himself as when He does. The saint is ever to remain submissive to God's will, whatever this may mean.[25]

There are large parts of the world where healing-miracles, in proof of a living and all-powerful Christ, may well be looked for; and it may confidently be anticipated, as the present apostasy increases, that Christ will manifest His deity and lordship in increasing measure through miracle-signs, including healings. We are not to say, therefore, that the Word is sufficient. It is so to those who know and believe it; but it is not so to those who have never heard of it or who, having heard, have disbelieved it. To these persons a dramatic appeal may have to be made, and on the plane where such will most easily be understood, the physical.[26]

SEVERAL OBSERVATIONS

One: God does not always heal the sick. The apostle Paul did not receive healing in answer to his prayers (2 Cor. 12:7–10). Being unable to heal Trophimus, Paul left him sick at Miletum (2 Tim. 4:20).

Two: Having given people the knowledge and means of treating many diseases, God usually uses these to heal people (cp. Paul's advice to Timothy, 1 Tim. 5:23).

Three: Some illnesses of the Lord's people may be divine corrective chastisement for their failure to deal with known sins in their lives (1 Cor. 11:30–32). When they deal with these sins, God forgives them their sins and removes their affliction.

Four: Other illnesses are for God's glory and our spiritual productivity. These debilitating afflictions allow the Lord to manifest His grace of ministry and life in us (2 Cor. 12:9–10; 4:7–10). God is more concerned with our fruitfulness than our bodily comfort (John 15:1–5; cp. James 1:2–4).

Five: The bodies of living gospel believers are still mortal, subject to disease and death (Rom. 7:17; 8:10–11, 23). Our bodies will not experience our Lord's redemptive work (deliverance from disease and death) until He changes them when He comes for His Church (1 Thess. 4:13–17; see Rom. 8:11; 13:11; Phil. 3:20–21; 1 Cor. 15:50–57).

Six: There is no command for us to rebuke Satan for any cause, including illness. Even the archangel Michael could only say to Satan, "The Lord rebuke you" (Jude 9). We can resist the Devil in God's strength when we first give ourselves to God (James 4:7). We can also pray for those who are possessed by demons (Matt. 17:21).

Seven: Unlike natural faith, which is a dependence upon self or human resources, biblical faith is an attitude of complete reliance upon God and His Word. We trust in God by relying upon His promises. However, we must be certain that the promises that we are trusting are those that He has given to us, not those for people of another time. Many people are looking to God for material prosperity and physical well-being, like that promised to obedient Israel in Leviticus 26:3–13 and Deuteronomy 28:1–14. While God assures us of His spiritual blessings and care as we walk in obedience to Him, He does not today promise us physical health and material affluence (Matt. 6:24–34; Phil. 4:19; note that the Macedonian Philippians were a generous people, 2 Cor. 8:1–5; 9:5–7). When He was on earth, the Lord Jesus was not materially wealthy as some expect to be today.

Eight: Whenever we, as saved persons, become ill, we should first examine our own hearts for any sins in our lives or in our relations with others that we have failed to deal with by repentance and confession (Rev. 2:5; 1 John 1:9; Matt. 5:23–24). If there are none, then God has allowed this illness for some purpose. Normally, we seek healing by the means that are at hand like medication and therapy. If these fail, then we may ask for anointing by the church's elders (see the next section). If the illness persists, then we must accept our affliction as being God's will and look to Him for the grace to bear it. As the apostle Paul attested, in these cases the Lord will provide spiritual strength, blessing, and joy in the midst of physical weakness and distress (2 Cor. 12:9–10). Physical weakness causes us to lean more heavily upon God, which allows Him to use us in a greater way.

ANOINTING THE SICK WITH OIL

A gospel believer who is seriously ill may ask his or her pastor for anointing, according to the teaching of James 5:14–16. This anointing with oil applies to saved people who are hopelessly ill and who no longer seem to have within them the power of recovery (cp. John 5:6–7). James 5:14 commands the sick to ask for this ministry.

Anointing with oil does not guarantee recovery, but it appears to be the formal commitment of the sick person to God for healing according to the divine will. Anointing does not rule out the use of medical means or therapy, for God can heal by these means as well as apart from them. If it is His will, God can heal people instantly or over a period of time.

The anointing oil, usually olive oil, is a symbol of the Holy Spirit who indwells the Lord's people (James 4:5; 1 John 3:24) and who is able to heal according to God's pleasure (Eph. 3:20). "The prayer of faith" is an expression of faith that God is going to heal, whether immediately or eventually. It is given by the Holy Spirit at those times when it is His intention to do this. It is not always God's will to heal (2 Cor. 12:8–9) or to heal immediately (2 Tim. 4:20). As we have seen, physical healing by faith is not guaranteed by the atonement (see "His Humiliation: The Atonement and Physical Healing" under Christology).

Because illness is sometimes due to unjudged sins (1 Cor. 11:28–31), the sick person should examine his heart and deal with any known sin in his life (James 5:15–16) or in his relations with other people (Matt. 5:23–24) by repentance and confession to God (Rev. 2:5; 1 John 1:9).

APPENDIX T

Classes of Books Relating to the Biblical Period

The following lists are classifications of both canonical and noncanonical literature relating to the Old and New Testament periods.[27]

THE OLD TESTAMENT PERIOD

THE CANONICAL BOOKS

The Undisputed Canonical Books
(Homologoumena—The Ones Confessed)

These were the Old Testament books that were not only received as canonical without dispute from the first but their place in the OT Canon was never later challenged by the Jews or the Church. This group consists of all the books of the OT Canon save those of the next group, which immediately follows.

The Disputed Canonical Books
(Antilegomena—The Ones Spoken Against)

At first, these books were recognized as being canonical, but later they were challenged by certain rabbis at Jamnia (c. A.D. 90). The outcome of their debates was their firm acknowledgment of the canonicity of these books. These disputed canonical books follow:

Esther, which does not have the name of God. The book shows God's providential care and sovereignty.

Ecclesiastes, which seems to oppose orthodox teaching (3:19–20). But the context shows that Solomon was speaking about death and the return of the bodies of humans and animals to dust. He does distinguish between the directions that the spirit of man and that of animals take upon death (v. 21).

Proverbs, which has an apparent contradiction (26:4–5). Ordinarily, it is better to ignore a fool, but occasionally he needs a suitable reply to remind him that he is a fool.

The Song of Solomon, for its erotic passages (chaps. 4, 7). This song of married love portrays the spiritual relationship that the Lord has with His people.

Ezekiel, which seems to differ from the Levitical ritual of the Mosaic Law (chaps. 40–48). These chapters appear to describe the millennial temple and its ritual, which will exist in the Kingdom Age.

THE NONCANONICAL BOOKS

These were religious compositions, written between 300 B.C. and A.D. 100, which generally were circulated under false titles or unsubstantiated claims of authorship. Never recognized as being divinely inspired or authoritative, this literature was apparently written by pious Jews (all of whom but one are unknown) about persons and events relating to the Old Testament and the intertestament periods. Their objectives appear to be filling in the gaps of Jewish history, strengthening the Jewish mind against the influence of paganism, and extolling the dignity and glory of Israel.

The value of this literature follows: *Historically,* it provides information about the intertestament period. *Religiously,* it sheds light on the spiritual, philosophical, and intellectual life of Judaism during this period, especially regarding the person and work of the Messiah, life beyond death, and the reality and activity of angels and demons.

The Hidden Books (Apocrypha)

Early Christians included fifteen noncanonical books in their Greek and Latin translations of the Old Testament. These were *I Esdras, II Esdras, Tobit, Judith, The Additions to Esther, The Wisdom of Solomon, Ecclesiasticus (The Wisdom of Jesus the Son of Sirach), Baruch, The Letter of Jeremiah, The Prayer of Azariah and the Song of the Three Young Men, Susanna, Bel and the Dragon, The Prayer of Manasseh, I Maccabees,* and *II Maccabees.*

At the Council of Trent (1546), the Roman Catholic Church declared these writings to be canonical, excepting *I Esdras (III Esdras in the Latin Vulgate), II Esdras (IV Esdras in the Vulgate),* and *The Prayer of Manasseh.* Other Apocryphal books were *The Epistle of Jeremy* and *III Maccabees.*

The False Writings (Pseudepigrapha)

This group consists of the rest of the noncanonical literature of this period that was circulated under false titles. It includes *The Book of Jubilees, The Letter of Aristeas, The Book of Adam and Eve, The Martyrdom of Isaiah, The Book of Enoch, The Testaments of the Twelve Patriarchs, The Sibylline Oracles, The Assumption of Moses, The Book of the Secrets of Enoch, Baruch, Ezra, The Psalms of Solomon, IV Maccabees, Pirke Aboth,* and *The Story of Ahikar.*

THE NEW TESTAMENT PERIOD

THE CANONICAL BOOKS

The Undisputed Canonical Books (Homologoumena)

These were the New Testament books that were universally received as being canonical from the first. These include the four gospels, Acts, the apostle Paul's epistles, 1 Peter, and 1 John.

The Disputed Canonical Books (Antilegomena)

At first, these were not universally received as being canonical.

Hebrews was questioned in the West on the point of authorship.

James was considered to be in conflict with the apostle Paul on the doctrine of justification (2:14–26; cp. Gal. 2:16; Eph. 2:8–9). James does not deny justification by faith, but he emphasizes that true faith is manifested by good works, or doing God's will.

Second Peter was questioned because of differences in vocabulary and style from 1 Peter. The apostle Peter may have used a different secretary (cp. 1 Peter 5:12) or may himself have written the epistle. Also, 2 Peter contains different subject matter.

Second John and *3 John* were questioned on the grounds of authorship.

Jude was questioned because of the possibility of his referring to the pseudepigraphical *Book of Enoch* (1:9; 5:4) in Jude 14–15. Even if true, Jude did not endorse this book anymore than the apostle Paul did the pagan writings of Aratus (Acts 17:28), Epimenides (Acts 17:28; Titus 1:12), and Menander (1 Cor. 15:33).

Revelation was questioned on the point of authorship.

In the West, the canonicity of the twenty-seven books of the New Testament was recognized by the Synods of Hippo (393) and of Carthage (397). The NT Canon was recognized in the East by the close of the fifth century.

THE NONCANONICAL BOOKS

The Writings of the Apostolic Fathers

These were noncanonical writings, produced by Christian men who were the immediate successors of the Lord's apostles. Their writings did not have false content as did the *NT Apocrypha,* but they lacked apostolic authority, for they were not divinely inspired. Written during A.D. 80–180, these books were intended for the edification of other gospel believers. For a time, some churches regarded several of these books to be canonical, but later they rejected them.

These writings include those of Clement (Bishop of Rome), *The Epistle to the Corinthians;* of Ignatius (Bishop of Antioch), *The Epistle to the Magnesians, The Epistle to the Trallians, The Epistle to the Ephesians, The Epistle to the Romans, The Epistle to the Philadelphians,* and *The Epistle to the Smyraeans;* of Polycarp (Bishop of Smyrna), *The Epistle to the Philippians;* of Barnabas (of Alexandria?), *The Epistle of Barnabas;* of Hermas, *The Shepherd;* and (author unknown) *The Teachings of the Apostles.*

The False Writings (Pseudepigrapha)

Sometimes called the *NT Apocrypha,* these were fictitious writings circulated under false titles of NT persons. Taking the canonical books as their models, they are absurd and impious writings. Written during A.D. 100–800, their authors, presumably Christians, are unknown.

Some of these writings are *The Protevangelium of James, The Gospel of Thomas, The Gospel of Peter, The Gospel of Philip, The Acts of John, The Acts of Peter, The Acts of Paul, The Acts of Andrew, The Acts of Thomas, The Epistle to the Laodiceans, The Epistle of the Apostles, The Apocalypse of Peter, The Apocalypse of Paul,* and *The Apocalypse of Thomas.*

The value of these noncanonical books is that they reflect the belief of their authors and the tastes of their readers. They also set forth certain ideals of the Christian life and concepts of the Christian faith that were widespread during the second century and thereafter.

APPENDIX U

Our Inward Desires

The Scriptures indicate that there are at least two kinds of inward desires (often called "lusts" in KJV) that we who are saved have. These are demand desires and need desires.

Let us consider these.

THE DEMAND DESIRES

These are desires that are expressed by those inner moral forces that would dominate our lives. These forces are God and sin.

GOD'S DESIRES FOR US (JAMES 4:5)

If "Spirit" here refers to the indwelling Holy Spirit, then He desires something to the point of envy. Other passages indicate that God desires that we voluntarily submit ourselves to His control that He might use us as His instruments of righteousness for His glory (cp. Rom. 6:11–22; Eph. 1:12; 2:10). He also desires that we allow Him to help us to refuse the demands of our spiritual enemies (James 4:7; Gal. 5:16–17) and to do His will (Rom. 12:2; Eph. 5:17). Finally, God impresses His desires for us upon our hearts as well as expresses them in His Word (Rom. 10:1; Phil. 2:13; Ps. 119:105; Col. 3:16).

THE SIN FORCE'S DESIRES FOR US

Our spiritual enemies desire to dominate us and use us for their evil expressions. These enemies are the sin force within (Rom. 6:12; Gal. 5:16–21; James 1:14–15) and Satan (1 Thess. 3:5) and the world (1 John 2:16–17) without.[28] As long as we live on earth, these enemies will solicit us to yield to their evil demands. Besides the inner urges of the sin force, we have those evil thoughts and desires that Satan puts into our minds. There is no way that we can prevent these evil desires from occurring. However, to defeat them we must immediately give ourselves to God, resist them in His strength, think holy thoughts, and do His will (James 4:7; 2 Cor. 10:5; Phil. 4:8).

Observe that 1 John 2:16 speaks about "all that is in the world" as being "the lust of the flesh, and the lust of the eye and the pride of life."[29] This may mean that the world solicits us to satisfy our physical and aesthetic desires in unholy ways. "The pride of life" ("life" means "goods," 3:17) may be the world's soliciting us to acquire and to regard material possessions and personal achievements as it does and to exalt their importance and value above God and His things (cp. Luke 12:15, 34).

THE NEED DESIRES

These are natural desires that arise from the needs of our physical and spiritual lives. For gospel believers these desires are in themselves not sinful, for our personhoods and inner human natures have been renewed (Col. 3:9–10; Titus 3:5; 1 Peter 1:22; Acts 15:9) and our bodies, though mortal, are no longer the proper tools of sin (Rom. 6:6–7). However, to avoid sinning, we must seek to satisfy these need desires in God's time and way (cp. Matt. 4:1–10).

THE NEED DESIRES OF OUR NATURAL LIFE

One, psychological desires: We have need for self-preservation, self-determination, self-expression, love, satisfying intellectual curiosity and reasoning, and social interaction.

Two, physical desires: We also have need for food, rest, activity, comfort, and sexual satisfaction. Newly created, Eve's desires for food, aesthetic satisfaction, and wisdom were not sinful (Gen. 3:6). Rising from her sinless, unfallen humanity, these desires were wholesome and natural. Our natural life desires are not in themselves sinful, unless they are being controlled by sin (see above). However, we must be on the alert against satisfying these desires in sinful ways or in obsessive amounts (Titus 2:12; 1 Peter 1:14–15). There are times when we cannot satisfy these desires within God's will drawing upon His sufficient grace (2 Cor. 12:7–10). In times of deprivation, we can learn to be content with the help of the Lord Jesus (Phil. 4:10–13; Heb. 13:5–6).

THE NEED DESIRES OF OUR SPIRITUAL LIFE

These desires include longings for God, spiritual knowledge, righteousness (doing right things), fellowship with other believers, engaging in ministry, victory over spiritual enemies, obedience to God, salvation of others, and being with Jesus (Pss. 42:1–2; 63:1; Matt. 5:6; Rom. 1:11; 7:21–25; 10:1; Phil. 1:23; 1 Thess. 2:17; 1 Peter 2:2). We can receive divine satisfaction of these needs by looking to Jesus, meditating on the Scriptures, doing God's will, and by faith allowing the Holy Spirit to minister to us (Pss. 1:1–3; 37:4; Heb. 12:2; Matt. 11:28–30; John 6:35, 63; 7:37–39).

APPENDIX V

The Human Body-Grid

In the light of what the Bible teaches about personhood and human nature, I propose the following description of the function of the human body, both now and in the future.

THE HUMAN MAKEUP

As human beings, our makeup consists of personhood (I, or self) plus our human nature (body, soul, and spirit; cp. Job 7:11). Our personhood brings to our human nature self-awareness, individuality, morality, and perpetuity. Without personhood, we would only be human animals or human clones, not human persons. On the other hand, our human nature makes us human beings and provides us with the capacity, capability, and mechanism for personal expression and impression, or perception.

In addition to presently animating the body, the soul and spirit give us the inner capacity for intellect (with its rational thinking and understanding), emotion (with its expressions of feelings), and will (with its ability to make decisions and choices).[30] The souls and spirits of all saved people appear to be the same in quantity and quality. In gospel believers, this part of our human nature is saved, that is, it is delivered from the inherent corruption of original sin and is renewed for spiritual life functions as well as retaining its physical life ones (1 Peter 1:22; Rom. 8:10; 2 Tim. 2:22; Acts 15:9; Eph. 4:24). Because of this, we can express holy emotions, think right thoughts, understand spiritual truth, make right moral decisions, and submit ourselves to God and His will for us.

THE HUMAN BODY-GRID

As an electrode controls the flow of electrons, so the body controls the flow of input and output data between people and their environments. It governs the transmission of one's personal expressions and the reception of one's environmental impressions.

Its Transmitting Human Expressions

The body provides the physical mechanism that allows one's inner soul-spirit capabilities to function in conjunction with one's personhood in human experience. This body mechanism itself is affected by certain internal and external factors that restrict or enhance the functions of the soul-spirit in human experience as in one's thinking, feelings, and decisions and exerting one's will. A factor that alters the body-grid is environmental conditions that act upon and impede the body's functions. Physical factors include the body's genetic code, physical development, physical disabilities, and state of health. For example, if one is mentally retarded or one's brain is damaged, then this may restrict one's ability to understand facts or to make decisions. In other cases, medication may help the body to function better. Thus, I see the body as a grid that directly acts upon, restricts, and affects the interactive functions involved in human expression and impression. When it is ill or damaged, the body affects us adversely by relaying to us and our inner nature partial or distorted information.

Because he or she has a human nature, a person has the potential of expressing human actions, thoughts, emotions, feelings, attitudes, understanding, decisions, evaluations, and the like. The quantitative and qualitative factors of these human experiences are determined, however, by the body-grid. Furthermore, the moral character of behavioral activity is determined by the moral force, whether God or sin, that energizes these activities for good or for bad (Luke 6:45; cp. Rom. 6; 8:1–13). If we act in the energy of God, we do holy human things; if we act in the energy of sin, we do sinful human things (Luke 6:45). It is impossible to act apart from one of these forces if we have morally developed to the point of being responsible for our behavior. Saved people act in the energy of sin whenever they give themselves to it or fail to yield themselves to the Holy Spirit and act in His power.

Thus, the body is a radio transmitter that provides the mechanism for expressing emotion, intellect, and will. For example, when a man sings a song, it is he (his personhood) who does it. With his soul-spirit, he sings understanding, emotion, and will. A woman may also sing by means of her body. It enables her to remember and sing the words according to the notes of the song. It also determines the quality of her voice, indeed, whether she can sing at all. Yielding oneself to God or to sin will determine the moral character of one's singing, whether it will glorify God or it will be sinful. A chart tracing human expressions of the saved person follows:

HUMAN EXPRESSIONS
(Direction: from within to without)

Personhood
Giving human nature:
1. Self-awareness
2. Individuality
3. Perpetuity
4. Morality for moral evaluation, decision, and conscience

Moral or Immoral Force
Controlling influence, or energy, consisting of the Holy Spirit or the sin force. These determine the moral character of human expressions when they possess the heart.

Soul-Spirit
The same in all people, giving them the dynamics for:
1. Emotion
2. Will for decisions
3. Intellect: understanding, memory, conscience
4. Physical life

Body-Grid Expressions
Differing with each person, these expressions are determined by the:
1. Body's senses
2. Genetic code
3. Development
4. Disabilities
5. Results of external stimuli and conditioning

Personal Human Expressions
Qualified by the grid:
1. Actions
2. Thoughts
3. Reasoning

4. Emotions
5. Attitudes
6. Communication
7. Understanding
8. Evaluation
9. Decisions

Moral Character

Righteous human expressions or sinful human expressions, as determined by the moral or immoral force that possesses the heart.

Its Receiving Human Impressions

The body also acts like a radio receiver, by which the reverse of this transmission process takes place in human impression or perception. It allows a person to receive any communication from his or her environment or from others. When a man hears a sermon, for instance, his body-grid, which provides the mechanism of perception in sight, hearing, and thought will affect his reception of the message. His soul-spirit, which provides the capability for understanding, emotional reaction, and volitional responses, will deal with the data that is relayed by the body-grid. This data, imbued with understanding and emotion, will then be relayed to and impressed upon his personhood, or self. If a woman is yielded to God and her body is functioning normally, she will understand the truth that God has for her in the message and will make a favorable response and will give praise. If she is dominated by sin, then she will sinfully react to the message. If a person's body-grid is defective in its sensory organs or mentality, then the communicated data will be distorted and perception will be faulty. If the body is seriously affected, that person may not comprehend or hear the message at all.

HUMAN IMPRESSIONS

(Direction: from without to within)

Outside Stimuli

1. Environment
2. People
3. Pictures
4. Literature
5. Odors
6. Things for body needs
7. Experiences
8. Holy influences
9. Evil influences

Body-Grid

1. The senses
2. The genetic code
3. Development
4. Disabilities
5. Conditioning
6. Body needs

Soul-Spirit
1. The emotions
2. The will
3. The intellect: understanding, memory, and conscience

Moral or Immoral Force
The Holy Spirit or the sin force acting upon one's inner nature and personhood.

Personhood
True or false impressions; holy or evil impressions.

With this in view, we can see that the body-grid directly affects one's received impressions and transmitted expressions. Because of this, no two people are alike in their reception and expression of data. This accounts for the variety of human personalities, opinions, and preferences that exist among people in this world.

THE FUTURE HUMAN BODY
Upon death, the gospel believer's personhood and his or her soul-spirit leaves the body and goes to heaven (2 Cor. 5:8; Phil. 1:23). Because he or she requires the soul-spirit for intellect, emotion, and will after death, these parts of human nature are perpetuated for the person's use. Moreover, because one needs a body-mechanism that will allow one to receive impressions and to transmit expressions, upon death the believer's personhood and soul-spirit are united to a heavenly intermediate body until the resurrection of his or her own body (see Luke 16:22–30; Rev. 6:9–11, "souls" is a synecdoche for people; 14:1–5). Without a body, dead people would have no means of receiving external stimuli or communication and of expressing their thoughts, emotions, and will.

Upon the resurrection of their own bodies, each gospel believer will be permanently reunited with his or her own renewed body-grid (1 Cor. 15:25–53), which will be changed and animated by the Holy Spirit (Rom. 8:11). Because the resurrection bodies of saved people will be like the Lord Jesus' glorified body (Phil. 3:20–21; 1 John 3:2; 1 Cor. 13:12; 15:49), this will give them the Lord's human body-grid. This will enable them to experience forever unimpeded expressions and impressions of Christlikeness in their thinking, emotions, and will.

With Jesus' kind of body-grid, all redeemed people will be the same in their thinking, feelings, and decisions. While this sameness would be intolerable in our present world, it will be perfect for the eternal state. Having the one divine nature and representing the quintessence of perfection, the Persons of the Godhead have had the same will, emotions, thoughts, qualities, and powers from all eternity. Thus there will be perfect harmony among the Lord's people forever as there is among the Father, the Son, and the Holy Spirit. With the renewal of our bodies and our having Jesus' kind of body-grid, we shall then fully experience all that eternal life is (Titus 1:2; Col. 3:4).

APPENDIX W

The Saved Person's Forgiveness of Others

THE BIBLICAL MEANINGS OF FORGIVENESS

The verb *forgive* means to release one from an obligation (Matt. 18:27) or from punishment for wrongdoing (1 John 1:9). "Forgiveness" is the act of forgiving or the state of being forgiven. In this study, the act of forgiving is in view.

ITS THEOLOGICAL MEANINGS

Only God can forgive sins or offenses against Him (Luke 5:21). This is God's releasing the repentant sinner from the guilt and punishment of his sins when he meets the condition of forgiveness. God is justly able to do this because of the substitutionary sacrifice of the Lord Jesus on behalf of sinners. There are two kinds of divine forgiveness.

One: God's *judicial forgiveness* of unsaved people (Acts 10:43). This is His canceling His judicial retribution against them, which was sending them to hell. To receive this forgiveness, the unsaved person must repent and trust in Jesus and His atoning work for his salvation (Acts 10:43; 16:31).

Two: God's *parental forgiveness* of saved people (1 John 1:9). This is His canceling His corrective chastisement of His people. To receive this, the saved person must repent and confess his sin to God (Rev. 2:5; 1 John 1:9).

ITS PRECEPTIVE MEANING (LUKE 17:3–4; EPH. 4:32; COL. 3:13)

This concerns God's command for His people to forgive one another. Like divine forgiveness, this forgiveness requires the offender to meet certain conditions. In response to this, the offended saved person acknowledges that the repentant offender has fulfilled the duty for his or her wrongdoing, and the offended person treats the matter as being forever settled. Let us look at this in more detail.

THE SAVED PERSON'S FORGIVENESS OF OTHERS

In our relations with others, we inevitably offend one another. This requires our forgiving those who have offended us and our securing the forgiveness of those whom we have wronged.

THE KINDS OF HUMAN OFFENSES

1. Sinful offenses

Offenses are sinful violations (Luke 17:3) of people's feelings, integrity, moral convictions, persons, property, rights and the like. If these are not dealt with immediately when they occur or become known, they will adversely affect the relationship between the offended person and the offender.

2. Sinless annoyances

We must distinguish between sinful offenses and sinless annoyances. An amoral annoyance, like singing off pitch, may be irritating to the choir director, but it does not have moral implication unless it is done with malice.

THE NEED FOR THE SAVED PERSON'S FORGIVENESS OF OTHERS

Because of their having the inner sin force, God's people often yield to its evil urges and sinfully treat others in nonloving ways or respond to ill-treatment in sinful ways (cp. 1 Cor. 3:3; Gal. 5:19–20; Eph. 4:31; Col. 3:8–9). This wrongdoing establishes the need for preceptive forgiveness (Eph. 4:32) for at least two reasons:

1. *That God may forgive us of our filial sins.*

When we have neglected to make right our offenses toward others, it is useless to worship God or to seek His fellowship until we have done so (Matt. 5:23–24). Also, when we are unforgiving toward a repentant offender, we condone the sin of an unforgiving attitude (cp. Matt. 6:14–15; 18:35). In this case, God will not forgive us of other filial sins that we confess to Him until we have dealt with the sin of being unforgiving toward repentant people (cp. Ps. 66:18).

2. *That there may be unity among God's people.*

Division and strife are marks of carnality (1 Cor. 3:3). This means that people who strive with one another are dominated by the sin force rather than by the Holy Spirit. Being vain and selfish, carnal believers are quarrelsome, spiteful, and inconsiderate of others. But people who are filled with the Holy Spirit have His fruit of love and peace in their lives and seek to promote the well-being of others (Eph. 4:1–3; Gal. 5:22; John 13:34; 1 Cor. 13:4–7). Our forgiving repentant offenders and our righting our wrongdoing contribute to the spiritual health, power, and unity of the local church, of which we are a part (cp. 2 Cor. 7:4–16). Failure here stifles God's blessing and power in our local churches (1 Thess. 5:19).

A DESCRIPTION OF THE SAVED PERSON'S FORGIVENESS OF OTHERS

Although forgiveness means to release a person from an obligation, in divine forgiveness and preceptive forgiveness, the offender must fulfill the conditions of forgiveness before he can be forgiven of his wrongdoing (Acts 10:43; Rev. 2:5; 1 John 1:9; Luke 17:3; Matt. 5:23–25). This forgiveness is the offended person's acknowledging that the repentant offender has fulfilled his duty and his treating the matter as forever settled (Luke 17:3). Our forgiving others as God has forgiven us (Eph. 4:32) concerns the offender's meeting the conditions of forgiveness. It is not the cancellation of his obligation before he fulfills it, as many people think. God does not forgive sinning people until they meet the requirements of forgiveness.

THE DUTIES INVOLVED IN THE SAVED PERSON'S FORGIVENESS OF OTHERS

These duties relate to the offender and to the offended person.

1. *The duties of the offender*

God will not receive worship of offenders until they have dealt with their sins against the offended persons (Matt. 5:23–24). What is one to do when one has knowingly offended another person?

a. *Repent of the wrongdoing (Luke 17:3–4; Rev. 2:5).*

This change of mind and attitude leads one to accept the responsibility of one's action and to see it as a sin against the person whom one has wronged.

b. *Confess the offense to God as a sin (Luke 17:3; 1 John 1:9).*

This is necessary for receiving divine parental forgiveness.

c. *Give oneself to God for help in making right the wrongdoing (Rom. 6:13; Eph. 5:18; Phil. 4:13).*

d. *Go to the offended person and make right the offense (Matt. 5:23–25).*

This is more than an apology. This requires the offender to confess the wrongdoing as a sin (cp. Luke 15:21) and to make restitution if there was bodily injury or property damage or loss (19:8; cp. Exod. 21:30–36; Prov. 6:30–31).

2. *The duties of the offended person*

What is one to do when one is offended by a saved person? [31]

a. Give oneself immediately to God.

This is for divine help and direction in having right attitudes toward the offender and in dealing with the matter in a biblical way rather than with sinful retaliation (Eph. 5:18; Gal. 6:1; Matt. 5:44).

b. Go to the offender and point out the wrongdoing.

One should do this if the offender delays making right the offense (Matt. 18:15; Luke 17:3). The purpose of going to the offender is lovingly to lead him or her to repentance and to restore the offender to God's fellowship and to that of His people; it is not to vindicate oneself. Only God can justly exact recompense for the wrongs of unrepentant people (Rom. 12:17–21).

c. Forgive the offender when the conditions of forgiveness have been fulfilled (Luke 17:3; cp. 2 Cor. 2:6–8).

When one sees that the offender has fulfilled his or her obligation, then the offended person must acknowledge that the offender has done this and accept the matter as being forever settled.

d. Do not forgive the unrepentant saved offender (Luke 7:3: note conj. "if").

If the offender does not carry out his or her duty for the wrongdoing, then the offended person must not forgive the offender. This does not mean that the offended person is to retaliate against the offender (Rom. 12:17–21), feel bitter (Matt. 5:44; John 13:34), or harbor resentment (1 Cor. 13:5), for these sinful reactions are not expressions of Jesus' love (John 13:34–35). Above all, it does not mean that the offended person is to ignore the offense or pretend that it did not occur. This hypocrisy fails to deal with the problem.

After giving ourselves to God, we as saved offended persons must lovingly confront the saved offenders and encourage them to deal with their sin and to put it away in the biblical manner (Matt. 18:15; Gal. 6:1). Again, this is for the purpose of leading offenders to repentance and restoring them to God's fellowship and to that of the Lord's people (cp. 2 Thess. 3:14; 2 Cor. 2:6–8). But if offenders do not fulfill this duty, then their offenses cannot be dropped, or forgiven, until they do. Moreover, the offended persons cannot have fellowship with the offenders until the wrong is righted (cp. 2 Thess. 3:14–15).[32] To ignore the situation is to condone the offenders' sin and to perpetuate disharmony among God's people.

SEVERAL OBSERVATIONS

One: If both persons are members of the same church and the offender or the offended person refuses to do his or her duty, then the procedure given in Matthew 18:16–19 and 2 Thessalonians 3:14–15 must be followed.

Two: Offenders are not released from their obligations to make right their offenses as long as they can do so.

Three: If the law allows, irresolvable legal disputes between saved people should be settled by competent saved people, who are appointed by the church or the denominational body which has jurisdiction over the disputing parties (1 Cor. 6:1–8). It appears that we can litigate against unrepentant unsaved people or saved people who unlawfully offend us, especially in matters of debt and property damage and loss, and who are not accountable to the same church authority. Matthew 5:40 concerns the decisions of unjust or corrupt courts.

Four: In the case of disagreement as to what constitutes the fulfillment of an obligation in addition to repentance and confession, it may be necessary to have the matter arbitrated by a mutually acceptable third person, who is spiritually minded.

THE MOTIVATIONS FOR THE SAVED PERSON'S FORGIVENESS OF OTHERS

How does God impel us to forgive repentant offenders even when we do not feel like it? He does this by:

One, His command (Luke 17:3)

Two, His having judicially forgiven us our sins (Eph. 1:7; cp. Matt. 18:32–33)

Three, His warning of withholding from us His parental forgiveness (Matt. 6:15; cp. 18:34–35)

Four, His example (Eph. 4:32–5:1)

God does not ask us to do what He Himself does not do. God never ignores people's sins or pretends that they do not occur. Moreover, He forgives only when sinners meet His conditions. To ignore the offensive situation is to condone the offender's sin and to perpetuate disunity among the Lord's people. Pretending that the wrong does not exist does not heal the sore. Also, harboring grudges or bitter resentments grieves the Holy Spirit and hinders God's blessing. Only the Holy Spirit can give us a right attitude toward people who have offended us and can help us to deal with the matter in the biblical way.

SEVERAL QUESTIONS ABOUT THE SAVED PERSON'S FORGIVENESS OF OTHERS

1. Did not Jesus teach that we are to turn the cheek?

Jesus' teaching in Matthew 5:39–41 concerns retaliation. We are to return good for evil (vv. 42–45), not evil for evil. Only God can avenge wronged persons justly (Rom. 12:17–21).

2. Did not Jesus ask God to forgive His crucifiers?

Jesus prayed for the Roman soldiers who had crucified Him (Luke 23:34), not for the Roman governor and Jewish leaders, who had delivered Him for execution. That these leaders remained guilty of their crimes against Jesus (Matt. 27:18, 24; John 19:11) is seen in the later charges of the apostles Peter and Paul, who declared that these people had murdered Jesus, for this was their intention (Acts 2:23; 3:15; 5:30; 7:52; 10:39).[33]

3. Is not our identifying people's offenses being judgmental?

Jesus' prohibition (Matt. 7:1–5) was against unrighteous judgment, which is made solely on the basis of appearance or superficial knowledge of the facts (John 7:24). Right moral judgments, which we must make daily, involve our learning the facts of the matter and evaluating its moral character in the light of Scripture. How else can we identify the "brother who is overtaken in a fault" (Gal. 6:1) or rebuke those who have wronged us (Luke 17:3)?

4. Is not breaking fellowship with an offender punitive?

Since fellowship is a friendly relationship where nothing exists to mar this congeniality, the offense has already broken this relationship. Second Thessalonians 3:14–15 gives the command, purpose, and extent of this action (see endnote 31). It is hypocritical to pretend that all is well when it is not.

5. Since God readily forgives us, should we not readily forgive others?

God only forgives unsaved people when they meet the conditions of repentance and faith in Jesus and His atoning work, and His people when they fulfill the conditions of repentance and confession. Likewise, we should forgive only when offenders fulfill their obligation to us (Luke 17:3).

6. Why should I forgive this person when I know that he will offend me again?

Jesus commanded us to forgive offenders for repeated offenses as long as they meet the condition of forgiveness (Luke 17:4). It is an act of Christian love to help these kinds of offenders to overcome their sinful habits by urging them to give themselves to God, to resist in God's strength the urge to offend others, and to do the holy alternative, which is doing God's will and expressing His love (James 4:7; Rom. 12:2; Gal. 5:13, 16, 22).

7. *Are we obligated to address offenses that are made known to us?*

Yes. If I am the offender, I must make right my wrongdoing. If another person has offended me and does nothing about it, I should strive to help him (Gal. 6:1). If one is not offended by the action of another person, then there is no obligation to be fulfilled. If the inoffensive action was with malice, then the person must settle with God.

8. *Should we not overlook offenses because "love covers a multitude of sins"?*

James 5:20 was speaking about lovingly turning a sinning brother away from his evil behavior (cp. Gal. 6:1). It is not loving to leave offenders to their sins without trying to help them to get right with God and with humankind.

9. *How can we forgive when the offense is "too great"?*

We can look to the Holy Spirit or to the Lord Jesus to help us to do what needs to be done as we give ourselves to Him for this purpose (John 14:16; Phil. 4:13; cp. 1 Peter 2:23).

10. *How can we forgive when we do not feel like it?*

We can do this with the help of the Holy Spirit and with the love that He gives (Gal. 5:22). God chose to love us when He did not like us, because we were sinners; and He provided a way by which He could forgive us through Jesus (1 John 4:9–10). God's commands to us are directed to our will, not to our feelings.

11. *How can we forgive ourselves?*

The Bible never speaks of our forgiving ourselves as though self were a separate entity that we have to deal with. When we (our total person including self) repent and confess our sins, we are divinely forgiven (Rev. 2:5; 1 John 1:9). God's forgiving us eliminates the need for self-forgiveness. Our duty to ourselves is to deny ourselves the usurpation of sin by yielding ourselves to God for His enablement to do those things that please Him (Rom. 6:11–13; 12:1–2; cp. Mark 8:34). In personal moral behavior, it is the total self (I, me) that acts, even in instances of self-affliction. However, our wrongdoing may bring us adverse consequences. Repentance leads us to accept the responsibility of our wrongdoing, to admit that it was sinful, and to resolve not to do it again.

12. *When we forgive, why do we still have wrong feelings?*

There are two kinds of wrong feelings that are related to forgiveness: *One,* guilty feelings for sins for which we have received God's forgiveness. These feelings come from Satan (cp. Rev. 12:10). *Two,* ill-feelings against offenders. These come from the sin force within us. We can turn these feelings over to the Lord (2 Cor. 10:5), claim the assurance of God's cleansing (1 John 1:9), ask the Holy Spirit to fill us with His love for those people who have hurt us (Matt. 5:44; Gal. 5:22; 1 Cor. 13:4–5), and set our minds on holy things (Phil. 4:4–8).

13. *If forgetting is a part of forgiveness, how can we forget the offenses of others against us?*

Forgetting is a figurative concept that is associated with divine forgiveness (Jer. 31:34). This conveys the idea that by "forgetting" our sins, God will never hold us responsible for the sins that He has forgiven us and will never bring these up to condemn us (Rom. 8:31–39). Memorywise, it is not possible to forget our wrongdoings or those of others. However, we can rejoice in the assurance of God's forgiveness and reject Satan's continuing accusations of these sins. When we forgive others who repent of their wrongdoings, we must not allow these memories to affect our relationships with these people and must treat them as though these offenses never occurred. God can help us with this (2 Cor. 10:5). On the other hand, until these people repent and make right their wrongdoings, we cannot forget them or pretend that everything is all right.

14. If we do not see our actions as offensive, how should we respond to people who do?

If someone is offended by our actions, then we must deal with the matter as being offensive, regardless how we may view it. We often offend people unknowingly or unintentionally; but when this is brought to our attention, we still must fulfill our obligation to them.

15. To what extent should we seek to satisfy those whom we have offended?

We must seek to satisfy them to the extent of our ability as required by the nature of the offense. If this is unsatisfactory, then the matter must be arbitrated by a third person, whom we and the offended person accept. The offended person must be careful not to yield to the inner urges of the sin force to make unfair demands and to have ill-feelings. A court must decide cases relating to law. If the offended person refuses to accept the repentant offender and to deal with the problem, then the offender can do no more. In this case, the offended person becomes the offender and must be dealt with. People who serve as arbitrators must avoid being biased in these cases. To my mind, it is better for the arbitrator to hear the complaints of both parties for the first time when he or she meets with them together rather than privately with each one alone.

APPENDIX X

Figures of Association: Synecdoche and Metonymy

There are many kinds of figurative expressions in the Bible.[34] These are words, phrases, or clauses that are used to convey meanings other than those that are literal, or natural, to them. Among these figures of speech are synecdoche and metonymy, which are figures of association. The recognition of these figures of speech, which are not commonly known to many Bible readers, is of utmost importance for interpreting the Bible and, thus, for understanding biblical doctrine. Study the following figures of association and their examples to become familiar with their use in the Scriptures.

THE SYNECDOCHE (GK. "TO RECEIVE JOINTLY")

KINDS OF SYNECDOCHE

1. A word or words that stand for the whole entity of which they are an essential part

For instance, if we said that we had bought a new *set of wheels,* this could mean a new car. The set of wheels, being an essential part of the car, would be a synecdoche for the whole car. Also, we might say that we counted *noses,* meaning people.

2. A word or words for the whole of an entity that stands for only an essential part

For instance, if a person said that he ate an *orange,* this would normally mean that he ate the edible part, not the rind and seeds, too. Also, one might say that all America was aroused, for only a part of the population.

In the Bible, the synecdoche of an essential part that stands for the whole of something is much more common than the synecdoche of a whole that stands for an essential part of something. "Essential parts" are parts that are inherent or basic to the nature or composition of the people or thing that it represents. For example, having a human nature is essential to one's humanity, but having an automobile is not.

EXAMPLES OF SYNECDOCHE

1. *An essential part of something standing for the whole of it*

   "Baptism" for John the Baptizer's ministry (Matt. 21:25). He preached the need for this.

   "Blood" for atonement (Eph. 1:7; Rom. 5:9). Offering blood was part of the atoning process (Lev. 17:11).

   "Body" for one's entire self (Rom. 12:1; Heb. 10:10)

   "Brass" for musical instrument (1 Cor. 13:1)

   "Bread" for food (Matt. 4:4)

   "Breaking bread" for eating (Acts 2:46; 20:7). This is part of the eating process.

   "Conversation" for manner of life (Eph. 2:3)

   "Death" for atonement (Rom. 5:10). Death of the sacrifice was part of the atoning process.

   "Death" for Jesus' death and resurrection (Heb. 2:14)

   "Dust" for one's body (Eccl. 12:7). The body was originally made from soil.

   "Ephraim" for Israel (Hos. 4:17; 5:13). This was a tribe for the whole nation.

   "Eyes" for inner self with its desires (2 Peter 2:14)

   "Flesh" for the person (Eccl. 5:6). The body is an essential part of us.

   "Justified" for saved (Gal. 2:16). Justification is a component of salvation.

   "Law" for the OT Scriptures (Matt. 5:17)

   "Mouth" for one's body (Eccl. 6:7)

   "Repent" for exercising salvational faith (Acts 17:30). Repentance is a part of this faith in Jesus and His atoning work.

   "Sanctified" for being saved (Heb. 10:10). Sanctification is a part of salvation.

   "Shedding blood" for offering it (Heb. 9:22; cp. Lev. 17:11). For an atonement for sins, the blood of the sacrifice had first to be shed, and then it was offered on an altar.

   "Soul" for people (Acts 27:37; James 1:21; Gen. 46:26). Humans have body, soul, and spirit.

   "Soul" for the whole person (Gen. 2:7; cp. 1:24 "creature"). Soul is a part of humans.

   "Spirit" for people (1 Cor. 5:5; 2 Tim. 4:22). Spirit is a part of humans.

   "Spirit" for the whole person (2 Cor. 7:13)

   "Walking" for one's conduct (Eph. 2:10; 4:17)

   "Word" for one's spoken or written words (Isa. 1:10; John 5:24)

2. *The whole of something standing for an essential part of it*

   "All Israel" for the elect Jewish remnant (Rom. 11:26; cp. 9:6)

   "Bread" for grain, from which flour is made (Eccl. 11:1)

   "Cities" for a particular city (Judg. 12:7)

   "Grace" for the spiritual gift of apostleship (Rom. 12:3; Eph. 3:2)

   "Israel" for the Messiah (Jesus), who was an Israelite (Isa. 49:3)

   "World" for the Roman Empire (Luke 2:1)

THE METONYMY (GK. "TO CHANGE NAME")

This is a word which is given in place of another word, to which it stands in a close relation; but unlike a synecdoche, a metonymy is not an essential part of what it represents. For instance, a policeman's badge represents the authority of the municipality, but it is not an essential part of that authority. Also, a wedding ring represents a marriage, but it is not an essential part of marriage. Or it is said that a kettle boils, meaning the contents boil. Study the following kinds of metonymy and their examples:

1. *Cause for its effect or result*
   "Arrow" for a wound (Job 34:6)
   "Crucifixion" for death (Gal. 2:20)
   "Death" for sheol, the destination of those who died during OT times (Isa. 38:18)
   "Mouth" for testimony, which consists of words (Deut. 19:15)
   "Soul" for physical life (Mark 8:35–37). The soul animates the body.
   "Spirit" for physical life (Eccl. 12:7). The spirit animates the body.
2. *Effect or result for its cause*
   "Breath" for physical life (Eccl. 3:19)
   "Call on . . . the Lord" for expressing salvational faith (Rom. 10:13)
   "Hell" (gehenna) for the sin force (James 3:6). Hell is the divine penalty for sinning.
   "Lust" for the indwelling sin force, which produces within us desires to sin (James 1:14; Rom. 13:14; Gal. 5:16)
   "Wrath" for the sin force, which causes sinful anger (James 1:20)
3. *Container for thing contained*
   "Cup" for the experience of physical death (Matt. 26:39)
   "Cup" for the product of grapes (1 Cor. 11:25)
   "Cup" for the experience of sufferings and death (Matt. 26:42)
   "Houses" for personal possessions (Matt. 23:14)
4. *Sign for thing signified*
   "Cross" for the Lord's atoning work (1 Cor. 1:18)
   "Darkness" for being in spiritual darkness of sin and ignorance (Eph. 5:8)
   "Darkness" for sin (1 John 1:5, 6)
   "Name" for Jesus' atoning work (John 1:12)
   "Name" for Jesus' interests, work, and will (John 14:13–14; 15:16)
   "Scepter" for political authority (Gen. 49:10)
5. *Author for his writings*
   "Moses and the prophets" for their OT writings (Luke 16:29)
6. *Instrument for cause*
   "Ears" for people's attention (2 Tim. 4:4).
   "Eye" and "hand" for the inner sin force (Matt. 5:30–31)
   "Flesh" for the inner sin force that uses the body for its evil expressions (Gal. 5:16)
   "Heart" for the control center of life (Prov. 4:23; Luke 6:45; Acts 5:3; Eph. 3:17)
7. *Cause for instrument*
   "The devil" (Satan) for his demon allies (Acts 5:3; James 4:7; 1 Peter 5:8). Observe that Satan personally attacked Jesus (Matt. 4:3–10; 16:22–23).
8. *Means for end*
   "Death" for resurrection (Heb. 2:14)
   "Faith" for the body of Christian truth that is believed (Jude 3, 20)
   "Stripes" for our Lord's atoning sacrifice (1 Peter 2:24)
9. *Place for people*
   "Death," "grave," and "pit" (sheol) for its inhabitants (Isa. 38:18)
   "Heavens" and "earth" for its inhabitants (Ps. 69:34; Isa. 1:2)
   "House" for its occupants or family (1 Sam. 3:12–14)
10. *Event for something related to it*
    "Passover" for a paschal lamb (Exod. 12:21)
11. *Ritual for its participants*
    "Circumcision" for male Jews (Acts 10:45; Gal. 2:9)

APPENDIX Y

The Kinds of English Bibles

The major distinction in the kinds of English translations is between word-for-word (formal equivalence) translations and idea-for-idea (functional equivalence) translations. Being largely based on the translator's understanding of the meaning of the text, the latter are more subjective translations. Many recent editions of the Bible combine both kinds.

KINDS ACCORDING TO TRANSLATION

LITERAL TRANSLATIONS

These are largely word-for-word (formal equivalence) translations of the Bible from the original languages (Hebrew OT and Greek NT) into English. These are most desirable for serious Bible study. Examples are *The King James Version, The New King James Version, The American Standard Version* (1901), and *The New American Standard Version*.

IDIOMATIC TRANSLATIONS

These are clause-for-clause or phrase-for-phrase (functional equivalence) translations, made with an effort to give the ideas, expressed by the original language words and phrases, in modern English form. An example is *The New Testament in Modern English* by J. B. Phillips.

COMBINED TRANSLATIONS

These are translations that are partly literal and partly idiomatic. Examples are *The New English Bible* and *The New International Version*.

EXPANDED TRANSLATIONS

Since a single Hebrew or Greek word cannot always be fully expressed by a single English word, an effort is made to express more completely the meaning or the force of the words of the original languages in these expanded translations. Examples of these are *An Expanded Translation of the New Testament* by Kenneth Wuest and *The Amplified Bible*.

SIMPLIFIED TRANSLATIONS

The purpose of these is to reach a wider readership by providing a Bible with the simplest vocabulary of spoken, colloquial English. Examples are *Today's English Version* by Robert Bratcher and *New Life Version*, with a basic controlled vocabulary of 850 words.

CONDENSED TRANSLATIONS

This deletes those parts of the Bible that the editor considers to be repetitious or superfluous material. An example of this is *The Reader's Digest Bible*, edited by Bruce M. Metzger.

PARAPHRASED TRANSLATIONS

To paraphrase is to say the same thing in other words. While any translation often requires some paraphrasing, this kind of translation is almost wholly paraphrased. Since a paraphrase is essentially an interpretation of Scripture, the value of a paraphrased version rests upon the accuracy of the translator's interpretation. This kind of translation is not desirable for serious Bible study, by which the student seeks his own Bible interpretation. An example is *The Living Bible* by Kenneth N. Taylor.

BIASED TRANSLATIONS

These are translations that incorporate and reflect the translator's theological bias. Examples of these are *The Revised Standard Version* which reflects religious liberalism, *The New World Bible* which reflects the doctrines of the Jehovah's Witnesses, and *The Revised King James Version* which reflects the doctrines of Mormonism.[35]

KINDS ACCORDING TO CONTENT

TEXT BIBLES

These give only the text of Scripture.

REFERENCE BIBLES

These have center and/or marginal Scripture references.

ANNOTATED BIBLES

Sometimes called "study Bibles," these have editorial comments, book summaries, charts, and other helps.

Many Bibles also have maps of biblical lands and a small concordance, or an alphabetical arrangement of the main words of Scriptures and their primary references.

APPENDIX Z

Our Loving God and Others

An authority in Jewish law asked Jesus a sincere question, "Which is the first [greatest] commandment of all?" (Mark 12:28). Jesus answered (vv. 29–30) by quoting Deuteronomy 6:4–5, "Hear, O Israel, the LORD our God is one LORD; and you shall love the LORD your God with all your heart, and with all your soul, and with all your mind, and with all your strength." The Lord also added the second greatest commandment (Mark 12:31), quoting Leviticus 19:18, "You shall love your neighbor as yourself." Let us see what these kinds of love mean, and how we are to express them.

OUR LOVE FOR GOD (Mark 12:29–30)

The foremost of the 613 Mosaic laws is to love God (cp. Deut. 10:12). It remains our greatest obligation today (cp. John 21:15; Rom, 13:8–9). Let us consider the love that we owe to God: its nature, manner, and benefits.

WHAT KIND OF LOVE DO WE OWE TO GOD?

We express various kinds of love: for country, for some pleasurable thing, for spouse, for friends, for children, for parents, and for other Christians. Are we to love God with these kinds of love? Because He is more than these objects of love, we are to love Him with a special affection that we do not share with other people or things. We see this special love in the Lord Jesus' love for the Father (John 14:31). Let us consider the ingredients that comprise this love.

1. One ingredient is obedience (John 14:31).

Loving obedience expresses true love for God (John 14:15, 21, 23). Jesus lived in continual obedience to the Father, for as man He was the Father's slave (Phil. 2:7). Our Lord sought to please the Father in everything (John 6:38; 8:28–29; 17:4), even in death (Phil. 2:8).

They who love God obey Him. They seek to please Him in everything.

2. Another ingredient is delight (John 4:32–34).

Jesus found His greatest delight and satisfaction in the Father. This satisfaction arose from an eternal relationship with the Father. This is seen in His prayer life (Luke 6:12) and in His association with the Father (John 8:28). He never acted independently of the Father (14:10). It was His chief delight to walk in the Father's fellowship (4:34).

Those who love God delight in many things (1 Tim. 6:17), but their greatest pleasure and satisfaction are found in God and in the things that relate to Him (Pss. 1:1–3; 122:1).

3. Another ingredient is trust (Matt. 27:43).

It was the scornful witness of Jesus' enemies that He trusted in God. He trusted the Father throughout His earthly lifetime. He knew that the Father had not left Him alone (John 8:29). He had absolute confidence in the Father's will and care, even when He was abused by His enemies (1 Peter 2:23) and died (Luke 23:46).

Those who love God accept His will for them and trust His loving wisdom even when they cannot understand what He is doing (cp. 2 Cor. 5:7; Job 13:15). God cannot lie; He is too wise to err.

4. A last ingredient is honoring God (John 8:49).

Revering the Father (Heb. 5:7), the Lord Jesus ever sought to honor Him (John 8:49). To honor people is to respect them, hold them in esteem, value them. Jesus showed the highest respect for His Father throughout His lifetime. He acknowledged that the Father worked and spoke through Him (John 14:10). His prayer was, "Father, glorify your name" (John 12:28).

Those who love God seek to honor Him in all that they do (1 Cor. 10:31). They give Him the credit for their achievements in life (15:10). They seek to exalt Him by doing His will. They revere Him for what and who He is (Heb. 12:28–29).

The Lord Jesus loved the Father. He expressed this by obeying Him, delighting in Him, trusting Him, and honoring Him. Our love for God must have these same components.

In What Manner Are We to Express These Ingredients of Love?

The Lord Jesus indicated this in Matthew 12:30b.

One: We are to love God heartily. This means with our total being (Col. 3:23; contra Matt. 15:8). Halfhearted love is not acceptable.

Two: We are to love God exclusively. Our love for God is like the commitment of married love, which is not to be shared with anyone else or with anything (1 John 2:15, this should read, "love for the Father"). We may love other people and things, but not with the love that we owe to God. To compromise this love is to be a spiritual adulterer or adulteress (cp. James 4:4).

Three: We are to love dependently. We cannot express this love by ourselves (Phil. 4:13; Gal. 2:20). We can only do this with the help of the Holy Spirit. As we rely on Him, He will give us the love that we owe to God and help us to express this love consistently and uncompromisingly.

WHAT ARE THE BENEFITS OF THIS LOVE?

The benefits of God's responses to this love are given in Psalm 91:14–16.

Do you really love God? Or is your affection just superficial sentimentalism? The Lord asked, "Simon, do you love Me more than these [things]" (John 21:15)? "We love God because He first loved us" (1 John 4:19).

OUR LOVE FOR OTHERS (Mark 12:31)

The Lord declared that the second greatest commandment was to love one's neighbor as oneself (cp. Lev. 19:18). Let us see what this means and what new dimension has been added to this love.

WHAT DOES IT MEAN TO LOVE ONESELF?

"Self " is not an enemy. "Self " is my personhood, I, me. There is a wrong kind of self-love which we must avoid (2 Tim. 3:2). This is selfishness—a self-seeking and self-serving kind of love that disregards the needs of others. Also, there is a right kind of self-love, which is expressed by self-respect and self-care. Let us look at these aspects.

1. One aspect of holy self-love is self-respect (Rom. 12:3).

"A sound-minded" view of self reasons to have a true view of one's self. How do you feel about yourself? Do you respect yourself?

Self-respect is based on self-acceptance, self-esteem, or a sense of self-value. People who respect themselves value themselves (Rom. 12:3). Recognizing their abilities and spiritual gifts, they know their function in the mystical body of Christ, the Church (vv. 4–6). They also recognize their limitations.

Some people overrate themselves. They believe that the local church could not carry on without them. However, most people underrate themselves because they sin, fall short of the expectations of others, and are told by Satan that they are no good.

Actually, all people have value. Unsaved people have a value that Christians often do not appreciate. Because they are made in the God's image (Gen. 9:6; James 3:9), they are persons, not animals. Also, they contribute in many ways to the well-being of human society. But these values do not earn them credit with God. Saved people have additional value. They are children of God (John 1:12), new creatures in Christ (2 Cor. 5:17), and God's gift to His Son (John 17:2, 6, 9, 11, 22, 24).

Are you aware of your value? You will not see this in a mirror. You must look at yourself as God sees you in Christ. It is this kind of value that gives us self-respect. Also, it is this kind of respect that we are to show to other saved people by considering them better than ourselves (Phil. 2:3). The other person may not be better morally or intellectually, but he is better functionally because of his exclusive work place in the Lord's mystical body, the Church (1 Cor. 12:14–25; note the underraters, vv. 15–20, and the overraters, vv. 21–25). Each saved person has a ministry that no one else can fulfill.

This law sets forth the principle that if we are to show respect for others, we must first have it for ourselves.

2. Another aspect of holy self-love is self-care (Eph. 5:28–29).

Self-care has to do with providing for one's well-being. When we love ourselves, we care for ourselves by providing for our needs, grooming ourselves, and protecting ourselves. Unsaved people are concerned about their temporal needs (Matt. 6:31–32). Saved people should also be concerned about their spiritual needs and priorities (v. 33).

When we love others as we love ourselves, we are concerned about their physical and spiritual needs (Gal. 6:9–10; 1 John 3:16–18).

This law sets forth the principle that, if we are to be concerned about the needs of others, we must first be concerned about our own needs, whether spiritual or physical.

In summary, to love others as we love ourselves means that we are to respect them as people and be concerned about their needs, both temporal and spiritual. However, this kind of love was limited to "neighbors," or friends. The Mosaic Law made no provision for loving enemies, for this was not humanly possible (John 15:13; Rom. 5:7).

WHAT NEW DIMENSION HAS BEEN ADDED TO SELF-LOVE IN THE PRESENT DISPENSATION?

The Lord Jesus taught that we should love our enemies as well (Matt. 5:43–44; note that v. 44b explains v. 44a). But how can we do this, for people do not naturally love their enemies?

Although we do not naturally love our enemies, God graciously chose to love us when we were His enemies (John 3:16; Rom. 5:8). When we consider God's love for the world, we must be careful not to equate this love with human friendship love, which is based on the pleasure that we receive from others. God's sacrificial love for the world is based wholly on His grace, or undeserved favor. God did not like unsaved people when He loved them; they were not His friends (Rom. 5:10). He did not love them spontaneously because of any pleasure He received from them. But He did deliberately, graciously choose to love them, despite their wretched condition. His love for unsaved people was expressed in His giving His Son to be their Savior (John 3:16). He now shows a compassionate love for the world (Matt. 5:45) so as to bring them to repentance and faith in Jesus (Rom. 2:4; 2 Peter 3:9). When people reject God's sacrificial love, there remains only His wrath (John 3:36). We must never convey to unsaved people the idea that God loves them with human friendship love, for this conveys the false message that things between God and them are not as bad as some people describe them to be. His love for them was shown in His sending His Son to be a sacrifice for their sins (1 John 4:9–10).

It is God's kind of love that we are to express toward others, even toward our enemies (John 13:34–35; Matt. 5:44–45). God does not ask us to like all people or to take pleasure in them. He does demand that we minister to their needs, even at personal sacrifice (1 John 3:16; 1 Cor. 13:4–7), and that we show them patience, kindness, and courtesy (1 Cor. 13:4–7). Needless to say, we can do this only by the power of the Holy Spirit (Gal. 5:22).

It is this love that is the mark of true discipleship (John 13:35; cp. 1 Cor. 13:4–7). The unsaved do not understand biblical doctrine, but they do recognize Jesus' unique love when they see it in His people.

In contrast to empty words and rituals, these two commandments, to love God and to love others, whether friend or foe, Christian or non-Christian (Mark 12:29–31), represent true religion (vv. 32–34; James 1:26–27), not only under the Mosaic Law but also under grace as well (Rom. 13:8–10). What kind of Christian religion do you have and display to others?

ENDNOTES

1. For the biblical purposes of speaking in tongues, see "His Relation to Spiritual Gifts: The gift of tongues" under Pneumatology.
2. See "His Relation to Spiritual Gifts: The seven spiritual gifts that are not operating today" under Pneumatology.
3. In the Scriptures, we find three images relating to man: *one,* God's image in man (Gen. 1:26–27), which is personhood; *two,* the image of Adam's fallen humanity, which unsaved people have (1 Cor. 15:49); and *three,* the image of Christ's glorified humanity, after which saved people are being fashioned (Rom. 8:29). The Lord Jesus is the image of the invisible God (2 Cor. 4:4;

Col. 1:15) in the sense that, being God manifest in the flesh (1 Tim. 3:16; John 1:14, 18), He essentially reveals God insofar as His human nature allows (John 14:9).

4. We must be willing to comply with people's customs, especially those of a foreign culture, except when these conflict with God's preceptive will for us (cp. 1 Cor. 9:19–23).

5. David Baron, *Rays of Messiah's Glory* (Grand Rapids: Zondervan Publishing House, 1886), 26f.; Sir Robert Anderson, *The Coming Prince* (London: Hodder Stoughton, 1895), chap. X.

6. A "prophetic year" of 360 days is referred to in several pasages that speak of 1,260 days (Rev. 11:3; 12:6) as being equal to "42 months" (11:2; 13:5) or to "time, times, and half a time," with "time" representing a period of 360 days (see 12:14 with v. 6; Dan. 7:25; 12:7; cp. vv. 11–12; 8:14).

7. Edwin Yamauchi, "Meshech, Tubal and Company: A Review," *The Journal of the Evangelical Theological Society,* vol. 19, no. 3 (1976), 239.

8. See Alexander Hislop, *The Two Babylons* (London: Partridge, 1926), 21–40.

9. Perhaps this alludes to the Lord's warning of the Beast's breaking his treaty with Israel in the middle of the Tribulation Age (Dan. 9:27; Matt. 24:15–21). It does not seem possible that there would be Jews living in Jerusalem at the end of the Tribulation Age.

10. Calvinists commonly regard the word *predestination* to include election and reprobation. See L. Berkhof, *Systematic Theology,* 113. I see predestination as following election and as God's predetermination of what He would do with the people whom He had chosen to save (Rom. 8:29; Eph. 1:5, 11–12). See "God's Part in the Application of Salvation" under Soteriology.

11. L. S. Chafer, *Systematic Theology,* 3:180ff.

12. W. G. T. Shedd, *Dogmatic Theology,* 1:444ff.

13. Interpreting Babylon to be Rome (Rev. ch 17), many belive that this historical period refers t the Romans, who conquered the Mediterranean nations. But this is not certain. The legs may refer to Babylon's being controlled by the Syrian Seleucids and then the Parthians during 312–55 B.C.

14. The number in brackets indicates the time of these future events as follows: [1], before the "seventieth week" of Daniel 9; [2], the first half of the "seventieth week"; [3], the middle of the "seventieth week"; [4], the second half of the "seventieth week"; [5], toward the close of the "seventieth week"; and [6], after the "seventieth week." See the chart, "The Prophetic Future," on page 552.

15. An interlude is a pause in the progress of the vision. It gives additional details relating to these times.

16. See "The Separation and Dedication of the Christian Life: Our separation from the things of the world" under Zoeology.

17. Giving is an essential part of worshiping God (see "The Ministries of the Christian Life: The Ministry of Worshiping God" under Zoeology).

18. Note that there is the spiritual gift of giving, which God uses in special ministry (see "His Relation to Spiritual Gifts: The twelve spiritual gifts that are operating today") under Pneumatology.

19. The word *angels* means "messengers." Perhaps this refers to human pastors of these local churches.

20. Philadelphia: The Judson Press, 1894, reprinted in 1944, chap. 1. Used by permission of the Judson Press. This edition is now published by Kregel Publications under the title, *Principles and Practices for Baptist Churches*.

21. See Paul R. Jackson, *The Doctrine and Administration of the Local Church* (Des Plaines, Ill.: Regular Baptist Press, 1968), chap. XVII.

22. Albertus Pieters, *The Seed of Abraham* (Grand Rapids: W. B. Eerdmans Pub. Co., 1950), 121.

23. Note that "All Israel" (v. 26) is a synecdoche (a figure of association) for the elect remnant of Israel.

24. See "His Relation to Spiritual Gifts: The seven spiritual gifts that are not operating today" under Pneumatology.

25. Henry W. Frost, *Miraculous Healing* (London: Marshall, Morgan & Scott, 1951), chap. XI, 115ff.

26. Ibid., chap. X, 109ff.
27. See "The Canonicity of the Bible" under Bibliology.
28. See Rom. 7:8; 13:14; Gal. 5:24; Eph. 2:3; 4:27; Titus 2:12; 2 Peter 2:18–19. Observe that "flesh" in these passages means the sin force's dominating us and our human nature. Unsaved people are completely dominated by the sin force (Eph. 2:3; 4:22; Titus 3:3; 2 Peter 3:3; Rom. 1:24). In principle, gospel believers have been delivered from this bondage so that they might give themselves over to God's command (Rom. 6:2, 6–7, 11–19; 1 Peter 2:11, 21).
29. Here "the world" is that system consisting of the total society, culture, and philosophy of unsaved mankind, which is headed by Satan (John 16:11) and whose works are evil (7:7).
30. Because of their having the same biblical functions, the soul and spirit may be the same thing, with their designations indicating the attachments of this immaterial part of human nature to the body—its association with blood being "soul" (Lev. 17:11, 14, "life" should read "soul") and its association with breath being "spirit" (Gen. 7:21–22; Isa. 42:5). See "Humans Are Complex Beings" under Anthropology.
31. When we are offended by unsaved people, they may not repent of their wrongdoing against us because of their hostility toward God and His people (John 15:18–21). If this is the case, we must accept this, treat them with Christian love, and seek ways to convey to them a gospel witness.
32. Note the command ("have no company with him"), purpose ("that he may be ashamed"), and extent ("yet count him not as an enemy but admonish him as a brother").
33. Their "ignorance" (Acts 3:17) related to Jesus' identity as being God (John 19:33; Acts 13:27; 1 Cor. 2:8). This was because of their spiritual blindness (Matt. 13:13–15). God does not forgive responsible people until they meet the conditions of forgiveness.
34. This is adapted in part from George H. Reibold, *Figurative Language* (Franklin, Ohio: James Knapp Reeve, 1925), chap. VI.
35. Some readers may be disturbed by my placing the RSV in this category. Because of the liberal bias of many of its translators, this version ignores references to the deity of the Lord Jesus in such OT messianic passages as Psalms 2:11; 45:6; Micah 5:2; and Zechariah 12:10. For other criticisms see Oswald T. Allis, *Critiques of the RSV of 1946 (NT) and the RSV of 1952 (OT)* (Philadelphia: The Presbyterian and Reformed Publishing Co., 1948, 1953).

THE PROPHETIC FUTURE

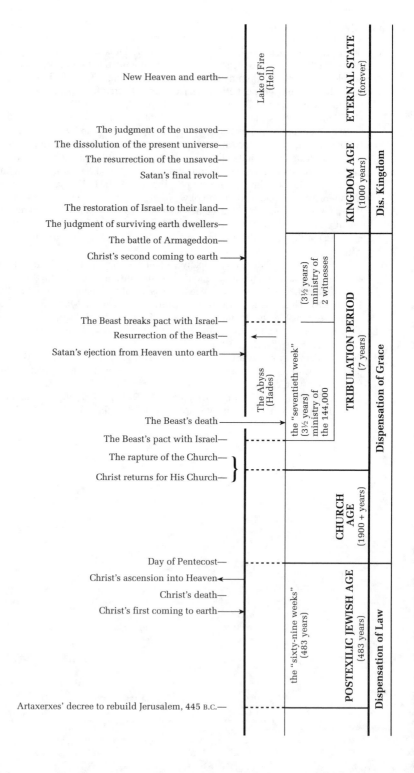

New Heaven and earth—

The judgment of the unsaved—
The dissolution of the present universe—
The resurrection of the unsaved—
Satan's final revolt—

The restoration of Israel to their land—
The judgment of surviving earth dwellers—
The battle of Armageddon—
Christ's second coming to earth —→

The Beast breaks pact with Israel—
Resurrection of the Beast—
Satan's ejection from Heaven unto earth —→

The Beast's death —
The Beast's pact with Israel—
The rapture of the Church— }
Christ returns for His Church— }

Day of Pentecost—
Christ's ascension into Heaven ←
Christ's death—
Christ's first coming to earth —→

Artaxerxes' decree to rebuild Jerusalem, 445 B.C.—

Lake of Fire (Hell)

ETERNAL STATE (forever)

KINGDOM AGE (1000 years)

Dis. Kingdom

(3½ years) ministry of 2 witnesses

TRIBULATION PERIOD (7 years)

the "seventieth week" (3½ years) ministry of the 144,000

The Abyss (Hades)

Dispensation of Grace

CHURCH AGE (1900 + years)

POSTEXILIC JEWISH AGE (483 years)

the "sixty-nine weeks" (483 years)

Dispensation of Law

ADDENDA

THE GENEALOGY FROM ADAM TO ABRAHAM*

(Genesis 5; 9:28f.)

	Born (date)	Lived (years)	Died (date)	1	2	3	4	5	6	7	8	9	10
				Lived with (in years)									
1. Adam	A.M. 0	930	A.M. 930	...	800	695	605	535	470	308	243	56	...
2. Seth	130	912	1042	800	...	677	587	647	582	365	225	168	...
3. Enos	235	905	1140	695	677	...	815	745	680	365	453	266	84
4. Cainan	325	910	1235	605	587	815	...	840	775	365	548	361	179
5. Mahalaleel	395	895	1290	535	647	745	840	...	830	365	603	416	234
6. Jared	460	962	1422	470	582	680	775	830	...	365	735	548	366
7. Enoch	622	365	987	308	365	365	365	365	365	...	300	113	...
8. Methuselah	687	969	1656	243	225	453	548	603	735	300	...	782	600
9. Lamech	874	777	1651	56	168	266	361	416	548	113	782	...	595
10. Noah	1056	950	2006	...	...	84	179	234	366	...	600	595	...

The Flood (A.M. 1656–1657)

(Gen. 11:1–26)

	Born (date)	Lived (years)	Died (date)	10	11	12	13	14	15	16	17	18	19	20
				Lived with (in years)										
10. Noah	1056	950	2006	...	448	348	309	283	249	219	187	157	128	...
11. Shem	1558	600	2158	448	...	438	465	435	401	371	339	309	280	150
12. Arphaxad	1658	438	2096	348	438	...	403	373	339	309	277	247	218	88
13. Salah	1693	433	2126	309	465	403	...	403	369	339	307	277	248	118
14. Eber	1723	464	2187	283	435	373	403	...	430	400	368	338	309	179
15. Peleg	1757	239	1996	249	401	339	369	430	...	209	177	147	118	...
16. Reu	1787	239	2026	219	371	309	339	400	209	...	207	177	148	18
17. Serug	1819	230	2049	187	339	277	307	368	177	207	...	200	171	41
18. Nahor	1849	148	1997	157	309	247	277	338	147	177	200	...	119	...
19. Terah	1878	205	2083	128	280	218	248	309	118	148	171	119	...	75
20. Abraham	2008	175	2183	...	150	88	118	179	...	18	41	...	75	...

---

* Adapted from J. B. Dimbleby, *All Past Time* (London: E. Nester, 1897), 15.
  A.M. = *Anno mundi*, Latin for "in the year of the world" or from the time of its creation. Deduct A.M. dates from 4004 to get B.C. dates.

COMMON GRACE

This is that general influence of the Holy Spirit on the unsaved that allows them, in spite of their depravity, to experience the features of their personhoods like morality and religious interests, as well as to strive for civil order. However, this grace does not effect or issue in their salvation. Apparently, this grace as well as the Holy Spirit's restraint on universal evil will be removed during the Tribulation Age (Matt. 24:12; 2 Thess. 2:7; Rev. 9:20–21).

THE TIMES OF THE GENTILES

This appears to refer to the time, perhaps from the days of the Babylonian Nebuchadnezzar (Dan. 2), during which the Gentiles have the preeminent place in God's present program for mankind. This will reach its climax in the world rule of the Beast during the second half of the Tribulation Age, when he tramples Jerusalem under foot for three and a half years (Rev. 11:2). At the close of this period, the Lord will return to earth and will restore Israel to her rightful place as the head of the nations (Acts 15:14–17; see "The Prophecy of Jesus' Second Coming to Earth" under Eschatology, and Appendix K: "Israel's Future As Described in Biblical Prophecy").

GOOD WORKS

In the Scriptures, "good works" means more than doing things that are good by human standards. Good works represent our doing God's will in Jesus' strength or the power of the Holy Spirit, for God's glory (Heb. 13:21; 1 Cor. 10:31). This is how we should understand James 4:17 and Romans 3:12. (See "The Prophecy of Jesus' Appraisal of His Church: The Criteria of This Appraisal" under Eschatology.) All other works are evil in His sight (Rom. 14:23; John 15:5).

CARNAL CHRISTIANS

Carnal means "fleshly," that is, acting in the energy of the sin force (1 Cor. 3:1; Rom. 8:4–5). This is in contrast to *spiritual,* which means acting in the energy of the Holy Spirit (1 Cor. 2:15; cp. Gal. 5:16). We gospel believers are either carnal or spiritual during every conscious moment of life, according to the moral force that is energizing us at the time (Luke 6:45). Needless to say, God wants us to walk in the energy of the Holy Spirit rather than of sin (Gal. 5:16, 25; Rom. 8:1–13). It is urgent that daily we give ourselves to God and to His management of our lives. Unsaved people are continually carnal, for they are living under the complete domination of the sin force (Eph. 2:3; 4:17–19).

AMILLENNIALISM AND POSTMILLENNIALISM

Amillenialism is the view that there will be no rule of the Lord Jesus on earth before the last judgment (Rev. 20:11–15). Based on an allegorical or spiritualizing interpretation of Revelation 20:1–6, conservative amillennialists hold two views of Christ's thousand-year reign. Some see it as fulfilled during the present time in the Church, either on earth (Augustine) or in heaven (B. B. Warfield). Others see it as referring to Jesus' rule over His people in the eternal state, immediately following His second coming to earth and the last judgment (O. T. Allis, L. Berkhof, F. E. Hamilton).

Postmillennialism is the view that the prophecies of the Lord's millennial rule will be fulfilled before His return, with the whole world being Christianized by gospel preaching and teaching and by Christian legislation. After He returns, the dead will be raised and judged (L. Boettner, W. G. T. Shedd, A. H. Strong). This view is held today by those who advocate dominion or theodicy theology. Like amillennialism, postmillennialism is growing in popularity, for dispensationalism, with its more biblical perspective, sees only the gloom and doom of the coming Tribulation Age (2 Tim. 3:1–5; 1 Thess. 5:1–10).

SHEOL, HADES

Hell, or the lake of fire, is not to be equated with OT sheol and NT hades, both of which refer to the same place.[1] During the time before Jesus' resurrection, all people went to sheol.[2] Luke 16:19–31, which records a historical event, reveals that hades was divided into parts: a place for the saved, or righteous, called "Abraham's bosom" (v. 23), or "paradise" (23:43); and a place for the wicked, separated by an impassable gulf (16:26; cp. Ps. 9:17). Upon His ascension, the Lord Jesus took the inhabitants of Abraham's bosom with Him to heaven (cp. Eph. 4:8). Today, gospel believers upon death do not go to hades but go directly to be with Jesus in heaven (Phil. 1:23; 2 Cor. 5:8). This is probably what the Lord had in mind when He said that the gates of hades (meaning its authority) would not prevail over the Church (Matt. 16:18). Some fallen evil angels (demons) are confined to another part of hades, called "Tartaros" (Gk. for "hell" in 2 Peter 2:4, KJV), to await their final judgment and doom.

The Scriptures indicate that sheol, or hades, is within the earth (Ezek. 26:20; 31:14–18; 32:18; cp. Ps. 63:9; Isa. 14:9, 15; Phil. 2:10; Rev. 5:3, 13). After the future resurrection of the unsaved and the dissolution of the universe, hades will be abolished, for it will no longer be needed, and its inhabitants, the unsaved, will be cast into the lake of fire (Rev. 20:13–14).

THE UNFORGIVABLE SIN (MATT. 12:31–32)

This unforgivable sin is one that only unsaved people can commit. It appears from our Lord's words that this is not just any sin, nor is it a quality that any sin can assume. It is a sin against the Holy Spirit. It is to blaspheme Him, that is, to speak abusively against Him.

Some Jewish religious leaders of Jesus' day deliberately and hatefully attributed the power of Satan to Jesus' casting out demons (Matt. 9:32–34; 12:22–24; Luke 11:15). Although this charge was directed to the Lord, it was an act of blasphemy against the Holy Spirit, in Whose power Jesus did His miraculous works (Matt. 12:28; Luke 4:1, 14; Acts 10:38). The reason for this sin's being so abhorrent to the Lord Jesus seems to be that He always sought to honor and to uphold the integrity of the Holy Spirit, in whose power He lived and served as the human Messiah.

A study of the character and attitudes of these blasphemers reveals that this sin cannot be committed ignorantly or mistakenly by a child of God. Despite their recognition of Jesus' divine commission, these religious leaders refused to accept Him and His ministry (cp. John 3:1–2; 5:31–39; 7:28). Also, boasting of their clever avoidance of being persuaded by Jesus, they sought to do away with Him (John 7:45–49; Matt. 12:14).

A saved person cannot commit this sin without doing two impossible things: *One,* he must overthrow his salvational faith in Jesus, which is God's gift (Acts 3:16; 2 Peter 1:1) and which is sustained by our Lord's prayers (Luke 22:31–32). And, *two,* he must render ineffective the sovereign work of God in his heart (Phil. 2:13; 1:6).

Some believe that this sin cannot be committed by anyone today, because the circumstances differ from those of Jesus' time; but this is not certain. Since our Lord is building His Church today through the ministries of the Holy Spirit in His people (1 Cor. 12:13; Acts 1:8), it may be that an unsaved person could commit this sin if he recognized the true nature of the Lord's work and deliberately, maliciously attributed it to Satan. Unsaved people will commit this sin in the middle of the Tribulation Age, after Satan's being confined to earth, when they choose to follow the Beast, Satan's human agent (Rev. 13:15–17; 14:9–11; 2 Thess. 2:10–12).

We who are saved should be acquainted with and be grateful for the ministries of the Holy Spirit in our lives. Daily, we should yield ourselves to His filling and direction and should walk in His fellowship and power.

THE SIN UNTO DEATH (1 JOHN 5:16)

Leading to premature physical death, this is a sin that saved people can commit. This sin appears to be hatred of God's reproof in His corrective and nurturing dealings with His people (Prov. 15:10; 29:1; Heb. 12:5–7, 9). Our heavenly Father constantly deals with us in order to keep us in the way of holiness and to develop our spiritual lives (John 15:2; James 1:2–4; Rev. 3:19). However, if we should refuse to respond favorably to this discipline and set our hearts against it to the extent of hating it, then we would render ourselves useless to God in this world. Consequently, He would prematurely remove us from earth and take us to heaven (John 15:2, 6).

This sin has no relation to the offender's salvation, but it does concern his fulfilling God's revealed will for his life (1 Cor. 5:5; 11:32). When we recognize that another believer has committed this sin, we are not to pray for his deliverance from God's disciplinary action, for our prayers will not be heard (1 John 5:16: cp. Jer. 7:13–16). On the other hand, we have an obligation toward those who commit other sins (Gal. 6:1). Obviously, we have to be cautious in our speculation of the reason for the trials and death of God's people. Only when we are closely associated with a person can we know his true attitude toward God.

Needless to say, it is important that we be submissive to God's corrective and nurturing disciplines in our lives. Knowing His purpose for us, He will do what it takes to bring this about in the best possible way. We should immediately deal with known sins by repentance and confession (Rev. 2:5; 1 John 1:9) so as to avoid His corrective chastisement. His grace is more than sufficient for our experiencing those divine dealings that would cause us to be more fruitful (2 Cor. 12:9–10).

HUMAN PHYSICAL MORTALITY

"Mortality" concerns the human body's being subject to physical death. As we examine this subject in the light of Scripture, it seems that we must distinguish between natural mortality and judicial mortality, or between the mortality that belonged to Adam's and Eve's newly created bodies and the judicial mortality that was divinely imposed upon them as a sentence for their sinning. It appears that the newly created body was naturally subject to death if certain life-sustaining practices, like eating, were not followed (Gen. 1:29). Even the Lord Jesus, who had a sinless body, would have died physically on two occasions had angels not ministered to Him. After being forty days without food, He would have died from starvation, for He was too weak to provide for Himself (Matt. 4:2, 11). On the other occasion, He would have died from an undefined overwhelming experience in Gethsemane on the eve of His atoning sacrifice (26:38–39; Luke 22:43).

On the other hand, when Adam and Eve sinned, God imposed on their bodies the sentence of judicial mortality (Gen. 3:19; Rom. 6:23; 8:10). This appointed their bodies to certain death by disease and deterioration. Apparently, God adversely affected their genes and immune systems, making their bodies vulnerable to harmful bacteria, viruses, toxins, and pollutants. It is this judicial death that is the product of man's initial sinning (original sin), that is transmitted to all mankind and that is a "bondage of corruption" to everyone in this world (Rom. 5:12; 8:10, 20–23; Heb. 2:14–15).

Vegetation and animals also are vulnerable to environmental harm, disease, predation, and death. This is due to a divine curse, which enables mankind to maintain a relative dominance over nature and which makes human life more difficult in this world (Gen. 1:28; 3:17–19; Rom. 8:19–22).

HUMAN CLONES

The recent scientific feat of cloning an adult sheep, reported in March 1997, has raised moral and theological questions about cloning humans. While certain theologians and scientists agree that a human clone and its DNA donor would be "separate persons," meaning that "each would have his or her own body, mind, and soul," this view is not in accord with my understanding of human makeup, which I believe consists of personhood and human nature (body, soul, and spirit; see under Anthropology).

Since cloning is a bizarre substitute for God's ordained way of producing humans by the union of sperm and ovum, this could create a species of human animals without personhood. This means that these products would have a human nature but not personhood (the image of God), with its self-awareness, sense of morality, and its accountability. In my view, human nature is propagated by the parents and personhood is created by God at the moment of conception (cp. Mal. 2:10). When humans reproduce their kind apart from God's ordained way, using a male and a female, then God may not cooperate by creating personhood for those human natures that are cloned.

Something like cloning may have occurred before the Noachic Flood when fallen angels (demons) "came in unto the daughters of men," commonly interpreted as their having sexual relations with human females (Gen. 6:1–4; cp. 1 Peter 3:19–20; Jude 6–7).[3] Renowned "fallen ones" (the meaning of KJV "giants") were produced, some of which may have been the celebrated and worshiped subjects of ancient mythology, that were grossly wicked and were divinely destroyed by the Flood (vv. 5–13). Since angels do not reproduce themselves, their having sexual relations with human women may be an anthropomorphic expression for a means of reproduction like cloning.

This may occur again in the second half of the Tribulation Age, in the days of the fourth kingdom of Daniel chapter 2 (vv. 33, 40–43), when Satan rules earth through the Beast. The "iron mixed with clay" suggests another unnatural union of demons with humans ("they" the iron being demons; "clay" being the "seed of men"). In this case, it may be that these humans will not be just demon-possessed people but demon-possessed human animals, derived from a process like cloning, who are used to do Satan's bidding. Modern science is creating instruments of wonder, devastation, and horror that will be unleashed during the coming Tribulation Age along with the supernatural activity of Satan and his demon allies.

GOD'S WILL REGARDING HUMAN GOVERNMENT

With his sinning, Adam lost a part of this authority over the earth to Satan, who as "the prince of this world" (John 12:31; 14:30; 16:11; cp. Heb. 2:5–8; Luke 4:5–6), became the invisible, spiritual ruler of unsaved people. However, human government still remained God's institution and its human rulers remained His agents to maintain an orderly and peaceful human society on earth (Rom. 13:1–5; Titus 2:1; 1 Peter 2:13–14), although this may at times be influenced by the Devil (cp. Dan. 10:12–20). With this in view, God's will regarding our duties to human government follows: we who have been saved by trusting in Jesus as our Savior are to honor government officials (1 Peter 2:17), obey government (Rom. 13:1; Titus 3:1; 1 Peter 2:13–14) insofar as this does not conflict with God's will for us (Acts 4:19–21; 5:29; see Dan. 3; 6:10), support the cost of government by paying taxes (Rom. 13:6–7), serve government in the will of God (Titus 3:1), and pray for governmental officials (1 Tim. 2:1–3).

ENDNOTES

1. The Hebrew *sheol* and the Greek *hades* are often translated "hell" in the KJV. The KJV translation "hell" for *sheol* occurs in Deuteronomy 32:22; 2 Samuel 22:6; Job 11:8; 26:6; Psalms 9:17; 16:10; 18:5; 55:15; 86:13; 116:3; 139:8; Proverbs 5:5; 7:27; 9:18; 15:11, 24; 23:14; 27:20; Isaiah 5:14; 14:9, 15; 28:15, 18; 57:9; Ezekiel 31:16–17; 32:21, 27; Amos 9:2; Jonah 2:2; Habakkuk 2:5. "Hell" for *hades* occurs in Matthew 11:23; 16:18; Luke 16:23; Acts 2:27, 31; Revelation 1:18; 6:8; 20:13–14.

2. *Sheol* is Hebrew for "grave" in Genesis 37:35; Job 7:9; Psalm 6:5; Isaiah 14:11 and for "pit" in Numbers 16:30, 33.

3. Jude 6–7 should read, "The angels that kept not their first place of power . . . Even as (did) Sodom and Gomorrha and the cities about them, in like manner these (angels, v. 6), having given themselves over to fornication and going after flesh of a different kind [KJV, "strange"], are set forth as an example of suffering the (divine) punishment of eternal fire." A sin of Sodom and Gomorrha was their engaging in unnatural sexual practices like homosexuality (Gen. 19:5, "know" refers to this).

SUBJECT INDEX

Entries are defined or explained on the pages whose numbers are in brackets or stand alone. Related entries are indicated by an asterisk (*) and n. = endnote.

SELECT SCRIPTURE
REFERENCE INDEX